STANDARD CHESS OPENINGS

STANDARD CHESS OPENINGS

Eric Schiller

CARDOZA PUBLISHING

ACKNOWLEDGEMENTS

This massive project was made possible with the advice and support of my friends, students and associates. I'd like to specially thank Avery Cardoza for helpful editing and Gabe Kahane for proofreading the manuscript, as well as Peter Kemmis Betty, Bob Dudley, Tony Gillam, Burt Hochberg, Ray Keene, Ken Smith, and Bob Wade without whom my career as a chess writer would never have gotten off the ground. Thanks also go to Jim McCawley, Jerry Sadock and Gerard Diffloth and the rest of the Department of Linguisitcs, who sharpened by research and academic skills at the University of Chicago.

Ultimately, however, credit goes to my parents, without whose support I wouldn't be doing the work I love.

First Edition

Libray of Congress Catalog Card No: 96-71754
ISBN: 0-940685-72-8
Front Cover Photograph by Paul Eisenberg

CARDOZA PUBLISHING
PO Box 1500 Cooper Station, New York, NY 10276
Phone (718)743-5229 • Fax(718)743-8284 • Email:cardozapub@aol.com
Web Site - www.cardozapub.com

ABOUT THE AUTHOR

Eric Schiller, widely considered one of the world's foremost chess analysts, writers and teachers, is internationally recognized for his definitive works on openings. He is the author of 77 chess books including definitive studies of many chess openings and more than two dozen USCF (United States Chess Federation) best-sellers.

His major works include the prestigious *Batsford Chess Openings* with World Champion Garry Kasparov and Grandmaster Raymond Keene, and Cardoza Publishing's definitive series on openings, *World Champion Openings*, *Standard Chess Openings*, and *Unorthodox Chess Openings* – an exhaustive and complete opening library of more than 1700 pages! He's also the author of *Gambit Opening Repertoire for White*, *Gambit Opening Repertoire for Black*, and multiple other chess titles for Cardoza Publishing. (For updated listings of all chess titles published by Cardoza Publishing, go online to www.cardozapub.com, or for those books and more by Eric Schiller, to www.chessworks.com)

Schiller has provided major content for Mindscape's *ChessMaster 5000*, Electronic Art's *Kasparov's Gambit*, and his own multimedia chess title (Zane Publishing), *Dr. Schiller Teaches Chess.*

Eric Schiller is a National and Life Master, an International Arbiter of F.I.D.E., and the official trainer for many of America's top young players. He has recently been appointed as official coach of America's best players under 18 to represent the United States at the Chess World Championships. He has also presided over world championship matches dating back to 1983, runs prestigious international tournaments, and been interviewed dozens of times in major media throughout the world. His games have been featured in all the leading journals and newspapers including the venerable New York Times.

To the memory of Grandmaster Miguel Najdorf, a unique and wonderful figure who will be greatly missed.

TABLE OF CONTENTS

1. INTRODUCTION

This book is an introduction to every standard opening strategy in common use in tournament and correspondence chess games. In all, more than 3,000 opening strategies are presented, and more than 250 of these openings are given special coverage with completely annotated games illustrating their principles so that you have a full picture of an opening, from the first moves right through to the endgame.

My emphasis is on understanding the openings and how they might apply to the games you'll play. Every opening includes a representative diagram of the opening position, the typical move order, clear explanations of the thinking behind the moves, the direction the opening is heading, and how the ideas behind the opening are influential not only in the first few moves, but later on in the development of the game.

You'll also learn the important variations that can develop out of these openings, and of course, be able to follow the full course of thinking by following the annotated games. In many cases, the illustrative game showcasing the opening is played by the inventor of the opening, a world champion, a great theoretician, or the player most closely associated with it. In fact, that game often is representative of the best ever played in these openings. A few particularly interesting and appropriate games by lesser players are also included, for often, the most appropriate examples of openings seen at amateur levels are better illustrated by the games of non-professional players themselves.

All the main games are complete, so that you can see how a small advantage can turn into a masterful brilliancy, or how opportunities can be squandered.

In short, you will learn enough of the general principles of the opening so that you'll be able to play strong chess right from the start of a game, even without detailed knowledge of the openings. And once you learn to achieve good positions, and have a game plan to proceed into the middle game and beyond, many of your opponents will start to crumble and you will have all you need to bring home the point!

2. OVERVIEW

It is impossible to provide detailed analysis of all the chess openings in a single book. Indeed, each of the openings discussed in this volume have been studied intensively, and have books devoted to their individual properties.

There are thousands of common chess openings strategies, with names ranging from Sicilian Dragon, Hedgehog, and Rat through the more esoteric Creepy-Crawly Opening. Most top chessplayers only play a dozen or so at a time, and make major changes only a few times in their professional career. Their choices are generally conservative, leaving experimental approaches for an occasional outing when the mood fits. The range of openings chosen by each player may be small, but there is a great deal of variety when comparing the repertoires of various superstars.

The openings cover a wide range of styles and applications. In some cases, I have gone into greater detail on an opening because I wanted to capture the variety of positions that are often seen. In other case, I have given additional examples because the opening is part of one of the recommended repertoires found in the last chapter of the book. Finally, a few openings get a little special attention just because I happen to like them and know more about them from my own personal experience.

Chess opening strategy still remains more of an art than a science, and fashion often dictates popularity, rather than any objective standard. Openings fade in and out. In the 1990s, for example, we have seen a revival of variations which were only common in the last century! Nowadays we find current champions Garry Kasparov and Anatoly Karpov adopting plans which have only rarely been seen since Paul Morphy in the 1850s and 60s.

WHAT IS A STANDARD OPENING?

There is no clear definition of a "standard" opening. I define the term as applying to any opening which an active chessplayer might reasonably expect to encounter frequently. This is not the same as an "orthodox" opening, which is an opening that complies with generally accepted principles of deploying one's forces early in the game. Thus, some of the openings in this book will also be treated in the companion volume *Unorthodox Chess Openings*, but are included here so that this volume will stand alone as a reference to all the standard chess openings.

To determine the frequency of an opening, the Caxton Chess Database of over one million games was used. This database was chosen because it also includes a significant number of amateur and correspondence games, so that the goal of treating openings which are frequently encountered in club and informal chess could be achieved.

Inclusion in the group of standard openings is not based on bare numbers alone. In some cases, openings branch off early into subvariations which differ dramatically in style. In these cases, several subvariations are presented in order to give a balanced picture of the opening as a whole

TRANSPOSITIONS

Often a game begins in one opening but shifts into another by reaching a position that is more typical of the latter. For example, suppose White plays 1.Nf3 and Black responds 1.c5. We would consider both of these moves typical of a flank game. But if White now plays 2.e4, then we have the Sicilian Defense, usually reached by 1.e4 c5; 2.Nf3.

Of course it does not matter at this point which move order was used, but it is sometimes the case that these transpositions are seen even late in the opening, perhaps at move 10 or 12. In addition, it is possible to reach the same position by a different number of moves!

For example 1.e4 d5; 2.exd5 Qxd5; 3.Nc3 Qd6; 4.d4 c6 is a variation of the Scandinavian Defense which I have frequently played, though it isn't quite respectable. It can also arise from the Alekhine Defense after 1.e4 Nf6; 2.e5 Ng8; 3.d4 d6; 4.exd6 Qxd6; 5.Nc3 c6. Same position, two move orders. Here is another I have used: 1.e4 c6; 2.d4 d5; 3.exd5 Qxd5; 4.Nc3 Qd6. Many paths, all leading to my own pet variation!

Because there are so many possible transpositions, it is not easy to determine which opening characterizes a particular game. When we talk about the King's Indian Defense, for example, we are not concerned with whether the game begins 1.d4 Nf6; 2.c4 g6; 3.Nc3 Bg7. If Black plays an early ...d5, we will be in Gruenfeld territory, while an early ...c5 may shift us to a Modern Benoni. It is only after Black has completed development, including ...d6 and ...0-0 (in most cases) that we can be fairly certain of remaining in the realm of the King's Indian.

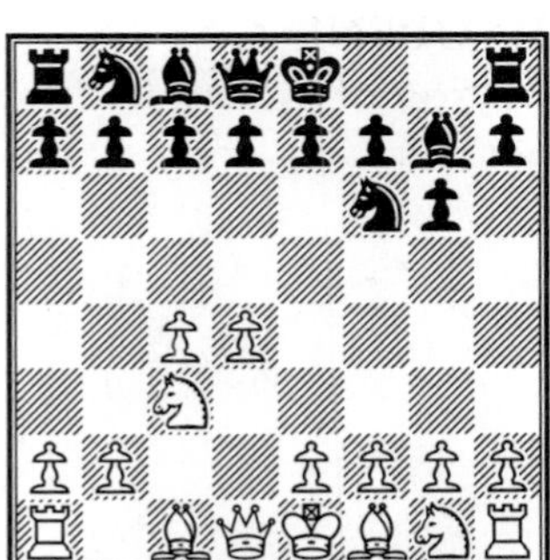

1.d4 Nf6
2.c4 g6
3.Nc3 Bg7

Opening Codes

To make it easy to refer to other sources of chess information for a more thorough examination of the openings, the standard codes for openings used in professional publications is included at the start of each game, right after the names of the players.

These codes have a letter, A through E, and a number, 00 through 99, which are used to identify the opening in the *Encyclopedia of Chess Openings, Chess Informant, Chess Life* and other important publications. These codes can also be used to search for games on the Internet or in chess databases such as *Caxton Chess Database*.

3. CHOOSING THE BEST OPENINGS

CHOOSING THE BEST OPENINGS AS WHITE

After many centuries of experience, it should be possible for scholars to determine the best openings strategies, but it is one of the pleasures of chess that this remains an impossible task. The complex interplay of the factors described above makes simplistic statements just seem vain. Nevertheless, we have been able to narrow the candidates. The first pair of obvious candidates are 1.e4 and 1.d4. Each occupies and controls important central territory and allows a bishop to get into the game. The pawn at d4 is protected by the queen, and this is sometimes used to argue for 1.d4.

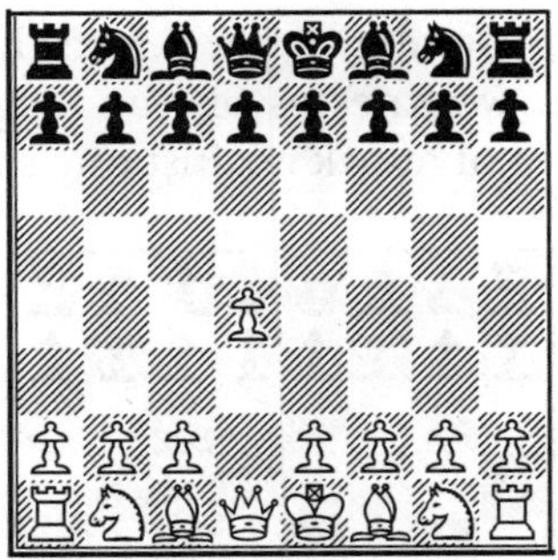

1.d4

But this is not an important factor, because the goal of either opening is to establish pawns at both squares. Here is the picture after 1.e4.

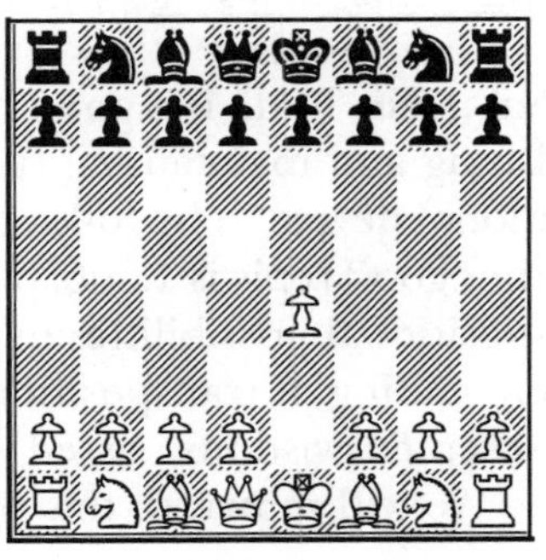

1.e4

Since the e4-square is slightly more difficult to control, it could be argued that White should seize this square first. Black can try to prevent the White pawn from safely occupying e4 by playing d5 as soon as possible. Of White's first moves, only 1.e4 and 1.c4 discourage this reply, while 1.d4 allows it.

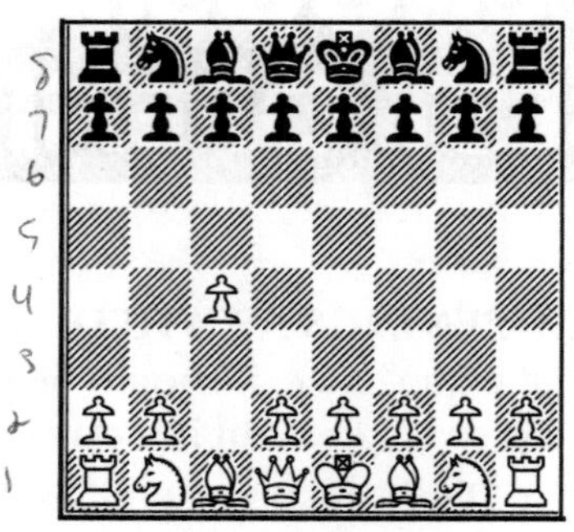

1.c4

1.c4 gets an honorable mention because it does hinder 1...d5, since 2.cxd5 Qxd5 3.Nc3 gives White a clear initiative and gains a tempo against the enemy queen. On the other side of the board, 1.f4 is not as useful, because Black can reply 1...d5 and control the e4 square. Controlling e5 is not as important, and in fact when White does play 1.f4, 1...e5! is a very strong reply, known as the From Gambit. After 2.fxe5 d6; 3.exd6 Bxd6 White already has to worry about weaknesses on the kingside. 1.c4, on the other hand, does not create lines of attack against one's own king.

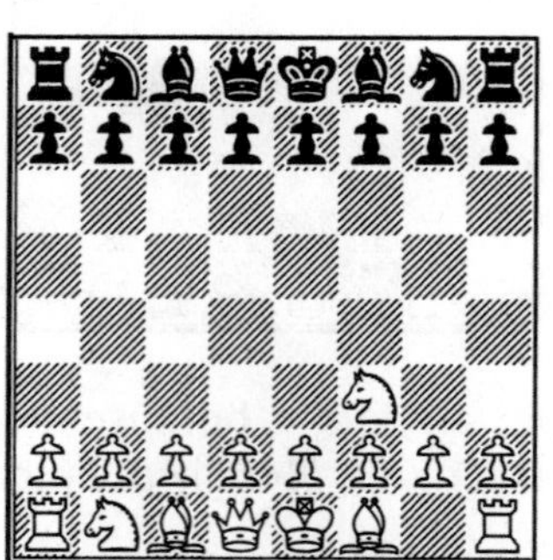

1.Nf3

1.Nf3 is often seen, but again 1...d5 is a good reply and then White has no real chance of establishing and maintaining the ideal pawn center. It is often used as a transpositional device to be followed by an early advance of White's pawn to d4. Another good reply is 1...d6, preparing 2...e5. One must keep in mind many transpositional possibilities in both cases.

Indeed, it is the understanding of transpositional pathways that has undermined much of the accepted wisdom passed down from the early decades of the 20th century. We will return to this point in our discussion of the best defenses, below.

For many years statistics were used to evaluate chess openings, especially in the early years of the computer age when computers were used to perform statistical analyses on openings. Even today there are some who persist in this largely irrelevant activity. Statistics are useless when evaluating chess openings, for the following reasons:

1. The result of a chess game is not directly tied to the result of the opening. Many twists, turns, blunders and brilliancies lie on the road between the opening and the endgame, and sometimes a game is lost by overstepping the time control in a winning position. Also keep in mind that the players may have been mismatched from the start.

2. An opening may win game after game until a refutation is found, and then disappear quickly. The database will simply show that one side won, say, 95% of the games with this opening. Yet once the refutation is established, no serious player will use the opening in competitive play.

3. Openings are sometimes used for psychological effect in an attempt to make the opponent suffer some discomfort regardless of the objective evaluation of the position.

CHOOSING THE BEST DEFENSES AS BLACK

Choosing a defense is a highly personal matter. The various openings have different characteristics. Some, such as the Spanish Game, are Classical in nature, relying on an early contest for control of the center. Others, including the Modern Defense, allow White to fulfill the opening ambition of creating an ideal pawn center, only to work against this formation later on. There are openings which create blocked centers, such as the Old Benoni, and those which ignore the center entirely, though those are considered rather unorthodox.

Therefore your choice of systems is based to some extent on stylistic preference. It is generally advisable for beginners and intermediate players to choose a classical opening, answering White's first move with a symmetrical choice, for example 1.e4 e5, 1.d4 d5, or 1.c4 c5. More advanced players can afford to break the symmetry immediately, for example with 1.e4 c5 (Sicilian Defense),1.d4 Nf6 (Indian Defense), and 1.c4 e5 (King's English).

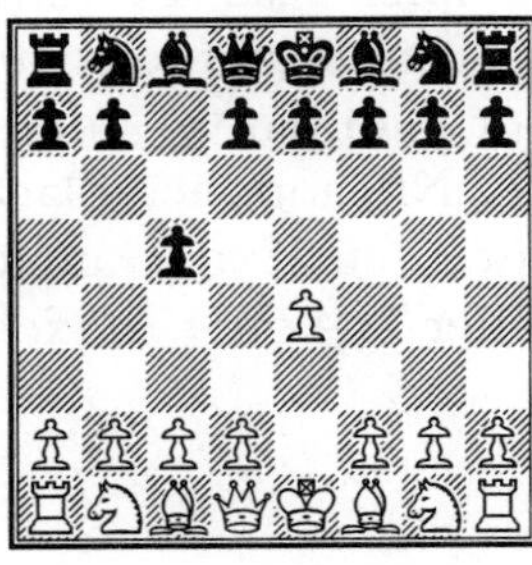

1.e4 c5
Sicilian Defense

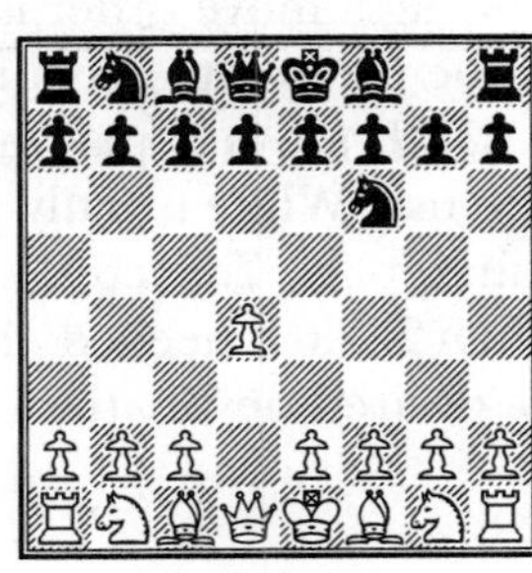

1.e4 Nf6
Indian Defense

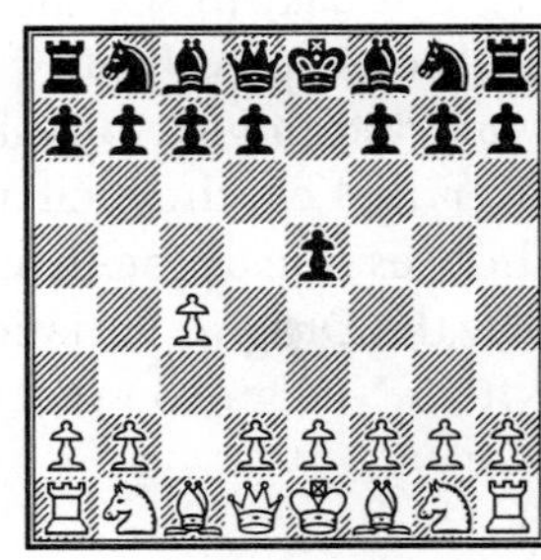

1.c4 e5
King's English

In the past few decades, a new appreciation of transpositions has led to a widening of the number of acceptable defenses early in the game. For example, moves such as 1...d6 and 1...g6, once condemned, are now quite normal. Even the move 1...a6, once considered a joke, has gained more respectability, when it was understood that the move ...a6 is part of many different defensive strategies, and that as long as one is planning to develop normally, the order of moves may not be terribly significant.

The major question these days is what additional possibilities are available to the opponent when one uses an unusual move order. Let's assume that you want to set up the following position for Black:

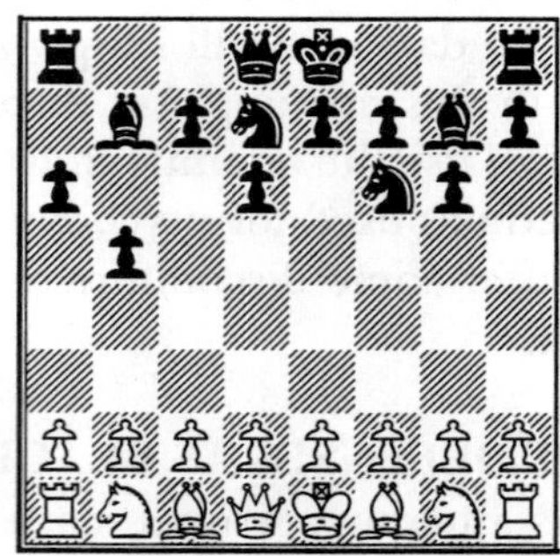

There are three basic components: kingside fianchetto with knight at f6 and castling; extended fianchetto on the queenside, and a pawn at d6. To reach the position you can begin with any of the elements. Your opponent will have different options depending on the move order you choose.

If you are prepared to allow the opponent to establish the ideal pawn center, which is normally the result of the defensive formation we are discussing, then any relevant move will do. After 1.e4, 1...Nf6 prevents White from playing 2.d4, unlike all the other replies for Black, but after 2.e5 our knight has to move. 1...g6 and 1...d6 are the normal moves to reach the desired position. 1...a6 is a strange move order, and White can thwart Black's plans with 2.c4 if desired. Then 2...c5 can transpose to the Sicilian Defense, or Black can try 2...e6 to be followed by ...d5 with a French Defense.

It is easy to see that choosing a move order is a complex task. All transpositional possibilities must be taken into account. It is important to try to avoid landing in positions which are not part of your plan. For example, after 1.e4 c5, the Sicilian Defense, White usually plays 2.Nf3 and then Black chooses one of the three main replies, 2...Nc6, 2...d6, or 2...e6. If you want to play the Dragon Variation, then 2...d6 is needed, then after 3.d4 cxd4; 4.Nxd4 Nf6; 5.Nc3 g6 you reach the desired destination.

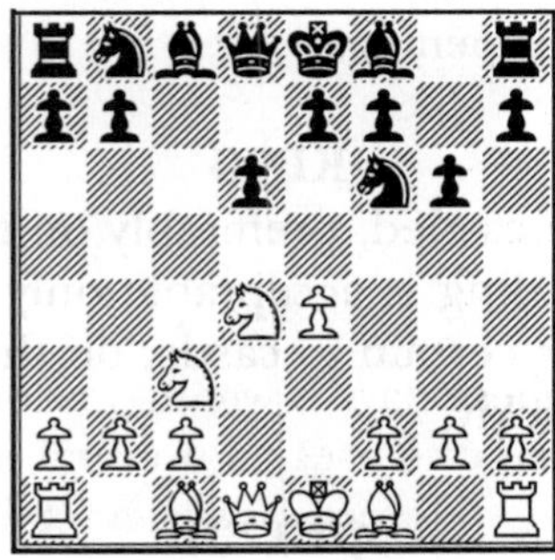

White can try to derail you with the cunning move order 2.Nc3, to which Black generally replies 2...Nc6. If White then plays 3.Nge2, then after, say, 3...Nf6 4.d4 cxd4; 5.Nxd4 Black cannot reach the Dragon, because 5...g6 is the Accelerated Dragon (since there is a knight on c6 rather than a pawn at d6), which is a very different opening strategically.

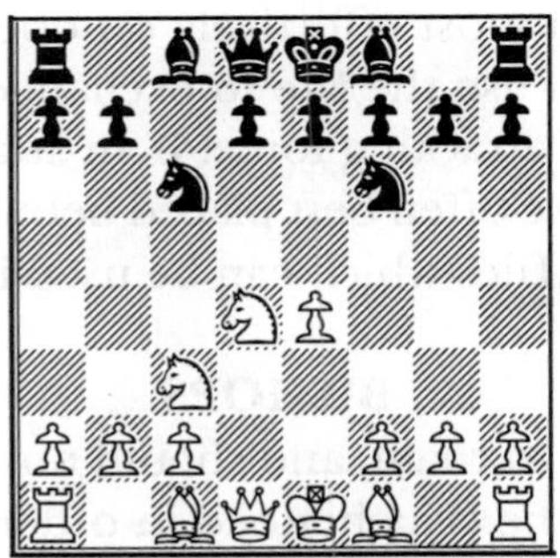

Such finesse in the opening is a hallmark of play in the late 20th century. Optimizing your chances of reaching familiar and acceptable positions is part of the hard work that goes into developing an opening repertoire.

CHOOSING THE BEST SQUARES FOR YOUR PIECES

We can evaluate openings from a slightly different perspective as well, asking where each piece will be most effective. Naturally it is not possible to configure your pieces perfectly in the opening. If it were that easy, chess would be a simple game! Instead, you have to make trade-offs, assisting some pieces to reach their desired posts while forcing others to wait their turn.

Most pieces can be repositioned throughout the opening, but special care should be taken with pawns, which cannot move backwards, and kings, which cannot move quickly. If you place a bishop on a the queenside when it belongs on the kingside, it might take two or three moves to get it into proper position, but a king could require six moves to remedy such a mistake, and if a pawn goes too far it cannot be brought back.

Let's take a brief look at each of the pieces to get a perspective on how we might use them in the opening.

KING

The King should be castled, preferably on the kingside, as soon as possible. Queenside castling is acceptable only when the enemy kings has already castled, or is certain to castle, on the kingside, when White can launch an attack quickly.

QUEEN

The queen should not be developed until it can perform a useful function. In general, she should not advance beyond the third rank, except to recapture a pawn at d4 or c4, the latter often by a check at a4.

ROOKS

The placement of the rooks is one of the trickiest questions in chess. The rooks will perform most effectively on open files, but in that case the opponent can often use the file to exchange the rooks, eliminating them as members of an attacking force. If an attack with pawns is appropriate, then the rooks are often best placed behind the advancing pawns, in anticipation of open files which can be used in an attack.

BISHOPS

Bishops need space to roam, and should not be locked behind barriers of pawns. They can be fianchettoed in order to operate on the long diagonals, or placed near the center to attack or defend important squares. For example, in the open games a bishop at c4 aims at the f7-square, often Black's most vulnerable point. On the other hand, bishops on the fourth rank are exposed to attack by enemy pieces and pawns, so they are often best placed on the third rank, at e3 and d3 (e6 and d6).

KNIGHTS

A knight's power is greatest at the center of the board, but to place a knight in the center where it can be attacked by enemy pawns is only going to help the enemy. Therefore, the knights should remain on the third rank, keeping an eye on important squares in the center. Usually one knight goes to f3, and the other to c3 or d2. The latter has less influence on the center, but is required if a pawn is desired at c3 to support the ideal pawn center.

PAWNS

Pawns are used to gain space in the opening. Each pawn in the center keeps enemy pieces from occupying critical squares. The ideal pawn center, discussed above, controls four important squares in the center. Since White moves first, it is much easier to establish the ideal pawn center. Black can usually do so only with a gambit of a pawn, so the second player should try simply to disrupt White's plan by establishing one strong pawn at d5 or e5. Otherwise, pawns should not be placed on squares intended for pieces, or blocking their lines.

Since pawns cannot move horizontally or backwards, great care must be made with each pawn move, as pawns cannot usually be repositioned easily. Because the absence of a pawn always opens up some file or diagonal for use, it is possible to sacrifice a pawn in the opening to gain rapid development and some positional goal, such as control of space. This privilege is not restricted to White, but the advantage of the first move makes it more likely that such a gambit approach will succeed.

It is important to remember that each advance of a pawn creates weaknesses in the pawn structure which can be exploited by enemy pieces. Both players should avoid doubling of pawns, though there are many exceptions when the open file can be used to good effect.

THE ROLE OF THE PAWNS

We can consider the role of each individual pawn in the opening act:

The a-Pawn

The a-pawn belongs at home, though it can advance one square to attack an enemy piece, or two squares if the enemy has advanced the a-pawn a single square with the intent of advancing the b-pawn two squares. This prophylactic maneuver is typical in the Benoni Defense, but much less so in the Sicilian Defense, where White almost always allows the advance of the b-pawn by Black.

The b-Pawn

The b-pawn should remain in place under most circumstances, though it can advance one square to create a niche for a bishop, or two squares if supported by an a-pawn on the third rank.

The c-Pawn

The choice of opening determines the role of the c-pawn, which can jump to c4 on the first move (English Opening), second move (Queen's Gambit and Indian Defenses), or later. Usually the c-pawn works in tandem with the d-pawn. Both can advance to the fourth rank, or either one can stay behind on the third rank to provide support for the other.

The d-Pawn and e-Pawn

In the case of the d-pawn and e-pawn, the best station is on the fourth rank, creating the ideal pawn center. This is not always achievable, however, so often one is relegated to a supporting role on the third rank. In this case, however, the bishop can be hemmed in, as in the French Defense or Queen's Gambit Declined. Therefore, it is advisable, when possible, to develop the relevant bishop first, as in the Modern Bishop's Opening.

The f-Pawn

The f-pawn does not take small steps. It remains on the second rank, since kingside castling is anticipated and any movement will weaken the diagonal leading to the king both immediately and after kingside castling. It can leap to the fourth rank in many cases because the battle for the e5-square sometimes requires it, or in order to advance to f5 to attack a Black pawn at e6 or g6. The f-pawn rarely sits comfortably on f3, except when White castles queenside, or at f6, except in certain cases where support of e5 is essential, as in the Exchange Variation of the Spanish Game.

The g-Pawn

The defense of a king which is castled on the kingside is often entrusted to the g-pawn, so generally it only advances if it will be replaced by a bishop in the fianchetto formation. Tarrasch considered the advance of the g-pawn two squares to be the "suicide move" and while modern theory allows for it in a number of specific circumstances, the general rule of keeping the g-pawn on the second or third rank during the opening is good advice.

The h-Pawn

Similarly, the h-pawn should stay at home for the first part of the game, unless it actually attacks an enemy piece and gains time. Sometimes it can be advanced if the enemy has already played the h-pawn forward two squares. This is seen in the Classical Variation of the Caro-Kann Defense and the Soltis Variation of the Yugoslav Attack in the Sicilian Dragon.

Let's now move on to the openings themselves.

4. THE OPEN GAMES

The term Open Game refers to openings which begin 1.e4 e5. This classical Black response is designed to discourage White from playing an early d4. Indeed, in those cases where White chooses to attempt to create the ideal pawn center with pawns at e4 and d4, the d4 is quickly captured, and White has little hope of obtaining a serious advantage. This is seen in such openings as the **Scotch Game** and **Göring Gambit**.

Instead, White usually chooses to develop the kingside forces, normally with 2.Nf3 and 3.Bb5 **Spanish Game** or **Ruy Lopez**, or 3.Bc4 **Italian Game**, also known as the Giuoco Piano followed by castling. The play often starts out slowly, but attacks can develop quickly, especially if Black does not find a safe haven for the king on one of the flanks.

We will start our examination with miscellaneous Open Games. The focus of our attention will be on the **Bishop's Opening** (1.e4 e5; 2.Bc4) and **Vienna Game** (1.e4 e5; 2.Nc3) where White rapidly deploys a minor piece on the queenside. Then we will examine some minor lines which are not as frequently encountered in tournament play, but which are seen more often in correspondence and amateur games. These include the **Latvian** and **Elephant Gambits** and the venerable **Philidor Defense** (1.e4 e5; 2.Nf3 d6).

Then we will move on to the romantic **King's Gambit** (1.e4 e5; 2.f4), which has been so exhaustively analyzed that it is becoming very difficult to inject new life into the old war-horse. There are many exciting sacrifices for both sides, but they are now well known and are rarely effective in professional circles.

The **Russian Defense** (1.e4 e5; 2.Nf3 Nf6) has a justifiable reputation as a boring opening, with a great deal of symmetry which makes it hard for either side to gain much of an advantage.

Next up is the **Scotch Game and Gambit** (1.e4 e5; 2.Nf3 Nc6; 3.d4 exd4) which resolves the situation in the center early in the game. The former, where White recaptures immediately with 4.Nxd4, tends to lead to sterile positions with at best a minuscule spatial advantage for White. The gambit approach with 4.Bc4, delaying the recapture of the pawn, is much more exciting, but with careful play Black can blunt White's initiative and obtain a good game.

The **Three Knights** (1.e4 e5; 2.Nf3 Nc6; 3.Nc3) and **Four Knights** (1.e4 e5; 2.Nf3 Nc6; 3.Nc3 Nf6) are usually adopted only to escape the paths of main line theory and are unambitious, but can present difficulties to an unprepared player of the Black side.

The **Italian Game** (1.e4 e5; 2.Nf3 Nc6; 3.Bc4) often involves a lot of subtle maneuvering, and short games are now the exception, rather than the commonplace result seen in the 19th century. Black needs to take care to guard the f7-square, but otherwise there are few difficulties to face.

Finally, we reach the **Spanish Game** (1.e4 e5; 2.Nf3 Nc6; 3.Bb5), one of the loftiest of the chess openings. This fertile territory has produced some of the greatest masterpieces of the Royal Game. Both sides retain their central pawns and pieces throughout the opening and sometimes no material is exchanged until after the first two dozen moves have been played.

MISCELLANEOUS OPEN GAMES

Although the openings in this section are not as popular as the Spanish Game, Italian Game, or even the King's Gambit it is nevertheless quite normal to see them in use at both professional and amateur levels of play.

One of the main motivations for using these rarer openings is the relative ease with which they can be learned. Less popular openings tend to acquire theory more slowly. Openings such as the Bishop's Opening and Vienna game are positionally sound and offer White some chances for an advantage, though with correct play Black should be able to equalize.

In general, however, White does not choose this sort of opening in order to achieve a substantial advantage early in the game. Any confrontation is postponed until the middlegame and patience is required on the part of both players.

BISHOP'S OPENING

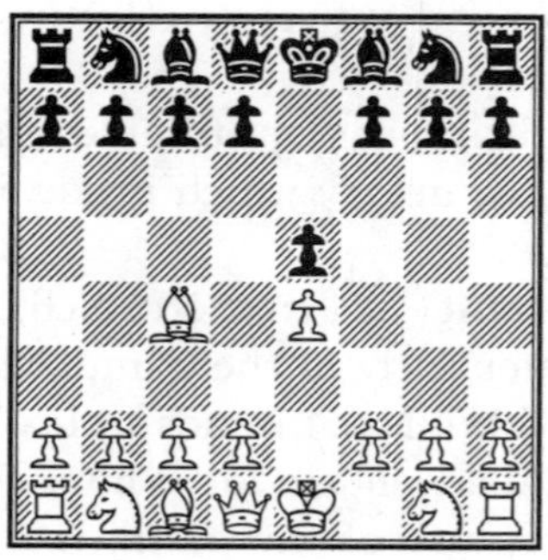

1.e4 **e5**
2.Bc4

The **Bishop's Opening** is a sound developing sequence which has many transpositional possibilities. It can lead to the Italian Game, King's Gambit, and Vienna Game, depending on next few moves. There are also some independent lines which involve an early d4 by White. In the 1980s it was sometimes favored by players seeking to avoid the massive amount of theory involved in the Spanish and Italian Games, but now the Bishop's Opening has developed into a major opening which requires almost as much study as the others. There is nothing wrong with this plan, which will often transpose to one of the other Open Games.

Another option for White is to mix the deployment of the bishop with a knight at c3, establishing a firm grip in the center. Some of the paths are fascinating, such as Prince Urusoff's gambit. The prince indulged his analytical fantasies in the mid–19th century. White sacrifices a pawn for rapid development, but loses control of the center at the same time. There is no clear consensus regarding Black's best plan of defense, but the Urusoff Gambit is nevertheless considered a bit suspect and is rarely encountered in professional tournaments.

(1) SPIELMANN - PRZEPIORKA [C23]
German Championship, 1906

1.e4 e5; 2.Bc4 Bc5. This is the Boi Variation, but it never has reached manhood, being universally condemned for most of its existence, which is a long one! **3.d3.** A quiet plan. Spielmann tried the gambit plan 3.b4!? against Duras, and often played an immediate 3.Nc3, though that simply transposes to positions we will look at below. 3.Nf3 Nc6; 4.c3 reached a Classical Variation of the Italian Game in Scovara - Boi, Madrid 1575, the first known game with 2...Bc5. Yet another plan is 3.c3, seen in Roca-Lorena, Greenhills 1996, where after 3...Nf6; 4.d4 exd4; 5.cxd4 Bb4+; 6.Bd2 Bxd2+; 7.Nxd2 White had complete control of the center.

3...d6. 3...c6 is considered correct, in order to achieve an early ...d5. 3...Nc6 or 3...Nf6 can lead to the Italian Game. **4.Nc3 Nc6.** Black can also play ...c6, but now that the pawn is at d6, a further advance to d5 will involve a loss of time. **5.Na4.**

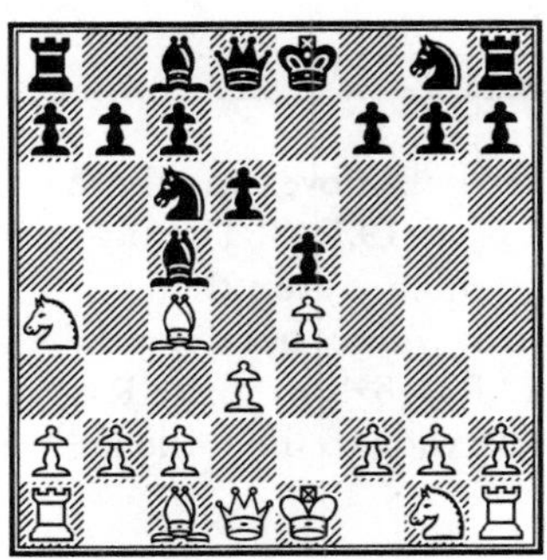

White wastes a tempo in order to eliminate the enemy cleric and gain the long-term advantage of the bishop pair. **5...Bb6.** Against Olland, Spielmann was permitted to capture at c5 after 5...Nf6. **6.Nxb6 axb6; 7.f4!** If you want to attack, you need open lines! **7...Nf6; 8.Nf3 Bg4; 9.c3!** This move keeps the enemy knight out of d4, but has two other advantages. It is now possible for the White queen to be developed at b3, and it also enables a later advance of the d-pawn. **9...d5.** Black takes action in the center before castling, which is acceptable in the Open Games, especially when White has not castled. **10.exd5 Nxd5; 11.h3 Bxf3; 12.Qxf3 Nxf4; 13.Bxf4 exf4; 14.0-0 0-0; 15.Qxf4.**

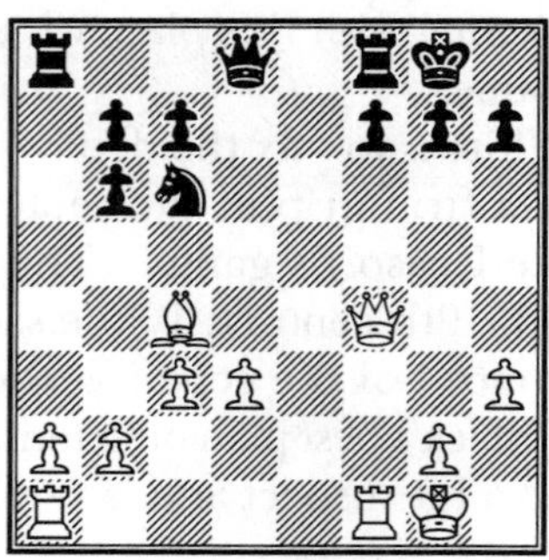

After a series of exchanges and liquidation of the center pawns, White has emerged with a clear advantage because of the queenside pawn majority and bishop versus knight, combined with pressure at the ever-vulnerable f7-square. **15...Qd7.** Black now has dealt with pressure at f7. Because Black will be able to add additional defenders with ...Nd8, and, or ...Re8-e7, White will not be able to win by direct means. **16.d4 Rae8; 17.Rf3 Re7; 18.Raf1 Nd8.**

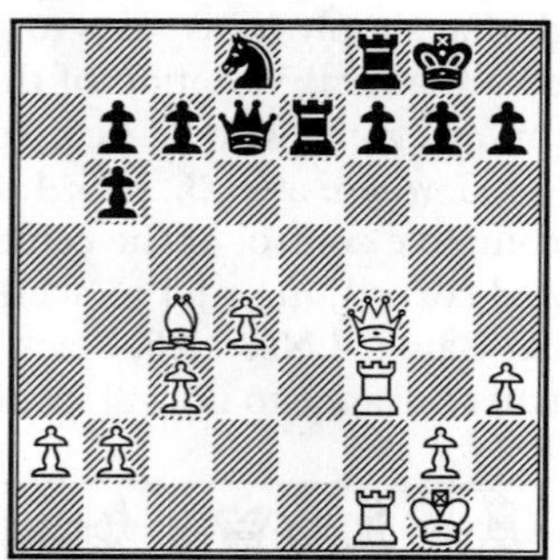

Both sides have played obvious moves and there is no way for White to add any more pressure at f7. So what now? **19.Rg3!** The threat is Qh6. **19...g6; 20.Qh6 Qc6.** Black must now watch the g6-square, even though that pawn seems to be strongly defended. Note that the pawn at f7 does not defend the g-pawn, because it is pinned. 20...c6? loses to 21.Rf6 b5; 22.Rfxg6+!! hxg6; 23.Rxg6#. **21.Bb3 Rfe8; 22.Rf4.** Now White threatens to transfer the rook to the h-file and work on h7. **22...Re4.**

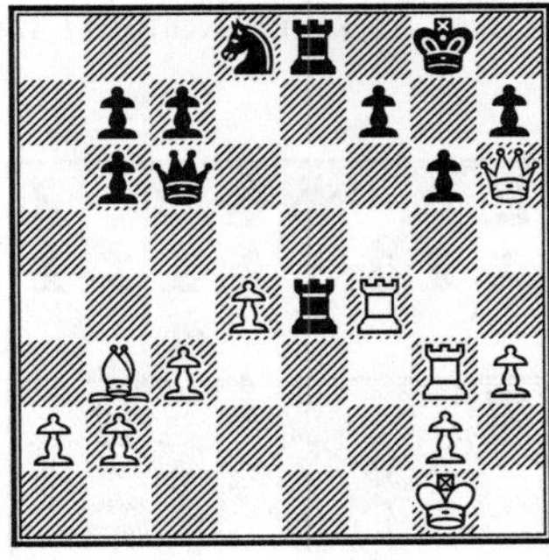

So far this has been a textbook example of a good attack. Now comes the flashy finish! **23.Bxf7+!! Nxf7; 24.Rxf7 Kxf7; 25.Qxh7+ Kf8; 26.Rf3+** and there is no stopping checkmate. **White won.**

(2) ALEKHINE - RETHY [C28]

Munich, 1941

1.e4 e5; 2.Bc4 Nf6; 3.d3 Nc6; 4.Nc3 Be7.

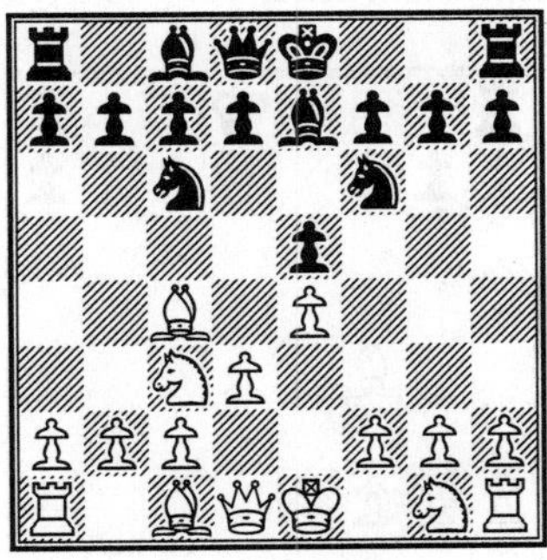

In this case we see a hybrid between the Vienna Game and the Bishop's Opening, an approach very popular with classical masters. Both sides are playing it safe, but now White opens up the game.

4...Na5; 5.Nge2 Nxc4; 6.dxc4 Bc5 is an interesting plan, seen in Kuijf-Garcia, Wijk aan Zee 1996. 4...d6; 5.f4 Na5 seems less effective, however. 6.f5 Nxc4; 7.dxc4 g6; 8.g4 Bd7; 9.Qf3 (9.Bg5 comes into consideration. 9.g5 Nxe4; 10.Nxe4 gxf5; 11.Ng3 f4; 12.Ne4 Bc6 may give Black enough for the piece.) 9...gxf5 10.gxf5 Bc6; 11.Nh3 Rg8; 12.Nf2 a6; 13.Be3 b5 led to some fascinating complications after 14.0-0-0 bxc4; 15.Qe2 Qb8; 16.Qxc4 Qb7; 17.Rhg1! Rxg1; 18.Rxg1 Rb8.

White ignored the threat at b2 and boldly continued 19.Ng4!? Nd7; 20.Nh6. After 20...Qxb2+; 21.Kd2 Qb4 the initiative swayed back and forth: 22.Qxf7+ Kd8; 23.Rb1 Qxc3+; 24.Kxc3 Rxb1 but here the rook and bishop were no match for the queen and White went on to win: 25.Ng4 d5; 26.exd5 Bb4+; 27.Kd3 Bxd5; 28.Qxd5 Rd1+; 29.Ke4, Morovic-Yurtayev, Yerevan Olympiad 1996.

5.f4 d6; 6.Nf3 Bg4; 7.0-0 Nd4? Black is too impressed by the pin on the knight at f3. Simply castling would have been wiser. Given that a World Champion was playing White, one would have thought Black might have shown a little more respect. If this move was effective, Alekhine wouldn't have allowed it. **8.fxe5 Bxf3; 9.gxf3 dxe5.**

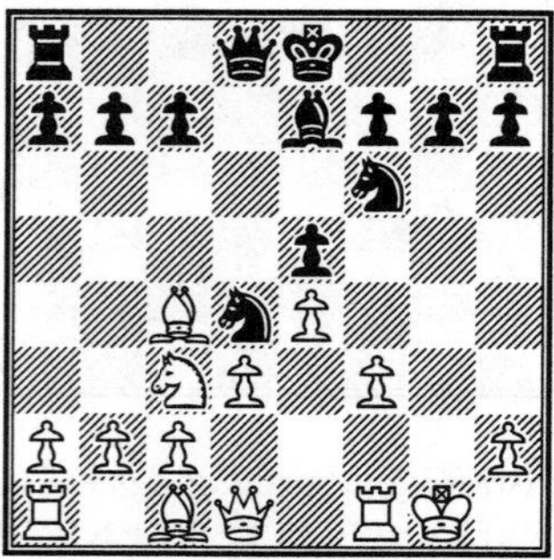

At first it looks as though Black's plan has succeeded, since the White king looks vulnerable. But none of Black's pieces are in a position to exploit it, and so the advantage of the bishop pair is significant. Alekhine now renews the pressure on the center and threatens to open up some lines in the center while Black's king has not yet found shelter. **10.f4! Bd6; 11.Be3 Nc6; 12.d4!** The pressure is unrelenting. White is clearly better. **12...exd4; 13.Bxd4 Nxd4; 14.Qxd4 Qe7.**

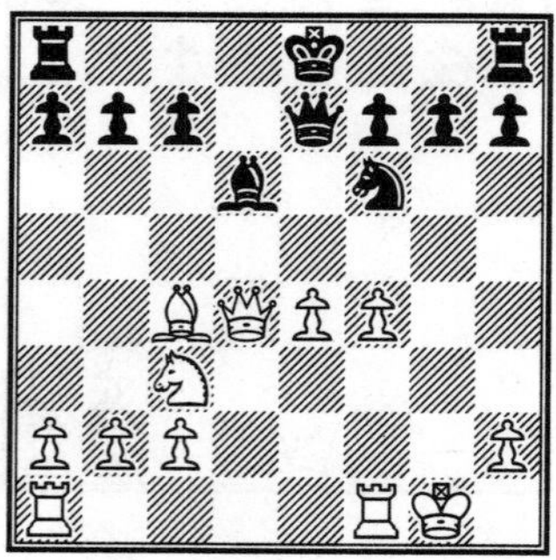

Black has survived immediate destruction and is close to castling. There is a serious threat of ...Bc5. For all that, however, White owns the center and threatens a nasty fork at e5. **15.Kh1 Bc5; 16.Qd3 Rd8; 17.Qe2.** After a few retreats, White is ready to bounce back. Meanwhile, Black is getting nervous. With queenside castling no longer an option, and an open g-file discouraging kingside castling, Black tries a reckless and wrongheaded attack. **17...h5?** Hoping to sink the knight at g4 and cause some damage in concert with the bishop at c5. **18.Rf3! Bd4; 19.e5 Bxc3; 20.bxc3.**

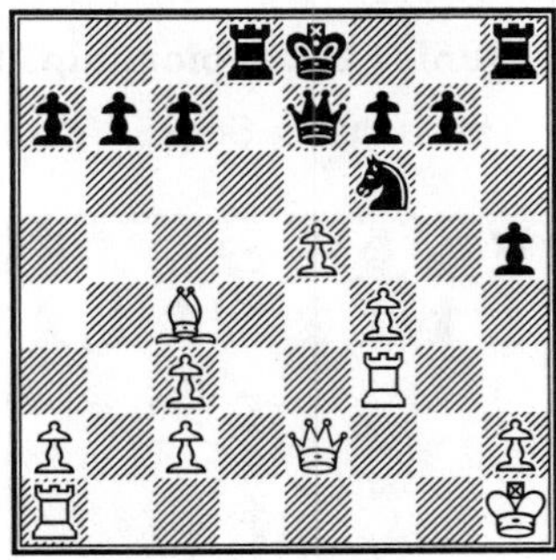

White's pawn structure is a mess, but that does not matter. Black's pieces have no coordination, and things aren't going to get any better. **20...Nd5; 21.Rg1 Kf8; 22.f5!** The White pawns control all the important squares. **22...f6.** This prevents the further advance of the f-pawn, but effectively locks the rook at h8 out of the game. **23.e6.**

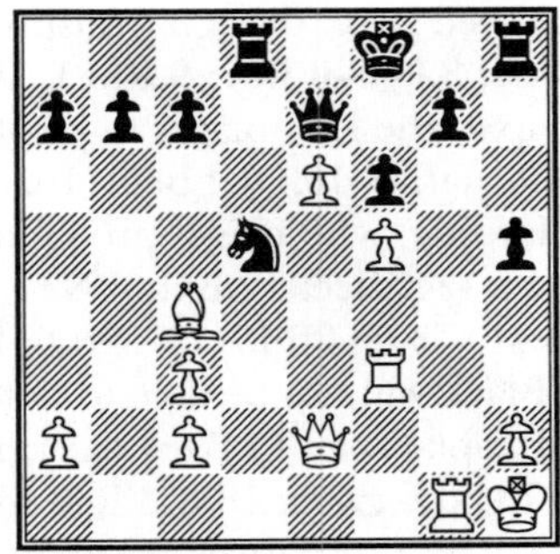

Black must have felt like a boxer awaiting the knockout punch, knowing it is just a matter of time before his head hits the canvas. **23...h4; 24.Qe4 c6; 25.Rd1 g5; 26.Rfd3!** The en passant capture would have been irrelevant. **26...Kg7; 27.Bxd5 cxd5; 28.Rxd5 Rxd5; 29.Qxd5.** Now suddenly the pawn structure favors White, decisively. **29...Rc8; 30.Qd7 Re8; 31.Qa4 Rd8; 32.Rxd8.** Black resigned. If the rook is captured, then Qd7+ ends it all. **White won.**

(3) TIMOSCHENKO - KARPOV [C24]

Soviet Junior Championship, 1967

1.e4 e5; 2.Bc4 Nf6; 3.d4. This is Prince Sergei Urusoff's gambit. **3...exd4; 4.Nf3.**

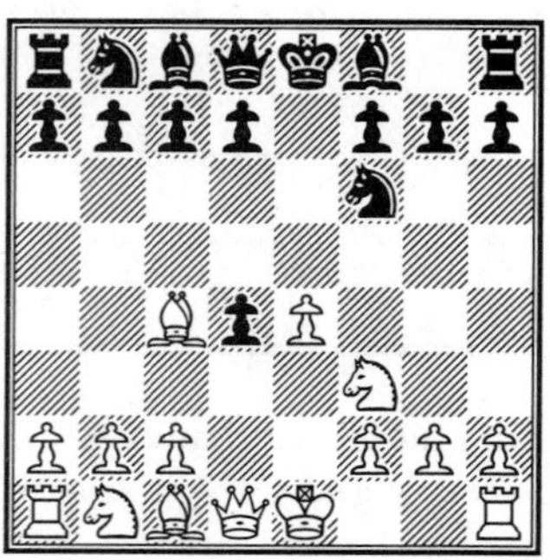

4...Nxe4. This is the critical move. Black can avoid the complications which follow by choosing 4...Nc6, transposing to the Two Knight's Defense. **5.Qxd4 Nf6; 6.Bg5 c6**. 6...Be7 is usually played here, though transpositions are possible, as seen in the present game. **7.Nc3 d5; 8.0–0–0 Be7; 9.Rhe1.** White is well mobilized, but Black has material and it is up to the first player to justify the investment. **9...Be6.**

9...0–0 is a reasonable alternative. 10.Qh4 Be6! (10...Bf5 11.Nd4 Bg6; 12.Bd3 h6 is evaluated as unclear by Harding, who cites Caro-Janowski, Berlin 1897.) 11.Bd3 h6 allows White to carry out a sacrifice: 12.Bxh6! Ne4 (12...gxh6; 13.Qxh6 Nbd7; 14.Ng5 leaves Black defenseless.) 13.Qf4 Bd6 (13...gxh6; 14.Bxe4 dxe4; 15.Nxe4 Qe8; 16.Nf6+ Bxf6; 17.Qxf6 and Black will not be able to defend the king.) 14.Qe3 Bc5; 15.Nd4 Qf6 (15...gxh6 is still unplayable: 16.Bxe4 dxe4; 17.Nxe4 Qb6; 18.Nf6+ Kh8; 19.Qxh6#) 16.Bxe4 Qxh6; 17.Qxh6 gxh6; 18.Bf3 Re8 with level chances.

10.Qh4 Nbd7; 11.Bd3 c5. The alternatives are no better. 11...Qa5; 12.Nd4 0–0–0; 13.Nxe6 fxe6; 14.Rxe6 Bb4; 15.Ne2! guarantees an advantage for White. 15...h6 (15...Qxa2?; 16.Qxb4 Qa1+; 17.Kd2 and White wins.) 16.Bxf6 Nxf6; 17.Kb1 (17.Bf5 also looks good.) 17...Bd6; 18.Nd4 with a clear advantage for White Estrin-Klaman, USSR 1946. 11...Nc5; 12.Nd4 Nfd7; 13.Bxe7 Qxe7; 14.Qxe7+ Kxe7; 15.f4 with a clear advantage for White in Neishtadt-Volkevich, Moscow Championship 1958. The game saw this instantiated in the form of a favorable ending after 15...Nxd3+; 16.Rxd3 g6; 17.g4 Nc5; 18.Rde3 Kd6; 19.b4! Ne4; 20.Nxe4+ dxe4; 21.Nxe6 fxe6; 22.Rxe4.

12.Ne5 Nxe5; 13.Rxe5. White has tremendous pressure on the center, and Black never gets enough time to extricate his king from its exposed position. **13...d4; 14.f4 Nd7.** 14...dxc3 15.Bb5+ Bd7; 16.Bxf6 and White wins. **15.Bb5 Bxg5; 16.fxg5 Qc7.** 16...dxc3 loses to 17.Bxd7+ Kf8; 18.Rxe6! fxe6; 19.Qf4+ Ke7; 20.Qd6+ Kf7; 21.Qxe6+ Kf8; 22.Rf1+ and Black can give up. **17.Bxd7+ Kxd7.**

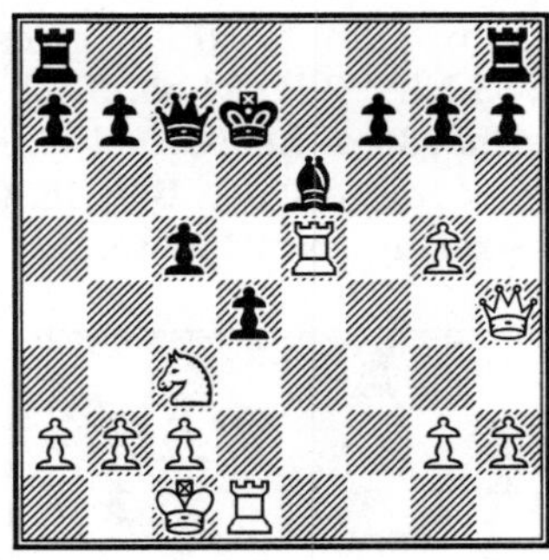

18.Qe4 Qc6? 18...b6 would have been better, but White retains the advantage on 19.Nb5 Qc6; 20.Nxd4! for example: 20...cxd4; 21.Rxd4+ Kc7; 22.Rxe6! fxe6; 23.Rc4 Qxc4; 24.Qxc4+ Kd7; 25.Qd4+ and White should win the endgame. 18...Rad8! was relatively best, for example 19.Nd5 Qd6; 20.c3 Kc8 attacking the knight at d5. 21.Nf4 Bxa2; 22.cxd4 cxd4; 23.Ra5 Qc7+; 24.Qc2 Bb3!; 25.Qxc7+ Kxc7; 26.Rd3 Be6; 27.Rxa7 leaves White with some pressure for the pawn. **19.Rxc5!**

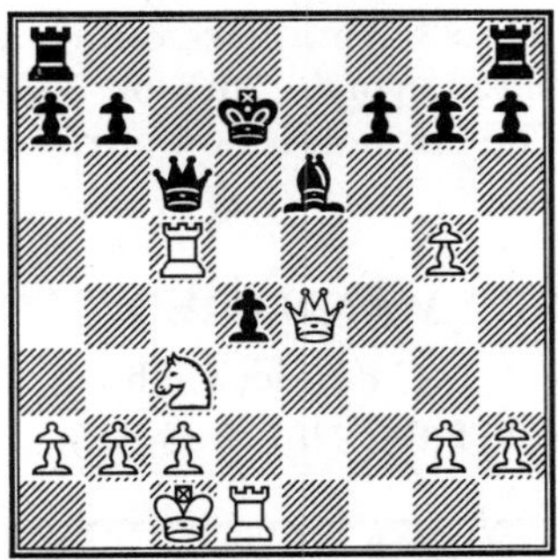

This fine move leads to a winning position for White. **19...Qxe4.** 19...Qxc5 loses to 20.Qxb7+ Qc7; 21.Rxd4+. **20.Nxe4 Rhc8.** Black tries to eliminate the most active enemy piece, after which he can chase the knight from its outpost at e4. The d-pawn was doomed in any event. **21.Rxd4+ Ke7; 22.a4! b6; 23.Rxc8 Rxc8; 24.Kd2!** Centralizing the king is an important component of White's endgame strategy. **24...Bf5; 25.c4 Rc6; 26.Ng3 Be6; 27.Kc3 Rc5; 28.h4.**

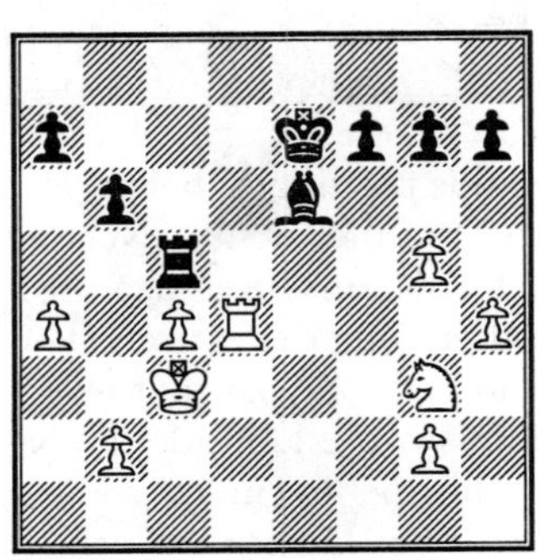

28...h6; 29.b4 Rc8; 30.Ne4! f5. 30...hxg5 31.Nxg5! gives White a potentially passed h-pawn. **31.Nf2!?** 31.gxf6+ gxf6; 32.Nf2 h5 gives Black more play on the g-file. **31...hxg5; 32.hxg5 Rh8; 33.Nh3! Bd7; 34.b5.** Black's bishop now seems to have little to do. **34...Rh5; 35.Kb4 Rh8; 36.a5 Be6; 37.a6!** White wants to keep all the files closed - except the one his rook controls! **37...Bf7; 38.Kc3 g6; 39.Kb4 Rc8; 40.Nf4 Rc5; 41.Nd3 Rc8.** The most straightforward move.

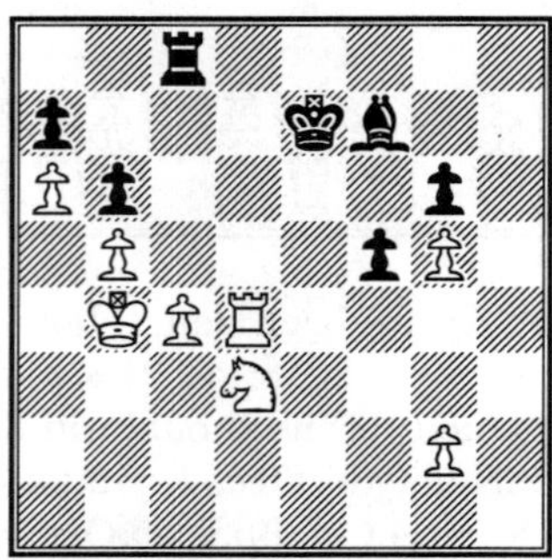

42.c5 bxc5+; 43.Nxc5 Be8; 44.Rd1 Rc7; 45.g3 Rc8; 46.Re1+ Kd8; 47.Nb7+ Kd7; 48.Re3 Bf7; 49.Rd3+ Ke7; 50.Rc3. Now Black cannot avoid the exchange of rooks without allowing a deadly infiltration of the 7th rank. **50...Rxc3; 51.Kxc3 Bd5; 52.Kd4! Bg2; 53.Kc5 Bf1; 54.Na5.** The position is now a trivial win, since the a-pawn falls after Nc6. **White won.**

(4) SPIELMANN - REGGIO [C26]

Ostende, 1906

1.e4 e5; 2.Bc4 Nf6; 3.d3 Bc5; 4.Nc3.

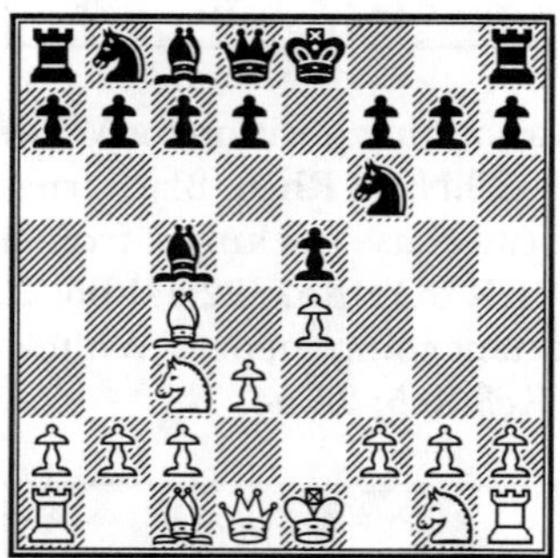

It is hard to characterize this position as belonging to any single opening, since it contains moves characteristic of the Vienna (Nc3) and Italian (Bc4) games. This was one of Spielmann's pet formations, used against many different move orders. **4...d6; 5.f4.** Spielmann also used 5.Bg5 effectively. The text is more in the spirit of the King's Gambit. White can keep the pawn at f4, to maintain pressure at e5, or advance it with evil intentions on the kingside. **5...Ng4.** It is generally unwise to move the same piece twice in the opening unless some specific goal can be achieved. Here the attack against f2 is trivial. Instead, Black should just play 5...Nc6 as in

Lehtinen-Sorsa, Tampere 1996. **6.f5 Qh4+ 7.g3 Qh5; 8.h3 Bxg1; 9.Qxg4 Qxg4; 10.hxg4.**

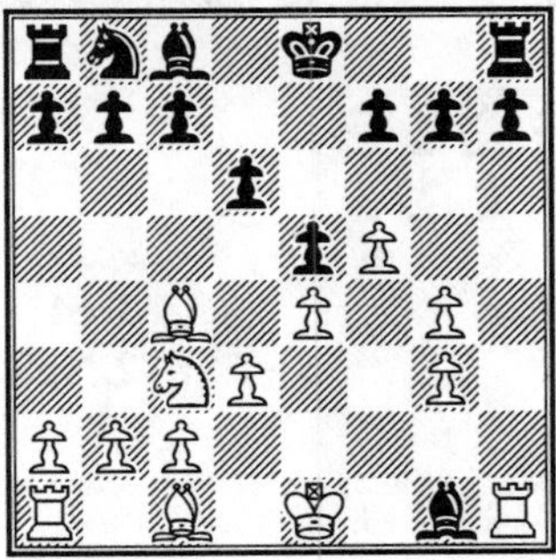

White's advantages are clear: better bishops, a powerful kingside, and more advanced development. **10...Bb6; 11.g5 Nc6; 12.g6!** Deftly exploiting the pin on the h-file. **12...fxg6; 13.fxg6 h6.**

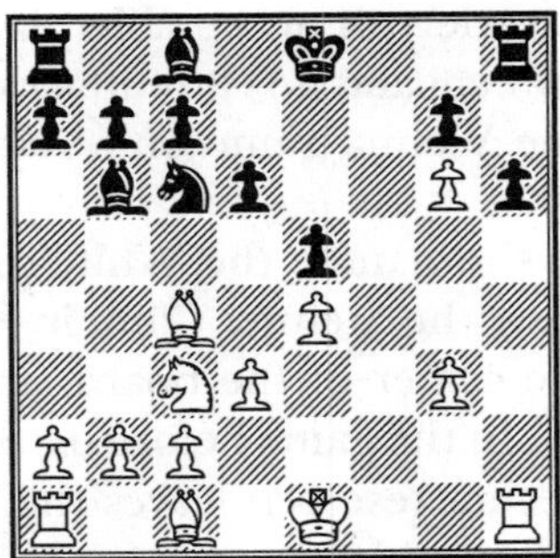

Now the stage is set. If only the g-pawn could move forward... **14.Rxh6!! Rxh6; 15.Bxh6 Ne7.** 15...gxh6 16.g7 and the pawn queens. **16.Bf7+ Kf8; 17.Bg5.** Although material is almost equal, the overwhelming kingside forces wrap this game up quickly. **17...Bg4; 18.Kd2 Bh5.** To block the h-file, but there is another highway to victory. **19.Rf1.** 19.g4 would have been quicker. **19...c6; 20.g4.** Black resigned, because the bishop cannot capture either pawn. 20...Bxg4 (20...Nxg6; 21.Bxg6+ Kg8; 22.gxh5) **21.Rh1. White won.**

VIENNA GAME

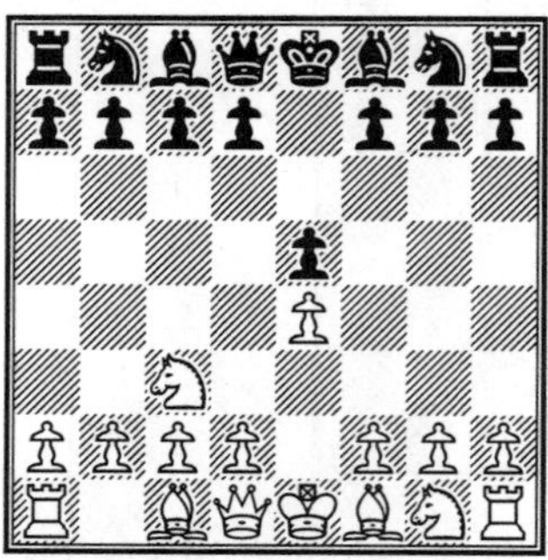

1.e4 e5
2.Nc3

The **Vienna Game** is not particularly ambitious. White develops the knight to c3 in order to control the important d5 square as well as to defend the pawn at e4. Black has a variety of acceptable plans. In general both sides will continue with development and no early attacks are common. At present, no leading player uses the Vienna game on a regular basis, but it is often seen in amateur games.

There are several ways to handle the White pieces. The f-pawn can be offered as a gambit. This is the Steinitz Gambit. Steinitz was not afraid of bringing his king into the center of the board, and this fearless approach attracted a lot of attention. In the game before us, Steinitz did not manage to find the best plan, but recent research leaves the question of the opening entirely unclear. Black will be able to aim a lot of forces at the White king, but they will all be driven back, eventually.

Another approach is a solid setup with Bc4 and d3 can be used to set the stage for a later attack. Sometimes White prefers to fianchetto a bishop at g2. Both sides normally castle on the kingside.

(5) STEINITZ - LIVERPOOL CHESS CLUB [C25]

Postal, 1899

1.e4 e5; 2.Nc3 Nc6; 3.f4 exf4; 4.d4.

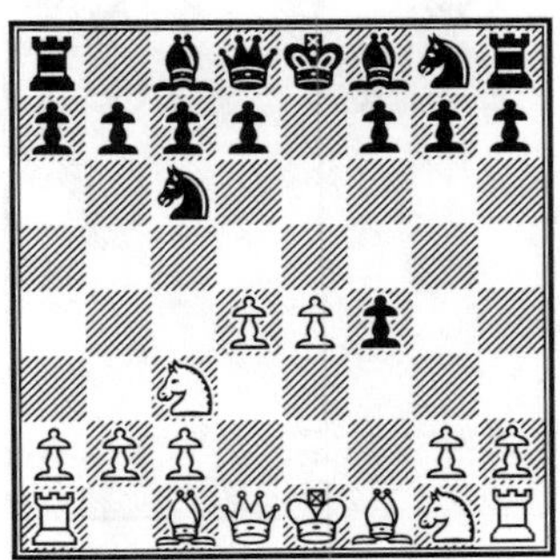

4...Qh4+; 5.Ke2 d5. 5...d6; 6.Nf3 Bg4; 7.Bxf4 is best met by 7...f5! and now 8.Be3 fxe4; 9.Nxe4 Be7; 10.Kd3! Qh5; 11.Kd2! gets the White king to safety. Play might continue 11...Nf6; 12.Nf2 Qa5+; 13.c3 Bf5; 14.Bd3 Bxd3; 15.Kxd3 Qf5+; 16.Kd2 Nd5; 17.Re1 Nxe3; 18.Rxe3 Na5 with massive complications. Further investigation is still required, even after almost a century!

5...b6 is popular now, for example 6.Nb5 Ba6; 7.a4 0-0-0; 8.Nf3 Qg4; 9.Kf2 Bb7; 10.Bd3 a6; 11.Nc3 Nf6; 12.Re1 g5; 13.e5 Nxd4; 14.Bxa6 Bxa6; 15.Nxd4 Qh4+; 16.Kg1 Ng4; 17.h3 Bc5; 18.hxg4 Bxd4+; 19.Qxd4 Qxe1+; 20.Kh2 h5 and Black won in Gavrilov-Potapov, Perm 1997.

6.exd5. 6.Nxd5 Bg4+; 7.Nf3 f5; 8.Kd2 Bxf3 (8...Qd8 seems best to me, but has not been tested in the tournament arena. I cannot find a convincing continuation for White. 9.Bd3 may be playable, for example 9...Nxd4; 10.Re1 Ne7; 11.c3 fxe4; 12.Bxe4 c6; 13.Nf6+! gxf6; 14.cxd4 and Black has to find some shelter for the king, which is no better off than his White counterpart.) 9.Qxf3 Qf2+; 10.Qe2 Qxd4+ and here White can choose either 11.Qd3 or 11.Ke1 with an interesting position which deserves practical tests. **6...Bg4+; 7.Nf3 0-0-0; 8.dxc6 Bc5!**

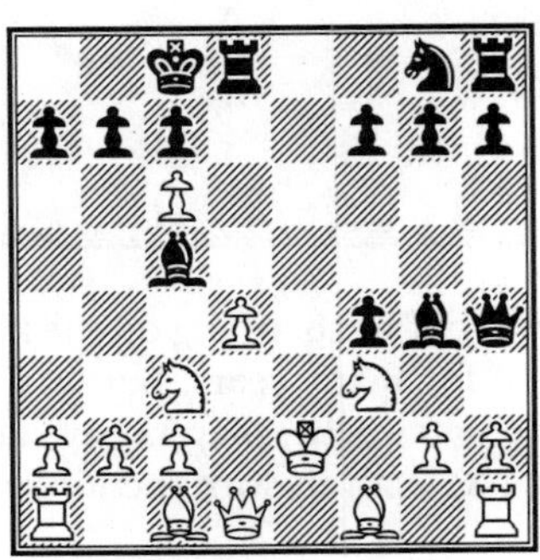

A delightfully messy position has arisen, which is typical of the line as a whole. **9.Qe1.** This move was recommended by l'Hermet in the 1880s, and the complications have yet to be worked out. 9.cxb7+ Kb8; 10.Qe1 transposes to the main line. **9...Qh5** if 9...Re8+; 10.Kd2 Rxel; 11.Nxh4 when white emerges a piece up. **10.cxb7+**

Kb8; 11.Kd1? 11.Kd2 is correct, for example 11...Bxf3; 12.gxf3 Bxd4; 13.Bd3 Qxf3; 14.Qf1 and what does Black do now? **11...Bxd4! 12.Bd2 Bxc3; 13.bxc3 Bxf3+; 14.gxf3 Qxf3+; 15.Be2 Qxc3.**

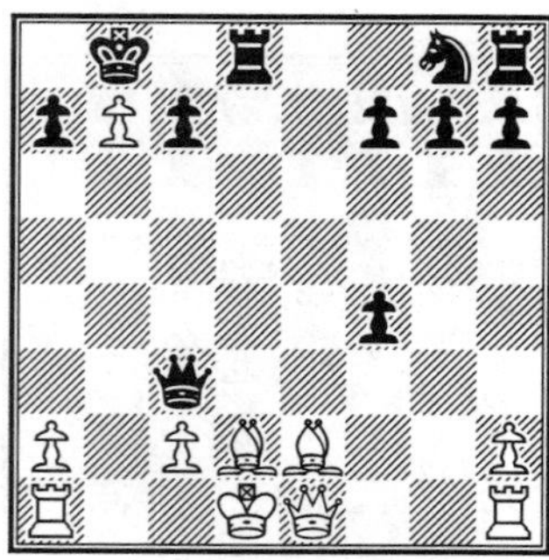

Black is still down a piece, but the White king cannot escape, and Black's forces mobilize quickly. **16.Rb1 Nf6; 17.Bd3 Qc6; 18.Rg1 Rhe8; 19.Qf2 Nd5; 20.Qd4.** Now the final assault begins. **20...Ne3+; 21.Bxe3 fxe3; 22.Qxg7 f5; 23.Qg2 Qc3; 24.Ke2 f4; 25.Rbe1.** The members of the Liverpool club finish the game with style and efficiency. **25...f3+; 26.Kxf3 Rf8+; 27.Kg4 Qg7+; 28.Kh4 Qh6+; 29.Kg3 Qg5+; 30.Kh3 Qh5+; 31.Kg3 Rf6; 32.h4 Rg8+; 33.Kh3 Qxh4+; 34.Kxh4 Rh6#. Black won.**

(6) MIESES - BLACKBURNE [C26]

Dresden, 1892

1.e4 e5; 2.Nc3 Nf6; 3.g3.

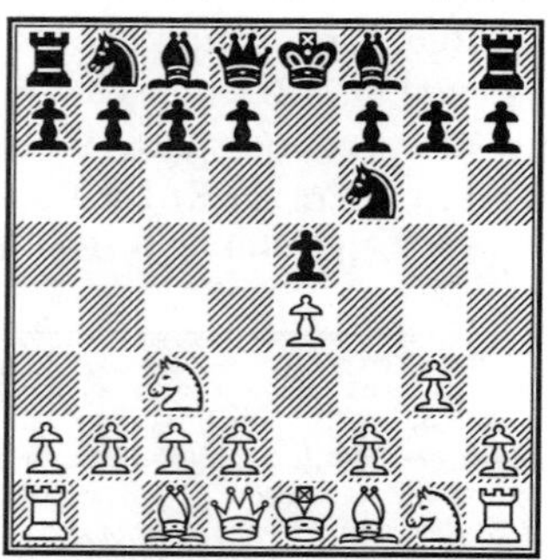

Mieses developed the idea of fianchettoing on the kingside in the Vienna Game. This plan remained dormant for many years, but was revived in the 1980s at the master level of chess. Still, no noteworthy players have taken it up on a regular basis. The bishop does not function effectively with the long diagonal blocked by White's own pawn at e4.

3...Nc6; 4.Bg2 d6; 5.d3 Be7; 6.Nge2 0-0; 7.h3 Ne8; 8.g4 g6; 9.Bh6 Ng7; 10.Qd2 Be6; 11.0-0-0 Nd4; 12.Nxd4 exd4; 13.Ne2 c5; 14.f4 f6; 15.f5 Bf7; 16.h4 a5. Black has a good position, with plenty of counterplay on the queenside. **17.Ng3?** White should have attended to the weak a-pawn by playing 17.Kb1. **17...Bxa2; 18.fxg6 hxg6; 19.h5 g5; 20.Nf5 Nxf5; 21.Bxf8 Ne3; 22.Bxe7 Qxe7; 23.Rdg1 a4; 24.Qe2 Be6; 25.Kd2**

Qd8; 26.Ra1 a3; 27.Rhb1. 27.bxa3 Qa5+! 28.Kc1 Qc3 leads to rapid ruin for White. **27...a2; 28.Rg1 Qb6; 29.Kc1 c4; 30.dxc4 Nxc4; 31.b3 d3; 32.cxd3.** 32.Qf1 d2+ 33.Kd1 Ne3+ also wins. **32...Qxg1+; 33.Bf1 Bxg4; 34.Qe1 Qd4. White won.**

(7) WYBE - BRYSON [C27]

Postal, 1985

1.e4 e5; 2.Nc3 Nf6; 3.Bc4 Nxe4.

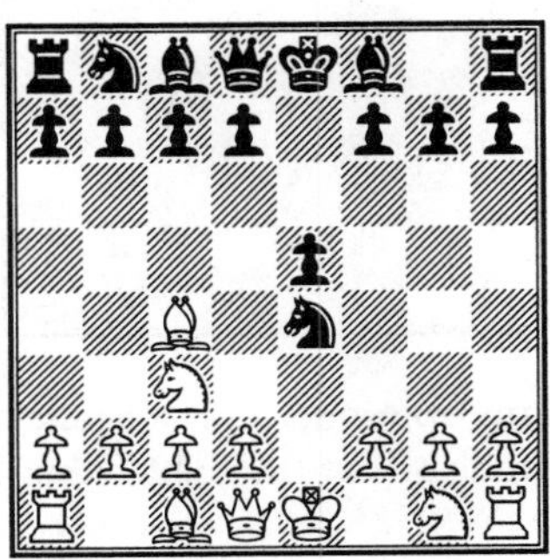

This variation of the **Vienna Game** can lead to very exciting play, and it gives rise to the Frankenstein-Dracula, or Monster Variation after **4.Qh5 Nd6; 5.Bb3 Nc6.** 5...Be7 takes all the fun out of the line, and leads to a somewhat boring equality. **6.Nb5.** White threatens to remove the knight at d6 which defends the pawn at f7, so the next few moves are forced. **6...g6; 7.Qf3 f5; 8.Qd5 Qe7; 9.Nxc7+ Kd8; 10.Nxa8.**

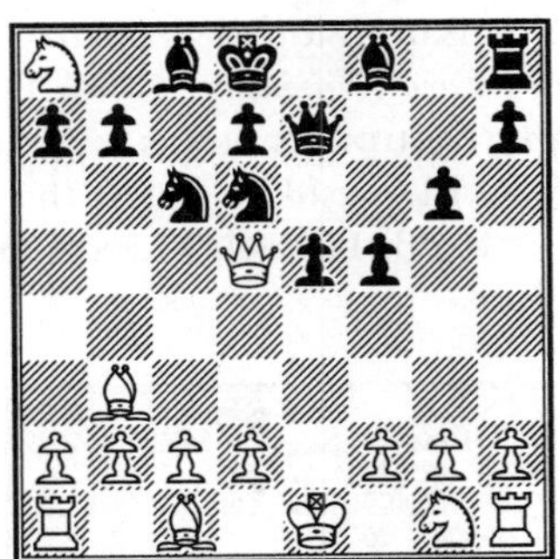

This is the start of the Frankenstein-Dracula Variation, which was named by Irish theoretician Tim Harding, who considered that this position might arise if the mad scientist and the Count sat down and played a game of chess. Indeed, the messy complications have not been solved even after decades of research, and the opening is seen far more frequently in correspondence play than over the board in normal competition. I have written a monograph on this opening, starting from the position in the diagram, and it is impossible to summarize all the complications of the position in a single game, so this is just a taste.

10...b6 is invariably played, and now White has eight different plans. Most authorities agree that advancing the d-pawn to d3 is best, to keep control of the important e4 square. **11.d3.** 11.Qf3 was tried by Weaver Adams, one of the early specialists in the variation. 11...Bb7; 12.Qh3 Nd4; 13.c3 Ne6; 14.Bxe6 Qxe6; 15.Ne2 Bg7; 16.0–

0 g5; 17.d4 g4; 18.Qh4+ Kc8; 19.dxe5 Bxe5; 20.Nf4 and White went on to win in Adams-Hesse, United States Championship 1948. **11...Bb7; 12.h4 f4.** 12...Kc8?!; 13.Bg5! gave White a strong attack in Adams-Jackson, Ventnor City 1943. **13.Qf3.**

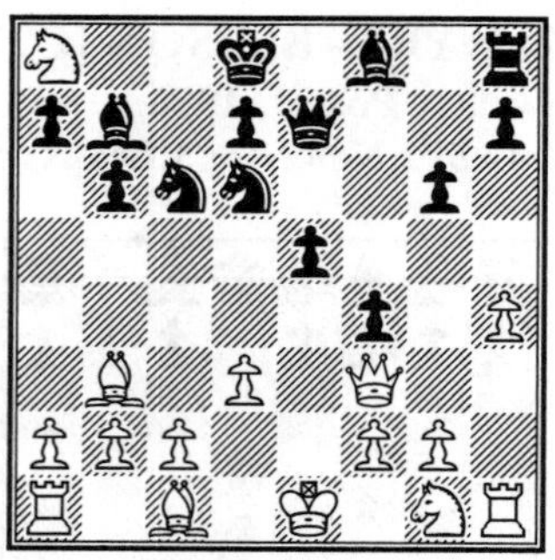

13...Bh6. 13...Nd4 is, in my opinion, a playable alternative. 14.Qg4 h5!; 15.Qxg6 Rh7 leads to very messy complications. 16.Nxb6 axb6; 17.Rh2 Rg7; 18.Qxh5 Bxg2; 19.c3 looks good at first.

I found the following an amazing line: 19...Be4!!; 20.cxd4 Rxg1+; 21.Kd2 Nf5!; 22.dxe4 Qb4+; 23.Kc2 Nxd4+; 24.Kd3 Nxb3; 25.Qxe5 Bg7!; 26.Qc7+ Kxc7; 27.Bxf4+ Be5!!; 28.Bxe5+ Kc6; 29.Rxg1 Qd2+; 30.Kc4 Na5#. I used some computers to analyze the complications, and none of the programs came close to finding this variation. It is something only a human fantasy can create!

Some authorities consider the position more promising for White after 16.Qg5 but I feel that after 16...Rg7; 17.Qxe7+; Bxe7; 18.c3 Bxg2; 19.Rh2 Bxa8; 20.cxd4 Rxg1+. Black has good compensation for the exchange. Details of the analysis can be found in *The Frankenstein-Dracula Variation*, Chess Enterprises 1997.

14.Qg4. 14.Bd2 is considered stronger. It was originally proposed by Soviet theoreticians Konstantinopolsky and Lepeshkin, but at the time they wrote their book no practical examples were at hand. **14...e4!; 15.Bxf4 exd3+; 16.Kf1 Bxf4; 17.Qxf4 Rf8; 18.Qg3 Ne4; 19.Qc7+ Ke8.**

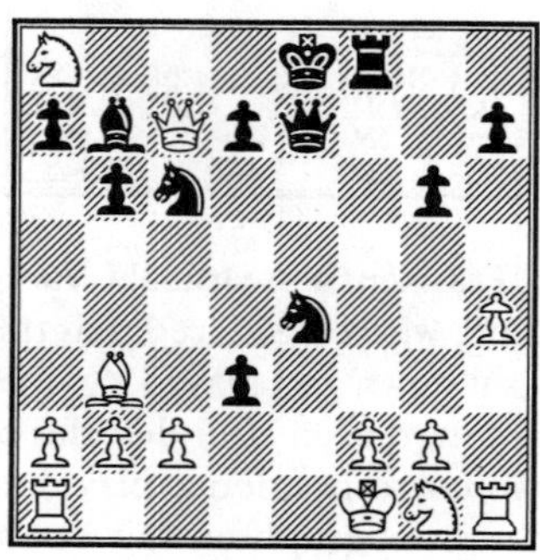

All this is forced, and was well-known from a famous game Ost-Hansen-Nunn, Teesside 1974. Wibe now improves on that game with **20.Nf3!** and after **20...Qc5; 21.Kg1 Rxf3!?** 21...Qxf2+; 22.Kh2 Rxf3; 23.Rhf1 Qxh4+; 24.Kg1 Rxf1+; 25.Rxf1 Ng3 comes into consideration. **22.Kh2.** 22.cxd3 Qxf2+; 23.Kh2 Rf4 wins for Black. 22.Rf1 Rxf2; 23.Kh2 Qh5; 24.Rxf2 Qxh4+; 25.Kg1 Qxf2+; 26.Kh2 d2 and the threat is ...Qh4+, followed by d1 Q+.

22...Qh5? Black missed a very complicated winning line here, after the stunning 22...d2!! and the analysis is complicated, but here is a sample: 23.Qxb7 (23.gxf3 Qxf2+; 24.Kh3 Qxf3+; 25.Kh2 Qe2+; 26.Kh3 Nf2+; 27.Kg3 Qe3+; 28.Kh2 Ng4+; 29.Kg2 Nd8+!; 30.Qxb7 Nxb7; 31.Rhf1 Qe2+; 32.Kh3 Ne3 and Black wins.) 23...Qd6+; 24.Kg1 d1Q+; 25.Rxd1 Qxd1+; 26.Kh2 Qd6+; 27.Kg1 Rxf2 and Black's attack is overpowering. **23.Rhf1 Nd4; 24.Rae1 d2; 25.Qxb7 dxe1Q; 26.Nc7+ Kf8; 27.Qc8+ Kg7; 28.Qxd7+ Kh6.**

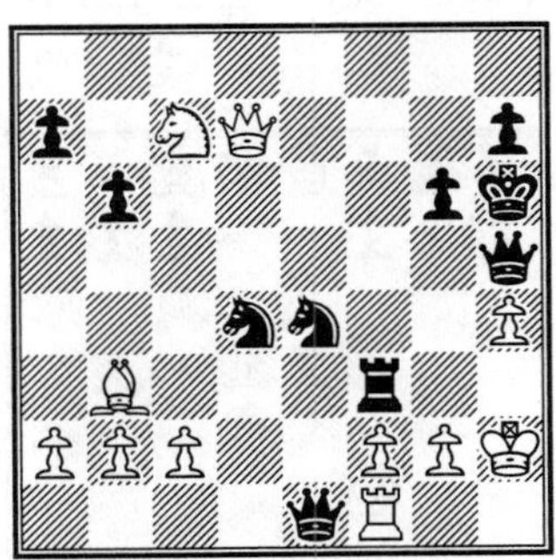

The Black king finds shelter all the way over on the kingside, and White's attack comes to a halt. Notice how effectively the Black knights control key squares. **29.Rxe1 Qxh4+; 30.Kg1 Qxf2+; 31.Kh2 Qh4+; 32.Kg1 Rf1+!!** and White resigned because of 33.Rxf1 (33.Kxf1 Qh1#) **33...Ne2#. Black won.**

(8) SPIELMANN - FLAMBERG [C29]

Mannheim, 1914

1.e4 e5; 2.Nc3 Nf6; 3.f4 d5.

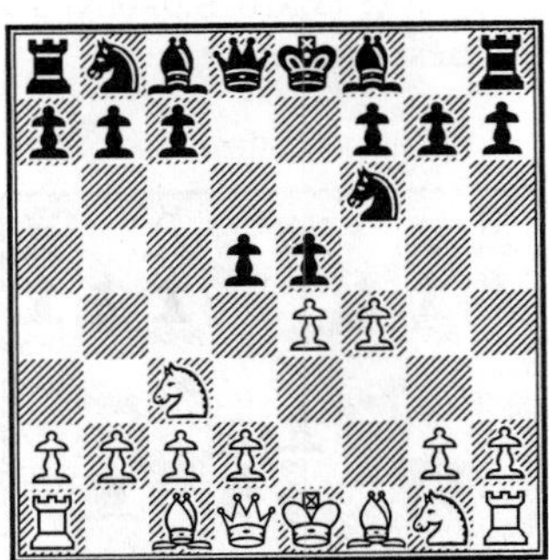

This is one of the main lines of the Vienna Game, though the entire opening has been semi-retired for decades and is rarely seen today. White clarifies the center too early in the game, and Black should be able to equalize without special difficulty.

3...exf4; 4.Nf3 leads to typical King's Gambit play, but Black's knight is not so well-posted at f6 (4.d4 Bb4; 5.Bd3 Qe7; 6.Qe2 Nc6; 7.e5 Nxd4; 8.exf6 Nxe2; 9.fxe7 Nxc3; 10.a3 Ba5; 11.Bd2 is 17th century analysis by Greco. Black can resign. 4.e5 Ng8; 5.Nf3 d6; 6.d4 dxe5; 7.dxe5 Qxd1+; 8.Kxd1 Bg4; 9.Nd5 Na6; 10.Bxa6 0–0–0 led to a win for Black in Zeigler-Schiller, Electronic Postal 1990.) 4...d6; 5.Bc4 Bg4; 6.d4 d5; 7.exd5 Bd6; 8.0–0 0–0; 9.Qd3 Nbd7; 10.Ng5 h6; 11.Nge4 g5; 12.Nxd6 cxd6; 13.g3 and the Black position fell apart: 13...fxg3; 14.Qxg3 Qb6; 15.Be3 Kg7; 16.h4 gxh4; 17.Qxh4 h5; 18.Qg5+ Kh8; 19.Rxf6 Nxf6; 20.Qxf6+ Kg8; 21.Bh6 and Black resigned in Alekhine-De Klerck, Tjepoe 1933.

4.fxe5. 4.d3 is the Steinitz Variation, now discredited because of such examples as 4...exf4; 5.e5 d4; 6.Nce2 Nd5; 7.Nxf4 Bb4+; 8.Kf2 Nc6; 9.Nf3 0–0; 10.Be2 Ne3!; 11.Bxe3 dxe3+; 12.Kxe3 Bc5+; 13.d4 Nxd4!!; 14.Nxd4 Qg5; 15.c3 Qxe5+; 16.Kf3 Rd8; 17.g3 Bxd4! and Black went on to win in Lombardy-Smyslov, Teesside 1975. **4...Nxe4; 5.Nf3.**

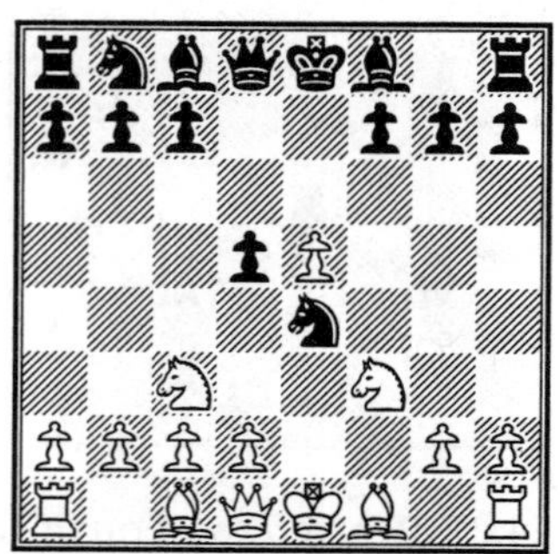

This is the most common move, though Spielmann also liked 5.Qf3. **5...Bg4.** This move is no longer considered playable, but at the time Black was still exploring many paths. 5...Nc6; 6.Bb5 is a powerful pin, and Black can no longer equalize. 6...Bb4; 7.Qe2 Bxc3; 8.dxc3 0–0; 9.Bf4 was good for White in Tarrasch-Schiffers, Hastings 1895. 5...Bc5; 6.d4 Bb4; 7.Qe2 Nxc3; 8.dxc3 0-0; 9.Bf4 a6; 10.Bxc6 bxc6; 11.0-0-0 Be6; 12.Nd4 Qd7; 13.Nxe6 Qxe6; 14.Rhe1 and White is better, with a firm grip on the center and stronger pawns, Turner-Morris, British Team Championship 1997. 5...Be7; 6.d4 0–0; 7.Bd3 f5; 8.exf6 Bxf6; 9.0–0 Nc6 was seen in several Spielmann games. 10.Ne2 is probably the best move.

6.Qe2.

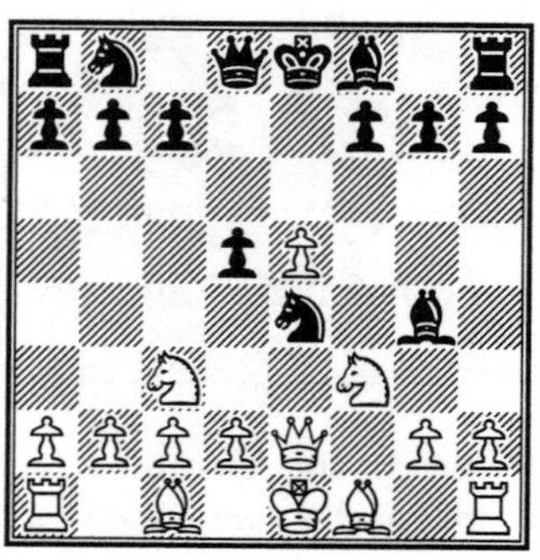

This position is more complex than it looks, and many plans have been tried for Black. Back in 1914, Spielmann's opponent tried an inferior one. **6...Nc5?!** 6...Nxc3 7.dxc3 is a little better for White. 6...Ng5; 7.d4 is possible with two branches:

A) 7...Ne6; 8.Be3 (8.h3 Bxf3; 9.Qxf3 Nxd4) 8...Nc6; 9.0–0–0 Bb4; 10.h3 Bxf3;

11.gxf3 Bxc3; 12.bxc3 Qe7; 13.Qb5! Qa3+; 14.Qb2 leaves White with powerful bishops against rather useless knights.

B) 7...Nxf3+; 8.gxf3 Be6; 9.Be3 Nc6; 10.Qg2 Qd7; 11.0–0–0 0–0–0; 12.Ne2 is better for White, according to Wienermeisters Konstantinopolsky & Lepeshkin. Translating their book was my introduction to this fascinating opening. 6...Nc6 7.Nxe4 dxe4 (7...Nd4; 8.Qd3 Bxf3; 9.Ng3 gave White a winning game in Euwe-Yates, Hague 1921.) **7.d4 Bxf3.** 7...Ne6; 8.Be3 c5; 9.Qb5+ Qd7; 10.Qxd7+ Nxd7; 11.Nxd5 Bxf3; 12.gxf3 cxd4; 13.Bd2 leaves White with the better game. **8.Qxf3 Qh4+; 9.g3 Qxd4; 10.Be3.**

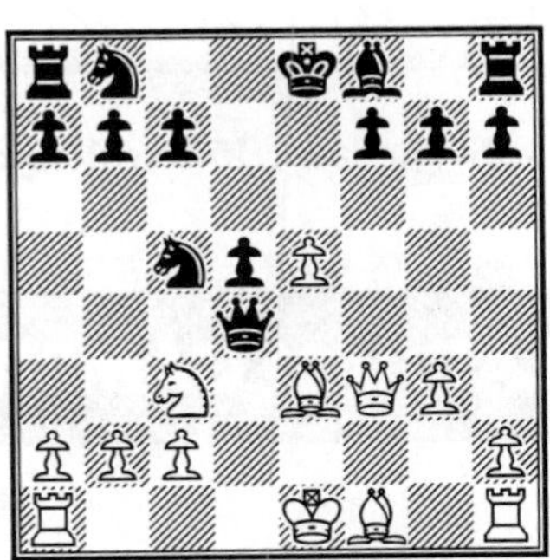

10...Qxe5? 10...Qb4; 11.0–0–0 Ne6; 12.Nxd5 Qa5; 13.Bc4 is clearly better for White. **11.0–0–0!** The pressure at d5 is intense, so Black must use the c6-square for a pawn. Black thinks that will provide sufficient defense, but White has a surprise in store! **11...c6 12.Nxd5!!; cxd5; 13.Rxd5 Qe6; 14.Bc4.**

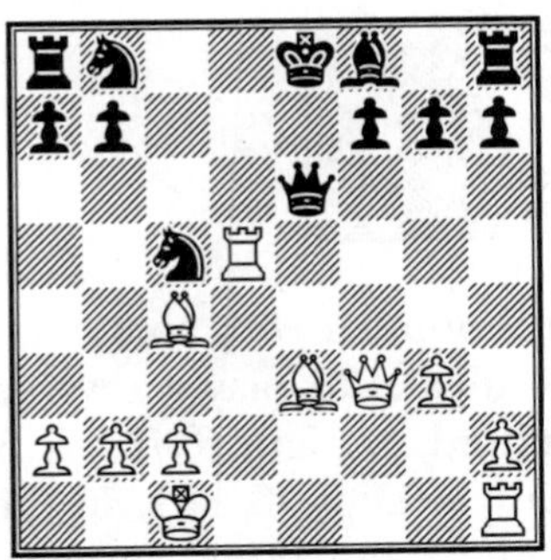

White's threats more than compensate for the piece. **14...Qe4.**

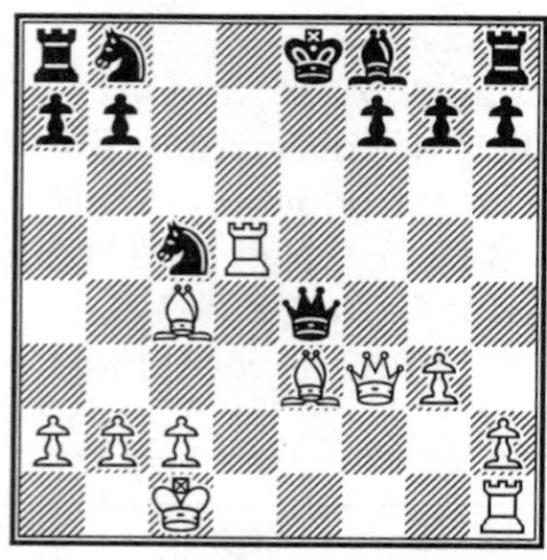

Now it is time to part with the lady! **15.Bxc5!! Qxf3; 16.Re1+ Be7; 17.Rxe7+ Kf8; 18.Rd8#. White won.**

LATVIAN GAMBIT

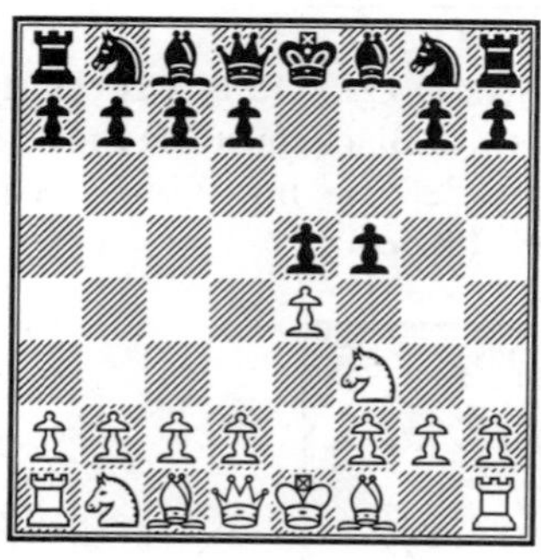

1.e4 e5
2.Nf3 f5

The **Latvian Gambit** is popular with amateurs but no professional players take it seriously. The idea is to play a reversed King's Gambit, where White has already committed a knight to f3. As Black in a King's Gambit, the knight does not usually occupy f6 early in the game. The Latvian can lead to exciting complications, but White comes out on top in most of the well-analyzed variations. It is often played for surprise value, or by die-hard gambiteers who insist on giving up a pawn for insufficient compensation.

(9) FISCHER - PUPOLS [C40]
US Junior Championship, 1955

1.e4 e5; 2.Nf3 f5; 3.Nxe5. The standard recommendation, and objectively the best move. The only practical problem is that White needs to be familiar with quite a lot of theory, as often, Black will slide into disreputable sidelines that are hard to figure out at the board. The reward however, is usually a full point at the chessboard.

3.exf5 e4; 4.Ng1 is my personal favorite, and will be discussed in *Unorthodox Chess Openings*. But here we follow the main lines, and we will look at the latest analysis. 4.Ne5 is more ambitious, and is recommended in *The Big Book of Busts*.

3...Qf6; 4.d4. 4.Nc4. This is Leonhardt's move, but you don't need the courage of a lion to play it, since it gives White a nice, clean, positional game which may frustrate the violent players of the Black side. On the other hand, Black doesn't have a bad game after 4...fxe4; 5.Nc3 Qf7 as promoted by Gunderam.

4...d6; 5.Nc4 fxe4; 6.Nc3. This is not the sharpest move, but it does give White a good game. 6.Be2 is the Bronstein Variation. It is a flexible move which should insure a small advantage for White, and no reliable equalizing methods are known. 6...d5; 7.Ne3! Qf7 (7...Ne7; 8.c4 dxc4; 9.Nc3 Bf5; 10.Bxc4 Nbc6; 11.d5 Ne5; 12.Qa4+ is a little better for White, as Black's pieces are awkwardly placed, Rittenhouse-Downey, Postal 1992.) 8.c4 c6; 9.Nc3 Nf6; 10.Qa4 Nbd7; 11.cxd5 Nb6; 12.Qb3 Nbxd5; 13.Nexd5 Nxd5; 14.Nxe4 Nb4; 15.Qxf7+ Kxf7; 16.Bc4+ Kg6; 17.Bb3 and White had a secure extra pawn in Enklaar-Holz, Amsterdam (IBM) 1979. **6...Qg6.** Black hopes to tie down the White bishop to the defense of the pawn at g2. Keep in mind that Bobby Fischer was just a kid at the time of this game. His opponent went on to become a highly respected master, though his openings became a bit less wild over time.

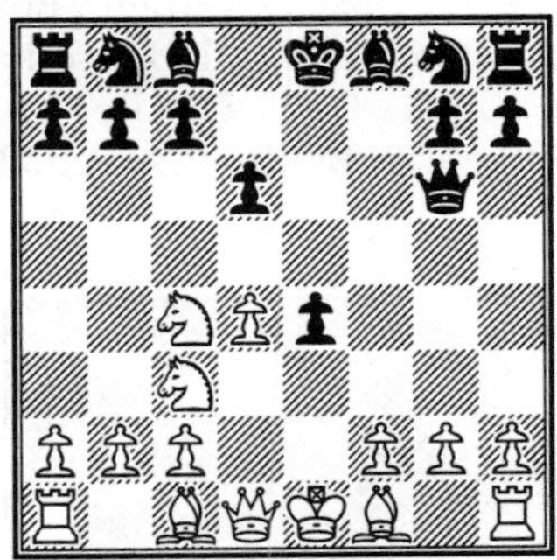

Now White has a choice between two main plans. **7.Ne3.** 7.f3 exf3; 8.Qxf3 Nc6 is now the main line, which continues 9.Bd3 Qg4; 10.Qe3+! Be7; 11.0–0 and now Black has nothing better than 11...Nf6 with a slight disadvantage because the bishop is useless at e7. Taking the d-pawn leads to a favorable endgame for White. 11...Qxd4?; 12.Nb5! Qxe3+; 13.Nxe3 Kd8; 14.Nd5 is horrible for Black. **7...Nf6; 8.Bc4 c6; 9.d5 Be7.** 9...Nbd7 is recommended by theoretician Tony Kosten in his recent book on the Latvian Gambit.

10.a4 Nbd7; 11.a5! Fischer already had deep positional understanding and is building up a good position. **11...Ne5; 12.Be2 0–0; 13.0–0 Bd7; 14.Kh1.** Fischer could have continued to push the a-pawn, and that might have provided more counterplay. **14...Kh8; 15.Nc4.** White has an advantage in space, and Black must seek chances on the kingside. **15...Nfg4; 16.Qe1 Rf7.** The rook would have been better placed at f5. **17.h3 Nf6; 18.Nxe5 dxe5; 19.Bc4 Rff8; 20.Be3 Nh5; 21.Kh2!?** The start of a clever plan to bring the rook to the h-file. But the idea is not without danger. 21.dxc6 Bxc6 deflects the bishop from the kingside, and buys valuable time. For example 22.Nd5 and at least White has a bit of an initiative. **21...Bd6; 22.Bb3 Nf4; 23.Bxf4 exf4.**

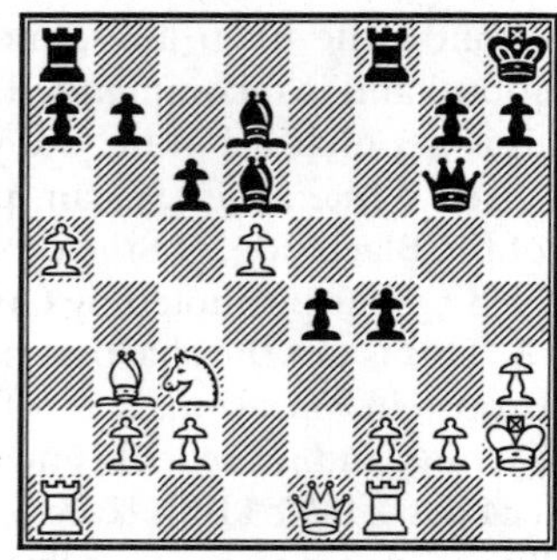

Most players would pay a little respect to Black's attack, but not Fischer. **24.Qxe4.** So Fischer takes the pawn and is willing to face the consequences. **24...f3+?** 24...Qh5! would have been very strong, and it is hard to see any way for White to survive. After ...Re8 all the Black forces will be attacking the king. **25.g3 Bf5; 26.Qh4 Rae8; 27.Rae1 Be5; 28.Qb4 Qh6; 29.h4 g5; 30.Rh1.** Now the opening of the h-file may prove more dangerous to Black. Then again, it may not. Fischer's plan is clever, but not correct. 30.Rxe5 Rxe5; 31.Qd4 Qg7; 32.dxc6 bxc6 is certainly not better for White. **30...gxh4; 31.Kg1! h3; 32.dxc6 bxc6; 33.Qc5.** Here Black overlooks a quick win. **33...Qg7?** 33...Bxg3!!; 34.Rxe8 Qc1+!; 35.Nd1 Qxd1+; 36.Re1 Qxe1#. **34.Kh2 Qf6; 35.Qxa7 Bd4; 36.Qc7 Bxf2; 37.Rxe8 Rxe8; 38.Rf1 Bd4; 39.Rxf3 Bxc3; 40.bxc3 Re2+; 41.Kh1 Be4; 42.Qc8+ Kg7.**

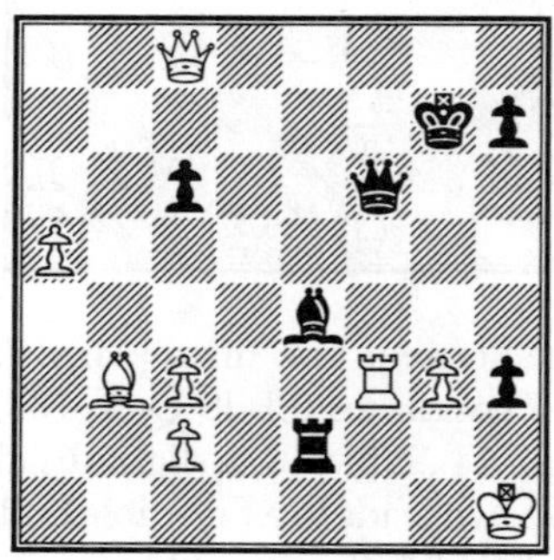

Here the great Bobby Fischer slips up. **43.Qg4+?** 43.Qd7+! Kh6 (43...Kg6; 44.Qg4+ also draws.) 44.Qxh3+ Kg7; 45.Qd7+ draws. **43...Qg6; 44.Qd7+ Kh6. Black won.**

ELEPHANT GAMBIT

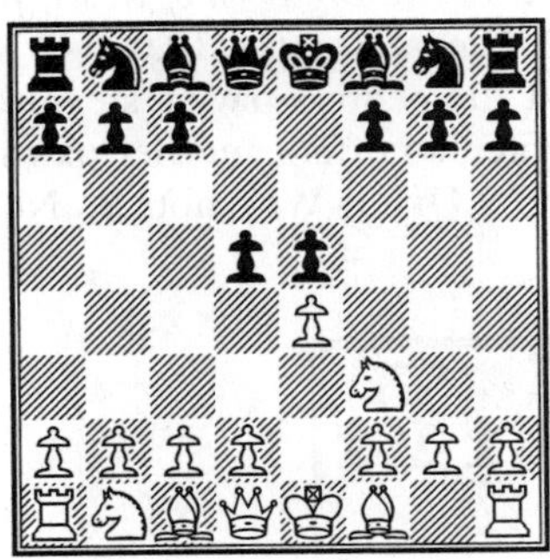

1.e4 e5
2.Nf3 d5

The **Elephant Gambit** is an ungainly opening where Black tries to simply stomp on White's opening privileges. Once relegated to the trash heap, new ideas have elevated the line to something approaching respectability, but White does seem to maintain the upper hand with calm and logical play.

(10) KONSTANTINOPOLSKY - HOVE [C40]

Telegraph Match, 1954

1.e4 e5; 2.Nf3 d5; 3.exd5 e4. 3...c6 might be a reasonable gambit if White were obliged to capture at c6, but there is no rule against declining! 4.Nxe5! Qxd5; 5.d4 c5; 6.Be3 Nc6; 7.Nc3 and White's development is gaining momentum. After 7...Qe6; 8.Nxc6 Black is lost. 8...cxd4 (8...bxc6; 9.d5 cxd5; 10.Nxd5 Bd6; 11.Bc4 Qg6; 12.Qe2 is just one of many pleasant possibilities, but it is better than the game.) 9.Nxd4 Qf6; 10.Bb5+ Bd7; 11.Bxd7+ Kxd7; 12.Qf3 and White, playing Black, resigned in Koltanowski-White, San Francisco (casual) 1960. **4.Qe2 Nf6.** 4...Qe7; 5.Nd4 Qe5; 6.Nb5 Bd6; 7.d4 gave White a great position in Morphy-Mongredien, Paris 1859. **5.d3! Be7.**

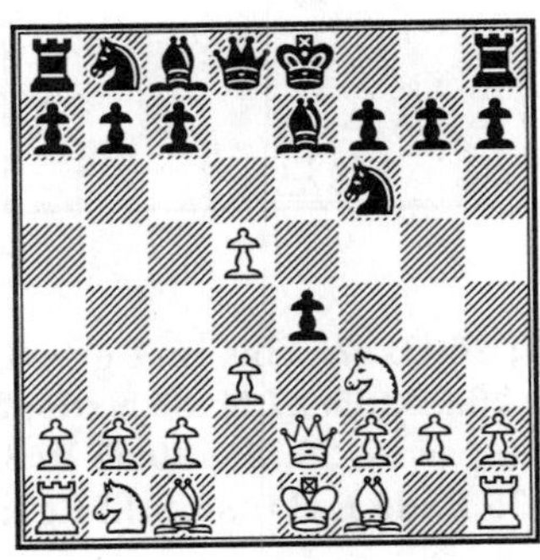

This is the recommended move in unorthodox opening circles. It is in fact a most orthodox approach, but Black can't escape an inferior position. 5...Qxd5 should be met by the strange looking 6.Nfd2! and after 6...Be7; 7.Nxe4 0-0; 8.Nbc3 White can be very happy with the lead in development and the initiative, Keres-Augustin, 1943. **6.dxe4 0-0; 7.Nc3.** 7.Bg5 is also good. In the *Big Book of Busts*, John Watson and I give 7...Nxe4; 8.Bxe7 Qxe7; 9.Nbd2 f5 The latest twist. 10.0-0-0 Nd7; 11.Nd4 Nb6; 12.f3 Qf6; 13.Nxe4 fxe4; 14.fxe4 and the central pawns steamroll forward. **7...Re8; 8.Bd2 b5.** Black is busted in the center, so offers another pawn to liven up the game. That's three, if you are counting. **9.Qxb5!** Why not? **9...Nbd7; 10.Nd4 Bc5; 11.Nc6 Nxe4.**

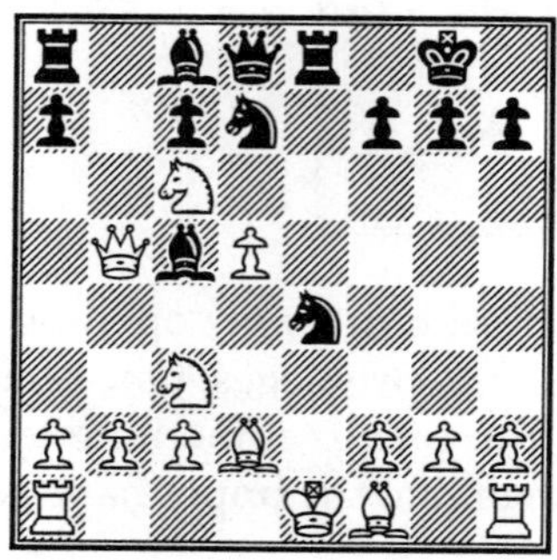

So now things are a little messy. **12.0-0-0.** 12.Nxd8 Nxc3+ regains the material with interest, but White doesn't fall for it. **12...Nxc3; 13.Bxc3 Qh4.** Black wants the f-pawn, but he can't have it! **14.g3! Qh5; 15.Bd4! Bxd4; 16.Nxd4 Rb8; 17.Qa5.** Black has an open file, but no real attack. **17...Rb6; 18.Be2 Qh6+; 19.f4 Bb7; 20.Bb5 Qd6; 21.Qc3 Rd8; 22.Rhe1 Nf6; 23.Nf5 Qf8.** Black is forced on the defensive, and never mind White's extra pawn!

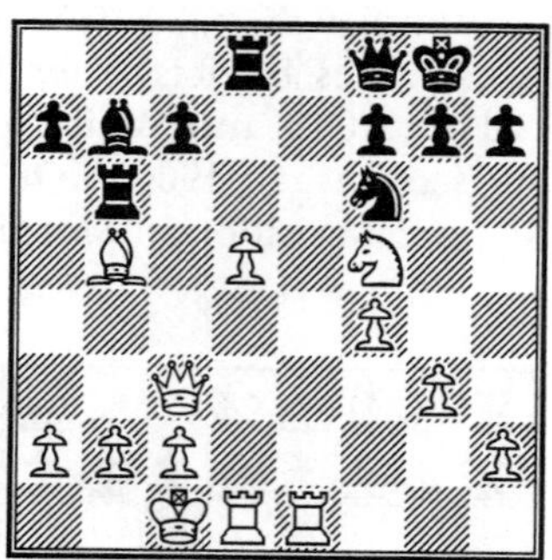

24.a4 h6; 25.Ne7+ Kh7; 26.Qxc7. This isn't greed, just taking advantage of a chance to win another pawn. **26...Bxd5; 27.Nxd5 Nxd5; 28.Qc4 Rbd6; 29.Rd3.** Black has no compensation for the pawns. **29...f5; 30.a5 Rc8; 31.Qb3 Rc5; 32.Re8 Qf6; 33.Re5 Qd8; 34.Bc4 Rxa5; 35.Bxd5 Ra1+; 36.Kd2 Rg1; 37.Bg8+. White won.**

PHILIDOR DEFENSE

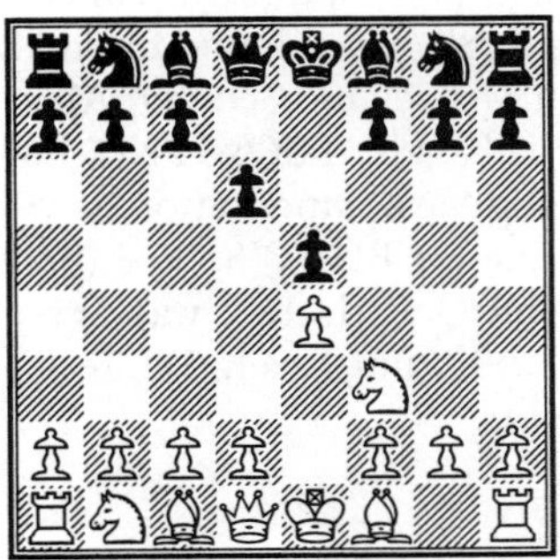

1.e4	**e5**
2.Nf3	**d6**

The **Philidor Defense** has a terrible reputation, even though some very strong players such as Bent Larsen have used it in important encounters. By locking in the bishop at f8, Black reduces the options for defensive formations. The only viable line is the one Larsen has promoted, involving the fianchetto of the dark-squared bishop combined with an early capture at d4. This can be very dangerous for White, as seen in the following game.

(11) HAZAI - SAX [C41]

Hungary, 1971

1.e4 e5; 2.Nf3 d6; 3.d4 exd4; 4.Nxd4 g6.

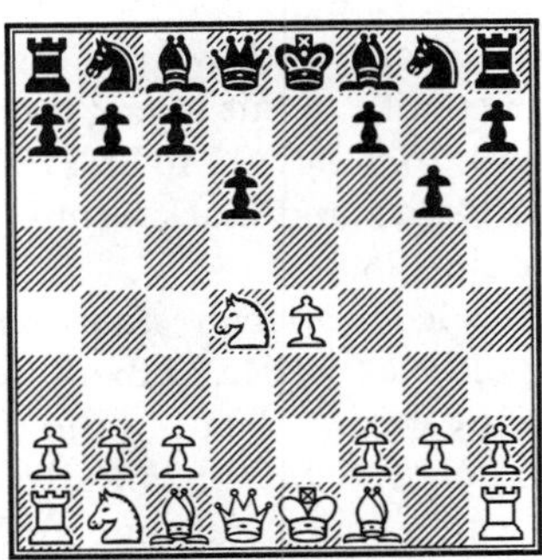

The Larsen Variation has a lot in common with the Sicilian Dragon, with the important difference that Black has a semi-open e-file instead of a c-file. This means that the pressure will be applied at e4, and that exchange sacrifices at c3, typical of the Dragon, are not available. For a long time it was thought that Black did not have enough firepower on the queenside to counter a kingside pawnstorm by White, but recently new ideas have been found to invigorate the Black position. This is one of the easiest openings to play for Black, since the ideas are simple: develop, castle kingside, place a rook at e8 an a knight at c6, and then let the pawns fly on the queenside. Play is very sharp, and there is nothing boring about this line of the Philidor!

5.Nc3 Bg7; 6.Bf4. 6.Be3 is probably best. Now after the natural 6...Nf6; 7.Qd2 0–0; 8.0–0–0. It is important to point out here some flawed analysis in the otherwise excellent book on the Philidor by Tony Kosten. (8.f3 is, Kosten claims, easily met by 8...d5 and now he claims that 9.e5 allows 9...Re8!! (sic). I found his analysis fascinating, and was rewarded with a good game in McClelland-Schiller, Alexandria 1996: 10.exf6 Bh6; 11.Nd1 c5; 12.Kf2 Bxe3+; 13.Nxe3 cxd4; 14.Qxd4 Nc6 but suppose he had just played 12.Ne2! I would have had negligible compensation then. Fortunately, the simple 9...Nh5 or 9...Nd7 will save the line for Black.) 8...Re8 (8...Nc6; 9.f3 a6; 10.h4 Ne5; 11.Bh6 Bxh6; 12.Qxh6 c6; 13.h5 Qe7; 14.Be2 was agreed drawn in Reindermann-Piket, Dutch Championship 1995, but surely White has the better chances here, with the attack well under way.)

9.f3 Nc6.

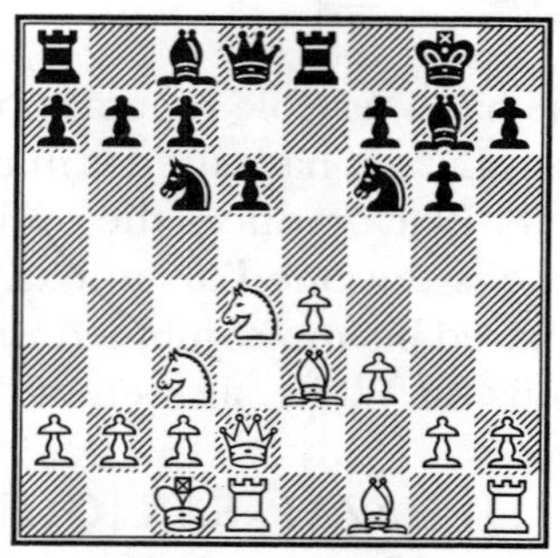

10. g4 Ne5; 11.Be2 a6. Black is ready to advance on the queenside with ...b5. White has tried many plans here. 12.Bg5.

(12.g5 Nh5; 13.Rhg1 b5 was analyzed by Larsen back in 1971. Kosten decries the lack of practical experience with it, but in fact there is an interesting game on record: 14.f4 Nc4; 15.Bxc4 bxc4; 16.f5 Bb7; 17.f6 Bf8; 18.Rg4 Rb8; 19.Qe2 c5; 20.Nf5! Qb6!; 21.Rh4 Bxe4; 22.Nxe4 Qxb2+ and Black went on to win in Fogarasi-Dreyev, European Junior Championship 1989.)

12...b5; 13.h4 Bb7; 14.h5 c5 led to an interesting sacrifice: 15.Nf5!? gxf5; 16.gxf5 Kh8; 17.Rhg1 Rg8; 18.f4 b4; 19.Na4 Nxe4; 20.Bxd8 Nxd2; 21.h6 Raxd8 and here White gained the advantage by greatly delaying the capture of the knight at d2: 22.hxg7+! Rxg7; 23.Rxg7 Kxg7; 24.f6+! Kh6; 25.Rxd2 Nf3; 26.Bxf3 Bxf3; 27.Nxc5 Re8; 28.Rh2+ Kg6; 29.Nxa6 with a better endgame for White in Sax-Adorjan, Hungary 1970.

6.Bc4 Nc6; 7.Nxc6 (7.Be3 Nf6; 8.f3 0–0; 9.Qd2 a6; 10.0–0–0 Ne5!; 11.Be2 c5; 12.Nb3 c4; 13.Nd4 b5; 14.Nd5 Nxd5; 15.exd5 Bd7 gave Black good counterplay in Morris-Alkaersig, Copenhagen 1993.) 7...bxc6; 8.0–0 Ne7; 9.f4 Be6; 10.Bd3 Qd7; 11.Qf3 f5; 12.Bd2 0–0; 13.Rae1 Rae8 with an even game, Browne-Larsen, San Juan 1969.

6...Nc6; 7.Nxc6 bxc6 is another possibility.

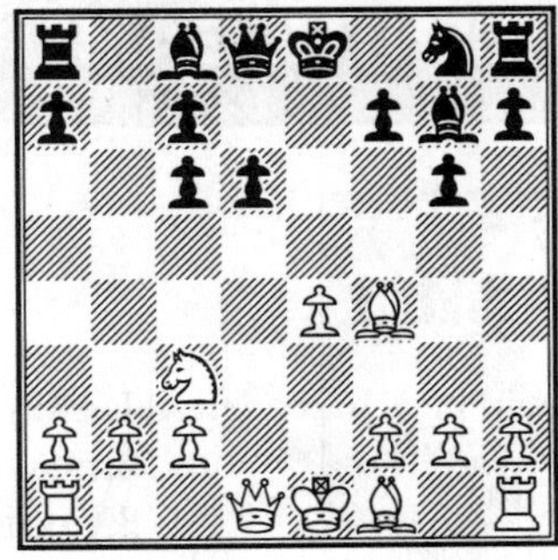

In the Larsen Variation Black often accepts the doubled pawns in return for an open b-file. Obviously, if White castles queenside, then the file will be useful in the attack, but even when that does not take place there will still be pressure at b2, where the lines of a rook at b8 and a bishop at g7 converge. **8.Bc4 Rb8; 9.Qc1?** The natural retreat of the bishop to b3 would have been much stronger. **9...d5!** Now Black's pieces mobilize at a furious pace. **10.exd5 Rb4!; 11.Bb3 Qe7+; 12.Be3 Ba6!** The White king cannot flee to the kingside. and the pin on the e-file is excruciating. **13.Qd2.**

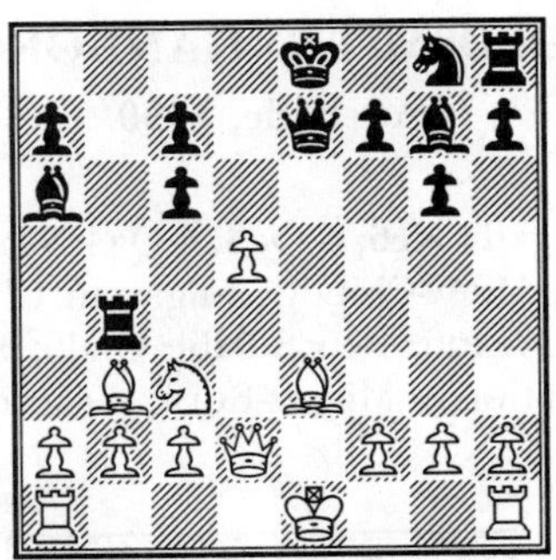

Now Black plays a stunning move, exploiting the pin. **13...Rd4!!; 14.Qc1 Nf6; 15.f3.** White tries to get the king to f2, but there is no safety there. **15...Bh6!; 16.Kf2 Ng4+!!** A brilliant finish to the miniature. **17.fxg4 Qf6+; 18.Kg1 Rd1+.** White resigned, since 19.Qxd1 loses to 19...Bxe3+ and 19.Nxd1 loses to Qf1 mate! **Black won.**

CENTER GAME

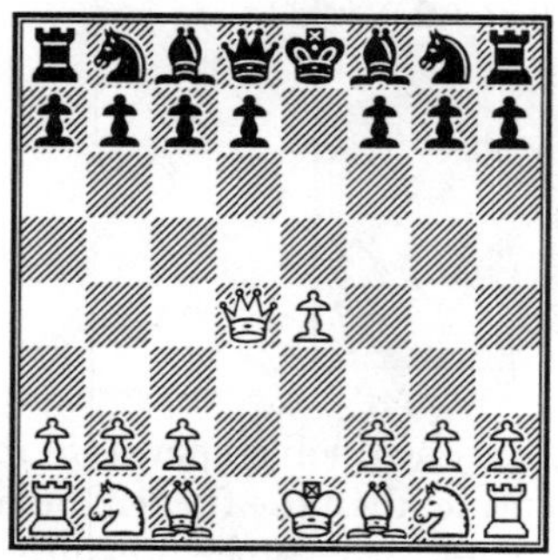

1.e4	**e5**
2.d4	**exd4**
3.Qxd4	

The old **Center Game** has fallen into complete disrepute. It is simply too slow, because White must lose time when Black attacks the queen at d4 while developing the knight from b8 to c6. It is still seen from time to time in amateur events, but no serious player uses it these days.

(12) GOLDSMITH - HANDOKO [C22]
Adelaide, 1990

1.e4 e5; 2.d4 exd4; 3.Qxd4 Nc6; 4.Qe3. 4.Qa4 Nf6; 5.Bg5 Be7; 6.Nc3 0–0 and Black had no problems in Milev-Chipev, Bulgarian Championship 1961. **4...Nf6; 5.Nc3.** 5.e5 Ng4; 6.Qe4 d5; 7.exd6+ Be6; 8.Ba6!? Qxd6; 9.Bxb7 Qb4+; 10.Qxb4 Nxb4 was the interesting continuation of Mieses-Burn, Wroclaw 1912. **5...Bb4; 6.Bd2 0–0; 7.0–0–0 Re8; 8.Bc4 Ne5!?**

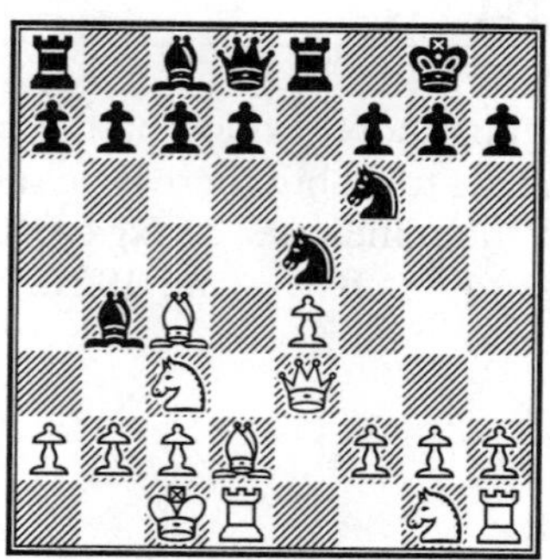

8...d6; 9.f3 Ne5; 10.Bb3 Be6 gave Black complete equality in Spielmann-Eliskases, Semmering 1937. **9.Bb3 d6; 10.Nf3.** 10.f3 would transpose into the previous note. **10...Be6; 11.Bxe6 Rxe6; 12.Nd4 Re8.** 12...Nc4?; 13.Nxe6 Nxe3; 14.Nxd8 Nxd1; 15.Rxd1 Rxd8; 16.f3 is pretty drawish.

13.Nf5 Nc4. White is now faced with tremendous pressure at e4, since the main defender, the knight at c3, is under attack. **14.Qg5 g6; 15.Be1 Bxc3; 16.Bxc3 Nxe4.**

Despite White's menacing pieces, the attack is not strong enough to worry Black, who has the advantage if there is no immediate disaster looming. **17.Qh6.**

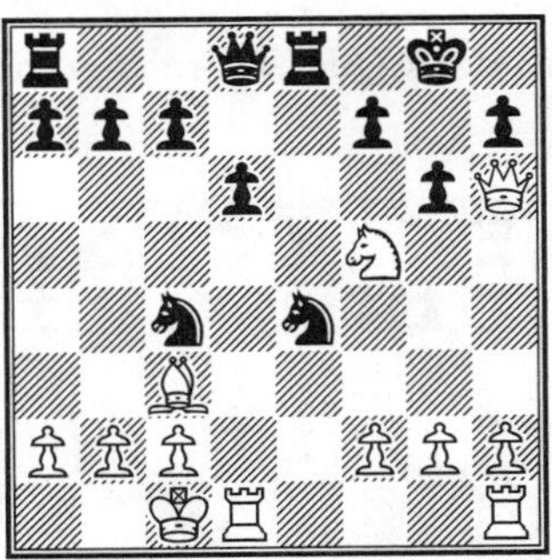

17...Qg5+; 18.Qxg5 Nxg5; 19.Nh6+ Kf8; 20.h4. White must put all his energy into the attack, since otherwise he is a pawn down for nothing. **20...Ne4.** But the Black pieces are too active! **21.Bh8.** 21.Bd4 c5; 22.Be3 Nxe3; 23.fxe3 Nf2?? (23...f5! would preserve Black's advantage.) 24.Rhf1 Nxd1; 25.Rxf7#. **21...Nxf2; 22.Rhf1 Re2; 23.Bd4.** 23.Rde1 Rae8; 24.Rxe2 Rxe2; 25.b3 Ne3 and Black wins. **23...Nxd1; 24.Rxf7+ Ke8; 25.Kxd1 Rd2+. Black won.**

PONZIANI OPENING

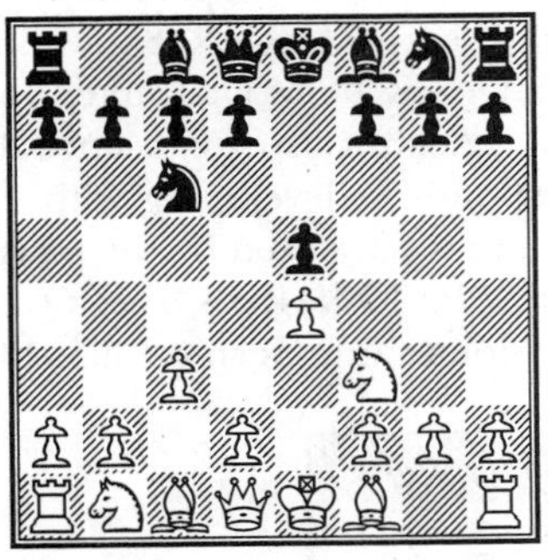

1.e4 e5
2.Nf3 Nc6
3.c3

The **Ponziani** is an unambitious opening. Taking time out to support the advance of the d-pawn with c3 is just too slow. Nevertheless, Black must be careful, because unless an appropriate defense is chosen, White can transpose to favorable positions in other openings. Therefore the correct reply is to immediately challenge the center, since White no longer has the c3-square for a knight to do combat at d5.

(13) MAKKROPOULOS - TOLNAI [C44]
Dortmund, 1988

1.e4 e5; 2.Nf3 Nc6; 3.c3 d5; 4.Qa4. There are other plans, but this is the most interesting. **4...Bd7.**

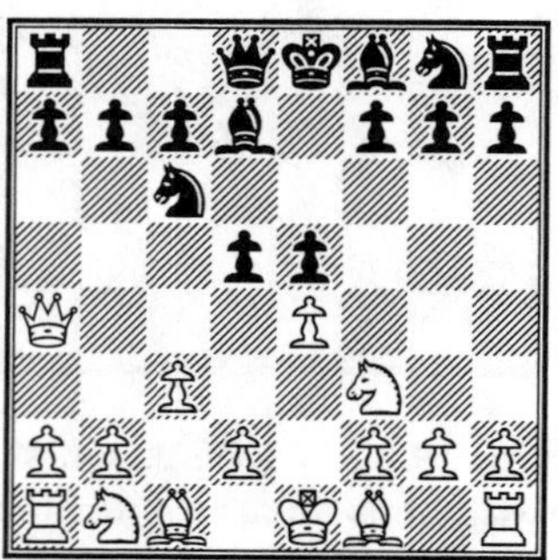

A sensible reply which leads to a simplification of the position. The Steinitz Variation, 4...f6, is not as common these days. **5.exd5 Nd4; 6.Qd1 Nxf3+; 7.Qxf3.** 7.gxf3 Qh4; 8.d4 0-0-0; 9.Be3 Re8; 10.dxe5 Rxe5; 11.Qd4 Qxd4; 12.cxd4 Rxd5 led to a better endgame for Black in Turner-Hebden, Hastings Masters 1995. **7...Nf6.** 7...Bd6!? is an interesting alternative. 8.Bc4 f5; 9.d3 Qf6 with a very solid position for Black.

8.Bc4. 8.c4 Bc5 leaves White very weak on the dark squares. 8.d4? falls into a trap: 8...exd4; 9.cxd4 Qe7+!; 10.Be3? Qb4+ and White drops a pawn. **8...e4!** The most aggressive continuation. **9.Qe2.** 9.Qg3 Bd6!; 10.Qxg7 Rg8 and Black is much better, according to Khristov. **9...Bd6!?** 9...Qe7 is beneficial, intending to castle queenside. **10.d4 0-0; 11.h3 Re8; 12.Be3 h6.** 12...a6 is also good, since Bg5 does not constitute much of a threat. White can respond by developing with 13.Nd2 Rb8; 14.Bb3 b5; 15.0-0 but now after 15...h6 White is paralyzed by the pawn at e4, and the attempt to eliminate it with 16.f3 Qe7; 17.fxe4 Nxe4; 18.Nxe4 Qxe4 left Black with the better bishops in Zelcic-Malaniuk, Montecatini Terme 1995. **13.Nd2.**

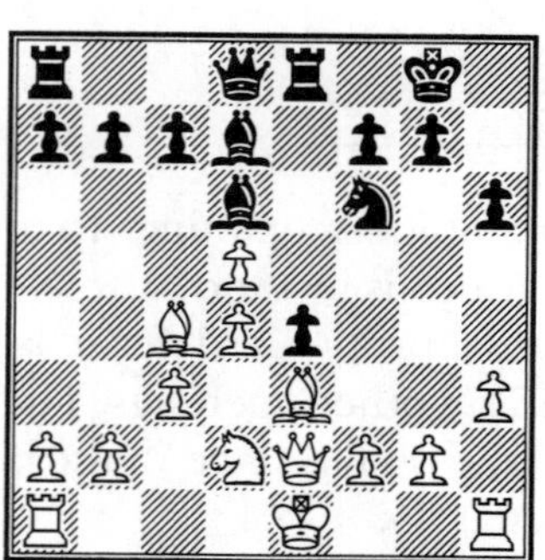

Black has a comfortable game. **13...Nh7.** 13...Qe7 is a reasonable alternative. **14.0-0-0 f5; 15.g3 Nf6; 16.f4.** Pretty much forced, in order to stop the kingside onslaught. But now Black can turn his attention elsewhere. **16...a6; 17.Rdg1 b5;**

18.Bb3 a5; 19.a3 h5! Black is careful to take time out to defend the kingside. **20.c4 a4; 21.Ba2 bxc4; 22.Nxc4 Bb5.**

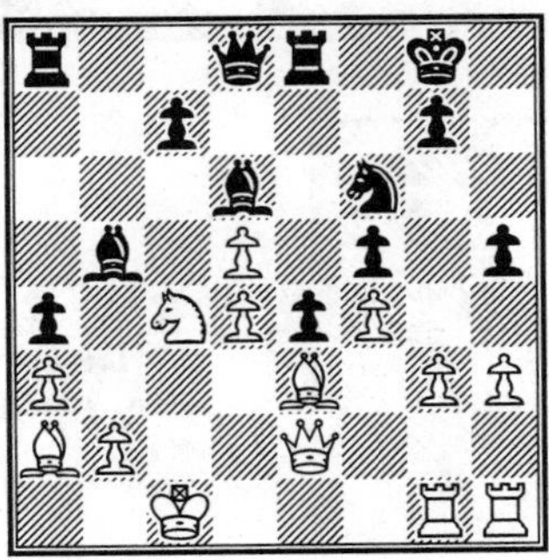

Black has a dominating position, so White decides to go for broke. **23.g4 hxg4; 24.hxg4 fxg4; 25.Rh4 Qd7; 26.Qh2 Bxc4; 27.Bxc4 Qf5!** From this vantage point the Black queen both defends the kingside and puts pressure at d5. **28.Be2 Qxd5; 29.Rhxg4.** 29.Rh8+ Kf7 achieves nothing for White. **29...Nxg4; 30.Rxg4 Qb3; 31.Qh6 Re7; 32.f5 Rf7; 33.f6 Bf8; 34.d5.** White hopes that one day the bishop will reach the a1–h8 diagonal, but this absorbs too much time. **34...Qxd5; 35.Qh4 Re8; 36.Bd2 Re6; 37.Bc3.** Finally, but the bishop will be ineffective once it is pinned. **37...Rc6; 38.fxg7 Bxg7; 39.Rxe4.**

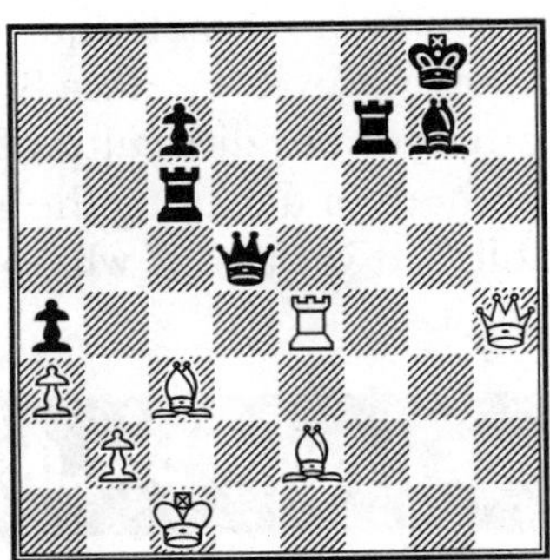

39...Rff6! A beautiful and subtle move which brings the game to a rapid conclusion. The threat is simply Rh6. **40.Re8+ Rf8; 41.Rxf8+ Kxf8. Black won.**

KING'S GAMBIT

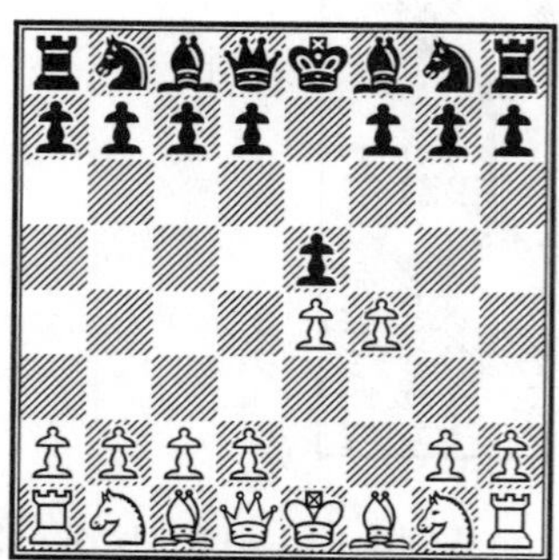

1.e4 e5
2.f4

The **King's Gambit** is an ancient opening and has been extensively analyzed for over a century. There have even been entire tournaments where the players were obligated to start the game with it. White offers a pawn to deprive the Black center of its anchor at e5. The pawn can be recaptured much later, either by the bishop at c1 (after the d-pawn advances) or even by a rook once White has castled on the kingside. In either case the open f-file can be used to attack f7, the most vulnerable square in the Black camp. The opening has fallen from favor, however, because Black has found a variety of effective defenses which often lead to difficulties for White.

We'll look at various methods of declining the gambit first, and work our way toward the most established variations where Black accepts the pawn, and then tries to hold on to it.

KINGS GAMBIT DECLINED

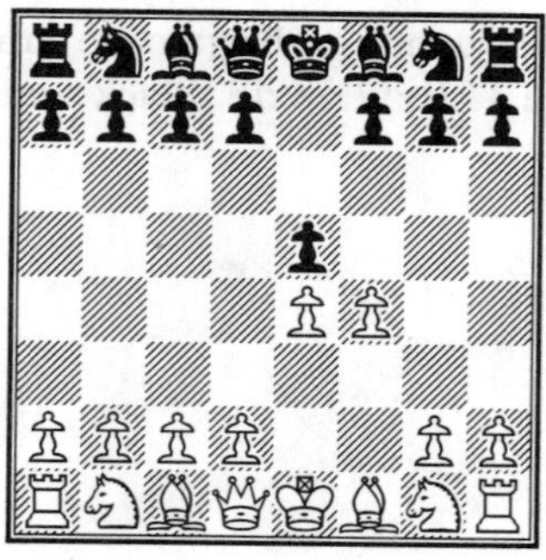

1.e4 e5
2.f4

Suppose Black decides not to capture the pawn at f4 Black can safely ignore the threat of fxe5 because then ...Qh4+ is deadly. This allows developing moves like 2...Bc5, 2...Nf6, and 2...Nc6 to be played. Black can also play aggressively in the center with 2...d5, the Falkbeer Countergambit. Even the early queen sortie 2...Qh4+; 3.g3 Qe7 is considered playable. The Classical King's Gambit Declined does not have a good reputation, despite the useful developing move.

(14) EUWE - MAROCZY [C30]

Amsterdam, 1921

1.e4 e5; 2.f4 Bc5.

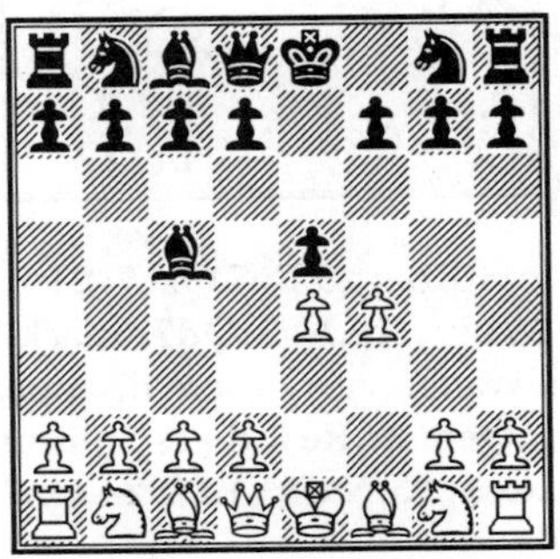

The King's Gambit Declined has been around a long time and fades in and out of popularity. When this game was played, it was, according to Euwe, the standard line. **3.Nf3 d6; 4.c3.** Euwe was following the fashion of the time, and had Maroczy reacted a little better, he would have paid a price for it. But modern thinking supports this move, as well as 4.Nc3. **4...Bg4.** 4...Nf6; 5.d4 (5.Bd3 is an old recommendation. 5...0–0; 6.Bc2 Re8 and White would be in a little trouble, unable to castle and behind in development.) 5...exd4; 6.cxd4 Bb4+; 7.Bd2 Bxd2+; 8.Nbxd2 is better for White, and has been played by female superstar Judith Polgar. **5.fxe5 dxe5; 6.Qa4+ Bd7; 7.Qc2 Qe7; 8.d4.** Finally! The ideal pawn center is established. Black tries to open up some lines but the center holds. **8...exd4; 9.cxd4.**

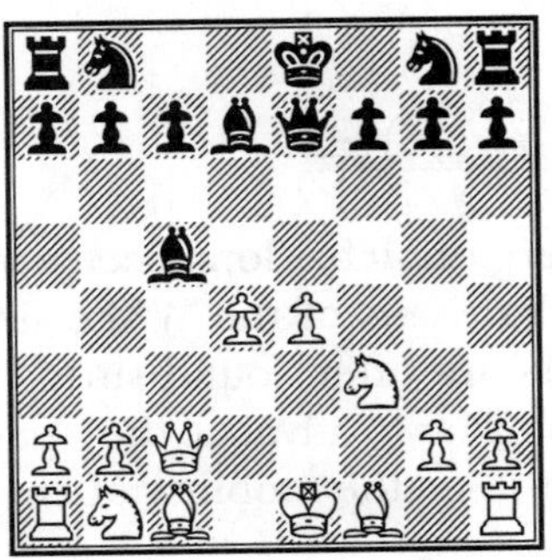

9...Bb4+; 10.Nc3 Bc6. The attempt to use piece pressure to work against the strong center fails because since the king is still at e8, Black cannot effectively use a rook on the e-file. **11.Bd3 Bxc3+?** Black should be developing, not exchanging his only active pieces. **12.bxc3 Bxe4.** A temporary sacrifice, thanks to the pin on the e-file. But the pin only lasts as long as the White king remains in the center. **13.Bxe4 f5; 14.0–0! fxe4; 15.Qb3!** The most precise move, threatening to capture at b7. **15...c5; 16.Ba3 Nf6; 17.Bxc5.** Black just doesn't have time to take the knight. **17...Qf7; 18.c4.**

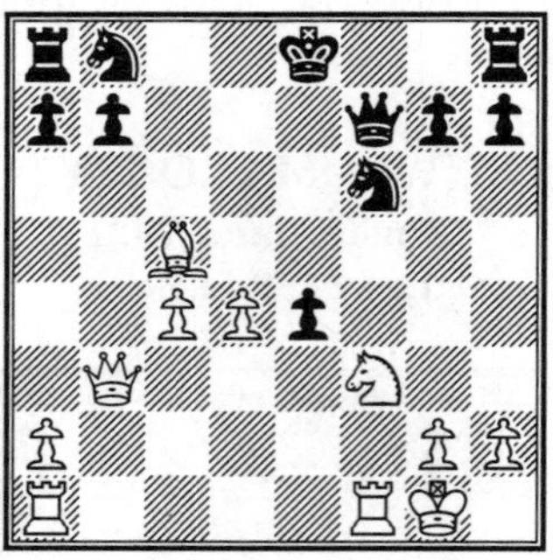

18...b6. 18...exf3; 19.Rae1+ Kd8; 20.Re7 Qxe7; 21.Bxe7+ Kxe7; 22.Qxb7+ Nbd7; 23.Qxf3 is an easy win for White. **19.Ng5 Qd7.** Black has just two defenders, the queen at d7 and knight at f6. Watch one of them disappear! **20.Rxf6!! gxf6; 21.Nxe4.** The threat is now Nxf6+. **21...Qe6; 22.Re1.** Re-establishing the threat, and now Black has no useful defense. **22...bxc5; 23.Nxf6+ Kf7; 24.Qb7+. White won.**

FALKBEER COUNTERGAMBIT

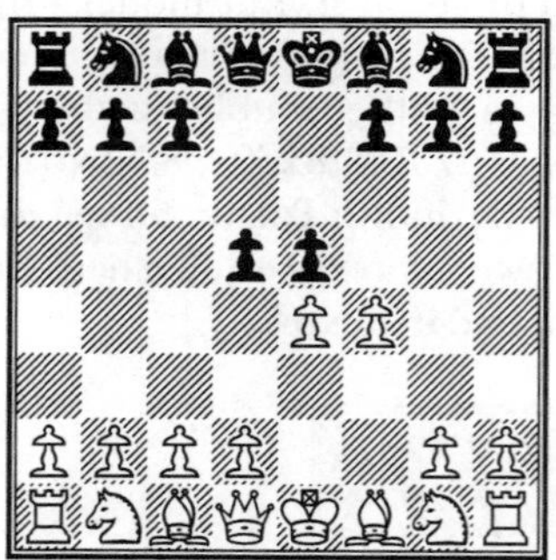

1.e4 e5
2.f4 d5

The **Falkbeer Countergambit** has long been a respected manner of greeting the King's Gambit. Partisans of the White side seem to hold it in low regard, yet strong players are often found sitting on the Black side. Black sacrifices a pawn at d5 in order to advance the e-pawn to e4, where it cramps White's forecourt and restricts the mobility of enemy forces.

(15) WELTEVREEDE - EUWE [C32]
Amsterdam 1926

1.e4 e5; 2.f4 d5; 3.exd5 e4; 4.d3. This is the move which is most preferred by

Joe Gallagher, one of the leading theoreticians of the King's Gambit from White's point of view. It immediately resolves the issue of the e-pawn. Black can capture at d3, but this just gives White an advantage in space and development. The most logical reply is ...Nf6, which begins the development of the kingside forces. **4...Nf6.** 4...Qxd5; 5.Qe2 Nf6; 6.Nd2 is better for White, since Black cannot easily cope with the pressure at e4. Developing the knight at c3 instead would be less effective because Black would pin the knight with ...Bb4.

5.Nc3. 5.dxe4 is Gallagher's choice. 5...Nxe4; 6.Be3 (6.Nf3 is the more conservative move, and is probably objectively better, though after 6...Be7!? I think Black has a fully playable game.) 6...Qh4+; 7.g3 Nxg3; 8.Nf3! (8.hxg3 Qxh1; 9.Qe2 Bb4+; 10.c3 Bd6; 11.Bg2 Qh6; 12.Bd4+ Kd8 and the e-file caused problems for White in Tal-Trifunovic, Havana 1963.) 8...Qe7; 9.hxg3 Qxe3+; 10.Qe2 Qxe2+; 11.Bxe2 was seen in Spassky-Matanovic, Belgrade 1964. White has some advantages that offset the loss of the bishop pair. **5...Bb4; 6.Bd2**

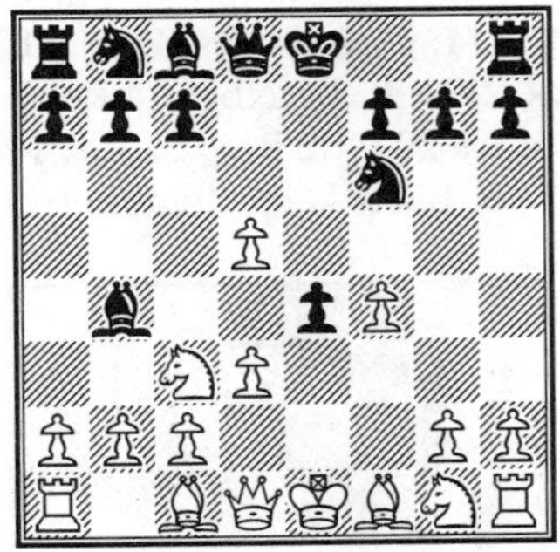

6.dxe4 Nxe4; 7.Qd4 Bxc3+; 8.bxc3 0–0; 9.Nf3 Re8 is another well established line, for example 10.Be2 Nd6 (10...Bg4; 11.0–0 Nxc3; 12.Qxc3 Rxe2; 13.Bb2 Qf8; 14.Nd4 Re4; 15.Qd3 Qe7; 16.Ne6 Re2; 17.Nd4 Re3; 18.Qd2 Na6; 19.f5 f6; 20.h3 Bh5; 21.Ne6 with a big advantage for White in Tarrasch-Walbrodt, Leipzig 1894.) 11.Bb2 Re4; 12.Qf2 Nc4; 13.0–0–0 Nxb2; 14.Kxb2 Qd6 and White had lots of weaknesses in Jaenisch-Staunton, London England 1851.

6...e3; 7.Bxe3. 7.Bc1?? is a horrible move: 7...Nxd5; 8.Nge2 Bg4; 9.h3 Bxc3+ and White resigned in Guilbert-Gedult, Paris 1974. **7...0–0; 8.Be2.** 8.Qf3 Re8; 9.Be2 Bg4; 10.Qg3 Bxe2; 11.Ngxe2 Qe7 gives Black compensation for the pawn, for example 12.Kf2 Qxe3+; 13.Qxe3 Ng4+; 14.Kf3 Nxe3; 15.Ne4 Nxd5; 16.c4 Nf6; 17.Nxf6+ gxf6; 18.d4 Nd7 and White resigned in Rohde-Brasket, New York 1978. **8...Re8; 9.Bd2 Bg4; 10.Nf3 Bxf3!** It is worth parting with the bishop pair to fracture White's pawns. **11.gxf3 Bxc3; 12.bxc3 Nxd5; 13.0–0.**

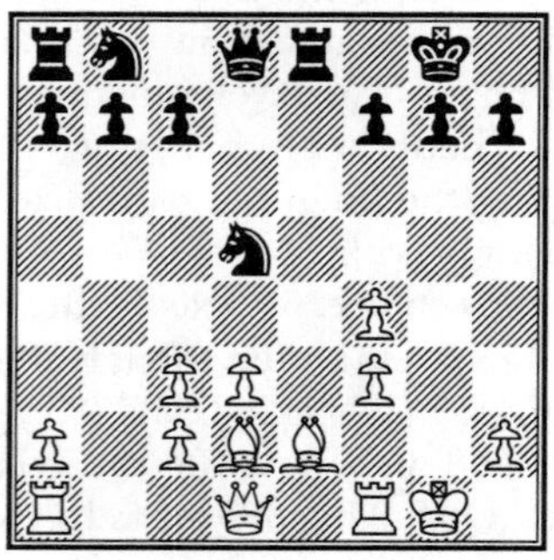

White has managed to castle and holds the bishop pair, but Black's position has fewer weaknesses. The extra pawn is doubled and meaningless. **13...Qf6.** Black regains the pawn now. **14.d4 Nxf4; 15.Bxf4 Qxf4; 16.Rb1 Nd7!** There is no need to defend the pawn at b7. **17.Rf2.** 17.Rxb7 Nb6; 18.Rxc7 Nd5; 19.Rc5 Ne3 would be most unpleasant for White, since 20.Qd2 Re6; 21.Re1 Rg6+; 22.Kh1 Rg2 is terminal. **17...Nb6; 18.c4 Rad8; 19.c3 c5.** Black keeps hammering away at the center. **20.d5.**

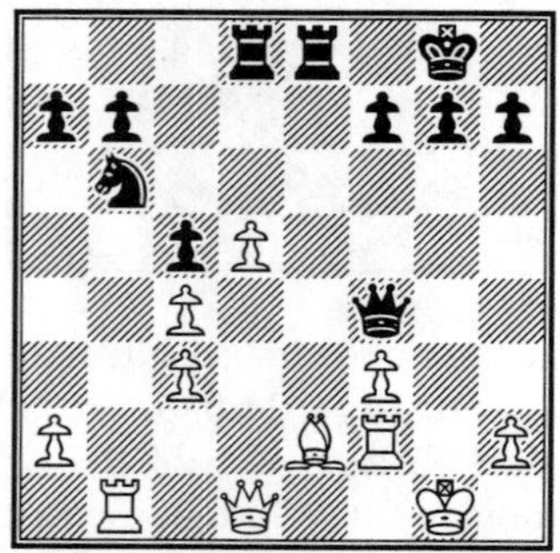

20...Nxc4!; 21.Qa4. 21.Bxc4 Qxc4; 22.d6 Qxc3 is much better for Black since the b-pawn is taboo due to the threat of ...Re1+. **21...Qf5; 22.Rxb7.** White has the pawn, but the kingside lacks sufficient defense. **22...Qg5+; 23.Rg2 Qc1+; 24.Bf1 Nd2; 25.Rxd2.** 25.Rf2 Re1 and the threats are unstoppable: 26.Qb5 Nxf1; 27.Rxf1 Qe3+; 28.Kg2 Re2+; 29.Kh1 Qe5; 30.f4 Qxd5+; 31.Kg1 Qg2#. **25...Qxd2; 26.Qh4 Rxd5; 27.Bc4 Re1+; 28.Bf1 Rg5+. Black won.**

BREYER GAMBIT

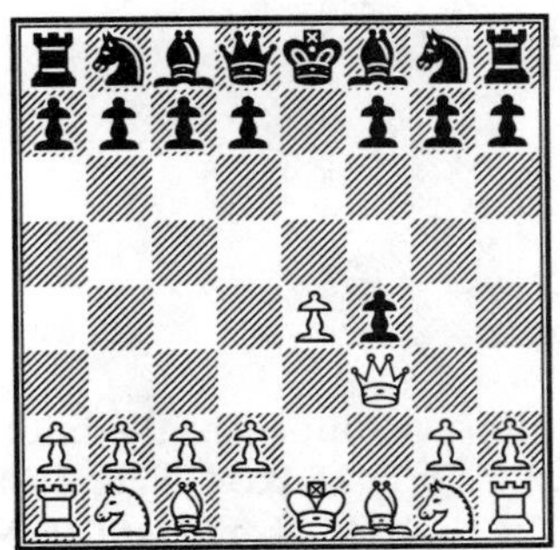

1.e4 e5
2.f4 exf4
3.Qf3

The **Breyer Variation** of the King's Gambit no longer enjoys a good reputation, but back in the Roaring Twenties it was still considered playable. White reckons that the queen is safe enough on f3, but the weakness of d4 and e5 is quickly exploited by a Black knight.

(16) SPIELMANN - MOLLER [C33]
Goteborg, 1920

1.e4 e5; 2.f4 exf4; 3.Qf3 Nc6; 4.c3 Nf6. 4...Ne5! 5.Qxf4 Bd6; 6.Qe3 Ng4; 7.Qh3 h5 gives Black a good game, Khamperupka-Blatny, Czechoslovakia 1962. **5.d4 d5; 6.e5 Ne4; 7.Bb5** White has a good game, with a strong center. **7...Qh4+; 8.Kf1! g5; 9.Nd2.** White moves to eliminate the powerful Black knight. **9...Bg4.**

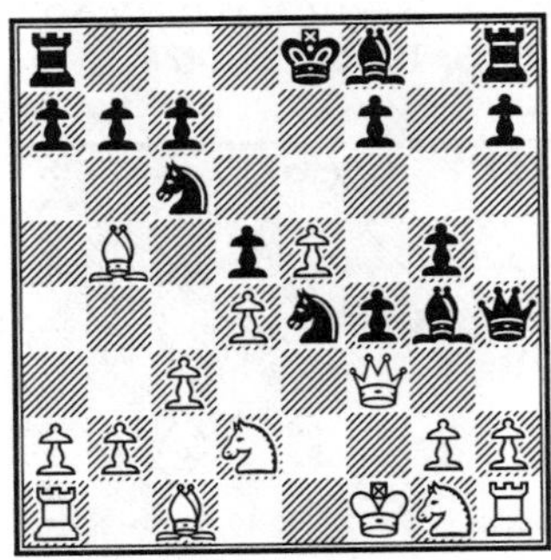

White seems to be in serious trouble here, but a queen sacrifice is coming. **10.Nxe4 Bxf3; 11.Nxf3 Qh6; 12.Nf6+ Kd8.**

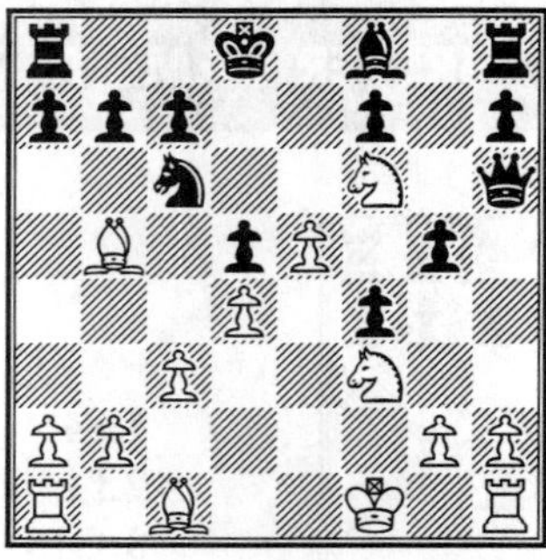

White has just two pieces for a queen and pawn, but keeps the initiative going. **13.h4! Be7.** 13...gxh4; 14.Bd3! Ne7; 15.Rxh4 Qg7; 16.Bxf4 Ng6; 17.Bh6 Nxh4; 18.Bxg7 Bxg7; 19.Nxh4 with two pieces for the rook. **14.Nxg5 Qg6; 15.Nxd5 Bxg5; 16.hxg5 Qc2.**

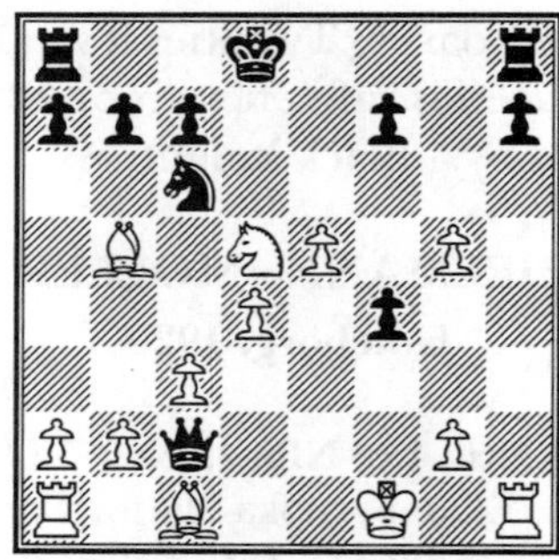

White does not have to worry. The queen can't do much harm alone, and White's pieces are very active. **17.Be2.** This retreat is made so that the other bishop can be developed. **17...Ne7; 18.Nxf4 c5; 19.Rh3 cxd4?**

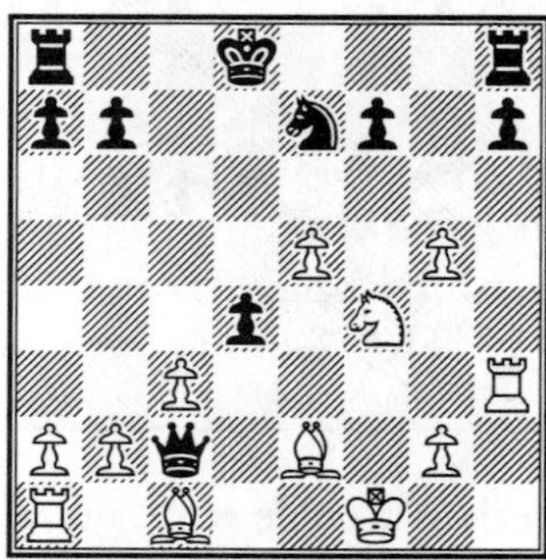

White has two pieces and two pawns for the queen, and Black's forces are uncoordinated. The last thing Black should be doing is opening lines! **20.Rd3!** Now the d-file will be open, and on top of that the Black queen has no retreat! **20...Kd7.** Hoping that White will capture on d4, which gives the queen some chance of escape.

20...Qa4 allows 21.Rxd4+. **21.Bd1! Qxd3+; 22.Nxd3 dxc3; 23.bxc3.**

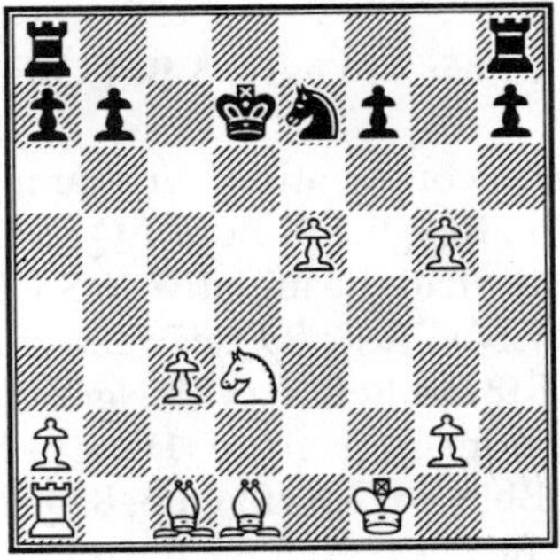

Now the position is an easy win, with two bishops and a pawn for a rook. **23...Rhd8; 24.Be2 Nf5; 25.Bf4 Kc7; 26.Rb1 b6; 27.e6+ Kc8; 28.Ne5. White won.**

BISHOP'S GAMBIT

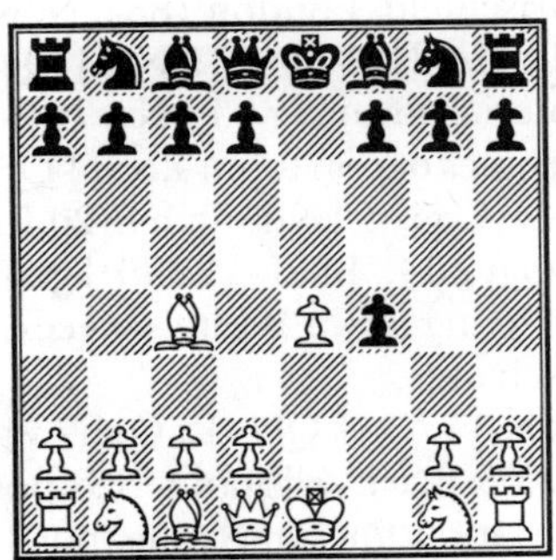

1.e4 e5
2.f4 exf4
3.Bc4

The **Bishop's Gambit** is a favorite of such leading players as Adolph Anderssen, Mikhail Chigorin and Bobby Fischer, and a particularly strong weapon in the hands of Finnish Grandmaster Heikki Westerinen. White is willing to let the king be discomfited by a check at h4, counting on the later gain of time in chasing back the enemy queen.

This is an exciting opening, though after a while the play may become calmer and more positional. The opening dates back to the early 17th century, and many different defenses have been tried. In fact, most of Black's major defenses were analyzed in a famous book by Ruy Lopez! Still, Black has finally developed a reliable defense. Black should not rush out with ...Qh4+, for reasons which will be made clear in the present game. An early ...d5 often helps Black develop, but there are additional interesting paths which still require further investigation.

(17) WESTERINEN - OFSTED [C33]

Gausdal, 1994

1.e4 e5; 2.f4 exf4; 3.Bc4 Qh4+.

3...d5 4.exd5 is a common continuation, for example:

A) 4...Nf6; 5.Nc3 Bd6 (5...Bg4; 6.Nf3 Bd6; 7.Qe2+ Kf8; 8.0–0 Nbd7; 9.d4 Nb6; 10.Bb3 Qd7; 11.Ne5 and White had the initiative in So. Polgar-Valenti, Val Maubuee France 1988.) 6.Qe2+ Qe7; 7.Nb5 Kd8; 8.Qxe7+ Bxe7; 9.d4 a6; 10.d6 cxd6; 11.Nc3 Bf5; 12.Bxf4 Bxc2; 13.Bxf7 Rf8; 14.Be6 Nc6; 15.Nge2 Ne4; 16.Nd5 Bd3 with a complex game in Westerinen-Kraidman, England (Duncan Lawrie) 1988.

B) 4...Qh4+; 5.Kf1 f3; 6.Bb5+ c6; 7.Nxf3 Qh5; 8.Qe2+ Be7; 9.dxc6 Nxc6; 10.Ne5 Qf5+; 11.Ke1 Qxc2; 12.Nc3 Bd7; 13.Nxc6 Bxc6; 14.Bd3 Bxg2; 15.Rg1 was a typical Westerinen quick finish in Westerinen-Franzen, Belgrade 1988. 3...f5 is the Lopez Countergambit, an aggressive defense advocated in my *Who's Afraid of the King's Gambit?* 4.Qe2 (4.h4 Qe7; 5.d3 fxe4; 6.dxe4 Qxe4+; 7.Qe2 Qxe2+; 8.Bxe2 Nf6; 9.Bxf4 c6 led to equality in Alekhine-Giese, Postal 1905.)

4...Qh4+; 5.Kd1 fxe4; 6.Qxe4+ Be7; 7.Nf3 Qh5 and the best I see for White is:

A) 8.Re1 is recommended by some authorities, but I believe that Black is doing fine after 8...Nc6; 9.Bxg8 Rxg8; 10.Nc3 d6!; 11.Nd5 Bf5; 12.Qc4 Bxc2+; 13.Ke2! Bh4!, a move which improves over Hoffer-Grischfeld, London 1882. Now the following possibilities present themselves: 14.Kf1+ (14.d4 0–0–0; 15.Nxf4 Qe8+!; 16.Be3 Bxe1; 17.Qxc2 g5 and Black has a serious material advantage. 14.Nxc7+ Kd7; 15.Nxa8 Re8+; 16.Kf1 Bxe1; 17.Nxe1 Qd1 and Black comes out on top. 14.Nxf4 Qf7; 15.Qxf7+ Kxf7; 16.Nxh4 Rae8+; 17.Kf1 Rxe1+; 18.Kxe1 g5; 19.Nd5 gxh4; 20.Kf2 Be4 and Black's active pieces lead to a material advantage.) 14...Bxe1; 15.Nf6+! gxf6; 16.Qxg8+ Kd7; 17.Qxa8 Bh4 with the threat of ...Bd3+, tying down White's pieces, gives Black more than enough compensation for the exchange.

B) 8.Bxg8 Rxg8; 9.Nc3 Nc6; 10.Nd5 Kd8; 11.Nxf4 Qf7; 12.Qxh7 was played in Cordel-Neumann, Paris 1867, and after 12...d5 Black fell into a bad position. This game has stood as the final word on the variation for some time, but I found that after 12...d6, keeping the d-pawn out of the range of the enemy knights. This position is still awaiting practical tests. 3...Nf6! is present considered the most reliable defense.

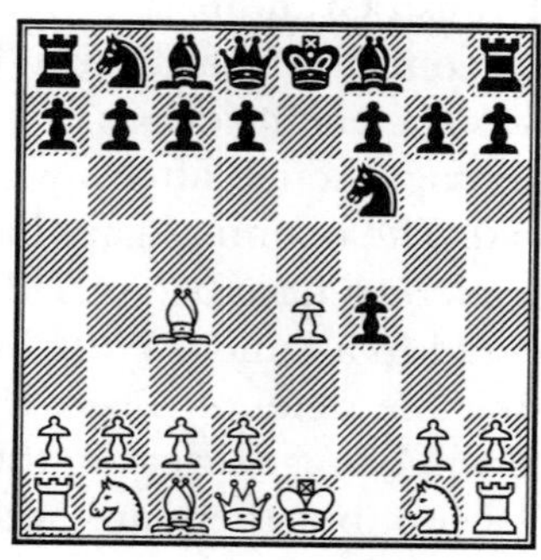

4.Nc3 c6.

A) 5.Bb3 d5; 6.exd5 cxd5; 7.d4 Bb4; 8.Nf3 0–0; 9.0–0 Bxc3; 10.bxc3 Qc7; 11.Qe1

Nc6; 12.Qh4 Ne7; 13.Bxf4 Qxc3; 14.Bd2 Qc7; 15.Ne5 Nf5; 16.Qf4 Be6; 17.Bb4 Rfc8; 18.g4 Nd6; 19.Rae1 Nfe4?

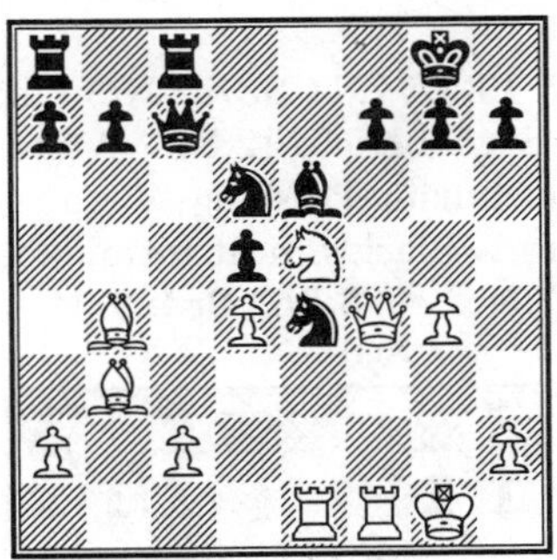

(19...a5!) 20.c4! dxc4 (20...Nxc4; 21.Bxc4 Qb6!; 22.Rxe4! Qxb4; 23.Nxf7 Rxc4; 24.Rxe6 Rxd4; 25.Qf5 Rxg4+; 26.Kh1 with a clear advantage for White) 21.Bc2 Nf6; 22.g5 Nh5? (22...Nd5; 23.Qh4 g6; 24.Nxg6 fxg6; 25.Rxe6 Nxb4; 26.Bxg6 Qg7; 27.Rxd6 hxg6; 28.Qe1!) 23.Qf3+ g6; 24.Nxg6! hxg6; 25.Bxg6 fxg6 (25...Ng7; 26.Bxd6 Qxd6; 27.Bxf7+ Bxf7; 28.Qxf7+ Kh8; 29.Re4) 26.Rxe6 Qf7 (26...Qg7 27.Bxd6!) 27.Qd5 Nf5; 28.Rxf5! White won. Morozevich-Anand, Intel Moscow Rapid GP 1) 1995.

B) 5.d4 Nxe4; 6.Nxe4 d5; 7.Qe2 Be7; 8.Bd3 dxe4; 9.Qxe4 Nd7; 10.Nf3 Nf6; 11.Qxf4 Nd5; 12.Qg3 Nb4; 13.Qxg7 Bf6; 14.Qh6 Nxd3+; 15.cxd3 Qe7+; 16.Kf2 Be6; 17.Bg5 Bxg5; 18.Qxg5 Qxg5; 19.Nxg5 0–0–0; 20.Ke3 Bd5; 21.Rhf1 Rhg8; 22.Nxf7 Rde8+; 23.Ne5 Rxg2; 24.Rf2 Reg8; 25.Raf1 Bxa2; 26.Nc4 Rxf2; 27.Rxf2 Re8+ was drawn in Stocek-Keitlinghaus, Lazne Bohdanec 1996.

4.Kf1

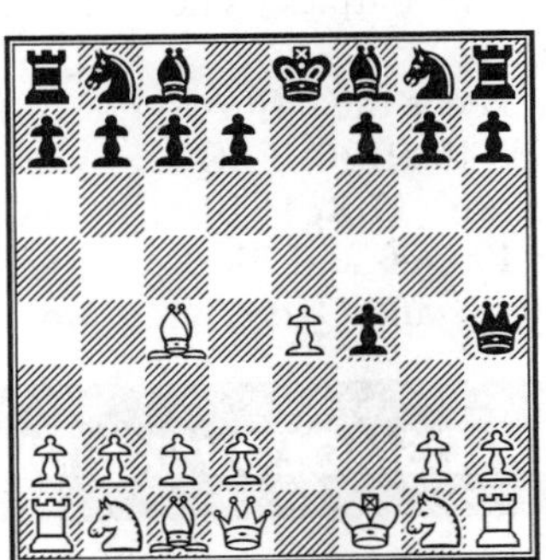

Black now has at least half a dozen plans, but they all fall short of equality. **4...d5.** 4...d6; 5.d4 g5; 6.g3 Bh3+; 7.Kf2 Qh6; 8.Nxh3 Qxh3; 9.Qf3 Bg7; 10.c3 and White recovered the pawn at f4 and went on to win in Westerinen-Bokan, Moscow 1989. 4...Nf6; 5.Nf3 Qh5; 6.Nc3 c6; 7.Qe2 Bb4; 8.e5 Ng4; 9.Ne4 0–0; 10.c3 Be7; 11.d4 Kh8; 12.Bxf4 Na6; 13.Re1 Nh6; 14.h3 Nc7; 15.Bd3 Ne6; 16.Ng3 Nxf4; 17.Qd2 Nxd3; 18.Nxh5 Nxe1; 19.Kxe1 and Black had insufficient compensation for the queen in Westerinen-Hebden, London (Natwest) 1988.

4...b5 is a famous move, because it led to one of the most famous games in the history of chess, the "Immortal Game" between Anderssen and Kieseritzky, London 1851: 4...b5; 5.Bxb5 Nf6; 6.Nf3 Qh6; Here 7.Nc3 brings White the advantage, but the brilliant game continued 7.d3 Nh5; 8.Nh4 Qg5; 9.Nf5 c6; 10.g4 Nf6; 11.Rg1 cxb5; 12.h4 Qg6; 13.h5 Qg5; 14.Qf3 Ng8; 15.Bxf4 Qf6; 16.Nc3 Bc5; 17.Nd5 Qxb2; 18.Bd6? Bxg1; 19.e5 Qxa1+; 20.Ke2 White won. 20...Na6; 21.Nxg7+ Kd8; 22.Qf6+ Nxf6; 23.Be7#.

5.Bxd5 Nf6. 5...g5; 6.Nc3 Bg7; 7.d4 Ne7; 8.Nf3 Qh5 seems to defend, but after 9.h4 h6; 10.Qd3 Nbc6; 11.Bxc6+! bxc6; 12.Na4 White has the center and Black's pawn structure is a mess, Teichmann-Pillsbury, Vienna (Gambit Tournament) 1903. 5...Bd6!; 6.Nc3 Ne7; 7.d4 f6 is Black's most formidable defense, Szekely-Nyholm, Abbazia 1912. **6.Nf3 Qh5; 7.Nc3 c6; 8.Bb3 Bg4; 9.d4.**

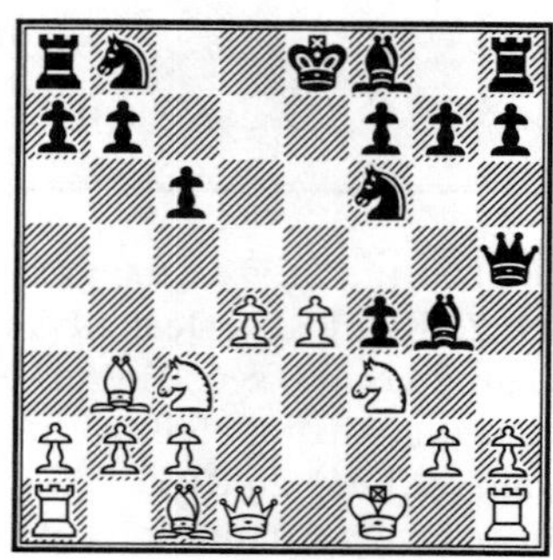

White owns the center and the king is perfectly safe. If White is allowed to regain the pawn at f4 without a fight, Black will be at a serious disadvantage. **9...g5; 10.e5 Nfd7; 11.Ne4.** White has a great advantage, because it is very difficult for Black to develop. The Black kingside can be smashed open by a timely h4. **11...Be7; 12.Qe2 0–0; 13.h4! c5; 14.Nf2!** This forces matters on the kingside, where Black's king, although not presently under attack, is nevertheless in great danger. **14...Bxf3; 15.gxf3.** Now the g-file is open.

15...gxh4. Black at least keeps the h-file closed. **16.e6!** Black has no satisfactory reply. **16...Bd6.** Desperation. 16...fxe6; 17.Qxe6+ wins a piece. 16...Nf6; 17.exf7+ Rxf7; 18.Qxe7 is equally painful. **17.Rg1+ Kh8; 18.exf7!** There is no need to settle for a mere piece! **18...Nf6; 19.Qe6** and Black resigned, since there is no defense against the dual threats of Rg8+ and Qxd6. **White won.**

BONCH-OSMOLOVSKY DEFENSE

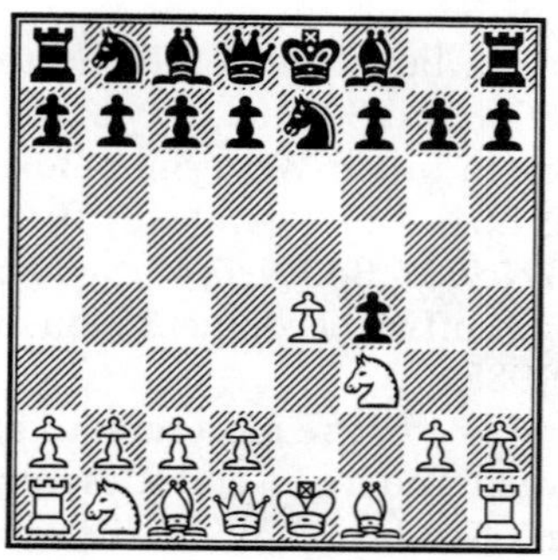

1.e4 e5
2.f4 exf4
3.Nf3 Ne7

The King's Gambit Accepted is one of the most heavily analyzed openings, with thousands of pages of analysis available for study. For this reason Black often tries to find a sideline that won't require too much preparation, given that the King's Gambit is rarely seen in professional play in modern tournaments. Boris Spassky has had a long love affair with this romantic gambit, however, and it comes as no surprise when he thrusts the f-pawn forward at move two. Opponents try to prepare refinements, but he never seems to have any difficulty meeting them at the board.

(18) SPASSKY - SEIRAWAN [C34]

Montpellier (Candidates), 1985

1.e4 e5; 2.f4 exf4; 3.Nf3 Ne7.

An unusual defense. 3...Be7 is very reliable, but placing the knight on that square, even if temporarily, just slows down the development. 3...g5 is the old main line, but it is almost never seen in top competition these days. This is probably due to the enormous amount of preparation required to master all the complications, which does not seem worth the effort when one considers how rare the King's Gambit is.

4.d4 d5. 4...Ng6 5.h4 forces Black to play 5...h5, with an ugly position. **5.Nc3 dxe4; 6.Nxe4 Ng6; 7.h4!** Spassky has played this opening before, and was familiar with the appropriate plan for White. **7...Qe7.** 7...Be7; 8.h5 Nh4; 9.Bxf4 gave White a good game in Kuznetsov vs. Bonch Osmolovsky, Moscow 1964. This defense (3...Ne7) is known as the Bonch Osmolovsky Variation. **8.Kf2.** The White king is treated differently, some might even say disrespectfully, in the King's Gambit. The large amount of breathing room on the kingside keeps it relatively safe. **8...Bg4; 9.h5 Nh4; 10.Bxf4 Nc6; 11.Bb5!** A useful pin, as is typical in the Open Games. White will disrupt the enemy pawn structure. **11...0–0–0; 12.Bxc6! bxc6; 13.Qd3 Nxf3; 14.gxf3.**

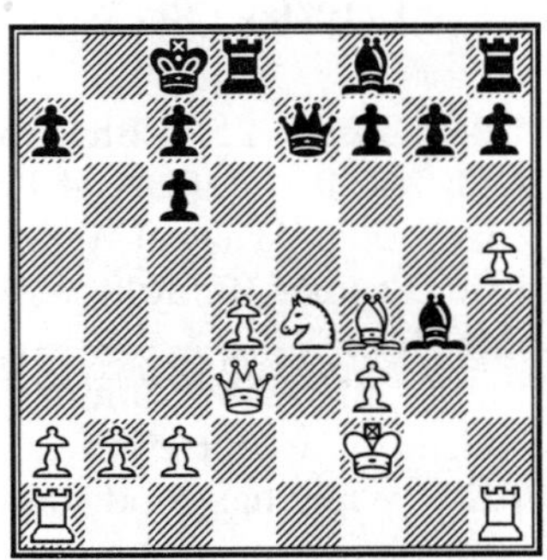

Whose king is safer? White's! **14...Bf5; 15.Qa6+ Kb8; 16.Nc5.** Queen and knight are often a dynamic duo. See how quickly they reach the queenside! **16...Bc8; 17.Qxc6 Rxd4.** There is nothing better, but now Spassky applies his formidable technique. Right now the attack features queen and knight, with assistance from the bishop. Now it is time for the heavy artillery to move into place in the center. **18.Rae1 Rxf4; 19.Qb5+ Ka8; 20.Qc6+ Kb8; 21.Rxe7 Bxe7.** In terms of material, Black's deficit is minor, and the bishop pair is enough compensation. But the king is still too exposed. It is ironic that the single pawn at f3 provides all the defense the White King needs, while not even the entire Black army can keep the queenside together. **22.Rd1 Rf6; 23.Nd7+ Bxd7; 24.Qxd7 Rd8; 25.Qb5+ Kc8; 26.Rxd8+ Bxd8.**

27.Qa4! There is a direct threat at a7, and an indirect threat at g7 via Qg4+. **27...g5.** 27...Kb8; 28.Qb4+ and White is going to win a pawn. If the king moves to a8, the key is Qe4+. If c8 is the choice, then Qg4+ works. Finally, if ...Rb6, then Qe8 attacks the bishop and the pawn at f7. **28.Qxa7 Rf4; 29.Qa6+ Kb8; 30.Qd3.** Another pawn falls. **30...Be7; 31.Qxh7 g4; 32.Kg3. White won.**

CUNNINGHAM DEFENSE

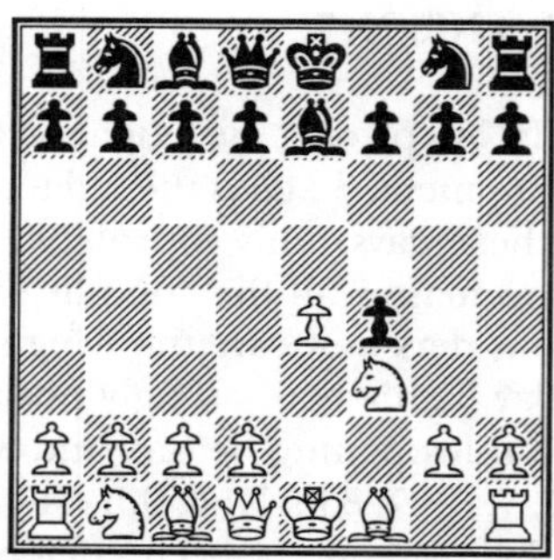

1.e4	**e5**
2.f4	**exf4**
3.Nf3	**Be7**

The **Cunningham** is a very reasonable defense to the King's Gambit. Black develops, but keeps available the option of delivering a check at h4.

(19) RIEMANN - TARRASCH [C35]
Leipzig, 1883

1.e4 e5; 2.f4 exf4; 3.Nf3 Be7; 4.Bc4. 4.Nc3 Bh4+; 5.Ke2 d5 is perhaps the best line for both sides. 6.Nxd5 Nf6; 7.Nxf6+ Qxf6; 8.d4 Bg4; 9.c3 gives White a solid center since 9...c5 allows 10.dxc5 as in Arnason-Wedberg, Randers 1985. Now an interesting move is 10...0–0 with the idea of ...Rd8, when it seems to me that Black stands a bit better. **4...Bh4+; 5.Kf1.**

5.g3 is the old-fashioned move, played by Cunningham himself, but it was only effective when players felt obliged to accept every sacrifice that came their way. After 5...fxg3; 6.0–0 gxh2+; 7.Kh1 White has good compensation, but if Black does not capture the pawn at h2, but plays instead the logical 6...d5, White must work hard to justify the investment. **5...d5; 6.Bxd5.**

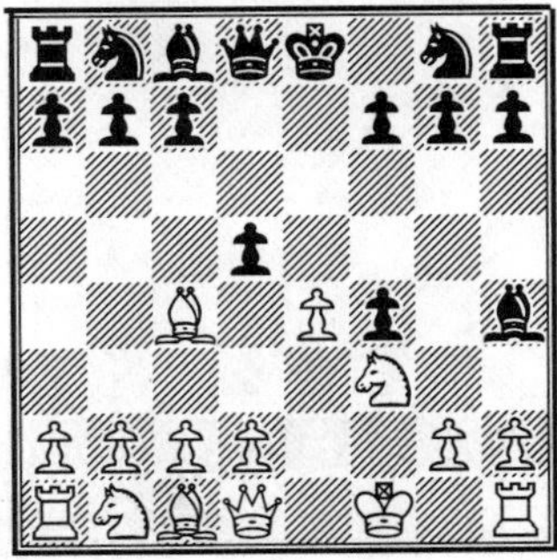

This keeps the bishop active. Capturing with the pawn is also possible, but it does block the bishop, at least temporarily. **6...Nf6; 7.Nc3.** 7.Nxh4 Nxd5; 8.exd5 Qxh4; 9.Qe1+ Qxe1+; 10.Kxe1 leads to an endgame in which White will be unable to accomplish much given the bishops of opposite colors. **7...Nxd5.** 7...0–0; 8.d3 c6; 9.Bb3 a5; 10.a4 Na6 seems reasonably comfortable for Black, who can follow up with ...Nc5 and ...Be6. **8.Nxd5 Bg4!; 9.Nxf4 Nc6.** The pin on the knight at f3 buys Black some time to complete development. **10.h3 Bxf3; 11.Qxf3 Nd4; 12.Qg4.** Black now regains the pawn with a superior game. **12...Nxc2; 13.Rb1.** 13.Qxg7?? loses to 13...Bf6. **13...0–0; 14.d4.**

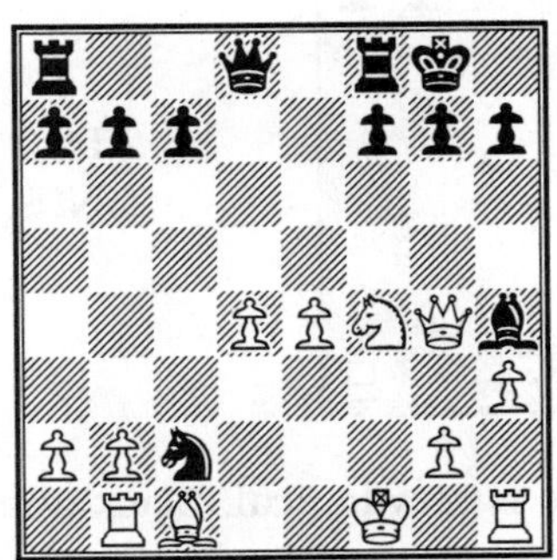

Black is comfortably developed and the exposed White king inspires Black to open up the f-file with a piece sacrifice. **14...f5!; 15.exf5 Qxd4; 16.Qxh4 Rae8.** The Black attack is worth much more than a piece,. and White's game quickly falls apart. **17.Bd2 Qxd2; 18.Qf2 Ne3+!; 19.Kg1 Qd4!** There will be no exchange of queens! **20.Ne2 Qd3; 21.Nc3 Rxf5.** Now the f-file is the highway to victory. **22.Qg3 Ref8; 23.Re1 Rf1+!; 24.Rxf1 Rxf1+; 25.Kh2.**

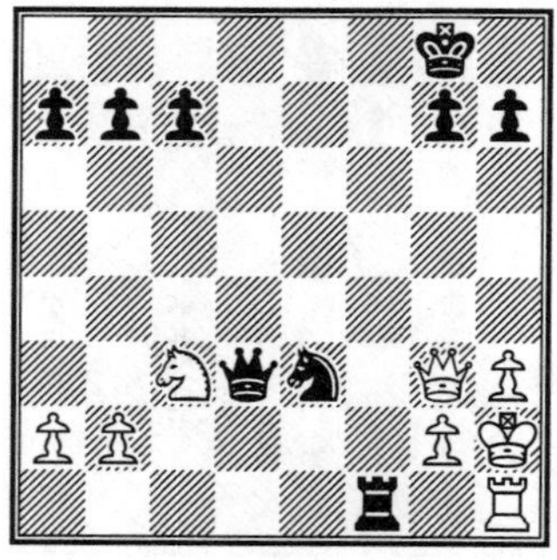

Now Tarrasch provides an elegant finish. **25...Ng4+; 26.Qxg4 Qd6+; 27.g3 Qd2+; 28.Ne2 Rf2+; 29.Kg1 Qe1#. Black won.**

MODERN DEFENSE

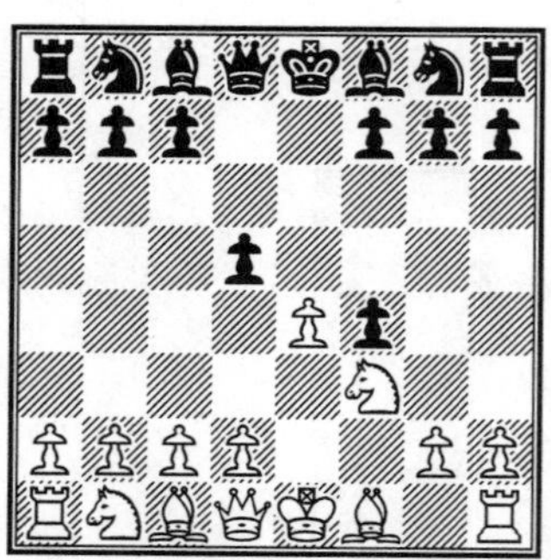

1.e4	**e5**
2.f4	**exf4**
3.Nf3	**d5**

The **Modern Defense** is very logical. Black opens up the center and obtains easy development. White can obtain a very small advantage with precise play, but the lack of any serious weaknesses in Black's position makes it difficult to achieve any major gains without a subtantial miscalculation. The defense is straightforward, with few tactical traps for either player. Nevertheless, it is possible for the play to liven up and some care is required on both sides.

(20) ILLESCAS - MUREY [C36]

Holon, 1987

1.e4 e5; 2.f4 d5

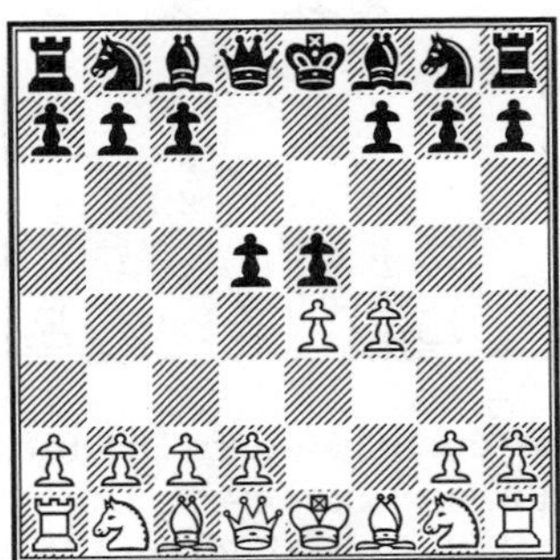

If White wants to play a gambit, why not offer a countergambit? The Falkbeer has a lot of interesting byways. We are going to examine one of them, a transposition to the Modern Defense, which usually arises via 1.e4 e5; 2.f4 exf4; 3.Nf3 d5.

3.exd5. We saw the normal Falkbeer earlier with 3...e4 while 3...c6 has been popular. But Black can also head into the paths of the Modern variation, sidestepping annoyances like the Bishop's Gambit, Breyer, and other divergence. 3.Nf3 exf4; 4.exd5 transposes below. **3...exf4; 4.Nf3 Nf6; 5.Bb5+.**

The most dangerous for Black, according to Korchnoi & Zak (1986). 5.Bc4 Bd6; 6.Nc3 0–0; 7.0–0 c6; 8.d4 cxd5; 9.Nxd5 Be6; 10.Nxf6+ Qxf6; 11.Bxe6 (11.Be2 Korchnoi & Zak consider this position more attractive for White, but I am not sure why. 11...Nc6 and Black will put his rooks in the center, with strong pressure. He can also look to the kingside for attacking possibilities.) 11...fxe6; 12.Ne5 Bxe5; 13.dxe5 Qxe5; 14.Bxf4 Qc5+; 15.Kh1 Nc6= Bronstein-Matanovic, Lvov 1962. 5.c4 c6; 6.d4 cxd5; 7.c5 Nc6; 8.Bxf4 Be7; 9.Nc3 0–0; 10.Bb5 Ne4; 11.0–0 Bg4; 12.Qa4 Bxf3; 13.gxf3 (13.Rxf3 Nxd4; 14.Qxd4 Bxc5) 13...Ng5; 14.Bg3 Ne6 with a comfortable game for Black, Tolush-Averbakh, Leningrad 1959. **5...c6.** 5...Bd7; 6.Be2!? Bd6; 7.c4 0–0; 8.d4 c5; 9.0–0 Re8; 10.Kh1 Na6; 11.Nc3 b6; 12.Bd3 h6; 13.Bc2 g5 led to complex play in Van der Plassche-Scheeren, Eindhoven 1987.

6.dxc6 Nxc6. 6...bxc6 This weakening of the pawn structure does not seem justified, but the move has been played frequently. 7.Bc4 Nd5; This defense was worked out by Botvinnik in preparations for the World Championship tourney of 1948. He didn't need it there, but had opportunity to test it out a few years later. 8.0–0 Bd6; 9.Nc3 (9.d4 was seen in Bronstein-Botvinnik, Soviet Championship 1952, but Black had a good game after 9...0–0; 10.Nc3 Nxc3; 11.bxc3 Bg4.) 9...Be6; 10.Ne4 Be7; 11.Bb3 and now Black must castle, with a slightly inferior game. If not, disaster can strike quickly, as in Tal-Winter, 1960: 11...Nd7; 12.d4 N7f6?; 13.Neg5 Bg4; 14.Qd3 Nd7; 15.Bxd5! cxd5; 16.Bxf4 h6; 17.Nxf7! and Black's position was indefensible.

7.d4 Bd6.

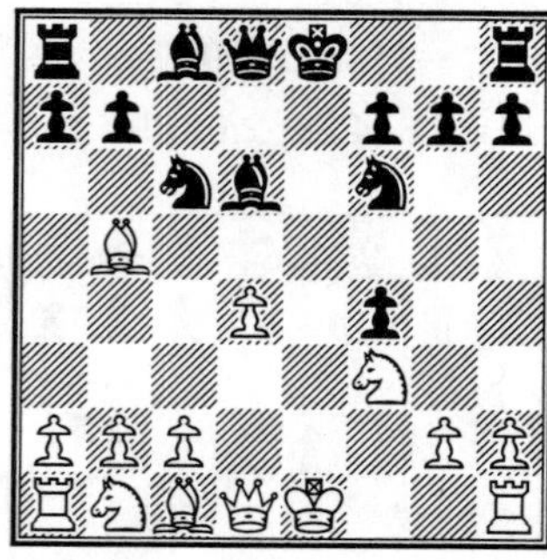

This is a typical position from the Modern Defense. White has a mobile central pawn majority with a passed pawn on the d-file. Black's pawns are on the kingside, and can become dangerous if allowed to advance, especially after White castles. White can choose between 8.Qe2+ and 8.0–0. The latter is safer, but the check is more fun.

8.Qe2+. 8.0–0 0–0; 9.Nbd2 (9.c3 Nd5! brings instant equality.) 9...Bg4; 10.Nc4 Bc7; 11.Bxc6 bxc6; 12.Qd3 Qd5 (Glaskov-Simitsyn, USSR 1972) (12...Bxf3; 13.Rxf3 Nh5; 14.Bd2 Qd5 analyzed by Gallagher, is an interesting alternative.) 13.Nfe5 Here Korchnoi claims an advantage for White. 13...Bh5; 14.Bxf4 Rfe8 This is a very complicated position, but the bishop pair and central pressure are probably worth the pawn.

8...Kf8!? A novelty, introduced in this game. 8...Be6; 9.Ng5 0–0; 10.Nxe6 fxe6; 11.Bxc6 bxc6; 12.0–0 leaves the situation far from clear. **9.Bxc6?** 9.0–0! is obvious and strong. White has the better chances here, since Black will find it difficult to mobilize the kingside. It is hard to understand why White chose to capture on c6, since the advantage is greater with a light-square weapon.

9...bxc6; 10.Ne5 Qb6!; 11.Nc4!? 11.c3 would allow 11...Ba6 with a better game for Black. **11...Qxd4; 12.Nxd6 Qxd6; 13.0–0 g5.** White has no real compensation here. **14.Bd2 Qc5+; 15.Kh1 Bg4.** Black has the initiative now. **16.Qe1 Kg7; 17.Bb4 Qf5; 18.Qc3 Rhe8; 19.Nd2 Kg8; 20.Rae1 Be2.** Now the final assault begins. **21.Rf2 Bb5; 22.Rxe8+ Rxe8; 23.h3 Re1+; 24.Kh2 g4; 25.g3 Qd5!** Here White resigned, as the kingside has fallen apart. **Black won.**

MUZIO GAMBIT

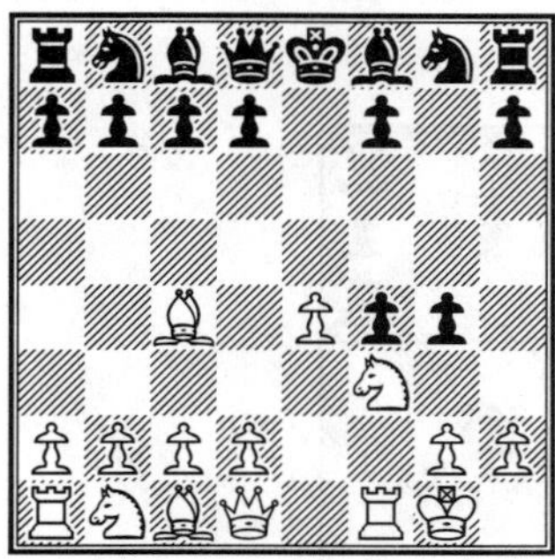

1.e4	**e5**
2.f4	**exf4**
3.Nf3	**g5**
4.Bc4	**g4**
5.0–0	

This is the **Muzio Gambit**, which sacrifices a full piece for a strong attack. The complexities of this line have been examined for over a century, but new ideas are still being discovered. The Muzio certainly qualifies as one of the most brutal of chess openings, with all forces targeted at f7.

(21) ZUKERTORT - ANDERSSEN [C37]
Breslau, 1865

1.e4 e5; 2.f4 exf4; 3.Nf3 g5; 4.Bc4 g4; 5.0-0 gxf3. Black should certainly accept the gambit, as otherwise White has a comfortable lead in development. **6.Qxf3 Qf6.** This is the best way to defend, since both f4 and f7 are covered, and the king can move to d8 if necessary. **7.e5.** White invests another pawn to deflect the enemy queen. 7.c3 Nc6; 8.d4 Nxd4; 9.Bxf7+ Qxf7; 10.cxd4 Bh6; 11.Nc3 is a more solid approach, which provides chances for both sides. **7...Qxe5; 8.d3.** This is the obvious and consistent move. White opens a path for the bishop at c1 and will capture the pawn at f4 with it. 8.Bxf7+ has been tried, but it is not sufficient against best play: 8...Kxf7. This is the Schumov Variation. 9.d4 Qxd4+; 10.Be3 Qf6 (10...Qxb2; 11.Qxf4+ Nf6; 12.Bd4 and White wins.) 11.Nc3 Bh6?!

(11...d6; 12.Bxf4 h5 is old analysis from the Bilguer Handbuch. White does not have much compensation here. 13.Ne4 Qf5; 14.Bxd6 Qxf3; 15.Rxf3+ Kg6; 16.Bxf8 Bg4; 17.Rf4 Nd7 and Black has a decisive material advantage.)

12.Nd5 Qe5; 13.Bxf4 Bxf4; 14.Qd3 Kg7; 15.Rxf4 h5 (15...Ne7; 16.Re4 Qxe4; 17.Qxe4 Nxd5; 18.Qe5+ is better for White.) 16.Qg3+ Kh6 (16...Kh7??; 17.Rf7+ Kh6; 18.Qxe5 Kg6; 19.Qg7#) 17.Rf6+ Qxf6; 18.Nxf6 Nxf6. Black has a rook and three pieces for a queen, which is more than enough. But the king must be defended. 19.Rf1 Rf8; 20.Qe3+ Kg6; 21.h4 Nc6 the obvious move, but the pawn at c7 turns out to be weak. (21...d6; 22.Qg5+ Kh7; 23.Rxf6 Rxf6; 24.Qxf6 Nd7; 25.Qg5) 22.Qg5+ Kh7; 23.Rxf6 Rxf6; 24.Qxf6 d6; 25.Qf7+ Kh8; 26.Qxc7 and White went on to win in Kurenkov-Vlasov, Russian Boys Under-12 Championship 1997.

8...Bh6. Other moves have not proven successful. For example, 8...Bc5+; 9.Kh1 Be3; 10.Bxf7+ Kxf7; 11.Bxe3 d6; 12.Bxf4 Qf6; 13.Qh5+ Qg6; 14.Be5+ Nf6; 15.Rxf6+

and Black resigned in Gedult-Gill, Paris 1974. 8...Bd6; 9.Nc3 c6; 10.Bd2 Ne7; 11.Rae1 Qg7; 12.Ne4 Be5; 13.Bxf4 Bxf4; 14.Qxf4 Kd8; 15.Nd6 f6; 16.Nf7+ Ke8; 17.Qc7 and the threat of Qd8 mate forced resignation in Ostmann-Svensson, Postal 1980. **9.Nc3 Ne7.** 9...c6 is too slow: 10.Bxf4 Qxf4; 11.Qh5 Qd4+; 12.Kh1 d5; 13.Qxf7+ Kd8; 14.Rae1 Bd7; 15.Bxd5 cxd5; 16.Nxd5 Nc6; 17.Re8+ Bxe8; 18.Qc7# Pulitzer-Marco, Gambit Tournament 1900. **10.Bd2.**

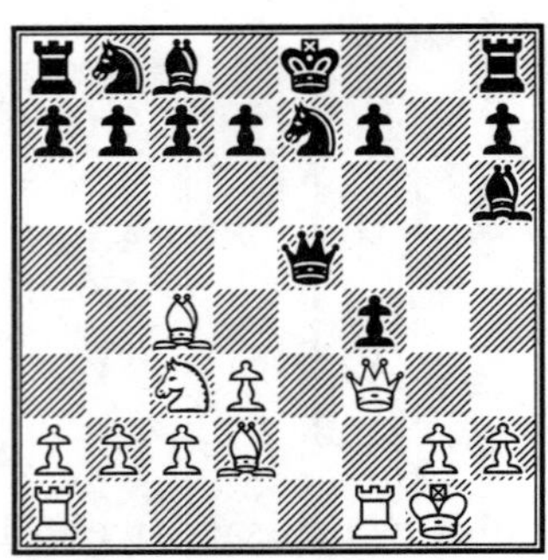

Now the question is, how should Black defend? Logically, Black should strive to advance d7-d5, cutting off the diagonals. To accomplish that, support is needed from a pawn at c6. **10...c6.** 10...Nbc6 is a different plan. Here Black hopes to gain enough time to move the queen from e5 and station the knight there, where it can fork the White queen and bishop. 11.Rae1 Qf5 (11...Qc5+; 12.Kh1 Nd4; 13.Qh3 d5; 14.Qxh6 Be6; 15.b4 Qc6; 16.b5 Qc5; 17.Na4 Qa3; 18.Bb3 f3 is an exciting option. 19.Qf6 Rg8; 20.g3 Nxb5; 21.Rxf3 0-0-0; 22.Bg5 Rde8; 23.Rfe3 Rg6; 24.Qf4 Qd6 and White had little to show for the pawn in Jonkman-Godena, Cannes 1993.) 12.Nd5 Kd8 and now White has tried all sorts of plans, for example

A) 13.Qe2 used to be considered best, but then a new defense was discovered: 13...b5! (13...Qe6; 14.Qf3 Qf5; 15.Qe2 Qe6; 16.Qh5 Qg6; 17.Qe2 was agreed drawn in Minic-Sokolov, Yugoslav Championship 1961.) 14.Nxe7 Qc5+; 15.Rf2 Nxe7 gives Black a clear advantage, according to Korchnoi.

B) 13.Re4 Nxd5; 14.Bxd5 Ne5; 15.Rxe5 Qxe5; 16.Bc3 Qd6; 17.Bxh8 Qc5+; 18.d4 Qxc2; 19.Bf6+ Ke8; 20.Qh5 Qg6; 21.Qe5+ Kf8; 22.Qe7+ Kg8; 23.Qe8+ Bf8; 24.Be7 Qg7; 25.Rxf4 and Black gave up in Caspero-Chiosso, Postal 1981.

C) 13.Bc3 13...Re8 (13...Rg8; 14.Bf6 Bg5; 15.Bxg5 Qxg5; 16.Nxf4 Ne5; 17.Qe4 d6; 18.h4 Qg4; 19.Bxf7 Rf8; 20.Bh5 Qg7; 21.d4 N5c6; 22.c3 a5; 23.Ne6+ Bxe6; 24.Rxf8+ Qxf8; 25.Qxe6 Ra6; 26.Rf1 Qg7; 27.Bg4 Nb8; 28.Rf7 and White won in a game attributed to, believe it or not, Karl Marx, against a player named Meyer in 1850. Was White's play capitalistic investment or socialist sacrifice?) 14.Bf6 Bg5; 15.g4 Qg6; 16.Bxg5 Qxg5; 17.h4 Qxh4; 18.Qxf4 d6; 19.Nf6 Ne5; 20.Rxe5 dxe5; 21.Qxe5 Bxg4; 22.Qd4+ Kc8; 23.Be6+ Kb8; 24.Nd7+ Kc8; 25.Nc5+ Kb8; 26.Na6+ bxa6; 27.Qb4# and Black was mated in Chigorin-Davidov, Saint Petersburg 1874. **11.Rae1 Qc5+; 12.Kh1 d5.**

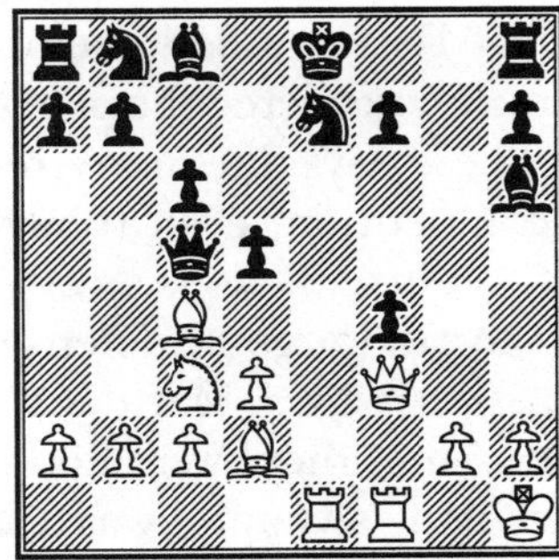

This position has been seen in a number of games. **13.Bxd5.** 13.Qh5 is also effective, pinning the pawn at d5 and attacking the bishop at h6. 13...Qd6; 14.Bxd5 cxd5; 15.Nxd5 Nbc6; 16.Bc3 Bd7; 17.Rxe7+ Nxe7; 18.Re1 Bf8; 19.Bb4 Qh6; 20.Qe5 Bc6; 21.Bxe7 Bxd5; 22.Bf6+ Be6; 23.Qb5# and once again White delivered the checkmate in Zukertort-Anderssen, Breslau 1865. **13...cxd5; 14.Nxd5 Be6.** 14...Qxd5 loses the queen to 15.Rxe7+ Kxe7; 16.Qxd5 **15.Nf6+ Kd8; 16.Qxb7 Nec6; 17.Rxf4!** Who needs the rook at a8? White is after the king! **17...Bc8.**

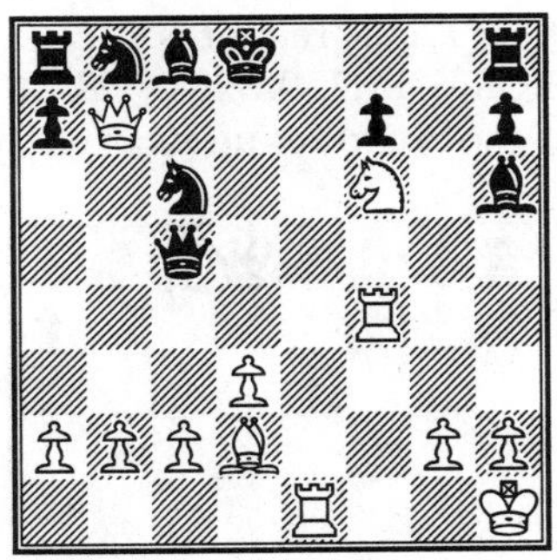

18.Rd4+!! Nxd4; 19.Ba5+ Qxa5; 20.Qe7#. White won.

FISCHER DEFENSE

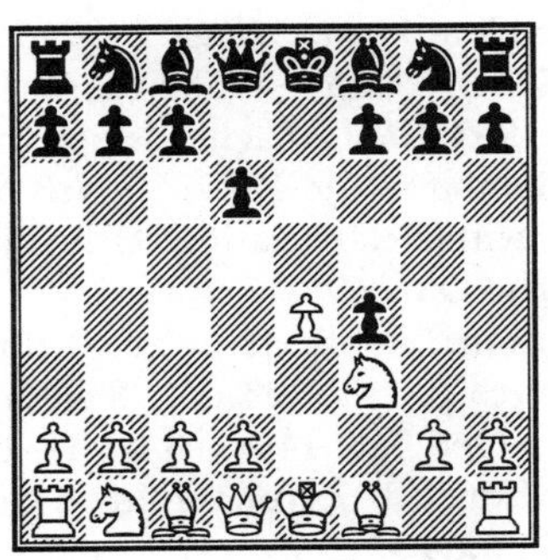

1.e4	**e5**
2.f4	**exf4**
3.Nf3	**d6**

This is the famous Bobby Fischer "bust" to the King's Gambit. For a little while the great influence of Fischer's endorsement had everyone fooled, but then for many years no one considered the plan a serious threat to White's ambitious opening plans. These days one more frequently finds the Fischer Defense used in serious competition, even though White obtains a good game with accurate play. Of course 3...d6 is a very logical move.

Fischer was motivated to find a good defense, because he had lost in humiliating fashion to Boris Spassky at Mar del Plata 1960. So Bobby went to work, publishing his ideas, since there were few opportunities to use them at the board, given that the King's Gambit was a fairly rare opening in the 60s. Fischer realized that a White knight at e5 is often the cornerstone of an attack, so this simple move eliminates that possibility, while also giving some scope to the bishop at c8.

(22) ARNASON - LARSEN [C38]

Reykjavik, 1978

1.e4 e5; 2.f4 exf4; 3.Nf3 d6; 4.Bc4. 4.d4 is considered the most important move for White. 4...g5; 5.h4 g4; 6.Ng1 This retreat is necessary. (6.Ng5 f6! gives Black a great game. 7.Nh3 gxh3; 8.Qh5+ Kd7; 9.Bxf4 Qe8!; 10.Qf3 Kd8 makes a strange impression on the eyes (was the board set up incorrectly?)

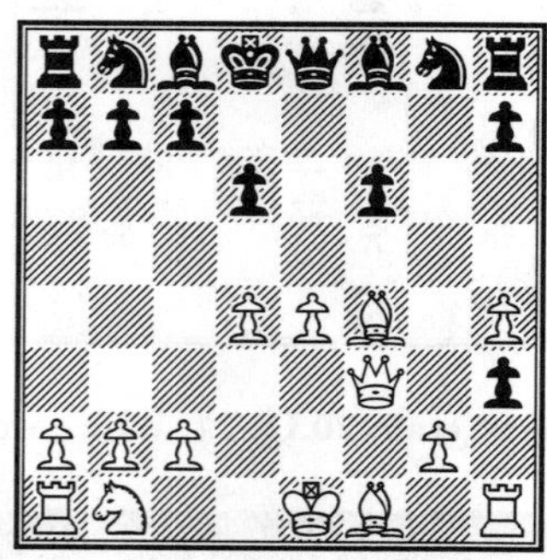

White has insufficient compensation for the piece. This is Fischer's analysis.) 6...Bh6 (6...Nf6; 7.Bxf4 Nxe4; 8.Bd3 Qe7; 9.Ne2 Bg7; 10.0–0 0–0; 11.Bxe4 Qxe4; 12.Nbc3 and White had a big initiative in Hebden-Borm, Orange 1987. 6...f3!?; 7.Bg5 Be7; 8.Qd2 h6; 9.Bxe7 fxg2; 10.Bxg2 Nxe7; 11.Nc3 gave White more than enough for the pawn in Gallagher-Ziatdinov, Lenk 1991. Joe Gallagher is perhaps the leading Grandmaster exponent of the King's Gambit in the 1990s.) 7.Nc3 Nf6; 8.Nge2 Nh5 and now White should have played g3, with a clarification of the kingside situation that works in White's favor, Cranbourne-Larsen, France 1981.

4...h6. 5.d3 has recently attracted attention, but after 5...g5 6.g3 Bh3 the situation is quite messy. 4...Be7?!; 5.d4 Nf6; 6.Nc3 0–0; 7.Bb3 d5?; 8.e5 Ne4; 9.Nxd5 Bh4+; 10.Kf1 b6; 11.c4 Nc6; 12.Bxf4 Nf2; 13.Qe1 Ba6; 14.Nxh4 Nxh1; 15.Kg1! and White won quickly in Arnason-Kuzmin, Reykyavik 1978 (played in an earlier round of the same tournament as our main game!). **5.d4 g5.**

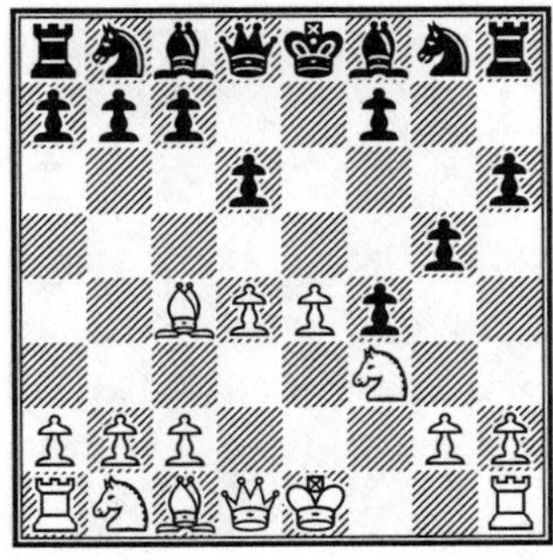

6.0–0 Bg7; 7.g3. 7.c3 Ne7; 8.g3 Ng6; 9.Qb3 0–0; 10.gxf4 gxf4; 11.Kh1 Nc6; 12.Qc2 Nce7; 13.Nbd2 Be6; 14.Rg1 Bxc4; 15.Nxc4 d5; 16.Nce5 dxe4; 17.Qxe4 Qd5; 18.Qxd5 Nxd5 gave Black a decent endgame, in Smith-Fischer, Chicago (Simultaneous) 1964. **7...Nc6.** 7...g4; 8.Nh4 f3; 9.Nc3 Nc6; 10.Be3 Nf6; 11.Qd2 Nxe4; 12.Nxe4 d5; 13.Nc3 dxc4; 14.Rae1 0–0; 15.d5 Ne7; 16.Bxh6 Ng6; 17.Nxg6 fxg6; 18.Bxg7 Kxg7; 19.Qd4+ Qf6; 20.Re7+ Kg8; 21.Qxf6 Rxf6; 22.Rxc7 gave White an endgame advantage in Spassky-Karpov, Hamburg (TV) 1982. **8.gxf4 g4; 9.d5 gxf3; 10.dxc6.**

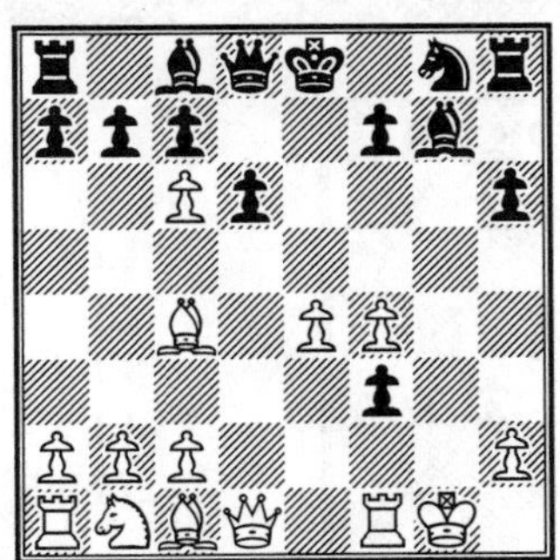

A typically messy position in the Fischer Defense! **10...Qf6!; 11.Bb5.** White sets up a killer discovered check, but must send his king on a journey to the middle of the board before the check can be delivered. **11...Qg6+; 12.Kf2 Qg2+; 13.Ke3 Kf8!** Suddenly the power of the discovered check is reduced to nil, and White must worry about that king at e3. **14.Rf2 Qg6; 15.Qxf3 Qg1!; 16.Nc3 Bxc3!; 17.bxc3 Nf6.** Although the White king is not under attack, it is still in the way. The pins at f2 and c1 are annoying, and three Black pieces have access to g4. The bishop at b5 and pawn at c6 seem irrelevant. **18.Kd3 Bg4; 19.Qg2 Qxg2; 20.Rxg2 Bf3.**

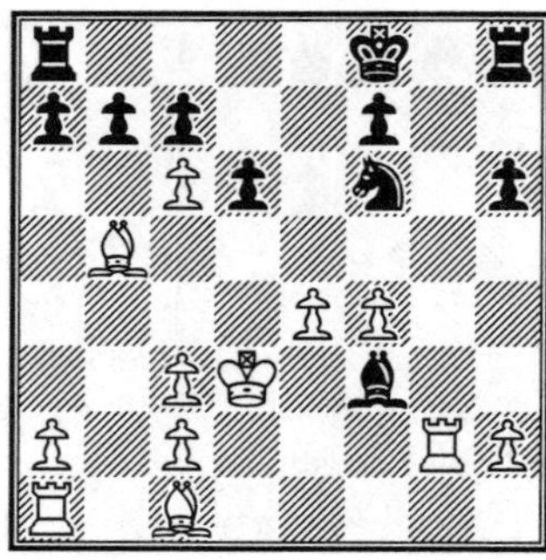

This is not an endgame. Black's attack continues relentlessly. **21.cxb7 Bxe4+!; 22.Kd4 c5+!; 23.Kc4 Bxb7; 24.Rg1 Be4.** White's pawns are falling, and White is forced on the defensive even in the endgame. **25.Ba4 Rb8; 26.Rd1 Ke7; 27.Ba3 Rhc8!** Now the threat of ...d5 forced resignation. An exciting game! **Black won.**

KIESERITZKY GAMBIT

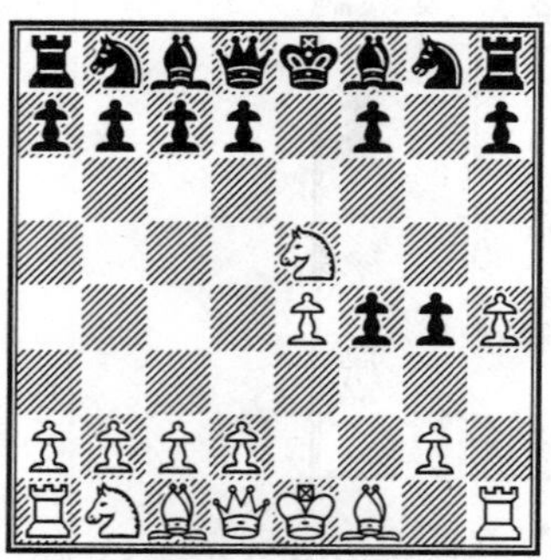

1.e4	**e5**
2.f4	**exf4**
3.Nf3	**g5**
4.h4	**g4**
5.Ne5	

The **Kieseritzky Gambit** is one of the oldest lines in the King's Gambit, but it retains its vitality even today, and is seen in encounters at the highest levels, as evidenced by this game. Black has many different replies, but I think that strong players will usually adopt 5...d6. Recent attempts to improve on established theory have been unsuccessful, in my opinion. From e5, the knight can capture the pawn at g4, which cannot be defended without great risk.

(23) NUNN - TIMMAN [C39]
Amsterdam, 1995

1.e4 e5; 2.f4 exf4; 3.Nf3 g5. This introduces the main lines of the King's Knight Gambit. **4.h4 g4; 5.Ne5 d6!**

5...h5 is the Long Whip Variation. It is no longer considered playable. 6.Bc4

Rh7; 7.d4 Bh6; 8.Nc3 Nc6 and now White storms in with 9.Nxf7!! Rxf7; 10.Bxf7+ Kxf7; 11.Bxf4! as in Bronstein-Dubinin, Leningrad 1947, which continued 11...Bxf4; 12.0–0 Qxh4; 13.Rxf4+ Kg7; 14.Qd2 d6; 15.Raf1 Nd8; 16.Nd5 Bd7; 17.e5! with an overpowering attack.

5...Qe7; 6.d4 d6; 7.Nxg4 Qxe4+; 8.Qe2 d5; 9.Nf2 Qxe2+; 10.Kxe2 Bd6; 11.Nd3 White will regain the pawn with a superior position, Kieseritzky-Dumonch, Paris 1849.

5...d5 is the Brentano Variation. White secures the advantage by taking control of the center. 6.d4 Nf6; 7.Bxf4 Nxe4; 8.Nd2! White exploits the initiative and lead in development by challenging the only Black piece which is taking part in the game. 8...Nxd2 is required, as otherwise White will capture at e4 and the Black pawn will become weak. 9.Qxd2 Bg7; 10.Bh6! The strength of the White attack was documented in Teschner-Dahl, Berlin 1946, which concluded 10...Bxh6?!; 11.Qxh6 Be6; 12.Bd3 Nd7; 13.Nxf7!! Bxf7; 14.0–0 Ne5; Black hopes for dxe5, which would close the e-file. 15.Rae1! and Black resigned.

6.Nxg4 Nf6. 6...Be7 is popular and beneficial. Gallagher concedes that 7.d4 is not effective, but his evaluation of the more modest 7.d3 as bringing advantage to White seems optimistic to me. 7.d3 Bxh4+; 8.Nf2 and now I think that 8...Bg3 should bring Black an equal game. (8...Qg5; 9.Qd2 Bg3; 10.Nc3 Nf6; 11.Ne2 works out well for White, if Black plays Gallagher's suggested 11...Bxf2+, but I think that 11...Qe5 deserves consideration.) 9.Qd2 Bg4; 10.Nc3 Nc6 with a complicated position that requires further tests. **7.Nxf6+ Qxf6; 8.Nc3.**

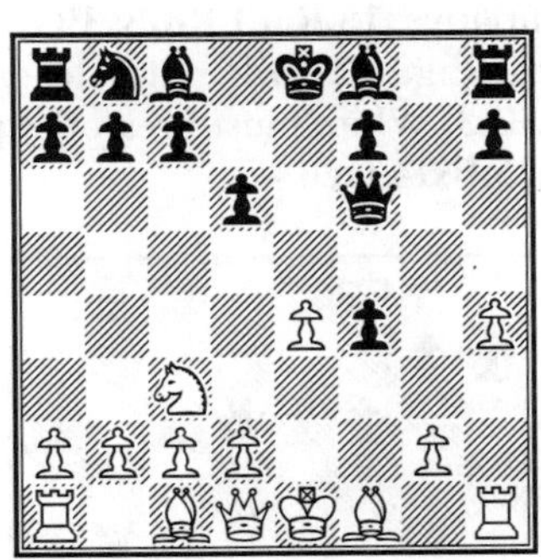

Now according to theory, Black's best is 8...Be6, but Timman, a well-prepared player, tried to work with another plan to control the d5-square. **8...c6!?** 8...Be6!?; 9.Qe2 Nd7; 10.b3 Rg8; 11.Bb2 Bg4!; 12.Qf2 d5 Black deftly exploits the pin on the knight at c3. 13.Be2 Bc5; 14.Qf1 Bxe2; 15.Qxe2 0–0–0; 16.0–0–0. White has an aggressive position, and Black will be on the defensive against threats in the center of the board. The game De la Villa-Fernandez, Barcelona 1990 eventually ended in a draw, but White did not make the most of his chances.

9.Qf3. 9.Be2 Rg8; 10.Bf3 Bh6; 11.d4 Na6; 12.e5 dxe5; 13.Ne4 Qe7; 14.0–0 gives White a strong attacking position, according to Gallagher's book, but Timman was surely prepared for that line. We will have to wait for another opportunity to see what he had in mind. **9...Rg8.** 9...Bh6?! loses to 10.g4 , according to Timman. 10...Bg7; 11.g5 Qd4; 12.d3 is definitely unpleasant for the second player. **10.Qf2 Bg4; 11.d3 Bh6; 12.Ne2.** White finally has enough firepower to reclaim the pawn at f4.

12...Nd7. 12...f3?! is a dubious attempt to create a desperado out of the f-pawn.

Timman gives 13.Bxh6 fxg2 (13...Qxb2? loses to 14.Qd4 .) 14.Qxf6 gxh1Q; 15.Bg5 with a clearly superior position for White. **13.Nxf4 0–0–0; 14.g3.** 14.Ne2!? is possible, against which Timman suggests 14...Bxc1; 15.Qxf6 Nxf6; 16.Rxc1 Rde8; 17.Kf2 Nh5 and Black will have compensation for the pawn when ...f5 gets played. **14...Qe5; 15.Bg2 f5; 16.0–0 fxe4.**

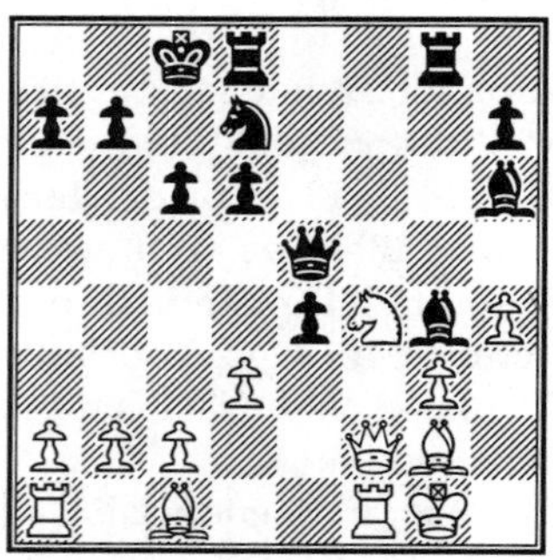

Things are already going downhill for White. There is really nothing better than recapturing at e4, though that is not impressive, either. **17.Bd2?** 17.dxe4 Nc5; 18.Nd3 Nxd3; 19.cxd3 Rdf8; 20.Bf4 Bxf4; 21.gxf4 Qh5 and Black is already better, with an active light-squared bishop. 17.Bxe4! is best. After 17...Rdf8 Black certainly has compensation, but White may not stand worse. **17...Bf3!** A superb infiltration which gives Black a tremendous initiative. **18.Rae1 Rdf8; 19.dxe4 Bxg2.** 19...Bxf4; 20.Bxf4 Rxf4; 21.gxf4 Qc5; 22.Qxc5 Rxg2+; 23.Kh1 Rf2+ leads to a draw, as analyzed by Timman. **20.Kxg2 Rg4; 21.Kh3.** White must break the pin. **21...Rfg8; 22.Rg1 Nf6; 23.Qf3 Qe7; 24.Rg2 Bxf4; 25.Bxf4 Qe6.**

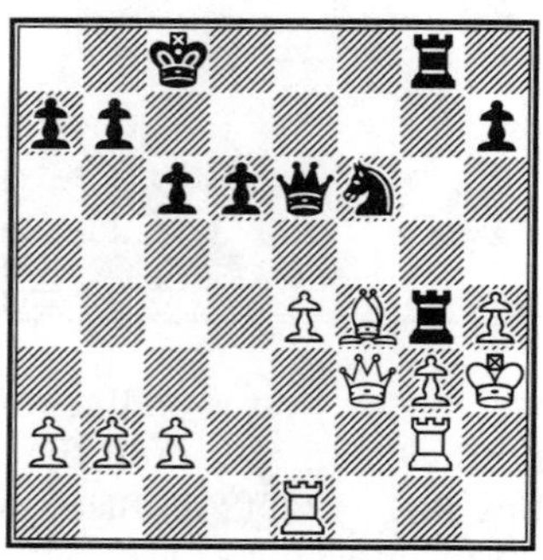

Black maintains the pressure, and White is squirming. **26.Kh2 Nh5; 27.Ree2 Rf8; 28.Ref2 Nxf4; 29.gxf4 Rxh4+; 30.Kg1 Qxa2; 31.Qg3?** An error in time pressure. After 31.f5 Qb1+ 32.Rf1 Qxb2; Black still has the threat of ...Qc5+ and a capture at e4, while the White f-pawn remains blockaded. **31...Qb1+; 32.Rf1 Rh1+.** This forces the win. **33.Kxh1 Qxf1+; 34.Rg1 Qxf4; 35.Qh3+ Kb8; 36.Qxh7 a6; 37.Rg8 Qc1+. Black won.**

RUSSIAN GAME

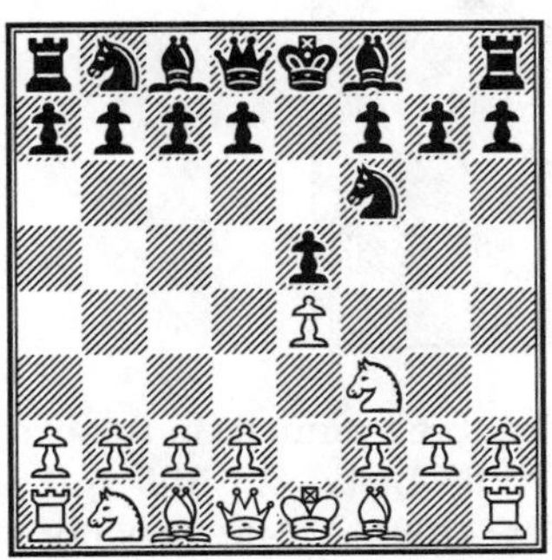

1.e4 e5
2.Nf3 Nf6

The **Russian Game**, also known as the **Petroff Defense**. Black starts out by mimicking White's moves, though that can't last for long. The Russian Game is very solid and it is unlikely that White can achieve a significant advantage with it, but on the other hand the sterile positions which arise are usually a bit more comfortable for White. Black has few ambitions early in the game but is content to postpone the main battle until after both sides have finished development.

The most heroic defenders of Russian territory, are, appropriately enough, FIDE World Champion Anatoly Karpov and Grandmaster Artur Yusupov, both Russians. They are willing to adopt this unpretentious defense, waiting for their opponents to make positional errors before trying to claim the full point. Both are capable of showing the extreme patience necessary to achieving success with the Black pieces in this opening.

(24) SPIELMANN - MARSHALL [C42]
San Sebastian, 1912

1.e4 e5; 2.Nf3 Nf6; 3.Nxe5 d6. 3...Nxe4; 4.Qe2 Qe7; 5.Qxe4 d6; 6.d4 dxe5; 7.dxe5 is better for White, because Black cannot quickly regain the pawn, for example 7...Nc6; 8.f4 f6; 9.Nc3 fxe5; 10.Nd5 Qd6?; 11.fxe5 Nxe5; 12.Bf4 Be6; 13.Nxc7+ Qxc7; 14.Bxe5. **4.Nf3.** 4.Nxf7 Kxf7.

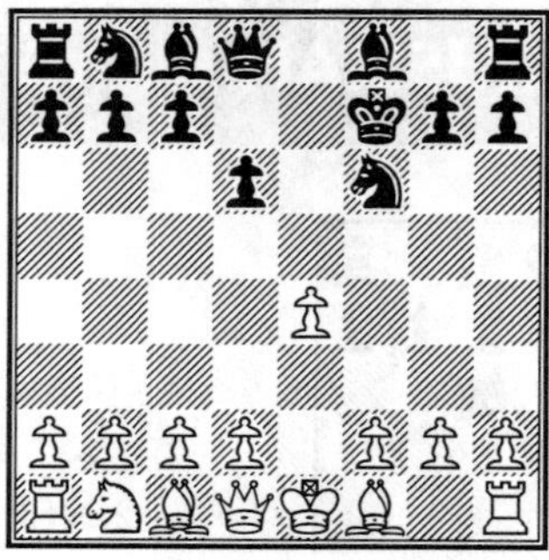

The Cochrane Gambit is now considered to be refuted on the basis of the following line: 5.d4 Qe8!; 6.Bd3 (6.Nc3 c6!; 7.Bd3 Bg4!; 8.f3 Bh5 and according to Watson and Schiller in *"The Big Book of Busts"* (1995) White does not have enough compensation for the sacrificed piece.) 6...c5; 7.dxc5 (7.d5 is met by 7...c4; 8.Bxc4 Qxe4+; 9.Be2 Qxd5) 7...d5!; 8.Nc3 dxe4; 9.Nxe4 Bf5!; 10.f3 Bxc5; 11.Qe2 Nxe4; 12.fxe4 Be6; 13.Rf1+ Kg8 with a winning position for Black, according to Hoeksma. **4...Nxe4; 5.d4.** 5.Qe2 Qe7; 6.d3 Nf6; 7.Bg5 Qxe2+; 8.Bxe2 Be7, the position is as equal as it is boring. **5...d5.**

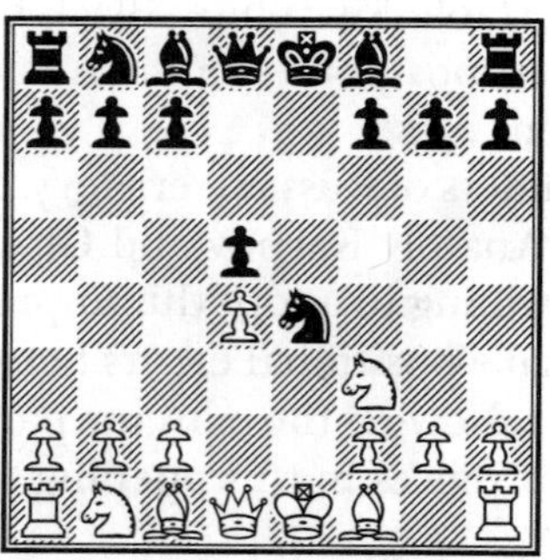

The pawn structure will retain its symmetry, and White has only the tiniest of advantages, inherited from the privilege of the first move. **6.Bd3 Bd6.** 6...Be7. The modest deployment of the bishop is also popular. The main line runs: 7.0–0 Nc6; 8.c4 Nb4; 9.cxd5 (9.Be2 0–0; 10.Nc3 Be6; 11.Be3 f5; 12.a3 Nxc3; 13.bxc3 Nc6; 14.cxd5 Bxd5 and Black was no worse, Belyavsky-Karpov, Barcelona 1989.) 9...Nxd3; 10.Qxd3 Qxd5 with an equal game. **7.0–0.** Both sides simply develop their pieces. White has the same advantage as at the start of the game-the privilege of moving first–but that is all. Players who choose this defense as Black count on White to make a mistake, or rely on their defensive skills.

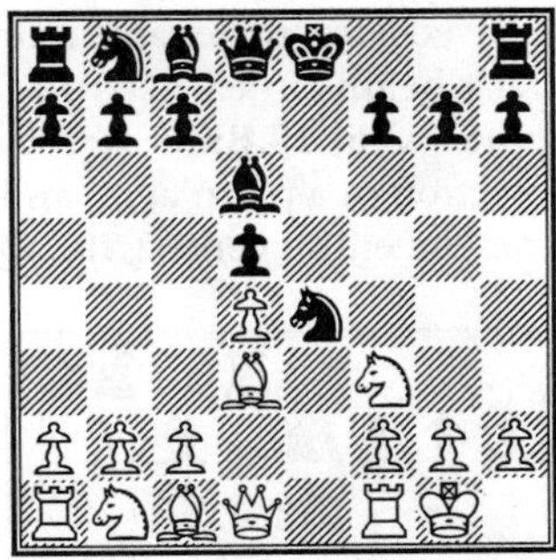

7...Bg4. 7...0–0; 8.c4 c6 is a popular alternative. 9.cxd5 cxd5; 10.Nc3 Nxc3; 11.bxc3 Bg4; 12.Rb1 b6; 13.Rb5 Bc7 position is defensible for Black, as in Wahls-Rozentalis, Germany 1992. 9.Nc3 Nxc3; 10.bxc3 dxc4; 11.Bxc4 Bg4 was fine for Black in Morozevich - Ippolito, New York Open 1997.

8.c4 0–0.

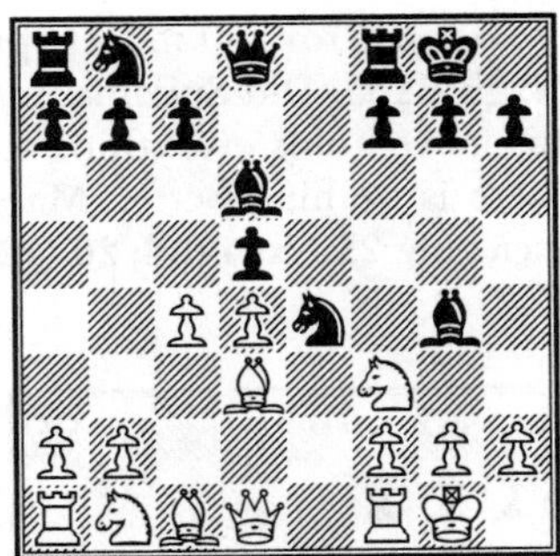

Marshall was also an aggressive player, and he loved gambits. Here he sacrifices a pawn for rapid development. Since White's extra pawn will be doubled and weak, it isn't a significant factor. **9.cxd5 f5?!** A new move at the time, and one which has been forgotten. Normally Black plays 9...Nf6 and then recaptures the pawn at d5 with that knight. **10.Nc3 Nd7; 11.h3 Bh5; 12.Nxe4 fxe4; 13.Bxe4.**

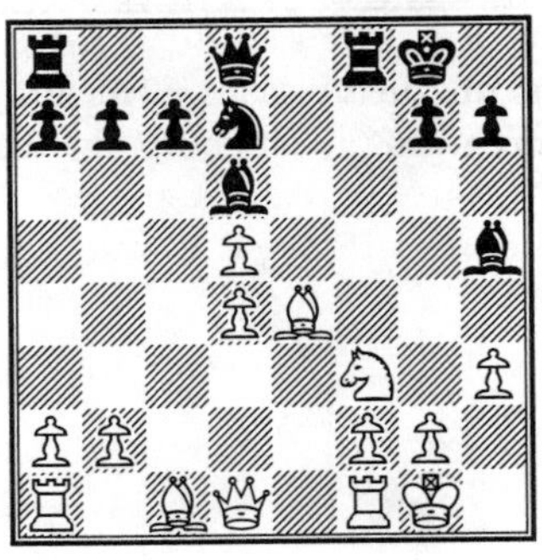

13...Kh8?! 13...Nf6; 14.Bf5! Kh8; 15.Qb3! Nxd5; 16.Bg5 gave White a great attack in Leonhardt - Marshall, played later in the same tournament. **14.Qd3 h6; 15.Bd2 Qf6; 16.g4.** Now White's attack begins in earnest. **16...Bf7; 17.g5 Qd8**. 17...hxg5; 18.Bxg5 wins instantly. **18.gxh6 gxh6; 19.Bxh6 Rg8+; 20.Kh1.** Both kings are exposed, but White has the protection of a pawn at h3 and his pieces are better placed to attack. Note that he controls the entire center! **20...Qf6; 21.Qe3 Rae8; 22.Bg5!**

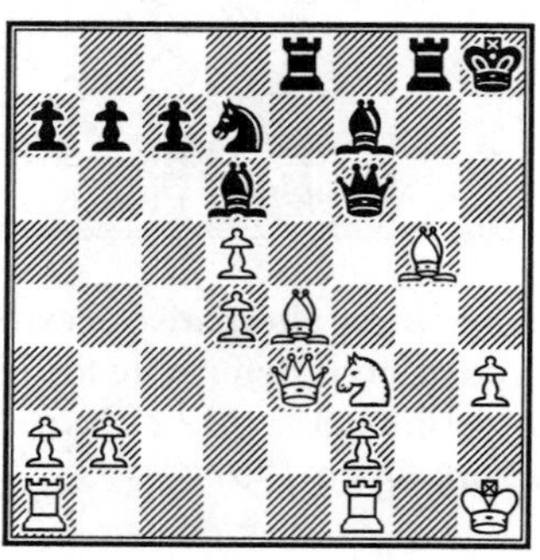

At first sight this seems to be an error, but in fact Spielmann knows exactly what he is doing. **22...Rxg5; 23.Nxg5 Bxd5.** Did Spielmann overlook that this bishop is pinned? Hardly. **24.Rg1!** This move holds everything together, and the game is effectively over. **24...Rxe4.** There is nothing better. Marshall tries to mix it up but Spielmann handles the game cleanly. **25.Nxe4 Bf4; 26.Qf3 Qf5; 27.Rae1 Nf6; 28.Qg2 Bxe4; 29.f3 Ng4.**

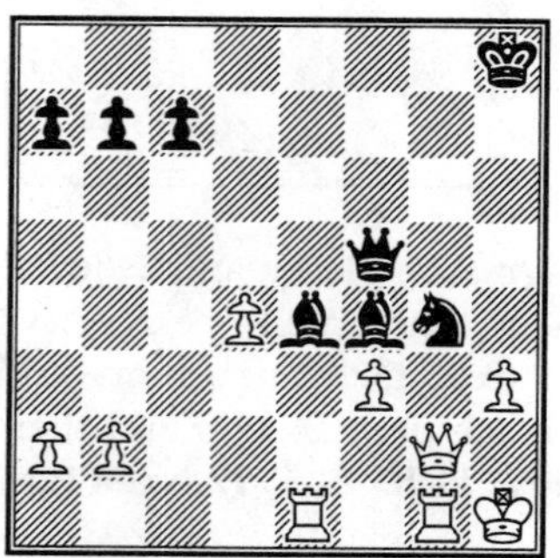

A pretty picture, but the puzzle is easy to solve. **30.Qxg4 Qxg4; 31.Rxg4 Bxf3+; 32.Kg1 Bxg4; 33.hxg4. White won.**

(25) KAMSKY - KARPOV [C43]

World Championship (6th match game), 1996

1.e4 e5; 2.Nf3 Nf6; 3.d4.

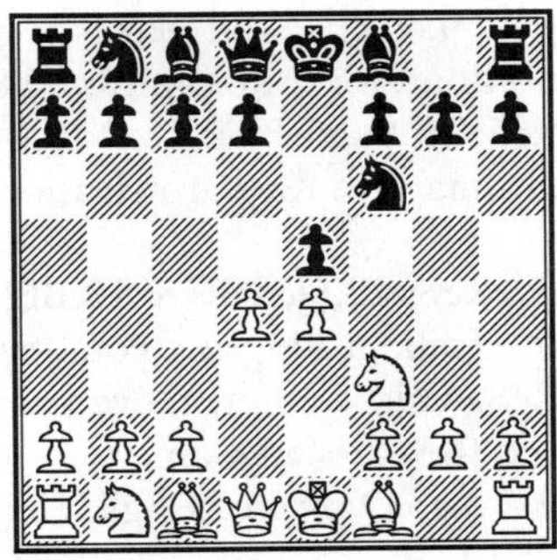

This move has faded in and out of popularity as a weapon against the Russian Game. **3...Nxe4.** 3...exd4 is less common, but is also playable, for example 4.e5 Ne4; 5.Qxd4 d5; 6.exd6 Nxd6; 7.Nc3 (7.Bg5 Nc6; 8.Qe3+ Be7; 9.Bxe7 Nxe7; 10.Bd3 0–0; 11.0–0 Bf5; 12.Nc3 Re8; 13.Bxf5 was agreed drawn in Shliperman-Bhat, United States Cadet Championship 1995.)

7...Nc6; 8.Qf4 and now the current favorite is 8...Nf5; 9.Bb5 Bd6; 10.Qe4+ Qe7 and White has not been able to make progress, no matter which side the king goes to: 11.0–0 (11.Bg5 f6; 12.Bd2 Bd7; 13.0–0–0 Qxe4; 14.Nxe4 Be7 and Black had no problems equalizing in the 10th game of the 1990 World Championship between Kasparov and Karpov.) 11...0–0; 12.Rd1 Ne5; 13.Bf4 Nxf3+; 14.Qxf3 Nh4; 15.Qg3 Bxf4; 16.Qxf4 Be6 led to a draw after a few more moves in Short -Akopian, Yerevan Olympiad 1996. **4.Bd3.**

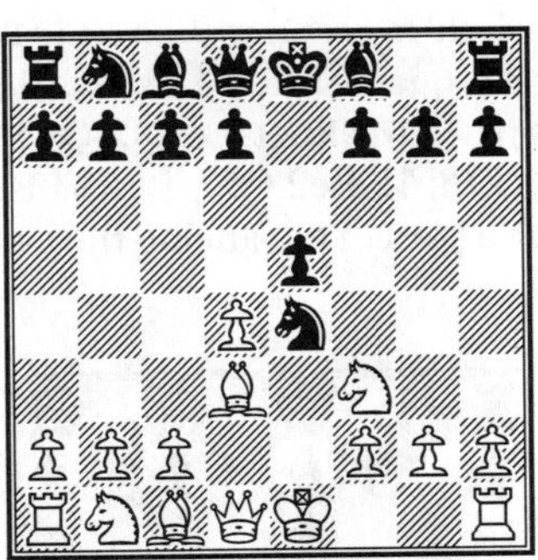

4...d5. The normal move, though 4...Nc6 is also in vogue. **5.Nxe5 Nd7.** This has become the most popular continuation in high level competition. Black immediately challenges the enemy knight. 5...Bd6 remains a solid alternative. The symmetry cannot be maintained forever, but it is still acceptable here. 6.0–0 Nc6; 7.Nxc6 bxc6; 8.c4 0–0; 9.c5 Be7; 10.f3 (10.Nc3 Bf6; 11.Qc2 Bxd4; 12.Nxe4 dxe4; 13.Bxe4 Qh4; 14.g3 Qf6; 15.Be3 Bxe3; 16.fxe3 Qh6; 17.Rf4 and White had the better position, with complete control of the center, in Ivanchuk-Yusupov, Horgen (Credit Suisse) 1995.) 10...Ng5; 11.Nc3 Re8; 12.Qa4 Bd7; 13.Bd2 Rb8; 14.Rab1 Bf6; 15.Kh1 h5; 16.Ne2 h4; 17.h3 Qc8; 18.Ba6 Qd8; 19.Bd3 Qc8; 20.Ba6 Qd8 was agreed drawn in

Kasparov-Yusupov, Horgen (Credit Suisse) 1995.

6.Nxd7 Bxd7; 7.0–0 Bd6. 7...Be7 is the major alternative. 8.c4 Nf6; 9.Nc3 Be6; 10.c5 Qd7; 11.Bf4 0–0; 12.Re1 Rfe8 brought Black approximate equality in J.Polgar-Yusupov, Vienna 1996. 7...Qh4 can be played, with malicious intent, but it carries a heavy commitment. 8.c4 0–0–0; 9.c5 g5! Bold play is required.

10.f3 (10.Be3 is more ambitious, for example 10...Re8; 11.Nd2 Bg7; 12.Nf3 Qh5; 13.Nxg5 Qxd1; 14.Rfxd1 Nxg5; 15.Bxg5 Bg4; 16.Rd2 Bxd4; 17.c6 Be5; 18.Bb5 b6; 19.Bh4 gave White a slight advantage in Kasparov-Ivanchuk, Debrecen 1992. Black's pawns are quite weak.)

10...Nf6; 11.Be3 Rg8 (11...Re8; 12.Qd2 Rg8; 13.Bf2 Qh6; 14.Qa5 Kb8; 15.Bg3 Rc8; 16.Nc3 Nh5 gave Black excellent kingside counterplay in A.Rodriguez-Lima, Guarapuava 1991.) 12.Nc3 Re8. This is a new move proposed by Russian specialist Artur Yusupov, who has played the Russian Game for most of his career. It received a baptism of fire in this game. 13.g3 Qh3; 14.Re1 g4; 15.f4 Qh5; 16.Qc2 Bg7; 17.Bf2 Ne4!? The start of a sacrificial plan. 18.Nxe4 dxe4; 19.Bxe4 Rxe4; 20.Rxe4 Qd5; 21.Rae1 Bc6 and Black regained the exchange with 22.Qb3 Qxb3; 23.axb3 Bxe4; 24.Rxe4 and was able to cope with the pawn deficit in Tiviakov-Schwartzman, Wijk aan Zee 1995.

8.Nc3. Kamsky tries something a little out of the ordinary here. 8.c4 is the alternative strategy, concentrating on the d5-square. 8...c6; 9.cxd5 cxd5; 10.Qh5 (10.Nc3 Nxc3; 11.bxc3 0–0; 12.Qh5 g6 solved Black's defensive problems in Tiviakov-Yusupov, Groningen 1994.) 10...0–0; 11.Qxd5 Bc6; 12.Qh5 g6; 13.Qh3 and here the new move 13...Qb6! led to a draw after 14.Nc3 Qxd4!; 15.Bxe4 Bxe4; 16.Qh4 f5; 17.Nb5 Qf6; 18.Qxf6 Rxf6; 19.Bg5 Re6; 20.Nxd6 Rxd6; 21.Rad1 in J.Polgar-Yusupov, Madrid 1995.

8...Qh4. 8...Nxc3; 9.bxc3 was a little better for White in Kharlov - P.Nielsen, Kemerovo 1995. **9.g3.** This is the strongest defensive formation against Black's kingside attack. Although Black is attacking with queen and three minor pieces, White can eliminate the knight at e4 when necessary. **9...Nxc3.** Black might as well inflict a little structural damage on the queenside. **10.bxc3.** 10.gxh4 Nxd1; 11.Rxd1 forces White to suffer from serious pawn weaknesses. **10...Qg4; 11.Re1+ Kd8!** A new move, introduced in this game. 11...Kf8; 12.Be2 Qf5; 13.Rb1 is better for White, according to Christiansen, who suggests a plan of advancing the c-pawn for White. **12.Be2 Qf5; 13.Rb1 b6; 14.c4.**

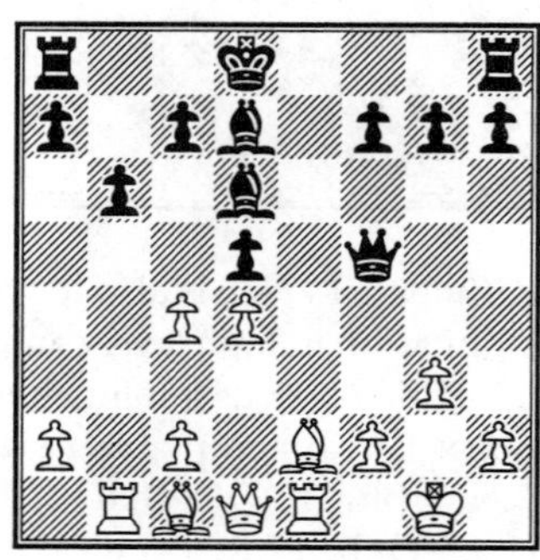

Black is now forced to capture, as otherwise might open up even more. **14...dxc4.** 14...c6; 15.c5! bxc5; 16.c4 is given by Karpov, who notes that the Black king is very vulnerable. **15.Bxc4 Re8.** Black would like to exchange rooks to ease the defensive burden. **16.Be3.** White declines, of course, since there are still chances to open up the game. **16...Bc6.** Black's threats on the diagonal must not be taken lightly. **17.d5 Bd7.** The maneuver has accomplished the strategic goal of making the c5 square available. **18.Bf1.** The bishop retreats to clear the way for the c-pawn to advance. **18...h6; 19.c4 Re7!** Black prepares to slide the king over to f8 and double rooks on the e-file. **20.Bd3 Qf6; 21.Kg2 Ke8!; 22.Bc2 Qc3; 23.Bb3?** This passive move gives Black the initiative. White should have offered an exchange of queens with Qd3. **23...Kf8; 24.Rc1 Qf6; 25.Bc2 Rae8; 26.Qd3.**

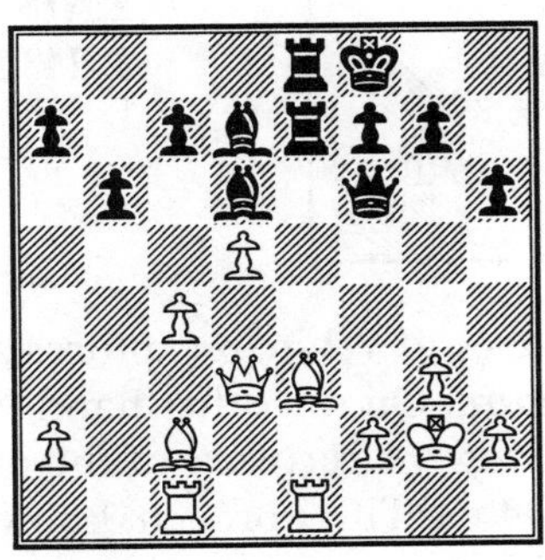

White is fixated on the Black kingside, but it is his own home that is threatened after **26...Bg4!** and there is a major threat of ...Qf3+, ...Bh3, and ...Qg2#. **27.Bd2?** White's position is already bad, but the damage could have been limited. 27.f4 Bc5; 28.Bxc5 bxc5; 29.Rxe7 Rxe7; 30.Bd1 Re1; 31.Rb1 Qf5; 32.Qxf5 Bxf5; 33.Rb8+ Ke7; 34.Bf3 Ra1; 35.Rb2 although after 35...Bb1 Black has a clear advantage, as analyzed by Karpov and Henley. **27...Re2!** This wins quickly. **28.Rxe2 Rxe2; 29.Rf1.** There is nothing better: the White queen cannot guard both d2 and f3 forever, so: **29...Rxd2!** White resigned. Karpov and Henley give the following possible conclusion: 30.Qxd2 Qf3+; 31.Kg1 Bh3; 32.Be4 Qxe4; 33.f3 Bc5+; 34.Kh1 Qf5; 35.g4 Qf6 and White can do no better than 36.Qe2 Bxf1; 37.Qxf1 Qb2 and Black wins without difficulty. **Black won.**

SCOTCH GAME AND GAMBITS

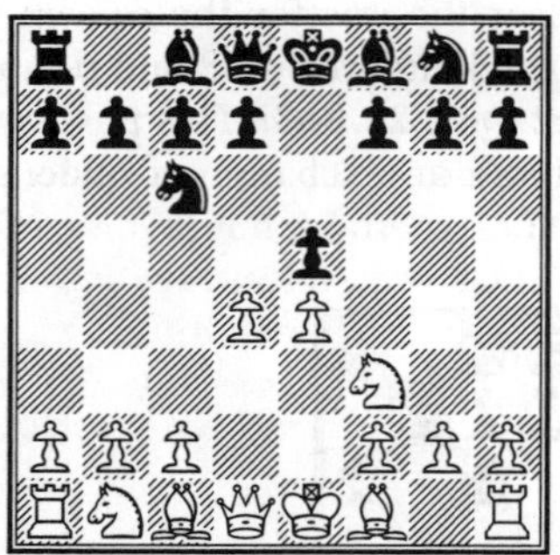

1.e4 e5
2.Nf3 Nc6
3.d4

The **Scotch** has two faces. If White recaptures at d4 with the knight, the game takes on a quiet nature. On the other hand, White can turn the opening into a gambit by delaying the recovery of the pawn, or making the gambit permanent by playing 4.c3. This aproach, known as the Göring Gambit, can lead to fierce play, and is very popular in amateur events.

GÖRING GAMBIT

In the Göring Gambit White invests a pawn in order to gain rapid development. It is important to note that the advance of the c-pawn gives the White queen access to the b3 square, and from there it can form a strong battery with a bishop at c4.

(26) GÖRING - PAULSEN [C44]

Leipzig, 1877

1.e4 e5; 2.Nf3 Nc6; 3.d4 exd4; 4.c3.

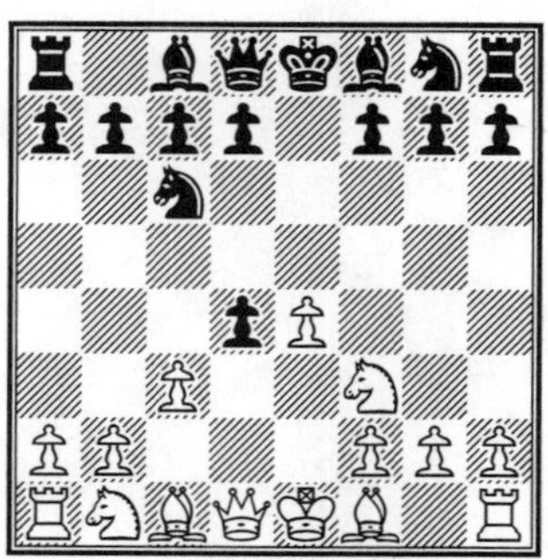

This game played a major role in the development of the Göring Gambit. It was played on the morning of July 16, 1877 in the Master tournament at Leipzig. Göring, a professor of philosophy at the University of Leipzig, made quite an impression on the home-town crowd.

4...dxc3; 5.Bc4 Schallop remarked in the tournament book that this double pawn sacrifice is incorrect, but that the refutation is not easy to find. Indeed, this sums up the situation well, save that after over a century of analysis Black has managed to find the best path, which, ironically, is the very defense used in this game! After the more prosaic 5.Nc3 White has good compensation for the pawn, and in my 1997 book on the opening I recommend it as the best method, but that is a minority view, since almost every other authority prefers 5.Bc4. Still, I don't see any way White can get enough for two pawns, and my arguments are put forth in this game.

5...cxb2. Accepting the pawn is the only way to play for the advantage. 5...c2; 6.Qxc2 Bb4+ is another old plan, for example 7.Nc3 Qf6; 8.0–0 Bxc3; 9.bxc3 Ne5; 10.Nxe5 Qxe5; 11.Ba3 d6; 12.f4 Qa5; 13.Bb4 Qb6+; 14.Kh1 Nh6; 15.f5 Ng4; 16.e5 Nxe5; 17.Bd5 c5; 18.Ba3 Qa6; 19.Bb2 c4; 20.a4 Bd7; 21.Ba3 0–0–0; 22.f6 g6; 23.Rf4 Bc6; 24.Rd4 Bxd5; 25.Rxd5 Qc6; 26.Qe4 Nd3; 27.Qd4 Rhe8; 28.Bxd6 Re4; 29.Qxa7 Qxd5; 30.Qb8+ Kd7; 31.Qc7+ Ke8; 32.Be7 Nf2+; 33.Kg1 Nd1; 34.Qg3 Qe5; 35.Qxe5 and Black gave up in Göring-Anderssen, Altona 1872.

6.Bxb2 Bb4+.

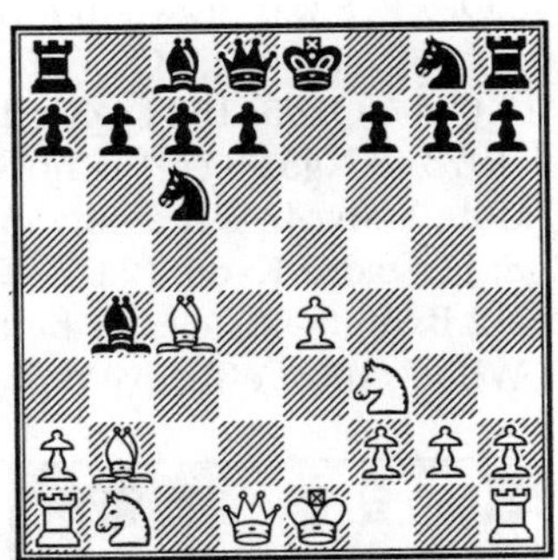

This is a logical move, developing with tempo. Nevertheless, it leaves the kingside without a defender of the dark squares. **7.Nc3.** 7.Nbd2 is rarely seen. 7...Kf8 (7...Nf6; 8.e5 Ne4; 9.a3 Nxd2; 10.Nxd2 Bxd2+; 11.Qxd2 0–0; 12.0–0 gives White some compensation for the pawn.) 8.0–0 d6; 9.Qb` 3 Nh6; 10.Rad1 gave White plenty of play. This historical game continued 10...Bg4; 11.a3 Bxd2; 12.Rxd2 Rg8; 13.Qe3 Bxf3; 14.Qxf3 Qe7; 15.Rfd1 Ne5; 16.Bxe5 Qxe5; 17.Rd5 Qf6; 18.Qb3 Rb8; 19.e5 dxe5; 20.Qb4+ Ke8; 21.Bb5+ c6; 22.Bxc6+ Qxc6; 23.Rxe5+ Qe6; 24.Qd6 White won. Tarrasch -Lasker, Berlin 1882. **7...Nf6.** This is not the best move, in my opinion. Black gets a good game with 7...d6.

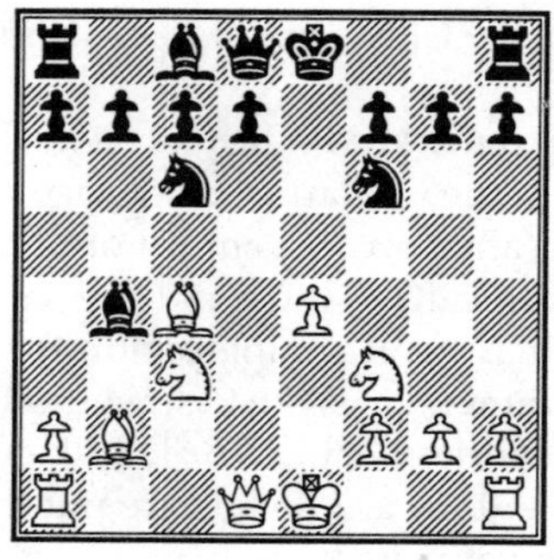

7...d6! and now

A) 8.0–0 is given by Smith & Hall. 8...Nf6 for some reason, Smith & Hall only consider 8...Bxc3?!, a move which makes very little sense. 8...Bg4 also comes into consideration. 9.Nd5 0–0; 10.Bxf6 gxf6; 11.Nxb4 Nxb4; 12.Qb3 a5; 13.Nd4 (13.Nh4 Qe7; 14.Qg3+ Kh8 and White can't really continue the attack.) 13...Bd7 and although White has some compensation, it does not seem to be enough.

B) 8.Qb3 Qe7!; 9.0–0 Bxc3; 10.Qxc3 f6; 11.Bd5 Bd7; 12.Qb3 Kf8; 13.Qxb7 Rb8; 14.Qxc7 Rc8; 15.Qb7 Rb8; 16.Qc7 Rc8 was drawn in Liptay-Kluger, , Hungary 1963. 7...Nge7 is possible, for example 8.Ng5 Ne5; 9.Qb3 d5; 10.Bb5+ c6; 11.Qxb4 cxb5; 12.0–0 0–0; 13.Rad1 N7c6; 14.Qxb5 Qxg5; 15.f4 Qh5; 16.fxe5 d4; 17.e6 was drawn in Richter-Oechslein, Postal 1973. **8.Ng5.** 8.e5?! is not nearly as good as Smith & Hall claim. 8...d5!; 9.exf6 Qxf6! (9...dxc4? is the only move given by Smith & Hall, but it is a blunder. 10.fxg7 Rg8; 11.Qxd8+ Kxd8; 12.0–0–0+ is much better for White.) 10.0–0 Bxc3; 11.Bxc3 Qxc3; 12.Bxd5 0–0 is clearly better for Black, Stein-Spassky, Tallinn 1959. 8.Qc2! This is White's most effective reply. 8...d6; 9.0–0–0 0–0!

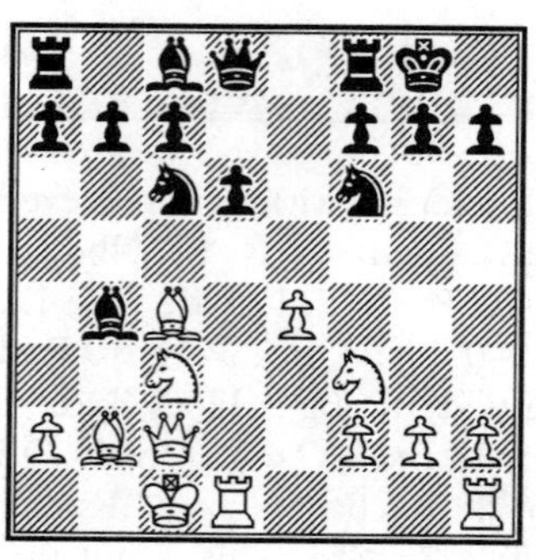

10.e5 (10.Ng5!? Ne5; 11.Bb3 Bg4; 12.f3 Bd7; 13.f4 provides White with a clear initiative. 13...Neg4; 14.h4 Bxc3; 15.Bxc3 h6; 16.Nf3 Qe7; 17.Nd4 gave White a very strong attack in Kusche-Baumbach, Postal 1984.) 10...Ng4; 11.Nd5! Bc5; 12.exd6 (12.Nf6+ Nxf6; 13.exf6 gxf6 gives up too much material. For example: 14.g4 Qe7; 15.g5 Ne5; 16.Rde1 Re8; 17.g6 Be6; 18.gxh7+ Kh8; 19.Nxe5 fxe5; 20.Bxe6 Qxe6; 21.Kb1 Qg6. Black won. McAllen-Harding, London 1972.) 12...cxd6.

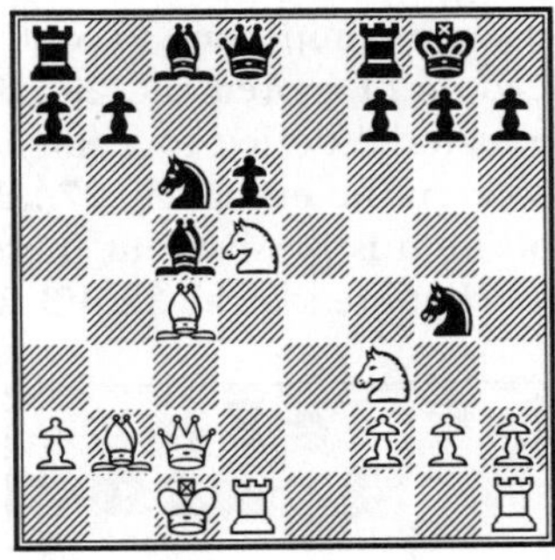

White is still down two pawns, and the open c-file could become dangerous. Still, Black's pieces are awkwardly placed, so White has time to attack the king, which has very little defense. 13.h4 Kh8; 14.Ng5 f5; 15.Nf4 Nce5; 16.Qc3 Bxf2; 17.Kb1 Qc7; 18.Bb3 Qxc3; 19.Bxc3 Bc5; 20.h5 b6 allows White to win with pure tactics. 21.Ng6+ hxg6; 22.hxg6+ Nh6; 23.Rde1 Rf6; 24.Nf7+ Rxf7; 25.Bxf7 Be6; 26.Rxe5 Bb4; 27.Ba1 Bxf7; 28.Rxh6+ and Black conceded in Dolgov-Mikhailchuk, Postal 1991.

8...Ne5; 9.Bb3 0–0; 10.0–0. White is in no hurry. Black's developed pieces are all exposed to attack, and White is almost completely mobilized. **10...d6.** 10...h6?!; 11.f4 Bc5+; 12.Kh1 Neg4; 13.e5 Nf2+; 14.Rxf2 Bxf2; 15.exf6 hxg5; 16.fxg7 Re8; 17.Qh5 wins for White. **11.f4 Bc5+; 12.Kh1 Neg4.** Black is trying to attack but has far too few pieces developed. This is a typical 19th century game, where the understanding of the balance between attack and defense has not yet been achieved. **13.Nd5.** A strong move, exchanging a knight which is not participating in the attack for a defender of the Black king. **13...Nxd5; 14.Qxd5 c6.** This move is only good if Black can achieve an early ...d5, but that square belongs to White. Now the pawn at d6 will require constant attention.

15.Qd3 h6. 15...Nf2+; 16.Rxf2 Bxf2; 17.e5 g6; 18.exd6 wins for White, as the Black king has no defense. **16.Nh3 Be6; 17.Qc3! Nf6; 18.Bc2!** White is hanging on to all attacking resources. **18...b5; 19.Rf3.** 19.e5! might have been more effective. **19...Nh5?!** This knight just sits helplessly on the edge of the board. **20.f5 b4; 21.Qd3 Bc8; 22.Bb3!**

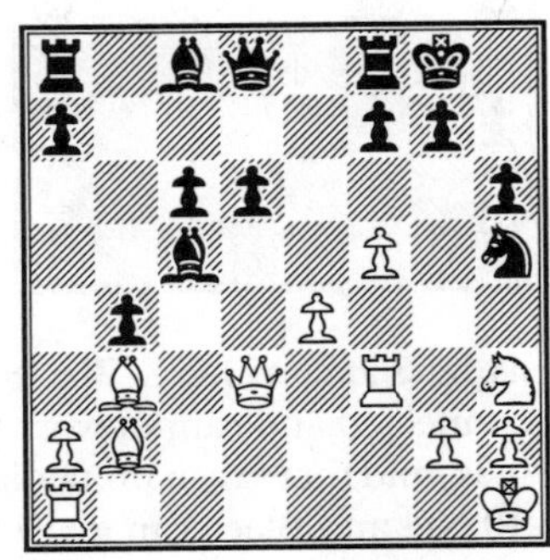

Now that the Black bishop has been driven back, White re-establishes the pin on the pawn at f7. **22...a5; 23.Bc4?!** An inaccuracy. White should just have continued with the attack. 23.g4 Nf6; 24.Rg1! would have been very strong. **23...a4; 24.Raf1 a3; 25.Ba1.** White decides that it is more important to control the long diagonal than to provide the bishop with freedom of movement. **25...d5; 26.exd5 cxd5; 27.Bxd5.** White has now reduced the material deficit to a single pawn, and has very active pieces. But Black can now pick up the exchange. **27...Ba6!; 28.Qe4 Bxf1; 29.Rxf1 Ra6; 30.Qc4 Ra5.** Black's position is passive, but there is a lot of extra material. **31.Rd1 Kh7?** 31...Qe7 was much more logical. **32.Bf3 Re8.**

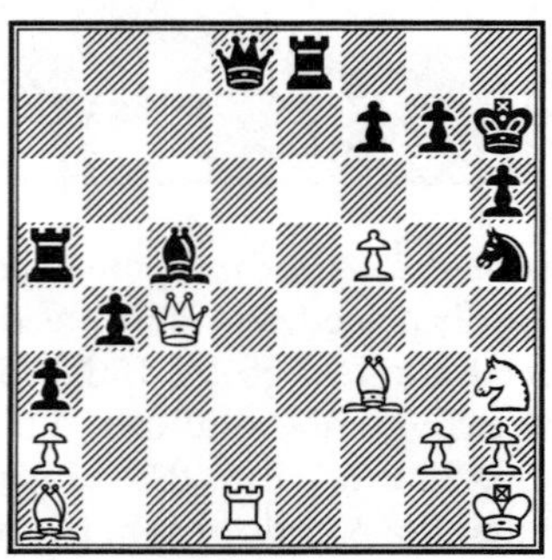

How should this position be evaluated? Black has the exchange and a pawn, and the threat on the queen is meaningless as long as the first rank is undefended. White therefore retreats the queen, but such a passive move does not make sense when the material is so lopsided. If White had properly appreciated the position, he would have realized that Black is threatening to take over the initiative on the kingside with ...Qh4 and threats of ...Ng3+ can arise. Therefore the correct plan is the prophylactic move g3, preventing the enemy queen from coming to h4, while simultaneously renewing the threat of Rxd8. **33.Qf1?** 33.g3 Qxd1+; 34.Bxd1 Re1+; 35.Kg2 Rxd1; 36.Qxf7 Rxa1; 37.Qxh5.

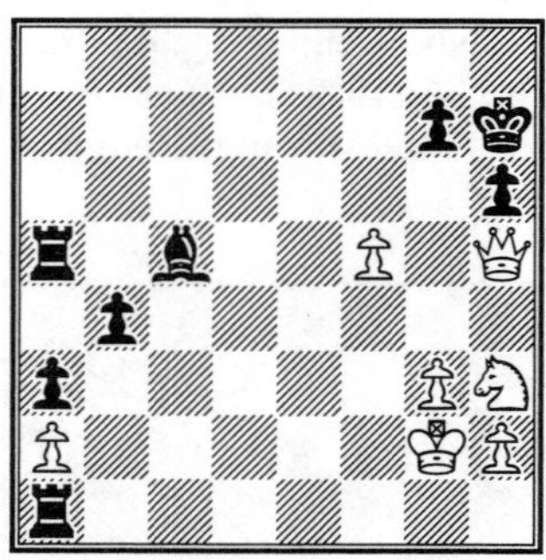

We are following analysis by Schallop here. Black has two serious problems. First of all the rooks are not connected and cannot work together. Second, the light-squares around the king are weak, and there is an immediate threat of Ng5+. 37...Be7; 38.Qg6+ Kg8; 39.Qe6+ Kf8; 40.Nf4 and Black can give up. Back to the game.

33...Qh4!; 34.g3 Nxg3+!; 35.hxg3 Qxg3; 36.Qg2 Re1+; 37.Ng1.

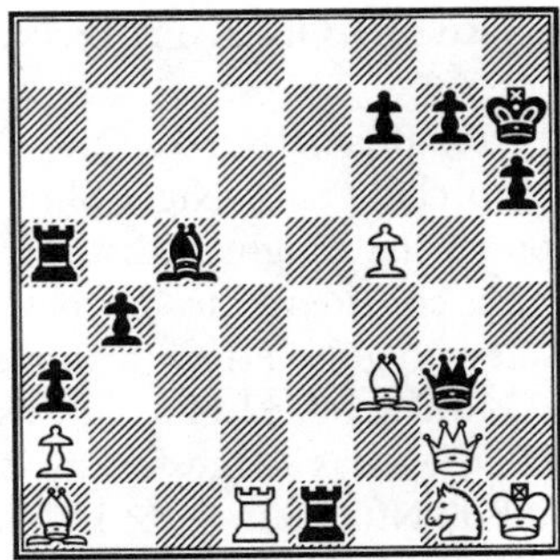

How things have changed! Black has a raging attack and a bunch of pawns to his credit. **37...Qh4+; 38.Qh2 Qxh2+; 39.Kxh2 Bxg1+; 40.Kg2 Rxd1; 41.Bxd1 Be3.** The endgame is hopeless for White. **42.Kf3 Bd2; 43.Bc2 f6; 44.Bd4 h5; 45.Ke2 Rd5; 46.Bf2 Bc3; 47.Be3 Re5; 48.Kf3 Rxe3+; 49.Kxe3 Kh6; 50.Bb1 Kg5; 51.Kf3 h4; 52.Kg2 g6; 53.fxg6 f5; 54.Kh3 Bf6; 55.Bc2 Kxg6; 56.Bd1 Kg5; 57.Ba4 Kf4; 58.Kg2 Ke3; 59.Kf1 f4; 60.Bd7 b3; 61.Be6 b2; 62.Bf5 Kd2. Black won.**

SCOTCH GAME

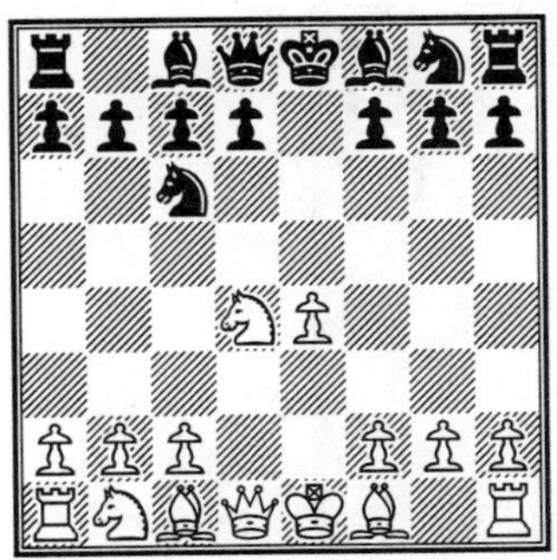

1.e4 e5
2.Nf3 Nc6
3.d4 exd4
4.Nxd4

The **Scotch Game** was considered harmless for most of the 20th century, but when Garry Kasparov resurrected it in his 1990 title defense against Anatoly Karpov it became popular again. The resolution of the tension in the center is premature. 4.Bc4 Nf6 leads to the Scotch Gambit which can also arise from the Two Knights Defense.

(27) SPIELMANN - RUBINSTEIN [C45]
Stockholm, 1919

1.e4 e5; 2.Nf3 Nc6; 3.d4 exd4; 4.Nxd4 Bc5. The main alternative is the development of the other knight. 4...Nf6; 5.Nxc6 bxc6; 6.e5 Qe7; 7.Qe2 Nd5; 8.c4 Ba6; 9.b3 was seen in games between Kasparov and Karpov. Here is part of their encounter at Tilburg 1991: 9...g6; 10.f4 f6; 11.Ba3 Qf7; 12.Qd2 Nb6; 13.c5 Bxf1; 14.cxb6 with an exciting position, where Karpov made a big mistake. 14...axb6?; Black had to try 14...Ba6!; 15.e6!! dxe6; 16.Bxf8 Rd8; 17.Qb2 Bxg2; 18.Qxg2 Kxf8; 19.Qxc6 and White went on to win.

5.Be3. 5.Nxc6 is a significant alternative. **5...Qf6.** This move was revived in the 1990s by World Championship challenger Nigel Short. An alternative is 5...Bb6. **6.Nb5.** Normally, White support the knight with the c-pawn. Spielmann plays the Blumenfeld Attack, which is not considered to be good enough for use in top level competition, but it can be used with good effect in amateur games. 6.c3 Nge7; 7.Bc4 0–0; 8.0–0 Bb6; 9.Nc2 d6; 10.Bxb6 axb6; 11.f4 as in Kasparov-Short, Linares 1992.

6...Bxe3; 7.fxe3 Qh4+. 7...Qe5 was suggested by Bronstein, but White has an effective reply: 8.Nd2! Kd8; 9.Bd3 Nf6; 10.0–0 d6; 11.Nf3 Qe7; 12.Qe1 Bd7; 13.Qg3 and White had a promising attacking position in Pinkas-Sokolov, Lublin 1974. **8.g3 Qd8.** This is the safe line for Black. Wild complications follow if Black takes the pawn: 8...Qxe4; 9.Nxc7+ Kd8; 10.Nxa8 Qxh1; 11.Qd6 Nf6; 12.Nd2 Ne4 (12...Ne8; 13.Qf4 Qd5; 14.0–0–0 is unclear.) 13.Qc7+ Ke7; 14.0–0–0 Nxd2; 15.Bb5 Qd5; 16.Bxc6 bxc6; 17.Rxd2 with a messy position.

9.Qg4. 9.N1c3 is a reasonable alternative. **9...g6.** 9...Kf8; 10.Qf4 d6; 11.Nd2 Nf6; 12.Be2 is interesting, so that White can castle queenside and attack on the kingside. Instead, in Mieses-Schelfhout, Amsterdam 1946, White placed a bishop on c4, where it was vulnerable to ...Ne5, and then castled kingside. This wrong-headed plan gave the whole line a dubious reputation for White. 9...Nf6; 10.Qxg7 Rg8; 11.Qh6 Rg6; 12.Qh4 d6; 13.N1c3 looks more promising for White. **10.Qf4 d6.**

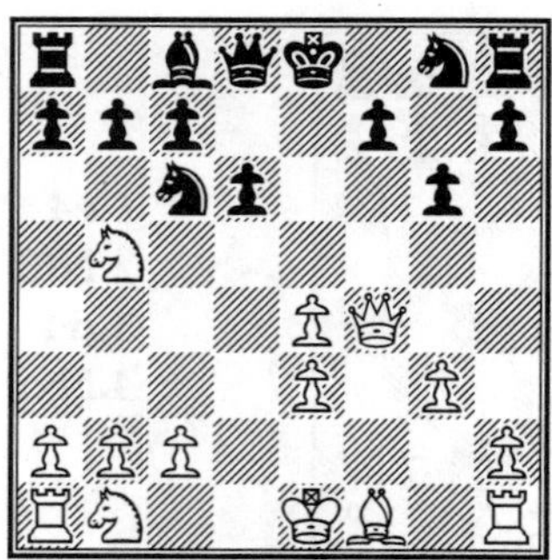

11.Bc4. White targets the weakest point in the Black camp-f7. **11...Be6.** 11...Ne5; 12.0–0 Qe7 (12...Nxc4??; 13.Qxf7#) 13.Nd2 is complicated, but White does have a lead in development and useful files for the rooks in return for the isolated doubled pawns on the e-file. **12.Bxe6 fxe6; 13.0–0.**

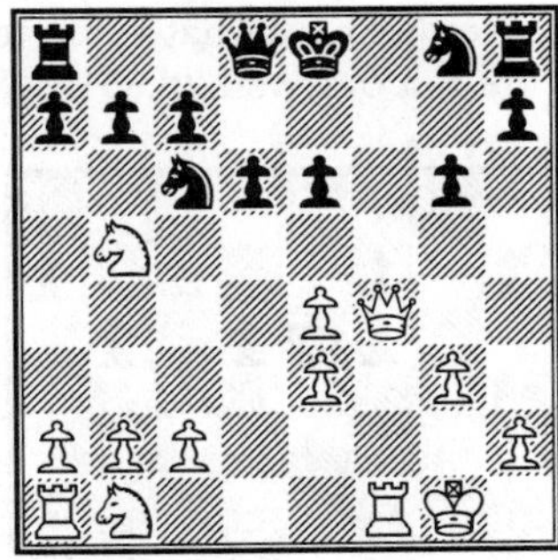

Now White has the advantage, and the Black king will not be able to castle to safety. Spielmann will now attack on both flanks! **13...Nge7; 14.N1c3 Ne5; 15.Qf6 Kd7; 16.Nd4 Qg8.** Black manages to respond to all the threats, but the position is very loose because the Black forces are uncoordinated. **17.Ncb5 N7c6?!** 17...Rf8 is the obvious move and it is stronger, for example: 18.Qxf8 Qxf8; 19.Rxf8 Rxf8; 20.Nxc7! Nf3+ (20...Kxc7?; 21.Nxe6+ Kc6; 22.Nxf8) 21.Nxf3 Rxf3; 22.Nb5 Rxe3; 23.Rd1 Nc8; 24.Nc3 with equal chances. **18.Nxc6 bxc6.**

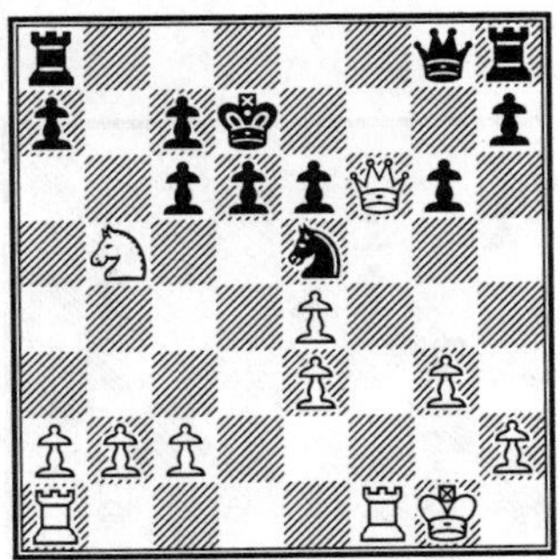

It seems that Black has consolidated here, but White has a trick! **19.Rad1! Rf8.** 19...cxb5; 20.Qxe5 a6; 21.Rf6 is better for White. **20.Qxe5 Rxf1+; 21.Kxf1 Qf7+; 22.Kg2 Rf8.**

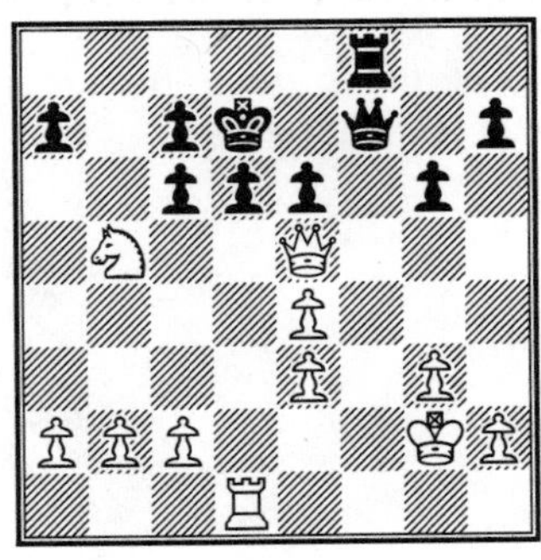

Black has threats on the f-file, but White can break down the fortress guarding the enemy king. Exciting stuff! **23.Nxd6! Qf3+; 24.Kh3 Qxd1; 25.Qg7+ Kxd6; 26.Qxf8+ Kd7; 27.Qf7+ Kd6.** Now we have what seems to be a quiet queen and pawn endgame, but the fireworks are not over yet! **28.e5+!**

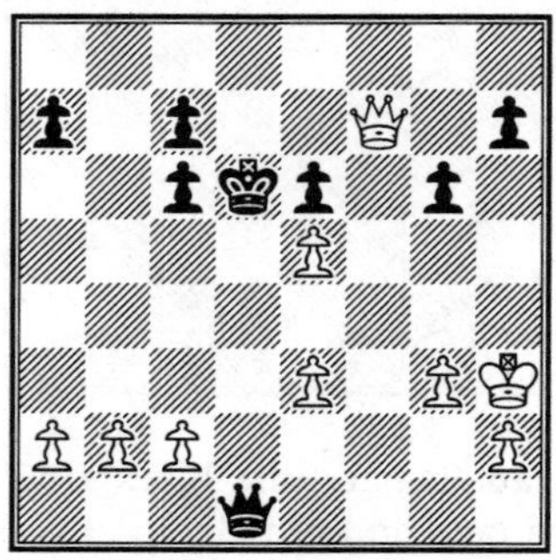

28...Kc5. 28...Kxe5; 29.Qxc7+ (29.Qf4+ Kd5; 30.e4+ Kd4; 31.Qf6+ Ke3 draws.) 29...Kf6; 30.Qf4+ Ke7; (30...Kg7; 31.Qd4+ Qxd4; 32.exd4 is a winning endgame for White.) 31.g4 Qxc2; 32.Qc7+ and White is better. **29.Qxh7 Qxc2; 30.Qe7+ Kb5; 31.Qxe6 Qxb2; 32.Qb3+!** Spielmann has accurately calculated the king and pawn endgame, so it is time to end the attack and finish Black off in the endgame. **32...Qxb3; 33.axb3.**

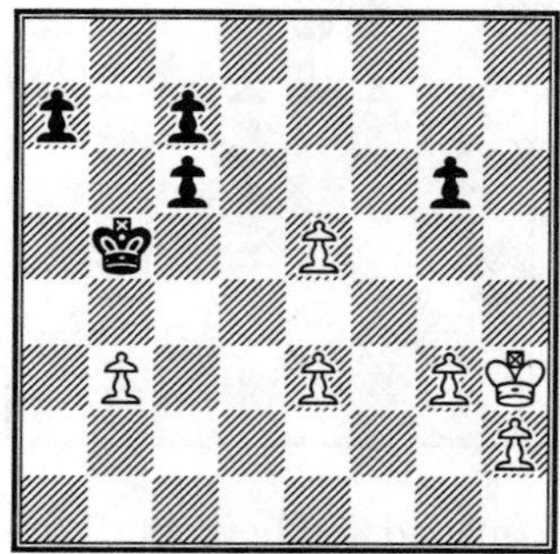

White wins. **33...c5; 34.Kg4 Kc6; 35.Kf3 g5; 36.h4 gxh4; 37.gxh4 Kd5; 38.Kf4 c4; 39.bxc4+ Ke6; 40.h5 a5; 41.h6 Kf7; 42.e6+. White won.**

MIESES VARIATION

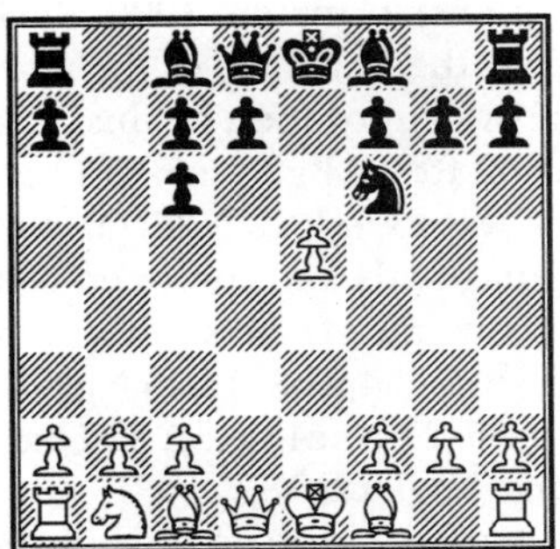

1.e4 e5
2.Nf3 Nc6
3.d4 exd4
4.Nxd4 Nf6
5.Nxc6 bxc6
6.e5

The **Mieses Variation** received a big boost when Garry Kasparov chose it in his 1990 match against Anatoly Karpov. White gains space and time by advancing the e-pawn, but later in the game this pawn can become vulnerable. Black has serious problems developing the bishop from c8, which usually lands on a6, to which White reacts by planting a pawn at c4. More recent games have seen Black rally to reach equal positions. The opening, however, is somewhat in decline at present.

(28) KASPAROV - KARPOV [C45]
Tilburg (Interpolis), 1991

6...Qe7. The only sensible reply, pinning the pawn. Black locks in the bishop at f8, for the moment, but White's reply will create an equal problem for his own bishop. **7.Qe2 Nd5; 8.c4.**

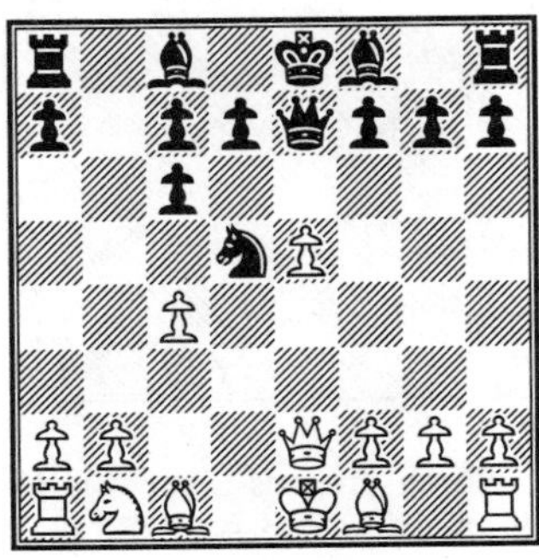

This has become the main line. Mieses himself tried it, but did not meet with great success until Kasparov brought it back. 8.Nd2 Bb7; 9.Nb3 was among other moves tried by Mieses without notable success. 9...0-0-0; 10.c4 Nb6; 11.Bd2 Re8; 12.f4 f6; 13.a4 Ba6; 14.Qe4 Qf7 and now 15.c5 led to some exciting play: 15...Bxf1;

16.cxb6 Qxb3; 17.bxa7 Kb7; 18.Rxf1 d5; 19.Rf3 Qb6; 20.Qc2 Qg1+; 21.Rf1 Qxg2; 22.Qb3+ Ka8 and Black had the attack and a better pawn structure in Mieses-Tarrasch, Berlin (match) 1916.

8...Ba6. 8...Nb6 is a less reliable defense. 9.Nd2 Qe6; 10.b3 a5; 11.Bb2 Bb4; 12.a3 Bxd2+; 13.Qxd2 and White had the more comfortable position in the 16th game of the Kasparov-Karpov World Championship match, 1990. **9.b3.** White secures the c4-square and is not concerned about the weakness of the a5-e1 diagonal. **9...g6.** 9...0–0–0; 10.Bb2 (10.g3!? was Kasparov's innovation against Karpov in the 14th game of the 1990 match. 10...Re8; 11.Bb2 f6; 12.Bg2 fxe5 and here Kasparov castled, but a year later an even stronger move was found: 13.Nd2! g6; 14.0–0–0 Bh6; 15.Kb1 and White's pressure on both long diagonals and the open central files is sufficient compensation for the pawn, especially since the bishop at a6 is idle.)

10...Nb6; 11.g3 Re8; 12.Bh3 f6; 13.0–0 fxe5; 14.a4 Kb8; 15.a5 Nd5; 16.Qd2 Nf6; 17.Re1 e4; 18.Na3 Qf7; 19.b4 Bxc4; 20.Bxf6 gxf6; 21.Nxc4 Qxc4; 22.Qxd7 and Black eventually won in Mieses-Teichmann, Hastings England 1895.

10.f4! Mieses had experimented with f4 earlier in the game, but the timing of such a move is critical, and here it works to White's advantage. **10...f6.** The standard method of attempting to undermine the pawn. 10...Qb4+; 11.Bd2 Qb6; 12.Nc3 Bb4 is an interesting alternative, adopted by Karpov against Gelfand at Linares 1992. **11.Ba3 Qf7!** A good defense, and perhaps the only one, since Black's position has many weaknesses.

12.Qd2. 12.exf6+ Kd8 doesn't lead to any advantage for White, because the Black king is safe behind the pawn barrier and the e-file can be used to good advantage against the White king, especially since Black has the better development. **12...Nb6.** 12...Bxa3; 13.cxd5 Bxf1; 14.Nxa3 Ba6; 15.Qa5 gives White the advantage, according to analysis by Speelman. **13.c5.** This forces matters, and considerably sharpens the game. **13...Bxf1; 14.cxb6.** Here Black should just have retreated the bishop to a6. Instead, Karpov launches a counterattack against the bishop at a3, but White has a surprise in store. **14...axb6?**

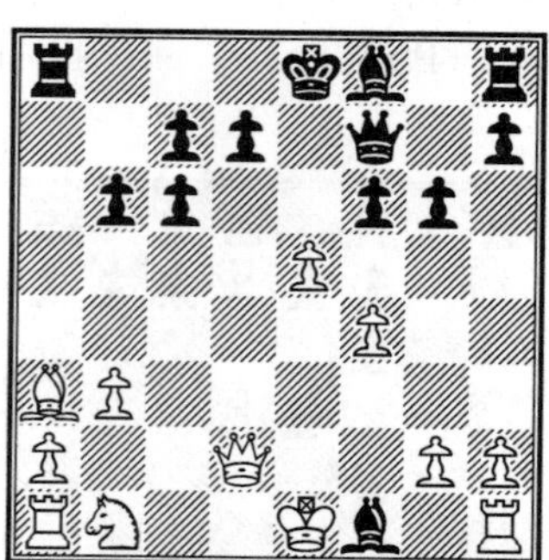

15.e6!! A brilliant move which creates a serious problem for Black, who must capture with the pawn. **15...dxe6.** 15...Qxe6+??; 16.Kxf1 Bxa3; 17.Nxa3 Rxa3; 18.Re1 wins the queen. **16.Bxf8 Rd8.** A very unusual position, with bishops occupying the home square of their enemy counterparts! Black is trying to take over the initiative, but White fights back. **17.Qb2! Bxg2.** 17...Bd3 would have been wiser. With bishops of opposite color the endgame would be more balanced and the possibility of trapping the White king in the center, or forcing him to the exposed queenside, is greater.

18.Ba3 g5 would have provided more compensation for the piece.

18.Qxg2 Kxf8; 19.Qxc6 Black has two pawns for the piece, but it is not enough. **19...Rd6; 20.Qc3 Kg7; 21.Nd2 Rhd8; 22.0-0-0.** The White king has escaped to relative safety, and Black has only a small amount of pressure. **22...Qe8?!** Karpov sets up the threat of ...Rc6, but gives up the pawn at c7, Better was 22...Rd5, threatening ...Rc5 directly.

23.Qxc7+ R8d7; 24.Qc2 Qb8; 25.Nc4. White has a winning position, but must play carefully. The queenside pawn majority is the key, preventing Black from exchanging queens. **25...Rd5; 26.Qf2 Qc7; 27.Qxb6! Qxf4+; 28.Qe3 Qg4; 29.Rdg1 Qh4; 30.Rg3** White's king is quite safe, and now the pawns are free to advance. **30...e5; 31.Rh3 Qg4; 32.Rg1 Rd1+; 33.Rxd1 Qxd1+; 34.Kb2 h5; 35.Rg3 Qh1; 36.Qf2** Kasparov manages to defend all the critical squares while also keeping pressure against the Black kingside. **36...h4; 37.Qg2.** This forces the queens off, and the rest is trivial. **37...Qxg2+; 38.Rxg2 g5; 39.a4 Kg6; 40.a5 e4; 41.b4 h3; 42.Rg3 Rh7; 43.a6 f5; 44.Ra3. White won.**

HAXO GAMBIT

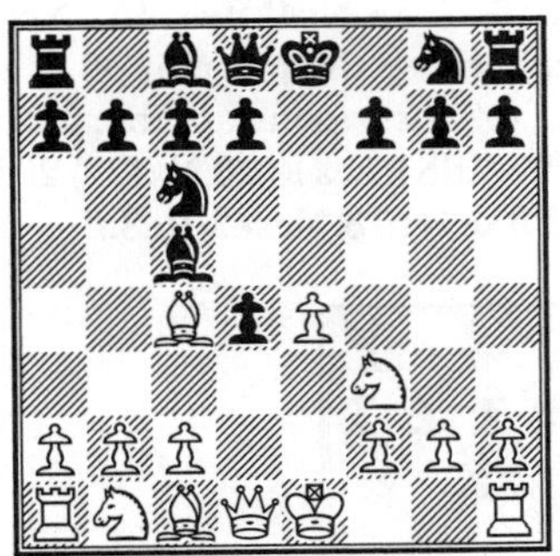

1.e4	**e5**
2.Nf3	**Nc6**
3.d4	**exd4**
4.Bc4	**Bc5**

This ancient and obvious developing move can be met by a gambit continuation which insures an initiative for White. The **Haxo Gambit** sees White get valuable queenside real estate for the sacrificed pawn.

(29) SCHLECHTER - NYHOLM [C44]
Baden bei Wien, 1914

1.e4 e5; 2.Nf3 Nc6; 3.d4 exd4; 4.Bc4 Bc5; 5.c3! 5.Ng5 Nh6; 6.Nxf7 Nxf7; 7.Bxf7+ Kxf7; 8.Qh5+ g6; 9.Qxc5 d6; 10.Qc4+ Be6 and Black was only very slightly worse in La Bourdonnais-Haxo, Gilvoisin 1837. The king is exposed but White has no development to take advantage of it. **5...d3; 6.b4! Bb6; 7.a4 a5.** 7...a6; 8.Qb3 Qf6; 9.a5 Ba7; 10.0-0 d6 Necessary, since 10...Ne5 fails to 11.Nxe5 and 12.Bxf7+. 11.b5

A) 11...axb5; 12.a6! bxa6; 13.Bd5 Bb7 (13...Nge7; 14.Bg5 is very annoying for Black.) 14.Rxa6! Bxf2+; 15.Rxf2 Rxa6; 16.Ng5 with an unstoppable attack.

B) 11...Ne5; 12.Nxe5 dxe5; 13.bxa6 bxa6; 14.Qa4+! A fine move which disrupts the Black position, since the bishop belongs at b7, not d7. 14...Bd7; 15.Qd1 Ne7;

16.Qxd3 and White was better in Sveshnikov-A.Petrosian, USSR 1974. **8.b5 Qe7.** 8...Nce7; 9.Ne5 d5; 10.exd5 Nxd5; 11.Nxf7 Kxf7; 12.Qf3+ Ke6; 13.Qe4+ and White recovers his piece with interest. **9.0–0.**

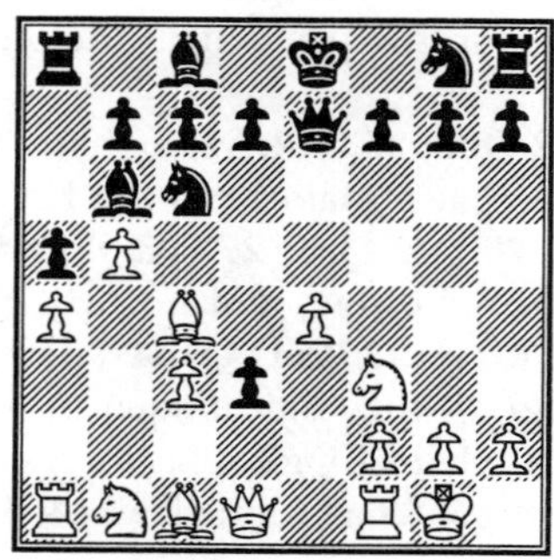

White is better developed with control of the center and more space. **9...Nd8; 10.Nd4!** Headed for f5. **10...d6; 11.Nf5 Qf6.** 11...Bxf5; 12.exf5 Qf6; 13.Qxd3 Ne7; 14.Re1 0–0; 15.Qe4 Re8; 16.g4 and Black cannot escape the pin on the e-file. 16...h6; 17.Ra2 White will transfer the rook from the a-file to the e-file, with tremendous pressure. **12.Bxd3 Ne6; 13.Qc2 Ne7; 14.Nd2 Bd7; 15.Nc4! Bc5.** 15...Nc8; 16.Ba3 0–0; 17.e5! brings White a decisive advantage, because the pawn at d6 is both pinned and under attack. **16.Be3 b6.** 16...Bxe3; 17.fxe3 just opens another hazardous file. 17...Qg5; 18.Ncxd6+ cxd6; 19.Nxd6+ Kf8; (19...Kd8 loses to 20.Nxf7+) 20.Rxf7+ Kg8; 21.Qf2 Rf8; 22.Rxf8+ Nxf8; 23.Qf7#. **17.f4! Bxe3+; 18.Ncxe3 Rc8.**

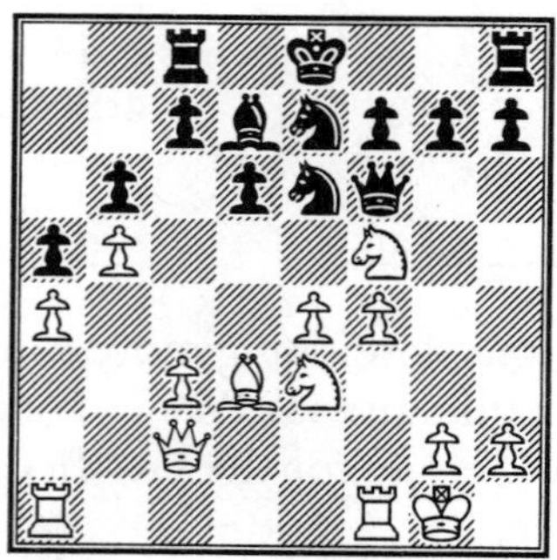

White's domination of the center and superior development are decisive here. **19.e5! Nxf5; 20.exf6 Nxe3; 21.Qe2. White won.**

SCOTCH GAMBIT

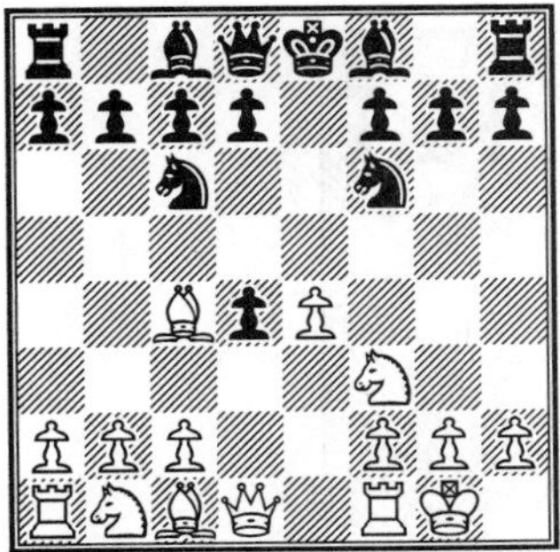

1.e4	**e5**
2.Nf3	**Nc6**
3.Bc4	**Nf6**
4.d4	**exd4**
5.0–0	

The Scotch Gambit can also be reached via 1.e4 e5; 2.Nf3 Nc6; 3.d4 exd4; 4.Bc4 Nf6; 5.0–0. White will regain the pawn eventually, but for the moment is preoccupied with developing the forces as quickly as possible.

(30) SPIELMANN - JOHNER [C55]
Carlsbad, 1907

1.e4 e5; 2.Nf3 Nc6; 3.Bc4 Nf6; 4.d4 exd4; 5.0–0 Bc5. 5...Nxe4 is the usual move these days, For example: 6.Re1 d5; 7.Bxd5 Qxd5; 8.Nc3 with exciting pins, which soon get resolved. 8...Qa5; 9.Nxe4 Be6; 10.Bd2 Bb4; 11.Nxd4 Nxd4; 12.c3 Be7; 13.cxd4 Qd5 with complex play. A typical example is: 14.Bb4 Bxb4; 15.Qa4+ Qc6; 16.Qxb4 0–0–0; 17.Nc3 Qb6; 18.Qxb6 axb6; 19.Rad1 with a level endgame. Black has bishop vs. knight and a better pawn structure but White has more active rooks and control of the center, Tinnes and-Konstantinopolsky, Postal 1958.

6.c3. Instead of this move, White usually chooses 6.e5, the Max Lange Attack, which leads to lots of complications and requires a good understanding of opening theory. But 6.c3 is a valid gambit in its own right, and is not as well known.

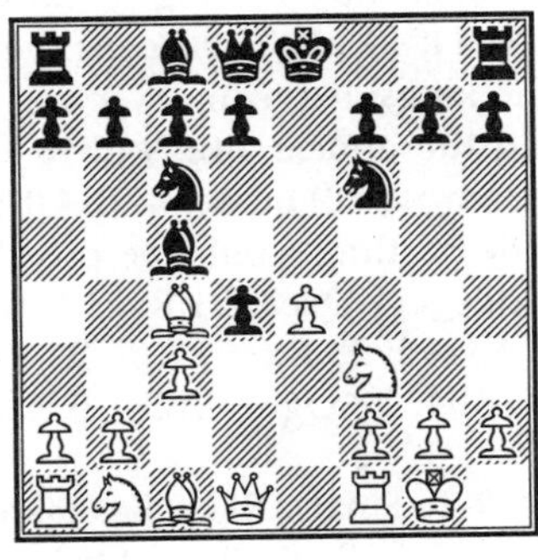

6...Nxe4, this is the best move for Black. Accepting the gambit can be dangerous, as are other methods of declining. 6...dxc3; 7.Nxc3 d6; 8.Bg5 gives White a lot of pressure, with the threat of Nd5 in the air. 6...d5; 7.exd5 Nxd5; 8.cxd4 Be7; 9.Bxd5

Qxd5; 10.Nc3 Qd8; 11.d5 gives White a strong initiative. 6...d3; 7.b4 Be7; 8.e5 Ng4; 9.Re1 leaves Black's pieces looking ridiculous, and the d-pawn can be captured at will. **7.cxd4 d5.** 7...Be7; 8.d5 is clearly good for White. Black must react more vigorously, which is why 7...d5 is correct here, as in most similar situations. **8.dxc5 dxc4.**

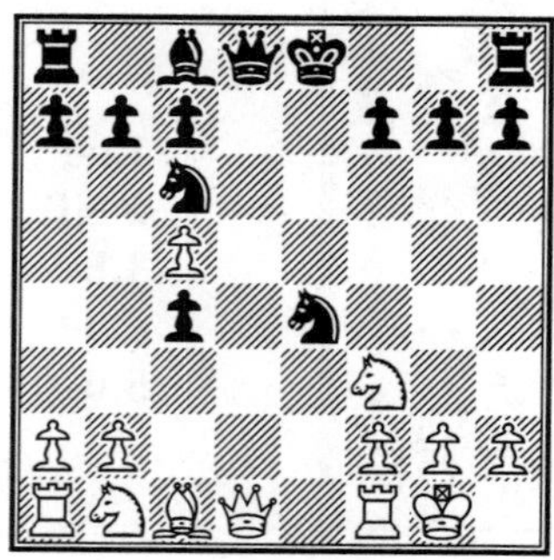

The pawn structure is messy but White has the advantage of being castled already. **9.Qe2.** 9.Qxd8+ Kxd8; 10.Rd1+ Bd7; 11.Be3 Ke7 is about equal. **9...Qe7?!** 9...Qd3! is better and offers good chances of equality, for example: 10.Re1 f5; 11.Nbd2 0–0; 12.Nxe4 fxe4; 13.Qxe4 Bf5! with a complicated position. **10.Qxc4 Nxc5; 11.b4 Ne6; 12.Ba3!**

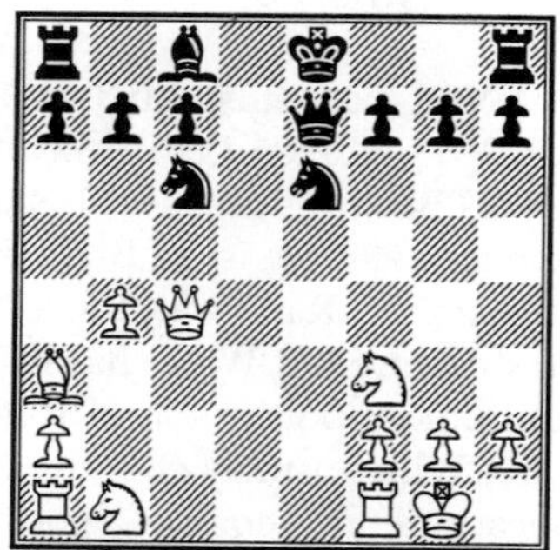

With this move Spielmann sets up the big threat of 13.b5 and maintains the initiative. **12...Qf6; 13.Nc3 Ncd4; 14.b5!** This keeps the enemy king trapped in the center. The disruption of the kingside pawn cover will not be important, as Black has no resources to back up the attack. **14...Nxf3+; 15.gxf3 Qd4** hoping for an endgame in which the White pawns will be weak. **16.Qb3! Nc5.** 16...Bd7 would have been wiser, so that queenside castling would be possible. **17.Qc2 Bh3.** 17...Qc4; 18.Rfe1+ Be6; 19.Re5 Na4; 20.Qxa4 Qxc3; 21.Rae1 leaves Black in big trouble, for example: 21...Qxf3; 22.Rxe6+ fxe6; 23.Rxe6+ Kf7; 24.Re7+ Kf6 (24...Kg6; 25.Qc2+ Kh6; 26.Bc1+ Kh5; 27.Qc5+ Kh4; 28.Qg5+ Kh3; 29.Re3) 25.Qd4+ Kg6; 26.Rxg7+ Kh6; 27.Rg3 Qh5; 28.Bc1+.

18.Ne2! Qf6; 19.Qxc5 0–0–0. Finally Black has managed to castle, but the king isn't much safer on the queenside! 19...Bxf1; 20.Qe3+ Kd8; 21.Rd1+ Kc8; 22.Kxf1 would be hopeless for Black. **20.Rfc1! c6?** 20...Qg6+; 21.Ng3 would win in the long run, but Black's move made it easy. 20...Kb8; 21.Qxc7+ Ka8; 22.Qg3 is also fairly simple. **21.Qxa7! White won.**

(31) KUPREICHIK - BELYAVSKY [C55]

Soviet Championship, 1981

1.e4 e5; 2.Nf3 Nc6; 3.Bc4 Nf6; 4.d4 exd4; 5.e5.

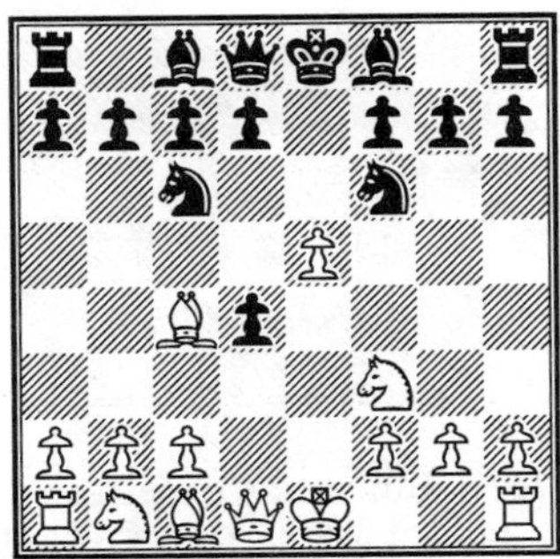

In the Scotch Gambit, White has as choice between castling or the immediate advance of the e-pawn, seen in this game. This is the most aggressive reaction to Black's defensive plans. The pawn at e5 forces the Black knight to evacuate, but the same pawn can become vulnerable and is usually exchanged off early in the game.

5...Ne4. For 5...Ng4 see the next game. **6.0–0 Be7.** 6...Nc5!? is an interesting, and perhaps undervalued alternative, since the knight can take up a solid position on e6. 7.Nxd4 Nxd4; 8.Qxd4 d6?! (8...Ne6 might be met by 9.Qg4 d6; 10.Rd1!?) 9.Bf4 d5 and now 10.Bxd5! is best, as noted by Zagorovsky: 10...Bf5 (10...c6?; 11.Bxf7+ Kxf7; 12.Qxd8) **7.c3 d5.** Black strives for central counterplay. The immediate plan is to get rid of the powerful White bishop. **8.Bb3 Nc5; 9.cxd4 Nxb3; 10.Qxb3 Rb8,** this is an ugly move, but defending the b-pawn with the rook has a venerable history dating back to Chigorin. Still, White's position must be preferred here, despite the bishop pair. **11.Nc3 Be6; 12.Be3 0–0; 13.Rad1 Na5; 14.Qc2 Bg4; 15.Qe2 Nc4.** Black now gets rid of the other White bishop. **16.h3 Nxe3; 17.Qxe3.**

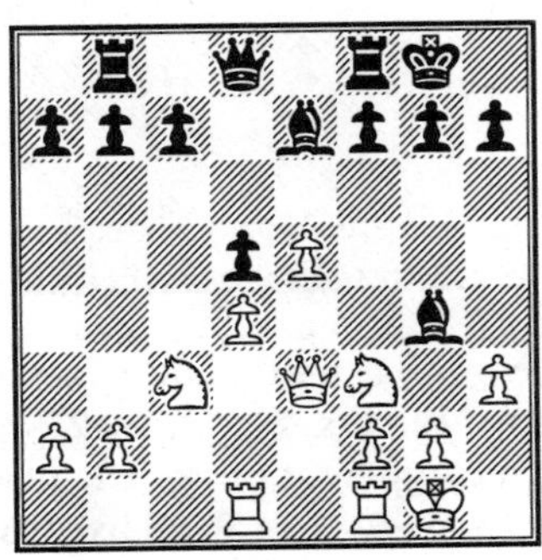

Black has a very passive position. **17...Be6; 18.Nh2 f6.** Opening up the position for the bishops seems to make sense, but White manages to make better use of the new structure. **19.exf6 Rxf6; 20.Nf3 Qd6; 21.Rde1!** This is the correct rook to place at e1, since the f-pawn will need the support of the other rook. **21...Re8; 22.Ne5 Bf8; 23.f4!** The assault begins! **23...c5; 24.Kh1 Qb6; 25.Ng4 Rf5; 26.Qg3 Kh8.** White threatened Nh6+. **27.Ne3 Rf7; 28.Nexd5.** The application of pressure has netted a pawn, and now White builds a juggernaut. **28...Qc6; 29.dxc5 Bxd5; 30.Rxe8.**

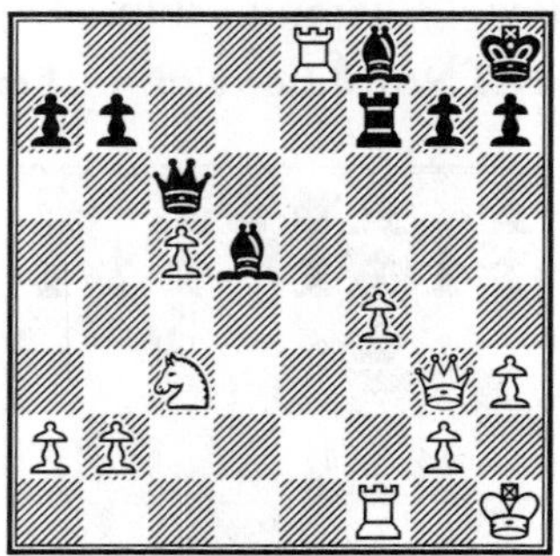

Black applies an intermezzo, but it has no effect on the final act. **30...Bxg2+; 31.Qxg2 Qxe8; 32.Ne4 Qd7; 33.Qf3 h6; 34.Rd1 Qc6; 35.Rd8.** White's advantage is too great, and the rest is simple. **35...Kh7; 36.Kh2 Be7; 37.Rd3 Bxc5; 38.Rc3 Qb6; 39.Rxc5 Qxb2+; 40.Kg3 Qd4; 41.Rc2. White won.**

(32) VALVO - LEVIT [C55]

Chicago, 1992

1.e4 e5; 2.Nf3 Nc6; 3.d4 exd4; 4.Bc4 Nf6; 5.e5 Ng4. The 5...Ng4 line is one of those openings where an early endgame is uncomfortable for black. **6.Qe2 Qe7; 7.Bf4 d6; 8.exd6 cxd6.**

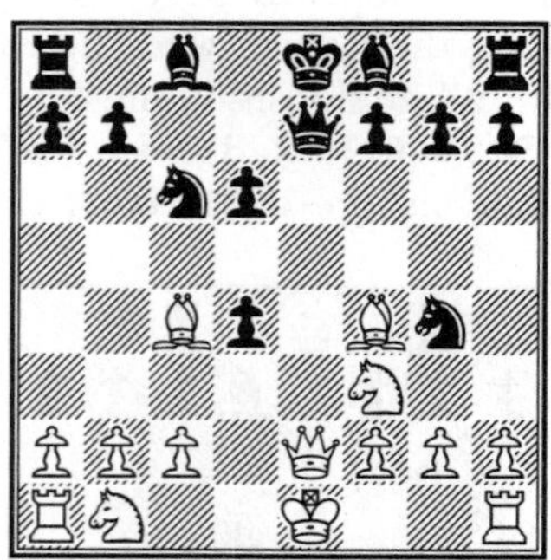

8...Qxe2+ is wiser, as the move is pretty much inevitable. **9.Nbd2 Bf5; 10.Nb3.** The knight is well-placed here. **10...Qxe2+; 11.Kxe2 Nge5; 12.Bb5 Nxf3; 13.Kxf3.** White has more than enough compensation for the pawn. Black's pawns are weak and development is lagging. **13...0–0–0; 14.Bxc6 bxc6; 15.Nxd4.**

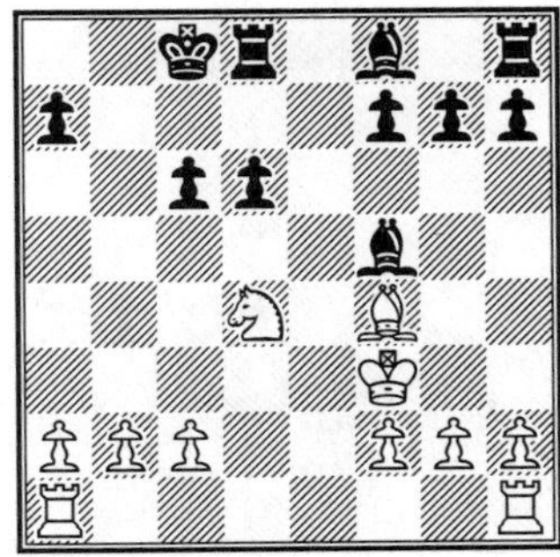

Now material equilibrium is restored. Black's bishop pair is offset by the weak pawn structure and the scope of White's pieces. **15...Bd7; 16.c4 c5.** A sign of Black's concern for the position. Now the d-pawn is backward. But alternative plans were hard to find. **17.Ne2 Bc6+; 18.Kg3 Be7.** 18...d5; 19.cxd5 Bxd5; 20.Rhc1 with a clear advantage for White. **19.Rad1?!** 19.h4! d5?!; 20.cxd5 Bxd5; 21.Rhc1. White has the initiative and the Black king is vulnerable. **19...g5; 20.Bd2 d5.** Black has now equalized, at least! **21.f3.** 21.cxd5 Bxd5; 22.Rc1 Bd6+. **21...dxc4; 22.Ba5 Rd3; 23.b3.**

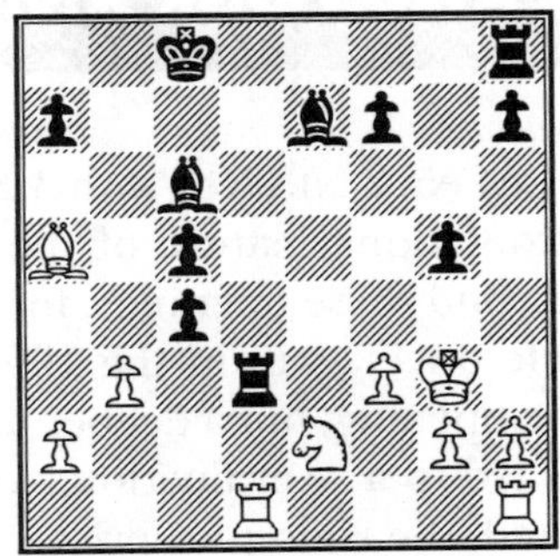

23...Bd8!? 23...Rxd1; 24.Rxd1 cxb3; 25.axb3. **24.Bxd8 Rhxd8; 25.Rc1 Rd2!; 26.Nc3 f5!** Black has firm control of the initiative. **27.Rhg1 R8d4; 28.h3!?** 28.bxc4? Rg4+!!; 29.fxg4 f4+; 30.Kh3 Rd6! and mate follows. **28...h5; 29.bxc4 h4+; 30.Kh2 Rxc4; 31.Rgf1.**

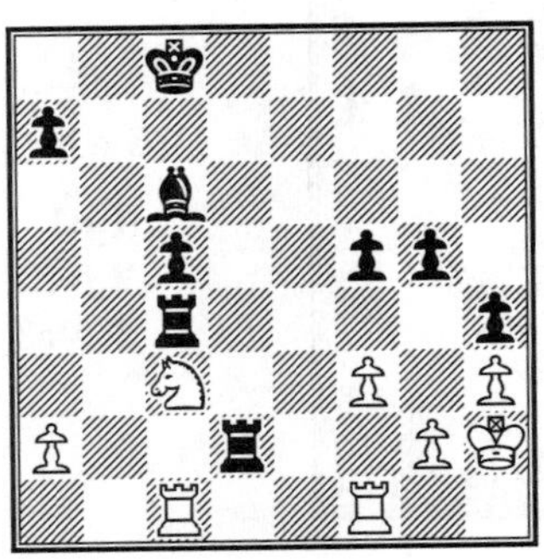

31...g4; 32.hxg4! fxg4; 33.Ne4! Rxc1; 34.Rxc1 Bxe4.

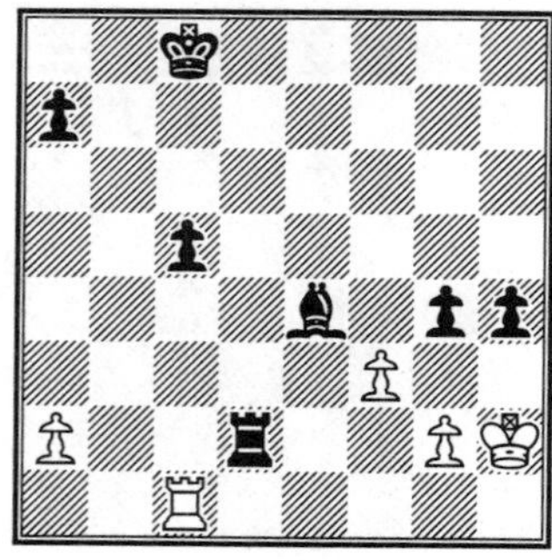

35.Rxc5+ Kb7; 36.fxe4 h3!; 37.Rg5 Rxa2. Another plan is 37...Rxg2+; 38.Kh1 Kc6; 39.a4 Kd6; 40.a5 (40.e5+!?) 40...Ke6; 41.a6 Kf6; 42.Rg8 g3; 43.Ra8 Ra2 and Black wins. **38.Rxg4 Rxg2+; 39.Rxg2?? hxg2; 40.Kxg2 a5.** White resigned and ended the game. Levit passed away in 1996, a dear man who will be greatly missed. **Black won.**

THREE AND FOUR KNIGHTS

When White follows 1.e4 e5; 2.Nf3 Nc6 with 3.Nc3, Black can take some comfort in the non-confrontational nature of the openings. Appearances can be deceiving, however, and these openings, formerly dismissed by theoreticians, have come to life once again in the 1990s. White has not really found new resources in the opening, but a deeper understanding of some of the positional factors has led to a re-evaluation. Among the enthusiasts of the White side is Tal Shaked, the young American star.

THREE KNIGHTS

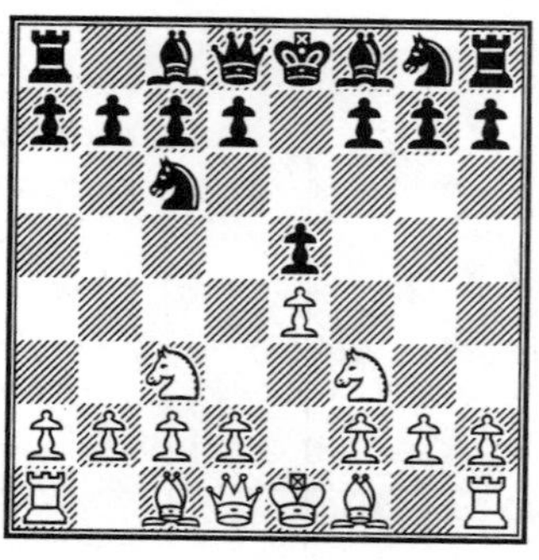

1.e4 e5
2.Nf3 Nc6
3.Nc3

White invites Black to enter the Four Knights Game with this move, but there is an interesting alternative which offers Black a lively game without much risk.

(33) BLACKBURNE - STEINITZ [C46]
London, 1883

1.e4 e5; 2.Nf3 Nc6; 3.Nc3 g6. This is the Steinitz Defense. The fianchetto is a typically modern positional device designed to maximize the power of a bishop without exposing it to attack. Steinitz was of course far ahead of his time, but Blackburne too played many games which would not be out of place in a contemporary tournament. 3...Bc5 looks like a logical developing move but the game can become quite trappy after 4.Nxe5 Nxe5; 5.d4 Bd6; 6.dxe5 Bxe5; 7.Bd3 for example this recent miniature: 7...Qh4?!; 8.Nd5! Ne7; 9.g3 Qh3; 10.Nxe7 Kxe7; 11.f4 Qg2; 12.Rf1 Bd4; 13.Qh5! d5; 14.Bd2 Rd8; 15.f5! Bxb2; 16.Rd1 dxe4; 17.Bc4 and Black resigned in Glek-Romanishin, Biel 1996.

4.d4. White occupies the center, however, this increases the scope of the bishop on g7. **4...exd4; 5.Nxd4 Bg7; 6.Be3 Nf6.** Black's plan is simple: castle kingside and play ...Re8, placing pressure on the pawn at e4. The formation is similar to that of the Larsen Variation of the Philidor Defense. **7.Be2!?** More restrained than 7.Bc4, but 7.Nxc6 bxc6; 8.e5 Ng8 (8...Nd5; 9.Nxd5 cxd5; 10.Qxd5 Rb8 gives Black some play for the pawn.) 9.Bd4 should also be considered, to further cramp Black. On 9...Qe7; 10.Qe2 and White will follow with queenside castling. **7...0–0; 8.0–0 Ne7?!** Pursuing a wrong plan. After 8...Re8!; 9.Bf3 (9.f3 is met by 9...d5!) 9...Ne5 is equal.

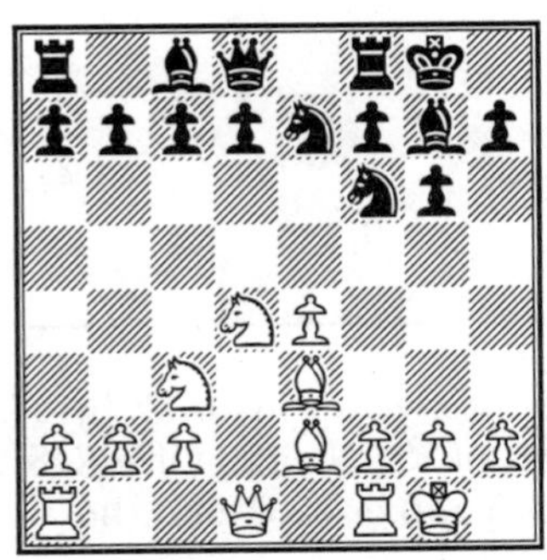

9.Bf3 d6. Black had undoubtedly prepared 9...d5 , but then 10.e5 Ne8; 11.Bg5! is awkward for him. **10.Qd2 Nd7; 11.Bh6!** White has a clear advantage in the center which allows him to turn his attention to the kingside. It is often advantageous for White to exchange the defender of the Black king and create long-term weaknesses on the dark squares, especially f6 and h6. **11...Ne5; 12.Bxg7 Kxg7; 13.Be2 f6!?** Creating a new weakness on e6 which Blackburne now aims to exploit. **14.f4 Nf7; 15.Rad1** Blackburne plays like a modern master and calmly accumulating advantages by developing all his pieces before attacking.

15...c6; 16.Bc4 Bd7; 17.Bxf7! An unexpected exchange for Black, giving up a powerful bishop for a passive knight. White, however, plans to break through in the center, and must eliminate the knight, so it can't return to its e5-post. **17...Rxf7; 18.f5.** Now Ne6 is threatened, since a Black capture will lose the d6 pawn. **18...Nc8.**

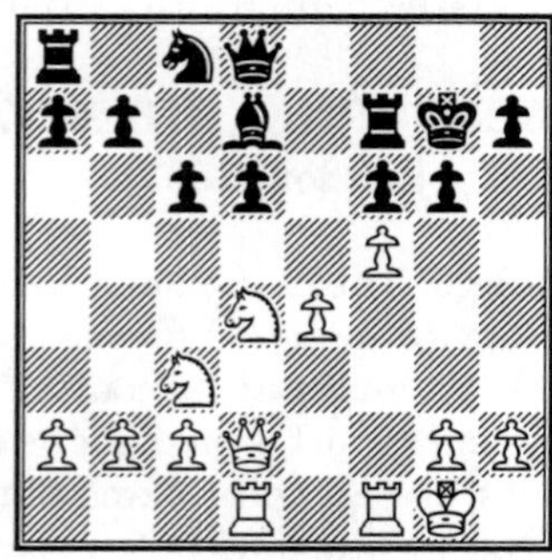

19.e5!! Brilliant! Every White piece is ready for the attack. Steinitz was not treated like this very often. **19...fxe5.** 19...dxe5? loses to 20.Ne6+ Bxe6; 21.Qxd8. **20.Ne6+! Bxe6; 21.fxe6 Re7.** Black, practically playing without his a8-rook, cannot afford to exchange rooks. Blackburne gives 21...Rf5; 22.g4 Qg5; 23.Qxg5 Rxg5; 24.h3 threatening Ne4, trapping the rook 24...d5; 25.Ne4! anyway! 25...dxe4; 26.Rf7+ Kh6; 27.Rdd7.

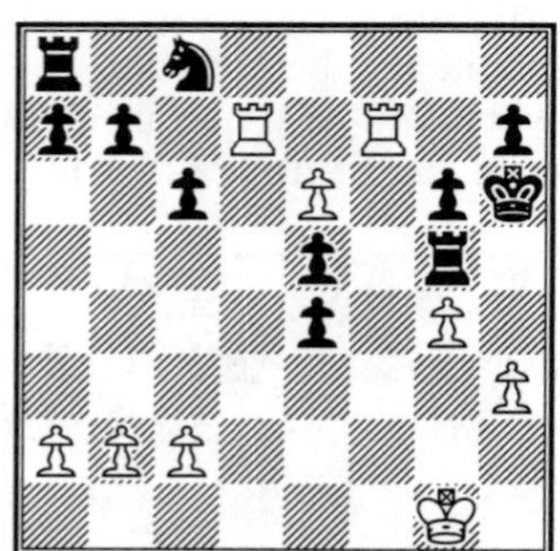

To avoid mate, Black must give up his rook by 27...Rxg4+. **22.Qg5.** White is threatening 23.Rf7+. **22...Qe8,** or 22...Nb6; 23.Qf6+ Kg8; 24.Ne4 gives White a strong attack. **23.Rd3!** The entry of another rook into the attack along the third rank is decisive. **23...Rxe6; 24.Rh3 Qe7.** There is no defense to Qh6+ and Qxh7, e.g. 24...Re7; 25.Qh6+ Kg8; 26.Rhf3! Nb6; 27.Ne4 and White invades via f6. **25.Qh6+ Kg8; 26.Rf8+! Qxf8; 27.Qxh7#. White won.**

FOUR KNIGHTS

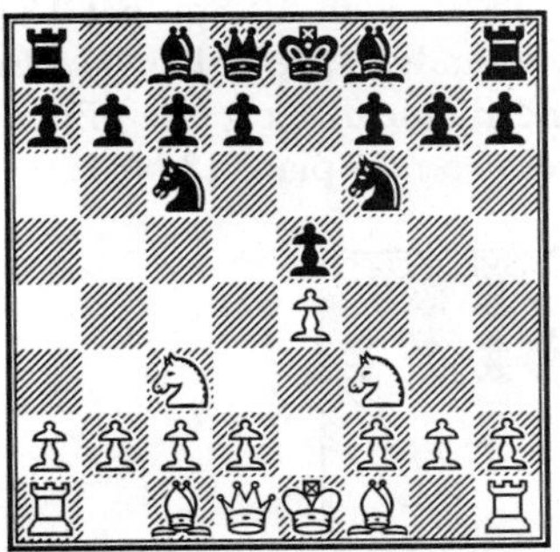

1.e4	**e5**
2.Nc3	**Nc6**
3.Nf3	**Nf6**

The **Four Knights** was considered a rather fuddy-duddy opening until recently, suitable for use only by ancient chessplayers huddled over some chessboard in the park. Thorough analysis seemed to have eliminated any chance of an advantage in this ponderous opening. Nevertheless, in recent years, new advocates such as young American Tal Shaked and experiments by leading European stars have somewhat rejuvenated the ancient plan.

(34) SPIELMANN - YATES [C47]

Semmering, 1926

1.e4 e5; 2.Nc3 Nc6; 3.Nf3 Nf6; 4.d4.

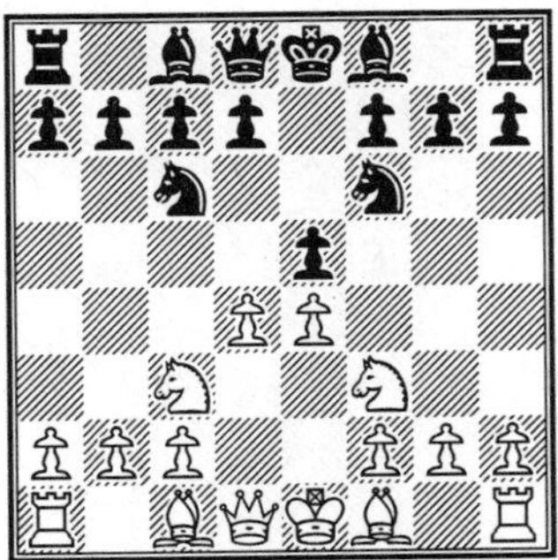

This is known as the *Scotch Four Knights*, since it combines the four knight moves with the central break at d4. The alternative is 4.Bb5, the Spanish Four Knights. **4...exd4.** This capture gives White an advantage in space. Instead, Black should pin the knight at c3. 4...Bb4; 5.Nxe5 Qe7; 6.Nxc6 Qxe4+; 7.Be2 Qxc6; 8.0–0 Bxc3; 9.bxc3 Qxc3; 10.Rb1 Qa5; 11.Rb5 gave White good prospects in Reefschlaeger-Hertneck, Bundesliga 1988. White does not have to recapture at d4, but can adopt the Belgrade Gambit with 5.Nd5!? Black can enter the complicated lines after 5...Nxe4 or can adopt the boring 5...Be7, which leads to an equal game.

5.Nxd4. 5.Nd5 is the once exciting Belgrade Gambit, which is not common today. However, recent literature suggests that it may be revived. **Bb4; 6.Nxc6 bxc6; 7.Bd3 d5.** Castling is a reasonable alternative. **8.exd5 cxd5; 9.0–0.** 9.Qe2+ Be7; 10.0–0 0–0; 11.Re1 Re8; 12.Bg5 Bg4; 13.Qe5 c6; 14.Qg3 Bh5; 15.Qh4 Bg6; 16.Bxg6 hxg6 is a more modern continuation, but Black's bishop maneuver brought equality in Istratescu-Krasenkov, Yerevan Olympiad 1996. **9...0–0; 10.Bg5 c6; 11.Qf3.** White tries to keep up the pressure, since that is the only advantage he has. **11...Be7; 12.Rae1 Rb8!** This move gives Black equality. That doesn't mean the game will end in a draw, however. Spielmann will simply have to develop a new plan. **13.Nd1.**

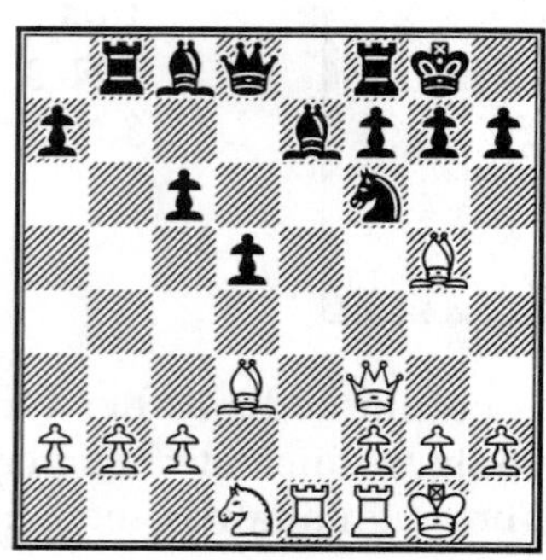

13...Re8. 13...h6 allows typical Spielmannesque fireworks: 14.Bxh6!! gxh6; 15.Qe3 Re8; 16.Qxh6 and Black will find it hard to defend against the threat of Re5-g5 or Re3-g3. Note that the knight cannot move because of threats at h7. 13...Bg4; 14.Bxf6 Bxf3; 15.Bxe7 Qd7; 16.gxf3 Rfe8; 17.Bc5 and the three pieces are worth more than the queen. **14.h3 Be6; 15.Re2 c5; 16.Rfe1.** The theme of Spielmann's attack is pressure at e7. It does not pay off until much later, but it succeeds in the end. **16...d4; 17.Bf5 Bc4; 18.Re5 Bb5; 19.b3 Bd6; 20.Rxe8+ Bxe8.**

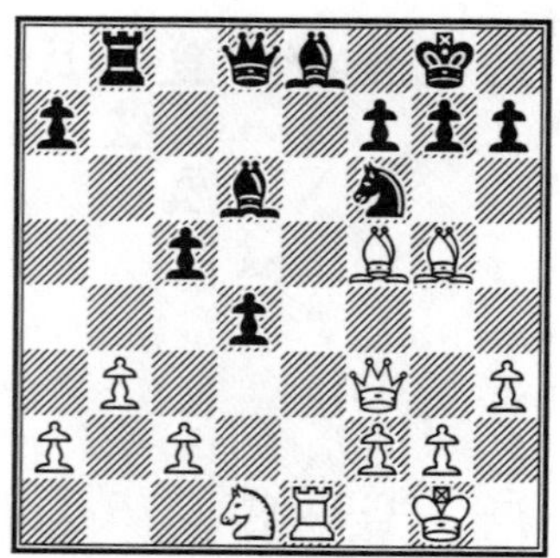

Now Spielmann takes time to attend to the queenside by sending his knight on an errand. It will later return to take part in the final assault. **21.Nb2 Bb5; 22.a4 Ba6; 23.Bd3.** At first sight this is a strange move, since it trades an attacking piece for one which is not actively participating in the defense. The key to this position is the Black rook, which cannot in any way help defend the king. This means that White should be able to bring superior attacking force to the kingside. **23...Bxd3; 24.Nxd3 h6; 25.Bh4 a5; 26.Ne5!** Keep your eye on this knight, which has returned from its queenside quest and positions itself to deliver the fatal blow! **26...Rc8; 27.Ng4! Be7.**

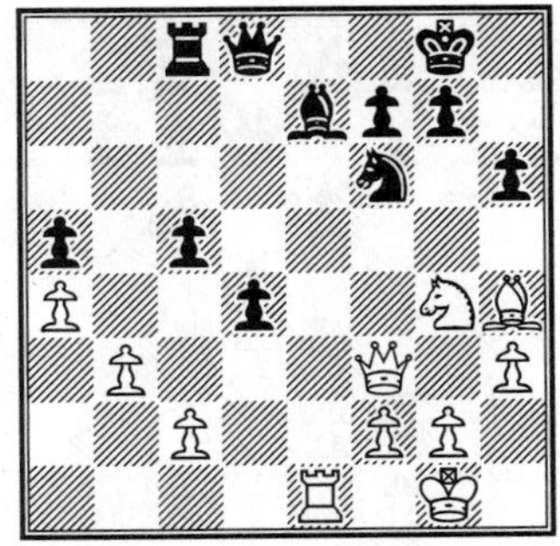

The way is prepared. The Black defense relies on the bishop at e7, so Spielmann sweeps it from the board with a sacrifice. **28.Rxe7!! Qxe7; 29.Nxf6+ gxf6.** Now a simple fork finishes the game. **30.Qg4+ Kh7; 31.Qxc8. White won.**

(35) SPASSKY-XIE JUN [C49]

Copenhagen,1997

1.e4 e5; 2.Nf3 Nc6; 3.Nc3 Nf6; 4.Bb5 Bb4.

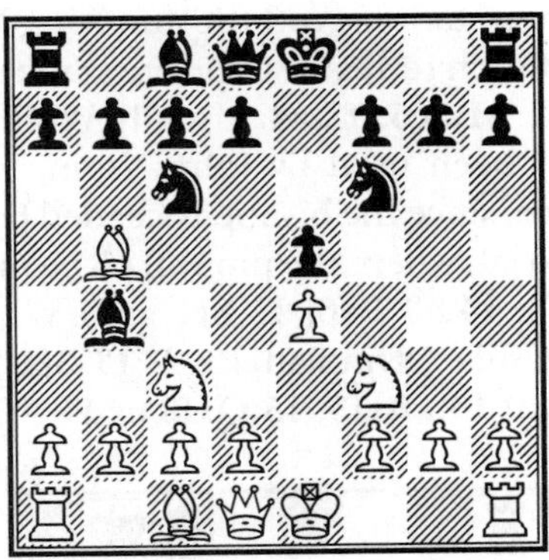

The Spanish Four Knights has a completely different nature from the Scotch Four Knights which we saw in the previous game. Here, possible captures at c3 lead to a very different and unbalanced pawn structure. The main lines have been established for almost a century, yet new twists are still being discovered. Here two former World Champions refine the theory a bit further. **5.0–0 0–0; 6.d3 d6.** Black can afford to maintain the symmetry for a bit, but will soon break it by capturing at c3. **7.Bg5 Bxc3; 8.bxc3 Qe7; 9.Re1 Nd8.**

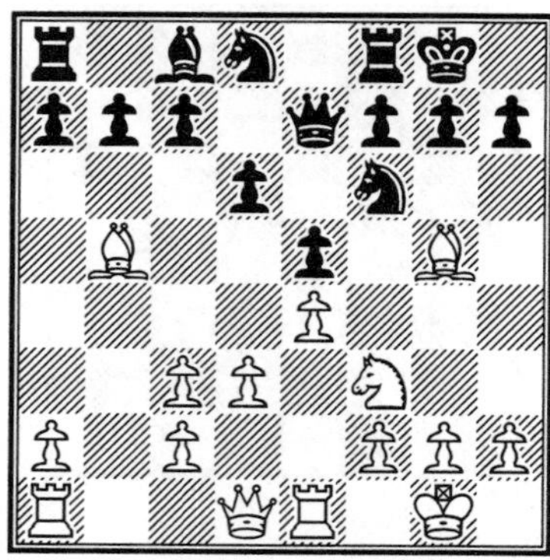

This may seem like an odd move, but the maneuver, known as the Metger Unpin, has a point. The knight will come to e6 and chase away the bishop, breaking the dangerous and annoying pin. Johannes Metger used this plan way back in 1893, and for a long time it was considered to shut down White's opening. The Four Knights as a whole went into a decline. Now however, new resources have been found.

10.d4 Ne6; 11.Bc1. An opening of retreats! No wonder the Four Knighs suffers from a cowardly reputation. And the annoying White bishop will return home soon. The point of each retreat is to position the piece on a better square, so it is not at all illogical. **11...c5; 12.a4.** Usually White plays Bf1 immediately, but this idea, which has been used by John Nunn, is a modern preference. **12...Nc7.** A strange choice, since the bishop is headed backward anyway. Xie Jun wants to get her bishop to g4, where the pin will place more indirect pressure on d4. 12...Rd8; 13.Bc4 Nf8; 14.h3 Be6; 15.Bf1 gave White a more comfortable game in Nunn-Norri, Manila Olympiad 1992. **13.Bf1 Bg4; 14.h3!** A surprise, Spassky gambits the pawn! **14...Bxf3; 15.Qxf3 cxd4; 16.cxd4 exd4.**

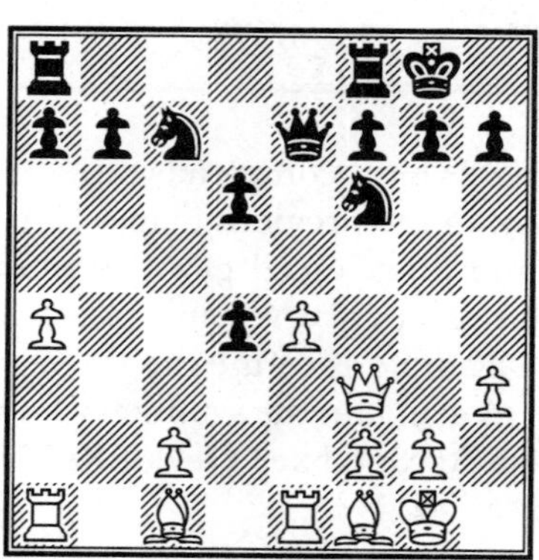

Play along the e-file is at the heart of the Four Knights, and Spassky wastes no time opening things up. **17.e5 Nd7; 18.Ba3.** A bit fancy. 18.Qxb7 is playable, since 18...Nxe5; 19.f4 allows 19...Nf3+! **18...Nxe5; 19.Qxb7 Qd7; 20.Qe4 Rfd8;**

21.Qxd4 Ne6; 22.Qe4.

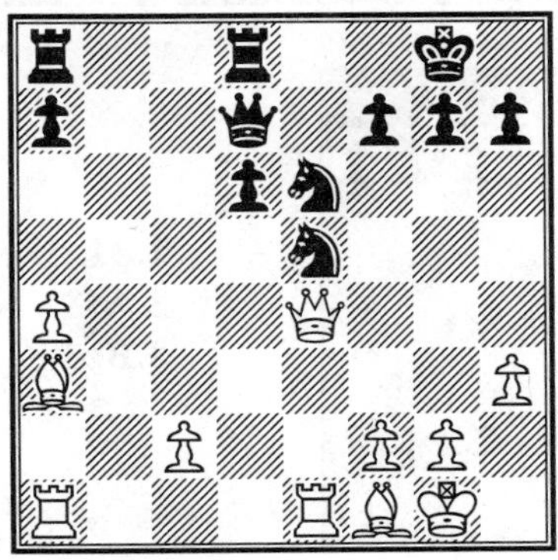

White is clearly better here, with the bishop pair and a juicy target at d6. But the former Women's World Champion hangs in. **22...Rac8; 23.Rad1 Qc7; 24.f4 Nc6; 25.Bd3 Nf8; 26.Kh1 Rb8; 27.Bc4 a5; 28.c3 Na7; 29.Rd4 Nc8; 30.Qf5 Nb6; 31.Ba2 Rb7; 32.Re3 Qc6; 33.Rg3?** 33.Qxa5 was simple and strong. Spassky gets distracted by the kingside attack. **33...d5!** A good move which starts to create a little counterplay and limits the power of the bishop at a2. **34.c4 Qe6.**

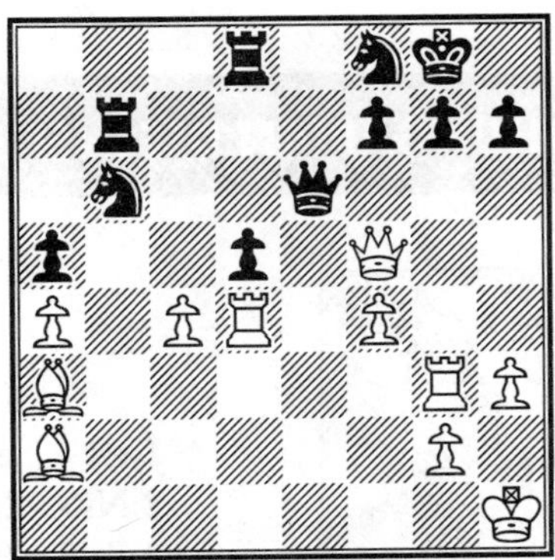

Spassky may have thought that he could close the game with a sacrifice at g7 here, but it doesn't work. In fact, there doesn't seem to be any way to maintain equality in the position! **35.Qg5.** 35.Rxg7+? Kxg7; 36.Qg5+ Ng6; 37.Qxd8 runs into 37...Qe1+; 38.Kh2 Qf2! attacking the bishop at a2 and rook at d4. **35...f6; 36.Qh5 Qe1+; 37.Kh2 Qf2; 38.Bxf8.** Black is losing in any case. **38...Qxd4; 39.Bb1 Kxf8; 40.Qxh7 Rf7; 41.Bg6 Qxf4; 42.Bxf7 Kxf7; 43.Qxg7+ Ke6; 44.c5 Nc4.** White resigned.

ITALIAN GAME (GIUCO PIANO)

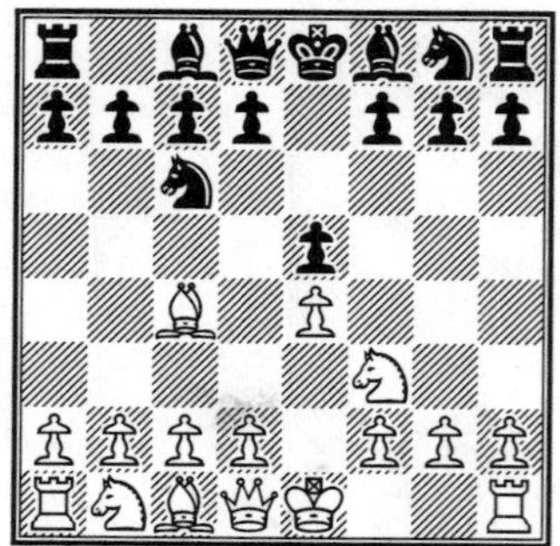

1.e4	e5
2.Nf3	Nc6
3.Bc4	

The **Italian Game**, also known as the **Giuco Piano**, is one of the oldest openings, but it retains its vitality in the hands of such stars as Anatoly Karpov. White is content to simply develop pieces on useful squares and postpones any confrontation until the middlegame.

The opening has been largely eclipsed by the more refined Spanish Game, but is still a staple of amateur games. In the following pages, we'll look at some of the important variations.

HUNGARIAN DEFENSE

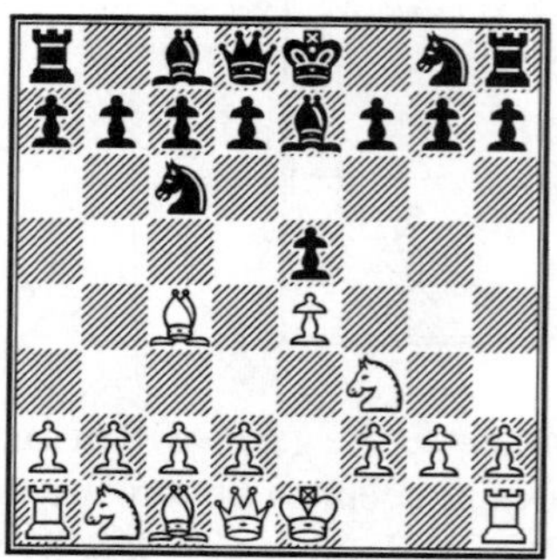

1.e4	e5
2.Nf3	Nc6
3.Bc4	Be7

The **Hungarian Defense** is a viable alternative to the Two Knights Defense or Italian Game. It is very solid and conforms to opening principles. Black accepts a somewhat cramped game, recognizing White's privilege of attacking first. Development takes place quietly and no challenges are issued early in the game.

(36) ZIULYARKIN - KARPOV [C50]

Zlatoust, 1962

1.e4 e5; 2.Nf3 Nc6; 3.Bc4 Be7; 4.d4 d6; 5.c3. This move is a logical way of supporting the center. 5.Nc3 Nf6; 6.h3 0–0; 7.0–0 h6; 8.Re1 Re8; 9.Be3 is the most logical continuation, as in Tal-Filip, Miskolc 1963. Black has nothing to do here, but Filip's subsequent capture at d4 yields a better center for White. **5...Nf6; 6.dxe5.** 6.Qe2 Bg4 puts a lot of pressure on White's center. **6...Nxe5; 7.Nxe5 dxe5; 8.Qc2.** 8.Qxd8+ Bxd8 gives White nothing. **8...0–0; 9.Bg5 c6; 10.Bxf6?!** This is a completely unmotivated exchange of a bishop for a knight, and the future World Champion must have been very happy as Black.

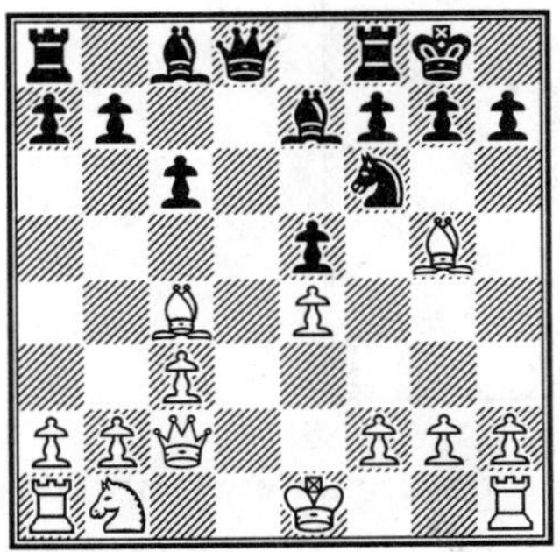

10...Bxf6; 11.Nd2 Qe7; 12.0–0–0. This invites a queenside attack, and Karpov is willing to oblige. **12...b5; 13.Be2 Be6; 14.Kb1 Rab8; 15.g4 c5; 16.h4.** The kingside pawnstorm cannot be effective because Black has not advanced any pawns in that area and has no weaknesses to attack.

16...Qc7; 17.g5 Be7; 18.c4. 18.Rdg1 Qa5; 19.c4 Rfd8; 20.Nb3 Qb4 gives Black a serious advantage, for example 21.cxb5 c4!; 22.Nc1 Rd2; 23.Qc3 Qxc3; 24.bxc3 Rxb5+; 25.Ka1 Ba3 and Black wins. **18...a6; 19.Ka1 Rb6; 20.Nf1 bxc4; 21.Ne3 Re8** to make room for the bishop to retreat. 21...Rfb8 would have made more sense. **22.Bxc4 Bxc4; 23.Nxc4 Rb4; 24.Rd5 f6; 25.gxf6 Bxf6; 26.a3 Rbb8; 27.Nd6?** A mistake, since the knight occupied an effective post at c4. **27...Red8; 28.Qc4.**

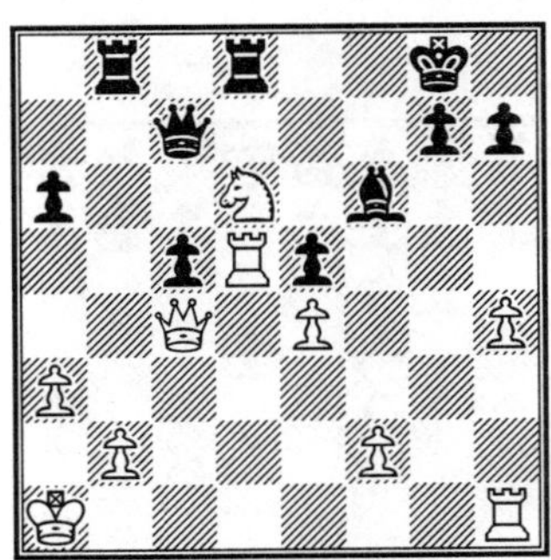

This seems to create major threats on the diagonal. **28...Kf8!; 29.Rhd1 Qb6.** Now White must have really wished the knight were still at c4! **30.R5d2??** 30.R1d2

would have kept White in the game, though Black is clearly better after 30...Bxh4; 31.Qa2 Qb3; 32.Qxb3 Rxb3; 33.Rxe5 Rb6; 34.Nc4 Rxd2; 35.Nxd2 Bf6; 36.Nc4 Bxe5; 37.Nxb6 Bd4 when the slow knight has a real challenge to keep pace with Black's h-pawn. **30...Rxd6; 31.b4 Rxd2; 32.Rxd2 cxb4; 33.Rd7 Be7; 34.a4 b3; 35.Kb1 Qxf2. Black won.**

EVANS GAMBIT

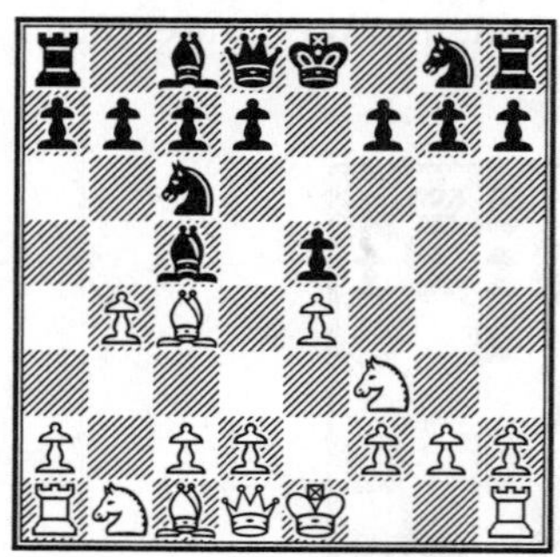

1.e4 e5
2.Nf3 Nc6
3.Bc4 Bc5
4.b4!?

The **Evans' Gambit** is enjoying a new round of popularity. White invests a pawn to gain complete control of the center, and whether Black accepts or declines, White will have good attacking chances. Recently some top Grandmasters have taken up the line, which had been relegated to the amateur ranks for decades. Several new monographs have appeared on the subject debating old and new analysis, and anyone who chooses to defend the Italian Game with 3...Bc5 had better be prepared to meet it!

(37) FISCHER - FINE [C52]
New York, 1963

1.e4 e5; 2.Nf3 Nc6; 3.Bc4 Bc5; 4.b4!? Bxb4. 4...Bb6; 5.a4 is the most common way of declining the gambit.

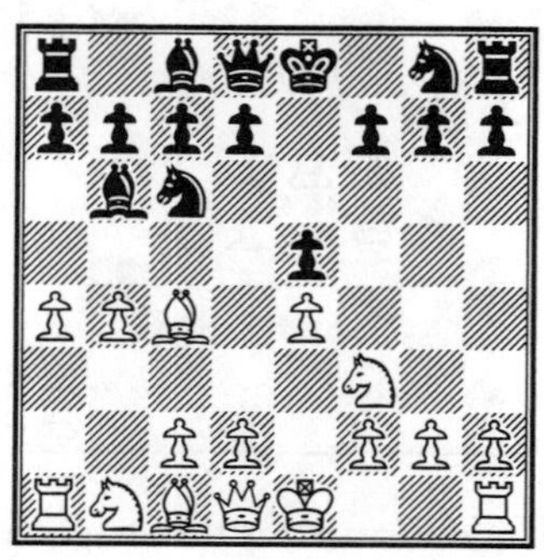

A) 5...a5; 6.b5 Nd4; 7.Nxd4 (7.Bxf7+ Kxf7; 8.Nxe5+ Kf8; 9.c3 is still considered unclear.) 7...Bxd4; 8.c3 Bb6; 9.d4 exd4; 10.0–0 Ne7; 11.Bg5 h6; 12.Bxe7. White can also try retreating the bishop. 12...Qxe7; 13.cxd4 Qd6?! Kasparov considers 13...Qb4 a better try. 14.Nc3 Bxd4; 15.Nd5! Bxa1; 16.Qxa1 0–0; 17.e5 Qc5; 18.Rc1 c6; 19.Ba2 Qa3; 20.Nb6 d5; 21.Nxa8 and White had a winning position in Kasparov-Piket, Amsterdam (Euwe)1995.

B) 5...a6; 6.Nc3 Nf6.

B1) 7.Nd5 Nxd5; 8.exd5 Nd4! seems to be doing well for Black here. 9.a5 Castling and capturing at e5 are options, but they are also not good enough to give White an advantage. 9...Ba7; 10.0–0?! (White should try 10.d6!? cxd6; 11.0–0 0–0; 12.Nxd4 Bxd4; 13.c3 with approximate equality.) 10...Nxf3+; 11.Qxf3 d6 and Black had the better pawn structure in Miranovic-Leko, Hungary 1995.

B2) 7.d4 is one brand new and very interesting idea for White, tested in Conquest-Winants, Amsterdam Open 1996.

5.c3 Ba5. 5...Be7 has soared to prominence on the basis of a recent game played at the highest level.

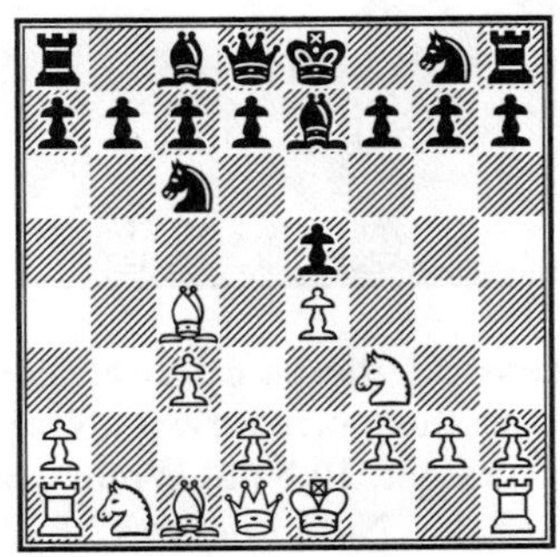

6.d4 Na5; 7.Be2 (7.Nxe5 Nxc4; 8.Nxc4 d5; 9.exd5 Qxd5; 10.Ne3 Qd8; 11.0–0 Nf6; 12.c4 0–0; 13.Bb2 c6; 14.Nc3 b5; 15.cxb5 cxb5; 16.Qf3 Rb8; 17.d5 Bc5; 18.Rad1 gave White the advantage in Nunn-Lukacs, Budapest 1978. 7.Bxf7+ Kxf7; 8.Nxe5+ Kf8; 9.Qf3+ Nf6; 10.g4 d6; 11.g5 dxe5; 12.gxf6 Bxf6; 13.dxe5 Nc4; 14.exf6 Qxf6; 15.Qxf6+ gxf6; 16.Bh6+ gives White good attacking chances, even in the endgame, Losev-Baikov, Moscow1989.)

Now Black releases the tension in the center. 7...exd4; 8.Qxd4 Here Black has a lot of defensive plans, including many dating back to the last century. This is hardly surprising, since there is a need to develop and reposition most of the pieces. We'll just consider the natural developing plan with ...Nf6 and take a brief look at the alternative with ...d6.

A) 8...Nf6; 9.e5 Nc6; 10.Qh4 Nd5; 11.Qg3 g6; 12.0–0 Nb6? (12...d6; 13.Rd1 Be6; 14.Bh6 gives White compensation for the pawn, but probably no more.) 13.c4 d6; 14.Rd1 Nd7; 15.Bh6! Ncxe5; 16.Nxe5 Nxe5 and here Bg7 looks good, but Kasparov chooses another plan. 17.Nc3 f6; 18.c5 and now Black played the natural but incorrect 18...Nf7? (18...Be6 is better, though Black is still suffering. 19.cxd6 Bxd6; 20.Ne4 gives White a strong attack, according to Blatny.) 19.cxd6 cxd6; 20.Qe3 Nxh6; 21.Qxh6 Bf8; 22.Qe3+ Kf7; 23.Nd5 Be6; 24.Nf4 Qe7; 25.Re1 and Black resigned in Kasparov-Anand Riga (Tal Memorial) 1995. The conclusion might have been 25...Re8; 26.Nxe6 Qxe6; 27.Qxe6+ Kxe6 (27...Rxe6; 28.Bc4) 28.Bb5+ and White wins easily.

B) 8...d6; 9.Qxg7 Bf6; 10.Qg3 Qe7 and here White must take care not to play 11.0-0?! Qxe4!; 12.Nd4! Be5!; 13.Qg5 Ne7 when White has no compensation for the pawns. 6.d4 exd4; Fine continues to play sharply. 6...Qe7; 7.0-0 Bb6; 8.Ba3 d6; 9.Bb5 Bd7; 10.Bxc6 Bxc6; 11.Nxe5 and White has an obvious advantage in space and in the center, Sveshnikov-Sofieva, Capelle la Grande 1995. 6...d6; 7.Qb3 Qd7; 8.dxe5 Bb6; 9.Nbd2 dxe5; 10.Ba3 Na5; 11.Qb4 c5; 12.Qb2 Nxc4; 13.Nxc4 f6; 14.Rd1 gave White the d-file as compensation for the pawn, and Black's vulnerable light squares provided even greater possibilities in Christiansen-Gretarsson, Yerevan Olympiad 1996. **7.0-0 dxc3?!** It is said that the only way to refute a gambit is to accept it, but this is a bit too much. Black really needs to develop, and even 7...Bb6 is logical, keeping some pressure in the center. **8.Qb3 Qe7; 9.Nxc3.**

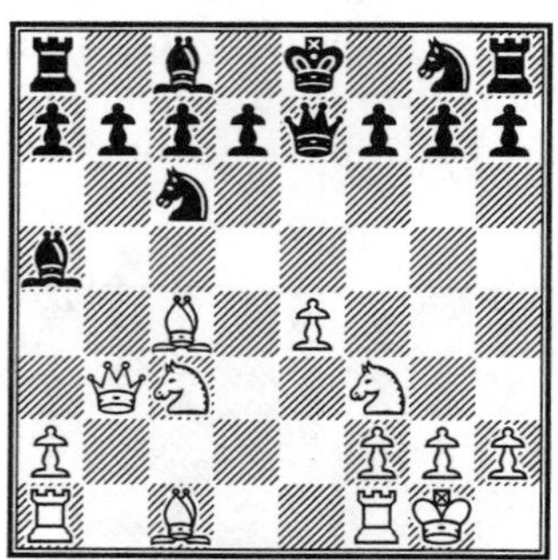

Black must get the queens off the board at all costs, so the correct move is 9...Qb4, even though it gives up the pawn at f7. **9...Nf6?** Black is already struggling but this knight just becomes a target. **10.Nd5!** White grabs the initiative and never lets go. **10...Nxd5; 11.exd5 Ne5.** 11...Nd8? loses to 12.Ba3 d6; 13.Qb5+ Bd7; 14.Qxa5 with big threats. **12.Nxe5 Qxe5; 13.Bb2 Qg5.** White must keep up the pressure or else Black's king will escape from the center.

14.h4! This deflects the enemy queen. **14...Qxh4.** 14...Qg4; 15.Rfe1+! Bxe1; 16.Rxe1+ Kd8; 17.Qe3 Qxh4; 18.g3! Black cannot keep control of e7. **15.Bxg7 Rg8; 16.Rfe1+ Kd8,** taking the rook leads to the same finish. **17.Qg3!** Black resigned, as there is no way to defend f6. **White won.**

CLASSICAL VARIATION

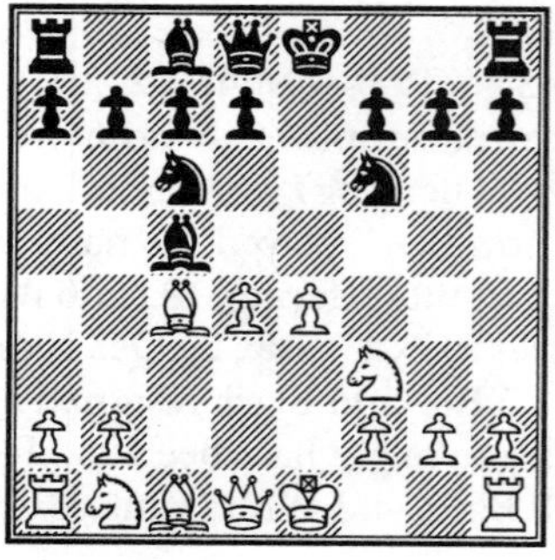

1.e4	**e5**
2.Nf3	**Nc6**
3.Bc4	**Bc5**
4.c3	**Nf6**
5.d4	**exd4**
6.cxd4	

White has established the ideal pawn center and is attacking the Black bishop. But note that Black already has three pieces developed to White's two, so the loss of time is not so significant. Black can pick up the tempo a bit with 6...Bb4+. White must then decide how to interpose.

(38) STEINITZ - VON BARDELEBEN [C54]

Hastings, 1895

1.e4 e5; 2.Nf3 Nc6; 3.Bc4 Bc5; 4.c3 Nf6; 5.d4 exd4; 6.cxd4 Bb4+; 7.Nc3!? After the safer 7.Bd2 Bxd2+; 8.Nbxd2 d5; 9.exd5 Nxd5 play is about equal. **7...d5!?** After years of study, theorists have found that 7...Nxe4 is best, with the main line being a temporary piece sacrifice: 8.0–0 Bxc3!; 9.d5!, leading to enormous complications. **8.exd5 Nxd5; 9.0–0!**

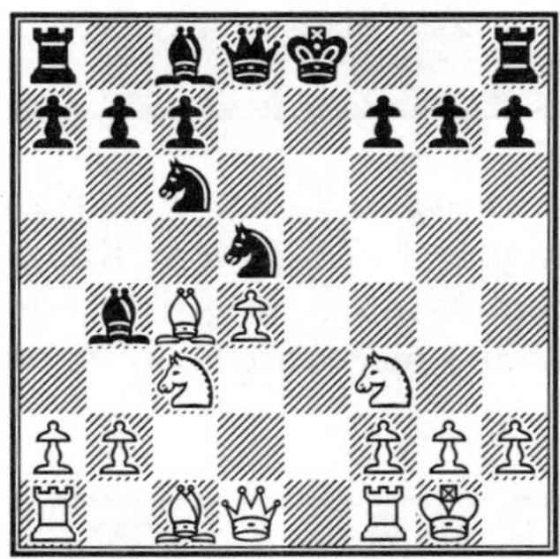

9...Be6. Black cannot take the pawn: 9...Nxc3; 10.bxc3 Bxc3?; 11.Qb3! Bxa1; 12.Bxf7+ Kf8; 13.Ba3+ Ne7; 14.Rxa1 followed by Re1. **10.Bg5 Be7; 11.Bxd5!** Steinitz recognizes that he needs to act fast if he is to achieve any advantage. His attack is based on keeping the Black king stuck in the center. He was justifiably recognized as the founder of modern positional chess, but in his younger days, he was known as 'The Austrian Morphy' for his brilliant attacks. **11...Bxd5; 12.Nxd5 Qxd5; 13.Bxe7 Nxe7; 14.Re1 f6.**

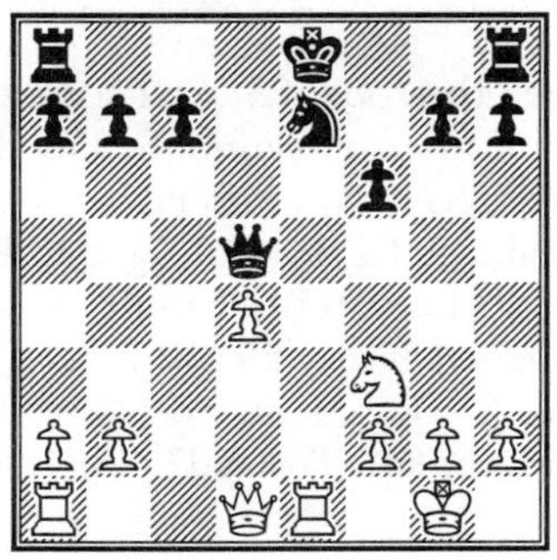

White now needs to maintain his edge in development or Black simply castle by hand with 15...Kf7 and 16...Rhe8, when he will have the better game because of

White's isolated pawn on d4. **15.Qe2 Qd7; 16.Rac1!** White might have tried 16.d5 followed by 17.Nd4. **16...c6?** Black's only move was 16...Kf7 to connect the rooks and defend the knight from behind. **17.d5! cxd5; 18.Nd4,** the knight enters the attack with devastating force. **18...Kf7; 19.Ne6 Rhc8; 20.Qg4 g6; 21.Ng5+ Ke8.** Now follows one of the great chess combinations.

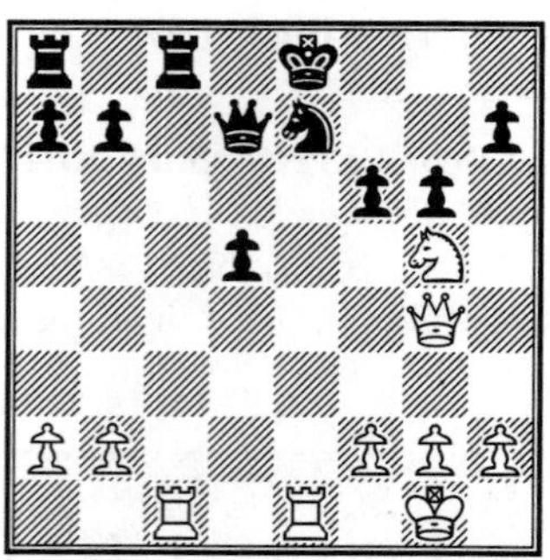

22.Rxe7+! Kf8. 22...Qxe7 loses to 23.Rxc8+, but 22...Kxe7 is not much better: 22...Kxe7; 23.Re1+ Kd6; 24.Qb4+ Kc7; 25.Ne6+ Kb8; 26.Qf4+ Rc7; 27.Nxc7. But after 22...Kf8, it looks as though White is in trouble, because back-rank mate threatens, and in fact all four of White's pieces are about to be captured! Steinitz has seen further. **23.Rf7+! Kg8.**

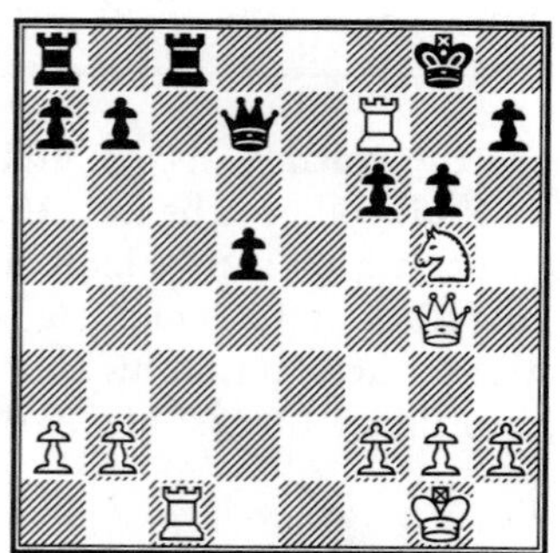

Black still cannot capture the rook: 23...Qxf7; 24.Rxc8+ Rxc8; 25.Qxc8+ Qe8 and White wins. **24.Rg7+!** This monster cannot be killed. **24...Kh8.** Black also loses after 24...Kf8; 25.Nxh7+! **25.Rxh7+.** Von Bardeleben resigned here not wanting to provide the pleasure of a beautiful finish. **25...Kg8; 26.Rg7+!** Once again, 26...Kf8; 27.Nh7+ or 26...Qxg7; 27.Rxc8+ lose, so Black must return to h8. But now the queen enters the attack via the opened h-file: **26...Kh8; 27.Qh4+! Kxg7; 28.Qh7+ Kf8; 29.Qh8+ Ke7; 30.Qg7+ Ke8.** Black gets mated after 30...Kd6; 31.Qxf6+. **31.Qg8+ Ke7; 32.Qf7+ Kd8; 33.Qf8+ Qe8; 34.Nf7+! Kd7; 35.Qd6#. White won.**

MODERN BISHOP OPENING

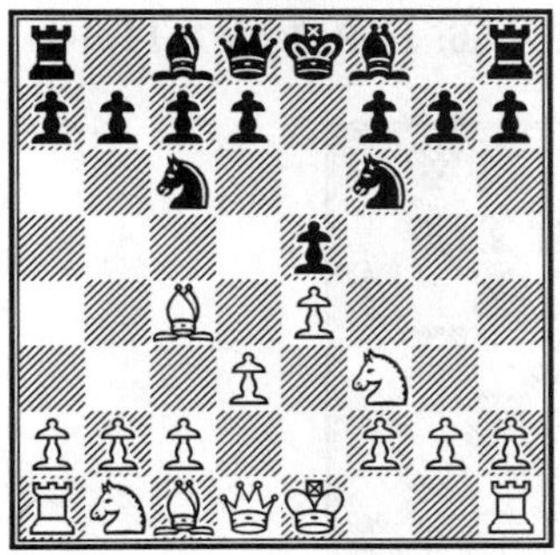

1.e4	**e5**
2.Bc4	**Nf6**
3.d3	**Nc6**
4.Nf3	

This quiet move can lead to excitement later on in the game. This opening is known as the **Modern Bishop's Opening**, although it most often arises from the Italian Game. The opening has reappeared in serious competition in the 1980s and 1990s. White cannot hope for quick victories in this opening, but has a solid position and Black has to work hard to create counterplay which poses any threat.

(39) SPEELMAN - YUSUPOV [C54]
Hastings, 1988

1.e4 e5; 2.Bc4 Nf6; 3.d3 Nc6; 4.Nf3 Bc5. This is the more active reply, reaching the Giuoco Piano. Black can also develop more conservatively. 4...Be7; 5.0–0 0–0; 6.Re1 d6; 7.Bb3 (7.c3 Na5; 8.Bb5 a6; 9.Ba4 c5; 10.Nbd2 Qc7; 11.Nf1 Be6; 12.h3 Rad8; 13.Bg5 h6; 14.Bh4 g6; 15.d4 Nh5; 16.Bxe7 Qxe7; 17.b4 Nc4; 18.Bb3 cxd4; 19.cxd4 Rc8; 20.Rc1 b5; 21.Ne3 Nf4; 22.Rc2 Nxe3; 23.Rxe3 Rxc2; 24.Qxc2 Rc8; 25.Qd2 Bxb3; 26.Rxb3 Rc4; 27.Ra3 Rxd4; 28.Qe3 Rxb4; 29.Rxa6 Qc7; 30.Qd2 Qc4; 31.Qe1 Nd3; 32.Qd1 Rb2; 33.Kh2 Qxe4; 34.Rxd6 Qf4+; 35.Kg1 Nxf2. Black won. Yudasin-Vladimirov, Tilburg 1994.)

7...Nd7; 8.c3 Nc5; 9.Bc2 Bg4; 10.Nbd2 d5; 11.h3 Bh5; 12.Qe2 a5; 13.Nf1 Bxf3; 14.Qxf3 d4; 15.Ng3 Bg5; 16.Nf5 g6; 17.Qg3 Bxc1; 18.Raxc1 Kh8; 19.Nh6 a4; 20.f4 exf4; 21.Qxf4 Kg7; 22.Ng4 h5; 23.Qh6+ Kg8; 24.Nh2 Ne5; 25.Rcd1 Ra6; 26.Rf1 Rb6; 27.Qc1 dxc3; 28.Qe3 Qe7; 29.bxc3 Rb2; 30.Bb1 Rd8; Yudasin-Kupreichik, Sverdlovsk Soviet Union 1984, Black won. (83)

5.c3 d6. 5...a6; 6.0–0 Ba7; 7.Re1 0–0; 8.Bb3 Kudrin-Korchnoi, Wijk aan Zee 1985 saw 8.Nbd2 Re8; 9.Bb3, but Black equalized with a quick ...d5. 8...d6; 9.h3 Be6; 10.Nbd2 Nd7; 11.Nf1 A standard maneuver, intending to bring the knight to the kingside via g3 or f3. 11...Bxb3; 12.Qxb3 Nc5; 13.Qc2 Ne6; 14.Be3 Bxe3; 15.Nxe3 Nf4 and Black's knight at f4 was very strong in Waitzkin-Adams, New York (CITS) 1996. 5...Bb6; 6.Nbd2 0–0; 7.0–0 d6; 8.Bb3 Ne7; 9.Nc4 Ng6; 10.Re1 c6; 11.Nxb6 axb6; 12.d4 Qe7 with a solid position for Black, Wolff-Sokolov, New York (CITS) 1996.

6.0-0 0-0; 7.Nbd2. 7.Bb3 a6; 8.Re1 Ba7; 9.h3 Be6; 10.Nbd2 Nd7 (10...Bxb3; 11.Qxb3 Rb8; 12.Nf1 Nh5; 13.Bg5 Qd7; 14.Rad1 Qe6 and now 15.d4 exd4; 16.cxd4 Qxb3; 17.axb3 f5 led to a very unbalanced position in Waitzkin-Xie Jun, San Francisco (Pan Pacific) 1995.) 11.Nf1 Bxb3; 12.Qxb3 Nc5; 13.Qc2 d5; 14.Rd1 Ne6; 15.Qb3 Nc5; 16.Qc2 Ne6; 17.Qb3 Nc5 was agreed drawn in Waitzkin-A. Ivanov, US Class Championship 1995. **7...a6; 8.Bb3 Be6; 9.Nc4 h6; 10.Re1 Ne7; 11.d4.**

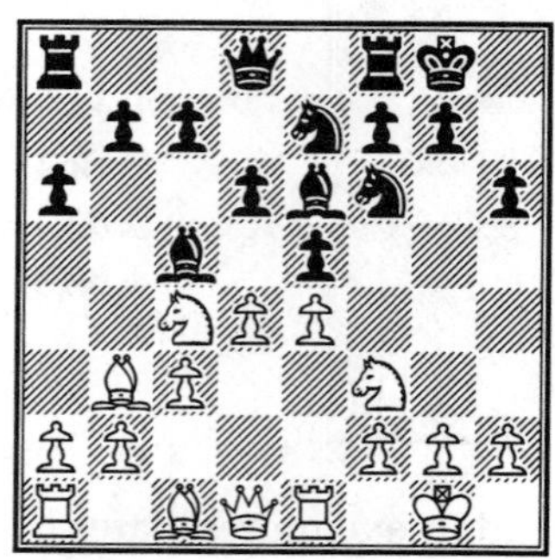

White has waited a long time to achieve this advance, but it now takes place with a full supporting cast. Black must capture. **11...exd4; 12.cxd4 Ba7; 13.d5.** White did not want to open up the a7-g1 diagonal while limiting the prospects of his bishop at b3, but otherwise Black could play ...a5. **13...Bg4; 14.Be3 Bxe3; 15.Nxe3 Bh5; 16.Nf1.** The knight uses this square to pivot to g3, after which Black will have nothing better than to exchange bishop for knight at f3. **16...Ng6; 17.Ng3 Bxf3; 18.Qxf3 Nd7.** Black will take the e5 square as compensation for the minor exchange. **19.Rac1 Nde5; 20.Qe3 c6; 21.dxc6 bxc6.**

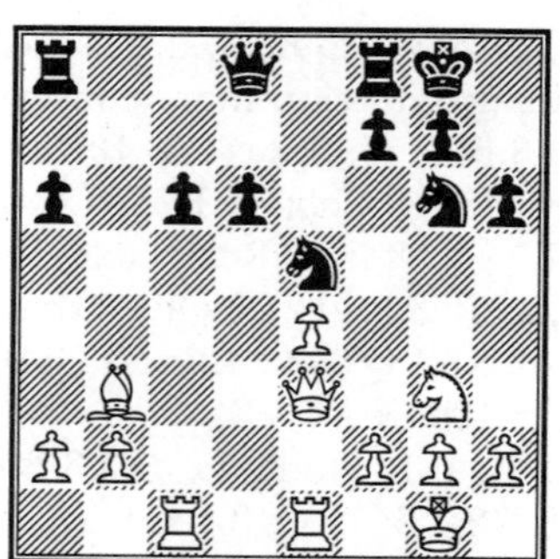

The strong knight at e5 defends the c6-square, and Black's position is not as precarious as it seems. White can try to drive the knight back with f4, but that would lead to disaster, if played immediately. **22.Nf5.** 22.f4 Ng4; 23.Qd4 (23.Qd3?? Qb6+ 24.Kh1 Nf2+; 25.Kg1 Nh3+; 26.Kh1 Qg1+ 27.Rxg1 Nf2#) 23...Qh4; 24.Nf1 c5; 25.Qxd6 Qf2+; 26.Kh1 Nxf4; 27.Qd2 Qxd2; 28.Nxd2 Nf2+; 29.Kg1 N2d3 and Black wins material. **22...Nh4; 23.Red1 Nxf5; 24.exf5 a5.** Now White must attend to the queenside.

25.Qd4 Re8; 26.Ba4 Rc8; 27.h3. White cannot make any further progress in the center or on the queenside, so now makes a move which has two useful points: there is no danger of a later back rank mate and the pawn at f5 can be supported by the g-pawn if necessary. **27...Qf6; 28.Rc3.** White exchanges the weak pawn at f5 for the pawn at d6, bringing more pressure to bear on the pawn at c6. **28...Qxf5; 29.Qxd6 Re6; 30.Qd2 Rce8.** The power of the knight at e5 continues to hold the Black position together, but any attempt to dislodge it with f4 would create serious weaknesses on the White kingside. **31.Bb3 R6e7; 32.Bc2 Qf6; 33.Re3 Qg5; 34.Qd4 c5** threatening a cheap trick. **35.Qc3.** 35.Qxc5?? drops the queen to 35...Nf3+.

35...g6. 35...Nc6 would have provided more chances. I suspect that both players were in their customary terrible time trouble. **36.Ba4 Rb8; 37.Rde1 f6; 38.Qxa5 Kf8; 39.Rd1 c4** Black lost on time, but the position was lost in any case. **40.Rd8+ Rxd8; 41.Qxd8+ Kf7; 42.b3** and Black has no good reply. **White won.**

WILKES BARRE VARIATION

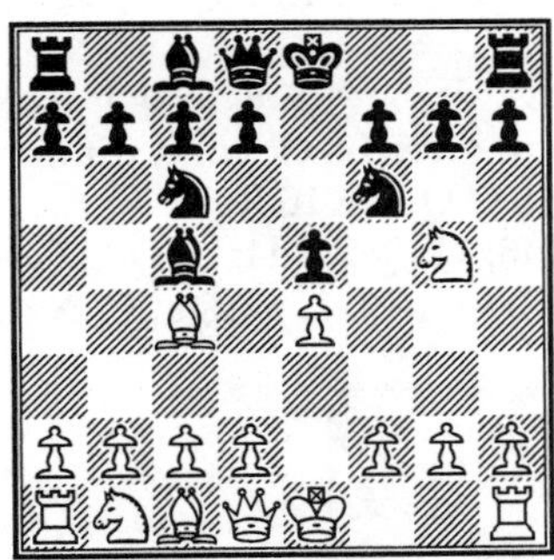

1.e4	**e5**
2.Nf3	**Nc6**
3.Bc4	**Nf6**
4.Ng5	**Bc5**

This is the very aggressive **Wilkes Barre Variation** in American, or the **Traxler Counterattack** as it is known in Europe. The latter is certainly more justified. By any name, it is a very sharp opening, but seems to be just too risky for Black. Even if one believes in some untested resource for Black, the amount of memorization and tactical skill required discourages many chessplayers from adopting it. The opening is rarely seen in professional competition, but is a favorite at the amateur level. Although White can play prosaically with 5.d4, most players prefer to capture at f7 with one of the minor pieces.

(40) MIKISTA - TRAXLER [C57]

Postal, 1896

1.e4 e5; 2.Nf3 Nc6; 3.Bc4 Nf6; 4.Ng5 Bc5; 5.Nxf7. 5.Bxf7+ is superior. 5...Ke7; 6.Bd5 Chigorin's contribution. The idea is to get rid of one of the enemy knights.

6...d6 (6...Rf8; 7.0–0 d6; 8.h3 keeps the enemy bishop off the useful g4-square. 8...Qe8; 9.Nc3 Qg6; 10.d4 Bb6! leads to a complex but well-investigated position.) 7.c3 Qe8!? (7...Rf8 resembles lines with 6...Rf8.) 8.d4 and in a game between super-grandmasters Karpov chose to take up the challenge with 8...exd4; 9.cxd4 Nxd4; 10.Nc3 Qh5; 11.Qd3 Rf8 with a sharp position, which did not quiet down after

12.b4! Bb6; 13.Na4 Nc6; 14.Nxb6 axb6; 15.Qc3 h6!; 16.Nf3 (16.Nh7 Nxh7; 17.Qxg7+ Rf7; 18.Bxf7 Qxf7; 19.Bxh6 Qxg7; 20.Bxg7 Nxb4 and Black's queenside pawns will advance more quickly than White's queenside pawns. For example 21.Kd2 Rxa2+; 22.Rxa2 Nxa2; 23.Rb1 Be6; 24.f4 Nf6; 25.Bxf6+ Kxf6; 26.h3 Bc4; 27.g4 b5; 28.g5+ Kg6; 29.h4 c5; 30.f5+ Kh7; 31.h5 b4; 32.g6+ Kg7 and the pawns are blockaded.

Of course this is just an extreme example, the ending is much too complicated for a cursory note.) 16...Bg4; 17.Bxc6 bxc6; 18.Nd2 Qb5 and Black has a better game in Karpov-Belyavsky, Soviet Championship 1983, because the king is trapped in the center and Black has useful open lines for the rooks. 5.d4 is best met by 5...d5!

5...Bxf2+; 6.Kf1. 6.Ke2? allows Black to carry out an effective and impressive attack, as Traxler himself demonstrated: 6...Nd4+; 7.Kd3 b5; 8.Bb3 Nxe4; 9.Nxd8 Nc5+; 10.Kc3 Ne2+; 11.Qxe2 Bd4+; 12.Kb4 a5+; 13.Kxb5 Ba6+; 14.Kxa5 Bd3+; 15.Kb4 Na6+; 16.Ka4 Nb4+; 17.Kxb4 c5#. Black won. Reinisch-Traxler, Prague Czechoslovakia 1896; 6.Kxf2? Nxe4+; 7.Kg1 (7.Ke3 Qe7! 8.Kxe4 Qh4+ and the best White can do is concede a pawn with 9.Ke3 Qf4+; 10.Ke2 Qxc4+; 11.Ke1 Qxf7; 12.Rf1 Qe7 and Black has a clear advantage.) 7...Qh4.

A) 8.g3 is stronger, but Black can at least draw with 8...Nxg3; 9.hxg3 Qxg3+; 10.Kf1 Rf8; 11.Qh5 Nd4 (11...d5 is better and gives Black good winning chances.) 12.Rg1 Qf4+; 13.Kg2 Qe4+; 14.Kg3 Nf5+; 15.Kf2 Qd4+; 16.Kg2 Nh4+; 17.Kh2 Qf4+.

B) 8.Qf1? 8...Rf8; 9.d3 Nd6; 10.Nxd6+ cxd6; 11.Qe2 Nd4; 12.Qd2 Qg4 and Black resigned in Perrin-Wilkes Barre Chess Club, Postal 1931. **6...Qe7; 7.Nxh8 d5!**

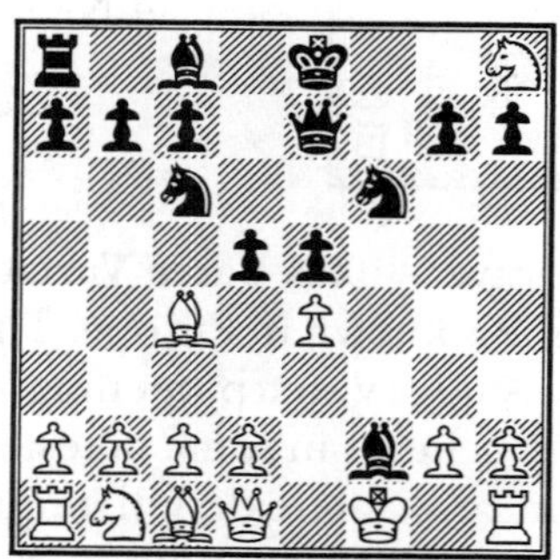

This accelerates Black's development and makes the attack all the more dangerous. **8.exd5.** 8.Qf3? loses to 8...Bh4!; 9.Bxd5 Nd4; 10.Qa3 Nxd5; 11.Qxe7+ Kxe7!; 12.exd5 Bh3!! and White resigned in Apartsev-I. Zaitsev, Moscow 1964. **8...Nd4.** This position has been analyzed for a century but no firm conclusions have been reached. **9.c3.** Now the advance of the d-pawn is preferred. 9.d6 was researched in the 1930s by D. Menovsky. 9...Qxd6; 10.c3 Bg4; 11.Qa4+ Nd7; 12.Kxf2 Qf6+; 13.Ke1 (13.Kg1 Be2!; 14.h3 Qf1+; 15.Kh2 Qf4+ is a draw, following analysis by Kabiyev.) 13...0-0-0.

A) 14.cxd4? exd4 and Black has an irresistible attack, according to Estrin. 15.Be2 Bxe2; 16.Kxe2 leaves White with two extra pieces and an extra rook, but there is no shelter for the king, for example 16...Qe6+; 17.Kf2 (17.Kd1 Qg4+; 18.Kc2 Qe4+; 19.d3 Qxg2+; 20.Kb3 Nc5+; 21.Ka3 Nxa4; 22.Rd1 Rxh8; 23.Kxa4 Qc2+ and Black cleans up.) 17...Rf8+; 18.Kg3 Qd6+; 19.Kh3 Qh6+; 20.Kg3 Qg5+; 21.Kh3 Rf4 and mate follows: 22.g3 Qf5+; 23.Kg2 Rf2+; 24.Kg1 Qf3 and White can only toss in a final move before getting mated.

B) 14.Rf1; 14...Qh4+; 15.Rf2 Nb6; 16.g3 Qh3; 17.cxd4 Nxa4; 18.Nf7 and according to Radchenko, White has a small advantage. **9...Bg4; 10.Qa4+ Nd7; 11.Kxf2.**

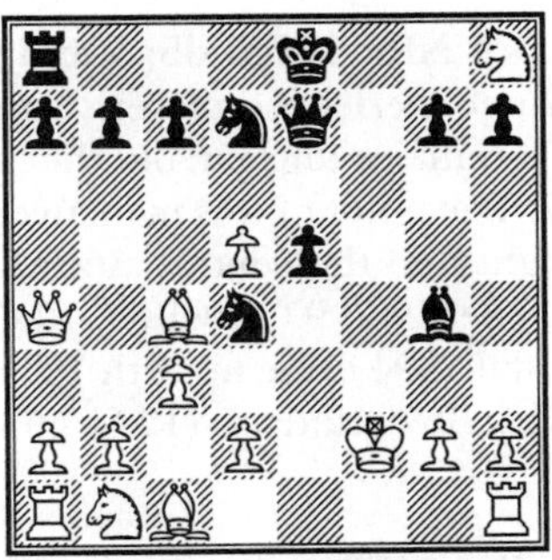

White has an extra rook and piece, but all of the pieces are huddled on the queenside or back rank and can't help defend the king against the coming onslaught. **11...Qh4+; 12.Ke3.** 12.Kf1 0–0–0; 13.Nf7 Rf8 and Black won in Smirnov-Ulanov, Moscow 1955. 12.g3 Qf6+; 13.Ke1 Qf5; 14.cxd4 Qe4+; 15.Kf2 Qf3+; 16.Ke1 Qxh1+; 17.Bf1 0–0–0; 18.d3 Rf8; 19.Be3 Qxf1+; 20.Kd2 Qe2+; 21.Kc3 Nb6; 22.Qa5 Qxe3; 23.Kb3 Bd1+ and Black resigned in Maasen-Stadler, Postal 1954. **12...Qg5+; 13.Kf2 Qf5+; 14.Kg1 0–0–0; 15.cxd4 Rf8; 16.h3 Qf2+; 17.Kh2 Bxh3; 18.Kxh3 g5.** White resigned. **Black won.**

FRITZ AND ULVESTAD VARIATIONS

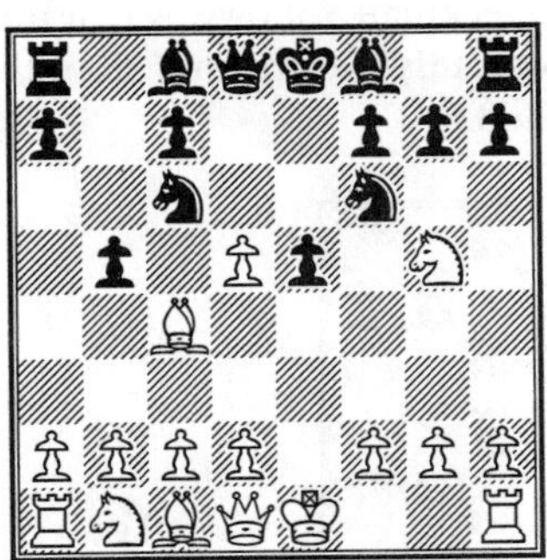

1.e4	**e5**
2.Nf3	**Nc6**
3.Bc4	**Nf6**
4.Ng5	**d5**
5.exd5	**b5**

This is the **Ulvestad Variation**, which is just a transpositional variation of the **Fritz Variation**, 5...Nd4 followed by ...b5. The two converge quickly in most cases, since the idea of 5...b5 is combined with the positioning of a Black knight at d4.

In any case, the play is lively and filled with massive tactical complications, which is why the opening has been played by the best correspondence players but is rarely seen in over-the-board events.

(41) ESTRIN - BERLINER [C57]
Correspondence World Championship, 1965

1.e4 e5; 2.Nf3 Nc6; 3.Bc4 Nf6; 4.Ng5 d5; 5.exd5 b5. 5...Nxd5 leads to risky play. Two examples familiar to experienced players from their youngest days are:

A) 6.d4 , the Lolli Attack, remains unclear, but the later word, from *The Big Book of Busts,* is 6...Bb4+; 7.c3 Be7; The point of this maneuver is to eliminate the possibility of White getting the knight into the central attack via c3. 8.Nxf7 (8.Qf3 Bxg5; 9.Bxd5 0–0 is fine for Black.) 8...Kxf7; 9.Qf3+ Ke6; 10.Qe4 was considered best for ages, but Kalvach-Drtina, Postal 1994 came up with 10...b5! which puts the question to the White bishop. 11.Bxb5 Bb7; 12.dxe5 (12.f4 g6; 13.fxe5 Rf8; 14.Qg4+ Rf5; 15.Bd3.

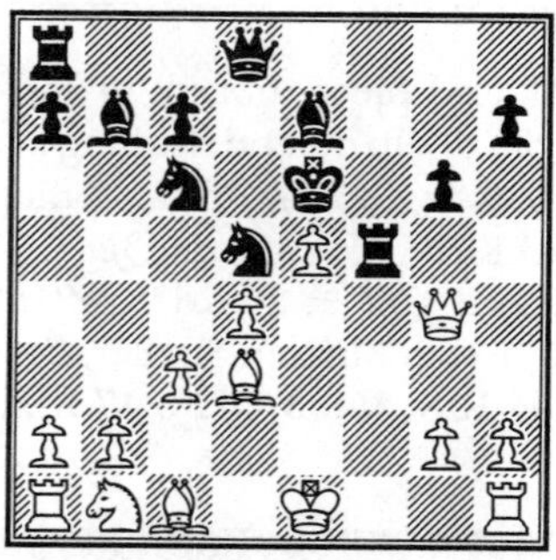

An amazing move follows, the start of a series of fireworks which will brighten the day or night of any chessplayer. 15...Nxd4!!; 16.Rf1 Ne3!!; 17.Bxe3 Nf3+; 18.gxf3 Qxd3; 19.Qd4 Bh4+!!; 20.Qxh4 Qxe3+ and checkmate follows. A magnificent game by two unknown players, and one which is presently overturning all of the theory in the Lolli attack.) 12...Rf8; 13.Qg4+ Rf5; 14.Bd3.

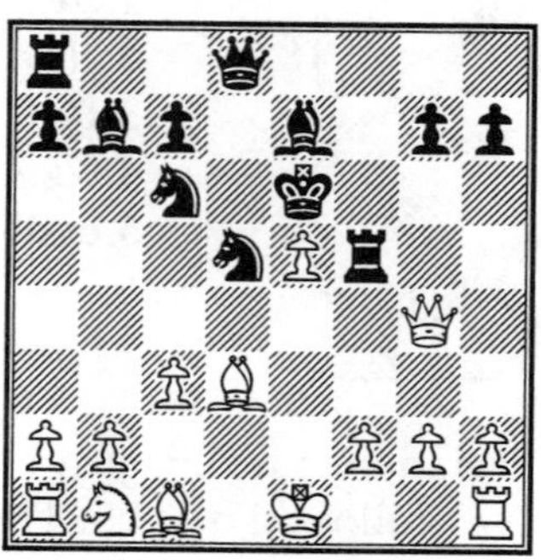

Black's next move is truly stunning! 14...Nd4!! What a move! Black defends the rook at f5 by offering a piece which can be captured by a pawn!! 15.Rf1? Ne3!!; 16.Bxe3 Nf3+; 17.gxf3 Qxd3; 18.Qd4;

B) 6.Nxf7, known as the Fried Liver or Fegattello Attack. Original analysis in The *Big Book of Busts* offers a new twist on the opening, which may turn out to be playable as Black after all. 6...Kxf7; 7.Qf3+ Ke6; It is universally recognized that this is the only playable defense. 8.Nc3 Ncb4 Again, the only move. 9.a3! Nxc2+; 10.Kd1 Nd4 (10...Nxa1; 11.Nxd5! Kd7; 12.d4! eliminates any hope for survival, according to analysis by Estrin, for example 12...c6; 13.Qf5+ Ke8; 14.Qxe5+ Be7; 15.Qxg7 Rf8; 16.Nxe7 Qxe7; 17.Re1 Qxe1+; 18.Kxe1 b5; 19.Ba2 and even if the Black king does not get checkmated, the knight at a1 can never escape,) 11.Bxd5+ Kd7; 12.Qf7+ (12.Qg3 Qf6; 13.Ne4 Qf5; 14.d3 c6; 15.Ba2 Kc7 and although the position is far from simple, Black's chances seem no worse.)

12...Qe7 and Black follows with ...c6. Chances seem to be about even. 5...Nd4; 6.c3 b5; 7.Bf1 is the Fritz move order, reaching the position at move 7 in the game. 5...Nd4; 6.c3 b5 is an alternative move order. White can enter the main lines with Bf1, and should do so, since 7.Bd3?! Bf5; 8.Bxf5 Nxf5; 9.Qf3 was played in Morozevich-Timman, Amsterdam 1996, where Black would have had the advantage after 9...Qd7. **6.Bf1 Nd4; 7.c3 Nxd5.**

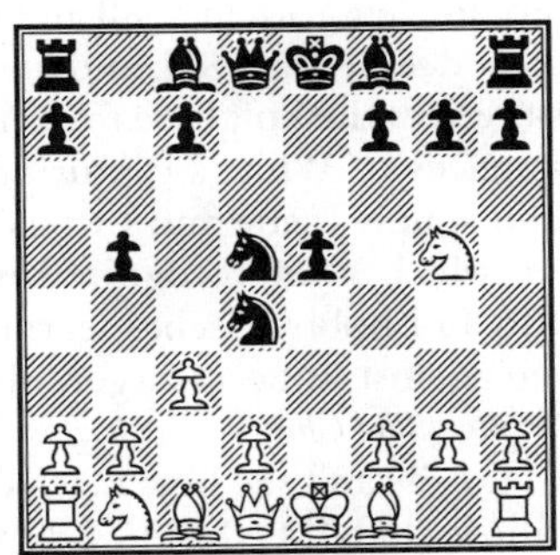

Here is where the fun begins. There are three horses running around on the field and each quickly finds itself in danger. This game has had a lasting influence on the theory of the Fritz Variation. **8.Ne4.** 8.cxd4 is met by 8...Qxg5 where...

A) 9.Nc3 should now be considered White's best plan. 9...exd4; 10.Bxb5+ Bd7; 11.Bxd7+ Kxd7; 12.0–0 and now the question is, can Black capture at c4? 12...dxc3 (12...Nf4; 13.g3 Nh3+; 14.Kg2 Nf4+; 15.Kh1 dxc3; 16.Qa4+ c6; 17.gxf4 Qd5+; 18.Kg1 cxb2; 19.Bxb2 Bc5; 20.Rae1 f6 is about equal, van der Wiel-Timman, Amsterdam 1980.) 13.dxc3 Qe5; 14.c4 Bd6; 15.f4! Nxf4; 16.Bxf4 Qc5+; 17.Kh1 Qxc4. Black probably does better with 17...f5, but White is better in any case. 18.Rc1 and White has a tremendous attack.

B) 9.Bxb5+ 9...Kd8; 10.Qf3 is a line which has brought Bobby Fischer both grief and joy. (10.0–0 Bb7; 11.Qf3 Rb8; 12.Qg3 Qxg3; 13.hxg3 exd4 gave Black a good game in Shabalov-A.Ivanov, United States Championship 1996.) 10...exd4 (10...e4; 11.Qxe4 Bd6; 12.0–0 Bb7; 13.d3 Nf4; 14.Bxf4 Qxb5; 15.d5 Qxb2; 16.Bxd6 cxd6; 17.Re1 Qf6; 18.Nc3 Rc8; 19.Qb4 Re8; 20.Qa5+ Kd7; 21.Qa4+ and Fischer's opponent in a simultaneous exhibition resigned just in time to avoid checkmate, Montreal 1964.) 11.Bc6.

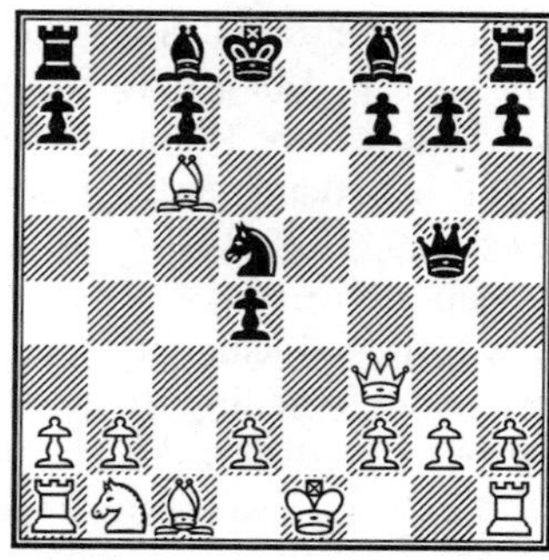

Here is a story of how an important theoretical novelty was found. I was playing in an international tournament in New York in 1980 and was defending the opening as Black. This position has been deeply analyzed, and I was familiar with the theory, which stated that I should just retreat the knight to f6. A huge amount of analysis had been devoted to the consequences of White's capturing at a8. But at the board I realized that White could then simply castle and I would have no useful reply. So I discovered an alternative move, which is now recognized as best. (11.0–0 Bb7; 12.Qxf7 allows the devastating 12...Nf6 and Bobby Fischer learned this when he was forced to resign a casual game played against Robert Burger, who later went on to write an excellent survey on Fischer's play, *The Chess of Bobby Fischer.*)

B1) 11...Nf6; 12.0–0! and now I can't see how Black can keep White from developing: 12...Rb8; 13.d3 Qc5 allows 14.b4! Qxb4; 15.Bd2 Qc5 (15...Qb6; 16.Bg5 and Black's king is in serious trouble.) 16.Rc1 Bg4; 17.Qg3 Qb6 is probably the best Black can do, but after 18.Bg5 White has more than enough compensation for the pawn.

B2) 11...Nb4!; 12.Bxa8 Nc2+; 13.Kd1 (13.Kf1 Ba6+; 14.Kg1 Nxa1 is more comfortable for Black.) 13...Bg4; 14.Kxc2 (14.Qxg4 Qxg4+; 15.Kxc2 Qg6+; 16.Kd1 c6 and White can resign.) 14...Bxf3; 15.Bxf3 Qc5+; 16.Kd1 d3; 17.Nc3 Qxf2. I don't have the rest of this game, but I went on to win without difficulty. Rothman-Schiller, New York 1981.

8...Qh4. 8...Ne6; 9.Bxb5+ Bd7; 10.Bxd7+ Qxd7; 11.0–0 f5 and Black had enough counterplay to compensate for the pawn in Estrin-Muir, Postal 1977. **9.Ng3 Bg4; 10.f3 e4!** leads to a much-discussed position after **11.cxd4 Bd6; 12.Bxb5+ Kd8; 13.0–0 exf3.**

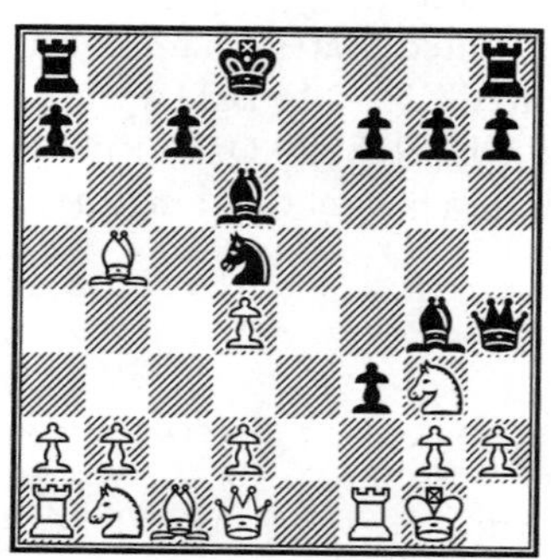

Two protagonists in this debate are the players of this game. The American so far seems to have the last word, but perhaps there is still more to be found. **14.Rxf3.** 14.Qb3 Nb4! leads to wonderful complications. Here is the main line, but note that there are plenty of tactics in all of the positions which follow! 15.Rxf3! White offers the rook, but if Black captures the light squares will be too exposed. 15...c6! takes care of some of the potential problems on the long diagonal. Here White should be patient, and not try to grab anything yet.

Another threat is established with 16.a3! Bxf3; 17.Qxf3 Re8 and now attend to development with 18.Nc3! Re1+; 19.Kf2 Nc2!; 20.Nce2 Bxg3+; 21.Qxg3 (21.hxg3 Qh1 and Black wins.) 21...Qxg3+; 22.hxg3 cxb5 and here Black's superior pawn structure and extra exchange provides a clear advantage. This is from Berliner's analysis, which comprehensively surveys the sidelines as well. **14...Rb8!; 15.Be2?** One thing everyone can agree with is that this is an error. 15.a4 a6!; 16.Bf1 Re8; 17.Nc3 c6; 18.d3 f5; 19.Be2 Bxf3; 20.Bxf3 Ne3 is assessed as even by Berliner, but of course the position remains very sharp. **15...Bxf3; 16.Bxf3 Qxd4+; 17.Kh1 Bxg3!; 18.hxg3 Rb6.**

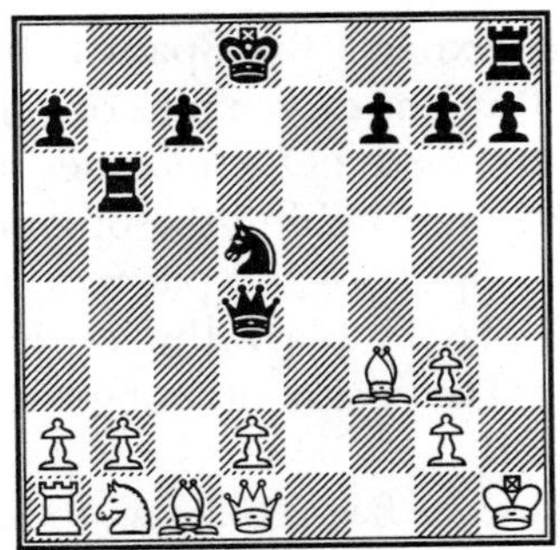

...and White was lucky even to survive for a few moves. **19.d3 Ne3; 20.Bxe3 Qxe3; 21.Bg4.** To guard against checks at h6 by retreating the bishop to h3. But Black has a better plan, involving trapping the bishop behind a wall of pawns. **21...h5!; 22.Bh3 g5!; 23.Nd2 g4!; 24.Nc4.**

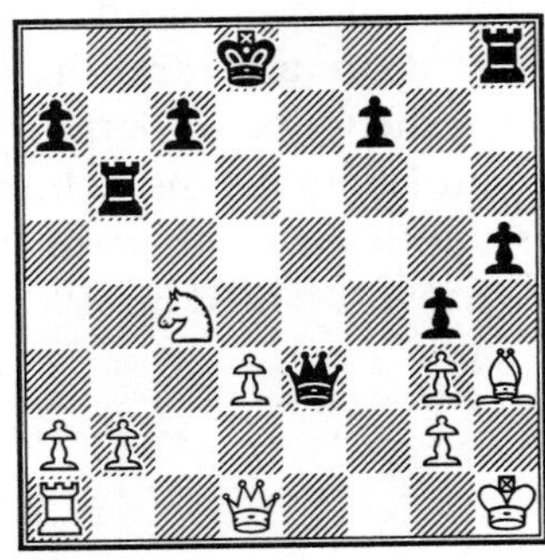

White goes after the rook but Black shows that it is irrelevant! **24...Qxg3!; 25.Nxb6 gxh3!; 26.Qf3 hxg2+; 27.Qxg2 Qxg2+; 28.Kxg2 cxb6** and the ending is winning for Black. The game concluded **29.Rf1 Ke7; 30.Re1+ Kd6; 31.Rf1 Rc8; 32.Rxf7 Rc7; 33.Rf2 Ke5; 34.a4 Kd4; 35.a5 Kxd3; 36.Rf3+ Kc2; 37.b4 b5; 38.a6 Rc4; 39.Rf7 Rxb4; 40.Rb7 Rg4+ 41.Kf3 b4; 42.Rxa7 b3. Black won.**

SPANISH GAME (RUY LOPEZ)

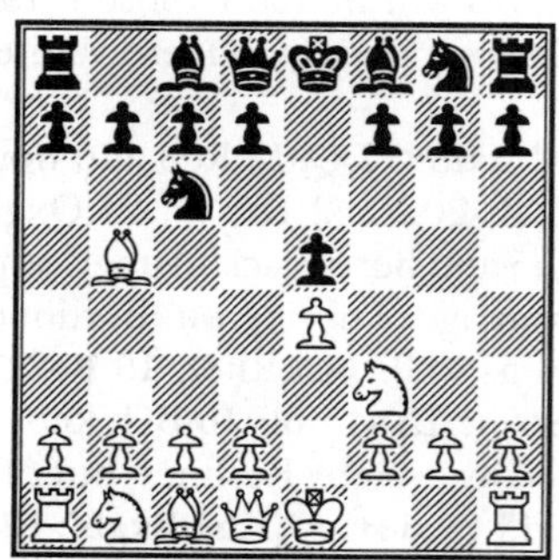

1.e4 e5
2.Nf3 Nc6
3.Bb5

These days everybody expects the Spanish Inquisition! The **Spanish Game**, also known as the **Ruy Lopez**, remains one of the most popular openings and thoroughly dominates the Open Games in both amateur and professional competition. The logic behind the opening is crystal clear. White wants to undermine the support of the pawn at e5, hopefully to win it at some point. With careful play by Black this never happens of course, but White can exact a positional price, maintaining a lead in development and a firm grip on the center.

For over a century Black has favored 3...a6, to immediately put the question to the bishop. White can respond by capturing at c6, but giving up a bishop for a knight is hardly likely lead to an advantage for the first player. Instead, the bishop usually retreats to a4, where it can still keep a hungry eye on the knight, but can also be repositioned at b3 or c2 with designs on the kingside.

In most cases, White will aim for a kingside attack while Black will play on the queenside and also prepare a central break. Sometimes Black will capture White's e-pawn, as in the Open Variation, but more frequently will be content to maneuver behind solid defensive lines.

We'll look at these possibilities and others in the more than one dozen variations of the Spanish Game presented here.

STEINITZ DEFENSE

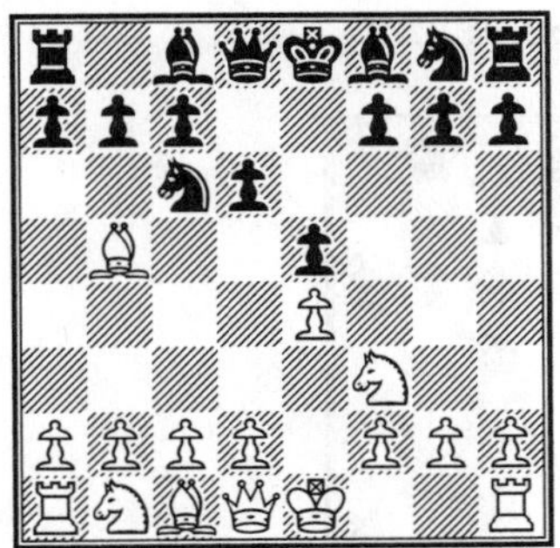

1.e4	**e5**
2.Nf3	**Nc6**
3.Bb5	**d6**

Steinitz's pet defense to the Spanish Game was popular at the end of the nineteenth century, but it has almost disappeared from view in its "pure" form. Instead, Black defers the advance of the d-pawn until after a preliminary 3...a6; 4.Ba4 (Modern Steinitz) or 3...Nf6; 4.0–0 (Improved Steinitz).

It is not the case that the immediate 3...d6 is unplayable, it is just that either of the other move orders makes Black's life a bit more comfortable, so that there is no reason to play the move right away.

(42) PONCE - STEINITZ [C62]

Havana, 1888

1.e4 e5; 2.Nf3 Nc6; 3.Bb5 d6.

4.d4 Bd7; 5.0–0. Surprisingly, this routine move is not best, and allows Black to carry out his plan. White can achieve more by developing the other knight here. 5.Nc3 Nf6 (5...exd4; 6.Nxd4 g6; 7.Be3 Bg7; 8.Qd2 Nf6; 9.0–0–0 0–0 leads to double-edged play, but White's attack should be faster than Black's. Compare this with the Larsen Variation of the Philidor Defense.) 6.0–0 Be7; 7.Re1 exd4; 8.Nxd4 0–0; 9.Bxc6 bxc6; 10.Bf4 gave White the more comfortable position in Geller-Welling, Holland 1986.

5...exd4!? Steinitz also successfully employed 5...Nge7, for example against Golmayo, also in Havana. **6.Nxd4 g6; 7.Nxc6 bxc6; 8.Bc4.** 8.Qd4 is met by 8...Qf6. **8...Bg7; 9.Qf3 Nf6; 10.Re1.** Steinitz noted that this is "A premature preparation for the attack which leaves the rook unprotected, and subsequently causes him embarrassment. It was for many purposes better to develop Nc3, followed by Bd2 and then Rae1."

10...0–0; 11.c3. Even here, Nc3 was preferable. **11...Re8.** 11...Nxe4; 12.Rxe4 d5; 13.Re1 dxc4; 14.Na3 with a better game for White, according to Steinitz. **12.Bb3 d5; 13.Bc2 Bf5; 14.Bg5 dxe4; 15.Qg3 Rb8.** Always a considerable compensation for allowing his pawns to be doubled, in the present and similar openings. By compelling White to advance the b-pawn, Black indirectly obtains greater command for his light-squared bishop, which can be easily unmasked by removing the knight that now blocks his action."–Steinitz.

16.b3 h6; 17.Rd1 Qe7; 18.Bxf6 Qxf6; 19.Qxc7. White gets the pawn back, but the queen is offside and Black quickly develops an attack which takes advantage of this fact. **19...e3; 20.Bxf5 exf2+; 21.Kxf2 Qxf5+; 22.Kg1 Be5!**

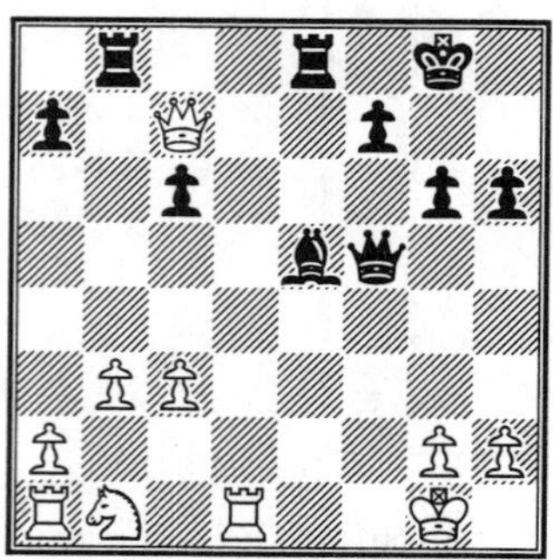

It is easy to see that White's poor development has left the king defenseless. **23.Qd7 Rbd8; 24.Qxd8 Rxd8; 25.Rxd8+ Kg7; 26.Na3.** 26.Nd2 Bf6; 27.Re8 Bxc3; 28.Rd1 Qc2 also delivers the game to Black. **26...Bxc3.** White resigned, as there is no way to hang on to the piece. The most obvious threat is ...Qc5+. **Black won.**

SCHLIEMANN VARIATION

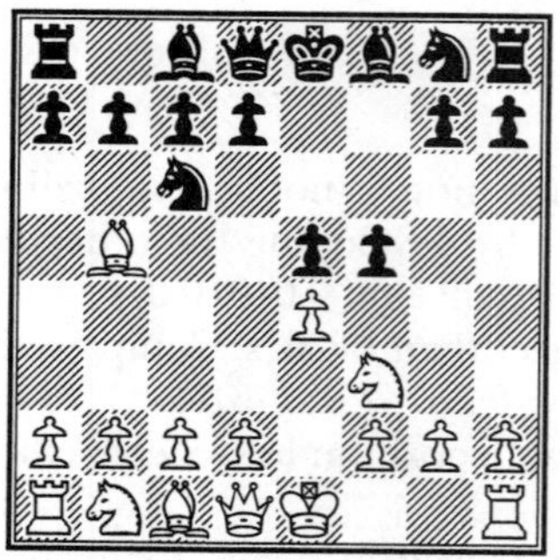

1.e4 e5
2.Nf3 Nc6
3.Bb5 f5

The **Schliemann Defense**, or **Jaenisch Gambit**, is one of the most dangerous lines of the Spanish Game. But dangerous for whom? Periodically refuted, the opening keeps resurfacing as new resources are found for Black. Black tries to smash open the center from the very first moves, even though this may create weaknesses and allow White to attack the king with malicious intent.

(43) GEORGIEV - INKIOV [C63]

Bulgarian Championship, 1988

1.e4 e5; 2.Nf3 Nc6; 3.Bb5 f5; 4.Nc3. This introduces the Dyckhoff variation, which is the main line. **4...fxe4; 5.Nxe4 d5.** The Tartakower Variation with 5...Nf6 is a modern alternative, but most players enjoy the messy complications which arise after this move. **6.Nxe5!** Of course! White is better developed and has the right to attack here. Now a lot of sacrifices are in the air, and the complications have been explored for many years. **6...dxe4; 7.Nxc6 Qg5.**

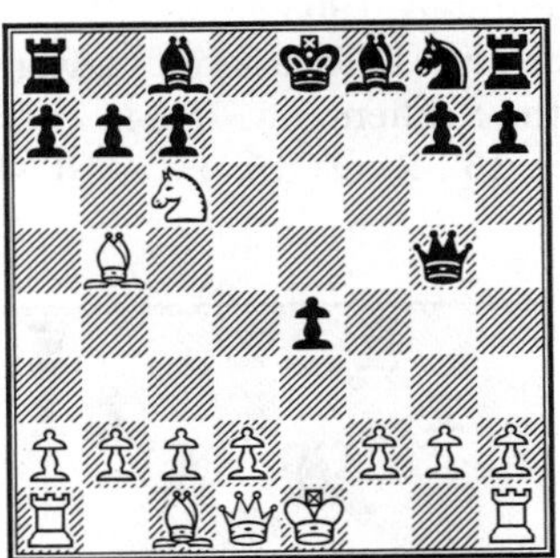

This is the Classical Variation. 7...Qd5, the Mohring Variation is rarely seen anymore, though it does make an occasional appearances in grandmaster play. **8.Qe2.** Patience is needed. This move protects the bishop at b5 and adds power to the discovered check which will be played sooner or later. **8...Nf6.** A developing move which also has the merit of defending the pawn at e4. Black is not afraid of a little discovered check! **9.f4.** White deflects the enemy queen. **9...Qxf4.** 9...Qh4+ is also seen. **10.d4.** The main line runs 10.Ne5+ c6; 11.d4 Qh4+; 12.g3 Qh3; 13.Bc4 Bd6; 14.Bg5 0-0-0 with massive complications. **10...Qd6.**

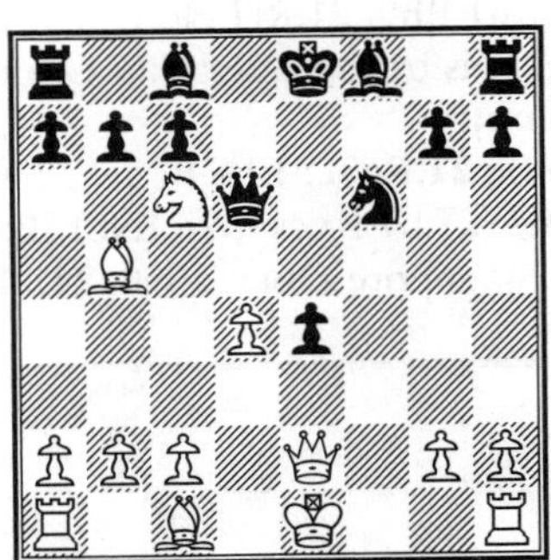

11.Nxa7+?! A dubious plan which re-emerged recently, probably because of ignorance by players of the White side, who certainly offered no improvements on standard theory! **11...c6; 12.Nxc8.** 12.Bf4?! Qxf4; 13.Nxc6 bxc6 (13...Bd7; 14.Ne5 gives White a strong attack against the exposed Black king.) 14.Bxc6+ Bd7; 15.Bxa8 Bb4+!; 16.c3 0–0. Now the White King is unsafe. 17.Bb7 Bg4; 18.Qf2 (18.Qc4+ Kh8; 19.cxb4 Qe3+; 20.Kf1 Nd5#) 18...Qxf2+; 19.Kxf2 Nd5+; 20.Kg3 (20.Ke1 Nxc3 and

Black wins. 20.Kg1 Nxc3; 21.bxc3 Bxc3 and the threat of ...Bxd4# is just too much.) 20...Bd6+!; 21.Kxg4 Ne3+; 22.Kh3 Rf6 Black threatens 23...Rh6#. 23.Kh4 Bf4. Black won., Kokotovic-Vajs, Postal 1971.

12...Qb4+; 13.c3. 13.Kd1 is refuted simply by 13...Qxb5; 14.c4 Qa4+; 15.b3 Qa5; Black won., Lazic-Lipski, Yugoslavia 1980. 13.Bd2 Qxb5!; 14.c4 Qxb2; 15.0–0 Rxc8; 16.Qe3 Bb4 (16...Bd6; 17.Rab1 Qxa2; 18.Rxb7 0–0; 19.Qg5 Rc7; 20.Rxc7 Bxc7; 21.Bb4 Qxc4; 22.Bxf8 Qxd4+; 23.Kh1 Kxf8; 24.Qf5 Qe5; 25.Qxh7 e3. Black threatens to advance the e-pawn, Doornbos-Bejar, World Under Sixteen Championship 1991. 16...Rd8; 17.Bc3 Qc2; 18.d5 Qd3; 19.Qxd3 exd3; 20.Rxf6 gxf6; 21.Bxf6 Bc5+ was drawn in , Rhodin-Berezovsky, Bern 1993.) 17.Qh3 0–0; 18.Be3 Bd2; 19.Bf2 Rce8 Black won, Spassov-Hennings, 1965.

13...Qxb5; 14.Qxb5 cxb5 gives Black a serious advantage as noted in Shamkovich & Schiller's 1983 book on the Schliemann. **15.a4.** 15.Nb6 is countered by 15...Ra6 where Black is clearly better. **15...Rxc8.** 15...bxa4 16.Nb6! and the knight escapes. **16.axb5 Bd6.**

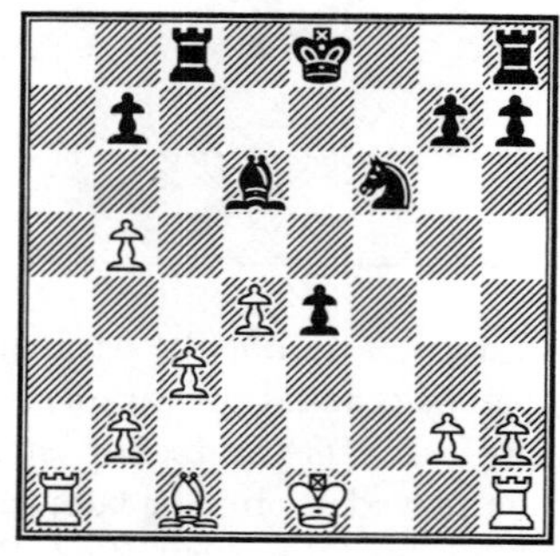

17.Ra7. 17.0–0 0–0 makes Black's life much easier, as the Dutch unorthodox openings specialist Gerard Welling demonstrated. 18.Bf4 Ne8; 19.Be3 Bb8; 20.Rxf8+ Kxf8; 21.Rf1+ Kg8; 22.Rf5 Nd6; 23.Re5 Kf7 and Black should win. **17...0–0! 18.Rxb7 Ng4; 19.Rf1.** 19.h3 Nf2; 20.Rg1 Bh2; 21.Rf1 Nd3+; 22.Ke2 Rxf1; 23.Kxf1 Nxc1 and Black wins, according to analysis by the Bulgarian Grandmaster Inkiov, a specialist in the Black side of this opening.

19...Bxh2; 20.Rxf8+ Rxf8; 21.Re7. 21.b6 Bg3+; 22.Kd1 Rf1+; 23.Kc2 e3; 24.Re7 Kf8; 25.Re4 Nf6; 26.Rxe3 Bf4; 27.b7 Rxc1+; 28.Kxc1 Bxe3+; 29.Kc2 Bf4; 30.c4 Ke7; Black won. Langier-Votava, Singapore Open 1990. **21...Rf2!**

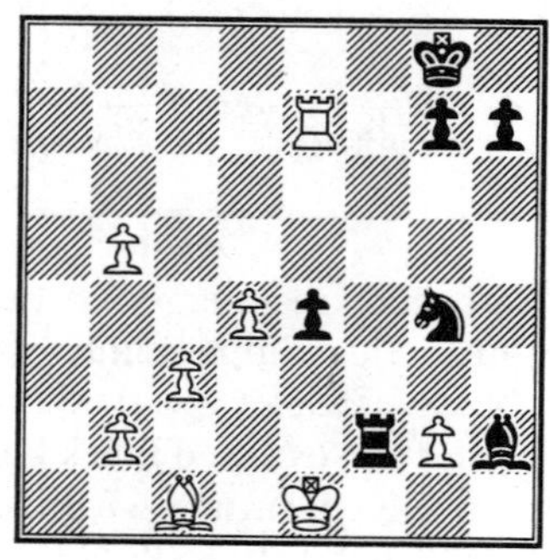

22.Rxe4. There is nothing better, but the Black rook wreaks havoc on the second rank. **22...Rxg2; 23.Bd2 Bg3+; 24.Kf1 Rf2+; 25.Kg1 Nh2. Black won.**

(44) SHORT - PIKET [C63]
Dortmund, 1995

1.e4 e5; 2.Nf3 Nc6; 3.Bb5 f5; 4.d4. This move leads to extraordinary complications, but Black seems to be able to hold the position together. The play is quite different from the Classical Variation, in that it is White who gets to enjoy the attacking privilege here.

4...fxe4; 5.Bxc6. An alternative is 5.Nxe5 Nxe5; 6.dxe5 c6; 7.Nc3.

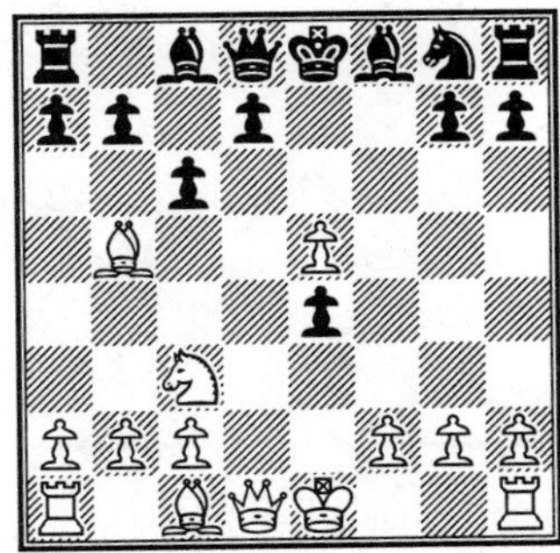

This leads to very complicated play. Black will grab a lot of material, but the price is the vulnerability of the king. The latest analysis shows that Black should win in the main lines. 7...cxb5; 8.Nxe4 d5!; 9.exd6 Nf6; 10.Qd4 (10.Qe2 Kf7! was better for Black in Rossman-Moehring, East Germany 1982.) 10...Qd7!; 11.0–0 Nxe4; 12.Re1 (12.Qxe4+ Qe6; 13.Qf3 Bxd6; 14.Bd2 Qf5; 15.Rfe1+ Kf7; 16.Qc3 Be6 and White resigned in Hansen-Briem, Aarhus 1965. This game remained in obscurity until 1983, when it was brought to prominence in a book by Leonid Shamkovich and Eric Schiller.) 12...Qxd6; 13.Qxe4+ Kf7; 14.Qe8+ (14.Qf3+ Kg6; 15.Bf4 Qf6; 16.Qg3+ Kf7; 17.Qb3+ Be6; 18.Qxb5 Qxf4; 19.Qxb7+ Be7; 20.Rxe6 Kxe6; 21.Re1+ Kf5; 22.Qxe7 Rae8; 23.Qf7+ Kg5; 24.Qxg7+ Kh5 and White has no more resources, since 15.Rxe8 is met by 15...Qc1+, winning instantly.) 14...Kg8; 15.Bg5 Qg6; 16.Rad1 Qxe8; 17.Rxe8 Kf7; 18.Rdd8.

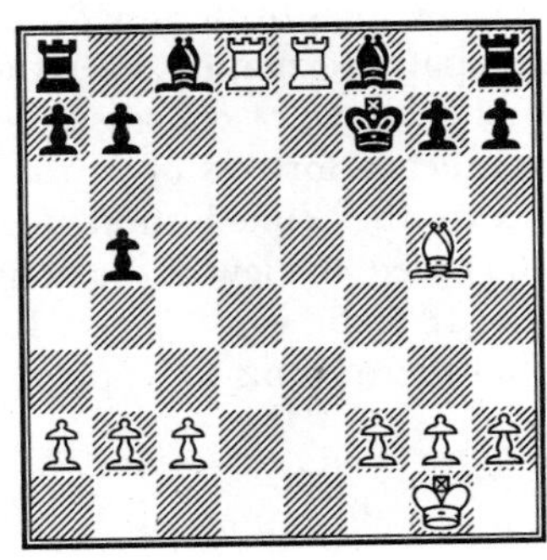

18...Bd7!!; 19.Rxf8+ Rxf8; 20.Rxd7+ Kg6; 21.Be3 Rfd8; 22.Rd4 Rxd4; 23.Bxd4 Rd8; 24.c3 a6; 25.Kf1 Kf5; 26.Ke2 g5. White resigned in Hergert-Grosshans, Postal 1986. **5...dxc6; 6.Nxe5 Qh4; 7.Nc3.** 7.0–0 Nf6; 8.f3 Bd6; 9.Qe1 Qh5; 10.Nc3 Bxe5; 11.dxe5 Qxe5; 12.Nxe4 0–0; 13.Nxf6+ Qxf6; 14.c3 was agreed drawn in Rellstab-Tolush, Vienna (European Team Championship) 1957.

7...Nf6; 8.h3. 8.Qe2 is still a viable option here. 8...Bb4; 9.Qc4 Bxc3+; 10.bxc3 Nd5; 11.Ba3 Qf6; 12.0–0 Be6; 13.Qc5 Nb6; 14.Qa5 Qd8; 15.Rfe1 Qd5; 16.Bc5 0–0–0; 17.Qxa7 Rde8; 18.c4 Qd8; 19.Rab1 Bf5; 20.Bxb6 cxb6; 21.Rxb6 Qc7; 22.Reb1 Qb8; 23.Rxc6+ and Black lost in Marco-Trenchard, Vienna 1898. **8...Nd5; 9.0–0 Nxc3; 10.bxc3 Bd6.**

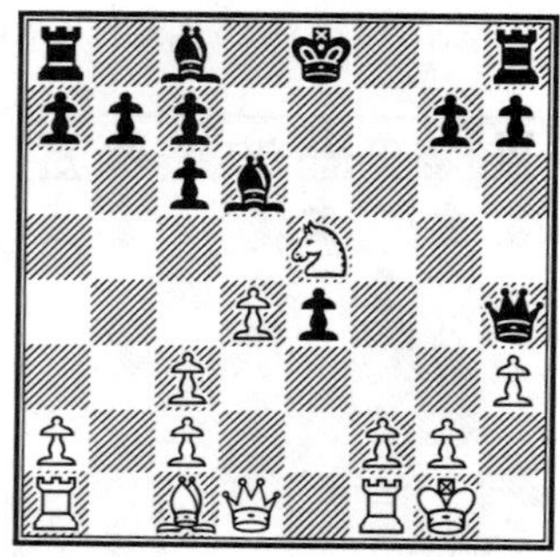

Black has the advantage of the bishop pair, and as long as the king can be brought to safety will enjoy a small advantage. **11.Qe1!?**

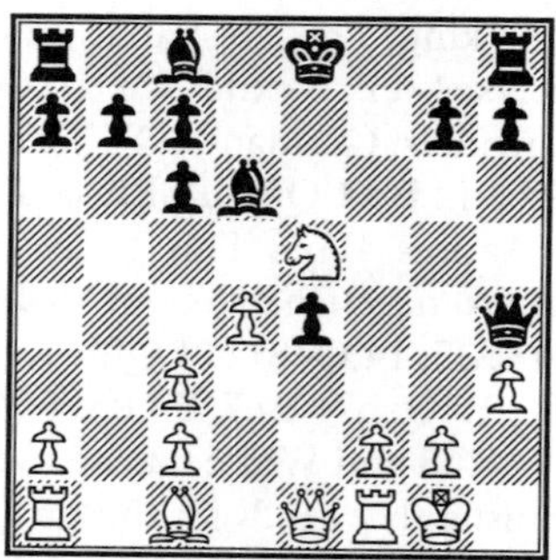

White threatens to open some lines by playing f3. Black takes advantage of the opportunity to destroy White's pawn formation, even though it means parting with the bishop pair. This is a good example of conversion of an advantage. **11...Bxe5; 12.dxe5 Bf5; 13.c4 c5.** Black erects a fortress of pawns on the dark-squares of the queenside, with no weaknesses for the White bishop to exploit. **14.Qe3 b6; 15.f4 h5.** 15...exf3 loses to 16.Qxf3 0–0 Forced, in view of the double-attack on the rook at a8 and bishop at f5. 17.Qd5+ Kh8; 18.Rxf5! wins a piece. **16.Bb2 0–0–0; 17.Rad1.** This position was agreed drawn, but there seems to be plenty of play left.

CORDEL DEFENSE AND GAMBIT

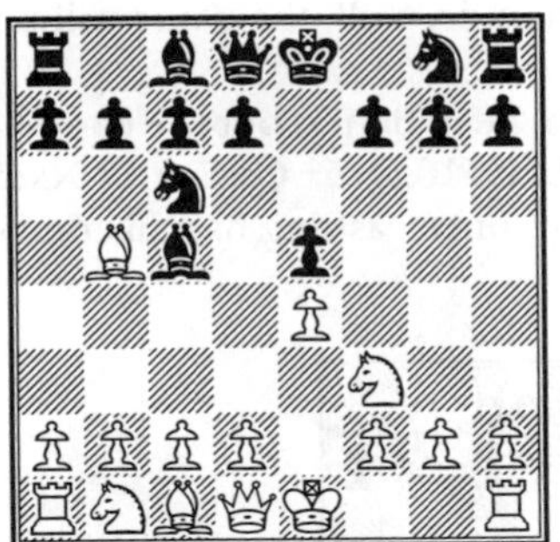

1.e4 e5
2.Nf3 Nc6
3.Bb5 Bc5

This is the **Cordel** or **Classical Variation** of the Spanish Game. Black ignores the indirect threat on the e-pawn and concentrates on developing as quickly as possible.

The Cordel Defense arises when Black plays 3...Bc5 and the game does not continue 4.0-0 Nf6, which is the Classical Variation. Black develops quickly, not fearing the exchange at c6, and in fact is willing to offer up the pawn at e5 in many different circumstances. Capturing at e5 is not usually to White's advantage, however. The primary risk here is that White will be able to take advantage of the placement of the bishop by a timely Nxe5 followed by d4. We can see this theme in many forms, some of which are shown in the following game.

(45) GILEZETDINOV - TOLUSH [C64]
Soviet Union, 1970

4.c3 Nf6. 4...f5 is the exciting Cordel Gambit. According to Spanish Gambits by Shamkovich and Schiller, White can get an advantage by capturing at e5. 5.Nxe5 Nxe5; 6.d4 fxe4; 7.Qh5+ Nf7; 8.Bc4 Qe7; 9.dxc5 Nf6; 10.Bxf7+ Kf8 (10...Qxf7; 11.Qe5+ Qe7; 12.Qxc7 0-0; 13.0-0 Ng4; 14.Qg3 is better for White, according to the *Encyclopedia of Chess Openings*.) 11.Qg5 Kxf7; 12.0-0 b6 (12...h6; 13.Qg3 Qxc5; 14.Be3 gave White the advantage in Suetin - Mikhnin, Soviet Union 1964.)

5.d4 Bb6; 6.Nxe5!? 6.Qe2! is stronger. **6...Nxe5; 7.dxe5 Nxe4; 8.Qg4 Bxf2+; 9.Ke2?!**

9.Kd1!? Qh4; 10.Qxg7 is an interesting alternative. 10...Rf8; 11.b4 prepares the way for Bh6, which would be premature if played immediately. (11.Bh6?! Bc5; 12.Rf1 Nf2+; 13.Rxf2 Qxf2; 14.Nd2 Qf5! and it is White who is in trouble.) 11...Qh5+ (11...f6? fails to 12.e6! Qh5+; 13.Kc2 .) 12.Kc2 Qg6 (12...Bh4!?; 13.Bh6 Be7; 14.Rf1 b6!; 15.e6 Nd6 led to unclear complications in Ree-Zuidema, Holland 1962.) 13.Qxg6 fxg6 and here Euwe claims that White stands better.

9...Qh4; 10.Qxg7 Rf8; 11.Nd2! 11.Bh6?! Bc5; 12.Rf1 c6; 13.Rf4 Qh5+; 14.Ke1 cxb5; 15.Rxe4 b6 and Black was clearly better in Florian-Forintos, Budapest 1961. **11...Bc5?!** 11...Nxd2 is correct. 12.Bxd2 Bc5; 13.Rhf1 Qe4+. After 13...c6 Short-Gulko, Linares 1989 ended in a draw. 14.Kd1 Qg6; Black's lack of development is not important here. 15.Qxg6 fxg6; 16.Rxf8+ Bxf8. The position is level, but Black has an easier time picking a target - the weak pawn at d5. Still, the game will probably end in a draw.

12.Nf3 Qh5; 13.Re1. 13.Rd1 would have been better, but the complications still favor Black. 13...b6!?; 14.Bd3 d5; 15.exd6 Nxd6; 16.Qe5+ Qxe5+; 17.Nxe5 Bb7 and I think that Black's position is to be preferred, once castling has taken place. **13...b6; 14.Kf1 Bb7.**

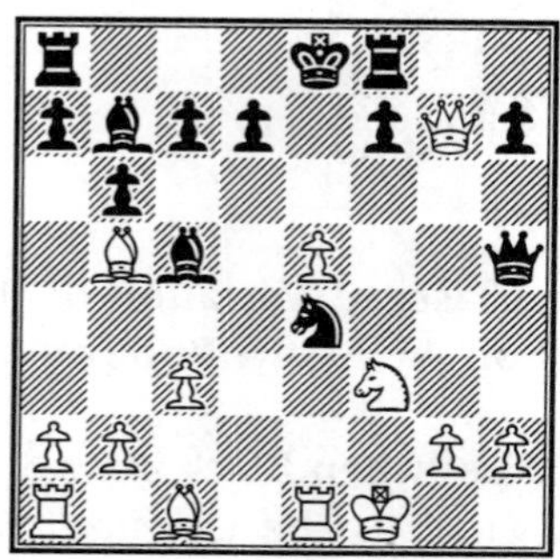

15.e6. 15.Qh6 Qg4 leaves the situation quite unclear. **15...0–0–0!** Now that the Black monarch has reached a safe haven, it is White who must worry about the safety of his king. **16.exd7+ Kb8; 17.Qe5 Qg6; 18.Nh4 Qg4; 19.Qf4.** 19.Nf3 Rxd7!; 20.Bxd7 Ba6+ is very strong for Black, for example 21.Re2 Bxe2+; 22.Kxe2 Qxg2+; 23.Kd3 Qxf3+; 24.Kc2 Rd8 and Black wins. **19...f5; 20.Nf3.** 20.Qxg4 fxg4+; 21.Ke2 does not save White: 21...Rf2+; 22.Kd1 c6; 23.Rxe4 Rxd7+; 24.Ke1 cxb5; 25.Bf4+ Kc8; 26.Re8+ Rd8; 27.Rxd8+ Kxd8; 28.Rd1+ Ke8 and the bishop pair gives Black a tremendous advantage. **20...Bd6; 21.Qh6 a6; 22.Bd3 Rxd7; 23.Re2 Rf6; 24.Qe3 Bc5; 25.Nd4 Bxd4; 26.cxd4.**

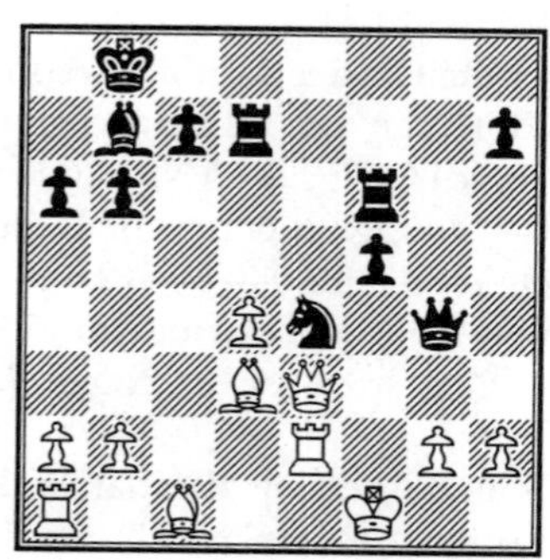

26...Rxd4!; 27.h3. 27.Qxd4 is no better after 27...Nd2+; 28.Bxd2 Qxd4. **27...Qh4; 28.Re1 Rxd3. Black won.**

CLASSICAL VARIATION

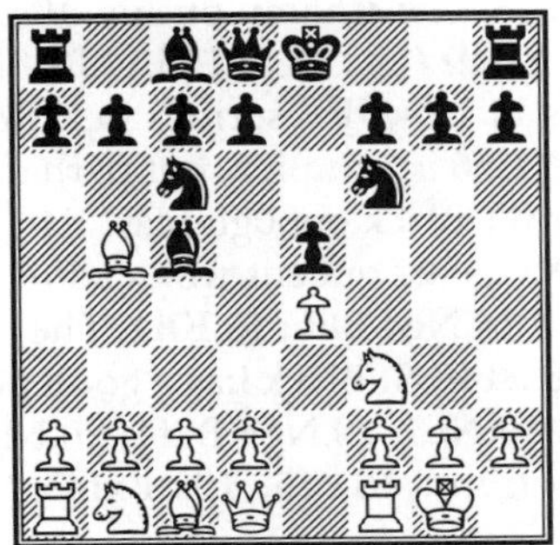

1.e4	e5
2.Nf3	Nc6
3.Bb5	Nf6
4.0–0	Bc5

The **Classical Defense**, also known in this form as the **Beverwijk Variation**, uses a bishop at c5 and knight at f6 to place immediate pressure on the White center. Again the tactical device of a capture at e5 followed by d4 plays a role. Boris Spassky is the best-known defender of the Black side. The defense is recommended to beginners, as once the first few moves are out of the way there are few tactical traps to avoid and play proceeds normally.

(46) KROGIUS - SPASSKY [C65]
Soviet Championship, 1959

1.e4 e5; 2.Nf3 Nc6; 3.Bb5 Nf6; 4.0–0 Bc5; 5.Nxe5.

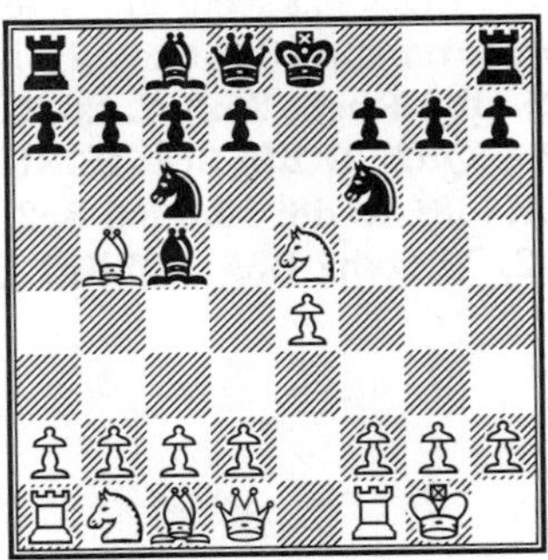

This is a very direct move by White, but it leads to complications which are not unfavorable for the second player. **5...Nxe5; 6.d4 c6!?** This move accomplishes two things. It challenges the Bb5 and also provides important support for the critical d5 square. **7.dxe5.** 7.Ba4 Nxe4; 8.Re1 d5 is good for Black, for example: 9.dxc5 0–0; 10.Qd4 Qf6! (threatening Nf3+) 11.Be3 Bh3! (renewing the threat) 12.Kh1 Bxg2+; 13.Kxg2 Qf3+!; 14.Kg1 Qg4+; 15.Kh1 Nf3; 16.Qd1 Qh3 and White resigned in Hofmann-Lambert, Vienna 1947.

7...Nxe4; 8.Bd3. 8.Qg4 has a bark that is worse than its bite. 8...Nxf2!; 9.Qxg7 Ne4+; 10.Kh1 Rf8 and Black should have little difficulty consolidating, after which an attack on the kingside is a distinct possibility. **8...d5; 9.exd6.** 9.Qf3 Qh4; 10.g3 Bg4!; 11.Qf4 g5 and the complications favored Black in DeGroot-O'Kelly, Beverwijk 1946.

9...Nf6!; 10.Qe2+. 10.Bf4 Bxd6; 11.Bxd6 Qxd6; 12.Nc3 Be6; 13.Qe2 0–0 gave rise to a balanced position in Aronin-Keres, Soviet Championship 1952. **10...Be6; 11.Bg5 Qxd6!; 12.Bxf6.** 12.Nc3 Ng4; 13.g3 Bd4!? (13...Ne5; 14.Bf4 f6; 15.Ne4 Qe7; 16.Nxc5 Qxc5; 17.Bxe5 fxe5; 18.Rfe1 leaves Black with a serious weakness at e5, as well as an insecure king.) 14.Ne4 Qc7; 15.c3 Bb6 is complex, but perhaps the weakening of the light squares on the kingside gives Black enough play.

12...gxf6; 13.Nd2 Qe5! Clearly an exchange of queens will lead to a favorable position for Black, who owns the bishop pair. **14.Ne4 Bb6; 15.Kh1.** The point of this move is to unpin the f-pawn. **15...0–0–0!; 16.a4 Kb8.** Black has a good position and is in no hurry here. **17.a5 Bc7; 18.f4 Qd4; 19.Nc3.** 19.Ng3 Bxf4; 20.Nh5 Be5 and Black's centralized clerics fire in all directions. **19...f5.** 19...Bxf4?; 20.a6! with counterplay. **20.a6.**

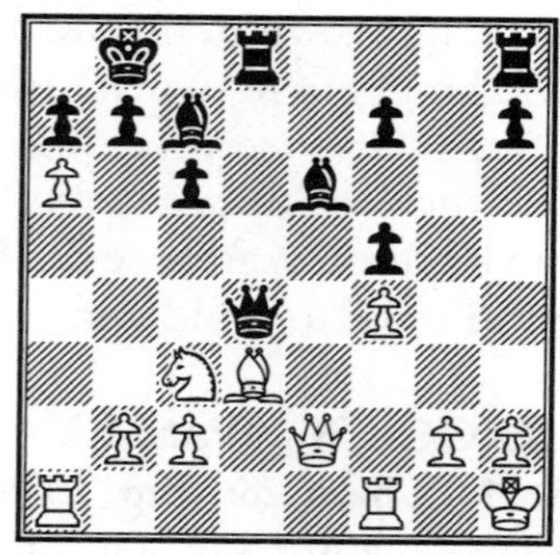

20...b5!; 21.Qf3 Qb6! Now Black has secured his defenses. **22.Qh3 Qc5; 23.Qf3 b4; 24.Na4 Qd6!** Black's forces remain coordinated while White's seem to be scattered all over the board. **25.Qh3 Rhg8; 26.Be2.** 26.Bxf5 Bxf5; 27.Qxf5 Qd2 and Black has a strong attack. **26...Qd2; 27.Bf3 Bc4; 28.Rfd1 Qxf4.** The game is effectively over at this point. **29.Rxd8+ Rxd8; 30.Bxc6 Be2; 31.Rg1 Rd1; 32.g4 Rxg1+; 33.Kxg1 Qc1+; 34.Kf2 Qxc2; 35.Qxh7 Bb5+; 36.Kg1 Qd1+; 37.Kf2 Qf1+; 38.Ke3 Qf4#. Black won.**

EXCHANGE VARIATION

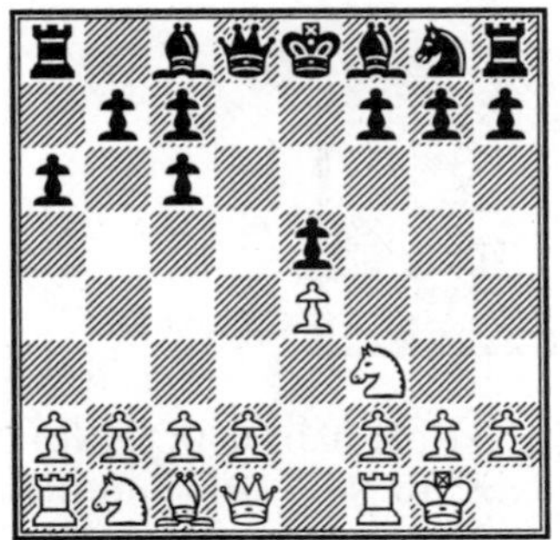

1.e4	**e5**
2.Nf3	**Nc6**
3.Bb5	**a6**
4.Bxc6	**dxc6**
5.0–0	

When White exchanges bishop for knight at move 4, the opening leads almost inevitably into an early endgame. White has a kingside pawn majority which can prove dangerous if it becomes mobile, but Black has the bishop pair, which can be a most dangerous weapon. White does not have to castle at move 5, but this is the only plan seen in modern tournament play. White will open up the center with an early d4, so it is best to get the king to safety right away.

(47) SCHUSSLER - WESTERINEN [C68]

Copenhagen, 1979

1.e4 e5; 2.Nf3 Nc6; 3.Bb5 a6; 4.Bxc6 dxc6; 5.0–0 Bd6.

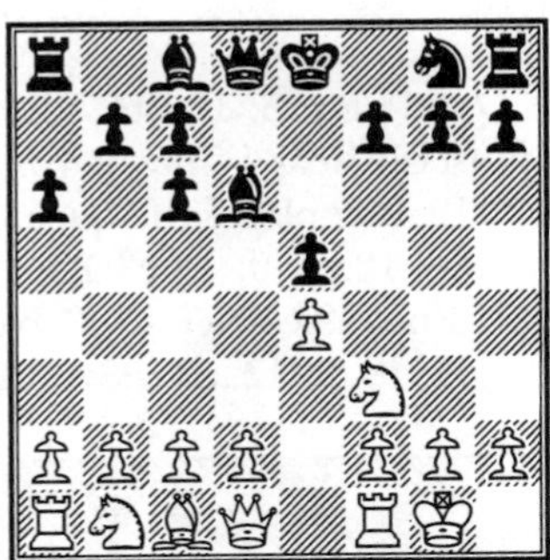

This is a very solid method of handling the Exchange Variation as Black. The main idea is to reinforce the e5-square with ...f6, and develop the knight at g8 via e7. The battle concentrates on the center, and Black must be careful not to allow a breakthrough by White, but if sufficient caution is exercised Black will achieve at least an equal position. **6.d4.** As usual, White cannot achieve anything without opening up the center. **6...exd4; 7.Qxd4 f6.**

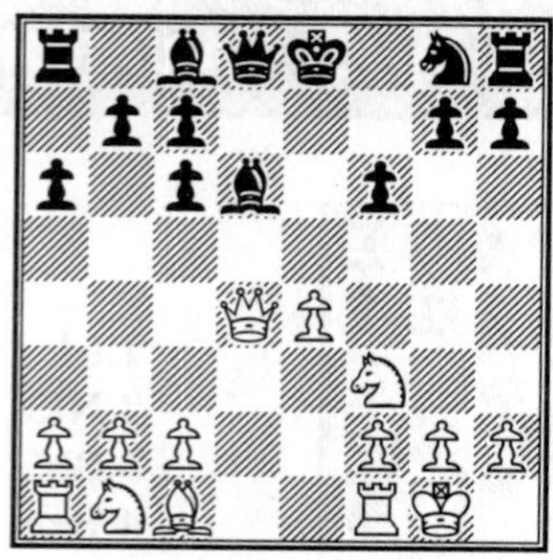

8.b3. 8.Nbd2 is too slow: 8...Be6; 9.Nb3 (9.h3 Ne7; 10.b3 0–0; 11.Nc4 Bb4; 12.Ne3 Qxd4; 13.Nxd4 Bf7; 14.Bb2 Rfe8; 15.Rad1 Nc8; 16.Ndf5 Nd6 and the e-pawn was under considerable pressure in Santo Roman-Nunn, Oviedo Action 1992.) 9...b6; 10.e5 fxe5; 11.Nxe5 Ne7; 12.Bg5 0–0; 13.Nxc6 Nxc6; 14.Bxd8 Nxd4; 15.Nxd4 Bc4; 16.Bg5 Bxf1; 17.Rxf1 Rae8; 18.Be3 Rxe3 and White resigned in Chevaldonnet-Pytel, Val Thorens 1977. **8...Ne7; 9.Nbd2 Be6.**

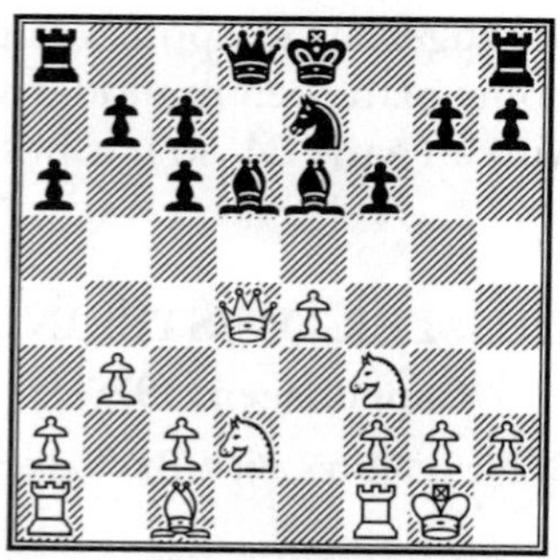

10.Nc4 Bb4; 11.Ne3. 11.Qxd8+ Rxd8; 12.Bb2 Bxc4; 13.bxc4 0–0; 14.Nd4 Kf7 and Black was able to work against the weak White pawns in Mulligan-Flear, Blackpool Zonal 1990. **11...c5; 12.Qxd8+.** 12.Qb2 places the queen in a very artificial situation and Black has no problems after 12...0–0; 13.c3 Ba5; 14.Qc2 Qe8; 15.Ba3 Qh5; 16.Rad1 Rae8; 17.Nd2 b5; 18.f4 Bb6; 19.c4 Nc6; 20.f5 Nd4 where a draw was agreed in Krnic-Westerinen, Copenhagen 1979. **12...Rxd8; 13.Bb2 0–0; 14.Rfd1 c6.**

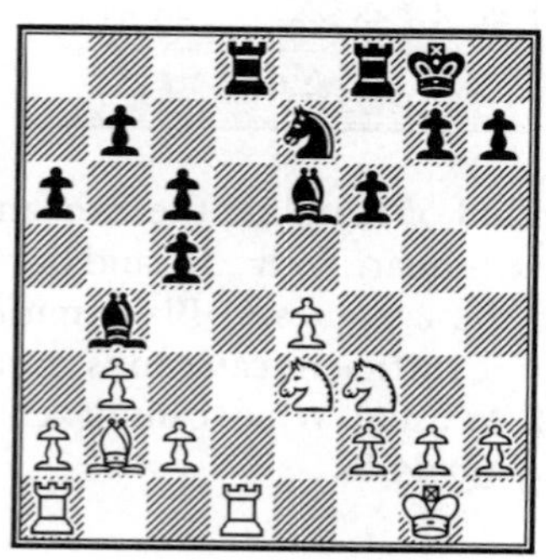

There is no way for White to make any real progress here, as Black has all the key squares covered. **15.Kf1 Nc8; 16.e5 Kf7; 17.Ke2 Ne7; 18.exf6 gxf6; 19.c4 Nf5!; 20.Nc2 Rfe8; 21.Kf1.** 21.Nxb4 cxb4 brings about an endgame with bishops of opposite colors, which should ensure a draw. **21...Ba5; 22.Nce1 b5; 23.Nd3.**

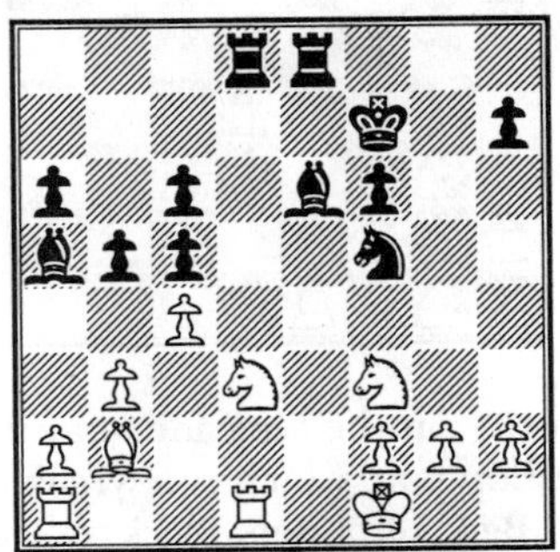

Now Black invests the exchange to pick off the c-pawn. **23...Rxd3!; 24.Rxd3 bxc4; 25.Rdd1 c3; 26.Ba3 c2.** White has nothing better than to return the exchange here, after which Black wins without difficulty. **27.Rd2 Bxd2; 28.Nxd2 Rd8; 29.Ke1 Nh4; 30.g3 Bg4; 31.Rc1 Nf3+. Black won.**

(48) FISCHER - SPASSKY [C69]

Sveti Stefan (9th Match game) 1992

1.e4 e5; 2.Nf3 Nc6; 3.Bb5 a6; 4.Bxc6 dxc6; 5.0–0 f6.

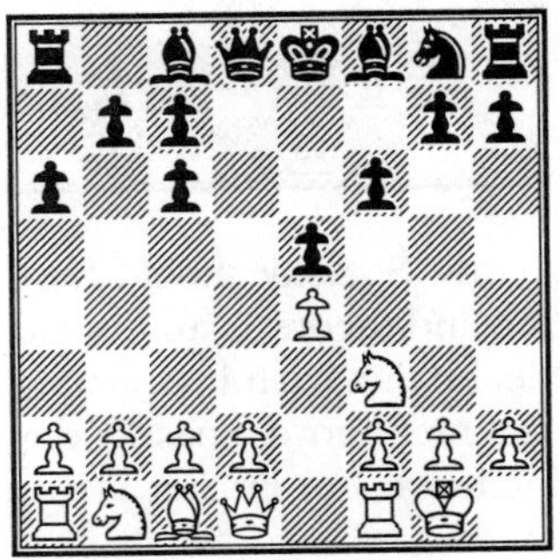

This move would be odd in most circumstances, but in the Exchange Spanish it is almost inevitable. **6.d4.** 6.Nxe5 fxe5; 7.Qh5+ Kd7 and despite the exposed position of the Black king, White cannot successfully conclude the attack. **6...exd4; 7.Nxd4 c5.** This lets Black exchange queens. Then in the endgame the bishops can be effective. A good plan, but the attack does not end when the queens leave the playing field! **8.Nb3 Qxd1; 9.Rxd1.**

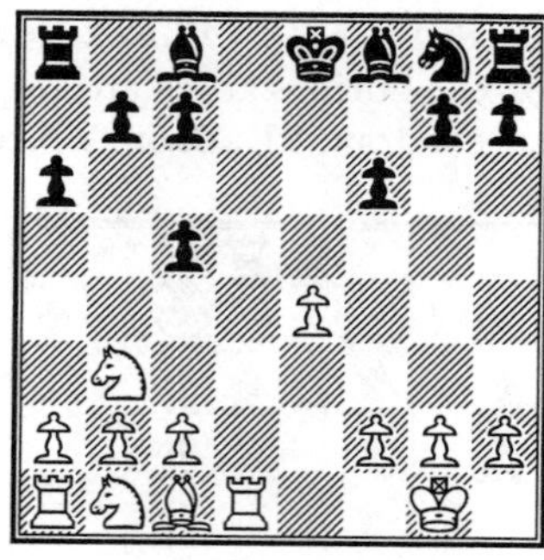

White has a pawn majority on the kingside, and this can be decisive in some endgames. Black has the bishop pair, which can wreak havoc in the middlegame if enough lines are opened. **9...Bg4; 10.f3 Be6.** Black provoked the weakness of the a7-g1 diagonal with this maneuver. **11.Nc3 Bd6; 12.Be3 b6.** Black's clerics are remarkably silent. Yet at the time this game was played, the position was considered quite reasonable. **13.a4.**

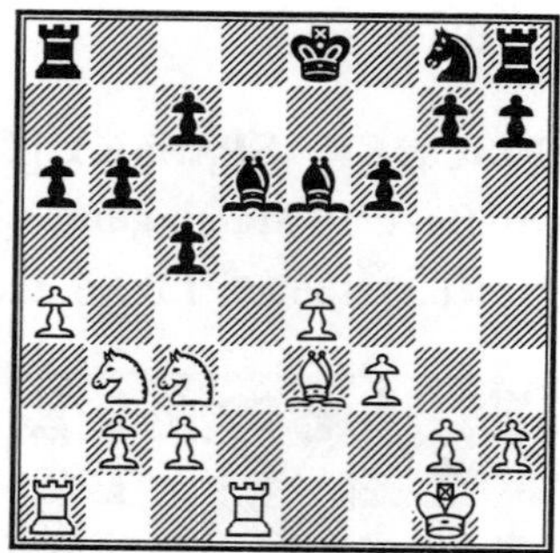

Now, according to Kasparov, Spassky should have played 13...Kf7 with equal chances. The brilliant tactician and theoretician Leonid Shamkovich points out that 13...a5 might also be playable. Shamkovich is probably right, since by allowing the White pawn to reach a5 at the next move, Spassky digs his own grave. **13...0-0-0.** The books said this was a fine move, but Fischer proves otherwise. **14.a5 Kb7.**

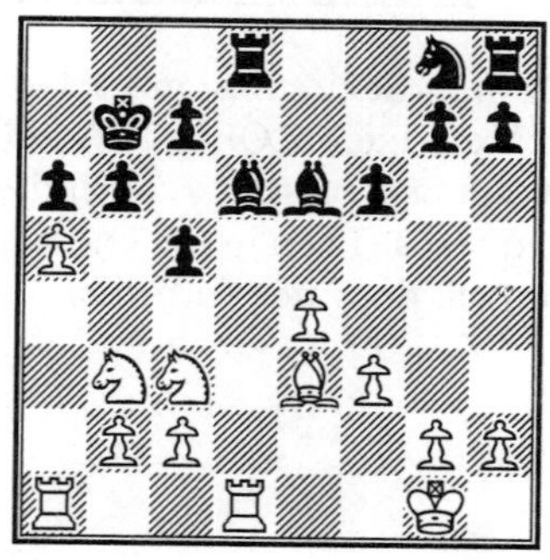

The whole point of the formation with pawn at f6 and bishop at d6 is to prevent the White pawn from reaching e5. Bobby Fischer is not so easily denied! **15.e5!!** The first sign of serious trouble for Black. The pawn cannot be taken. Curiously, this is not the first time this position has been reached. We are still in known territory. **15...Be7.** 15...fxe5; 16.axb6 cxb6; 17.Ne4 Bc7 and White can win material with a small sacrifice. 18.Nbxc5+ bxc5; 19.Nxc5+ Kc8; 20.Rxd8+ Bxd8; 21.Nxe6 is gruesome. **16.Rxd8 Bxd8; 17.Ne4.** An improvement on 17.axb6 cxb6, which had been seen back in 1976.

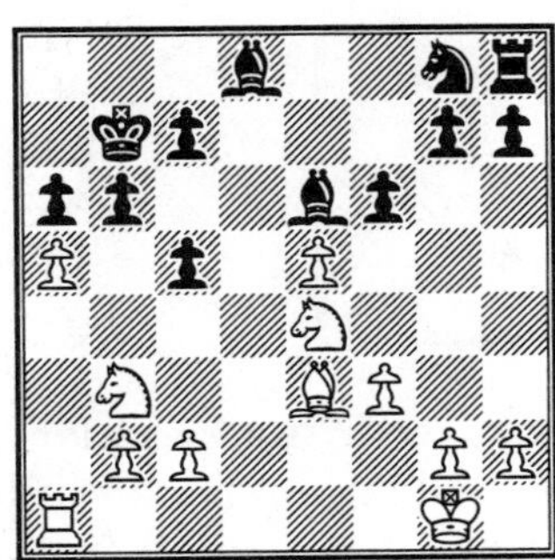

Now Spassky blunders away the game, yet we are still following a game which was over a decade old at the time. Spassky is a creative genius, but has never been known as a particularly hard worker, especially in the opening. **17...Kc6??** 17...Bxb3; 18.cxb3 f5; 19.Rd1 Ne7; 20.Ng5 Nc6; 21.axb6 Bxg5; 22.Bxg5 Kxb6; 23.Rd7 Re8; 24.Rxg7 Rxe5; 25.Rxh7 Re1+; 26.Kf2 Rb1; 27.h4 gave White a substantial advantage in a 1980 game played by Fischer's friend Peter Biyiasas as White. Fischer may have known the game from Biyiasas, or may have read about it in a 1992 book on the opening in which considerable analysis of the position was published, **18.axb6 cxb6.**

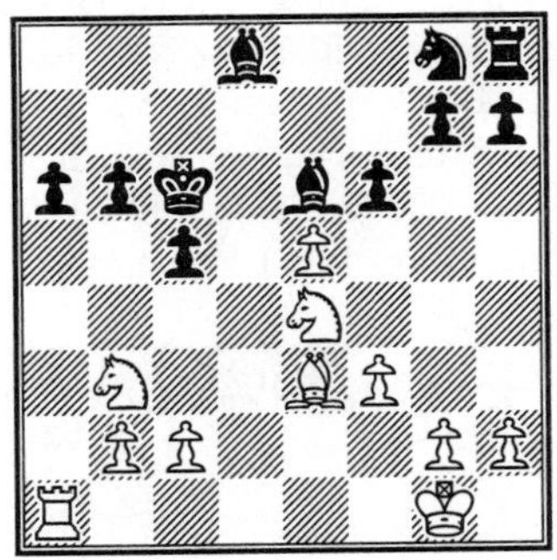

Now the heavily defended pawn at c5 is blown away. **19.Nbxc5! Bc8.** 19...bxc5; 20.Rxa6+ Kd7; 21.Nxc5+ Ke7; 22.Nxe6 g6; 23.Bc5+ Ke8; 24.Ra8 and White wins the bishop. **20.Nxa6 fxe5; 21.Nb4+. White won.**

NORWEGIAN VARIATION

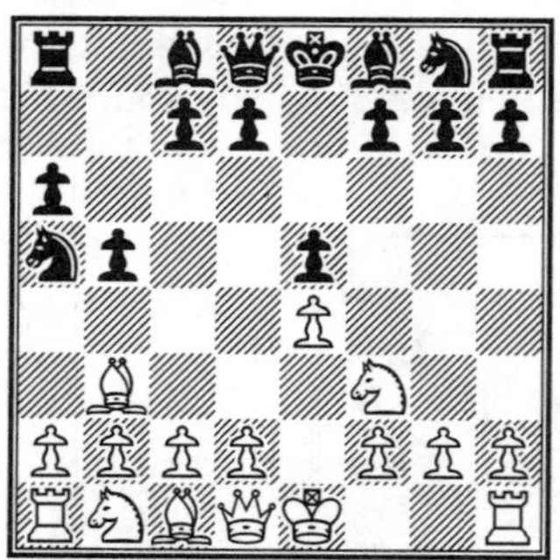

1.e4	**e5**
2.Nf3	**Nc6**
3.Bb5	**a6**
4.Ba4	**b5**
5.Bb3	**Na5**

This was once known as the **Wing Variation**, but so much theory has been flowing in from the fjords that it is now called the **Norwegian Variation**. Black aims to assassinate the Spanish bishop as quickly as possible. This takes valuable time, but it may be that Black can get away with it.

(49) LEHMANN - DONNER [C70]
Beverwijk, 1965

1.e4 e5; 2.Nf3 Nc6; 3.Bb5 a6; 4.Ba4 b5; 5.Bb3 Na5; 6.0–0. The main line, for good reason. There is nothing to be done about the bishop at b3, so White goes for maximum mobilization of the remaining forces. 6.Bxf7+ is the wild Swedish Variation. White goes for the kill immediately, but Black can survive. 6...Kxf7; 7.Nxe5+ Ke7; 8.Nc3 Qe8!; 9.Nd5+ Kd8; 10.Qf3 Bb7!; 11.Nf7+ Kc8; 12.0–0 Nf6; 13.Nxh8 Nxe4; 14.d3 Bxd5; 15.dxe4 Be6 and Black stood better in Nilsson-Hoen, Sweden 1970.

6...d6; 7.d4. The appropriate move, opening up the game before Black has a chance to develop. **7...exd4; 8.Nxd4 Nxb3.** 8...Bb7; 9.Qe1 is a bit better for White, as in Platonov-Savon, Soviet Championship 1969. **9.axb3.**

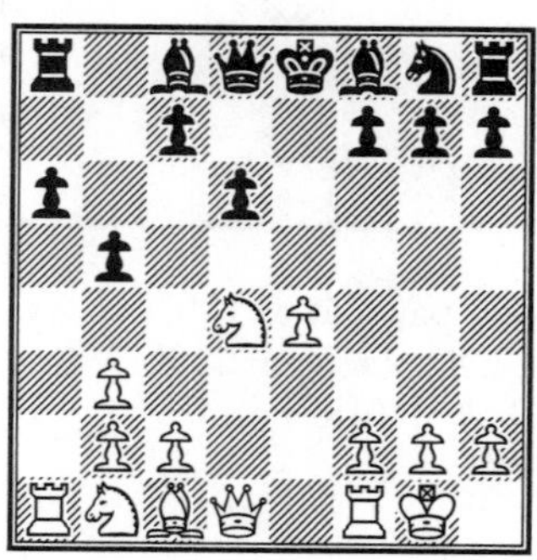

White has an advantage in development and semi-open files to work with. **9...Bb7;**

10.Re1. The problem with this position for Black is that White has too much control of the center, and can infiltrate via d5, since if Black plays c7-c6 the pawns will be weak. A good alternative is 10.Nc3. **10...Ne7.** Black does better with 10...g6, but the White position still makes a better impression.

11.Nc3 Qd7; 12.Nd5! c5. Giving up the exchange is the only way to alleviate the pressure, but White not only wins the exchange, he also goes for the Black king, which is stranded in the center. 12...Nxd5!?; 13.exd5+ Be7; 14.Nc6 Bxc6; 15.dxc6 Qxc6; 16.Bg5 f6; 17.Qh5+ led to nothing more than a draw in Prandstetter-B.Stein, Dortmund 1987. **13.Nb6 Qd8; 14.Nf5! Nxf5.** 14...Qxb6; 15.Nxd6+ Kd7; 16.Nxf7+ is a deadly discovered check. **15.exf5+ Be7; 16.Nxa8 Qxa8??** 16...Bxa8 was the only move, though White is clearly better after 17.Rxa6 0–0; 18.Rxa8 Qxa8; 19.Rxe7 Qd8; 20.f6. **17.Qxd6. White won.**

MODERN STEINITZ VARIATION

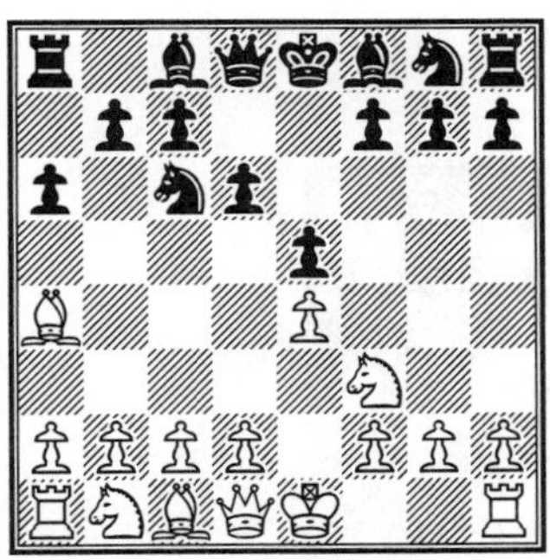

1.e4	**e5**
2.Nf3	**Nc6**
3.Bb5	**a6**
4.Ba4	**d6**

This is the Modern handling of the Steinitz Defense. Black pushes back the bishop before playing ...d6, so that ...b5 will be available, if needed, breaking the pin against the knight at c6. Boris Spassky has been among the advocates of the Black side. It has strong appeal to strategic planners who like to work against weak squares in a methodical positional manner, but sometimes attacking play livens things up.

(50) LASKER - STEINITZ [C87]
St. Petersburg, 1895

1.e4 e5; 2.Nf3 Nc6; 3.Bb5 a6; 4.Ba4 d6; 5.d4 Bd7. 5...b5; 6.Bb3 Nxd4; 7.Nxd4 exd4; 8.c3 Bb7; 9.0–0 Nf6; 10.cxd4 is fine for Black, but the pawn at e4 is taboo: 10...Nxe4?; 11.Re1 Be7; 12.Qf3 d5; 13.Rxe4! dxe4; 14.Qxf7+ with a very promising attack for White in Velimirovic-Maynard, Thessaloniki Olympiad 1988. **6.c3.** This position is usually reached via 5.c3 Bd7; 6.d4. **6...Nf6.**

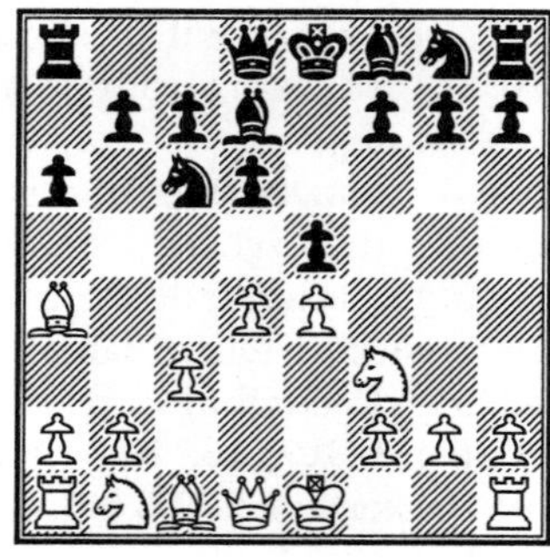

6...Nge7 looks strange, but it is a promising defense, for example 7.Bb3 h6; 8.Nbd2 Ng6; 9.Nc4 Be7; 10.Ne3 Bg5; 11.Nxg5 hxg5 and Black has the h-file to play with, Sax-Portisch, Skelleftea 1989. **7.Nbd2 Be7; 8.0–0 0–0.** White has a stronger center. but Black's position is quite solid. **9.Re1 Re8; 10.Nf1 Bf8; 11.Ng3 g6.** A necessary concession, since otherwise the White knight could get into f5. **12.h3 Bg7; 13.Bc2 Bc8; 14.d5 Ne7; 15.Be3.** White controls a lot more space and has the advantage in the center, **15...Rf8.**

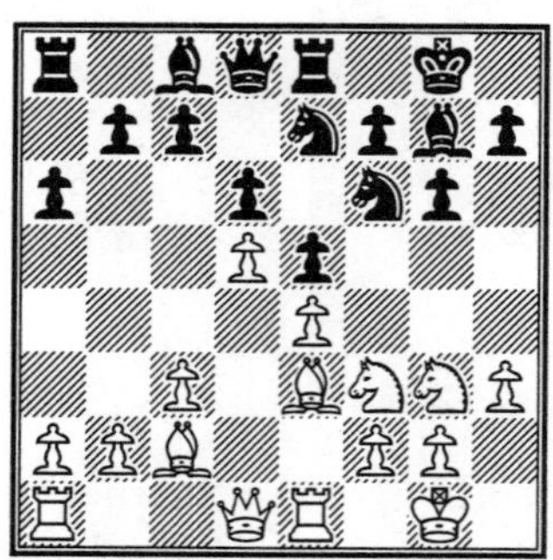

The rook had to leave f8 so that the bishop could transfer to g7 and keep an eye on the weak squares, but a lot of time has been wasted. **16.Qd2 Ne8; 17.Bh6 Kh8; 18.Rad1 Ng8; 19.Bxg7+.** Whenever you can eliminate a fianchettoed bishop, your opponent is going to have a hard time defending. **19...Nxg7; 20.c4 f5; 21.Qc3 fxe4; 22.Bxe4 Nf6; 23.Qe3 Nxe4; 24.Nxe4.**

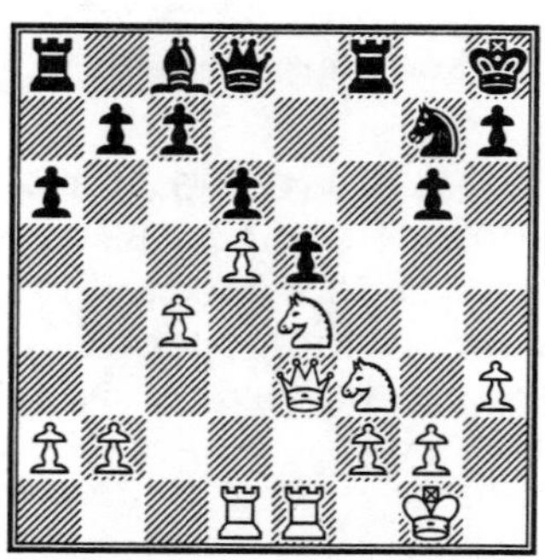

24...Rf4. This looks like a logical move, but the vulnerability of the Black king is now exposed by a brilliant combination which also exploits the weakness of the 7th rank. First Lasker puts more pressure at d6. **25.c5 Bf5.** Black has a simple threat, to capture at e4, and an indirect threat at c5, because if the knight moves away, then the pawn at c5 can be captured. So White defends one knight with the other. **26.Nfg5 Qd7.** This answers the threatened fork at f7. But now White clears the path for his pieces with a queen sacrifice. **27.Qxf4 exf4; 28.Nf6.** Notice that the Black queen must guard the f7-square, otherwise 29.Nf7 will be checkmate **28...Ne6; 29.Nxd7 Nxg5.** White is now ahead in material, with an extra exchange. But even more importantly, he can invade the 7th rank. **30.Re7 Kg8; 31.Nf6+ Kf8; 32.Rxc7.** Here Black resigned, because the rook will continue his pillage of the 7th rank, and there isn't anything he can do about it. **White won.**

(51) RETI - CAPABLANCA [C74]
Berlin, 1928

1.e4 e5; 2.Nf3 Nc6; 3.Bb5 d6. The old and discredited Steinitz defense, but the game quickly transposes to a more popular line. **4.c3,** laziness, perhaps. 4.d4 is the correct way to get an advantage for White. **4...a6; 5.Ba4.** We are now in the Modern Steinitz Variation. **5...f5.** This is the famous Siesta Variation. It is not considered fully playable for Black, but is a fun surprise weapon and demonstrates some of the exciting possibilities of the Spanish Game.

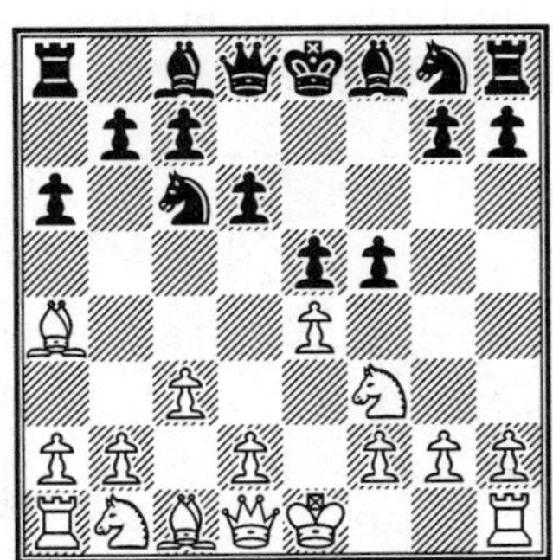

6.d4. Modern authorities prefer capturing at f5, which leads to rapid development for White. 6.exf5 Bxf5; 7.0–0 Bd3 to try to prevent d4, after which White would have a clear advantage. 8.Re1 Be7 and here a couple of strong players, Lautier and Yusupov, have been found on the Black side recently.

A) 9.c4?! Rb8!; 10.Qb3 e4; 11.Ng5 Nf6 (11...Bxb1? loses to 12.Ne6 Qc8; 13.Rxb1 Qxe6; 14.Bxc6+ because of the pin on the b-file. 11...Bxg5? is also defeated by a pin: 12.Qxd3 Nf6; 13.Nc3 and White has a clear advantage.) 12.Nc3 0–0; 13.Ncxe4 Nxe4; 14.Nxe4 (14.Ne6? is refuted in spectacular fashion: 14...Bh4!! and now if White takes the queen with 15.Nxd8 then after 15...Bxf2+; 16.Kh1 Bxe1 the White king is in deep trouble.) 14...Ne5; 15.Re3 was seen in Topalov-Lautier, Linares 1995 and here Black could have obtained a slight advantage by capturing at c4 with the bishop.

B) 9.Bc2! is strong 9...Bxc2; 10.Qxc2 Nf6; 11.d4! and White has the initiative. 11...e4; 12.Ng5 d5; 13.f3 h6; 14.Nh3 0–0; 15.Nd2 exf3; 16.Nxf3 Qd7; 17.Qg6 and White obtained a slight advantage in Leko-Yusupov, Vienna 1996. **6...fxe4; 7.Ng5**

exd4; 8.Nxe4. White might do better to castle and make a gambit of the opening. **8...Nf6.** Black uses the exposed White knight to develop with tempo. **9.Bg5 Be7; 10.Qxd4.** White miscalculates that Black won't be able to take advantage of his exposed queen. **10...b5.** Winning material, but White must have felt that Black's many pawn moves would give White enough counterplay. **11.Nxf6+ gxf6; 12.Qd5 bxa4.**

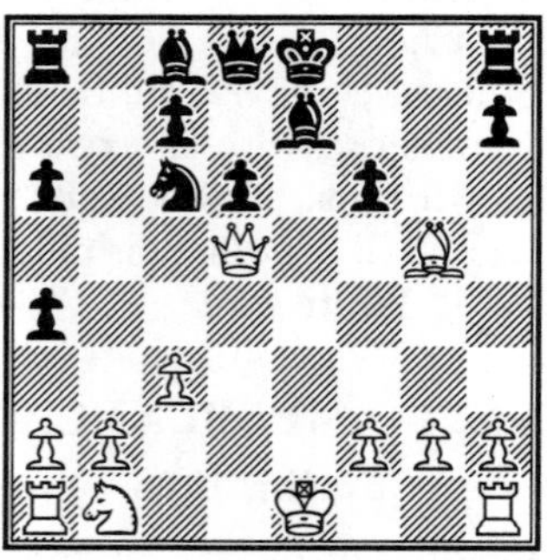

13.Bh6. 13.Qxc6+ achieves nothing against 13...Bd7. **13...Qd7.** This fine move defends the knight as well as the bishop on e7, prepares to attack White's kingside by a later ...Qg4 or Qh3 and gets Black ready to castle queenside. **14.0–0 Bb7.** Aiming his extra piece straight at White's king position. **15.Bg7 0–0–0.** Another fine move. Black is willing to give back a little material to take the initiative. After White takes the rook Black will have his bishop, knight, queen and rook all aiming at White's king, which has no defenders. **16.Bxh8.**

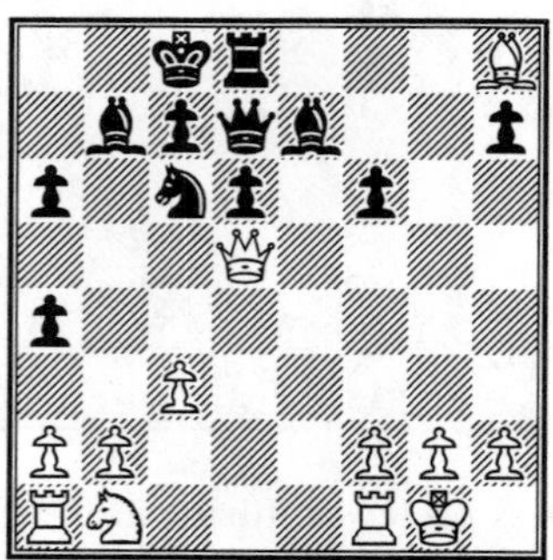

16...Ne5. Now White's queen won't be able to get back to defend the kingside. **17.Qd1 Bf3,** very powerful; Black wins a tempo on White's queen while not allowing the counterplay White might hope for after, e.g. 17...Qf5; 18.Qxa4. **18.gxf3 Qh3.** White has no defense to threats like 19...Nxf3+ and 19...Rg8, so Reti gave up. **Black won.**

(52) ONISCHUK - MALANIUK [C76]

Nikolayev Zonal, 1995

1.e4 e5; 2.Nf3 Nc6; 3.Bb5 a6; 4.Ba4 d6; 5.c3 Bd7; 6.d4 g6; 7.0–0 Bg7.

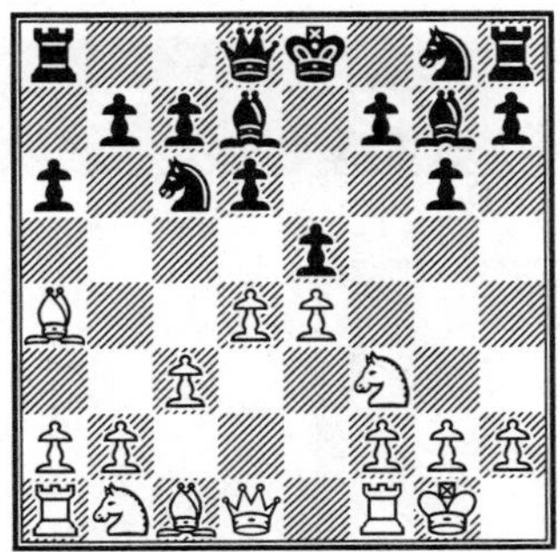

This is the main line of the Modern Steinitz Defense. White has a strong center but Black, by delaying the development of the knight from g8 to f6, keeps up the pressure from g7. Recent developments have been favoring White, who is able to conquer a great deal of territory early in the game.

8.d5. 8.Be3 Nf6; 9.Nbd2 0–0; 10.dxe5 Nxe5; 11.Nxe5 dxe5; 12.f3 is another solid plan, which gave White a small advantage in Topalov-Azmaiparashvili, Madrid 1996. **8...Nce7; 9.c4.** 9.Bxd7+ Qxd7; 10.c4 is another way to play the position. After 10...Nf6; 11.Nc3 0–0. Black can take advantage of Black's awkward pieces with 12.c5! and White has an initiative. **9...h6!?** Black has been trying several plans to free the position. 9...f6!? looks ungainly, but Black can perhaps defend with ...Nh6-f7. 9...b5!? should be met by retreating the bishop to b3. **10.Nc3 f5; 11.exf5 gxf5; 12.Nh4!?** The knight is exposed here, but it is more active than at e1. **12...Nf6; 13.f4 e4; 14.Ne2 Bxa4; 15.Qxa4+ Nd7; 16.Be3 0–0.** 16...Bxb2? would be a serious error because of 17.Bd4 Bxa1; 18.Bxa1 0–0; 19.Qd1 Rf7; 20.Nd4 and the f-pawn is threatened because White can employ a timely check at g4. **17.Bd4 c5!; 18.Bxg7 Kxg7; 19.Ng3.**

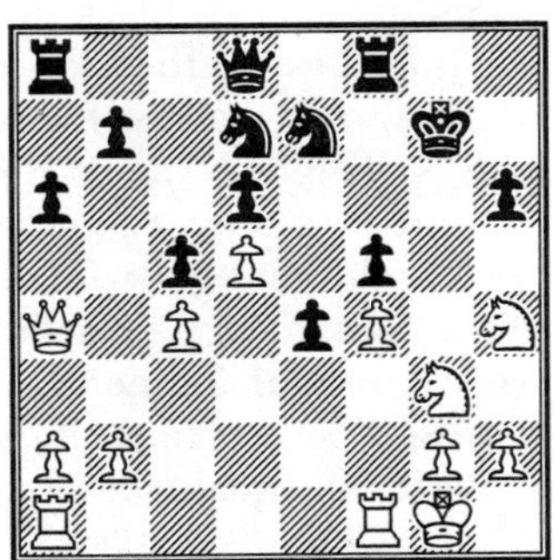

Here the queen should remain on the queenside, which is the only place that Black can whip up some counterplay. From c8, it can slo help with the defense of the pawn at f5. **19...Qe8?!; 20.Rae1 Rd8?!** Black is playing too passively. This was the last chance to carry out the thematic advance of the b-pawn. 20...b5!; 21.cxb5 axb5; 22.Qxb5 Rb8 gives Black some counterplay on the queenside. **21.Qa5! Rc8; 22.Qc3+**

Kh7; 23.Qc2 Kg8. Black was in time pressure, and missed the tactical finish. **24.Nxe4! fxe4; 25.Qxe4.** White is ready to lift a rook to the third rank to create a mating attack. **25...Rf7.** This defends g7, but overlooks the pin on the e-file which is immediately exploited with **26.Ng6!** and Black resigned. **White won.**

MACKENZIE ATTACK

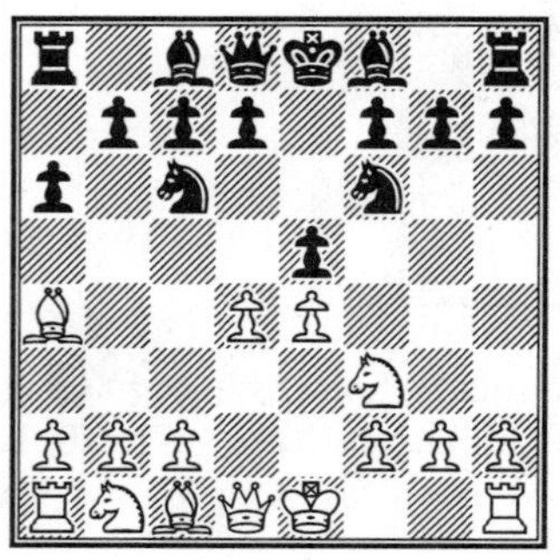

1.e4	**e5**
2.Nf3	**Nc6**
3.Bb5	**a6**
4.Ba4	**Nf6**
5.d4	

The **Mackenzie Attack**, or **Spanish Gambit**, follows established opening principles, and White can expect either to recapture the pawn soon or to obtain positional compensation in the form of an initiative.

(53) MACKENZIE - HOSMER [C60]
Cleveland (American Chess Congress), 1871

1.e4 e5; 2.Nf3 Nc6; 3.Bb5 a6; 4.Ba4 Nf6; 5.d4 exd4. White threatens to capture at e5, so Black is advised to accept the offer. 5...Nxe4 is weaker. 6.Qe2 b5; 7.Qxe4 d5; 8.Qe3 bxa4; 9.Nxe5 Nxe5; 10.0–0! Be6; 11.dxe5 Qd7; 12.Nc3 was better for White in Kholmov-Khasin, Soviet Championship 1961. Black cannot advance the d-pawn because White can reply Qe4 or Qf3, attacking the rook at a8.

6.0–0 Be7! This position can also be reached from 5.0–0 Be7; 6.d4 dxe4. **7.e5.** 7.Re1 is a solid alternative. **7...Ne4; 8.Nxd4 Nxd4.** In the original notes to this game in the tournament book, an immediate retreat to c5 was preferred, but almost a century later this idea was tried and found guilty of a small advantage for White. 8...Nc5; 9.Nf5 0–0; 10.Qg4 g6; 11.Bxc6 dxc6; 12.Nxe7+ Qxe7; 13.Qg3! Re8; 14.Nc3 Bf5; 15.Re1 and Black had no compensation for the weak pawn structure in Robatsch-Minev, Maribor 1967. 8...0–0 is also a good plan. 9.Nf5 d5; 10.Nxe7+ Nxe7; 11.c3 c6; 12.Nd2 Nc5; 13.Bc2 Bf5 gave Black full equality in Ljubojevic-Karpov, Milan 1975.

9.Qxd4 Nc5; 10.Bb3 Nxb3. This is not necessary. Black should just castle. 10...0–0; 11.Bf4 Ne6!; 12.Bxe6 dxe6 was good enough for equality in Pachman-Gligoric, Saltsjöbaden (Interzonal) 1948. **11.axb3.**

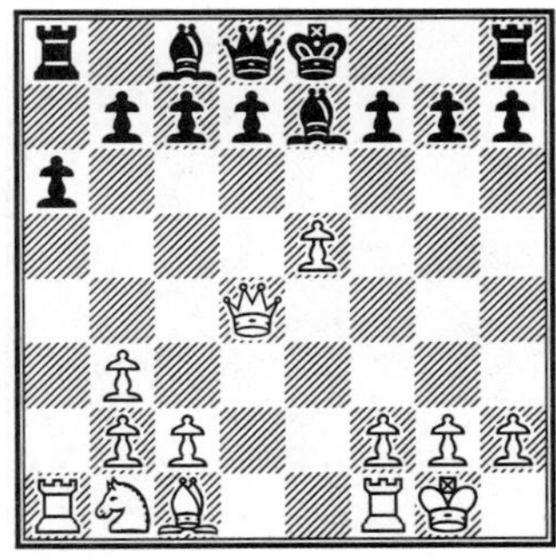

Black fails to see the danger on the dark squares. Castling was a better plan. **11...d6?; 12.exd6 Qxd6; 13.Qxg7 Bf6; 14.Re1+ Kd8; 15.Bg5. White won.**

WORRAL ATTACK

1.e4	**e5**
2.Nf3	**Nc6**
3.Bb5	**a6**
4.Ba4	**Nf6**
5.Qe2	

This is the **Worral Attack**, a simple line for White in the Spanish Game. The idea is simply to castle and then slide a rook to d1, after which any opening of the d-file can leave the Black queen vulnerable to attack

(54) SCHILLER - ARNE [C60]
Foster City, 1995

1.e4 e5; 2.Nf3 Nc6; 3.Bb5 a6; 4.Ba4 Nf6; 5.Qe2 b5. 5...Be7. 6.0–0 0–0? is a blunder: 7.Bxc6 dxc6; 8.Nxe5 Qd4; 9.Nf3 and if 9...Qxe4 then 10.Qxe4 Nxe4; 11.Re1, winning a piece. **6.Bb3 Bc5.**

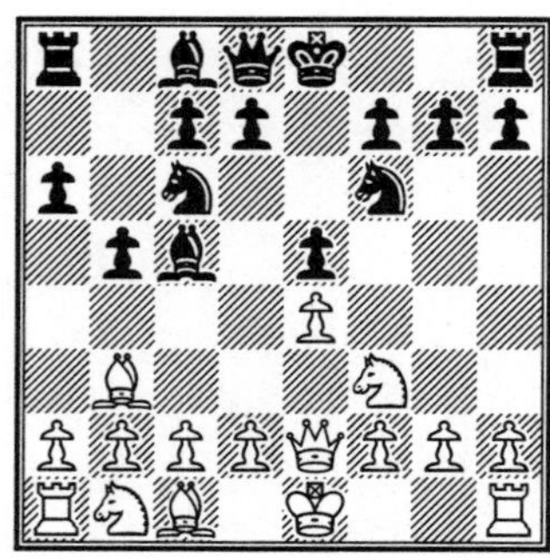

The sharpest continuation. 6...Be7; 7.c3 0–0; 8.0–0 d5; 9.d3 Bb7. This is a popular and conservative defense, and has served Black well recently, for example in Ehlvest-Anand, Riga (PCA) 1995. **7.c3.** 7.a4 is another plan, trying to undermine b5. **7...0–0; 8.0–0.** I could have settled for equality with 9.d3, but felt like taking a few chances.

8...d6. 8...d5; 9.exd5 e4; 10.Ng5 (10.dxc6 exf3; 11.Qxf3 Bg4; 12.Qg3 Be2. Black has good attacking chances, according to analysis in *Spanish Gambits* by Shamkovich & Schiller.) 10...Bg4; 11.Qe1 Ne5; 12.d4 Nd3; 13.Qe3 Bd6; 14.Nxe4 Nxc1; 15.Rxc1 Re8; 16.f3 Bxh2+; 17.Kxh2 Bxf3; 18.Qxf3 Nxe4. Black had a good game in Milev-Karaklajic, Belgrade 1957. **9.h3.** This is probably not necessary, as Black's bishop is headed to b7, but I wanted to make sure it was kept off of g4, where the pin on the knight would weaken my control of d4.

9...Bb7; 10.Rd1 Re8; 11.a4 b4; 12.a5 Qb8?! In retrospect, this is an error. The simple 12...Qe7 would have given Black an equal game. **13.d4!?**

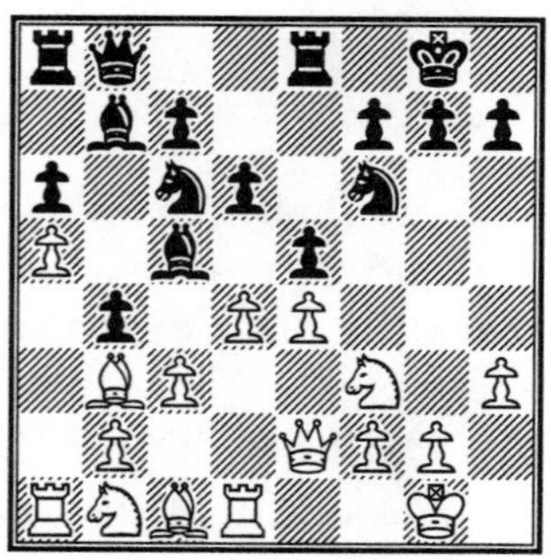

This is a deliberate sacrifice. I saw the Black forces huddled on the queenside and felt that a pawn could safely be invested for good attacking chances. **13...exd4; 14.cxd4 Ba7.** 14...Rxe4 was certainly playable, but I felt that I would then have sufficient compensation. 15.Be3!? Ba7; 16.Nbd2 Re7; 17.Qd3. White has good play for the pawn. Whether it is enough is not entirely clear, but as a practical matter I would have been satisfied with the position. **15.e5! d5.** 15...Nd7; 16.Ng5 gives White a strong attack. 15...dxe5; 16.dxe5 Nd8; 17.Ng5 threatens Rxd8 followed by an assault at f7. 15...Re7; 16.Bg5 Threatens to smash open the kingside. **16.Qd3!** Now Black must try for complications. **16...Ne4.** 16...Nd7; 17.Bxd5 Ne7; 18.Bc4 is simple and strong. **17.Bxd5 Nxf2.**

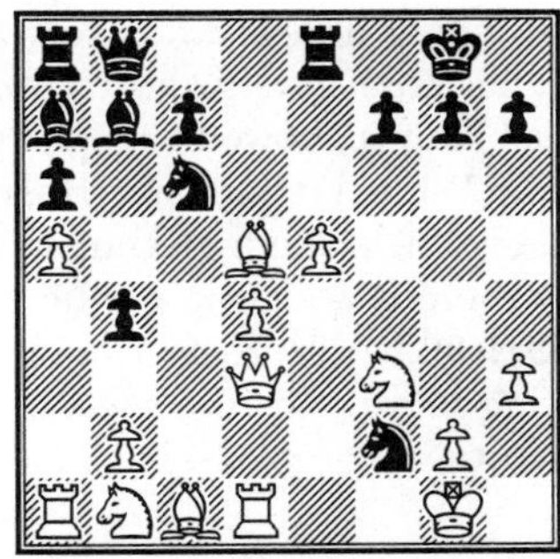

The idea is that if White captures the knight the pin the d4 allows captures at e5 with counterplay. Instead, I sacrifice a bishop and a rook to go after the undefended Black king. **18.Bxf7+!!** 18.Kxf2 Nxe5; 19.Qb3 Bxd5; 20.Qxd5 Nxf3 (20...c6; 21.Qe4 Nxf3; 22.Qxf3 Qd6; 23.Be3 Re6 also provides a little counterplay.) 21.gxf3 c5 leaves the White king vulnerable to attack. **18...Kxf7; 19.Qf5+ Kg8; 20.Ng5 Nxd1.**

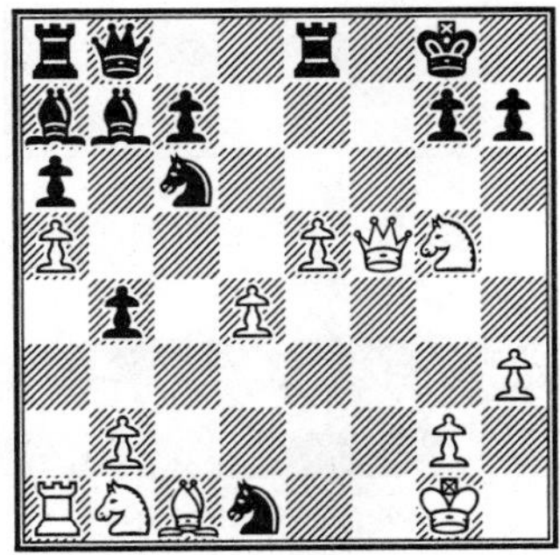

20...Nxh3+ would have put up more resistance. 21.Qxh3 Bxd4+; 22.Rxd4 Nxd4; 23.Qxh7+ Kf8; 24.Qh8+ Ke7; 25.Qxg7+ Kd8; 26.Be3 c5; 27.Bxd4 cxd4; 28.Qf6+ Kd7; 29.Qf5+.

A) 29...Kd8; 30.Ne6+ Rxe6; 31.Qxe6 and White should win, for example: 31...Qc7; 32.Nd2 Rc8 (32...Qg7 33.g4; 32...Qc6 33.Qg8+ Kc7; 34.Qg7+ Kb8; 35.Re1) 33.Rf1.

B) 29...Kc6; 30.Na3! and the knight cannot be captured because of 31.Rc1+ and mate follows quickly. **21.Qxh7+ Kf8; 22.Qh8+ Ke7; 23.Qxg7+ Kd8; 24.Nf7+ Kd7.**

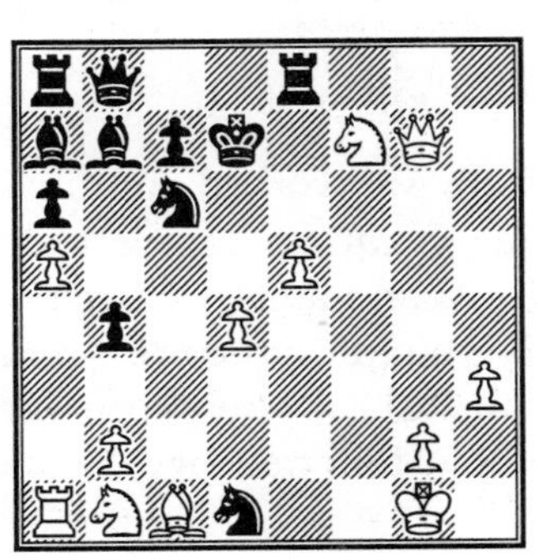

This position looks great for White, but it is not so simple. **25.e6+!** This is the only move to effectively continue the attack. **25...Kxe6.** Now there is a long series of forced moves. **26.Ng5+ Kd5.** 26...Kd6; 27.Nd2 also leaves the Black king with many worries. **27.Qd7+.** If the Black king is allowed to capture the d-pawn, then the next time it moves it will expose the White king to check from the bishop at a7, and that may, in some circumstances, give Black enough time to regroup. **27...Kc4; 28.Nd2+ Kd3; 29.Qf5+! Kxd4.** Surely there is a mating net here! There is, but it involves a problem-like move. **30.Ngf3+!** 30.Ndf3+ Kc4+ would have prolonged the game. **30...Ke3; 31.Kf1!!** A quiet king move ends the spectacular combination. The final position deserves its own picture.

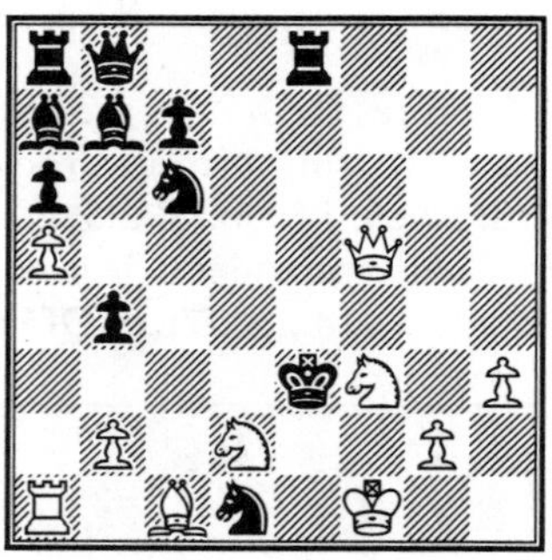

White won.

ARKHANGELSK VARIATION

1.e4	**e5**
2.Nf3	**Nc6**
3.Bb5	**a6**
4.Ba4	**Nf6**
5.0–0	**b5**
6.Bb3	

The **Arkhangelsk** system was worked out in its namesake city by a number of Soviet theoreticians. It can lead to very sharp positions and is very popular in both professional and amateur circles. White can adopt a number of strategies, including building the ideal pawn center with c3 and d4, defending the e-pawn with Re1, or straightforward development with Nc3 or d3. Black will play ...Bb7, followed by ...Bc5 in most cases, and castle kingside.

(55) ASTROM - SHIROV [C78]

Stockholm, 1989

1.e4 e5; 2.Nf3 Nc6; 3.Bb5 a6; 4.Ba4 Nf6; 5.0–0 b5; 6.Bb3 Bb7. 6...Bc5 is the Neo-Arkhangelsk, which often transposes into the Arkhangelsk, but where Re1 is discouraged because of the vulnerability of the f2-square. White has been exploring a variety of paths, seeking an advantage. 7.a4 (7.d3 0–0; 8.a4 Rb8!? is a new plan that looks promising for Black. 9.Nbd2 d6; 10.c3 Bb6; 11.h3 Nh5; 12.axb5 axb5; 13.Re1 Nf4; 14.Nf1 Qf6; 15.Be3 Ne7; 16.N1h2 c5; 17.Ng4 Qg6; 18.Nh4 Qg5; 19.Nf3 Qg6 was agreed drawn in Adams-Shirov, Madrid 1996.) 7...Bb7; 8.d3 d6; 9.Nc3 b4; 10.Nd5 Na5; 11.Nxf6+ Qxf6; 12.Ba2 h6 gave Black a solid position in the 12th game of the 1995 PCA World Championship match between Kasparov and Anand.

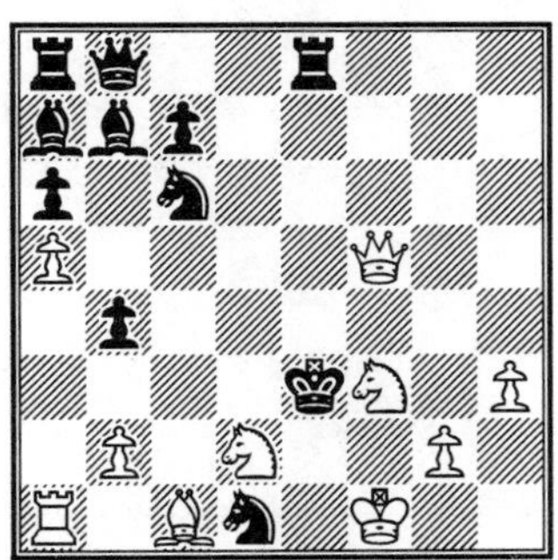

7.c3. This is a very challenging plan, threaten to establish the ideal pawn center quickly. Black's threat to capture the e-pawn is simply ignored. 7.d3 is a more timid plan. 7...Be7; 7...Bd6 is actually playable here, and is used by several top players, including Belyavsky and Malaniuk. 8.Nc3

(8.a4 0–0; 9.Nc3 b4; 10.Nd5 Na5; 11.Nxe7+ Qxe7; 12.Ba2 d5; 13.exd5 Bxd5; 14.Bxd5 Nxd5; 15.Re1 f6 gave Black a good game in Reeh-Shirov, Gausdal 1991.)

8...0–0 (8...d6; 9.a4 b4; 10.Nd5 0–0; 11.a5 Nxd5; 12.Bxd5 Nxa5; 13.Rxa5 c6! and with the rook at a5 and bishop at d5 under attack, the best move was 14.Bxf7+ but after 14...Rxf7; 15.Ra1 a5 Black was better in Christiansen-Larsen, Mar del Plata 1981.) 9.Bd2 (9.Re1 d6; 10.a4 Na5; 11.axb5 axb5; 12.Nxb5 Nxb3; 13.Rxa8 Bxa8; 14.cxb3 h6; 15.Qc2 c5 with a solid position for Black, Mokry-Shirov, Brno 1991.)

9...d6; 10.Nd5 (10.a4 Na5; 11.Ba2 b4; 12.Nd5 Nxd5; 13.exd5 c5; 14.dxc6 Nxc6; 15.Bd5 Qa5; 16.Ba2 d5 and Black had the ideal pawn center in Bologan-Shirov, Moscow 1991.) 10...Nxd5; 11.Bxd5 Qd7; 12.a4 Bf6; 13.Bg5 Bxg5; 14.Nxg5 Nd8; 15.Bxb7 Nxb7; 16.axb5 Qxb5; 17.Qd2 with a superior pawn structure for White in Faibisovich-Mikhalchishin, Soviet Championship 1975.

7.d4 is premature. 7...Nxd4; 8.Nxd4 exd4; 9.e5 Ne4; 10.c3 dxc3; 11.Qf3 d5; 12.exd6 Qf6; 13.Re1 0–0–0! and Black has the better of the brawl, Tseshkovsky-Belyavsky, Lvov 1978. 7.Re1 Bc5; 8.c3 is a similar line, except that the pawn at d4 is defended. On the other hand, the f2-square is weak and Black can attack with pawns on the kingside. 8...0–0. Black can choose ...d6 instead, but the text is more popular. 9.d4 Bb6; 10.Be3 d6; 11.Nbd2 h6; 12.h3 and two recent plans look good for Black:

A) 12...Rb8!? gets the rook off a potentially dangerous activity. 13.Bc2 (13.d5

Bxe3; 14.dxc6 Bxd2 and White cannot capture at b7, because the pawn does not attack the rook, as it would if the rook were still on a8. 15.Qxd2 Bxc6 and Black wins a pawn.) 13...Re8 with a solid position in Ki. Georgiev-Belyavsky, Yugoslavia 1996.

B) 12...Qd7!? leaves White hunting for a plan after 13.Bc2 Rae8 with the idea of exchanging pawns at d4 and then ...Nb4, as in the Zaitsev Variation. White should probably take time out of a3. 14.d5 Ne7; 15.Bxb6 cxb6; 16.Bd3 when Black played the strongly prophylactic 16...Rb8! aimed at defending the queenside if White plays a4, but that is what White should have done, as 17.Bf1?! Ne8; 18.Qb3 Kh8 gave Black excellent prospects on the kingside in Pikula-Petronic, Belgrade 1996.

7...Nxe4; 8.d4 Na5; 9.Bc2. 9.Nxe5 Nxb3; 10.Qxb3 Qf6; 11.f3 Nc5; 12.Qd1 Ne6; 13.a4 Bd6 allows Black to establish good counterplay, Anand-Mikhalchishin, Moscow (GMA) 1989. **9...exd4.**

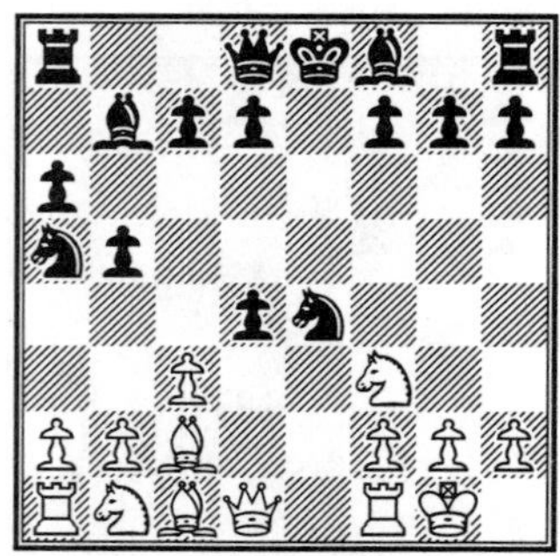

White must play carefully here. In any case, results have not been promising. **10.Re1.** 10.b4 Nc4; 11.Bxe4 Bxe4; 12.Re1 d5; 13.Nxd4 c5; 14.bxc5 Bxc5; 15.f3 0–0; 16.fxe4 dxe4; 17.Rxe4 Qd5; 18.Qf3 Ne5; 19.Qf5 Rae8 was better for Black in Hellers-Shirov, Stockholm 1990. 10.Qe2 d5; 11.Nxd4 c5; 12.Nb3 Nxb3; 13.axb3 Be7; 14.Re1 0–0; 15.f3 f5!; 16.fxe4 fxe4 gives Black compensation for the pawn, for example 17.c4 Bd6; 18.Qg4 Qf6; 19.Be3 d4; 20.Nd2 Qe5 and Black won quickly in Mortensen-Shirov, Kerteminde 1991. 10.Nxd4 c5; 11.Nf5 Qf6; 12.Qf3 Nd6; 13.Qe3+ Kd8; 14.Qxc5 gets the pawn back but 14...Ne4; 15.Qd4 Qxf5; 16.Nd2 Qf6; 17.Nxe4 Qxd4; 18.cxd4 f6; 19.Nc5 Bd5 was fine for Black in Renet-Shirov, France 1991. **10...d5; 11.Nxd4 c5.**

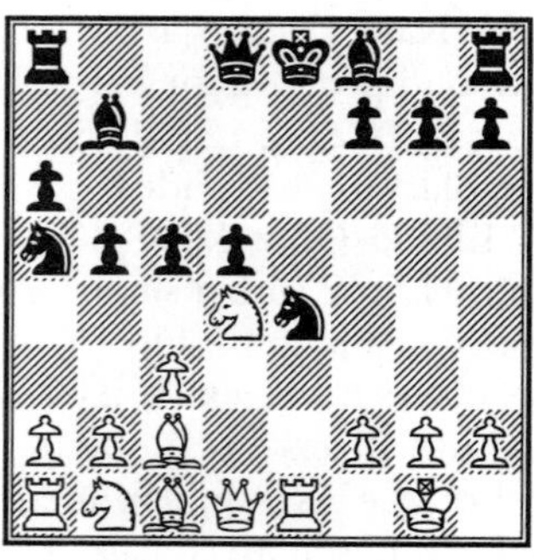

This move may seem risky, since the Black king must head to the queenside. But there are enough pieces around to defend the king, and the knight at e4 is a real asset. **12.Nf5?!** 12.f3 cxd4; 13.fxe4 d3!; 14.exd5+ Be7; 15.Qxd3 Qxd5 is slightly worse for White, according to Lane, but after 16.Qxd5 Bxd5; 17.Be4 Bxe4; 18.Rxe4 should lead to a draw. **12...Qd7; 13.Ng3 0–0–0.** Black's king is relatively safe here, but the center begins to crumble. **14.Nxe4 dxe4; 15.Qe2 f5; 16.a4.** The thematic queenside advance comes rather late, but still plays an important role. In any case, no better move comes to mind. **16...b4.** Black cannot afford to open lines. The knight is offside and there are weaknesses on the dark-squares. **17.Bg5.**

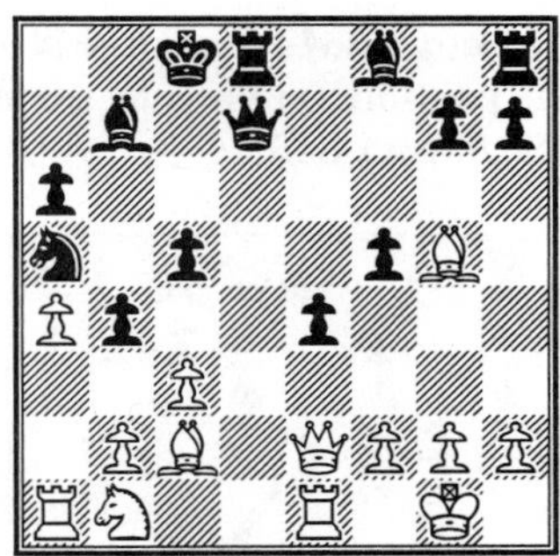

17...b3! 17...Be7; 18.Bxe7 Qxe7 would have been a second-best plan but Black would still have a good game. **18.Bxd8 Qxd8; 19.Bd1 c4.** In return for the exchange Black has a healthy extra pawn and the White pieces are pathetic, lying around on the home rank. **20.Nd2 Qc7; 21.Qf1 Bd6; 22.g3 Bc5; 23.Qh3 Kb8; 24.Nf1.** White would like to pivot the knight to e3, but Black gets there first! **24...e3!; 25.Rxe3 Bxe3; 26.Nxe3 Qc6.** The mating threat forces White's hand. **27.Qg2 Qxg2+; 28.Nxg2 Rd8.** Black infiltrates the seventh rank, and the game is effectively over. **29.Ne3 Rd2; 30.Nxf5 Rxb2; 31.Nd6 Bc6. Black won.**

OPEN VARIATION

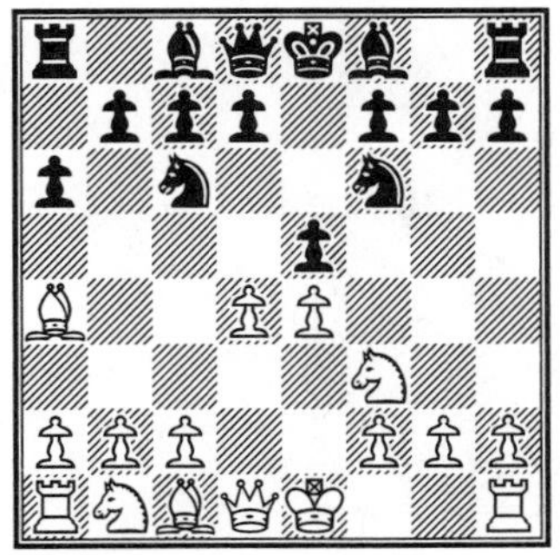

1.e4	**e5**
2.Nf3	**Nc6**
3.Bb5	**a6**
4.Ba4	**Nf6**
5.0–0	**Nxe4**

In the **Open Variation**, Black captures the e4 pawn, giving up the pawn at e5 in return. The knight has a powerful post at e4, controlling important squares such as d2 and f2. On the other hand, White can create pressure at d5, and has a variety of attacking plans. Viktor Korchnoi has long been a leading advocate of the Black side. Bent Larsen was also known for his aggressive handling of the defense. More recently, Viswanathan Anand has taken up the torch.

(56) KASPAROV - ANAND [C80]

New York (PCA World Championship, game 10, 1995

1.e4 e5; 2.Nf3 Nc6; 3.Bb5 a6; 4.Ba4 Nf6; 5.0–0 Nxe4; 6.d4 b5. This counterattack is designed to release the pressure on the queenside. **7.Bb3.** White threatens to move the bishop to d5. **7...d5; 8.dxe5 Be6.**

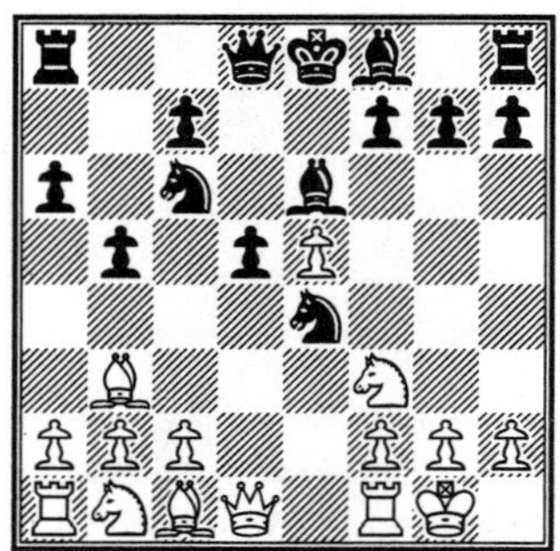

The last few moves are firmly established as best, but now White has several plans. **9.Nbd2.** This move has moved up to an equal position with 9.c3 as the main line of the Open Spanish. **9...Nc5; 10.c3 d4.** The most aggressive, but also the riskiest line. After 10...Bg4, intending to retreat the knight to e6, Black has a decent game. **11.Ng5.** This introduces a piece sacrifice which leads to unclear complications if accepted. Anand had prepared an alternative line. **11...dxc3.** 11...Qxg5; 12.Qf3 0–0–0; 13.Bxe6+ fxe6; 14.Qxc6.

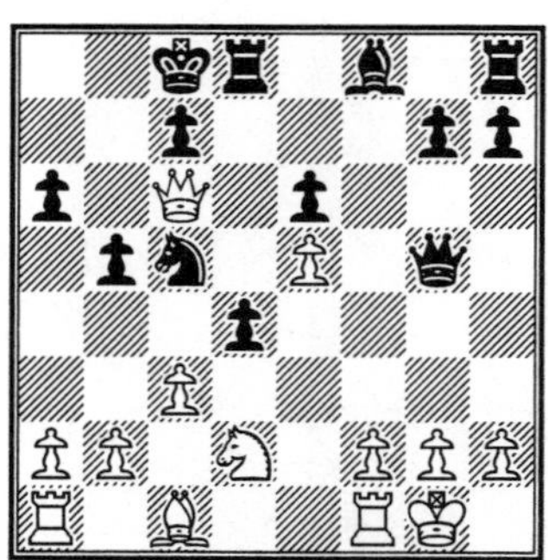

This is a well-explored alternative for Black. The jury is still out, but Korchnoi and Timman seem to agree on the best plan for Black: 14...Qxe5; 15.b4 Qd5; 16.Qxd5 exd5; 17.bxc5 dxc3; 18.Nb3 d4; 19.Ba3 g6! and Black has plenty of compensation for the piece. **12.Nxe6 fxe6; 13.bxc3 Qd3.** This much had been seen in game #6 of the match, but in this game Kasparov was ready with an old new move from the magical hand of Mikhail Tal.

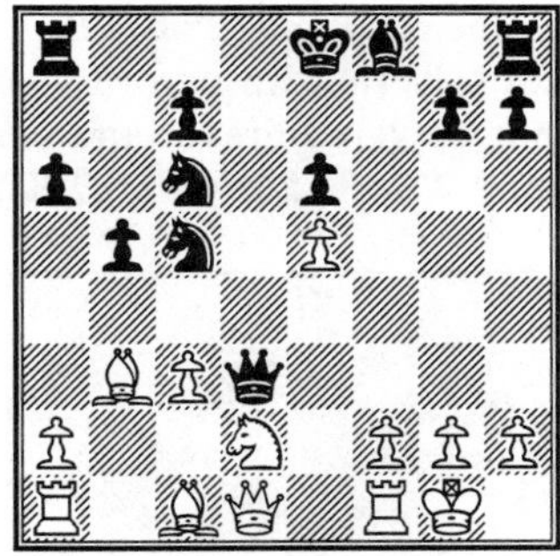

14.Bc2!! Tal's idea is to set up a magnificent rook sacrifice. Kasparov claimed that the idea had only come to his attention a few days before this game. **14...Qxc3.** Anand responded quickly and seemed to be well within his own preparation. **15.Nb3.** This seemed to catch Anand by surprise. Kasparov sacrifices the rook at a1 for a fierce attack. **15...Nxb3.** Amazingly, even this much is not new. An obscure postal game between Berg and Nevestveit in 1990 reached the same position, and varied with 15...Rd8. After 16.Bd2 Qxc5; 17.Re1 Qd5, Kasparov would have played not 18.Nxc5, as in the cited game, but rather 18.Qg4! which would have brought victory quickly. **16.Bxb3.**

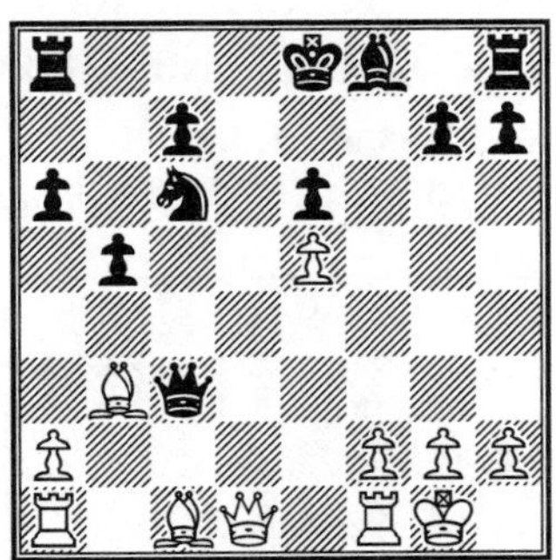

16...Nd4. Anand defers acceptance of the sacrifice until the next move. After 16...Qxa1; 17.Qh5+, it is hard to find a defense for Black. **17.Qg4 Qxa1; 18.Bxe6 Rd8.** At this point there doesn't seem to be any way to save the game for Black.

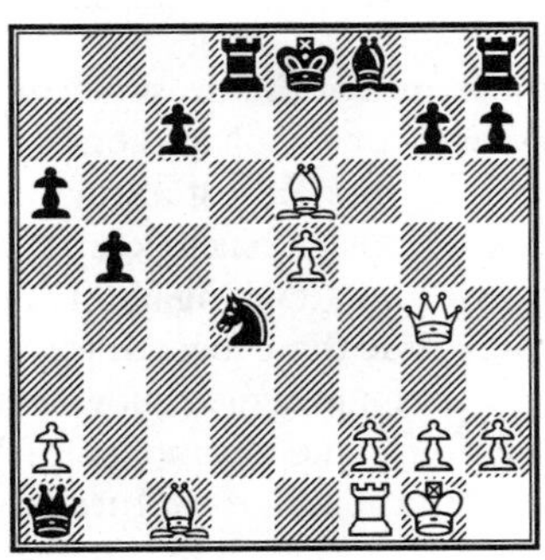

19.Bh6 Qc3. Not 19...Qxf1+?; 20.Kxf1 gxh6; 21.Qh5+. **20.Bxg7 Qd3; 21.Bxh8 Qg6.** 21...Ne2+ only postpones the inevitable. **22.Bf6 Be7; 23.Bxe7 Qxg4** or 23...Kxe7; 24.Qh4+. **24.Bxg4 Kxe7; 25.Rc1.** By now Kasparov is out of his opening preparation and has a winning position, but it still requires accurate play, which the World Champion carries out with efficiency. **25...c6; 26.f4 a5; 27.Kf2 a4; 28.Ke3 b4.**

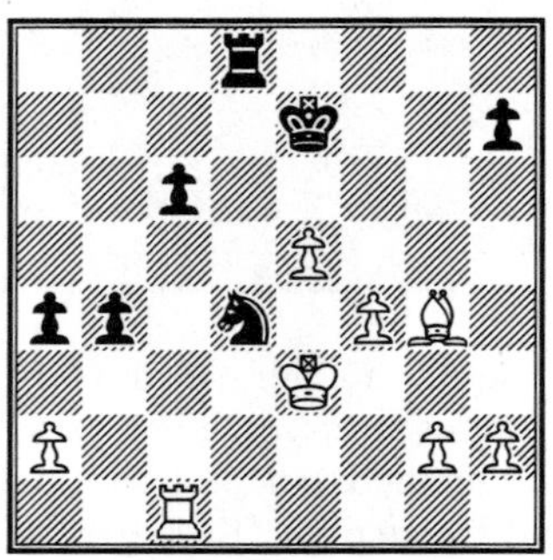

29.Bd1. The bishop gets out of the way so that the g-pawn can advance. **29...a3; 30.g4 Rd5; 31.Rc4 c5; 32.Ke4 Rd8; 33.Rxc5 Ne6; 34.Rd5 Rc8; 35.f5 Rc4+; 36.Ke3 Nc5; 37.g5 Rc1; 38.Rd6. White won.**

(57) GELLER - CHEKHOV [C82]

Soviet Championship, 1980

1.e4 e5; 2.Nf3 Nc6; 3.Bb5 a6; 4.Ba4 Nf6; 5.0–0 Nxe4; 6.d4 b5; 7.Bb3 d5; 8.dxe5 Be6; 9.c3 Bc5; 10.Nbd2 0–0; 11.Bc2 Nxf2; 12.Rxf2.

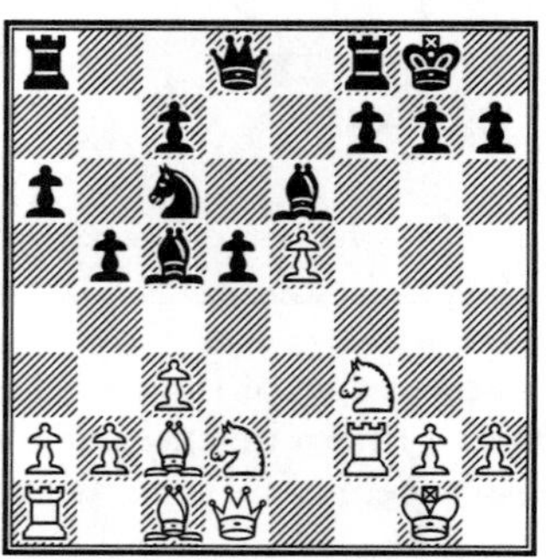

This is the Dilworth Attack, one of the most fascinating variations in the Open Spanish. Black gives up two pieces for a rook and one or two pawns, and exposes the White King to a furious attack. White almost always manages to survive, however, and then an endgame arises where Black has to keep the White minor pieces at bay. Therefore both endgame finesse and attacking ability are required to play the opening as Black. Although for some time the Dilworth was considered suspect, it was reevaluated in the early 1980s, and the judgment now seems to be that the endgames remain unclear, with at best a minuscule advantage for White.

12...f6; 13.exf6 Bxf2+. The immediate capture is generally considered better than 13...Qxf6, because in the latter case White can respond 14.Qf1. Recent analysis has shown that Black has good chances in those lines, as well. **14.Kxf2 Qxf6; 15.Kg1.** The normal move, though many others have been tried. 15.Nf1 Ne5; 16.Be3 Rae8; 17.Bd4 Karpov approves of this move, citing the present game, where White develops a dangerous initiative. But Black has ways to improve on Chekhov's play. 17...Qh4+; 18.Kg1 Nxf3+; 19.gxf3 Qg5+?! Black overlooks a simple resource (19...Bf5; 20.Nd2 Bxc2; 21.Qxc2 Re2 and Black wins. Still, had Black seen that plan we would have been deprived of the following interesting developments.) 20.Ng3 Bh3; 21.a4 Re6; 22.axb5 axb5; 23.f4 Rxf4; 24.Qh5 Qxh5; 25.Nxh5. This endgame seems to be okay for White, who will pick up the pawn at g7. But even here Black has a lot of counterplay, since the knight, by leaving its post at g3 to capture the queen, allows the rook to penetrate the seventh rank, where it will grab the b-pawn. 25...Rf3; 26.Bxg7 Kf7! A clever move, threatening to play 27...Rg6+; 28.Bxg6 Kxg6 attacking both knight and bishop. 27.Bd4 Re2; 28.Bxh7 Rxb2; 29.Ng3 Rd2 was played in Enders-Chekhov, Dresden 1985. Black now has only one extra pawn, but it is enough. White's pieces are uncoordinated and the constant threat of back rank mates is annoying.

15.Nb3? seeks to conquer the d4 square, but it fails: 15...Ne5; 16.Nbd4 Bg4; 17.b4 Rae8; 18.Bd2 Qh4+; 19.Kg1 Qh5; 20.a4 bxa4; 21.Rxa4 Bxf3; 22.Nxf3 Rxf3!; 23.Bf4 Rf8; 24.Qxd5+ Kh8 and White gave up in K.Thomas-Schiller, New York 1980.

15...Rae8; 16.Nf1 Ne5; 17.Be3. This is a common position, since it can arise from various move orders at move 15, 16, and 17. Black's best plan now is to head for the endgame. **17...Nxf3+; 18.Qxf3 Qxf3; 19.gxf3 Rxf3; 20.Bd1.** The retreat to d1 was popular for a while, but it really just inhibits the rook at a1, and after the Black rook moves, the bishop usually gets out of the way again. 20.Bf2 brings about a very important position for the evaluation of the opening. From here the reader should pay a great deal of attention to the various types of endgames presented in the endgame chapters. 20...Bh3! Clearly best, since the pressure on the kingside and free access to the e-file are essential to Black's plans. 21.Nd2 Rf6; 22.Bd3 h5!; 23.Re1 Forced, according to Chekhov. 23...Rxe1+; 24.Bxe1 c5 with chances for both sides in Kaminsky-Chekhov, Zubniewice 1993. **20...Rf7!; 21.Bb3 c6; 22.Bd4.** 22.Ng3 Bh3; 23.Bd4 transposes to the game. **22...Bh3; 23.Ng3.**

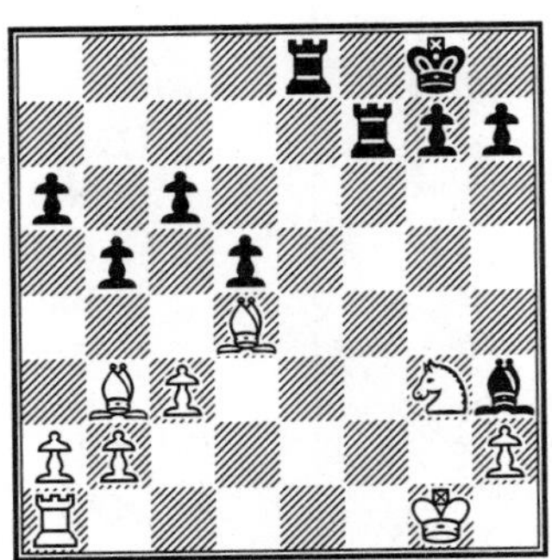

The knight can also move to d3, but it only seems to get in the way there. 23.Ne3 This is the alternative to 23.Ng3. Black has done well from this position, by using the standard plan of advancing the h-pawn. 23...Rf4; 24.Re1 Re6. Black can probably play 24...h5 immediately. 25.Bc2 h5; 26.Bd3 h4; 27.Bc5 a5! A useful move which contests control of b4. 28.Bf1 Bf5; 29.Re2 Be4; 30.h3. White needs to make some room on the kingside. Although the Black attack seems ferocious, in reality it is just the prelude to a favorable endgame. The idea is to build the pressure until White is forced to exchange a pair of rooks to reduce it. This must be combined with optimal piece placement so that the resulting endgame, where Black has rook and two pawns for the minor pieces, is winnable. 30...Rf3; 31.Rf2 Rxf2; 32.Kxf2 Rf6+; 33.Ke1 Rf3. All of White's pieces are tied down, but there is a lot of hard work ahead before a the full point was awarded in Arnason-Petursson, Reykjavik 1980.

23...g6; 24.Bc2. Again, Black's plan involves h7-h5-h4 to drive away the knight. **24...Re6; 25.Bd3 h5; 26.Bf1.** A sensible plan, since the bishop at h3 is involved in the attack and the one at d3 is not participating in the defense. As usual, White employs a strategy of exchanging off minor pieces in order to use the power of the minor pieces against a rook in the endgame. **26...Bxf1; 27.Rxf1 h4; 28.Rxf7.** Otherwise the knight has to retreat to h1. **28...Kxf7; 29.Nf1 Re2.** Black's counterplay, as is so often the case, is based on the occupation of the seventh rank. **30.b4 Rxa2; 31.h3.** Pretty much forced, as otherwise Black gains control of g2. **31...Ke6; 32.Ne3 a5; 33.bxa5 Rxa5; 34.Kf2 Kd6.** It is clear that Black's pawns are not vulnerable, especially since White's bishop is confined to the dark squares and the knight has only one useful target–e5. **35.Bf6.** 35.Ng4 c5; 36.Bf6 Ra3; 37.Ne5 Ke6; 38.Bg7 Rxc3; 39.Nxg6 Rxh3 and the Black pawns win.

35...Ra4; 36.Ke2 b4!; 37.cxb4 Rxb4; 38.Ng4 Rb3. Here we can see White's problem. The king had to move to the center to stop the passed pawns, but now the h-pawn is vulnerable, and can be defended only by the knight. But if the knight stays home, the bishop has no help, and the rook can operate on both flanks, assisting the queenside pawns while at the same time keeping the pressure on h3. **39.Nf2 c5; 40.Bxh4 d4; 41.Bg5 c4; 42.h4 Kd5; 43.Nh3.** Presumably White resigned during the adjournment, or after the time control had been cleared. The endgame is now utterly hopeless. **Black won.**

MARSHALL ATTACK

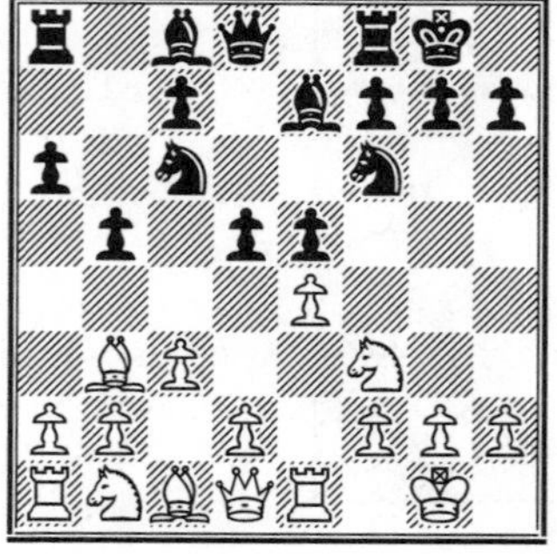

1.e4	**e5**
2.Nf3	**Nc6**
3.Bb5	**a6**
4.Ba4	**Nf6**
5.0–0	**Be7**
6.Re1	**b5**
7.Bb3	**0–0**
8.c3	**d5**

The famous **Marshall Attack**, still popular in contemporary chess, boasts Michael Adams and Viswanathan Anand as the leading advocates. It was quite a shock when this game was played, with the inventor handling the Black pieces. In return for a pawn, Black gains rapid development and strong attacking chances against the White king. The opening has been deeply analyzed, with some lines worked out to the end of the first time control at move 40! On the other hand, new life has been pumped into the Anti-Marshall move 8.a4, which leads to slower play which is now held to be slightly better for White. There are still plenty of players willing to take up the Marshall on either side of the board, so it is unlikely to disappear soon.

(58) Capablanca - Marshall [C89]

New York, 1918

1.e4 e5; 2.Nf3 Nc6; 3.Bb5 a6; 4.Ba4 Nf6; 5.0–0 Be7; 6.Re1 b5; 7.Bb3 0–0; 8.c3 d5!? 9.exd5 Nxd5; 10.Nxe5 Nxe5. This bold move usually leads to the following exchanges. **11.Rxe5.**

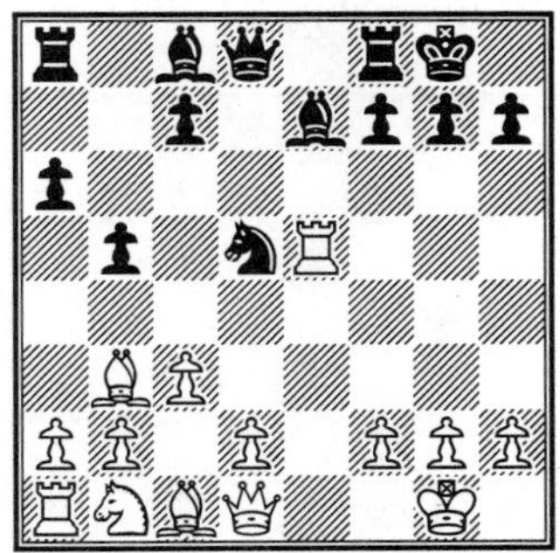

11...Nf6. As a result of this game, 11...Nf6 fell out of favor, and 11...c6 has become the standard continuation and has been analyzed well past move 30. A typical line is 12.d4 Bd6; 13.Re1 ah4; 14.g3 ah3; 15.Be3 Bg4; 16.ad3 Rae8; 17.Nd2 Re6; 18.a4 f5; 19.af1 ah5; 20.f4 bxa4 which has been played hundreds of times! The evaluation of the Marshall remains unclear, but as noted in the note to move 8, White may have a way of avoiding it and obtaining an advantage at the same time. **12.Re1 Bd6; 13.h3 Ng4; 14.Qf3!** 14.hxg4 Qh4; 15.g3 Bxg3; 16.fxg3 Qxg3+; 17.Kf1 Bxg4 and Black wins. **14...Qh4; 15.d4!** 15.Re8 is met by 15...Bb7! **15...Nxf2; 16.Re2.** 16.Qxf2? would be a blunder because of 16...Bh2+ 17.Kf1 Bg3; 18.Qxf7+ Rxf7+ and, because it is check, White has no time for 19.Re8#.

16...Bg4. 16...Ng4; 17.Nd2. Taking the rook leads to disaster because Black infiltrates with the queen at g3. 17...Bd7; 18.Nf1 Nf6; 19.Be3 and White is clearly better. **17.hxg4 Bh2+; 18.Kf1 Bg3.** 18...Nh1; 19.Be3 Ng3+; 20.Ke1 Nxe2+; 21.Kxe2 Rae8; 22.Nd2 is a position Black wouldn't wish on his mother-in-law. The h-file will be an expressway to disaster, and the pressure on the e-file is irrelevant. **19.Rxf2 Qh1+.**

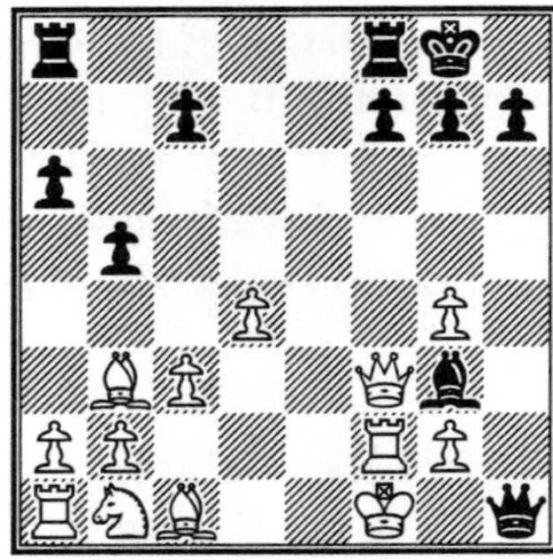

20.Ke2. Capablanca is conducting the defense with utmost precision and Black's attack is falling apart. **20...Bxf2.** 20...Qxc1. 21.Rf1 Qxb2+; 22.Nd2 Bd6; 23.Bxf7+ and White wins. **21.Bd2 Bh4; 22.Qh3.** If Black exchanges queens, then there is no more attack and resignation is inevitable. **22...Rae8+; 23.Kd3 Qf1+; 24.Kc2.**

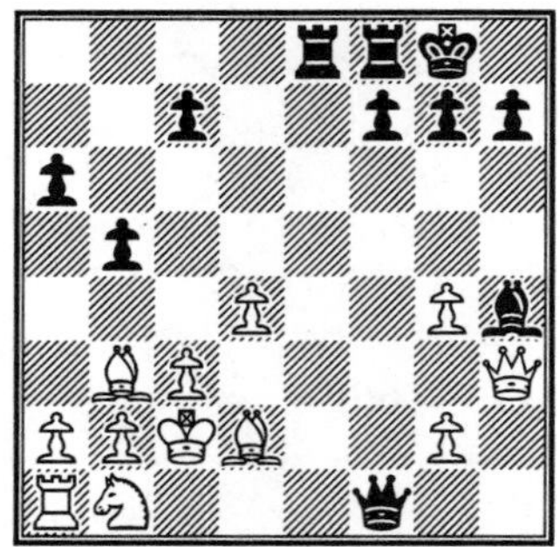

White is not worried. Black has too little in the way of attacking force, and all Capablanca has to do is activate the rook at a1. **24...Bf2; 25.Qf3 Qg1; 26.Bd5 c5; 27.dxc5 Bxc5; 28.b4 Bd6.** White has two pieces for a rook, but the rook has been sitting on a1 the entire game.

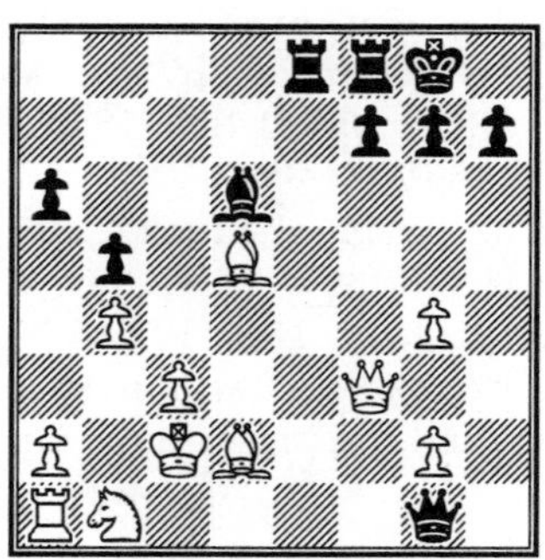

Now Capablanca brings it out. **29.a4! a5; 30.axb5 axb4; 31.Ra6! bxc3; 32.Nxc3 Bb4.** Capablanca's king is completely safe, and his attack is stronger than it looks. **33.b6 Bxc3; 34.Bxc3 h6; 35.b7 Re3.** Here Capablanca finished off the game with a brilliant move, announcing mate in 6. **36.Bxf7+.** 36.Qxf7+!? Rxf7; 37.b8Q+ Kh7;

38.Rxh6+ Kxh6; 39.Qh8+ Kg5; 40.Qh5+ Kf4; 41.Qxf7+ would have been pretty, but much slower. **36...Rxf7.** 36...Kh8; 37.Rxh6#. **37.b8Q+.** A new queen brings the game to a swift conclusion. **37...Re8; 38.Qxe8+ Kh7; 39.Qfe4+ Rf5; 40.Qxf5+ g6; 41.Qexg6#. White won.**

CLOSED VARIATIONS

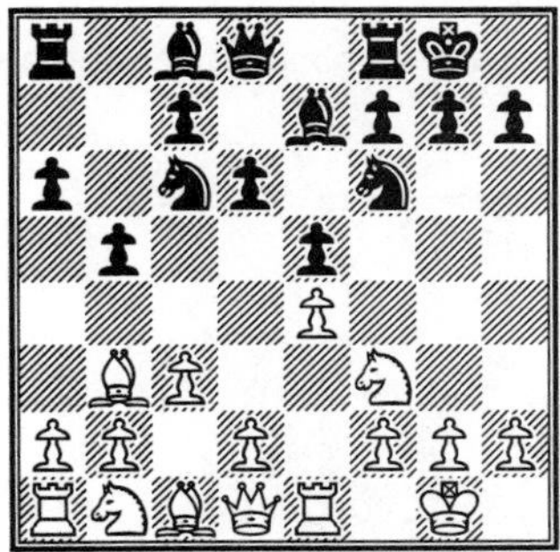

1.e4	**e5**
2.Nf3	**Nc6**
3.Bb5	**a6**
4.Ba4	**Nf6**
5.0–0	**Be7**
6.Re1	**b5**
7.Bb3	**d6**
8.c3	**0–0**

Although technically all variations stemming from 5...Be7 are considered **Closed Variations**, the term usually refers to the positions after 1.e4 e5; 2.Nf3 Nc6; 3.Bb5 a6; 4.Ba4 Nf6; 5.0–0 Be7; 6.Re1 b5; 7.Bb3 d6; 8.c3 0–0. White normally plays 9.h3, to prevent ...Bg4 with an annoying pin on the knight at f3, but this is not absolutely necessary.

Play in the Closed Spanish tends to be slow, with White allowing the attack to simmer for a long time before uncovering it on the kingside. Black can react in the center or on the queenside. There is a great deal of behind the scenes maneuvering, and the placement of each piece, especially the minor pieces, is critical.

(59) CAPABLANCA - BOGOLJUBOW [C91]

London 1922

1.e4 e5; 2.Nf3 Nc6; 3.Bb5 a6; 4.Ba4 Nf6; 5.0–0 Be7; 6.Re1 b5; 7.Bb3 d6; 8.c3 0–0; 9.d4.

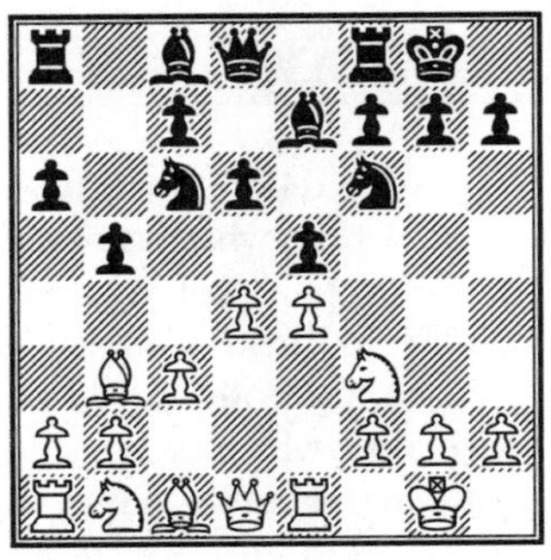

The Yates Variation went out of fashion after it was discovered that Black can get a reasonable game. Later, however, it was reinvigorated with new ideas by Romanishin and others and although Black is able to equalize, the play is lively and 9.d4 remains a playable alternative to 9.h3.The only objection to White's plan is that Black can play ...Bg4, pinning the knight. **9...exd4?!** The release of tension in the center is premature. 9...Bg4 is the contemporary reply. 10.h3 Bh5; 11.Be3 Bg6; 12.Nbd2 Nxe4?; 13.Bd5! Nxd2; 14.Nxd2 Qe8; 15.Qf3 and the pressure at c6 wins material.

10.cxd4 Bg4; 11.Be3 Na5; 12.Bc2 Nc4; 13.Bc1. Is this a loss of time? Not really, since the knight will eventually be forced back with b2-b3 and then the bishop can be profitably employed at b2. **13...c5.**

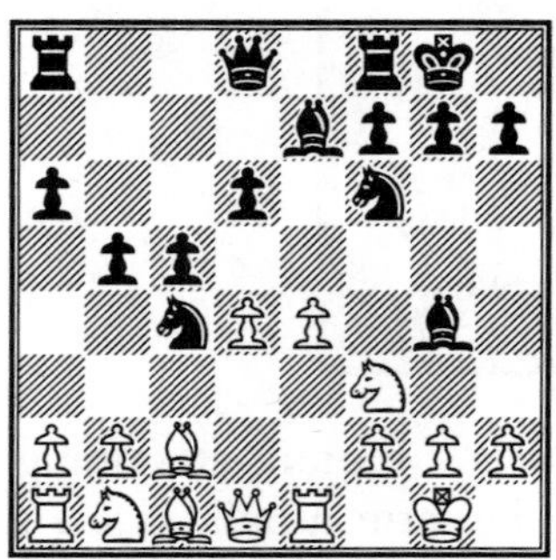

Classical Spanish play–Black will expand on the queenside and White will attempt to keep control of the center and attack on the kingside. **14.b3 Na5; 15.Bb2.** As promised. It would have been wrong to push the d-pawn, because then Black would simply swing his knight from f6 to d7 and stick the bishop on the long diagonal. **15...Nc6; 16.d5 Nb4.**

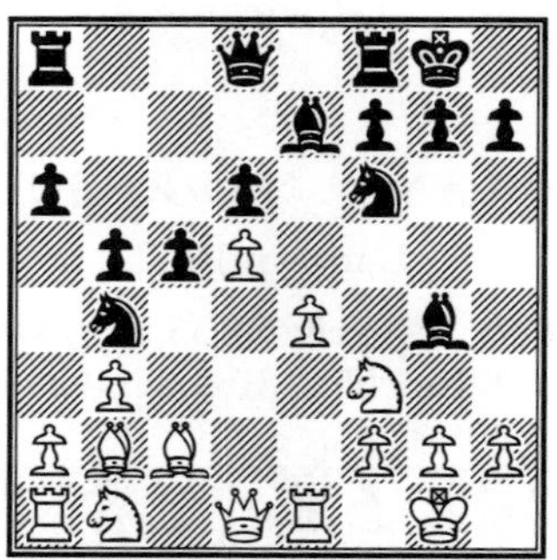

Black has lured White into playing d4-d5, but it has cost him some time. He now attempts to eliminate the Spanish bishop, which can be dangerous after e5. **17.Nbd2 Nxc2; 18.Qxc2.** Black has the bishop pair, but White controls the center and has a strong bishop at b2. Should he play on the kingside, as usual, or perhaps undermine the Black pawn structure with a2-a4. Or both? And how to time all of this?

18...Re8; 19.Qd3. A very nice move which increases the pressure on the queenside while making it easier for the queen to get to the kingside via the third rank. Before making a concrete plan, White strives to improve the position of his pieces. **19...h6.**

If Black was worried about e4-e5, he could have played Nf6-d7, but White isn't ready for such action yet. 19...Nd7; 20.e5 Bxf3; 21.Nxf3 dxe5; 22.Nxe5 Nxe5; 23.Bxe5 Bd6; 24.Bxd6 Qxd6; 25.Rad1 is not likely to be enough to win, given the blockade of the pawn. **20.Nf1 Nd7; 21.h3 Bh5?!** Black is a little too attached to his bishop pair. He should have captured and then played Bf6, to take control of the e5 square which has been the center of attention for some time. **22.N3d2! Bf6; 23.Bxf6 Qxf6.**

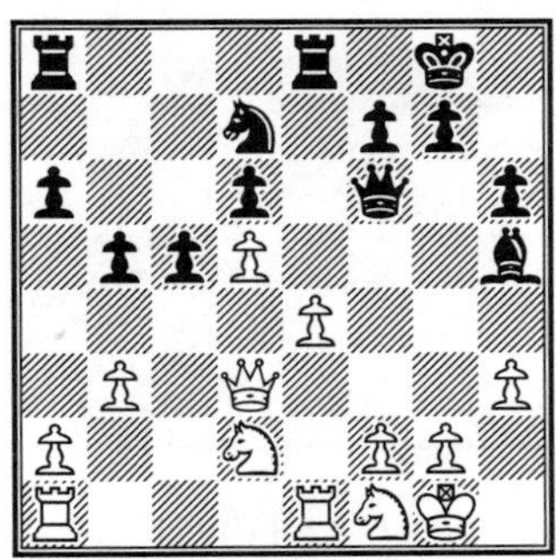

Black seems to have secured the central squares, but now White deflects the Black knight to the queenside, and then launches his attack. **24.a4! c4; 25.bxc4 Nc5; 26.Qe3 bxa4.**

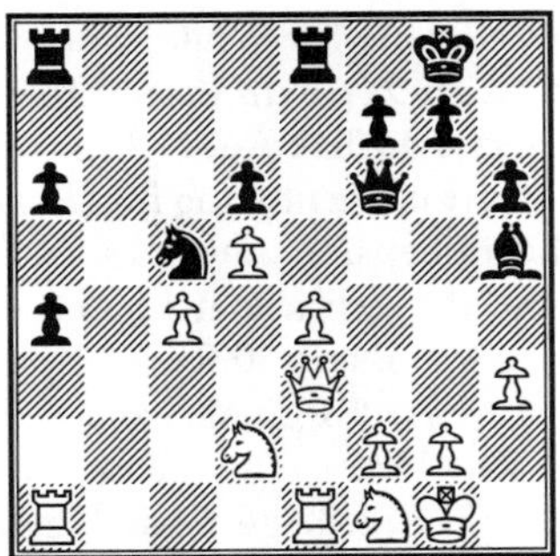

The position has changed considerably. Black has some valuable assets on the queenside and a seemingly well-placed knight, but it is actually offside. **27.f4!** White is prepared to bring a pawnstorm against the enemy king. The Nc5 cannot come to the aid of its monarch. The attack can be repelled, but only by going into a complicated endgame.

27...Qe7; 28.g4 Bg6; 29.f5 Bh7; 30.Ng3 Qe5; 31.Kg2 Rab8; 32.Rab1 f6?! This is a passive move which creates further holes in Black's position. Since all of his chances lay on the queenside, he should have continued with his infiltration of the White position. 32...Rb2; 33.Rxb2 Qxb2; 34.Rb1 Qc2; 35.Kf3 Nb3; 36.Ngf1 f6 would have been appropriate, since in this position the White pieces cannot occupy any of the holes on the kingside. Indeed, Black's advanced pawn can be dangerous, and the Bh7 might eventually enter the game via a4.

33.Nf3! Rb2+; 34.Rxb2 Qxb2+; 35.Re2. This is a much more comfortable position for White. The hole at e6 will be a nice landing site for the Nf3, and the passed pawn is not important. **35...Qb3; 36.Nd4! Qxe3.** 36...Qxc4; 37.Ne6! is good for White.

Black cannot take the knight, because then the bishop at h7 is permanently out of the game. The best continuation would be to seize the open file. 37...Rb8; 38.Nxc5! dxc5; 39.Rd2 Rb3; 40.Qf2! and White has a powerful passed pawn, which cannot be stopped by the Black king since 40...Kf8 would be met by 41.Qf4! **37.Rxe3 Rb8.**

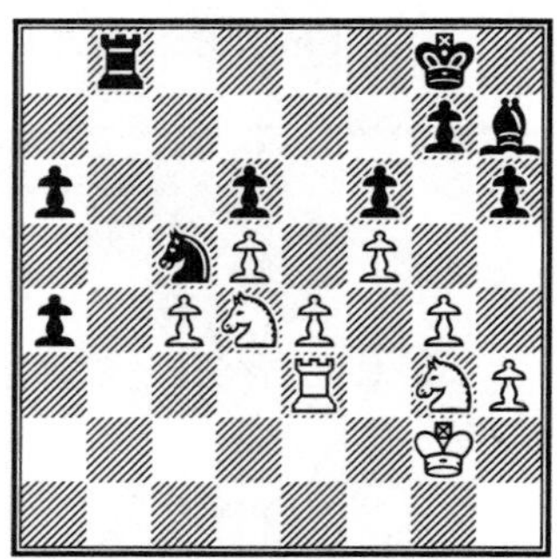

At first sight it seems that Black has all the chances with his open file and passed pawn. But White sees the potential of a passed d-pawn! **38.Rc3 Kf7; 39.Kf3 Rb2; 40.Nge2 Bg8.** Now White, keeping in mind the theme of the previous variations, sees that he can achieve his goal of a passed d-pawn. He notices that the pawn at e4 is not a material consideration in this position. **41.Ne6! Nb3.** Of course Black cannot even think about exchanging at e6 and entombing the bishop. 41...Nxe4; 42.Kxe4 Rxe2+; 43.Kd4 is a winning endgame for White, since the bishop is useless and the king is close enough to pick off the a-pawns even if the rooks leave the board.

42.c5!! dxc5; 43.Nxc5 Nd2+; 44.Kf2 Ke7?! Again Black finds himself unthinkingly following conventional wisdom by moving his king to the center. But he needed to invest more thought in his queenside advantage. 44...Nb1!; 45.Rc4! a3; 46.Ne6! Ke7! (46...a2; 47.Rc7+ Ke8; 48.d6 with a mating net.) 47.Rc7+ Kd6; 48.Rc6+ Ke7; 49.Rxa6 (49.Rc7+ Kd6 draws.) 49...Bxe6; 50.Rxe6+ Kd7; 51.Ra6 a2; 52.Ke1 and the king gets over in time. **45.Ke1 Nb1; 46.Rd3 a3?!** and here Black should have stuck to his plan, instead of belatedly switching to the queenside advance. 46...Kd6! 47.Nxa4 Rb4; 48.Nac3 Nxc3; 49.Nxc3 Bf7; 50.Kd2 g6; 51.Ke3 gxf5; 52.gxf5 Be8 with drawing chances, although the kingside pawns remain very weak. **47.d6+ Kd8.**

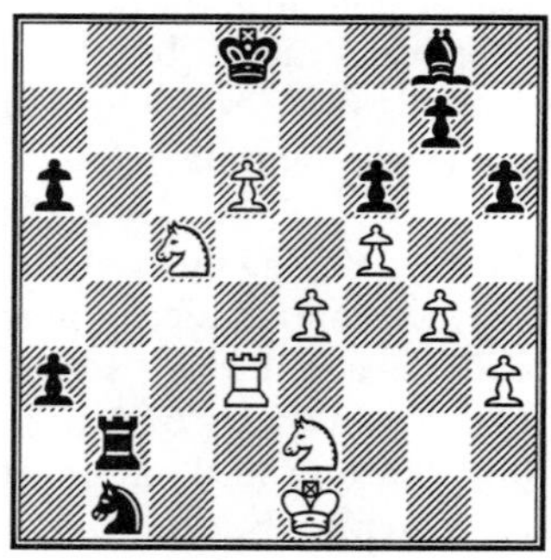

At this point White is concentrating on mate rather than a longwinded endgame. The idea is that a knight at c6 would force the king off the queening square. **48.Nd4! Rb6; 49.Nde6+ Bxe6; 50.fxe6 Rb8; 51.e7+ Ke8; 52.Nxa6. White won.**

(60) ANAND - KAMSKY [C92]

Las Palmas (1st Match Game), 1995

1.e4 e5; 2.Nf3 Nc6; 3.Bb5 a6; 4.Ba4 Nf6; 5.0–0 Be7; 6.Re1 b5; 7.Bb3 d6; 8.c3 0–0; 9.h3 Bb7; 10.d4 Re8; 11.Nbd2 Bf8; 12.a4 h6; 13.Bc2 exd4; 14.cxd4 Nb4; 15.Bb1 g6.

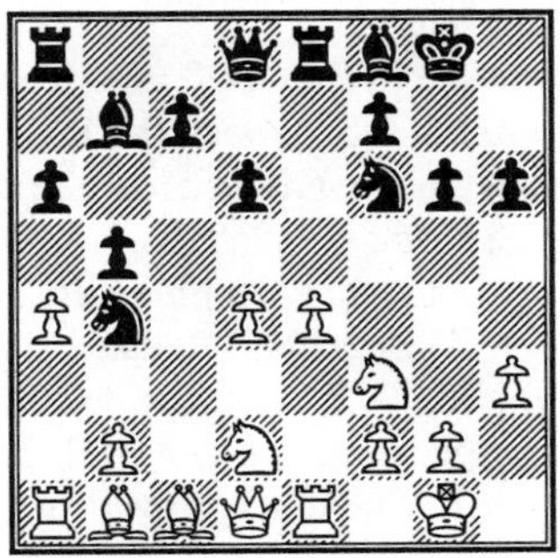

This is the standard continuation of the Zaitsev Variation. Black has tried a few plans here, but only 15...g6 and 15...c5 are seen regularly. It is truly amazing how deeply this position has been analyzed, and yet fresh new ideas are constantly being introduced in high level games. The basic ideas are clear: the battle will take place primarily in the center, though if the central situation is resolved then Black can work on the queenside while White concentrates on the kingside.

The Zaitsev continues to attract many of the best players in the world, but also has a solid following at lower levels, too. The high learning curve of all the complex and subtle variations is a discouragement to some, but for others, the intriguing task of finding new ideas after two dozen or so moves is a tempting challenge. After all, only a single pair of pawns have been removed from the board, so it is not surprising that there remains much to be discovered. 15...c5; 16.d5 Nd7; 17.Ra3 has been a standard continuation for some time now.

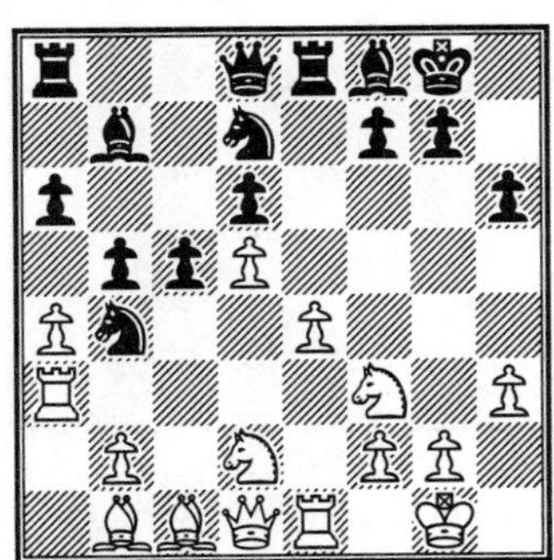

Black has two distinct strategies here. The c-pawn can advance, controlling the d3 and b3 squares while freeing up a nice outpost for a knight. Alternatively, Black can challenge the White center with 18...f5, which was featured in the 1990 World Championship match.

A) 17...c4; 18.Nd4 (18.axb5 axb5; 19.Nd4 Ne5!?; 20.Rxa8! Qxa8; 21.Nxb5 Qa5; 22.Na3 Ba6; 23.Re3 Qc5 was seen in the 7th game of the match, which was eventually drawn.) 18...Qf6; 19.N2f3 Nd3 (19...Nc5; 20.axb5 axb5; 21.Nxb5 Rxa3; 22.Nxa3

Ba6; 23.Re3 Rb8; 24.e5 dxe5; 25.Nxe5 and now Black must play the correct knight to d3: 25...Ncd3! after which Black's position has withstood practical testing and the conclusion is that there is certainly enough compensation for the pawn, Nunn-Psakhis, Hastings 1987.) 20.Bxd3 (20.Rxd3!? cxd3; 21.axb5 might be worth a try.) 20...b4; 21.Bxc4 bxa3; 22.b3 Nc5; 23.Qc2 Qg6; 24.Nh4 Qf6; 25.Nhf3 Qg6; 26.Nh4 Qf6 was drawn in the fifth game of the match.

B) 17...f5 was Karpov's choice in the 1990 match against Kasparov.

B1) 18.exf5 was seen in the 4th game of the Kasparov-Karpov match. 18...Nf6 (18...Bxd5; 19.Ne4 Bf7 was an improvement that Karpov unleashed in game 22.) 19.Ne4 Bxd5; 20.Nxf6+ Qxf6; 21.Bd2 Qxb2; 22.Bxb4 and here Karpov had prepared the retreat 22...Bf7 and was prepared to decline Kasparov's sacrificial 23.Re6 with 23...Qxb4. After 24.Rb3 Qxa4; 25.Bc2 Rad8 Black had equalized.

B2) 18.Rae3 Nf6; 19.Nh2 Qd7 (19...Kh8?!; 20.b3 bxa4; 21.bxa4 c4; 22.Bb2 gave Kasparov good attacking prospects in the 20th game of the match.) 20.exf5 Rxe3; 21.fxe3 Bxd5; 22.Ng4 Be7; 23.e4 Bf7 proved playable for Black in Kasparov-Karpov, Amsterdam 1990.

B3) 18.Nh2; 18...Nf6 (18...c4; 19.Rf3 Re5; 20.Rg3 gives White good attacking chances, Timman-Piket, Amsterdam 1995.) 19.Rf3 Re5; 20.Rxf5 Rxf5; 21.exf5 Bxd5 and here White went wrong with 22.Ne4?! and after 22...Bxe4; 23.Bxe4 d5; 24.Bf3 c4; 25.Re6 Nd3; 26.Be3 d4! Black had a powerful position in Khalifman-Karpov, Reggio Emilia 1991. Kamsky switched to 15...Qd7 in the 9th game. 16.b3 g6; 17.Bb2 Bg7; 18.Qc1 Rac8; 19.Bc3 c5; 20.d5 Qe7; 21.Nf1 and here Black should have played 21...Nd7.

16.Ra3. 16.Nh2 is also possible. **16...Bg7.** 16...Qd7 17.Rae3 c5; 18.dxc5 dxc5; 19.e5 Nfd5; 20.e6 fxe6; 21.Re4 Nf6; 22.Ne5 Qd5; 23.Ng4 Nh7; 24.Ne3 Qd7; 25.Rg4 g5 left the kingside weak, but Black managed to survive in Wolff-Ivanov, United States Championship 1995. **17.e5!**

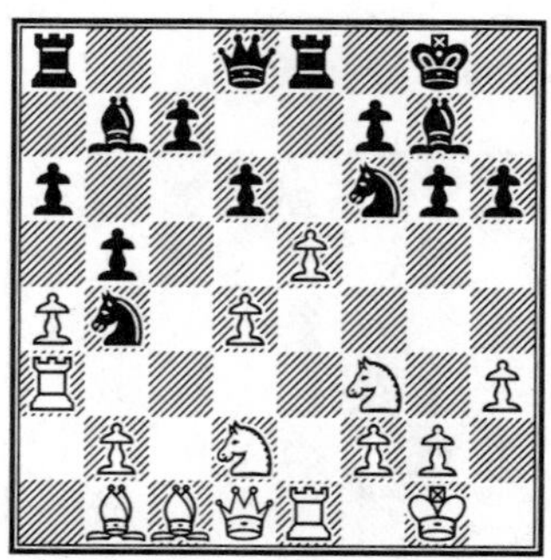

This bold move was introduced in the present game. White had tried a number of other plans, with mixed degree of success. 17.Nh2 c5; 18.d5 and now Black should play 18...c4, since 18...Nd7; 19.Ndf3 Nb6; 20.axb5 axb5; 21.Ng4 Kh7; 22.h4 gave White a strong attack in Khalifman-Gavrilov, St. Petersburg 1994. 17.Rae3 is also consistent with White's plans. **17...dxe5.** 17...Nfd5; 18.Ne4 gives the knight a powerful central post which will assist a future kingside attack. **18.dxe5 Nh5.** Unfortunately, there is no better square for the knight: 18...Nh7; 19.Qb3 c5 allows a simple attack based on the pin on the f-pawn: 20.Bxg6 Bd5; 21.Bxh7+ Kxh7; 22.Qc3 Na2; 23.Rxa2 Bxa2; 24.axb5 axb5; 25.Qxc5 gives White two pawns for the exchange and

Black's king is still weak.

19.axb5 axb5; 20.Qb3 c5; 21.Ne4. 21.Rxa8 Qxa8; 22.e6?! Bd5; 23.exf7+ Kxf7 is better for Black, according to Ftacnik. **21...Bxe5; 22.Nxc5!** This is an improvement over 22.Bxh6 Bd5; 23.Qe3 Bxb2; 24.Rxa8 where Black must recapture with the queen, or else face the following disaster: 24...Bxa8; 25.Qxc5 Nd3; 26.Bxd3 Qxd3; 27.Nf6+ Nxf6; 28.Rxe8+ Kh7; 29.Ng5+ Kxh6; 30.Rh8+ and Black resigned in Blees-Edvardsson, Hafnarfjordur 1995. 22.Rxa8 should, in this case, be captured by the bishop: 22...Bxa8; 23.Nxc5 Bxf3; 24.Qxb4 Bc6; 25.Bxh6 and White has the advantage.

22...Bxf3; 23.Qxf3 Rc8; 24.Ne4! White is building a strong attack against the weak Black kingside. **24...Kg7; 25.Rd1 Qe7; 26.Be3 Red8.** 26...Bxb2 fails to 27.Ra7 Rc7; 28.Bc5 and White grabs the knight at b4. **27.Ra7 Qe6.** 27...Rxd1+ 28.Qxd1 Rd8; 29.Qf3 Qe6; 30.Nc5 is also better for White. **28.Nc5.** In time pressure, White misses 28.Rxd8! Rxd8; 29.g4 Anand recommends 29.Nc5 29...Nf4 30.Bxf4 Bxf4; 31.Qxf4 Rd1+; 32.Kg2 Rxb1; 33.Nd6! Qd5+; 34.f3 Rxb2+; 35.Kg3+- Nd3; 36.Ne8+ was pointed out by Anand. Black cannot survive.

28...Rxd1+; 29.Qxd1 Qd5?! Putting the queen at d6 would have been somewhat stronger. **30.Qg4!** White has the advantage here, because of the tactical threats on the kingside, where both the f-pawn and g-pawn are pinned. **30...Rc7.** 30...Rxc5?? loses instantly to 31.Qxg6+ Kf8; 32.Bxc5+. **31.Rxc7 Bxc7.**

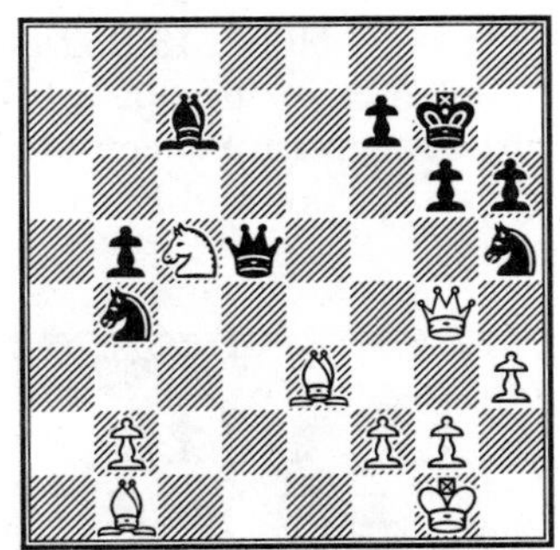

32.g3. 32.Bd4+ might have been more efficient, for example 32...Kf8 (32...Kg8; 33.Bxg6! fxg6; 34.Qxg6+ Kf8; 35.Ne6+ Ke7; 36.Nxc7! Qxd4; 37.Qe8+ Kf6; 38.Qh8+ Ng7 and now Ftacnik gives 39.Qxg7+! Kxg7; 40.Ne6+ Kf6; 41.Nxd4 and White wins easily.) 33.Bxg6! fxg6; 34.Ne6+ Kf7; 35.Nxc7 Qc6; 36.Qf3+ Qxf3; 37.gxf3 and the pawn at b5 falls. **32...Qc4.** White lost on time here, but would have had the better position after **33.Bd4+.** Exchanging queens sould also have been good, with White enjoying the bishop pair. 33...Nf6; 34.Bxg6! Be5 (34...fxg6; 35.Qd7+ Qf7; 36.Ne6+ Kg8; 37.Qxf7+ Kxf7; 38.Nxc7 as given by Yusupov.) 35.Bxe5 Qxg4; 36.hxg4 Kxg6; 37.f3 with a much better endgame for White according to Yusupov.

(61) TIMMAN - KASPAROV [C93]

Hilversum, 1st match game, 1985

1.e4 e5; 2.Nf3 Nc6; 3.Bb5 a6; 4.Ba4 Nf6; 5.0–0 Be7; 6.Re1 b5; 7.Bb3 d6; 8.c3 0–0; 9.h3 Bb7; 10.d4 Re8; 11.Nbd2 Bf8; 12.a3 h6.

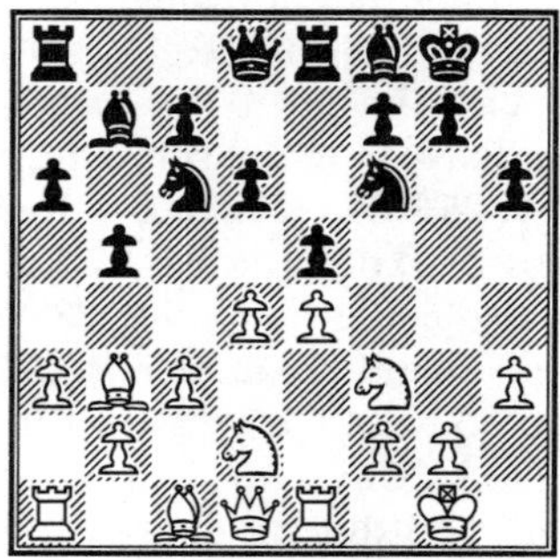

This is a form of the Smyslov Defense which also involves the moves typical of the Zaitsev Variation. With the following two moves, Black also employs the knight maneuver which characterizes the Breyer Variation! You can see why we call this the Hybrid Variation. **13.Bc2 Nb8; 14.b4 Nbd7; 15.Bb2 g6.** A typical position in the Zaitsev, Smyslov, and Breyer defenses to the Spanish Inquisition. White has two options–quiet play with 16.Qb1 or aggressive queenside action. **16.c4!?** Timman has played this bold line against both Karpov and Kasparov. **16...exd4; 17.cxb5 axb5; 18.Nxd4 c6.**

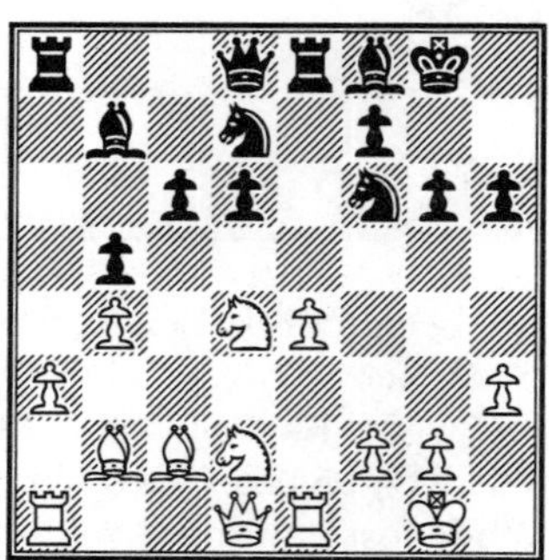

In this position, White aims at the targets on the queenside, and therefore the best move is probably 19.Bd3, but that hadn't been discovered yet. **19.a4 bxa4; 20.Bxa4 Qb6.** Kasparov's innovation, prepared for this game. Black's plan is illustrated nicely by the present game. He will aim for the liberating advance d6-d5 when his pieces will be better placed than their White counterparts. **21.b5?!** With this move White hopes to highlight the weakness at d6, but the plan fails and in the third game of the match Timman improved with 21.Nc2 which became the standard move in 1986.

21...cxb5; 22.Bxb5 d5! This move eliminates Black's only weakness and puts strong pressure on the center. White already suffers from a pin on the b-file and his pieces do not seem to be doing anything. **23.Rxa8 Bxa8; 24.Qa4 Nc5!** More pressure on the center. And in addition, Black has taken the initiative. **25.Qc2 Rb8.** Because of the pin, this move allows the rook to escape without losing time, because sooner or later White will have to waste a move to break it.

26.exd5 Nxd5. A strange sight–most of the pieces remain on the board but the queenside pawns have been swept clear. One would assume that the position is equal, but in fact Black still holds a slight initiative. **27.Nc4?! Qc7; 28.Ne5?!** The final chance for equality lie in 28.Re8, exchanging off the dangerous Black rook. But now Kasparov was able to develop a plan to exploit his spatial advantage, based on control of the b-file and the h8-a1 diagonal. **28...Bg7!; 29.Nec6.** 29.Bc6? would have met with an impressive refutation: 29...Bxe5!; 30.Qxc5 Rxb2; 31.Qxd5 Bxd4; 32.Re8+ Kh7; 33.Qxd4 Rb1+. **29...Bxc6; 30.Bxc6 Nf4.**

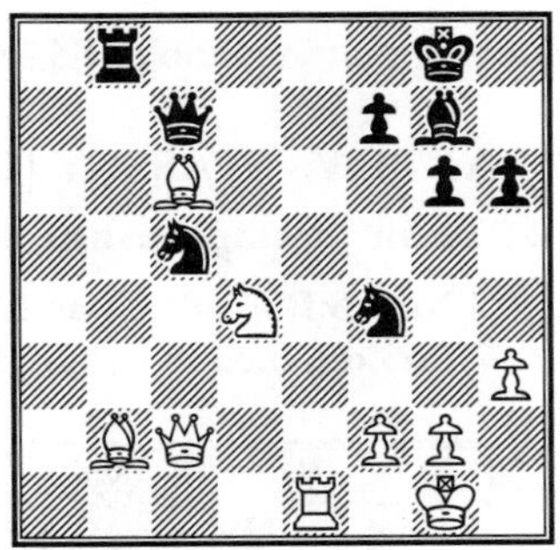

Black's control of the b- and c-files, combined with the pin on the diagonal and more active knights gives him a decisive advantage! **31.Bb5.** Timman tries to cut off the b-file, establish his own pin on the c-file, and free his game with Rc1. Black would just love to get his queen onto the a8-h1 diagonal with deadly threats at g2. This is easily done! 31.Re8+ Rxe8; 32.Bxe8 Nce6 exploits the pin at d4, with a little help from the threatened fork at e2. 33.Qxc7 Nxc7; 34.Bd7 Bxd4; 35.Bxd4 Ne2+; 31.Qxc5 Rxb2; 32.Nb5 Qa5; 33.Qe3 meets with quiet refutation: 33...Kh7!

31...Rxb5!; 32.Nxb5 Qc6; 33.f3 Qxb5. and Black has a decisive material advantage. But with the symmetrical pawn structure the win still requires the creation of an effective plan. It is easy to see that a knight planted at g3 would be nice, but it needs support. **34.Bxg7 Kxg7; 35.Qc3+ Kg8; 36.Qe5 Nfe6; 37.Ra1 Qb7.** First Black organizes his defense. The next step is to advance the h-pawn so that the eventual infiltration of the knight to g3 can be accomplished. **38.Qd6 h5; 39.Kh1 Kh7; 40.Rc1 Qa7; 41.Rb1 Ng7; 42.Rb8 Nce6; 43.Qe5 Nd4; 44.Rb1 h4.** Watching this game I remember being impressed by the ease with which the World Champion achieved his objectives. The maneuvering of the knights makes sense only in hindsight. **45.Qb8 Qe7; 46.Qb4 Qf6; 47.Qf8 Ne2; 48.Rd1 Nf5; 49.Qb8 Ne3; 50.Qd8 Qf4.** Black has properly declined all offers to exchange queens–it is mate he is after! **51.Re1.**

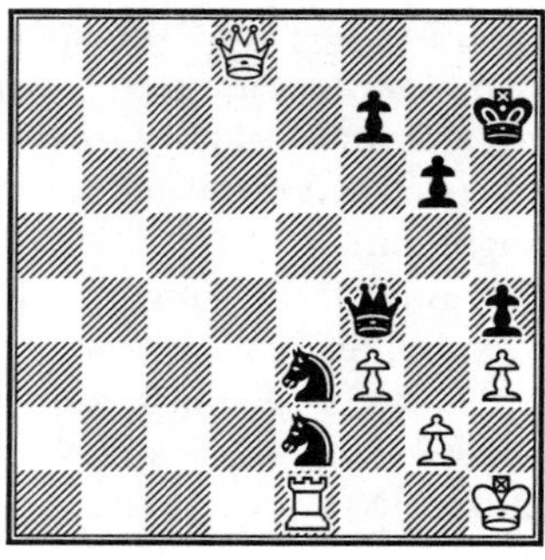

51...Nf1! And Timman, seeing that inevitable Nf1–g3-e2-f2, gave up. **Black won.**

(62) KARPOV - SPASSKY [C94]

Soviet Team Championship, 1973

1.e4 e5; 2.Nf3 Nc6; 3.Bb5 a6; 4.Ba4 Nf6; 5.0–0 Be7; 6.Re1 b5; 7.Bb3 d6; 8.c3 0–0; 9.h3 Nb8; 10.d3.

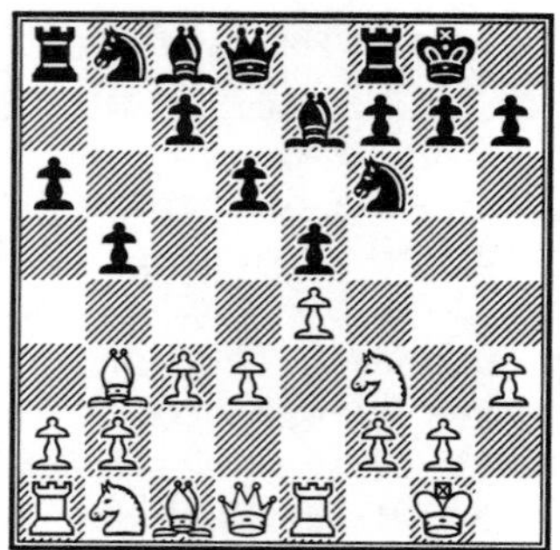

For a long time Karpov preferred this quiet move to the standard 10.d4. It leads to quite different position, since Black cannot mount a counterattack using a pawn at d4 as a target. **10...Bb7; 11.Nbd2 Nbd7; 12.Nf1.** This move is typical of the Closed Spanish in general, but is particularly common in the Breyer. White pivots the knight to the kingside where it can leap from g3 to f5 and aim right at the heart of the enemy camp.

12...Re8; 13.Ng3 Nc5; 14.Bc2 Bf8. These are the normal moves in the position. White want to target the enemy king eventually, but first must invest some time insuring that Black does not obtain significant counterplay on the queenside.

15.b4 Ncd7; 16.d4 h6; 17.Bd2 Nb6; 18.Bd3 g6?! Too passive. Black should stake a claim on the queenside before it is too late and the best way of doing so would be to aim for c7-c7 with a preparatory Rc8. That plan is not without risk, but it is better than treading water. **19.Qc2 Nfd7; 20.Rad1.** Karpov carefully completes his mobilization before launching his attack. More importantly, he recognized the potential usefulness of this rook on the d-file, despite the fact that the file is almost filled with pieces! **20...Bg7.**

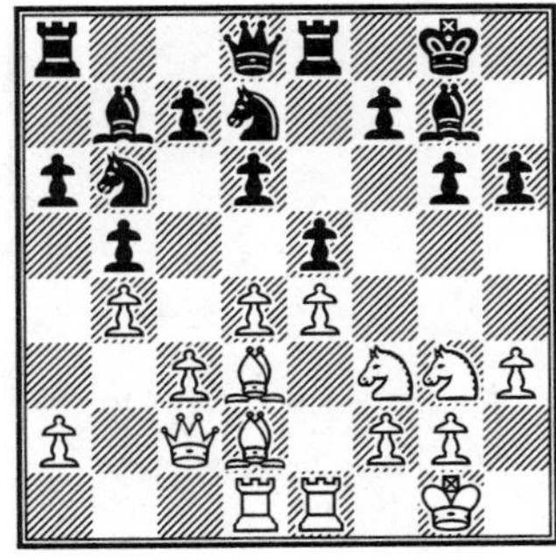

Now Karpov must create his plan. The center is still filled with tension. The Rd1 has distant "man-on-man" coverage against the Black queen. **21.dxe5!** A well-timed exchange. Black should now recapture with the knight, even though after 22.Nxe5 Bxe5; 23.f4 White will have a strong central position. **21...dxe5?!; 22.c4!** This forces the weakening of Black's queenside pawn structure. **22...bxc4; 23.Bxc4 Qe7?!** Spassky wants to play c7-c5 as soon as possible, eliminating his weak pawn. But he should have taken the opportunity to exchange his knight for White's powerful light-squared bishop.

24.Bb3! c5; 25.a4! Karpov already has the idea of a plan in which he will sacrifice the exchange by allowing Black to play Bb7-c6-a4 after the Bb3 is chased back to a2. This plan is based on an evaluation of the Re1 as relatively useless. **25...c4.** 25...cxb4; 26.a5 Rac8; 27.Qa2 Na8; 28.Bxb4! is a decisive blow. **26.Ba2 Bc6.**

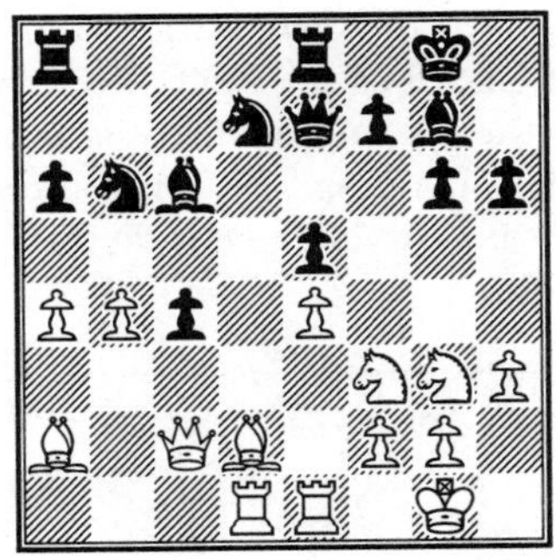

27.a5! Ba4; 28.Qc1 Nc8; 29.Bxh6! The superior activity of White's forces which results from the sacrifice of the exchange will enable him to attack on the kingside. **29...Bxd1; 30.Rxd1 Nd6?!** Understandably, Black wants to get this knight into a position to help with the defense of the king. Best was 30...Ra7, though that would have parted with the c-pawn after 31.Bxg7 Kxg7; 32.Qxc4. **31.Bxg7 Kxg7.**

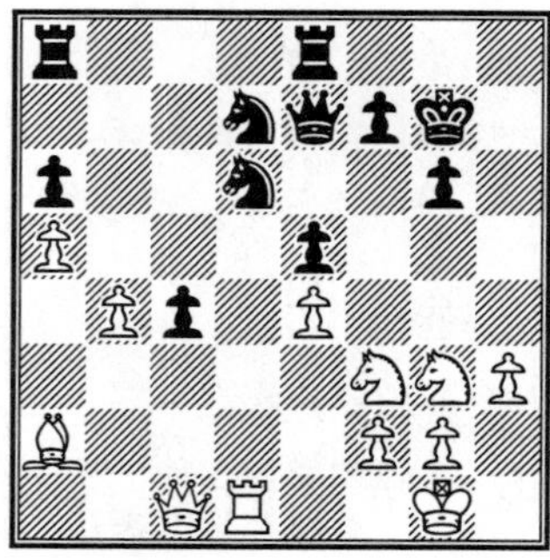

White now observes that the horses are guarded only by the queen, which can be deflected. **32.Qg5!** with the amusing point that 32...Qxg5; 33.Nxg5 leaves Black with no way to stop the loss of one of the knights, while 32...Nf6?? drops the queen to 33.Nf5+. **32...f6; 33.Qg4,** maintaining the threat of Nf5+. **33...Kh7; 34.Nh4** and Black resigned rather than invite 34...Rg8; 35.Bxc4! or 34...Nf8 35.Nxg6! Nxg6; 36.Qh5+ Kg7; 37.Rxd6! and the thematic Nf5+ follows. The entire plan was based on play along the d-file which Karpov anticipated with 20.Rad1! **White won.**

(63) UNZICKER - TAL [C95]

Hamburg (W. Germany vs. USSR), 1960

1.e4 e5; 2.Nf3 Nc6; 3.Bb5 a6; 4.Ba4 Nf6; 5.0-0 Be7; 6.Re1 b5; 7.Bb3 0-0. Black should play 7...d6 if the Breyer is the goal, because against this move Kasparov has demonstrated the power of 8.a4! **8.c3 d6; 9.h3.** White plays this to keep the enemy bishop away from g4, when the pin on the knight is annoying. Now Black has many different strategies, including combining ...Bb7 and ...Re8, repositioning minor pieces with ...Nd7 and ...Bf6, or playing on the queenside with ...Na5. Tal chooses another, very respectable path. **9...Nb8.**

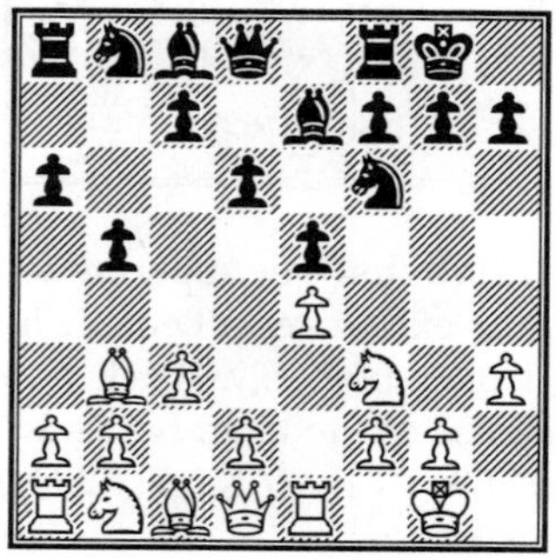

The Breyer Variation, which has held up well throughout the century. **10.d4 Nbd7; 11.Nbd2 Bb7; 12.Bc2 Re8; 13.Nf1 Bf8; 14.Ng3 g6; 15.b3.** An old fashioned line. Now 15.Bg5 and 15.a4 are preferred. **15...Bg7; 16.d5 Nb6; 17.Qe2?** A serious error which allows Tal to undermine White's center. The best plan is to play Be3, in order to put pressure on the dark squares and bring the other rook to a more active position. **17...c6; 18.c4 cxd5; 19.cxd5.**

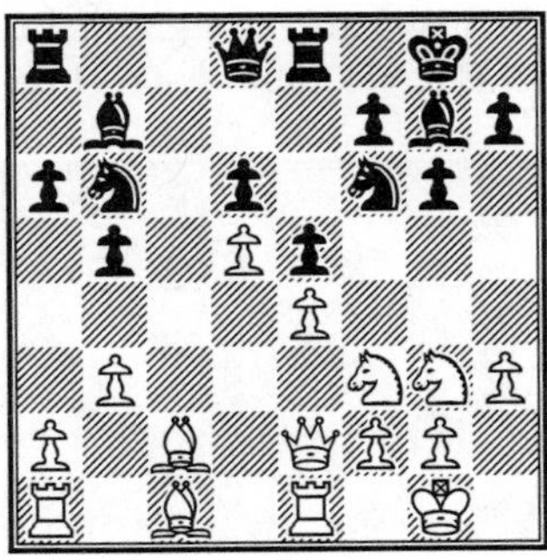

Time for Tal to create some fireworks. White's center looks very strong, but it crumbles quickly. **19...Nfxd5; 20.exd5 e4.** The bishop on g7 now springs to life. **21.Nxe4 Bxa1; 22.Bg5 f6; 23.Be3.** Some people never learn. Over three decades later, White tried to improve with 23.Bh4 but suffered a similar fate after 23...Bxd5; 24.Rxa1 Bxe4; 25.Bxe4 d5 and Black, in another game played in Germany, had a big advantage. **23...Nxd5; 24.Rxa1 Nxe3; 25.Qxe3 Bxe4; 26.Bxe4 d5.**

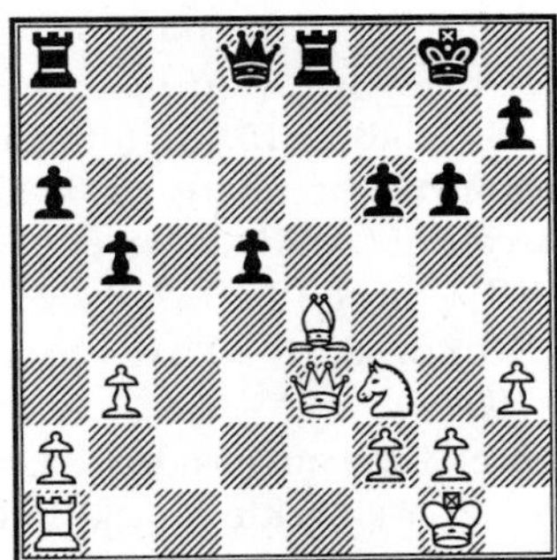

White resigned, since the bishop is lost. Note that Rd1 doesn't help because Black can capture the bishop with the rook anyway, with a decisive advantage. **Black won.**

(64) VERLINSKY - PANOV [C99]

Moscow Championship, 1945

1.e4 e5; 2.Nf3 Nc6; 3.Bb5 a6; 4.Ba4 Nf6; 5.0-0 Be7; 6.Re1 b5; 7.Bb3 d6; 8.c3 Na5; 9.Bc2 c5; 10.h3 0-0; 11.d4 Qc7; 12.Nbd2 Bb7.

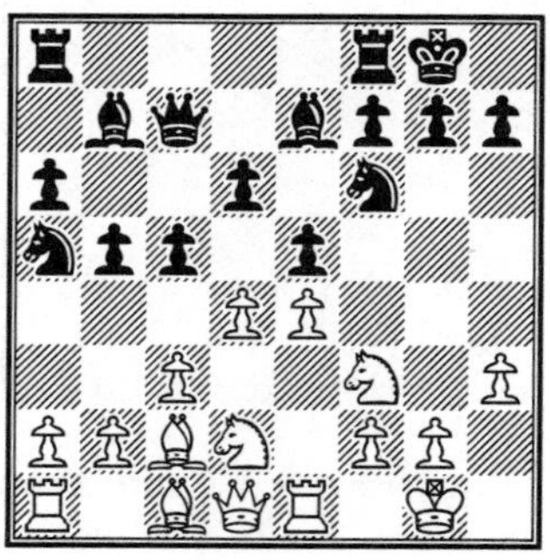

This is a basic position of the Panov's Variation, a popular line in the Chigorin Defense that was worked out in the 1940s, though it was originally seen in Cohn-Johner, Vienna 1908. Actually, Panov's plan entails a capture by Black at d4, which can be played on this move or later on, as in the present game. 12...Kh8 is an example of Mikhail Chigorin's handling of the position. 13.Nf1 (13.b4! cxb4; 14.cxb4 Nc6; 15.a3 exd4; 16.Bb2 left Black with too many weaknesses in Smyslov-Filip,. Amsterdam 1956.) 13...Ng8; 14.Ne3 Be6; 15.Nf5 Bf6; 16.d5 Bd7; 17.g4 g6 and Black had no worries in Duras-Chigorin, Nurenberg 1906. 12...cxd4; 13.cxd4 Bb7 is the more accurate move order, because it avoids a variety of options which are otherwise available to White at move 13 against 12...Bb7. 14.d5 Bc8; 15.Nf1 Bd7; 16.N3h2 Rfc8; 17.Bd3 Nb7; 18.b4 a5; 19.Bd2 axb4; 20.Bxb4 brought about a messy position in Bronstein-Keres, Moscow 1951.

In general, the open nature of the queenside means that White will not be able to devote sufficient resources to a kingside attack, but the weak pawn at b5 will require constant attention. **13.Nf1.** White could choose instead advance the d-pawn, sidestepping the possibility of the Panov, but it is a harmless move. 13.d5 Bc8 and it will be harder for White to open up the game and attack the Black king.

13...cxd4; 14.cxd4 Rac8; 15.Bd3. 15.Bb1 is a common alternative, tucking away the bishop on a safer square. Still, experience has shown that Black can equalize with a standard maneuver of deploying both knights on the queenside. 15...Nd7 (15...d5 is an interesting move, though it is now considered somewhat suspect. 16.exd5! exd4; 17.Bg5 h6; 18.Bxh6!! is a tremendous sacrifice worked out by the Czech theoretician Thelen. Here is one sample line: 18...gxh6; 19.Qd2 Rfd8; 20.Qxh6 Rxd5; 21.Re4! and Black cannot survive.) 16.Ne3 exd4; 17.Nxd4 g6; 18.a4 b4; 19.Ba2 Nf6; 20.Bd2 Qb6; 21.Nef5 gxf5; 22.Nxf5 Qd8; 23.Bxb4 Nc6; 24.e5 Nxb4; 25.exf6 Bxf6; 26.Qg4+ Kh8; 27.Qxb4 Rc5; 28.Qxb7 Rxf5; 29.Qxa6 Bd4 and Black has the initiative and attacking chances which compensate for the pawns, Unzicker-Keres, Hamburg 1956.

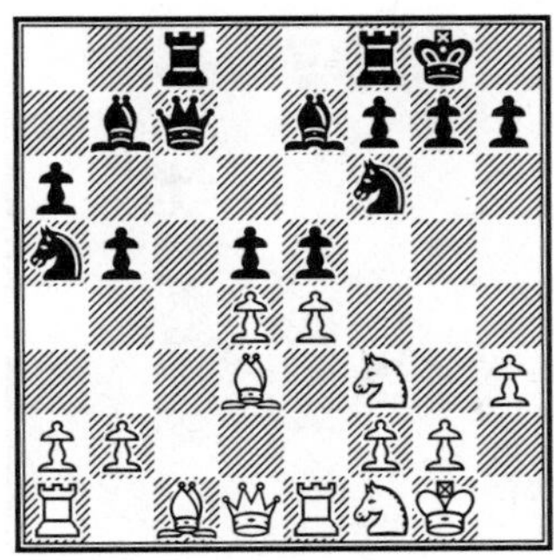

15...d5. 15...Nd7 is the more cautious approach. 16.Ne3 exd4; 17.Nxd4 Bf6; 18.Ndf5 g6; 19.Nh6+ Kh8; 20.Rb1 Bg7; 21.Nhg4 h5; 22.Nh2 Nc5; 23.Nd5 Bxd5; 24.exd5 Nxd3; 25.Qxd3 Qc2 gave Black sufficient counterplay in Smyslov-Keres, Yugoslavia 1959.

15...Nc6; 16.Ne3 Rfe8; 17.Nf5 Bf8; 18.Bg5 Nd7; 19.Rc1 Qb8; 20.Bb1 Nxd4; 21.N3xd4 Rxc1; 22.Bxc1 exd4 encouraged Bobby Fischer to invest a piece in an attack: 23.Nh6+ gxh6; 24.Qg4+ Kh8; 25.Qxd7 Bd5; 26.Qf5 Re5; 27.Qf3 f5; 28.Bf4 Re8; 29.Qh5 Bxe4; 30.f3 Bc6; 31.Rc1 Bd7; 32.Bxh6 Re6; 33.Bxf8 Qxf8; 34.Qh4 Qf6; 35.Qxf6+ Rxf6; 36.Kf2 and despite being a pawn down, White has better chances in the endgame because Black's pawns are so weak. 36...Kg7; 37.Rc7 Rf7; 38.Ke2 f4; 39.Ra7 Kf6; 40.Rxa6 and White went on to win in Fischer-Keres, Zurich 1959.

16.exd5. Now most of the attention is concentrated on the other capture. 16.dxe5 Nxe4; 17.Ng3! f5 (17...Rfd8 did not work out well for Panov: 18.Qe2 Bb4; 19.Rf1 Qc6; 20.Ng5 Nxg5; 21.Bxg5 Re8; 22.Qg4 Bf8; 23.Rac1 Qb6; 24.Nh5 Rxc1; 25.Rxc1 Qe6; 26.Bf5 Qxe5; 27.Nf6+ Kh8; 28.f4 Qe2; 29.Nxe8 Qxe8; 30.Qh4 h6; 31.Re1 Qc6; 32.Be7 Bc8; 33.Bxc8 Qxc8; 34.Bxf8 Qxf8; 35.Qe7 Kg8; 36.Qd7 Qc5+; 37.Kh2 Nc4; 38.Re8+ Kh7; 39.Qf5+ and Black resigned in Bronstein-Panov, Moscow City Championship 1946.) 18.exf6 Bxf6; 19.Nxe4 (19.Nf5?! Nc4; 20.Re2 allowed Panov to use tactics to gain the advantage with 20...Nxb2!; 21.Bxb2 Bxb2; 22.Nh6+ gxh6; 23.Rxb2 Qg7 and Black's attack proved successful in Ravinsky-Panov, Moscow 1947.) 19...dxe4; 20.Bxe4 Rfd8; 21.Qe2 Re8; 22.Nd2 Qd7; 23.Qf1 Nc6; 24.Nb3 Nd4; 25.Bxb7 Qxb7; 26.Nxd4 Bxd4 was drawn in Geller-Keres, Amsterdam 1956.

16...e4! A key move, which destroys the coordination of White's pieces. **17.Bxe4 Nxe4; 18.Rxe4 Bxd5; 19.Re1 Qb7; 20.Bf4.** 20.Ne3 Bxf3; 21.Qxf3 Qxf3; 22.gxf3 Nc6; 23.Nd5! Bh4! and the weakness of the White pawns gave Black the advantage in Unzicker-Euwe, Germany vs. Holland Match 1951. **20...Rfd8; 21.N1d2 Bb4!** A minor but annoying pin. **22.Re3 f6; 23.b3 Ba3; 24.Qe2 Nc6.**

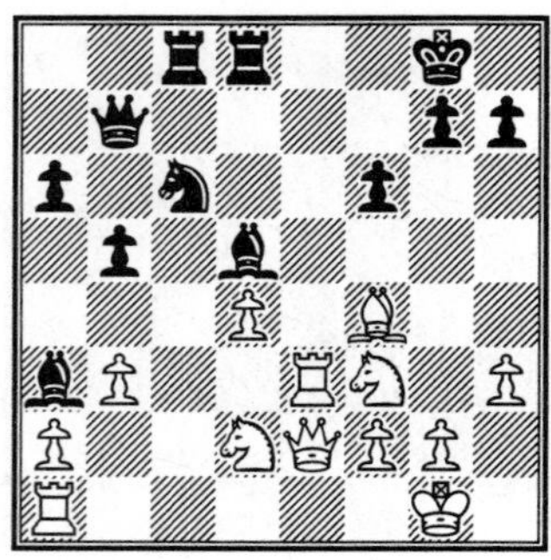

Black has the advantage. White not only has an isolated pawn, blockaded by the bishop at d5, but also has very little room to maneuver. **25.Ne4 Qb6; 26.Rd1 Bf7; 27.Qd2 Bb4; 28.Qb2 Qa5; 29.Re2 h6; 30.Bd2 Qb6; 31.Bxb4 Nxb4; 32.Red2 Nd5; 33.Nc5 Bh5; 34.Rd3.** A poor move, but there was no real hope of salvation. **34...Nf4; 35.g4.0** 35.Re3 loses instantly to 35...Rxc5! **35...Nxh3+; 36.Kh2 Bxg4; 37.Re1 Qd6+; 38.Kh1 Rxc5. Black won.**

5. THE SEMI-OPEN GAMES

The Semi-Open Games is a broad category covering all responses to 1.e4 except for 1...e5. In professional chess, the Semi-Open Games are generally preferred, because they relieve the symmetry earlier in the game and lead to more open central pawn formations.

The most popular Semi-Open Games are the **Sicilian Defenses** which begin 1.e4 c5. Most of the recent World Champions have relied heavily on one or more of the major variations of the Sicilian. Bobby Fischer and Garry Kasparov use it almost exclusively, and all the leading contenders for the crown use it regularly. The play tends to be very sharp, with White launching a full-scale attack on Black's king. Black has chances for an assault on White's king, especially when Black is castled on the kingside while White's monarch is stationed on the queenside. The Sicilian Defense has one of the smallest ratios of draws of all openings, and is very useful in must-win situations.

The next most important opening in this group is the **French Defense** (1.e4 e6). Black prepares ...d5 and is willing to accept a "bad bishop" at c8 for much of the game as the price of central stability. The French is not for everyone, because it requires Black to maneuver in limited space for a long time, but it is an effective weapon for those who like to counter-attack. No World Champion since Petrosian has used it regularly, but many of the top contenders use it, and among Grandmasters in general there are many Francophiles.

The **Caro-Kann Defense** supports ...d5 in a different way. After 1.e4, Black plays 1...c6. The point is that after an inevitable ...d5, the Black bishop at c8 can get into the game. This is quite different from the situation in the French, where a pawn at e6 is in the way. There is a drawback, however, in that advancing the c-pawn to c6 does not directly lead to easier development. White will be able to mobilize more quickly and usually enjoys an advantage in space. Endgames are typical in the Caro-Kann, and therefore the opening appeals to endgame specialists.

The reputation of the **Modern Defenses**, which involve an early fianchetto against 1.e4 with ...g6 on the first or second move, has been rising for many years, though it has now stabilized just short of full respectability. White is allowed to establish the ideal pawn center with 2.d4, and Black will often have difficulty equalizing. Nevertheless, the serpent at g7 has a long range, and the powerful bishop can support many tactical operations in the center and on the queenside. The very best players in the world do not often use a Modern Defense in important games, but they do face it frequently in top competitions. A more conservative approach is the Pirc Defense, where after 1.e4 d6 2.d4 Nf6 White is usually going to play 3.Nc3, after which 3...g6 leads to positions where Black's eventual central counterplay will not have to worry about White advancing a pawn to c3 in support of the center, because the knight sits at that square.

The **Alekhine Defense** offers White the opportunity to gain space and time after 1.e4 Nf6; 2.e5. After 2...Nd5 White can sooner or later play c4, attacking the knight once again. The idea for Black is that White's center can easily be overextended. Former United States Champion Lev Alburt played the Alekhine almost exclusively, but few top players use it as anything but a surprise weapon now.

The only other significant Semi-Open Game is the **Scandinavian Defense** (1.e4 d5). After White captures at d5 Black can either recapture with the queen or play ...Nf6 and pick up the pawn later. In either case White enjoys an advantage in space, but without good technique this advantage can slip away quickly.

SICILIAN DEFENSES

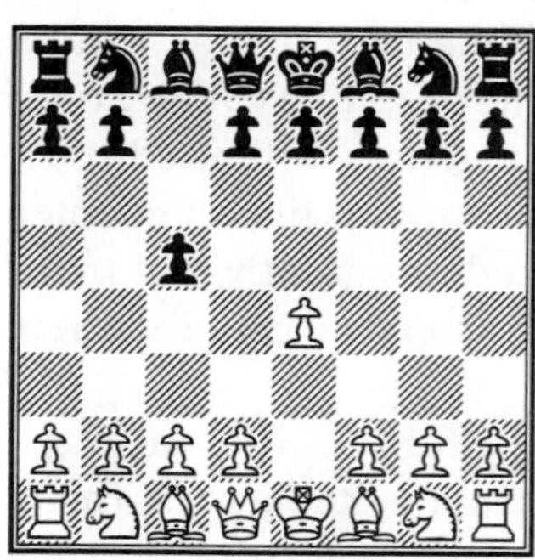

1.e4 c5

There are many different Sicilian Defenses, and they have very different histories and personalities. Some date back to the 18th century, while others have been developed only in the 1990s. Most "normal" Sicilians continue 2.Nf3 and Black now chooses between three moves: 2...d6, 2...e6 and 2...Nc6. Although these can lead to quite a variety of positions, there are also many places where the lines intersect, and calculating transpositional possibilities is a required skill if you want to play either side of the Sicilian.

You will meet many different Sicilians in the pages that follow, but let's get acquainted with a few of the most important variations.

The dangerous Dragon Variation is the head of a constellation of related lines where Black fianchettoes the bishop at g7. Usually it is reached via 2...d6; 3.d4 cxd4; 4.Nxd4 Nf6; 5.Nc3 g6. White normally castles queenside and launches a pawnstorm on the kingside, while Black aims everything at the White king. The Dragon attacks frequently on the chessboards of major tournaments, and a lot of theory has been accumulated. Dragoneers are known for spending many hours in their caves, preparing new traps.

The notorious Najdorf Variation sees Black secure the b5 square by stationing a pawn at a6, both to keep out enemy knights and also to prepare for a queenside attack with ...b5. After 2...d6; 3.d4 cxd4; 4.Nxd4 Nf6; 5.Nc3 a6 White has many options, but none have been effective enough to discourage top players from using it. It is in the repertoires of many leading players and is the backbone of World Champion Garry Kasparov's repertoire.

The Classical Variation is reached by two paths 2...d6; 3.d4 cxd4; 4.Nxd4 Nf6; 5.Nc3 Nc6 or 2...Nc6; 3.d4 cxd4; 4.Nxd4 Nf6; 5.Nc3 d6. This is most directly confronted by 6.Bg5, the Richter-Rauzer Attack, where Black usually replies 6...e6 so that if White captures at f6, Black can recapture with the queen. For some reason, this opening is almost exclusively seen in top-level competition. It leads to longer, more positional struggles than the Najdorf or Dragon. White can also try 6.Bc4, which leads to the Sozin Variation, part of the Scheveningen complex we'll turn to next.

The Scheveningen Variation, named for a town in Holland, combines ...e6 with ...d6, instead of the ...Nc6/...d6 combination of the Classical. The pawn at e6 can serve as target for White's tactical operations. Sacrifices of a knight or bishop on that square are almost routine. The most exciting lines start with 6.Bc4 and are known as the Sozin Variation. Opposite wing castling can lead to very double-edged games. There are other plans. White can continue with simple development or go for broke on the kingside with the dangerous Keres Attack, which begins 2...d6; 3.d4 cxd4; 4.Nxd4 Nf6; 5.Nc3 e6; 6.g4. Often Black plays this Sicilian defensively, trying to create impregnable barriers. A hedgehog position is often the result.

Black does not have to play an early ...d6 at all. The Kan Variation 2...e6 3.d4 cxd4; 4.Nxd4 a6 has long been popular, with the pawns serving to patrol the important squares at b5, d5 and f5. The play can transpose to the Najdorf or Scheveningen, but usually either ends up in a hedgehog or follows its own path. The weaknesses of the dark squares at b6 and d6 is indisputable, but does not deter players from adopting the Black side.

Finally, we have the structurally odd variations with an early ...e5, most prominently, the Lasker-Pelikan Variation. After 2...Nc6; 3.d4 cxd4; 4.Nxd4 Nf6; 5.Nc3 e5 there is a glaring hole at d5, and the battle will be waged primarily on the light squares. White has an advantage in space, but Black will be able to create counterplay on the light squares with ...b5 and ...f5. The variation has recently become fully respectable and has a following among many top players. The most persistent advocate of the Black side has been

Evgeny Sveshnikov, a passionate defender of the variation which now bears his name.

We'll start with some of the peripheral variations and work our way to the core of the Sicilian repertoire. You can observe the almost infinite variety offered by the Sicilian.

MCDONNELL ATTACK

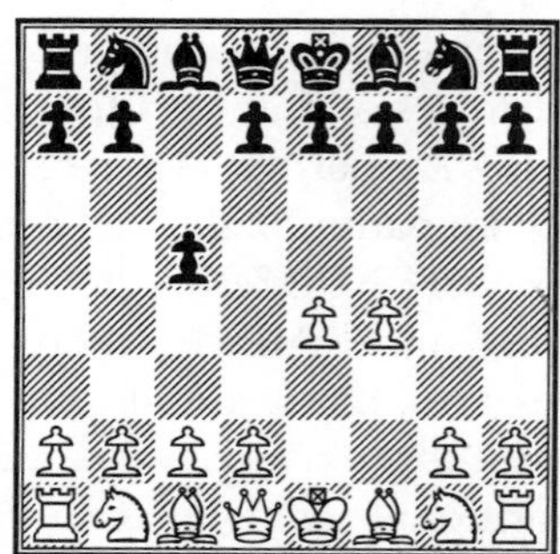

1.e4 c5
2.f4

The **McDonnell Attack** has a long history, dating back to the classic match between McDonnell and De La Bourdonnais in 1834, but it wasn't until the 1980s that it became a serious opening, when it was integrated into the Grand Prix Attack which dominated the British chess scene for some time. The idea is to avoid any direct confrontation with Black's pawn at c5, choosing instead to build an attack on the f-file, where an advance to f5 can challenge a Black pawn at e6 or g6. After racking up a tremendous score for White in the early 1980s, players of the Black side eventually discovered that the "Sicilian Break" with 2...d5 was not only playable, but would in fact insure at least equality. For this reason the McDonnell Attack has fallen from favor and the Grand Prix positions are reached iafter 2.Nc3 followed by 3.f4.

(65) MCDONNELL - DE LA BOURDONNAIS [B21]
London (14th Match Game) (14), 1834

1.e4 c5; 2.f4 e6. 2...d5! the Tal Gambit, is now considered a virtual refutation of the line. Black is able to develop quickly. 3.exd5 Nf6; 4.Bb5+ Nbd7 (4...Bd7; 5.Bxd7+ Qxd7; 6.c4 e6; 7.Qe2 Be7; 8.dxe6 Qxe6; 9.Qxe6 fxe6; 10.Nf3 Nc6 and Black's piece play compensated for the pawn in Smit-Colias, USA 1990.) 5.c4 a6.

A) 6.Bxd7+ Bxd7; 7.Nf3 (7.Nc3 e6; 8.Qe2 Be7; 9.dxe6 Bxe6; 10.Nf3 0–0 was fine for Black in Lazzeri-Yermolinsky, U.S. Open 1996.) 7...e6; 8.Qe2 Be7; 9.dxe6 Bxe6; 10.0–0 0–0; 11.Nc3 Re8; 12.Ne5 Nd7; 13.Kh1 Nxe5; 14.fxe5 Qd4; 15.b3 Rad8 and Black had plenty of play for the pawn in Zhuravlev-Yermolinsky, Soviet Championship 1988.

B) 6.Ba4; 6...b5 7.cxb5 Nxd5; 8.Nf3 g6; 9.Nc3 N5b6; 10.d4 Nxa4; 11.Qxa4 Bg7; 12.Be3 Nb6; 13.Qa5 0–0; 14.0–0–0 axb5; 15.Qxb5 Ba6; 16.Qxc5 Nc4; 17.Rhe1 Qb8; 18.b3 Rc8; 19.Qxc8+ Bxc8 and White resigned in Hodgson-Yrjola, Tallinn Soviet Union 1987.

3.Nf3 d5. 3...Nc6; 4.c3 d5; 5.e5 f6; 6.Be2 Be7; 7.Na3 Qb6; 8.Nc2 Nh6; 9.d4 cxd4; 10.cxd4 Bd7 gave Black a flexible position in the 7th game of the match. **4.e5.** The position now shows fundamental characteristics of the French Defense. **4...Nc6; 5.c3 f6; 6.Na3.** After using this move for a while McDonnell tried 6.Bd3 in the 68th game of the marathon match and earned a full point, but in the 70th game Bourdonnais rebounded and won with Black, and also gained victory in game 76. **6...Nh6.**

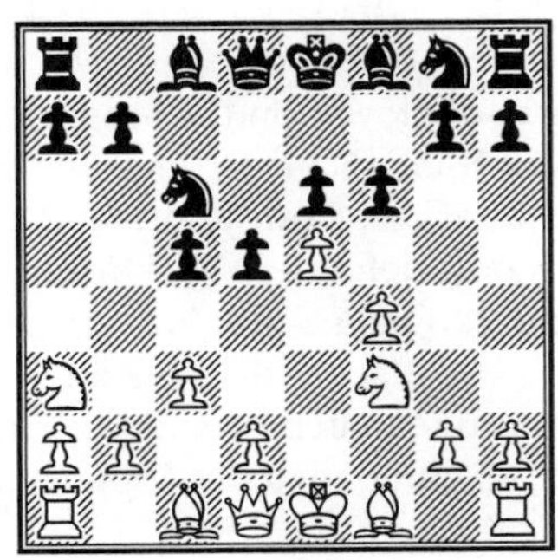

6...fxe5; 7.fxe5 Nxe5; 8.Nxe5 Qh4+; 9.g3 Qe4+; 10.Qe2 Qxh1; 11.Qb5+ leads to interesting complications which haven't been fully worked out yet. **7.Nc2 Qb6.** 7...Be7; 8.d4 0–0; 9.Bd3 was seen in the 5th game of the match and after 9...c4?; 10.Be2 Bd7; 11.0–0 b5; 12.Ne3 a5; 13.Kh1 fxe5; 14.fxe5 Nf5; 15.g4. White had a strong attack. 7...Nf7; 8.d4 Qb6; 9.Ne3 cxd4; 10.cxd4 Bb4+; 11.Kf2 fxe5; 12.fxe5 0–0; 13.Kg3 was White's ambitious plan in the 9th game, but the exposed king got White into trouble after 13...Qc7; 14.h4 Nfxe5!!; 15.dxe5 Nxe5; 16.Kh3 Nxf3; 17.gxf3 d4.

8.d4. 8.Be2 is a stronger move, suggested long ago by Mikhail Chigorin. 8...Bd7; 9.0–0 c4+; 10.Kh1 Ng4; 11.d4 cxd3; 12.Bxd3.

A) 12...fxe5 13.fxe5 (13.Nxe5 Ncxe5; 14.fxe5 Nf2+!) 13...Ncxe5?; 14.Nxe5 Nxe5; 15.Qh5+ and White wins.

B) 12...Nf2+?; 13.Rxf2 Qxf2; 14.Be3+- winning the queen. **8...Bd7.** 8...cxd4; 9.cxd4. Staunton considered capturing with the knight to be superior. 9...Bb4+; 10.Nxb4; 10.Kf2 fared no better in game 28.) 10...Qxb4+ was played in game 13, and White should have just offered an exchange of queens with 11.Qd2 Qxd2+ instead of running away with the king.

9.Ne3. 9.h4 cxd4. Black preferred to castle queenside in the 34th game. 10.cxd4 Nf5; 11.Kf2 h5; 12.g3 0–0–0; 13.Kg2 Be7; 14.a3 Be8; 15.b4 led to a sharp conflict in the 32nd game of the match. **9...cxd4; 10.cxd4 Bb4+ 11.Kf2.** 11.Bd2 is clobbered by 11...Nxd4! **11...0–0; 12.Kg3.** 12.Be2 fxe5; 13.fxe5 Nxe5! 14.dxe5 Ng4+ and White has nothing better than resignation.

12...fxe5. 12...Rac8; 13.h4 fxe5; 14.fxe5 was seen in game 16, but Black had a strong reply: 14...Rxf3+!; 15.gxf3 Nxd4; 16.Bd3 Rf8; 17.f4 Bc5; 18.Rf1 Bb5!; 19.Bxb5 Qxb5; 20.Kh3 Ne2; 21.Ng2 Nf5!; 22.Kh2 Neg3; 23.Rf3 Ne4; 24.Qf1 Qe8; 25.b4 Bd4; 26.Rb1 Qh5; 27.Rbb3 Rc8; 28.Be3 Rc2; 29.Kg1 Nxe3; 30.Rfxe3 Nd2; 31.Qd3 Rc1+; 32.Kh2 Nf1+; 33.Kh3 Nxe3; 34.Nxe3 Qf3+; 35.Kh2 Rh1#. **13.fxe5.**

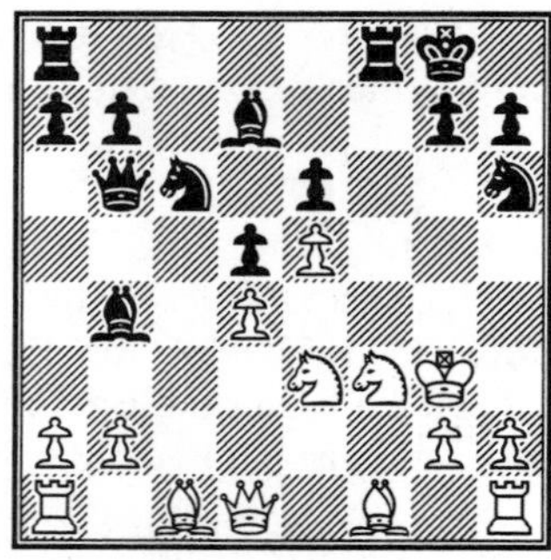

13...Be8! The bishop is re-deployed on the kingside. White suffers from having to defend the d-pawn. **14.Kh3 Bh5; 15.g4.** Otherwise the pawn at d4 falls. **15...Bg6; 16.Bg2 Be4!** The knight is attacked from another direction. **17.g5 Nf5; 18.Nxf5 Rxf5; 19.Be3.** The d-pawn is now defended, but the e-pawn is vulnerable! **19...Bxf3; 20.Bxf3 Nxe5; 21.Bg4 Nxg4; 22.Qxg4 Raf8.** Now it is not the mere pawn, but the exposed White king which gives Black a decisive advantage. **23.Rhg1 Bd6; 24.Bc1 Rf3+; 25.Kh4 R8f4.** Rarely has one match provided so much theoretical material on a single line, but then again, 85-game matches (Bourdonnais won 51.5-33.5) are not very common! **Black won.**

SMITH-MORRA GAMBIT

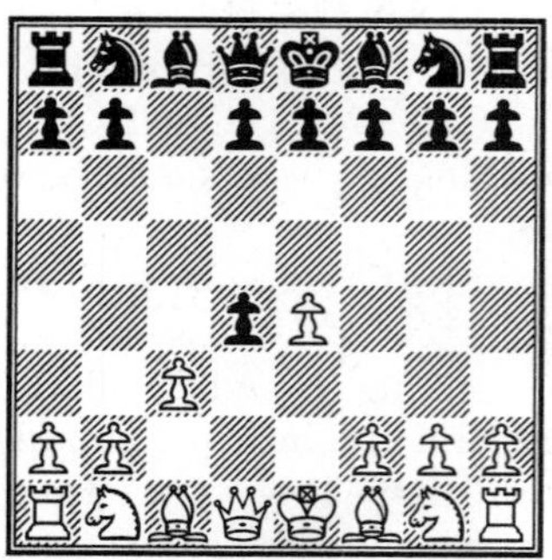

1.e4	**c5**
2.d4	**cxd4**
3.c3	

The **Smith-Morra Gambit** is almost exclusively used by amateurs. It is not that the opening is unsound that discourages professionals, it is the view that at best White can achieve an equal game with sufficient compensation for the pawn, provided that Black follows one of the accepted defensive plans. One easy option for Black is to transpose to the Alapin Sicilian with 3...Nf6. Other methods of declining the gambit are not as successful.

American Ken Smith, publisher, author and excellent poker player, almost single-handedly revived this gambit, playing it and analyzing it constantly over the latter decades of this century. He demonstrated that White's open lines and lead in development pose serious problems for Black should the second player lack requisite defensive and tactical skills. Many games end in quick kills for White. Yet properly prepared, the player of the Black side has nothing to fear. In this game we look at the main lines, and also at some recommended defenses which are growing in popularity.

(66) SMITH - MCGUIRE [B21]

Colorado, 1978

1.e4 c5; 2.d4 cxd4; 3.c3 dxc3; 4.Nxc3 Nc6. Usually this is an automatic move, but Black has a defensive alternative which strives for more active counterplay: 4...e6!?; 5.Nf3 Bc5! (5...a6; 6.Bc4 Qc7; 7.Qe2 Nc6; 8.0–0 Bd6 is a somewhat awkward, but in practice highly effective defense.) 6.Bc4 d6; 7.0–0 a6; 8.a3 Ne7; 9.b4 Ba7 and Black has a solid defense, Down-Chandler, Walsall 1992. **5.Nf3 d6; 6.Bc4 e6.**

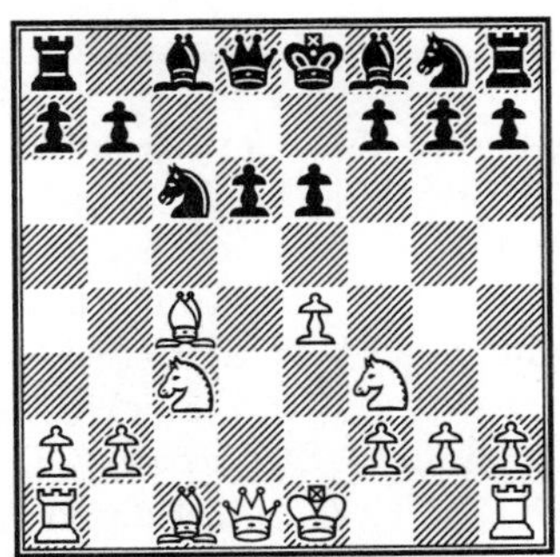

6...a6; 7.0–0 Nf6; 8.a3.

8.Bg5 e6; 9.Qe2 h6; 10.Bh4 g5; 11.Bg3 Nh5; 12.Rfd1 Nxg3; 13.hxg3 g4; 14.Ne1 Ne5; 15.Bb3 h5; 16.Nd3 Bg7; 17.Nf4 h4; 18.Qd2 hxg3; 19.fxg3 Qb6+; 20.Kf1 Bd7; 21.Rac1 Rd8; 22.Ke2 Nf3; 23.Qd3 Nd4+; 24.Kd2 Nxb3+; 25.axb3 Qf2+; 26.Nce2 Bb5; 27.Qe3 Qxe3+; 28.Kxe3 e5; 29.Nd5 Bh6+; 30.Kf2 Bxc1; 31.Rxc1 Bc6; 32.Nec3 Kd7; 33.Nf6+ Ke6; 34.Nxg4 f5; 35.exf5+ Kxf5; 36.Ne3+ Ke6; 37.g4 d5; 38.Ne2 d4; 39.Nc4 Rdg8; 40.Kg3 Rg5. Black won. Smith-Evans, San Antonio 1972

8...e6; 9.Qe2 h6; 10.Rd1 e5; 11.Nd5 Be7; 12.Be3 Nxd5; 13.exd5 Nb8; 14.Nxe5 dxe5; 15.f4 exf4; 16.d6 fxe3; 17.Qxe3 Nc6; 18.Bd5 0–0; 19.Bxc6 Bg5. Black won. Smith-Mecking, San Antonio 1972.

7.0–0 Nge7. 7...Be7 is the traditional approach, though it gives Black virtually no winning chances and requires tenacious defense just to get a draw. 8.Qe2 Nf6; 9.Rd1 e5; 10.Be3! This is the most promising move. 10.h3 used to be standard, but it now seems that White has nothing to fear by letting Black play ...Bg4. 10...0–0 11.Rac1 Bg4; 12.h3 Bh5; 13.g4. Players with a lower stock of courage can switch to the queenside now with a3 and b4, but true gambiteers will prefer this move. 13...Bg6; 14.Bc5 Nxg4? (14...Rc8! was seen in Monokroussos-I.Ivanov, Reno 1985, where White should have tried 15.Bd5! with compensation for the pawn.) 15.hxg4 Qc8; 16.Nxe5 dxc5; 17.Nd5! The knight at c6 is overworked. If it leaves c6 by choice or capture, then Nxe7+ wins on the spot. 17...Bg5; 18.Nxg6 hxg6; 19.f4 and White had more than enough for the pawn in Smith-Ramirez, San Francisco California 1972.

8.Bg5 a6; 9.Rc1. 9.Qe2 h6; 10.Bh4?!. 10.Be3 is more promising. 10...Qa5; 11.Bg3 Ng6; 12.Qd2 Nge5; 13.Nxe5 dxe5; 14.a3 Be7; 15.b4 Qd8; 16.Qa2 b5; 17.Bb3 0–0 and White had no real compensation for the pawn, Smith-Byrne, San Antonio 1972. **9...h6; 10.Bh4 Qd7.** 10...g5; 11.Bg3 Ng6; 12.Nd4 Bd7; 13.Nxc6 Bxc6; 14.f4 opened up the game in White's favor in Atarintsev-Syamidi, Soviet Union 1978. **11.Qd2 Ng6; 12.Bg3 b5?!**

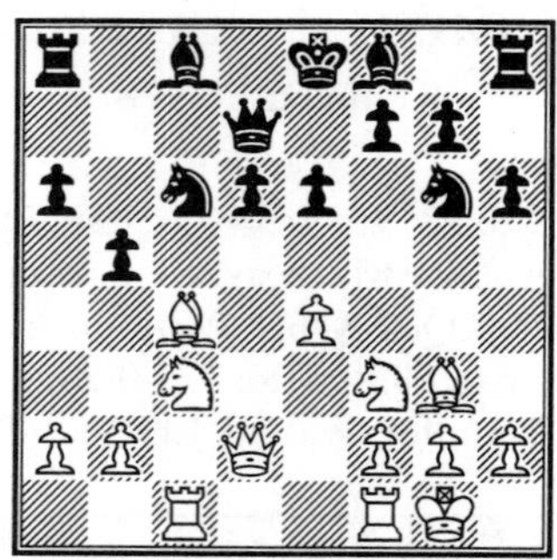

This is certainly an invitation to a sacrifice at b5, and Smith is not about to decline! **13.Nxb5! axb5; 14.Bxb5 Bb7; 15.Nd4 Rc8; 16.Rfd1!** White is in no hurry. Black's development is lagging and there are two connected passed pawns on the queenside which provide lasting compensation. **16...e5.** Black chooses to erect a pawn barrier, but the knights might have desired the use of th e5 square at some point. Moreover, the holes at f5 and d5 are quickly filled. Black's problem is that White threatens Nxc6 and then the d-pawn would fall, so some positional sacrifice was necessary. **17.Nf5 f6; 18.Qd5 Rc7; 19.f3 Kd8; 20.Qd2 Qc8; 21.Bf2 Nd4.** This finally resolves the tension, but the price is high. **22.Nxd4 exd4; 23.Bxd4 Rxc1; 24.Rxc1.**

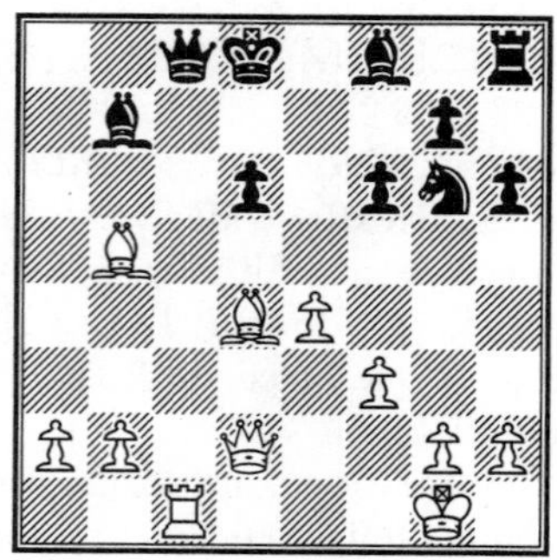

The Black king is too exposed. Black is playing a rook down, because the castle at h8 is not even a spectator. **24...Qb8; 25.Bb6+ Ke7; 26.Rc7+ Ke6; 27.Bc4+ d5; 28.Bxd5+ Ke5; 29.Rxb7** and Black had enough and resigned. **White won.**

SICILIAN: ALAPIN

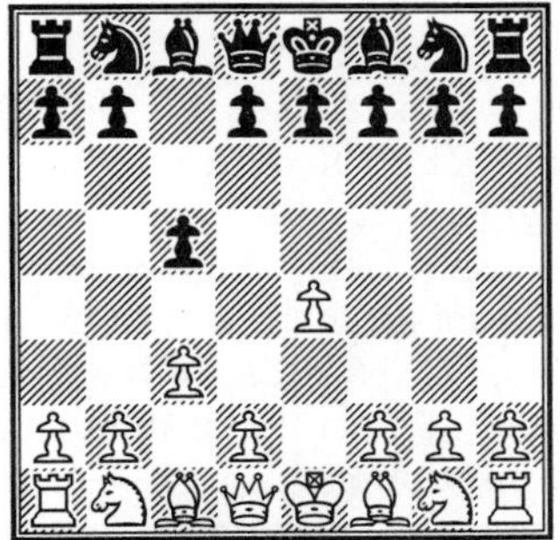

1.e4 c5
2.c3

The **Alapin Sicilian** is an old and quiet reaction to the Sicilian Defense, which lay in obscurity until Societ theoretician Evgeny Sveshnikov started to annoy people with it in the last few decades. The idea is to build the ideal pawn center in spite of Black's pawn at c5. The appeal of the line in recent times is due in part to the fact that it avoids most of the main lines and therefore requires much less preparation than the normal Sicilians. It is also a favorite opening of computers. This unambitious variation seems to have run its course and is starting to fade from the tournament scene, as Black now has several ways of reacting to it that bring about fully playable games.

(67) EKSTROEM - DUMITRACHE [B22]

Yerevan Olympiad, 1996

1.e4 c5; 2.c3 d5; 3.exd5 Qxd5; 4.Nf3 Nf6; 5.d4 Bg4.

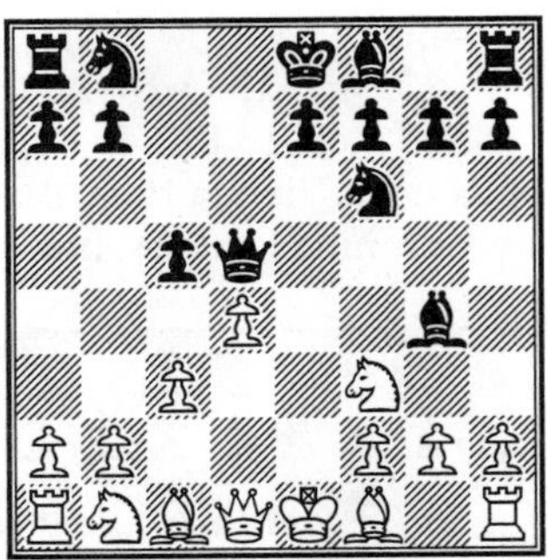

This has become the most popular way of dealing with the Alapin Sicilian in top-level competition. Black plays along the lines of the Scandinavian Defense, but has a better form of that opening since White cannot attack the Black queen with Nc3. This logical system is undergoing practical tests on an almost daily basis, so it is only possible to present a snapshot of current theory.

6.Qa4+. There are several common plans for White here, each dealing with the pin in a different way. The text simply abandons the knight at f3 to its fate, yet this seems to be quite playable for White. The newcomer Nbd2 supports the c4 square for a bishop and gives White the most flexibility. The boring old Be2 unpin is still seen, too. 6.Be2 e6; 7.0–0 Nc6; 8.Be3 White can interpolate h5, to which Black must retreat ...Bh5, here or at several points in the future. 8...cxd4; 9.cxd4 Be7; 10.Nc3 Qd6; 11.h3 Bh5; 12.Qd2.

12.Nb5 Qb8; 13.Nc3 0–0; 14.Ne5 Bxe2; 15.Qxe2 Nxe5; 16.Bf4 Nf3+; 17.Qxf3 Qc8; 18.Rac1 Qd7; 19.Rfd1 Rfd8; 20.Be5 Rac8; 21.d5 Nxd5; 22.Nxd5 exd5; 23.Rxc8 Rxc8; 24.Rxd5 Rc1+; 25.Kh2 Qc6; 26.Qd3 h6; 27.Rd7 and in A.Nakamura-Bourmistrov, World Boys Under–10 Championship 1996, White managed to squeeze a full point out of the position, though his advantage is slight. 12.Qb3 0–0; 13.Rfd1 Rfd8; 14.Rac1 Qb4; 15.Qxb4 Nxb4; 16.g4 Bg6; 17.Ne5 Nfd5; 18.Nxd5 Nxd5 and the position is level. In Estrada Gonsalez-Ljubojevic, France 1995, White made the mistake of capturing at g6 and fell into a worse position.

12...0–0; 13.Rfd1 Rfd8; 14.Rac1 Rac8 and the position resembles a reversed Tarrasch Defense, and White has enough defense to hold on to the weak d-pawn. 6.Nbd2 Nc6; 7.Bc4 Bxf3; 8.gxf3 Qf5; 9.Qb3 0–0–0.

A) 10.Bxf7 Nd5; 11.Bxd5 Rxd5; 12.Rg1! (12.Ne4?! e6; 13.Ng3 Qxf3; 14.Be3 cxd4; 15.Bxd4 Bd6 and Black was on his way to a quick win: 16.Qd1 Qg2; 17.Qg4 Nxd4; 18.cxd4 Bb4+; 19.Ke2 Rf5; 20.Rhf1 Rhf8; 21.Kd3 Kb8; 22.Rac1 Rf3+; 23.Kc4 Bd2 and White resigned in Votava-Lutz, Yerevan Olympiad 1996.) 12...e6; 13.Rg3 cxd4; 14.Ne4 Be7 was better for Black in Shaked-De Firmian, United States Championship 1996.

B) 10.Bb5! looks like a big improvement for White. 10...cxd4; 11.Bxc6 bxc6; 12.0–0! e6; 13.Qa4 Qb5; 14.Qxb5 cxb5; 15.cxd4 Rxd4; 16.Nb3 with a complex position in which the exposed Black king and rapid White development compensate for the missing pawn and fractured pawn structure, Antonio-Huebner, Yerevan Olympiad 1996. **6...Nc6.** 6...Bd7; 7.Qb3 cxd4; 8.Bc4 Qe4+; 9.Kf1 e6 is a logical continuation, and it has been seen a number of times recently:

A) 10.Nbd2!? Qc6; 11.Nxd4 Qc7; 12.N2f3 Be7N; 13.Ng5! 0–0; 14.Bxe6 fxe6; 15.Ndxe6 Bxe6 (15...Qb6!; 16.Nxf8+ Qxb3; 17.axb3 Bxf83) 16.Nxe6 Qc6!; 17.h4! was good for White in Vlassov-Shipov, Moscow 1995;

B) 10.Nxd4; 10...Nc6; 11.Nd2 Qg6; 12.Qxb7 Rb8; 13.Qc7 Rc8; 14.Qg3 Nxd4; 15.Qxg6 hxg6; 16.cxd4 Bb4; 17.b3 Bc3; 18.Rb1 Bxd4; 19.Bb2 Bc5 with a slight advantage to White in Stevic-Galliamova, Vienna 1996. Black has sufficient counterplay to deprive White of any serious winning chances, however. **7.Bc4 Qd7.**

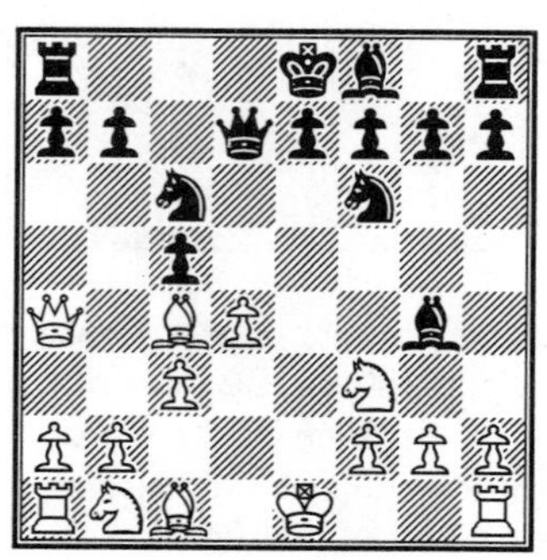

The position is filled with tension on all sides of the board. 7...Qe4+; 8.Be3 (8.Be2 cxd4; 9.Nbd2 Qd5; 10.cxd4 is a typical isolated d-pawn game where the queen is not the most efficient blockader of the isolani.) 8...Bxf3; 9.Nd2 is interesting: 9...Bd1!; 10.Qxd1 Qxg2; 11.Qf3 Qxf3; 12.Nxf3 cxd4; 13.Nxd4 Nxd4; 14.Bxd4 gives White considerable compensation for the pawn. In addition to the bishop pair and better development, White has the threat of Bb5+. **8.dxc5 Bxf3.** Black can also try 8...e5. **9.gxf3 Qf5.** Again the advance of the e-pawn comes into consideration. **10.Be3.** 10.Qb3 0-0-0; 11.Bxf7 gives Black excellent counterplay after 11...Qxf3; 12.Be6+ Kb8; 13.0-0 Ne5;. **10...e6.**

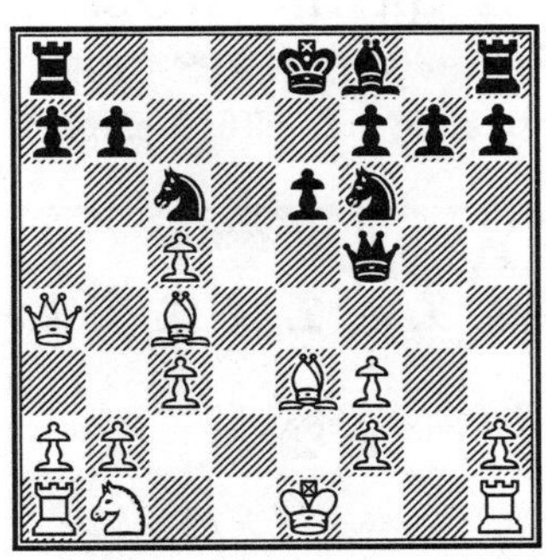

11.Ba6!! This leads to sacrificial fireworks. Obviously Black cannot capture at a6, because of Qxc6+, but Black can defend the knight while simultaneously attacking the rook at h1. **11...Qxf3; 12.Bxb7!** The point, White is going to sacrifice both rooks! **12...Qxh1+; 13.Ke2 Kd7; 14.Nd2!!** This is a classic example of a double-rook sacrifice. White will have queen and three minor pieces to use in the attack against the enemy king, which has at best two knights and a pawn for defense. **14...Qxa1; 15.Bxc6+ Ke7; 16.Bxa8.** Now White has a guaranteed material advantage, but more importantly Black has no way to get the bishop and rook into the game.

16...Qxb2; 17.Qxa7+ Kd8; 18.c6! White now threatens mate via Bb6+, Qb8+ and Qd8#. **18...Bd6; 19.Qxf7?** 19.Bb6+ Ke8; 20.Qa6 was simplest, keeping in mind that Black cannot castle because the King has moved. 20...Ke7; 21.Qb7+ Kf8; 22.c7 Qb5+; 23.Kd1 Qa4+; 24.Nb3 and Black quickly runs out of checks. **19...Qb5+; 20.Ke1 Qe5?**

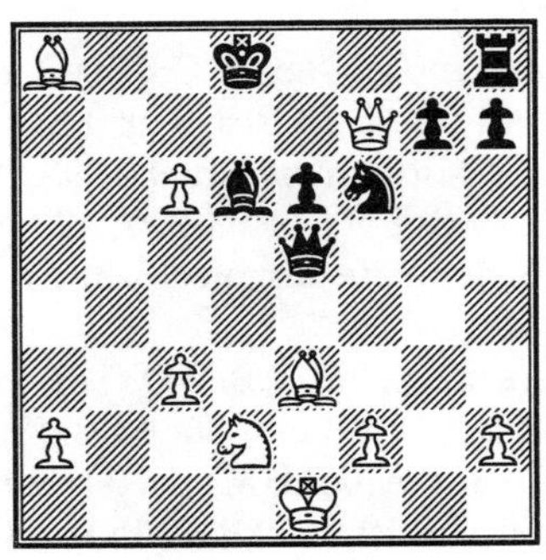

This move does not make much sense. Black had to mobilize the rook for the defense. 20...Re8! puts up the stiffest resistance. 21.Qxg7 Be7 and the White queen is shut out of the attack. 22.Bb7 binds the Black queen to the b6-square, because of the threat of Bb6+. White can then play Qg5. 22...Kc7; 23.Bd4 e5; 24.Be3 Qd5; 25.a4 Qh1+; 26.Ke2 Qxh2; 27.a5 Qh5+; 28.f3 Nd5; 29.Ne4 Nxe3; 30.Kxe3 and White is only a little better, with insufficient escorts for the a-pawn. **21.Kf1 Bc5; 22.Nf3 Qc7; 23.Ng5 Kc8; 24.Bb7+ Kb8; 25.Qxc7+.** Black resigned, as the endgame is hopeless: **25...Kxc7; 26.Nxe6+ Kb8; 27.Bxc5 Nd5; 28.c4 Nc3; 29.Ba6** was drawn in.

(68) BENJAMIN - WOLFF [B22]

New York (CITS), 1996

1.e4 c5; 2.c3 Nf6; 3.e5 Nd5.

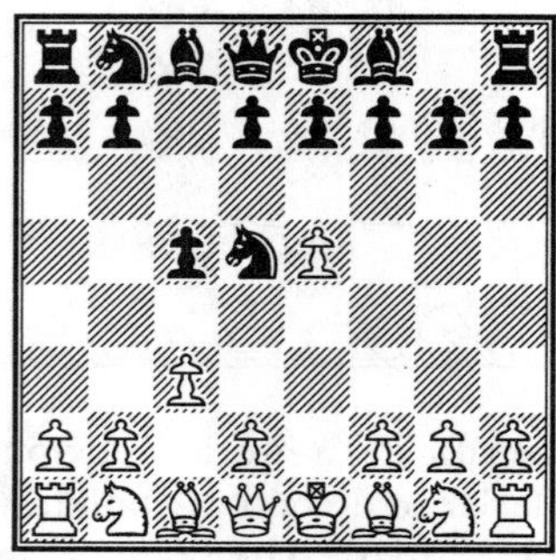

This used to be the main line of the Alapin Sicilian. The position is not unlike the Alekhine Defense, except that the White pawn at c3 is less useful (the move c3 is almost never seen in the Alekhine) and Black already has a pawn at c5 to capture at d4 when desired.

4.d4. 4.Nf3 gives Black additional options, for example 4...Nc6 (4...e6; 5.Bc4 Nb6; 6.Be2 Be7; 7.d4 0–0; 8.0–0 Nc6; 9.Bf4 Nd5; 10.Bg3 cxd4; 11.c4 Ndb4; 12.a3 d3; 13.Bxd3 Nxd3; 14.Qxd3 and the Black position is very cramped, Sveshnikov-Mauro, Amantea 1995. 4...d6; 5.d4 cxd4; 6.cxd4 Nc6; 7.Bc4 e6; 8.0–0 Be7; 9.Qe2 0–0; 10.Qe4 dxe5; 11.dxe5 b6; 12.Bd3 g6; 13.Bh6 Re8; 14.Nbd2 Ndb4; 15.Bc4 Bb7; 16.Qf4 Nd3!? and Black had counterplay in Chernyayev-Neverov, St. Petersburg 1995.) 5.Bc4 Nb6; 6.Bb3.

A) 6...d5 is the traditional move. 7.exd6 Qxd6 (7...exd6; 8.d4 Bg4; 9.0–0 cxd4; 10.h3 Bh5; 11.g4 Bg6; 12.Nxd4 Be7; 13.Re1 0–0; 14.f4 Nxd4!; 15.Qxd4 Bh4! with counterplay for Black in Afek-Mittelman, Israel 1995. The Black bishops are very active.) 8.Na3 Be6; 9.0–0 c4; 10.Bc2 g6; 11.b3 Bg7; 12.Qe2 cxb3; 13.axb3 0–0; 14.d4 and White had managed to untangle his pieces in Sveshnikov-Kveinys, European Club Championship 1996.

B) 6...c4!? is a more interesting plan. 7.Bc2 Qc7 (7...d6; 8.exd6 Qxd6; 9.0–0 Bg4; 10.Re1 e6; 11.h3 Bh5; 12.b3 Bg6; 13.Ba3 Qd5; 14.Bxf8 Kxf8 led to a complex, but probably balanced game in Nunn-Anand, Monaco (rapid) 1994.) 8.Qe2 g5; 9.Nxg5 Qxe5; 10.d4 cxd3; 11.Bxd3 Qxe2+; 12.Bxe2 Bg7; 13.0–0 0–0 was about even in Torre-Ivanchuk, Yerevan Olympiad 1996. **4...cxd4; 5.Nf3.** 5.cxd4.

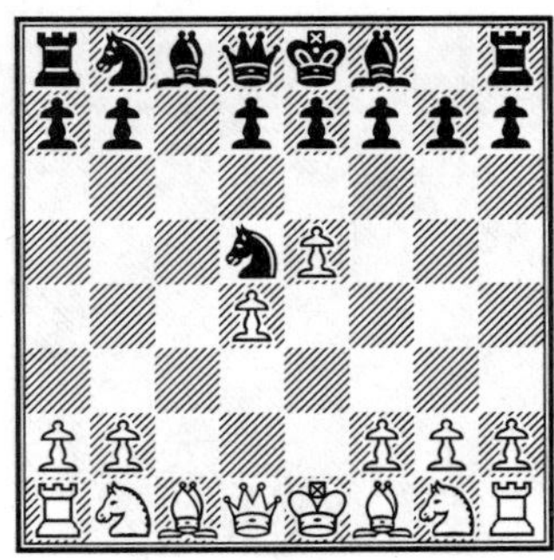

This position can also be reached via the Smith-Morra Gambit Declined with 1.e4 c5; 2.d4 cxd4; 3.c3 Nf6; 4.e5 Nd5; 5.cxd4, as in the Adams-Anand game referenced below, but it is seen more frequently in the canonical move order 1.e4 c5; 2.c3 Nf6; 3.e5 Nd5; 4.d4 cxd4; 5.cxd4. Many theoreticians have contributed to the White side, include Sveshnikov, a long-time advocate of 2.c3 against the Sicilian, Benjamin, the theoretician on IBM's DEEP BLUE team, and Czech theoretician Pavel Blatny. 5...e6; 6.Nf3

A) 6...b6 is a logical alternative, because the bishop will find a way to participate in the game from the queenside.

A1) 7.Nc3 Nxc3; 8.bxc3 Qc7! It is important to keep pressure on the dark squares. 9.Bd2 (9.Be2!? is an interesting sacrifice. 9...Qxc3+; 10.Bd2 Qa3; 11.Rc1 gave White sufficient play for the pawn in Van Mil-Krasenkov, Budapest 1989.) 9...Bb7; 10.Bd3 d6; 11.0–0 Nd7 (11...dxe5; 12.Nxe5 Nc6; 13.f4 Bd6; 14.Qh5 g6; 15.Qh4 Qe7; 16.Qh3 forced Black to castle queenside in Waitzkin-Tisdall, San Francisco (Pan-Pacific) 1995. with a very double-edged position.) 12.Re1 dxe5; 13.Nxe5 Nxe5; 14.Rxe5 Bd6 is another very sharp position, Rizzitano-Miles, USA 1980.

A2) 7.Bd3 Bb4+; 8.Bd2 Bxd2+; 9.Qxd2 Ba6; 10.Nc3 Nxc3; 11.bxc3 0–0 is slightly better for White, but the advantage is not likely to grow unless Black makes serious errors, Barlov-Rajkovic, Kragujevac 1977.

A3) 7.Bc4 Ba6; 8.Bxa6 Nxa6; 9.0–0 Be7; 10.Nbd2 0–0; 11.Ne4 Nac7; 12.Bg5 f6; 13.exf6 Nxf6; 14.Bxf6 gxf6; 15.Rc1 d5; 16.Ng3 Qd7; 17.Nh4 Bd6; 18.f4 f5. This position was reached in Adams-Benjamin, New York (CITS) 1996 and Black's position is as bad as it looks. 18...f5 Black's position is as bad as it looks. 19.Nh5 Qf7; 20.Rf3 Kh8; 21.Rh3 Rg8; 22.Nf3 Qe7; 23.Qe2 Ne8; 24.Rc6 Qd7; 25.Ne5 Qe7; 26.Rxd6! Nxd6; 27.Nc6 White won. Adams-Benjamin, New York (CITS) 1996).

B) 6...d6 is another well-traveled path.

C) 6...Nc6; 7.Bd3.

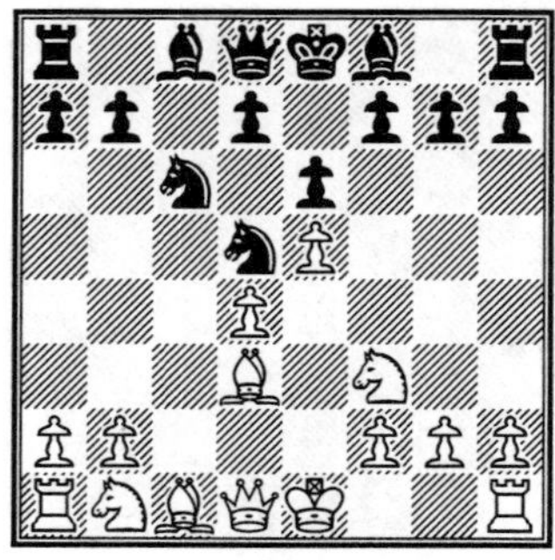

Now Black starts to work on the center. 7...d6; 8.a3. This keeps enemy knights off of b4. This keeps enemy knights off of b4. This keeps enemy knights off of b4. 8...dxe5 (8...Nde7; 9.Nc3 Ng6; 10.Qe2 dxe5; 11.dxe5 Ncxe5; 12.Bb5+ Nd7; 13.h4 gave White an initiative on both flanks in J.Shahade-Mazzarelli, US Open 1995.) 9.dxe5 g6; 10.0–0 Bg7; 11.Qe2 0–0; 12.Re1 b6; 13.Bd2 Bb7; 14.Nc3 Na5; 15.Rad1 Nb3; 16.Ne4 Nxd2; 17.Qxd2 Qe7; 18.Nd6 and White was better in Adams-Anand, Paris (Immopar) 1992. 5.Bc4 Qc7 is presently considered sufficient for equality. Now Bxd5 fails to ...Qxe5+. 5.Qxd4 e6; 6.Nf3 Nc6; 7.Qe4 f5 leads to sharp positions in which Black's chances are no worse.

5...Nc6; 6.Bc4 is very popular, especially at amateur levels where White's temporary attacking chances are more easily exploited. is very popular, especially at amateur levels where White's temporary attacking chances are more easily exploited. **6...Nb6; 7.Bb3 d6; 8.exd6 Qxd6; 9.0–0.** 9.Na3!? is an interesting plan which has been advocated at the board by young American star Tal Shaked. **9...Be6; 10.Na3.**

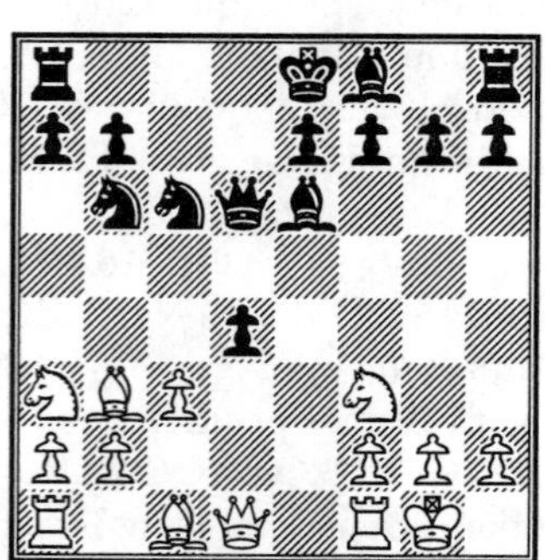

This has been the popular plan for about a decade. 10.Bxe6 Qxe6; 11.Nxd4 Nxd4; 12.Qxd4 Rd8 has been worked out to Black's satisfaction. **10...Bxb3.** 10...dxc3 led to some wild play in Benjamin-Iljinic, Yerevan Olympiad 1996: 11.Qe2 Bxb3; 12.Nb5 Qb8; 13.axb3 e5; 14.bxc3 Be7; 15.Bg5 f6; 16.Be3 Nc8; 17.Nh4 0–0; 18.Qg4 a6; 19.Nf5 g6; 20.Nxe7+ N6xe7; 21.Qc4+ Kg7; 22.Nc7 Nd6; 23.Qc5 Rc8; 24.Nxa8 Rxc5; 25.Bxc5 Ne4; 26.Bxe7 Qxa8; 27.Bb4 Kf7 and Black eventually won. **11.Qxb3 Qd5; 12.Nb5 Rc8; 13.Nfxd4 Nxd4; 14.Nxd4 e6; 15.Rd1 Bc5; 16.Qb5+ Ke7; 17.Qe2 Rhd8; 18.Be3 Qe5; 19.Qg4 Kf8; 20.Bf4.**

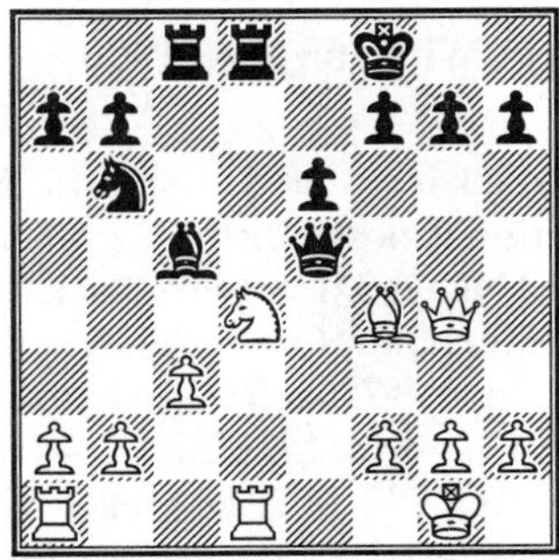

20...h5? This is a blunder. Up to here we were still in the deep preparation that Joel had prepared when working on the Deep Blue vs. Kasparov match. After 20...Qd5, Black would only have been slightly worse. **21.Qh4 Qd5.** Too late. **22.Nxe6+ fxe6; 23.Rxd5 Rxd5; 24.Be3 Nd7; 25.Bxc5+ Nxc5; 26.c4 Rf5; 27.Rd1. White won.**

GRAND PRIX ATTACK

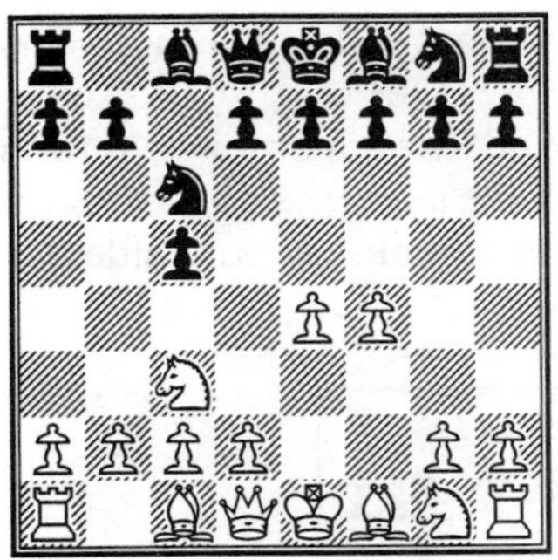

1.e4 c5
2.Nc3 with 3.f4

1.e4 c5; 2.Nc3 with 3.f4 is the **Grand Prix Attack**, which got its name from the patronage of many strong British players on the grand prix circuit in the 1980s. White avoids any direct confrontation in the center but chooses instead to operate on the flank. The further advance of the f-pawn can be overwhelming, but Black must also take note of attacks on the dark squares supported by the maneuver Qe1–g3 or f4.

For some time Black struggled to find ways to blunt White's attack, but as with most peripheral lines experience eventually led Black to find the most solid defensive formation, and the Grand Prix Attack has faded in Grandmaster chess, but is still quite popular in amateur play.

(69) ANAND - GELFAND [B23]

Wijk aan Zee, 1996

1.e4 c5; 2.Nc3 d6. The attack is reached even more frequently after 2...Nc6; 3.f4, which allows for some additional possibilities, e.g., 3...g6; 4.Nf3 Bg7; 5.Bb5 Bd4; 6.Bc4 e6; 7.Nxd4 cxd4; 8.Ne2 Nge7; 9.d3 where Black had to worry about the holes on the queenside in Zhelnin-Mochalov, Orel 1996. Another approach is 2...e6; 3.Nf3 a6; 4.g3 d6; 5.Bg2 Nf6; 6.e5 dxe5; 7.Nxe5 Ra7; 8.d3 b6; 9.0–0 Be7; 10.Be3 Bb7; 11.Bxb7 Rxb7; 12.Qf3 Qc8; 13.d4 cxd4; 14.Bxd4 0–0; 15.a4 Nfd7; 16.Rfd1 Nxe5; 17.Bxe5 Nc6; 18.Bd6 Bxd6; 19.Rxd6 Rc7; 20.Qe2 Na5; 21.Rxb6 Nc4; 22.Rb4 a5; 23.Rb5 Nxb2; 24.Nd5 exd5; 25.Rxb2 Rc5 which was drawn in Anand-Ivanchuk, at the same event.

3.f4 g6. 3...Nc6; 4.Nf3 Nf6; 5.Bb5 e6?; 6.Bxc6+ bxc6; 7.d3 Nd7; 8.0–0 Be7; 9.Qe1 0–0; 10.Kh1 a5; 11.b3 Nb6; 12.a4 left White in control of both flanks in Short-Azmaiparashvili, Yerevan Olympiad 1996.

4.Nf3 Bg7. 4...Nc6; 5.Bb5 Bd7; 6.0–0 Bg7; 7.d3 Nf6; 8.Bxc6 (8.a4 0–0; 9.Kh1 Nd4; 10.Be3 Bg4; 11.Bc4 e6; 12.Ba2 Bxf3; 13.gxf3 Nh5; 14.Rg1 Qh4; 15.Bxd4 cxd4; 16.Ne2 Kh8; 17.c3 dxc3; 18.bxc3 Qf2; 19.Rf1 Qe3; 20.f5 exf5; 21.Rb1 b6; 22.exf5 Rae8; 23.Rb2 Re5; 24.fxg6 fxg6; 25.d4 Re7; 26.Qb3 Ree8; 27.Qd5 Nf6; 28.Qc6 Ne4; 29.Ng3 Nxc3; 30.f4 Qxd4; 31.f5 Nd1; 32.Rg2 Ne3. Black won. Conquest-King, Ireland 1996)

8...bxc6? Black should certainly have captured with the bishop. Doubling the c-pawns is one of the goals of White's strategy. 9.Qe1 0–0; 10.b3 Ne8; 11.Bd2 Nc7; 12.Qh4 prepares a kingside attack, and in Yuldachev-deFirmian, Yerevan Olympiad 1996, Black over-reacted with 12...f5? where White increased the pressure with 13.Rae1 fxe4; 14.Nxe4 h6; 15.Ba5! and Black was in trouble on both sides of the board. **5.Bc4.**

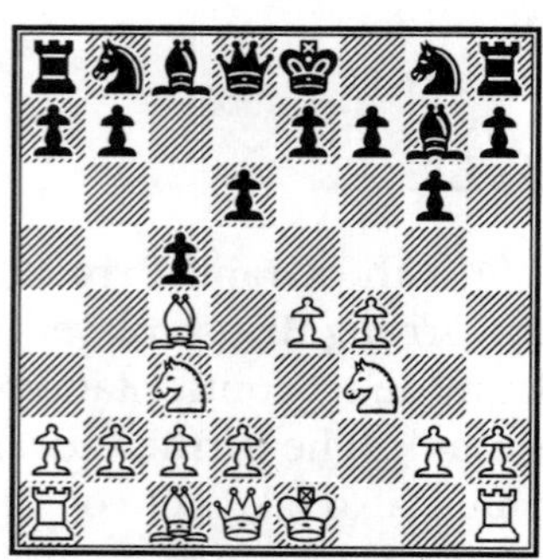

5.Bb5+ Bd7; 6.Bxd7+ Qxd7; 7.0–0 Nc6. This is the most popular line of the Grand Prix Attack. 8.d3 Nh6; 9.Kh1 f5 placed a strong barrier in the path of the White attack in Adams-Gelfand, Dortmund 1996. **5...Nc6; 6.d3 e6; 7.0–0 Nge7; 8.Qe1 h6; 9.Bb3 a6.** 9...Nd4; 10.Nxd4 cxd4; 11.Ne2 0–0; 12.Kh1 was a little better for White in Topalov-Van Wely, from the same tournament as our main game. **10.e5 Nf5; 11.Kh1 Nfd4; 12.Ne4 Nxf3; 13.Rxf3 dxe5; 14.fxe5 Nxe5; 15.Rf1 g5; 16.Qg3 0–0; 17.Bxg5 hxg5; 18.Nxg5 Ng6; 19.Rae1 Qe7.**

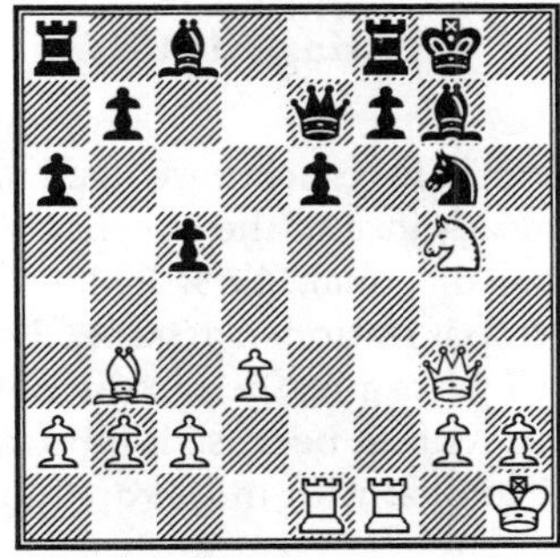

20.Rf5! This sets up the threat of Qh3, since the knight at g5 is defended. Of course the rook cannot be captured because the e-pawn is pinned by the rook at e1. **20...Bf6.** The knight is once again under attack and must now retreat or receive additional protection, right? **21.Nxe6!!** Wrong! The knight leaps forward, into the attck, smashing the protective barrier surrounding the enemy king. **21...fxe6; 22.Rxe6 Kg7.** 22...Qg7; 23.Rexf6+ and White wins. **23.Rxe7+ Bxe7; 24.Rxf8 Bxf8; 25.h4** and Black resigned, as there is no defense against the advance of the h-pawn: **25...Kh7.** 25...Kf6; 26.Qg5+ Kg7; 27.h5; 25...Kh6; 26.Qg5+ Kh7; 27.h5 Ne7; 28.Qf6. **26.h5 Ne7; 27.Qf4 Bg7; 28.h6 Bxh6; 29.Qf7+ Kh8; 30.Qxe7. White won.**

CLOSED SICILIAN

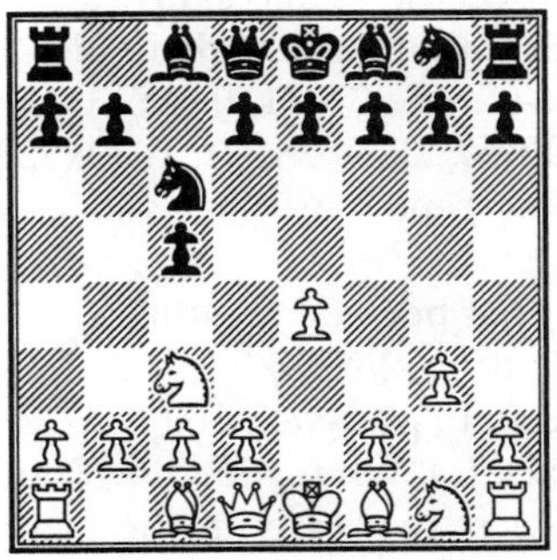

1.e4 c5
2.Nc3 Nc6
3.g3

The traditional **Closed Sicilian** is a popular way of avoiding the main lines while still anticipating an exciting game. Typically, White will attack on the kingside and Black will try to advance on the queenside, with both kings on the kingside. If Black fails to choose an appropriate formation, the game can be brutally short, but if the correct setup is employed it is White who may have to suffer as the Black queenside pawns march up the board.

(70) THOMAS - DEVOS [B24]
Hastings, 1946

1.e4 c5; 2.Nc3 Nc6; 3.g3 g6. This is acknowledged to be the best move, because a bishop at g7 can support the advance of the queenside pawns and exercise a great deal of influence on the long diagonal. **4.d3.** It does not matter whether this is played before or after the bishop is stationed at g2. **4...Bg7; 5.Bg2 Nf6?** This is a bad idea. The knight belongs at e7, as can be seen in the notes to 5...e6. But we choose the move as the focus of our attention because it illustrates almost the only danger that Black must be prepared to deal with in the opening. 5...e6 is a very common reply.

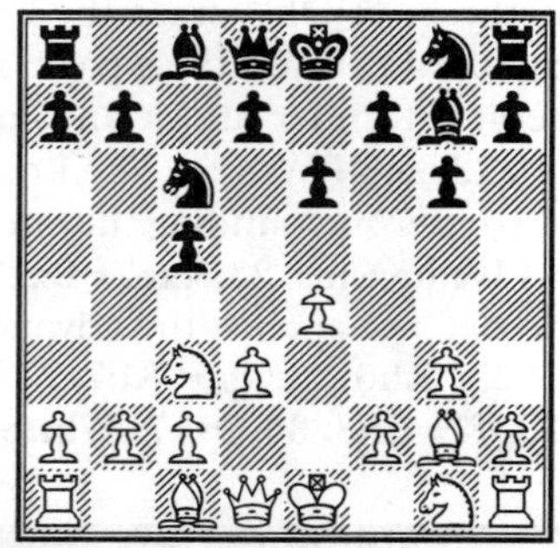

Now White has several plans, including Be3, Nge2 and f4. All of them are fully playable, but none should frighten a well-prepared opponent.

6.Be3 is the best move in the position, because White gains time by attacking the pawn at c5. (Anatoly Karpov scored well with 6.Nge2 early in his career, as the following example shows. 6...Nge7; 7.0-0 0-0; 8.Be3 Nd4; 9.Qd2 Qa5; 10.Nf4 d6; 11.Rab1 Nec6; 12.a3 a6; 13.Qd1 b5; 14.Nce2 Bb7; 15.c3 Nxe2+; 16.Qxe2 Rac8; 17.h4 b4; 18.axb4 cxb4; 19.d4 gave White a strong center in Karpov-Palatnik, Moscow 1967.)

6...Nd4 is a quite different plan. Smyslov has been devastatingly effective on the White side, for example (6...d6; 7.Qd2 Qa5; 8.Nge2 Nd4; 9.0-0 Ne7; 10.Kh1 Bd7; 11.f4 Rb8; 12.g4 h5; 13.f5 Be5; 14.fxg6 Nxg6; 15.g5 Nxe2; 16.Qxe2 Bxc3; 17.bxc3 Qxc3; 18.Qf2 Qg7; 19.d4 with a strong attack for White, Smyslov-Kottnauer, Moscow 1946.) 7.Nce2! It is unusual that such a retreat early in the game will bring rewards, but in this specific position it is justified by tactical considerations. White offers up the b-pawn, but Black should not be so reckless as to accept the invitation. 7...d6; 8.c3 Nc6; 9.d4 cxd4; 10.Nxd4 Nxd4; 11.Bxd4 e5.

Black intends to advance the d-pawn or f-pawn in the near future, but as it turns out, this is not possible. 12.Be3 Ne7; 13.Ne2 0-0; 14.0-0 Be6. Black has good development and is ready for ...d5, but Smyslov prevents it with 15.Qd2! Qc7 (15...d5; 16.Bc5 and now the d-pawn cannot leave the d-file because of the threat of an exchange of queens followed by Bxe7.) 16.Rfc1 White is going to clamp down on the center with 17.c4, so Black switches to plan B. 16...f5? Black had to play on the queenside with ...b5. 17.c4! fxe4; 18.Nc3 This offers up the pawn at c4, but Smyslov was prepared to meet 18...Nf5 (18...Bxc4 with 19.Nxe4 d5; 20.Ng5 d4; 21.Ne6 dxe3;

22.Qxe3 and the bishop at e4 is pinned, so White will be able to capture the rook at f8, though that is hardly the end of the story!

22...Qd6; 23.Nxf8 Bf7 and now the knight is still trapped, so it looks as though Black will have two pieces for the rook. Not quite! 24.Rd1 Nd5; 25.Qb3 Rd8; 26.Nxg6 hxg6; 27.Bxd5 Bxd5; 28.Rxd5! and after 28...Qxd5 White has the miraculous 29.Rd1!! forcing 29...Qxb3; 30.Rxd8+ Bf8; 31.axb3 with a winning endgame for White!) 19.Nxe4 Nxe3; 20.Qxe3 h6; 21.Rd1 and White eventually converted the positional advantage to a win in Smyslov-Denker, USSR vs. USA Match, 1946.

5...d6! is the most accurate move order, since this move is almost always played at some point. The attempts to get the pawn to d5 in one turn are almost always thwarted by a timely Be3. 6.Nge2 This is one of several popular plans. The development of the knight at h3 was preferred by Smyslov but is now rarely seen. 6.Be3 and 6.f4 are other available options. Of course there are certainly plenty of opportunities for transpositions, as White decides which parts of the plan to reveal first.

6...Rb8 (6...Nf6 can be played with the idea of bringing the knight to d7, but it isn't a very healthy choice. 7.h3 0–0; 8.0–0 Nd4; 9.Nxd4 cxd4; 10.Ne2 Nd7; 11.f4 f5; 12.Kh2 Kh8; 13.exf5 gxf5; 14.c3 dxc3; 15.bxc3 with a more active position for White in Spassky-Gipslis, Soviet Championship 1961. 6...Qd7; 7.Be3 b6; 8.f4 Bb7 is a rather artificial formation and after 9.0–0 Nd4; 10.Qd2 h5; 11.h3 f5; 12.Bf2 0–0–0; 13.Nxd4 Bxd4; 14.Bxd4 cxd4; 15.Ne2 e5; 16.c3 White undermined the enemy center in Karpov-Schaufelberger, European Junior Championship 1967. 6...Nd4; 7.Nxd4 cxd4; 8.Ne2 is also better for White. 8...Bg4; 9.f3 Bd7; 10.h4 Rc8; 11.Bd2 Qb6; 12.Qb1 e6; 13.0–0 Ne7; 14.a4 0–0; 15.b4 and White had the initiative and more space in Spassky-Brochet, French Team Championship 1991.)

7.0–0 b5; 8.f4 e6; 9.e5 d5; 10.Be3 Qb6; 11.a4 a6; 12.axb5 axb5; 13.Bf2 and here White had much better development with well-posted pieces, Smyslov-Boleslavsky, Soviet Team Championship 1952.

6.Nge2. 6.Be3 is a very popular approach, for example 6...d6; 7.h3 Nd4; 8.Nce2 Qb6; 9.c3 Nxe2; 10.Qxe2 Bd7; 11.Nf3 Qa6 with prospects for an interesting middlegame, Karpov-Sukhanov, Moscow 1968. **6...0–0; 7.Be3 d6; 8.h3.**

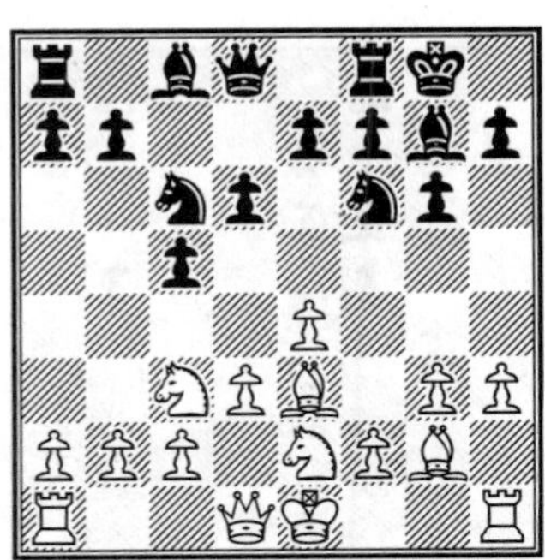

White prevents the enemy from using the g4-square. **8...Bd7.** 8...e5; 9.0–0 Be6; 10.f4 Nd4; 11.Qd2 Ne8; 12.fxe5 dxe5; 13.Nd5!? Bxd5; 14.exd5 Nxe2+; 15.Qxe2 b6; 16.Rab1 Nd6 and the position was dynamically balanced in Spassky-Simagin, Soviet Championship 1961. **9.0–0.** White's plan now is to attack the Black kingside, targeting the bishop at g7 by setting up a battery of queen and bishop on the c1–h6 diagonal. This theme is seen in many forms.

9...Qc8 Black forces the White king to occupy h2. 9...Rb8 allows White to carry out the plan right away: 10.Qd2! b5; 11.Bh6 (11.Nd1 Qa5; 12.c3 can be played before undertaking kingside play, for example 12...Rfc8; 13.Bh6 Bh8; 14.g4 Ne8; 15.f4 b4; 16.f5 bxc3; 17.bxc3 Ne5; 18.Nf4 Qd8; 19.Ne3 Nc7; 20.Qf2 Qe8; 21.Rad1. White went on to win, Karpov-Tsamriuk, Leningrad 1967.)

11...Ne8; 12.Bxg7 Kxg7. Now the advance of the f-pawn begins. 13.f4 e6; 14.f5 b4; 15.Nd1 Nd4; 16.Ne3 gxf5; 17.exf5 Nxf5; 18.Nxf5+ exf5 and White went on to vigorously exploit the weaknesses on the kingside with 19.Rf4 Rh8; 20.Raf1 Kf8; 21.g4! h5; 22.Ng3! hxg4; 23.Nxf5. It was only a matter of time before Black's kingside collapses. 23...Be6; 24.Nh6 f6; 25.Nxg4 Bxg4; 26.Rxg4 Ke7; 27.Bc6 Qb6; 28.Re1+ Kd8; 29.Qg2 Rc8; 30.Bxe8 Rxe8; 31.Rxe8+ Kxe8; 32.Rg8+. Black resigned in Thomas-Norman, Hastings 1934. **10.Kh2 Ne5; 11.f3 b5; 12.Qd2 b4; 13.Nd1 Rd8; 14.Bh6.**

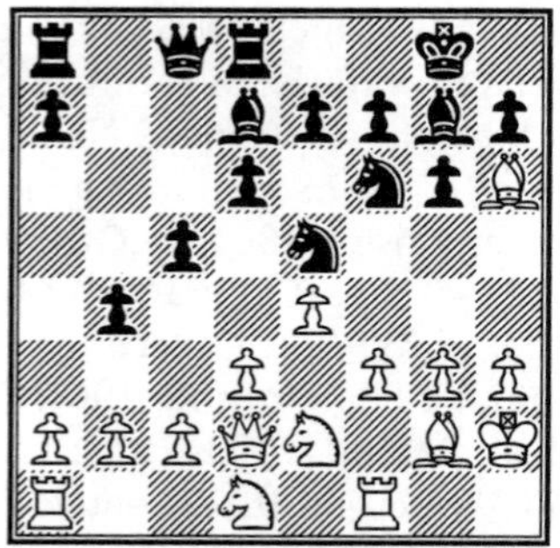

Here Black can preserve the bishop by retreating to h8, but White will show us how this plan is dealt with. **14...Bh8; 15.Bg5 Bc6; 16.Ne3 Qb7; 17.Rad1 Rac8.** Now it is time to advance the f-pawn. **18.f4 Ned7; 19.f5 Nb6.** It is not easy for White to make progress, as the kingside is guarded by a bishop and a knight. **20.Bxf6 Bxf6; 21.Ng4 Rf8.** 21...Bg7; 22.f6 exf6; 23.Nxf6+ and White will be able to double rooks on the f-file and attack. **22.Nxf6+ exf6; 23.Qh6 Nd7; 24.Rf4! g5.**

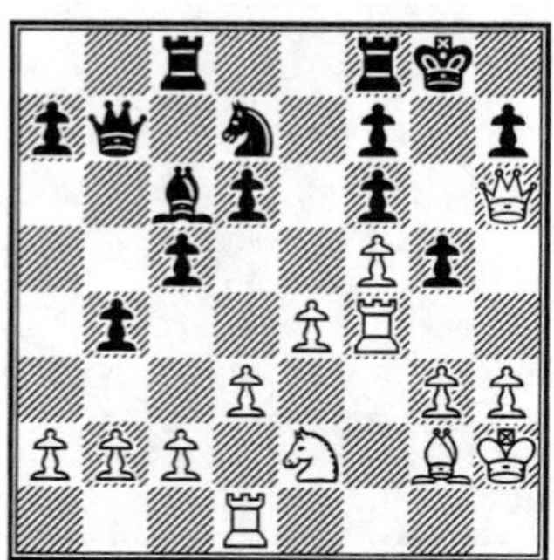

White is only attacking with queen and rook, but the Black king has little breathing room and the attack must be taken seriously. **25.Rg4 Kh8; 26.Nf4! Rg8; 27.Nh5.** The Black pawns on the kingside suddenly look very weak. **27...Qc7; 28.Nxf6** and Black resigned because of **28...Rg7; 29.Rxg5 Rcg8; 30.Nxg8 Rxg8; 31.f6 Qd8; 32.e5 Bxg2; 33.Rg7 Nf8; 34.Rxg8+ Kxg8; 35.Qg7#. White won.**

NIMZOWITSCH SICILIAN

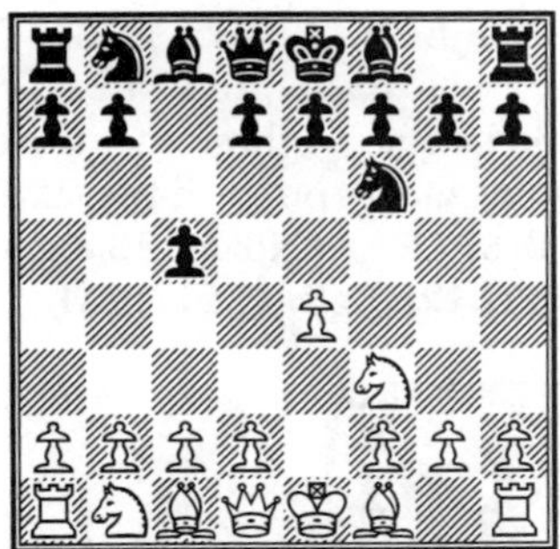

1.e4	**c5**
2.Nf3	**Nf6**

The **Nimzowitsch Sicilian** is an aggressive plan which has remained just below the level of respectability for most of its existence. The prevailing view is that White will obtain a small advantage in the main lines, but players of the Black side continue to find new and challenging resources. The position resembles that of the Alekhine Defense, but with the important difference that Black has committed the c-pawn to c5, and that radically changes the nature of the struggles, since if White advances the d-pawn to d4 it can be captured by the c-pawn.

(71) YATES - NIMZOWITSCH [B29]
London, 1927

1.e4 c5; 2.Nf3 Nf6 3.e5. 3.Nc3 d5 is often seen, for example 4.exd5 Nxd5; 5.Bb5+ Bd7; 6.Ne5 Nf6; 7.Nxd7 Nbxd7; 8.d4! cxd4; 9.Qxd4 a6; 10.Be2 e6; 11.Bf4 with a slightly more comfortable position for White in Kramnik-Seirawan, Amsterdam 1996. After 11...Qa5!, however, White would have nothing significant other than the bishop pair. **3...Nd5; 4.Bc4.**

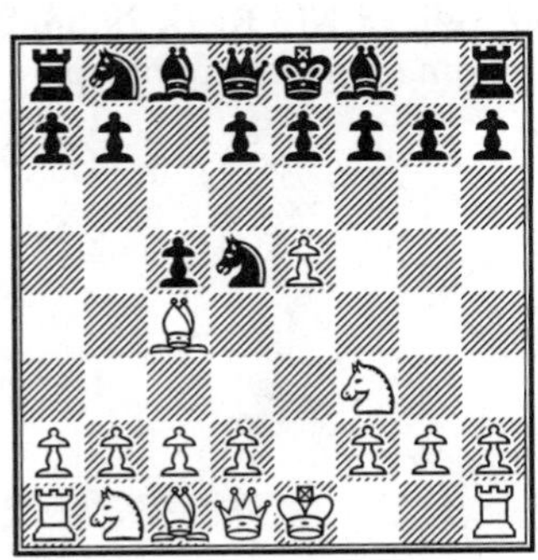

4...Nb6; 5.Be2. Nimzowitsch notes that the loss of tempo by the bishop is offset by the fact that b6 is not a good square for the knight. **5...Nc6; 6.c3.** White prepares to occupy the center by advancing the pawn to d4, but this must not be done too hastily. **6...d5; 7.d4?!** Obvious, but not best. White should capture instead. 7.exd6 exd6; With the bishop sitting on e2, Black has nothing to fear on the e-file. **7...cxd4; 8.cxd4 Bf5; 9.0–0 e6.** Black has a solid position with well-placed pieces. Already it is hard to find an effective plan for White. **10.Nc3 Be7; 11.Ne1?!** 11.Be3 0–0; 12.Rc1 was suggested by Nimzowitsch, who offered the plan a3, b4, and Nd2-b3-c5. 12...Rc8; 13.a3 Na5; 14.Nb5 Rxc1; 15.Bxc1 a6; 16.Nc3 Nac4 and I think that the chances are about level. **11...Nd7!** Nimzowitsch lines up some tactics on the d-file. **12.Bg4.** 12.f4?? is a blunder that loses to 12...Nxd4; 13.Qxd4 Bc5;. 12.Be3 Ndxe5; 13.dxe5 d4; 14.Bd2 dxc3; 15.Bxc3 Qc7 gives Black the better game. **12...Bg6; 13.f4 Nxd4.**

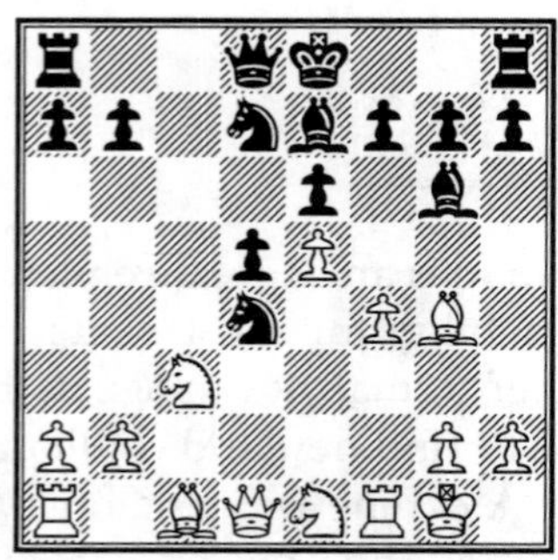

The pawn at d5 is not as strong as it seems. **14.Nxd5!** 14.Qxd4?? loses to 14...Bc5. **14...Nc6.** 14...exd5; 15.Bxd7+ Qxd7; 16.Qxd4 leaves Black with a disgusting game where the advance of White pawn on the kingside is inevitable. **15.Nxe7 Qb6+!; 16.Kh1 Nxe7.** White's pawns are weak and the bishops are ineffective. Now Yates takes his eye off the center and gets punished. **17.Qa4?** 17.Qe2! was necessary. The threat is Be3, and White is hanging on to a small initiative. 17...Nd5; 18.Bf3 Qc5; 19.Bd2 N7b6; 20.Rc1 Qe7 is given by Nimzowitsch. 21.Qb5+! Qd7; 22.Qxd7+ Kxd7 is probably about equal. **17...h5!** Black's plan is to play Nf5-g3 as soon as possible. This forces White to bring the bishop back to h3, so that the h-file can remain closed. **18.Bh3 Bf5; 19.Qa3.** This prevents Black from castling, but frees up an important sqaure. **19...Qb5!; 20.Kg1 Nb6; 21.Qf3 Nbd5; 22.b3 Qb6+!; 23.Rf2 Rc8; 24.Bd2 Rh6?!.** 24...0–0 was objectively better, given Black's domination of the center. **25.Rd1 Bxh3; 26.Qxh3 Nf5; 27.Qd3 Rg6; 28.Nf3 Rg4!; 29.h3.** 29.a4!? might have been better, in an attempt to obtain some sort of counterplay. **29...Rg3; 30.a4 Nh4.** The threat is Rxg2+. **31.Kf1.**

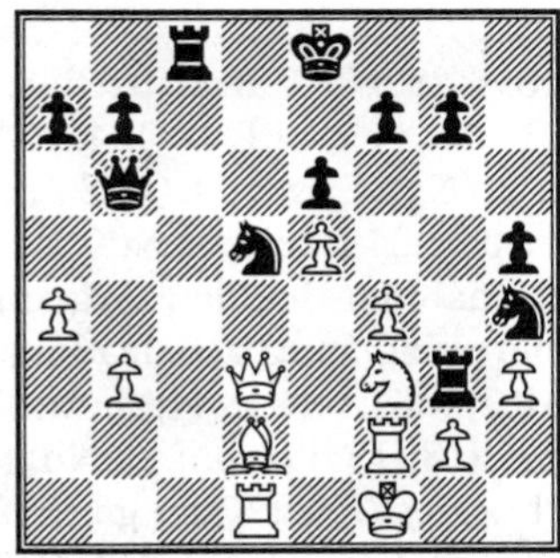

31...Rc6! Prophylaxis against the threat of Qh7 followed by Qh8+. **32.a5 Qd8; 33.Kg1 Nf5; 34.Kh2 a6; 35.Qb1 Qe7!** The queen invades on the dark squares. **36.Nd4 Qh4; 37.Be1** There is nothing better. 37.Nxf5 Rxh3+; 38.gxh3 Qxf2+; 39.Kh1 exf5 and Black wins. 37.Nxc6 gets mated after 37...Rxh3+; 38.gxh3 Qxf2+; 39.Kh1 Ng3#. **37...Nxf4!; 38.Rxf4 Rxh3+; 39.gxh3 Qxf4+; 40.Kg2 Ne3+ 41.Kg1 Qf1+** and Yates resigned. Nimzowitsch won the award for the best-played game in the event, and received ten pounds for this sterling effort. **Black won.**

ROSSOLIMO VARIATION

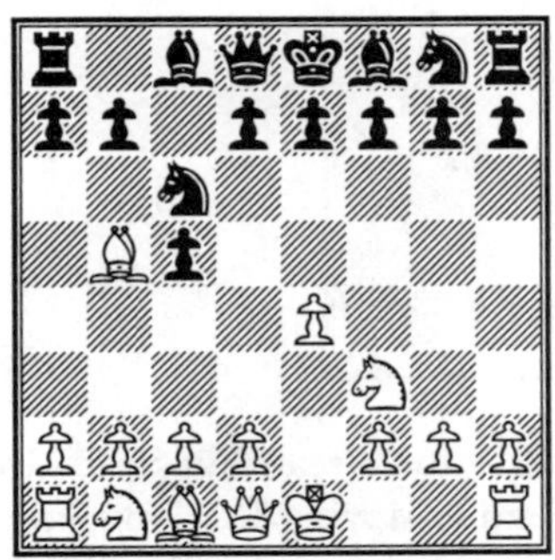

1.e4	**c5**
2.Nf3	**Nc6**
3.Bb5	

This opening is known as the **Anti-Sicilian**, but is often known as the **Rossolimo Attack** or **Nyezhmetdinov Attack** after the two romantic attacking artists who have wielded it effectively. The present game, one of Rossolimo's best, shows the possibilities inherent in the line.

(72) ROSSOLIMO - ROMANENKO [B31]

Bad Gastein, 1948

1.e4 c5; 2.Nf3 Nc6; 3.Bb5 g6. Theory considers this to be the best reply. If Black wants to avoid the doubled pawns at c6 that can arise after an early capture, then 3...Qc7 and 3...Qb6 and 3...Nd4 are playable, but in these cases Black will have a difficult time achieving equality. **4.0–0.** The immediate capture at c6 has risen in popularity lately.

4...Bg7; 5.Re1. 5.Nc3 Nf6; 6.d3 0–0; 7.Bxc6 bxc6; 8.Nd2 d5; 9.Nb3 c4; 10.dxc4 Nxe4; 11.Nxe4 dxe4; 12.Qe2 f5; 13.c3 e5; 14.Rd1 Qh4; 15.Nc5 a5; 16.b4 axb4; 17.cxb4 f4; 18.Nxe4 f3; 19.gxf3 Qh5; 20.Ng3 Qxf3; 21.Qxf3 Rxf3; 22.Rd8+ Rf8; 23.Rxf8+ Kxf8; 24.a4 e4; 25.Ra3 Be6; 26.Nxe4 Bxc4; 27.Nd6 Bd5; 28.a5 Ke7; 29.Nb7 Bd4; Rossolimo-Castillo Larenas, Zonal Mar del Plata Argentina 1950, White won. 5.c3 Nf6; 6.Re1 0–0; 7.h3 is an interesting approach, leading in many cases to positions typical of the Spanish Game. 7...d6; 8.d4 cxd4; 9.cxd4 a6; 10.Bf1 e5; 11.Nc3 b5; 12.a3 Bb7; 13.Bg5 h6; 14.Be3 Rc8; 15.d5 Na5; 16.Nd2 Nd7; 17.a4 f5; 18.axb5 f4; 19.Ba7 Ra8; 20.bxa6 Bc8; 21.b4 Rxa7; 22.Rxa5 g5; 23.Nb5 Rxa6; 24.Rxa6 Bxa6; 25.Nxd6 Bxf1; 26.Rxf1 Qb6; 27.Nf5 Qxb4; 28.Qc2 Qc5; 29.Qxc5 Nxc5; 30.Rc1 Nxe4; 31.Ne7+ and Black resigned in Nyezhmetdinov-Radulov, Varna Bulgaria 1967.

5...Nf6. 5...e5; 6.Bxc6 dxc6; 7.d3 Qc7; 8.Be3 b6; 9.a4 Nf6; 10.a5 Rb8; 11.Qc1 Nd7; 12.axb6 axb6; 13.Bh6 0–0; 14.Nc3! (14.Bxg7 Kxg7; 15.Nbd2 Re8 was equal in Hecht-Adorjan, Hungary 1974.) 14...Re8; 15.Bxg7 Kxg7; 16.Ne2 and White stood better in Rossolimo-Deze, Vrsac 1969. **6.Nc3.** Usually White puts a pawn on this square, but this is also a playable line. **6...Nd4?!** Black needs to complete development and get the king to safety. 6...0–0; 7.e5 Ne8; 8.Bxc6 dxc6; 9.h3 Nc7 leaves White with at best a very small advantage. **7.e5 Ng8; 8.d3 Nxb5; 9.Nxb5 a6.**

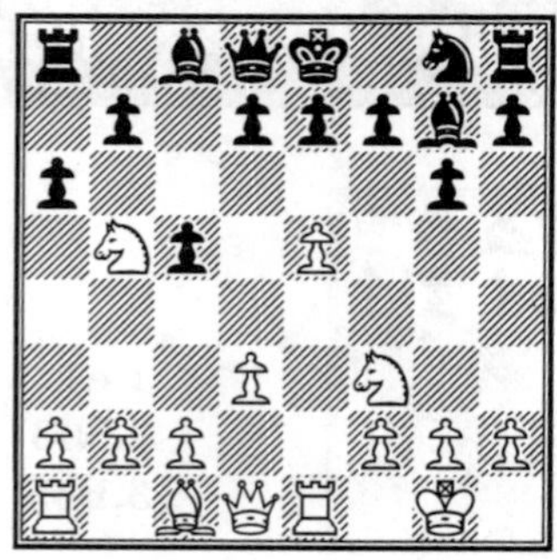

Here Black must have expected the knight to retreat, but instead runs into a typical Rossolimo combination. **10.Nd6+!! exd6;** Moving the king was better, but Black's position would still have been terrible. **11.Bg5 Qa5; 12.exd6+ Kf8.** Now it looks as if the attack is slowing, but Rossolimo throws more fuel on the fire! **13.Re8+!! Kxe8; 14.Qe2+ Kf8; 15.Be7+ Ke8; 16.Bd8+!** A final sacrifice brings the game home. **16...Kxd8; 17.Ng5** and Black resigned, since the only way to defend f7 is to move the knight from g8 to h6, but that allows Qe7#. **White won.**

KALASHNIKOV VARIATION

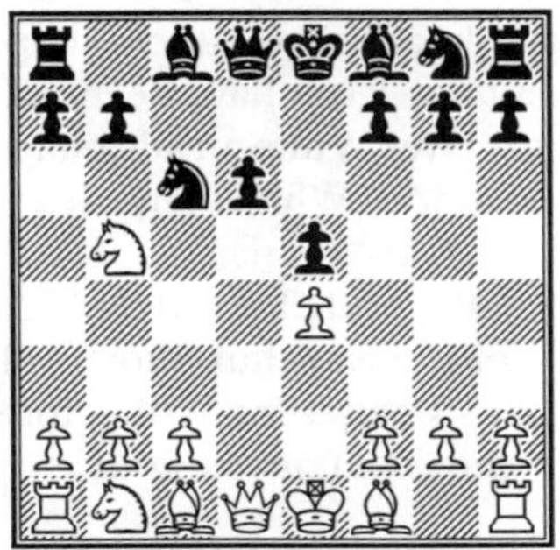

1.e4 c5
2.Nf3 Nc6
3.d4 cxd4
4.Nxd4 e5
5.Nb5 d6

The **Kalashnikov** is a relatively recent addition to the Sicilian arsenal. Once held to be unplayable because of the binding effect of 6.c4, it is now a reasonably respectable opening as ways have been found to counter White's plan. The ideas behind the opening are similar to that of the Lasker-Pelikan Variation, into which this line can transpose after 6.N1c3 Nf6. Theory on the Kalashnikov is still advancing at a rapid pace.

(73) LEKO - KRAMNIK [B32]

Dortmund, 1995

1.e4 c5; 2.Nf3 Nc6; 3.d4 cxd4; 4.Nxd4 e5; 5.Nb5 d6; 6.c4.

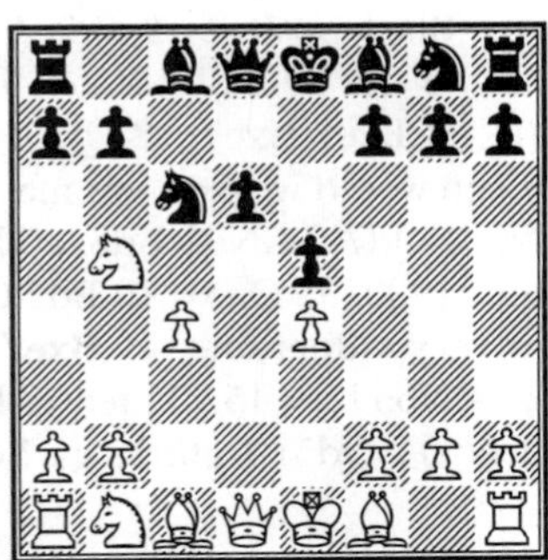

The Maroczy Bind is still considered the best approach for White, and White has been finding ways to establish a small advantage. The present game shows an interesting new plan for Black. **6...Be7.** Black can kick the knight immediately with ...a6, and this is a popular option. 6...a6; 7.N5c3 Nf6 (7...f5; 8.exf5 Bxf5; 9.Bd3 Bxd3; 10.Qxd3 is structurally better for White.) 8.Bg5 h6; 9.Bxf6 Qxf6; 10.Nd5 is also a little better for White. 6...Be6 is also seen, for example 7.N1c3 a6; 8.Na3 Rc8; 9.Be2 Nf6; 10.Be3 Be7; 11.0–0 0–0; 12.Rc1 h6; 13.Qd2 Ne8; 14.Rfd1 Bg5; 15.Nc2 Bxe3; 16.Qxe3 Qg5; 17.Qxg5 hxg5; 18.f3 with a better endgame for White in Damljanovic-

Ivanovic, Yugoslav Championship 1966.

7.Be2. This move is presently more popular than placing one of the knights at c3. White wants to retain some flexibility on the queenside. 7.N1c3 a6; 8.Na3 Be6; 9.Nc2 Bg5!; 10.Be2 Bxc1; 11.Rxc1 Nf6; 12.0–0 0–0; 13.Qd2 Qb8! allowed Black's defenses to hold in Almasi-Milov, Buenos Aires 1996. **7...f5!?** This is an interesting try, taking advantage of the fact that White has already moved the bishop to e2. Now if White captures at f5 and then plays Bd3, a tempo will have been wasted. 7...a6; 8.N5c3 Bg5; 9.Nd2! Nd4; 10.Nf3 Bxc1; 11.Rxc1 gives White an advantage, thanks to the weakness of Black's pawn structure combined with White's large lead in development.

7...Be6 is a common move. 8.0–0 a6 (8...Nf6; 9.N1c3 a6; 10.Na3 Nd4; 11.Be3 Nxe2+; 12.Nxe2 0–0; 13.f3 led to an edge for White in Ivanchuk-Short, Tilburg 1990.) 9.N5c3 Bg5; 10.Bxg5 Qxg5; 11.f4 exf4; 12.Qxd6 is better for White, for example in Mainka-Klinger, Vienna 1991. **8.exf5.** White should in any case take up this challenge. **8...Bxf5.**

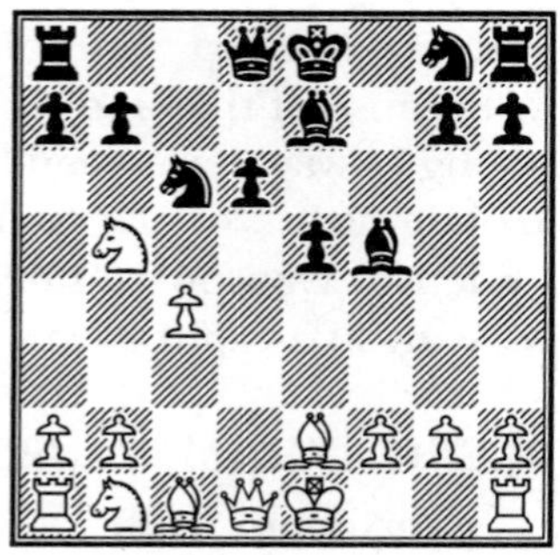

9.Bg5. This is the strongest move, undermining the protection of the d6-square which is the weakest pawn in the Black position. **9...a6.** Although some theoreticians criticize this move, it seems to be the best Black has. 9...Nf6? is actually a serious error. 10.Bh5+! Kf8 (10...Nxh5; 11.Bxe7 Nxe7; 12.Qxh5+ Bg6; 13.Qd1 Nf5; 14.Qd5 is clearly better for White. 10...g6 would weaken too many squares on the kingside.) 11.0–0 a6; 12.Bxf6 gxf6; 13.N5c3 Qd7; 14.Nd5 Bd8; 15.Nbc3 and White was better in Belikov-Sherbakov, Kuybishev 1990. 9...Qa5+; 10.Bd2 Qd8; 11.Bg4 Bxg4; 12.Qxg4 leaves the Black dark-squares very vulnerable. **10.Bxe7 Kxe7.** 10...Qa5+; 11.N1c3 axb5; 12.Bxd6 Rd8; 13.c5 b4; 14.Nb5 b3+; 15.Kf1 leaves Black in a lot of trouble, for example 15...bxa2; 16.Nc7+ Kf7; 17.Qd5+ Kg6; 18.g4 Bd7; 19.Bd3+. **11.N5c3 Nf6; 12.0–0.**

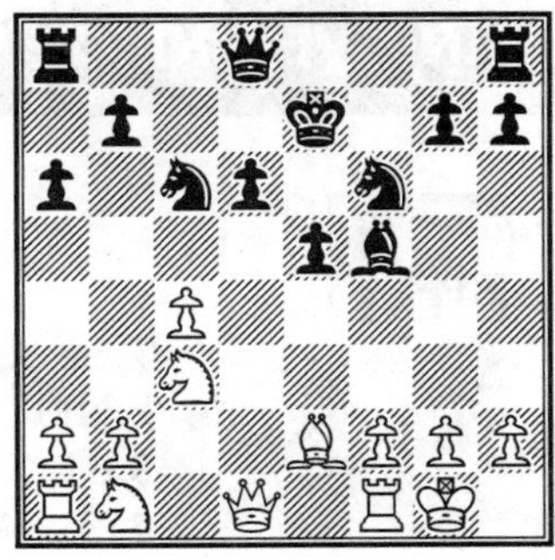

12...Qb6. 12...Nd4; 13.Bd3 Be6 is also good for White, since Black's king is in a very ugly position. **13.b3.** 13.g4!? might be more promising. For example: 13...Bxb1 (13...Be6; 14.b3 Rad8 should be acceptable for Black.) 14.g5 Bf5; 15.gxf6+ Kf7! (15...gxf6; 16.Nd5+) 16.fxg7 Rhg8; 17.Bh5+ Kxg7 and it is the White king that is in greater danger. **13...Rhd8; 14.Bd3.** 14.Nd2 d5; 15.g4 dxc4; 16.gxf5 **14...Be6; 15.Be4 Qd4.** 15...Qa5!? is an interesting alternative. **16.Qe2.** 16.Qxd4? would be a mistake because of 16...exd4 and if 17.Nd5+ then simply 17...Bxd5; 18.cxd5 Nb4 and Black has nothing to worry about. **16...Nxe4.**

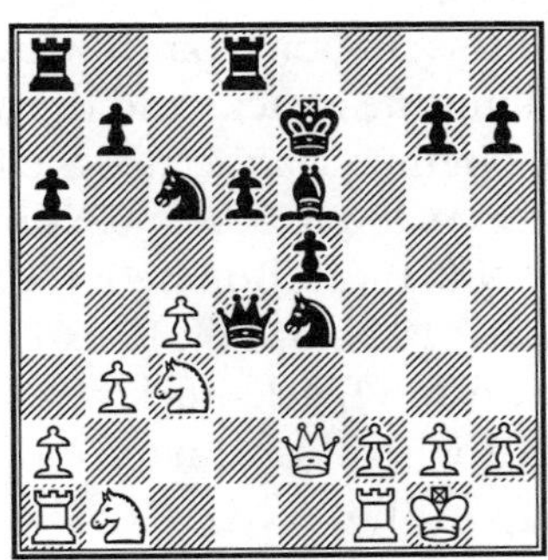

17.Nxe4. 17.Qxe4 Qxe4; 18.Nxe4 b5! gives Black sufficient counterplay to hold the endgame. **17...Qxa1.** Black will settle for two rooks in exchange for the queen. **18.Nbc3 Nd4; 19.Qd2 Qxf1+.** 19...Nxb3? 20.Qg5+ Kf8; 21.Rxa1 Nxa1; 22.Qc1 with a clear advantage for White **20.Kxf1 h6; 21.Ne2 Nxe2; 22.Kxe2.** Here the game was agreed drawn, though the endgame would be far from boring.

LASKER-PELIKAN: SVESHNIKOV VARIATION

1.e4	**c5**
2.Nf3	**Nc6**
3.d4	**cxd4**
4.Nxd4	**Nf6**
5.Nc3	**e5**

The **Lasker-Pelikan**, with its awkward advance of the e-pawn and gaping hole at d5, did not achieve respectability easily. For many years it was considered positionally suspect. Evgeny Sveshnikov is almost single-handedly responsible for taking the obscure Lasker-Pelikan Sicilian and turning it into a major branch of the Sicilian Defense. For over 30 years he has passionately defended the Black side of this ungainly pawn structure, finding compensation for the hole at d5 in kingside attacks and dynamic piece play.

Black can also play the opening via the ...e6 Sicilians, and Sveshnikov has often adopted that path, for example 5...e6; 6.Ndb5 d6; 7.Bf4 e5; 8.Bg5 a6; 9.Na3 b5; 10.Bxf6 gxf6; 11.Nd5 f5; 12.Bd3 Be6; 13.0–0 Bg7; 14.Qh5 f4; 15.c3 0–0; 16.Nc2 f5; 17.Ncb4 Nxb4; 18.Nxb4 d5!; 19.exd5 Bd7; 20.Bc2 Be8; 21.Qe2 Kh8; 22.Rad1 Qh4; 23.f3 Rf6 and Black quickly closed in on the enemy king. This is a good example of the explosive nature of the Sveshnikov. 24.Qe1 Qg5; 25.Qxe5 Bd7; 26.Qe7 Rg8; 27.Qxd7 Rf7. White resigned, Zinn-Sveshnikov, Decin 1974.

(74) KORSUNSKY - SVESHNIKOV [B33]
Soviet Union, 1977

1.e4 c5; 2.Nf3 Nc6; 3.d4 cxd4; 4.Nxd4 Nf6; 5.Nc3 e5; 6.Ndb5. 6.Nb3?! was seen in Lasker's day, though it has been abandoned in serious chess. 6...Bb4; 7.Bd3 d5; 8.exd5 Nxd5; 9.Bd2 Nxc3; 10.bxc3 Bd6; 11.Qh5 Qc7; 12.0–0 Be6; 13.Bg5!? h6; 14.f4 exf4; 15.Rae1 Kd7 and now White unleashed 16.Bf5!! which threw Lasker off balance. 16...Raf8 (The correct defense was 16...Qb6+!? 17.Kh1 g6; 18.Bxe6+ fxe6; 19.Qxg6 hxg5; 20.Qxe6+ Kc7; 21.Qf7+ Kb8; 22.Nd4 and Black has a small advantage, now that the king is safe.) 17.Bxf4 Bxf4; 18.Nc5+ Kc8; 19.Bxe6+ fxe6; 20.Nxe6 Bxh2+; 21.Qxh2 Rxf1+; 22.Rxf1 Qd7 and White had a very small advantage in Schlechter-Lasker, World Championship (9th Match Game) 1910.

6...d6; 7.Bg5. This is the normal move, though 7.Nd5 is also seen. **7...a6; 8.Na3 b5.** This is the Chelyabinsk Variation named after a Russian city where much of the theory was worked out. **9.Bxf6.** 9.Nd5 is the major alternative, but Sveshnikov has developed ways of handling it, for example 9...Be7; 10.Bxf6 Bxf6; 11.c3 0–0; 12.Nc2 Bg5 (12...Rb8; 13.b4 Ne7; 14.Nce3 Bg5; 15.Nxe7+ Qxe7; 16.Nd5 Qb7; 17.h4 Bd8; 18.g3 Be6; 19.Bg2 Bxd5; 20.Qxd5 Qxd5; 21.exd5 e4 and Black had the better endgame, since the e-pawn cannot be captured due to ...Re8.Bojkovic-Sveshnikov, Novi Sad Yugoslavia 1979. 13.a4 (13.Be2 Kh8; 14.0–0 f5; 15.Bf3 Ra7; 16.a4 bxa4; 17.Rxa4 a5; 18.exf5 Bxf5; 19.b4 Raf7; 20.b5 Ne7; 21.Nxe7 Rxe7; 22.Bd5 Qb6 and Black had the more flexible position in Muratov-Sveshnikov, Soviet Championship 1981.) 13...bxa4; 14.Rxa4 a5; 15.Bc4 Rb8; 16.b3 Kh8; 17.0–0 f5; 18.exf5 Bxf5; 19.Qe2 Qd7; 20.Nce3 Be6; 21.Rd1 Bd8; 22.Ra2 Qf7; 23.Qd3 Qh5; 24.Nf1 e4; 25.Qc2 Bh4 and Black had a strong kingside attack in Geller-Sveshnikov, Soviet Championship 1978. **9...gxf6; 10.Nd5 f5.**

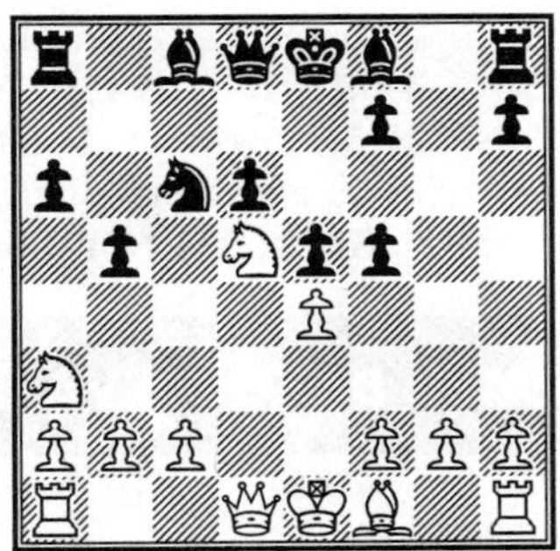

This is the start of the Sveshnikov Variation proper. White has many plans, including two possible sacrifices at b5. It is essential for Black to be well-prepared, and if so, then it is by no means easy for White to obtain an advantage. Note that there is no safe haven for the White king, since the g-file is available to Black if the king slides to the kingside, but the queenside is also exposed. It is worth noting that 10...Bg7 is a major alternative move order. Usually the play will transpose, but there are some independent lines, for example 10...Bg7; 11.Bd3 Ne7; 12.Nxe7 Qxe7; 13.c3 f5; 14.0–0 0–0; 15.Nc2 Rb8; 16.exf5 e4; 17.Re1 Bxf5 as in Kramnik-Nunn, Monaco 1994.

11.exf5. 11.Bxb5 axb5; 12.Nxb5 has worn out its welcome. Sveshnikov defended it this way: 12...Ra7; 13.Nxa7 Nxa7; 14.Qf3 Nc6; 15.0–0–0 Bh6+; 16.Kb1 fxe4; 17.Qxe4 0–0; 18.g4 Kh8; 19.Rhg1 f5; 20.gxf5 Bxf5 and Black had the initiative, Peresypkin-Sveshnikov, Soviet Union 1973. 11.Bd3 is a calmer move which is preferred by most top players. 11...Be6

A) 12.0–0 is less ambitious, but stronger: 12...Bg7; 13.Qh5 f4; 14.c4 bxc4; 15.Bxc4 0–0; 16.Rac1 Rb8; 17.b3 is the most topical variation, and even here there is plenty of experience. Even after 17...Qd7; 18.Rfd1 Kh8; 19.Qh4 there are quite a number of games, for example 19...Bxd5 (19...f5; 20.Nxf4! exf4; 21.Bxe6 Qxe6; 22.Rxc6 fxe4 with unclear complications in Turzo-Shaked, World Under–16 Championship 1994.) 20.Bxd5 Nb4 as in Renet-Korchnoi, Lugano 1988, where 21.Rc3! would have been best, according to Renet (20...Nd4; 21.Rc4! f5; 22.Nc2 fxe4; 23.Nxd4 exd4; 24.Bxe4 gives White a strong attack, and that is what Sveshnikov chose as White against Vyzhmanavin at Protvino 1987.)

B) 12.Qh5; 12...Bg7; 13.c3 (13.f3 Rc8; 14.c3 fxe4; 15.fxe4 b4; 16.cxb4 Nxb4;

17.Nxb4 Qa5; 18.Nac2 Rxc2; 19.0–0 Rxb2 and Black is in control, Diaz-Sveshnikov, Bucharest 1976.) 13...0–0; 14.g4 (14.exf5 Bxd5; 15.f6 e4; 16.fxg7 Re8!; 17.Be2 Re5; 18.Qh6 Rg5!; 19.Rd1 Qe7; 20.Nc2 Rg6; 21.Qf4 Bxa2 and Black was better in Tukmakov-Sveshnikov, Moscow 1975.) 14...fxg4; 15.Nc2 f5; 16.Nde3 f4; 17.Nxg4 Kh8; 18.Rg1 Rb8; 19.a3 a5; 20.Kf1 Qd7; 21.Ne1 Qf7; 22.Qh4 Qe7; 23.Qh5 Bf7; 24.Qh3 Bc4; 25.Rd1 Nd8; 26.Nf3 Bf6; 27.Bxc4 bxc4; 28.Nxf6 Rxf6 consolidated Black's position in Tseshkovsky-Sveshnikov, Sochi 1974.

11...Bxf5; 12.c3 Bg7; 13.Nc2. This is White's most common strategy, bringing this knight to e3 to support its comrade at d5. **13...0–0.** 13...Be6; 14.Nce3 Ne7; 15.Be2 (15.g3 Nxd5; 16.Nxd5 0–0; 17.Bg2 a5; 18.0–0 Rb8; 19.Qe2 Qd7 is comfortable for Black., Yakovich-Sveshnikov, Sochi 1986.) 15...Nxd5; 16.Nxd5 0–0; 17.0–0 Rc8; 18.a4 Rc5; 19.Bf3 a5; 20.axb5 Rxb5; 21.b4 axb4; 22.Nxb4 d5; 23.Qa4 and White controls more space on the queenside, Ricardi-Sveshnikov, Brazil 1986. **14.a4.** White strikes at the weak square on the queenside, but is seriously neglecting development of the kingside. **14...bxa4; 15.Nce3 Bd7; 16.Qh5 f5; 17.Bd3 e4! 18.Bc4 Kh8.** The Black king is perfectly safe. **19.Nf4 Ne5;** Now White had nothing better than retreating the bisho to e2, but instead tries an ambitious plan that meets with immediate rejection. **20.Ne6? Bxe6; 21.Bxe6 Nd3+; 22.Kf1 Nf4. Black won.**

ACCELERATED DRAGON VARIATION

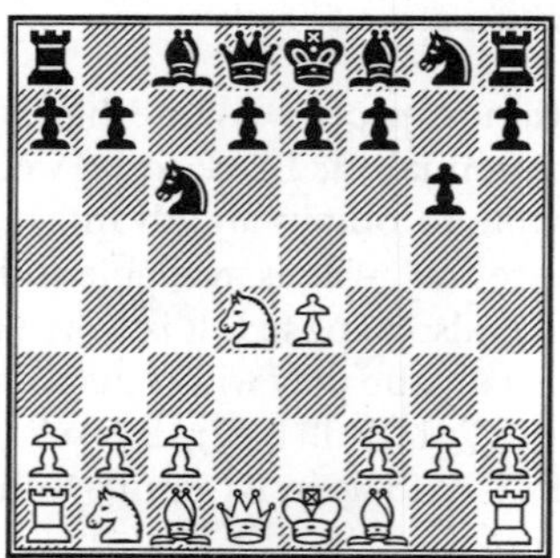

1.c4	**c5**
2.Nf3	**Nc6**
3.d4	**cxd4**
4.Nxd4	**g6**

When Black plays ...Nc6 instead of ...d6 and then fianchettoes the bishop at g7 before playing ...Nf6, we have the **Accelerated Dragon**. The point behind this plan is to save time by advancing the d-pawn to d5 (the Sicilian break) in one move, if permitted to do so by White. The drawback to this plan is the lack of pressure at e4, which allows White to create the dreaded Maroczy Bind by playing 5.c4. Although Black suffers from some lack of maneuvering room, the opening remains popular, in part because it is fairly simple to play. Black can use the dark squares effectively, often bringing a knight to c5 via d7.

(75) KARPOV - KAVALEK [B36]

Nice (Olympiad), 1974

1.c4 c5; 2.Nf3 g6; 3.d4 cxd4; 4.Nxd4 Nc6; 5.e4 Nf6; 6.Nc3 d6.

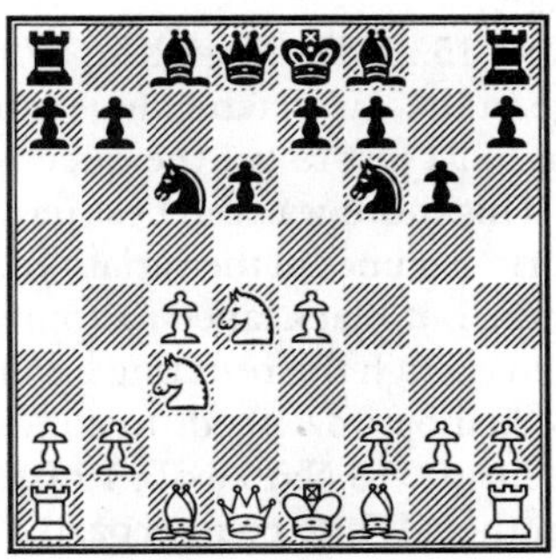

By a circuitous route starting with the English Opening and continuing through the Anglo-Indian, we have finally arrived at the Maroczy Bind lines of the Accelerated Dragon. **7.Be2 Nxd4.** 7.Nb3 Bg7; 8.Be2 0-0; 9.Be3 b6; 10.0-0 Bb7; 11.f4 Rc8; 12.Bf3 is another plan. Black can swing the knight to the queenside with 13...Nd7 and achieve a solid position, as in Korchnoi-Andersson, Ubeda 1997. **8.Qxd4 Bg7; 9.Bg5.** 9.Be3 is also quite common. 9...0–0; 10.Qd2 Be6; 11.0–0 a6; 12.f3 Qa5; 13.Rab1 led to a more promising game for White in Kramnik-Anand, Amsterdam 1996.

9...0–0. This position has the canonical move order 1.e4 c5; 2.Nf3 Nc6; 3.d4 cxd4; 4.Nxd4 g6; 5.c4 Nf6; 6.Nc3 Nxd4; 7.Qxd4 d6; 8.Bg5 Bg7; 9.Be2 0–0 or 9.f3, with the development of the bishop coming later. **10.Qd2 Be6.** This is the natural resting place for the bishop. White usually places a pawn at f3, so all of the squares on the kingside are denied to the Black cleric. Black can play ...a6 here and then ...Be6 on the next turn, as in Marciano-Pavlovic, Ubeda 1997. **11.Rc1.** The rook is not destined to hide behind the pieces! The idea is that eventually the White knight will leap to d5, and if Black captures, then White recaptures with the c-pawn, leaving the rook at c1 smiling down an open file. **11...Qa5.** Now if the knight moves to d5, Black can exchange queens with check and go into an endgame. **12.b3.**

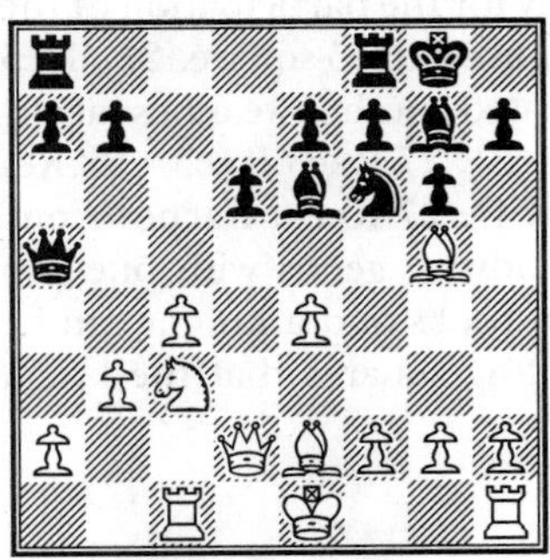

There is simple logic behind this move. Black is going to attack the c4-square with ...b5 at some point. White prepares for this by making sure that the c4-square is overprotected. **12...Rfc8.** This move directly counters White's plan, since now if the c-file is opened Black also has a rook occupying the file. **13.f3.** In a game Averbakh-Popov, Polanica Zdroj 1976, the same position was reached by 1.c4 c5; 2.Nf3 Nf6; 3.Nc3 d6; 4.d4 cxd4; 5.Nxd4 Nc6; 6.e4 Nxd4; 7.Qxd4 g6; 8.Bg5 Bg7; 9.f3 0-0; 10.Qd2 Be6; 11.Rc1 Qa5; 12.b3 Rfc8; 13.Be2! **13...a6; 14.Na4.** White enters an endgame which holds a small advantage.

14...Qxd2+; 15.Kxd2 Rc6. 15...Nd7; 16.g4 Kf8; 17.h4 Nc5; 18.Nc3 a5; 19.Nd5 gave White a clear advantage in the Averbakh game mentioned in the note to move 13. **16.Nc3.** The knight went to a4 just to get the queens off the board, so now it is time to return to the game. This move was the best move played in this position in 1974, which saw several important games in the variation under discussion. **16...Rac8; 17.Nd5 Kf8.** A natural reaction, but Black failed to appreciate that the knight had to be captured immediately, even though the resulting ending would have been uncomfortable at best. **18.Be3!** The bishop now needs to concentrate on the dark squares in the center and on the queenside. 18.Nxf6 exf6; 19.Be3 f5 is fine for Black, whose bishops are more active than their White counterparts.

18...Nd7; 19.h4! The advance of the kingside pawns is the key to this position. They must advance up the board, leaving empty space behind which can be used by the bishops. **19...Bxd5.** While this would have been effective at move 17, now it is too late. 17...f5 would have offered better chances for a successful defense. **20.exd5 R6c7; 21.h5.**

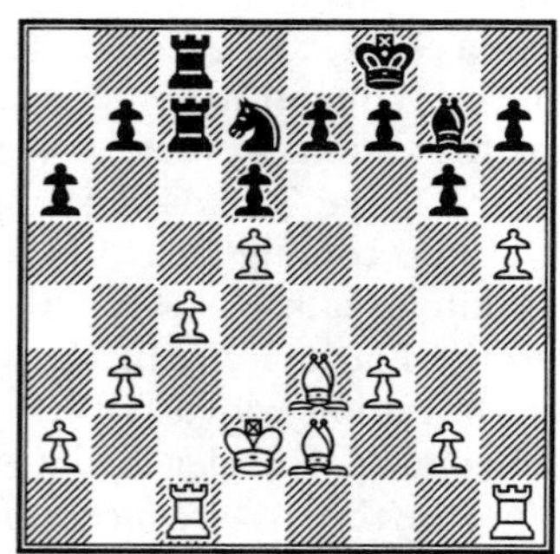

21...Kg8. White threatened to capture at g6, and then double rooks on the h-file. **22.f4!** This clears the way for the participation of the bishop at g4, and also robs Black of the opportunity to use the e5-square. **22...Nc5; 23.Bg4 Ne4+; 24.Kd3 f5.** Black has secured e4, but created another weakness at e6. **25.Bf3 b5; 26.g4!** 26.cxb5?? would lose by force to 26...Rc3+; 27.Rxc3 Rxc3+; 28.Ke2 Ng3+; 29.Kd2 Nxh1 gives Black an extra rook. **26...bxc4+; 27.Rxc4.** Karpov's endgame knowledge tells him that this endgame is more advantageous with one rook each. Single rooks work better with bishops, but two rooks and a knight can be very formidable partners, with the extra rook controlling squares that the knight cannot reach. **27...Rxc4; 28.bxc4.**

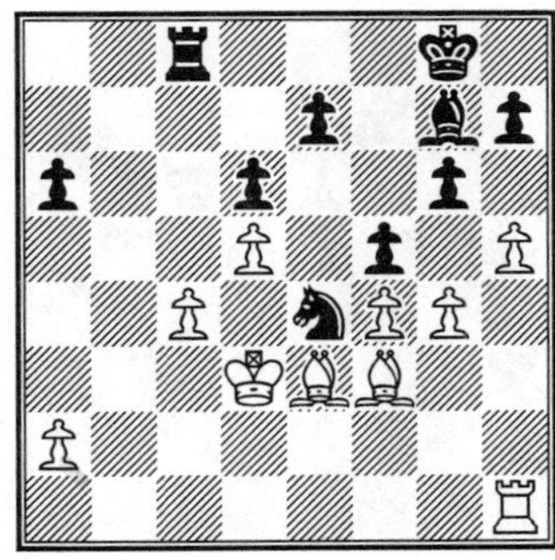

White's advantage is growing. Black now encourages White to at least part with the bishop pair. **28...Nc5+; 29.Bxc5! Rxc5.** In positions with rooks, bishops of opposite colors do not lead to drawish games. Instead, the bishops are unstoppable attackers, and the kings become targets. **30.h6!** Black must now retreat to f8 and give up the great diagonal, because otherwise the White rook infiltrates via the b-file with devastating effect. **30...Bf8.** 30...fxg4; 31.Bxg4 Bf8 loses to the following moves, pointed out by Karpov. 32.Be6+ Kh8; 33.f5 Ra5; 34.Rb1 Ra3+; 35.Ke2 Rxa2+; 36.Kf1 Bxh6; 37.f6! exf6; 38.Rb8+ Kg7; 39.Rg8#! **31.Kc3.** After the game, Karpov and Geller discovered that White would have won more quickly by closing the kingside with 31.g5. Black takes advantage of the small inaccuracy. **31...fxg4!; 32.Bxg4 Kf7; 33.Be6+ Kf6.**

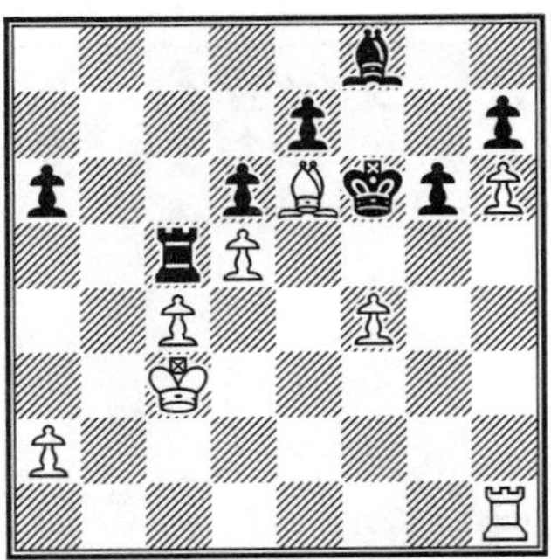

The king is now in an active position, and the White rook is tied down defending the weak h-pawn. This is a good illustration of how sacrificing a pawn in the endgame can bring a great a deal of freedom of movement, which provides significant compensation. In general, it is better to be a pawn down in an active position than to have even material but suffer from immobility. **34.Bg8.** Kavalek knew that this pawn is doomed, but has a clever move. **34...Rc7; 35.Bxh7 e6!; 36.Bg8 exd5; 37.h7!**

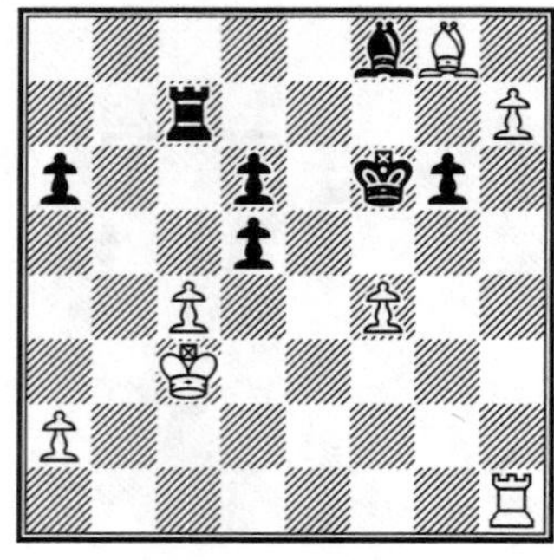

37.Bxd5 Bxh6 would have been a dead draw. **37...Bg7??** In time pressure, Kavalek lets the draw slip. It was necessary to capture at c4: 37...Rxc4+; 38.Kd3 Bg7; 39.h8Q? (39.Bxd5 Rc5 and the game would likely end in a draw.) 39...Bxh8; 40.Rxh8 Rc8 and the piece will be regained after ...Kg7. **38.Bxd5!** White gets to keep the passed pawn now, and the game is effectively over. **38...Bh8; 39.Kd3 Kf5; 40.Ke3 Re7+; 41.Kf3 a5; 42.a4 Rc7; 43.Be4+ Kf6; 44.Rh6 Rg7; 45.Kg4.** Black resigned, since there is no defense to the advance of the f-pawn and win of the g-pawn. **White won.**

(76) ARONSON - GURGENIDZE [B36]

Soviet Championship, 1957

1.e4 c5; 2.Nf3 Nc6; 3.d4 cxd4; 4.Nxd4 g6; 5.c4 Nf6; 6.Nc3 Nxd4; 7.Qxd4 d6.

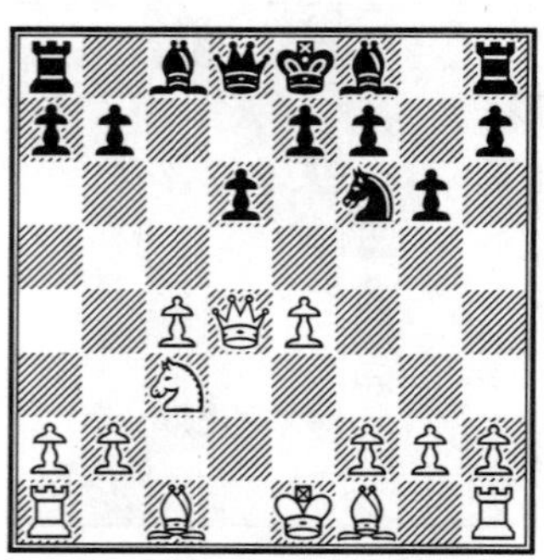

In the Gurgenidze Variation Black, exchanges knights on d4 in order to eventually gain time by attacking the White queen and using the c-file to work against the pawn at c4. The bishop at g7 will be a valuable asset in this fight. At the same time, Black must be wary of kingside attacks. White can respond with classical development, or can try to build a battery by deploying the dark-squared bishop at g5 and then retreating the queen to d2. The pawn at e4 can be supported by another pawn at f3. This makes it difficult for Black to achieve typical Sicilian counterplay, as ...d5 and ...b5 breaks are difficult to achieve. The opening was actually seen even in the Classical era, but it was Bukuti Gurgenidze who made it his patent, using it in the 1957 Soviet Championship, where this game took place.

8.Be2. 8.Be3 Bg7; 9.f3 Qa5 (9...0-0; 10.Qd2 Be6; 11.Rc1 Qa5; 12.Bd3 Rfc8; 13.b3 a6; 14.Ne2 Qxd2+; 15.Kxd2 leads to a typical Maroczy Bind endgame, J. Polgar

-Antunes, Yerevan Olympiad 1996.) 10.Qd2 a6; 11.Be2 Be6; 12.Rc1 Rc8; 13.b3 Nd7; 14.0–0 0–0; 15.Nd5 Qd8; 16.Qb4 Bxd5; 17.cxd5 Rxc1; 18.Rxc1 and the bishop pair and control of the c-file gave White the advantage in Capablanca-Colle, Barcelona 1929. 8.Qd2 Bg7; 9.Bd3 Nd7; 10.b3 Nc5; 11.Bb2 0–0; 12.0–0 a6; 13.Be2 Bd7; 14.b4 Ne6; 15.Nd5 Bxb2; 16.Qxb2 Bc6 gave Black a solid position in Krogius-Gurgenidze, Soviet Championship 1956.

8...Bg7; 9.0–0. 9.Be3 0–0; 10.Qd2 is an alternative, which Tal has played from both sides of the board.

A) 10...Ng4!?; 11.Bd4 Bh6 (11...e5; 12.Be3 Nxe3; 13.Qxe3 f5; 14.Rd1 Bf6; 15.0–0 b6; 16.Bf3 f4; 17.Qd3 and the d-pawn was doomed in Tal-Ghitescu, Leipzig Olympiad 1960.) 12.Qd1 Ne5; 13.Bxe5 dxe5; 14.Qxd8 Rxd8 and the bishop pair compensated for the doubled pawns in Cardoso-Tal, Portoroz Interzonal 1958.

B) 10...Be6; 11.0–0 a6; 12.f3 Qa5; 13.Rab1 Rfc8; 14.Rfc1 Rab8; 15.b4 Qd8; 16.c5 a5 is an alternative, complex plan, seen in Kramnik-Anand, Amsterdam (VSB) 1996.

9...0–0; 10.Bg5. 10.Qe3 is rather slow, making it hard to develop the bishop from c1 to a useful square. 10...a6; 11.Bd2 Bd7; 12.Rfd1 Bc6; 13.b4 b6; 14.Rab1 Nd7; 15.h4 b5; 16.a3 bxc4; 17.Bxc4 Ne5; 18.Bb3 Bb7; 19.h5 gxh5; 20.Qh3 Bc8; 21.Qg3 Bg4; 22.f3 Be6; 23.Nd5 Bxd5! This eliminates the powerful knight and replaces it with a less useful bishop. 24.Bxd5 Qb6+; 25.Kh2 Rac8 Salov-Dzindzichashvili, New York (CITS) 1996 gave Black promising attacking paths in the form of open c- and g-files.

10...h6; 11.Bh4 g5; 12.Bg3 Nh5; 13.Qd2 Nxg3; 14.hxg3 Bd7. This is a typical maneuver by the light-squared bishop, which is headed to c6 to put pressure on the center. Black's only serious problem is the weakness of the kingside, the price paid for obtaining the bishop pair. **15.Rad1 Bc6; 16.Bd3 e6; 17.Qe2.** White has cleverly rearranged the pieces to be able to exploit the weak light squares on the kingside. Now Black has to worry about the queen getting to h5 and then the eventual advance of the e-pawn will open up dangerous firing lines. **17...Qb6; 18.Kh1.** The f-pawn is unpinned so that it may advance. **18...h5,** desperation perhaps. Exchanging the h-pawn for the b-pawn must take into account White's kingside aspirations. **19.Qxh5 Qxb2.**

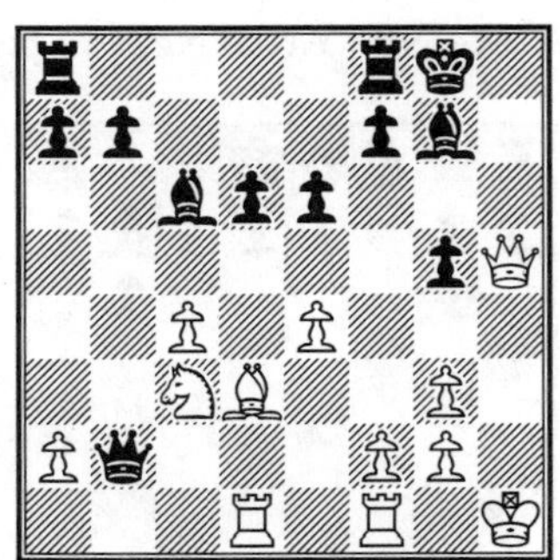

It looks as though Black has the initiative here, with two powerful bishops. White responds with a fine sacrifice that blows open the game. **20.Nd5! exd5; 21.exd5.** The threat of checkmate at h7 recovers the piece with interest. **21...f5; 22.dxc6 bxc6; 23.Qxg5.** White has an extra pawn, but in an endgame, the bishops of opposite color might lead to a draw. In fact, Black, with the extra central pawn, would stand no worse. But there is a long way to go before the endgame is reached, and opposite colored bishops give rise to additional attacking chances. The initiative is what is important, and White owns it.

23...Qf6; 24.Qh5. No endgame! **24...Rf7; 25.g4 fxg4; 26.Bg6! Re7; 27.Qxg4 Re6; 28.Be4 Kf7!; 29.g3.** 29.Bxc6 Rh8+; 30.Kg1 Qh6; 31.Qh3 Qxh3; 32.gxh3 Rxh3; 33.Kg2 Reh6 leaves White with no serious winning chances. **29...Rc8; 30.Kg2 Rc7; 31.Rh1 Re5.** Black has stationed the pieces on dark squares, and it is not easy for White to break through. The rook at e5 is a great defender, so White offers an exchange. **32.Rh5 Rxh5; 33.Qxh5+ Ke7; 34.Re1! Kd8.** The king has been driven to the queenside, but there is not enough safety there, either. **35.Bc2 Kc8; 36.Bf5+ Kb7; 37.Rb1+ Ka6.**

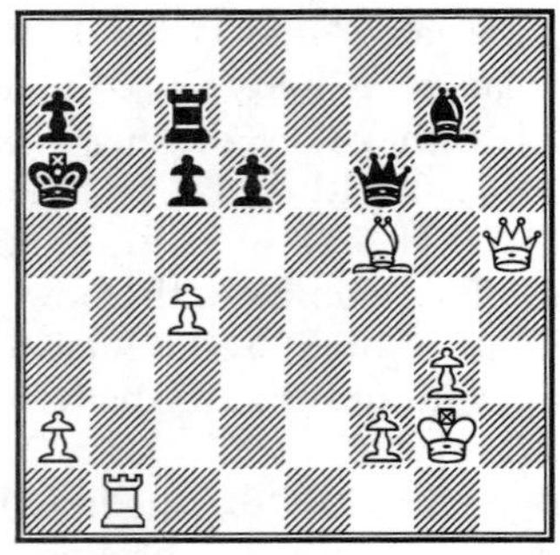

Now the king is cornered, and White opens lines for the kill! **38.c5 Qe5; 39.cxd6 Qxd6; 40.Qe2+.** This is the start of a long mating variation. **40...Ka5; 41.Qe1+ Ka6; 42.Rb3 c5; 43.Ra3+ Kb5; 44.Qa5+ Kc6; 45.Qa6+ Kd5; 46.Qd3+ Bd4; 47.Qe4+ Kc4; 48.Be6+ Kb4; 49.Qb1+. White won.**

(77) LARSEN - PETROSIAN [B39]

Santa Monica, 1966

1.e4 c5; 2.Nf3 Nc6; 3.d4 cxd4; 4.Nxd4 g6; 5.Be3 Bg7; 6.c4 Nf6; 7.Nc3 Ng4; 8.Qxg4 Nxd4.

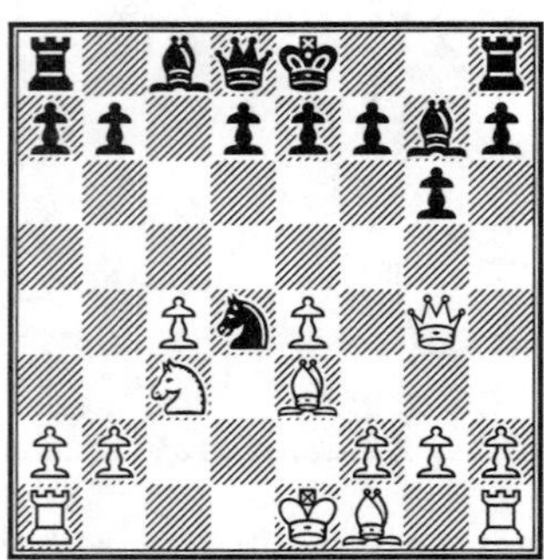

This is one of the standard lines in the Accelerated Dragon. After a flurry or tactics, we see that White has a Maroczy Bind formation, but the position is somewhat simplified because of the exchange of knights. This opening is quite topical and new developments are constantly taking place in the tournament arena. **9.Qd1 Ne6.** 9...e5 is inferior as after 10.Nb5 0-0. White has been doing well, for example 11.Be2!? (11.Qd2 Qe7; 12.f3!? f5; 13.Bd3 d6; 14.Bg5! Bf6; 15.Bxf6 Qxf6; 16.Nxd4 exd4; 17.0-0 and White was much better because the doubled d-pawns are weak, Yemelin-Silman, Budapest 1994.) 11...Nxb5; 12.cxb5 d6; 13.0-0 Be6; 14.Qa4 Qd7; 15.Rfd1. White is better, thanks to better bishops and pressure against the backward pawn at d6, Ivanchuk-Kortchnoi, Monaco (rapid) 1994.

10.Qd2. White also frequently plays 10.Rc1 d6; 11.Bd3 Bd7; 12.0-0 0-0; 13.Bb1 a5 has been defended several times by Larsen, who has often been seen on the Black side of the 7...Ng4 variation. **10...d6.** 10...Qa5!?; 11.Rc1 Bxc3; 12.Rxc3 Qxa2; 13.Bd3 may lead to difficulty for Black on the kingside, as the rook at c3 may find its way to h3. White will be able to castle and then launch a serious attack. **11.Be2 Bd7.** 11...Qa5; 12.Rc1 Bd7; 13.0-0 Nc5; 14.Bh6! 0-0; 15.Bxg7 Kxg7; 16.b3! left Black truly regretting the absence of the dark squared bishops in Korchnoi-Petrosian, Candidates match 1973. Clearly Petrosian still had confidence in the opening! **12.0-0 0-0.**

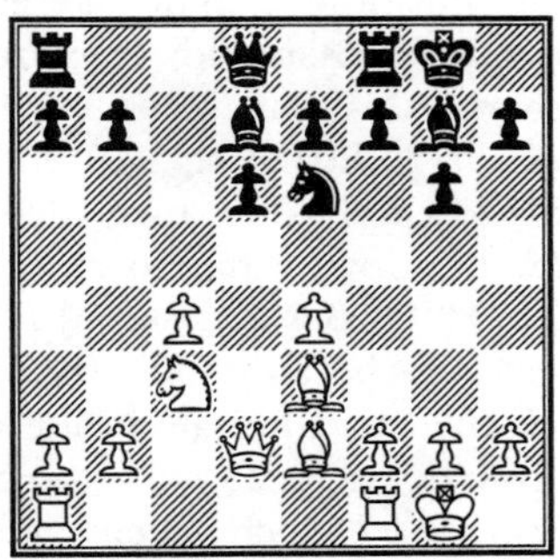

The question of rook placement is always important in the Maroczy bind, and several approaches have been tried here. **13.Rad1!** 13.Rac1 Bc6; 14.Rfd1 Nc5; 15.f3 a5; 16.b3 Qb6; 17.Nb5 Rfc8; 18.Bf1 Qd8 was for Black in Keres-Petrosian, Candidates Tournament 1959. **13...Bc6; 14.Nd5 Re8?!** Swinging the knight to c5 would have been more efficient. 14...Nc5; 15.f3 a5; 16.Bg5 (Not 16.Bd4? Bxd4+; 17.Qxd4 e5; 18.Qd2 Ne6 and Black has a good game, Porath-Larsen, Amsterdam 1964. Presumably Petrosian was aware of that game, but Larsen had clearly found something better for White, as he switched sides for this game.) 16...Re8; 17.b3. This position is analyzed by Donaldson and Silman, who confirm that White has a "minimal" advantage.

15.f4 Nc7; 16.f5 Na6; 17.Bg4?! Larsen didn't find the correct plan of queenside expansion here. This is a critical position, one in which the advantage will either be increased or significantly diminished by the very next move. Even the best players sometimes fail to recognize critical positions, and suffer the consequences. 17.b4! Nb8; 18.b5 Bd7. If Black takes the knight, White recaptures with the queen with a dominating position. 19.Bg5 and Black is under considerable pressure. Fortunately, White still has a lot of interesting possibilities and Black can still easily go wrong. **17...Nc5; 18.fxg6 hxg6.** 18...fxg6; 19.Bxc5 dxc5; 20.Be6+ also gives White a strong attack, yet after 20...Kh8 Larsen considered only 22.Qg5, when 22...Bxd5 might hold on. Petrosian, however, feared 22.Rf7. **19.Qf2 Rf8.**

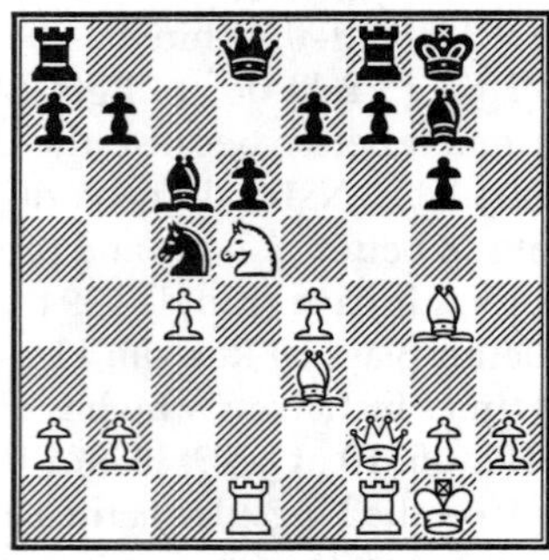

Now comes a move of pure genius! **20.e5!!** How is such a move found? Larsen admitted that it was simply matter of all of the alternatives being inadequate. Many brilliant moves are discovered this way. **20...Bxe5; 21.Qh4 Bxd5; 22.Rxd5 Ne6?** Petrosian had misevaluated this position when he entered the variation with ...hxg6. 22...e6 was the correct move, but Petrosian didn't realize what was coming at move 25 in the game, so didn't choose this plan. Later both players analyzed 23.Qxd8 Rfxd8; 24.Rxe5 dxe5; 25.Bxc5 f5; 26.Bd1 Rd2; 27.Bb3! Rad8 (27...Rxb2; 28.Rd1 is thoroughly unpleasant for Black who has no open files to create counterplay with the rooks.) 28.Re1! Rxb2 (28...e4 allows White to reorganize with 29.Be7! and the bishop will transfer to e5 via f6.) 29.Ba3 Rbd2; 30.Bc1 R2d3; 31.Bg5 R8d7; 32.Rxe5 and the rooks have no entry squares because the bishops rake the diagonals.

23.Rf3 Bf6? Petrosian claimed that he saw White's coming combination just after his bishop had beed deposited on f6. 23...f5 is the only move. 24.Rh3 and now Petrosian wanted to play his king to g7 which he felt would provide some chances to defend.

A) 24...Kg7; 25.Qh7+ Kf6; 26.Bxf5!! may have been overlooked by Petrosian. I don't see any defense, since capturing the bishop is out of the question. 26...Kxf5 (26...gxf5; 27.Rh6#) 27.Rf3+ Ke4; 28.Qxg6+ Rf5; 29.Qxf5# is such a pretty mate, it looks more like a composition than a game!

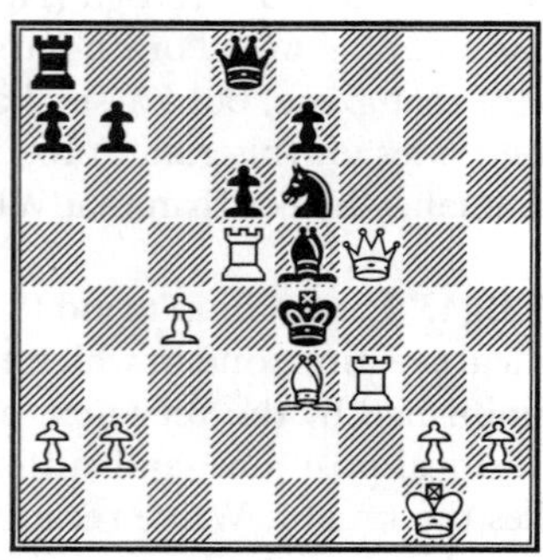

B) A pretty variant is 24...Ng7; 25.Bf3!! Kf7 (25...e6; 26.Qh7+ Kf7; 27.Rb5 and either the a-pawn or b-pawn falls.) 26.Rb5! Rh8 (26...b6; 27.Bxa8 Qxa8; 28.Bd4 and Black doesn't have enough for the exchange.) 27.Bd5+ Ne6; 28.Qg5 Rxh3; 29.Bxe6+ Kxe6; 30.Qxg6+ Bf6; 31.Qxf5+ Kf7; 32.Qxh3 and White has a clear extra pawn and good attacking chances on both flanks. **24.Qh6 Bg7.**

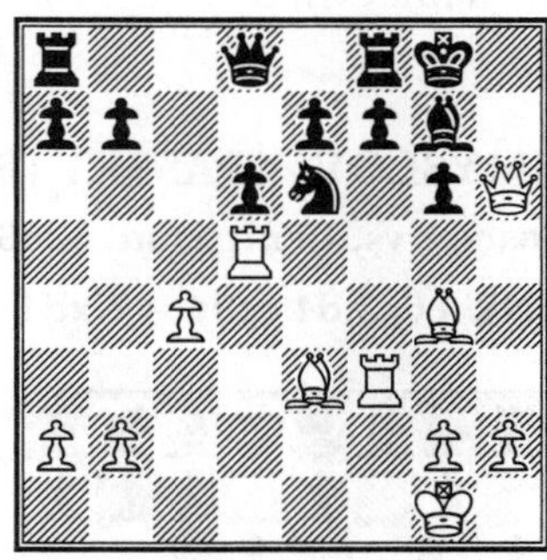

25.Qxg6! Larsen modestly said that it was not hard to find this combination because the calculations are too simple. The audience seemed taken aback, however. **25...Nf4.** 25...Nc7; 26.Qxg7+ Kxg7; 27.Rg5+ and mate next move with Rh3. 25...fxg6; 26.Bxe6+ Rf7; 27.Rxf7 Kh8; 28.Rg5! and the rook continues its journey to g3 and h3. **26.Rxf4 fxg6; 27.Be6+ Rf7.** 27...Kh7; 28.Rh4+ Bh6; 29.Bxh6 Rf5 (29...g5; 30.Rxg5 Qb6+; 31.c5! and Black can only delay checkmate by sacrificing all of his pieces.) 30.Rxf5 gxf5; 31.Bf7 e5; 32.Rh3 and Black has no defense against Bf8#, which can be delayed only slightly by ...Qh4.

28.Rxf7 Kh8. 28...Be5; 29.Rf5+ Kh8; 30.Rfxe5 and the position after 30...dxe5; 31.Rxd8+ Rxd8 is lost, as after 32.Bd5 there is nothing better than 32...e6 and now 33.Bg5 Rd7; 34.Bf6+ Kh7; 35.Bf3 Black starts losing pawns. **29.Rg5! b5; 30.Rg3** and Black resigned, as checkmate follows quickly. We have been able to obtain many insights into this great game from the players themselves, in the wonderful tournament book on the Second Piatigorsky Cup, edited by Isaac Kashdan. This book belongs in every chessplayer's library. **White won.**

KAN VARIATION

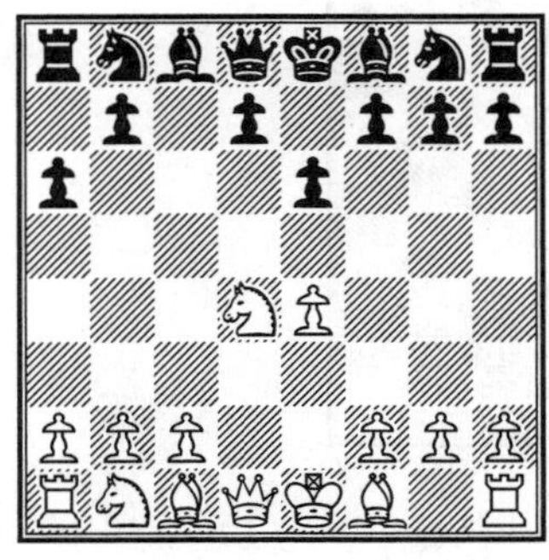

1.e4	**c5**
2.Nf3	**e6**
3.d4	**cxd4**
4.Nxd4	**a6**

The **Kan Variation** can transpose into a Scheveningen or Paulsen Sicilian, though there are also independent paths. The idea is to keep the enemy knights out, the pawns at e6 and a covering the b5 and d5 squares respectively. In modern play a hedgehog position often arises, too. In the present game, however, we examine a line where White intervenes early in the game to prevent transpositions.

(78) SMYSLOV - SPASSKY [B41]

Moscow vs. Leningrad, 1959

1.e4 c5; 2.Nf3 e6; 3.d4 cxd4; 4.Nxd4 a6; 5.c4.

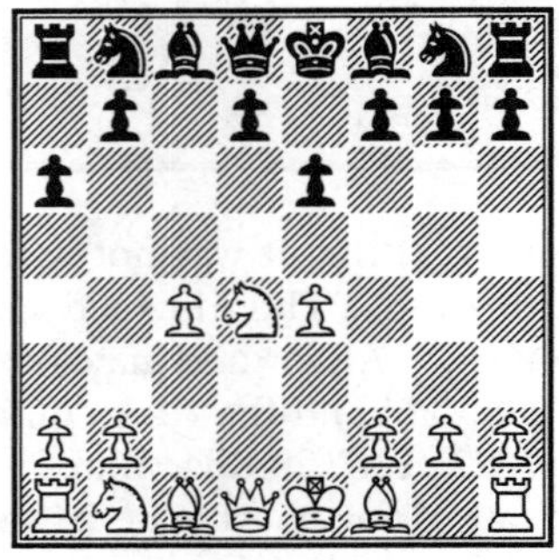

Setting up the bind is not such a common strategy these days, as Black has better resources than we see in this game. **5...Nc6.** Spassky leaves the well-known paths of 5...Nf6. A third option, perhaps best, is to station the queen at c7. For example 5...Qc7; 6.a3 Nf6; 7.Nc3 Nc6; 8.Be3 Be7; 9.Rc1 Ne5; 10.Be2 Ng6; 11.0–0 b6; 12.f4 0–0; 13.b4 Bb7 with a balanced game in Torre-Karpov, Bad Lauterberg 1977. **6.Nc3 Bc5.** The bishop nudges the horse backwards, and then sets up a pin. **7.Nb3 Bb4; 8.Bd3 Nge7; 9.0–0 0–0.** Both sides have been developing, but now Black adopts a typical plan for this type of formation. He captures on c3, and then advances his d-pawn. But his artificial position (Ne7) helps White. **10.Qc2 Bxc3; 11.Qxc3.**

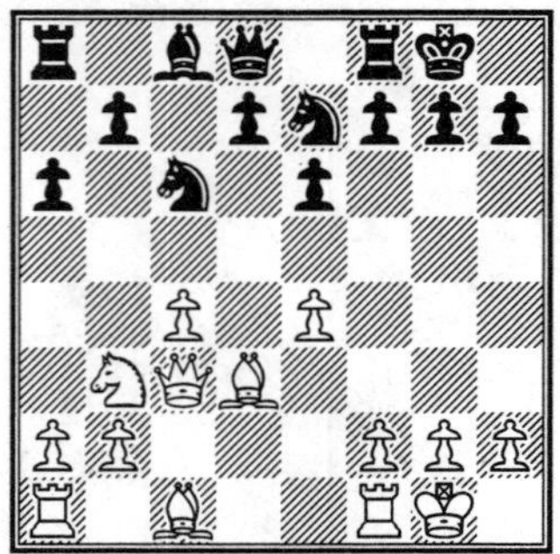

Black can now get in the ...d5 break, which is usually the goal of the Sicilian. Spassky was willing to give up the minor exchange (bishop for knight) in order to get this in. Had he seen what was coming at move 16, he might have adopted a different strategy. **11...d5; 12.Be3 dxc4; 13.Bxc4 Qc7; 14.Rac1 Rd8; 15.f4 Bd7.**

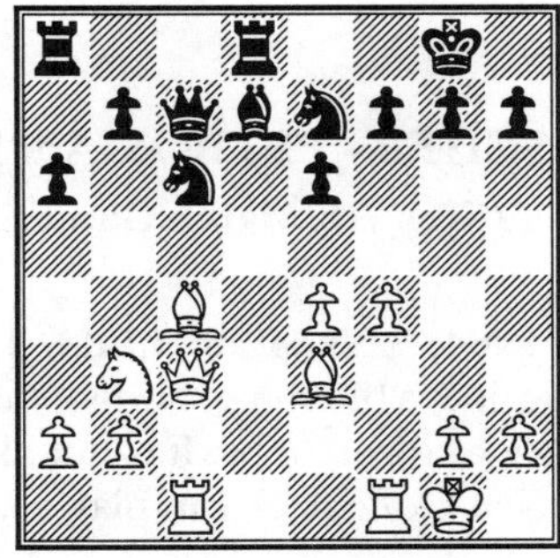

Black seems ready to claim equality, after Ra8-c8. But the weakness of the dark squares on the queenside give White an inviting target for the Be3. **16.Qe1!** White transfers his queen to f2, where it will not only support the g1–a7 diagonal, but also gives more impetus to an advance of the f-pawn, since f7 is no longer guarded by the Black rook. **16...b6.** 16...b5; 17.Be2 Be8; 18.Qf2 Rab8; 19.Nc5 exploits the dark squares in a different way. **17.Qf2 Rab8; 18.f5! Qc8.**

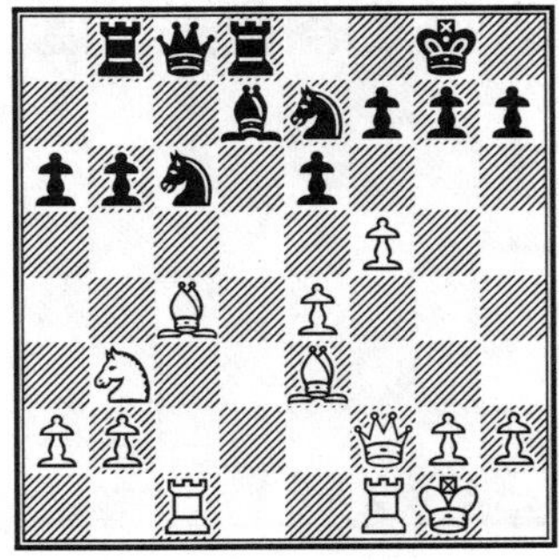

Examining this diagram we see that the pressure point is e6, and the next few moves are aimed directly at the target. They prove to be the last moves! **19.Nd4! Nxd4.** 19...e5 opens a line, but more importantly allows White to advance the f-pawn further. 20.Nxc6 Nxc6; 21.Bd5; 19...exf5; 20.exf5 b5; 21.f6! **20.Bxd4 Nc6; 21.fxe6 Bxe6; 22.Bxe6.**

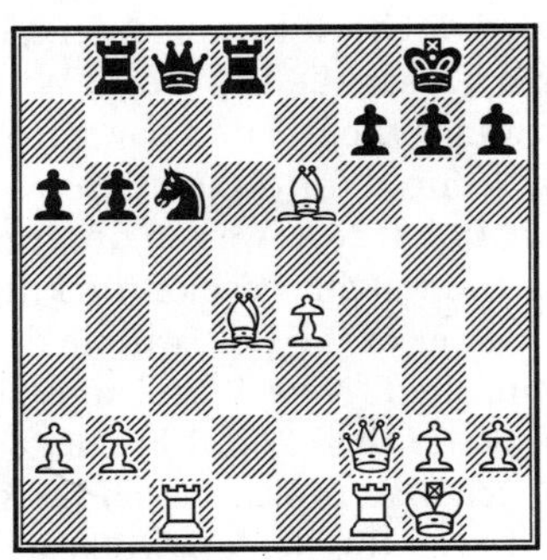

Black resigned, because mate is inevitable after 22...Qxe6; 23.Rxc6 Qxc6; 24.Qxf7+. **White won.**

(79) FISCHER - PETROSIAN [B42]

Buenos Aires 7th Match Game, 1971

1.e4 c5; 2.Nf3 e6; 3.d4 cxd4; 4.Nxd4 a6; 5.Bd3. This is the most principled continuation. Although the d-file is a bit over-crowded, the support of e4 gives White a lot of flexibility in the choice of formations. It is not always necessary to station a knight at c3, for example. 5.Nc3 Qc7. Black can play 5...b5, which is more exciting but does carry a fair degree of risk. 6.Bd3 Bc5; 7.Nb3 Be7; 8.Qg4 g6; 9.Bg5 gave White an initiative in Van der Wiel-Nijboer, Netherlands Championship 1996.

5...Nc6. 5...Nf6 is the most common, and at the same time most transpositional continuation. 6.0–0 d6; 7.c4 g6; 8.Nc3 Bg7; 9.Bg5 Nbd7; 10.Rc1 Qc7 is a hedgehog, as in Timman-Kengis, Yerevan Olympiad 1996. **6.Nxc6 bxc6; 7.0–0.** 7.f4 is sometimes played here. **7...d5; 8.c4!?** White adds to the central pressure with this move. **8...Nf6; 9.cxd5 cxd5; 10.exd5 exd5.**

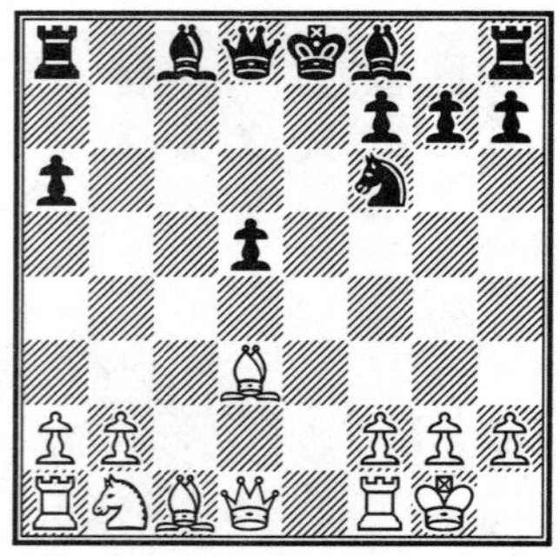

Clearly the isolated queen pawn is going to play a significant role in the game. Part of White's strategy will be to dominate the adjacent files. **11.Nc3 Be7; 12.Qa4+ Qd7; 13.Re1!** Fischer doesn't engage in cheap theatrics: 13.Bb5?! axb5!; 14.Qxa8 0–0 and the follow up with Bb7 and an eventual advance of the d-pawn will give Black an excellent game. **13...Qxa4; 14.Nxa4.** The isolated pawn is even weaker in the endgame, and White is halfway toward achieving his goal of dominating the c- and e-files. The pawn at a6, defended doubly for the moment, is also a potential weakness. **14...Be6; 15.Be3 0–0; 16.Bc5!** This is the key move. With the dark-squared bishops off the board, the rooks can attack the isolated pawn from the side. In addition, the c5-square will be more easily secured for occupation by the knight.

16...Rfe8; 17.Bxe7 Rxe7; 18.b4! Now we can observe the weakness of the pawn at a6, which will come under the watchful eye of the knight from its new outpost at c5. This, combined with the power of the Be2, will tie down Black's forces. **18...Kf8; 19.Nc5 Bc8.** Mission accomplished. Now White must find a way to increase the pressure on d5 but how can he do this? **20.f3!** Fischer's plan is almost brutal in its simplicity - he threatens to exchange rooks, march his king up the diagonal to d4, chase the knight from f6 and grab the weak pawn at d5. **20...Rea7; 21.Re5.** Just as planned back at move 13! **21...Bd7; 22.Nxd7+!** There comes a time in every plan when the immediate goal is achieved, and it is time to capitalize. The knight, though well placed, has done its job and now the domination of the remaining open file is the primary objective. **22...Rxd7; 23.Rc1.**

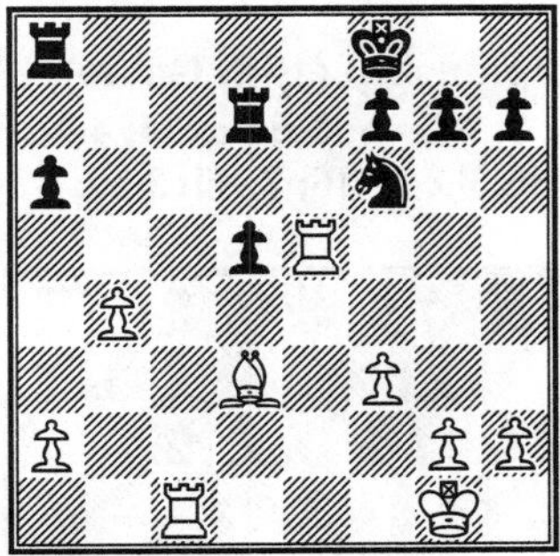

The weakness of the pawns continues to plague Black, who must now worry about the threat of Rc1–c6. **23...Rd6; 24.Rc7.** The sixth is protected - but the seventh rank is now available. Black quickly runs out of moves. **24...Nd7; 25.Re2 g6; 26.Kf2 h5; 27.f4!** A precise move which further limits Black's options. **27...h4; 28.Kf3 f5; 29.Ke3.** Black is virtually in zugzwang, so he advances his prized pawn, and opens up more lines for White. **29...d4+; 30.Kd2 Nb6; 31.Ree7 Nd5; 32.Rf7+ Ke8; 33.Rb7** This appears to drop a a pawn, but in fact it guarantees victory. **33...Nxb4; 34.Bc4!** and Petrosian resigned, because after 34...Nc6; 35.Rh7 Rf6; 36.Rh8+ Rf8; 37.Bf7+. **White won.**

PAULSEN VARIATION

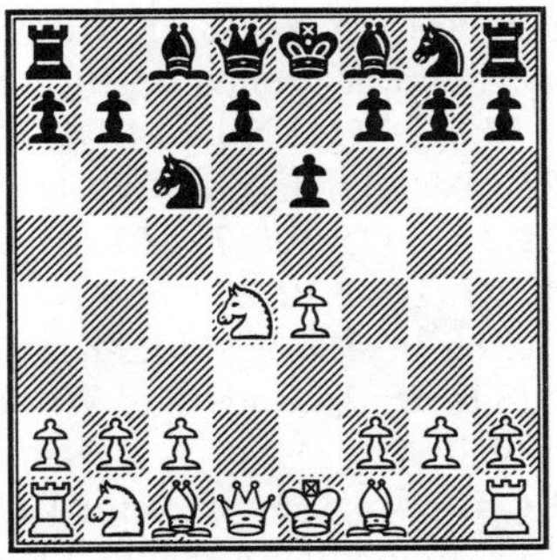

1.e4	**c5**
2.Nf3	**e6**
3.d4	**cxd4**
4.Nxd4	**Nc6**

The **Paulsen** is also a highly transpositional opening. It can merge with the Kan, Scheveningen and other variations. From the diagrammed position play, can also lead to non-Paulsen paths. For example, after, 5.Nc3 Nf6; 6.Nb5 d6; 7.Bf4 e5; 8.Bg5 we reach the Lasker-Pelikan, with each side having taken an extra move (e6-e5 for Black, Bf4-g5 for White). A true Paulsen usually involves the moves ...a6 and ...Qc7. The flexibility of Black's formation makes this a popular defensive choice. One of the most fascinating lines is a gambit used by Garry Kasparov against Anatoly Karpov in their 1985 World Championship match.

(80) KARPOV - KASPAROV [B44]

World Championship (16th Game), Moscow 1985
1.e4 c5; 2.Nf3 e6; 3.d4 cxd4; 4.Nxd4 Nc6; 5.Nb5 d6; 6.c4 Nf6; 7.N1c3 a6; 8.Na3 d5.

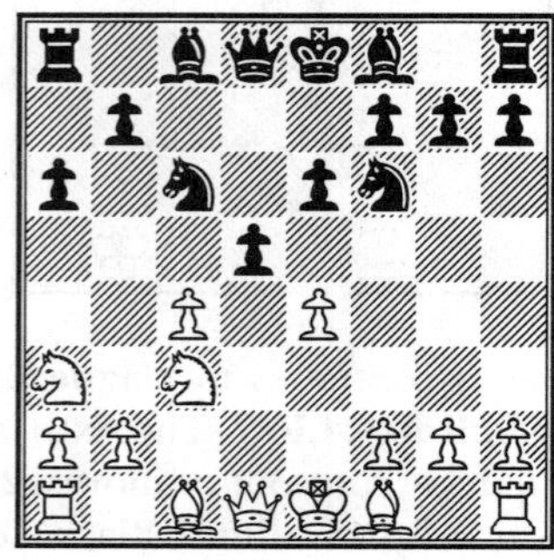

This is known as the Gary Gambit, because of the enormous impact his 1985 match games against Karpov caused at the time. Hungarian master Peter Dely is credited in much of the literature, and he tells the story of how he came up with the idea of this sacrifice while preparing to play his arch-rival Honfi at the 1965 Hungarian Championships, with Dely on a roll scoring 6 out of 7 points to start the event. In any case, the idea is to temporarily sacrifice the d-pawn in order to blast open the center and get active piece play. The theoretical battles in the variation took place mostly in the mid–1980s, but the line has not died out yet.

8...Be7 is the more traditional move, for example 9.Be2 0–0; 10.0–0 b6; 11.Be3 Bb7 (11...Ne5; 12.Rc1 Bb7; 13.f3 Rb8; 14.Bd4 Re8; 15.Qd2 Ra8; 16.Rfd1 Nfd7; 17.Bf1 Rc8; 18.Kh1 Qc7; 19.Qf2 Qb8 and Black had a good hedgehog position in a training game Nikitin-Kasparov, 1981.) 12.Qb3 (12.f3 Rb8; 13.Qe1 Nd7; 14.Qf2 Nc5; 15.Rfd1 f5; 16.exf5 Rxf5 and Black's pieces were better placed than their White counterparts in Saren-Karpov, Skopje Olympiad 1972.) 12...Na5 (12...Nd7; 13.Rfd1 Nc5; 14.Qc2 Qc7; 15.Rac1 Rac8; 16.Nab1 Ne5; 17.Nd2 Ncd7; 18.a3 Rfe8; 19.b4 Nf6; 20.h3 Ng6; 21.Qb1 Ba8; 22.Na4 Rb8 with a solid hedgehog position, Jadoul-Karpov, Brussels 1986.) 13.Qxb6 Nxe4; 14.Nxe4 Bxe4; 15.Qxd8 Bxd8; 16.Rad1 and White was better in Karpov-Kasparov, World Championship 1984.

9.cxd5 exd5; 10.exd5 Nb4; 11.Be2. 11.Qa4+ was seen in Peter Dely's original game, which we present in full as it shows a swashbuckling effort by Black: 11...Bd7; 12.Qb3 Be7?! Later it would become known that the bishop should be stationed at c5. 13.Bf4 Bg4; 14.f3 Nfxd5? The wrong knight! Black would have had excellent prospects after (14...Nbxd5 when it is hard to find a good move for White. If 15.fxg4 Nxf4; 16.Qa4+ b5; 17.Naxb5 0–0; 18.Qxf4 axb5; 19.Bxb5 then 19...Qb6 gives Black an excellent game.) 15.Nxd5 Nxd5; 16.fxg4 Nxf4; 17.Qa4+ b5; 18.Qxf4 0–0; 19.Qd2 Re8; 20.Kd1 Bg5; 21.Qxd8 Raxd8+; 22.Kc2 Rd2+; 23.Kc3 Rc8+; 24.Kb3 Bf6; 25.Rb1 Rc1; 26.Bxb5 Rxh1; 27.Rxh1 Rxb2+; 28.Kc4 axb5+; 29.Nxb5 Rxg2; 30.h3 Rxa2; 31.Re1 h5; 32.gxh5 Ra4+; 33.Kd5 Rh4; 34.Re3 Rxh5+; 35.Kc6 Bh4 was drawn in

Honfi-Dely, Hungary 1965.

11.Bc4 attempts to hold on to the pawn by rather crude means. 11...Bg4; 12.Be2 is a quiet move which does not challenge the validity of the gambit. (12.Qd4 b5 leads to an outright brawl after 13.Ncxb5!? axb5; 14.Bxb5+ Bd7; 15.d6 Nc2+; 16.Nxc2 Qa5+; 17.Bd2 Qxb5 and the fun is just beginning! 18.0–0–0 Rxa2; 19.Rhe1+ Be6; 20.Bb4 Qc6; 21.Kb1 Ra8; 22.f4 Kd7; 23.Re5 Ba2+; 24.Kc1 Bd5; 25.Rd3 Bxd6; 26.Bxd6 Rhc8; 27.Re7+ Kd8; 28.Rc3 Qxd6; 29.Rxf7 Rxc3; 30.bxc3 Ne8 and Black went on to win in Santo Roman-Kouatly, Cannes 1986. 12.f3 Bf5; 13.Qe2+ Be7; 14.0–0 0–0; 15.Rd1 Bc5+; 16.Kh1 Re8; 17.Qf1 b5 gave Black a fine game in Stanca-Crisan, Baile Herculane 1986.) 12...Bxe2; 13.Qxe2+ Qe7; 14.Be3 Nbxd5; 15.Nc2 (15.Nxd5 Nxd5; 16.0–0 was more ambitious.) 15...Nxe3; 16.Nxe3 Qe6; 17.0–0 Bc5; 18.Rfe1 0–0 was agreed drawn in the 12th game of the match between Karpov and Kasparov.

11...Bc5. 11...Nfxd5; 12.0–0 Be6; 13.Qa4+ (13.Nxd5 Qxd5; 14.Bc4 Qxd1; 15.Rxd1 Bc5; 16.Bxe6 fxe6; 17.Nc4 Nc2; 18.Rb1 0–0 was equal in Korneyev-Horvath, Velden Open 1993.) 13...b5 allows the thematic sacrifice 14.Naxb5 axb5; 15.Bxb5+ Ke7; 16.Nxd5+ Nxd5; 17.Qe4 with a lot of compensation for the piece. Here is an exciting example: 17...f5; 18.Qf3 Kf7; 19.Rd1 Rc8; 20.Ba4 Qh4; 21.Bb3 Nf6; 22.Bxe6+ Kxe6; 23.Re1+ Ne4; 24.g3 Qh3; 25.Be3 Bb4; 26.Bd4 Bxe1; 27.Qb3+ Ke7; 28.Rxe1 Rhd8; 29.Qb7+ Ke6; 30.f3 Rxd4; 31.Qxc8+ Kf7; 32.fxe4 Rd2; 33.Qc4+ Kg6; 34.exf5+ Kh5; 35.Qf7+ Kh6; 36.Re6+ Kg5; 37.Qxg7+ Kxf5; 38.Re5# Almasi-Horvath, Hungarian Championship 1993.

12.0–0. 12.Be3 Bxe3; 13.Qa4+ Nd7; 14.Qxb4 Bc5; 15.Qe4+ Kf8; 16.0–0 b5; 17.Nc2 Nf6; 18.Qd3 g6; 19.Bf3 Bf5; 20.Qd2 h5 with a complex game in Karpov-Van der Wiel, Brussels 1986. **12...0–0.**

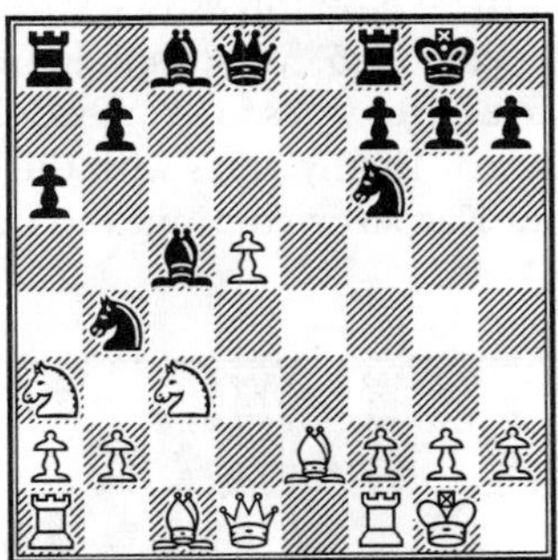

A great deal of research has gone into this position. **13.Bf3!** 13.Bg5 Nbxd5; 14.Nxd5 Qxd5; 15.Qxd5 Nxd5 brought about an even endgame in Barbulescu-Wirthensohn, World Team Championship 1985. **13...Bf5; 14.Bg5!?** A somewhat ineffective plan, given that Karpov finds the best defense. 14.Be3 Bxe3; 15.fxe3 Re8; 16.Qd4 a5; 17.e4 and White stood better in Turzo-Ivanovic, World Under-16 Boys Championship 1994. **14...Re8!** Kasparov has his eye trained on the critical e4 square. **15.Qd2.** 15.Nc4 Bd3; 16.a3 Bxc4; 17.axb4 Bxb4; 18.Re1 Rxe1+; 19.Qxe1 was an alternative continuation pointed out by Kasparov. **15...b5!** This pawn controls important squares which keep the White knights in a state of discomfort. **16.Rad1 Nd3!**

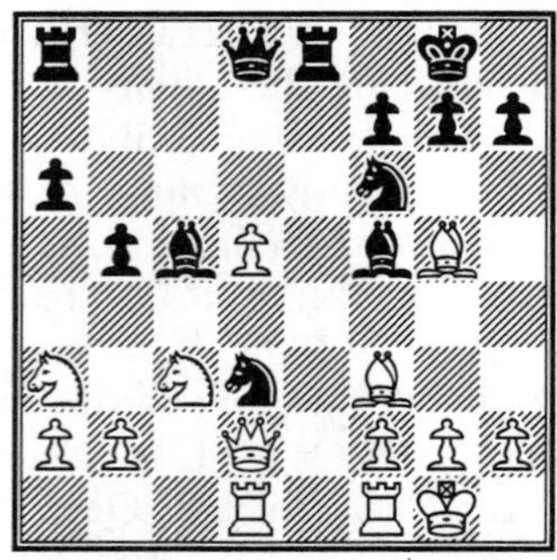

Here Karpov makes an obvious move which winds up getting him into deep trouble. **17.Nab1?** 17.d6 was best, according to Kasparov, though it is by no means clear what the evaluation should be after 17...Ra7!? (17...Qxd6; 18.Bxa8 Rxa8 is an interesting sacrificial plan.) 18.Nd5. **17...h6; 18.Bh4 b4!** Black now contains the enemy knights in a different manner. **19.Na4 Bd6; 20.Bg3 Rc8.** 20...Ne4 was an alternative which also looked good for Black. **21.b3 g5!** This prevents White from redeploying the knight at b2 because after exchanging knights there Black would have the strong move ...g4!

22.Bxd6. 22.h4 Ne4!; 23.Bxe4 Bxe4; 24.hxg5 Bxg3; 25.fxg3 Qxd5; 26.gxh6 Rc6 gives Black a strong attack, according to Kasparov. **22...Qxd6; 23.g3.** 23.Be2 just helps Black after 23...Nf4! **23...Nd7; 24.Bg2.** Bringing the knight to b2 would have led to massive complications but if Black steps through the minefield carefully he would have been rewarded with 24.Nb2 forces Black to find the amazing 24...Qf6!! and after 25.Nxd3 Bxd3; 26.Qxd3 Ne5. White's lady finds herself in a position of extreme embarrassment, since 27.Qe3 loses to 27...Nxf3+! **24...Qf6; 25.a3 a5; 26.axb4 axb4; 27.Qa2 Bg6; 28.d6.** Karpov finally parts with the extra pawn, hoping to gain some scope for his pieces, but Kasparov continues to clamp down on the position. **28...g4! 29.Qd2 Kg7; 30.f3 Qxd6.**

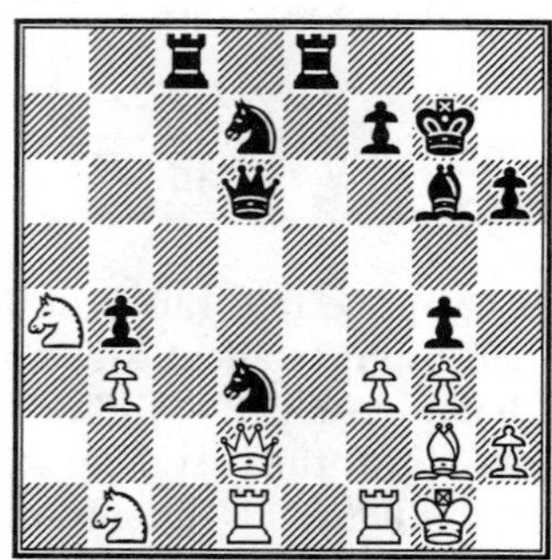

Black has an overwhelming positional advantage which culminates in an effective kingside attack. **31.fxg4 Qd4+; 32.Kh1 Nf6; 33.Rf4 Ne4; 34.Qxd3.** The queen has been staring at this horse for far too long, and now sacrifices herself to eliminate it, but after **34...Nf2+ 35.Rxf2 Bxd3; 36.Rfd2 Qe3; 37.Rxd3.** Kasparov has the final word with **37...Rc1!!** and the game was over: **38.Nb2 Qf2; 39.Nd2 Rxd1+; 40.Nxd1**

Re1+. White resigned. Kasparov considered this game his "supreme creative achievement" and although he has gone on to win many impressive games, this is surely one of his best. **Black won.**

(81) KASPAROV - KENGIS [B47]

Riga (Tal Memorial), 1995

1.e4 c5; 2.Nf3 e6; 3.d4 cxd4; 4.Nxd4 Nc6; 5.Nc3 Qc7. This is a more typical Paulsen Variation. Black develops slowly but creates a formation that is hard to crack. **6.Be2 a6; 7.0–0 Nf6.**

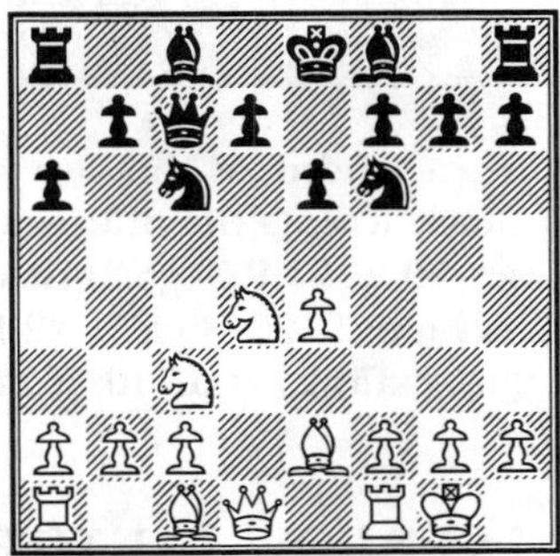

8.Kh1. White plays this move so that the f-pawn can advance. **8...Nxd4; 9.Qxd4 Bc5.** The exchange of knights allows the bishop to develop with tempo. Black should follow this with ...b5 and ...Bb7. **10.Qd3 h5?!** This is premature. Black should first play ...b5 and ...Bb7, and only then begin the kingside assault, as Ivanchuk demonstrated against Anand at the Buenos Aires Thematic Tournament, 1994. **11.Bg5!?** How real is the threat to capture the knight? Not very substantial, since that would only open another line to the White kingside. **11...b5; 12.f4.**

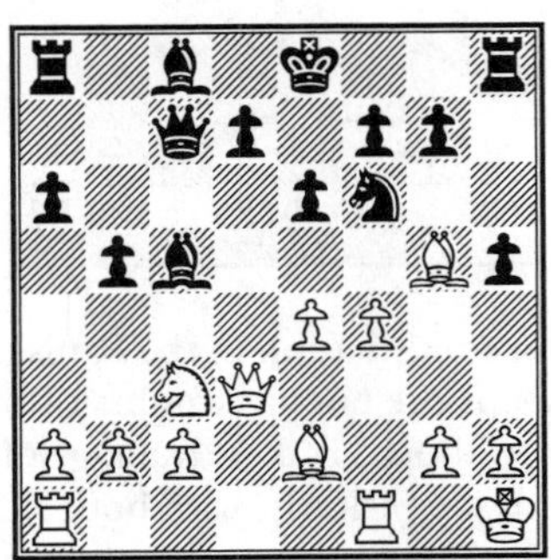

12...Bb7. Black fails to appreciate the danger. There is a White pawn at f4 and that means that the e5-square is under White's control. **13.e5! Nd5.** 13...Ng4 can be met by 14.Bf3!, since 14...Nf2+ fails to 15.Rxf2 Bxf2; 16.Bxb7 Qxb7; 17.Ne4 as pointed out by Dolmatov. **14.Nxd5 Bxd5; 15.a4.** 15.Bf3 would have been more to the point. **15...Qc6; 16.Bf3 Bxf3; 17.Rxf3.** White's forces are in place, and if Black castles anytime soon, the sacrificial move Bf6! is in the offing. **17...bxa4; 18.f5 Rb8; 19.Raf1 0–0?** This is an invitation that will not be refused!

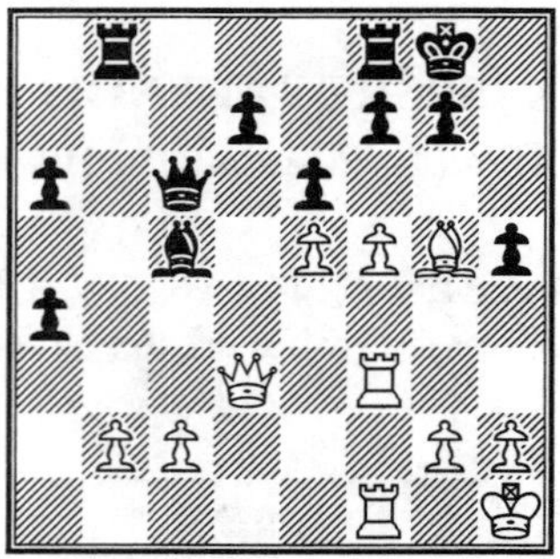

20.Bf6! The bishop can be sacrificed, as the heavy artillery remains aimed at the enemy king. **20...Qb5.** If Black accepts the offer with 20...gxf6 then 21.Rg3+ is followed by Qe2 and mate is inevitable. **21.Rg3 g6.** If Black captures the queen at d3, then White wins with a typical motif: 21...Qxd3; 22.Rxg7+ Kh8; 23.Rg5+ Kh7; 24.Rxh5+ Kg8; 25.Rh8#. **22.Qd1 exf5; 23.Rxf5 Rb6; 24.Qxh5.** Checkmate cannot be prevented. **White won.**

(82) KASPAROV - LAUTIER [B48]

Amsterdam (Euwe Memorial), 1995

1.e4 c5; 2.Nf3 e6; 3.d4 cxd4; 4.Nxd4 Nc6; 5.Nc3 Qc7; 6.Be3 a6.

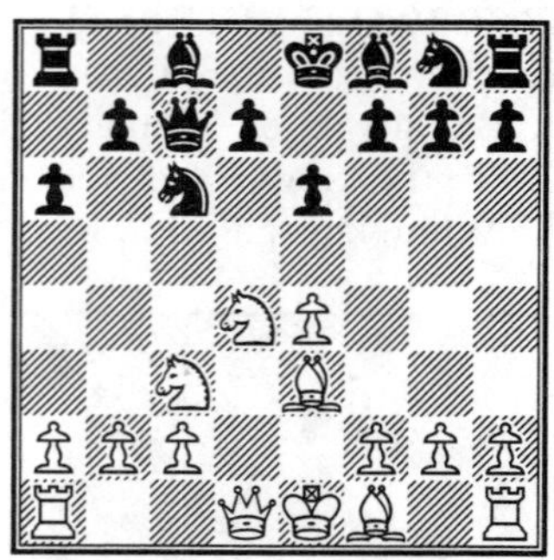

This is the most common continuation in the Paulsen. It is sometimes called the Bastrikov Variation. Black keeps the enemy knights off of b5 and d5, and will catch up in development later. White hopes to take advantage of the weakened dark squares. The opening usually proceeds fairly slowly, with both sides castling on the kingside. White can try many different plans of attack, but the key battle is for the d4 square. White will often exchange knights and then station a bishop there. Black seeks counterplay through pawn advances on the queenside.

7.Bd3 Nf6. 7...b5; 8.0–0 Bb7; 9.Nxc6 Qxc6; 10.Re1 Nf6; 11.Bd4 Be7 is another plan. Now 12.Qf3 can be met by the new move 12...b4! and however the knight retreats, Black responds with d6 and has a solid position. For example 13.Nd1 d6; 14.b3 0–0; 15.Bb2 as in J.Polgar-Leko, Dortmund 1996, where Black could have equalized with 15...Rfe8. **8.0–0 Ne5.** 8...Nxd4; 9.Bxd4 Bc5; 10.Be2 Qd6!? is now an interesting continuation. White seems to have the better prospects after exchanging on c5, Kozakov-Poluyakhov, Krasnodar 1996.

9.h3 Bc5; 10.Kh1 d6; 11.f4 Ned7. 11...Ng6; 12.Qe2 0–0; 13.Rae1 e5; 14.fxe5 dxe5; 15.Nf3 Nf4; 16.Qf2 Bxe3; 17.Rxe3 Be6; 18.Ng5 h6; 19.Nxe6 fxe6!; 20.Rf3 was agreed drawn in Ivanovic-Pikula, Yugoslav Championship 1996. **12.a3 b5.** 12...0–0 is also an option. Now White can sacrifice at b5. **13.Bxb5!? axb5; 14.Ndxb5 Qb6?!**

14...Qc6 is a better choice. 15.Bxc5 dxc5; 16.e5 Ba6; 17.a4 (17.Nd6+!? Ke7; 18.Rf2 Rhd8; 19.Rd2 gives White compensation, according to Kasparov.) 17...Nd5; 18.Nxd5 exd5; 19.Nd6+ Ke7; 20.Re1 h5; 21.Qf3 and White's threat of c4 gives enough compensation–Kasparov. **15.Bxc5 dxc5; 16.Nd6+?!** This is too optimistic, and Kasparov should have advanced the e-pawn instead. 16.e5 Ba6; 17.a4! Bxb5; 18.Nxb5 Nd5 and here White could explore both 19.c4 and the check at d6. **16...Ke7; 17.Nxc8+?** Another error from the World Champion. The need to advance the e-pawn just hadn't sunk in. 17.e5 Ba6; 18.Rf2 Rhd8; 19.Rd2 Qxb2!? 20.Na4 Qb8 and Black would be a a little better if he could find a way to untangle the pieces. **17...Rhxc8; 18.e5 Ne8.**

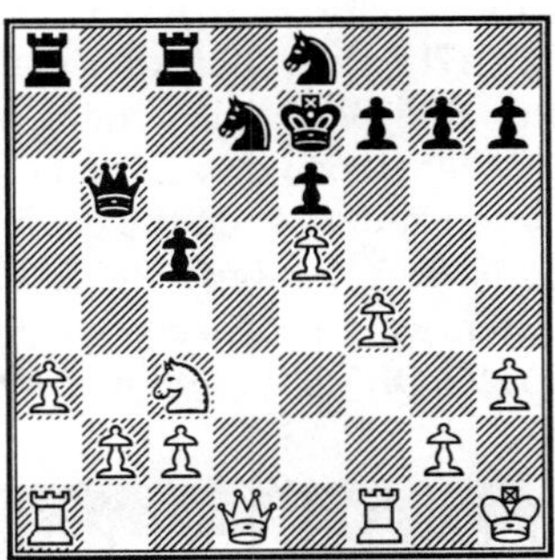

There can be no doubt that Black has the advantage here. White has only two pawns for the piece, and the Black king has plenty of protection. It just takes too long now for White to get an attack going. Note how well-defended the d6-square is. **19.Qh5.** White might have tried Knaak's idea of b3 here. **19...h6.** 19...Qxb2!?; 20.Qh4+! f6; 21.Ne4 Qxc2; 22.Rae1 gives White a powerful attack, according to Knaak. **20.Rae1.** 20.f5? fails to 20...Nxe5; 21.fxe6 Qxe6; 22.Rae1 f6. **20...f5!** Now White will never advance the f-pawn, and the Black king is safe. **21.Rf3.** 21.exf6+ fails to open up any significant lines. 21...Nexf6; 22.Qg6 Kf8 and there is no way to continue the attack. **21...c4?!** Black should have cold-bloodedly grabbed the b-pawn.

22.g4! Now White has some fighting chances. **22...fxg4.** 22...Qc6 comes into consideration, pinning the enemy rook and reducing its effectiveness. **23.Qxg4.** White at least has a plan now. The f-pawn can advance. **23...Ra5!** Black constructs a defense along the fifth rank. 23...Qxb2? would come too late now, as after 24.f5 Black's king is under fire.

24.Ne4 Qc6?! The idea here is to set up a pin against the White king. Still, the position of the knight at e4, though well-centralized, means that the e-pawn is no longer protected by the rook at e1. Therefore Black could take the opportunity to capture at b2, with ...Qxe5 a real threat. For example 24...Qxb2! 25.Nd6 Nxd6; 26.exd6+ Kxd6 (26...Kf8?; 27.f5!,) 27.Qxe6+ Kc7; 28.Rd1 (28.Qxc4+ Rc5) 28...Nb6; 24...Qxb2; 25.Nd6 Rc6 and there is no way to continue the attack. 26.Nxe8 Kxe8;

27.Qxg7 Rxa3 and White is lost.

25.Nd6! The pawn at g7 becomes a target now, since the Black knight must evacuate e8. **25...Nxd6; 26.exd6+ Kf8.** 26...Qxd6; 27.Qxg7+ Kd8; 28.Qxh6 would give White three pawns for the piece.

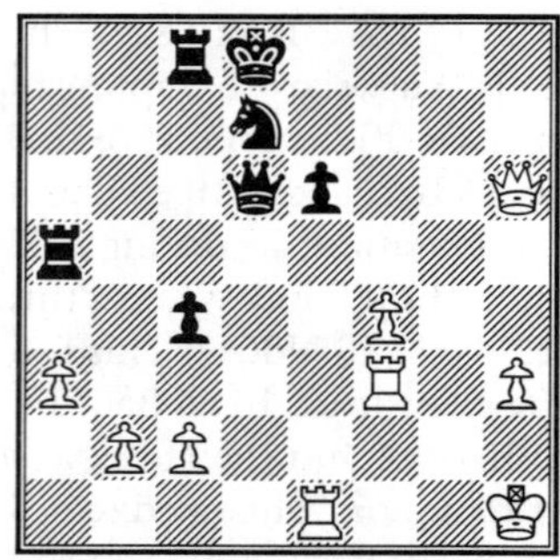

Time pressure now plays a major role. **27.Rg1?** White just did not have enough time left to properly assess the situation. 27.Rxe6! was the correct plan. 27...Re8 (Not 27...Nf6?? because of 28.d7! Qxd7; 29.Rxf6+ gxf6; 30.Qxd7 .) 28.Re7 Rxe7; 29.dxe7+ Kxe7; 30.Qxg7+ Kd8 and Black still retains a small advantage, though it would be much greater if the White b-pawn wasn't on the board. **27...g5!** The finishing touch! Black relies on the pin at f3 to keep the enemy rook at bay, and keeps the g-file closed. **28.Rgg3.** 28.fxg5+ Rf5; 29.Rgg3 Ne5; 30.Qh5 Rxf3; 31.Qxh6+ Kg8; 32.Qxe6+ and Black ends matters with the discovered check 32...Rf7+ when it is time for White to resign. **28...Rf5; 29.Qh5 Nf6; 30.Qxh6+ Kf7; 31.Kg1 Rg8.** White resigned. **Black won.**

CANAL VARIATION

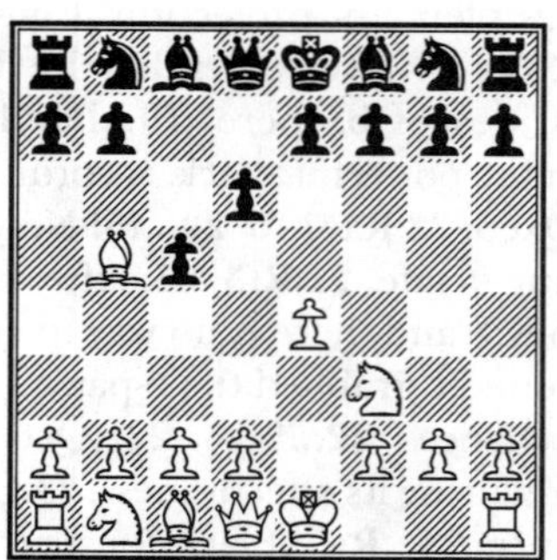

1.e4 c5
2.Nf3 d6
3.Bb5+

The **Canal Variation** goes by many names. It shares, with 1.e4 c5; 2.Nf3 Nc6; 3.Bb5, the uninformative title **Anti-Sicilian**, but has also been attributed to Rossolimo. Canal, who was a major theoretician in his day, also deserves some credit for the line. White's idea is to trade off the light-squared bishop if Black plays 3...Bd7, and can then set up a Maroczy Bind formation with c4, as we will see in the next game. The most interesting defense, however, is to block the check with a knight, later driving back the bishop with ...a6 and continuing to develop in normal Sicilian fashion.

In this game we see the inventor of the Najdorf handling the Black pieces in a manner which is equally approved of today. Notice that the game takes on many Spanish characteristics in the middlegame, and the ease of playing Spanish position is one of the factors that appeals to players of the White side.

(83) CANAL - NAJDORF [B51]
Venice, 1948

1.e4 c5; 2.Nf3 d6; 3.Bb5+ Nd7. 3...Nc6 is an alternative method of dealing with the check. 4.0–0 and now Black has many options. 4...Bd7 (4...Nf6; 5.Re1 e5; 6.c3 Bd7; 7.d4 Qc7; 8.Bg5 Be7; 9.Bxf6 Bxf6; 10.dxc5 dxc5; 11.Bxc6 worked out better for White in O'Kelly-Najdorf, Amsterdam 1950, since if Black takes back with the bishop, then c4 is strong.

4...a6 just encourages the move that White was going to play anyway, the capture at c6. 5.Bxc6+ bxc6; 6.d4 cxd4; 7.Qxd4 gives White a big lead in development, Aronin-Kotov, Moscow 1949. 4...Bg4; 5.h3 Bh5; 6.Bxc6+ bxc6; 7.d3 e5; 8.Nbd2 Be7; 9.Nc4 gave White an active position in Govashelichvili-Tukmakov, Soviet Union 1978.)

5.c3 can be played as a gambit after (5.c4 Nf6; 6.Nc3 gives White a favorable Maroczy Bind formation, Gurgenidze-Timoschenko, USSR 1977.) 5...a6; 6.Bxc6 Bxc6; 7.Re1 Nf6; 8.d4 Bxe4; 9.Bg5 and now Black's best defense is 9...Bd5!; 10.Nbd2 c4; 11.b3 b5; 12.bxc4 bxc4; 13.Nf1 with compensation for the pawn in Fetter-Ruban, Miskolo 1990.

White has three basic plans here. One is to open up the game with 4.d4, the second is simply castling, and the third is to attempt to create the ideal pawn center by supporting the d4 advance with a preliminary c3. **4.c3** 4.0–0 a6!? (4...Ngf6; 5.d4 Nxe4 may be a bit risky for Black, but 5...cxd4, entering open Sicilian lines, is better, as in Ivanchuk-Kasparov, Linares 1991.) 5.Bxd7+ Bxd7; 6.d4 e6; 7.Nc3 Ne7; 8.dxc5 dxc5; 9.Ne5 Nc6; 10.Nxd7 (10.Nxc6 Bxc6; 11.Qg4 Qf6; 12.Rd1 Be7; 13.Qg3 0–0; 14.Bf4 Rfd8; 15.Bc7 Rxd1+; 16.Rxd1 Qg6; 17.Qxg6 hxg6; 18.Bd6 Bxd6; 19.Rxd6 Kf8 led to a better endgame for Black in Rossolimo-Najdorf, Havana 1952.) 10...Qxd7; 11.Qxd7+ Kxd7; 12.Be3 Ne5; 13.Rad1+ Kc6 with equal chances in Kostic-Najdorf, Bled 1950.

4.d4 Ngf6; 5.0–0 a6; 6.Bxd7+ Nxd7; 7.Nc3 e6 of course Black can also open up the game with ...cxd4, leading to Scheveningen positions where White does not suffer from the lack of a light-squared bishop but Black may miss the knight, which is an effective queenside attacker. 8.Bg5 Qc7; 9.Re1 cxd4; 10.Qxd4 Ne5! and Black had a decent game in Ljubojevic-Kasparov, Amsterdam 1991, because White does not dare to capture at e5, which would only open more lines for the enemy bishop pair.

4...a6; 5.Ba4!? A plan in true Spanish style. In fact, play can easily transpose to Spanish territory if Black plays ...e5, as occurs in this game. **5...Ngf6; 6.Bc2 e5; 7.d4.**

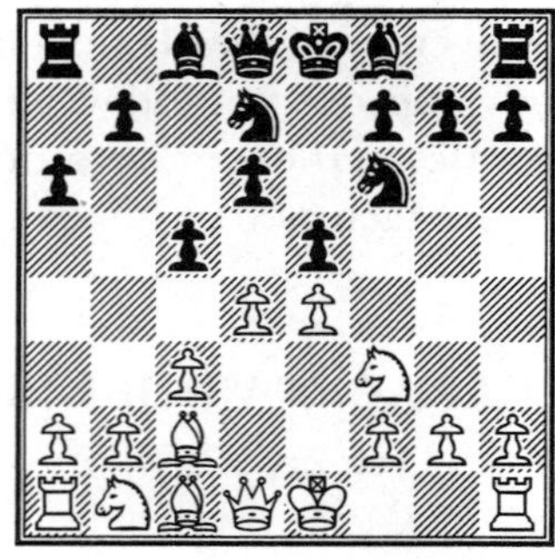

The only thing that makes this position different from a normal Spanish is that Black hasn't played ...b5, but that move is in any case inevitable. **7...Be7; 8.0–0 0–0; 9.Nbd2 Qc7; 10.Re1 Re8; 11.Nf1 Bf8; 12.h3 g6.** Each move has conformed to standard Spanish play. **13.Ne3 b5; 14.d5 c4.**

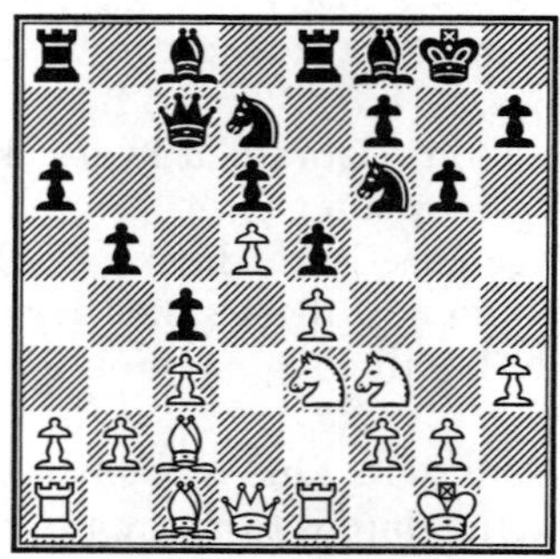

We have now reached a typical Closed Spanish position. White has gained a little time by playing Bb5-a4-c2 rather than Bb5-a4-b3-c2, but on the other hand Black has played ...Nbd7 instead of ...Nc6-b8-d7 as in the Breyer Variation of the Spanish. Indeed, the bishop at c8 also stands better than if it were on b7, as is typical in the Breyer.

15.Nh2 Nc5; 16.Qf3 Bg7; 17.g4 h6; 18.Nef1. The f1 square sees a lot of action in this game as a transfer square for knights and even the king. **18...Nh7; 19.Be3 a5.** Black must try to attack on the queenside, as otherwise White will have a free hand on the kingside. **20.Ng3 Qe7; 21.Qg2.** White seems to have difficulty coming up with a coherent plan. **21...Kh8; 22.Kf1 b4; 23.Nf3 bxc3!** Black is creating some roon to operate on the queenside. **24.bxc3 Nd3!** Black is going to get a weak pawn at d3, but it is remarkably difficult for White to get at it. **25.Bxd3 cxd3.**

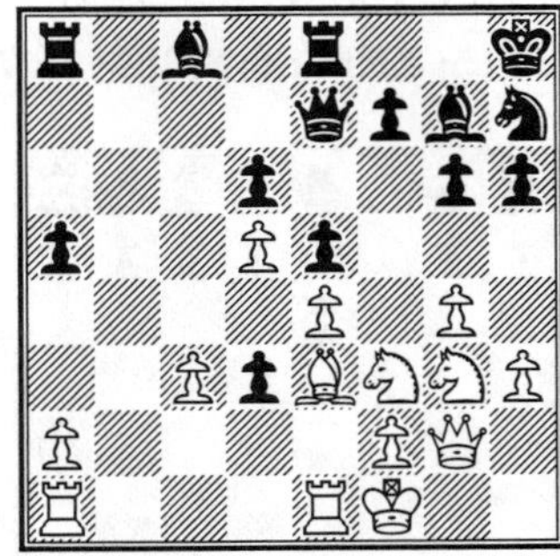

26.Nd2 Rf8! Now Black is ready to strike not on the queenside, but back on the kingside! **27.Reb1.** Perhaps the other rook would have been wiser. Another option is Kg1, so that the opening of the f-file will not be so dangerous. **27...h5!; 28.f3 f5!** Black temporarily sacrifices a pawn to keep the initiative going. **29.exf5 h4; 30.Nge4 gxf5; 31.gxf5 Bxf5; 32.Ke1.** White could have initiated counterplay with Rb6 immediately. **32...Nf6; 33.c4 Qc7; 34.Rb6 Nxe4; 35.fxe4 Bh7.** Black's bishop pair is walled off from the game, for the moment. **36.Rab1 Rf7; 37.Qg4 Rg8!** Black has not given up on the kingside attack. **38.Rc6 Qe7; 39.Qe6.**

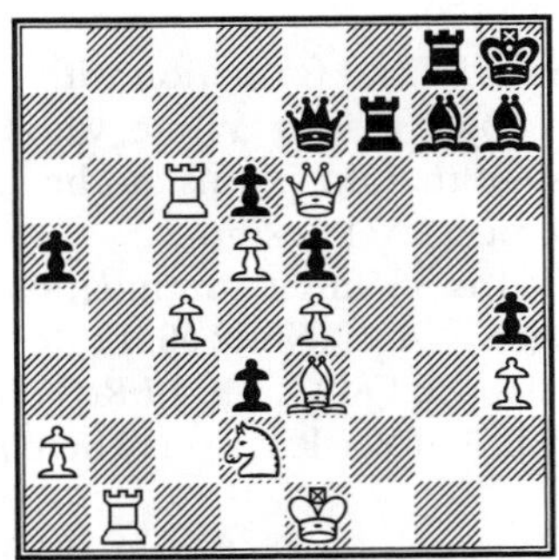

White tries to exchange the queens, hoping that the healthier pawn structure will find a future in the endgame. **39...Bf8; 40.Qxe7 Bxe7; 41.Rb3** why bother with the pawn? 41.Rb7 seemed much more to the point. This was likely the first move White made after time control, and that is always a dangerous moment, psychologically. **41...Rg3! 42.Rxd3 Rxh3.** Black now has the more dangerous passed pawn and a nasty pin. Still, White has counterplay. **43.Rb3! a4; 44.Rb8+ Kg7; 45.Ke2?** White had to play c5 here, to keep some sort of counterplay going. **45...Bg6; 46.Rcc8 Bf8; 47.c5** A bit late now. **47...dxc5; 48.Re8 Rg3.**

Now things are looking very grim for White. The best practical chance was to play Kd3, retreat a rook to the first rank, and prepare to sacrifice a piece for the flying h-pawn at some point, hoping to pick off the remaining weak Black pawns and find some sort of drawing line. White panics here, and plays a useless sacrifice. **49.Rxf8 Bh5+!; 50.Kd3 Rxf8; 51.Rb7+ Rf7; 52.Rb6 h3; 53.Rb1 h2; 54.Rh1 Rf2!** A final, elegant exploitation of the theme of pins that has run throughout the game. **Black won.**

(84) BENJAMIN - GUREVICH, I [B52]

New York Open, 1991

1.e4 c5; 2.Nf3 d6; 3.Bb5+ Bd7.

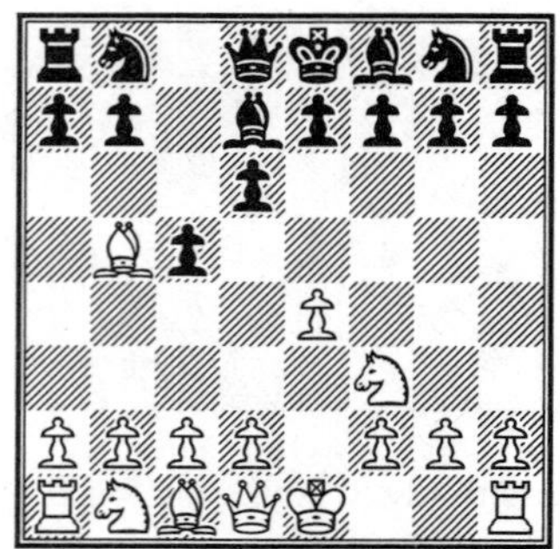

This is the most common way of greeting the bishop check. **4.Bxd7+ Qxd7.** 4...Nxd7 is also possible, but the knight does not stand all that well there. 5.0–0 (5.c4 is possible here as well, for example 5...Ngf6; 6.Nc3 g6; 7.d4 cxd4; 8.Nxd4 Bg7; 9.0–0 0–0; 10.Be3 a6; 11.Rc1 Rc8; 12.b3 with a typical hedgehog position in Shamkovich-Browne, USA Championship 1980.) 5...Ngf6; 6.Qe2 e6; 7.b3 Be7; 8.Bb2 0–0; 9.d4 cxd4; 10.Nxd4 Qc7; 11.c4 a6; 12.Nc3 Rfe8; 13.f4 and White controlled more space in Tal-Miles, Riga Interzonal 1979.

5.c4. This sets up a Maroczy Bind formation with the light-squared bishops removed from the board. This ought to favor White, who has eliminated the problematic bad bishop, but it turns out that the pawns on the light squares are a bit vulnerable, so this is considered to be a level position.

5.0–0 Nc6; 6.c3 Nf6; 7.d4 is a gambit continuation that seems to have run its course. 7...cxd4; 8.cxd4 d5; 9.e5 Ne4; 10.Nbd2 e6; 11.Re1 Nxd2; 12.Bxd2 Be7; 13.Bg5 Bxg5; 14.Nxg5 Qe7; 15.Nf3 0–0; 16.Qd2 Rac8; 17.Re3 b6; 18.Rc1 Na5; 19.Rec3 Qd7; 20.Qc2 Rxc3; 21.Qxc3 h6; 22.b3 left Black in a small bind in Hakki-Mohamed, Yerevan Olympiad 1996.

5...Nc6 is the most common move, even though Black is inviting the full Maroczy Bind. 5...e5 is a radical departure from the usual Maroczy Bind, but the point is that White cannot play d4 now, and that means the center will remain closed. This system has been seen even in quite recent tournaments.

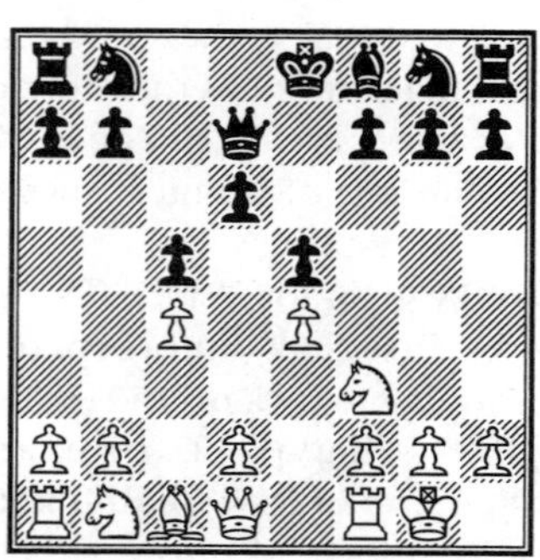

6.0–0 (6.Nc3 Nc6; 7.0–0 Nge7; 8.Nd5 Nxd5; 9.cxd5 Nd4; 10.Nxd4 cxd4; 11.d3 Be7; 12.Qb3 0–0; 13.f4 and White had the initiative, Karpov-Ribli, Bath 1973.) 6...g6; 7.Nc3

A) 7...Bh6; 8.Nd5 Nc6; 9.a3. It is true that White does not want to advance the d-pawn to d3, allowing the exchange of bishops. White has a surprising plan in store for the d-pawn, however. 9...Nce7; 10.b4 Nxd5; 11.cxd5 cxb4.

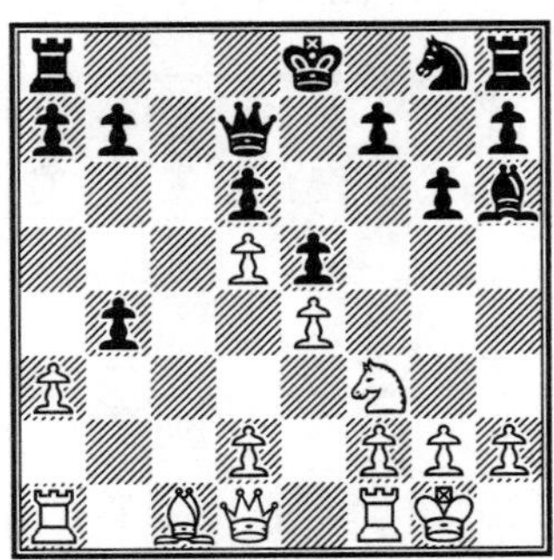

Here Black must have surely counted on White's recapturing at b4, but with the enemy king still trapped in the center, Larsen comes up with a surprising plan. 12.d4!!

A1) 12...Bxc1; 13.Rxc1! and now if 13...bxa3 (13...exd4; 14.Qxd4 f6; 15.e5! dxe5; 16.Nxe5 fxe5; 17.Qxe5+ Qe7; 18.Qxh8 and White wins.) then 14.dxe5! dxe5; 15.Nxe5 Qe7; 16.Qa4+ Kf8 (16...Kd8; 17.Qd4 f6; 18.Nc4 leaves the Black king in a most precarious position.) 17.Nd7+ Kg7; 18.Qd4+ f6 (18...Nf6; 19.Nxf6 Qxf6; 20.e5 Qd8; 21.d6 and Black cannot defend against threats of Rc7 or e6+.)

A2) 12...f6; 13.dxe5 fxe5; 14.axb4 Bxc1; 15.Rxc1 Nf6; 16.Ng5 0–0; 17.f4 and White had a good attack and a big target at e6 in Larsen-Suboticanec, Zagreb 1955.

B) 7...Bg7 is more sensible, but after 8.Rb1 Nc6; 9.d3 Nge7; 10.Bd2 0–0; 11.Nd5 Nxd5 (11...Rab8; 12.b4 Nxd5; 13.exd5 Nxb4; 14.Bxb4 cxb4; 15.Rxb4 Rfe8; 16.Re1 Qc7; 17.Qb3 and White's knight is more powerful than the Black bishop, Schmid-Andersson, Nice Olympiad 1974.) 12.cxd5 Nd4; 13.b4 Black must not sit still, but should open things up with 13...f5! with unclear complications in Shaked-Kaidanov, United States Championship 1996.

5...g6 is a completely different approach. 6.d4 (6.Nc3 was played in one of the early Sokolsky games in the line: 6...Bg7; 7.d3 Nc6; 8.Be3 Nh6; 9.h3 f5; 10.Bxh6 Bxh6; 11.exf5 gxf5; 12.d4 Qe6+; 13.Qe2 Qxe2+; 14.Nxe2 0–0; 15.d5 Nb4; 16.0–0 with a superior pawn structure for White in Sokolsky-Goldberg, Soviet Championship 1947.) 6...cxd4; 7.Nxd4 Bg7; 8.0–0 Nc6 sets a clever trap. 9.Ne2?? is now a major mistake. (9.Be3 Nf6; 10.f3 is a much more solid approach, where White has the usual small advantage typical of the Maroczy Bind.) 9...Ne5! and now White has nothing better than trying a pawn sacrifice, as b3 is out of the question and Nd2 leads to too much congestion. 10.Nbc3 Nxc4; 11.b3 Nb6; 12.a4 Qd8; 13.Be3 Nf6; 14.Rc1 0–0; 15.h3 Nbd7; 16.g4 Ne5; 17.f4 Nc6; 18.f5 Rc8; 19.Nf4. White stood better in Morozevich-Topalov, Pamplona Open 1995

On the other hand, 5...Qg4; 6.0–0 Qxe4; 7.d4 cxd4; 8.Re1! gives White plenty of compensation for the pawns, for example 8...Qc6; 9.Nxd4 Qxc4; 10.Na3 Qc8; 11.Bf4 Qd7; 12.Nab5 e5; 13.Bxe5 dxe5; 14.Rxe5+ Be7; 15.Rd5 Qc8; 16.Nf5 Kf8; 17.Nxe7

Kxe7; 18.Re5+ and Black resigned in Browne-Quinteros, Wijk aan Zee 1974.

6.d4. 6.Nc3 g6; 7.d4 Bg7!? was tried by Kasparov against Shirov at the 1996 Olympiad in Yerevan. Black got the upper hand after (7...cxd4; 8.Nxd4 Bg7 transposes below.) 8.d5 Bxc3+! 9.bxc3 Na5; 10.0–0 f6! 11.Nd2 b6; 12.Qe2?! (12.Rb1 Nh6; 13.Nb3 Nxb3; 14.axb3 Nf7; 15.f4 0–0 is assessed as equal by Shirov.) 12...Qa4; 13.f4 Nh6; 14.e5 0–0–0. 6.0–0 g6; 7.d4 cxd4; 8.Nxd4 Bg7; 9.Be3 (9.Ne2 Ne5;) 9...Nf6; 10.f3 0–0; 11.Nc3 transposes below. **6...cxd4.**

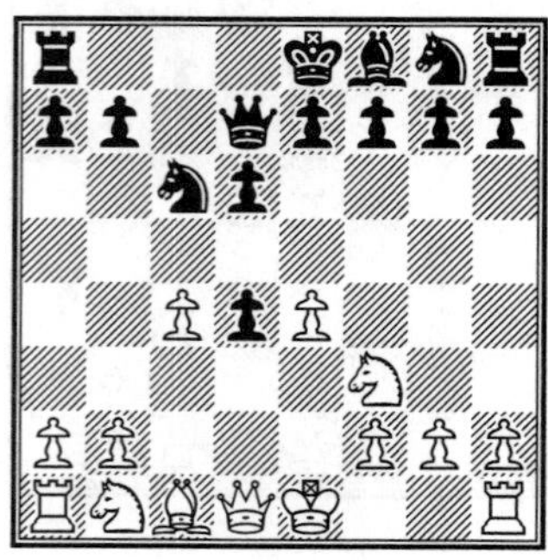

6...Qg4 is a strange, and ultimately unsuccessful plan: 7.d5 Nd4; 8.Nbd2 Nxf3+; 9.Qxf3 Nf6; 10.Qxg4 Nxg4; 11.Nf3 e5; 12.dxe6 fxe6; 13.h3 Nf6; 14.e5 dxe5; 15.Nxe5 leaves Black with an inferior pawn structure, as in Tal-Balashov, Soviet Championship 1974. **7.Nxd4 g6; 8.Nc3 Bg7; 9.Be3.** 9.Nde2 Nf6; 10.0–0 0–0; 11.f3 a6; 12.a4 e6 (12...Rfc8; 13.b3 Qd8; 14.Kh1 Nd7; 15.Bg5 Qa5; 16.Qd2 Nc5; 17.Rab1 e6; 18.Rfd1 Rab8; 19.Bh4 Qb6; 20.Qxd6 brought White the advantage in Kramnik-Gelfand, Match 1994.) 13.Bg5 Qc7 was about equal in Shirov-J.Polgar, Vienna 1996. **9...Nf6; 10.f3 0–0; 11.0–0.**

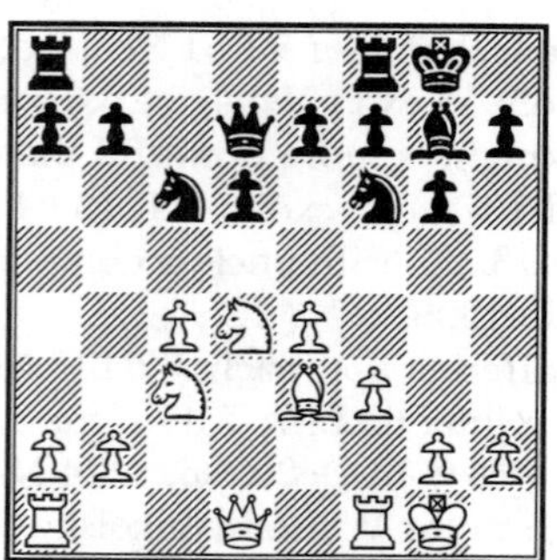

This is a very typical hedgehog position, except that the light-squared bishops are gone from the board. This works somewhat to White's advantage, because a light-squared White bishop would find itself frustrated sitting behind the pawn chain. If Black had such a bishop, it might operate effectively from e6 or play a supporting role at b7.

11...e6. A new plan, intending to force through ...d5 as soon as possible. There are no less than six alternatives, but none are known to guarantee equality. 11...Rac8; 12.b3 Rfd8; 13.Rc1 e6 shows the same plan executed a bit later. 14.Kh1 (14.Qd2 b6;

15.Nxc6 Rxc6; 16.Rfd1 Qb7; 17.Bg5 Rd7; 18.Qf4 Ne8; 19.Qh4 a6 and Black's hedgehog formation held up well in a game between the two Andrade brothers at the 1995 World Under-16 Championship.) 14...d5; 15.exd5 exd5; 16.c5 Ne8; 17.Ncb5 a6; 18.Nc3 Nc7; 19.Na4 Qe7; 20.Re1 Ne6; 21.Nb6 Rb8; 22.Nxc6 bxc6; 23.b4 and White had a strong position in Kasparov-Zelkind, Simultaneous Exhibition 1994.

11...a6 can be played immediately, since a hedgehog is intended. For example 12.a4 Rac8; 13.Nb3 and now again 13...e6 is playable, as in Platonov-Polugayevsky, USSR 1971, which saw further 14.Rc1 Rfd8; 15.Qd2 Na5 with sufficient counterplay for Black. **12.Qd2 Ne5; 13.b3.**

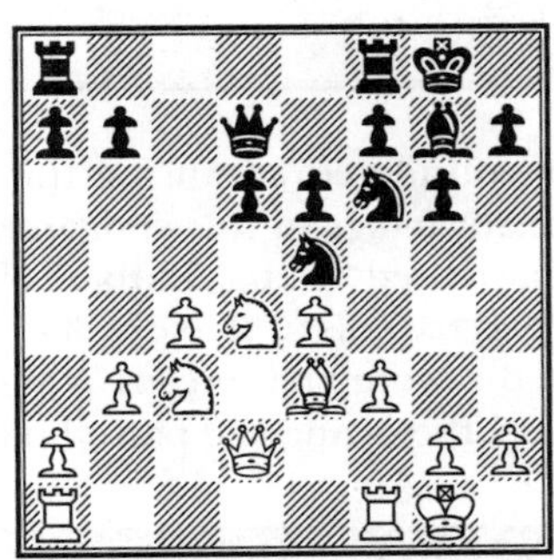

Black now seizes the opportunity to carry out the Sicilian break. **13...d5!?; 14.exd5 exd5; 15.c5.** White leaves Black with a weak pawn at d5, and has a mobile queenside pawn majority. **15...Rfd8; 16.Rfd1 Rac8; 17.Ndb5 Bf8.** This sets up a tactical trap, but while White walks in the general direction, the trap is avoided. **18.Nxa7!?** This looks reasonable enough, as there is no way to directly exploit the position of the knight at a7 but there are indirect threats based on the weakness of the g1-a7 diagonal. 18.Qf2 a6; 19.Qg3 is an interesting alternative.

18...Rxc5; 19.Bd4!? 19.Bxc5 Bxc5+; 20.Kh1 Bxa7 and Black has a virtually winning position. 19.Na4! looks strong too, and may be less complicated than the text. **19...Qf5; 20.Qe3 Ned7; 21.Nab5.** This did not have to be played immediately, but it makes sense to extricate the knight immediately. **21...Rcc8; 22.Qd3 Qh5.** 22...Qxd3; 23.Rxd3 Bc5 would have left Black a bit worse in the endgame because of the weak pawn. **23.Re1.** 23.Ne2 is a logical alternative, opening up a lot of possibilities for both of White's knights. **23...Rc6; 24.Rad1 Bg7; 25.Re7.** 25.Bxf6 Nxf6; 26.Re7 is also better for White. **25...b6; 26.Na7.**

Doubling rooks on the e-file might have been more natural. Of course White could try the more ambitious 26.g4 Qg5; 27.Be3 Qh4 after which play could become quite lively, for example 28.g5 Ng4 (28...d4; 29.Qxd4! Qxd4; 30.Bxd4 Nh5; 31.Bxg7 Nxg7; 32.Rdxd7) 29.fxg4 Qxg4+; 30.Kf2 Qh4+; 31.Kf1 Qh3+; 32.Ke1 Qh4+; 33.Bf2 Qb4; 34.Re3 Rdc8; 35.Rc1 and White has an extra piece, but is very tied down. **26...Re6; 27.Rxe6 fxe6; 28.Nc6 Re8; 29.Re1.**

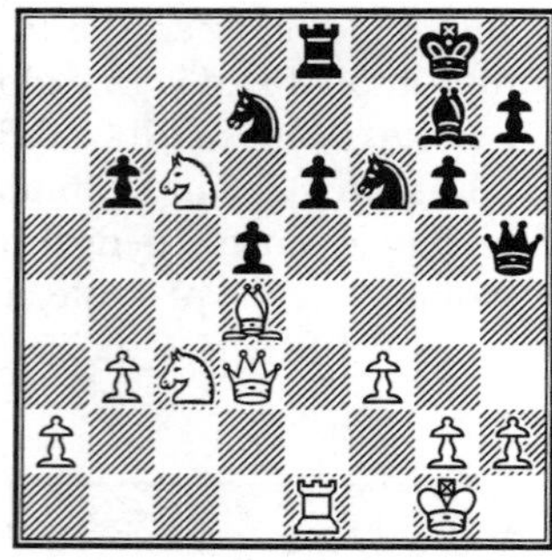

Here Black might have considered advancing the e-pawn. **29...Qf5; 30.Qxf5 gxf5; 31.Na4.** White has the advantage in this endgame, because Black's b-pawn is weak. **31...e5.** Black should have tried 31...b5. **32.Bxb6 Nxb6; 33.Nxb6 Re6; 34.Nc8!** This saves the piece, since 34...Rxc6 fails to 35.Ne7+. **34...Bf8; 35.N8a7 Bc5+; 36.Kf1.** White has an advantage, but the score I have reads White won at this point. Perhaps Black lost on time. In any case, the connected passed pawns were ready to advance. **White won.**

CLASSICAL VARIATION

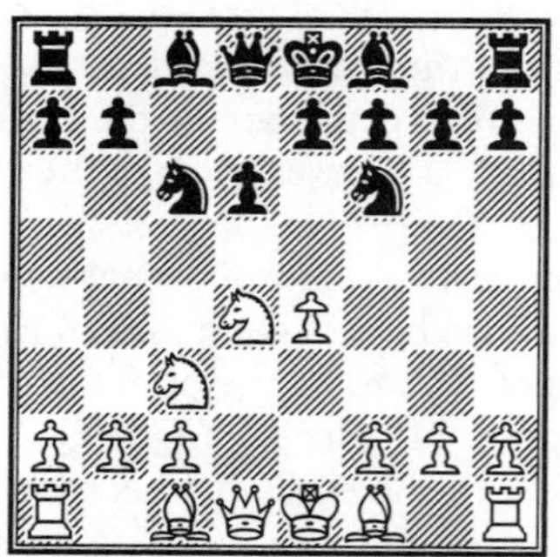

1.e4	**c5**
2.Nf3	**d6**
3.d4	**cxd4**
4.Nxd4	**Nf6**
5.Nc3	**Nc6**

The **Classical Variation** relies on solid and rapid development with a focus on the center of the board. There are two main lines in the Classical Variation. White can go on the offensive immediately with 6.Bc4, leading to the Sozin Variation, invite the Boleslavsky Variation (or a transposition to the Scheveningen Sicilian) with 6.Be2 or play more subtly with the Richter-Rauzer after 6.Bg5. We will examine an example of each approach.

SOZIN VARIATION

The **Sozin Variation** appears in several Sicilian Defenses, including the Najdort, Sahevening and Classical Variations. Each move order involves different options for White and Black. The next game shows a special possibility in the Classical.

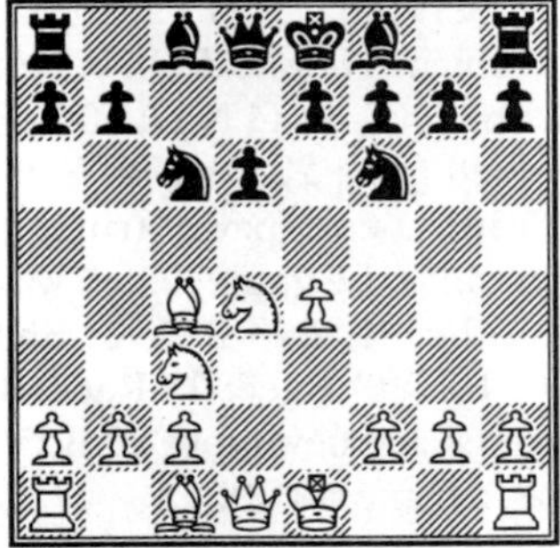

1.e4 c5
2.Nf3 d6
3.d4 cxd4
4.Nxd4 Nf6
5.Nc3 Nc6
6.Bc4

(85) KUPREICHIK - TAL [B57]

Sochi, 1970

1.e4 c5; 2.Nf3 d6; 3.d4 cxd4; 4.Nxd4 Nf6; 5.Nc3 Nc6; 6.Bc4 Qb6.

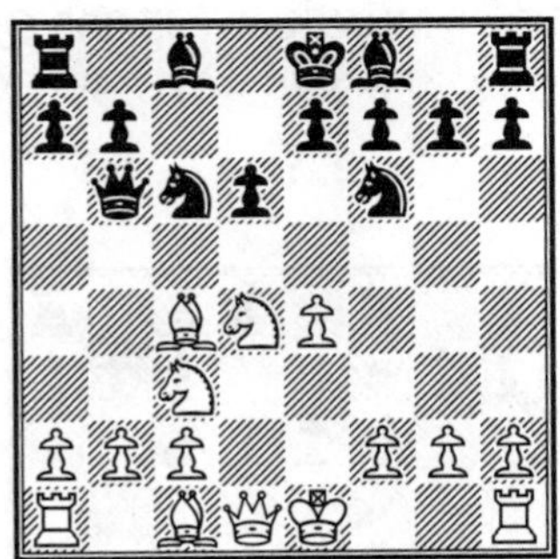

6...e6 is the normal reply, in which case the game transposes to normal lines of the Sozin Attack. Black has a serious alternative in 6...Qb6, which immediately puts the question to the knight at d4. Inevitably, the Black queen will be driven back to c7, or go there voluntarily, since otherwise the pawn at b7 cannot advance to b5, which is an integral part of Black's strategy in the Classical Sicilian. This opening is known as the Anti-Sozin Variation.

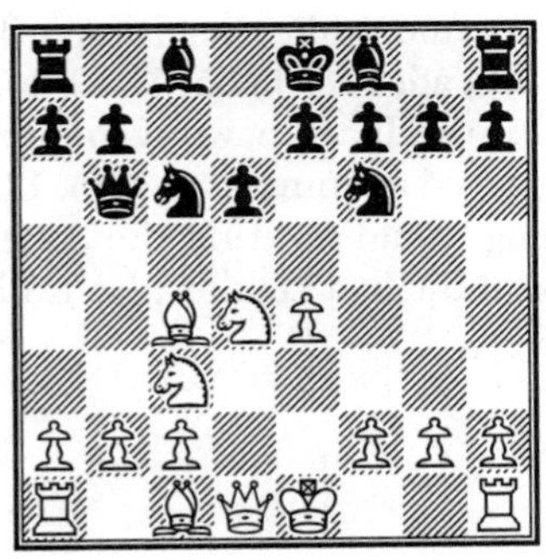

7.Nb3. 7.Ndb5 is a very popular alternative, with Nick DeFirmian often found on the White side, and Vladimir Kramnik as Black. 7...a6; 8.Be3 Qa5 (8...Qd8; 9.Nd4 Ng4; 10.Nxc6 bxc6; 11.Bd2 g6; 12.h3 Nf6; 13.Bg5 Bg7; 14.Qd2 0–0; 15.0–0–0 led to messy complications in DeFirmian-So. Polgar, Bermuda 1995.) 9.Nd4 Ne5

(9...Ng4 led to a lively game in DeFirmian-Smirin, New York (Intel) 1995. 10.Nxc6 bxc6; 11.Bd2 g6; 12.Qe2 Bg7; 13.h3 Ne5; 14.Bb3 Qc7; 15.f4 Nd7; 16.Be3 0–0; 17.0–0 a5; 18.Qf2 e6; 19.f5 d5; 20.exd5 cxd5; 21.fxe6 fxe6; 22.Qh4 Bb7; 23.Bh6 Bxh6; 24.Qxh6 Rxf1+; 25.Rxf1 Rf8; 26.Rxf8+ Nxf8 with a better pawn structure for White, though White's bishop at b3 had to work to get into the game. 9...e6 was seen when two of the leading protagonists battled each other: 10.0–0 Be7; 11.Bb3 0–0; 12.f4 Bd7; 13.f5 Nxd4; 14.Bxd4 exf5; 15.exf5 Bc6; 16.Qd3 Rae8; 17.Rad1 Bd8; 18.Kh1 Nd7; 19.Qg3 Bf6 and now White unsheathed the sharp new move 20.Bd5! and gained the advantage in DeFirmian-Kramnik, Yerevan Olympiad 1996.)

10.Bd3 (10.Nb3 Qc7; 11.Be2 e6; 12.f4 Nc4; 13.Bxc4 Qxc4; 14.Qf3 Bd7; 15.0–0–0 Rc8; 16.Bd4 b5; 17.a3 Be7; 18.Bxf6 gxf6 led to a position resembling the Richter-Rauzer Variation in Ivanchuk-Kramnik, Paris (Intel) 1995.) 10...Neg4; 11.Bc1 g6; 12.Nb3 Qb6; 13.Qe2 Bg7; 14.f4 Nh5; 15.Nd5 Qd8; 16.Bd2 e6; 17.Ba5 Qh4+; 18.g3 Nxg3 led to an absolute brawl, which deserves to be quoted in full: 19.Nc7+ Ke7; 20.hxg3 Qxg3+; 21.Kd1 Nf2+; 22.Kd2 Nxh1; 23.Nxa8 Qxf4+; 24.Qe3 Qh2+; 25.Qe2 Qf4+; 26.Qe3 Qh2+; 27.Qe2 Bh6+; 28.Kc3 Qe5+; 29.Kb4 Ng3; 30.Qe1 Bg7; 31.Nb6 d5; 32.Ka4 Bd7+; 33.Nxd7 b5+; 34.Kb4 Kxd7; 35.Bb6 Qxb2; 36.exd5 Rc8; 37.dxe6+ Ke8; 38.Bc5 Bc3+; 39.Qxc3 a5+; 40.Kxb5 Qxc3 and White resigned in Topalov-Kramnik, Belgrade 1995.

7...e6; 8.Be3 Qc7.

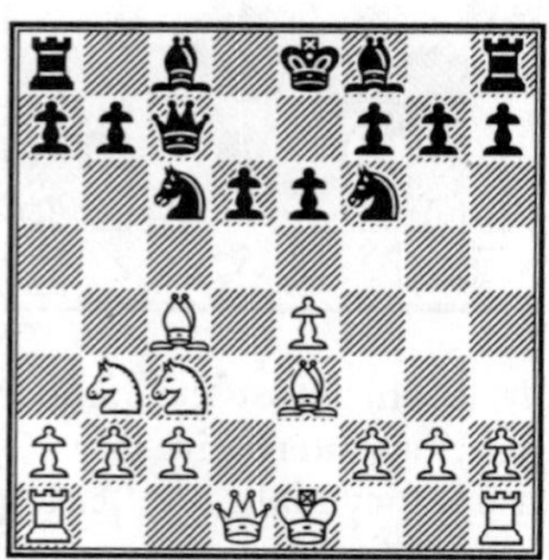

Now the position resembles a Scheveningen Variation, but White's knight at b3 and bishop at c4 are somewhat misplaced and uncoordinated. The knight will sit at b3 for most of the rest of the game, while the bishop will have to be repositioned at d3 to play an effective role. **9.f4 a6; 10.Bd3 b5; 11.a3.** It is not clear that this move is needed, since the advance of the Black pawn to b4 does not carry any particular strength. White could have played an immediate Qf3. **11...Be7; 12.Qf3 Bb7; 13.0–0.** It is clear that the White king would not find the queenside a comfortable homestead. **13...Rc8.** Black's typical Sicilian counterplay is down the c-file, especially at c3. **14.Rae1! 0–0.**

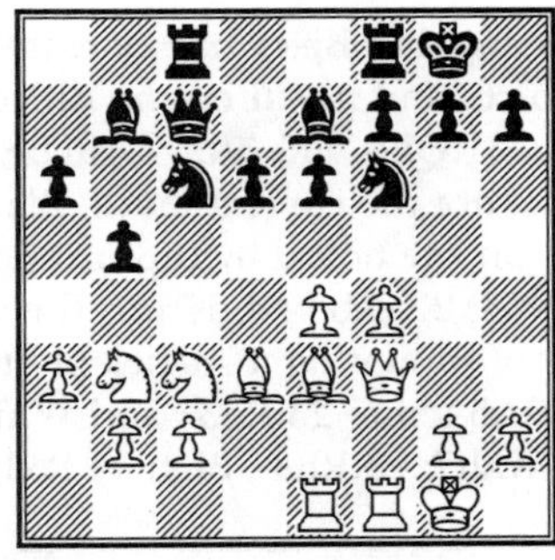

15.Qh3. A pawnstorm would not work here. 15.g4? b4; 16.axb4 Nxb4; 17.g5 Nd7; 18.h4 Nxd3; 19.cxd3. **15...b4!** In the Sicilian, it is important to control the initiative. **16.Nd5.** 16.axb4 Nxb4; 17.Nd4 would have given Black an acceptable game, according to Keres. **16...exd5; 17.exd5 Nb8.**

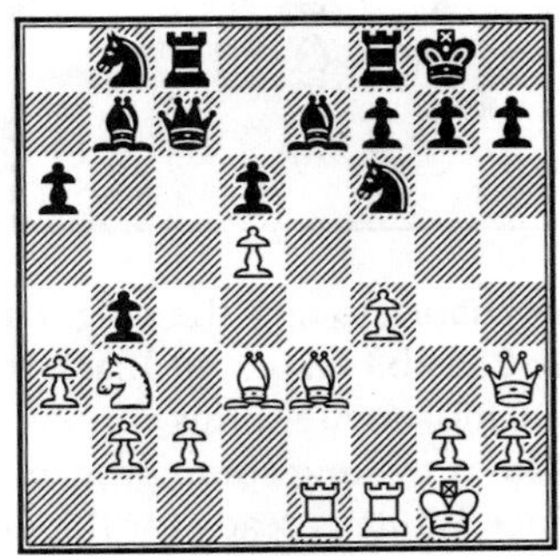

This is a very good move. White wanted to play 18.Nd4, but Black could meet that by shifting the rook from c8-d8, after which Black could challenge the c8-h3 diagonal with ...Bc8. **18.Bd4 g6.** Black must be careful. The threat is to capture on f6 and then at h7. If the h-pawn advances, however, there is a nasty surprise in store. 18...h6?; 19.Bxf6 Bxf6; 20.Qf5. The threat at h7 forces Black to return the piece. 20...g6; 21.Qxf6 bxa3; 22.bxa3 and the missing pawn is the least of Black's worries.

19.Rf3. White improves the attacking position by lifting the rook to the third rank, where it can join its colleague on the e-file (or vice-versa). It does not seem that White has any effective method of continuing the attack here, for example: 19.Re3 Bxd5; 20.Qh4 Bxb3; 21.cxb3 Nc6!; 22.Bxf6 Bxf6; 23.Qxf6 Qb6 and Black has a deadly pin, following analysis by Keres. **19...Bxd5; 20.Rfe3 Bd8.**

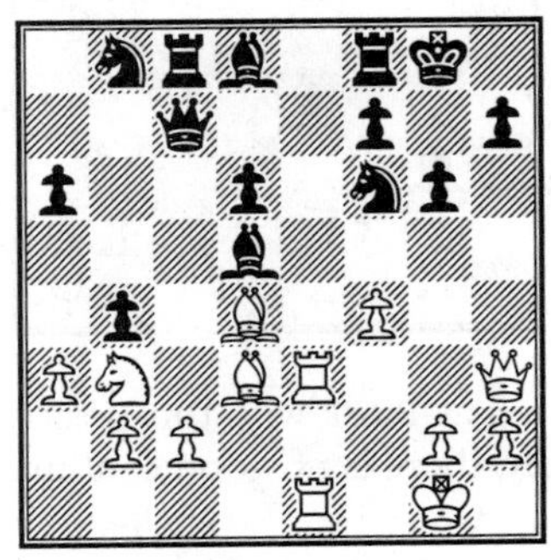

White's forces are menacing, but Black has an extra piece. All that is needed is to get the knight from b8 to c6, and it will not be difficult to arrange a protective shield for the Black monarch. **21.Qh4.** The attack will be strengthened by bringing a rook to h3. **21...Nbd7?** This is not the correct move. Black should have reduced the amount of fighting material on the board by capturing at b3. Later, Tal will regret delaying the capture. 21...Bxb3; 22.cxb3 Nbd7 was the appropriate response, after which White has little hope of mounting a sufficient attack. 21...Nh5? would have been rudely punished: 22.Qxh5 gxh5; 23.Rg3+ and White wins. 21...Ne8? gets polished off quickly: 22.Qxh7+ Kxh7; 23.Rh3+ Bh4; 24.Rxh4+ Kg8; 25.Rh8#. **22.Qh6.**

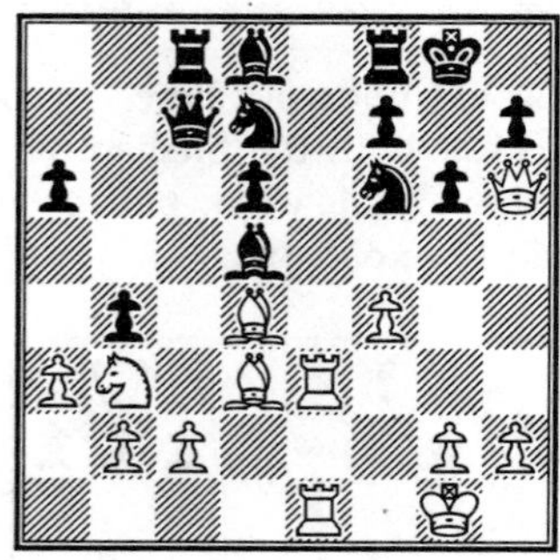

Now again Tal misses his chance to take the knight at b3, which would have won quickly. **22...Qb7?** 22...Bxb3; 23.cxb3 Qa5! and Black is powerless against the dual threats of ...Qh5 and ...Bb6! Unfortunately, this continuation was not revealed until after the game. **23.Rg3!** White is making some progress now, and there is no time for Black to capture at b3 since White is ready for the demolition sacrifice at g6.

23...Nc5?! Another mistake, but a natural one. Keres later conducted a thorough analysis and demonstrated that 23...Bb6! would have provided Tal with many winning chances. 23...Bxb3; 24.Bxg6 hxg6; 25.Rxg6+ fxg6; 26.Qxg6+ Kh8; 27.Qh6+ and White slides out with a draw. 23...Bb6; 24.Re7 Bxb3; 25.Bxg6 Bxd4+; 26.Kh1 Kh8; 27.Bxf7 Both of the players had seen this possibility during the game, and rejected it, but deeper analysis shows that there is a light at the end of the tunnel. 27...Ng4!; 28.Bg6! Rf7!! (28...Nf2+; 29.Kg1 Ng4+ would merely draw.) 29.Rxf7 (29.Rxg4 runs into 29...Rxe7 .) 29...Nxh6; 30.Rxh7+ Kg8.

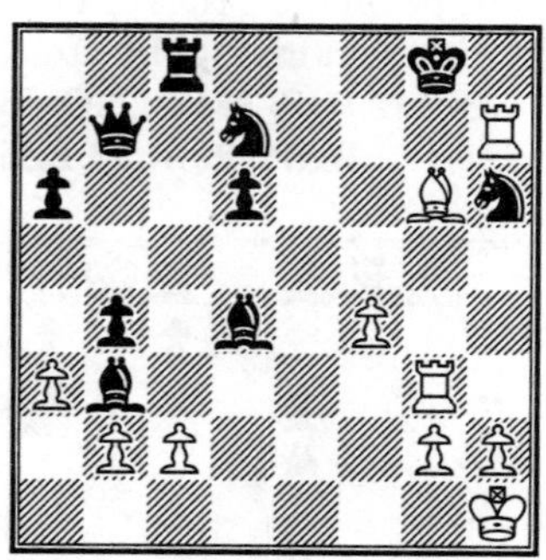

Anyone would be worried as Black with this position, far from the actual position on the board. Amazingly, there is no good continuation for White. Keres gives a sample: 31.Be4+ regains the queen, but it isn't enough. 31...Kf8; 32.Bxb7 Rxc2. Black threatens a back rank mate, and has three pieces for a rook. **24.Nxc5 dxc5.**

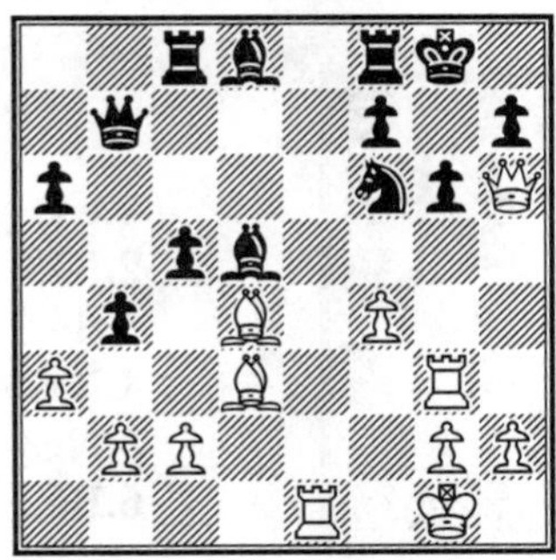

25.f5! White keeps piling on the pressure, and Tal cracks. **25...cxd4?** Black could still have saved the game. 25...Rc7!; 26.Bxc5! The threat of mate at f8 is imposing, yet there is a way out. 26...Re7!! A brilliant interference which leaves the situation less than clear. 27.fxg6 (27.Rxe7 Bxe7; 28.fxg6 fxg6 and now 29.Bxg6 fails to 29...Kh8 .) 27...fxg6 Keres stops here. 28.Bxe7 Bxe7; 29.axb4 Bxb4; 30.c3 Bc5+; 31.Kh1 Qg7 and Black's two pieces are worth more than the enemy rook. **26.fxg6 fxg6; 27.Bxg6!**

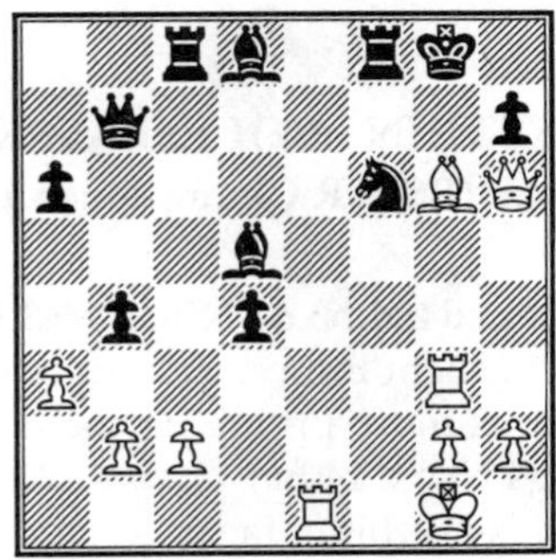

This is the breakthrough. The cleric threatens to impudently approach the enemy king at either f7 or h7. **27...Kh8; 28.Qxf8+ Ng8; 29.Bf5 Rb8; 30.Re8 Qf7; 31.Rh3.**

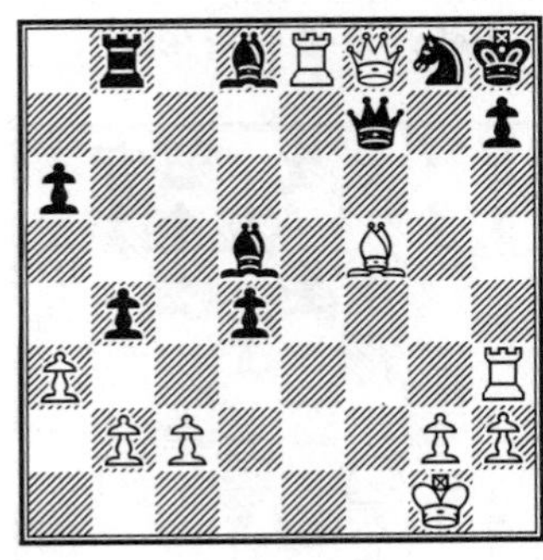

The final position is a pretty picture. Black can no longer guard all the critical squares surrounding the king. **White won.**

BOLESLAVSKY VARIATION

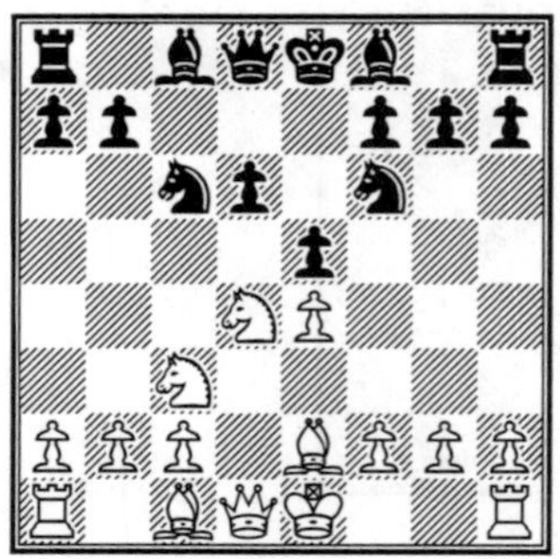

1.e4	**c5**
2.Nf3	**Nc6**
3.d4	**cxd4**
4.Nxd4	**Nf6**
5.Nc3	**d6**
6.Be2	**e5**

This is the **Boleslavsky Sicilian**, developed by Isaak Boleslavsky before and after the Second World War. The advance of the e-pawn leaves a gaping hole at d5, but as the present game shows it is not easy to take advantage of it. The present evaluation of the opening is that it is acceptable for Black, though a bit riskier than the transposition to the Scheveningen Sicilian with 6...e6.

(86) ESTRIN - BOLESLAVSKY [B59]
Sverdlovsk (RSFSR Championship), 1958

1.e4 c5; 2.Nf3 Nc6; 3.d4 cxd4; 4.Nxd4 Nf6; 5.Nc3 d6; 6.Be2 e5; 7.Nb3. White has experimented with other knight moves, without much success. 7.Nf3 h6; 8.Bc4 (8.0–0 Be7; 9.Re1 0–0; 10.h3 is more promising these days, for example 10...Re8; 11.Bf1 Bf8; 12.Nh2 a6; 13.Ng4 Nxg4; 14.hxg4 Be6; 15.Nd5 with control of the center and kingside prospects in Glek-Volzhin, Linares 1996.)

8...Be7; 9.Qe2 0–0; 10.h3 Be6!; 11.0–0. If White exchanges on e6, Black has a strong center and useful open file. 11...Rc8; 12.Bb3 Na5; 13.Rd1 Qc7; 14.g4 Nxb3; 15.axb3 a6; 16.Kh1 b5; 17.b4 and now in Stoltz-Boleslavsky, Groningen 1946, Black could have cemented the advantage with 17...Qb7! (17.Rxa6 b4; 18.Nd5 Bxd5; 19.exd5 Qxc2 and Black is better.) **7...Be7; 8.0–0 0–0; 9.f4.**

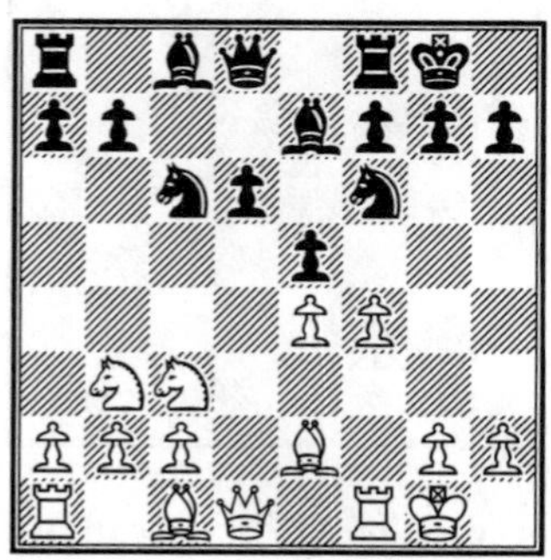

Here Black has a choice. Capturing at f4 opens up the game and entails a certain amount of risk, but 9...a5 is a good alternative. **9...exf4.** 9...a5; 10.Be3 a4; 11.Nd2 a3; 12.b3 Nd4 demonstrated the efficiency of Black's plan in Luboshitz-Boleslavsky, Minsk 1955. **10.Bxf4 Be6.** Black has a comfortable position, with the weakness at d6 under control. Of more concern is the d5-square, so Black aims as much firepower as possible in that direction. **11.Bf3?!** White responds in kind, looking at d5. As it turns out, however, Black was not threatening to advance the pawn to that square. The quiet 11.Kh1, eliminating later problems on the a7-g1 diagonal, would have been more prudent.

11...Ne5; 12.Nd5? This is a serious positional mistake. As Boleslavsky himself noted, it is unwise to occupy the d5-square in this opening unless the capture by Black in response leads to a position which is favorable for White, it should be held back. In the present position, White must recapture with a pawn, and that gives Black fewer problems. **12...Nxd5!; 13.exd5 Bd7.**

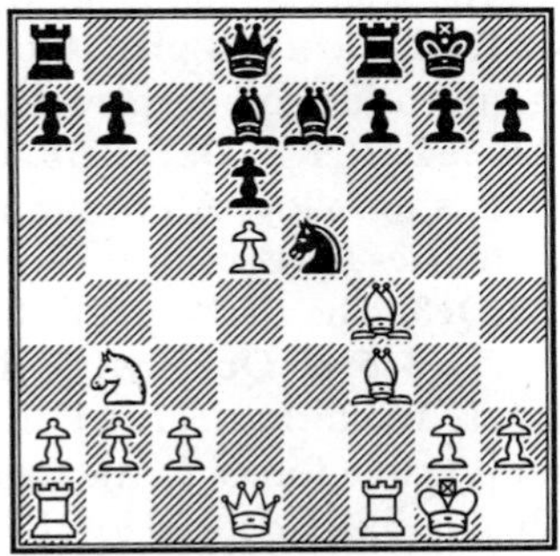

White has achieved nothing in the opening and the dark squares will soon belong to Black. With a growing feeling of desperation, White takes radical action to make sure there will be no trouble on the a1–h8 diagonal. **14.Bxe5?** The correct plan was still Kh1, getting the king off the dangerous dark-square. **14...dxe5; 15.c4 Ba4!**

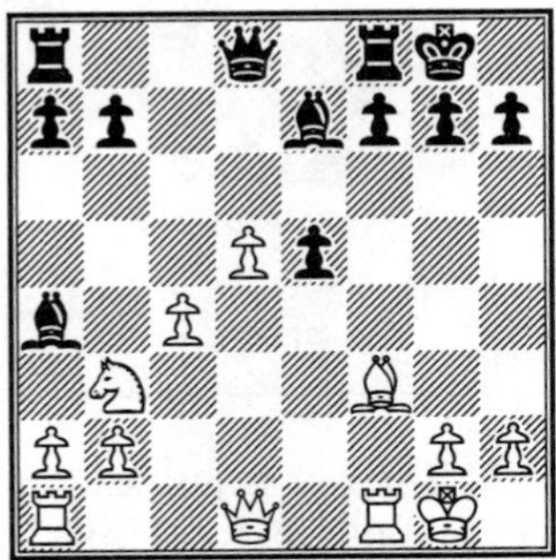

An annoying pin which may have been overlooked by Estrin. **16.Kh1.** Finally, but now Black's positional advantage is too great. For better or worse, the d-pawn had to advance. 16.d6 Bxd6; 17.Bxb7 and now 17...Qb6+ exploits the position of the enemy monarch. 18.Kh1 Qxb7; 19.Qxd6 Bxb3; 20.axb3 Qxb3; 21.Qxe5 Qxc4. The endgame is much better for Black, who has an extra pawn. Nevertheless, White could put up quite a struggle, as the major pieces are very useful for keeping pawns at bay. **16...Bd6; 17.Qe2 b6!**

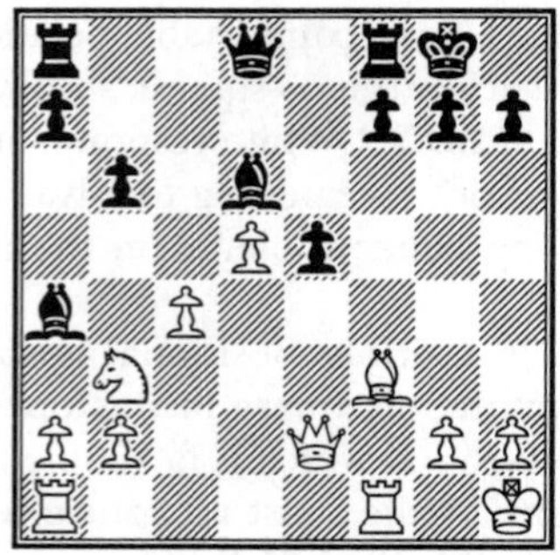

A fine move, keeping control of all the important dark squares. Now it is White who has a hole, at c5. **18.Nd2 f5!** The correct plan is to advance the e- and f-pawns. White has no corresponding queenside counterplay. **19.b3 Bd7; 20.g3.** White must make room for the bishop. **20...e4; 21.Bg2 Qe7; 22.Rae1 Rae8!** A quiet move, but necessary preparation for what is to follow. All of Black's forces will participate in the final assault. **23.Nb1.** White tries to regroup.

23...Rf6; 24.Nc3 Rh6; 25.Qe3. The dark-squares become the staging area for the new and important battle. **25...Bc5; 26.Qc1 Bb4; 27.Re3 Ba3.** 27...Qg5?; 28.Rxe4! Qxc1; 29.Rxe8+ Bxe8; 30.Rxc1. White has earned an extra pawn. **28.Qd2 Qg5; 29.Ne2.** White is bringing all possible forces to the defense of the king, but Black rules the dark-squares. **29...Bc5.** Forced, to avoid loss of the exchange. **30.Nd4 Qf6!** Now White should have given up on the idea or preserving the material balance and conceded the exchange by retreating the knight. Instead, he tries to hang on to his rook, but pays a higher price. **31.Rd1? f4!**

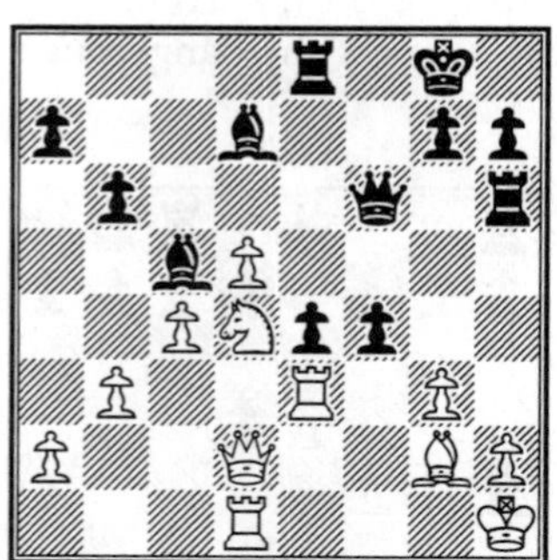

The decisive breakthrough. The rest is just a mopping-up operation. **32.Rxe4** 32.gxf4 Qxf4; 33.h3 Bd6; 34.Bf1 Bg4; 35.Rde1 Bxh3 and Black wins, as demonstrated by Boleslavsky. **32...Rxe4; 33.Bxe4 fxg3; 34.Nf3 Bf2!** A pretty move, cutting off the queen from the defense of h2. **35.h4.**

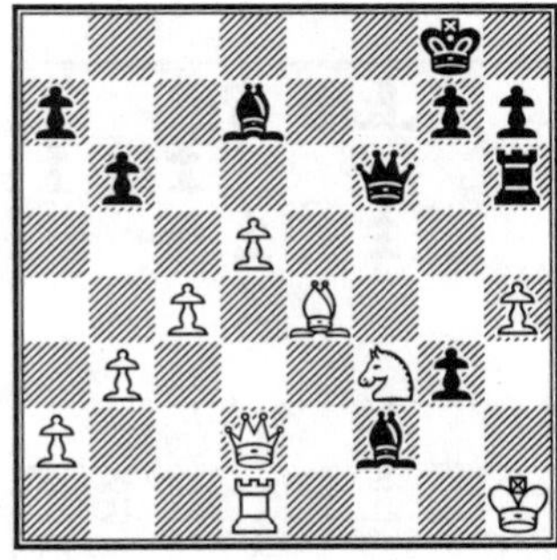

This allows a fine combination to bring the game to a close. **35...Qxf3+!!; 36.Bxf3 Rxh4+; 37.Kg2 Bh3+. Black won.**

RICHTER ATTACK

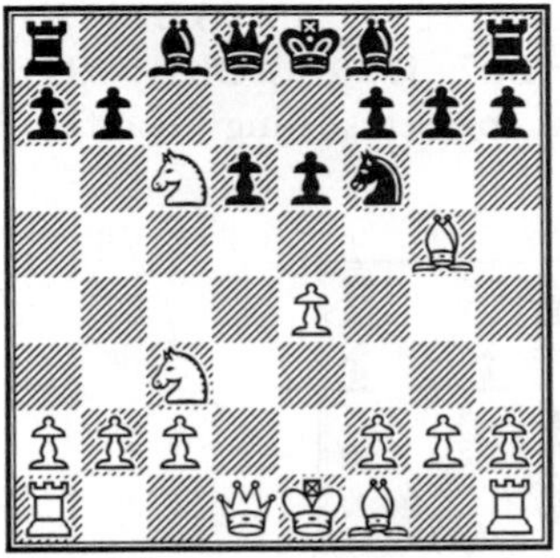

1.e4	**c5**
2.Nf3	**Nc6**
3.d4	**cxd4**
4.Nxd4	**Nf6**
5.Nc3	**d6**
6.Bg5	**e6**
7.Nxc6	

This is the **Richter Attack**, which is often confused with the Rauzer Attack (7.Qd2!). The present game was quite influential, and until World War II broke out the opening was heavily analyzed in major chess centers. Eventually, however, remedies were found and it has found few followers lately.

(87) RICHTER - WAGNER [B62]
Hamburg, 1932

1. e4 c5; 2.Nf3 Nc6; 3.d4 cxd4; 4.Nxd4 Nf6; 5.Nc3 d6; 6.Bg5 e6; 7.Nxc6 bxc6; 8.e5 dxe5?! 8...Qa5! pins the e-pawn to the bishop, and this is the correct plan. 9.Bxf6 gxf6; 10.exd6 Qe5+ (10...Rb8 is also good.) 11.Qe2 Bxd6; 12.0-0-0 Rb8; 13.Qxe5 Bxe5 and the bishop pair provided an endgame advantage in Dahlquist-Lundin, Stockholm 1934.

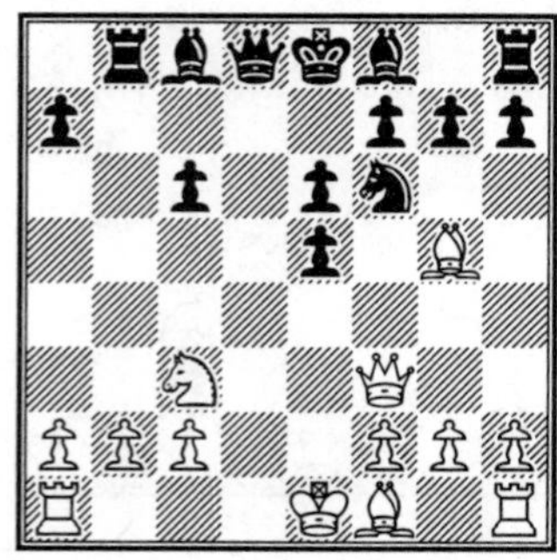

9.Qf3 Rb8. 9...Be7! is better, and Black has a comfortable game, for example 10.Qxc6+ Bd7; 11.Qf3 e4!; 12.Nxe4 Nxe4; 13.Bxe7 Qa5+ and Black is already good, but if White is not careful the game can come crashing to a close with 14.b4?? Qe5 and White, faced with the loss of a piece, can resign, as in Troianescu-Samarian, Bucharest 1940. The player of the Black pieces went on to become a leading theoretician. **10.Rd1 Qc7; 11.Ne4 Bb4+.** 11...Nxe4; 12.Rd8+ (12.Bd8 Qb7; 13.Qxe4 Qb4+; 14.Qxb4 Bxb4+; 15.c3 Bd6 and Black is better.) 12...Qxd8; 13.Bxd8 Kxd8; 14.Qxe4 Rxb2; 15.Qxe5 Rb1+; 16.Kd2 f6; 17.Qd4+ Bd7; 18.Qxa7 Bb4+; 19.c3 Bd6; 20.g3 Ke7; 21.Bg2 and White is better. 11...Nd5! is correct, sealing the d-file. **12.c3 Nxe4; 13.Bd8!**

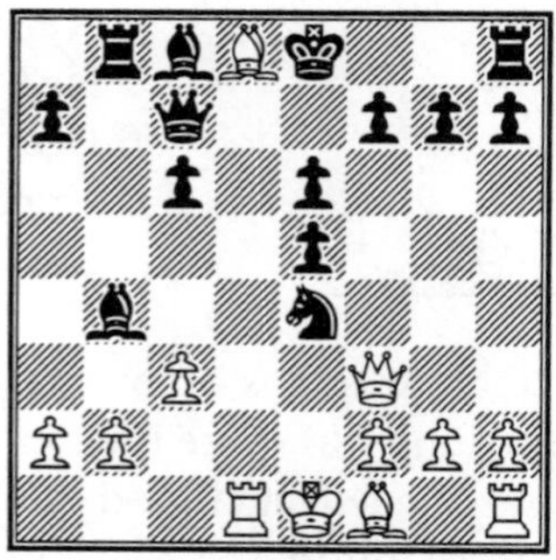

Finally White makes good use of the d8-square! **13...Qb7; 14.Qxe4 Bf8.** There is nothing better, but Black's pieces are pathetic. **15.Qxe5 Bd7; 16.Ba6 f6; 17.Bxf6! gxf6; 18.Qh5+ White won.**

RICHTER-RAUZER VARIATION

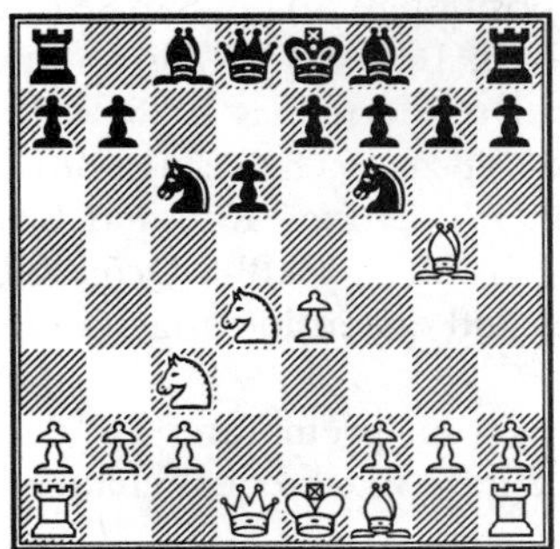

1.e4 c5
2.Nf3 Nc6
3.d4 cxd4
4.Nxd4 Nf6
5.Nc3 d6
6.Bg5

The **Richter-Rauzer** may look like an ordinary Sicilian, but appearances are deceiving. Here you will find no vicious flank attacks. Positional play is the order of the day, and the ability to evaluate the importances of weak pawns and squares, especially in the endgame, is essential. This is not to say that fireworks never appear, only that they are comparatively rare, considering that opposite wing castling is normal.

Even most of the sacrificial lines have positional goals. Black usually plays 6...e6, and after 7.Qd2 can play either 7...a6 or 7...Be7. White will castle on the queenside, and Black will head toward the kingside. There are some minor alternatives at move 6 for Black, but they are rarely seen these days. That may be just a matter of fashion.

(88) KASPAROV - HRACEK [B66]

Yerevan Olympiad, 1995

1.e4 c5; 2.Nf3 Nc6; 3.d4 cxd4; 4.Nxd4 Nf6; 5.Nc3 d6; 6.Bg5 e6; 7.Qd2 a6.

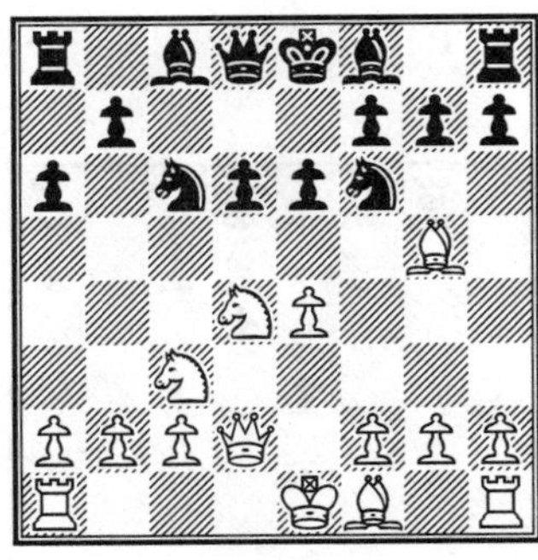

This is the more common handling of the Black side for most of the past few decades. Black takes care of the b5 square and prepares to occupy it with a pawn. Before developing, Black will clarify the central situation with an exchange of knights at d4, and may leave the king in the center for a long time. The Classical line with

7...Be7 is also quite popular, but 7...a6 is generally preferred. **8.0–0–0 Nxd4;** 8...h6; 9.Be3 Nxd4 (9...Be7; 10.f4 Nxd4; 11.Bxd4 b5 transposes below.) 10.Bxd4 b5; 11.f4 Be7.

A) 12.Qe3 Qc7 (12...Bb7; 13.Bxf6 gxf6; 14.Bd3 Qa5; 15.Kb1 b4; 16.Ne2 Qc5; 17.Nd4 Bc6; 18.Rhe1 Bd7 gave Black a solid position in Adams-San Segundo, Madrid 1996.) 13.e5 dxe5; 14.Bxe5 Ng4; 15.Qf3 Nxe5; 16.Qxa8 Nd7 is an interesting exchange sacrifice, seen in Ivanchuk-Kramnik, Dos Hermanas 1996.

B) 12.Bd3 b4; 13.Ne2 Qa5; 14.Bxf6 Bxf6; 15.Bc4 (15.e5 dxe5; 16.Be4 Ra7; 17.Qd6 Be7; 18.Qc6+ Bd7; 19.Rxd7 Rxd7; 20.Rd1 Qc7; 21.fxe5 Kd8 and Black is okay,) 15...0–0!; 16.Qxd6 Bb7; 17.Qd3 Rfd8; 18.Qe3 Rdc8!; 19.Bb3 Qc5; 20.Qxc5 Rxc5; 21.Ng3 a5; 22.Ba4 Bh4! and Black's bishops and queenside attack were a large advantage in Short-Salov, Madrid 1995.

9.Qxd4 Be7; 10.f4 b5; 11.Bxf6. 11.e5 is a bit premature: 11...dxe5; 12.Qxe5 Bd7; 13.Be2 Rc8; 14.h4 Qc7; 15.Qxc7 Rxc7 gave Black equal chances in Tseitlin-Khalifman, Ischia 1996. **11...gxf6.**

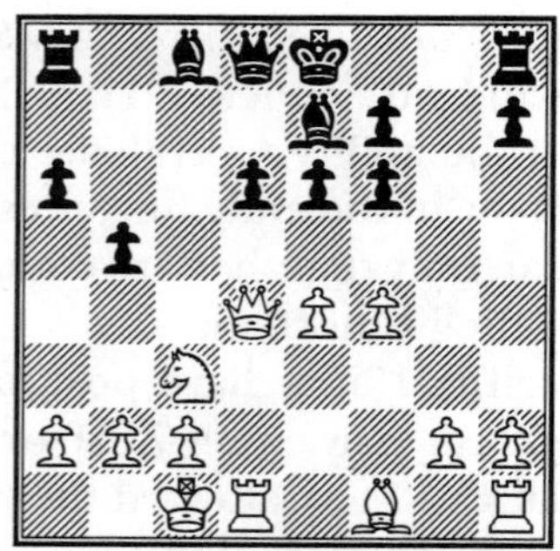

This position was quite popular in 1996, but Kasparov came up with a powerful new plan that calls Black's strategy into question. **12.e5! d5.** The pawn cannot be captured. 12...dxe5; 13.Qe4 Bd7; 14.Rxd7! Kxd7; 15.Bxb5+ axb5; 16.Rd1+ and White wins material. 12...fxe5; 13.fxe5 d5 leaves the f7-square too weak, according to Kasparov. **13.Kb1 b4?** Black is still under-developed, so placing the bishop at b7 might have been wiser. **14.Ne2 a5; 15.Ng3 f5.** Black seems to be battening down the hatches on both flanks, but each pawn advance creates a weakness in its wake. **16.Nh5 Rb8.**

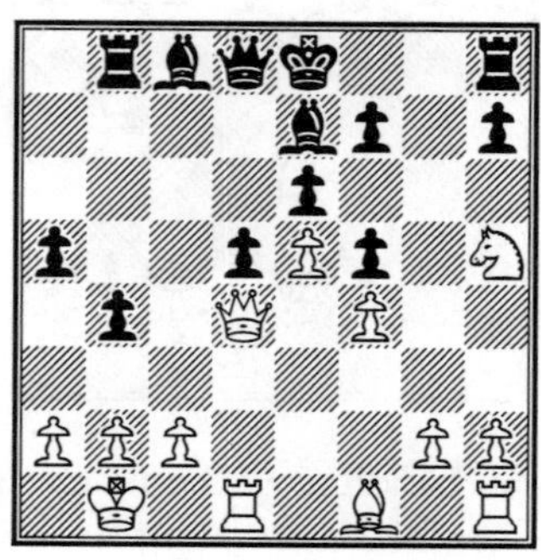

17.g4! White does not need any additional pieces to launch the attack. The queen, knight and pawns are an effective fighting force, and before the game is over the bishop will also have something to say. **17...fxg4; 18.f5! Rg8; 19.Nf6+! Bxf6; 20.exf6.** As a result of White's initiative the pathways to the Black king have been opened. All that stands in the way are a couple of pawns. **20...Qd6; 21.Bg2!** The long range weapon is loaded.

21...Rg5; 22.Bxd5! A direct hit on the pawn chain. The bishop cannot be captured. **22...Bd7.** 22...Qxd5. 23.Qf4 hits both rooks while also attacking the queen!; 22...exd5; 23.Qe3+ Kf8; 24.Qxg5 and it is all over. **23.Rhe1 h6.** 23...Rxf5; 24.Bxe6 Qxd4; 25.Bxf5+ Kf8; 26.Rxd4 Bxf5; 27.Re5 was an alternative way of losing, as pointed out by Kasparov. **24.fxe6 fxe6; 25.Qa7.** Black resigned. **Black won.**

DRAGON VARIATION

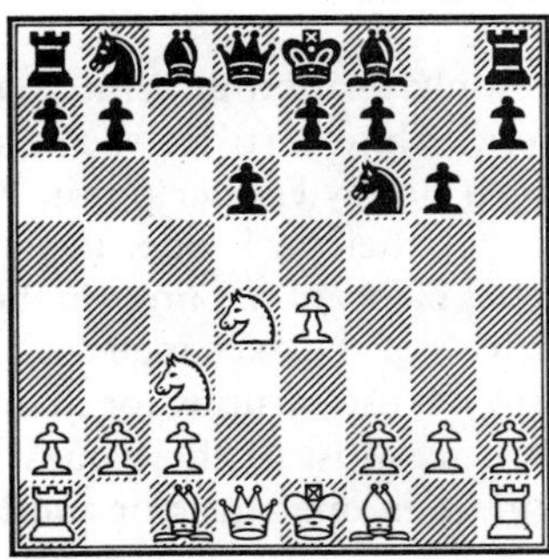

1.e4	**c5**
2.Nf3	**d6**
3.d4	**cxd4**
4.Nxd4	**Nf6**
5.Nc3	**g6**

This is the **Dragon** formation. The tongue of the serpent is the bishop at g7, which can lash out all the way across the board to inflict serious damage. Black will castle kingside and use the combined power of the bishop at g7 and a rook on the c-file to create tremendous pressure at c3, often sacrificing the exchange, either to win the pawn at e4 or to disrupt the White king's defenses should White castle on the queenside.

Indeed, queenside castling is the most aggressive reaction by White. When this is combined with support of e4 by advancing a pawn to f3, we have the Yugoslav Attack, one of the most deeply studied openings in all of chess. Most games these days do not enter new territory in the first two dozen moves. Our examples will concentrate on this popular plan. For more information, check out the forthcoming book *Secrets of the Sicilian Dragon.*

(89) KARPOV - KORCHNOI [B78]

Candidates Match (2nd Game), 1974

1.e4 c5; 2.Nf3 d6; 3.d4 cxd4; 4.Nxd4 Nf6; 5.Nc3 g6 6.Be3 Bg7; 7.f3.

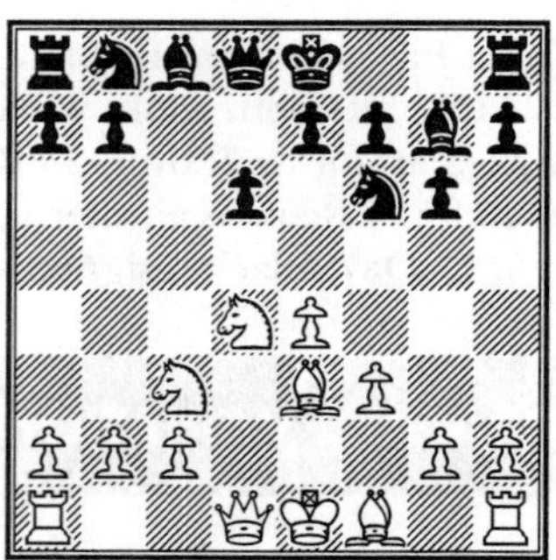

This is the dreaded Yugoslav Attack, the only weapon in White's arsenal that poses a serious threat to the Sicilian Dragon. White fortifies the center, castles queenside, and then attacks along the h-file. As Bobby Fischer put it, White's play was simply sac, sac and mate! Well, stalwarts of the Black side, including recent convert Garry Kasparov, have found that Black has plenty of resources in the queenside counterattack, which usually involves the sacrifice of the exchange at c3.

The Yugoslav Attack has been subjected to intense scrutiny for many years, but it is still not clear which side gets the advantage. Most of the games are bloody, though draws by perpetual check can be found when one attack or another is about to run out of steam.

Openings this sharp often find players on both sides of the position, and I must admit that I enjoy playing Black just as much as I do when I have the White pieces. There is something invigorating about the Dragon, and the over-the-board debates are a lot of fun, with post-mortems often running several hours. This sets up the Yugoslav formation, which is one of the most popular methods of greeting the Dragon.

7...Nc6; 8.Qd2 0-0.

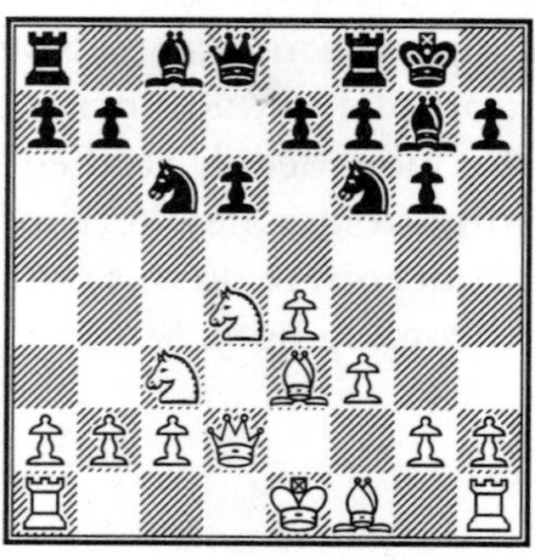

9.Bc4. This is the first place where White must make a serious decision. There are two alternative plans, 9.g4 and 9.0-0-0, which lead to positions which are quite different from the main lines. The point is that the bishop at c4 is a useful weapon, but at the same time is exposed to enemy attack. **9...Bd7.** 10.h4. Most of the time it makes little difference whether White castles now or advances the h-pawn, since both moves are an essential part of the plan. 10.0–0–0 Rc8; 11.Bb3 Ne5; 12.h4 h5 is the Soltis Variation discussed in the next game.

10...Rc8. 10...Qa5 is the oldest line, and it was thought to be dead and buried, but young English theoretician Chris Ward, among others, has brought it back to life. 11.0–0–0 Ne5; 12.Bb3 Rfc8 with several branches:

A) 13.Kb1 Nc4; 14.Bxc4 Rxc4; 15.Nb3 Qa6; 16.Bd4 Rac8; 17.h5 Be6; 18.hxg6 hxg6 was not dangerous for Black in Borge-Ward, Copenhagen 1995.

B) 13.g4 can be met by 13...b5!?; 14.h5 Nc4; 15.Bxc4 bxc4. This capture is usually not possible, but it brings very different positions from those with ...Rxc4. 16.hxg6?! (16.Bh6 Bh8; 17.Nf5 Re8; 18.hxg6 fxg6; 19.Bg7 remains unclear. Ward writes that he is not sure he "believes" in it.) 16...fxg6; 17.Rdg1 Rab8; 18.Bh6 Bh8; 19.Nf5 gxf5; 20.g5 Nxe4; 21.fxe4 Rxb2; 22.g6 Qxc3; 23.gxh7+ Kf7 is a typical example of Black's defensive resources in this line. White's attack has run out of steam and Black threatens the simple ...Rb1+, as Kxb1 is mated by ...Qa1#. Therefore White must remove the queens from the board, but even though this wins material, Black's attack is far from over. 24.Qxc3 Bxc3; 25.Bd2 Bxd2+; 26.Kxb2 Rb8+; 27.Ka3 (27.Ka1 Bc3#) 27...Bb4+; 28.Kb2 Bc5+; 29.Kc3 and now Black recovers the material. 29...Bxg1; 30.h8Q Rxh8 and in Olesen-Tisdall, Gausdal (Troll Masters) 1995 White resigned, as 31.Rxh8 fxe4; 32.Kxc4 Be6+; 33.Kc3 Bxa2 is hopeless.

C) 13.h5 Nxh5 (13...Nc4; 14.Bxc4 Rxc4; 15.Nb3 Qc7; 16.hxg6 hxg6; 17.Bh6 Bh8 gave Black a good game in Porras-Berntsen, Yerevan Olympiad 1996.) 14.Nd5 (14.Nde2 Be6; 15.Kb1 Nc4; 16.Bxc4 Rxc4; 17.g4 Ng3! undermines the support of the knight at c3, and White went down quickly after 18.Nxg3 Rxc3; 19.b3 Rac8; 20.Rc1 Bxb3!; 21.cxb3 Rxb3+ and White resigned in Morris-Ward, London (Lloyds Bank) 1983.) 14...Qxd2+; 15.Rxd2 Kf8; 16.g4 Nf6; 17.Nxf6! Bxf6; 18.Rxh7 Kg8; (18...Nc4; 19.Bxc4 Rxc4; 20.g5 Bg7; 21.Rdh2 Rac8; 22.f4 Bg4; 23.c3 Kg8; 24.R7h4 Bh5 is evaluated as about even by Ward.) 19.Rh1 a5; 20.a3 a4; 21.Ba2 b5; 22.Kb1 b4; 23.g5 Bg7; 24.axb4 a3 with good counterplay for Black in Glek-Hodgson, Bundesliga 1995.

11.Bb3.

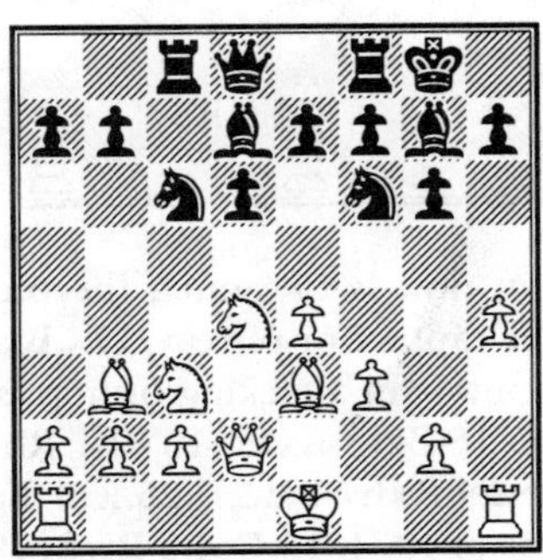

11...Ne5. 11...h5 returns to the Soltis Variation, considered in our next game. **12.0–0–0 Nc4; 13.Bxc4 Rxc4.**

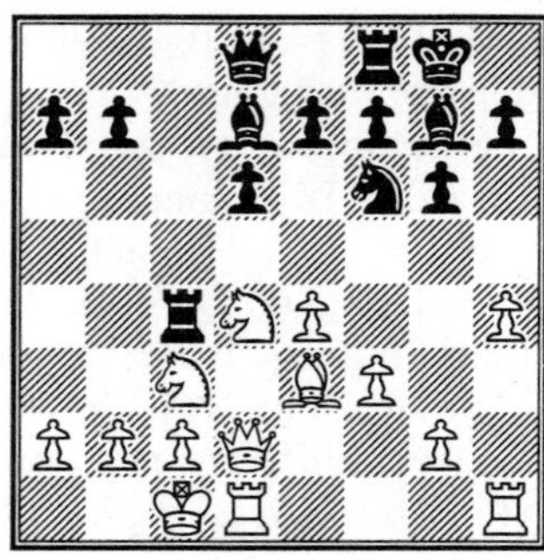

Now White has the traditional choice between king safety and all-out attack. **14.h5.** 14.Kb1 Qc7; 15.g4 Rc8; 16.h5 b5; 17.hxg6 fxg6; 18.Nd5 Nxd5; 19.exd5 Be5; 20.Qd3 Qb7; 21.Qe4 leaves the White queen overloaded. After 21...e6 White can try a sacrificial path with 22.Rxh7 Kxh7; 23.Rh1+ Kg7; 24.Bh6+ but after 24...Kf6; 25.Bg5+ Kxg5; 26.f4+ Bxf4. White's attack has run out of steam, Djurhuus-Tisdall, Reykjavik (PCA 1996.)

14...Nxh5; 15.g4 Nf6; 16.Nde2. 16.Bh6! is considered best, and recent developments have confirmed this evaluation, for example 16...Nxe4; 17.Qe3 Rxc3; 18.bxc3 Nf6; 19.Bxg7 Kxg7; 20.Qh6+ Kh8; 21.Ne2 Rg8; 22.Qe3 Be6; 23.Qxa7! and now perhaps the quiet ...Qc7 is best, since active play on the a-file does not seem to work: 23...Qa8; 24.Qxa8 Rxa8; 25.Nf4 Bxa2; 26.Rhe1 and White was clearly better in Haba-Dobias, Austria 1994. **16...Qa5.**

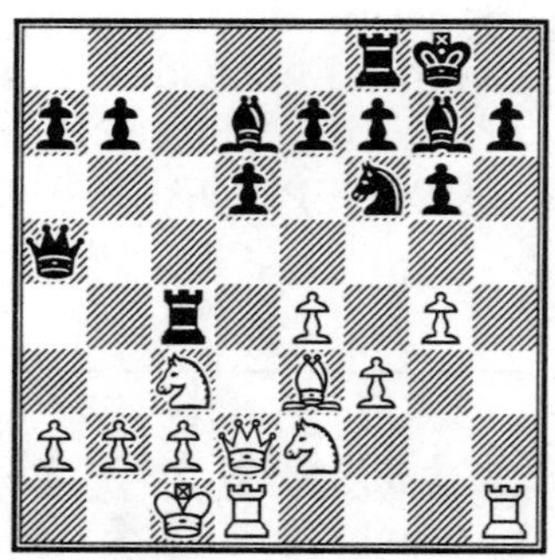

White's only logical plan now is to launch the piece attack on the kingside. **17.Bh6.** Now Black can either capture or retreat. **17...Bxh6.** 17...Bh8 involves a typical exchange sacrifice. The powerful attacking bishop is traded for a rook which is not of great defensive value. 18.Bxf8 Kxf8; 19.Kb1 Rb4; 20.g5 Nh5; 21.Nc1 Be6; 22.Nb3 Qe5; 23.Rxh5 Bxb3; 24.Rxh7 Bxa2+; 25.Kc1 Bg7 and Black's attack looks stronger, Almrot-Gernud, Postal 1974. **18.Qxh6 Rfc8; 19.Rd3.** 19.g5 Nh5; 20.Rxh5 gxh5; 21.Nd5 Rxc2+; 22.Kb1 is good for White, who can concentrate on the attack. 22...Qd8. The e7-square only gets temporary support. 23.Nef4 Qf8; 24.Nxe7+! Qxe7; 25.Nd5 and the threat of Nf6+ is too much, Dobsa-Reinhardt, Postal 1982.

19...R4c5? This is now known to be a serious error. 19...Be6; 20.g5 Nh5; 21.Ng3 Qe5! is the best defense, though White's attacking chances must be preferred. **20.g5 Rxg5; 21.Rd5 Rxd5; 22.Nxd5 Re8; 23.Nef4 Bc6.**

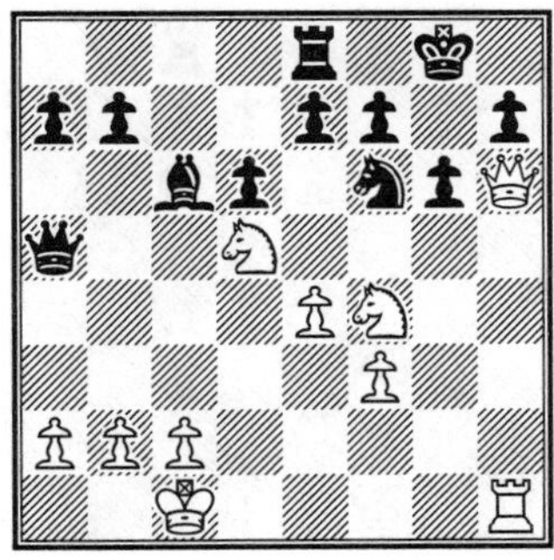

24.e5! This breaks down the enemy defenses, and the game is soon over. **24...Bxd5.** 24...dxe5; 25.Nxf6+ exf6; 26.Nh5 and mate is inevitable. **25.exf6 exf6; 26.Qxh7+ Kf8; 27.Qh8+.** Here Black resigned, but the end would have come soon enough after 27...Ke7; 28.Nxd5+ Qxd5; 29.Re1+ Kd7; 30.Qxe8+. **White won.**

(90) PRITCHETT - SOLTIS

Haifa 1970

1.e4 c5; 2.Nf3 d6; 3.d4 cxd4; 4.Nxd4 Nf6; 5.Nc3 g6 6.Be3 Bg7; 7.f3 Nc6; 8.Qd2 0–0; 9.Bc4 Bd7; 10.h4 h5.

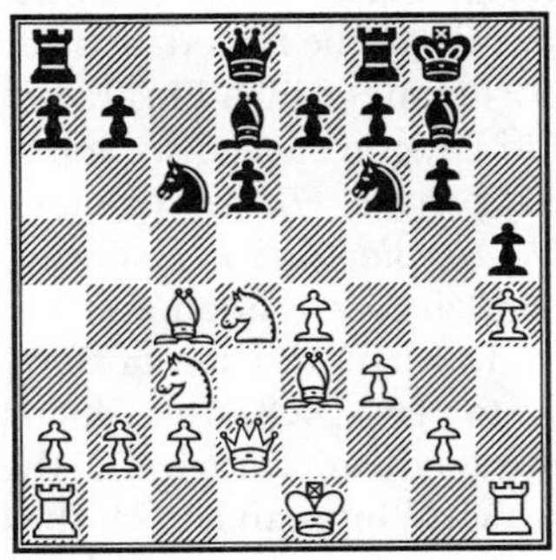

This is the Soltis Variation, developed by American Grandmaster and chess writer Andy Soltis during the 1970s. The present game is one of the first to bring the variation to the attention of the public, and contains all of the strategic elements we have come to expect from the line. White will try to attack on the kingside, but the pawn at h5 slows down the assault. In the meantime, Black will sacrifice an exchange at c3 to expose the White king, which invariably is castled queenside. **11.0–0–0 Rc8; 12.Bb3 Ne5.**

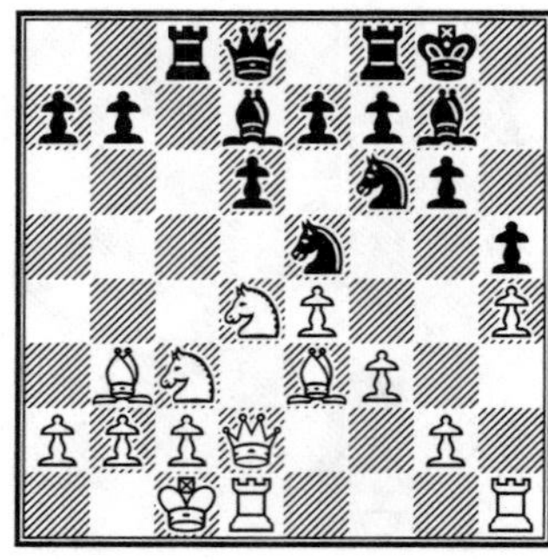

This position can be reached by several move orders, but it is the gateway to the main lines of the Soltis Variation. Here White has several plans. I choose 13.Bh6 as our main line because it was played in this seminal game and also because I prefer it myself as White. 13.Bg5 and 13.Kb1 are equally popular. The position in the diagram has been subjected to exhaustive analysis, and is the subject of a book spanning more than 300 pages. What follows is just a taste of the tactical possibilities. In this opening, tactics are everything. Strategically, little more need be said than that Black will attack with all possible fury on the queenside, while White will hack away at the kingside.

Both sides can sacrifice pawns or pieces to speed up the attack. Black sacrifices an exchange at c3, and White will give up the g-pawn in most lines, advancing it to g4 to try to open lines. The goals are clear, but the subtle effects of move orders and brilliant surprise sacrifics are seen in the forced tactical variations. Therefore I have chosen to present a lot of short games which illustrate the main ideas. With players such as Kasparov, Karpov and Dragon specialists Soltis and Nunn involved, I think this gives a good introductory picture. For more detail, see Steve Mayer's excellent book *The Soltis Variation of the Yugoslav Attack*, Hypermodern Press 1995.

13.Bh6. There are many plans for White here. The most popular options are 13.Bh6, 13.Bg5 and the quiet 13.Kb1. The aim of Bh6 is to exchange dark squared bishops before Black has time to play ...Re8, after which the bishop can safely retreat to h8. Therefore it is in many ways the most logical of the three plans. 13.Bg5 is most often met by 13...Rc5 after which White can launch the kingside attack or take time out for Kb1. The latter course is preferred by top players.

A) 14.g4 hxg4; 15.f4 Nc4 (15...Nf3 fails to 16.Nxf3 gxf3; 17.Bxf6 Bxf6; 18.e5 Bg7; 19.Ne4 Rc6; 20.h5 Bf5; 21.Ng3 and Black resigned in Rybin-Zichner, Postal 1988.) 16.Qe2 and here Black must react vigorously with 16...b5! Now White advances to undermine the pawn at g6. 17.f5 Qa5 Black now threatens to open things up with ...Nxb2, and White has tried several moves. (17...a5 is too slow. 18.h5 gxf5; 19.h6 Bh8; 20.h7+ Anderson,Perez,Las Vegas 1994)

A1) 18.fxg6 allows 18...Nxb2 but after 19.gxf7+ Rxf7; 20.Kxb2 Qxc3+; 21.Kb1 Black must not try 21...d5? (21...Re5 is stronger.) 22.Bxf6 Rxf6; 23.Rd3 Qa5; 24.exd5 Rc4; 25.Nc6 Qb6; 26.Nxe7+ Kh8; 27.h5 Rf2; 28.Ng6+ Kg8; 29.Qe7 Rh2; 30.Rf1 Bf5; 31.h6 Bf6; 32.h7+ and Black resigned in Gofshtein-Mestel, Hastings 1991.

A2) 18.Bxc4 Rxc4; 19.Nb3 Qa6; 20.h5 Nxe4 leads to unclear complications.

A3) 18.Bxf6 Bxf6; 19.Qxg4 Nxb2? (19...Kg7!; 20.Rh3 Rfc8; 21.Nd5 Rxd5!; 22.exd5 Qb6 was thought to be good for Black but I think that after 23.Rg3! Rh8;

24.c3. White will play Bc2 with a strong attack.) 20.Qxg6+ Bg7; 21.Rhg1 Nd3+; 22.Rxd3. Black resigned, Eriksson-Djeno, Moscow Olympiad 1994.

B) 14.Kb1.

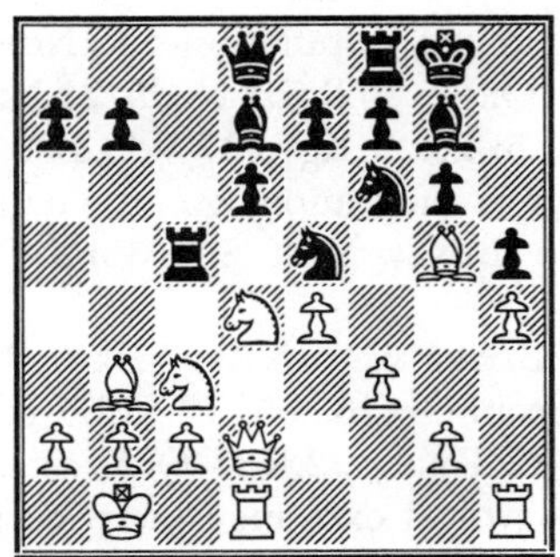

This safeguards the White king and is now the more popular move.

B1) 14...Re8 is Jonathan Mestel's speciality.

B1a) 15.g4 is the most radical reply, but White's attack is unconvincing. 15...hxg4; 16.h5 Nxh5; 17.Bh6 (17.Nd5 Rxd5; 18.exd5 Nxf3; 19.Nxf3 gxf3; 20.Rdg1 Bf5; 21.Qe3 Qb6; 22.Qxf3 Qd4; 23.Bc1 Be4 and White is in trouble, Martin-Mestel, London 1994.) 17...e6; 18.Rdg1 Nxf3; 19.Nxf3 gxf3; 20.Bxg7 Kxg7; 21.Qxd6 Rg5; 22.Qd4+ Qf6; 23.e5 Qxe5; 24.Qxd7 Rxg1+; 25.Rxg1 f2 and Black had a winning attack, Kaplan-Mestel, Oviedo 1993.

B1b) 15.f4 is probably best, though Black has decent chances.

B1c) 15.Bh6 allows Black to play 15...Bh8! which is the point of ...Re8. 16.g4 a5; 17.gxh5 Nxh5; 18.f4 Ng4; 19.f5 Rxc3; 20.bxc3 a4; 21.fxg6 axb3; 22.gxf7+ Kxf7; 23.cxb3 Qa5; 24.Rdf1+ Kg6; 25.Rhg1 Qe5; 26.Bf8 Bf6; 27.Qe2 Ng3; 28.h5+ Kh7; 29.Rxg3 Qxg3; 30.e5 Qxe5; 31.Qd3+ Kh8. White resigned, Finn-Mestel, Hastings 1991.

B2) 14...b5 is the normal move, and both sides play for flank attacks as White answers with 15.g4. 15...a5 is the natural continuation and it has been seen many times. 16.Bxf6 Bxf6; 17.gxh5 is normally seen now, though White has in the past advanced the a-pawn. (17.a3 hxg4; 18.f4 Nc4; 19.Qd3 has been retired ever since the following game: 19...Qc8; 20.Nd5 Rxd5; 21.exd5 Bf5; 22.Nxf5 Qxf5; 23.c3 Ne3; 24.Qxf5 gxf5; 25.Rd2 a4; 26.Ba2 Rc8; 27.h5 Nc4; 28.Re2 Rc5; 29.Rd1 Kg7; 30.Kc1 Nb6; 31.Rd3 Kh6 with an eventual draw in Karpov-Georgiev, Dubai Olympiad 1986.) 17...a4; 18.Bd5! e6.

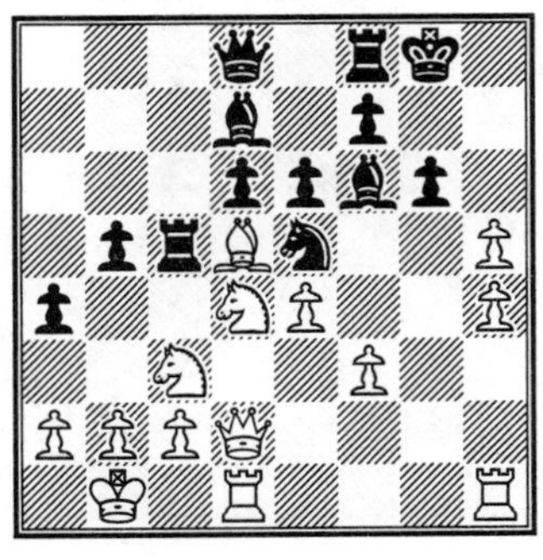

The tactical possibilities in this position have been well explored. 19.hxg6! exd5; 20.h5 Bg5 (20...Rxc3; 21.bxc3 Bg5 is already too slow. 22.f4 Bh6; 23.Rdg1 Qe7; 24.Qg2 Bxf4; 25.g7 Rb8; 26.h6 Ng6; 27.Nf5 Bxf5; 28.exf5 Qe5; 29.fxg6 f5 and Black resigned. Here Mestel was on the White side, against Kudrin at Hastings 1986.) 13.Kb1 Nc4; 14.Bxc4 Rxc4 is a very popular line. 15.Nde2 b5; 16.Bh6 Qa5; 17.Bxg7 Kxg7; 18.Nf4 Rfc8; 19.Ncd5 Qxd2; 20.Rxd2 Nxd5; 21.Nxd5 Kf8; 22.Re1 Rb8; 23.b3 Rc5; 24.Nf4 Rbc8; 25.Kb2 a5; 26.a3 Kg7; 27.Nd5 Be6; 28.b4 axb4; 29.axb4 Rc4; 30.Nb6 Rxb4+; 31.Ka3 Rxc2 is the famous game Anand-Kasparov from the 1995 PCA World Chanmpionship in New York. See *World Champion Openings* for commentary on this game.

13...Bxh6. 13...Nc4; 14.Bxc4 Rxc4; 15.Bxg7 Kxg7; 16.Kb1 leaves Black without sufficient counterplay, for example 16...e5; 17.Ndb5 Bxb5; 18.Nxb5 Qb6; 19.Nc3 Rfc8; 20.Qxd6 R8c6; 21.Qe7 Rxc3; 22.Rd8 Qc5. Ernst Winsnes, 1994 Sweden. **14.Qxh6 Rxc3!** This is the typical exchange sacrifice which provides Black with compensating attacking chances on the queenside. **15.bxc3.**

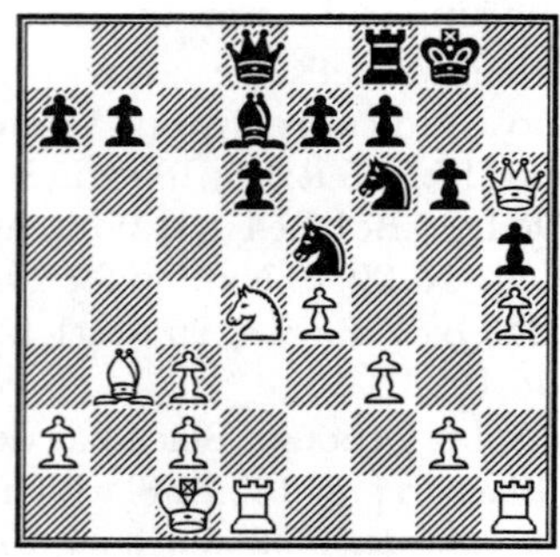

15...Qa5. 15...Qc7; 16.g4 (16.Kb2 a5; 17.Ne2 a4; 18.f4 Nc4+; 19.Bxc4 Qxc4; 20.f5 a3+; 21.Kc1 Schiller-Goldman, Morgan Park 1986) 16...Qxc3; 17.Kb1 Rc8; 18.gxh5 Nxh5; 19.Rhg1 Nc4; 20.Bxc4 Rxc4; 21.Qxh5 Rxd4; 22.Rxg6+ 1-0 Gruenfeld-Findlay, Toronto 1984 **16.Qe3.** 16.Kb1 is the main line now. 16...Rc8; 17.g4 Nc4; 18.gxh5 Qxc3; 19.Bxc4 Rxc4; 20.Rd3 Qb4+; 21.Nb3 Nxh5; 22.Qg5 (22.Rd5 Qc3; 23.Rxh5 Qxc2+; 24.Ka1 Qc3+; 25.Kb1 Qd3+; 26.Ka1 was drawn in Gallagher-Mestel, Swansea 1987.) 22...Nf6; 23.Rhd1 Rc5; 24.Qe3 a5; 25.Qe1 Qb6; 26.Kc1 Re5 with unclear complications in Schiller-Herbst, Pan American Intercollegiate Championship 1986. **16...Rc8; 17.Kb2.**

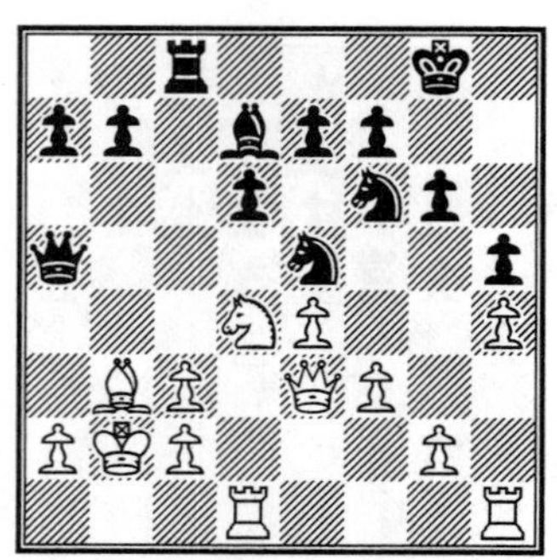

17...Qb6. Black pins the knight at d4 and prepares to advance the a-pawn. **18.Ka1 Qc5; 19.g4 a5!** The feathers are flying now! **20.gxh5 Nxh5; 21.Qh6?** 21.f4 Ng4; 22.Qf3 Qxc3+; 23.Qxc3 Rxc3 is certainly no worse for Black, but it is better than the text. **21...a4; 22.Bxf7+.** There is nothng better, but Black is winning now. **22...Kxf7; 23.Qh7+ Ng7; 24.Ne2 Qc4; 25.h5 Be6; 26.hxg6+ Nxg6; 27.Kb1 Rh8; 28.Qxg6+ Kxg6; 29.Rdg1+ Kf7; 30.Rxh8 Qb5+; 31.Kc1 Qxe2. Black won.**

(91) PLASKETT - WATSON,W [B76]

Brighton, 1996

1.e4 c5; 2.Nf3 d6; 3.d4 cxd4; 4.Nxd4 Nf6; 5.Nc3 g6; 6.Be3 Bg7; 7.f3 0-0; 8.Qd2 Nc6; 9.g4.

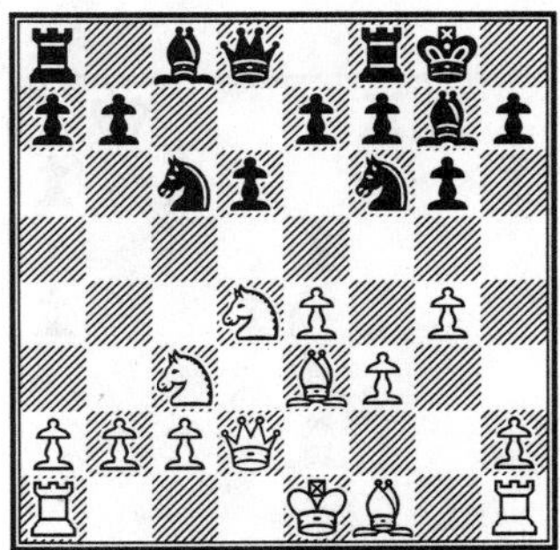

This move also introduces some exciting chess, if the players are so inclined. In contrast to the usual lines with 9.Bc4, here the bishops remains safely at home, for most of the game! **9...Be6; 10.0-0-0 Nxd4; 11.Bxd4 Qa5; 12.a3 Rfc8; 13.h4 Rab8; 14.h5 b5; 15.h6.** Now the fireworks begin! **15...b4!?** Black can also retreat to f8, with a playable game, but that plan has not been sufficiently explored yet. **16.hxg7 bxa3; 17.Qh6.**

Dragoneers hate to abandon a plan, and this position arose again in Fernandez-Gonzales, Barcelona 1985. White's fate there was no better than in our main game. 17.Nd5 axb2+; 18.Bxb2 Rxb2!; 19.Nxe7+ Kxg7; 20.Qh6+ Kh8; 21.Nxc8 Qb4 and White was forced to resign. **17...axb2+; 18.Kd2.**

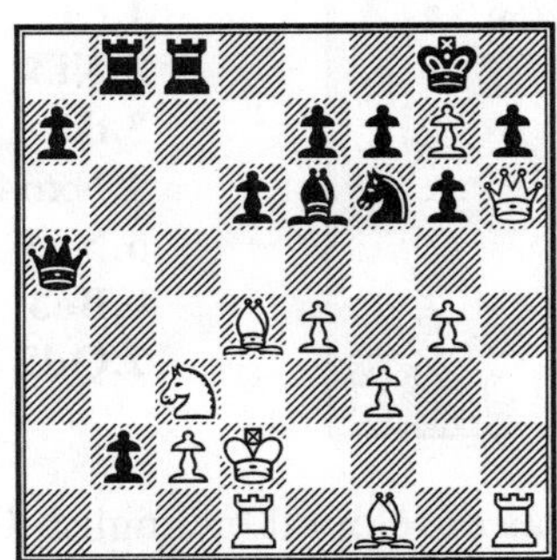

18...Bxg4!! This smashes apart the kingside. The idea is credited to Jonthan Mestel, one of the greatest theoreticians in the Dragon, and it is put into practice by

William Watson, who has risen to an equal rank in the Dragon lore. **19.Bxf6.** 19.fxg4 e5! and White cannot escape the pressure of the Black forces on the queenside. **19...Bh5.** This bishop only temporarily blockades the h-file, but it buys Black enough time to bring the queen into attacking formation and a relentless pursuit of the White monarch.

20.Bd4. White must try to improve here, but so far the theoreticians have been convinced by analysis from Chris Ward, the newest member of the inner circle of Dragon wisdom. Here is just a sample: 20.Ke3 Rxc3+!; 21.Bxc3 Qxc3+; 22.Bd3 a5; 23.Rxh5 gxh5; 24.e5 Qxe5+; 25.Kf2 Qd4+; 26.Ke2 f5; 27.Bxf5 Qxd1+; 28.Kxd1 b1Q+ and Black has only to arrange to get the queen back to the kingside, for example 29.Kd2 Qb4+; 30.Ke2 (30.Kc1 Qe1#) 30...Qb5+; 31.Bd3 Qe5+; 32.Kf2 Qxg7. **20...e5!; 21.Rxh5.** What else? White must open some lines! **21...gxh5; 22.Qg5 Qb4; 23.Bd3 Qxd4; 24.Nd5.**

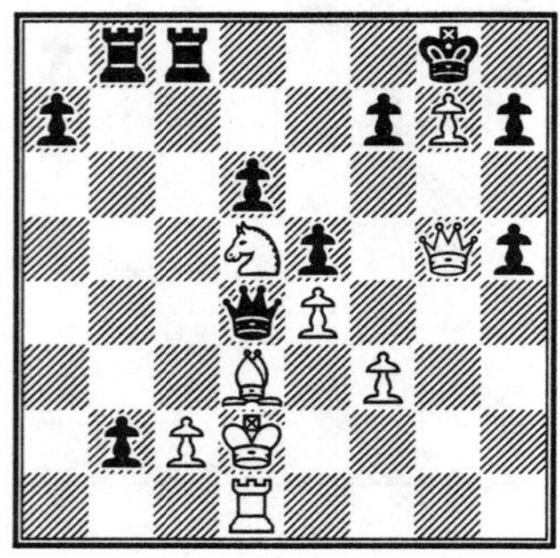

White threatens mate in one, but that is one move too slow! **24...Qf2+; 25.Be2 Rxc2+; 26.Kxc2 Qxe2+; 27.Kc3 Qxf3+; 28.Kc4 Qb3#. Black won.**

ENGLISH ATTACK

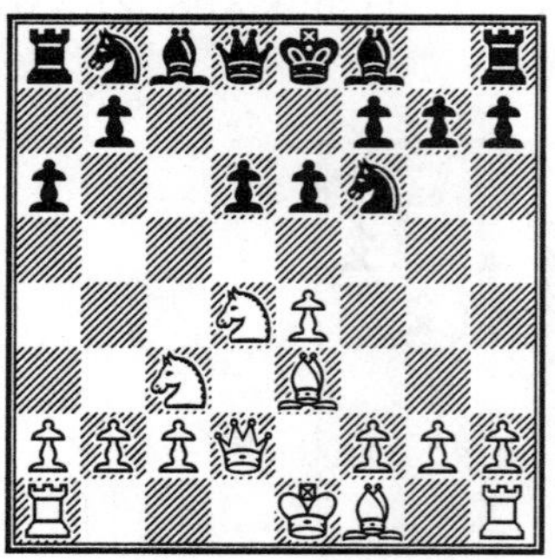

1.e4 c5
2.Nf3 d6
3.d4 cxd4
4.Nxd4 Nf6
5.Nc3 a6
6.Be3 e6
7.Qd2

The **English Attack** was developed by English Grandmasters, especially Michael Adams, John Nunn and Nigel Short, in the late 1980s and soon became a common position in top competitions. The ideas are similar to those of the Yugoslav Attack in the Dragon Variation, except that Black has not fianchettoed on the kingside and instead has played ...e6. White will castle queenside and launch a pawnstorm with g4 and h4.

Unlike the Yugoslav Attack, however, the onslaught takes longer to reach the enemy king, who has not weakened his protective pawn barrier. Black will therefore have extra time to attack on the queenside, but does not have the power of a bishop at g7 to call on, so it is much harder to create sufficient pressure at c3.

(92) NUNN - MARIN [B80]

Szirak Interzonal, 1987

1.e4 c5; 2.Nf3 d6; 3.d4 cxd4; 4.Nxd4 Nf6; 5.Nc3 a6; 6.Be3 e6; 7.Qd2 b5. 7...Ng4; 8.Bg5 leaves the knight offside and Black is far behind in development. **8.f3.**

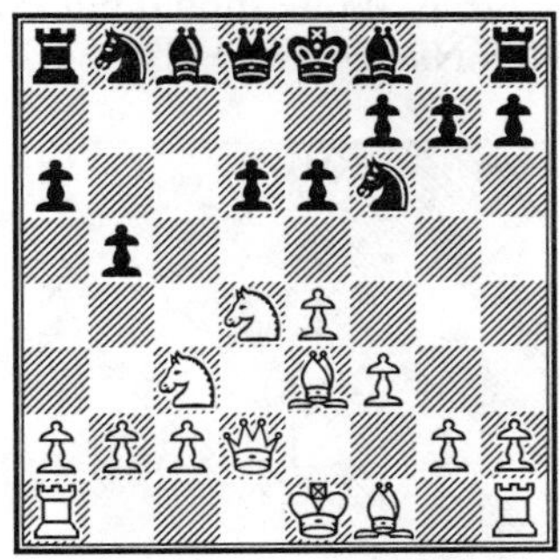

8...Nbd7. Black can also fianchetto the bishop at g7 in support of development of the knight at c6. 8...Bb7; 9.g4 Nc6; 10.Nxc6 Bxc6; 11.g5 Nd7; 12.0–0–0 Qc7; 13.h4 Rc8 (13...b4; 14.Ne2 d5; 15.Nd4 Bb7 is unclear, according to Huebner.) 14.a3 Bb7; 15.Bd4 (15.h5 might be more to the point.) 15...Ne5; 16.Qe3 Nc4; 17.Bxc4 Qxc4 was played in Short-Ribli, Montpellier Candidates 1985. 18.b3 Qc6; 19.Kb2 Rg8 followed by ...Be7 is still unclear–Huebner. **9.g4 h6.** 9...Nb6; 10.0–0–0 Bb7; 11.g5 Nfd7; 12.h4 Be7; 13.h5 b4 gave Black counterplay in Anand-Kr. Georgiev, Palma de Mallorca 1989. **10.0–0–0 Bb7; 11.Bd3.**

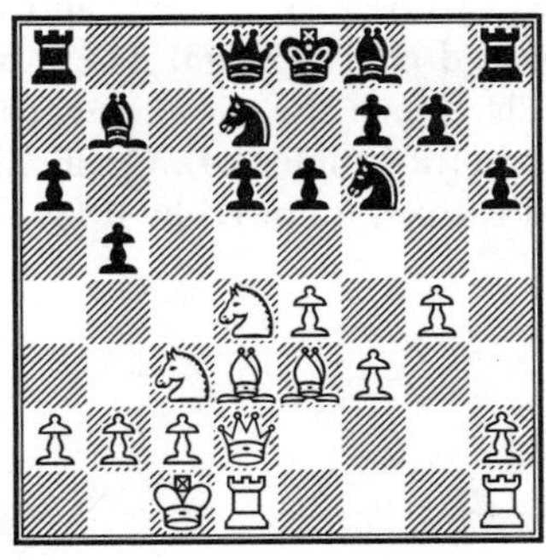

White has completed development, and Black cannot sit still. Though ...Be7 and kingside castling seems logical, it is too slow and walks right into White's attack. Therefore Black has concentrated on play in the center or on the queenside. **11...Ne5.** 11...b4; 12.Nce2 d5; 13.exd5 Nxd5 allows 14.Nxe6!! fxe6; 15.Bg6+ Ke7; 16.Nf4! Ne5; 17.Rhe1! Kf6; 18.Nxe6 Kxe6 (18...Qd6; 19.Nc5 Qc6; 20.Nxb7 Nxe3; 21.Qxe3 Nxg6; 22.Rd6+) 19.Bd4 Bd6; 20.f4 so that line seems to be dead, thanks to the analysis provided by Huebner.

12.Rhe1 Nfd7. 12...b4; 13.Na4 d5; 14.exd5 Nxd5 is a more active plan, Mainka-Olafsson, Dortmund 1988. **13.f4 b4.** 13...Nxg4; 14.e5 Nc5; 15.Ndxb5 Nxd3+; 16.Qxd3 axb5; 17.exd6 is evaluated by Nunn as unclear. Black has great difficulty developing the kingside, but White only has one pawn for the piece. Still, if the b-pawn falls, then White will have four connected passed pawns, one already on the sixth rank. 17...Qa5 looks interesting.

A) 18.Bc5 Kd8; 19.b4 (19.Qd4 Ra6) 19...Qa3+; 20.Kb1 Bc6 and Black consolidates.

B) 18.Qxb5+ 18.Qxb5; 19.Nxb5 Nxe3; 20.Rxe3 Rxa2; 21.Kb1 Ra4 and White is running out of pawns for the piece. White should not capture at b5, but it is hard to find other good moves. **14.Nd5 Nxd3+; 15.Qxd3.**

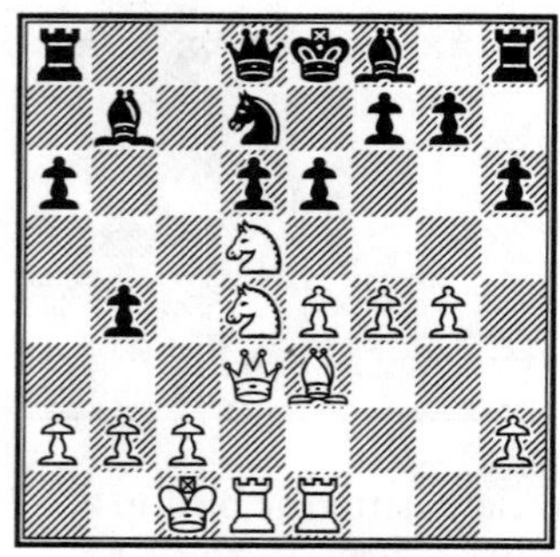

15...exd5. 15...Nc5; 16.Qc4 Rc8; 17.Qxb4 exd5; 18.exd5 Bxd5; 19.Nf3 Be6 and White didn't have enough compensation for the piece in Short-Sax, 5th match game 1988. **16.exd5 Be7; 17.Nc6 Bxc6; 18.dxc6 Nf6?** Castling is long overdue. 18...0–0 19.cxd7 Qxd7; 20.Bd4 is considerably better for White, but it is not nearly as bad as the game.

19.Bb6 Qxb6. Now White, with only three attacking pieces left, sacrifices again! **20.Rxe7+!! Kf8.** 20...Kxe7; 21.Qxd6+ Ke8; 22.Re1+ and White mates. **21.Qxd6 Kg8;** Black must avoid the discovered check. **22.g5!** The attack is relentless. **22...hxg5; 23.fxg5 Rc8.** Black will gladly return the piece to get rid of the monster c-pawn. **24.c7!** Nunn is not interested in the knight! **24...Qxd6; 25.Rxd6 Ng4; 26.Rd8+ Kh7; 27.Red7.** Black cannot avoid Rxh8+, followed by Rd8+, so it was time to topple the king. **White won.**

KERES ATTACK

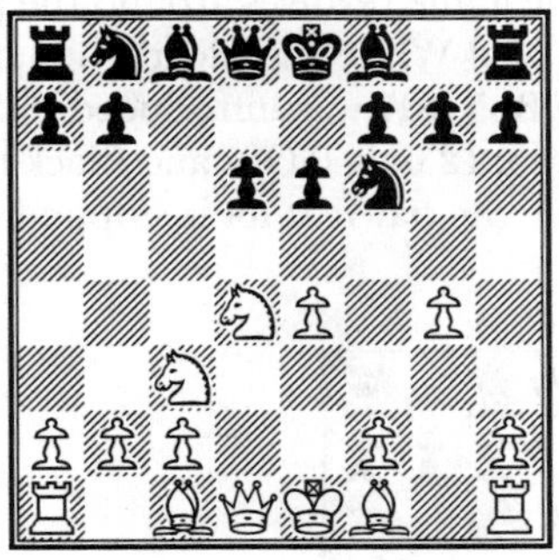

1.e4 c5
2.Nf3 d6
3.d4 cxd4
4.Nxd4 Nf6
5.Nc3 e6
6.g4

This is the much-feared **Keres Attack**, the greatest disincentive to Black's move order. It is by no means clear that White has a guaranteed advantage, but the results overwhelmingly favor the first player. So even Kasparov, who loves to defend the Scheveningen, often arrives via a Najdorf route to avoid the Keres.

(93) KARPOV - HORT [B81]
Moscow, 1971

1.e4 c5; 2.Nf3 d6; 3.d4 cxd4; 4.Nxd4 Nf6; 5.Nc3 e6; 6.g4 Nc6.

There are two significant alternatives in 6...e5 and 6...h6, while 6...a6 is also possible, as are transpositions among the systems. Let's consider a few examples from a recent tournament where top stars were compelled to begin each game with the Sicilian Defense. It was held in Buenos Aires, and greatly enriched the theory of the opening.

6...e5; 7.Bb5+ Bd7; 8.Bxd7+ Qxd7; 9.Nf5 h5; 10.Bg5 Nh7; 11.Bd2 hxg4; 12.Qxg4 g6; 13.Ne3 Qxg4; 14.Nxg4 led to an eventual draw in the game between Ljubojevic, one of the stars of the 1970s, and young Judith Polgar, the most accomplished female chessplayer ever. 6...h6 is also very popular.

A) 7.g5 hxg5; 8.Bxg5 Nc6; 9.Bg2 Bd7; 10.Nb3 a6; 11.Qe2 Qc7; 12.0-0-0 0-0-0; 13.h4 Kb8; 14.h5 Be7; 15.f4 was seen in Polgar's game against 1994 World Championship candidate Valery Salov, who surprised her with 15...Ng8! a new move with a lot of venom.

The game continued 16.Nd4 Bf6; 17.Nf3 Nge7; 18.Bxf6 gxf6; 19.Qd2 and now a remarkable defensive maneuver should have led to an advantage for Black, even though White gained a pawn with 19...Rh6; 20.Qxd6 Qxd6; 21.Rxd6 Kc7; 22.e5 and here 22...Rg8 would have given Black a slight advantage.

B) 7.h3 is a bit slow, and there are two reliable plans for Black, both involving ...a6 but differing in the placement of the knight at b8. 7...a6 (7...Nc6; 8.Be3 a6; 9.f4 Be7; 10.Qd2 g5; 11.Nf3 Nd7; 12.f5 Nde5; 13.Nxe5 Nxe5; 14.0-0-0 b5 with sufficient counterplay for Black, Shirov-Andersson, Yerevan Olympiad 1996.) 8.Bg2 g5; 9.Qe2

Nbd7; 10.Nb3 Ne5; 11.f4 gxf4; 12.Bxf4 Nfd7; 13.0–0–0 b5 and Black had plenty of counterplay here, too, in Leko-Ivanchuk, Wijk aan Zee 1996.

C) 7.h4 Be7 (7...Nc6; 8.Rg1 d5; 9.Bb5 Bd7; 10.exd5 Nxd5; 11.Nxd5 exd5; 12.Be3 Qxh4; 13.Qe2 Nxd4; 14.Bxd4+ Qe7; 15.Bxd7+ Kxd7; 16.Be3 Rd8; 17.0–0–0 Kc8; 18.Qf3 Both sides have "castled" and now the game revolves around the pawn at d5. 18...a6; 19.Rd3 Qf6; 20.Qxf6 gxf6; 21.Rgd1 and White was clearly better in Ashley-Salov, New York (CITS) 1996.) 8.Be3 Nc6; 9.Bb5 Bd7 was introduced by Salov in his game against Shirov. 10.Qe2 h5; 11.gxh5 Nxh5; 12.0–0–0 Qc7 and Black had a promising position, with no real weaknesses, while the pawn at h4 is stopped in its track. 7.g5.

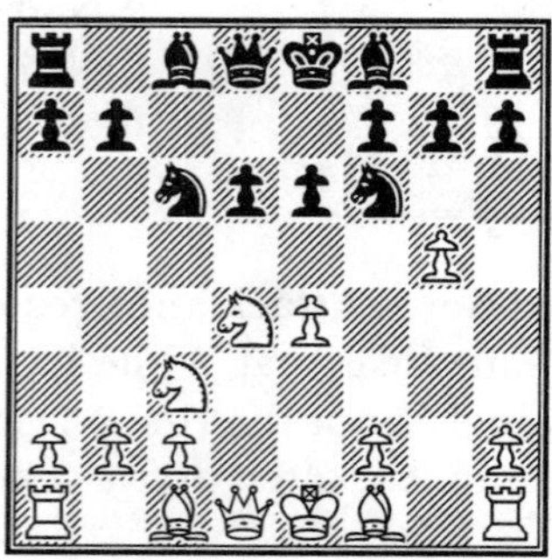

7...Nd7; 8.Be3 a6; 9.f4. White's advancing pawns look menacing, but there is not much piece action to support the kingside attack yet. **9...Be7; 10.Rg1 Nxd4.** Hort, one of the top stars of the 1960s and 1970s played this reluctantly, since it concedes the center to White, who now has better control of e5. Therefore Black will have to occupy that square while he can. **11.Qxd4.**

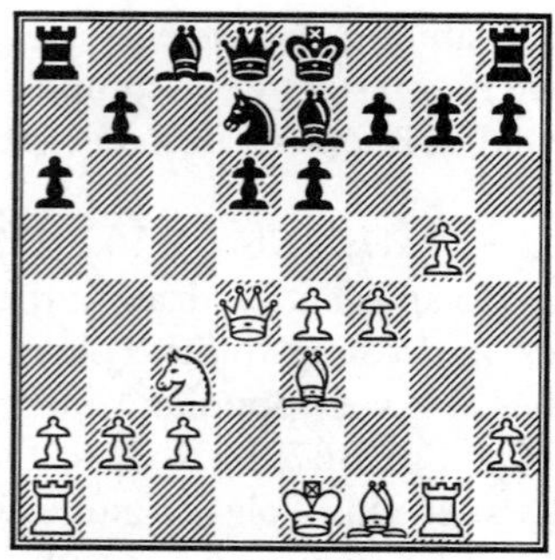

11...e5!; 12.Qd2 exf4; 13.Bxf4 Ne5. Black has executed his plan to take over the e5-square, but has had to accept a weak pawn at d6 in return.

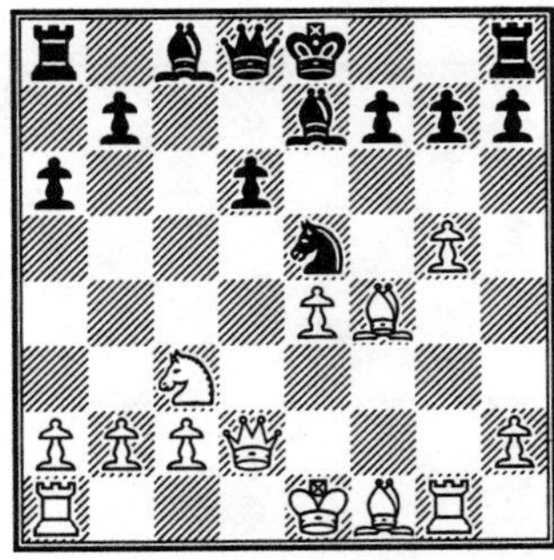

14.Be2 Be6; 15.Nd5! White correctly establishes a blockade at d5. If he had castled first, then Black would have been able to thwart this plan with 15...Qa5! **15...Bxd5; 16.exd5.** A difficult choice. Generally, one uses a piece to blockade a pawn, but here the weakness at d6 would have a counterpart at e4. Karpov's choice also gives more scope to his light-squared bishop. **16...Ng6.** Hort tries to mix it up. The threat is the capture at f4 followed by Qa5+. **17.Be3 h6?!** This is an error of judgment. Black reasoned that White would not capture, because that would result in a displacement of his king. But with the d-file sealed, the White king will rest comfortably at d1. **18.gxh6 Bh4+; 19.Kd1 gxh6; 20.Bxh6.**

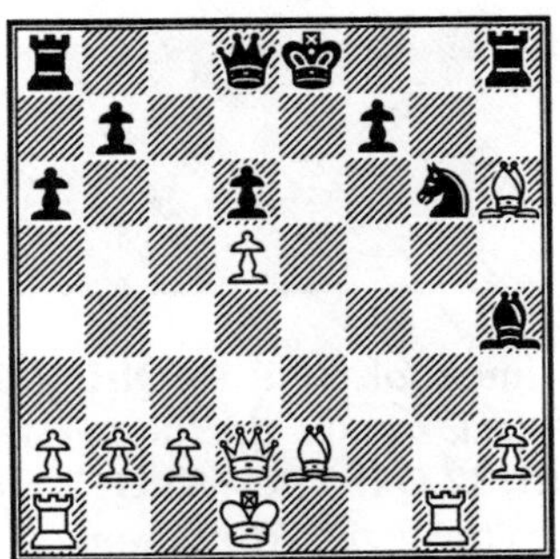

Never mind White's insignificant extra pawn at c2. The question is, where should the Bh4 be posted? **20...Bf6; 21.c3 Be5.** This is clearly a good square for the bishop, and there is a serious threat here of kingside infiltration with 22...Qh4, e.g., 23.Bg5 Qb6; 24.Be3 Qc7. But Karpov, recognizing the danger, puts a stop to Black's plans. **22.Rg4! Qf6?!** Despite White's advantages (bishop pair, open lines in the center) Hort should have taken the opportunity to restore the material balance with 22...Bxh2. Instead, he chose to play for complications.

23.h4! A strong positional move, saving and advancing the h-pawn. It is based on the tactical point that 23...Nxh4? would be countered by 24.Bg7. **23...Qf5; 24.Rb4.** This rook performs the double duty of protecting the fourth rank and attacking on the queenside. **24...Bf6; 25.h5 Ne7.** Not 25...Ne5?, which drops a piece to 27.Rf4! **26.Rf4.** 26.Rxb7?? Rxh6!; 27.Qxh6 Qxd5+ picks up the Rb7. **26...Qe5.**

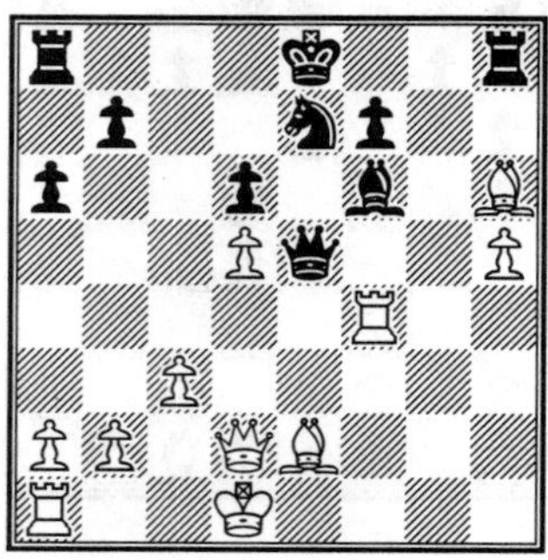

Black still hasn't castled, and will not be allowed to do so! **27.Rf3! Nxd5; 28.Rd3 Rxh6.** No better was 28...Ne7; 19.Bf4! **29.Rxd5!** White had to avoid the tactical trick 29.Qxh6 Bg5 when 30...Ne3+ would have been very powerful. **29...Qe4.**

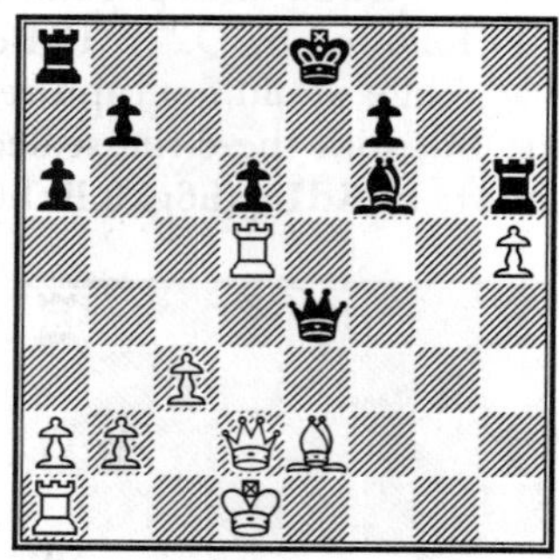

Keep your eye on the White rook. **30.Rd3! Qh1+.** The threat of Re3, combined with pressure at h6, force Black to take this desperate measure. He was in time pressure as well. **31.Kc2 Qxa1; 32.Qxh6 Be5; 33.Qg5.** Hort ran out of time, but that just brought a merciful end to the game. **White won.**

(94) SCHILLER - PAOLOZZI [B81]

Ramsgate (Regency Masters), 1981

1.e4 c5; 2.Nc3. This is not only an entry into the Closed Sicilian, but is also an attempt to transpose into a normal Open Sicilian which normally is reached via 2.Nf3. Therefore Black must be careful to choose a reply which keeps open the possibilities of transposing into the main lines. **2...e6; 3.Nge2 d6; 4.d4 cxd4.** Now we have reached the standard positions in the opening. **5.Nxd4 a6.** The Najdorf Variation is one of Black's most popular options, and it will be reached after Black plays ...Nf6. **6.Be3 Nf6; 7.g4.**

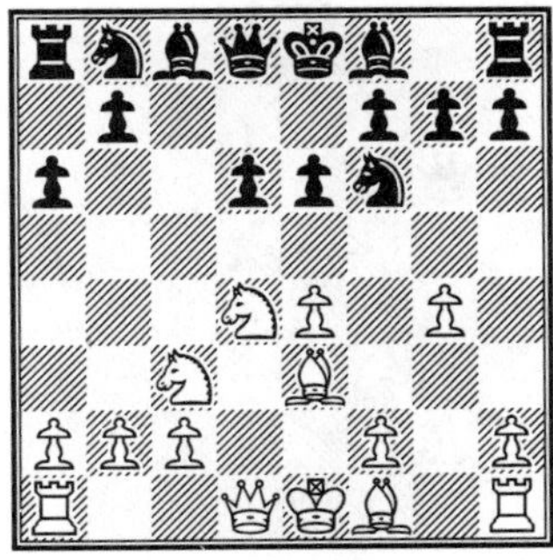

This move transposes to the Keres Attack Deferred. Many players would simply transpose to normal lines by playing either 7...h6 or 7...Nc6. But some players will also consider the significance of the fact that the bishop has already been developed at e3. My opponent reasons that there is another possibility which suggests itself because of the position of the bishop. In fact, the same reasoning led Swedish Grandmaster Ulf Andersson to the same conclusion back in the 1970s, and both played the same reply, advancing the pawn to h5.

This entire system is very popular now, but few players seem to be aware of its history. At the Groningen GM Open of 1996, one Grandmaster excitedly showed me his "new idea" with ...h5 and I had to let him know he was reinventing a wheel which I had already personally experienced.

7...h5. 7...h6 transposes to more normal Keres Attack lines, though these are by no means harmless for Black, as shown in Anand-Kasparov, Dos Hermanas 1996: 8.f4 e5? (8...Qb6 is stronger, e.g., 9.a3 Bd7 and now the pin on the a7-g1 diagonal forces White to retreat: 10.Bg1 Qc7! , wisely declining the offer of a poisoned pawn at b2. 11.Qe2 Nc6; 12.0–0–0 and in Hracek-Stocek, Cesko 1996, Black should have played 12...Be7 instead of castling queenside.)

9.Nf5 Nc6; 10.Qf3! g6; 11.0–0–0 gxf5; 12.exf5 when White had more than enough compensation, with the enemy king struggling to get out of the center. After 12...e4; 13.Nxe4 Nxe4; 14.Qxe4+ Qe7; 15.Qd3 Bg7 Kasparov points out that White could have obtained a much superior game with 16.Bb6! 0–0; 17.Qxd6 and Black will find it nearly impossible to mobilize the queenside. **8.g5 Ng4; 9.Bc1 Qb6.**

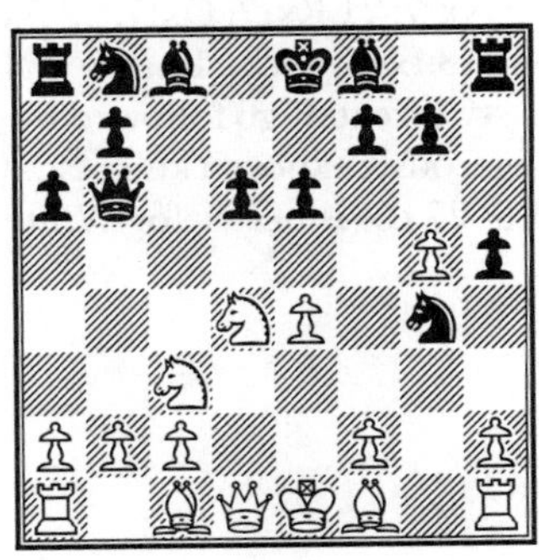

This is a departure from the plan adopted by Andersson, but it is not bad. **10.h3 Ne5; 11.Be2 g6; 12.Nb3 Nbc6; 13.f4!?**

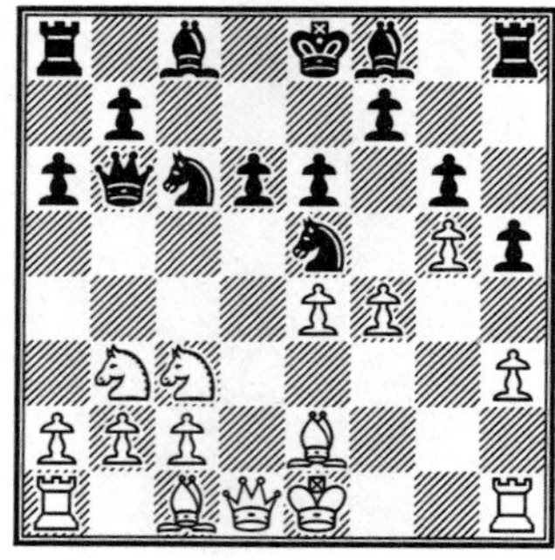

This entails a bit of risk, exposing a lot of territory near my king. In return, however, I keep the initiative. The obvious alternative was to chase the queen away with Be3, and that is what the computers prefer. I don't like to chase the queen away from an awkward square. Thematically, Black must strive for ...b5, and that entails moving the queen. So why push it in the right direction? **13...Nd7; 14.Rf1 Qc7; 15.Be3 b5; 16.f5!?**

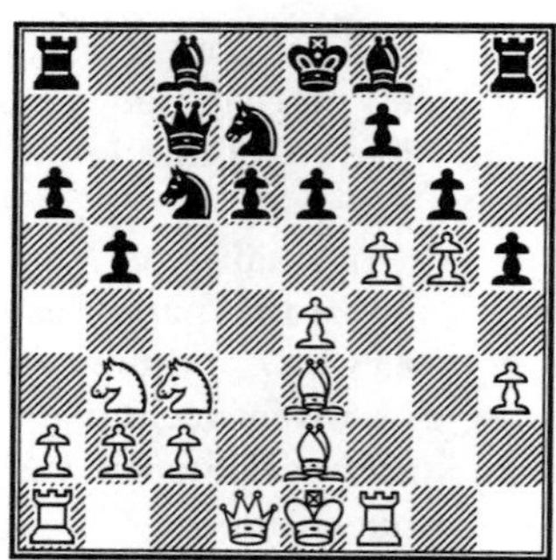

This is the kind of move you hold your breath while playing. I keep the initiative and weaken the enemy kingside, but I give up control of the e5-square, which is probably the most important square on the board. **16...Nde5; 17.Nd4 Bd7.** 17...Nxd4; 18.Bxd4. White threatens to capture at e5, establishing a queenside pawn majority. 18...b4; 19.fxg6 bxc3; 20.gxf7+ Nxf7; 21.Rxf7! Qxf7; 22.Bxh8 and the threat of Be2xh5 is terrible to behold. 17...b4; 18.fxg6 bxc3; 19.gxf7+ Nxf7; 20.Nxc6 cxb2; 21.Rb1 Qxc6; 22.Bxh5 creates the nasty threat of g6 followed by g7. Black will have to return material and is left with a dangerously exposed king. 22...Qxe4; 23.Bxf7+ Ke7; 24.Qf3 Qxf3; 25.Rxf3 Bg7; 26.g6 Bf6; 27.c3! is better for White. **18.fxe6 fxe6; 19.Rf6!**

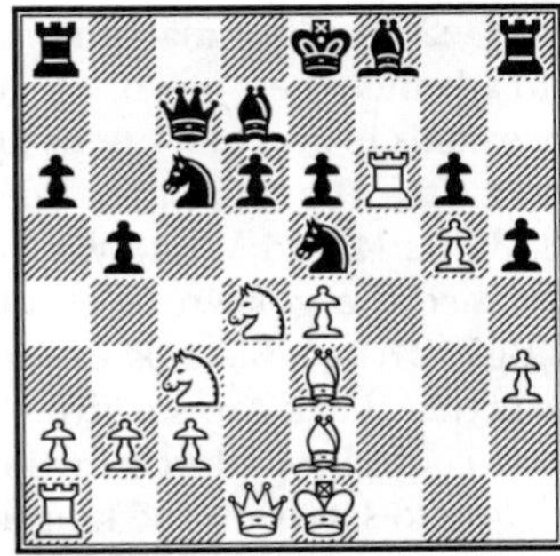

This move looks stronger than it is. Many humans would reject it quickly, since the rook will be chased away before it can do any harm. **19...Nd8.** Now all Black needs to do is play ...Be7 and the White rook will have to retreat, leaving White with an inferior game. Or so it seems. **20.Rxg6! Nxg6; 21.Bxh5 Nf7.** This position has been used to test computer evaluation functions. Almost all of the machines fail to find the correct continuations. 21...Kf7?? loses instantly to 22.Qf3+. **22.Bxg6.** This is the only reasonable move. **22...Rxh3.**

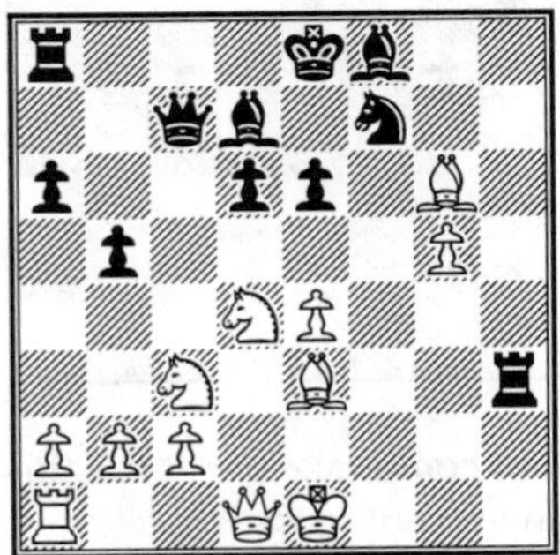

There is now a nasty threat of ...Rh1+. **23.Bxf7+?!** This is not the most accurate plan, since it gives Black more defensive possibilities. 23.Kd2! was correct, but I missed it.

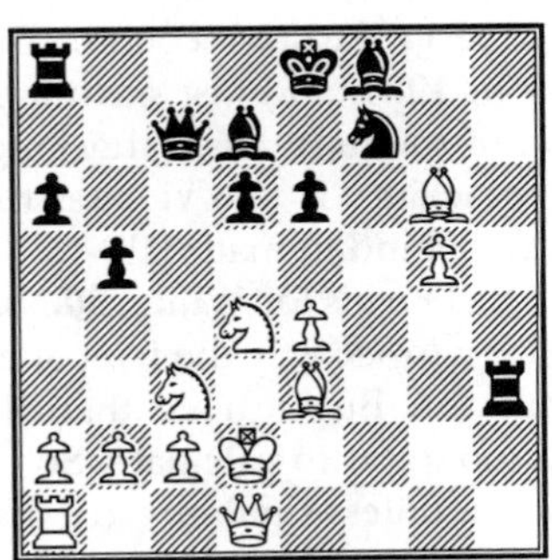

This clever, but seemingly reckless move, would have given me a very strong attack. 23...Rh2+ (23...Bc8; 24.Qe2 e5 is the machine line, and it is absolutely horrible. No human master would advance the e-pawn, because: a) it means that the Bf8 has no future, b) it critically weakens f5 and c) it opens up a huge hole at d5; 25.Nd5 Qb7; 26.Rf1! is much stronger than the computer line. 26...exd4; 27.Rxf7 Qxf7; 28.Bxf7+ Kxf7; 29.Qf1+ Kg8; 30.Bxd4 and White wins easily.) 24.Kc1 Bc8; 25.Qf3 Rb8; 26.Bh5 threatens to advance the g-pawn to g6 and then g7, so Black must blockade the g7-square. 26...Bg7; 27.Bg1 Black is in serious trouble. White has so many threats that it is not clear that Black can survive.

23...Kxf7; 24.Qe2!? Here I could have played my king to d2 instead, but I had hopes of castling to bring my king to safety on the kingside. **24...Qc4?!** This move is an obvious attempt to exchange queens, and would be played by most players. White's resources are buried quite deeply and are hard to find, especially in a tournament situation. 24...Rh1+ would lead to a very long series of relatively forced moves. I only present the main line here. 25.Kd2 Rxa1; 26.Qh5+ Ke7; 27.Nf5+! exf5; 28.Nd5+ Kd8; 29.Qf7 Kc8; 30.Qxf8+ Kb7; 31.Qxa8+! Kxa8; 32.Nxc7+ Kb7; 33.Nd5.

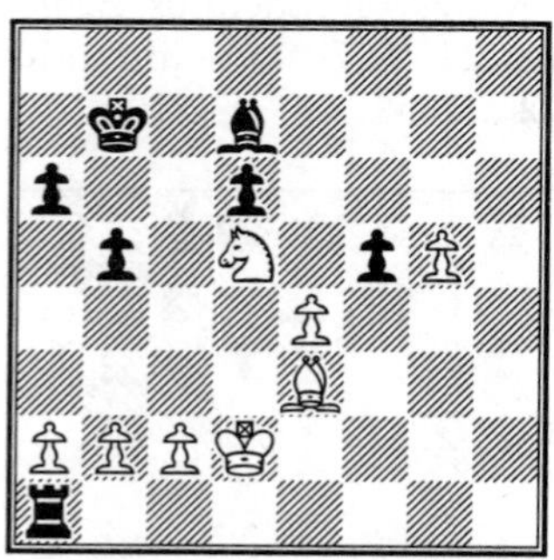

This was as far as my brain could take me at the time. I had confidence that the g-pawn was worth the exchange (rook vs knight).

25.Qf2+. Exchanging queens is certainly out of the question. **25...Kg8; 26.g6 Bg7?** A time-pressure error. 26...Rh1+?; 27.Kd2 Rxa1?!; 28.Qf7+ Kh8; 29.Qh7#. 26...Be8 was safest, guarding the critical f7-square. **27.Qf7+ Kh8; 28.0–0–0!** It was finally time to castle!

28...Be8. Now what can White do? 28...Rxe3 loses to 29.Rh1+. **29.Qxe6!!** This changes everything, and even Garry Kasparov couldn't find this in 4 minutes (though he was a mere Grandmaster in 1981, and just starting his climb to the championship. Here we see a violation of the most basic attacking principle: don't exchange the powerful queens when attacking. It also violates the near-cardinal rule: don't exchange pieces when you are behind in material!

29...Qxe6. 29...Rxe3; 30.Rh1+ wins for White. **30.Nxe6 Rxe3?** Black should simply capture at g6 here, but failed to see why the fruit at e3 is forbidden. 30...Bxc3! is correct, and then Black should win. But with less than 30 seconds per move remaining, the complications were too great to calculate. So it is hard to say how a computer would handle the position unless similar restrictions on depth of search were enforced. 31.Bf4 Bg7; 32.Rxd6 is actually not so simple to win for Black. White will have three pawns for the rook. 32...Rh4; 33.Nxg7 Rxf4; 34.Nh5! (34.Nxe8 Rxe8; 35.Rxa6 Rfxe4; 36.Rb6 R4e5 should win for Black, eventually.) 34...Rf1+; 35.Kd2

Rg1; 36.g7+ Kh7; 37.Nf6+ Kxg7; 38.Nxe8+ Rxe8; 39.Rxa6 Rxe4; 40.Rb6 Rg5. **31.Rh1+ Kg8; 32.Nd5!**

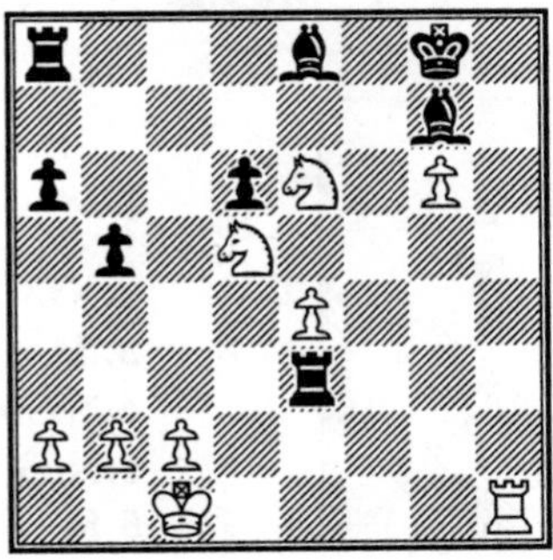

The threat is Ne7 and checkmate! **32...Bxg6.** The machines still consider this position better for Black. **33.Nxe3 Bxe4; 34.Rg1 Ra7; 35.Rg4 Bh7?** 35...d5!; 36.Kd2! d4; 37.Rxe4 dxe3+; 38.Kxe3 Bxb2. White has all the winning chances here, but it is not clear how many there are. **36.Nd5!** This wins by force. Black cannot prevent the liquidation of pieces that leads to a winning endgame for White. **36...Kh8; 37.Nxg7 Rxg7; 38.Rxg7 Kxg7.**

Any decent player can quickly conclude that resignation is inevitable for Black. **39.Nc7.** This wins a pawn. **39...Kf6.** If the a-pawn had advanced, then the b-pawn would have fallen. **40.Nxa6 Ke5; 41.Nc7.** My opponent resigned, since if the pawn advances to b4, then the knight returns to a6 attacking it, and any further advance would run into the wall of White pawns. The ending is such a trivial matter that few masters would bother even trying to defend. **White won.**

SCHEVENINGEN/NAJDORF WITH F4

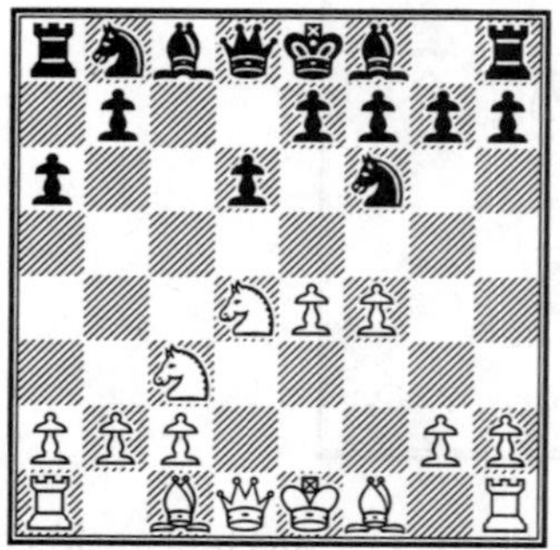

1.e4	**c5**
2.Nf3	**d6**
3.d4	**cxd4**
4.Nxd4	**Nf6**
5.Nc3	**a6**
6.f4	

This has become a popular way of meeting the Najdorf, largely due to the patronage of British theoretician John Nunn, who has featured it in his popular *Beating the Sicilian books*, published by Batsford. It is also a common strategy in the Scheveningen, and play usually converges when Black plays ...e6, as is the case in the present game. The pawn on f4 battles for control of e5, though Black can sometimes advance the e-pawn to that square later.

(95) POLGAR, J - VAN WELY [B82]

Amsterdam (Donner Memorial), 1995

1.e4 c5; 2.Nf3 d6; 3.d4 cxd4; 4.Nxd4 Nf6; 5.Nc3 a6; 6.f4 e6; 7.Qf3 Qb6; 8.Nb3 Qc7; 9.g4.

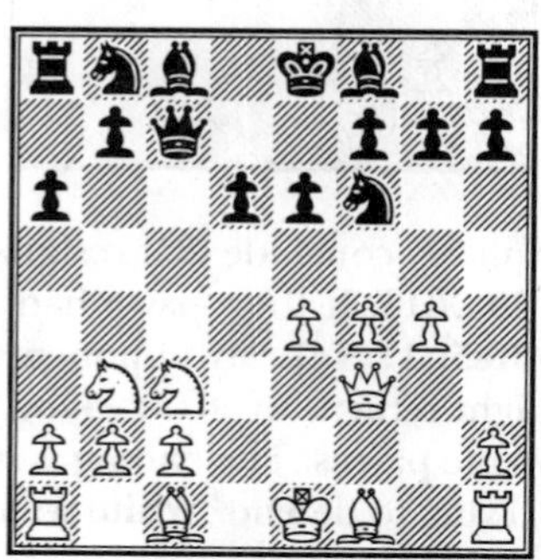

9.Bd3 b5; 10.g4 Bb7; 11.g5 Nfd7; 12.Bd2 Nc5 allows 13.Ne2! with a fluid position for White in Leko-Oll, Ter Apel 1996. **9...b5; 10.g5.** The logical continuation of the attack. **10...b4; 11.Nb5!** Sometimes we see White sacrifice a piece at b5, but usually capturing a pawn or two in the process. Here, the attack on f6 makes this move less of a sacrifice than a positional maneuver. **11...axb5; 12.gxf6 Nd7?!** 12...gxf6; 13.Nd4 Bd7; 14.f5 Nc6; 15.Nxb5 Qa5; 16.fxe6 fxe6; 17.Bd2 Ne5; 18.Qe2 Rc8 was even in Timman-Tal, Hilversum (match) 1988. **13.Bxb5 gxf6.** 13...Ba6!? is an interesting option. **14.f5** and now Black must leave the king in place. **14...Ke7?** 14...Qb6;

15.Qe2 Rb8; 16.c4 bxc3; 17.a4 Ba6; 18.Bxa6 Qxb3 provided counterplay in Gipslis-Van Wely, Gausdal (Peer Gynt) 1992.

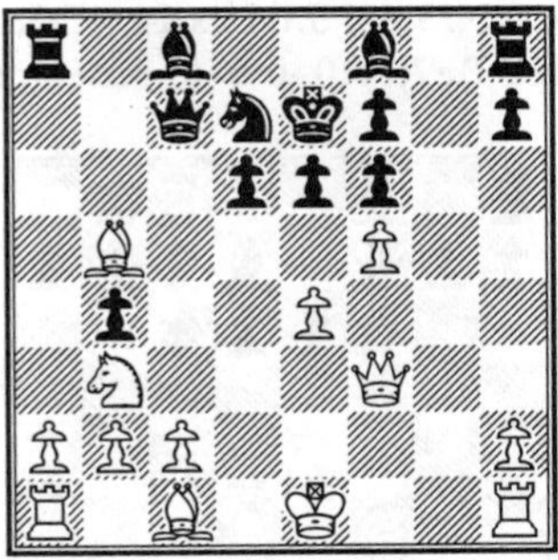

15.Bxd7 Bxd7; 16.fxe6 fxe6; 17.Rf1! The most efficient move, since 17.e5? allows Black to escape with 17...dxe5; 18.Qxa8 Bc6 and Black holds the advantage. **17...Bb5. 18.Qxf6+ Kd7.** 18...Ke8; 19.Qxh8 Bxf1 loses to 20.Bh6 Qf7; 21.Qxf8+ Qxf8; 22.Bxf8 Kxf8; 23.Kxf1. **19.Qxh8 Be7.** 19...Bxf1 gets demolished by 20.Qxh7+ Be7; 21.Bg5. There is no longer a way to save the game. **20.Qxa8 Qc4; 21.Qb7+ Ke8; 22.Rf2 Bh4; 23.Qf7+ Kd8; 24.Bg5+. White won.**

SCHEVENINGEN VARIATION

The **Scheveningen** features the "small center" for Black, with the pawns at d6 and e6 keeping the enemy pieces at bay. For the most part, Black pawns will remain behind the front lines, mostly on the third rank. White will not have very many weaknesses to work against, and precision is required by both sides. For this reason the top players in the world are frequently seen on both sides of the opening.

White has a number of different plans, from the quiet waters of e-lines with Be2, Be3 and kingside castling, to the wilder variations with opposite wing castling as in the English Attack, and of course the Keres Attack, which we have already seen.

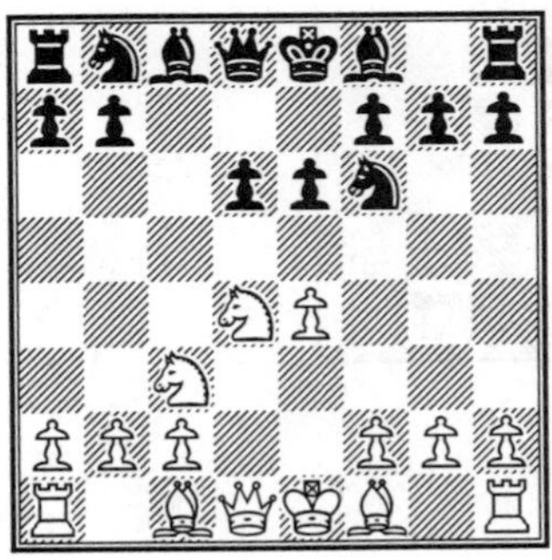

1.e4 c5
2.Nf3 e6
3.d4 cxd4
4.Nxd4 Nf6
5.Nc3 d6

(96) SMYSLOV - RUDAKOVSKY [B83]

Soviet Championship, 1945

1.e4 c5; 2.Nf3 e6; 3.d4 cxd4; 4.Nxd4 Nf6; 5.Nc3 d6; 6.Be2 Be7;. 7.0-0 0-0; 8.Be3 Nc6; 9.f4 Qc7.

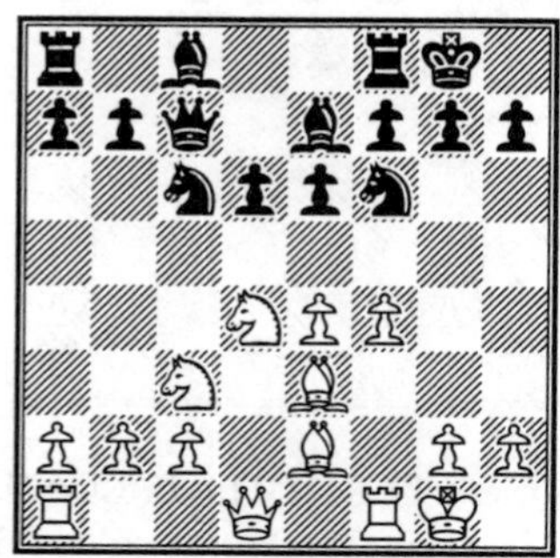

This is a Modern handling of the Scheveningen Variation, where Black delays the advance of the a-pawn to a6. Lines with an early ...a6 are known as the Classical lines. Ironically, for the past couple of decades the classical approach has come to dominate, but that is mostly due to the fact that many Scheveningens are reached from the Najdorf move order 1.e4 c5; 2.Nf3 d6; 3.d4 cxd4; 4.Nxd4 Nf6; 5.Nc3 a6, avoiding the Keres Attack. In either approach, both sides develop quickly and castle kingside. White enjoys a bit more space but the Black position is very solid.

10.Qe1. The queen often shifts to this square, from which it can leap to h4 and participate in a kingside attack. **10...Nxd4.** It is common to exchange knights at d4. Here Black has the added advantage that this can be followed by a strong thrust in the center. **11.Bxd4 e5!** Although this creates some holes at d5 and f5, it gives the bishop at c8 some breathing room. **12.Be3 Be6.** 12...exf4; 13.Bxf4 is also possible, but Black should not get greedy. 13...Qb6+; 14.Kh1 Qxb2?; 15.Qg3 Kh8; 16.e5 dxe5; 17.Bxe5 and White threatens to play Nd5! **13.f5 Bc4; 14.Bxc4 Qxc4.** Black has eliminated the light-squared bishops but the kingside belongs to White.

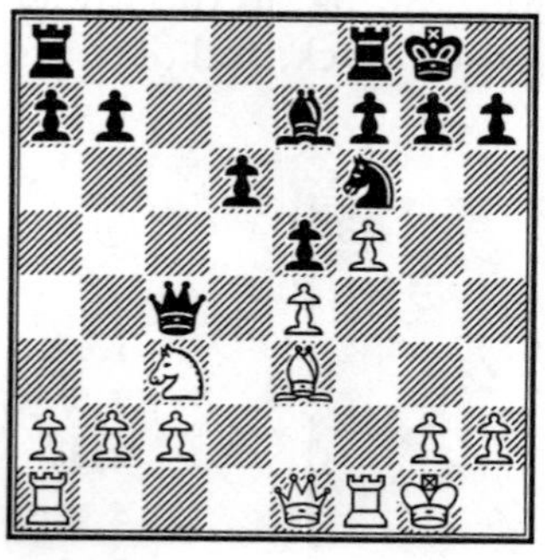

15.Bg5 Rfe8; 16.Bxf6 Bxf6. In exchanging bishop for knight, White counts on the tremendous outpost at d5 to bring home the point. **17.Nd5 Bd8; 18.c3 b5; 19.b3 Qc5+ 20.Kh1 Rc8.** Black has no targets. White can now freely pursue the enemy king. **21.Rf3 Kh8.**

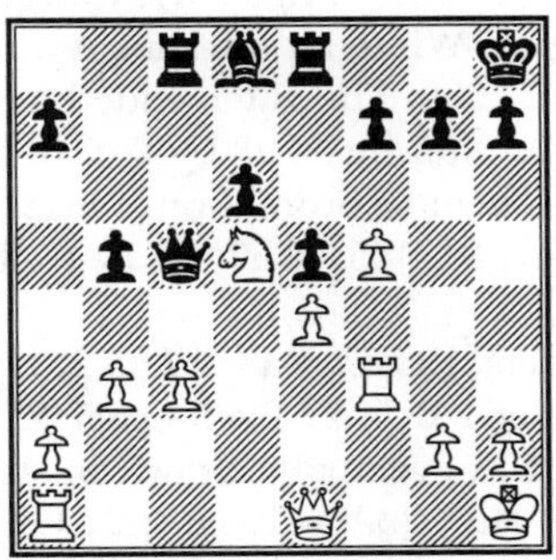

22.f6! The barriers start to fall. **22...gxf6; 23.Qh4 Rg8; 24.Nxf6 Rg7; 25.Rg3 Bxf6; 26.Qxf6.** Black resigned. White will bring the rook at a1, which has not yet moved, into the game with devastating effect. **26...Rcg8; 27.Rxg7 Rxg7; 28.Rd1 Qxc3; 29.h4 Qc7; 30.Rxd6. White won.**

(97) ANAND - KASPAROV [B85]

PCA World Championship (3rd match game, 1995)

1.e4 c5; 2.Nf3 d6; 3.d4 cxd4; 4.Nxd4 Nf6;
5.Nc3 a6; 6.Be2 e6; 7.0–0 Be7; 8.a4 Nc6; 9.Be3 0–0; 10.f4 Qc7; 11.Kh1.

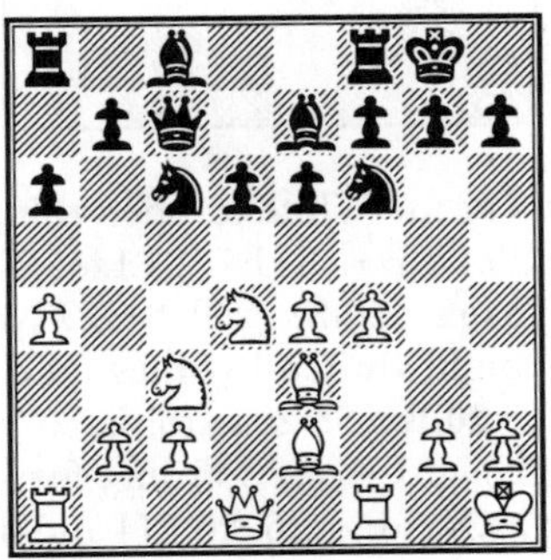

This is the Modern Scheveningen. To reach this position many paths have been traveled, and it takes a full eleven moves for White to set up the basic formation, typified by the usual small center pawn formation, Sicilian placing of minor pieces, and the inclusion of the prophylactic moves Kh1 and a4, each designed to limit Black's counterplay. Many top players are found on both sides of these positions, including Kasparov, Anand and Topalov during 1996.

11...Re8. Now White has to decide the future of the bishop at e2. Which diagonals are more important? The question remains open. **12.Bd3.** 12.Bf3.

A) 12...Na5; 13.Bg1 Bf8; 14.Qe1 Rb8; 15.h3! Nd7; 16.Bh2 is an interesting new plan. 16...Nc6; 17.Rd1 Nxd4; 18.Rxd4 b5; 19.axb5 (19.e5!? comes into consideration.) 19...axb5; 20.e5! f5!?; 21.exd6! Bxd6; 22.Nd5 Qa7; 23.Rd1! and White was slightly better in Kasparov-Topalov, Dos Hermanas 1996.

B) 12...Rb8; 13.g4 Nxd4 (13...Bf8; 14.g5 Nd7; 15.Bg2 Nxd4; 16.Bxd4 b5; 17.axb5 axb5; 18.Ra7 Qd8; 19.b4 gave White an advantage on both sides of the board in Ivanchuk-Topalov, Novgorod 1996. The game ended in spectacular fashion: 19...e5; 20.Be3 exf4; 21.Bxf4 Ne5; 22.Nd5 Bg4?! 23.Qd2 Nc6; 24.g6!! Nxa7; 25.gxf7+ Kh8; 26.Bg5!! Qd7; 27.fxe8N. A little underpromotion to liven things up! 27...Rxe8; 28.Qf2 Kg8; 29.e5!! h6; 30.Nb6 Qc7; 31.Bd5+ Kh7; 32.Be4+ Kg8; 33.Nd5 Qd7; 34.Ne7+! and Black resigned.)

14.Bxd4 e5; 15.fxe5 dxe5; 16.Ba7 Ra8; 17.g5 Rd8; 18.Qe2 Ne8; 19.Be3 Be6; 20.Qf2 Qc4 (20...Rdc8; 21.Rad1 Bc5; 22.Bxc5 Qxc5; 23.Nd5 Bxd5; 24.Rxd5 Qxc2; 25.Rxe5 Qxf2; 26.Rxf2 g6 was eventually drawn in Anand-Kasparov, Las Palmas 1996.) 21.Bb6 Rdc8; 22.Be3 Bc5; 23.Rad1 Bxe3; 24.Qxe3 Qb4; 25.Rd3 Rd8; 26.b3 Rd4; 27.Rfd1 Rc8; 28.R1d2 Qc5; 29.Kg2 b5; 30.axb5 axb5; 31.Nd1 Rxd3; 32.Qxd3 f6; 33.gxf6 Nxf6 and Black was better in Topalov-Kasparov, Yerevan Olympiad 1996.

12...Nb4; 13.a5 Bd7; 14.Nf3 Bc6; 15.Bb6 Qc8!? A new idea. Previously the queen had been stationed at d7. **16.Qe1 Nd7; 17.Bd4 Nc5!? 18.Qg3 f6.**

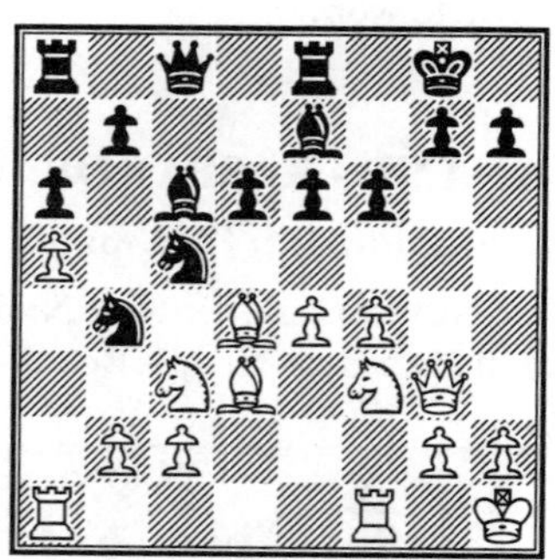

Now is the proper moment for White to open things up. **19.e5! Rf8.** 19...dxe5 allows the typical sacrifice 20.Bxh7+! Kxh7; 21.fxe5 Nxc2; 22.exf6 Bxf6; 23.Bxf6 gxf6; 24.Qh4+ Kg7; 25.Ne5! Bxg2+; 26.Kxg2 Ne3+; 27.Kh1 Nxf1; 28.Rxf1 and White if Black dares to take the knight the end comes quickly 28...fxe5; 29.Qg5+ Kh7; 30.Rf3 and mate next move. **20.Bxc5?** 20.exf6! is correct. 20...Bxf6 and now the sacrifice 21.Bxh7+! Kxh7; 22.Ng5+ is very strong, for example 22...Kg8 (22...Kg6; 23.f5+! exf5; 24.Nge4+ Kh7; 25.Nxf6+ gxf6; 26.Rf4 and mate on the h-file. 22...Bxg5; 23.fxg5! Kg8; 24.g6 and White has a strong attack, since Black's pieces are too far away to be of much help.) 23.Qh4 Bxg5; 24.fxg5 Qe8; 25.Rxf8+ Kxf8; 26.Rf1+ Kg8; 27.Bxg7 Kxg7; 28.Qh6+ Kg8; 29.Rf6! and Black's two extra pieces are useless in defense of the king.

20...dxc5; 21.Bc4 Bd5. 21...Bxf3; 22.Rxf3 is better for White since 22...Nxc2? allows 23.f5! Nd4; 24.fxe6! Nxf3; 25.Nd5 Qd8; 26.exf6 Bxf6; 27.e7! Bxe7; 28.Nc7+! Kh8; 29.Ne6 with a powerful attack. **22.Nxd5 exd5; 23.Bb3 c4; 24.Ba4 Nc6; 25.c3.** 25.Rad1 fxe5!; 26.fxe5; Qe6; 27.Bxc6 Qxc6; 28.Nd4 Qg6; 29.Qxg6 hxg6 gives White a slight positional advantage, but it is hard to do anything with it.

25...fxe5; 26.Nxe5! Nxe5; 27.fxe5 Qe6; 28.Bc2 Rxf1+; 29.Rxf1 Rf8; 30.Rxf8+

Bxf8; 31.Qf4 g6; 32.Bd1 Qf7; 33.Qd4! A strong move, planning to place a bishop at f3, where it will attack the weak pawn at d5. **33...Qf1+.** Black succeeds in getting queens off the board, and relies on the bishops of opposite color to hold the endgame. **34.Qg1 Qxg1+; 35.Kxg1 Kf7; 36.Bg4 b6!** This is the easiest drawing method. If White captures, then ...Bc5+ regains the pawn and there are no significant winning chances for either side.

SOZIN ATTACK

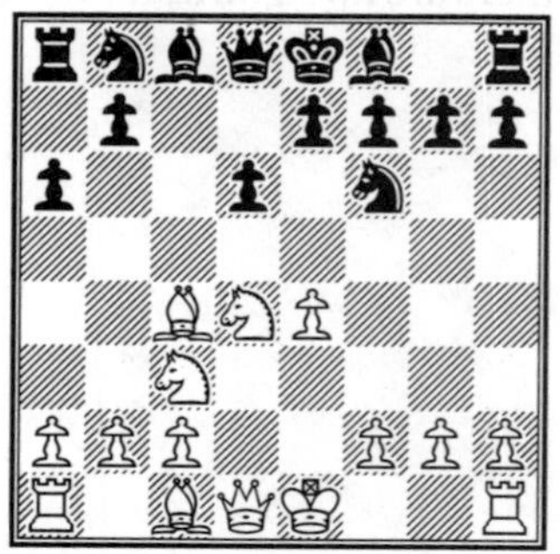

1.e4	**c5**
2.Nf3	**d6**
3.d4	**cxd4**
4.Nxd4	**Nf6**
5.Nc3	**a6**
6.Bc4	

Bobby Fischer loved the White side of the **Sozin Attack**, which was also featured in the 1993 PCA World Championship match between Nigel Short and Garry Kasparov.

White aims right at the Black king's forecourt, opening up options of sacrifices at e6 or f5. Kingside castling and a rapid advance of the f-pawn are common. Black will operate on the queenside, usually advancing the b-pawn to b5. The knight at b8 can be deployed at c6, or at d7 and later at c5.

(98) SHORT - KASPAROV [B87]

PCA World Championship, 16th Game, 1993

1.e4 c5; 2.Nf3 d6; 3.d4 cxd4; 4.Nxd4 Nf6; 5.Nc3 a6; 6.Bc4 e6; 7.Bb3 b5.

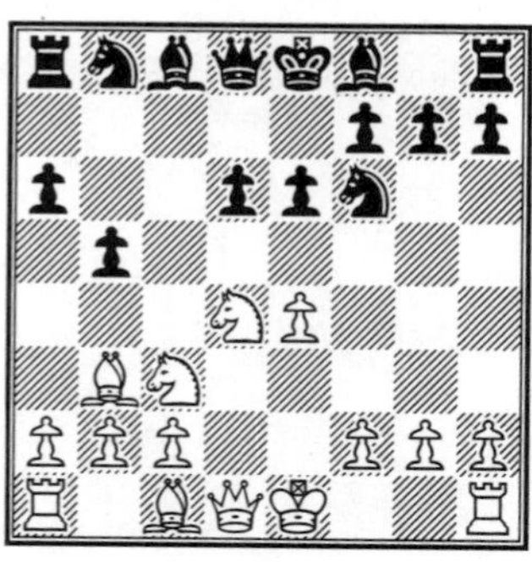

Black has other plans, including bringing the knight from b8 to either d7 or c6, but this is Kasparov's choice. **8.0–0 Be7.** 8...Bb7 is a promising alternative. 9.f4 Nc6; 10.Nxc6 Bxc6; 11.f5 e5; 12.Qd3 Be7; 13.Bg5 Qb6+; 14.Kh1 0–0; 15.Bxf6 Bxf6; 16.Bd5 secured the d5-square, and the advantage, for White in Fischer-Gadia, Mar del Plata 1960. Black should play 9...b4; 10.Na4 Bxe4 with a reasonable game.

9.Qf3. White has a number of alternative plans. 9.f4 0–0; 10.f5 b4; 11.Nce2 e5; 12.Nf3 Bb7 and White couldn't take advantage of the d5-square, so Black was better in Fischer-Smyslov, Yugoslavia (Candidates Tournament) 1959. **9...Qc7; 10.Qg3!** The weakness at g7 is now a target. **10...Nc6.** 10...Nbd7 is probably the best move, for example 11.Re1 Nc5; 12.Nf5 and Black dare not take the knight, because then after Qxg7 the pawn at f7 is in danger.

11.Nxc6. This exchange is still the recommended path. **11...Qxc6; 12.Re1.** 12.f3 is an interesting alternative which may give a slight advantage to White. **12...Bb7.** This is acknowledged as the best plan, putting more pressure at e4. **13.a3 Rd8; 14.f3.** 14.Qxg7 is just too risky. Short later demonstrated the power of the attack with the following variation. 14.Qxg7 Rg8; 15.Qh6 d5; 16.exd5 Nxd5; 17.Bxd5 Rxd5; 18.Ne4 Rd1; 19.Rxd1 Qxe4; 20.f3 Rxg2+; 21.Kxg2 Qxf3+; 22.Kg1 Qg2#.

14...0-0; 15.Bh6 Ne8; 16.Kh1. Short's improvement over a previous game which saw 16.Ne2. The move is useful because it prevents annoying checks on the a7-g1 diagonal. **16...Kh8; 17.Bg5 Bxg5; 18.Qxg5 Nf6; 19.Rad1 Rd7; 20.Rd3 Rfd8; 21.Red1 Qc5; 22.Qe3 Kg8; 23.Kg1 Kf8.** Black can be satisfied with this position. **24.Qf2 Ba8; 25.Ne2.**

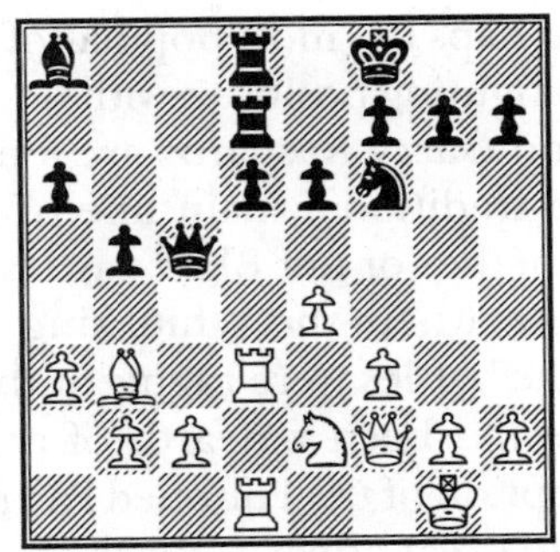

Short said later that he was too embarrassed to offer a draw here. Kasparov's next move is a major error, and the exchange of queens should have led to a draw. **25...g6?; 26.Nd4. Qe5;** Black can't play 26...e5 because of 27.Rc3!, e.g., 27...Qa7; 28.Nc6 Qxf2+; 29.Kxf2 Rc8; 3.Nxe5 Rxc3; 31.Nxd7+ Nxd7; 32.bxc3.

27.Re1 g5; 28.c3 Kg7; 29.Bc2 Rg8; 30.Nb3 Kf8; 31.Rd4 Ke7; 32.a4! Black has strong queenside play and a much better bishop. **32...h5; 33.axb5 axb5; 34.Rb4 h4; 35.Nd4 g4; 36.Rxb5 d5; 37.Qxh4 Qh5; 38.Nf5+.** Kasparov resigned here. Play might have continued: **38...exf5; 39.exf5+ Kf8; 40.Qxf6 Bb7; 41.Rxb7 Rxb7; 42.Qd8+ Kg7; 43.f6+ Kh8; 44.Qxg8+ Kxg8; 45.Re8#.**

NAJDORF VARIATION

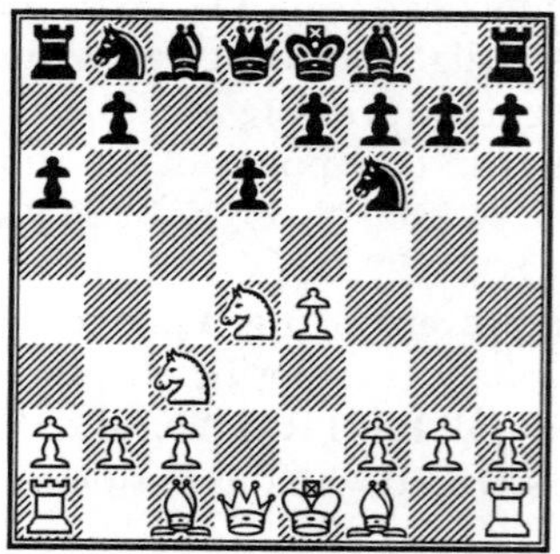

1.e4	c5
2.Nf3	d6
3.d4	cxd4
4.Nxd4	Nf6
5.Nc3	a6

The **Najdorf** is the perhaps the most popular of all of Black's defenses to 1.e4. It inevitably leads to fighting positions with unclear complications. Such stars as Bobby Fischer and Garry Kasparov are found on both sides of this exciting opening. In the traditional main line of the Najdorf, White will attack on the kingside, whether or not Black castles there, and Black in turn will work on the queenside, where the White king inevitably takes shelter.

For several decades the battles were raging at the highest levels of chess, but in recent years there has been a dearth of activity in the main lines, primarily because of the option of the Poisoned Pawn Variation which Fischer and Kasparov have used to great effect as Black. Therefore 6.Bg5 as a whole is in a bit of a slump, with the Sozin and English Attack in ascension. Nevertheless, the winds of fashion shift regularly, and we can expect to see a resurgence of the 6.Bg5 lines, and therefore also the traditional main lines, in the near future.

The Najdorf as a whole remains very popular, and all that is needed is a few strong advocates of the White side of 6.Bg5 to bring back the action and excitement that invariably accompanies the variation.

(99) FISCHER - GELLER [B97]

Monte Carlo, 1967

1.e4 c5; 2.Nf3 d6; 3.d4 cxd4; 4.Nxd4 Nf6; 5.Nc3 a6; 6.Bg5 e6; 7.f4 Qb6.

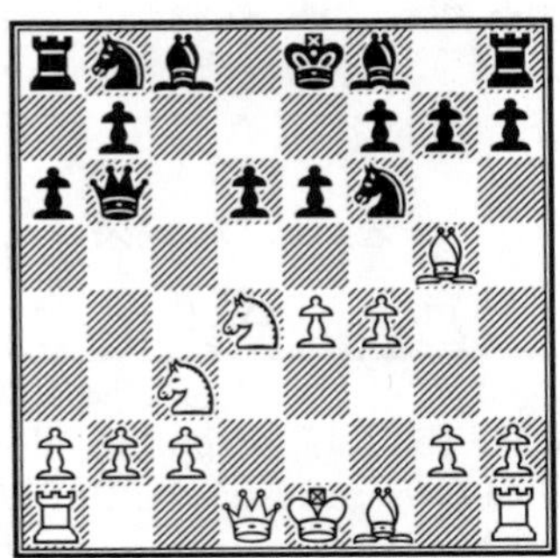

This is the wild Poisoned Pawn Variation, Fischer's speciality as Black. Here is one game where he shows how to handle the White side. Even though he lost, he completely outplayed his opponent in the opening.

8.Qd2 Qxb2; 9.Rb1. There is one worthy alternative: 9.Nb3 Qa3; 10.Bxf6 gxf6; 11.Be2 h5; 12.0–0 Nd7; 13.Kh1 h4! and Black threatens to advance to h3. 14.h3 Be7; 15.Rad1 b6; 16.Qe3 Bb7; 17.f5 Rc8; 18.fxe6 fxe6; 19.Bg4 Qb2! gave Black excellent counterplay in a contest between 1993 PCA World Championship challenger Nigel Short and Garry Kasparov, played at the 1995 tournament in Riga. **9...Qa3; 10.f5.** White has also thoroughly investigated 10.Be2. **10...Nc6.** Black must get some pieces off the board, in order to be prepared to handle the fierce White attack against the king, which is stranded in the center. **11.fxe6 fxe6; 12.Nxc6 bxc6; 13.e5 Nd5.**

13...dxe5; 14.Bxf6 gxf6; 15.Ne4 is also exciting. Black can capture the pawn at a2 or play more conservatively with a developing move. For example 15...Be7; 16.Be2 h5; 17.Rb3 Qa4; 18.Nxf6+ (18.c4 f5; 19.0–0 fxe4; 20.Qc3 Bc5+; 21.Kh1 Rf8; 22.Bxh5+ Kd8; 23.Rd1+ Bd4; 24.Rxd4+ exd4; 25.Qxd4+ Bd7; 26.Qb6+ Ke7; 27.Qc5+ Kf6; 28.Qd4+ e5; 29.Qxd7 was agreed drawn in Gorky-Spassky, USSR 1968.)

18...Bxf6; 19.c4 Ra7; 20.0–0 Be7; 21.Rb8 Rc7; 22.Qd3 Bc5+; 23.Kh1 Ke7; 24.Qg6 Kd6; 25.Rd1+ Bd4; 26.Rxd4+ exd4; 27.Qg3+ e5; 28.c5+ Kd5; 29.Bf3+ e4; 30.Qg5+ Kc4; 31.Qc1+ Kd5; 32.Qg5+ was also drawn, in Kasparov-Rashkovsky, USSR 1979. Kasparov played this theoretically important game before he even earned his Grandmaster title. These days only the very best players in the world dare to "discuss" this variation with him at the board! **14.Nxd5 cxd5.**

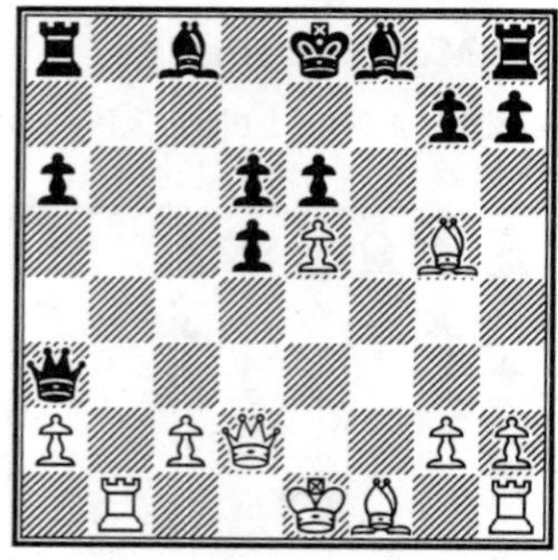

15.Be2 dxe5; 16.0–0 Bc5+. 16...Ra7, defending along the second rank, is now considered more reliable. 17.c4 Qc5+; 18.Kh1 d4; 19.Bh5+ g6; 20.Bd1 Be7; 21.Ba4+. This effective bishop journey has been seen in many games. The end of opening theory is still well beyond the horizon. 21...Kd8; 22.Rf7 h6; 23.Bxh6 e4. This position has been reached in dozens of games. White seems to get the upper hand on 24.Be3! e5; 25.Bg5 e3; 26.Bxe3 although the verdict is still out on 26...Rb7; 27.Re1 Be6; 28.Rg7 Kc8; 29.Bf2 Qb4; 30.Qd1 with a very messy position. **17.Kh1 Rf8; 18.c4.** It is normal for White to try to break up Black's central pawn mass. **18...Rxf1+; 19.Rxf1 Bb7.**

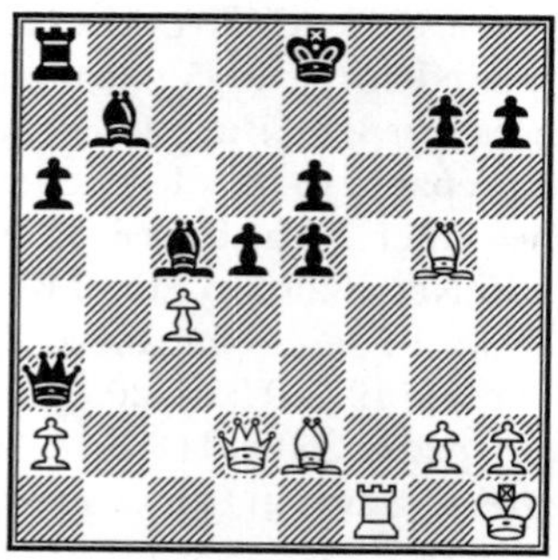

This is where Fischer fell. **20.Bg4?** 20.Qc2! e4; 21.Bg4 gave Tal a good position as White against Bogdanovic at Budva 1967. **20...dxc4; 21.Bxe6 Qd3; 22.Qe1 Be4!** A fine move from the Soviet star and Najdorf specialist. The lines are closed, the Black king is safe, and White is simply two pawns down. **23.Bg4 Rb8; 24.Bd1 Kd7; 25.Rf7+ Ke6. Black won.**

(100) SPASSKY - ELISKASES [B99]

Mar del Plata, 1960

1.e4 c5; 2.Nf3 d6; 3.d4 cxd4; 4.Nxd4 Nf6; 5.Nc3 a6; 6.Bg5 e6; 7.f4 Be7; 8.Qf3 Qc7.

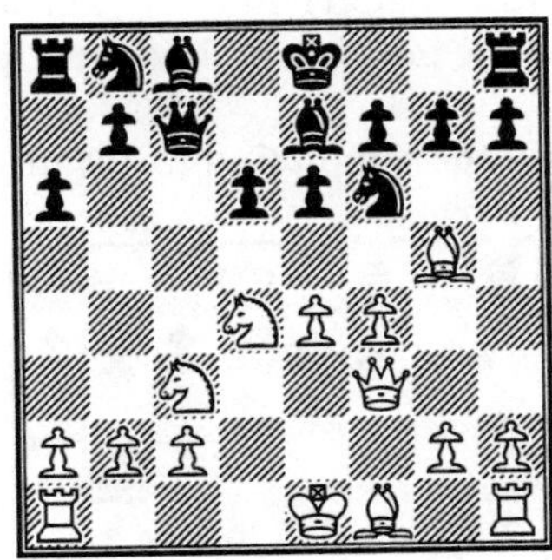

9.0–0–0 Nbd7; 10.g4. 10.Bd3 is equally popular: 10...h6; 11.Qh3 Nb6; 12.f5 e5; 13.Nde2 Bd7; 14.Kb1 Bc6; 15.Be3 d5; 16.Bxb6 Qxb6; 17.exd5 Ba3; 18.b3 Bxd5; 19.Nxd5 Nxd5; 20.Bc4 Nf6; 21.Nc3 0–0 led to an eventual draw in Nunn-Browne, Tilburg 1982. 10.Qg3 h6; 11.Bh4 g5!? is an interesting line. 12.fxg5 Rg8; 13.Nf3 Nh5; 14.Qe1 hxg5; 15.Bf2 b5; 16.a3 Bb7 gives Black good counterplay, Timman-Van Wely, Wijk aan Zee 1996.

10...b5; 11.Bxf6 Nxf6. Recently the capture with the pawn has been revived, but it is likely to be a temporary phenomenon. 11...gxf6; 12.f5 Ne5; 13.Qh3 0–0; 14.Qh6 (14.Nce2 Kh8; 15.Nf4 Rg8; 16.Rg1 is Gligoric-Fischer, Candidates Tournament 1959, where Fischer claims that 16...Qb7! provides the best defense.) 14...Kh8; 15.Rd3! gives White a very strong attack, for example 15...Nxd3+; 16.Bxd3 e5; 17.Nd5 Qb7; 18.Nc6!! Qxc6; 19.Nxe7 and Black cannot defend against the threats at f6 and f8, according to analysis by Popescu.

12.g5 Nd7; 13.a3. Later 13.f5!? would become the primary choice. This remains a viable alternative, however, and remains a major alternative. 13.f5

A) 13...Nc5; 14.f6 gxf6; 15.gxf6 Bf8; 16.Bh3 (16.Rg1 is the legacy of the late Hungarian theoretician Perenyi, and it is now the main line. The secrets of this line have been studied by professional and amateur theoreticians alike, and Daniel Olim of Las Vegas, an amateur player, has fed many ideas into the mainstream through his work with several top grandmasters.

The latest word from the tournament scene is 16...Bd7; 17.Rg7 b4; 18.Nd5! exd5; 19.exd5 0–0–0; 20.Rxf7 Bh6+ 21.Kb1 Rdf8 and now the new move is 22.Rxf8+ Rxf8; 23.Ne6! Nxe6; 24.dxe6 Bxe6; 25.Bh3 as in Shmuter-Kaspi, Tel Aviv 1996, where Black was unable to withstand the attack, despite the extra piece. The game concluded 25...Qc4 There is nothing better than giving up the piece, as analysis by Shmuter demonstrated. 26.b3 Qc5; 27.Bxe6+ Kc7; 28.Bd5! Kb6; 29.Qf5 Be3)

16...b4; 17.Nd5 exd5; 18.exd5 Bxh3; 19.Rhe1+ Kd8; 20.Nc6+ Kc8; 21.Qxh3+ Kb7; 22.Nxb4 and the attack ran out of steam, leaving Black with few problems to solve: 22...Qd7; 23.Qh5 Rg8; 24.Nc6 a5; 25.Qxh7 Rg6; 26.Kb1 Rh6; 27.Qg8 Rxf6; 28.Qg2 Kb6; 29.Rd4 Qf5; 30.b4 axb4; 31.Rxb4+ Kc7 and White resigned in Ciocaltea-Fischer, Netanya 1968.

B) 13...Bxg5+; 14.Kb1 is not as common now.

B1) 14...Ne5!; 15.Qh5 Qd8 (15...Qe7; 16.Nxe6 Bxe6; 17.fxe6 g6; 18.exf7+ Kxf7; 19.Nd5 is similar, and recently White has been doing well.) 16.Nxe6 is an interesting sacrifice. 16...Bxe6; 17.fxe6 g6!; 18.exf7+ Kxf7; 19.Qe2 Kg7! Black must play precisely, or the h-pawn will fly up the board and open up the position. 20.Bh3 Re8; 21.Rhf1 Ra7; 22.Qf2 Rf7; 23.Qd4 Bf6; 24.Nd5 was played in Thorhallsson-Browne, Reykjavik 1988 and the position looks a little better for White, though it is still quite messy.

B2) Black must avoid the temptation to advance the b-pawn: 14...b4?

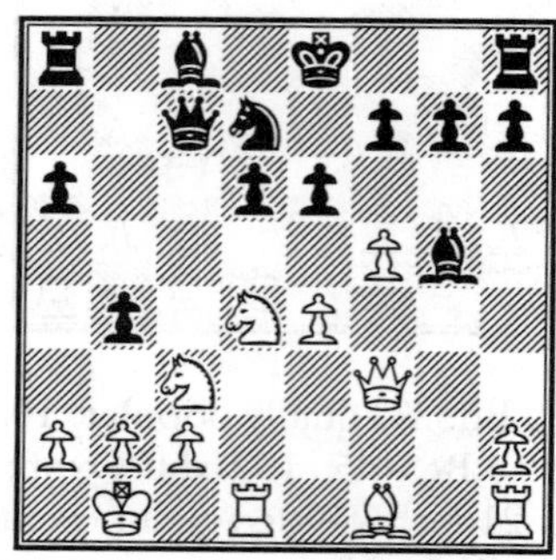

White now wins with a fine combination ending in a smothered mate! 15.fxe6 bxc3; 16.Qxf7+ Kd8; 17.e7+ Bxe7; 18.Ne6#. White won. Schiller-Klemm, Manhattan Chess Club Championship 1971

13...Bb7? An obvious move, but not best. 13...Rb8 is the main line. Black keeps the b-file open for operations. 14.h4 b4; 15.axb4 Rxb4; 16.Bh3 0–0 is one main line. Bobby Fischer demonstrated that 17.Nf5 Nc5!; 18.Nxe7 Qxe7 is fine for Black, in a game against Minic from Zagreb 1970. But White can get the advantage by sacrificial means. 17.Nxe6 fxe6; 18.Bxe6+ Kh8; 19.Nd5 and Black is in serious trouble. **14.Rg1.**

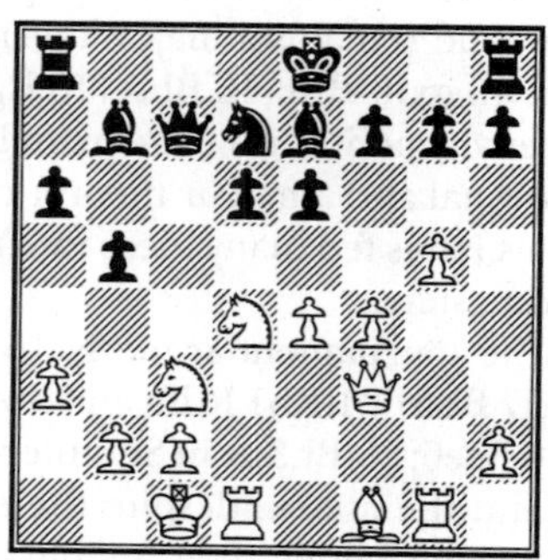

14.Bh3 is more promising. Tal used it successfully against Gligoric at Moscow 1963: 14...0–0–0; 15.Bxe6! fxe6; 16.Nxe6 Qc4; 17.Nd5 Bxd5; 18.exd5 Kb7; 19.b3 Qc8; 20.Rd3 Nb6; 21.Rc3 Qd7; 22.Rc7+ Qxc7; 23.Nxc7 Kxc7; 24.Qc3+ gave him a significant advantage. **14...g6.** A good alternative is 14...d5! 15.exd5 Nb6 as played by Fischer against O'Kelly at the 1960 Olympiad in Leipzig.

15.Bh3 0-0-0? This is a serious error. 15...Nc5! 16.Qe3 Qb6 is assessed as equal by John Nunn, one of the world's leading theoreticians. **16.Bxe6!** This small sacrifice leads to an overwhelming position. **16...fxe6; 17.Nxe6 Qb6; 18.Nxd8 Rxd8; 19.Qh3.**

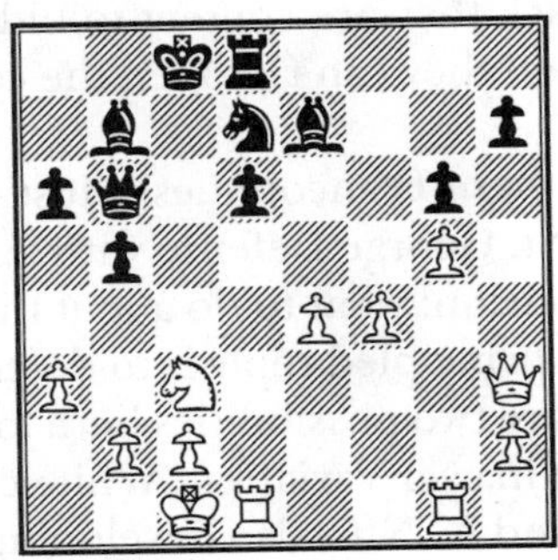

Black has two bishops for a rook, but White has two extra pawns, a pin on the knight at d7 and an attack at h7. Black must try to get an attack going very quickly. **19...b4; 20.axb4 d5; 21.Nxd5 Bxd5; 22.exd5 Bxb4.** The White king still has two healthy defenders, and three extra pawns are just too much of an advantage. **23.Rg3 Re8; 24.d6!** This keeps the Black pieces from getting coordinated. **24...Qc6; 25.Qxh7 Qe4; 26.Kb1 Rf8; 27.Rgd3!** White takes control of d4. **27...Rxf4.** 27...Bc5; 28.Rc3 Qxf4 would have led to immediate disaster after 29.Rxc5+! Nxc5; 30.Qc7# **28.Rd4 Qe5; 29.Rxf4 Qxf4; 30.Qxg6.** As pieces leave the board, White's advantage grows and the defense becomes more an exercise in futility. **30...Qe5; 31.Qg8+ Kb7; 32.Qd8 Qb5; 33.Qc7+ Ka8; 34.g6 Ba3; 35.Qc3 Bc5; 36.g7. White won.**

FRENCH DEFENSE

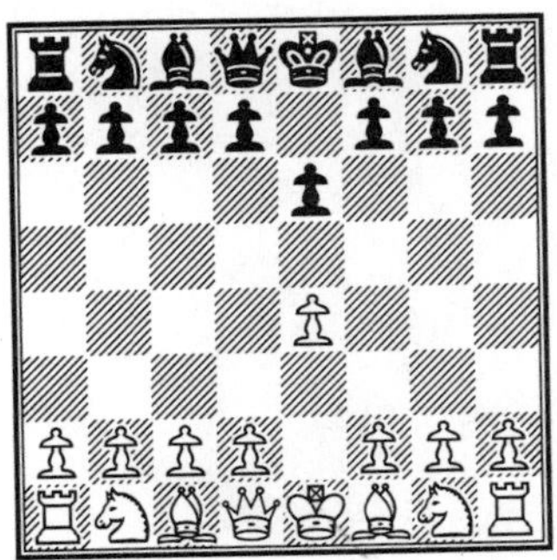

1.e4 e6

The **French Defense** is an opening which most players either love or hate. With the very first move Black tells the bishop at c8 that it is going to be a long time before that piece will play an active role in the game, at least on the kingside. White will be granted an advantage in the center and an advantage in space. Why then, should anyone want to play it as Black? In particular, why should such superstars as Mikhail Botvinnik, Tigran Petrosian, Viktor Korchnoi, Nigel Short and many other top players choose to defend it? These are patient players. They don't feel the need to attack from the very start of the game. As Black they are content to bide their time and wait for White to overextend. Then they can rip open the center and close in for the kill.

Dangerous animals, these Francophiles! Most games continue 2.d4 d5 (Black can slide into the St. George Defense with 2...a6 instead) when White is faced with a serious decision: what to do about the vulnerable pawn at e4?

In general, the most principled reply is to defend the pawn while developing a piece, and there are two possibilities here for the knight at b1. In the Classical Variation and Winawer Variation, White chooses 3.Nc3. The Classical approach is to respond 3...Nf6, also developing a knight, but the dominant line has been Winawer's 3...Bb4, which pins the knight at c3 and threatens to capture it. In the Tarrasch Variation White plays 3.Nd2, which temporarily blocks the bishop at c1 but which does not allow the pin.

There are other options for White, but they are of lesser importance. We will begin by examining these minor lines and work our way toward the glorious complexities of the main line.

ADVANCE VARIATION

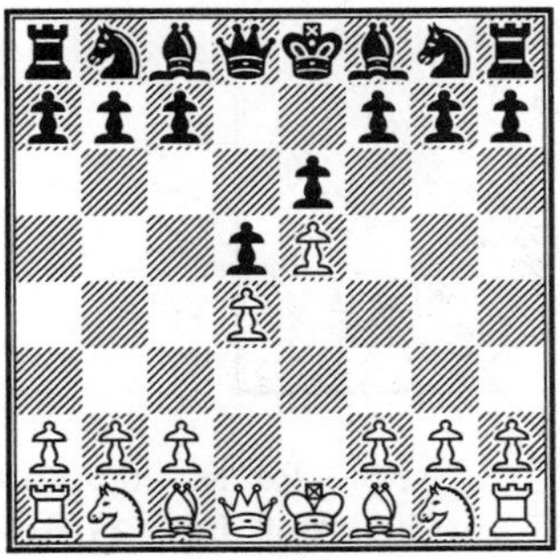

1.e4	e6
2.d4	d5
3.e5	

When White advances the pawn to the fifth rank, the tension in the center disappears, but White has secured an advantage in space. The bishop at c8 can suffer a very cramped and dull life if Black is not careful, and this led to many victories early in the history of the opening. This approach was widely adopted in the last century, but eventually it seemed to have exhausted itself. Steinitz's atempt to play an early e5 had worn out its welcome, and the advance of the e-pawn was now postponed until after 3.Nc3.

The great Aron Nimzowitsch revived the plan and turned it into an attacking weapon. Sir Stuart Milner-Barry, one of the best British players of his time, added a gambit continuation for White which remains in use today, though the chances are judged to be approximately level.

(101) MILNER-BARRY - BARDEN [C02]
British Championship, 1960

1.e4 c5; 2.c3 e6; 3.d4 d5; 4.e5 Qb6. 4...Nc6; 5.Nf3 Bd7; 6.Be2 (6.Bd3 see below.) 6...f6 is a reasonable alternative for Black. The normal move order is 1.e4 e6; 2.d4 d5; 3.e5 c5; 4.c3 and now either 4...Nc6 or 4...Qb6. Both moves are part of Black's strategy. **5.Bd3 Bd7.** 5...Nc6; 6.Nf3 cxd4; 7.cxd4 Bd7; 8.0–0 Nxd4 is the Milner-Barry Accepted. The most important continuation now is 9.Nxd4 Qxd4; 10.Nc3 Qxe5; 11.Re1 Qb8; 12.Nxd5 Bd6; 13.Qg4 Kf8 which has been seen in many games, including Smith-Watson, Los Angeles 1993.

6.dxc5. 6.Nf3 Nc6. **6...Bxc5; 7.Qe2 a5; 8.Nf3 Ne7; 9.Nbd2 Ng6.** This just creates a target on the kingside. Black should have advanced the a-pawn instead, taking b3 away from White. **10.Nb3 Be7; 11.h4 f6; 12.h5 Nxe5; 13.Nxe5 fxe5; 14.h6 g6;**

15.Qxe5 Rg8; 16.Be3 Qd6.

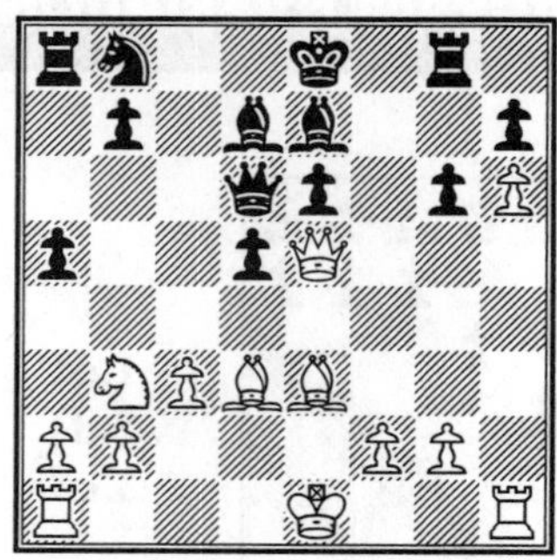

17.Bxg6+ Rxg6. 17...hxg6; 18.h7 Rf8; 19.h8Q Rxh8; 20.Rxh8+ Kf7; 21.Rh7+ and White wins. **18.Qh8+ Bf8; 19.Qxh7 e5; 20.0–0–0 Bc6; 21.Bc5 Rxh6; 22.Qg8 Rg6; 23.Qh8 Qf6; 24.Bxf8 Qxf8?** This shortens the game considerably. Black should have exchanged queens, though the position would still have been very bad. **25.Qxe5+ Kd8; 26.Rh8 Rg8; 27.Nc5 Bd7; 28.Nxd7 Nxd7; 29.Qxd5 Kc7; 30.Qxd7+ Kb6; 31.Qd4+ Ka6; 32.Qd6+ Qxd6; 33.Rxd6+ b6; 34.Rxg8 Rxg8; 35.g3 Rh8; 36.Kc2. White won.**

TARRASCH VARIATION

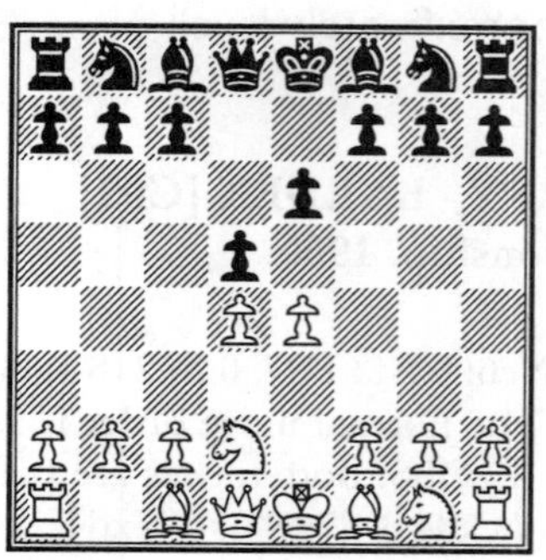

1.e4	**e6**
2.d4	**d5**
3.Nd2	

This modest deployment of the knight at d2 indicates that White is not out for a quick kill. In the **Tarrasch Variation**, White wants to determine the positional contour of the struggle first. Black is deprived of the Winawer strategy with ...Bb4, which can be met by the advance of a pawn to c3, but must still contend with a variety of other strategies. Black can capture at e4, returning the game to the Rubinstein Variation.

Another option is to develop the knight at f6, attacking the pawn at e4 and luring it forward. More in the true Tarrasch spirit are the systems with

...c5, where one side or the other winds up with an isolated d-pawn. Tarrasch loved to have isolated d-pawns, and was not pleased to discover that in his pet variation, it is sometimes Black who gets the isolated pawn!

(102) TARRASCH - ECKART [C05]

Nurenberg, 1889

1.e4 e6; 2.d4 d5; 3.Nd2 Nf6; 4.e5 Nfd7; 5.Bd3.

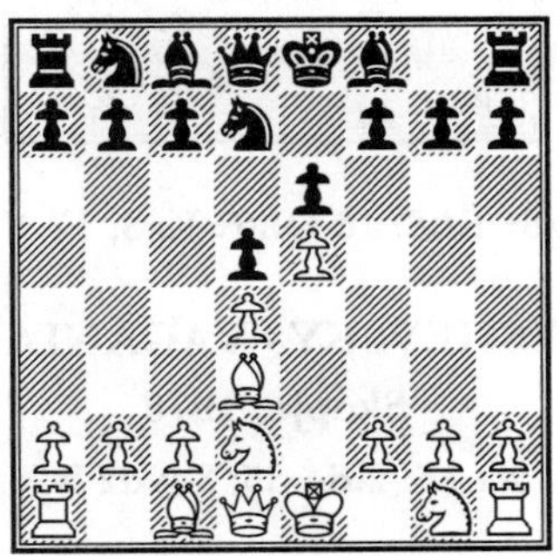

This is the way that Tarrasch wanted to handle the White side of his variation, known as the Closed Variation. The White forces are trained on the kingside, where the Black king must inevitably seek shelter. **5...c5; 6.c3 Nc6; 7.Ne2.** 7.Ngf3 is also common. **7...Qb6.** Black should exchange in the center instead and only then play ...Qb6.**8.Nf3 Be7.** 8...cxd4 9.cxd4.

9...f6!; 10.exf6 Nxf6; 11.0–0 Bd6 gives Black a reasonable game. White has tried many plans, but none seem to have any strong effect. Here is just one sample line: 12.Bf4!? This sacrifices the b-pawn in return for play on the dark squares. 12...Bxf4; 13.Nxf4 Qxb2; 14.Ng5 Ke7 and White has to justify the material investment.

10.Kf1 Be7. In this sharp line of the French, opening lines with 10...f6 is a wiser move. 11.a3 Nf8; 12.b4 Bd7; 13.Be3 Nd8. Black does have a plan: to play Bb5 and exchange the light-squared bishops. But this is easily parried, and turns out to be just a waste of time. 14.Nc3 a5. Black challenges White's queenside formation and forces White to determine his short-term plans. Alekhine decides to plant a pawn at b5. 15.Na4 Qa7; 16.b5 Alekhine-Capablanca, Holland (AVRO) 1938. Now the scope of the Bd7 is severely limited, and Black's plan, beginning with 13...Nd8, is exposed as faulty.

9.0–0 0–0. Black should just play ...f6 here. **10.Nf4 Nd8.** This defends f7 and e6, but ruins the communication between the kingside and the queenside. Black now has no way to use the minor pieces to defend the king, and White builds an attack by straight forward moves. **11.Qc2! f5.** 11...g6; 12.h4 c4; 13.Bxg6 hxg6; 14.h5 g5; 15.Ng6! fxg6; 16.Qxg6+ Kh8; 17.Bxg5 Bxg5; 18.Nxg5 Rf7; 19.Nxf7+ Nxf7; 20.Qxf7 Qxb2; 21.h6 and Black gets mated. **12.exf6 Nxf6; 13.Ng5.** White's pieces are swarming on the kingside, and Black just can't get enough defensive pieces to rescue the king. **13...g6.**

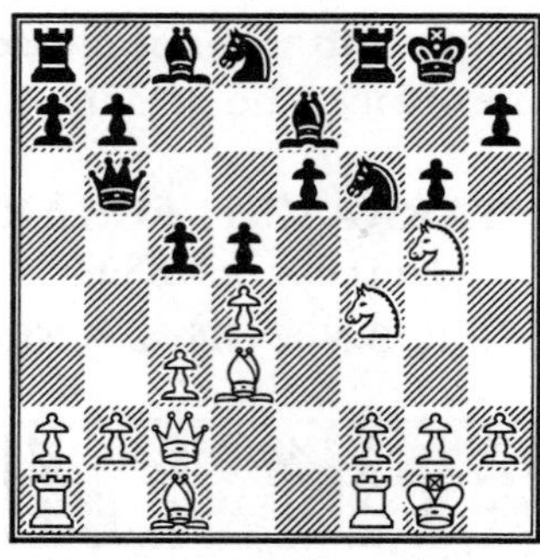

14.Bxg6! hxg6; 15.Qxg6+ Kh8; 16.Qh6+ Kg8; 17.Ng6. White won.

(103) RESHEVSKY - VAGANIAN [C05]

Skopje, 1976

1.e4 e6; 2.d4 d5; 3.Nd2 Nf6.

With this move Black invites the White pawn forward after which the knight will be forced to retreat. The position will remain closed for some time, but Black will always suffer from a lack of space. On the other hand, the White pawn chain can be undermined by such moves as ...c5 and ...f6. The plan is similar to the Classical French, except that the White knight at d2 is not as vulnerable as when it stands on c3. At the same time, however, the bishop at c1 has no clear path into the game. For this reason the knight at d2 is often maneuvered to f3. **4.e5 Nfd7; 5.f4.** In this system White gains a lot of space, but his formation can be undermined by counterattacks involving c7-c5 and f7-f6. **5...c5; 6.c3 Nc6; 7.Ndf3 Qa5?!**

This system is no longer considered playable, as it can be met by the strong reply 8.dxc5! Qxc5; 9.Bd3 and then White will occupy d4 with a knight, and there will be no source of counterplay for Black. 7...Qb6 has become the main line recently. 8.h4 (8.g3 Be7; 9.Bh3 cxd4; 10.cxd4 f6 leads to massive complications, for example as in Huebner-Mohr, Bundesliga 1988. Black is doing well in these lines at the moment.) 8...cxd4; 9.cxd4 Bb4+; 10.Kf2 f6; 11.Be3 Be7 is fully playable for Black, Belyavsky-Kindermann, Munich 1991.

8.Kf2? This radical method of breaking the pin is not needed. **8...Be7.** Black can also play expansively with b7-b5, but the text is safe and good. **9.Bd3.** Speelman suggests that 9.g3 is more logical, making room for the king. **9...Qb6!** Black returns to the main theme of the opening - pressure at d4 combined with f7-f6, which he will play on the next move.

10.Ne2 f6! 11.exf6. When Black sees a move like that, he can sit back and plan his victory speech. Now the pressure at d4 will become unbearable, and Vaganian gives a textbook lesson on how to completely fulfill the strategic goal. 11.Rf1 cxd4; 12.cxd4 fxe5; 13.fxe5 Ndxe5; 14.Nxe5? Nxe5; 11.Kg3 is a wild alternative, and it may be the best White can do in the position. Vaganian defeated Adorjan when the latter tried the plan against him in 1974, but the game was very complicated. Still, it hardly seems safe for White!

11...Bxf6! When one understands the strategic goal, the choice of recapture is simple. **12.Kg3.** Perhaps Reshevsky had prepared this as an improvement on the aforementioned Adorjan game, which saw Black pry open the kingside with g7-g5. But with the f-pawn gone, this is no longer a reasonable plan. So all eyes on d4! **12...cxd4; 13.cxd4 0–0; 14.Re1?**

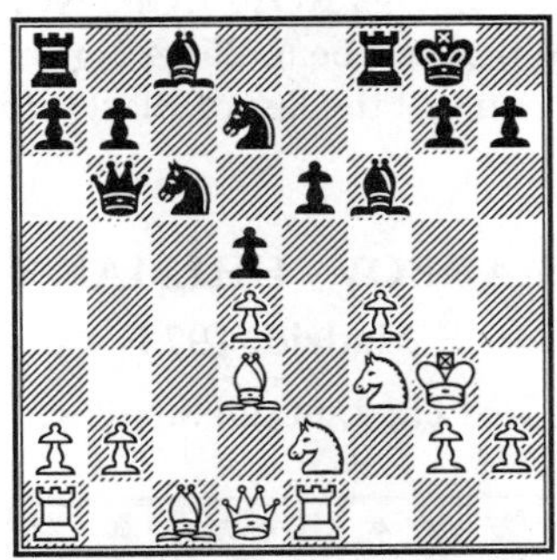

White should have attended to his king safety by advancing the h-pawn. Now Black sees that with the d-pawn gone, the king cannot retreat. 14.h4 Nxd4? 15.Nexd4 Bxd4; 16.Nxd4 Qxd4?? 17.Bxh7+ **14...e5!!; 15.fxe5 Ndxe5; 16.dxe5.**

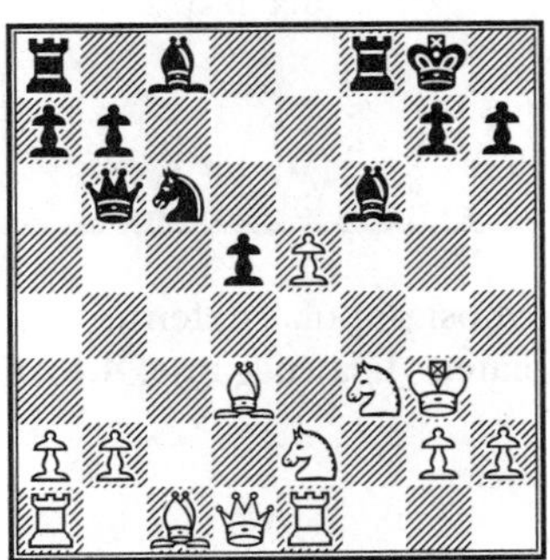

Imagine, if you will, both the Nf3 and Bf6 removed from the board. Then Qf2 is mate. Consider, as well, that the Nf3 is the only defender the king has. **16...Bh4+!!; 17.Kxh4.** 17.Nxh4 Qf2# **17...Rxf3!!; 18.Rf1.** 18.gxf3? Qf2+; 19.Kg5 h6+; 20.Kg6 Nxe5+; 21.Kh5 Qxh2# is a pretty mate. Notice how the Bc8 plays an important role without ever leaving home! **18...Qb4+; 19.Bf4 Qe7+; 20.Bg5 Qe6!**

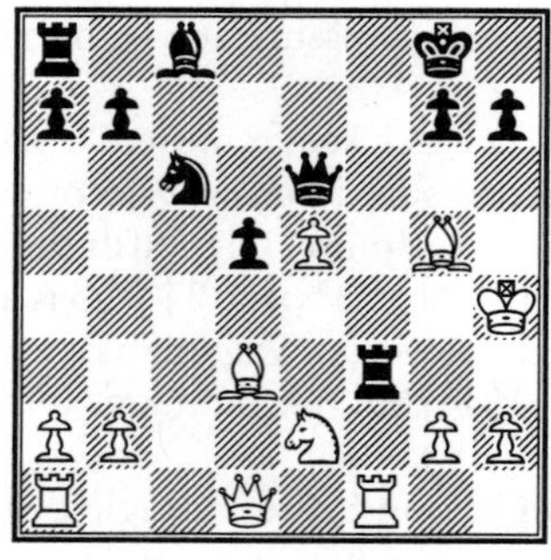

The attack has not led to mate, but since 21.h3? is met by 21...Qxh3+!; 22.gxh3 Rxh3 mate, White must return the piece, and then it is just mopping up time. **21.Bf5 Rxf5; 22.Nf4.** 22.Rxf5 Qxf5; 23.Qxd5+ Be6; 24.Qf3 Qxe5; 25.Bf4 g5+!; 26.Bxg5 Qxh2+ - Speelman. **22...Qxe5; 23.Qg4 Rf7; 24.Qh5 Ne7!** The addition of the knight to the attack is more than White can bear. **25.g4 Ng6+; 26.Kg3 Bd7; 27.Rae1 Qd6; 28.Bh6 Raf8.** And with the entry of the last of Black's forces, White resigned. **Black won.**

(104) KARPOV - UHLMANN [C09]

Madrid, 1973

1.e4 e6; 2.d4 d5; 3.Nd2 c5.

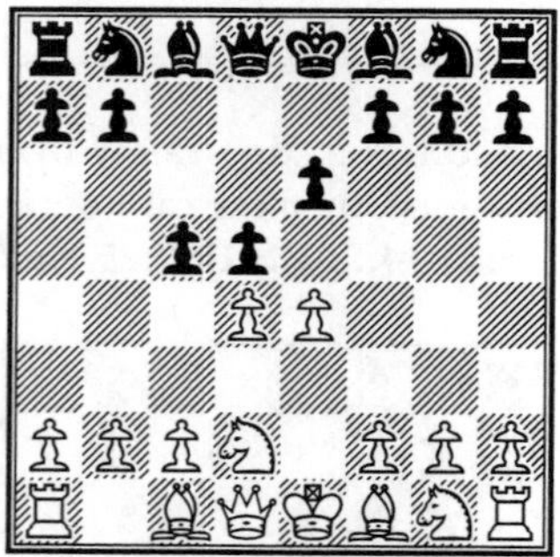

This remains one of the most popular defenses to the Tarrasch Variation of the French. Black invites an isolated d-pawn game. **4.exd5 exd5.** Black can also play 4...Qxd5.

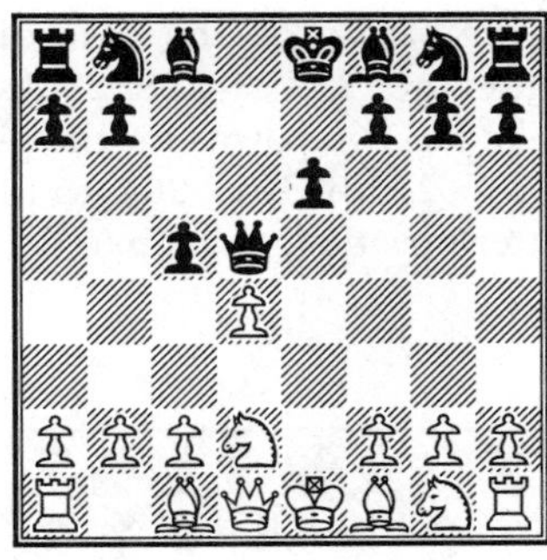

When Black recaptures with the queen, then the center is likely to be cleared of pawns quickly. White will enjoy a queenside pawn majority and Black is saddled with the usual bad bishop, but the slow nature of the struggle makes Black's defensive task manageable. 5.Ngf3 cxd4; 6.Bc4 Qd6. This is the correct post for the queen, though Dreyev has tried to resurrect the retreat to d8. 7.0–0 Nf6; 8.Nb3 Nc6; 9.Nbxd4 Nxd4; 10.Nxd4 (10.Qxd4 Qxd4; 11.Nxd4 should lead to a draw with correct play.)

10...a6. 10...Bd7 is a playable alternative. 11.c3 White has many choices here, including 11.Bb3, 11.b3 and 11.Re1. (11.Re1 Qc7; 12.Bb3 Bd6; 13.Nf5 Bxh2+; 14.Kh1 0–0; 15.Nxg7 Rd8; 16.Qf3 Kxg7; 17.Bh6+ Kg6; 18.c3 Nd5; 19.Rad1 f5; 20.Bc1 Bd6; 21.Bxd5 exd5; 22.Rxd5 and White is in a position to win, despite the missing bishop. 22...Bd7; 23.Qh3 Bf8; 24.Re3 Kg7; 25.Rg3+ Kh8; 26.Qh4 Be6; 27.Bf4 Be7; 28.Bxc7 and Black resigned in Adams-Dreyev, Wijk aan Zee 1996.)

11...Qc7; 12.Qe2 Bd6; 13.h3. White guards the g4-square and gets the h-pawn out of the line of attack of the Black battery on the b8-h2 diagonal. It is possible to sacrifice the pawn, but this does not bring White a superior position. For example (13.Bg5 Bxh2+; 14.Kh1 Bf4; 15.Bxf6 gxf6 and now if 16.Bxe6 fxe6; 17.Nxe6 Bxe6; 18.Qxe6+ Kf8; 19.Qxf6+ Kg8. White is fighting for a draw at best, Liang Jinrong-Brunner, Lucerne 1989.) 13...h6!? Normally Black castles here, but Spassky invigorates the variation with a new idea. (13...0–0. 14.Bb3 h6! is a new plan that turned out well for Black in Mohr-Belyavsky, Maribor 1996.) 14.Nf5 Bf8. Spassky's idea is to fianchetto the bishop at g7, not a usual strategy in the Tarrasch French. 15.a4 g6; 16.Nd4 Bg7.

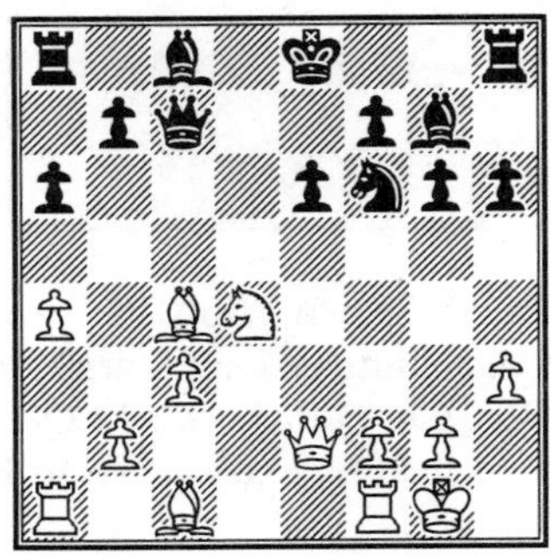

Since White is almost fully mobilized, and there is no really good square for the bishop at c1, the former Women's World Champion boldly sacrifices against her former World Champion opponent. 17.Bxe6!? fxe6; 18.Nxe6 Bxe6; 19.Qxe6+ Kf8; 20.b3! Black intends to use the bishop on the a3-f8 diagonal, which could prove devastating. 20...Qf7; 21.Qd6+ Kg8; 22.Re1 Re8; 23.Rxe8+ Nxe8; 24.Qb4. Things have calmed down a bit. White has two pawns for the piece but the Black monarch has plenty of defenders. 24...Nf6; 25.Bb2 Nd5; 26.Qc5 Kh7; 27.Re1 Rf8; 28.Re2 Qf5; 29.Rd2. There is nothing better now than going into the endgame. Xie Jun-Spassky, London 1996, Black won.

5.Ngf3 Nc6.

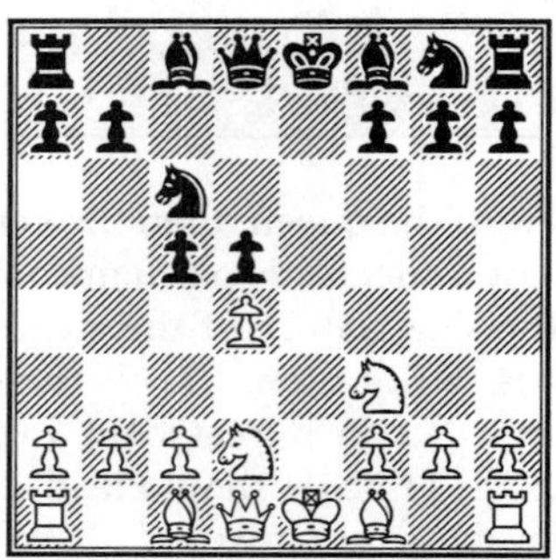

6.Bb5 Bd6; 7.dxc5 Bxc5. Tarrasch, who developed this approach for White, loved isolated pawns. He was disappointed to discover that Black would have that "luxury" in his own pet line. On the other hand, most strong players consider the isolated pawn a slight weakness unless accompanied by a strong intitiative or good piece play, so many players have favored the White side. 7...Qe7+; 8.Qe2 Bxc5; 9.Nb3 Bb6; 10.Ne5 Kf8; 11.Bf4 Qf6; 12.Bg3 h5; 13.h4 Nge7; 14.0-0-0 Nxe5; 15.Bxe5 Qxf2; 16.Bxg7+ Kxg7; 17.Qxe7 Bf5; 18.Qe5+ left the Black kingside too vulnerable in Karpov-Korchnoi, Candidates Match 1971. **8.0-0 Nge7; 9.Nb3 Bd6.**

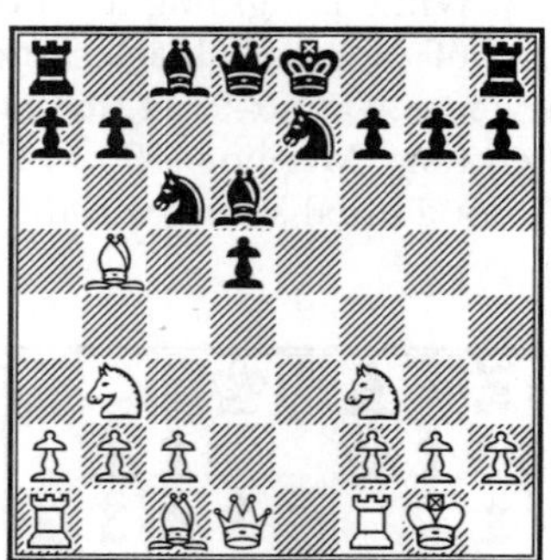

In positions with an isolated d-pawn White has two main objectives: the blockade of the isolated pawn and the elimination of Black's dark-squared bishop. 9...Bb6; 10.Re1 0-0; 11.Bg5 h6; 12.Bh4 g5; 13.Bg3 Nf5; 14.Qd2 Nxg3; 15.hxg3 Qf6; 16.c3 Bf5; 17.Qxd5 and White had a healthy extra pawn in Karpov-Vaganian, Budapest 1973.

10.Bg5! This move directly implements White's plan by transferring the bishop to a post from which it can reach the h2-g8 diagonal (via h4 to g3).

10.h3 0-0; 11.c3 a6; 12.Bd3 Bc7; 13.Bc2 Nf5; 14.Qd3 Qd6; 15.g4 g6; 16.gxf5

Bxf5; 17.Qd2 Bxh3; 18.Qh6 Qd7; 19.Qh4 Bxf1; 20.Kxf1 Ne5; 21.Nfd4 Rfe8; 22.Bf4 Nc4; 23.Nc5 Qc8; 24.Nd3 Bxf4; 25.Nxf4 Nxb2; 26.Nh5 Qc4+; 27.Kg2 Re6; 28.Nf6+ Rxf6; 29.Qxf6 Qxc3; 30.Rh1 Rf8; 31.Rh3 Qd2; 32.Nf5. White won. Tal-Short, Blitz Brussels 1987. Or 10.Bxc6+ bxc6; 11.Qd4 0–0; 12.Bf4 Nf5; 13.Qa4 Qb6; 14.Bxd6 Nxd6; 15.Ne5 c5; 16.Qc6 Ba6; 17.Rfd1 c4; 18.Nc5 Rfc8; 19.Qxb6 axb6; 20.Ncd7 f6; 21.Rxd5 Ne4; 22.Nxb6 fxe5; 23.Nxa8 c3; 24.b4 Rxa8; 25.Rxe5 Bb7; 26.a4 Kf7; 27.f3 Nd2; 28.Rc5. White won. Tal-Zaitshik, Tbilisi Soviet Union 1988

10...0–0; 11.Bh4 Bg4. 11...Qc7; 12.Bg3 Bxg3; 13.hxg3 Bg4; 14.Re1 Rad8; 15.c3 Qb6; 16.Bd3 Ng6; 17.Qc2 Bxf3; 18.gxf3 with Black saddled by a weak d-pawn, Karpov-Kuzmin, Leningrad Interzonal 1973. **12.Be2 Bh5?!** The superior 12...Re8! had already been introduced by Uhlmann, but he was probably afraid of a prepared innovation. **13.Re1 Qb6; 14.Nfd4!**

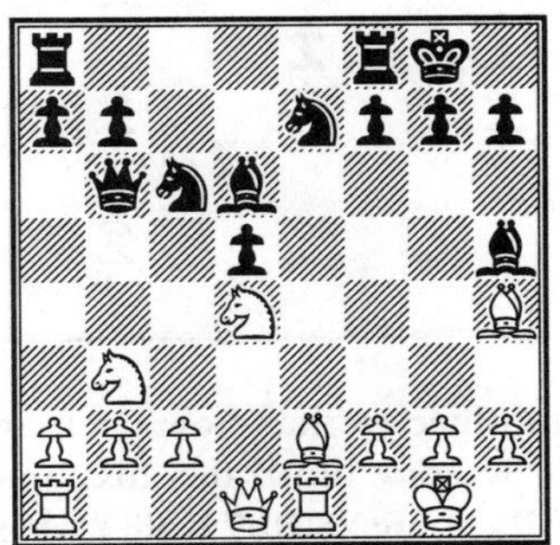

Black must now do something about the bishop at h5. **14...Bg6.** If Black had exchanged bishops the isolated pawn would have less protection. Uhlmann decides that the bishop may be of use at e4, since any eventual f2-f3 will weaken the a7-g1 diagonal. **15.c3 Rfe8; 16.Bf1!** Karpov realizes that this is the best square for the bishop, since on f3 it could be attacked by Nc6-e5. As we will see, the control of the e-file plays an important role in the remainder of the game. **16...Be4; 17.Bg3!** Now that all of White's pieces have been properly positioned, the exchange of bishops is appropriate. **17...Bxg3; 18.hxg3.**

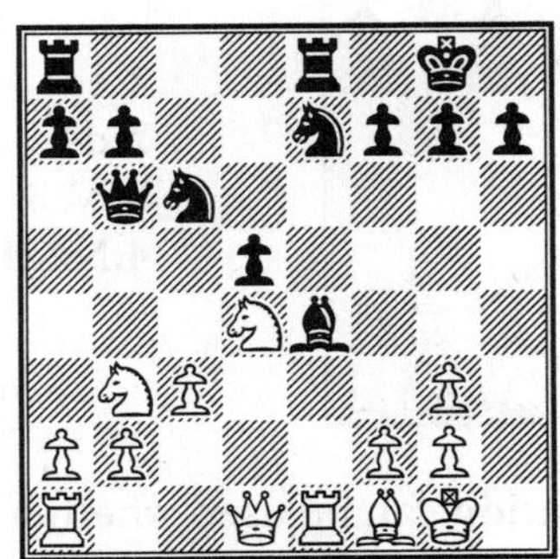

The cluster of pawns in front of the king creates an insurpassable protective barrier. **18...a5!?** The weakening of b5 is probably more significant than Black's mild initiative, but perhaps the move was played without taking into consideration White's potential sacrifice of the b-pawn. **19.a4 Nxd4; 20.Nxd4!** Karpov correctly maintains the blockade with the piece, since if 20...Qxb2 then 21.Nb5! threatens both 22.Nc7 and 22.Re2.

20...Nc6; 21.Bb5! The pin encourages Black's rook to leave the e-file. Probably 21...Bg6 would have been best here. **21...Red8?! 22.g4!** A very clever move, the point of which is to create threats of trapping the enemy bishop should it retreat to g6 (with f2-f4-f5). **22...Nxd4.** Now White gets a superior endgame. **23.Qxd4 Qxd4; 24.cxd4 Rac8.** 24...Kf8 Would not have prevented infiltration by the White rooks: 25.Re2 Rac8; 26.f3 Bg6; 27.Rae1 Rc7??; 28.Re8+ Rxe8; 29.Rxe8#. **25.f3 Bg6.**

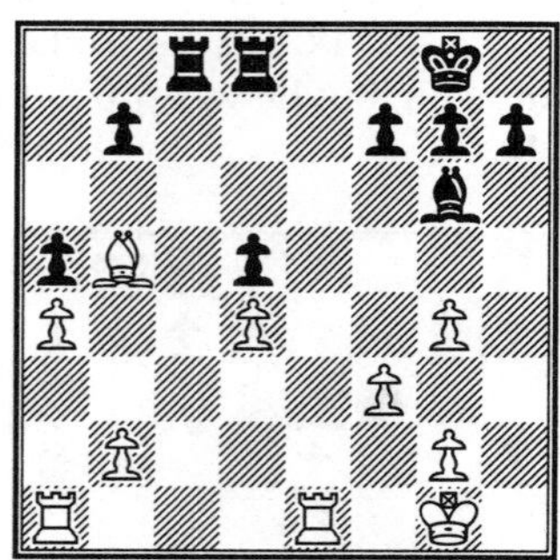

26.Re7. The immediate objective has now been achieved, and after the doubling of rooks on the e-file Karpov illustrates his famous endgame technique to secure the point. **26...b6; 27.Rae1 h6; 28.Rb7 Rd6; 29.Ree7 h5; 30.gxh5 Bxh5; 31.g4 Bg6; 32.f4 Rc1+; 33.Kf2 Rc2+; 34.Ke3 Be4; 35.Rxf7 Rg6; 36.g5 Kh7; 37.Rfe7 Rxb2; 38.Be8!; Rb3+ 39.Ke2 Rb2+; 40.Ke1 Rd6; 41.Rxg7+ Kh8; 42.Rge7. White won.**

RUBINSTEIN VARIATION

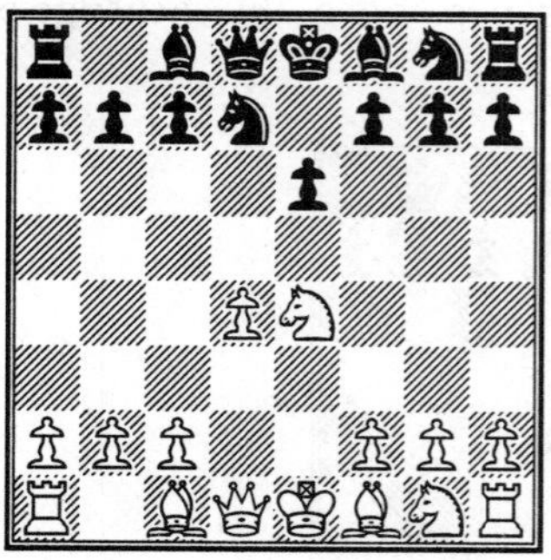

1.e4 e6
2.d4 d5
3.Nc3 dxe4
4.Nxe4 Nd7

The **Rubinstein Variation** can be used whether White chooses 3.Nc3 or 3.Nd2. Black concedes the center and will have to deal with the problem of the bishop at c8, but if these can be overcome then Black's life is easy indeed. On the other hand, if White can develop a serious initiative, Black's position can quickly go down in flames. The opening appeals to players with strong defensive skills, but none of the top stars use it.

(105) MATULOVIC - CANAL [C10]

Reggio Emilia, 1968

1.e4 e6; 2.d4 d5; 3.Nc3 dxe4; 4.Nxe4 Nd7.

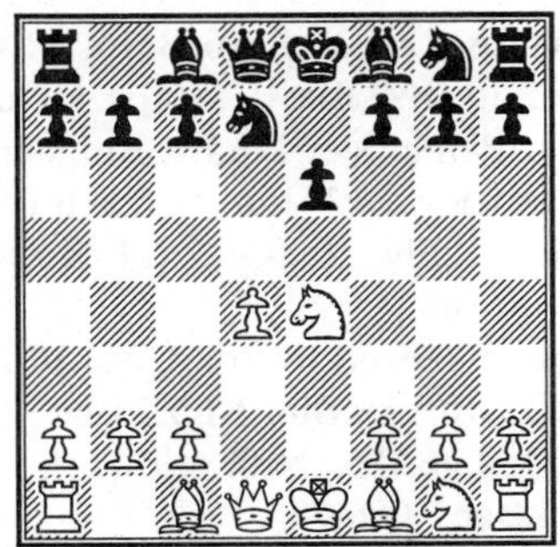

This is a popular continuation for Black, who prepares to develop the other knight at f6. Rubinstein used the defense effectively, but now it is appeals only to people who love defending positions that are slightly worse. 4...Bd7; 5.Nf3 Bc6 has been a popular plan for Black, who takes measures early in the game to eliminate his problematic bishop. 6.Bd3 Bxe4 (6...Nd7; 7.Ne5 gives White the advantage, according to Suetin, though play might develop on lines similar to that of the game. 7...Bxe4; 8.Bxe4 c6; 9.0–0 Ngf6; 10.Bd3 Bd6; 11.Qe2 with a Caro-Kannish position.)

7.Bxe4 c6. Although Black has made a lot of moves with his now-departed bishop, and now has no pieces developed, his structure is quite sound. White must now secure his spatial advantage. 8.0–0 Nf6; 9.Bd3 Nbd7; 10.c4 Bd6; 11.b3!? Spassky is fond of fianchettoing his dark-squared bishop. Here it is a very logical plan, and the power of the bishop will be seen in the concluding phase of the game. 11...0–0; 12.Bb2 Qc7; 13.Qc2 Rfe8; 14.Rfe1 Bf8; 15.Rad1. This position was reached in Spassky-O'Kelly, San Juan 1969. Both sides have completed their development and it is time to develop a plan. Black's problem is that if he opens up the position, then the bishop pair will be a significant factor. White stands better.

5.Nf3 Ngf6; 6.Nxf6+ Nxf6; 7.Bg5 Be7; 8.Bd3 0–0. 8...b6 is considered best by Harding, based on some games from the early part of the century. But in those games White failed to complete his development before launching an attack, tempted by the weak light squares on the queenside. 9.Qe2! Bb7; 10.0–0–0 Qd5; 11.Kb1 with an interesting and unbalanced position. **9.Qe2.**

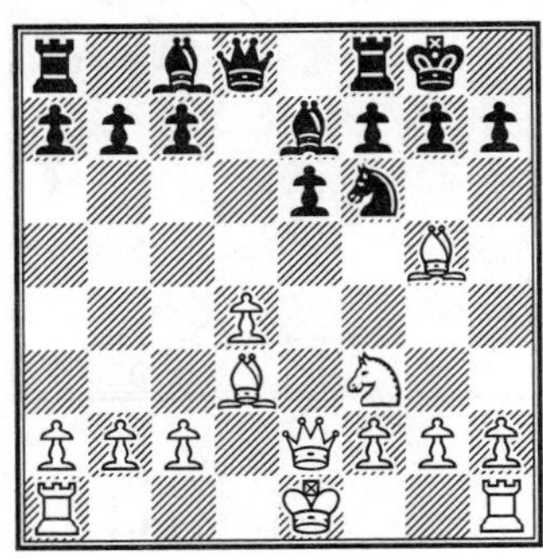

9...Qd5; 9...Nd5; 10.h4 h6; 11.Bxe7 (11.Bd2 is even stronger, according to Littlewood.) 11...Qxe7; 12.0-0-0 c5; 13.g4 cxd4 was played in Tatai-Andersson, Las Palmas 1972. Here Littlewood gives a very strong line for White. 14.g5!? Nf4; 15.Qe4 Nxd3+; 16.Rxd3 h5 and it almost looks like Black is out of the woods - but not quite! 17.g6! f6; 18.Nxd4 e5; 19.Nf5 and Black is in serious trouble on the kingside.

9...b6? is a mistake that loses to 10.Bxf6 Bxf6; 11.Qe4. 9...Rb8; 10.0-0-0 b6; 11.Rhe1 Bb7; 12.Bxf6 Bxf6; 13.Be4 Bxe4; 14.Qxe4 Qd5; 15.Qxd5 exd5; 16.Ne5! gave White the advantage in Panataleev-Popov, Bulgaria 1972. 16...Bxe5; 17.Rxe5 Rfd8; 18.Re7 with a clear advantage for White; 9...c5! is recommended by Littlewood. 10.0-0-0 is probably the best reply. 10...Qd5; 11.c4 Qd6; 12.Kb1 and White has more space and an active position.

10.0-0. 10.Bc4 would be answered by 10...Qe4! **10...h6; 11.c4!** This is effective now that Qa5+ is not on. **11...Qd6; 12.Bh4 Nh5?!** Black should have attended to his backward development. **13.Qe4 g6.** 13...Nf6? allows the defender of h7 to be blown off the board by 14.Bxf6. **14.Bxe7 Qxe7.**

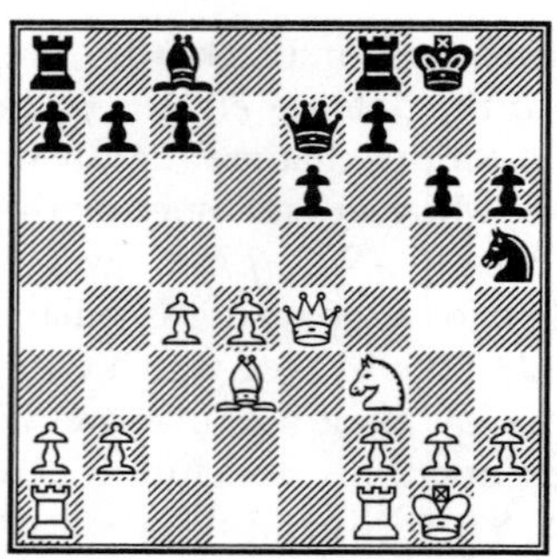

15.Ne5! Nf6. 15...Rd8; 16.Rae1 c5; 17.Nxg6! fxg6; 18.Qxg6+ Ng7; 19.d5 Qf7; 20.Qh7+ Kf8; 21.Bg6 Qf6; 22.dxe6 Nxe6; 23.Re3 Qg7; 24.Rf3+ Ke7; 25.Rf7+ and White wins. **16.Qe3 Kg7; 17.f4 Rd8; 18.Rad1!** Strong players generally try to activate all of their pieces before moving in for the kill. **18...Bd7; 19.g4 Be8; 20.f5! exf5; 21.gxf5 g5; 22.h4!** White is simply peeling away the defensive layers. **22...gxh4.** 22...g4; 23.Qg3 h5; 24.Rfe1 Qf8; 25.Qf4 Nh7; 26.f6+! Kg8 (26...Nxf6; 27.Qg5+) 27.Rd2 Kh8; 28.Rg2 Qg8; 29.Nxg4 hxg4; 30.Rxg4 Qf8; 31.Rg7 Nxf6; 32.Qh6+ and it is all over.

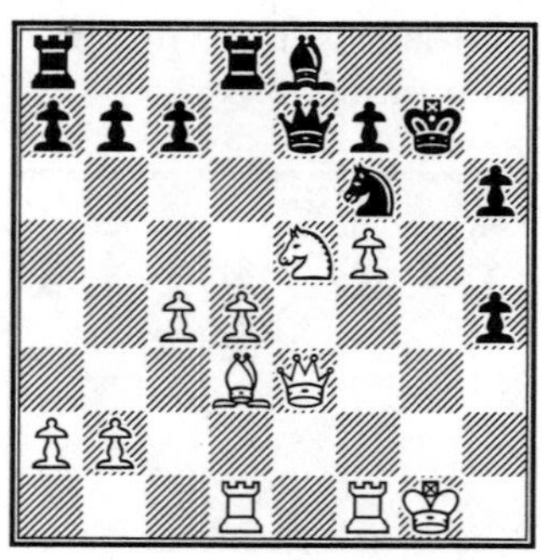

23.Rd2 Bc6; 24.Qf4 Rg8; 25.d5 Kh8+; 26.Kh1 Be8; 27.Rh2 Rg5; 28.Qxh4 and

Black resigned, because there is no defense. **28...Rh5; 29.Qg3 Rxh2+; 30.Qxh2 Ng8.** 30...h5 31.Qf4 Qf8; 32.Rg1! and Qg5 is coming. **31.f6 Qf8; 32.Qh4.** Black resigned, there being no defense to the threat of Rg7. **White won.**

CLASSICAL VARIATION

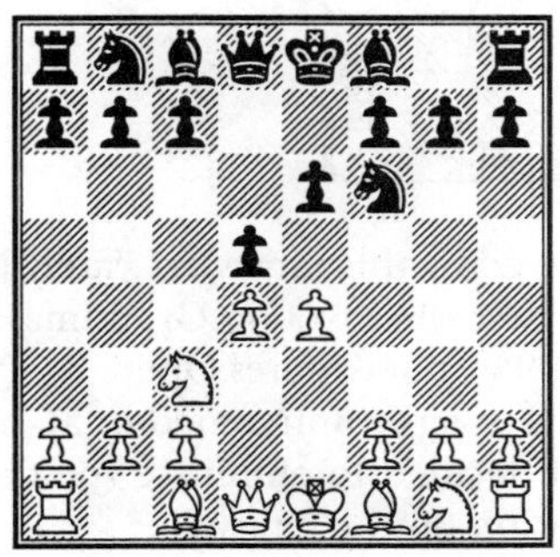

1.e4	**e6**
2.d4	**d5**
3.Nc3	**Nf6**

This is the **Classical Variation** of the French Defense. Black's plan is to firmly defend the light squares in the center, and then try to undermine the e4-square with moves such as ...c5. White now chooses between 4.Bg5 and 4.e5. For many years 4.Bg5 was considered more popular, but not anymore.

The Classical Variation is enjoying a renaissance these days, and World Championship challenger Nigel Short is leading the charge. Now White can play 4.Bg5, which allows either a pure Classical with 4...Be7, or a MacCutcheon with 4...Bb4. Often White avoids both by putting the question to the knight immediately with 4.e5.

(106) KASPAROV - SHORT [C11]
Amsterdam (Euwe Memorial), 1994

1.e4 e6; 2.d4 d5; 3.Nc3 Nf6; 4.e5. The old Steinitz variation is enjoying renewed popularity these days. A game between Kasparov and Short at the 1994 Euwe Memorial in Amsterdam had made a deep impression on me, and I was hoping to make use of a plan involving h4, Rh3-g3 and a kingside attack that worked well for Kasparov. **4...Nfd7; 5.f4 c5; 6.Nf3 Nc6.** This is the normal continuation. The battle rages for control of the d-pawn. **7.Be3 cxd4.**

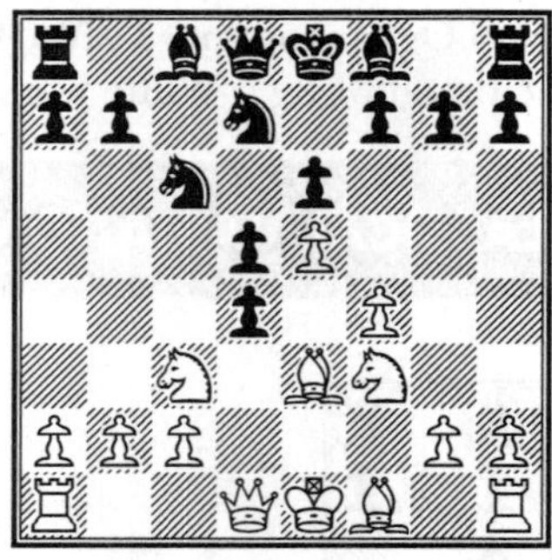

7...Qb6; 8.Qd2. The pawn sacrifice offered by this move has rarely been tested in the tournament arena. I was quite surprised when young Grandmaster Gabriel Schwartzman accepted it against me at the 1994 United States Open. 8...Qxb2; 9.Rb1 Qa3; 10.dxc5. This was my own idea. 10.Be2 was recommended in an old book by Harding, but it did not impress me at all. I decided to eliminate the dark-squared bishops and use Kasparov's attacking formation on the kingside.

10...Bxc5; 11.Bxc5 Qxc5; 12.Bd3 a6; 13.h4 Nb6; 14.Rh3! Nc4; 15.Bxc4 Qxc4; 16.a3! This is a very important move. I need to free the knight from the need to hang around at c3 just to defend the poor pawn. 16...b5; 17.Ne2 Bd7; 18.Nfd4! This eliminates the enemy knight, and I have a decent endgame even without the pawn, because Black is left with a very bad bishop. 18...Nxd4; 19.Nxd4 Rc8; 20.Rbb3! There are two points to this move. One is to be ready to transfer to the kingside at a moment's notice, and the other, more subtle, will be revealed shortly. 20...0-0 21.Rhg3 f6. Standard French counterplay. 22.f5!? I hadn't worked out all the tactics here. But I had a great deal of confidence and had seen some pleasant long variations, beginning at move 27!

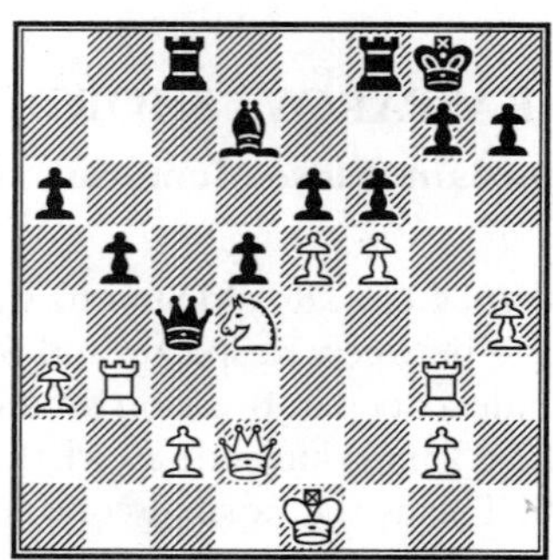

22...exf5. This fell in with my plans. But what about the alternative? Could I have held the position following: (22...fxe5; 23.Qh6 Rf7; 24.Rb4 Qc5!; 25.fxe6 Re7!; 26.exd7 exd4+; 27.Kf1 Rf8+; 28.Kg1 d3+; 29.Kh2 Kh8!; 29...dxc2? allows 30.Rbg4! with devastating threats at g7! 30.Qf4! Rxd7; 31.Qg4 Rdf7; 32.cxd3 Qc1. It might not have been easy, but neither would it have been a simple matter to find all these moves at the board!) 23.Rbc3! A critical preparatory move before the real attack begins. 23...Qa4; 24.Qh6 Rf7; 25.exf6 g6; 26.Rxg6+ hxg6; 27.Qxg6+. I had already worked out the rest of the game, and didn't bother to look for any alternative plans. 27...Kf8;

28.Qh6+; Ke8; 29.Qh8+ Rf8; 30.Re3+ Kd8; 31.Qxf8+ Kc7; 32.Qc5+ Kb8; 33.Qd6+ Rc7; 34.Rc3 Qa5; 35.Qxc7+ and my opponent resigned. This was one of the biggest upsets of the Open.

8.Nxd4 Bc5; 9.Qd2 0–0; 10.0–0–0 a6; 11.h4.

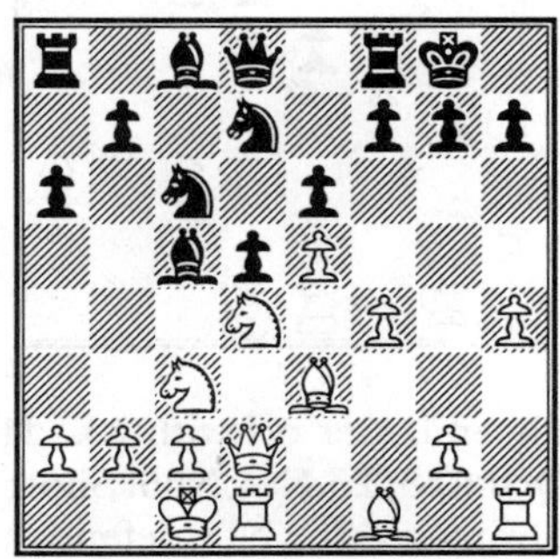

The point of this move is to provide a route to the third rank for the rook. In the game cited at move seven we saw this idea at work. **11...Nxd4; 12.Bxd4 b5; 13.Rh3 b4; 14.Na4 Bxd4; 15.Qxd4 f6.** This was an original idea, but 15...Qa5 would have been a better choice. **16.Qxb4 fxe5; 17.Qd6!** 17.fxe5 Nxe5 gives Black fewer headaches. **17...Qf6.**

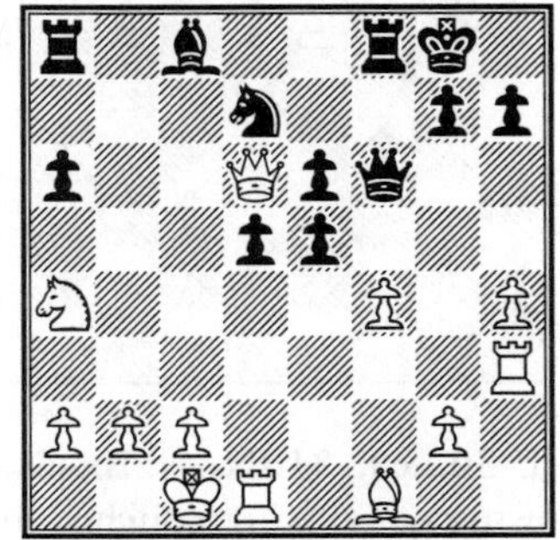

Now Kasparov plays a brilliant and unexpected move. **18.f5!!** The pawn cannot be captured. **18...Qh6+;** 18...exf5; 19.Qxd5+ Kh8; 20.Qxa8 wins a rook. 18...Qxf5; 19.Rf3 Qg4; 20.Rxf8+ Nxf8; 21.Nb6 Bb7; 22.Nxa8 Bxa8; 23.Bxa6 Qxg2; 24.Rf1 and Black can resign. **19.Kb1 Rxf5.** The pawn is gone, but another file is open! Against 19...Nf6 White could try 20.fxe6. **20.Rf3 Rxf3; 21.gxf3 Qf6; 22.Bh3 Kf722.** There was little choice, as Kasparov pointed out that 22...Nf8; 23.Nb6 Qxf3 loses to 24.Rf1 Qxh3; 25.Rxf8#. **23.c4.**

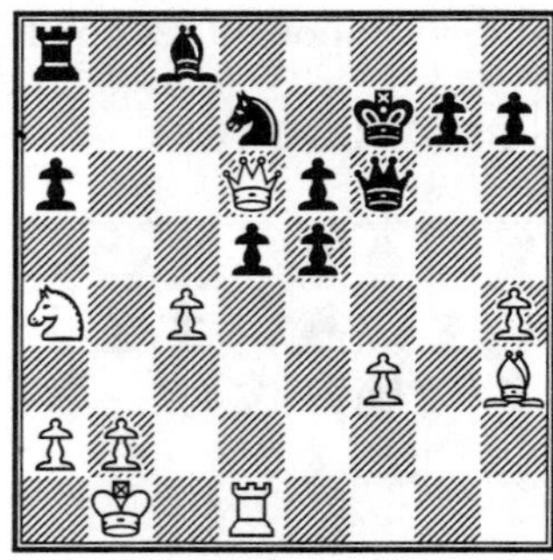

Here Short might have been better off with 23...d4, keeping the d-file closed. **23...dxc4; 24.Nc3 Qe7; 25.Qc6 Rb8; 26.Ne4 Nb6!** Short finds the only defense, but Kasparov still has a huge advantage. 26...Nf8 defends the e-pawn but White wins with 27.Nd6+ Kg8; 28.Nxc8 Qb4; 29.Bxe6+ Kh8; 30.b3! as given by Kasparov. After 30...cxb3; 31.Bxb3 Black has no more attack. **27.Ng5+ Kg8; 28.Qe4 g6; 29.Qxe5 Rb7; 30.Rd6.**

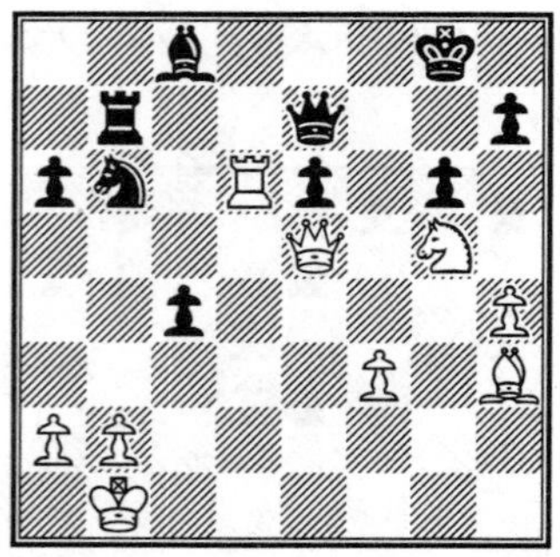

The e-pawn is doomed. **30...c3; 31.Bxe6+ Bxe6; 32.Rxe6.** Black resigned. Kasparov provided the following convincing conclusion: **32...Nc4; 33.Qxc3 Na3+. 34.Kc1 Qd7; 35.Rc6** and the threat of Rc8+ is fatal.

BURN VARIATION

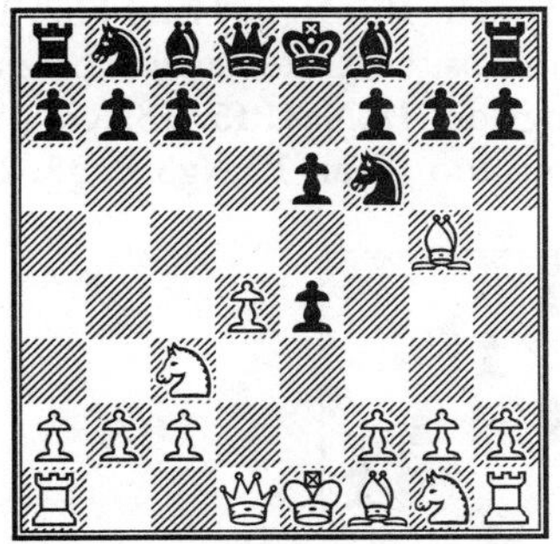

1.e4	**e6**
2.d4	**d5**
3.Nc3	**Nf6**
4.Bg5	**dxe4**

The **Burn Variation** has been suffering for most of its existence, and though some players enjoy the simplicity of the game as Black, there can be no doubt that White obtains a serious advantage. The problem is that the premature resolution of tension in the center allows White to develop quickly, and Black is not given time to establish a strong defensive formation.

The open center makes it easy for White to transfer pieces from the queenside to attacking positions on the kingside.

(107) GARBER - LAUTIER [C11]
New York Open, 1991

1.e4 e6; 2.d4 d5; 3.Nc3 Nf6; 4.Bg5 dxe4 5.Nxe4 Be7. 5...Nbd7; 6.Nxf6+ Nxf6; 7.Nf3 Be7; 8.Bd3 is slightly better for White, who controls more space. **6.Bxf6 gxf6; 7.Nf3 b6.** There are other methods of dealing with the problem of the light-squared bishop but they, too, leave White with a pleasant position. **8.Bb5+!?** 8. Bc4 is the most common move, but recently White has been scoring heavily with the check, including the major upset of a grandmaster in the present game. **8...c6; 9.Bd3 Bb7; 10.Qe2 Qc7; 11.0-0-0 Nd7; 12.Kb1 0-0-0.**

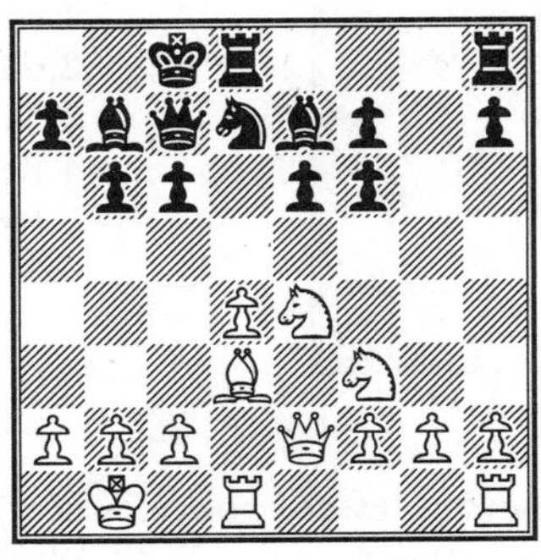

Black's king seems safe enough, but White now comes up with a surprising positional strategy of exchanging light-squared bishops. At first, this seems daft, since clearly the bishop at d3 has more scope than its counterpart at b7, but the logic soon reveals itself. **13.Ba6 Rhe8; 14.Bxb7+ Kxb7.** Black no longer has any compensation for his shattered pawns.

15.c4! The d5-square is now a flash point. **15...Nf8; 16.g3.** The position now looks much more like a Caro Kann than a French! **16...Ng6; 17.h4 h5?!** This creates a permanent weakness. In similar Caro Kann positions the pawn is often offered as a sacrifice, but there White has castled kingside. **18.Ne1! f5.** 18...c5; 19.d5! exd5; 20.cxd5 Bd6; 21.Qf3! and the pressure at f6 is too great. **19.Ng5 Bxg5; 20.hxg5 f4.**

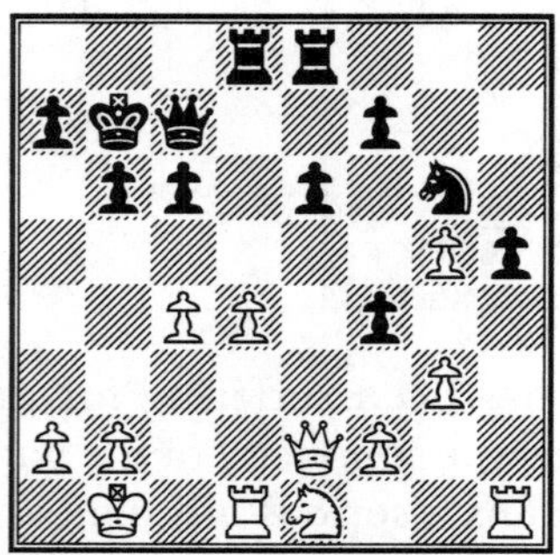

21.g4! hxg4; 22.Qxg4 e5; 23.d5! This is not just a passed pawn, it has a significant impact in the coming queenside attack. **23...cxd5.** 23...Qd7; 24.Qg2 e4; 25.Rh7 f3; 26.Qh2 leaves White in control. The h-file is already pocketed and when a White knight gets to e3 there will be a lock on the key light-squares in the center. **24.cxd5 e4; 25.Rh7 Qd7; 26.Qe2! Qf5; 27.d6 Rd7; 28.Nc2 Qxg5; 29.Nb4.** Black's queenside looks mighty naked now. **29...Qa5; 30.Qc4 Qc5; 31.Qa6+ Kb8; 32.Qa4 Qf5; 33.Qc6 e3+ 34.Ka1 a5; 35.Qxb6+ Rb7; 36.Nc6+ Kc8; 37.Qa6. White won.**

RICHTER ATTACK

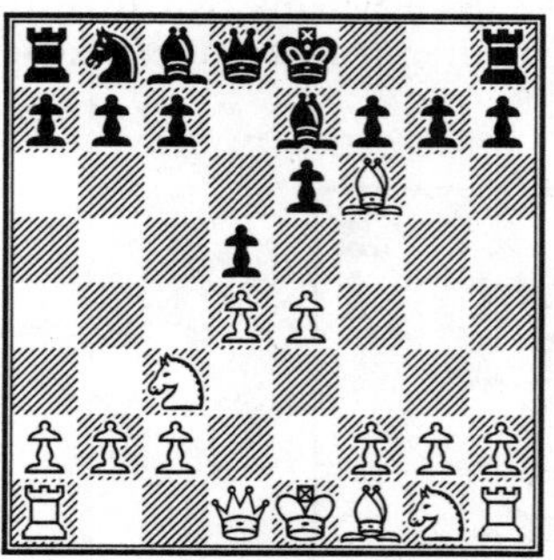

1.e4	**e6**
2.d4	**d5**
3.Nc3	**Nf6**
4.Bg5	**Be7**
5.Bxf6	

This is the **Richter Attack**, a lesser-known variation which is easy to play for White but which can be quite dangerous for Black. With 5.e5 under intense investigation, the sideline has found a new following among players who do not wish to invest a lot of time and money keeping up with the main lines.

(108) MASON - BIRD [C13]
Hastings, 1895

5...Bxf6; 6.e5. 6.Nf3 is also seen, for example 6...a6; 7.Bd3 Nc6; 8.e5 Be7; 9.Ne2 Nb4; 10.0-0 b6; 11.Nf4 Nxd3; 12.Qxd3 a5; 13.Rfe1 Ba6 with dynamic equality in Sokolov-Bischoff, Bad Swesten 1997. Exchanging the the center is another plan: 6...dxe4; 7.Nxe4 Nd7; 8.Bd3 b6; 9.0-0 Bb7; 10.Qe2 0-0; 11.Rad1 Qe7; 12.Rfe1 Rfd8 and Black was able to consolidate the kingside with ...Nf8 in Leonardo-Alexandre, Lisbon Masters 1997. **6...Be7; 7.Qg4.**

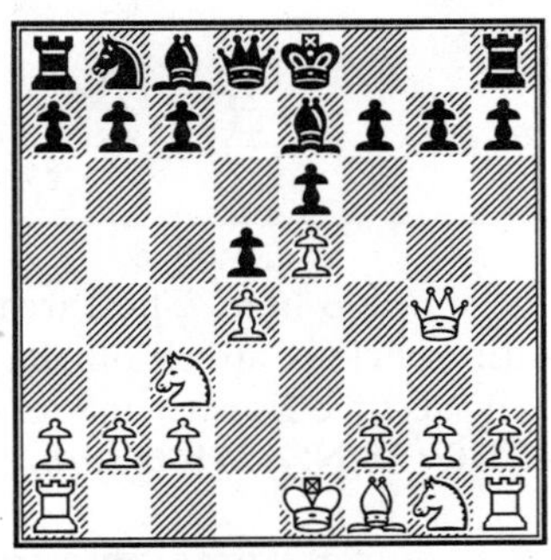

A typical French attacking motif. Black must now choose between weakening his kingside with Kf8 or g6, or castling into a precarious situation. **7...Kf8.** 7...g6 8.h4 h5; 9.Qf4 b6; 10.Nf3 Ba6; 11.Bxa6 Nxa6 was eventually drawn in Devcic-Josipovic, Zagreb 1997.

8.Bd3 c5. 8...f5; 9.Qf3 c5; 10.g4! cxd4; 11.gxf5 Kg8 (11...dxc3; 12.fxe6+ Kg8; 13.Qf7#) 12.Nce2 Nc6; 13.Qh3 with a big advantage for White in Schwarz-Haber, 1948. 8...b6!? was suggested by Tarrasch. It may be the best Black has, but it does seem a bit slow. 9.h4 Ba6; 10.0–0–0! c5; 11.Nh3 c4; 12.Be2 b5; 13.f4 b4; 14.Nb1 c3; 15.Bxa6 Nxa6; 16.f5 and White's attack is supported by a lot more firepower than Black's. **9.dxc5 Nc6; 10.Nf3.** 10.f4! is probably stronger, Schwarz-Schmidt, 1948. **10...h5; 11.Qg3 h4; 12.Qg4 Bxc5; 13.0–0.**

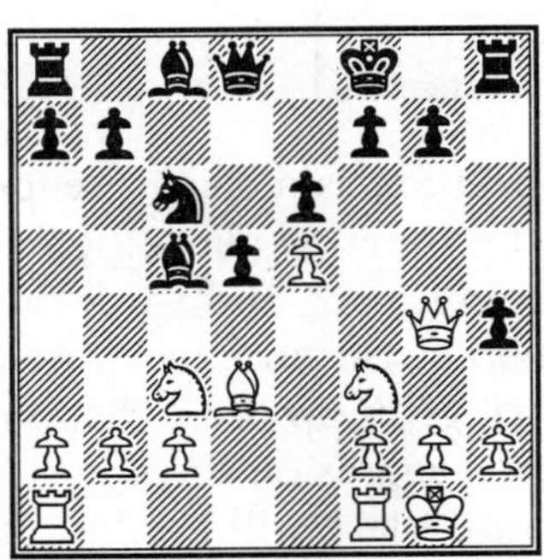

Black seems to be playing aimlessly, and White's well coordinated pieces will be more effective. **13...Bd7; 14.a3 Kg8; 15.Rae1 Be7; 16.Ne2 Rh6; 17.Ned4! Rc8; 18.c3.** There will be no counterplay on the c-file! **18...Kh8; 19.Re2 a6; 20.Rfe1 Na5; 21.Kh1 Nc6.** Obviously Black has no plan. **22.Nxc6 Rxc6; 23.Nd4 Rc8; 24.f4.** Now we can see what White had in mind when he doubled rooks on the e-file. **24...g6.** Pretty much forced. **25.Qh3 Bc5; 26.Nf3 Kg7; 27.Ng5 Be7; 28.Nf3 Qb6; 29.Qg4 Bb5; 30.Bxb5 Qxb5; 31.Nd4.**

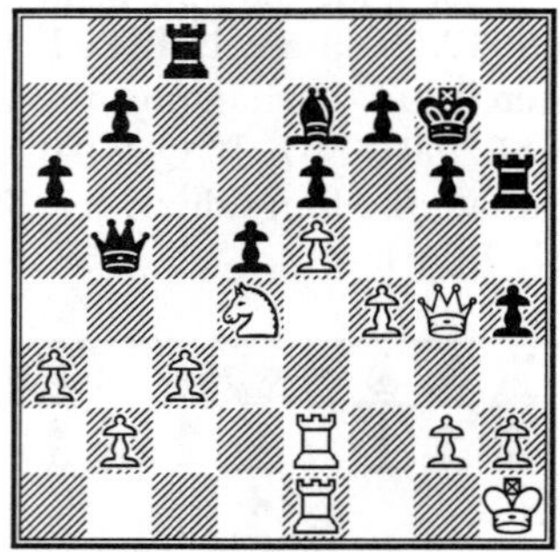

The knight keeps finding a home here. The threat of f5 has been renewed. White will break through with a vicious attack on the kingside. **31...Qd7; 32.f5! exf5; 33.e6! fxe6.** Now a small sacrifice finishes matters. **34.Nxf5+! Kh7; 35.Nxh6 Rc4; 36.Qxe6 Qxe6; 37.Rxe6 Bf8; 38.Nf7. White won.**

MACCUTCHEON VARIATION

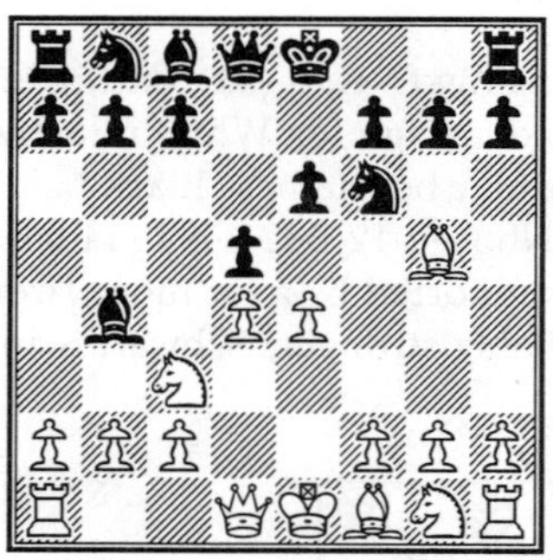

1.e4 e6
2.d4 d5
3.Nc3 Nf6
4.Bg5 Bb4

The **MacCutcheon Variation** is a sharp weapon which must be taken into account by anyone who dares to play 4.Bg5 against the French. Black intends to capture the knight at c3 and work on the weakness of the e4 square which is undermined by the absence of that knight.

In return for this, Black gives up the right to castle in most cases, and also has to weaken the dark-squares on the kingside, which is a long-lasting advantage for White because Black will not have a dark-squared bishop to defend those squares.

(109) KURAJICA - DVORETSKY [C12]
Wijk aan Zee, 1976

1.e4 e6; 2.d4 d5; 3.Nc3 Nf6; 4.Bg5 Bb4; 5.e5 h6; 6.Be3. The Janowski Variation 6.Bd2 is the older and more common move, and it is also good. Some recent examples are 6...Bxc3; 7.bxc3 Ne4; 8.Qg4 g6; 9.Bd3 Nxd2; 10.Kxd2 c5; 11.Nf3 Nc6 (11...c4; 12.Be2 Bd7; 13.Rhb1 Bc6; 14.Qh4 Qxh4; 15.Nxh4 a5; 16.h3 Nd7; 17.f4 Ke7; 18.g4 Rag8; 19.Rg1 and White controlled a lot more space and had a much better bishop in RogerI-Galiana, Oropesa del Mar 1996.)

12.Rhb1 c4; 13.Be2 Qe7; 14.a4 Kd8; 15.h4 Kc7; 16.h5 g5; 17.Qg3 Bd7; 18.Nh2 Rag8; 19.Ng4 Nb8; 20.Rf1 Be8; 21.Nf6 Rf8; 22.f4! gxf4; 23.Qh4 with a strong initiative for White in So. Polgar-Baginskaite, Yerevan Olympiad 1996. **6...Ne4; 7.Qg4 g6.**

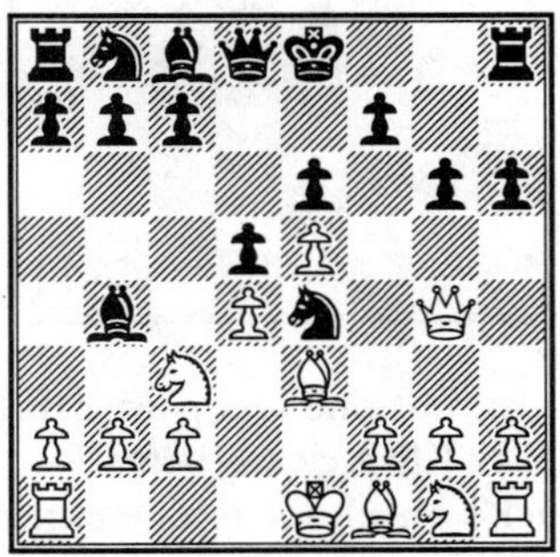

This is considered to be the most reliable defense. **8.a3! Bxc3+; 9.bxc3 Nxc3.** 9...c5; 10.Bd3 Qa5 (10...Nxc3; 11.dxc5 Qa5; 12.Bd2! Qa4; 13.Qb4! is the clever path to the advantage advocated by Suetin.) 11.Ne2 cxd4; 12.Bxd4 Nc6; 13.0–0 Nc5; 14.Bxg6! Rg8; 15.Bxf7+ Kxf7; 16.Qh5+ Ke7 gives White a ferocious attack, for example: 17.Qxh6 Kd8; 18.Nf4 Ne7; 19.Rfd1 Bd7; 20.c4! and Black eventually fell victim in Shamkovich-Chistyakov, USSR 1961. **10.Bd3 Nc6.**

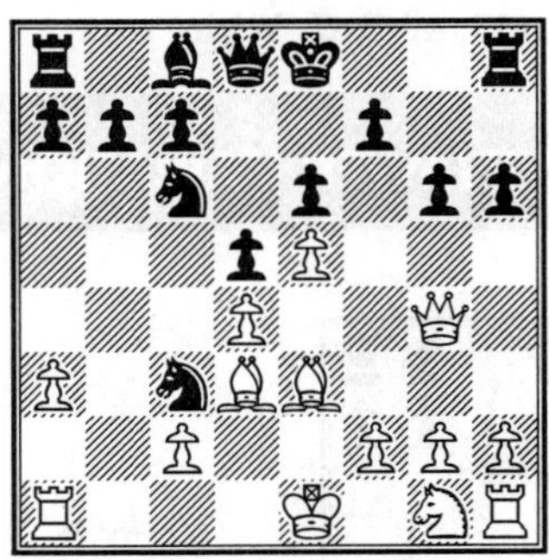

Although the great tactician Spielmann was of the opinion that Black stands better, modern theory holds that Black is in real trouble. 10...Qe7; 11.h4! b6; 12.h5 g5; 13.f4! cracks open the kingside. 13...gxf4; 14.Qxf4 and White has a dangerous initiative, Tolush-Sandin, Correspondence 1959.

11.h4! Ne7?! 11...Qe7; 12.h5 g5; 13.f4 gxf4; 14.Qxf4 Bd7; 15.Nh3! 0-0-0; 16.0-0 Rdf8; 17.Qf6! is better for White, according to Ubilava. Black will always have to attend to the weakness of his § at f7. 11...Bd7; 12.Bxg6!? Rg8 (12...fxg6?; 13.Qxg6+ Ke7; 14.Qf6+ Ke8; 15.Qxh8+) 13.Bxf7+ Kxf7; 14.Qh5+ Rg6; 15.Nh3! given by Eade, looks very strong for White, with the threat of Nf4. Black does not seem to have any real counterplay, and therefore White has time to build the attack. 15...Qe7; 16.Nf4 Rag8; 17.Rh3! and the rook will move to f3 where it will menace the enemy king.

12.f3 Bd7; 13.Qf4 Nf5; 14.Bf2 c5. It is too late to establish any real counterplay. **15.dxc5 d4; 16.Bxf5! gxf5; 17.Bxd4 Nd5; 18.Qd2.**

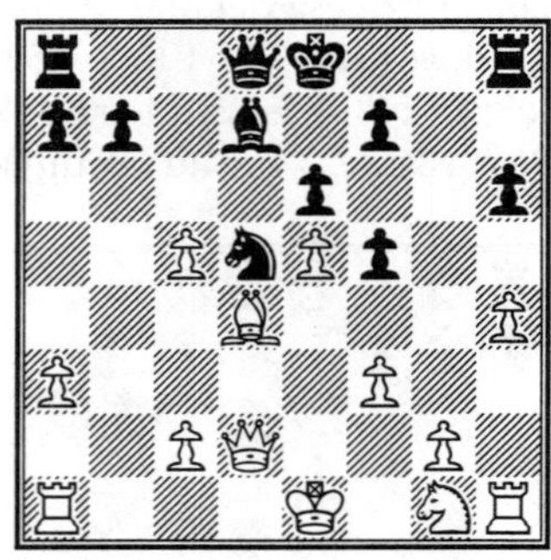

Black has a strong outpost, but one less pawn. **18...Qe7; 19.Ne2 Bb5; 20.Nc3 Nxc3.** 20...Ba6; 21.Nxd5 exd5; 22.Kf2 is clearly better for White. **21.Qxc3 Rg8; 22.Kf2.** The outpost is gone, and Black's only hope is an endgame with bishops of opposite colors. But as the saying goes, before the endgame the gods have placed the middlegame!

22...0-0-0; 23.Be3 Rd5; 24.Qb4 Bc6; 25.Rad1 a5; 26.Qf4! h5; 27.Rxd5 Bxd5; 28.c4 Bc6; 29.Rd1. White has a clear advantage in space and Black has more weaknesses. **29...f6; 30.g3 Qg7; 31.Bd4! fxe5.** 31...Rd8; 32.exf6 Qf7; 33.Rd2 and White consolidates. **32.Bxe5 Qf7; 33.Qd2.** The pressure on the d-file is now decisive. **33...Qe7; 34.Qxa5 b6; 35.Qxb6 Qb7; 36.Rd6! Bxf3.** 36...Qxb6; 37.cxb6 Kb7; 38.Rxe6 and Black has no chances to survive, despite bishops of opposite color. **37.Qxb7+ Bxb7; 38.Rxe6 Be4; 39.c6! Bd3; 40.Re7. White won.**

WINAWER VARIATION

1.e4	**e6**
2.d4	**d5**
3.Nc3	**Bb4**

The **Winawer Variation** got its name in this game, but the player of the Black pieces hardly deserves the full credit, as the ideas of the system were not worked out properly until well into the next century. The opening has also been named for Aron Nimzowitsch, who dabbled in it. The real heroes of the line are Mikhail Botvinnik and Wolfgang Uhlmann. The latter has built an entire career on the variation. Still, the designation of the defense as the Winawer Variation is too firmly entrenched to be changed.

Black's basic idea is to put pressure on the White center, usually with ...c5, giving up the bishop for the knight at c3, as in the Nimzo-Indian. Black is often forced to defend against a kingside attack for a long time, seeking counterplay in the center or simply waiting until the attack is exhausted and then preying on the weaknesses created by White. It takes a certain kind of personality to be willing to defend the Winawer. Professionals either love it or hate it, and no World Champion since Botvinnik has relied on it for important encounters. Still, many challengers for the crown have used it extensively, for example Viktor Korchnoi. It is a dynamic opening which is unlikely ever to disappear from the tournament scene.

(110) STEINITZ - WINAWER [C01]
Paris, 1867

1.e4 e6; 2.d4 d5; 3.Nc3 Bb4; 4.exd5. When the Winawer was young, this was considered the correct move, on the grounds that the Black bishop is misplaced in the exchange variation. Although this view was abandoned by the end of the 19th century, I still think that there is a solid positional basis for it. It is true that White will be able to obtain only the tiniest of positional advantages with best play, but the line does avoid all of the complexities and counterplay of the normal move 4.e5. There are many other options for White here.

4.Bd2 has been called, rather offensively, the "fingerslip" variation. I prefer to think of it as the Anti-Winawer. Theory holds that Black can draw with accurate play, so it is rarely seen in high-level chess. For amateurs, however, it can lead to some spectacular results. Here are examples from my own games; 4.Bd2

A) 4...Nc6; 5.Bb5 dxe4 (5...Nge7; 6.a3 Bxc3; 7.Bxc3 dxe4; 8.Qg4 0-0; 9.Qxe4 e5; 10.Bxc6 exd4; 11.Bb4 Nxc6; 12.Bxf8 Qxf8; 13.Nf3 and White was better in Schiller-Johansen, Loneon 1985.) 6.a3 Ba5; 7.Qg4 Nf6; 8.Qxg7 Rg8; 9.Qh6 Rg6; 10.Qh4 Rg4; 11.Qh6 Qxd4; 12.0-0-0 Rg6; 13.Qh4 Bd7; 14.Nge2 Qe5 led to unclear complications in Schiller-Lindsay, Chicago (Midwest Masters) 1988.

B) 4...b6; 5.Qg4 Bf8; 6.Bd3 Nf6; 7.Qe2 dxe4; 8.Nxe4 Be7; 9.Nf3 Bb7; 10.Neg5 Nc6; 11.Nxf7!! Nxd4; 12.Nxd8 Bxf3; 13.gxf3 Nxe2; 14.Nxe6 Kd7; 15.Bf5 g6; 16.Bh3 Kc6; 17.Kxe2 Rhe8; 18.Rhe1 Bd6; 19.Kf1. White won. Schiller-Gazmen, Illinois 1987;

C) 4...dxe4; 5.Qg4 Nf6; 6.Qxg7 Rg8; 7.Qh6 Qxd4; 8.0-0-0 Bf8; 9.Qh4 Rg4; 10.Qh3 Qxf2; 11.Be3 Qf5; 12.Be2 Rg6; 13.g4 Qe5; 14.Bd4 Qg5+; 15.Be3 Qa5; 16.g5 Rxg5; 17.Qh4 Rg6; 18.Nh3 Bd6 (A novelty. 18...Be7; 19 Nf4 and 18...Nbd7; 19 Nf4 give White an attack.) 19.Rhf1 Be5; 20.Nf4 (Not 20.Bh5 which allows the brilliant reply 20...Bg3!!) 20...Bxc3!; Not 20...Nbd7; 21.Nxg6 and White wins. 21.bxc3 Nd5! 22.Rxd5! exd5; 23.Nxg6 Qa3+!; 24.Kd2 hxg6; 25.Qh8+? (I missed the terminal 25

Rxf7!!, winning.) 25...Qf8; 26.Qe5+ Qe7; 27.Qh8+ Qf8; 28.Qe5+ and a draw was agreed in Schiller-N.Thomas, Brighton (Tranmer Memorial) 1985.

4...exd5; 5.Bd3 Be6? A horrible move, positionally. The bishop should aim for a more active post. 5...Nc6; 6.a3 Bxc3+ (6...Be7; 7.Nce2 Bg5; 8.f4 Bh4+; 9.g3 Bf6; 10.c3 Nge7; 11.Nf3 was slightly better for White in Glek-Hertneck, Germany 1996. Black weakened the kingside here with 11...h5, but it is not clear that there is a better plan.) 7.bxc3 Qf6; 8.Rb1 Nge7; 9.Ne2 Ng6; 10.0–0 0–0; 11.f4 Bf5? Black misses the threat. 12.Bxf5! Qxf5; 13.Ng3 Perhaps Black thought that White would be tempted by the pawn at b7, but that has very little to do with the game. 13...Qd7; 14.f5 Nge7; 15.f6! Usually white can only dream about such attacking moves. 15...Nc8; 16.fxg7 Re8; 17.Nh5 Re6; 18.Qg4 and Black resigned, since retreating the queen to d8 is met by Bg5, Short-Belyavsky, Dortmund 1995.

6.Nf3 h6; 7.0–0 Bxc3; 8.bxc3 Nd7. This is a strange move, because the normal plan involves advancing a pawn to c5 and then placing the knight at c6. **9.Rb1 Nb6; 10.Ne5!** Black's artificial formation makes it hard to dislodge this knight. **10...Ne7; 11.f4 Bf5.** Black must try to prevent the f-pawn from advancing to f5. **12.Bxf5 Nxf5; 13.Ba3 Nd6; 14.f5 Ne4.**

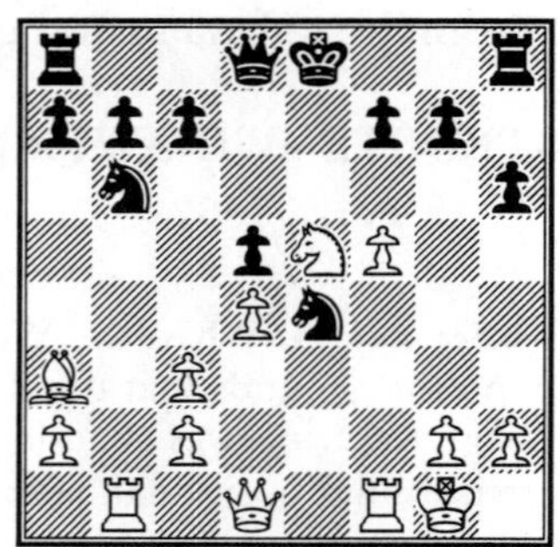

15.f6! This forces Black to weaken the kingside. **15...g6; 16.Qg4 Qc8; 17.Qxg6! Qe6.** 17...fxg6; 18.f7+ Kd8; 19.f8Q+ Rxf8; 20.Rxf8#. **18.Qg7 0–0–0.** The king escapes, but the price is rather high, as White wins material. **19.Nxf7 Nxc3; 20.Nxd8 Rxd8; 21.f7 Nd7.** Black can't allow White to get another queen! **22.Rbe1 Ne2+; 23.Kh1 c5; 24.Bxc5 Qe4; 25.f8Q.** Now it is all over. **25...Nxf8; 26.Rxf8 Ng3+; 27.Qxg3 Rxf8; 28.Bxf8. White won.**

(111) BRONSTEIN - UHLMANN [C18]

Tallinn, 1977

1.e4 e6; 2.d4 d5; 3.Nc3 Bb4; 4.e5 Ne7; 5.a3 Bxc3+; 6.bxc3 c5; 7.Qg4.

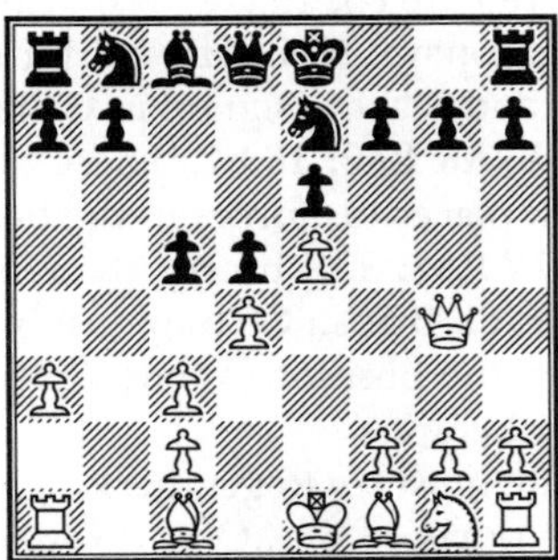

This leads to the Poisoned Pawn Variation of the Winawer French. Black gives up the g-pawn in return for rapid development, and will then play in the center. The White king is usually stuck in the center, where it can become a target for an attack. **7...Qc7; 8.Qxg7 Rg8; 9.Qxh7 cxd4; 10.Ne2.** The alternative is 10.Kd1, known as the "Life or Death" Variation. **10...Nbc6; 11.f4 Bd7; 12.Qd3 dxc3.**

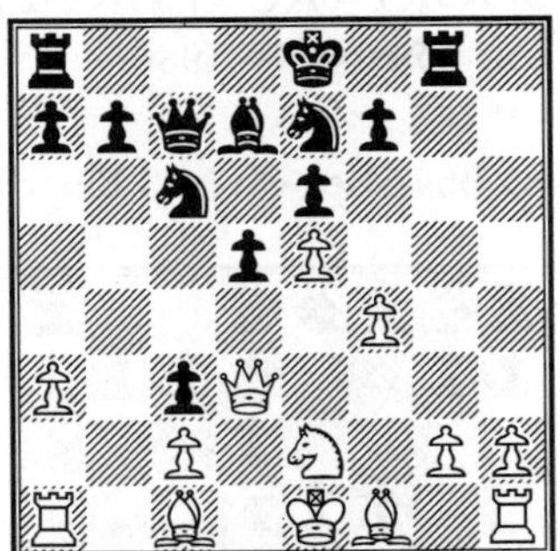

Here White has tried many moves, which flow in and out of fashion. At present, both of the captures at c3 continue to received a great deal of attention.

13.h4. 13.Qxc3 Nf5 prepares the advance of the d-pawn, for example 14.Rb1 d4; 15.Qc4 Qa5+; 16.Bd2 Qxa3; 17.Rxb7 Qa1+; 18.Kf2 Rc8; 19.Qd3 Nce7; 20.c4 Qa6; 21.Rb2 Qxc4; 22.Qxc4 Rxc4 led to a messy endgame in Portisch-Uhlmann, Monte Carlo 1968. 13.Nxc3 a6; 14.Rb1.

(14.Ne2 Nf5; 15.h3 Na5; 16.g4 Bb5; 17.Qc3 Qxc3+; 18.Nxc3 Bxf1; 19.Rxf1 Nd4; 20.Ra2 Rc8 is a well analyzed position, but a recent and innovative plan brought White the advantage in Morgado-Echeguren, Postal 1996: 21.Ne2! Rxc2; 22.Rxc2 Nxc2+; 23.Kd1 Na1; 24.Rf3! which forces 24...N1b3 but now 25.Rc3 gave White control of the important c-file.)

14...Na5; 15.h4 Nf5; 16.Rh3 0-0-0; 17.h5 Rg4; 18.h6 Rh8; 19.h7 Rg7; 20.Rb4 Nc4; 21.Qxf5 exf5; 22.Nxd5 Qa5; 23.Bxc4 Rhxh7; 24.Rc3. White threatens discovered checks, but it is Black's attack that proves decisive. 24...Rh1+; 25.Bf1+ Kd8; 26.Nb6 Bb5; 27.Nc4 Bxc4; 28.Rcxc4 Rxg2; 29.Be3 Qa4; 30.Bb6+ Ke7 and White resigned in Dueball-Uhlmann, Raach 1969.

13.Rb1 is one of the most popular moves at present. 13...0–0–0; 14.Nxc3 Na5 and here in addition to 15.Nb5 and 15.g3, a new plan has recently been introduced. 15.Ne2!? Nec6 (15...a6 is probably wiser, compare 13.Nxc3 a6 in Dueball-Uhlmann above.) 16.h4 Be8; 17.h5 f6; 18.exf6 e5; 19.fxe5 Nxe5; 20.Qc3 Qxc3+; 21.Nxc3 Ng4; 22.Bd3 Nxf6 and White's extra pawn is significant, for example 23.h6 Bd7; 24.0–0 Ng4; 25.Nxd5 Be6; 26.Ne7+ and Black resigned in Callet-Olivier, Paris 1996.

13...0–0–0; 14.h5 Nf5; 15.h6 Rg6; 16.h7. These are logical moves. White advances the pawn, while Black places his forces in the best positions to support central counterplay. **16...Rh8; 17.Rh3.** 17.Rh5 f6; 18.exf6 Be8 gave Black sufficient counterplay in Carleton-Botterill, British Championship 1978. **17...d4; 18.Rb1 Be8;** Black now retreats to solidify the position. White's pieces are not doing anything, and patience is an affordable luxury.

19.Qf3 Qd8; 20.g4. White must try to get this knight out of its outpost, but this costs a pawn. **20...Nh4!** The purpose of ...Qd8 is revealed! **21.Qh1 Rxg4; 22.Ng3 Rxh7.** Now that White's prize possession is gone, Black can concentrate on the center. **23.Ne4 Nxe5!; 24.fxe5 Bc6.** Black's temporary sacrifice exposes the miserable positions of the White pieces. **25.Bd3 Kc7; 26.Kf2.** White foresees a Black rook getting to e5. **26...Rh5; 27.Rf3.** A pitiful counterattack, easily repulsed. **27...Qg8! 28.Bf4 Nxf3; 29.Qxh5 Rxf4; 30.Qh6 Ng5+. Black won.**

(112) SHORT - KORCHNOI [C19]

Brussels 1986

1.e4 e6; 2.d4 d5; 3.Nc3 Bb4; 4.e5 c5; 5.a3 Bxc3+; 6.bxc3 Ne7; 7.Nf3.

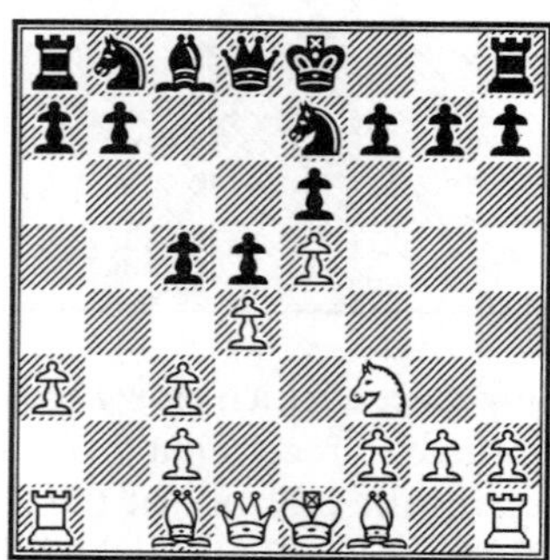

This is the "positional" treatment of the Winawer. Instead of engaging in the wild and double-edged battles that arise in the "poisoned pawn" lines with Qg4, White continues with development and supports the center. White has an advantage in space which is not going to disappear, and can afford to play calmly. Black must strive for pressure at all three points along the c3-e5 pawn chain.

7...Qa5. 7...Bd7 is the preference of the American theoretician John Watson, who has played the French for most of his career. He notes however, that this is largely a matter of taste, since other lines are also doing well for Black. 8.a4 Qa5;

A) 9.Qd2 Nbc6; 10.Be2 Rc8; 11.dxc5 Ng6; 12.0–0 0–0 (12...Ncxe5; 13.Nd4 a6 is suggested by Watson in his classic book *Play the French.*) 13.Qe3 Qc7; 14.Nd4 Qxe5;

15.Nb5 Qxe3; 16.Bxe3 led to complicate play in Smyslov-Uhlmann, Mar del Plata 1966, where White eventually prevailed.

B) 9.Bd2 Nbc6; 10.Bb5 is an idea from former United States Champion, New York Times columnist Robert Byrne. 10...f6 (10...Qc7; 11.0–0 0–0; 12.Bc1 b6; 13.Ba3 Na5; 14.dxc5 Bxb5; 15.cxb6 axb6; 16.axb5 Rfc8; 17.Bb4 Nc4; 18.Rxa8 Rxa8; 19.Re1 Ng6 and chances were level in Nunn-Yusupov, Belgrade 1991.) 11.Qe2 fxe5; 12.Nxe5 Nxe5; 13.Qxe5 Bxb5; 14.c4 Qd8; 15.cxb5 cxd4; 16.0–0 0–0; 17.Qxe6+ with more than enough compensation for White in Nunn-Brenninkmeijer, Groningen 1988. 7...Nbc6; 8.Bd3 Qa5; 9.Qd2 c4; 10.Be2 Qa4; 11.0–0 Bd7; 12.Ng5 h6 was fine for Black in Pogrebysssky-Botvinnik, Soviet Championship1934.

8.Bd2 Nbc6; 9.Be2. White can also try a flank approach with either 9.h4 or 9.a4. **9...cxd4; 10.cxd4 Qa4.** It takes a certain kind of player to be happy with the queen sitting on such an unusual square! Nevertheless, it is odd maneuvers such as this, where the mighty queen acts as a blockader of the a-pawn and keeps an eye on the pawn at d4. **11.Be3 b6; 12.Qd3.**

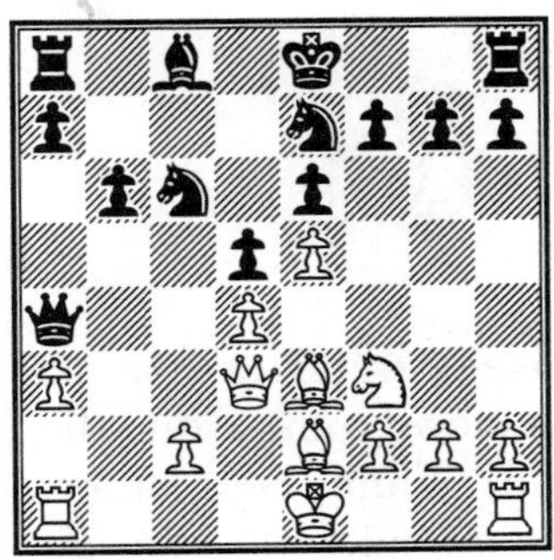

Now the knight can move from c6 to either a5 opr b4. **12...Nb4.** 12...Na5; 13.Nd2 Bd7; 14.0–0 Rc8; 15.Rfc1 0–0; 16.Rab1 Nc4; 17.Rb3 Rc7; 18.Nf3 Rfc8; 19.Bg5 Ng6; 20.h4 and White carried out an effective kingside attack in A.Sokolov-Yusupov, Candidates Match 1986. **13.Qb5+ Qxb5; 14.Bxb5+ Nbc6.** White's bishop pair is an asset, but the weaknesses in the pawn structure are significant. **15.Bd2 Bd7; 16.Ba6 f6!** The typical French break. placing unbearable pressure on the White center. **17.exf6 gxf6; 18.Bc3 h5; 19.Nh4 Kf7;** Black's king is perfectly safe here, since White has no forces in position to attack. In fact, White's pieces seem to be wandering aimlessly, while Black's are well-coordinated. **20.0–0 Rag8; 21.f4 Rg4; 22.g3.**

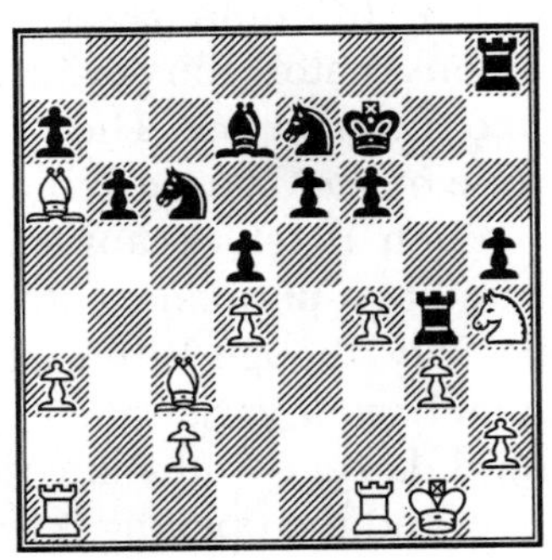

Now Korchnoi invests the exchange to obtain a strong attack. **22...Rxh4!; 23.gxh4 Nf5; 24.Kf2 Ncxd4; 25.Bxd4 Nxd4; 26.c4 Nb3.** Black's marauding knight continues to attack. **27.Rad1 Nc5; 28.Bb5 Bxb5; 29.cxb5 Kg6.** Typical Korchnoi (and French) play! The king takes an active role. **30.Rg1+ Kf5; 31.Ke3 Rc8; 32.Rg7 Nb3.** Now the d-pawn decides the game. **33.Rd3 d4+; 34.Kf3 Rc3; 35.Rxc3 dxc3; 36.Rc7 c2. Black won.**

CARO-KANN DEFENSE

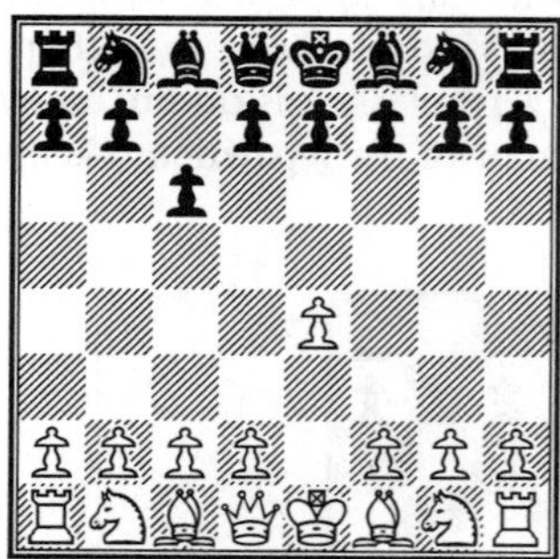

1.e4 c6

The **Caro-Kann Defense** is strategically simple: Black will advance the d-pawn to d5 on the second move, confronting the White pawn at e4. Unlike the French Defense, the Caro-Kann does not force Black's bishop to sit idly at c8. Instead, it has an open road to the kingside, and is usually developed there quite early in the game.

Even though players often castle on opposite wings, the Caro-Kann cannot usually be defeated by direct attacks. The Black position can usually absorb whatever White throws at it, and complex endgame play is typical. The result of the game may depend on the relative skill in endgame play.

The main lines of the opening continue 2.d4 d5; 3.Nc3 dxe4; 4.Nxe4, though the Advance Variation (3.e5) and Panov Attack (3.exd4 cxd5 4.c4) are very popular alternatives at both amateur and professional levels of play.

After 3.Nc3 dxe4; 4.Nxe4 Black has a choice of four different systems. The Classical Variation with 4...Bf5 dominated the opening until the late 1980s, when World Champion Anatoly Karpov turned 4...Nd7, now known as the Karpov Variation, into the main line. The systems with 4...Nf6 are not seen in top level play because of the damage White can inflict on the pawn structure with 5.Nxf6+. When Black recaptures with the e-pawn, the Tartakower Variation, White has a permanent structural advantage thanks to the queenside pawn majority, though with careful play Black can often grovel a draw. The Bronstein-Larsen Variation, 5...gxf6, is more ambitious, but the permanent structural damage to the kingside forces the Black king to evacuate to the queenside, and the opening remains suspect among professionals.

ACCELERATED PANOV ATTACK

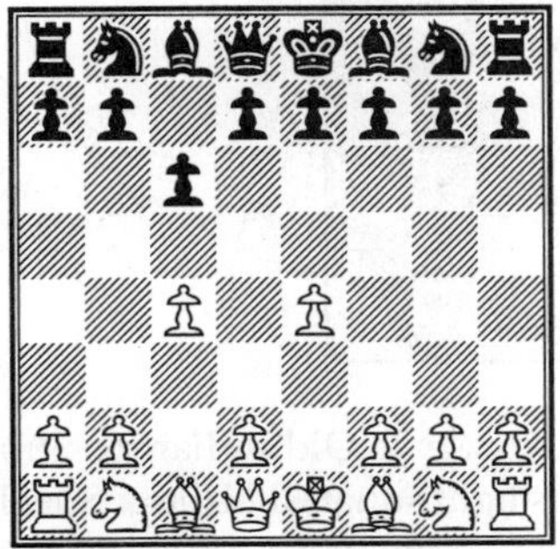

1.e4 c6
2.c4

The **Accelerated Panov** defines the contour of the middlegame quickly. If Black plays a quick ...d5, transposition to normal Panov Attack positions are likely, but there are several alternative plans for Black. This variation has grown in popularity in the past decade. Pure Caro-Kann players usually continue with 2...d5, but Larsen, who likes the Old Indian, prefers to advance the e-pawn, giving the game a quite different character.

(113) SPEELMAN - LARSEN [B10]
Lone Pine, 1978

1.e4 c6; 2.c4 e5. 2...d5; 3.exd5 cxd5; 4.cxd5 (4.d4 transposes to a standard Panov Attack.) 4...Nf6 is the other main option for Black. White is now considered to have the better chances after 5.Qa4+ Nbd7; 6.Nc3 g6; 7.Nf3 Bg7; 8.Qb3 0-0; 9.Bc4 Nb6; 10.d3 Bf5; 11.0-0 Rc8; 12.Re1, as in Am.Rodriguez-Pogorelov, Mondariz Balneario 1996. Usually White cannot get away with such greed, holding on to the weak extra pawn at d5, but in this case it seems to be acceptable.

3.Nf3 d6; 4.d4. Black can transpose to Old Indian positions immediately with ...Nbd7, but prefers to play a guessing game with White wondering what sort of formation Black will adopt. **4...Bg4.** Black places indirect pressure at d4. White should now develop calmly, as rash action in the center will not be effective. **5.Be2.** 5.dxe5? Bxf3!; 6.gxf3 dxe5; 7.Qxd8+ Kxd8; 8.f4 f6! is fine for Black, since White's bishop pair is limited in effectiveness by his bad pawn structure, Seirawan-Nikolic, Tilburg 1990. **5...Nd7; 6.Nc3 Be7; 7.0-0.**

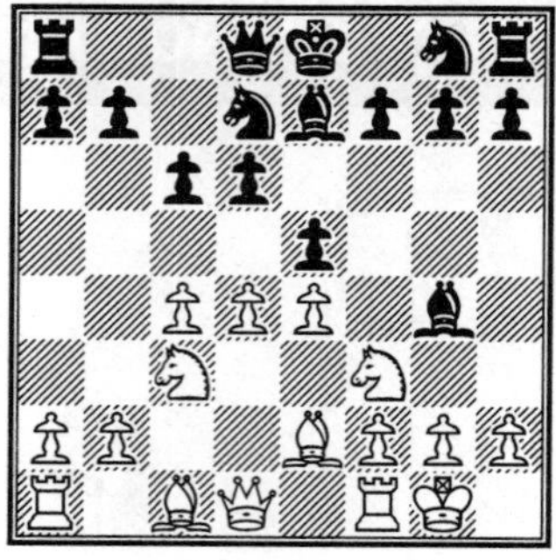

7...Ngf6. The game has now transposed to a true Old Indian position, but with the twist that Black has already developed his light-squared bishop. Speelman noted that it was difficult to come up with a good strategy here, so he fakes it. **8.Rb1** "I decided to wait whilst kidding Black that b4 is good - I don't think that it is very special." wrote Speelman, who noted that 8...a5 was by no means necessary. **8...0–0; 9.Re1 Re8.**

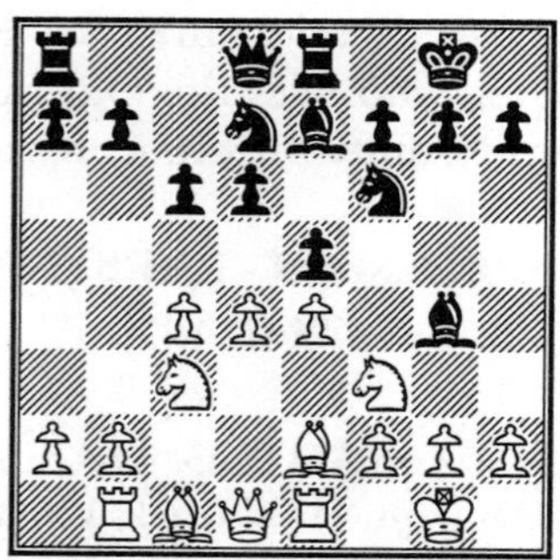

Now Speelman decides that an exchange of light-squared bishops would work to his advantage, so after developing the Bc1 he extends the standard invitation. **10.Be3 Bh5.** Larsen wants to keep his options open. **11.Nd2 Bg6!** The pin on the pawn at e4 gives rise to possible scenarios for a d6-d5 break, so Speelman wisely closes the center. **12.d5! a6; 13.b4 h5.** Larsen, who hates passive play, realizes that his has no chances to achieve anything on the queenside, and so he makes a threatening gesture on the other wing. **14.a4 h4?!** It turns out that by ceding g4 to White, Black gets into serious difficulties later in the game. **15.h3 Qc7; 16.Rb3 a5?!** A quiet waiting move like shifting a rook to b8 would have been preferable. **17.b5.**

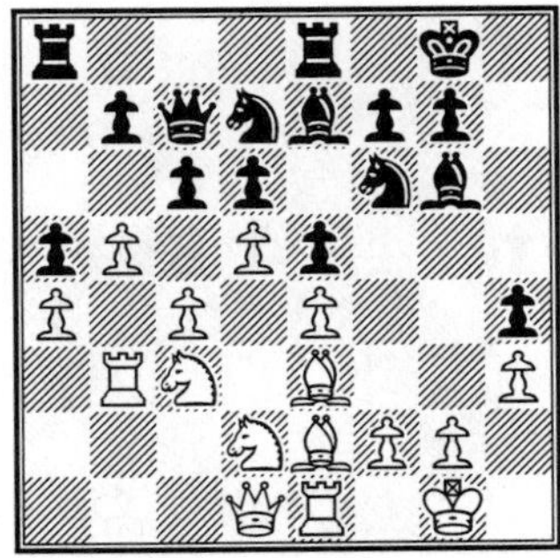

A critical position. One might think that it makes no difference whether the capture is made at c5 or d5, but it does. **17...cxd5?!; 18.Nxd5! Nxd5; 19.cxd5.** The elimination of a pair of knights would seem to help Black, who now has a little more room to maneuver. But in addition in giving White easier access to the c-file, it allows White to use the g4-square. **19...Rec8; 20.Bg4!** And now the advance of the h-pawn comes back to haunt Black. The Nd7 can no longer leap to c5 without wasting more time, but Black has no better plan. **20...Rf8; 21.Qc1.**

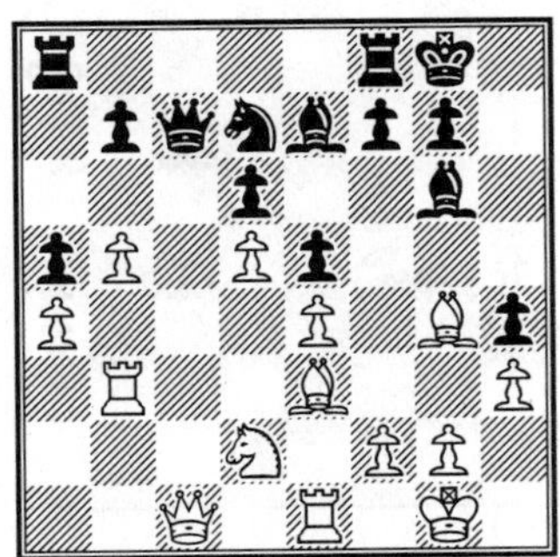

Now moving a rook to c8 loses material after the exchange of queens and b5-b6, so Black must allow White a passed pawn. **21...Nc5; 22.Bxc5 dxc5.** The plan now is to nail down the queenside and then continue to exploit the light squares on the h3-c8 diagonal, the theme that runs throughout the game. White's next move prevents the consolidating b7-b6. **23.b6! Qd8; 24.Nc4.** Black's position is hopeless, so he introduces some tactical complications. **24...Bxe4; 25.Rxe4 f5; 26.Bxf5.** In keeping with the general strategy. 26.d6 Bg5; 27.Qd1 fxe4; 28.Qd5+ Kh8; 29.Nxe5 would have been more effective, as suggested by Seirawan. **26...Rxf5; 27.d6 Bf6; 28.Qd1 Qd7.**

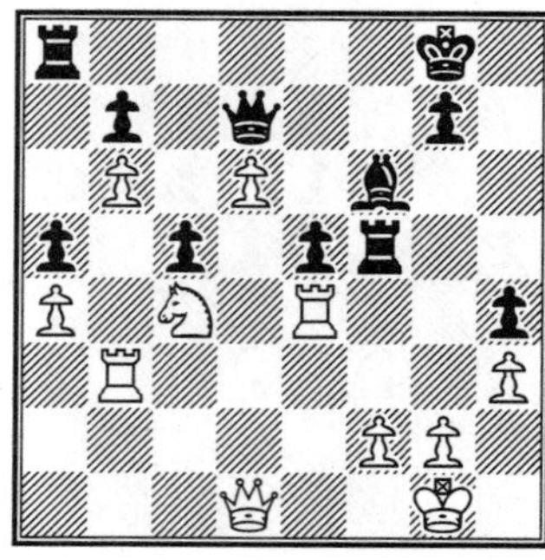

29.Qg4! Rd8. 29...Qxa4; 30.Ra3 Qd7; 31.Ne3. **30.Rb5.** The result of White's correct decision at move 23. **30...Qc8; 31.Rxa5 Rf4.** The threat was Ra8! **32.Qxc8 Rxc8; 33.Rxf4 exf4; 34.Ra7.** The b-pawn falls and the game ends quickly. **34...Re8.** 34...Rb8; 35.a5 Kf7; 36.Rxb7+!! Rxb7; 37.a6 and there is no stopping the pawns. **35.Rxb7 Kh7.** And now White exploits the theme of the previous note to bring the game to a brilliant conclusion.

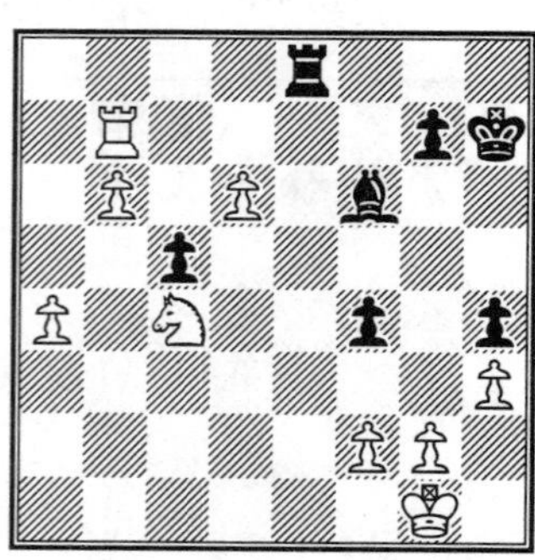

36.Re7! and Black resigned because of 36...Bxe7; 37.dxe7 Rxe7; 38 a5 etc. **White won.**

FANTASY VARIATION

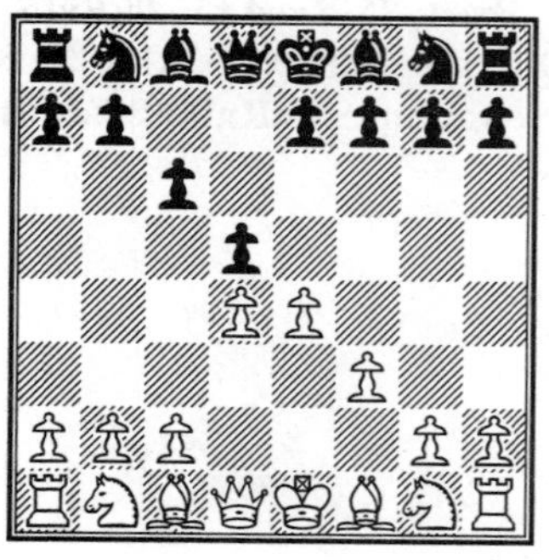

1.e4	**c6**
2.d4	**d5**
3.f3	

The **Fantasy Variation** was used at the turn of the century by Maroczy, and although it has never gotten the respect its results would merit, remains very much a viable system for White. It is also known as the **Maroczy Variation.**

There are several ideas behind the advance of the f-pawn. First of all, it supports the e4 square, but there is a cunning additional idea. If Black captures at e4, White will not necessarily recapture, but may instead continue development, leading to gambit play similar (or even transposing) to the Blackmar-Diemer Gambit. It is interesting that the very lines suggested in the 1980s, where Black captures at e4 and follows with ...e5, are now considered very risky.

The oldest line, where Black solidly defends with ...e6, was criticized for many years, but is now considered one of the most reliable defenses! A quite different reaction is 3...g6, leading to positions from the Gurgenidze Defense. This, too, is fully acceptable for Black.

(114) SMYSLOV - GEREBEN [B12]
Moscow vs. Budapest, 1949

1.e4 c6; 2.d4 d5; 3.f3 e6.

3...dxe4; 4.fxe4 e5; 5.Nf3 is best met by 5...Be6 (5...exd4; 6.Bc4 f6; 7.0–0 Bg4; 8.e5 gave White sufficient compensation for the pawn in Maroczy-Cohn, London 1899.) 6.c3 Nf6; 7.Bd3 Nbd7; 8.0–0 Bd6; 9.Kh1 Qe7; 10.Be3 Bc7; 11.Nbd2 0–0; 12.Bg5 h6; 13.Bh4 Kh8; 14.Qe2 Rg8; 15.c4 Rad8; 16.d5 Bg4; 17.h3 g5; 18.hxg4 gxh4; 19.Nxh4 Nxg4; 20.Nf5 Qg5; 21.Nf3 Qh5+; 22.N3h4 Rg5; 23.g3 Bb6; 24.Rf3 Rdg8; 25.Kg2 Bc5; 26.Rh1 Nf8; 27.Nxh6 Qxh6; 28.Nf5 Qxh1+; 29.Kxh1 Rh5+; 30.Nh4 Ng6; 31.Rf5 Nf4; 32.Rxh5+ Nxh5; 33.Nf5 Nf2+; 34.Kh2 Ng4+ was the exciting conclusion to Zelkind-Schiller, Pan American Intercollegiate Championship 1986. A nervous encounter in a critical team competition, this draw helped propel the University of Chicago to the Pan American Championship.

3...g6; 4.Nc3 Bg7; 5.Be3 Qb6; 6.Qd2 Qxb2; 7.Rb1 Qa3; 8.exd5 Nf6; 9.dxc6 bxc6; 10.Bd3 Nbd7; 11.Nge2 0–0; 12.0–0 proved solid for Black in Adams-Leko, Tilburg 1996.

4.Be3 dxe4. Black accepts the gambit, which is not the safest path. 4...Nf6; 5.Nd2 c5 Capturing at f3 would transpose below. 6.dxc5 Nc6; 7.c3 e5; 8.exd5 Nxd5; 9.Bf2 Be6; 10.Qa4 Be7; 11.h4 0–0; 12.Nh3 f6; 13.0–0–0 Qc7; 14.Bd3 Kh8; 15.g4 b6; 16.Ne4 bxc5; 17.Nxc5 Bxc5; 18.Bxc5. Black has some compensation for the pawn, but White's kingside attack is just as dangerous as Black's queenside attack, Conquest-Pinkus, Reykjavik 1996. **5.Nd2 exf3; 6.Ngxf3 Nf6; 7.Nc4 Nd5.** The knight takes up a nice post, but Black should be concerned with developing some of the other pieces! 7...Be7; 8.Bd3 Nd5; 9.Bd2 transposes.

8.Bd2 Be7; 9.Bd3 Bh4+? A critical mistake. The check achieves nothing more than a loss of time. 9...Bf6 is the most logical move, and Black has a solid position. Still, White has sufficient compensation for the pawn. 9...c5; 10.0–0 Nd7; 11.Nce5 gave White the better game in Rubens-Rause, Latvian Championship 1985. **10.g3 Bb6; 11. Qe2 a5; 12.a3 0-0.**

Bf6 Bf6:;

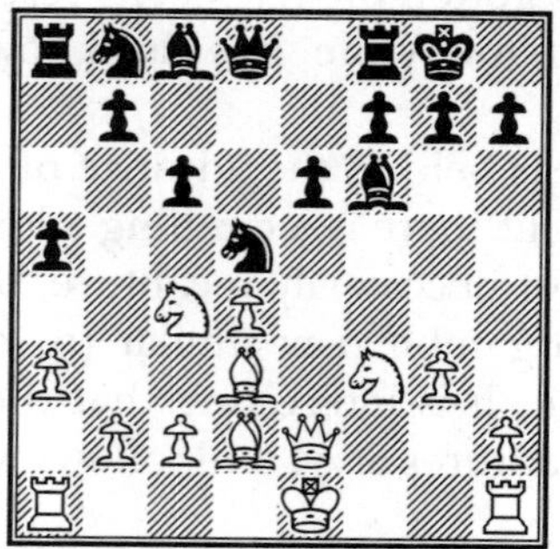

10.g3 Bf6; 11.Qe2 a5; 12.a3 0–0;13.h4! Be7. 13...Nd7; 14.Bxh7+!! Kxh7; 15.Ng5+ Bxg5; 16.hxg5+ Kg8; 17.Qh5 and White wins. **14.Ng5.** Now the sacrifice would fail: 14.Bxh7+ Kxh7; 15.Ng5+ Kg8; 16.Qh5 Nf6 and Black defends. **14...Nf6; 15.Ne5 b5.** 15...Qxd4 gives White a strong attack after 16.Bc3! Qc5; 17.Rf1 h6; 18.Rxf6!!

A) 18...Bxf6; 19.Ne4 (19.Qe4 g6; 20.Bd4 Qd6; 21.Ngxf7 Rxf7; 22.Qxg6+ Rg7; 23.Qxf6 Nd7) 19...Qe7; 20.Nxf6+ gxf6; 21.Qe4 f5; 22.Qf4 and White's attack will break though.

B) 18...gxf6; 19.Ne4 Qg1+; 20.Kd2 Qxa1; 21.Qg4+ Kh8; 22.Nxf6 Bxf6; 23.Qe4 and Black cannot avoid mate! **16.Rf1 h6.**

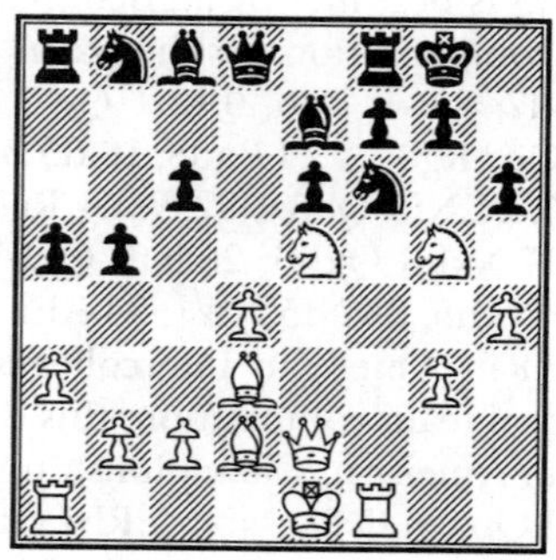

17.Rxf6! The typical sacrifice works here, as well. **17...gxf6; 18.Qh5 fxg5; 19.Qxh6.** Now all White has to do is open the h-file and bring the rook there. This is not difficult to achieve. **19...f5; 20.Qg6+ Kh8; 21.hxg5 Bxa3; 22.Ke2 Qd5; 23.Nf3. White won.**

ADVANCE VARIATION

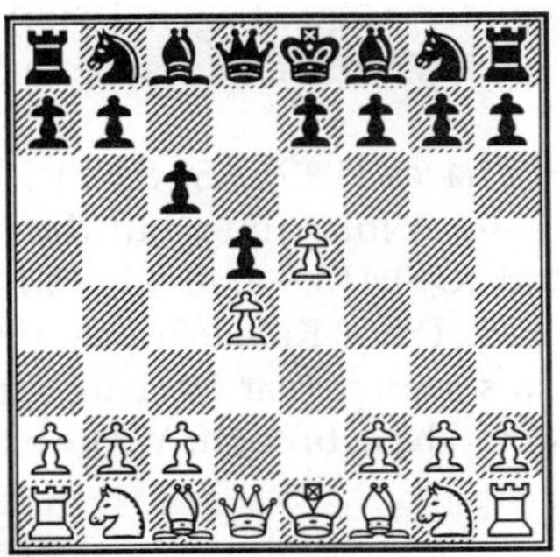

1.e4	c6
2.d4	d5
3.e5	

The **Advance Variation** gains space but commits White to an inflexible pawn formation. Black almost always replies 3...Bf5, so that the light squares can be sealed with ...e6. A later ...c5 will try to undermine White's pawn center. White can choose from among several plans. Simple development, with Nf3, Be2 and kingside castling, leads to a quiet game with a lot of maneuvering.

At the other extreme we have the variation which rose to prominence in the hands of John van der Wiel of the Netherlands, a top theoretician who has contributed new ideas in many different openings. In the early 1980s this approach, with 4.Nc3 and 5.g4, was all the rage, and it still has an entusiastic following.

(115) VAN DER WIEL - TIMMAN [B12]

Wijk aan Zee, 1982

1.e4 c6; 2.d4 d5; 3.e5 Bf5; 4.Nc3 e6; 5.g4.

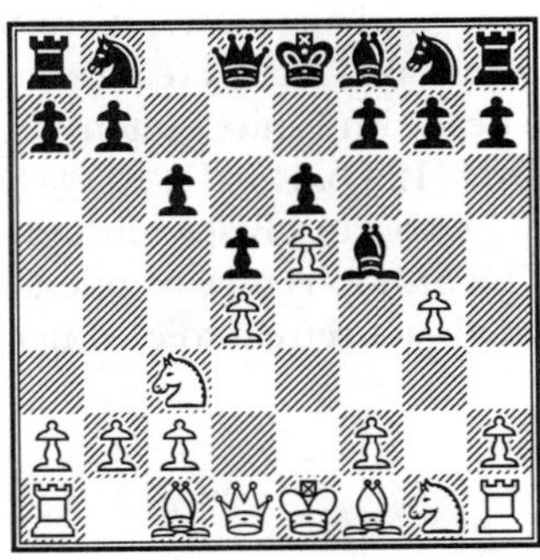

This is the starting position of the Van der Wiel Attack, which soared in popularity in the 1980s, partly due to his success in this game. **5...Bg6; 6.Nge2.** The future of the knight lies at f4 or g3, as circumstances dictate. **6...c5.** This is one of many approaches which have been tried by Black.

6...Bb4; 7.h4 Be4; 8.Rh3 is better for White, Vasyukov-Razuvayev, Soviet Union 1981. 6...Be7; 7.Be3 Nd7; 8.Qd2 h5; 9.Nf4! hxg4; 10.Nxg6 fxg6; 11.Bd3 is better for White, Kamsky-Miles, New York 1989. 6...f6; 7.h4 fxe5; 8.h5 Bf7; 9.dxe5 Nd7 (9...Bb4 led to complicated play in Westerinen-Groszpeter, Copenhagen 1988.) 10.f4 Qb6; 11.Nd4 0-0-0 12.a3 c5; 13.Nf3 Ne7; 14.b4! gave White the initiative in Marjanovic-Campora, Nis 1985.

7.Be3. A common alternative is 7.h4!? 7.h4 cxd4 (7...h5; 8.Nf4 Bh7; 9.Nxh5 cxd4 10.Qxd4 Nc6; 11.Bb5 has been around for a long time, but the most recent examples favor Black, e.g., 11...Nge7; 12.Bh6 Rg8!; 13.0-0-0 a6; 14.Bxc6+ Nxc6; 15.Qf4 Qa5 with dangerous counterplay for Black, David-Kallai, France 1996.) 8.Nxd4 h5; 9.f4! hxg4; 10.Bb5+ Nd7; 11.f5! Rxh4 was seen a year later in Van der Wiel-Speelman, Wijk aan Zee 1983. Here 12.Rf1 would have brought White a clear advantage. **7...Nc6.**

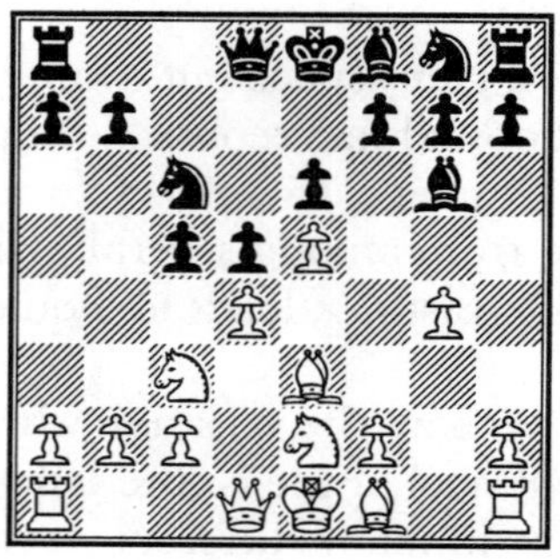

7...Nd7; 8.dxc5 leaves the knight somewhat misplaced at either d7 or c5. **8.dxc5.** This move seems anti-positional, since the pawn at e5 is weak and Black's d-pawn will be permitted to advance. Normally, such captures are only made when Black has no e-pawn at e7 or e6, in which case the Black d-pawn becomes isolated. Van der Wiel's insight was that this position is an exception to the rule. The bishop at g6 is too far from the queenside to support any offensive or defensive operations, and the pressure at c2 is not that significant, as pointed out long ago by Boleslavsky.

8...Nxe5; 9.Nd4. 9.Nf4 is a good alternative from Shabalov-Adianto, New York Open 1993. **9...a6?!** This is a mistake. Black create serious holes on the queenside, but more importantly fails to deal with White's intention to advance the f-pawn to f5. **10.f4 Nc4.** 10...Nc6; 11.f5 Nxd4; 12.Qxd4 exf5; 13.Qa4+ is clearly better for White, since 13...Qd7 can be met by 14.Bb5 and Black must give up the exchange. **11.Bxc4 dxc4; 12.f5! exf5; 13.gxf5.** The bishop is now trapped. **13...Qe7; 14.Kd2!** The king is perfectly safe here, and can always retreat to c1 if necessary. **14...0-0-0; 15.fxg6.**

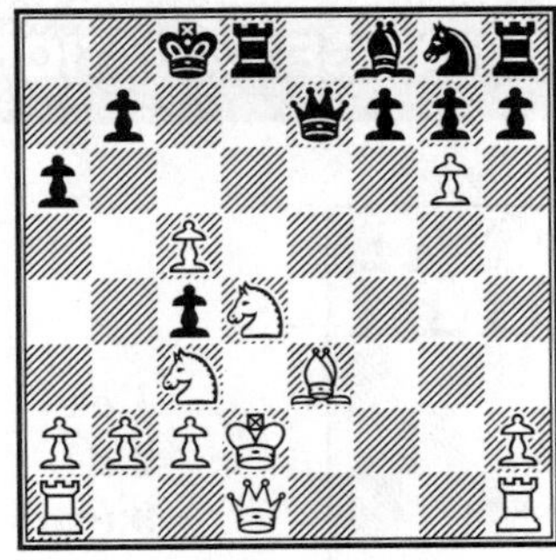

Here Black must try centralizing the queen. **15...hxg6?** 15...Qe5; 16.gxf7 Nh6; 17.Nce2 Nf5; 18.Qg1! and the knight at d4 has sufficient defense. **16.Qg4+.** Black has no defense now. **16...f5.** 16...Rd7; 17.Na4 and the weakness at b6 brings ruin. 16...Kb8; 17.Rhe1 Nf6; 18.Bf4+ Ka7; 19.Rxe7 Nxg4 (19...Rxd4+; 20.Ke3 Nxg4+; 21.Kxd4 Bxe7; 22.Kxc4 and White is a better in the endgame, since the queenside pawns can advance quickly. Black must avoid 22...Nxh2??; 23.Rh1 and White wins.) 20.Rxb7+ Kxb7; 21.c6+ Kc8; 22.Nce2 Nxh2; 23.Kc3 Ng4; 24.Kxc4 and White has more than enough compensation for the exchange. **17.Qxg6 Qe5.** Better late than never. **18.Raf1! Bxc5.** It looks as though Black's pressure at d4 gives him the initiative, but White has a killer move. **19.Rxf5.**

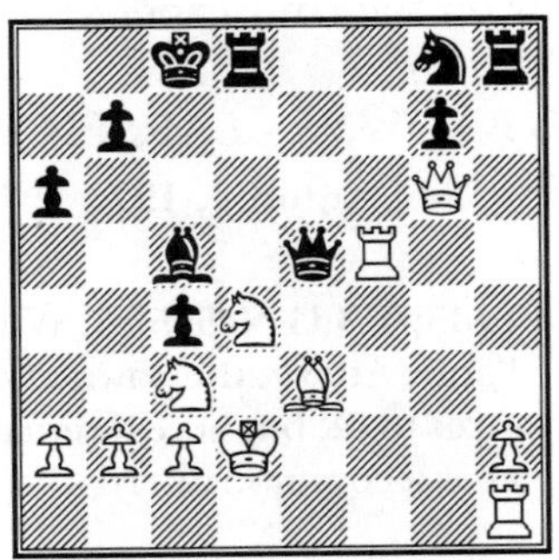

19...Rxh2+. 19...Rxd4+; 20.Bxd4 Qxd4+; 21.Kc1 Ne7; 22.Qe6+ Kb8; 23.Rff1 and Black has no compensation for the exchange. **20.Rxh2 Qxh2+; 21.Kc1 Qh1+; 22.Nd1.** The White king is safe. **22...Bd6.** 22...Bxd4; 23.Qe6+ Kb8; 24.Bxd4 Rxd4; 25.Qe5+ wins easily. **23.Qe6+ Kb8; 24.Rd5 Nf6; 25.Rxd6 Re8; 26.Qxc4 Ng4; 27.Bf4 Ka8; 28.Rxa6+. White won.**

EXCHANGE VARIATION

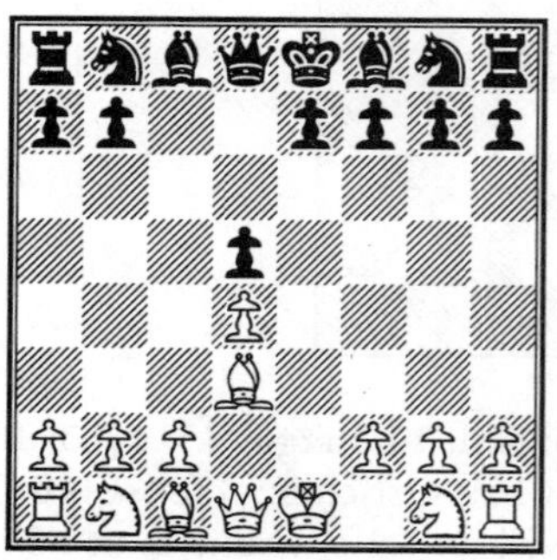

1.e4 c6
2.d4 d5
3.exd5 cxd5
4.Bd3

In the **Exchange Variation** the bishop takes up an active position. Black cannot do likewise, because his cleric remains locked in behind the barrier of pawns. The simplicity of the position, similar to that of the Advance Variation with 3...Bf5; 4.Nf3, appeals to some players who do not like to introduce complications early in the game. The dull symmetry does not prevent volcanic eruptions later in the game, especially if Black's concentration slips and weaknesses start to appear on the landscape.

(116) BROWNE - LARSEN [B13]
San Antonio, 1972

1.e4 c6; 2.d4 d5; 3.exd5 cxd5; 4.Bd3 Nc6; 5.c3. White is content to solidify the position in the center. In the Panov Attack, the pawn at d5 is an immediate target of the White c-pawn, which advances to c4, but here it remains at the more modest post on c3. **5...Nf6; 6.Bf4 Bg4.** 6...g6 is a common alternative which is also acceptable for Black.

7.Qb3! Whenever Black develops his light-squared bishop, the b7-pawn becomes weak. **7...Qc8; 8.Nd2 e6; 9.Ngf3 Be7.** 9...Nh5? is a poor idea, because Black has not completed his development yet. 10.Be3 Bd6; 11.Ne5! is a powerful pawn sacrifice, as the following variations show: 11...Bxe5 (11...Nxe5; 12.dxe5 Bxe5; 13.Qa4+ is hopeless for Black.) 12.dxe5 Nxe5 (12...0–0; 13.h3 Nxe5; 14.Bxh7+! Kxh7; 15.hxg4 also wins for White.) 13.Bb5+ Kf8; 14.f3 Bf5; 15.g4 and White has a sizable advantage. **10.0–0 0–0.**

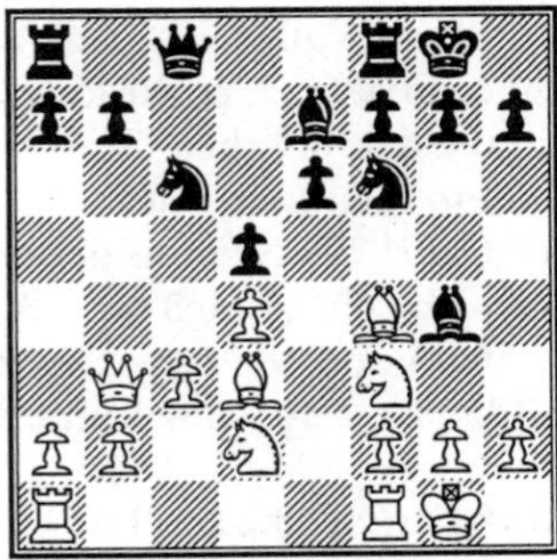

White has completed his development and is ready to take the initiative. **11.Ne5 Bh5.** 11...Nxe5; 12.dxe5 Nd7; 13.Qc2 g6; 14.h3 Bf5; 15.Bxf5 gxf5; 16.Bh6 and White has very good prospects for an effective kingside attack, since Black's forces are uncoordinated and cannot quickly come to the defense of their monarch. **12.Qc2.**

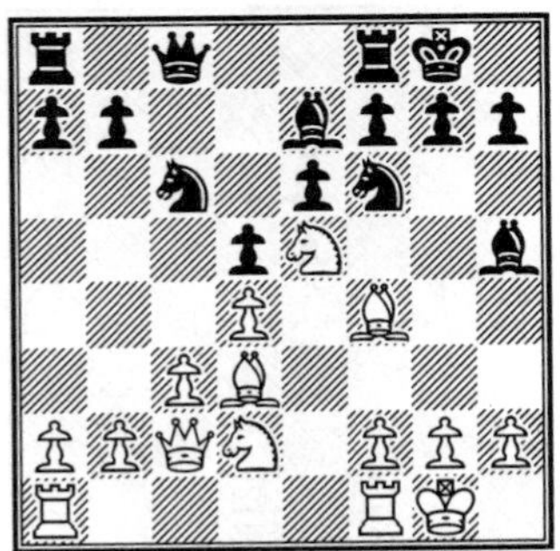

An important position, which Black must handle with great care. **12...Bg6?** A logical move, but one which allows White to obtain a clear positional edge. A decade later, Black found a more resistant plan: 12...Bd6!; 13.Nxc6 Qxc6; 14.Be5 Bg6 and now that White can no longer capture this piece with his knight, Black has a playable game, Timman-Huebner, Bugojno 1982. **13.Nxg6 hxg6; 14.Nf3.** Notice that White now has complete control of e5. **14...Nh5; 15.Be3 Qc7.** The queen was useless at c8, and now takes a role in the discussion of the dark squares.

16.g3! Browne recognizes the importance of the dark-squares, and in particular f4. The weakening of the light-squares is not so important, because Black has no pieces with which to exploit it. **16...Rfc8?!** A natural move, but Browne claims that the rooks would have functioned more appropriately on the a- and b-files, supporting a pawn storm which might have taken some of the heat off the kingside. **17.Qe2.** White has achieved a dominating position.

17...a6?! Evidently Larsen simply failed to appreciate the rapidity of White's attack. This is much too slow. One must admit, though, that White's position is already approaching domination. **18.Rae1 Re8; 19.Bc1!** An instructive pair of moves. White develops potential energy along the e-file. The idea is to play Ne5 and then go after the wayward enemy knight at h5. **19...Nf6; 20.Ng5!** Now that the diagonal is closed, this is possible. **20...Bd6; 21.f4.** Putting an end to any thoughts of advancing the e-pawn.

21...Nd7; 22.Nf3. White could have started advancing the h-pawn here instead. **22...Nf8; 23.Ne5.** White has a strategically won game here. There is simply no way for the Black pieces to coordinate in defense of the king. **23...Ne7; 24.Kg2 f6; 25.Nf3 Rab8; 26.h4 b5.** Rather late in the day, but there is no counterplay elsewhere. **27.a3!** The Grandmasters know when to take time out for a little preventative medicine. **27...Nc6; 28.Qf2 Ne7; 29.Qe2 Qc6?!** 29...Nc6 was better, but Browne showed that it too would have led to defeat: 30.Rh1 e5; 31.fxe5 fxe5; 32.dxe5 Nxe5; 33.Nxe5 Rxe5; 34.Qf3 Qb7; 35.Rxe5 Bxe5; 36.h5 and the attack is unstoppable, e.g., 36...Bxc3; 37.hxg6 d4; 38.Be4 Qe7; 39.Bd5+ Ne6; 40.Rh8+ Kxh8; 41.Qh5+ Kg8; 42.Qh7+ Kf8; 43.Qh8#.

30.Rh1 a5; 31.h5 b4; 32.cxb4 axb4; 33.a4! White is planning to plant a bishop at b5. **33...Qxa4; 34.Nh4 gxh5.** There is nothing better: 34...g5; 35.fxg5 Nf5; 36.Nxf5 exf5; 37.Qf3 and the pawns on the light squares are too weak. 34...Nf5; 35.hxg6 Nxd4; 36.Qh5 and the Black king is ready to topple. 34...e5; 35.fxe5 fxe5; 36.dxe5 Nc6; 37.hxg6 Rxe5; 38.Qf3+- with both f7 and d5 as potential targets. **35.Qxh5 Rec8; 36.f5!**

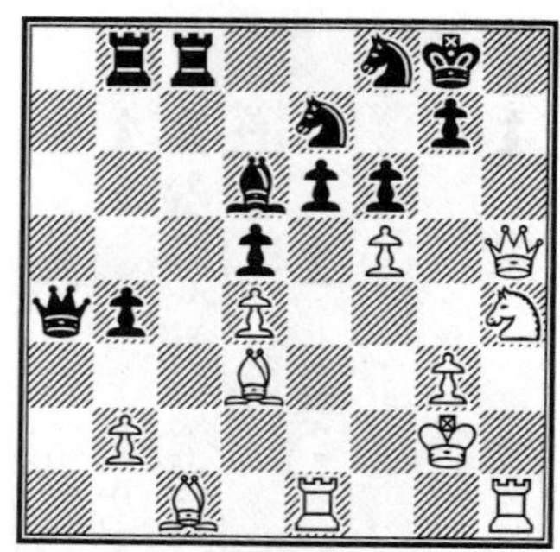

36...Qb3?! Not the most resistant, but Black is lost anyway. **37.fxe6 Nxe6.** 37...Qxd3 runs into 38.Qh8+!! Kxh8; 39.Ng6+ Kg8; 40.Rh8#. **38.Qh7+ Kf7; 39.Qh5+ Kf8.** 39...Kg8; 40.Rxe6 Qxd3; 41.Rxd6 Rc2+; 42.Kh3 and White wins. **40.Ng6+ Ke8; 41.Rxe6.** This was the sealed move, but the resumption of the game didn't take long. **41...Kd7; 42.Rxe7+ Bxe7; 43.Qf5+. White won.**

PANOV ATTACK

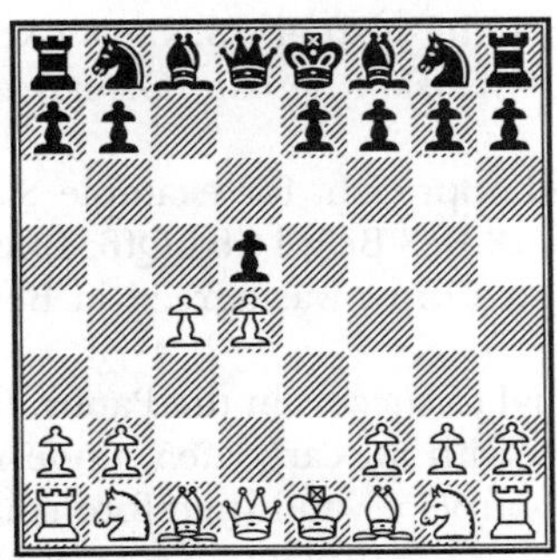

1.e4	**c6**
2.d4	**d5**
3.exd5	**cxd5**
4.c4	

The **Panov Attack** was introduced in this game. It led to widespread interest in the opening, which was explored deeply in the 1930s. The Panov remains one of the most principled reactions to the Caro Kann, but Black is considered to have sufficient defensive resources.

There are now three branches to the Panov. The most common positions arise after 5...e6, but that is largely due to the transpositional possibilities leading into the Panov from such diverse openings as the Nimzo-Indian, Tarrasch, English etc. The fianchetto defense with 5...g6 is a popular alternative, usually leading to complex endgames. For a middlegame fight, however, 5...Nc6 remains the leading choice.

(117) PANOV - MUDROV [B13]

Moscow Championship, 1929

1.e4 c6; 2.d4 d5; 3.exd5 cxd5; 4.c4 Nf6; 5.Nc3Nc6; 6.Nf3.

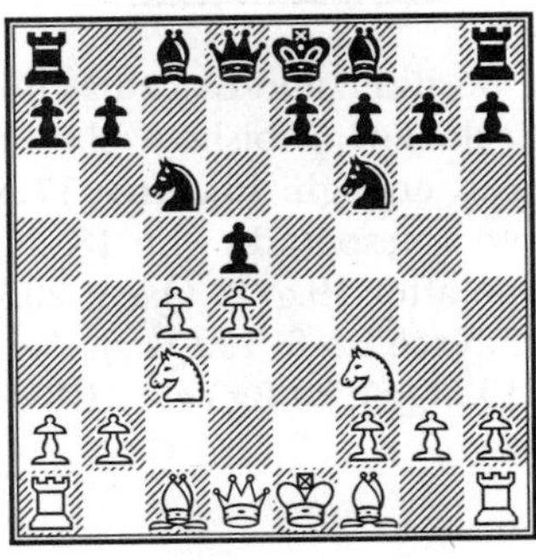

6.Bg5 Be6 is a very interesting line, developed by Tony Miles among others. 7.a3 Bg4; 8.f3 Be6; 9.c5 g6; 10.Bb5 Bg7; 11.Nge2 0–0; 12.0–0 Bf5; 13.b4 a6; 14.Ba4 h6; 15.Be3 Ne8; 16.Qd2 Kh7; 17.Ng3 e6; 18.Nge2 g5; 19.Bc2 Bxc2; 20.Qxc2+ f5; 21.Rab1 led to unclear complications in Kasparov-Dreyev, Moscow (Kremlin) 1996.

6...Bf5. It was eventually discovered that this bishop must move to g4 if Black is to count on sufficient counterplay, and that is the move seen in many recent games. Another option is 6...e6, creating a hybrid of the 5...e6 and 5...Nc6 lines. 6...e6; 7.c5 Ne4; 8.Qc2 Qa5 has been popular, but there is a challenging new approach for White in 9.a3! Be7; 10.Rb1 f5; 11.b4 Qc7; 12.b5 Nxd4!? 13.Nxd4 Bxc5; 14.Nxe4 fxe4; 15.b6! and White went on to win in Gdanski-Khenkin, Osterskars Havsbad 1995.

6...Bg4; 7.cxd5 Nxd5; 8.Qb3 is a sound approach, for example 8...Nb6; 9.d5 Bxf3; 10.gxf3 Nd4; 11.Qd1 e5; 12.dxe6 fxe6; 13.Be3 Bc5; 14.b4 Qf6; 15.bxc5 Nxf3+; 16.Ke2 0–0; 17.cxb6 Rad8; 18.Qc2 Nd4+ and a draw was agreed in Benjamin-Oll, New York (Marshall) 1995.

7.c5! The timing of this advance is crucial to success in the Panov. Under most circumstances Black can react in the center with an early ...e5, undermining the White pawns. In the present case, White controls e5 and therefore counterplay is harder to come by. **7...e6; 8.Bb5.** Now White has the threat of Ne5, creating unbearable pressure at c6. Therefore Black breaks the pin.

8...Nd7. 8...Be7; 9.Ne5 Qc7; 10.Qa4 Rc8; 11.Qxa7 and Black loses material. **9.Bf4 Be7; 10.h3 0–0; 11.0–0 a6; 12.Ba4 Rc8?!** 12...Bf6 would have been more helpful, keeping an eye on the e5 square. **13.Qe2 Re8; 14.Rfe1 Nf8.** 14...Bf6 comes too late now: 15.Bxc6 Rxc6; 16.Nxd5! exd5; 17.Qxe8+ Qxe8; 18.Rxe8+ Nf8; 19.Bd6 and White wins. **15.Rad1 Ng6; 16.Bh2.**

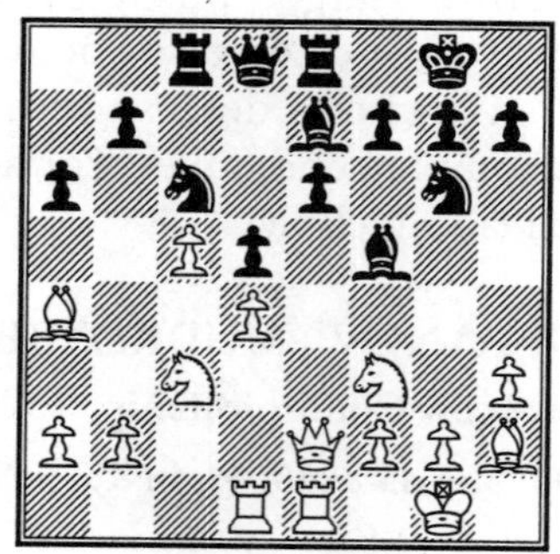

White has a lock on the position, and Black has no source of counterplay. The threat is simply g4, harassing the enemy bishop. Black tries to get a kingside attack going, but White repels it easily enough. **16...Nh4; 17.Ne5 Bf8.** 17...Nxe5; 18.Bxe8 lets Black turn the knight into a desperado with 18...Nef3+! but in any case White emerges with the better game after 19.gxf3 Qxe8; 20.Kh1 Bxh3; 21.Rg1 and it is Black who is under attack. **18.Nxc6 bxc6; 19.Qxa6.** Pawns are falling and the result of the game is already clear. **19...Qg5; 20.Bg3 e5; 21.Bxc6 Qh6; 22.Bb7 Re6; 23.Qf1 Bxh3; 24.Bxh4. White won.**

KARPOV VARIATION

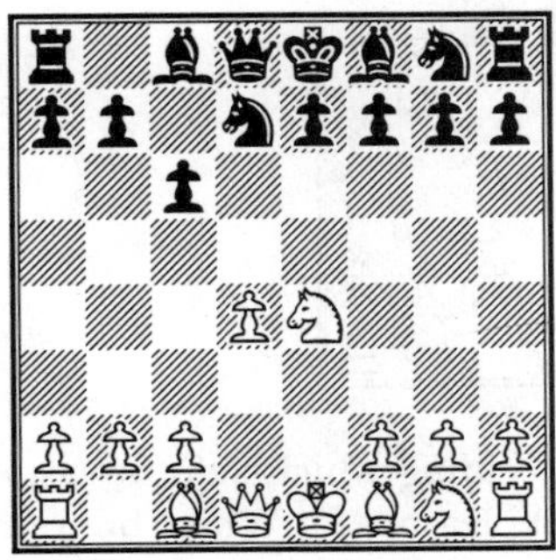

1.e4 c6
2.d4 d5
3.Nc3 dxe4
4.Nxe4 Nd7

This is the Filip-Flohr-Petrosian-Smyslov-Karpov Variation! That gives some idea of the appeal of this quiet move to positional players. Black uses this awkwardly placed knight to prepare Ng8-f6, when a White capture will not cause Black to double the kingside pawns. This variation has supplanted 4...Bf5 in tournament play, which still baffles me somewhat, unsurprisingly since I am a strong partisan of the ...Bf5 defense. The ...Nd7 system is a solid defense, but basically a counterpunching one, and patience is required to execute the plans available to Black.

(118) KAMSKY - KARPOV [B17]
Dortmund, 1993

1.e4 c6; 2.d4 d5; 3.Nd2 dxe4; 4.Nxe4 Nd7; 5.Ng5. This is the most aggressive reply and the one which is most often seen these days. Strangely, it was considered a minor option as recently as a decade ago. 5.Bc4 Ngf6; 6.Ng5 e6; 7.Qe2 Nb6 is the other main line. Karpov got a good position with it against Topalov at Belgrade 1995: 8.Bd3 h6; 9.N5f3 c5; 10.dxc5 Bxc5; 11.Ne5 Nbd7; 12.Ngf3 Qc7; 13.Bf4 Bb4+; 14.Nd2 Bxd2+; 15.Kxd2 0–0; 16.Rhd1 Nc5; 17.Ke1 Nd5; 18.Bg3 Nxd3+; 19.Rxd3 b5; 20.a4 Ba6!

5...Ngf6; 6.Bd3 e6; 7.N1f3 Bd6. Black has several options here, and 7...h6 and 7...Be7 are often seen. Karpov's rival Garry Kasparov got into deep trouble against the IBM Deep Blue computer when he dared the complications of 7...h6; 8.Nxe6 Qe7; 9.0-0 fxe6; 10.Bg6+ Kd8 and went down to a devastating defeat in just 19 moves. 11.Bf4 b5 (A dubious novelty.) 12.a4 Bb7; 13.Re1 Nd5; 14.Bg3 Kc8; 15.axb5 cxb5; 16.Qd3 Bc6; 17.Bf5! exf5; 18.Rxe7 Bxe7; 19.c4 and Black resigned in Deep Blue-Kasparov, 6th Match Game, New York 1997. In losing this game Kasparov also lost the match.

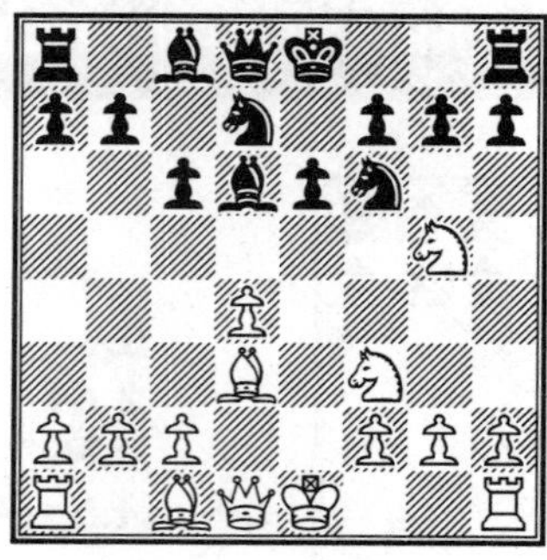

8.Qe2. White often plays this before deciding which side to castle to. **8...h6; 9.Ne4.** The removal of a pair of knights is not pleasant for White, but retreating with 9.Nh3 allows Black to attack with 9...g5. 9.Nxe6 fxe6; 10.Bg6+ Ke7 is fine for Black. **9...Nxe4; 10.Qxe4 Nf6; 11.Qh4.** Usually the queen retreats to e2, which is a somewhat safer post. Kamsky is going all-out for the win. **11...Ke7.** This move had been prepared by Karpov years in advance of this game. Black's forces are well-placed, and Karpov can contemplate a kingside attack.

12.Ne5. White sacrifices a pawn, hoping to build an attack against the exposed Black king. **12...Bxe5; 13.dxe5 Qa5+; 14.c3 Qxe5+; 15.Be3.** In return for the pawn White has the bishop pair and some potential for an attack against th Black king. **15...b6; 16.0–0–0 g5; 17.Qa4 c5; 18.Rhe1 Bd7!** The Black pawns keep the bishop on e3 at bay, and there are no discoveries to be feared. **19.Qa3 Rhd8; 20.g3 Qc7.** Overprotecting c5 against any sacrificial possibilities. **21.Bd4 Be8; 22.Kb1 Rd5.** A good move, but Karpov remarked that 22...Bc6 might be even stronger.

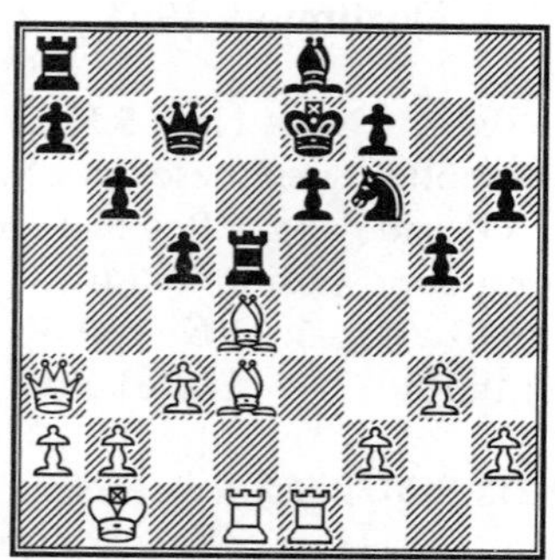

23.f4 Rad8; 24.Bc2 R5d6; 25.Bxf6+ Kxf6; 26.fxg5+ hxg5; 27.Rxd6 Rxd6. Many pieces have left the board, and White has less to show for the investment of a pawn. **28.c4 Ke7; 29.Qe3 f6; 30.h4 gxh4.** Kamsky's offer of a draw was politely refused. For Karpov, a pawn is a major advantage! **31.gxh4 Qd7; 32.Qh6 e5?**

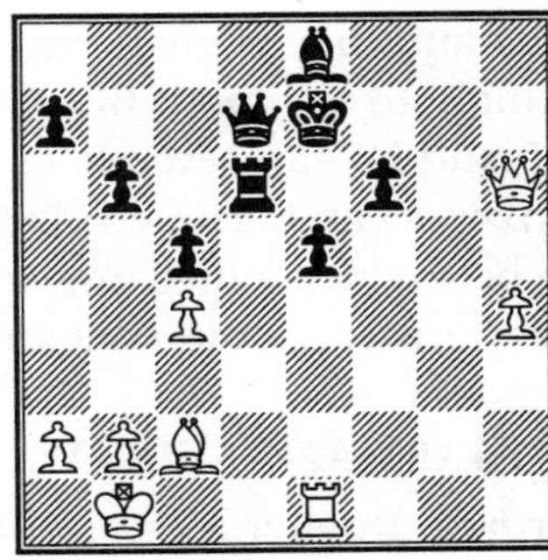

Karpov was drifting into time pressure, and missed the simple 32...Rd2! 33.Rf1 Qd4! which would have quickly put an end to the game. **33.h5 Qg4; 34.Qh7+ Kd8; 35.h6 Rd2; 36.Qf5 Qxf5; 37.Bxf5 Bd7?** A serious time pressure blunder. Kamsky could now play 38.Kc1! after which Karpov admitted that Black would be fighting for the draw, despite the extra pawn. The rook would have to retreat along the d-file, to prevent White from playing Rd1, and then the h-pawn would be hard to stop. **38.Bg6?** Kamsky returns the favor and misses his chance. **38...Rh2.** The h-pawn will no longer be a problem, and can be captured eventually.

39.h7 Ke7; 40.Bd3 Be6; 41.Rg1 f5; 42.Rg7+ Kf6; 43.Rxa7 e4! White's piece are completely out of play, and the material balance is unimportant. **44.Be2 f4; 45.b3 f3; 46.Bd1 Bf5; 47.Kc1 Bxh7; 48.Rb7 Ke5; 49.Rxb6 Rxa2. Black won.**

CLASSICAL CARO-KANN

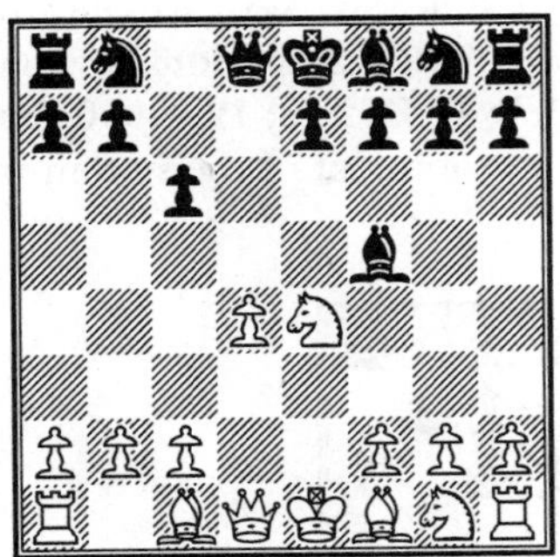

1.e4	**c6**
2.d4	**d5**
3.Nd2	**dxe4**
4.Nxe4	**Bf5**

The **Classical Caro-Kann** is one of the most solid defenses available to Black. In fact, it has been generally so successful that it became known as a "drawing variation". This is misleading, however, because although the Caro-Kann does not usually feature combinational pyrotechnics in the middlegame, it does lead to rich and complex endgames, often with knights and one or two major pieces for each side, with a large complement of pawns.

The nature of the pawn structure limits the advantage of a bishop pair, so White must find a strategy that permanently secures an advantage in space.

This is usually accomplished by harassing the Black bishop on the kingside, advancing the h-pawn to h5 and then exchanging bishops at d3. White can then aim to maneuver a knight to e5, and if Black exchanges at that square, then the twin pawns at e5 and h5 can severely cramp the kingside. In the endgame, however, these pawns can become vulnerable.

The dynamic balance between middlegame space and endgame structural weakness is the characteristic positional feature of the opening.

(119) KHALIFMAN - SEIRAWAN [B19]

Amsterdam (Donner Memorial), 1995

1.e4 c6; 2.d4 d5; 3.Nd2 dxe4; 4.Nxe4 Bf5.

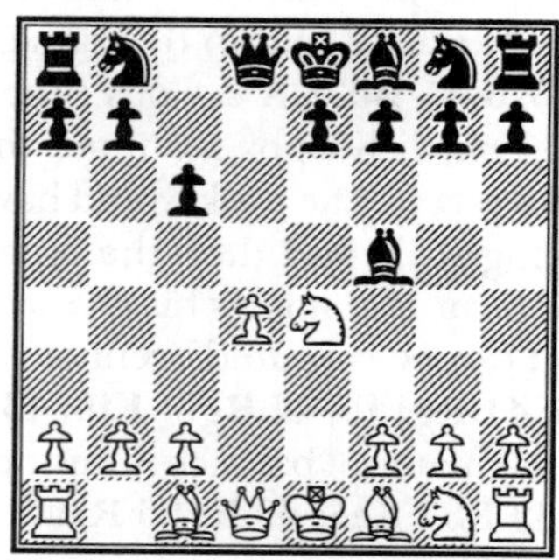

5.Ng3 Bg6; 6.h4. White carries out the first part of the plan. Black's reply is virtually forced, to make room for the bishop to retreat. **6...h6; 7.Nf3 Nd7; 8.h5!** This is one of Boris Spassky's most significant contributions to opening theory. Although the plan was by no means new at the time, Spassky gave the advance of the h-pawn a boost by adopting it in his 1966 World Championship match against Petrosian. **8...Bh7; 9.Bd3 Bxd3; 10.Qxd3 Qc7; 11.Bd2 e6; 12.0-0-0 Bd6.** 12...Ngf6 is the older line. Yasser Seirawan has been a proponent of the system with an early ...Bd6.

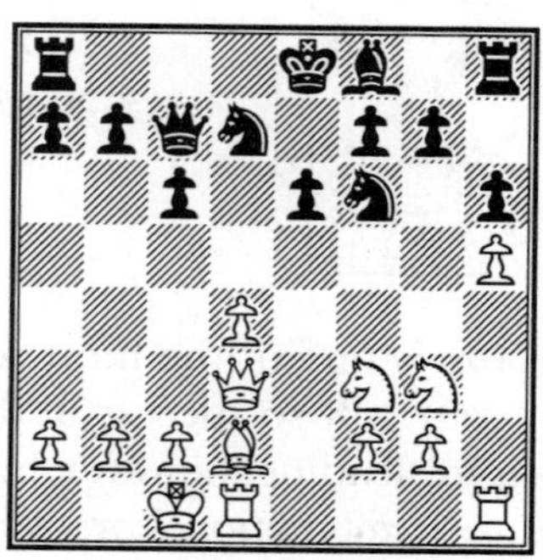

13.Qe2 is intended to support a later Ne5. (13.Ne4 0-0-0; 14.g3 Nxe4; 15.Qxe4 Nf6; 16.Qe2 Bd6; 17.Kb1 Rhe8 is a typical continuation, with an equal position, agreed drawn in a game between Sofia and Zsuzsa Polgar, Vejstrup 1989.) 13...0-0-

0; 14.Ne5 Nxe5; 15.dxe5 Nd7; 16.f4 Be7; 17.Be3 Nb6!?; 18.c4 Rxd1+; 19.Rxd1 Rd8 was equal in Keene-Schiller, Chicago 1985. Keene had prepared the position from a book by Kasparov, which did not consider 17...Nb6. 12...0–0–0 is another traditional move order.

A) 13.Qe2 Ngf6; 14.Ne5 Nxe5; 15.dxe5 Nd7 was the continuation in the 13th game of the 1966 Spassky-Petrosian match, which had previously seen only the inferior 8.Bd3?! 16.f4 Be7; 17.Ne4 Nc5; 18.Nc3 f6!; 19.exf6 Bxf6; 20.Qc4! Qb6; 21.b4 Na6; 22.Ne4! (22.Qxe6+?! would set White up for a combinational fall: 22...Kb8; 23.a3 Rxd2!; 24.Kxd2 Qd4+; 25.Ke2 Qxc3; 26.Rd2 Nc7; 27.Qd6 Re8+; 28.Kd1 Qa1#) 22...Nc7; 23.Rhe1 and White eventually prevailed.

B) 13.c4!? is a solid alternative, planning to shift the bishop to a more useful post at c3. 13...Ngf6; 14.Bc3!? Bd6; 15.Ne4 Bf4+; 16.Kc2 Ne5; 17.Nxe5 Bxe5; 18.Nc5 Bd6 and Black was still a bit short of equality in Bronstein-Kotov, Amsterdam (IBM) 1968.

13.Ne4 Ngf6; 14.Kb1! 14.Nxd6+ Qxd6 doesn't give White anything special: 15.Qe2 (15.Rh4?! b5; 16.Kb1 a5; 17.g4 Qd5; 18.Re1 c5! gave Black a strong initiative in Zapata-Seirawan, Wijk aan Zee 1995.) 15...b5; 16.Kb1 Qd5; 17.Rh4 a5 gave Black counterplay in Wolff-Seirawan, United States Championship 1992. 14.g3 is a logical alternative, keeping enemy pieces off of the f4-square. 14...b5!

A) 15.Ba5 Qxa5; 16.Nxd6+ Ke7; 17.Nxf7 Kxf7; 18.Ne5+ Kg8; 19.Qg6 Qxa2; 20.Qf7+ Kh7 was drawn immediately in Sherzer-Seirawan, United States Championship 1992, and a couple of moves later in Spangenberg-Seirawan, Buenos Aires 1993. (20...Kh7; 21.Qg6+)

B) 15.Kb1 15...a5; 16.Nxf6+ Nxf6; 17.Ne5 Bxe5; 18.dxe5 Qxe5; 19.Bc3 Qc7 gave Black compensation for the pawn, but no more, in Chandler-Seirawan, London 1984. **14...Bf4.**

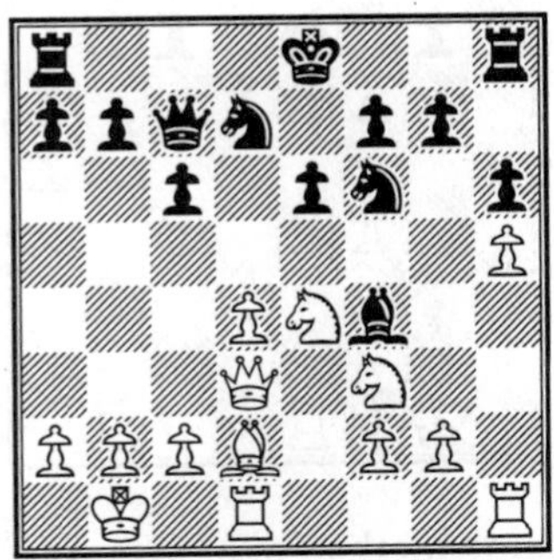

14...Nxe4; 15.Qxe4 fails to equalize after 15...0–0–0; 16.c4 c5; 17.Bc3 Arnason-Thorsteins, New York Open 1989. **15.Nxf6+.** 15.Bb4 is countered by 15...a5!; 16.Ba3 Nxe4; 17.Qxe4 Bd6; 18.Bxd6 Qxd6 with equal chances in Ivanchuk-Seirawan, Biel Interzonal 1993. **15...Nxf6.** On 15...gxf6 White plays 16.Bc3 with a better game. **16.Bxf4 Qxf4; 17.Qa3 Qc7; 18.Ne5 Qe7; 19.Qe3.** 19.Rh3 Qxa3; 20.Rxa3 Ke7! **19...Nd7; 20.Nd3! Qg5.** White can attack the Black king on either side of the board, so castling does not seem like a good idea, but this move allows White to develop a dangerous initiative. **21.f4 Qxg2; 22.Rhg1 Qd5.** 22...Qh2; 23.f5 0–0–0; 24.Nf4+!; **23.Ne5.**

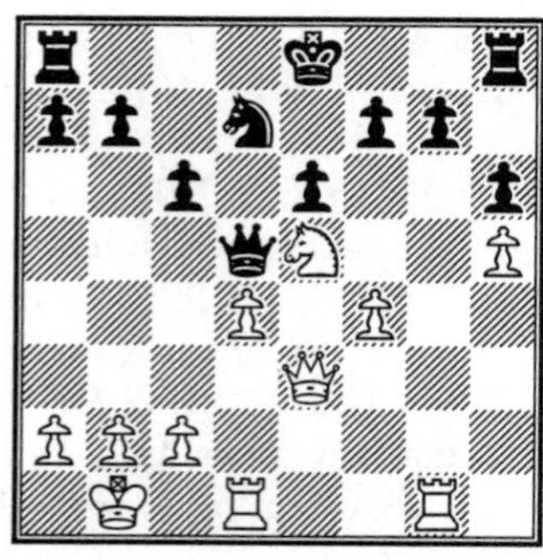

This is a critical position. Black cannot castle because of Qg3, but should the g-pawn be protected with king or rook? Or should Black just let it go? **23...Rg8.** 23...Kf8; 24.Qa3+ Kg8; 25.Qe7 Nxe5; 26.dxe5 and Blatny points out that Rxg7+!! is threatened. 23...Nf6 might give some counterplay if White simply captures the g-pawn, but there is a more powerful reply!

24.Rxg7 Rf8; 25.f5! Nxh5; 26.c4 Qd6; 27.Nxf7! Rxf7; 28.Rxf7 Kxf7; 29.Qxh6 as analyzed by Blatny, who gives the following variations which win for White. 29...Nf4 (29...Ng3; 30.Qh7+; 29...Qh2; 30.fxe6+ Kg8; 31.d5! cxd5; 32.cxd5 Rc8; 33.Qg6+ Ng7; 34.d6 Qh7; 35.Qxh7+ Kxh7; 36.d7) 30.fxe6+ Nxe6; 31.d5! cxd5; 32.cxd5 Ke7; 33.Qh4+ Ke8; 34.Qh5+ Ke7; 35.dxe6 and White wins after 35...Qxe6; 36.Qh7+ Qf7 (36...Kf8; 37.Qh8+ Qg8; 38.Rh1 Re8; 39.Qf6+ Qf7; 40.Rh8#) 37.Rd7+ Kxd7; 38.Qxf7+.

24.c4 Qd6.

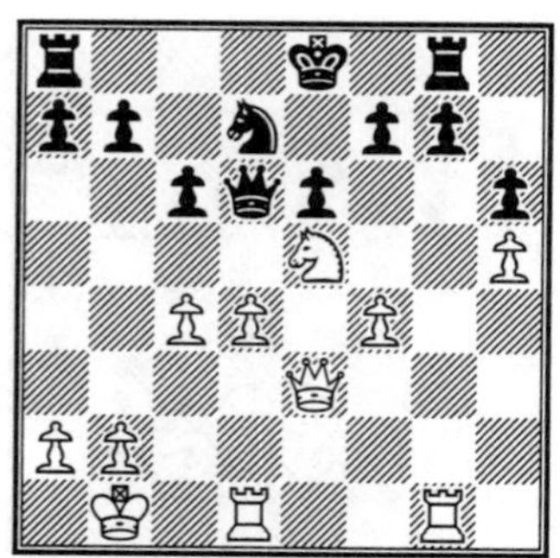

Now White uses as common method of breaking down the Caro-Kann defensive structure by playing d5! **25.d5! cxd5.** 25...Qc5 gives White the advantage as long as no exchange of queens is permitted. 26.Qb3! Qb6; 27.Qc3! Nxe5; 28.dxe6 is given by Blatny. 25...Nxe5; 26.fxe5 Qe7 and White threatens to advance the d-pawn, and also has threats of Qxh6. **26.Nxd7 Qxd7.** 26...Kxd7; 27.cxd5 exd5; 28.Qf3 Kc6; 29.Rd4! and Black's position is precarious. **27.cxd5 Rd8; 28.f5 e5; 29.Qxe5+ Qe7; 30.Qd4** and the rest is simple: **30...Kf8; 31.d6 Qf6; 32.Qc5 b6; 33.Qd5 Rh8; 34.d7 Qh4; 35.Rge1.** Black has only one defense against Re8+. **35...Kg8; 36.Re8+ Kh7; 37.Qxf7 Rhxe8; 38.Qg6+. White won.**

(120) KUPREICHIK - LOBRON [B19]

Ljubljana, 1989

1.e4 c6; 2.Nc3 d5; 3.d4 dxe4; 4.Nxe4 Bf5; 5.Ng3 Bg6; 6.h4 h6; 7.Nf3 Nd7; 8.h5 Bh7; 9.Bf4 Ngf6; 10.Bd3 Bxd3; 11.Qxd3 e6; 12.0–0–0.

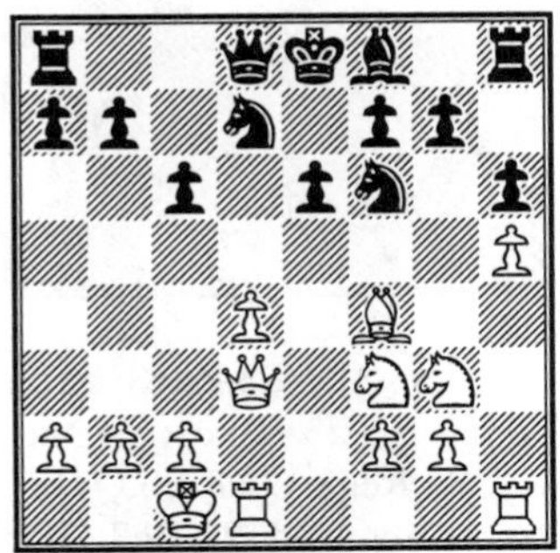

In addition to the classical plan with queenside castling for Black, there is a modern approach, spearheaded by Larsen and Lobron, which involves kingside castling and then rapid pawn advances on the queenside. **12...Be7; 13.Kb1.** 13.Qe2 0–0; 14.Rhe1 c5; 15.Nf5 cxd4!; 16.N3xd4 (16.Nxe7+ Qxe7; 17.Nxd4 is stronger.) 16...Bc5; 17.Nxh6+!? is an enterprising sacrifice. 17...gxh6; 18.Bxh6 Re8; 19.Qf3 Bf8; 20.Bg5 Rc8; 21.Kb1 Rc5; 22.Bh4 was seen in Tiviakov-Magem, Buenos Aires 1996, and here Black would stand better after the simple 22...Bg7. **13...0–0.**

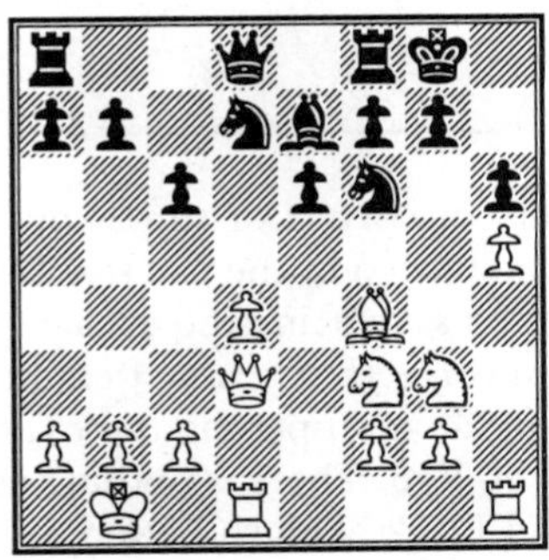

This is the newer approach from Lobron, one of the most successful employers of the Classical Caro-Kann, who knows when to push his a-pawn! **14.Ne4 Nxe4; 15.Qxe4 Nf6; 16.Qe2.** We now have a line similar to that which arises after 13.Ne4, which is not a promising line for White, though Karpov seems to think that White has an advantage here, if Black plays his queen to d5. **16...Qd5.** Evidently, Lobron disagrees. **17.Ne5 Qe4!** This queen maneuver lies at the heart of many of Black's games. In the endgame Black's chances are quite good, because the pawn at h5 is generally a liability. **18.Qd2.** 18.Qxe4; Nxe4 does not give White anything - see Thorsteins-Lobron, Reykjavik 1984. **18...Nd5.** Lobron deftly exploits the d5-square. **19.Bg3 Rfd8; 20.Rde1 Qf5.**

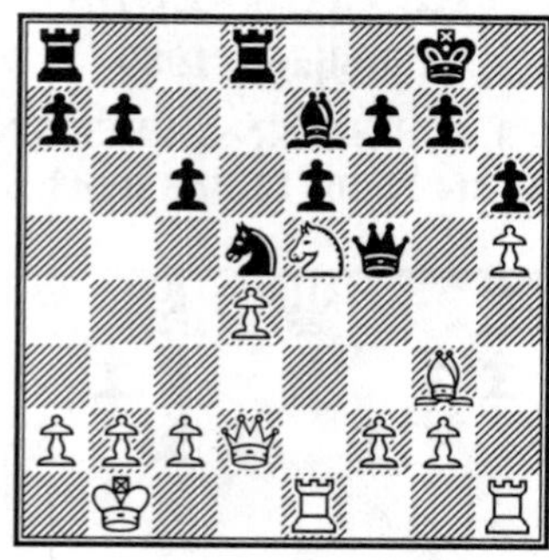

Black has achieved full equality. **21.Nd3 Rac8; 22.Be5 c5.** The thematic advance has been well-prepared. **23.dxc5 f6!** 23...Bxc5; 24.Nxc5 Rxc5; 25.g4!? **24.g4 Qf3.** 24...Qxg4 would be very risky. 25.Reg1 Qb4; 26.Qxh6 Bf8; 27.Bd6. **25.Bd4 Qxg4;** But now there is a gain of tempo involved. **26.Be3 Qf5; 27.Bxh6!?**

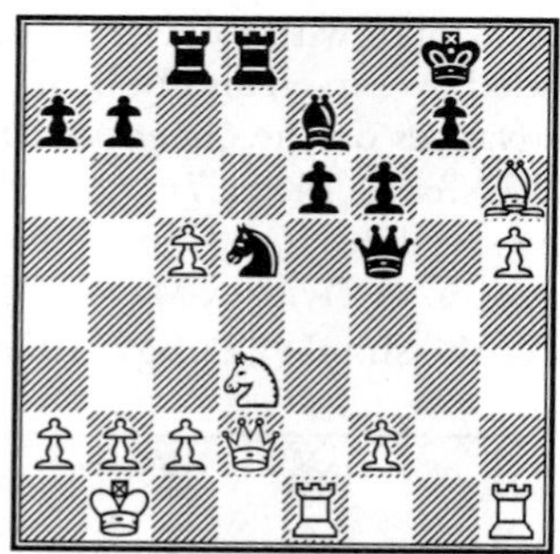

Is this sacrifice necessary or correct or simply optimistic? **27...gxh6; 28.Qxh6 Kf7; 29.Qc1.** The retreat is motivated by the fact that Black is getting ready to attack by moving his Knight and then sacrificing the exchange on d3. Clearly Kupreichik did not evaluate the position correctly when he went in for the sacrifice. **29...Bxc5; 30.Reg1 Bd6!** Overprotecting f4 and opening the c-file which can be useful if the rooks stay on the board. **31.h6 Rg8.** There is nothing else. **32.Qd1 Rxg1; 33.Rxg1.** 33.Qxg1 allows 33...Qg6 and Black is much better. **33...Rg8; 34.Rh1 Rh8; 35.Rh5 Qe4; 36.a3 Bf8.** Black is simply winning now. **37.Qd2 b6; 38.f3 Qg6; 39.Qh2 Rxh6; 40.Rxh6 Qxh6; 41.Qb8 Qh1+; 42.Ka2 Qxf3; 43.Qxa7+ Be7; 44.Qa4 Ne3; 45.Qh4 Nxc2; 46.Nf4 Nd4. Black won.**

MODERN DEFENSES

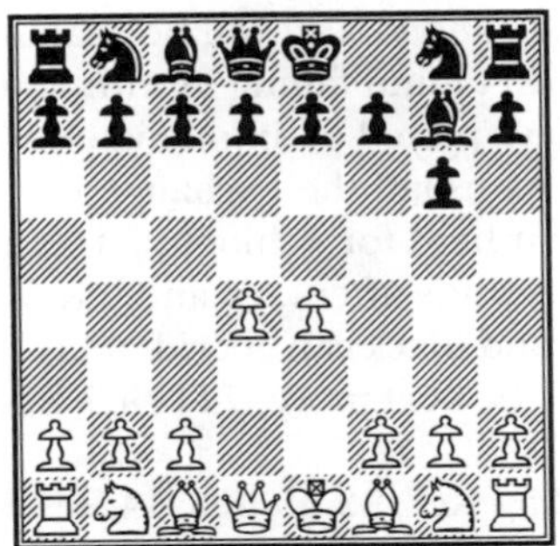

1.e4	**g6**
2.d4	**Bg7**

Once rejected as bizarre, the **Modern Defense** is now quite respectable. Black concedes the entire center and allows White to occupy it with pieces and pawns, hoping to use a hypermodern strategy to attack the center from the flank. The bishop at g7 can be a powerful weapon, as it is not blocked by a knight, as is the case in the Pirc Defense.

AVERBAKH VARIATION

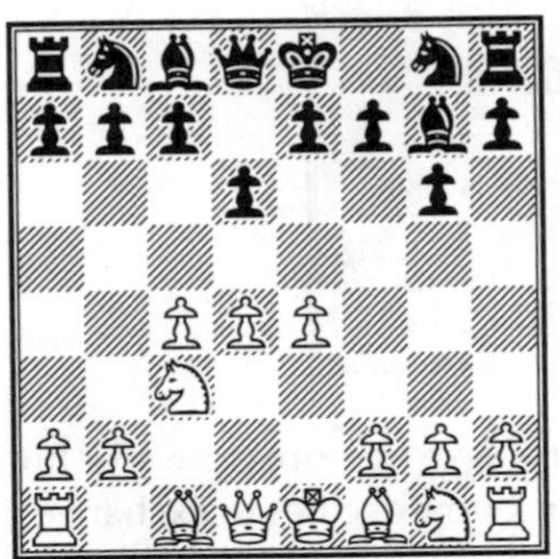

1.d4	**g6**
2.e4	**Bg7**
3.c4	**d6**
4.Nc3	

The **Averbakh Variation** invites a simple transposition to the King's Indian Defense after 4...Nf6, but there are several alternative plans which are now considered respectable. Black can attack the center directly with ...c5, ...Nc6 or ...e5. This last plan is the one seen most often at the highest level of chess, whether the move is played right away or after a preliminary ...Nd7.

The present game illustrates the key ideas of this plan, with a rapid ...f5 coming as soon as the center is closed.

(121) BOTVINNIK - SUTTLES [A42]

Belgrade, 1969

1.d4 g6; 2.e4 Bg7; 3.c4 d6; 4.Nc3.

4...e5. Other plans such as 4...Nc6, 4...c5 and 4...f5?! will be examined in *Unorthodox Chess Openings*. **5.Nge2.** Botvinnik didn't mind falling in with Suttles scheme. In fact, he wrote that he probably should have played d5 immediately! 5.dxe5 dxe5; 6.Qxd8+ Kxd8 is not at all bad for Black. As usual, the exchange of queens at d8 when White alredy has a pawn at c4 makes it hard for White to attack the exposed king, which quickly finds shelter on the queenside after ...c6 and ...Kc7. The pawns at c4 and e4 render the bishop at f1 useless, and Black can get rid of his "bad" bishop by moving it to h6. White prevents that with the next move. 7.f4 Nc6; 8.Nf3 Nd4 and Black has an initiative, for example 9.Kf2

9.Bd3 Nxf3+; 10.gxf3 c6; 11.c5 Ne7; 12.h4 Kc7; 13.h5 Be6; 14.Be3 Bh6; 15.Ne2 Rad8; 16.0–0–0 Bxa2; 17.Kc2 Be6; 18.hxg6 hxg6 and now the exchange sacrifice 19.Rxh6 Rxh6; 20.f5 was refuted by 20...Rh3; 21.Bg5 Rxd3; 22.fxe6 Rxd1; 23.Kxd1 f6! 24.Bxf6 Kd8; 25.Bxe5 Rxf3 and Black had a decisive advantage in Vaisser-Ivanchuk, Paris (Intel) 1995. 9...exf4; 10.Bxf4 Ne6; 11.Bd2 Nf6; 12.h3 Nd7; 13.Bd3 Ne5 with a strong position for Black in Petursson-Ehlvest, Yerevan Olympiad 1996. 5.d5 Ne7; 6.h4 is a radical attempt to storm the kingside, but after 6...h5!; 7.Be2 Nd7; 8.Nf3 Nf6. Black has a solid position.

5...Nc6; 6.d5 Nce7; 7.f3 f5.

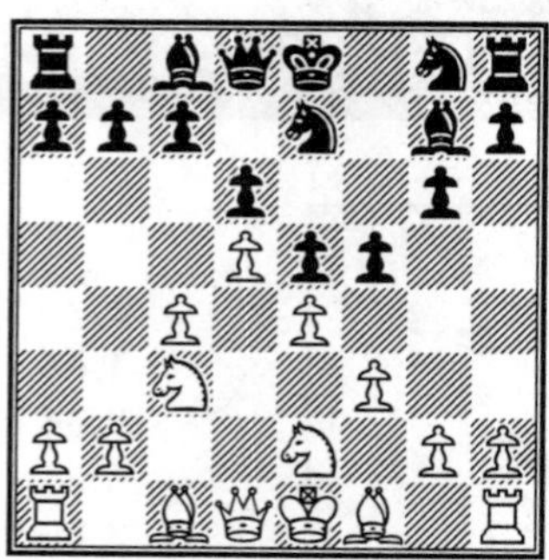

This move is at the heart of Black's strategy. The pressure will build at e4, because Black can follow with ...Nf6. **8.Be3.** Black now decides to exchange dark-squared bishops, though this may later make kingside castling more risky. **8...Bh6; 9.Bxh6 Nxh6; 10.Qd2 Nf7.** The knights stand guard around the king, and cover many important squares. Suttles frequently adopted this setup. **11.g3.** Keeping an eye on the f4-square. **11...0–0; 12.Bg2 c6; 13.0–0 cxd5; 14.cxd5 Qb6+; 15.Kh1 Bd7; 16.Rae1.**

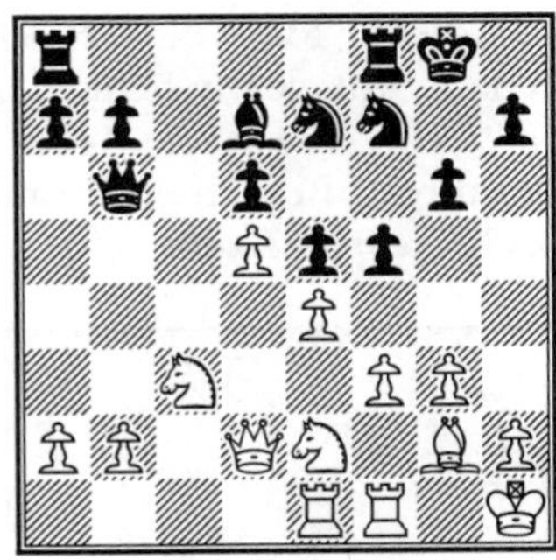

Both sides have played logically. The weakness at d6 is not significant as long as the barrier at e5 and f5 stays intact, but Botvinnik formulates a plan to undermine it. **16...Kg7; 17.f4! Rae8; 18.Nc1!** A cunning move, even if Botvinnik says so himself. One point is that if Black captures at f4, then the knight can get to the d4-square via b3, while additional breathing room on the e- and f-files adds to the pressure on Black's position. **18...exf4; 19.gxf4 fxe4; 20.Nxe4 Nf5.**

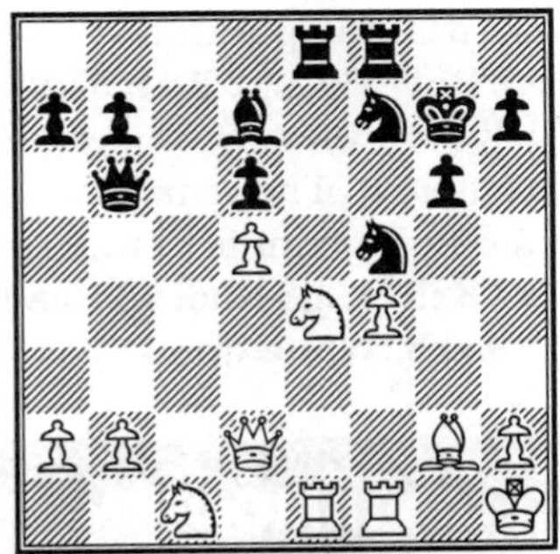

Unfortunately there is no direct attack here, since 21.Qc3+ is parried by 21...Qd4. Nevertheless, Black is really starting to miss that dark-squared bishop! **21.Nb3 Rc8; 22.Bh3 Ng3+; 23.hxg3 Bxh3; 24.Nd4.** Black's light squares are so weak that he cannot afford to take the rook.

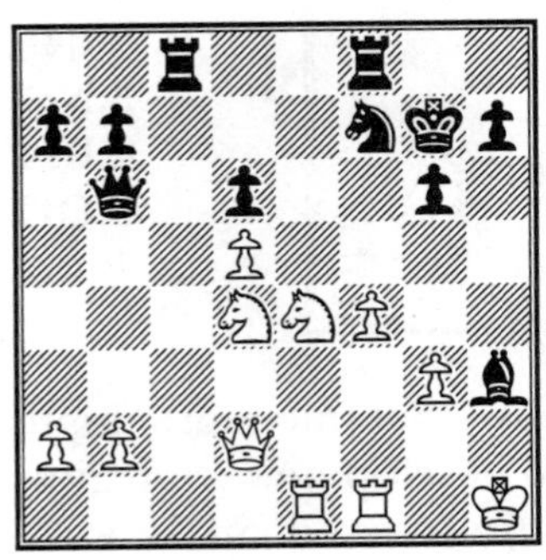

24...Rfe8. 24...Bxf1; 25.Ne6+ wins, for example 25...Kh8 (25...Kg8; 26.Nf6+ Kh8;

27.Nd7) 26.Nxf8 Bh3 (26...Rxf8; 27.Qc3+ Kg8; 28.Nf6+ Kg7; 29.Ne8+ Kh6; 30.Qg7+ Kh5; 31.Nf6#) 27.Ne6 is much better for White. **25.Rf3 Rc4; 26.Rd3 Qb4; 27.b3 Qxd2; 28.Rxd2.** The endgame is still clearly better for White. **28...Rc7; 29.Rde2 Bg4.** 29...Rce7; 30.Nxd6 Rxe2; 31.Nxe8+ Rxe8; 32.Rxe8 and White wins. **30.Re3 Bf5?** This fails to address the threat. Botvinnik recommended 30...Bd7. **31.Nxd6 Nxd6; 32.Nxf5+ gxf5; 33.Rxe8 Nxe8; 34.Rxe8.**

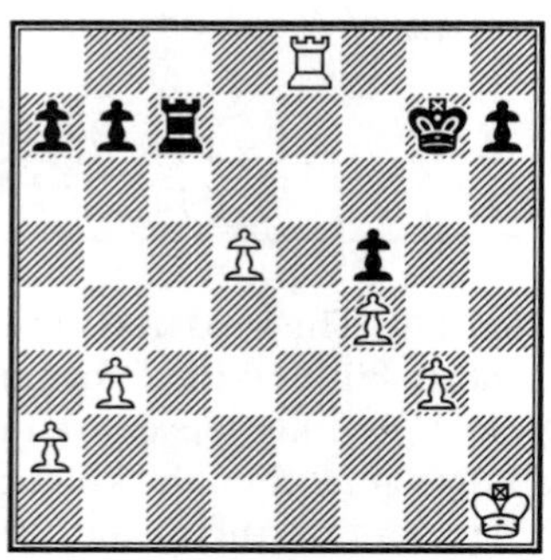

This endgame is not a simple win, becuase the pawns at d5, g3 and a2 are all possible targets. Botvinnik clarifies the position by exchanging the pawn at d5 for the one at h7. **34...Kg6; 35.Re2 Rc1+; 36.Kg2 Rd1; 37.Re6+ Kf7; 38.Rd6 Ke7; 39.Rh6 Rxd5; 40.Rxh7+ Kd6; 41.Kh3.** Now the plan is clear. White will establish a passed pawn on the kingside and promote it. The remainder of the game is a magnificent display of endgame technique by Botvinnik. **41...Ra5; 42.Kh4 b5; 43.Kg5 Rxa2; 44.Kxf5 a5; 45.g4 Ra3; 46.Ra7 Kc5; 47.g5 Kb6; 48.Ra8 Rxb3; 49.g6 Rg3; 50.Kf6 b4; 51.g7 Kb5; 52.g8Q Rxg8; 53.Rxg8. White won.**

ANTI-MODERN

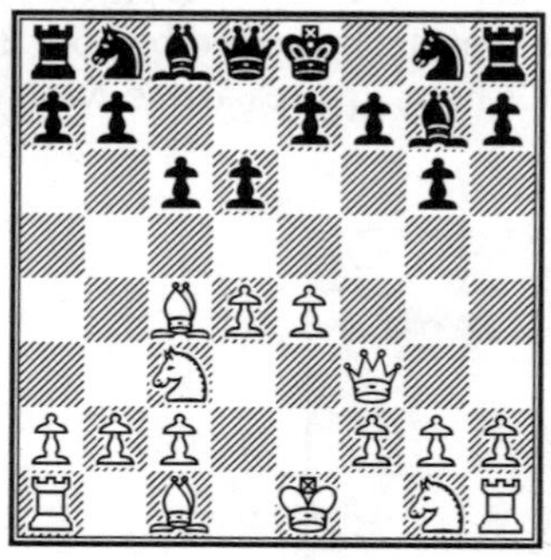

1.e4	**g6**
2.d4	**Bg7**
3.Nc3	**d6**
4.Bc4	**c6**
5.Qf3	

As the Modern Defenses became more popular inthe 1970s, players of the White pieces tried to develop new strategies against them. One of the most interesting was the direct assault on the weak f7-square. The **Anti-Modern** system scored well for a while, and although the initial enthusiasm has wavered, top stars like Judith Polgar and Viswanathan Anand still use it.

(122) POLGAR, J - SHIROV [B06]

Amsterdam (Donner Memorial), 1995

1.e4 g6; 2.d4 Bg7; 3.Nc3 c6; 4.Bc4 d6; 5.Qf3 e6; 6.Nge2 b5.

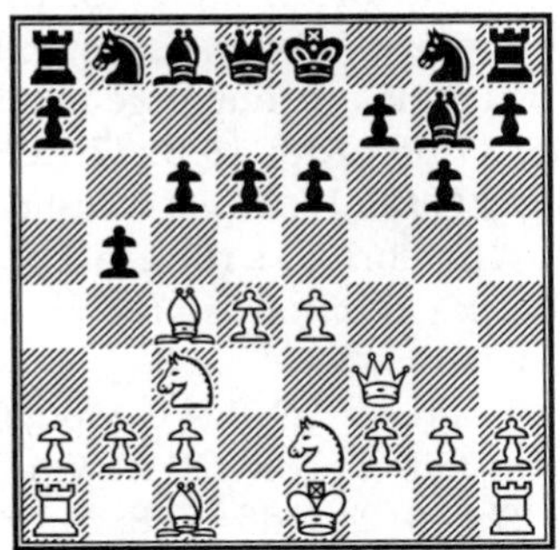

6...Nd7 is too passive: 7.0–0 Ngf6; 8.Bb3 0–0; 9.Bg5 h6; 10.Bh4 e5; 11.Rad1 Qe7; 12.Qe3 Re8; 13.f4 exd4; 14.Qxd4 Nxe4; 15.Bxe7 Bxd4+; 16.Rxd4 Nxc3; 17.Nxc3 Rxe7; 18.Rxd6 Kg7; 19.f5 gxf5; 20.Rxf5 Nf8; 21.Rf3 Be6; 22.Rg3+ Kh8; 23.Ne4! and White held a clear advantage in Nunn-Ehlvest, Skelleftea 1989.

7.Bb3 a5. Black's pawn moves are a bit excessive, and the lack of development will cause serious problems. Still, it is not all that easy for White to prove an advantage. 7...Ne7; 8.0–0 0–0; 9.Bf4 a5 is a better move order, as in Delgado-Perez, Santa Clara 1996. **8.a3.** White makes room for the bishop without giving up the b4-square, as would be the case on 8.a4?!

8...Ba6; 9.d5! Black is so far behind in developing the kingside that White can launch an immediate attack in the central. Even in this modern opening, ancient principles still apply! **9...cxd5.** 9...exd5!? is also possible, but White is better after 10.exd5 c5; 11.a4 b4; 12.Nb5 Bxb5; 13.axb5 Nf6; 14.c4 and Black will always suffer from a lack of space and a weak a-pawn. **10.exd5 e5.** This is a logical move, but Black's weaknesses are becoming permanent. **11.Ne4 Qc7.** 11...h6 is possible. 12.g4 Nf6; 13.N2g3 Nxe4; 14.Nxe4 0–0; 15.Qh3 f5!; 16.gxf5 Bc8!; 17.Ng3 Rxf5!; 18.Qg2 a4; 19.Ba2 Rf4 with counterplay for Black in Anand-Shirov, Dos Hermanas 1996. **12.c4!** It is time to halt Black's queenside initiative by forcing the issue on the a6-f1 diagonal. **12...bxc4; 13.Ba4+! Nd7; 14.N2c3.**

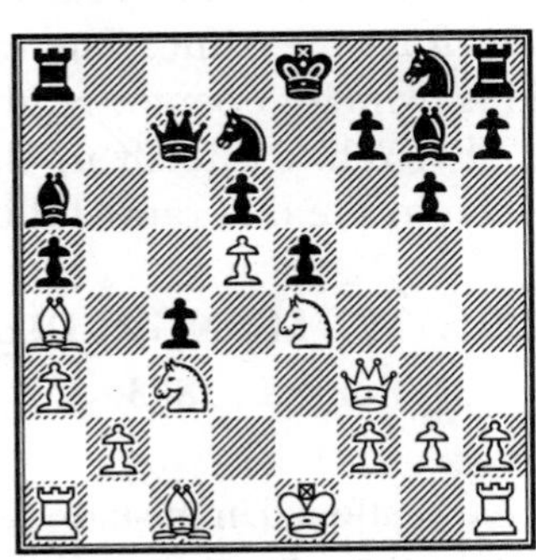

Black's bishops have limited scope, and White has sufficient compensation for the weak pawn. Note that the knight at d7 is pinned, so that ...Ngf6 is not on. Black tries to remedy this by moving the king, but that just leads to more trouble. **14...Ke7?!** 14...h6!?; 15.Nb5 Bxb5; 16.Bxb5 f5; 17.Nd2 Ngf6 allows White to build a strong attack with 18.Bc6 Rb8; 19.Nxc4, for example 19...e4; 20.Qg3! **15.Nxd6! Qxd6.** 15...Kxd6? loses to 16.Ne4+ Kxd5; 17.Qxf7+ Kxe4; 18.Bc2+ Kd4; 19.Be3#. 15...f5; 16.Ndb5 gives the White pawn at d5 a strong urge to advance.

16.Ne4 Qxd5. 16...Qb6; 17.d6+ Kf8; 18.Bxd7 Rd8; 19.Be6 f5; 20.Bg5 Qxb2; 21.0-0 is overpowering. **17.Bg5+ Ndf6.** 17...f6 gets crushed by 18.Rd1 Qxd1+; 19.Qxd1 and White will win. **18.Rd1.** White brings a rook to a powerful post at d7. **18...Qb7; 19.Rd7+ Qxd7; 20.Bxd7.** Black's position is critical, and the pressure is intense. Shirov fails to find the best defense.

20...h6? 20...Bb7 is forced, and now 21.Ba4 is good, for example 21...h6; 22.Qg3! hxg5; 23.Qxe5+ Kd8 (23...Kf8 fails to solve Black's problems after 24.Qd6+ Ne7; 25.Nxf6 Bxf6; 26.Qxf6 Rh4; 27.0-0) 24.Qd6+ Kc8; 25.Nc5 and Black cannot save the king without further material loss. **21.Qd1!** Black resigned here, rather than tolerate the humiliation of **21...hxg5; 22.Qd6+ Kd8; 23.Bb5+ Kc8; 24.Qc6+ Kb8; 25.Qb6+ Bb7; 26.Nd6 Ra7; 27.Qd8+ Bc8; 28.Qxc8#. White won.**

MONGREDIEN DEFENSE

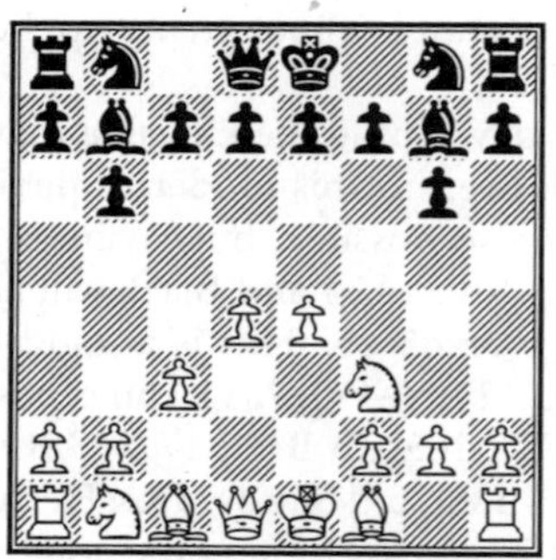

1.e4 g6
2.d4 Bg7
with ...b6
and ...Bb7

The **Mongredien Defense** uses a double fianchetto, and Black makes no effort to contest the center for some time. The diagram above represents only one of White's options, which depend greatly on move order. For example, after 1.e4 b6 2.d4 Bb7, White is likely to play 3.Nc3, and then 3...g6 avoids the strong center seen in the diagram and in our illustrative game.

(123) STEINITZ - MONGREDIEN [B06]
London, 1863

1.e4 g6; 2.d4 Bg7; 3.c3. As mentioned in the introduction, there are many other plans for White. Here is a sample of recent action: 1.Nf3 b6; 2.e4 Bb7; 3.Nc3 g6; 4.d4 Bg7; 5.Bc4 e6; 6.0-0 Ne7 (6...d6; 7.Bg5 Ne7; 8.Qd2 h6; 9.Be3 a6 is something like a hedgehog formation if Black later opts for ...c5, but in Rausz-Kovacs, Hungarian Team Championship 1995 Black opted to respond to 10.a4 with 10...d5, and after mass exchanges on d5 achieved an equal game.) 7.Re1 0-0; 8.e5 d6; 9.Bg5 Bxf3; 10.Qxf3 d5 and now the game got wild with 11.Bxe5 exd5; 12.Bxe7 Qxe7; 13.Nxd5 Qd8; 14.Nf6+ Bxf6; 15.Qxa8 Bg7; 16.Rad1 a5; 17.c4 and White's pawns and rook were better than the minor pieces in Otwinowska-Lebel, French Team Championship 1996.

3...b6; 4.Be3 Bb7; 5.Nd2. The problem with Black's approach at that time is that it acted as if White were not a participant in the game. Here Steinitz erects a solid center with plenty of support, and he does not overextend, so Black has no targets. **5...d6; 6.Ngf3 e5.**

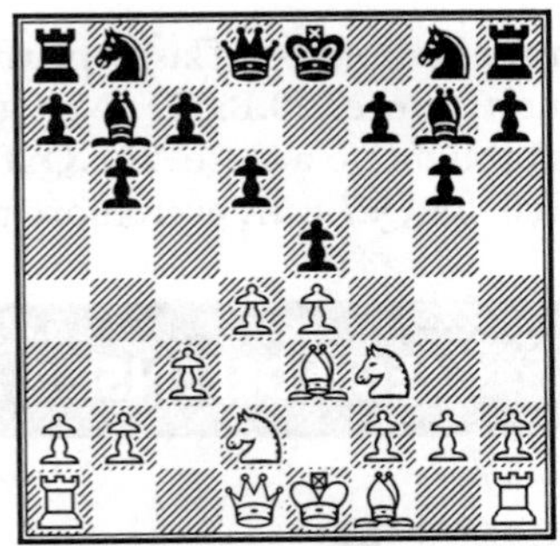

7.dxe5! Steinitz did not like to provide targets for Black's pieces. 7.d5 c6; 8.c4 Ne7; 9.Be2 f5 gives Black good counterplay. **7...dxe5; 8.Bc4 Ne7; 9.Qe2!** This clears the d1-square for a rook. **9...0–0; 10.h4! Nd7.** The general rule is that one reacts to flank activity with a counter-thrust in the center, but here Black has nothing to do in the middle of the board. **11.h5 Nf6; 12.hxg6! Nxg6.** 12...hxg6 would lose a pawn to 13.Nxe5 **13.0–0–0 c5?!** Black does not appreciate the danger he is in on the kingside. **14.Ng5 a6.** Black wants to drive back the enemy bishop, but has no time for such luxuries. **15.Nxh7! Nxh7.**

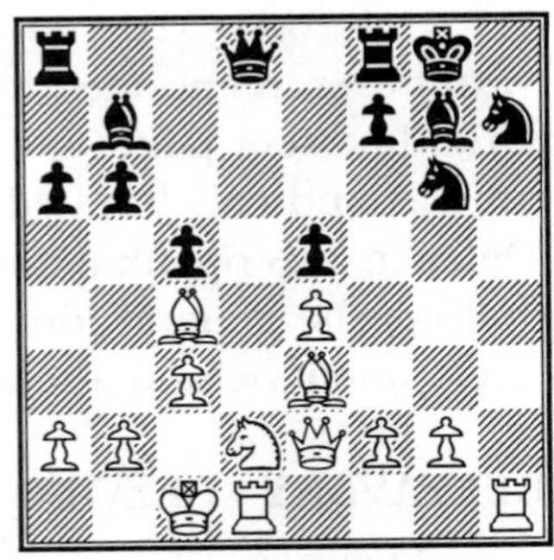

Having sacrificed a knight, White now shows that the fireworks are just beginning. **16.Rxh7!! Kxh7; 17.Qh5+ Kg8; 18.Rh1.** 18.Qxg6 is well met by 18...Qf6! **18...Re8.** The only way to avoid mate at h7. **19.Qxg6 Qf6.**

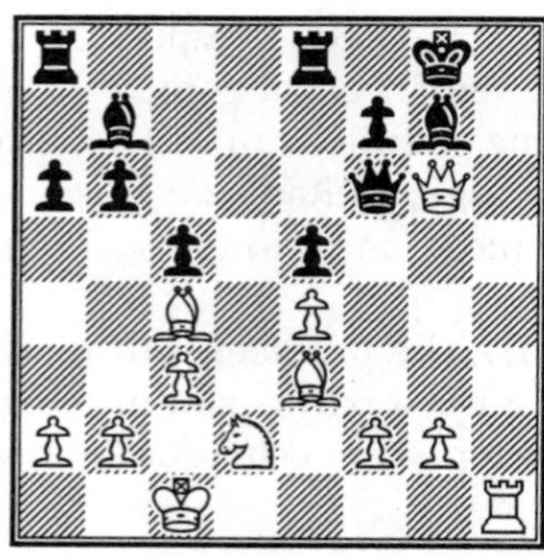

Steinitz did not have a reputation as a flashy player, but he did uncork some fine finishes when opportunity arose. **20.Bxf7+.** Now that the rook has been displaced from f7, the game is brought to a close. **20...Qxf7; 21.Rh8+! Kxh8; 22.Qxf7** Black resigned. After 22...Bc6, 23.Qc7 wins even more material. **White won.**

CZECH DEFENSE

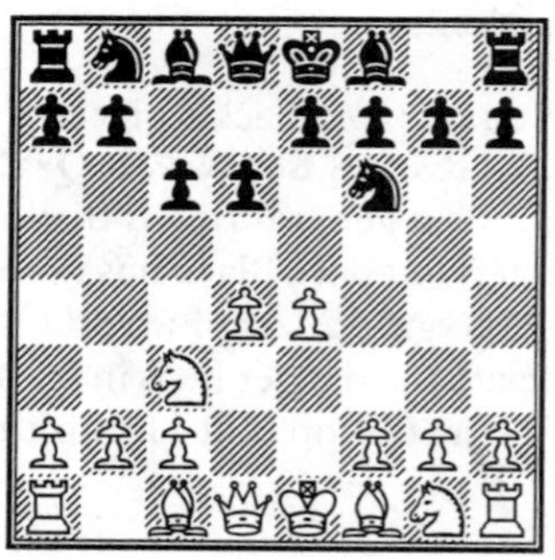

1.d4	**d6**
2.e4	**Nf6**
3.Nc3	**c6**

The **Czech Defense** wasn't even mentioned in serious circles until the late 1980s, when Czech Grandmasters Jansa and Prybil started to play it regularly in strong tournaments and collaborated on a small book on the opening. Unlike the Pirc Defence, this opening does not necessarily place a bishop at g7. Instead, it follows the general ideas of the Old Indian and Philidor Defenses: slow development behind a solid defensive formation.

(124) BELYAVSKY - BEZOLD [B07]

Portoroz, 1996

1.d4 d6; 2.e4 Nf6; 3.Nc3 c6; 4.f4. This is the logical move if White wants to try for a significant opening advantage. **4...Qa5.** This move puts pressure on White's center by pinning the knight at c3, which is the sole supporter of the pawn at e4. 4...Qb6 is an alternative which has been tested in recent events.

5.a3!? is Topalov's choice. (5.e5 Nd5; 6.Nxd5! cxd5; 7.Bd3 Nc6; 8.c3 g6; 9.Qe2 h5; 10.h3 Bf5!?; 11.Bxf5 gxf5; 12.e6 Qa6; 13.Qe3 Rh6; 14.exf7+ Kd7! and White was fighting for equality in Morozevich-Rivas Pastor, Pamplona 1995.) 5...Bg4; 6.Qd2 e5; 7.h3 exd4?; 8.Na4 Qc7; 9.hxg4 b5; 10.Qxd4 bxa4; 11.g5 Nfd7; 12.Qxa4 Nc5; 13.Qd4 Nbd7; 14.Nf3 Rb8; 15.Bc4 and White had the bishop pair and greater control of the center in Topalov-Rivas Pastor, Pamplona 1995.

5.e5. 5.Bd3 allows Black to play 5...e5, staking a claim in the center. 6.Nf3 Bg4 .

A) 7.Be3 leaves Black in a quandary about what to do next. 7...Nbd7 (7...exd4; 8.Bxd4 Qb4; 9.Be2 Nxe4; 10.0–0 d5; 11.Nxe4 dxe4; 12.c3 Qe7; 13.Ne5 Bxe2; 14.Qxe2 f5; 15.Qh5+ and Black was in serious trouble in Kindermann-Dorfman, Debrecen 1990. 7...exf4; 8.Bxf4 Qb6; 9.Ne2! Bxf3; 10.gxf3 Qxb2; 11.Rb1 Qxa2; 12.Rxb7 Qa5+; 13.Bd2 Qd8; 14.Qa1! a5; 15.d5 left Black squirming in Shirov-Rivas Pastor, Manila Olympiad 1992.) 8.0–0 Be7; 9.h3 Bh5.

(9...Bxf3; 10.Qxf3 0–0; 11.Ne2!? c5; 12.dxe5 dxe5; 13.Nc3 and White enjoys the advantage of the bishop pair, Yakovich-Mokry Pardubice 1994. 9...exf4; 10.Bxf4 Bxf3; 11.Qxf3 Qb6; 12.Ne2 was better for White in Glek-Tseshkovsky, Philadelphia 1990. Black must worry about the safety of the king, since a kingside attack by White is easy to arrange.)

10.Qe1 exf4; 11.Bxf4 Bg6; 12.e5 dxe5; 13.dxe5 Nd5; 14.e6 leads to exciting complications: 14...Qb6+; 15.Kh1 fxe6; 16.Bxg6+ hxg6; 17.Bg5 N5f6; 18.Qxe6 Qxb2; 19.Bxf6 gxf6; 20.Rab1 Qxc3; 21.Rxb7 0–0–0; 22.Rfb1 Black now returns material to slow down White's attack. 22...Rxh3+; 23.Qxh3 f5; 24.Qh2! f4; 25.Qxf4 Qa5; The only defense against mate at c7. 26.g3 g5; 27.Qe4 Qc3; 28.Rxa7 Bd6; 29.Ra8+ Bb8; 30.Qd3 and White eventually won in Browne-Benjamin, United States Championship 1995.

B) 7.dxe5 is less effective: 7...dxe5; 8.fxe5 Nfd7 (8...Bxf3; 9.Qxf3 Qxe5; 10.Bf4 gives White the initiative, Parkanyi-Horvath, Budapest (Schneider) 1995.) 9.Bf4 Nxe5; 10.Bxe5 Bxf3; 11.Qxf3 Qxe5; 12.0–0 Bc5+; 13.Kh1 0–0; 14.Qh3 g6; 15.Bc4 Kg7; 16.Rf3 b5; 17.Bb3 a5; 18.Raf1 Ra7 and White had no way to continue the attack in Cooper-Houska, Hastings (Challengers) 1996. **5...Ne4.**

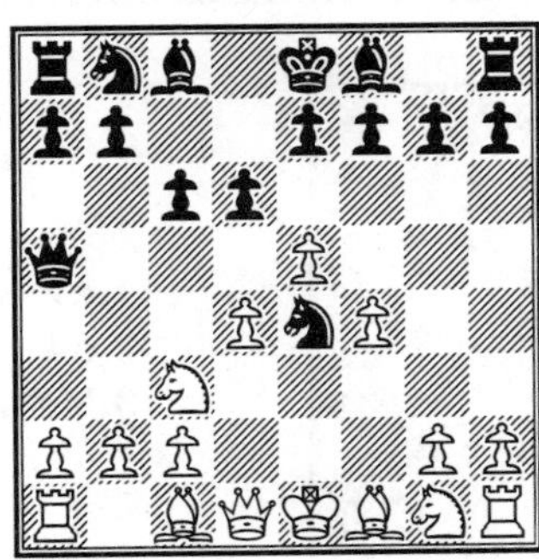

6.Qf3. 6.Bd2 Nxd2; 7.Qxd2 d5 is an alternative, giving White a clear spatial advantage. **6...Nxc3.** 6...d5; 7.Bd3 Na6; 8.Bxe4 dxe4; 9.Qxe4 Nb4 was played in Okhotnik-Conquest, French Team Championship 1996, and now White should consider 10.Nge2, so that after 10...g6, White can play 11.Ng3, keeping the enemy bishop off of f5. The immediate 10.f5 is not good, however, since Black can reply 10...g6, and if 11.f6, then 11...Bf5!

7.Bd2 Qd5. 7...Bf5; 8.Bd3 (8.Bxc3 Qd5; 9.Qxd5 cxd5; 10.0–0–0 Nc6; 11.Nf3 e6; 12.Bd3 g6; 13.Rhe1 Bg4; 14.Be2 h5; 15.g3 Bh6 gave Black good counterplay in P.Chandler-Pribyl, Schwaebisch Gmuend 1995.) 8...Bxd3; 9.cxd3 Qd5; 10.bxc3 Qxf3; 11.Nxf3 e6; 12.Ke2 dxe5; 13.fxe5 c5; 14.Rhb1 b6; 15.a4 Nc6; 16.a5 bxa5; 17.Rb7 gave White plenty of compensation for the pawn in Johansson-Agrest, Sollentuna 1995. **8.Qxc3 Bf5; 9.Nf3 dxe5; 10.Bc4 Qd8?** 10...Qe4+; 11.Kd1 Bg4; 12.Qb3 e6; 13.Re1 Bxf3+; 14.gxf3 Qxd4; 15.Qxb7 Qxc4; 16.Qxa8 Qb5 is probably the best Black can do, and it is a pretty horrible position. After the text, however, White built up an overwhelming position without difficulty. **11.Qb3 e6.**

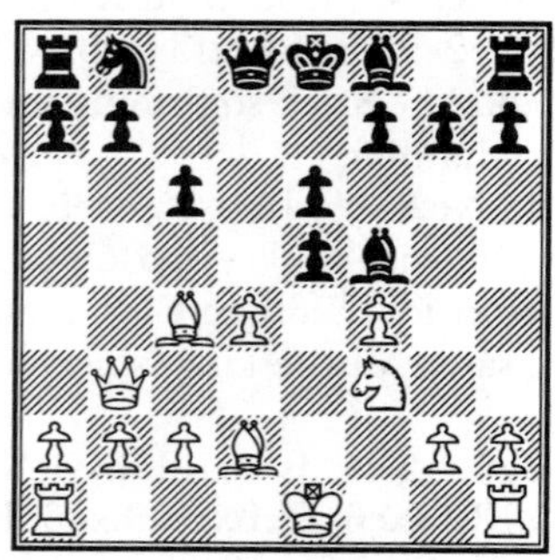

12.Qxb7 Be7. 12...Nd7; 13.Nxe5! Nxe5; 14.fxe5 Be4; 15.0–0–0! and taking the pawn at g2 is suicide: 15...Bxg2; 16.Rhg1 Rb8 (16...Bf3; 17.Rdf1 and the bishop is critically overworked, having to protect both f7 and c6.) 17.Qxa7 Bf3; 18.Rdf1 Bh5; 19.Rg5 Bg6; 20.Rxg6 hxg6; 21.Qxf7# **13.Qxa8 Qb6; 14.0–0–0 0–0; 15.Nxe5 Bd6; 16.Rhe1 Bxe5** and Black resigned without waiting for **17.dxe5 Nd7; 18.Be3 Nc5; 19.Bxc5 Qxc5; 20.Rd8.**

PIRC DEFENSE

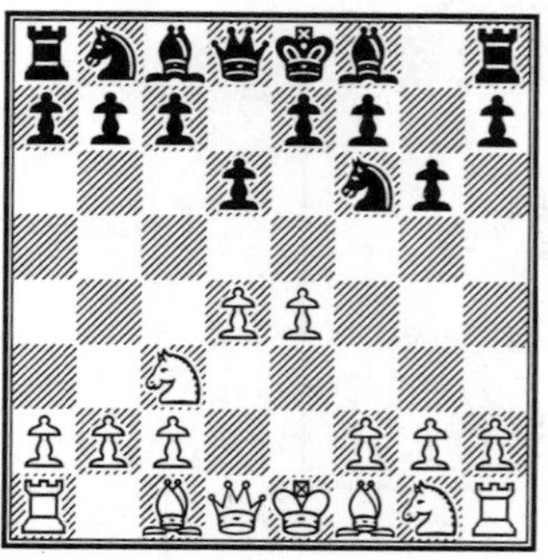

1.e4	**d6**
2.d4	**Nf6**
3.Nc3	**g6**

The **Pirc** intends to improve on the Modern Defense by forcing White to play 3.Nc3 (there are minor alternatives, but they do not achieve anything for White). Only then does Black fianchetto the bishop. The drawback here is that the bishop must sit impatiently behind the knight, waiting for it to move before gaining any influence in the game.

The Pirc is a little stodgier and Black often suffers from a lack of space. This is especially true in the Classical Variation with 4.Be2, where Black often gets squeezed to death in colorless, boring struggles. Here we look at two plans commonly found in amateur games. In the next game we see one of the early adopters of the Pirc/Modern complex defend the Pirc by transposition from the Modern Defense.

(125) ESTRIN - UFIMTSEV [B08]

Leningrad, 1949

1.e4 d6; 2.d4 g6; 3.Nf3 Bg7; 4.Bc4.

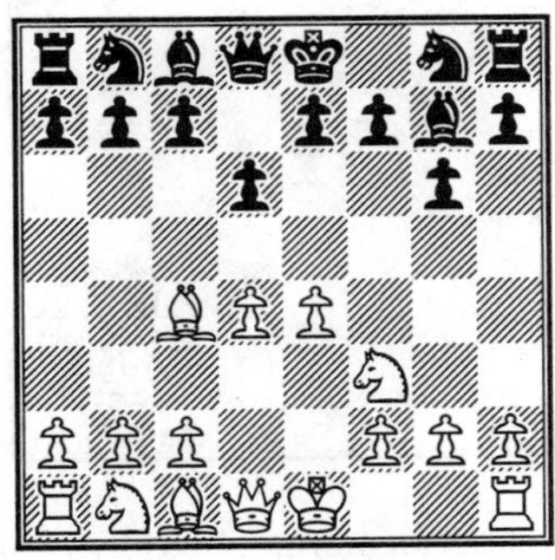

The Kholmov Variation is a popular method of playing against the Modern Defense. White simply develops normally, and will attack against the vulnerable f7 square. Black can usually defend against this direct plan, and counts on White to overextend so that the center will be vulnerable in the late middlegame and endgame. Ufimtsev is a player who received a lot of credit for the Modern Defense in Communist countries, but the name never caught on in the West.

4...Nf6; 5.Nc3. This transposes back into the normal Pirc lines. White can play differently, however, by defending the e-pawn with the queen and later supporting the center with c2-c3, a plan which is in keeping with the pure Modern Defense lines. 5.Qe2 is almost universally seen these days.

5...0–0 (5...c6; 6.Bb3 0–0; 7.0–0 Na6; 8.Nbd2 Qc7; 9.Rd1 e5; 10.Nc4 Bg4; 11.h3 Bxf3; 12.Qxf3 b5; 13.dxe5 dxe5; 14.Bg5 Nh5; 15.Ne3 Nf4; 16.Rd2 Nc5; 17.Ng4 Nxb3; 18.Qxb3 Ne6; 19.Bf6 h5; 20.Bxg7 Kxg7; 21.Nh2 Rad8; 22.Rad1 Rxd2; 23.Rxd2 Rd8; 24.Qe3 Qa5; 25.Rxd8 Qxd8; 26.Qe1 Qd4; 27.c3 Qd3; 28.Nf3 Kf6; 29.Kh2 g5; 30.Nd2 Shamkovich-Sowray, Bermuda-B 1995, Black won.)

6.0–0 Bg4 (6...c6; 7.Re1 d5; 8.exd5 cxd5; 9.Bd3 Nc6 is another acceptable defensive plan, Denker-Gufeld, United States Senior Open 1995.) 7.e5!? This is the sharpest line, leading to exciting complications. (7.Nbd2 Nc6; 8.c3 e5; 9.h3 Bxf3; 10.Nxf3 exd4; 11.cxd4 d5; 12.exd5 Nxd5 is nothing special, Ivanchuk-Anand, Moscow (Intel Rapid) 1995.)

7...dxe5 (7...Ne8 is preferred by most theoreticians. After 8.Rd1 Nc6; 9.Bd5 Qd7; 10.Bf4 Black should avoid the 10...e6? of Adorjan-Hort, Budapest 1973 in favor of 10...Qf5 with unclear complications.) 8.dxe5 Nd5; 9.Nbd2 Nb6; 10.Bd3 Nc6; 11.h3 Be6; 12.Rd1 Nd7; 13.Bc4 Nc5; 14.Bxe6 Nxe6; 15.Nb3 Qc8; 16.Qe4 and Black was able to reconfigure the back rank with 16...Rd8; 17.Be3 Rxd1+; 18.Rxd1 Qe8; 19.c4 Rd8 and a draw eventually resulted in Leko-Shirov, Vienna 1996.

5...0–0; 6.0–0. White can still opt for the Qe2 plan here. **6...c6.** Now it is known that Black can equalize with 6...Nxe4; 7.Nxe4 (7.Bxf7+? Rxf7; 8.Nxe4 h6; 9.Be3 Bg4 was better for Black in Basman-Nunn, London 1973 as White has insufficient compensation for the bishop pair.) 7...d5 is now known to equalize, on the basis of 8.Bd3 dxe4; 9.Bxe4 Nd7; 10.c3 c5, Lechtynsky-Sax, Tallinn 1979. **7.e5 Ne8; 8.h3 b5!?** White has not been able to sustain an initiative so Black takes over and attacks on the queenside. It is exactly this kind of counter-punching that appeals to players who adopt the hypermodern approach to chess. **9.Bb3 a5; 10.a4.** The Black bishop was about to be suffocated! **10...b4; 11.Ne4 d5; 12.Nc5.**

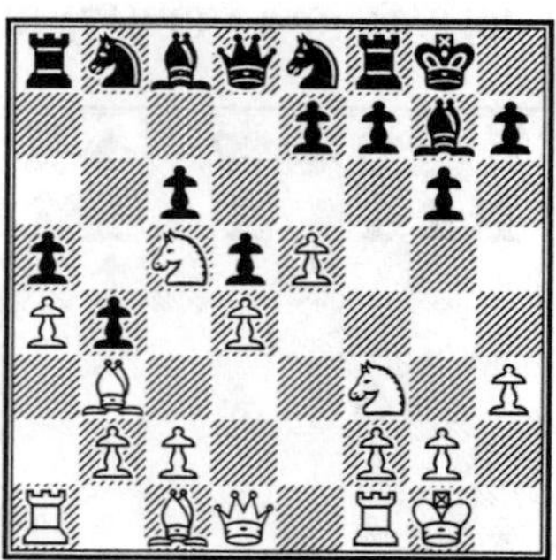

Objectively, White stands better here. The only problem is that it is not easy to come up with a convincing long-term plan. The knight occupies a wonderful outpost at c5, but can hardly contribute to a kingside attack, since the e4 square is guarded by a Black pawn. **12...Nd7; 13.Nd3 Nc7; 14.Re1 Ne6; 15.c3.** White could have played Be3 first, but wanted to keep open the option of deploying the bishop at a3. **15...bxc3; 16.bxc3 Rb8; 17.Ba3 Nb6; 18.Rb1.** White might have played the queen to d2 instead, connecting the rooks, since no effective discovered attacks against the bishop at b3 are to be found. **18...Re8; 19.Re2 Nc4; 20.Bxc4 Rxb1; 21.Qxb1 dxc4; 22.Nb2 Nf4.**

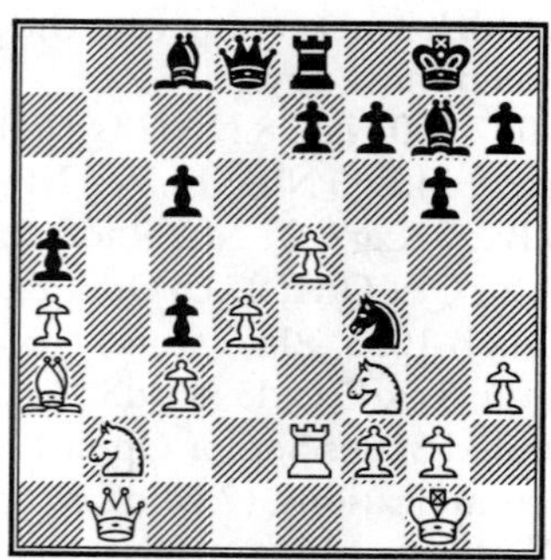

Now the picture has changed considerably. Both sides have weaknesses to work on, and Black has the bishop pair, which may be useful later in the game if the position gets opened up. The chances are about equally divided here, but a draw is by no means likely. **23.Re1 Bf5; 24.Qa2.** White is obsessed with the weak c-pawn, but such pawns are to be gathered in endgames, not in middlegames, when the king cannot afford to send a powerful force so far from home just to get a mere pawn.

24...Qd5!; 25.Qxc4. White must have overlooked the obvious reply: **25...Nxh3+!; 26.gxh3 Qxf3; 27.Re3 Qd5; 28.Qxd5 cxd5.** Now it is White who owns a weak pawn in the endgame, and Black has the bishop pair as well. Moreover, there is only one open file, which is of no use to either rook right now. **29.c4.** White eliminates the weakness. **29...Bh6!; 30.Re1 e6; 31.Bd6?** This loses material. 31.c5 Bf8 makes life very awkward for the bishop at a3. Note that White can never occupy the b-file because the Black bishop owns the light squares. **31...Bd2; 32.Re2.** 32.Rd1 Bc3; 33.Ba3 Rb8 and the knight is trapped.

32...Bc3; 33.Nd1 Bxd4; 34.Rd2 Ba7; 35.c5. 35.cxd5 exd5; 36.Rxd5 Bb8; 37.Bxb8 (37.Rxa5?? Bxd6; 38.exd6 Re1+ ;39.Kg2 Rxd1) 37...Rxb8; 38.Rb5 (38.Rxa5 Rb1; 39.Rd5 Bc2) 38...Rxb5; 39.axb5 a4; 40.b6 Bc8; 41.Nc3 a3 is a winning endgame for Black, for example 42.Kf1 Kf8; 43.Ke2 Ke7; 44.Kd2 Ke6; 45.f4 Kf5; 46.Kc2 Kxf4; 47.Nb5 a2; 48.Kb2 Kxe5; 49.Kxa2 Kd5 and the b-pawn falls.

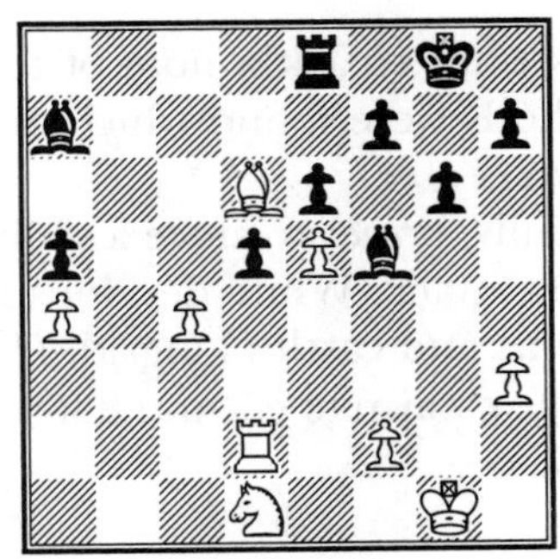

35...Rc8; 36.Ne3 Be4. Black could have, and should have, grabbed the h-pawn here, though that is so weak it can wait. **37.Ng4 Kg7; 38.Nf6.** The knight doesn't really accomplish anything here. Black can take the c-pawn whenever it is desirable, but there is no hurry. **38...Bf5; 39.Nd7 Be4; 40.Nf6 Bf3.** I suspect that one or both players were in severe time trouble here. **41.Nd7 g5; 42.Kh2 h5; 43.Kg3 g4; 44.h4.** Moving the king to f4 might have offered more practical chances to save the game.

44...Kg6; 45.Kf4 d4? Black has let a few opportunities slip, and should have eaten either the c-pawn or h-pawn earlier. Now some radical action is needed to provide winning chances. The problem is, this move should have lost! **46.Rxd4 Bc6; 47.Nb6 Re8; 48.Nc4 Bd5; 49.Nxa5 Rc8; 50.Rd3 f6!; 51.Rc3.** A very strange conclusion. The result is reported as a win for Black, and the only explanation is either a time forfeit or perhaps White mistakenly thought that the position is lost after **51...Bb6; 52.Nb3 Bxb3; 53.Rxb3 Bxc5; 54.Rc3.** 54.Bxc5 Rxc5; 55.exf6 Rc4+; 56.Kg3 Rxa4; 57.f7 Kxf7; 58.Rb5 Kg6; 59.Rg5+ Kh6; 60.Re5 Ra6; 61.Kf4 would be very tough to crack! **54...fxe5+; 55.Ke4!** and White wins! **Black won.**

AUSTRIAN ATTACK

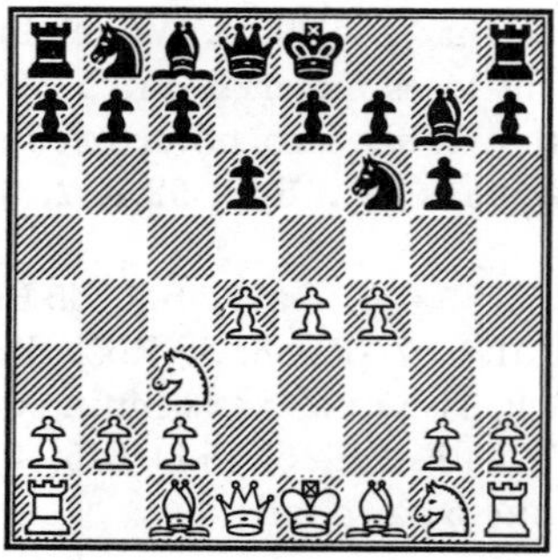

1.e4	d6
2.d4	Nf6
3.Nc3	g6
4.f4	Bg7

The **Austrian Attack** once struck a note of fear into defenders of the Pirc, but eventually methods were found which enabled Black to do battle with White's mighty pawn center.

Black must play carefully, however, since a slight error may allow White to build an overwhelming attack. White develops minor pieces behind the protective barrier of pawns and castles kingside. If appropriate, the attack can begin by advancing the e-pawn to e5, and Black must always be on guard against that central break.

(126) BARETIC - PIRC [B09]
Yugoslav Championship, 1968

1.e4 d6; 2.d4 Nf6; 3.Nc3 g6; 4.f4 Bg7; 5.Nf3 0–0; 6.Bd3. 6.Be3 Nc6; 7.Be2 e6; 8.Qd2 Ne7 and now the advance of the e-pawn allows Black to plant a knight at d5: 9.e5 Nfd5; 10.Nxd5 Nxd5; 11.Bf2 Bh6; 12.g3 b6; 13.h4 dxe5; 14.dxe5 Bb7; 15.h5. Now a flurry of tactics brings Black a better game. 15...Nxf4; 16.gxf4 Qxd2+; 17.Kxd2 Bxf4+; 18.Be3 Rad8+; 19.Bd3 Bxf3; 20.Bxf4 Bxh1; 21.Rxh1 Rd5 and Black has brought about a much superior endgame, because White cannot create any serious checkmating threats, Olafsson-Benjamin, Yerevan Olympiad 1996.

6.e5 is premature: 6...Nfd7; 7.h4 c5; 8.h5 cxd4; 9.hxg6 dxc3; 10.gxf7+ Rxf7; 11.Ng5 cxb2; 12.Bxb2 Qa5+; 13.c3 Nxe5; 14.Qb3 Qc5; 15.Be2 Qe3; 16.Bc1 Qg3+; 17.Kd1 Bg4; 18.Re1 Qd3+; 19.Bd2 Nc4 and White resigned in Bronstein-Conquest, Reykjavik 1996.

6...Nc6. The traditional method of handling the defense is to aim for ...e5, permanently preventing the advance of White's e-pawn. Therefore the knight is developed at c6, to support the e5-square. 6...Na6 is a popular alternative. After 7.0–0 c5; 8.d5 White has been doing well, for example 8...Bg4; 9.h3 Bxf3; 10.Rxf3 Nc7; 11.a4 Rb8; 12.Qe1 Nd7; 13.Bd2 Na6; 14.Nd1! and White quickly managed to neutralize the power of the enemy bishop after 14...e6; 15.dxe6 fxe6; 16.Bc3! when 16...Bxc3 17.Nxc3 Nb4; 18.Rd1 gave White a small advantage in S.Polgar-Hodgson, Amsterdam (Open) 1995. **7.Be3.**

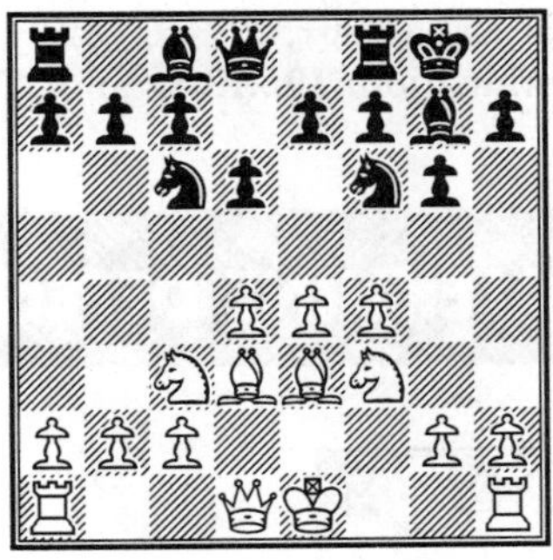

This used to be the most popular move, but now White normally either castles or advances to e5. 7.0–0 e5; 8.fxe5 dxe5; 9.d5 Ne7; 10.Nxe5 is well-established, but Black has found adequate counterplay in 10...c6; 11.Bg5 cxd5; 12.Bxf6 Qb6+; 13.Kh1 Bxf6; 14.Nxd5 Nxd5; 15.Nc4 Qd8; 16.exd5 b5; 17.Na5 Bh4!; 18.Qd2 Qxd5; 19.Qf4 and now the endgame after 19...Qg5; 20.Qxg5 Bxg5; 21.Bxb5 Rb8; 22.a4 a6; 23.Bc4 Rxb2; 24.Bb3 Be6! should be drawn, and was after 25.Nc4 Bxc4; 26.Bxc4 Rxc2; 27.Bxa6 Ra8; 28.Bd3 Rc5; 29.Bb5 Kg7; 30.Rad1 Ra7; 31.Rf2 in Hector-Hansen, Copenhagen 1995.

7.e5 dxe5; 8.fxe5 Nh5; 9.Be3 Bg4; 10.Be2 f6; 11.exf6 has been used effectively by Jan Timman: 11...exf6 (11...Bxf6; 12.Ne4 Bxf3; 13.Nxf6+ Nxf6; 14.Bxf3 e5; 15.dxe5 Nxe5; 16.0–0 was clearly better for White in Timman-Kuzmin, Yugoslavia 1979, since White retains at least one bishop against enemy knight in an open position.) 12.Qd2 Qe7 (12...f5! is best: 13.0–0–0 f4; 14.Bf2 Qd7 was unclear in Barczay-Nagy, Hungary 1973.) 13.0–0–0 Rfe8; 14.Rhe1 Kh8; 15.Bh6 Bxh6; 16.Qxh6 Qg7; 17.Qxg7+ Kxg7; 18.h3 and White had a more comfortable game in Timman-Nijboer, Netherlands 1985.

7...e5; 8.fxe5 dxe5; 9.d5 Nd4?! Pirc played the opening aggressively, but the simple retreat to e7 would have been wiser. **10.Nxe5 Nxd5; 11.Bxd4 Nf4; 12.Bf1?** This cowardly retreat makes no sense. The bishop would have been better stationed at c4. **12...Ne6.**

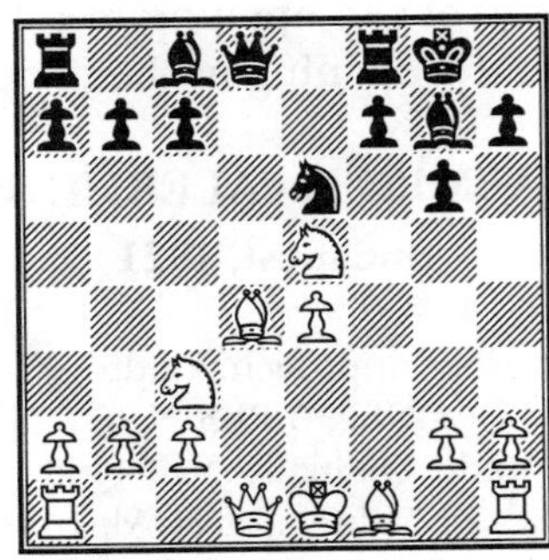

Here White miscalculates the tactical sequence. **13.Nxg6?** 13.Nc6 bxc6; 14.Bxg7 Kxg7 would have left White only very slightly better in the endgame. **13...Bxd4!** Now Black takes the initiative. Suddenly the White king is a target. **14.Nxf8 Qh4+; 15.Kd2 Qf4+; 16.Kd3 Qe3+; 17.Kc4 Bxc3; 18.bxc3.** 18.Qd5 loses elegantly to 18...b5+!;

19.Qxb5 Qd4+; 20.Kb3 Nc5+; 21.Ka3 Bxb2+; 22.Qxb2 Qa4#. **18...b5+; 19.Kxb5.** 19.Kb3 Nc5+; 20.Kb4 a5+; 21.Kxb5 Ba6+; 22.Kc6 Qh6+!; 23.Kd5 Qd6# is a beautiful alternative to the game continuation. **19...Rb8+** and White finally resigned. **Black won.**

ALEKHINE DEFENSE

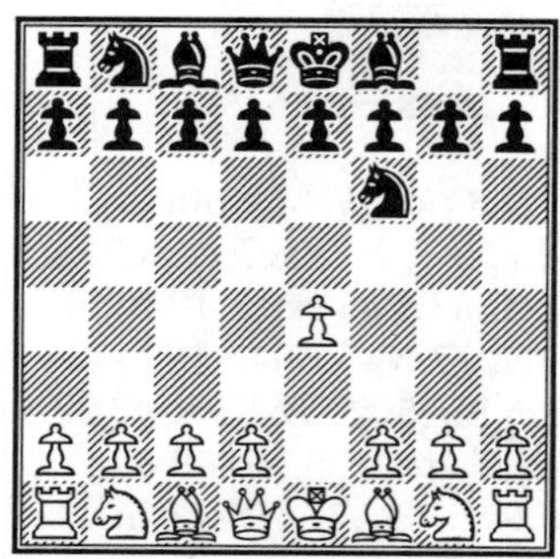

1.e4 Nf6

When Alekhine adopted 1...Nf6 in the following game it was quite a shock, and although he only used it less than two dozen times, the entire opening bears his name. The idea is quite hypermodern. White is tempted to advance pawns in the center, which can later be attacked by Black. At the same time, Black must suffer a cramped position and against a strong positional player may never achieve any significant counterplay.

Perhaps the greatest advantage of the Alekhine lies in the fact that the best lines for White require a great deal of work to learn, yet are only needed on those rare occasions when one's opponent plays 1...Nf6. As a result, many players on the White side prefer simple side-lines which provide a small, but not usually significant advantage.

We'll look at the theory of the opening in other games, but here, let's just introduce ourselves to the opening in the hands of Alekhine himself.

(127) SAEMISCH - ALEKHINE [B02]
Budapest, 1921

2.e5. 2.Nc3 is an unambitious approach. 2...d5

A) 3.exd5 Nxd5; 4.d4 (4.Bc4 Nb6; 5.Bb3 Nc6; 6.Nf3 Bf5; 7.d4 e6; 8.Bf4 Bd6; 9.Qd2 0–0; 10.0–0 Bg4; 11.Bxd6 Qxd6; 12.Ne4 Qd8; 13.c3 Bxf3; 14.gxf3 e5 and White's pawns were too weak in Milner Barry-Alekhine, Hastings 1933.) 4...Nc6; 5.Bb5 Nxc3; 6.Bxc6+ bxc6; 7.bxc3 Qd5; 8.Qf3 Bf5; 9.Qxd5 cxd5 was already better for Black in Factor-Alekhine, United States Championship 1932.

B) 3.e5 Nfd7; 4.d4 (4.Nxd5 Nxe5; 5.Ne3 Nbc6; 6.Nf3 Nxf3+; 7.Qxf3 Qd6; 8.Bb5 Bd7; 9.0–0 e6; 10.c3 Qe5; 11.a4 Bd6; 12.g3 Qf6; 13.Qxf6 gxf6; 14.d4 Na5; 15.Bxd7+ Kxd7 with good prospects for Black in Mieses-Alekhine, Baden Baden 1925. 4.f4 e6;

5.Nf3 c5; 6.g3 Nc6; 7.Bg2 Be7; 8.0–0 0–0; 9.d3 Nb6; 10.Ne2 d4; 11.g4 and White had the initiative in Nimzowitsch-Alekhine, Semmering 1926.) 4...c5; 5.Bb5 (5.Nxd5 e6; 6.Nc3 cxd4; 7.Qxd4 Nc6; 8.Qd1 Ncxe5; 9.Nf3 Nxf3+; 10.Qxf3 Be7; 11.Bd3 0–0; 12.0–0 was perhaps a little more comfortable for White in Aurbach-Alekhine, Bern 1925.)

5...Nc6; 6.Nf3 a6; 7.Bxc6 bxc6; 8.e6 fxe6; 9.0–0 e5; 10.dxe5 e6; 11.Ng5 Qe7; 12.f4 and the doubled pawns caused serious problems for Black in Bogoljubow-Alekhine, Carlsbad 1923. 2.d3 allows Black to transpose into a variety of openings, for example 2...e5 is good, since White rarely plays d3 in an Open Game. (2...c5; 3.f4 Nc6; 4.Nf3 delivered a Closed Sicilian formation in Thomas-Alekhine, Baden Baden 1925.)

3.f4 Nc6; 4.Nf3 (4.fxe5 Nxe5; 5.Nf3 Nxf3+; 6.Qxf3 d5; 7.e5 Qe7; 8.d4 Ne4; 9.Bd3 Qh4+; 10.g3 Qg4; 11.Nd2 Qxf3; 12.Nxf3 Be7; 13.Be3 Bh3; 14.Bxe4 dxe4; 15.Nd2 0–0–0 was fine for Black since the pawn at e4 cannot be captured due to the threat of ...Bg2, Nimzowitsch-Alekhine, New York 1927.) 4...d5; 5.exd5 Nxd5; 6.fxe5 Bg4; 7.Be2 Bxf3; 8.Bxf3 Qh4+ and Black had more than enough compensation for the pawn in Maroczy-Alekhine, New York 1924. **2...Nd5.**

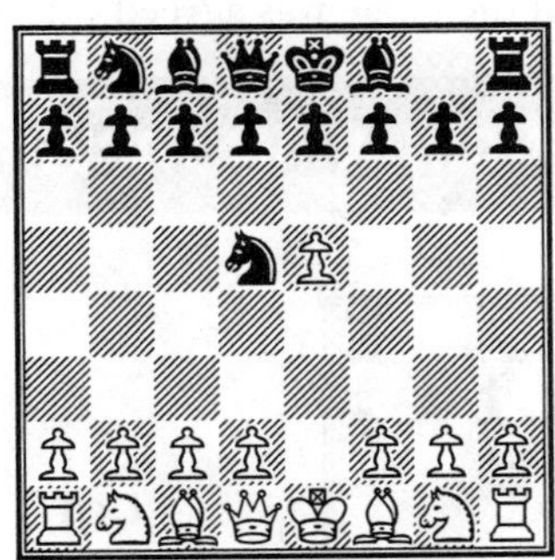

Now 3.d4 is usually seen, but other moves have been popular from time to time. **3.Nc3.** 3.Bc4 Nb6; 4.Bb3 c5; 5.d3 Nc6; 6.Nf3 e6; 7.Nc3 d5; 8.exd6 Bxd6; 9.Ne4 Be7 gave Black a solid position in Sergeant-Alekhine, Hastings 1926. 3.d4 d6 and here 4.Nf3, 4.c4 and 4.exd6 are the main lines, explored in games presented later, but there is also the odd 4.Bg5 which gets nowhere after 4...dxe5; 5.dxe5 Nc6; 6.Bb5 Bf5; 7.Nf3 Ndb4; 8.Na3 Qxd1+; 9.Rxd1 Nxc2+; 10.Nxc2 Bxc2; 11.Rc1 Be4 as in Steiner-Alekhine, Budapest 1921. **3...e6; 4.Nxd5 exd5; 5.d4 d6; 6.Nf3 Nc6.** The outline of Black's strategy is already clear: pressure on the center! **7.Be2 Be7; 8.Bf4 0–0; 9.0–0 f6!**

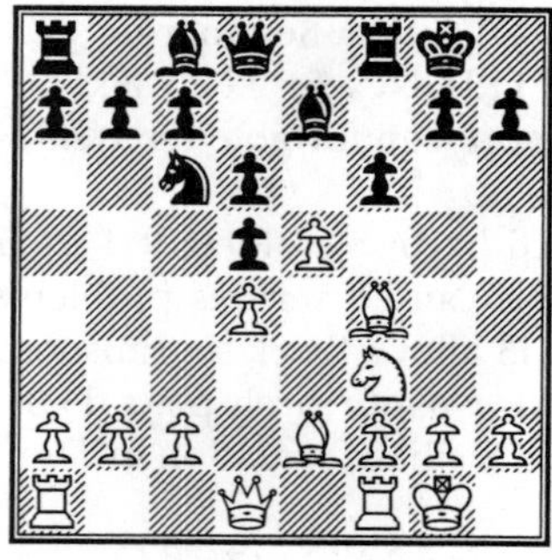

Black will not allow the White center to stand. **10.exd6 Bxd6; 11.Qd2 Bg4; 12.Rfe1 Re8.** Black has a comfortable game in a position resembling the Exchange Variation of the French Defense. **13.c3 Ne7; 14.Bxd6 Qxd6; 15.Nh4 Bd7.** Black avoids exchanges, but a draw is already the likely result of the game. **16.g3 Nf5; 17.Nxf5 Bxf5; 18.f3 Re6; 19.Bf1 Rae8; 20.Kf2 Kf7; 21.Rxe6 Qxe6; 22.Re1 Qxe1+; 23.Qxe1 Rxe1; 24.Kxe1** and the game was agreed drawn.

SCANDINAVIAN VARIATION

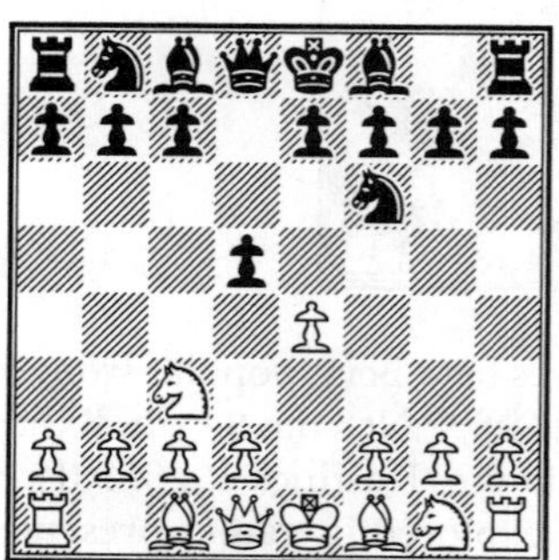

1.e4 Nf6
2.Nc3 d5

When confronted with the Alekhine Defense, some players think that they might as well avoid the main lines. After all, why work so hard to learn good lines for White when you will rarely encounter this plan at the board. One of the most common approaches among the standard openings is to refrain from advancing the e-pawn. Black can, of course, transpose to the Vienna Game with 2...e5, but this is not usually seen, since the Vienna is an Open Game, and Black's strategy from the first move has been to avoid such positions.

(128) VOROTNIKOV - KENGIS [B02]

Soviet Union, 1973

1.e4 Nf6; 2.Nc3 d5.

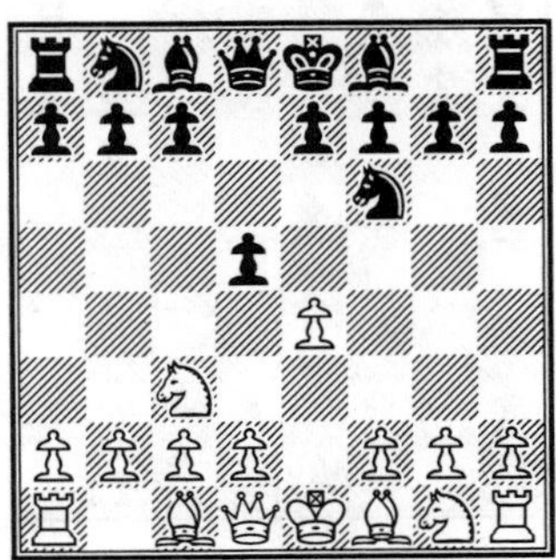

3.e5. White does not achieve anything by capturing at d5, which leads to positions similar to the Scandinavian Defense, Modern Variation. **3...Ne4.** Black has other moves, but this is the most aggressive. **4.Nce2.** If White exchanges knights, then there is no hope for an advantage. Allowing Black to make the exchange at the next move is not better. Therefore White retreats, planning to chase away the invader by playing c3.

4...f6. This is the old plan, which has been retired. It is fine in principle to try to attack White's pawn, but now attention is being focused on the strange advance of Black's d-pawn. 4...d4 is designed to discourage White from playing c3, but as we will see, many of the opening manuals err in condemning the most obvious plan. 5.c3 Nc6.

At one time it was claimed that Black could not afford to capture at c3, but in fact this plan may be fully playable. After (5...dxc3; 6.Qa4+ Black actually resigned in another game from the same year, thinking that the knight is lost without compensation, but this is not a clear position. 6...Nd7; 7.Qxe4 Nc5 and Black threatens ...Nd3+ followed by Nxf2+, winning the rook at h1. It is not easy to find a defense. 8.Qf3 Nd3+; 9.Kd1 cxb2; 10.Bxb2 Nxb2+; 11.Kc2 Nc4 is fine for Black.) **5.d3 Ng5.**

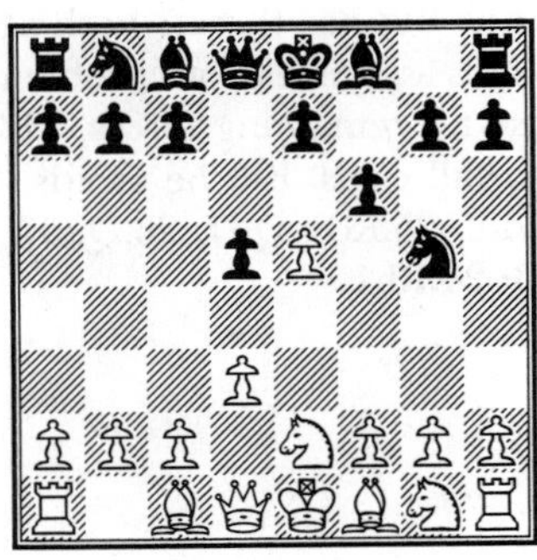

6.Bxg5!? 6.Nf4 is more common. This move is not dangerous, if handled correctly by Black. **6...fxg5; 7.h4 gxh4?!** This is the move which introduces all the complications. 7...g4 is better, but Black still has weaknesses to cope with and cannot develop comfortably, so White's chances must be judged as slightly preferable. **8.Nf4 g6; 9.Rxh4 Bg7.** Naturally Black cannot afford to expose the h5-e8 diagonal with ...g5. **10.d4 c5; 11.Bd3 Qa5+; 12.Kf1 cxd4.**

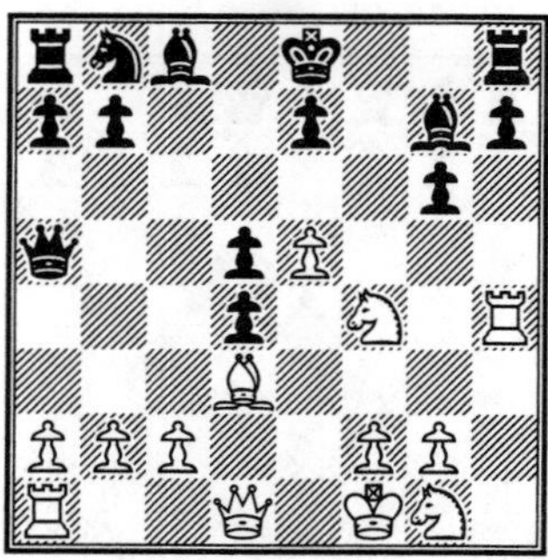

This is not mere pawn grabbing. Black follows the standard strategy of undermining the center. At the same time, White strikes on the kingside. **13.Rxh7 Rxh7; 14.Bxg6+ Kd8; 15.Bxh7 Bxe5.** The material is balanced, but Black must find a safe haven for his king. **16.Qf3 Nc6; 17.Nxd5.** Black would have been very happy to see the queens leave the board, since the knight on d5 would be very embarrassed after 17.Qxd5+ Qxd5; 18.Nxd5 e6. **17...Be6; 18.Qf8+ Kd7; 19.Qxa8 Qb5+; 20.Bd3 Qxb2.**

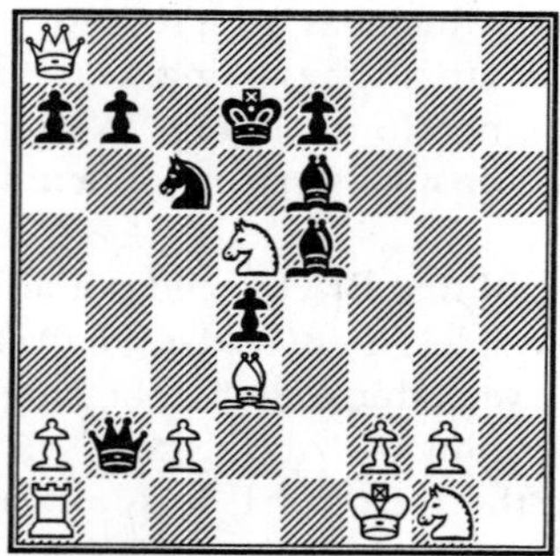

Black has sacrificed a rook but has threats both at a1 and d5. White finds an elegant solution. **21.Nb6+!!** This addresses both problems. By returning some material, White is able to mobilise his remaining forces. **21...Qxb6; 22.Nf3 Bb8; 23.c3!** White strives to open lines at all costs. But he avoids the reckless 23.Nxd4 Qxd4; 24.Qxb7+ when after 24...Kd8!; 25.Rd1 Qd7; 26.Qxd7+ Kxd7. Black would have a comfortable game. **23...dxc3; 24.Rb1.**

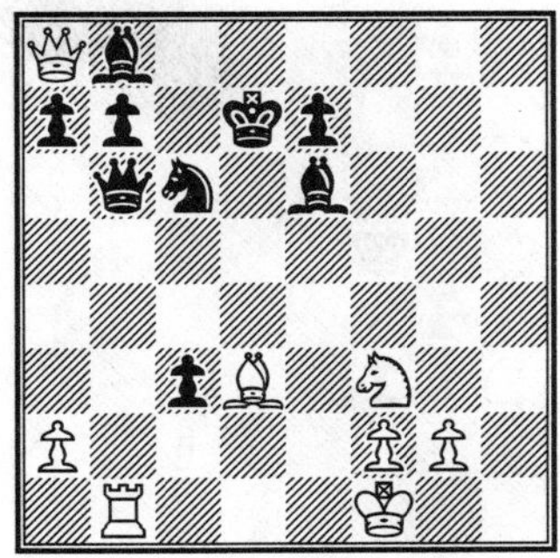

24...Qxb1+!; 25.Bxb1 Kc7. Black has cleverly sacrificed his queen in order to achieve a position where his opponent's queen lies uselessly in the corner. He also relies on his 'secret weapon' - the pawn on c2. Now if White had played 26.Ke1 that weapon would have been rendered harmless and White would be able to win without too much difficulty, but White is careless. **26.Be4? Bd5!; 27.Bh7.** Obviously Black will promote the c-pawn if the bishop on e4 leaves the long diagonal. **27...e6; 28.Ng5 Nb4?** Now Black misses his chance. After 28...Na5!; 29.Ke2 Nc4. Black stands better, for example 30.Be4?

30...Bxe4; 31.Nxe4 c2. **29.Ke2 b5; 30.Nxe6+! Kc8; 31.Qxd5 Nxd5; 32.Bf5.**

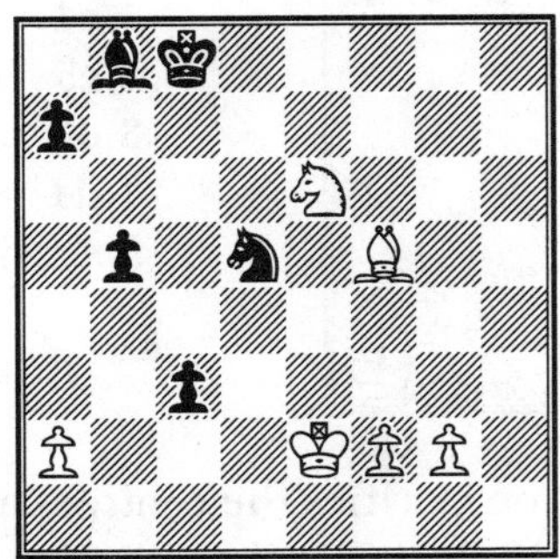

After all that, material is even again! However, White has a loaded battery at f5 and e6. **32...Kd7?** Kengis attributes this mistake to time pressure. Better was 32...Kb7; 33.Be4 Kc6; 34.Nd4+ Kc5; 35.Nb3+! (35.Nxb5? c2!; 36.Kd2 Nb4 and Black wins) 35...Kc6 with a probably draw. **33.Nd4+.** Now White wins. **33...Kd6; 34.Nxb5+ Kc5; 35.Na3 Nb4.**

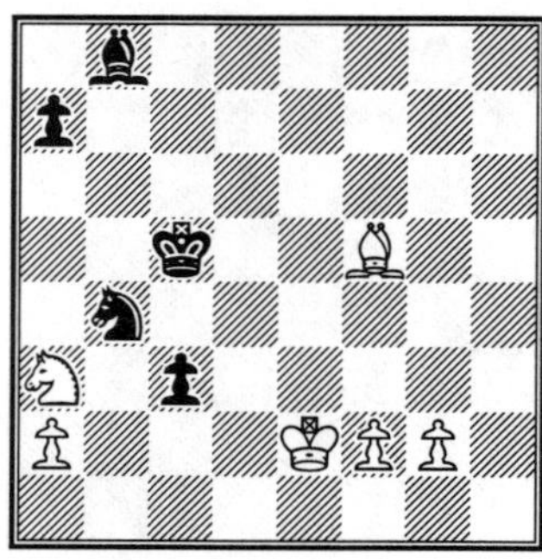

36.Bb1! Bd6; 37.g3 a6; 38.f4 Bc7; 39.Kf3 Kd4; 40.Nc2+ Nxc2; 41.Bxc2 a5. White won.

EXCHANGE VARIATION

1.e4	**Nf6**
2.e5	**Nd5**
3.c4	**Nb6**
4.d4	**d6**
5.exd6	

The **Exchange Variation** clarifies the central pawn structure early in the game, and insures that White will enjoy an advantage in space for some time. The opening does not require thorough preparation by White, and this is a definite plus, since the Alekhine Defense is not seen frequently in the tournament arena. All White needs to know is where to place the pieces, and even that is fairly obvious. The knights will come to c3 and either f3 or e2, and the bishops are deployed at e3 and d3. Castling will take place on the kingside.

Black can respond with one of two plans, either accepting a somewhat inferior structure after ...exd6, where exchanges can take place on the e-file, or the more interesting ...cxd6, which unbalances the position and gives Black counterplay on the c-file. The latter is the preference of most players, and is discussed in the present game.

(129) FISCHER - BERLINER [B02]

New York, 1960

1.e4 Nf6; 2.e5 Nd5; 3.c4 Nb6; 4.d4 d6; 5.exd6 cxd6; 6.Nc3 g6. Black will use the power of the fianchettoed bishop to place pressure on d4, which is the target of Black's operations in the early middlegame. **7.Bd3.** 7.Be3 is a common alternative, but Fischer's choice has logic behind it. White wants to castle quickly, so the kingside pieces get developed first. **7...Bg7; 8.Nge2.**

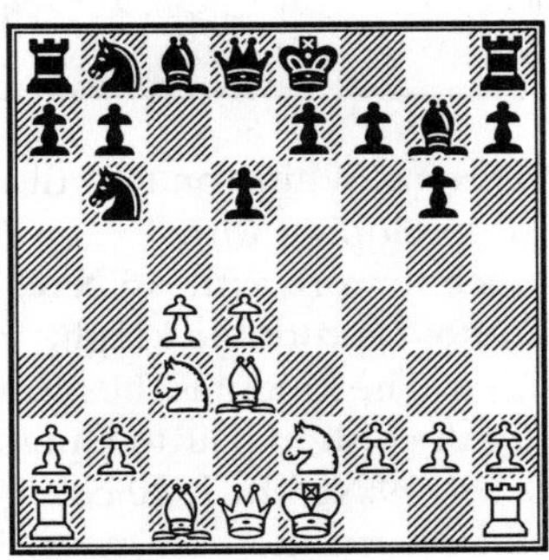

The knight goes to e2, because if it is placed at f3, it is subject to a pin with ...Bg4. **8...Nc6; 9.Be3.** Modern theory considers an advance to d5 to be more effective, but the text is also good. 9.d5 Ne5; 10.0–0 Nxd3; 11.Qxd3 Bf5; 12.Qd1 looks like a fine line for Black, who has gained the bishop pair and is developing with tempo. However, Black is ill-equipped to deal with the coming kingside attack, for example 12...0–0; 13.b3 Nd7; 14.Be3 Ne5; 15.h3 Qd7; 16.f4 Nd3; 17.g4 with a crushing position in Rogers-Duijenbade, The Hague 1960.

9...0–0; 10.0–0 e5. This is the best plan for Black. White now must decide what to do about the d-pawn, which is under attack from three enemy forces. White must advance, since the capture at e5 leads nowhere. **11.d5 Ne7; 12.b3 Nd7; 13.Ne4.**

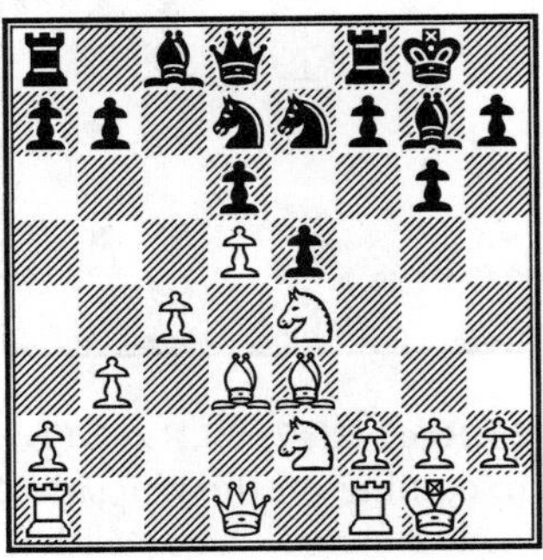

The knight takes up this active position, not fearing ...f5, which would critically weaken the e6-square. **13...Nf5; 14.Bg5.** White must preserve this bishop to try to infiltrate the kingside on the dark squares. **14...f6; 15.Bd2.**

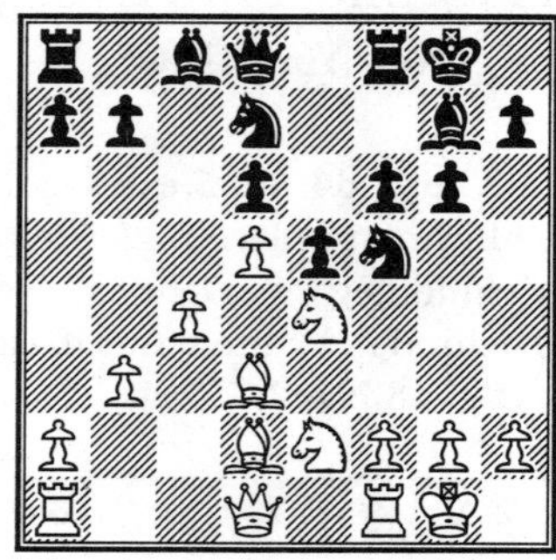

15...Nc5? This is a serious error. White can now disrupt Black's pawn structure. Black should have continued developing with 15...Qc7, after which White has an advantage in space but not much to work with. **16.Nxc5 dxc5; 17.Bxf5!** A fine positional decision. If Fischer did not capture the knight, Black would station it at d6, blockading White's passed pawn. The knight is the most effective blockading piece, and White is willing to give up the bishop pair to eliminate it.

17...Bxf5; 18.f4 exf4. 18...e4; 19.Ng3 Bd7; 20.Nxe4 f5; 21.Nc3 and White is just a pawn up. 18...Qd6 would have been the best move. **19.Nxf4 Qd6; 20.Nh5!** It is clear that Black's bishops are ineffective, but without them, the king would have no defense, so White eliminates one. **20...Rae8; 21.Nxg7 Kxg7; 22.Bf4 Qd7; 23.Qd2.** White cannot count on an endgame victory, despite the passed pawn, since the bishops of opposite color make that goal almost unachievable, especially since the pawn chain on the queenside can be attacked by the enemy bishop in the ending. The opposite colored bishops give rise to attacking chances, however, and Fischer deftly exploits them.

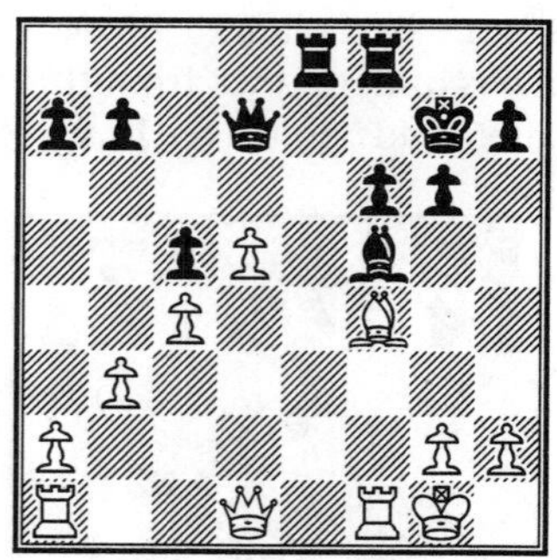

23...Rf7; 24.Bh6+ Kg8; 25.Rae1 Rfe7; 26.Rxe7 Qxe7. Black now controls the e-file, but there is a pawn storm coming on the kingside. **27.h3 Qe4; 28.Qf2!** 28.g4 is premature because of 28...Bxg4; 29.hxg4 Qxg4+ with a draw. **28...Qe7; 29.g4 Bd3; 30.Rd1 Be4; 31.d6! Qe5; 32.Bf4 Qc3; 33.d7 Rd8; 34.Qe2.** The White pieces are capable of both attack and defense, and there are no chances for Black to escape with an attack on White's king.

34...Qf3. 34...Qxh3; 35.Qxe4 Qxg4+; 36.Kf2 Qxd1; 37.Qe6+ Kg7; 38.Qe7+. White wins. **35.Qxf3 Bxf3; 36.Bc7.** Black resigned here, as if each side captures a rook, the White pawn cannot be prevented from promoting to a queen at d8. **White won.**

FOUR PAWNS ATTACK

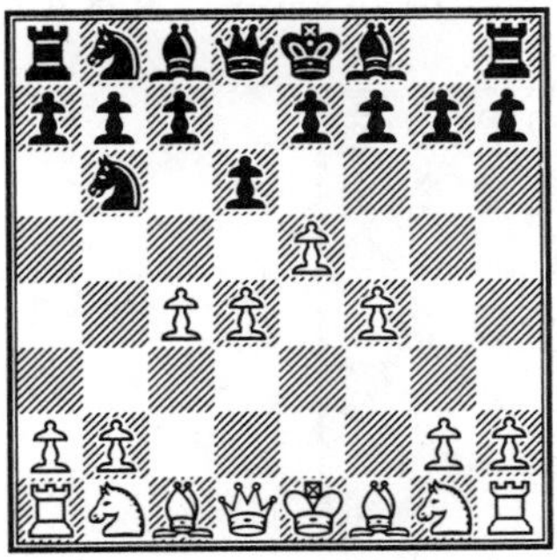

1.e4	**Nf6**
2.e5	**Nd5**
3.d4	**d6**
4.c4	**Nb6**
5.f4	

The **Four Pawns Attack** is what Black really wants to see in the Alekhine. Although White can manage a small positional advantage if all the complicated streams are navigated properly, it is enormously difficult to keep track of all the finesses.

In the Four Pawns Attack the first player attempts to seize the maximum amount of territory in the center and hold on to it. From Black's point of view, this is a welcome prospect, since it gives rise to maximal opportunities for hypermodern counterplay against the broad pawn front. Theoretical judgment varies from time to time, but at present it seems that White retains a slight advantage with proper play.

(130) DE WIT - NIJBOER [B03]

Dutch Open Championship, 1981

1.e4 Nf6; 2.e5 Nd5; 3.d4 d6; 4.c4 Nb6; 5.f4.

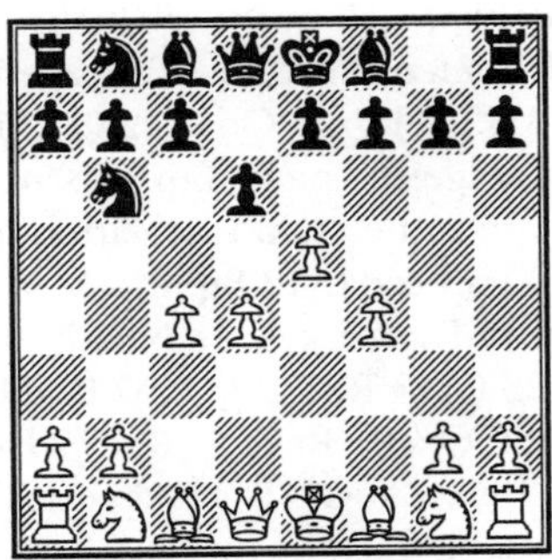

5...dxe5; 6.fxe5 Nc6. Black can also try the wild and complex move 6...c5, but it is now considered weak because it involves a queen sacrifice which is not sufficient for Black. 6...c5; 7.d5 e6; 8.Nc3 exd5; 9.cxd5 c4 and now 10.d6 Nc6; 11.Nf3 Bg4; 12.Bf4 g5; 13.Ne4! forces Black to give up the queen or face certain ruin. The main line continues 13...gxf4; 14.Nf6+ Qxf6; 15.exf6 0–0–0 and now Darius Pour's 16.Qc1, played in a blitz game, looks like the end of the line for Black. There are many complicated variations, but the most resistant is 16.Qc1 Re8+; 17.Kf2 Bxd6; 18.Bxc4 Bc5+; 19.Kf1 Bxf3; 20.gxf3 Re3; 21.Be6+! fxe6; 22.Qxc5 Rxf3+; 23.Kg2 Re3; 24.Rhe1 Rg8+; 25.Kh1 when the White king has reached a safe haven. **7.Be3 Bf5; 8.Nc3 e6.**

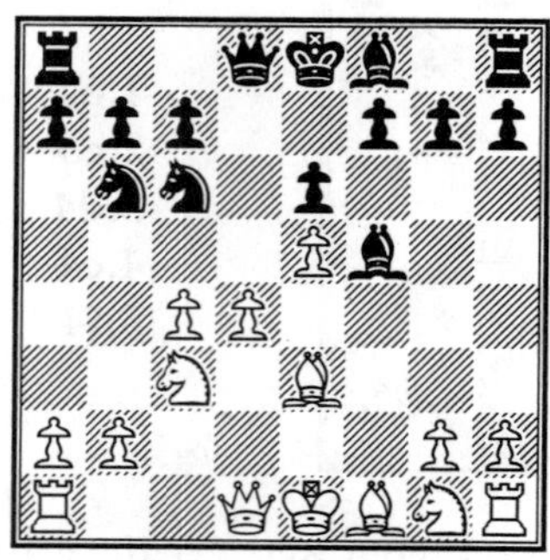

This is a typical formation in the Four Pawns Attack. The best move for White is now 9.Be2!, which prevents any pin after White plays Nf3 and Black responds with ...Bg4. White then has a slightly better game. **9.Nf3.** 9.Be2 Be7; 10.Nf3 0–0; 11.0–0 leaves Black with no real plan other than to try to undermine the center by striking at the head of the pawn chain at e5. 11...f6; 12.exf6 Bxf6; 13.Qd2 Qe7; 14.Rad1 Rad8; 15.Qc1 and White has better positioned pieces, Narciso-Mellado, Spanish Championship 1993.

9...Be7. There are three important variations for Black here. Black can simply develop, as in our main line, or can pin the enemy knight, despite the loss of tempo, or can try to castle queenside, which is very risky. 9...Qd7; 10.Be2 0–0–0; 11.0–0 and now 11...Bg4 is considered necessary, to indirectly prevent the advance of White's d-pawn. But White has another plan available here: 12.c5! Nd5; 13.Nxd5 Qxd5; 14.b4 Qe4; 15.Qb3 Nxd4; 16.Nxd4 Bxe2; 17.Nxe2 and while Black takes time to recover the piece, White can attack. 17...Rd3; 18.Qa4 Qxe3+; 19.Kh1 Qxe2; 20.Qxa7 Rd2; 21.Qa8+ Kd7; 22.Qxb7 and White, who has now sacrificed a piece, has a powerful attack as in Minasian-Donchenko, Neberezhnye Chelny 1988.

Note that the queen at b7 defends the pawn at g2, eliminating Black's checkmating threat. 9...Bg4; 10.Be2 Bxf3; 11.gxf3 Qd7; 12.Qd2 is a little more comfortable for White, who has an advantage in space, but it is not by any means critical for Black. Avoiding lines like these is the main motivation for the move order finesse

9.Be2 Nb4; 10.Rc1 c5; 11.a3 cxd4; 12.Bg5 dxc3; 13.Bxd8 Rxd8; 14.Qb3 cxb2; 15.Qxb2 Na4; 16.Qa1 Nc2+; 17.Rxc2 Bxc2; 18.Nd4 Bg6; 19.c5 Nxc5; 20.Bb5+ Nd7; 21.Qc3 a6; 22.Bxd7+ Rxd7; 23.Qc8+ Rd8; 24.Qxb7 Rxd4; 25.Qc6+ Rd7; 26.0–0 Bd3; 27.Rxf7 Bc5+; 28.Kh1 Bb5; 29.Qxe6+ Re7; 30.Rxe7+ Bxe7; 31.Qc8+ Bd8; 32.Qe6+ Be7; 33.Qc8+ Bd8; 34.Qe6+ Line Znosko Borovsky-Alekhine, Paris France 1925.

10.d5! This is more promising than the quiet 10.Be2. **10...Nb4.** 10...exd5; 11.cxd5 can be played first, for example: 11...Nb4; 12.Nd4 Bd7; 13.e6! fxe6; 14.dxe6 Bc6; 15.Qg4 Bh4+; 16.g3 Bxh1; 17.0–0–0 0–0; 18.gxh4 is a very complicated position, whose mysteries have not been fully explored yet. **11.Rc1.**

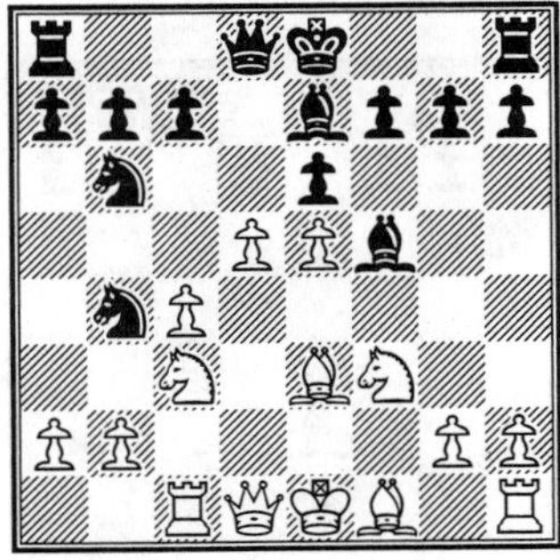

11...f6. This move tries to break up the White center immediately, but does not lead to equality. **12.a3 Na6; 13.exf6?!** White should play 13.g4 Bxg4 (13...Bg6; 14.dxe6! gives White an indisputable advantage.) 14.Rg1.2 Now Black is in trouble after either 14...f5 or (14...Bh5; 15.Be2 fxe5; 16.Ng5! Bxe2; 17.Qxe2 Bxg5; 18.Rxg5 Mestrovic-Cafferty, Postal 1973.) 15.h3 Bxf3; 16.Qxf3 0–0; 17.Rc2!

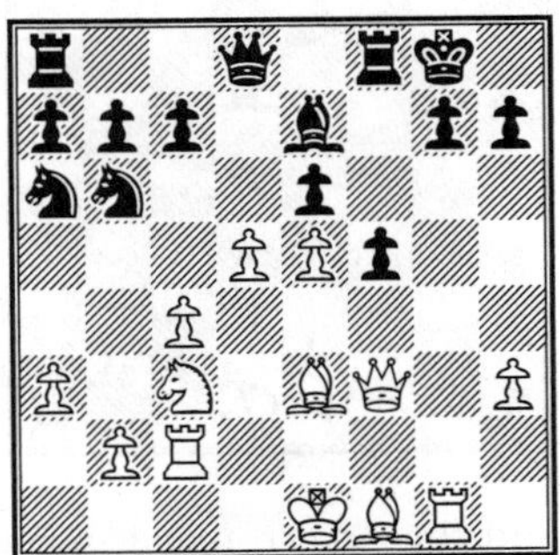

Velimirovic-Gipslis, Havana 1971. **13...Bxf6; 14.Nd4 0–0; 15.dxe6.** Black has a clear advantage after 15.Nxf5 exf5; 16.Be2 Qe7; 17.Bxb6 axb6; 18.0–0 Nc5; Minic-Vaganian, Erewat 1971. **15...Bxd4; 16.Qxd4 Qe7!**

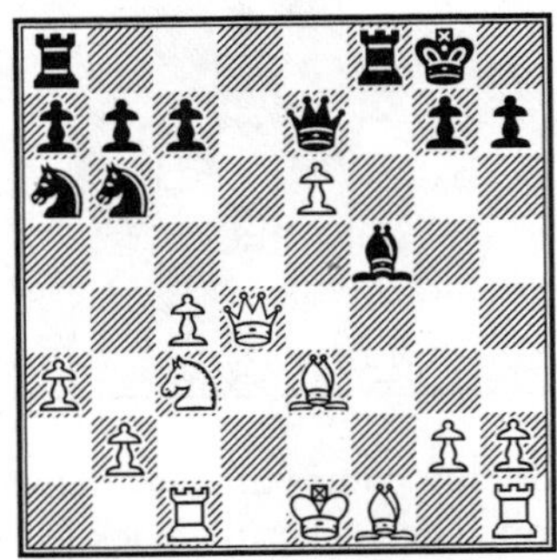

Black wisely keeps the queens on the board, cognizant of the fact that White is going to have real problems defending his king. **17.c5 Rad8; 18.Qe5 Nd7!; 19.Nd5.** In a difficult situation White plays for complications. If 19.Qg3 Qxe6; 20.Nd5!? Ne5!?

21.Nf4 Qe7; 22.Be2, Black can play 22...Nd3+; 23.Bxd3 Bxd3.

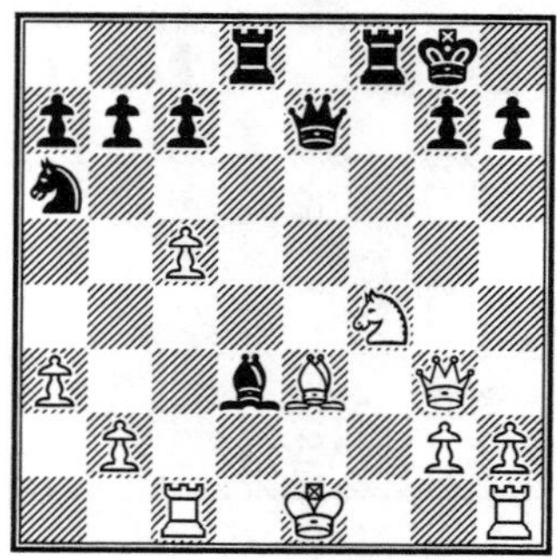

with a better position. **19...Qe8.** After 19...Qh4+; 20.Qg3 Qxg3+; 21.hxg3 Bxe6; 22.Bxa6 bxa6; 23.Nxc7.

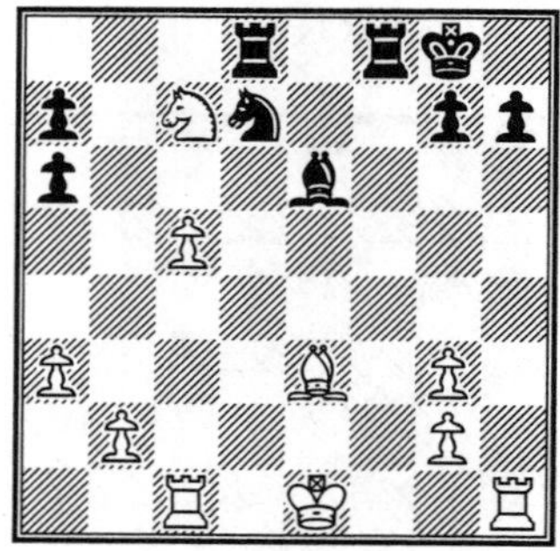

White is much better, and the c-pawn may prove unstoppable. **20.Qg3 Bxe6; 21.Nf4 Naxc5!**

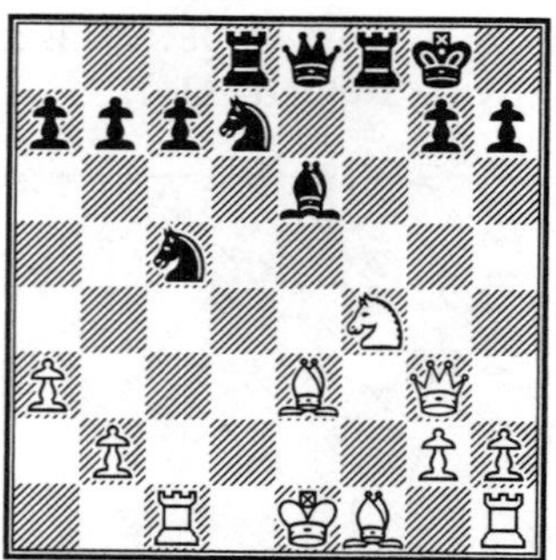

The 'useless' ...Na6 suddenly comes alive to deliver the decisive blow against White's overextended position. The back-rank black forces are poised to control the three central diagonals, and White's king is still a sitting duck at e1! **22.Bxc5** On 22.Rxc5 Black wins with 22...Nxc5; 23.Bxc5 Qd7; 24.Be3 Qd1+; 25.Kf2 Rd2+.

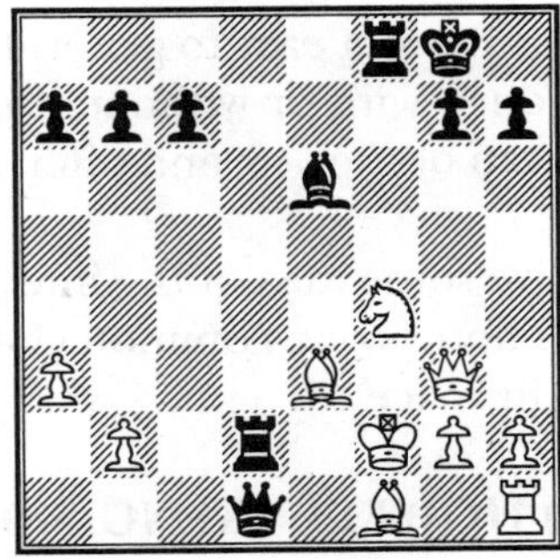

...and now 26.Kg1 (26.Bxd2 Qxd2+; 27.Kf3 h5.) 26...Bc4. **22...Nxc5; 23.Rxc5 Bc4+; 24.Kf2.** 24.Be2 would allow 24...Rxf4, while 24.Ne2 loses to 24...Rf1. **24...Rd2+; 25.Kg1 Bxf1; 26.Rxc7 Qe5; 27.Qb3+ Kh8; 28.Qc3 Qxc3; 29.bxc3 g5!**

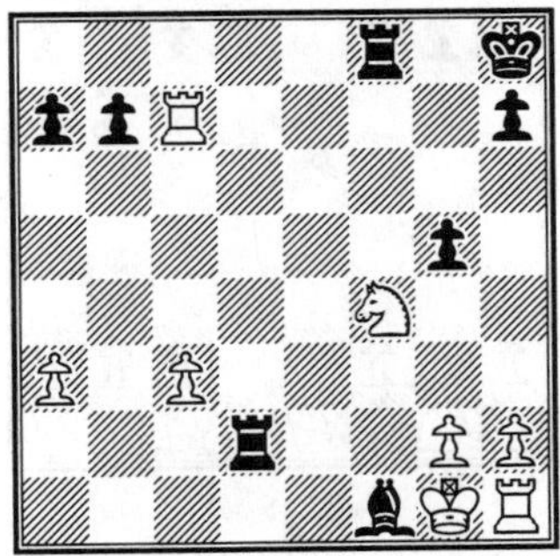

Now it's all over. **30.Kxf1 Rxf4+; 31.Ke1.** White's flag fell, but there would have been no point in playing on after **31...Rb2; 32.g3 Re4+; 33.Kf1 Ra4; 34.Re7 Rxa3** (Notes based on commentary by Frans Borm.). **Black won.**

MODERN VARIATIONS

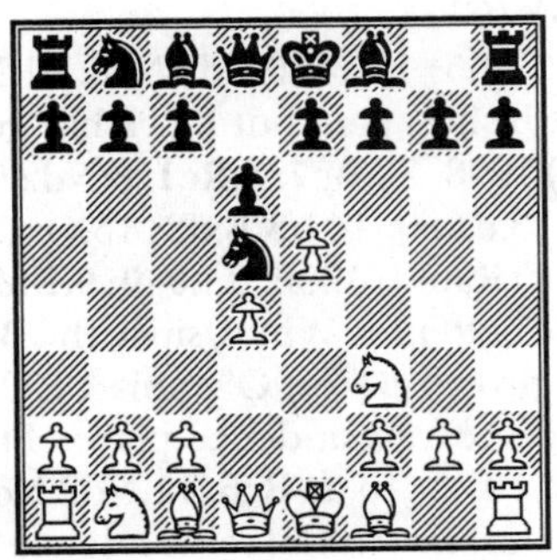

1.e4 Nf6
2.e5 Nd5
3.d4 d6
4.Nf3

The **Modern Variations** of the Alekhine Defense display a number of different personalities, and it is not easy to generalize. Black can apply pressure along the a1-h8 diagonal, with or without a preliminary capture at e5. Either a knight or a pawn can occupy c6, and often the bishop emerges from c8 to take roost at g4.

The following gaves give some idea of the internal diversity of the Modern Variations Alekhine. There is one common characteristic, however, and that is White's advantage in space.

(131) HOWELL - KENGIS [B04]

London, 1991

1.e4 Nf6; 2.e5 Nd5; 3.Nf3 d6; 4.d4 dxe5; 5.Nxe5 g6.

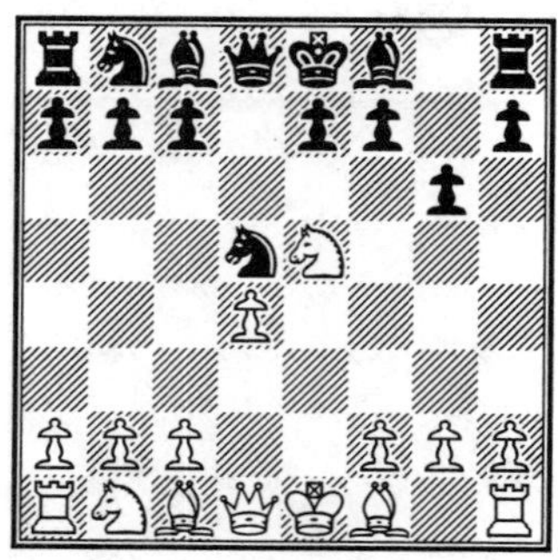

The Kengis Variation is a refinement on the Alburt Variation. Before fianchettoing, Black clarifies the central situation. This approach for Black had been doing quite well until 1996, when it ran into a couple of firestorms.

6.Bc4. 6.Nd2!? is possibly the strongest move. Miles-Pons, Andorra 1996 continued 6...Bg7; 7.Ndf3 0–0; 8.c4 Nb6; 9.Be2 N8d7; 10.Bf4 Nxe5; 11.Nxe5 Nd7; 12.Qd2! Nxe5; 13.Bxe5 Bxe5; 14.dxe5 Qxd2+; 15.Kxd2 and White had a significantly better endgame. This plan requires additional tests, but it looks very strong. 6.g3 is another new try. 6...Nd7; 7.Bg2 Nxe5; 8.dxe5 c6; 9.0–0 Bg7; 10.Qe2 Be6; 11.b3 Qc8; 12.Bb2 Bh3; 13.Nd2 Bxg2; 14.Kxg2 0–0; 15.c4 Nc7; 16.Ne4 and White enjoyed a large spatial advantage in Wolff-deFirmian, New York (CITS) 1996.

6...c6; 7.0–0. 7.Nc3 Bg7; 8.Nxd5 cxd5; 9.Bb5+ Bd7; 10.Bd3 Nc6; 11.Nxd7 Qxd7 is minimally better for White, thanks to the bishop pair, but Black has good central counterplay, Zie Jun-Hort, London (Foxtrot) 1996. **7...Bg7; 8.Re1.** 8.Nd2 0–0; 9.Ndf3 Nd7; 10.Nd3 a5; 11.a4 N7b6; 12.Bb3 Bg4; 13.c3 e6; 14.h3 Bxf3; 15.Qxf3 was nothing special for White in Almasi-Kengis, Bern (Rapid) 1996. **8...0–0; 9.Bb3.** 9.c3 Be6; 10.Nd2 Nd7; 11.Nxd7 Qxd7; 12.Ne4 is a little better for White, since the Black bishop sits a bit awkwardly on e6, Van der Wiel-Bagirov, Yerevan Olympiad 1996.

9...Be6. 9...a5 is preferred by the Dutch correspondence player Etmans, who likes an early advance of the a-pawn as Black. 10.c3 (10.a4 Be6; 11.Nd2 Nd7; 12.Ndf3 Nxe5; 13.Nxe5 Nc7 equalized in De Wit-Etmans, Dutch Correspondence Championship 1980.) 10...Be6; 11.Nd2 Nd7; 12.Nef3 Bg4; 13.h3 Bxf3; 14.Nxf3 e6; 15.Qe2 a4; 16.Bxd5 cxd5 gave Black a reasonably solid position in Oomen-Etmans, Dutch Correspondence Championship 1996.

10.c3. 10.Nd2 Nd7; 11.Nef3 Nc7; 12.Ne4 Bxb3; 13.axb3 Ne6; 14.c3 Re8; 15.h4 launched a kingside attack in Adams-Tu Hoang, Yerevan Olympiad 1996. **10...Nd7; 11.Nf3.** 11.Nd3 b5; 12.a4 Re8; 13.Nd2 a6; 14.Nf3 Bg4; 15.axb5 axb5; 16.Rxa8 Qxa8; 17.h3 Bxf3; 18.Qxf3 e6; 19.Bg5 h6; 20.Bh4 Qa7; 21.Bg3 was agreed drawn in Van Buuren-Etmans, Dutch Correspondence Championship 1985, but I prefer White's chances in the final position. **11...Nc7; 12.Bxe6 Nxe6; 13.Qb3 Qb6; 14.Qc4 c5; 15.d5 Nc7!**

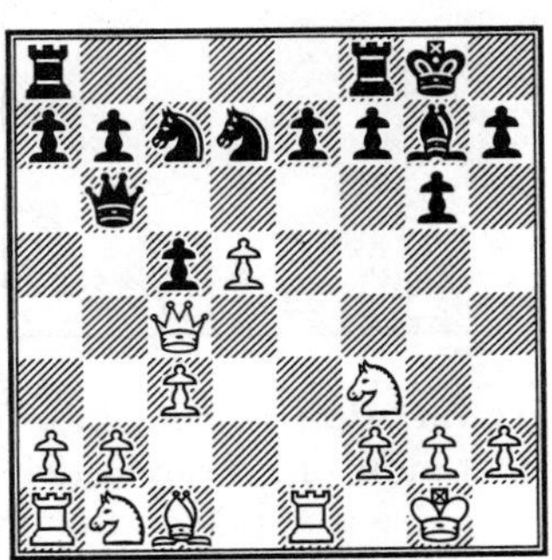

Black temporarily sacrifices the e-pawn but will get the d-pawn in return. **16.Rxe7 Qd6; 17.Re1 Qxd5; 18.Na3 Nb6; 19.Qxd5 Ncxd5.** The position is now perhaps a little better for Black, who has the more active bishop. **20.Bg5 h6; 21.Bd2 Na4; 22.Rab1 Rfe8; 23.Kf1.** 23.Nc4 looks more sensible, since the knight is more actively posted there and can come to e3 if needed. 23.Nb5 is also interesting. The text is logical, however, protecting the rook at f1.

23...a6; 24.Nc4 b5; 25.Ne3 Red8!? An interesting move, though the simple retreat of the knight to f6 would also have been strong. **26.Rec1?** This is a very ugly move and White's first rank is becoming a mess. 26.Ng4 would have been better, encouraging the Black king to step further from the center with ...Kh7. Later, Nge5 will be possible. **26...Nf6; 27.c4 Ne4; 28.Rc2 Rd3; 29.Be1 Re8; 30.Nd2 Nd6; 31.Ke2 Rdxe3+ 32.fxe3.** Now White is clearly worse. **32...Nf5; 33.Bf2 Nd4+; 34.Kd1 Nxc2; 35.Kxc2 f5; 36.a3 Kf7; 37.b3 Nc3; 38.Rf1 h5; 39.h3 Ne4; 40.Nxe4 Rxe4; 41.cxb5 axb5.**

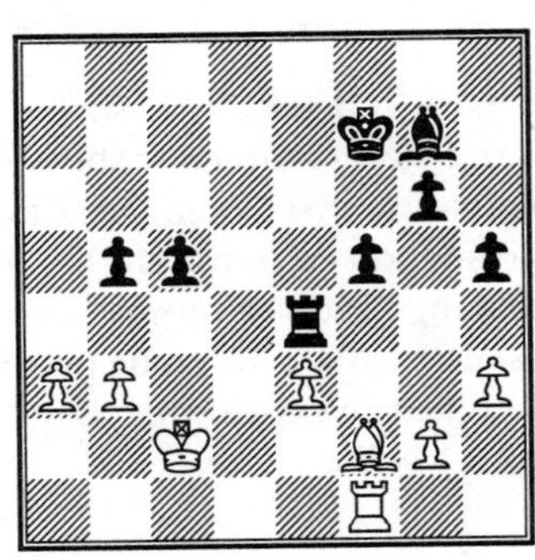

Black has a much better bishop in this endgame. **42.Rd1 Bh6; 43.Kd3 Ke6; 44.Ke2 Bg5; 45.Kf3 h4; 46.Rd2 Bf6; 47.Ra2 Kd5; 48.a4 b4; 49.a5 c4; 50.bxc4+ Kxc4; 51.a6 b3; 52.Ra4+ Kb5. Black won.**

(132) IVANOVIC - ALBURT [B04]

Reykjavik, 1982

1.e4 Nf6; 2.e5 Nd5; 3.d4 d6; 4.Nf3 g6.

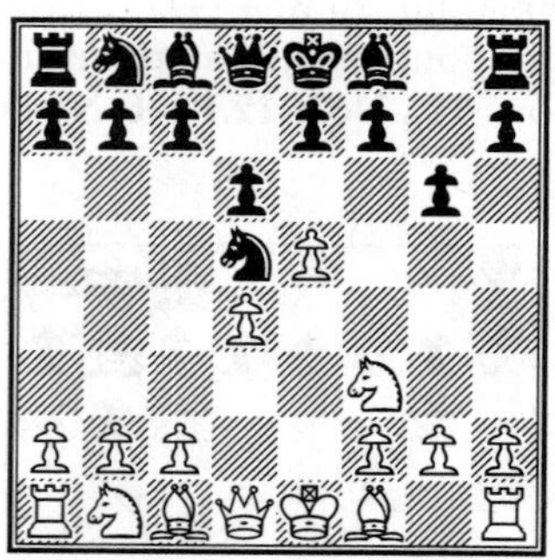

This variation, the **Albert Variation**, is named for former United States Champion Lev Alburt, who has spent most of his career defending the Black side of the Alekhine Defense. The primary idea is to pile on the pressure at e5, and White can either attempt to refute the plan with vigorous actions or simple transpose to the quieter waters of the Exchange Variation. **5.Be2.** 5.Bc4 is more ambitious, for example 5...Nb6; 6.Bb3 Bg7; 7.exd6 cxd6; 8.0–0 0–0; 9.Re1 and White has a small advantage, because it is difficult to find a way to get Black's pieces into the game, Anand-Timman, Linares 1992. **5...Bg7; 6.c4 Nb6.**

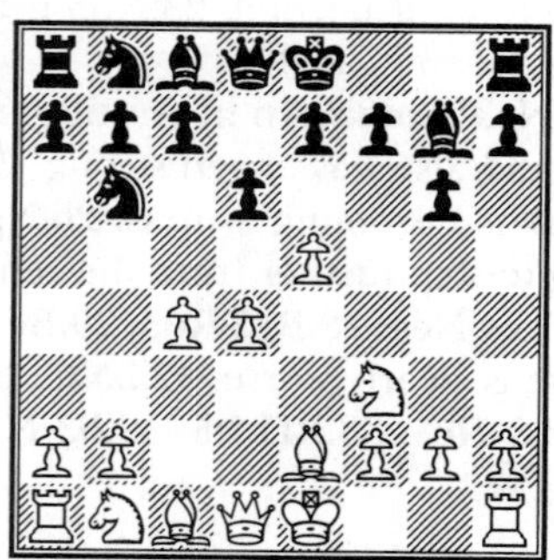

7.Be3? You may find it hard to believe that such a solid developing move is a mistake - but it is! The initiative now completely shifts over to Black. 7.exd6 would have been wiser, transposing into the Exchange Variation. **7...dxe5; 8.Nxe5 Bxe5!** It is highly unusual for Black to spend two tempi in the opening on the fianchetto of his king's bishop, only to exchange it three moves later for a mere knight. Perhaps this is why Ivanovic had not seen 8...Bxe5! when he played 7.Be3. There is a valuable chess and human lesson to be learned from this: Beware of stereotyped thinking. **9.dxe5 Qxd1+; 10.Kxd1 Nc6; 11.Nd2.**

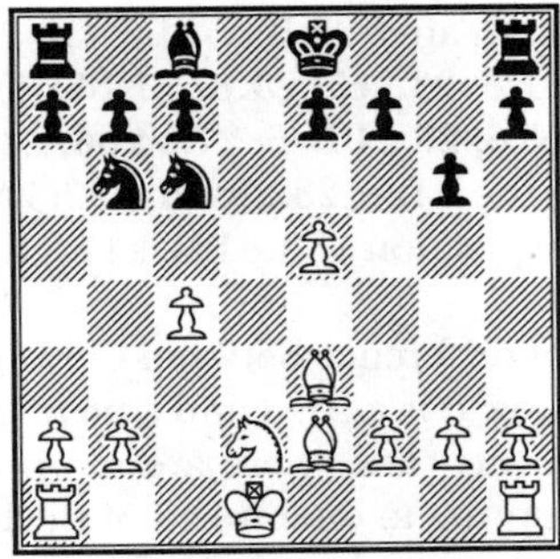

Black has a clear advantage. His initiative is of greater value than White's bishop pair. In addition, Black has the more compact pawn structure and safer king position.

11...Be6. 11...Bf5, which is the most active post for the bishop is also possible. After 12.g4 Be6; Black's 11th move becomes a zwischenzug to provoke another White pawn weakness. However, White would be able to use the extra g4 push to his advantage after 13.f4, followed by Rf1 and f5. Analysis (see below), however, proves 11...Bf5 to be the superior move. Note that 11...Nxe5 is inferior, giving away Black's advantage since Black's extra pawn would be valueless. 11...Bf5!?; 12.g4 Be6; 13.f4 0–0–0; 14.b3 Nd4; 15.Bxd4 Rxd4 works out well for Black. 11...Nxe5?!; 12.Bd4 f6; 13.Bxe5! fxe5 provides level chances.

12.f4 0–0–0; 13.b3 Rd7?! On 13...Nd4, 14.g3! gives White a solid position which is difficult to crack. Thus the difference between 11...Bf5!; 12. g4 Be6 and 11...Be6 becomes apparent. By inserting the zwischenzug 11...Bf5, Black would have provoked a fatal weakness in the pawn structure. Nevertheless, after 13...Rd7 the game actually peters out into a drawing equality. Black should play 13...f6!, but even here the black bishop would be better placed on f5. 13...f6! is the best move, since after 14.exf6 exf6; Black has a strong attack.

14.Ke1 Bf5. This is necessary in order to prevent 15.Ne4 followed by 16.Nc5 or 16.Ng5. **15.Kf2 Rhd8; 16.Nf3 f6.** Black stops 17.Ng5 and even threatens to penetrate with 17...Nb4. His control of the open d-file is illusory, since all potential invasion points along that file are adequately guarded by enemy pieces. White's bishop pair neutralizes Black's temporary initiative. The game remains evenly balanced. **17.Bc5 fxe5; 18.Nxe5 Nxe5; 19.fxe5 Rd2; 20.Ke3 Rc2; 21.Rhc1!**

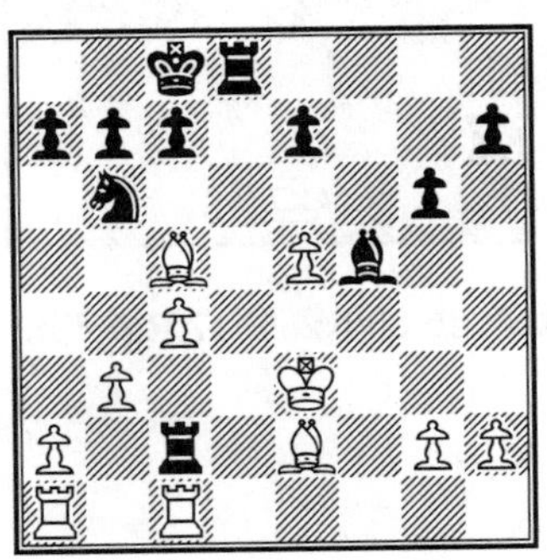

This prevents Black from doubling on the second rank. **21...Rxc1; 22.Rxc1 Nd7; 23.Bd4.** The bishop gets shut in after 23.Bxa7? b6. On 23.Bxe7? Re8 and 24...Nxe5, when Black seizes the initiative. **23...c5; 24.Bc3 Nb8!** The knight is headed for the strong outpost at d4. **25.a3 Nc6; 26.g4 Be6; 27.b4 b6; 28.bxc5.** White is anticipating a future rook invasion along the b-file. **28...bxc5; 29.h3 Nd4.** Threatening 30...Nxe2 and 31...Bxc4+. The powerful position of the Black knight compensates for the White bishop pair.

30.Bd3 h5. The essential difference between the White and Black armies is the bishop versus the knight factor. It is a tried and true maxim that bishops are preferable to knights when, as in this case, there are pawn clusters on both wings. By playing 30...h5 Black is attempting to dissolve all of the kingside pawns and create a more favorable situation for his knight. **31.Bxg6 hxg4; 32.hxg4.** 32.h4! is correct, reaching an even position after 32...Nf5+; 33.Bxf5 Bxf5;. **32...Bxg4; 33.Rf1 Be6; 34.Bd3 Nb3!**

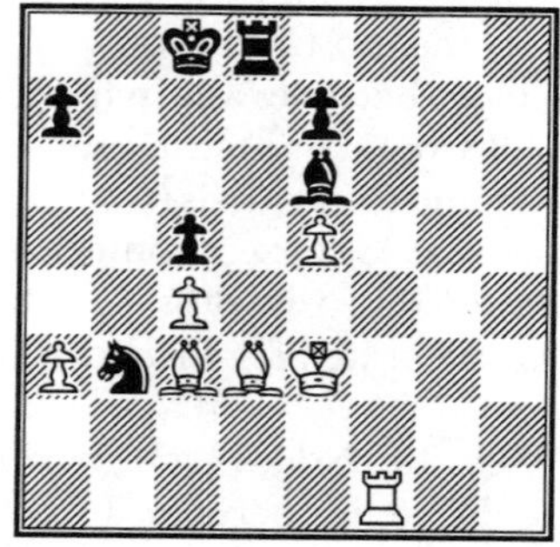

Black starts to take control of the game with, limiting the squares available to White's rook and king. **35.Rg1.** 35.Rb1? Rxd3+; 36.Kxd3 Bf5+ wins for Black. **35...Rh8** The game concluded: **36.Bf1 Rh4!; 37.Rg3 Kd7; 38.Bd3 Nd4; 39.Kd2 Rh2+ 40.Kd1 Ra2; 41.Bxd4 cxd4; 42.Be2 Bf5; 43.Rg5 Ke6.**

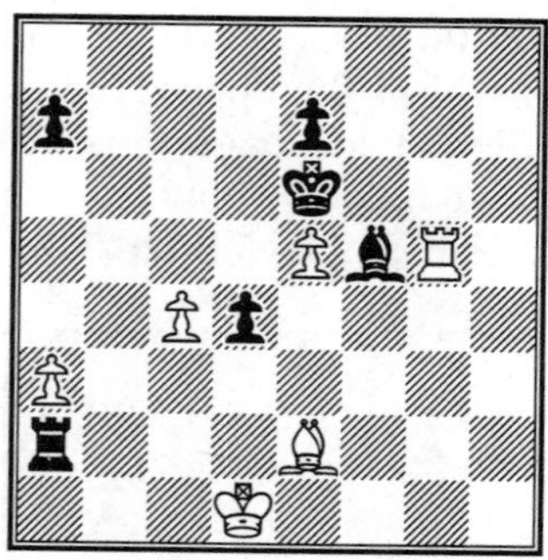

44.c5? Rxa3; 45.Bb5 Rc3; 46.c6 Kxe5; 47.Rg2 Rb3. Black won.

(133) KARPOV - ALBURT [B05]

Malta (Olympiad), 1980

1.e4 Nf6; 2.e5 Nd5; 3.d4 d6; 4.Nf3 Bg4.

This is the Modern Variation of the Alekhine Defense. It leads to a small but persistent advantage for White, and Black has been turning to alternatives such as former U.S. Champion Lev Alburt's pet line with 4...g6, which he perhaps should have adopted for this important encounter. **5.Be2 Nc6.** This is a divergence from the main line with 5...e6; 6.0–0 Be7; 7.c4 Nb6; 8.Nc3 0–0; 9.Be3 d5; 10.c5 Bxf3; 11.gxf3 which is a typical continuation. But Alburt had an unpleasant experience earlier in the year against the well-prepared theoretician Leonid Shamkovich at the Heraldica tournament in New York. 11...Nc8; 12.f4 and this position remains topical.

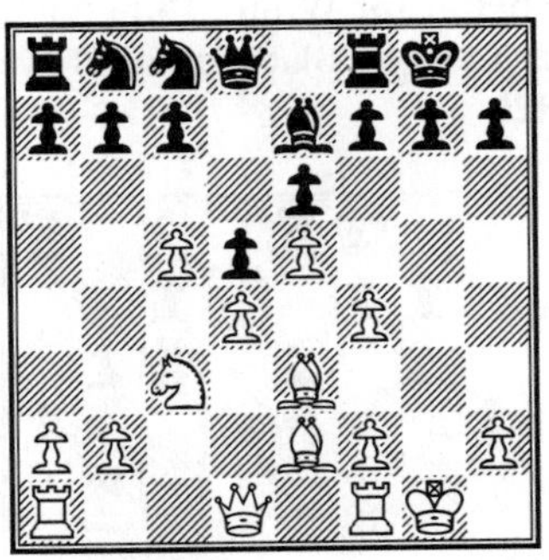

A) 12...f5; 13.Kh1 has been doing well for White: 13...Bh4 (13...Kh8; 14.Rg1 Rg8; 15.Qd2 allowed White to control too much space on the queenside in Herrera-Diaz Perez, Cuba 1995.) 14.Rg1 g6; 15.b4 Rf7; 16.b5 Nd7; 17.a4 Nf8; 18.Qf1 b6; 19.a5 Rb8; 20.axb6 axb6; 21.c6 and Black was being strangled in Glek-Kertesz, Bonn 1995.

B) 12...g6; 13.Kh1 Kh8 and now 14.f5 is critical. (14.Rg1 Bh4; 15.Rg4 Nc6; 16.Qg1 Rg8 is not bad for Black, Leko-Blatny, Brno 1993.) 14...gxf5; 15.Rg1 Rg8; 16.Rxg8+ Qxg8; 17.Bh6 and according to British theoretician Graham Burgess, Black may be be able to weather the storm in the short term, but will have long-term problems.

C) 12...b6; 13.Bd3!? and Alburt went wrong with 13...Bxc5?!, though 13...g6 leads only to messy complications for which Karpov might well have been prepared. 13...g6; 14.Qg4 f5; 15.Qh3 and Shamkovich suggests that White will build an attack by playing Kh1 and then Rg1.

6.c4 Nb6; 7.exd6. This transposes to the Exchange Variation, which is usually reached via 4.c4 Nb6; 5.exd6. 7.e6!? is an interesting alternative. 7.e6!? fxe6; 8.Be3 Bxf3; 9.Bxf3 Nxc4; 10.0–0 is a very promising alternative, seen in Gildardo Garcia-Pogorelov, Albacete 1995. **7...exd6.** This is better than capturing with the c-pawn, after which the advance to d5 is even more effective for White. **8.d5! Bxf3; 9.Bxf3 Ne5; 10.Be2 Qh4.**

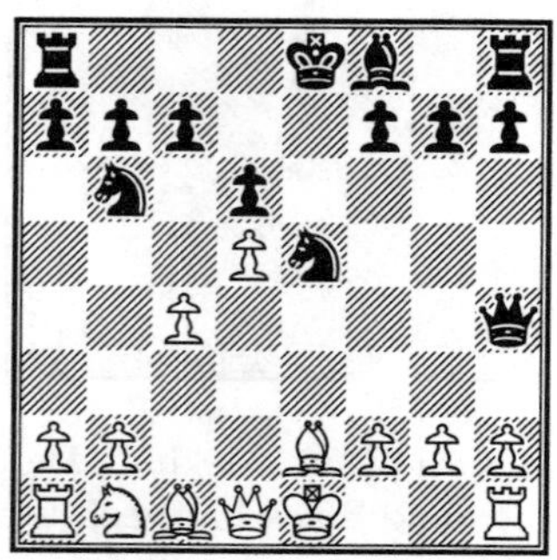

It is possible that 10...g6 is stronger than this ambitious move. 10...Be7; 11.Be3 0–0; 12.Nd2 Bf6; 13.Qc2 Ng6; 14.0–0 Re8; 15.Bd3 Bg5; 16.Bd4 Bxd2; 17.Qxd2 Ne5; 18.b3 Nxd3; 19.Qxd3 Qg5; 20.f4 Qh4; 21.Rf3 f6; 22.Raf1 Qh5; 23.g4 Qg6; 24.Qxg6 hxg6; 25.Re3 Rxe3; 26.Bxe3 Nd7; 27.Bd4 a5; 28.a4 was drawn in Sion Castro-Pogorelov, Zaragoza 1995. **11.0–0 h5; 12.Nd2 g6.** An attempt to improve on 12...Be7; 13.f4 which is known to be better for White. **13.f4 Ng4; 14.Nf3 Qf6; 15.Re1 0–0–0; 16.a4 a5.** This just presents a target. Black should have done something about the bishop at f8 instead. **17.Qd2!**

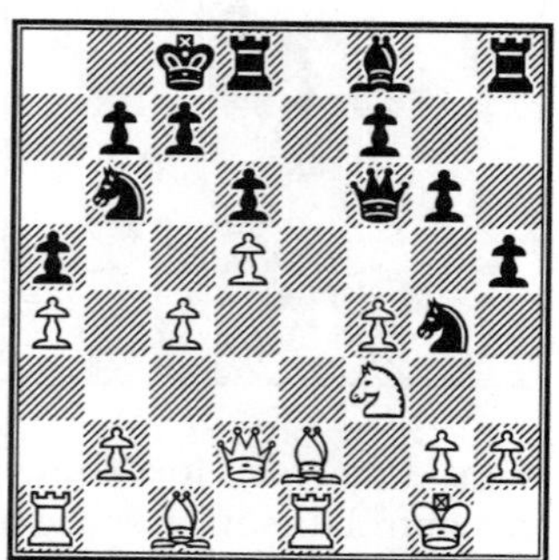

The dark squares are covered, and the White queen will sooner or later grab the weakling at a5. **17...Bg7; 18.h3 Rde8; 19.Bf1 Nh6; 20.Qxa5.** I was watching this game from time to time, since I was working at the Olympiad as one of the arbiters. Of course I was hoping the American team would do well, and was disappointed to see such a quick massacre on board one. But I knew this game would not last too much longer. **20...Nf5; 21.Rd1 Kb8; 22.Ra3 Re4; 23.Qb5 Nc8.**

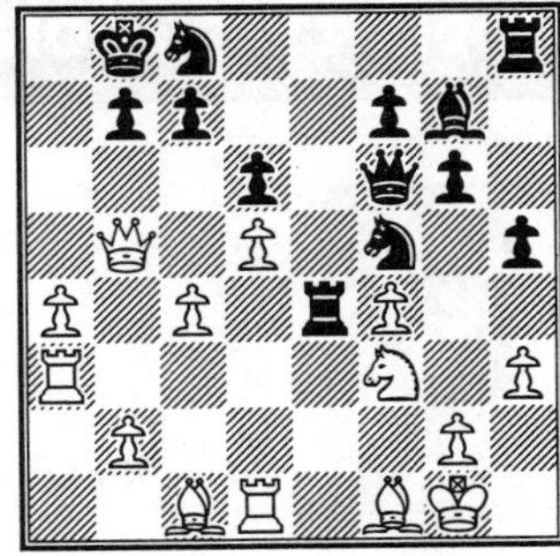

24.Rb3. Even a beginner could find the correct attacking method here! **24...b6; 25.a5! Qe7; 26.Qa6 Re8.** Now Karpov smashes through the final barrier. **27.c5! dxc5; 28.Bb5.** The light squares provide all the illumination needed for victory. **28...c6; 29.Bxc6 Bd4+; 30.Nxd4 Nxd4; 31.axb6 Nf3+; 32.Rxf3 Re1+; 33.Rxe1. White won.**

SCANDINAVIAN DEFENSE

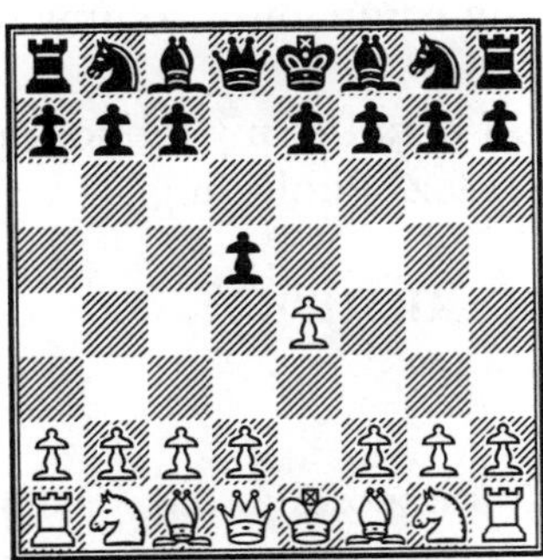

1.e4 d5

The **Scandinavian** has finally achieved a degree of respectability, thanks to its appearance in the 1995 PCA World Championship match between Garry Kasparov and Viswanathan Anand. The challenger used it effectively as a surprise weapon, but the opening has shown that it may be more than just a fad as it is seen more and more frequently in professional and amateur contests.

After 1.e4 d5 White is free to capture the pawn at d5. If Black recaptures immediately with 2...Qd5, then White develops a knight with tempo by playing 3.Nc3, which attacks the queen. If Black delays the capture and plays 2...Nf6, then White is free to develop while Black takes time for ...Nxd5, after which the knight at d5 can itself become a target. It is the former approach which has gained the most attention recently.

MODERN VARIATION

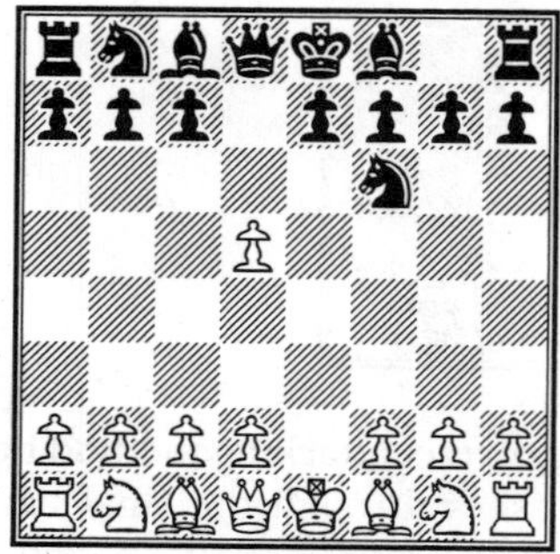

1.e4 d5
2.exd5 Nf6

The **Modern Variation**, or **Scandinavian Gambit**, is commonly seen. It temporarily concedes a little space in the center but that is not a major concession. Most top players do not have confidence in the opening, though they often reach similar positions from the Caro-Kann or Alekhine Defense. Black does not rush to recapture the pawn. It is not easily supported, and radical attempts such as 3.c4 encourage radical reactions, such as 3...e6!?, the Scandinavian Gambit discussed in the companion volume, *Unorthodox Chess Openings.*

The Modern Variation is discussed in detail in my monograph *Gambit Opening Repertoire for Black*, also from Cardoza Publishing.

(134) GELLER - MARIC [B01]
Yugoslavia, 1968

1.e4 d5; 2.exd5 Nf6; 3.d4. 3.Nc3 Nxd5 transposes to the Alekhine Defense, though the variation chosen by White is not among the strongest. **3...Nxd5; 4.Nf3 g6.** This is the Richter Variation. 4...Bg4 is the Gipslis Variation. 5.Be2 (5.Bb5+ c6; 6.Be2 is a slight improvement, since the pawn at c6 just gets in Black's way.)

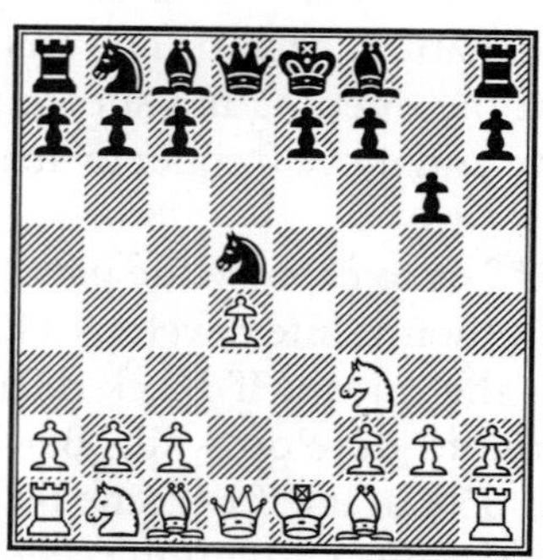

A) 5...e6; 6.0–0 Be7; 7.h3 (7.Ne5 Bxe2; 8.Qxe2 0–0; 9.Rd1 Nd7; 10.c4 N5f6; 11.Bf4 c6; 12.Nc3 Re8; 13.Rd3 Nf8; 14.Rad1 Qa5; 15.a3 Ng6; 16.Bg3 Rac8; 17.Qf3 Bd6; 18.Ng4 Nxg4; 19.Bxd6 Nf6; 20.Ne4 Nxe4; 21.Qxe4 was drawn in Leko-Kamsky, Groningen 1995) 7...Bh5; 8.c4 Nb6; 9.Nc3 Nc6; 10.d5 exd5; 11.Nxd5 Nxd5; 12.cxd5 Bxf3; 13.Bxf3 Ne5; 14.Be4 Bd6; 15.Qh5 Ng6; 16.Bg5 Qd7; 17.f4 f5; 18.Bc2 0–0; 19.Rae1 Nh8; 20.Bh4 g6; 21.Qf3 Qb5; 22.Bb3 a5; 23.a4 Qb4; 24.Kh1 b5; 25.Ra1 Rfe8; 26.Be1 Qc5; 27.Bf2 Qb4; 28.Be1 Qc5; 29.Bc3 Nf7; 30.Qd3 Re4; 31.Qxb5 Qxb5; 32.axb5 Rxf4; 33.Rxf4 Bxf4; 34.Rxa5 Rxa5; 35.Bxa5 Kg7; 36.Ba2 Kf6; 37.b6 cxb6; 38.Bxb6 Bd6; 39.Kg1 Ke5; 40.Kf2 Ke4; 41.Ke2 Ne5; 42.Ba5 Nd7; 43.b4 Kd4; 44.h4 Nf6; 45.Bb6+ Kc3; 46.b5 Kb4; 47.Bd4 Nd7; 48.b6 Kb5 was drawn in Peng Xiaomin-Wong Meng Kong, Beijing (Tan Chin Cup) 1995;

B) 5...Nc6; 6.c4 Nb6; 7.0–0 e6 (7...Bxf3; 8.Bxf3 Nxc4; 9.d5! N6e5; 10.Be2 Nd6; 11.Nc3 and White has more than enough for the pawn.) 8.Nc3 Bxf3 (8...Bb4; 9.d5 Ne7; 10.h3 Bxf3; 11.Bxf3 exd5; 12.cxd5 and the powerful pawn at d5 constricts Black's game, giving White a clear advantage. 8...Be7; 9.c5 Nd5; 10.Qb3 Rb8; 11.Nxd5 Qxd5; 12.Qa4 0–0; 13.h3 Bh5; 14.Be3 Bf6; 15.Rad1 Rfd8 and Black had some pressure in the center in McShane-Bryson, Hastings 1995, and White found it difficult to make progress.) 9.Bxf3 Nxc4 (9...Nxd4; 10.Bxb7 Rb8; 11.Ba6 Be7; 12.Be3 Nf5; 13.Bb5+ Kf8; 14.Qf3 Nxe3; 15.fxe3 and White was clearly better in Biyiasis-Green, Canada 1978.) 10.d5! exd5; 11.Re1+ Be7; 12.Nxd5 Nd6; 13.Bf4. The bishop pair and pressure on the e-file were worth much more than a pawn in Whitehead-Peters, USA 1978.

5.Be2. 5.c4 Nb6; 6.Nc3 Bg7; 7.c5 is another interesting approach. 7...N6d7 (7...Nd5; 8.Bc4 Nxc3; 9.bxc3 0–0; 10.0–0 Nc6 is more resilient for Black, I.Zaitsev-Smagin, Moscow 1995.) 8.Bc4 0–0; 9.0–0 c6; 10.Re1 Nf6; 11.h3 b5; 12.Bb3 a5; 13.a3 Na6; 14.Qe2 gave White control of the center and pressure on the e-file in DeFirmian-Azmaiparashvili, Yerevan Olympiad 1996. **5...Bg7; 6.0–0 0–0; 7.h3.** 7.c4 Nb6; 8.Nc3 Nc6; 9.d5 Ne5; 10.Nxe5 Bxe5; 11.Bh6 Re8; 12.f4 kept the initiative in White's hands in Smyslov-Thorhallsson, Reykjavik (Olafsson) 1995.

7...c6. 7...Nc6; 8.Re1 Nb6; 9.c3 a5; 10.Na3 a4; 11.Bb5 Bd7; 12.Bg5 Re8; 13.Qe2 Qc8; 14.Rad1 Na5; 15.Bd3! Bf5; 16.Bf4 c6; 17.Ne5 Nd5; 18.Bc1! White had a flexible game and a small advantage in Sigurjonsson-Tuzhovsky, Tbilisi 1974. **8.Re1 Nd7; 9.Bf1! Re8; 10.c4** Now! **10...Nc7; 11.Nc3.**

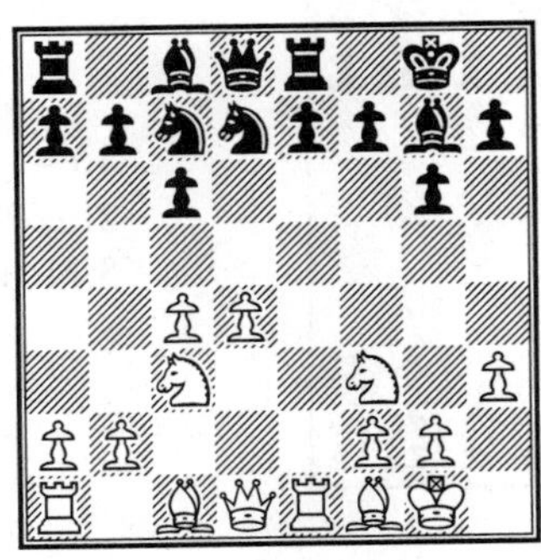

White has a better game here, with complete domination of the center and good development. Now play gets a bit sloppy. **11...e5?** This should have met with a tactical refutation. **12.d5?** 12.dxe5! Nxe5; 13.Rxe5! is the simple tactic that Geller missed. 13...Qxd1 14.Rxe8+ Nxe8; 15.Nxd1 and White has an extra piece. **12...f6;**

13.Be3 f5. Black could have achieved this in a single move. **14.Bg5 Bf6; 15.Bxf6 Qxf6; 16.Qd2 Kg7.** 16...e4; 17.Nd4 Ne5; 18.dxc6 Nxc6; 19.Nxc6 Qxc6; 20.Nd5. This must be evaluated as better for White, as the Black pawn chain is vulnerable to attack at f3 or g4, and the queenside pawn majority is a long-term asset. **17.Rad1.**

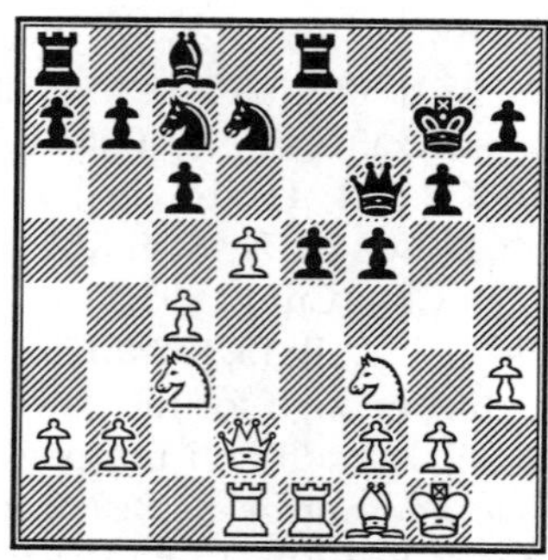

White has again built up a dominating position, as there is no way for Black to untangle his pieces. **17...cxd5; 18.cxd5 Qd6.** 18...e4; 19.Nd4 Ne5; 20.Ndb5 Nxb5; 21.Nxb5 Qb6; 22.Qc3 is clearly better for White, according to Maric. **19.Nb5! Nxb5; 20.Bxb5 Re7; 21.Qc3!** From this post her majesty oversees an important file and a crucial diagonal. **21...Kg8; 22.Bxd7! Bxd7; 23.Rxe5** and by adding material to positional advantages, White has a decisive edge.

23...Rae8; 24.Rde1 Rxe5; 25.Rxe5 Rc8; 26.Qd2 Be8; 27.Qf4. Threatening Rxe8+. **27...Qc5; 28.Ng5?!** Inefficient. 28.d6! would have been quicker, for example: 28...Qc1+; 29.Qxc1 Rxc1+; 30.Kh2 Bc6; 31.Rd5! as given by Maric. **28...h6; 29.Ne6 Qc1+; 30.Kh2 Qxf4+; 31.Nxf4 Kf8; 32.d6 Bf7; 33.Ne6+ Bxe6; 34.Rxe6 Kf7; 35.Re7+ Kf6; 36.Rxb7 a5; 37.d7 Rd8; 38.Ra7. White won.**

SCANDINAVIAN DEFENSE: MAIN LINE

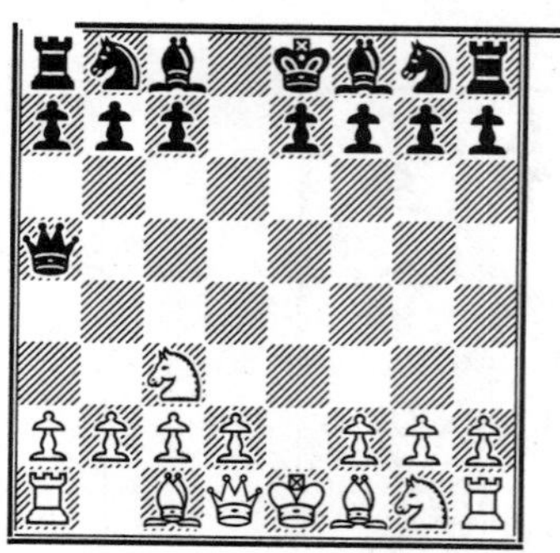

1.e4	**d5**
2.exd5	**Qxd5**
3.Nc3	**Qa5.**

When Black recaptures at d5 with the queen, an important opening principle regarding early development of the queen is violated. The queen is exposed on d5, and indeed she is usually attacked immediately by Nc3. Then the queen must move again, violating the general recommendation that a piece should not be moved twice in the opening.

Despite all that, the exchange of central pawns means that White cannot establish an ideal pawn center, and the slight positional advantages White gains can easily vanish into thin air unless backed up by exceptionally strong technique. Even the World Champion has some problems with it, as seen in our illustrative game.

(135) KASPAROV - ANAND [B01]

PCA World Championship, 1995

1.e4 d5; 2.exd5 Qxd5; 3.Nc3 Qa5 4.d4 Nf6. 4...e5, the Anderssen Counterattack, is now considered to be refuted. 5.Nf3 Bb4; 6.Bd2 exd4; 7.Qe2+ Ne7; 8.Nxd4 is better for White, as Tal has demonstrated. 8...0–0 9;.a3 Bd6; 10.Ndb5 Qb6; 11.0–0–0 Be6; 12.Bg5 Ng6; 13.Nxd6 cxd6; 14.h4 Nc6; 15.Be3 Qa5; 16.h5 Nge5; 17.Rh4 d5; 18.h6 g6; 19.f4 Nc4; 20.f5 Nxe3; 21.Qxe3 Bxf5; 22.Nxd5 Rad8; 23.b4 Qa4; 24.Qc3 Ne5; 25.Ne7+ Kh8; 26.Qxe5+ f6; 27.Qxf6+ and Black resigned in Tal-Skuja, Latvian Championship 1958.

5.Nf3 c6. The systems with the development of the bishop at f5 or g4 are too ambitious and White can obtain an advantage. 5...Nc6 is bad: 6.d5 Nb4; 7.Bb5+ c6; 8.dxc6 bxc6; 9.Ba4 Ba6; 10.a3 Rd8; 11.Bd2 Rd6; 12.axb4 Qf5; 13.Bb3 Ne4; 14.Rxa6 Rxd2; 15.Qa1 Nxc3; 16.bxc3 Rd6; 17.0–0 and Black gave up in Fischer-Seidman, New York (Rosenwald Memorial) 1959. 5...Bf5 has been defended by Larsen, but not with great success. 6.Bd2 Nbd7; 7.Bc4 c6; 8.Qe2 e6; 9.d5 cxd5; 10.Nxd5 and White has a strong initiative, Spassky-Larsen, Montreal 1979.

5...Bg4; 6.h3 Bh5; 7.g4 Bg6; 8.Ne5 (8.b4 Qb6; 9.Bg2 c6; 10.Bd2 Nbd7; 11.Ne5 Nxe5; 12.dxe5 Rd8; 13.Qe2 Nd5; 14.Na4 Qc7; 15.c4 and White was much better, in Kasparov's only previous game in the opening, from a 1991 simultaneous exhibition.) 8...e6; 9.h4 Bb4; 10.Rh3 c6; 11.Bd2 Qb6; 12.h5 Be4; 13.Re3 Bxc3; 14.Bxc3 Bd5; 15.g5 and White has a strong attack, Karpov-Rogers, Bath 1983. Australian Grandmaster Ian Rogers has been a leading advocate of fringe defenses such as the Scandinavian and Budapest Defenses.

6.Ne5. 6.Bd2 was Tal's preference, and it also looks a little better for White. 6.Bc4 Bf5; 7.Ne5 e6; 8.g4 Bg6; 9.h4 Nbd7; 10.Nxd7 Nxd7; 11.h5 Be4; 12.Rh3 is a hotly debated line, and the latest word is 12...Bg2!; 13.Re3 Nb6; 14.Bd3 Nd5 with a solid position for Black, Bauer-Prie, French Championship 1996.

6...Be6!? At present, this is considered Blacks best. **7.Bd3 Nbd7; 8.f4?!** A new move, but not a good one. Kasparov was probably taken by surprise, since he had so little experience with the Scandinavian. 8.Nxd7 Nxd7; 9.0–0 is surely a bit better for White. **8...g6!** This is the best way of developing the bishop. **9.0–0 Bg7.**

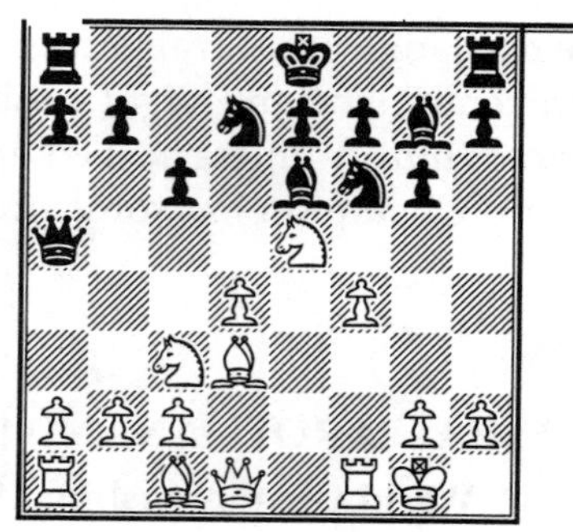

10.Kh1 Bf5!; 11.Bc4?! Kasparov tries to preserve the bishop but should have been more concerned with maintaining the balance, to which end 11.Be3 was called for. **11...e6; 12.Be2?!** Here Kasparov might have captured at d7, but it seems that Black could just capture with the king, and then bring rooks to a center and retreat the king to safety on either side of the board. **12...h5; 13.Be3 Rd8; 14.Bg1 0–0; 15.Bf3.**

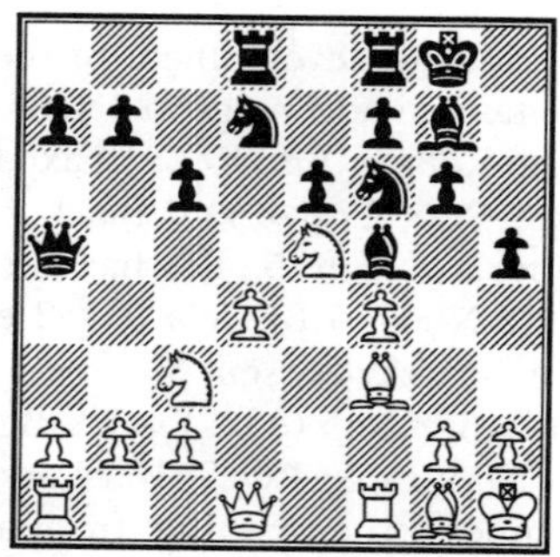

15...Nd5! 16.Nxd5 exd5. Capturing with the c-pawn would have given White a structural advantage, and eventually the bishop at g1 would run all over the dark-squares. **17.Bf2 Qc7; 18.Rc1 f6; 19.Nd3 Rfe8; 20.b3 Nb6; 21.a4! Nc8; 22.c4 Qf7; 23.a5! Bf8; 24.cxd5 cxd5; 25.Bh4 Nd6; 26.a6! b6; 27.Ne5! Qe6!; 28.g4! hxg4; 29.Nxg4 Bg7.** The bishop could also have been stationed effectively at e7, since the check at h6 would not accomplish much. **30.Rc7 Ne4?!** Capturing at g4 would have been wiser. 30...Bxg4; 31.Bxg4 f5! 32.Bxd8 fxg4 with a complicated position in which Black's chances are no worse. **31.Ne3.**

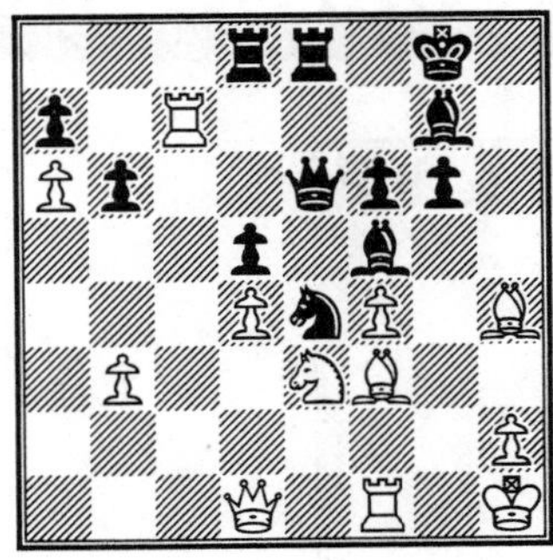

Anand cracks under the pressure. Here, and at move 32, he could have gotten a good position by heading for complications after ...Qd6. **31...Bh3?** 31...Qd6! is fine, since the sacrifice at g7 does not work: 32.Rxg7+? Kxg7; 33.Nxf5+ gxf5 is solid, for example 34.Rg1+ Kf8!; 35.Bxe4 Qxf4!; 36.Qh5 Qxe4+; 37.Rg2 Rd6 and White has exhausted all attacking possibilities. **32.Rg1 g5?!** A serious mistake. The correct plan was to exchange the a-pawn for the f-pawn with 32...Qd6! 33.Rxa7 Qxf4 for example 34.Rxg6 Rd7; 35.Rxd7 Bxd7; 36.Ng2 Qf5; 37.Bxe4 dxe4; 38.Rg3 e3 with counterplay. **33.Bg4! Bxg4; 34.Qxg4 Qxg4; 35.Rxg4 Nd6; 36.Bf2 Nb5; 37.Rb7 Re4; 38.f5!**

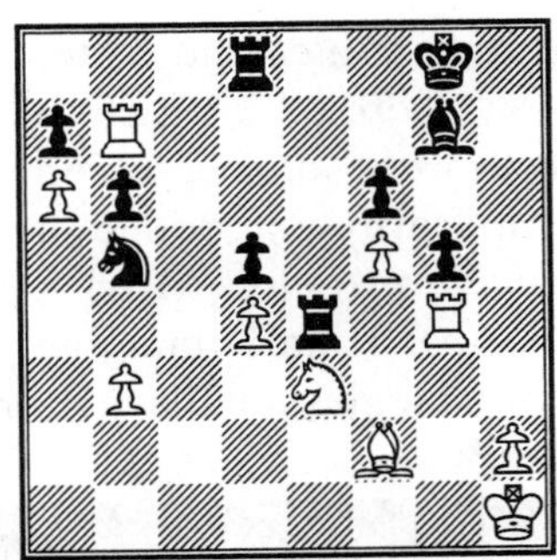

Here Anand should have played 38...Rc8, although after the rooks come off at e4 White will be able to advance the d-pawn. **38...Rxg4?!; 39.Nxg4 Rc8; 40.Rd7 Rc2?** A blunder in time pressure, but Black was in trouble anyway. **41.Rxd5** Anand resigned, since the White rook will get to the seventh rank soon. **White won.**

NIMZOWITSCH DEFENSES

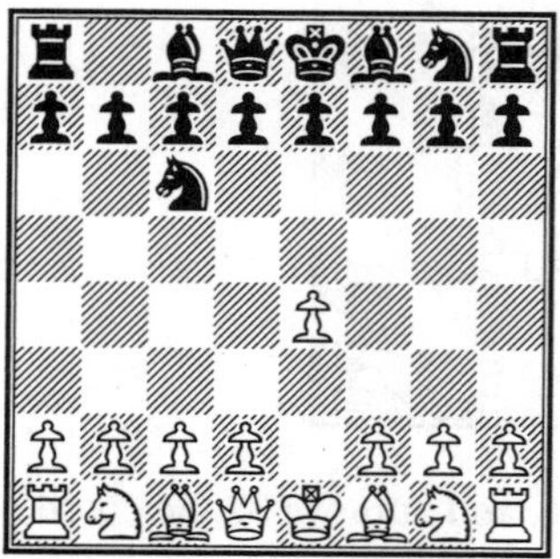

1.e4 Nc6

Nimzowitsch's pet defense, answering 1.e4 with 1...Nc6, allows White to build a strong center. This is true of most of his openings, as Nimzowitsch was one of the leading exponents of the Hypermodern school. Thanks largely to the efforts of such Grandmasters as Vlastimil Hort, Joel Benjamin and Tony Miles, it has gathered a fairly large following in amateur and even professional ranks.

After 2.d4, Black can either contest the center by advancing ...d5 or ...e5, or concede it with 2...e6 or 2...d6. In any case the struggle revolves around the d5 square. White has more resources to control this square, especially since Black has at least temporarily abandoned the idea of ...c6 by stationing the knight on that square. Nevertheless, Black's position is very solid and White's advantages are not particularly tangible. We will examine several quite different varieties of strategies for Black in this opening.

WILLIAMS VARIATION

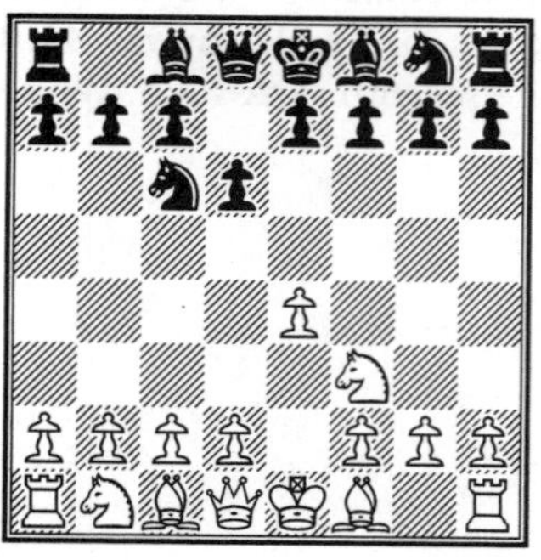

1.e4 Nc6
2.Nf3 d6

This is a plan that has been popular in recent years. Black can opt to return to an Open Game after ...e5, but the pawn at d6 will restrict the possible transpositions.

(136) ILLESCAS CORDOBA - MILES [B00]

Linares (Zonal), 1995

1.e4 Nc6; 2.Nf3 d6; 3.d4 Nf6; 4.Nc3 Bg4; 5.Be3.

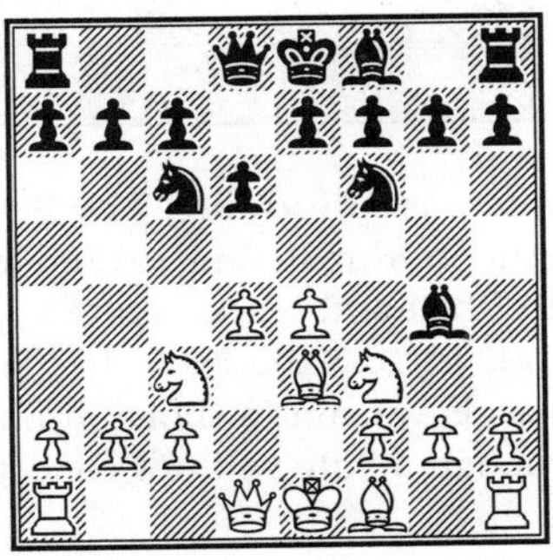

5...e6. 5...a6 6.h3 Bh5; 7.d5 Nb8 is an interesting alternative, seen in Yagupov-Hodgson, Linares (open) 1996. **6.h3 Bh5; 7.d5 Ne7.** 7...exd5; 8.exd5 Ne5 (8...Bxf3; 9.Qxf3 Ne5; 10.Qe2 threatens Qb5+ and Qxb7. 10...a6; 11.0-0-0 Black had great difficulty developing and eventually lost in Golubev-Markowski, Biel (Open) 1995.) 9.g4 Bg6 (9...Nxf3+; 10.Qxf3 Bg6; 11.0-0-0 White has an excellent game, and has been successful from this position, for example in Spraggett-Mohr, Ubeda (Open) 1996.) 10.Bb5+ Ned7; 11.Qe2 Be7; 12.0-0-0 a6; 13.Bd3 Bxd3; 14.Qxd3 looks a little better for White, Ivanov-Nesterov, Moscow 1995.

8.Bb5+! c6; 9.dxc6 bxc6. 9...Nxc6 would leave Black with a weak pawn structure, but it might have been better than the text. **10.Ba4 Qc7; 11.Qe2 Nd7; 12.g4.**

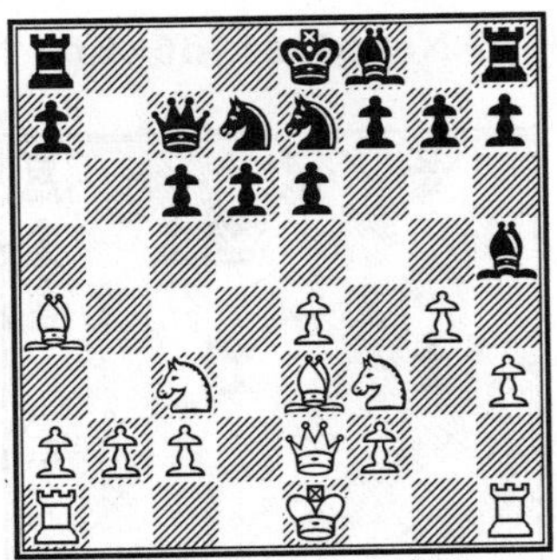

It is clear that White controls the play on both flanks and in the center. **12...Bg6; 13.0-0-0 e5; 14.Qc4.** There was no better news in another game from the same round at the same event: 14.Nh4 Nc8; 15.Qc4 Nc5? (15...Ncb6; 16.Qxc6 Qxc6; 17.Bxc6 Rc8 would have been relatively better.) 16.Bxc5 dxc5; 17.Qd5 and in the game Apicella-David, Black resigned right here. **14...Rc8; 15.Nh4 Nb6; 16.Bxb6 axb6.**

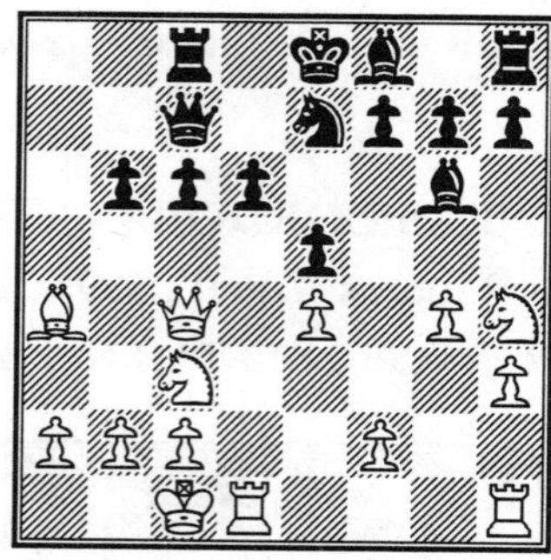

Black's lack of development is suffocating. The Black forces are sitting targets. Illescas now adds to the pressure by threatening to double rooks on the d-file. **17.Rd3! d5.** 17...f6; 18.Nxg6 hxg6; 19.Rhd1 and Black cannot survive, for example: 19...Rd8; 20.Nb5!; 17...b5 loses instantly to 18.Nxb5 cxb5; 19.Qxb5+ Kd8; 20.Qe8#. **18.exd5 Bxd3; 19.Qxd3.** The pawn at d5 remains a thorn in Black's side. **19...Rd8; 20.Rd1 g6; 21.d6.** The fork wins, though White will not collect the bounty for a few more moves.

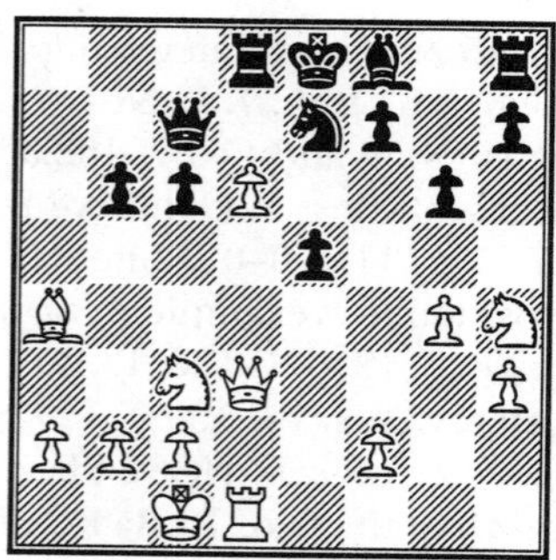

21...Bh6+; 22.Kb1 Qb8; 23.Ne4 b5; 24.Nf6+ Kf8; 25.dxe7+ Kxe7.

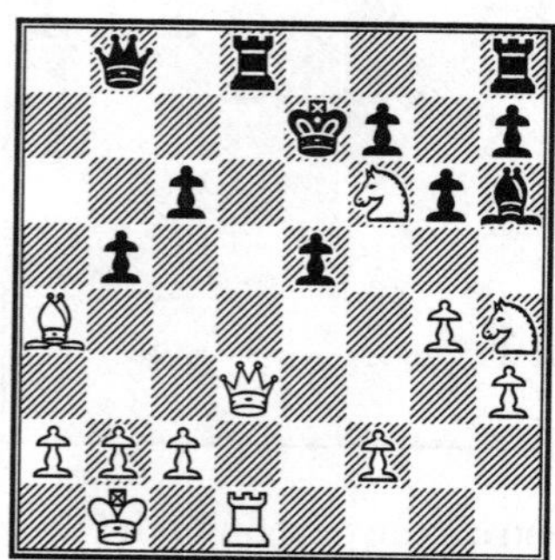

Now what? Illescas finds a clever move to wrap things up. **26.Nd7!! bxa4; 27.Nf5+!** The relentless pursuit of the king brings the game to an end. **27...gxf5; 28.Qa3+ Ke6; 29.gxf5+ Kxf5; 30.Qf3+.** Black resigned, since checkmate is inevitable. **White won.**

FRANCO-NIMZOWITSCH

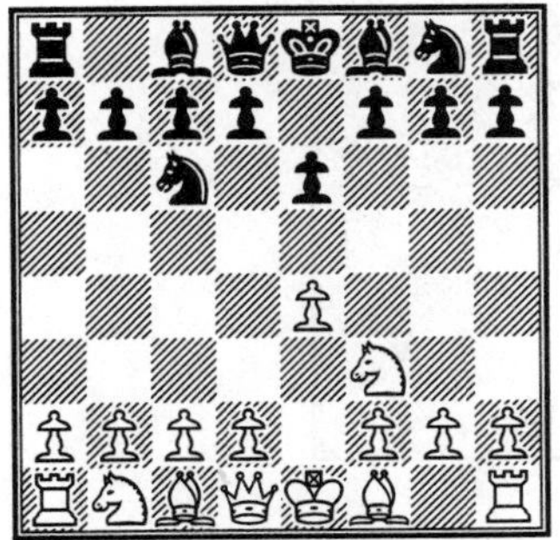

1.e4 Nc6
2.Nf3 e6

Nimzowitsch prepares to treat the opening as a form of the French Defense, but this line is generally criticized since in French positions the knight belongs on c6 only after the c-pawn has advanced to c5.

(137) SPIELMANN - NIMZOWITSCH [B00]
New York, 1927

1.e4 Nc6; 2.Nf3 e6; 3.d4 d5; 4.e5. The advance of the e-pawn is especially appropriate because Black needs more time to establish counterplay with ...c5 since the knight at c6 blocks the c-pawn. **4...b6.** Black needs to get the light-squared bishop into the game, but it really has no prospects. **5.c3 Nce7; 6.Bd3 a5!** This inhibits b2-b4, which would otherwise be an effective weapon in the battle for c5. **7.Qe2 Nf5; 8.h4 h5; 9.Ng5.**

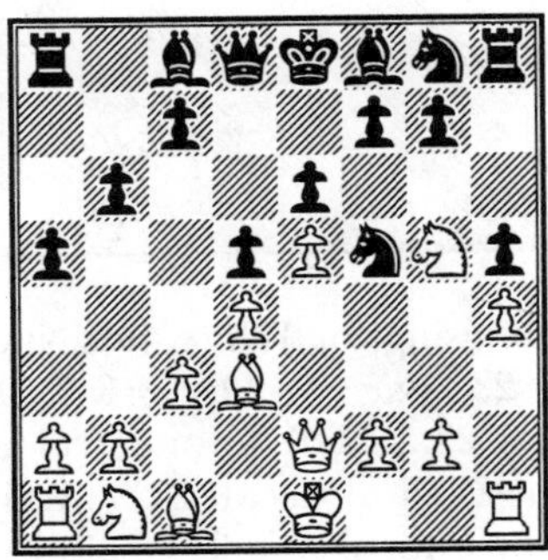

9...g6?! 9...Nge7; 10.Nd2 Ng6; 11.Ndf3 Be7 is a more reliable line, leading to a position which is roughly level. **10.Nd2 Nge7; 11.Nf1 c5; 12.f3 c4; 13.Bc2 b5.** Forced, because otherwise 14.a4 would have been annoying. **14.g4 Ng7.** 14...hxg4; 15.fxg4 Nxh4; 16.Qf2 wins for White. **15.Ng3 Nc6; 16.Qg2 Be7.** 16...Ra7 defends f7 but there is action on the h-file. 17.gxh5 Nxh5 (17...gxh5; 18.Nh7 Be7; 19.Bh6 Rg8; 20.Nxh5) 18.Nxh5 Rxh5; 19.Nxf7! Rxf7; 20.Bxg6 Rxh4; 21.Bxf7+ Kxf7; 22.Rg1 and the Black king has a very short life expectancy. **17.gxh5 gxh5.** 17...Nxh5 fails to

18.Nxf7! Kxf7; 19.Bxg6+ Kxg6; 20.Nxh5+ Kxh5; 21.Qg4#. **18.Rg1.** 18.Nh7 allows Black to escape with 18...Kd7! **18...Ra7!**

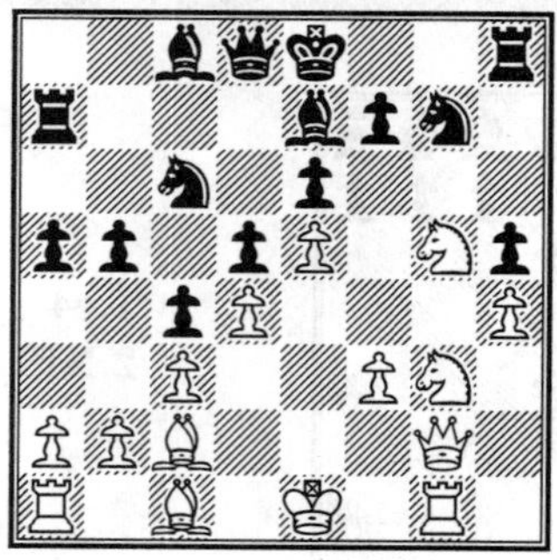

White should now have won with an effective sacrifice, and it is rather surprising that the normally combinative Spielmann mishandled it. **19.Nxf7! Kxf7; 20.Nxh5?** Tartakower has subjected this position to deep analysis, and found a way to win for White. 20.Ne2! is the beginning of a journey which will bring the knight to g6. 20...Bxh4+; 21.Kd1 Kg8 (21...Kf8; 22.Nf4; 21...Rg8; 22.Bh7) 22.Nf4 Rf7; 23.Ng6 Be7; 24.Nxh8 Kxh8; 25.Qg6! Qg8; 26.Qh6+ Qh7; 27.Qxh7#. **20...Bxh4+!** 20...Nxh5? loses quickly to 21.Qg6+ Kf8; 22.Bh6+ Rxh6; 23.Qg8# **21.Ke2?** 21.Kd1 would have been better, as will be clear later, when Black gets in an extra check. **21...Nxh5; 22.Bg6+ Ke7; 23.Bxh5.**

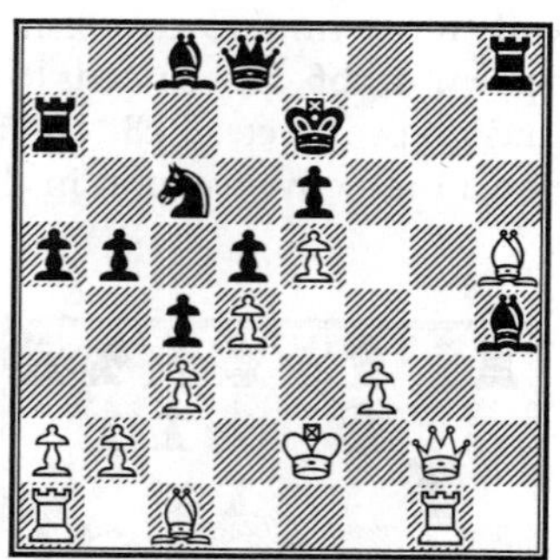

This position seems promising for White, but Nimzowitsch finds a clever defense. 23.Bg5+ doesn't work: 23...Bxg5; 24.Qxg5+ Kd7; 25.Bxh5 Qxg5; 26.Rxg5 Ne7 and Black is just a piece ahead. **23...Kd7!!** A wonderful move, spurning the bishop at h5, whose capture would have led to disaster. 23...Rxh5?; 24.Qg7+ Ke8; 25.Qg6+ Rf7; 26.Qxh5 and White wins, for example 26...Be7; 27.Rg8+ Bf8; 28.Bg5 Ne7; 29.Rxf8+ Kxf8; 30.Qh8+ Ng8; 31.Bxd8.

24.Qg7+ Be7; 25.Bf7 Rh2+. Now we see why White should have retreated the king to d1. **26.Kd1.** 26.Rg2 Rxg2+; 27.Qxg2 Qh8 and Black defends. **26...Kc7; 27.Bf4 Rxb2.** White no longer has any significant compensation for the piece, especially since there is no way to get the rook at a1 into the game. **28.Qh7 Kb6; 29.Rg8 Qc7; 30.Qh8 Nd8; 31.Bg6 Rg2; 32.Qh1 Rxg6; 33.Rxg6 b4; 34.Rg7 Qc6; 35.Qh8 Qa4+; 36.Ke1 Nc6; 37.Qxc8 Bh4+; 38.Bg3 Rxg7; 39.Bxh4 Qc2; 40.Bd8+ Nxd8; 41.Qb8+ Nb7.** White resigned. **Black won.**

SCANDINAVIAN VARIATION

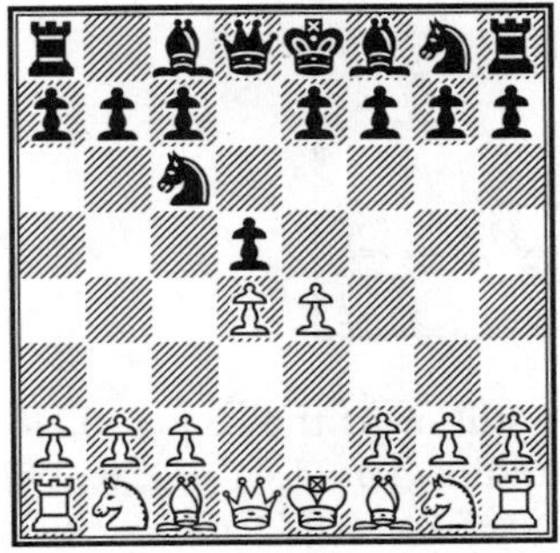

1.e4 Nc6
2.d4 d5

The defense with 2...d5 leads to an open game similar to the Scandinavian Defense, into which it can transpose. The knight is not necessarily well positioned at c6, however, and Black has fewer strategies available than in the 1...d5 lines.

(138) MAROCZY - SPIELMANN [B00]
Carlsbad, 1907

1.e4 Nc6; 2.d4 d5; 3.exd5. 3.Nc3 is the Bogoljubow Variation. 3...dxe4 (3...e5 will be treated in *Unorthodox Chess Openings*, as will many other sidelines of the Nimzowitsch Defense.) 4.d5 gives White an advantage in space. After 4...Nb8 White can try 5.f3, for example 5...e6 (5...exf3; 6.Qxf3 Nf6; 7.Bc4 Bg4; 8.Qg3 g6; 9.Bf4 with an excellent game for White.) 6.fxe4 Bb4; 7.Nf3 Nf6; 8.Qd4 where White's powerful center provides a solid advantage, Schlenker-Basquin, Lugano 1981.

3...Qxd5; 4.Nf3. 4.Nc3 Qxd4 (4...Qa5 would be a form of the Scandinavian Defense.) 5.Qe2 is an interesting gambit alternative, but there is insufficient practical experience yet. Benjamin & Schiller (1987) give the following analysis: 5...e6; 6.Nb5! Qd8; 7.Bf4 Bd6; 8.Bxd6! cxd6; 9.0–0–0 d5; 10.Rxd5!

4...Bg4. 4...e5; 5.Nc3 Bb4; 6.Be3! (6.Bd2 Bxc3; 7.Bxc3 e4 gave Black a good game in Tarrasch-Nimzowitsch, Bad Kissingen 1928.) 6...e4; 7.Nd2 Bxc3; 8.bxc3 Nf6; 9.Rb1!? and if Black takes the pawn, White gets good counterplay. 9...Qxa2; 10.Bc4 Qa5; 11.0–0 Qxc3; 12.Rb3 Qa5; 13.f3 0–0; 14.fxe4 Ng4; 15.Bf4 and the superb center and open files are more than enough compensation for the pawns. **5.Be2 0–0–0.**

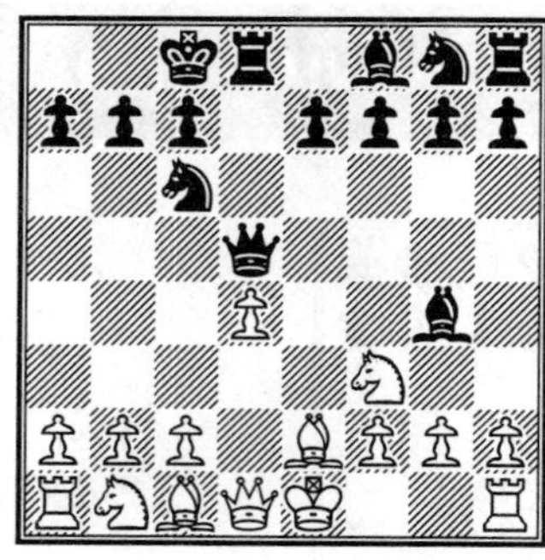

Black has developed quickly, but White still owns the center. **6.Nc3 Qa5.** This sort of position can also arise from the Scandinavian (1.e4 d5). 6...Qf5; 7.Be3 e5; 8.h3! is better for White. **7.Be3 Nf6.** 7...e5 8.Nxe5 Bxe2; 9.Qxe2 Nxe5; 10.dxe5 Qxe5; 11.0-0 is better for White, according to Zukertort.

8.Nd2. is a safe move which gives White excellent chances of obtaining an advantage even though Black can equalize with best play. 8.a3?! Qf5; 9.0-0 e5; 10.d5 Ne7; 11.h3 Bxf3; 12.Bxf3 h5. This position should favor White who holds the bishop pair and a strong presence in the center. But can he hold the pawn at d5? 13.Nb5?! a6; 14.Na7+ Kb8; 15.c4 b6; 16.a4 e4; 17.Be2 a5; 18.b4 Kxa7; 19.bxa5 c5; 20.axb6+ Kb8; 21.Bxc5 Ng6; 22.Bxf8 Nf4; 23.Ra3 Rhxf8; 24.a5 N6xd5; 25.cxd5 Rxd5; 26.Qe1 h4; 27.a6 Rc5; 28.Ra4 Nxh3+; 29.gxh3 Qxh3; 30.Qd2 Qe6; 31.Qf4+ Ka8; 32.Qxe4+ Qxe4; 33.Rxe4 Rc6; 34.Bf3 Kb8; 35.a7+. White won, Tisdall-Castro, Orense 1977.

8...Bxe2; 9.Qxe2 Qf5. 9...e6; 10.Nb3 Qf5; 11.0-0-0 Bd6; 12.h3 Na5. Tarrasch wrote that he played this in order to gain some space for his queen, which is barely able to move. 13.g4 Nxb3+; 14.axb3 Qa5; 15.Kb1 Nd5; 16.Na4 Nxe3. Tarrasch suggested that this was based on a miscalculation, and that 16...c6 and 16...h5 were preferable. 17.fxe3 and White was able to dominate the center in Chigorin-Tarrasch, Ostende 1907.

10.Nf3 e6. 10...e5; 11.0-0-0 exd4; 12.Nxd4 Nxd4; 13.Bxd4 and White has a small amount of annoying pressure. Black cannot afford to go pawn-grabbing here. 13...Qg5+?; 14.Kb1 Qxg2; 15.Bxf6 gxf6; 16.Rxd8+ Kxd8; 17.Rd1+ Bd6; 18.Qe3! a6; 19.Qd4 Qf3; 20.Ne4 with a clear advantage for White **11.0-0-0 Bb4; 12.Qc4 Bxc3.** 12...Nd5. Myers claims equality here. 13.Na4!? It seems to me that White has excellent attacking chances on the queenside. 13...Nce7 (intending to capture at e3 and place the other knight at d5) 14.Rd3 **13.Qxc3 Nd5; 14.Qd3 Qxd3; 15.Rxd3 h6.**

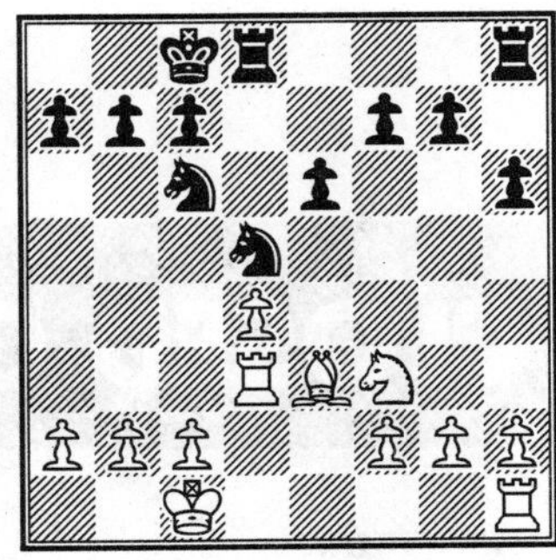

Now there begins a long and interesting positional middlegame, where Maroczy takes advantage of his slightly superior pawn structure. **16.a3 Rhe8; 17.Rhd1 Nxe3; 18.Rxe3 Re7; 19.b4! Red7; 20.c3 a6; 21.a4 Rd5.** Black must try to stop White's progress on the queenside, but a rook is not the best piece for this task, but there is nothing else available. The struggle now centers around the e5-square, which White would like to occupy with a knight.

22.Rde1 Ne7?! 22...b5!; 23.axb5 axb5; 24.Kc2 Kb7 was best, according to Marco. **23.Ne5! Nf5; 24.Rf3 f6.** A necessary weakening of the kingside, but in the long run a fatal one. **25.Ng6 Kd7.** 25...R5d6; 26.g4! corrals the horse. **26.g4 Ne7; 27.Nf4 Rd6; 28.Rfe3** and now White converts positional advantage into material advantage.

28...Nd5; 29.Nxd5 Rxd5; 30.Rxe6 Kc8; 31.Re7 R5d7; 32.h4 c6; 33.a5 Kc7; 34.Kc2 Rf8; 35.Re8 Rff7; 36.f4 g5; 37.hxg5 fxg5; 38.fxg5 hxg5; 39.Rg8 Rf3; 40.Kd2 Rh7; 41.Re3 Rh2+; 42.Kd3 Rf4; 43.Rxg5 Rg2; 44.Rg7+ Kb8; 45.Re8+ Ka7; 46.Rgg8. White won.

6. THE CLOSED GAMES

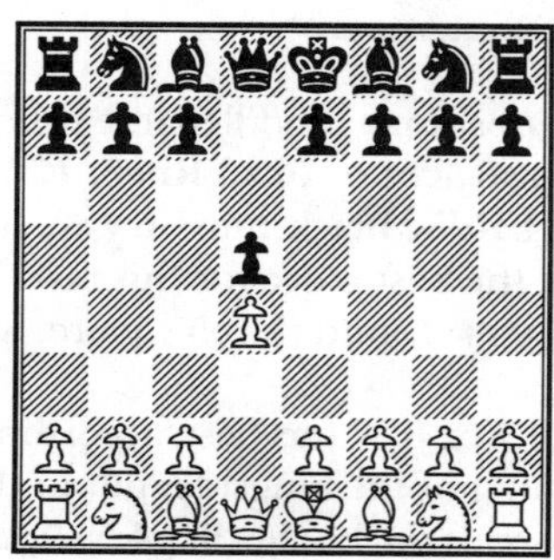

1.d4 d5

The **Closed Games** normally begin 1.d4 d5, although there are some transpositional lines from the Dutch Defense and some other openings. Playing 1...d5 right away effectively rules out the advance of either e-pawn to the center.

In general, these openings lead to quieter, longer struggles. For Black, they have the advantage of being very solid. White may be able to squeak out a small initiative, but the ideal pawn center remains only a dream. The vulnerable f7 square is well shielded from activity by White's bishop or queen on the a2-g8 diagonal.

Although the Closed Games all feature the same structure on the d-file, the wide variety of defensive approaches gives them less in common with each other than is the case in the Open Games. After 2.c4, Black can defend with ...e6, ...c6, or ...dxc4, all of which are quite normal. A system with ...e6 locks in the bishop at c8 but strongly supports the center. Working from the other side with ...c6, keeps the bishop mobile but is slower in developing the bishop from f8, and this delays castling. Capturing at c4 concedes the center to White, who must however take some time in regaining the pawn, and that allows Black to develop in comfort.

The typical pawn structures of the Queen's Gambit are well established. The **Exchange Variation** leads to opportunities for White on the queenside. The famous isolated d-pawn structure is the hallmark of the **Tarrasch Defense.** There are still other well-studied formations.

A related opening is the **Classical Dutch**. Although it is typically described as involving 1.d4 f5 2.c4 e6 and only later ...d5, it is more common to see it these days after 1.d4 d5; 2.c4 e6; 3.Nf3 c6; 4.e3 f5 or 4.g3 f5. The Stonewall formation is hard to crack, and if Black can solve the problem of the bad bishop at c8, prospects are good.

QUEEN'S GAMBIT ACCEPTED

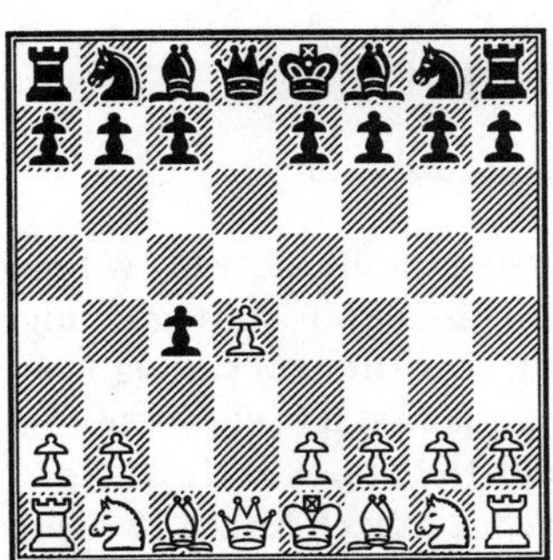

1.d4 d5
2.c4 dxc4

By accepting the Queen's Gambit, Black shows a willingness to concede the center for rapid development. This is a dangerous strategy, but it has remained playable throughout the 20th century.

(139) ZUKERTORT - STEINITZ [D26]
St. Louis (World Championship), 1886

1.d4 d5; 2.c4 e6; 3.Nc3 Nf6; 4.Nf3 dxc4. The Showalter Variation is considered part of the Queen's Gambit Accepted complex, but Steinitz hated that opening and did not want to capture the pawn at the second move in the normal order 1.d4 d5; 2.c4 dxc4. In fact, his idea was advanced for its time. He aimed for an isolated pawn position typical of the Panov Attack in the Caro Kann which lay far in the future.

5.e3. 5.e4 could be met by 5...Bb4, according to Steinitz, but modern theory considers 6.Bg5! to be better for White, classified as a Ragozin Defense. **5...c5; 6.Bxc4 cxd4; 7.exd4.** White could avoid the isolated pawn by capturing with the knight. **7...Be7; 8.0–0 0–0.** Black might do better to play ...Nc6 first, as in Pillsbury-Steinitz St. Petersburg 1895, 96.

9.Qe2 Nbd7; 10.Bb3. White could have gotten rid of the isolated pawn by playing d5 here, but after exchanges there wouldn't be much play left in the game. **10...Nb6; 11.Bf4.** 11.Rd1! is stronger. The bishop belongs at g5 in any case. For example: 11...Nbd5; 12.Bg5 Qa5; 13.Rac1 Bd7 and Black is no worse. **11...Nbd5; 12.Bg3.** The bishop performs no useful function here. **12...Qa5; 13.Rac1 Bd7; 14.Ne5 Rfd8; 15.Qf3.** 15.Nxd7 Rxd7 is fine for Black.

15...Be8; 16.Rfe1 Rac8; 17.Bh4. 17.Nxd5 Nxd5; 18.Rxc8 Rxc8; 19.Nc4 (19.Bxd5?? Qxe1#) 19...Qd8 is safe for Black. **17...Nxc3; 18.bxc3.** This pawn structure is typical of the Panov Attack. It gives White a stronger center but the hanging pawns can easily become a target. **18...Qc7; 19.Qd3?!** 19.Bg3 Bd6; 20.c4 was stronger, as pointed out by Lasker. **19...Nd5.**

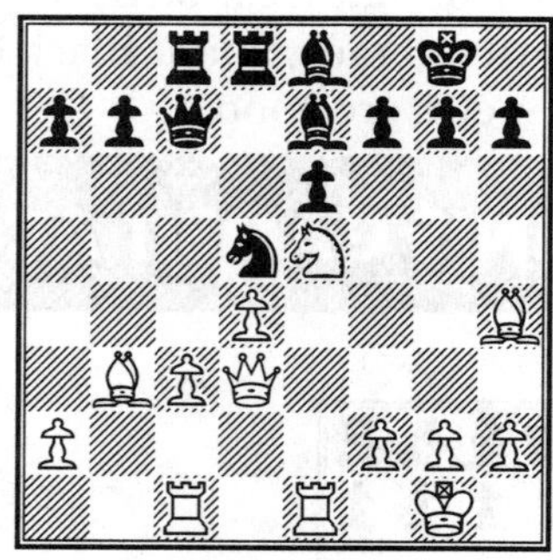

20.Bxe7. 20.Bc2 g6; 21.Bxe7 Qxe7 is good for Black, who will secure the c4-square by playing ...b5. **20...Qxe7; 21.Bxd5?** This is poor strategic judgment. White gives up the bishop for the knight, assuming that the blockading knight at d5 is a better value. In fact, the bishop could have remained a useful weapon. 21.Bc2! was best, since 21...Nf6 allows White to carry out the attack with 22.Ng4 g6; 23.Nh6+ Kg7; 24.Qh3 Nd5; 25.Be4 Nxc3; 26.Rxc3 Rxc3; 27.Qxc3 Kxh6; 28.d5 exd5; 29.Bxd5 Qxe1+; 30.Qxe1 Rxd5; 31.Qe3+ Kg7; 32.h3 Bc6; 33.Qxa7 and White is slightly better.

21...Rxd5; 22.c4 Rdd8; 23.Re3?! The d-pawn should be supported by a rook at d1. **23...Qd6; 24.Rd1.** Now the c-pawn is less well supported. 24.Rh3 accomplishes nothing. 24...h6!; 25.Rd1 f6 and Black is clearly better, according to Neistadt. **24...f6; 25.Rh3.** This is met by the same mechanism discussed in the previous note. **25...h6!** 25...fxe5 is too dangerous. 26.Qxh7+ Kf8; 27.Rf3+ Bf7; 28.Qh5 and now: 28...Rc7 (28...Qd7; 29.Qh8+ Ke7; 30.Qh4+ and White has the advantage, according to Steinitz.) 29.c5 is given by Steinitz, but it does not seem to offer more than a draw. 29...Qd5; 30.Qh8+ Ke7; 31.Qh4+ Ke8; 32.Qh8+.

26.Ng4. 26.Ng6 loses to 26...Bxg6; 27.Qxg6 Rxc4! and now 28.Rxh6 runs into 28...Qxd4!; 29.Qh7+ Kf8; 30.Qh8+ Kf7 which allows the elegant finish 31.Qxd8 Qxd8! and White cannot capture the queen because of the back-rank mate. **26...Qf4!** This is an excellent spot for the queen, and pressure is building on the White center. Black's next move will activate the bishop. **27.Ne3.**

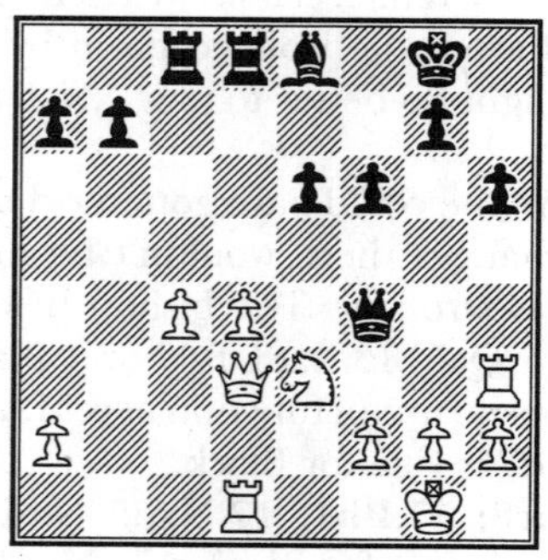

27.Rg3 b5; 28.cxb5 Rxd4!; 29.Nxh6+ Kf8; 30.Qa3+ Qd6 wins for Black, as noted by Steinitz. **27...Ba4!; 28.Rf3.** 28.Rd2!? would be countered by 28...b5. **28...Qd6; 29.Rd2** 29.Rxf6?? loses to 29...Bxd1! **29...Bc6.** 29...b5! would have been more efficient.

30.Rg3. 30.Rxf6? gxf6; 31.Qg6+ Kf8; 32.Qxf6+ fails to 32...Ke8 and the king escapes to the queenside. 30.d5 loses to 30...Qe5! as analyzed by Euwe. 31.Rg3 exd5; 32.Qg6 Rc7 and the Black rooks will come to the e-file. **30...f5!** White has run out of threats. **31.Rg6 Be4; 32.Qb3 Kh7! 33.c5 Rxc5; 34.Rxe6.** 34.Qxe6 was easily refuted by Steinitz himself: 34...Rc1+; 35.Nd1 (35.Nf1 Qxe6; 36.Rxe6 Bd5; 37.Re7 Bc4 is equally hopeless.) 35...Qxe6; 36.Rxe6 Bd5; 37.Re1 Bxa2; 38.Rxa2 Rxd4 and Black wins. **34...Rc1+; 35.Nd1.** 35.Nf1 would have been met by 35...Qf4! when the rook at d2 is threatened. **35...Qf4; 36.Qb2 Rb1; 37.Qc3 Rc8; 38.Rxe4 Qxe4. Black won.**

(140) GLIGORIC - PORTISCH [D27]
Pula, 1971

1.d4 d5; 2.c4 dxc4; 3.Nf3. This is the normal move. 3.e4 is also possible, but is generally considered a bit drawish. It was first seen in Saduletoi-Benavides, a game from the 16th century given in Polerio's manuscript.

The defense with 3...Nc6 is a recent development. (3...b5; 4.a4 c6; 5.axb5 cxb5; 6.b3 a5; 7.bxc4 b4; 8.f4 is given as Saduleto-Benavides by Polerio. Although the position bears a superficial resemblance to the Noteboom Variation of the Semi-Slav, White's domination of the center gives Black a lot to worry about. 3...c5 and 3...e5 are also common responses.) 4.Be3 Nf6; 5.f3 e5; 6.d5 Nd4; 7.Bxd4 exd4; 8.Qxd4 c6; 9.Nc3 Bb4; 10.Qe5+ Qe7; 11.Qxe7+ Kxe7; 12.dxc6 bxc6; 13.Bxc4 and White was slightly better in Karpov-Piket, Groningen 1995.

3...Nf6; 4.e3 e6; 5.Bxc4 c5; 6.0–0 a6.

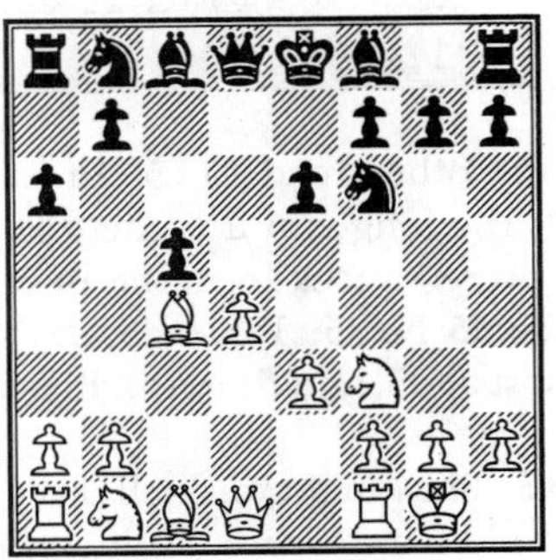

The main lines of Queen's Gambit Accepted are rich in strategic themes, but the most important one is queenside expansion by Black against central occupation by White, who can take time out to delay b7-b4 if he chooses. **7.a4.** This move slows down Black's plans, but it costs time and weakens b4. Now Black switches strategy to take aim at the center, since his queenside ambitions have been stopped for the moment.

7...Nc6; 8.Qe2 cxd4. 8...Qc7 is preferred by young Matthew Sadler, one of the rising stars of the chess world and an acknowledged master of the Queen's Gambit Accepted. Dzhangava-Sadler, Yerevan Olympiad 1996 continued 9.Nc3 Bd6; 10.Rd1 0–0; 11.h3 b6; 12.d5 exd5; 13.Bxd5 Bb7; 14.e4 Rae8; 15.Be3 Bf4; 16.Rac1 h6 where White jettisoned both bishops by capturing at f4 and c6 and soon came to regret the lack of defensive capability.

9.Rd1. A typical theme in the opening. White transfers the rook to a file where it will have "man-on-man" coverage of the enemy queen. But eventually White will recapture with the pawn, reducing the rook to a supporting role. **9...Be7; 10.exd4 0–0; 11.Nc3.** White will use his control of the center to attack the kingside, and the move d4-d5 may be useful, so Black acts quickly to blockade the pawn. **11...Nd5; 12.Bd3!** This bishop will find a haven at b1, where it can pressure the kingside from a safe distance.

12...Ncb4; 13.Bb1 b6! When one has an isolated pawn it is useful to station rooks on the files immediately adjacent to the pawn. Then minor pieces can be stationed on the squares diagonally in front of the pawn. Black's move takes control of c5. **14.a5!** With the preceding positional considerations in mind, White decides to try to place his knights at e5 and c5. To do this he must divert the b-pawn from b6. Once the outposts are established, White will have the basis for an attack. **14...Bd7.** Robbing White of an access point to c5 (with Na4). **15.Ne5.** White restores the threat by attacking the Bd7, guardian of a4. **15...bxa5.**

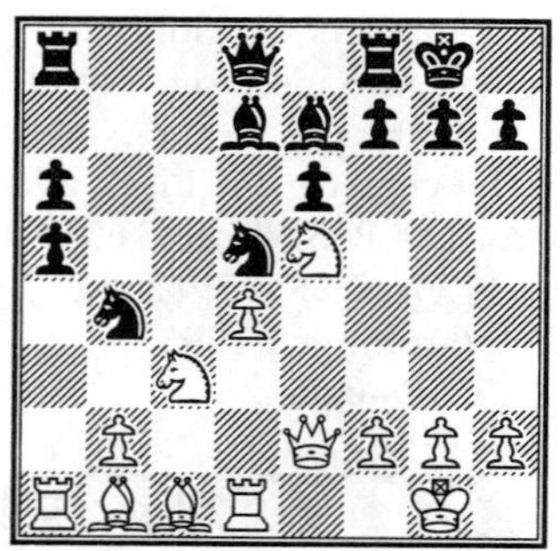

15...b5; 16.Ne4 takes the other road to c5. **16.Ra3!** White's short term plan involves the knights, but in the long run it is the enemy king which is the target. Since there is no good discovered attack from the Be7, Black decides to cut off the powerful Bb1. **16...f5; 17.Nxd5 Nxd5.** 17...exd5; 18.Nxd7 Qxd7; 19.Bf4 gets the bishop to a wonderful outpost at d5, and the weak Black pawns are also juicy targets for White's bishop.

18.Nxd7 Qxd7; 19.Rxa5. The knight was well placed at e5 but that was a temporary condition and Black could have eventually attacked it with a minor piece. But after the exchange at d7 White can now attack pawns that have no clerical support. **19...Nc7; 20.Ba2!** One of the themes we see in this game collection is that of shifting plans. It is to be expected that the opponent will counter a strategy most of the time, so one must be prepared to develop new plans in new situations. **20...Bd6;**

21.Bc4! Target: e6 Kh8; A defensive move with a tactical point. **22.Qf3!** 22.Bxa6? Bxh2+! 23.Kxh2 Qd6+; 24.Kg1 Nxa6. **22...Bb4; 23.Ra1 a5; 24.Bf4! Nd5; 25.Be5.** We saw this idea in the note to move 17. This bishop will dominate the dark squares for the rest of the game. The pressure at g7 cannot be exploited immediately, but it will play a role later.

25...Rfc8; 26.Qe2 Qb7; 27.h3! White has no immediate breakthrough and may need to worry about back-rank mate in the future, so he takes time out to create a flight-square. Thinking about potential threats from the opponent is an important part of planning! **27...Rc6; 28.Rac1 Rac8.** The bishop at e5 is stronger than its counterpart at b4, so it is logical to remove the other minor pieces from the board. **29.Bxd5! exd5; 30.Rxc6 Qxc6; 31.Rd3!**

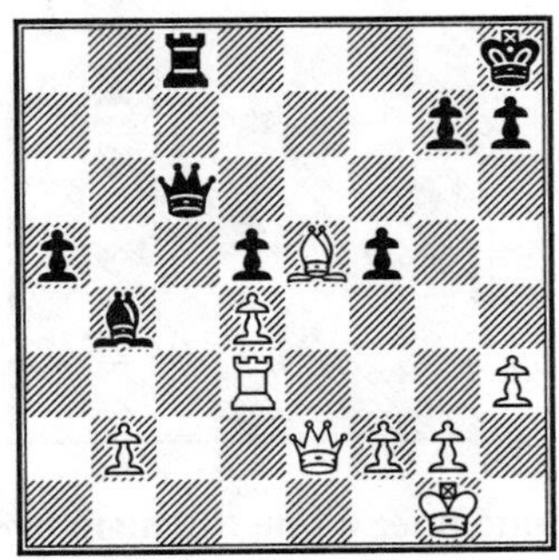

31...Qd7. 31...Qc2 allows the stunning 32.Bxg7+!! Kxg7; 33.Qe5+ Kf7; 34.Qxd5+ with complications which favor White. **32.Rg3 Bf8; 33.b3!** This not only prevents a5-a4, but it also places the pawn in a position where it is defended by the rook, which is more likely to remain in place than the queen. **33...Ra8.** Black's plan is obvious - eliminate the queenside pawns and concentrate on defense. **34.Qc2.** Threatens Rf3.

34...Rc8; 35.Qd2 Ra8; 36.Qg5 Kg8; 37.Rf3! White exploits the same theme. It will not win a pawn this time, but it does force Black to critically weaken his defensive formation. **37...g6; 38.Rc3.**

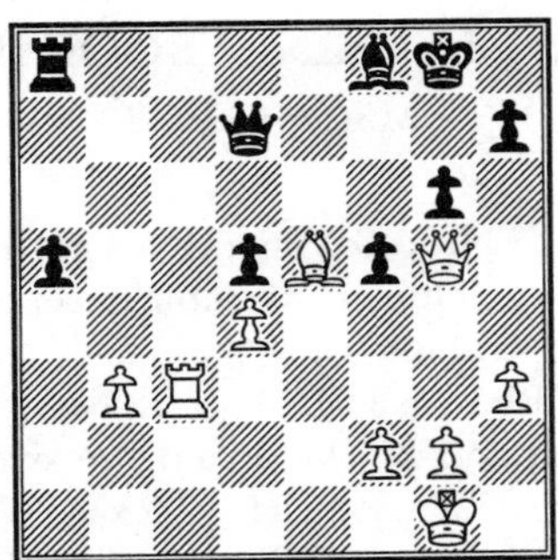

Here Black must try to exchange pieces. White must retain as much attacking force as possible. **38...Qd8.** 38...Rc8?; 39.Rxc8 Qxc8; 40.Qf6 **39.Qc1!** This takes control of the c-file. Black succeeds in removing the bishops from the board but White retains both a spatial advantage and attacking chances. **39...Bd6; 40.Qf4 Bxe5; 41.Qxe5 Ra7; 42.Rc5 Re7.** Black could not avoid losing a pawn. 42...Rd7; 43.Rb5 Qe7; 44.Rb8+ Kf7; 45.Qh8. **43.Rxd5! Qc7; 44.Qxc7 Rxc7; 45.Rxa5 Rb7; 46.Ra3 Rb4; 47.d5 Kg7; 48.Kf1 Kf6; 49.Ke2 Ke5; 50.Kd3 Kxd5; 51.Kc3 Re4.**

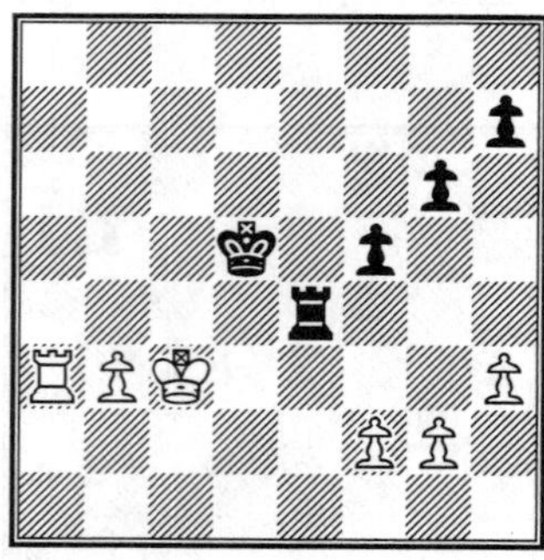

This is a classical rook endgame. White will maneuver his rook to d2, in order to defend the pawns along the second rank. Then he will use his king to gain additional space. **52.Ra4! Re2; 53.Rd4+ Kc5; 54.b4+ Kb5; 55.Rd5+ Kc6; 56.Rd2 Re1; 57.f3 Rg1; 58.Kd4!** White realizes that he cannot make progress on the queenside without giving up his kingside pawns, but with the Black king tied down keeping an eye on the b-pawn, White sends his own monarch after the Black pawns.

58...Re1; 59.Rc2+ Kb6; 60.Kd5! Re3; 61.Rc6+ Kb5; 62.Rc7 h5; 63.Rb7+ Ka4?! 63...Ka6; 64.Rg7 would have lasted longer. **64.Kc4!** and now the b-pawn will be able to advance. **64...Ka3; 65.Ra7+** and Black resigned, since his king can no longer keep pace with the pawn. **White won.**

(141) ALEKHINE - BOOK [D28]

Margate, 1938

1.d4 d5; 2.c4 dxc4; 3.Nf3 Nf6; 4.e3 e6; 5.Bxc4 c5. This is the Classical Defense, the most common form of the Queen's Gambit Accepted. **6.0–0.** 6.Qe2 a6; 7.dxc5 Bxc5; 8.0–0 Nc6 is a very topical line.

A) 9.e4 Qc7 (9...b5; 10.Bb3 e5; 11.h3 0–0; 12.Nc3 Nd4; 13.Nxd4 Bxd4; 14.Nd5 Nxd5; 15.Bxd5 Ra7; 16.Be3 and Black carried the symmetry a little too far with 16...Be6 and after 17.Bxe6 fxe6; 18.a4 bxa4; 19.Rxa4. White had the better game in Brenninkmeijer-Jonkman, Groningen 1996.) 10.e5 Nd7; 11.Bf4 and now Black prematurely attacked, without having insured the safety of her king, with 11...Nd4?!; 12.Nxd4 Bxd4 but after 13.Rd1 Qc5; 14.Nd2 b5 ws duly punished by 15.Ne4! Qb6; 16.Nd6+ Kf8; 17.Qh5 g6; 18.Qh6+ and was forced to resign in Bobrowska-Danielian, Yerevan Olympiad 1996.

B) 9.Nbd2 0–0; 10.Bd3 Be7; 11.b3 Nb4; 12.Bb1 b5; 13.Bb2 Bb7; 14.Rd1 Rc8 gives Black active queenside play, Astrom-Sadler, Yerevan Olympiad 1996.

C) 9.a3 can lead to interesting play on the queenside, e.g., 9...Bd6; 10.Nbd2 0–0; 11.Bd3 b5!; 12.Ne4 Nxe4; 13.Bxe4 Bb7; 14.Rd1 f5; 15.Bb1 Qc7; 16.a4!? bxa4; 17.Rxa4 Nb4; 18.e4 a5 with a complicated position in Topalov-Lautier, Amsterdam 1996.

6...Nc6; 7.Qe2 a6; 8.Nc3. 8.a4 would lead to more common lines. **8...b5; 9.Bb3.** Alekhine correctly keeps the bishop on the queenside, as the lack of a rook at d1 means that 9.Bd3 leaves d4 without sufficient protection. **9...b4.** This came as a surprise to Alekhine, who expected Black to play 9...Be7, as in an encounter with Euwe.

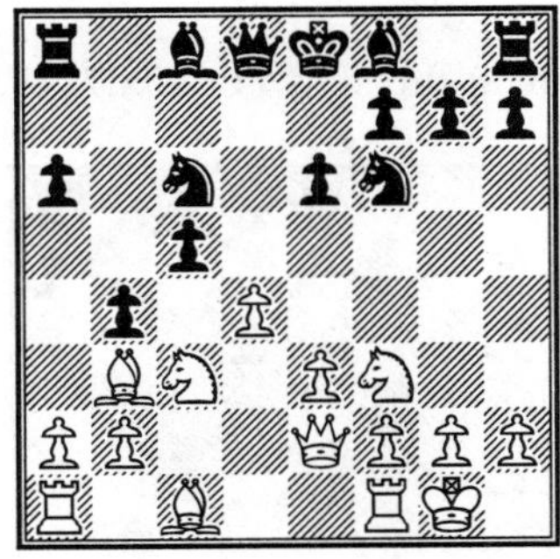

10.d5! Alekhine's judgment is probably correct, though Taimanov's preferred 10.Na4 is a worthy alternative. White's goal is to advance the e-pawn, and to do this he must somehow release the pressure at d4. **10...Na5.** 10...exd5; 11.Nxd5 Nxd5; 12.Rd1 followed by e3-e4 gives a clear advantage to White. **11.Ba4+ Bd7.** White has achieved quite a lot, but wouldn't it be great if he also had a rook on an open d-file? With this idea in mind, we can easily see how Alekhine creates one of his impressive combinations. **12.dxe6.**

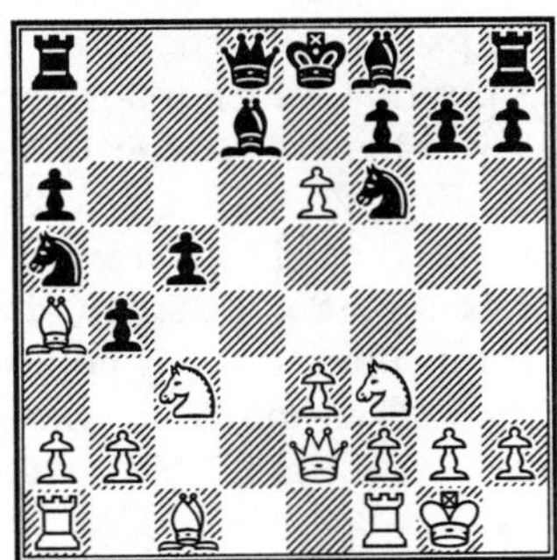

12...fxe6. 12...Bxa4; 13.exf7+ Kxf7; 14.Nxa4 **13.Rd1.** White is playing without the help of the rook at a1 and bishop at c1, but Black's pieces are even less active. **13...bxc3.**

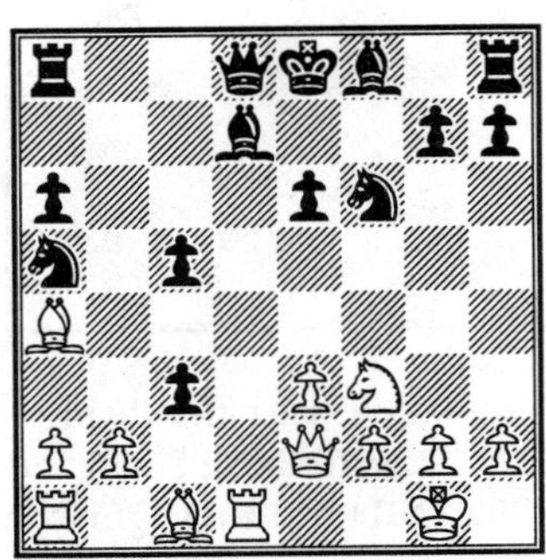

13...Be7; 14.Bxd7+ Nxd7; 15.Ne5 Ra7; 16.Qh5+ g6; 17.Nxg6 is a line given by Brinckmann. **14.Rxd7!!** Alekhine describes this as the high point of the combination. The main reason why the White attack is consequential is the position of the Na5 which cannot participate in the play. **14...Nxd7; 15.Ne5 Ra7; 16.bxc3.**

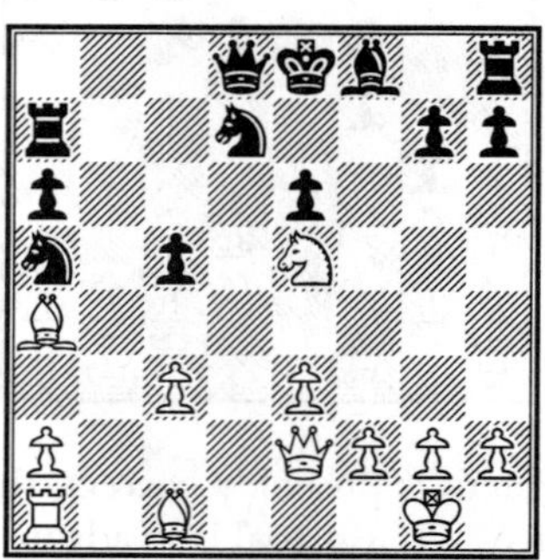

White's goal now is to get the bishop at c1 into the attack. **16...Ke7.** A strange looking move, but the alternatives are not pleasant. 16...Be7; 17.Qh5+ g6; 18.Nxg6 hxg6; 19.Qxh8+ Bf8; 20.Bc2 Qf6; 21.Qxf6 Nxf6; 22.Bxg6+ Kd8; 23.Bd2 Nc4; 24.Be1 and it is not clear that the three pawns and bishop pair will be enough to win though White is not likely to lose this position, which follows analysis by Brinckmann.

17.e4! This sets up tricks with Bg5+. **17...Nf6; 18.Bg5.** And now Qh5+ is in the air. **18...Qc7; 19.Bf4 Qb6.** 19...Kd8; 20.Nc6+ Qxc6; 21.Bxc6 Nxc6; 22.Rd1+ Nd7; 23.e5 and the queen will pillage on the light squares. 19...Qb7; 20.Qe3! and White is threatening to win quickly, for example 20...Kd8; 21.Qd3+ Kc8; 22.Rb1 Qxe4; 23.Nf7 Rxf7; 24.Rb8# **20.Rd1 g6.** At this point there is nothing better. 20...Nb7; 21.Nc4; 20...Ra8; 21.Bg5 Rd8; 22.Nd7 Qc7; 23.e5 and White wins. 20...Rg8; 21.Bg5 h6; 22.Qh5 g6; 23.Nxg6+ Rxg6; 24.Qxg6 hxg5; 25.e5! Nd5; 26.Qe8# was pointed out by Brinckmann. **21.Bg5 Bg7.**

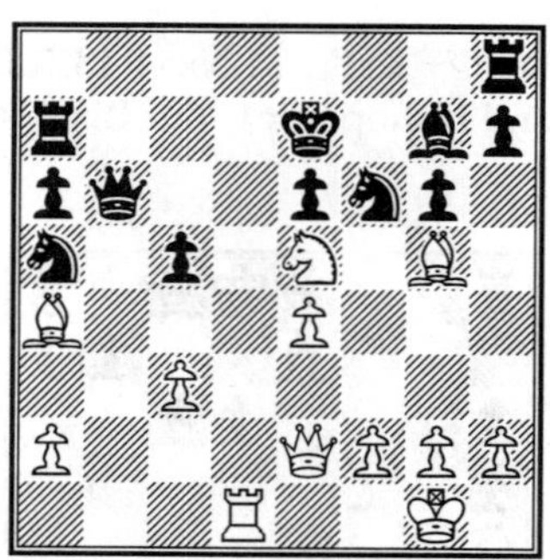

22.Nd7! The decisive, thematic thrust that brings the game to a swift conclusion. **22...Rxd7; 23.Rxd7+ Kf8; 24.Bxf6 Bxf6; 25.e5** and Black resigned, rather than walk into the obvious line: **25...Qb1+; 26.Rd1 Qf5; 27.exf6 Qxf6; 28.Qxa6 Qxc3; 29.Qxe6** to which there is simply no defense. **White won.**

QUEEN'S GAMBIT DECLINED

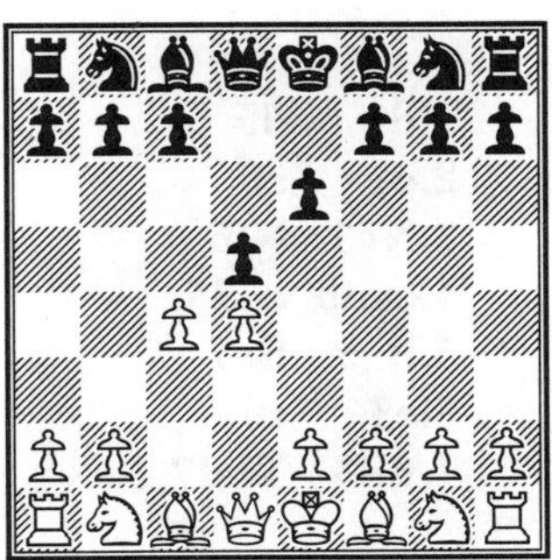

1.d4 d5
2.c4 e6

One of the oldest and most classical of defenses, the **Queen's Gambit Declined** is found on the chessboard about as frequently as the Spanish Game. Black will fight vigorously for control of the central squares, and develop quickly with ...Nf6, ...Be7, and kingside castling. The lack of open lines makes it very difficult for White to mount an effective attack.

The only serious disadvantage of the opening is the blocking of the bishop at c8, which can lead to a bad bishop in the endgame. After suitable development, Black will work toward advancing the e-pawn to e5 in the early middlegame. Players who are impatient to see the light-squared bishop get into the game generally prefer the Slav Defense or the Tarrasch Defense.

The most common continuations in the Queen's Gambit Declined (often known by the initials QGD) develop in one of two ways. White can play classically with 3.Nc3 Nf6; 4.Bg5 Be7; 5.Nf3 0-0; 6.e3. The alternative is the Exchange Variation 5.cxd5 exd5; 6.e3.

In the latter case Black no longer has to worry about the bishop at c8, which has a clear path to the enemy kingside. White, on the other hand, has a wide range of choices, and can adopt a strategy known as the minority attack where the queenside pawns will advance and undermine the enemy pawn structure. We will begin by examining this approach.

EXCHANGE VARIATION

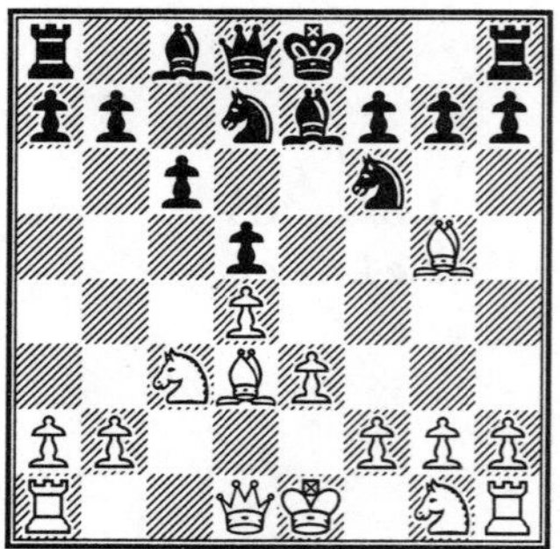

1.d4 d5
2.c4 e6
3.Nc3 Nf6
4.cxd5 exd5
5.Bg5 Be7
6.e3 c6
7.Bd3 Nbd7

This is the basic formation of the **Exchange Variation**. White wants to undermine the pawn chain which extends from b7 to d5, while Black will try to organize an attack against the White king. To achieve the queenside goals, White will often launch a minority attack by advancing the queenside pawns and creating weaknesses in Black's pawn formation.

An alternative plan for White is to seek a kingside attack, using the b1-h7 diagonal. Black must be careful not to get overwhelmed on either flank, and this defensive burdens makes some amateur players fear the opening, although professional players have no such reservations about sitting on the Black side.

(142) KARPOV - LJUBOJEVIC [D36]

Linares, 1989

1.d4 Nf6; 2.c4 e6; 3.Nc3 d5; 4.cxd5 exd5; 5.Bg5 c6; 6.e3 Nbd7; 7.Bd3 Be7; 8.Qc2 0-0.

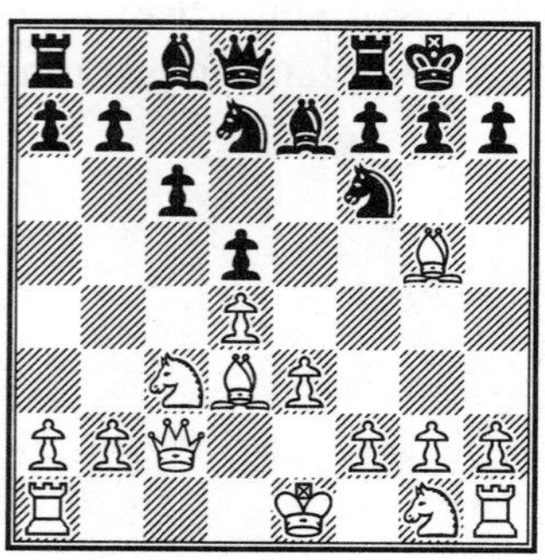

9.Nf3. This is the main line, if only because the position is reached frequently by transposition. The alternative, move order permitting, is 9.Nge2 and now the most common move is 9...Re8, making room for a knight to retreat to f8 and protect h7 from the rear. Three plans are now seen:

A) 10.0–0 Nf8; 11.Rab1 Ng4; 12.Bf4 Bd6; 13.b4 Bxf4; 14.Nxf4 g5; 15.Nh5 Qd6; 16.Ng3 Qh6; 17.h3 Nf6; 18.Nf5 Bxf5; 19.Bxf5 a6; 20.a4 Ng6; 21.b5 axb5; 22.axb5 Ne7; 23.Rfc1 Nxf5; 24.Qxf5 Qg6; 25.Qc2 Re6; 26.Ne2 Ne4; 27.bxc6 bxc6; 28.Rb6 Rc8; 29.Qa2 Kg7; 30.Qa6 Rc7; 31.Qa8 Qf5; 32.Rf1 Nf6; 33.g4 Qf3; 34.Ng3 Re8; 35.Rb8 Rce7; 36.Nf5+ Kg6; 37.Nxe7+ Rxe7; 38.Qxc6 Re6; 39.Qc2+ Kg7; 40.Qf5 White won. Hodgson-Murugan, British Championship 1993;

B) 10.h3 Nf8; 11.g4 a5; 12.Ng3 h6; 13.Bxf6 Bxf6; 14.Nce2 g6; 15.Kf1 Qd6; 16.Rc1 Bd7; 17.Kg2 b6; 18.h4 c5; 19.dxc5 bxc5; 20.Qxc5 Qxc5; 21.Rxc5 Bxg4; 22.h5 and White was a bit better in Salov-Van der Sterren, Hilversum 1993.

C) 10.0–0–0 a5; 11.g4 Nf8; 12.h3 a4; 13.Ng3 Qa5; 14.Kb1 b5; 15.Nce2 Bd7; 16.Nf5 Bxf5; 17.gxf5 Rac8; 18.Rhg1 Kh8; 19.Nf4 N8d7; 20.Qe2 a3; 21.b3 c5; 22.Bxf6 Nxf6; 23.Bxb5 Red8; 24.Rc1 Rb8; 25.Bd23 c4; 26.Bc2 Bd6; 27.Qe1 Bb4; 28.Qf1 Bd2; 29.Qg2 Rg8; 30.Ne2 Bxc1; Black won. Nielsen-Van der Sterren, Lloyds Bank Masters London England 1993.

We return to the position after 9.Nf3.

9...Re8; 10.0–0 Nf8; 11.Rab1. 11.Rae1 Ne4; 12.Bxe7 Qxe7; 13.Bxe4 dxe4; 14.Nd2 was better for White in Botvinnik-Robatsch, Amsterdam Netherlands 1966. **11...Ne4; 12.Bxe7 Qxe7; 13.b4.**

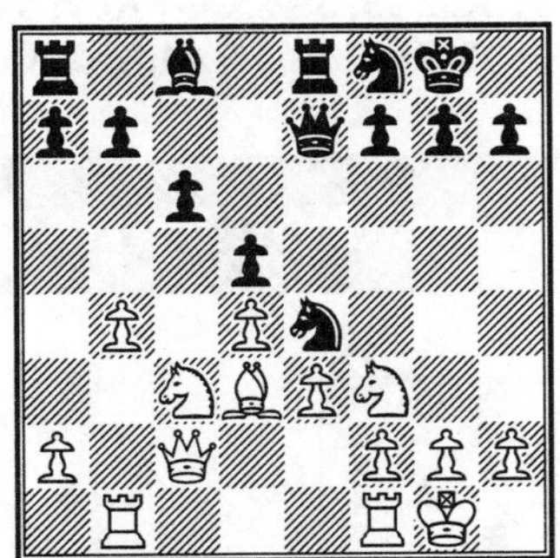

This is the famous Minority Attack. White advances the a- and b-pawns to attack the three Black pawns on the a-, b-, and c-files. After both pawns are exchanged, Black is left with a weak remaining pawn, which can be the target of attention by White. The pawn can often be won, and then the endgame is just a matter of technique.

Black should respond by aiming pieces at the kingside. If White wants to support queenside operations with pieces, fine, but how then to defend the White king? If Black fails to play actively, the fate that awaits is illustrated in all its gore in the present game.

13...a6; 14.a4 Bf5. The bishop can become a bit nervous on this square, but the b1-h7 diagonal must be guarded at all costs because it aims right at the heart of the Black king. **15.Ne5 Rad8; 16.Rfc1 Ng6.** The key to understanding the Minority Attack is to appreciate the endgame possibilities. In the present game we head right for an ending with no minor pieces, which are eliminated in the following flurry.

17.Bxe4 Bxe4; 18.Nxe4 dxe4; 19.Nxg6 hxg6; 20.b5. White carries out the thematic advance, and the structural deficiencies in Black's position are immediately exposed. This is exactly the sort of endgame that Black must avoid in the Minority Attack.

20...cxb5; 21.axb5 Rd6; 22.bxa6 bxa6.

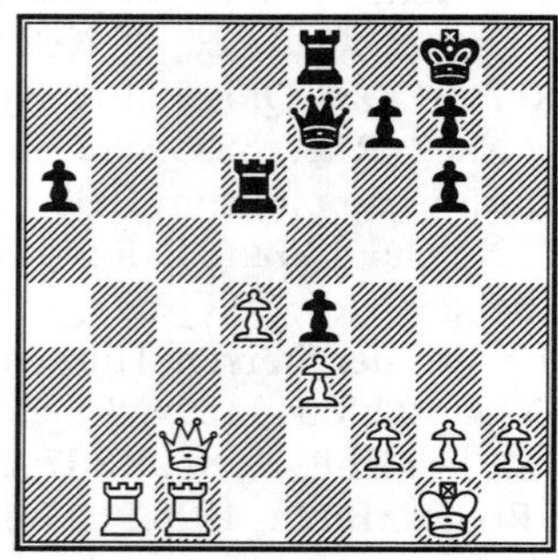

The game was effectively over at this point. The a-pawn is too weak, and there is no source of counterplay. Karpov displays his formidable technique to convert his positional advantages into a win.

23.Qa4 Qd7; 24.Qxd7 Rxd7; 25.Rc5 Ra7; 26.Ra5 Kf8; 27.Rb6 Rea8; 28.h4 Ke7; 29.Kh2 Kd7; 30.Kg3 Kc7; 31.Rb2 Rb7; 32.Rc5+ Kb8; 33.Ra2 Re7; 34.Kf4 Kb7; 35.Rb2+ Ka7; 36.Rc6 Rh8; 37.Ra2 a5; 38.Rxa5+ Kb7; 39.Rca6 Rxh4+; 40.Kg3 Rh5; 41.Ra7+ Kc6; 42.R5a6+ Kb5; 43.Rxe7 Rg5+; 44.Kh2 Kxa6; 45.Rxf7. White won.

THE HARRWITZ ATTACK

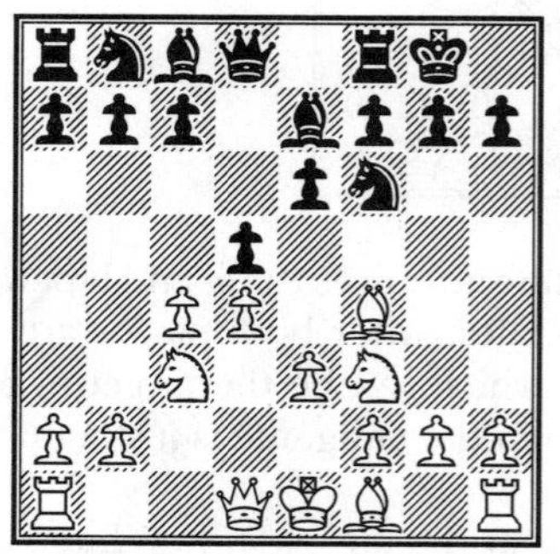

1.c4	**e6**
2.Nf3	**d5**
3.d4	**Nf6**
4.Nc3	**Be7**
5.Bf4	**0–0**
6.e3	

This solid formation has never had an enormous following, but it is being investigated more and more these days. White creates no weaknesses but simply concentrates on the dark squares in the center. The pawn at c4 gives White some light-square play to, by contrast with the London System, where the pawn stays on c2 or c3 for the duration of the opening. What gives this seemingly quiet position a real bite is the plan of queenside castling, which leads to opposite wing attacks that can be a lot of fun, and dangerous for both sides.

(143) KASPAROV - VAGANIAN [D37]

Novgorod, 1995

1.c4 e6; 2.Nf3 d5; 3.d4 Nf6; 4.Nc3 Be7; 5.Bf4 0–0; 6.e3 c5 is the normal reply, as otherwise White can advance to c5, for example 6...a6; 7.c5 Nh5; 8.Bd3 Nxf4; 9.exf4 Nc6; 10.a3 f5; 11.h4 Bf6; 12.Ne2 Bd7; 13.Rc1 Qe7; 14.h5 Nd8; 15.Ne5 with control of the center and good prospects on both flanks, Kasparov-Speelman, Moscow (Kremlin Stars) 1995. 6...dxc4; 7.Bxc4 is a favorable Queen's Gambit Accepted, because White has managed to develop the dark-squared bishop to a useful square before playing e3.

7.dxc5 Bxc5; 8.Qc2. 8.a3 Nc6; 9.Rc1 is another popular line. 9...a6 (9...d4; 10.Nxd4 e5!; 11.Nb3 Bxa3; 12.bxa3 exf4; 13.Qxd8 Rxd8; 14.exf4 was a little better for White in Kramnik-Belyavsky, Belgrade 1993.) 10.cxd5 exd5; 11.Bg5 d4!; 12.Nb5?! (12.Ne4 is stronger, though the position, which now resembles a Tarrasch Defense, is fine for Black.) 12...dxe3!; 13.Qxd8 exf2+; 14.Ke2 Rxd8; 15.Bxf6 Re8+; 16.Kd1 gxf6; 17.Rxc5 Bg4! and Black won quickly after 18.Nc3 Nd4; 19.Bc4 Nxf3; 20.Kc2 Bf5+; 21.Kb3 Nd2+; 22.Ka2 Be6! and in Dreyev-Short, Linares 1995 White resigned because the Black rook would soon infiltrate e1 and escort the pawn home. **8...Nc6.**

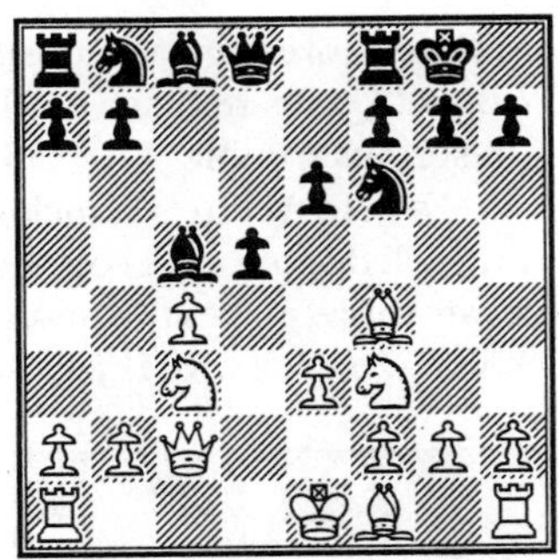

8...Qa5 is generally considered riskier. **9.a3 Qa5; 10.0–0–0**. A well established line, but with a pawn on a3, the defender can reasonably hope to strike back. 10.Nd2 Bb4; 11.cxd5 Nxd5; 12.Nxd5 exd5; 13.Bd3 h6; 14.Rc1 is an interesting option, Kramnik-Huebner, Bundesliga 1993. **10...Be7.** 10...Ne4; 11.Nb5 a6; 12.Nc7 e5; 13.Rxd5 f5 allowed 14.Rxe5!! Nxe5; 15.Bxe5 Ra7; 16.Nd5 b6; 17.Bd3 Bd7; 18.b4 and White controlled most of the board after 18...Qxa3+ 19.Bb2 Qa4; 20.bxc5 bxc5; 21.Ne5 Qxc2+; 22.Bxc2 Be6; 23.Nf4, Kasparov-Vaganian, European Team Championship 1992.

11.h4!? This is Kasparov's preferred plan of attack, though it remains to be seen whether it will withstand the test of time. 11.g4 dxc4; 12.Bxc4 e5; 13.g5 exf4; 14.gxf6 Bxf6; 15.Nd5 Ne7; 16.Nxf6+ gxf6; 17.Rhg1+ Kh8; 18.e4 b5 led to a very complicated game in Akopian-Short, Groningen 1996. 11.Bg5 Rd8; 12.Bd3 dxc4; 13.Bxc4 Bd7; 14.Kb1 Rac8; 15.h4 Ne5; 16.Nxe5 Qxe5; 17.Rd4 Bc6 gave Black sufficient counterplay in Kveinis-Klovan, Groningen 1991.

11...dxc4. 11...Rd8 looks like the best move. 12.Nd2 (12.g4 Bd7; 13.Kb1 dxc4; 14.Bxc4 Rac8; 15.g5 Nh5; 16.Bd6 g6; 17.Be2 Bxd6; 18.Rxd6 Ne7; 19.Qb3 gave White a small advantage in Kasparov-Ehlvest, Novgorod 1995.) 12...Rd7!? is an interesting but controversial defense. (12...e5; 13.Bg5 d4; 14.Nb3 Qb6; 15.c5 Qc7; 16.Nb5 Qb8; 17.exd4 a6; 18.Nd6 Bxd6; 19.cxd6 Qxd6; 20.dxe5 Qxd1+; 21.Qxd1 Rxd1+; 22.Kxd1 Nxe5 settled into a draw in Cifuentes Parada-Van der Sterren, Netherlands Championship 1995.) 13.Bd3 White will work up a kingside attack, but Black does have counterplay in the center. 13...Qd8; 14.cxd5 exd5; 15.Nf3 (15.Nb3!?) 15...Qf8; 16.g4

A) 16...Nxg4; 17.Bxh7+ Kh8; 18.Bf5 Rd8; 19.Bxg4 Bxg4; 20.Ng5 Qg8; 21.Rxd5 with a clear advantage for White;

B) 16...g6; 17.g5 (17.h5 Nxg4; 18.hxg6 fxg6; 19.Bxg6 hxg6; 20.Qxg6+ Qg7; 21.Qxg7+ Kxg7; 22.Rhg1 Rd8; 23.Nh2 with a clear advantage for White) 17...Nh5; 18.Bh2

C) 16...Ne4; 17.Ne5 Nxe5; 18.Bxe5 was played in Agdestein-Short, Isle of Lewis 1995. Now according to Korchnoi the best continuation is 18...g6; 19.Nxe4 dxe4; 20.Bxe4 Rxd1+; 21.Qxd1 since 21...Bxa3!; 22.bxa3 Qc5+ gets back the piece with good attacking chances against the exposed White king.

12.Bxc4 b6. 12...e5; 13.Bg5 Bg4; 14.Nd5 Bxf3; 15.gxf3 Nxd5; 16.Bxd5 Rac8; 17.Kb1 is a little better for White, but the play can become very sharp with attacks on both flanks. **13.Ng5 Ba6.** 13...h6 14.Nge4 **14.Nce4! g6.** This is a logical defense, but now Kasparov becomes fixed on the idea of advancing the pawn to h5 and opening up some lines for an attack. **15.Nxf6+ Bxf6; 16.Ne4.** The knight must retreat, as it is too early to attack.

16...Be7. The bishop might be more logically positioned at g7, but there is a flaw in that plan. 16...Bg7; 17.Bxa6! Qxa6; 18.Qxc6 e5; 19.Nf6+ Bxf6; 20.Qxf6 exf4; 21.exf4 and the Black king is in serious trouble. **17.Bxa6 Qxa6; 18.Kb1 Qb7; 19.h5!** The opening of the h-file is the key to White's attacking plan. **19...Rac8.** 19...e5; 20.hxg6 hxg6; 21.Rh6 and White will double rooks on the h-file. **20.hxg6 Nb4?** Black is losing anyway, but this desperate move makes the task simpler for White. **21.gxh7+ Kh8.** 21...Kg7; 22.Be5+ f6; 23.Nxf6 Nxc2; 24.Rd7! wins. **22.Be5+ f6.**

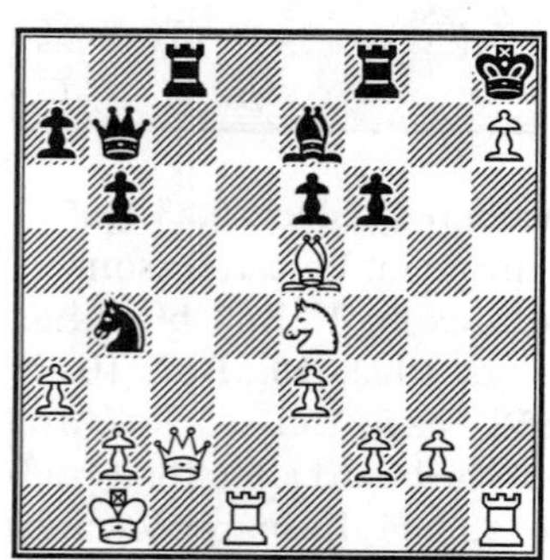

Now a final combination brings the game to a close. **23.Nxf6 Bxf6.** 23...Nxc2; 24.Nd5+ Bf6; 25.Nxf6 Qg7; 26.Ng4 Qxe5; 27.Nxe5 Rf6; 28.Rd7 leaves Black with no defense. 23...Rxf6 loses to 24.Qg6 Nd5; 25.Rxd5 Qxd5; 26.Qxf6+ Bxf6; 27.Bxf6#; 23...Rxc2; 24.Ng4+! Rf6 allows White to capture the knight at b4 with 25.axb4! since after 25...Qe4 White wins with 26.Bxf6+ Bxf6; 27.Nxf6 and amazingly there is no useful discovered check, for example 27...Rxb2+; 28.Kxb2 Qe5+; 29.Kb3 Qxf6 and now 30.Rd7 sets up an eventual back rank mate.

24.Bxf6+ and Black resigned, since after 24.Bxf6+ Rxf6; 25.axb4 Rxc2; 26.Rd8+ is no less painful. **24...Rxf6; 25.axb4.** White has too many extra pawns, and Black cannot capture the queen: **25...Rxc2??; 26.Rd8+ Kg7; 27.h8Q+** and mate follows quickly. **White won.**

RAGOZIN SYSTEM

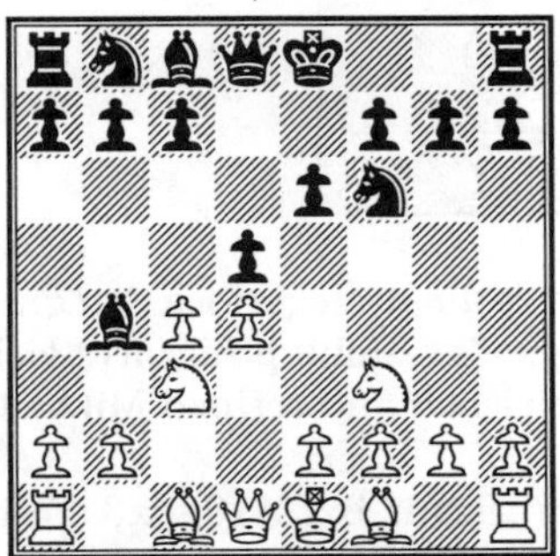

1.d4	**Nf6**
2.c4	**e6**
3.Nf3	**d5**
4.Nc3	**Bb4**

The **Ragozin Defense** can be reached from a number of openings including The Queen's Gambit, Nimzo-Indian and Panov Attack. It has never been considered a reliable path to equality, but has a fighting character which has attracted such advocates as Mikhail Tal. The variation earned its name in the 1934 Soviet Championship and in many subsequent events where Ragozin defended the Black side. The opening shares many ideas with the Nimzo-Indian. Black will often give up the bishop at b4 for the knight at c3, but the benefit of the position of the bishop is that the knight is pinned, so that White cannot take control of the e4-square.

(144) FREIMAN - RAGOZIN [D38]
Soviet Championship, 1934

1.d4 Nf6; 2.c4 e6; 3.Nf3 d5; 4.Nc3 Bb4; 5.Qa4+. 5.Bg5 h6; 6.Bxf6 Qxf6; 7.Qb3 (7.e3 c5; 8.cxd5 exd5; 9.Bb5+ Bd7; 10.Qa4 a6; 11.Bxd7+ Nxd7; 12.Ne5 Qd6; 13.Nxd7 Qxd7; 14.Qb3 Bxc3+; 15.Qxc3 c4 was soon drawn in Timman-Sosonko, Dutch Championship 1996.) 7...Nc6; 8.cxd5 Nxd4; 9.Nxd4 Qxd4; 10.Rd1 Qb6; 11.a3 Bxc3+; 12.Qxc3 0–0; 13.e3 exd5; 14.Rxd5 Be6; 15.Rb5 Qd6; 16.Be2 Rfd8; 17.0–0 Qd2 and Black had a strong game in Rabinovich-Ragozin, Soviet Union 1934.

5.cxd5 exd5; 6.Bg5 is a good plan, transposing to the Exchange Variation. For example: 6...Nbd7; 7.e3 (7.Qc2 c5; 8.a3 Bxc3+; 9.Qxc3 c4; 10.Nd2 h6 and Black was fine in Avrukh-Greenfeld, Beersheva 1996.) 7...c5; 8.Bd3 Qa5; 9.Qc2 c4; 10.Bf5 0–0; 11.0–0 Re8; 12.Nd2 g6; 13.Bxd7 Nxd7; 14.h4 Nb6; 15.f3 Bxc3; 16.bxc3 which was considered better for White, but in Sokolov-Sosonko, Dutch Championship 1996, a new idea for Black brought a playable game after 16...Qa4!; 17.Qc1 Bf5; 18.Re1 Qc6.

5...Nc6.

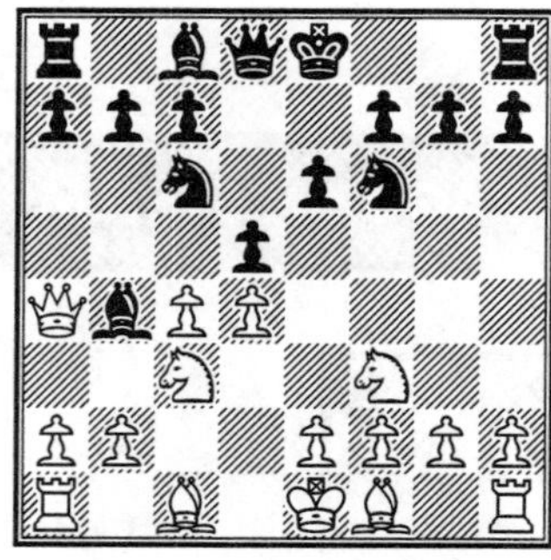

Although this move is obviously forced, it is the strategic idea that gives Ragozin's plan its particular flavor. In most of the Queen's Gambit positions Black strives for an early ...c5. In some ways, Ragozin has enriched and refined Mikhail Chigorin's defense with 1.d4 d5; 2.c4 Nc6.

6.Ne5. 6.Bg5 dxc4; 7.e3 Qd5; 8.Bxf6 gxf6; 9.Nd2 Bxc3; 10.bxc3 b5; 11.Qc2 Bb7; 12.Rb1 Rb8; 13.e4 gave White more than enough for the pawn in Rabinovich-Ragozin, Moscow 1935. 6.e3 0–0; 7.Bd2 a6; 8.Qc2 dxc4; 9.Bxc4 Bd6; 10.a3 e5; 11.d5 Ne7; 12.h3 b5; 13.Ba2 Qd7; 14.e4 a5; 15.0–0 b4 kept the initiative in Black's hands in Reshevsky-Ragozin, Semmering 1937. 6.cxd5 Nxd5; 7.Bd2 0–0; 8.e3 a6; 9.Qc2 Bd6; 10.a3 Nf6; 11.Be2 Bd7; 12.0–0 Qe7; 13.e4 allowed White to dominate the center in Gothilf-Ragozin, Soviet Union 1934. **6...Bd7; 7.Nxc6 Bxc3+; 8.bxc3 Bxc6.**

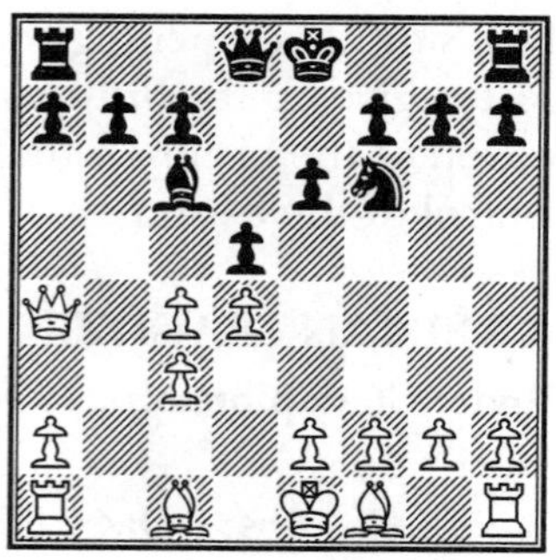

Black's bishop at c6 will turn out to be very strong. **9.Qb3 dxc4; 10.Qxc4 Ne4; 11.Be3 0–0; 12.f3.** White must try something to free the kingside, but that need not be done immediately. 9.Qb3 comes into consideration. **12...Nd6; 13.Qd3 Bb5; 14.Qc2.** Now Black invests a pawn to open up the game. **14...e5!?** 14...c5 was another interesting possibility. Black's game is very comfortable.

15.dxe5 Nc4; 16.Bf4. The bishop could also have been played to d4 or c5, but this is the best choice. **16...Qh4+; 17.g3 Qh5.** Black acts to keep White from playing e4. **18.Bg2.** 18.Qe4 might have been better, but it is optically difficult to play such a move when you are concentrating on getting a pawn to that square. The point is that the knight at c4 is a bit vulnerable. In fact, it is entirely possible that White stands better here.

18...Nxe5; 19.0–0. It is logical to get the king to a safe position, as we are well into the middlegame. White could have played in the center with 19.a4 followed by queenside castling, and then a fight could take place on opposite wings. There are no open lines on either flank, and White's pawnstorm will gain momentum quickly.

19...Ng6; 20.Bc1. White had no desire to part with the dark-squared bishop, which is his only effective fighting piece. 20.Bxc7?? would blunder a piece to 20...Qc5+. **20...Rfe8; 21.Rf2 Qc5; 22.e4.** White finally gets this move in, but now there is an important weakness at d3.

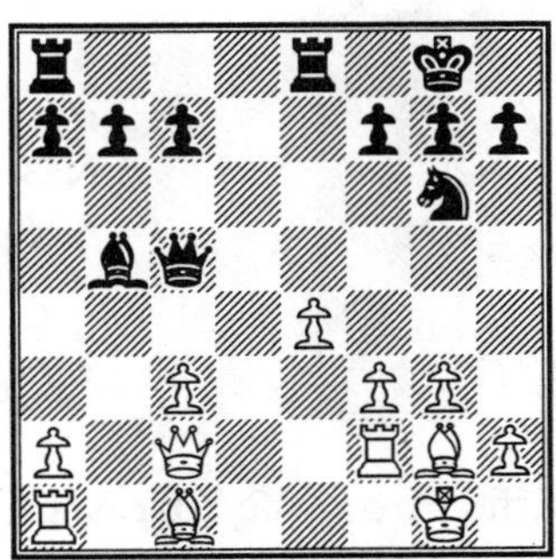

22.Kf1 loses to the surprising 22...Rxe2!! since 23.Rxe2 Re8 exploits the pin. **22...Ne5!; 23.a4 Bd3; 24.Qb3 Rad8; 25.Qb4 Qc6; 26.Bf4 h6; 27.Bxe5.** It is now clear that the knight is stronger than the bishop, so this exchange makes sense. **27...Rxe5; 28.Rd1 a5; 29.Qb2 Re7; 30.Rfd2 Red7; 31.h4 b6; 32.Bh3 Rd6; 33.Qa3.**

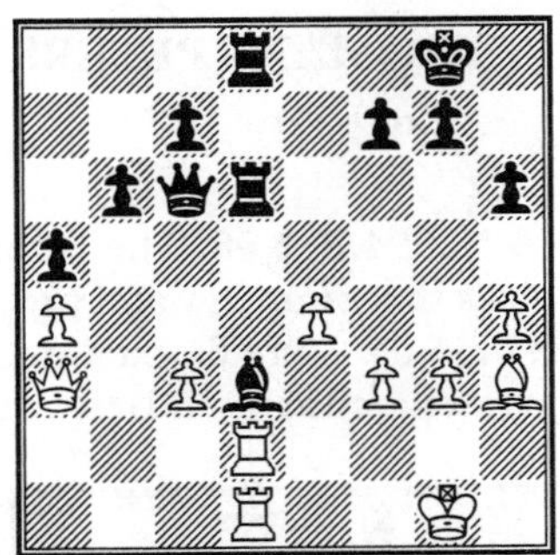

33.Qa1 Bc2; 34.Rxd6 Rxd6; 35.Rxd6 Qxd6; 36.Qb2 Qd1+; 37.Kf2 Qd2+; 38.Kg1 Qe3+; 39.Kg2 Bxa4 and Black wins. **33...Bc2!; 34.Rxd6 Rxd6; 35.Rd4 Rxd4; 36.cxd4 Qxa4** and Black went on to win without difficulty. **37.Qc3 Bb3; 38.d5 Qc4; 39.Qe5 Qc5+; 40.Kg2 Ba4; 41.h5 Bb5; 42.Qf5 Be8; 43.f4 a4; 44.Bg4 a3; 45.Qe5 Bb5. Black won.**

SEMI-TARRASCH DEFENSE

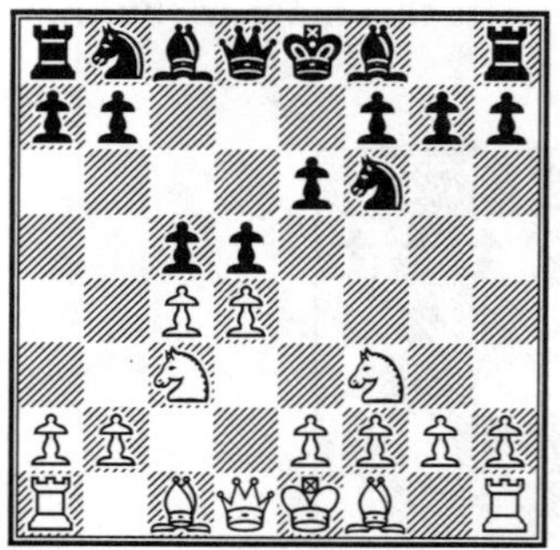

1.d4	**d5**
2.c4	**e6**
3.Nf3	**Nf6**
4.Nc3	**c5**

The **Semi-Tarrasch** differs from the Tarrasch Defense in that both sides have developed the kingside knights. This eliminates many options for Black, including the sharp Schara Gambit. On the other hand, it also means that Black can reply to cxd5 with ...Nxd5, avoiding the isolated d-pawn. In these cases, it is White who often winds up with the isolated pawn. The Semi-Tarrasch is most often reached by transposition from a Flank Opening.

(145) PETROSIAN - PETERS [D41]
Lone Pine, 1976

1.c4 Nf6; 2.Nc3 c5; 3.g3 Nc6; 4.Bg2 e6. The Semi-Tarrasch approach to the English works well. Black breaks the symmetry and prepares to stake a claim to the center with ...d5. **5.Nf3 Be7; 6.d4 d5.** Here 6...cxd4 might lead to a hedgehog, but this move leads to a Semi-Tarrasch or Tarrasch Defense. **7.cxd5.**

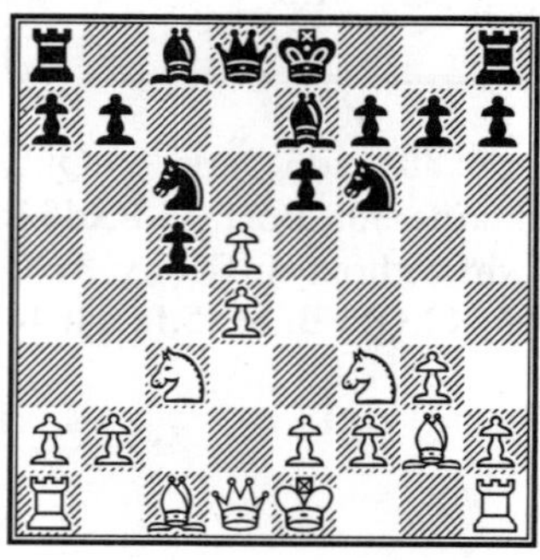

7...Nxd5. Capturing with the pawn would transpose to the Classical Tarrasch. **8.0–0 0–0.** White has several plans here. **9.Nxd5.** 9.Rb1 Bf6; 10.dxc5 Bxc3; 11.e4 Bf6; 12.exd5 Qxd5; 13.Qxd5 exd5; 14.Bf4 Bf5; 15.Rbd1 Bxb2; 16.Rxd5 Be6; 17.Rd2 Ba3; 18.Bd6 and White as better in Marin-Komljenovic, Ubeda 1996. 9.e4 forces Black to make a decision regarding the knight, which can either retreat or capture at c3. 9...Nb6; 10.dxc5 Qxd1; 11.Rxd1 Bxc5; 12.Bf4 f6; 13.Rac1 e5; 14.Nb5 exf4; 15.Rxc5 fxg3; 16.hxg3 Bg4; 17.Rd2 Rad8; 18.Nd6 and again White is better, Kortchnoi-Brunner, Zurich (2nd Match Game) 1996.

9...exd5. If there were still knights at c3 and f6, then we would be in the main lines of the Tarrasch, but this is a Semi-Tarrasch, which is easier to defend for Black because the knight at c3 gives rise to more possibilities than the one at f6. Their absence also gives Black more freedom to maneuver. **10.dxc5 Bxc5.** This is the main line of the formation known as the Keres-Parma Variation.

11.a3. There are no less than eight reasonable moves for White here, and of course transpositions are possible later on. 11.Bg5 f6; 12.Bd2 Bf5 (12...Qe7; 13.Bc3 Rd8; 14.e3 and the blockade is permanent.) 13.Qb3 Bb6; 14.Be3 Na5 (14...Bxe3; 15.Qxe3 d4; 16.Qf4 Be6; 17.Rfd1 Bc4; 18.Rd2 and the d-pawn must eventually fall.) 15.Qc3 Bxe3; 16.Qxe3 Re8; 17.Qc5 b6; 18.Qb5 a6; 19.Qa4 b5; 20.Qf4 Be4; 21.Rac1 Nc4; 22.b3 Ne5; 23.Nd4 Bxg2; 24.Kxg2 Qb6; 25.Rfd1. White has achieved a dominating position, thanks to the strong blockade at d4. This is exactly the kind of position Black must avoid. White went on to win in Kramnik-Kengis, Riga (Tal Memorial) 1995.

11...a5. This is a rather strange reaction, prompted no doubt by the fear of an advance of the White b-pawn to b4. 11...Bf5; 12.b4 Bb6 is roughly level, and Boris Spassky has defended the Black side. For example, here is a bit of his game against Portisch at Bugojno 1978: 13.Ra2 Be4; 14.Rd2 Qe7; 15.Bb2 Rfe8; 16.Qa1 f6; 17.Rfd1 Qe6 with full equality. **12.Ne1 d4; 13.Nd3 Bb6.** Black's pieces are awkwardly placed, and White has a blockade in place. **14.Bd2 Re8; 15.Rc1 Bg4.** The pawn at e2 is a natural source of counterplay, just as in a Tarrasch Defense. **16.Re1 Rc8; 17.h3.** The pressure at e2 is diminished.

17...Bf5; 18.Qb3 Be4. The exchange of light-squared bishops helps maintain the pawn at d4, since the knight at c6 cannot be eliminated by the bishop. At the same time, however, there are fewer resources for Black to use in any attack. **19.Bxe4 Rxe4; 20.Qb5.**

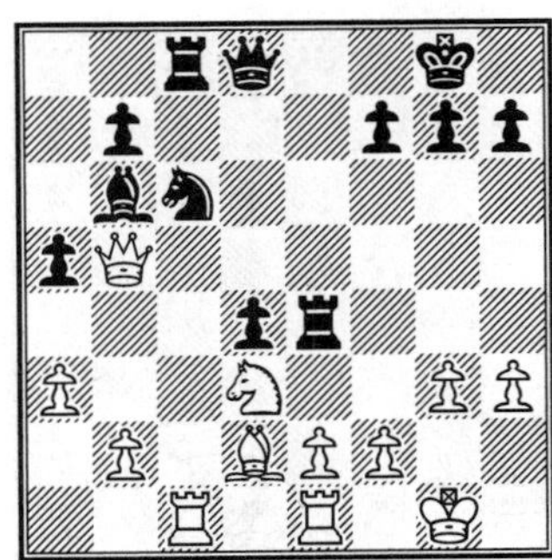

White stands better because the d-pawn is permanently blockaded and Black has no realistic attacking chances. **20...Na7; 21.Rxc8 Nxc8; 22.Bg5 Qd6; 23.Rc1.** All of White's pieces are on good squares while Black's pieces are scattered and uncoordinated. **23...Na7; 24.Qf5 Re8; 25.Bf4 Qd8; 26.Rc2.** White's position improves all the time. Still, good technique is required to convert the advantage into a win.

26...Nc6; 27.h4 h6; 28.Qb5 Na7; 29.Qf5. Petrosian marks time, trying to figure out a way to make further progress. **29...Nc6; 30.Kf1 Re6; 31.Qb5 Na7; 32.Qb3**

Nc6; 33.h5 Ne7; 34.Ke1. Now a plan is developed. The king will head to the queenside, and then a real kingside attack can be mounted. **34...Nd5; 35.Qb5 Nf6; 36.Kd1 Nd5; 37.Be5 Ne7; 38.g4 Nc6; 39.Bg3 Na7; 40.Qb3 Nc6; 41.Kc1 Re4; 42.f3** The slight weakening of e3 is not important. **42...Re3; 43.Kb1 Ne7; 44.Bh4 Qd6.**

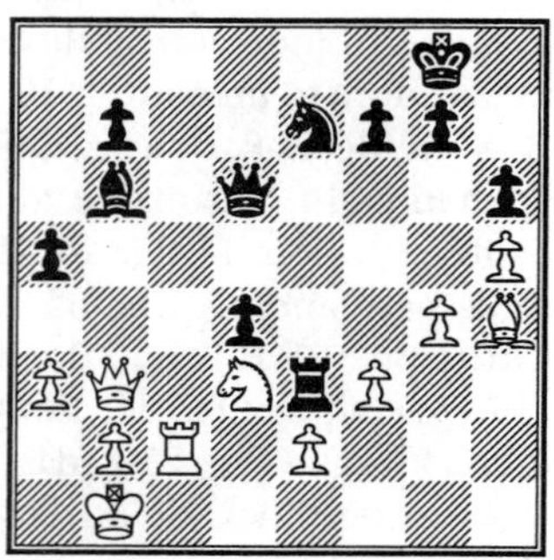

Petrosian has been slowly working out a plan, but often one needs a little help from the opponent. Perhaps Peters didn't think that White would be willing to part with the bishop, but Petrosian saw an opportunity and grabbed it. **45.Bxe7! Rxe7.** Black cannot capture with the queen because that would leave the bishop at b6 hanging. **46.Rc8+ Kh7; 47.Rf8.** The f-pawn falls and the game is quickly over. Note that this was made possible by the White pawns at g4 and h5, and those advances were made possible only after Petrosian walked the king to the queenside. **47...Qc7; 48.f4 Bc5; 49.Qd5 Re5; 50.Rxf7. White won.**

(146) KERES - FINE [D41]

Ostende, 1937

1.Nf3 d5; 2.d4 Nf6; 3.c4 e6; 4.Nc3 c5; 5.cxd5 Nxd5

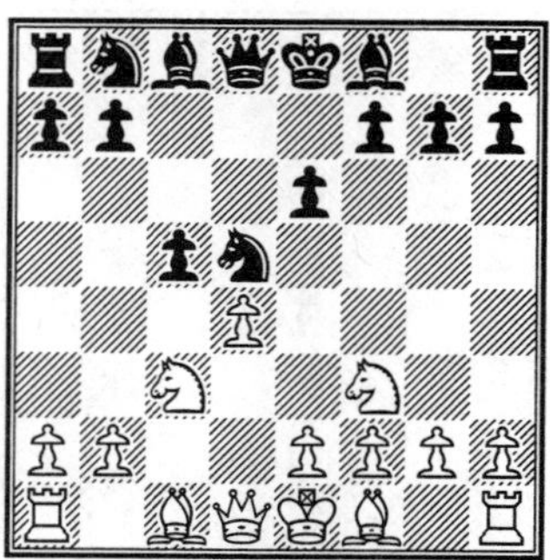

By recapturing with the Knight, Black chooses the Semi-Tarrasch. White can now apply pressure on the long diagonal by fianchettoing a bishop at g2, as we saw in the last game, or directly confront the enemy knight with e4. This is the Exchange Variation. **6.e4 Nxc3; 7.bxc3 cxd4; 8.cxd4 Bb4+; 9.Bd2 Bxd2+; 10.Qxd2.**

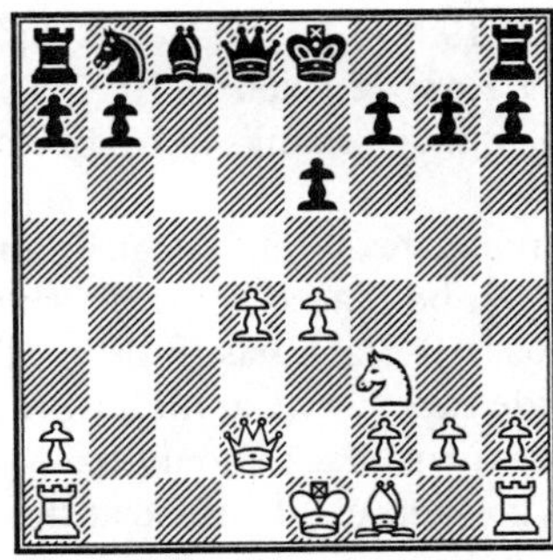

A common position in the Semi-Tarrasch. Black aims for an endgame, where he can take advantage of the queenside majority. White controls the center. **10...0–0; 11.Bc4.** Part of White's strategy lies in advancing his d-pawn at the appropriate time. The other component is a kingside attack. The two plans can be joined if the a2-g8 diagonal is part of the attack. **11...Nd7.** This is the more flexible move, which allows the knight to participate in the defense. 11...Nc6 places pressure on the center, but eventually the knight will be attacked by an advance of the d-pawn. Both moves are played these days

12.0–0 b6; 13.Rad1 Bb7; 14.Rfe1 Rc8; 15.Bb3 Nf6. This is the active continuation, which targets the e4-square and keeps an eye on d5, thus directly aimed at countering White's strategy. This knight could also have been posted at f8 (after Rf8-e8), adopting a purely defensive plan. **16.Qf4 Qc7.** Black would be delighted to see the queens leave the board, but White is still interested in a kingside attack. **17.Qh4 Rfd8.**

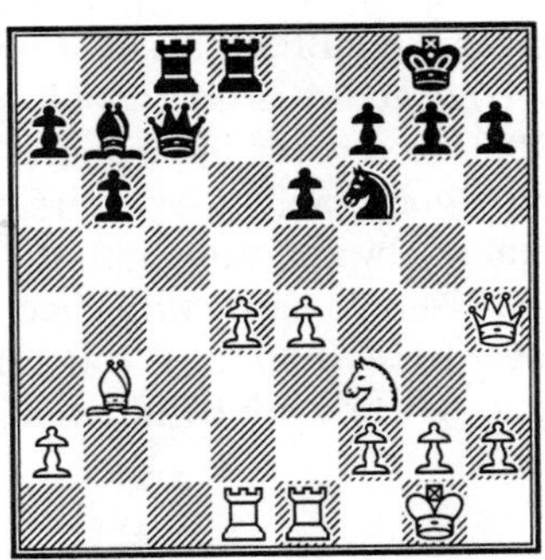

The developmental phase of the game is concluded, and it is time for decisions with regard to long-term strategy. **18.Re3?!** White has a difficult time planning here. The immediate advance of the pawn fails, but White sees that it can be made to work once the Ra1 is removed from the d-file. Yet the correct plan is a kingside attack, so he should kick the horse 18.d5? exd5; 19.e5 would be a reasonable plan, coupled with an exchange sacrifice. But it doesn't work. 19...Ne4; 20.Rxe4 dxe4 leaves the Rd1 loose. 21.Ng5 Rxd1+; 22.Bxd1 h6 and White has no compensation for the exchange. 18.Ne5 Qc3!; 19.Re3? Qxd4!; 20.Rxd4 Rc1+; 18.e5! is correct, depriving the kingside of its only defender.

Keres demonstrated the effectiveness of this plan with the following concrete variations: 18...Nd7 (18...Nd5; 19.Ng5 h6; 20.Ne4 Nc3; 21.Nf6+!; 18...Bxf3 19.exf6! Bxd1; 20.Qg5 Kf8; 21.Qxg7+ Ke8; 22.Rxe6+!) 19.Ng5 Nf8; 20.Ne4 Bxe4; 21.Qxe4 and White has a positional advantage thanks to his bishop and the ready availability of d4-d5.

18...b5! Black correctly anticipates White's strategy and prepares b6 for the queen, so that immediate pressure can be placed at d4 if White advances e4-e5. **19.Rde1 a5?!** But this is overambitious. All Black has to do is eliminate the kingside attack and he can enjoy his queenside superiority at his leisure. **20.a4! b4?** A critical strategic error. Here, or at the last turn, Black should have played h7-h6, so that White would not be able to use the g5-square. Of course at this point 20...bxa4 would have to be interpolated, but after 20.Bxa4 h6 it is a better position for Black. **21.d5!**

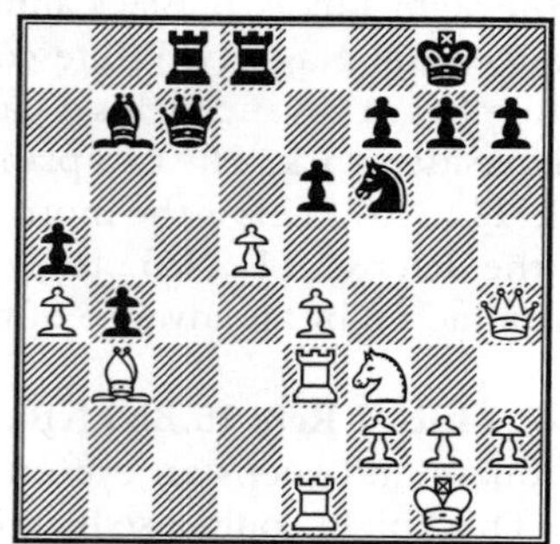

The same theme returns. After Black captures, White will push the e-pawn and then play Ng5 with a strong attack. **21...exd5.** 21...e5 22.Ng5 Rd6; 23.f4 with a strong attack. **22.e5 Nd7.** 22...Ne4 is helpful to White in that it allows him, via an exchange sacrifice, to open the diagonal for the Bb3. This has no immediate effect, but with a preliminary pawn sacrifice White adds considerable force to the attack. 23.e6! fxe6; 24.Rxe4! dxe4; Now Bxe6+ fails to recover the material, but the kingside, deprived of its principal defender, is now vulnerable to a powerful zwischenzug. 25.Ng5! Qc3! This move almost turns the tables, by attacking both the Bb3 and Re1 while simultaneously defending g7. But the bishop escapes with check. 26.Bxe6+ Kf8; 27.Rf1! and here White will at least recover his exchange, or can aim for f7 via f4. **23.Ng5 Nf8?** This was Black's last chance to defend with h7-h6, though this is already too late to achieve equality.

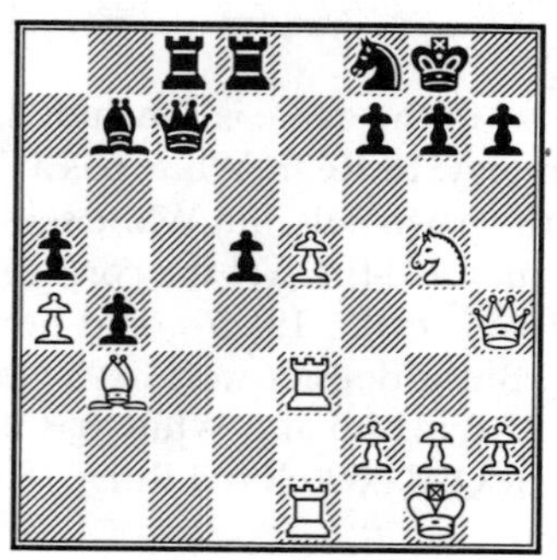

23...h6; 24.e6! hxg5; 25.exf7+ Kxf7; 26.Re7+ Kg8; 27.Qxg5 Qc3; 28.h3! Qf6; 29.Bxd5+ Bxd5; 30.Qxd5+ Kh8; 31.Rxd7 Rxd7; 32.Qxd7 Rf8 with an advantage to White, although it will not be easy to win the position. **24.Nxh7!** White single-mindedly carries out his attack. The material is not important because neither the Bb7 nor the rc8 can participate in the defense, but the Bb3 can play a role. In any event, the material is recouped quickly. **24...Nxh7; 25.Rh3 Qc1.** Obviously the knight cannot move because of mate at h8. **26.Qxh7+ Kf8; 27.Rhe3 d4; 28.Qh8+ Ke7; 29.Qxg7 Rf8.** 29...Bd5; 30.Qf6+ Ke8; (30...Kd7; 31.Bxd5) 31.e6! Bxe6; 32.Rxe6+ fxe6; 33.Qxe6+ Kf8; 34.Qe7# **30.Qf6+ Ke8; 31.e6!**

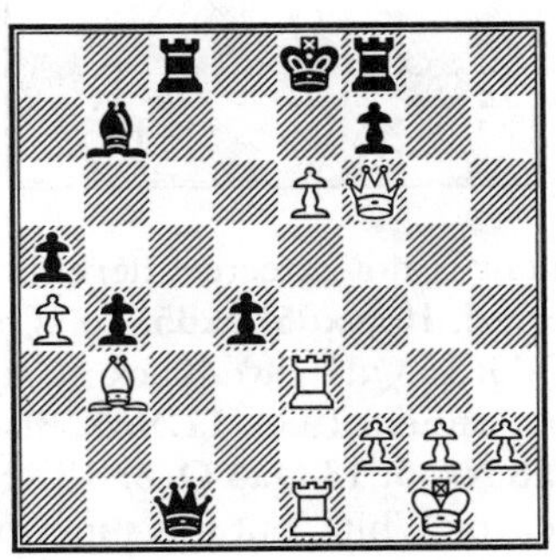

Black resigned because of 31...dxe3; 32.exf7+ Rxf7; 33.Bxf7+ Kd7; 34.Qe6+. The combination of d4-d5 and a kingside attack was played to perfection. **White won.**

(147) LARSEN - POMAR SALAMANCA [D41]

Spain, 1978

1.e4 c6; 2.d4 d5; 3.exd5 cxd5; 4.c4 Nf6; 5.Nc3 e6; 6.Nf3 Be7.

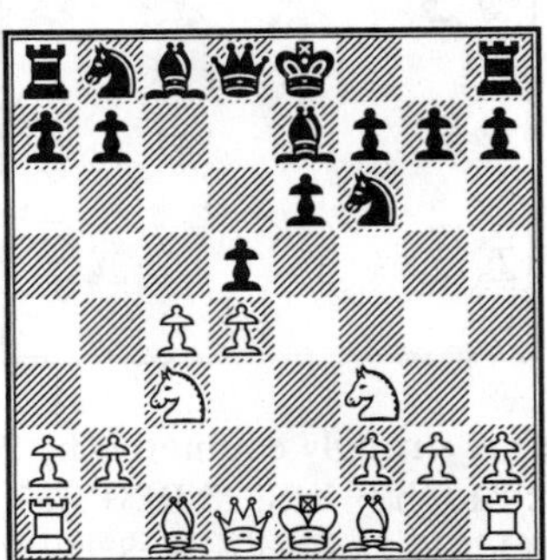

This is a pure Panov Attack, which is also part of the Semi-Tarrasch, although it is most typically reached from a Caro-Kann. When Black plays the bishop to b4 instead, we have a position common to the Nimzo-Indian Defense. In those cases, however, the bishop often winds up retreating to e7 anyway, so many players prefer to station it there in the first place. Black plans to calmly develop with kingside castling and then choosing a formation for the queenside pieces. **7.cxd5 Nxd5.** The position could be reached from a Semi-Tarrasch 1.d4d5; 2.c4e6; 3.Nc3 Nf6; 4.Nf3 c5; 5.cxd5 Nxd5; 6.e3 cxd4; 7.exd4 Be7. **8.Bd3 0–0; 9.0–0 b6.**

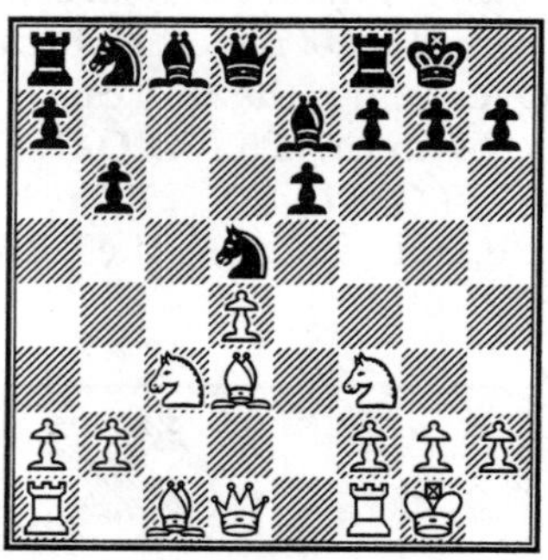

This plan of development is not effective here, because of White's reply. Instead, 9...Nc6 is to be preferred. **10.Nxd5! exd5.** 10...Qxd5; 11.Qc2 Bb7; 12.Bxh7+ Kh8; 13.Bd3 Nc6; 14.Be4 Qd6; 15.Qd1 gave Black no significant compensation for the pawn in Borm-Grooten, Arnhem 1983. **11.Ne5.** Black has serious holes on the queenside. **11...Ba6; 12.Bxa6 Nxa6; 13.Qa4 Qc8?** 13...Nc7; 14.Nc6 Qd7; 15.Nxe7+ Qxe7; 16.Bf4 is clearly better for White, but it is superior to the text.

14.Bf4 Qb7; 15.Qc6 Rab8. 15...Qxc6 16.Nxc6 Rfe8; 17.Rfc1 Bf8; 18.a3 leaves the Black pieces awkwardly placed. **16.Rfc1 Nb4; 17.Qd7! Na6** 17...Qxd7; 18.Nxd7 Rbd8; 19.Nxf8 Nd3; 20.Rc7 and in infiltration of the seventh rank gives White a significant advantage. 17...Rfd8; 18.Qf5 is similar to the game. **18.Rc3 Bf6; 19.Qf5 Rfe8.** 19...Bxe5; 20.Bxe5 Rbc8; 21.Qf6! –Larsen. **20.Rh3 h6.**

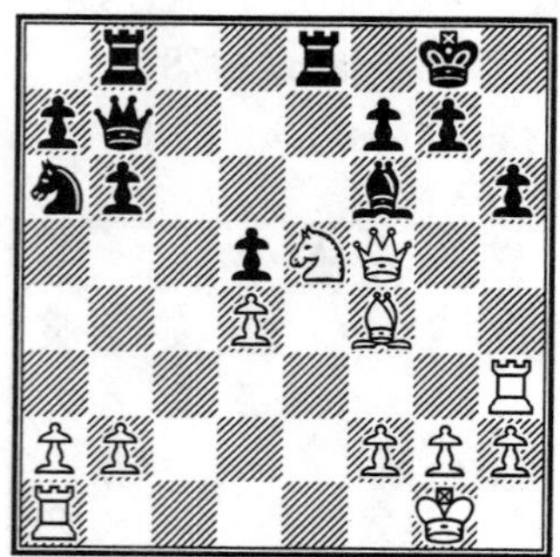

21.Bxh6! Qc8. 21...Bxe5 is strongly countered by 22.Bg5! f6 (22...Bf6; 23.Bxf6 gxf6; 24.Rg3+) 23.dxe5 fxg5; 24.Qh7+ Kf8; 25.Rf3+ Ke7; 26.Qxg7+ Kd8; 27.Rf7 Qc6 (27...Re7; 28.Qf8+ Re8; 29.Qd6+) 28.Qxg5+ Kc8; 29.Rc1 Nc5; 30.b4 and the pin wins. **22.Nd7! Re6; 23.Bxg7!!** Black resigned. Mate follows quickly at h7. **White won.**

CAMBRIDGE SPRINGS

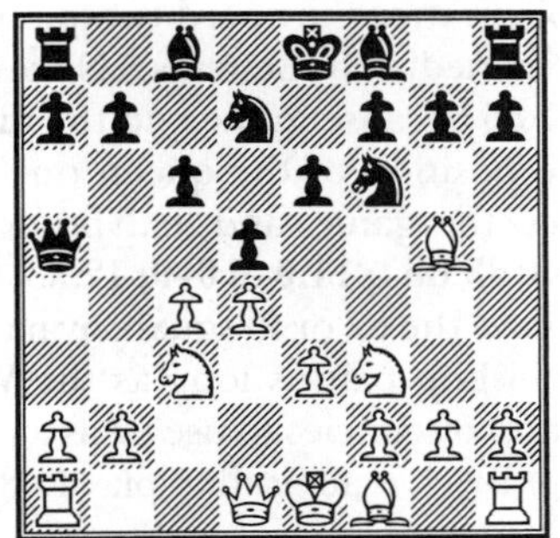

1.d4	**d5**
2.c4	**e6**
3.Nc3	**Nf6**
4.Bg5	**Nbd7**
5.Nf3	**c6**
6.e3	**Qa5**

The **Cambridge Springs** is one of American's most lasting contributions to opening theory. Black develops most of the forces quickly, with only the minor problem ofthe bishop at c8 to be solved. The bishop at f8 is stationed not defensively at e7, but at the active square b4, where pressure at c3 can free up the e4 square for occupation by a kngiht. The opening retains its solid reputation.

(148) MARSHALL - TEICHMANN [D52]
Cambridge Springs, 1904

1.d4 d5; 2.c4 e6; 3.Nc3 Nf6; 4.Bg5 Nbd7. 4... c5 is the Canal Variation. 5.cxd5 Qb6; 6.Nf3 (6.Bxf6 Qxb2; 7.Qc1 (7.Rc1 gxf6; 8.e3 cxd4; 9.Bb5+ Bd7; 10.Bxd7+ Nxd7; 11.exd4 Bb4; 12.Nge2 Rc8; 13.0–0 Bxc3; 14.Qd3 Nb6; 15.Rxc3 0–0; 16.dxe6 fxe6; 17.Ra3 was better for White in Hansen-Zsu.Polgar, Debrecen 1990.) 7...Qxc1+; 8.Rxc1 gxf6; 9.Ne4 Nd7; 10.dxe6 fxe6; 11.dxc5 f5; 12.Nd6+ was drawn in Tartakower-Canal, Venice 1948.) 6...cxd4; 7.Nxd4 Bc5; 8.Bxf6 gxf6; 9.e3 Qxb2; 10.Ndb5 Bb4; 11.Qc1 Qxc1+; 12.Rxc1 Na6 and play eventually led to a draw in Enevoldsen-Canal, Dubrovnik Olympiad, 1950.

5.Nf3 c6; 6.e3 Qa5; 7.Nd2.

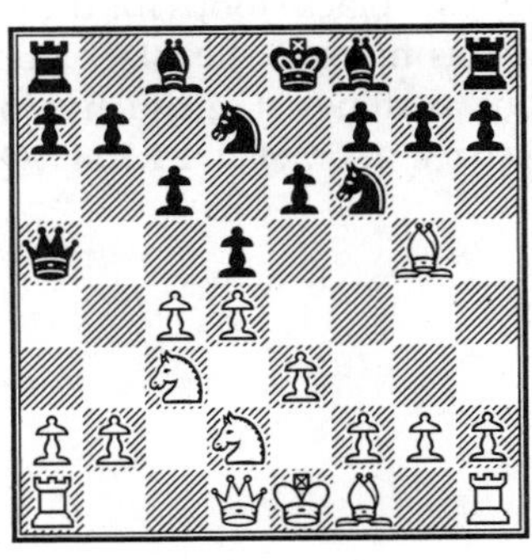

7...Ne4!? Even after all of these years there is no consensus on the merit of this plan. Samarian (1974) considers it the most important line for Black, while Euwe and van der Sterren (1980) dismiss it as "dubious". Since White must find the right move twice (at move 8 and move 9) in the opening in order to obtain any significant advantage, it may still be considered playable in over-the-board competition.

8.cxd5? This throws away the advantage immediately. Better is 8.Ndxe4! **8...Nxd2; 9.Qxd2.** White cannot afford to interpose dxe6 because in the end the bishop on g5 will hang. That's just a typical effect of the position of the queen on a5. **9...exd5** Naturally Black wants to get his bishop into the game, and 9...Nb6 doesn't work because 10.e4! defends the bishop on g5. **10.Bd3 Bb4; 11.0–0 0–0; 12.a3.** Oftentimes White plays this move when Black does not have the e7 or f8 square available. Nevertheless, Black need not fear giving up the bishop pair as long as the White dark-squared bishop is limited in scope. That bishop often tries to use e7 as a pivot square to swing over to the queenside, and therefore Black is advised to play Re8 early, as in the present game.

12...Bxc3; 13.bxc3 Re8!; 14.f4. This old-fashioned style of attack is still seen frequently in the Cambridge Springs. It is hard to attack the weak pawns at e3 and c3, while the rook can now enter the game via f3. **14...Nb6.** 14...Nf8 would have been more cautious, but then Black would have little to do on the queenside. **15.f5 f6; 16.Bf4 Nc4; 17.Qe2.**

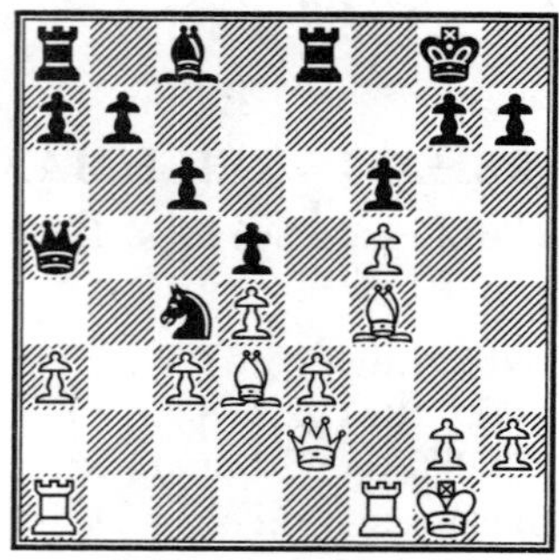

This does not hang the c-pawn, since White will answer 17...Qxc3 with 18.Rfc1 and 19.Bxc4. **17...b5; 18.Bxc4 bxc4.** 18...dxc4; 19.a4! brings White a clear advantage. **19.Qh5 Bd7; 20.Rf3,** abandoning the c-pawn on general principles. The fact that there are bishops of opposite color on the board makes this proceeding less hazardous." - Marshall **20...Qxc3.** "Black stoops for the gauntlet." - Marshall. It would be easier to find fault with this move if the Black queen were able to rejoin her husband on the kingside, but as things stand such a journey would take too long. This illustrates another drawback of 6...Qa5. **21.Raf1 Qd3; 22.g4.**

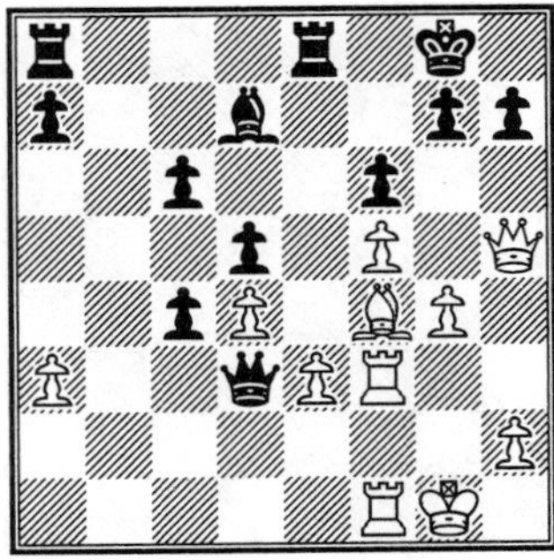

White has all of his pieces poised for the attack, and his king is well secured, so the pawn storm is the appropriate strategy. **22...Re7; 23.g5 Bxf5; 24.gxf6 gxf6.** Despite Marshall's comment, the Black queen is useful on d3, as it supports the bishop on f5 which holds together the light squares on the kingside. **25.Bh6 Bg6; 26.Qh4 Qe4; 27.Rxf6.**

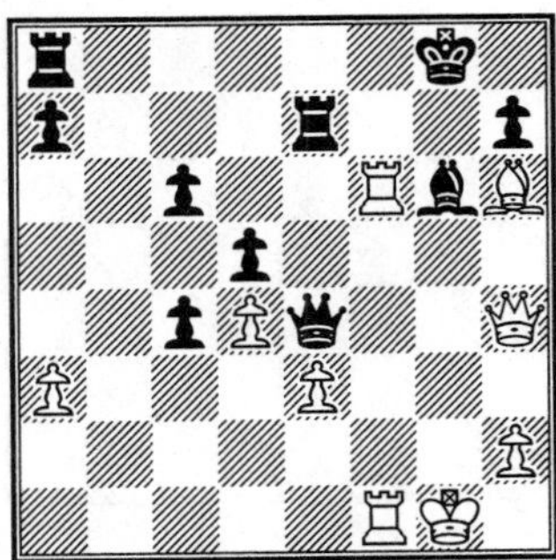

27...Rg7? According to Marshall, 27...Rf7 was the right move here, but it seems that Black did not like his chances after 28.Rxf7 Bxf7; 29.Qxe4 dxe4.

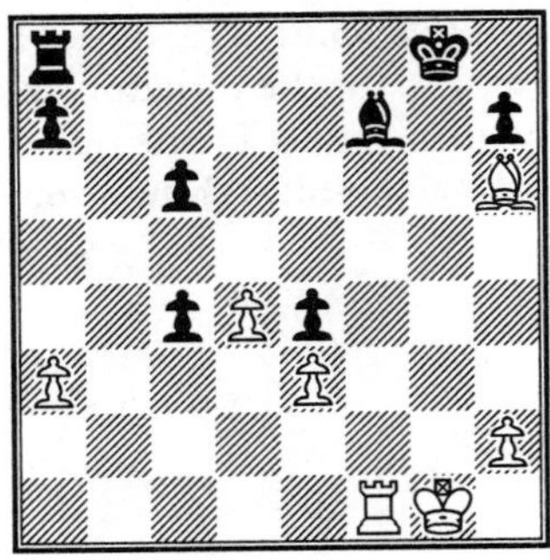

This judgment was surely wrong, as Black would have strong threats involving c3-c2 and Bf7-d5 would always do for a defense. The exchange sacrifice was certainly not necessary. **28.Qxe4 Bxe4+; 29.Bxg7 Kxg7; 30.Rxc6 Rb8; 31.Rc7+ Kh6; 32.Kf2 Rb2+; 33.Kg3 Rb3; 34.Kf4.**

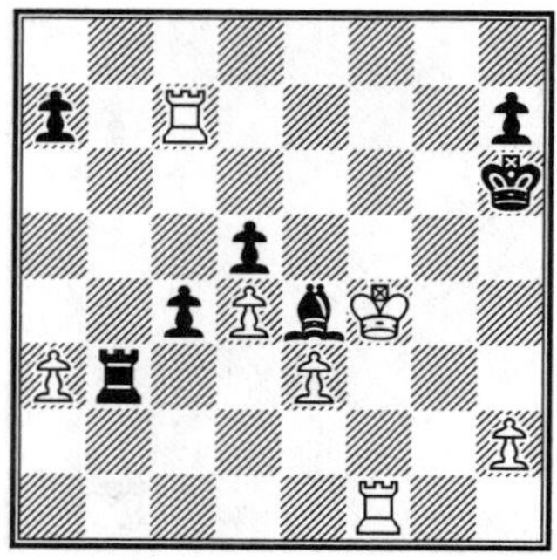

Black cannot cope with the power of the two rooks and the advancing king. **34...Bd3.** 34...Rxa3; 35.Rxc4! dxc4; 36.Kxe4 with a clear advantage for White since the Black king is cut off. **35.Rg1 Rb6; 36.Ke5 Be4; 37.Rg3 Rb8; 38.Rc6+ Kh5; 39.Rf6 Rb1; 40.Rc6 Rb8; 41.Rg7 Re8+ 42.Re6 Rc8; 43.Rf6 Bg6?**

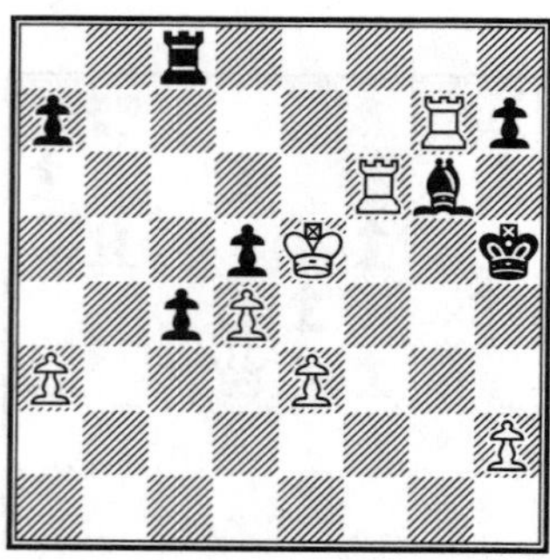

"The position is perilously close to a mate, yet this move was not immediately necessary, and the advance of the bishop pawn might temporarily have drawn the hostile fire. From now on the game plays itself." - Marshall. The remaining moves were: **44.Rgxg6 hxg6; 45.Kxd5 c3; 46.Rf1 Kg4; 47.Ke4 c2; 48.Rg1+ Kh3; 49.Rc1 g5; 50.d5 g4; 51.d6 Kxh2; 52.Ke5 Rc3; 53.e4 Kg3; 54.Kd4 Rc8; 55.e5 Kf4; 56.d7 Rd8; 57.e6 Kf5; 58.Kd5.** Not a great start for the variation, but perhaps this was just a case of the stronger player winning. In round 11 the opening was seen for the second time, with an even more disastrous result. **White won.**

LASKER DEFENSE

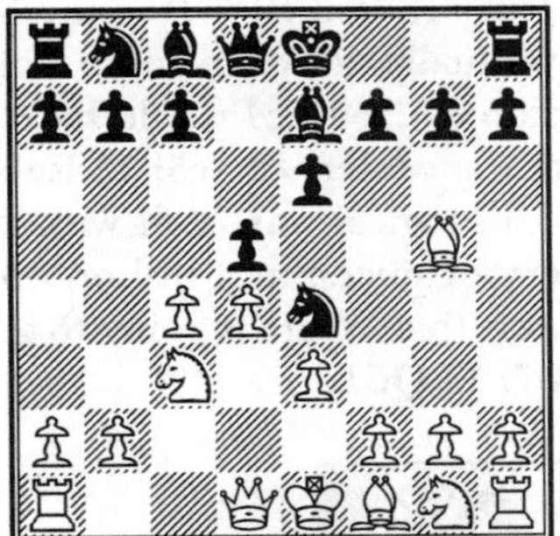

1.d4	**d5**
2.c4	**e6**
3.Nc3	**Nf6**
4.Bg5	**Be7**
5.e3	**Ne4**

Lasker's Defense to the Queen's Gambit challenges White to demonstrate an advantage after an early exchange of dark-squared bishops. Of course the remaining Black bishop is hemmed in by the pawn at e6, but that is typical of the Queen's Gambit Declined. Black's strategy is to resolve the tension in the center and then open up the game on the queenside. White must play very accurately to maintain even a small advantage.

(149) MARSHALL - LASKER [D53]
World Championship (3rd Match game), 1907

1.d4 d5; 2.c4 e6; 3.Nc3 Nf6; 4.Bg5 Be7; 5.e3 Ne4. The move ...h6 is often inserted before moving the knight to e4. 5...h6; 6.Bh4 Ne4; 7.Bxe7 Qxe7; 8.Nf3 0-0; 9.Rc1 c6; 10.Bd3 is a typical modern handling of the opening. After 10...Nxc3; 11.Rxc3 dxc4; 12.Rxc4! Nd7; 13.Bb1 e5; 14.Qc2 White had a promising attack in Polugayevsky-Augustin, Lugano Olympiad 1968. **6.Bxe7 Qxe7; 7.Bd3.**

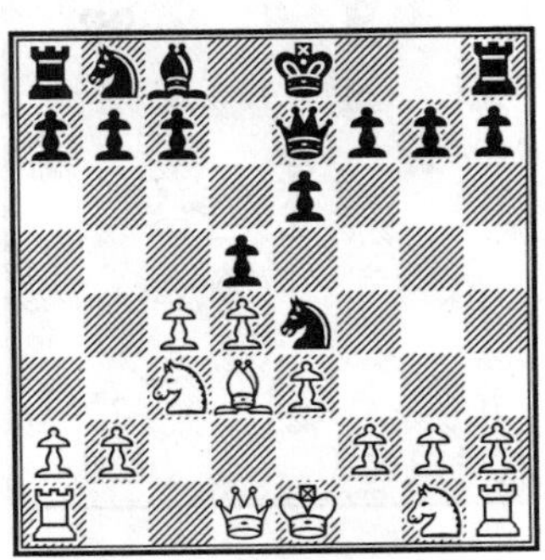

7.cxd5 is the more modern treatment, but it was seen in another game from this match! 7...Nxc3; 8.bxc3 exd5; 9.Qb3 c6; 10.c4 0-0; 11.Nf3 Qc7; 12.Rc1 Qa5+; 13.Rc3 Nd7; 14.Nd2 c5; 15.cxd5 cxd4; 16.exd4 Re8+; 17.Re3 Rxe3+; 18.fxe3 Nf6; 19.Be2

Ne4 and the re-occupation of e4 brought Black the advantage in the 15th game of the match. **7...Nxc3; 8.bxc3 Nd7?!** 8...dxc4; 9.Bxc4 c5 would have brought instant equality.

9.Nf3 0–0. Here too Black should have captured at c4 and then aimed for a rapid ...c5. 9...e5; 10.dxe5 dxc4; 11.Bxc4 Nxe5; 12.Nxe5 Qxe5; 13.Qd4 Qxd4; 14.exd4 Be6; 15.Bxe6 fxe6; 16.0–0 0–0–0; 17.Rfe1 Rd6; 18.Re3 Rf8; 19.Rae1 Kd7; 20.Rb1 Rb6; 21.Rxb6 axb6 and the endgame was eventually drawn in game 5 of the match.

10.0–0 Rd8; 11.Qc2 Nf8; 12.Ne5. 12.cxd5 exd5; 13.c4 would have been much stronger, as White is beginning to dominate the center. **12...c5; 13.Rab1.** Marshall seems uncertain which side to attack on. More logical was 13.f4 with an attack on the kingside, taking advantage of the battery of queen and bishop on the b1–h7 diagonal. **13...Qc7; 14.Qb3 b6.** There is no way that White is going to get anywhere on the queenside. **15.cxd5 exd5; 16.Qa4 Bb7; 17.Qd1.**

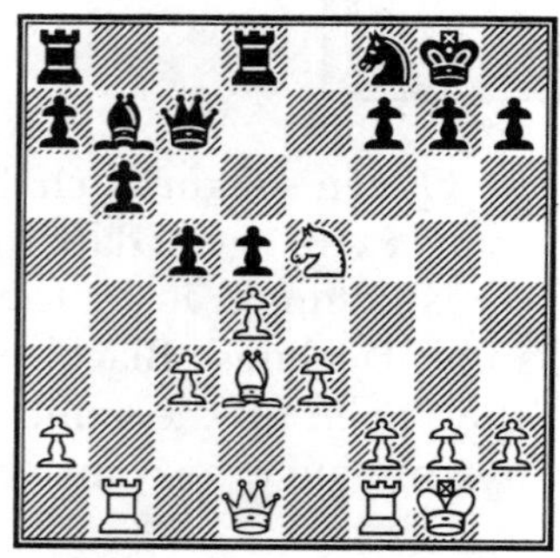

This ignominious retreat indicates that White's plans have failed. Now Black takes over the initiative. **17...Rd6; 18.Qg4 Re8; 19.Qg3 Rde6!; 20.Bf5 R6e7.** Black has a very solid position. **21.f4.** White has no basis for an attack here, and Black methodically repels the invaders and aims at the weakness created by the reckless advance of the f-pawn. **21...Bc8!; 22.Bxc8 Rxc8; 23.Qf3 Qd6; 24.Rfc1 Rec7; 25.h3 h6; 26.Kh2.** White still dreams of a kingside attack. **26...Nh7; 27.Qh5 Nf6; 28.Qf5 cxd4; 29.exd4 Ne4.**

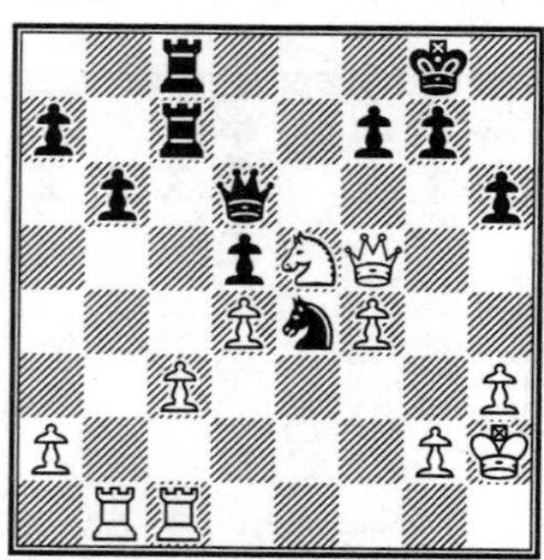

Another knight infiltrates e4, and this time it cannot be dislodged. From this mighty post it controls valuable dark squares in the White camp. **30.Nxf7.** White wins the exchange now, but the knight at e4 is worth more than either of White's rooks. **30...Rxf7; 31.Qxc8+ Rf8; 32.Qb7 Qxf4+; 33.Kg1.** 33.Kh1 Nf2+; 34.Kg1 Nxh3+;

35.gxh3 Qg3+; 36.Kh1 Rf2 and checkmate follows. **33...Qg5; 34.Kh2 Qg3+; 35.Kg1 Nd2; 36.Qxd5+ Kh8; 37.Kh1 Nf3!** The mighty steed delivers the final blow. **38.gxf3 Qxh3+; 39.Kg1 Qg3+; 40.Kh1 Rf4; 41.Qd8+ Kh7; 42.Rf1 Rf5 Black won.**

ANTI-TARTAKOWER ATTACK

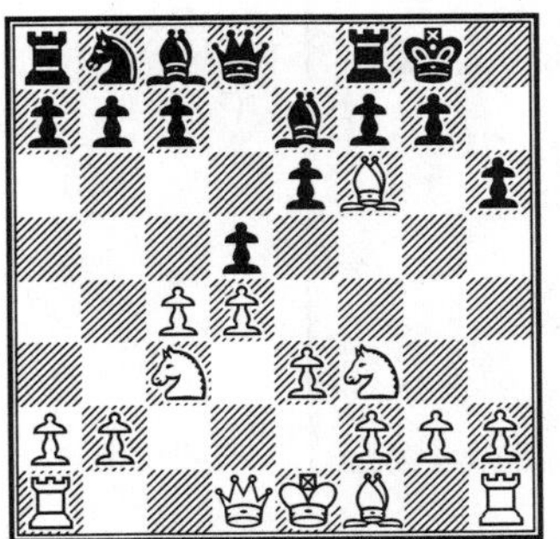

1.d4	**Nf6**
2.c4	**e6**
3.Nf3	**d5**
4.Nc3	**Be7**
5.Bg5	**0–0**
6.e3	**h6**
7.Bxf6	

This is the Anti-Tartakower system, designed to prevent Black from setting up the Tartakower formation with ...b6 and ...Bb7. White gives up the bishop pair, but maintains the initiative.

(150) KASPAROV - TIMMAN [D55]

London (USSR vs. World), 1984

1.d4 Nf6; 2.c4 e6; 3.Nf3 d5; 4.Nc3 Be7; 5.Bg5 0–0; 6.e3 h6; 7.Bxf6 Bxf6; 8.Qc2! 8.Qd2 has become less popular lately but placing the queen at c2 retains its sting. **8...c5; 9.dxc5 Qa5.**

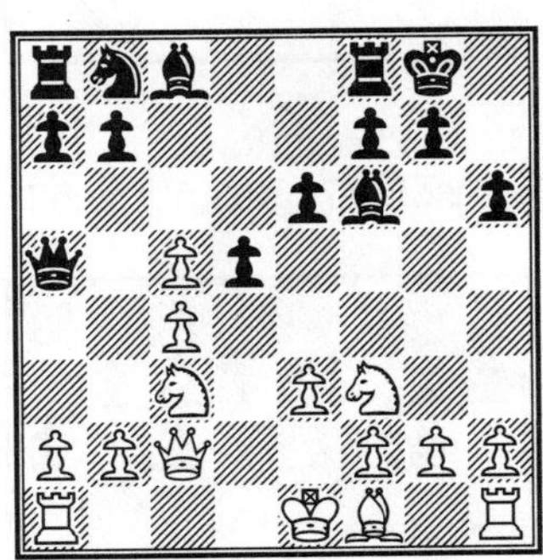

9...dxc4; 10.Bxc4 Qa5; 11.0–0 Bxc3; 12.Qxc3 Qxc3; 13.bxc3 Nd7; 14.c6 bxc6; 15.Rab1 Nb6 brought Kasparov close to equality in the 27th game of the 1984-85 World Championship match against Karpov. 9...Nc6; 10.0–0–0 Nb4; 11.Qa4 a5; 12.cxd5 exd5; 13.Nd4 Bg4; 14.Be2 Bxe2; 15.Ndxe2 Qe7; 16.a3 Qxc5; 17.Qb5 Na2+; 18.Kb1 Nxc3+; 19.Nxc3 Qc6; 20.Qxd5 Qa6; 21.Qd6 Bxc3; 22.Qxa6 Rxa6; 23.bxc3. White had enough to win the endgame in Van Wely-Vaganian, Yerevan Olympiad 1996.

10.cxd5! With this move Kasparov find his way out of the aforementioned difficulties and sets real problems for Timman. This move was played several times in the semifinals of that year's USSR Championship by Konstantin Lerner. Kasparov was no doubt familiar with these games, but Timman had not seen them. **10...exd5; 11.0-0-0** Kasparov's innovation. **11...Be6; 12.Nxd5 Rc8; 13.Kb1 Bxd5.** 13...Rxc5 would have been met strongly by 14.b4! **14.Rxd5 Nc6; 15.Bc4 Nb4.**

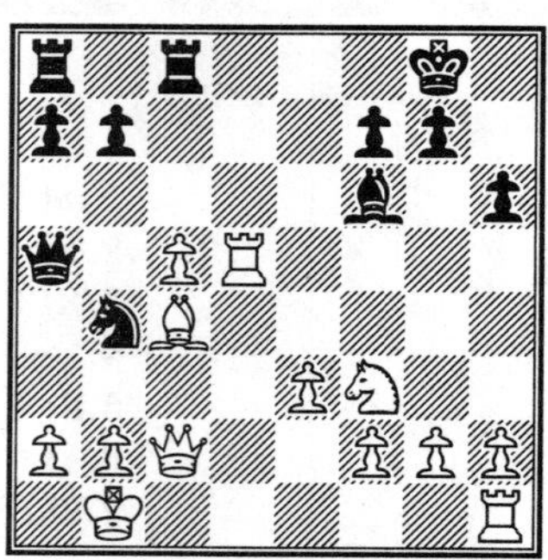

On 15...Ne7; 16.Qd2! is even stronger. **16.Qd2 Rxc5; 17.Rxc5 Qxc5; 18.Rc1 Qb6?!** Kasparov later said that 18...Qe7 would have provided decent drawing chances.

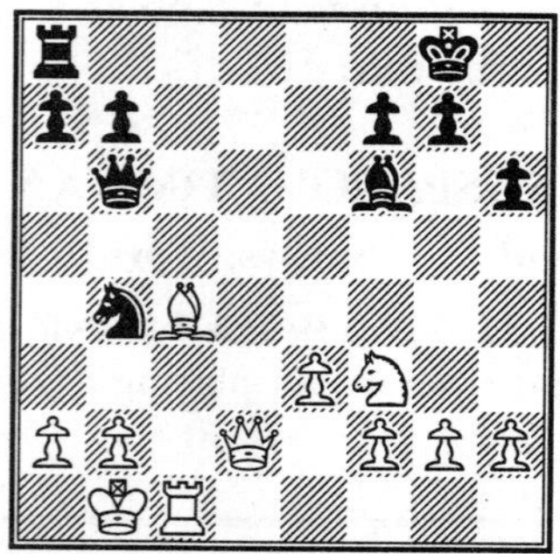

19.Qd7 Rf8. 19...Nxa2; 20.Rc2! and now...
A) 20...Nc3+; 21.Kc1 Ne4; 22.Bxf7+ Kh8; 23.Ne5!!

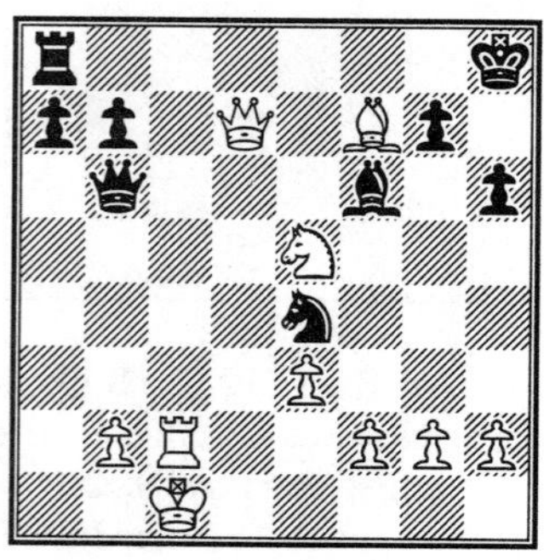

23...Rd8 (23...Bxe5; 24.Rc8+ etc.) 24.Ng6+ Kh7; 25.Qf

B) 20...Rd8; 21.Qxf7+ Kh7; 22.Kxa2 Qa5+; 23.Kb1 Rd1+; 24.Rc1 Qf5+; 25.e4! Qxe4+; 26.Ka2 Rxc1; 27.Qg8+ Kg6; 28.Bf7+ Kf5; 29.Qh7+ Kf4; 30.g3+ Kxf3; 31.Bh5+ and White wins the queen. **20.Qb5 Qd6; 21.e4 Nc6; 22.Bd5 a6?!**

Even after 22...Ne5! Black is in trouble, but the text leads to a quick resolution of the game. On 22...Nd4 Kasparov planned 23.Qd3! Nxf3 (23...Qb6; 24.e5 Nxf3; 25.exf6 Ne5; 26.Qf5 Qxf6; 27.Qxf6 gxf6; 28.Bxb7 with an easily won endgame.) 24.Bxf7+ **23.Qxb7 Ne5; 24.Rc8 Rxc8.** The light squares are still vulnerable: 24...Nxf3? ; 25.Qxf7+ etc. **25.Qxc8+ Kh7; 26.Qc2 Kg8.** 26...Nxf3?? 27.e5+ wins. **27.Nd2 g5; 28.a3 Kg7; 29.Nf1 Qb6; 30.Ng3 Kg6; 31.Ka2 h5; 32.Qc8 h4; 33.Qg8+ Bg7; 34.Nh5. White won.**

TARTAKOWER DEFENSE

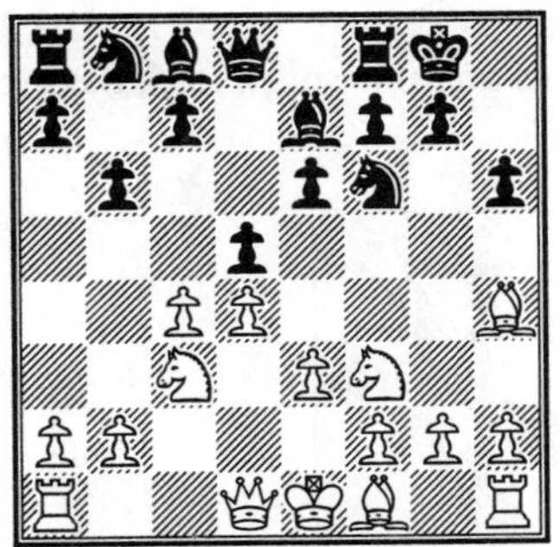

1.d4	**d5**
2.c4	**e6**
3.Nc3	**Nf6**
4.Nf3	**Be7**
5.Bg5	**h6**
6.Bh4	**0–0**
7.e3	**b6**

This is the Tartakower-Makagonov-Bondarevsky Variation, to name just a few of the designations in common use. The idea is to build a solid position. Karpov has battled Kasparov many times in this opening, and we'll look at some of those positions as we go along.

(151) KARPOV - GEORGIEV [D58]
Tilburg, 1994

1.d4 Nf6; 2.c4 e6; 3.Nf3 d5; 4.Nc3 Be7; 5.Bg5 h6. This is played to give Black additional options, such as ...g5, and has become the normal move. **6.Bh4 0–0; 7.e3 b6; 8.Be2 Bb7; 9.Bxf6 Bxf6; 10.cxd5 exd5; 11.b4.**

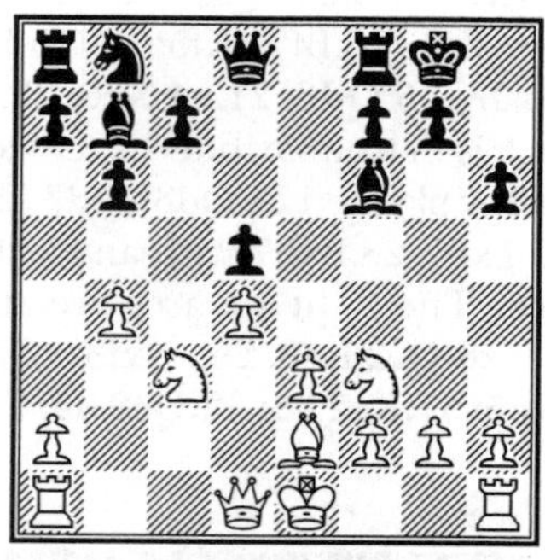

11...c6. This is often thought to be necessary, otherwise an advance of White's pawn to b5 might constrict the queenside. However, Black has a more aggressive plan, and that is the one that Kasparov, not surprisingly, prefers. 11...c5 has been seen in a number of Kasparov-Karpov games. 12.bxc5 bxc5; 13.Rb1 Bc6 Karpov tried 13...Qa5 in game 40, but it was an experiment he regretted, having to struggle for a draw. 14.0–0 Nd7; 15.Bb5 Qc7 and now:

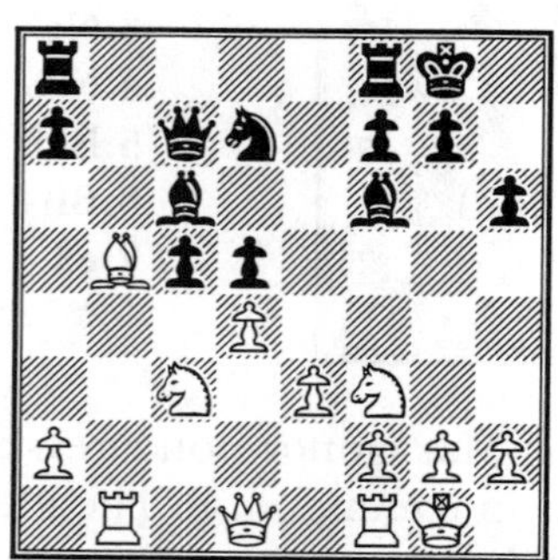

A) 16.Qd2 Rfd8; 17.Rfc1 Rab8; 18.Bxc6 Rxb1; 19.Nxb1 Qxc6; 20.dxc5 Nxc5; 21.Qc2 was agreed drawn in the 12th game of the 1984 match.

B) 16.Qc2

B1) 16...Rfd8; 17.Rfc1 Rab8; 18.a4 Qd6; 19.dxc5 Nxc5; 20.Bxc6 Qxc6; 21.Nb5 Be7; 22.Qf5 (22.Nxa7 was Karpov's choice as White in game 39 of the same match, and he squeezed out a small advantage on 22...Qa6!; 23.Nb5 Qxa4; 24.Qxa4 Nxa4; 25.Nfd4 but it was not difficult for Kasparov to hold the position.) 22...Qe8 and in the 38th game of the 1984 match Kasparov realized that capturing the pawn at a7 would allow too much counterplay after 23...Ra8, and White would get nowhere, so he tried another plan and the game ended in a draw after 23.Ne5 Rb7; 24.Nd4 Rc7; 25.Nb5 Rb7.

B2) 16...Rfc8; 17.Rfc1 Bxb5; 18.Nxb5 Qc6; 19.dxc5 Nxc5; 20.Qf5 Qe6; 21.Nfd4 Qxf5; 22.Nxf5 Ne6; 23.Rxc8+ Rxc8; 24.Nxa7 Rc2!; 25.Nb5 Rxa2; 26.h3 Ra5 was agreed drawn in game 42 of the 1984 marathon match.

C) 16.Qd3 Rfc8 (16...Rfd8; 17.Rfd1 Rab8; 18.Bxc6 Qxc6; 19.Rxb8 Rxb8 led to an even position in game 8 of the 1985 match.) 17.Rfc1 Rab8; 18.h3 was seen in game 18 of the 1987 match. Karpov played ...g6 here, and got a slightly worse position. **12.0–0.**

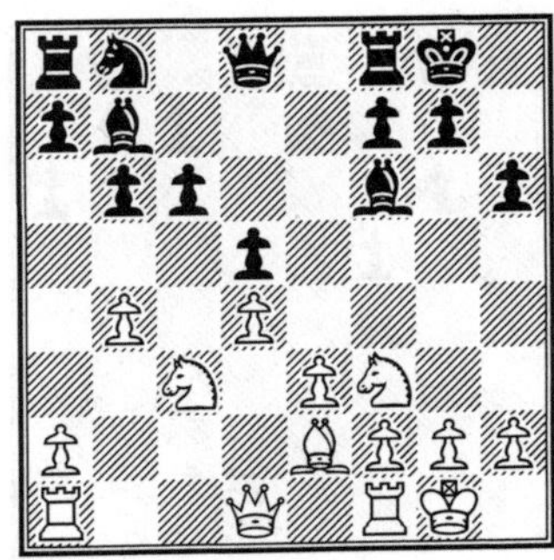

12...Qd6. There is no shortage of alternatives. 12...Re8 is considered acceptable, as are others. 12...a5; 13.a3 Qd6; 14.Qb3 axb4; 15.axb4 Nd7 was Karpov's choice as Black against Estevez at the 1973 Interzonal, en route to his first World Championship title. **13.Qb3 Nd7; 14.Rfe1.** Karpov had previously preferred 14.e4 against Ljubojevic in a rapid game at Roquebrune 1972. The text is the normal move, however. **14...Be7.** 14...Rfe8; 15.Bf1 Be7; 16.Rab1 a5; 17.bxa5 Rxa5; 18.a4 gave Karpov and advantage against Boensch, at Baden-Baden 1992. **15.Rab1 a5; 16.bxa5 Rxa5; 17.a4.** White is a little better, as in the Estevez game mentioned above. **17...Re8; 18.Bf1 Bf8; 19.Qc2 g6.**

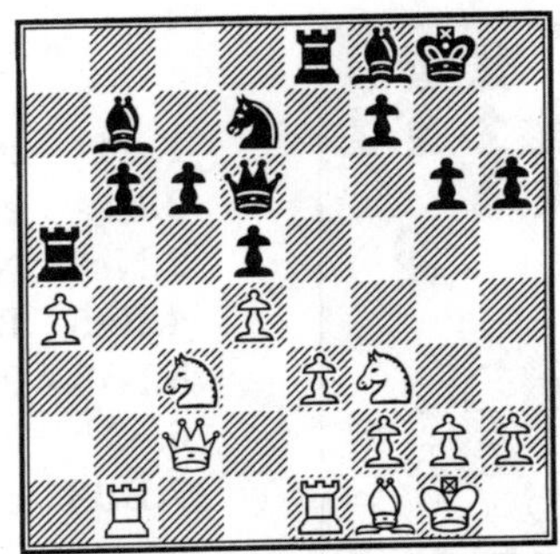

The quiet nature of the opening does not mean that play can be imprecise. Karpov demonstrates his sense of timing by blasting open the center now, and then going to work on Black's hanging pawns. **20.e4 dxe4; 21.Nxe4.** The hanging pawns at b6 and c6 are restrained by the White pawns at a4 and d4. **21...Qf4; 22.Bc4 Bg7; 23.Re2 c5.** An attempt to gain counterplay, but Karpov shuts it down. **24.d5! Raa8; 25.Rbe1.** White is setting up tactical threats. Black now tries to reorganize to go after the pawn at d5. **25...Rad8; 26.Qb3 Ba8; 27.g3 Qb8.**

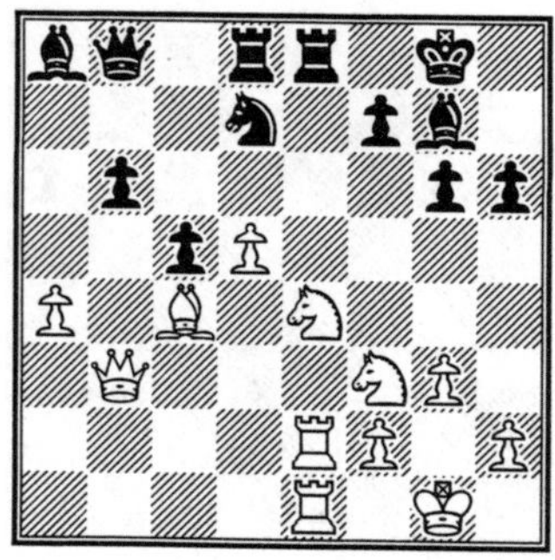

28.d6! Suddenly the age-old weakness at f7 plays a role. **28...Rf8; 29.Bxf7+ Rxf7; 30.Neg5!!** Karpov is known for positional play, but can explode some fireworks when the position calls for them. **30...hxg5; 31.Nxg5 Rdf8.** Black is trying to hang on, but Karpov finishes with a series of hammer blows. **32.Re8 Qxd6; 33.Qxf7+ Kh8; 34.Ne6. White won.**

BOTVINNIK COUNTERATTACK

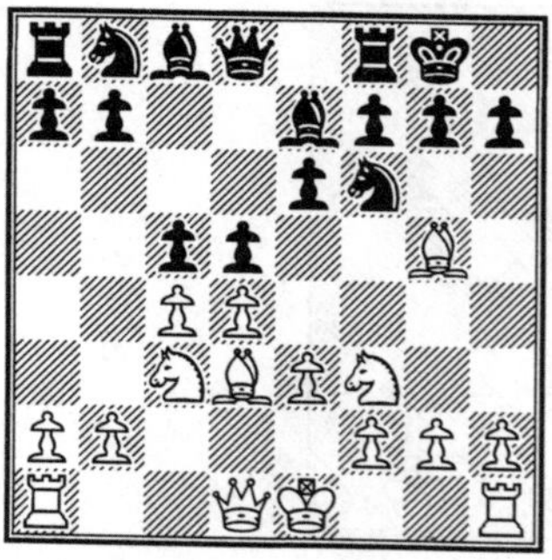

1.d4	**d5**
2.c4	**e6**
3.Nc3	**Nf6**
4.Bg5	**Be7**
5.Nf3	**0-0**
6.e3	**Nbd7**
7.Bd3	**c5**

We have seen the move ...c5 played in the Queen's Gambit Declined in the form of the Semi-Tarrasch and will meet the full Tarrasch Defense later. Here Black delays the advance until after castling and after White has played e3, so that a kingside fianchetto, often effective against the Tarrasch, will not be effective. Either side can exchange central pawns, with a Tarrasch transposition still possible if a c-pawn captures a d-pawn and is recaptured by an e-pawn.

(152) BOTVINNIK - VIDMAR [D60]

Nottingham, 1936

1.c4. The game starts out in the English. **1...e6; 2.Nf3 d5; 3.d4 Nf6; 4.Bg5 Be7; 5.Nc3 0–0; 6.e3 Nbd7; 7.Bd3 c5.** This is the Botvinnik Counterattack. 7...dxc4; 8.Bxc4 leads to a position from the Queen's Gambit Accepted which is also fine for Black. **8.0–0 cxd4; 9.exd4 dxc4; 10.Bxc4.** A standard isolated d-pawn position has been reached.

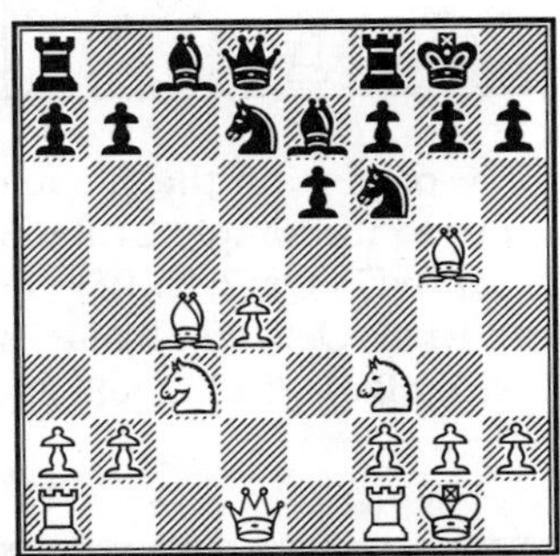

10...Nb6; 11.Bb3. White already enjoys a comfortable position, and Black should have taken some measures to reduce the pressure. 11...Nd5 is called for. **11...Bd7.** 11...Nfd5; 12.Bxe7 Qxe7; 13.Re1 Rd8; 14.Rc1 Nxc3 and White gets a small advantage whichever way the recapture is made. Timman chose to take with the knight against Ree at Amsterdam 1984, but with correct play Black could have equalized. So probably best is 15.bxc3 and then the knight can leap to e5. **12.Qd3 Nbd5.** Black blockades the pawn, which is the correct positional reaction, but some commentators suggested that the other knight would have been the correct one. After 12...Nfd5; 13.Bc2 g6 White would still have enjoyed a small advantage.

13.Ne5 Bc6; 14.Rad1. The interdependence of Black's forces is both an asset and a liability. White is going to attack on the kingside, so Black must strive for activity. **14...Nb4?!** Continued development was called for, with either 14...Qa5 or 14...Rc8. The knight will not accomplish anything more than encouraging White's queen to move to a more effective post on the kingside. **15.Qh3 Bd5.** Black spends more time jousting with the Bb3, but this problem is easily solved. On the other hand, 15...Nfd5; 16.Bc1! would also have been very strong for White.

16.Nxd5 Nbxd5. Now it is time for White to create a concrete plan based on his positional advantages. The target is f7. One would like to have a semi-open f-file, and also eliminate the pawn at e6. Two concepts equal one plan! **17.f4! Rc8.** 17...g6 is not playable because of 18.Bh6 Re8; 19.Ba4 and the bishops combine from a great distance to win the exchange. **18.f5 exf5.** Forced, since 18.Qd6; 19.fxe6 fxe6 leaves the pawn at e6 much too weak. **19.Rxf5 Qd6?!** This allows White to achieve his strategic goal by tactical means, but 19... Rc7; 20.Rdf1 and 21.Qh4 would have left Black in despair.

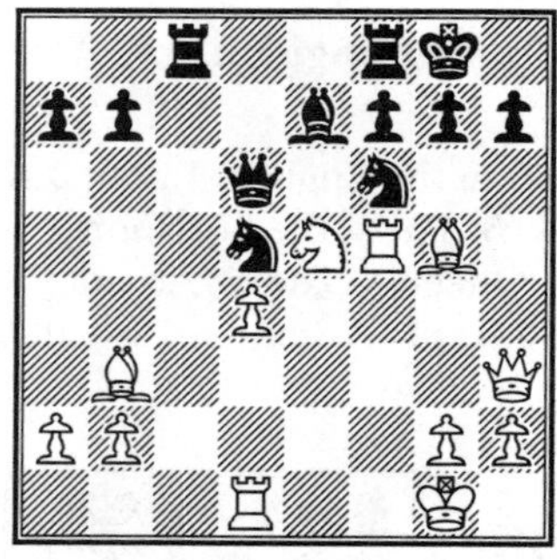

20.Nxf7!! The combination of pins on the file and on the diagonals reap rewards. **20...Rxf7.** 20...Kxf7 loses to the simple 21.Bxd5+. **21.Bxf6 Bxf6.** 21...Nxf6; 22.Rxf6! Qxf6; 23.Qxc8+ Bf8; 24.Bxf7+ Qxf7; 25.Rf1 Qe7; 26.Rxf8+ Qxf8; 27.Qxf8+ Kxf8; 28.Kf2 is an easy win. **22.Rxd5 Qc6.** 22...Bxd4+ is refuted by 23.Kh1! **23.Rd6** Avoiding the final trap of 23.Rc5?? Bxd4+! **23...Qe8; 24.Rd7.** Black resigned. **White won.**

ORTHODOX VARIATION

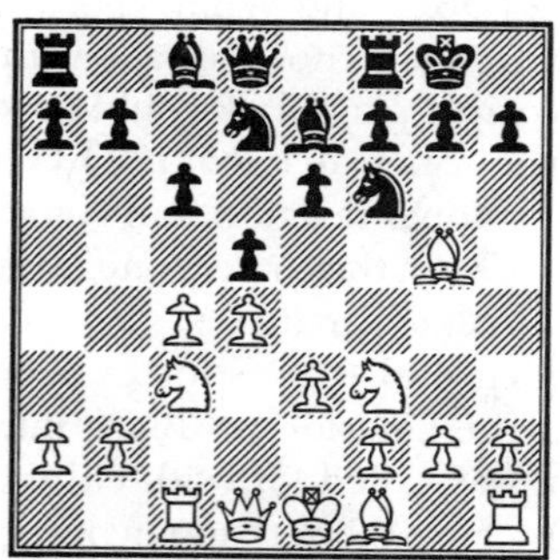

1.d4	**d5**
2.c4	**e6**
3.Nc3	**Nf6**
5.Bg5	**Nbd7**
5.e3	**Be7**
6.Nf3	**0–0**
7.Rc1	**c6**

The **Orthodox Variation** was once considered the pinnacle of correct opening play, but it has lost a lot of its popularity as White seems to maintain a small but persistent advantage if played accurately. Black's bishop on c8 can be truly miserable in this variation, and without it it is hard for Black to launch an ambitious action anywhere on the board. Still, it is a good opening for those with strong defensive and endgame skills.

(153) RUBINSTEIN - TAKACS [D65]

Budapest Hungary, 1926

1.c4 Nf6; 2.d4 e6; 3.Nc3 d5; 4.Bg5 Nbd7; 5.e3 Be7; 6.Nf3 0-0; 7.Rc1 c6; 8.Qc2 a6; 9.cxd5 exd5; 10.Bd3.

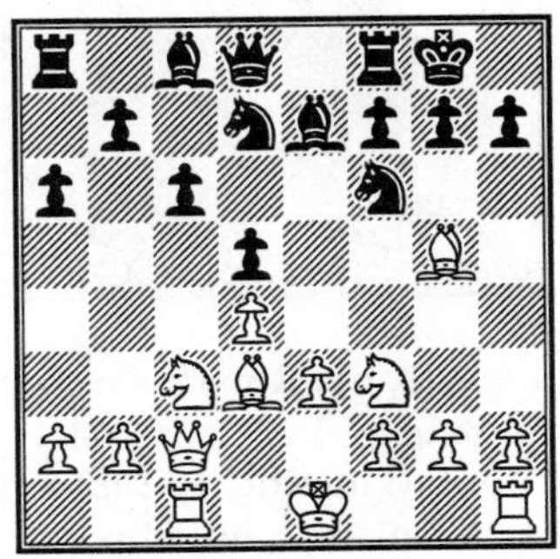

This common position in the Queen's Gambit Declined is known as the "fight for the tempo" and is part of the Rubinstein Attack. White has so far maintained a lead in development, which will be complete as soon as castling takes place. Black, on the other hand, has no rapid prospect of getting the bishop at c8 into the game. The bishop is no longer a "bad bishop", thanks to the exchange of pawns at d5 that has opened up the c8-h3 diagonal.

10...Re8; 11.0-0 Nf8. Now the bishop will be able to escape, but White has a choice of many plans, several of which may extract a very small advantage but nothing which should discourage Black from playing the line. **12.Rfe1.** I don't hold a high opinion of this move, and in my 1984 book on the Orthodox Queen's Gambit Declined, I relegated it to the lowest position on the totem pole. 12.Rb1 is the most aggressive, and perhaps best, move. 12.Bxf6 Bxf6; 13.b4 Be7; 14.Rb1 Bd6 gave Black a good game in Grabliauskas-Sulskis, Pardubice 1996. 12.h3 Ne4; 13.Bf4 Ng5; 14.Nxg5 Bxg5 brought White nothing special in the opening in Benjamin-Ziatdinov, New York Open 1995.

12...Bg4. 12...Ne4 is no better, since after 13.Bf4 Nxc3; 14.bxc3 Be6; 15.Nd2 b5; 16.e4 White has a strong game, Bielicki-Gruenberg, Germany 1995. The best move is 12...Be6!; 13.Na4 N6d7; 14.Bxe7 Qxe7; 15.Nc5 Nxc5; 16.Qxc5 Qc7! avoids an inferior endgame. 17.b4 Rad8! is a suggestion of Alekhine, as an improvement over 17...Nd7, played in the 25th game of his 1927 World Championship match against Capablanca. **13.Nd2 N6d7; 14.Bf4 Bg5.**

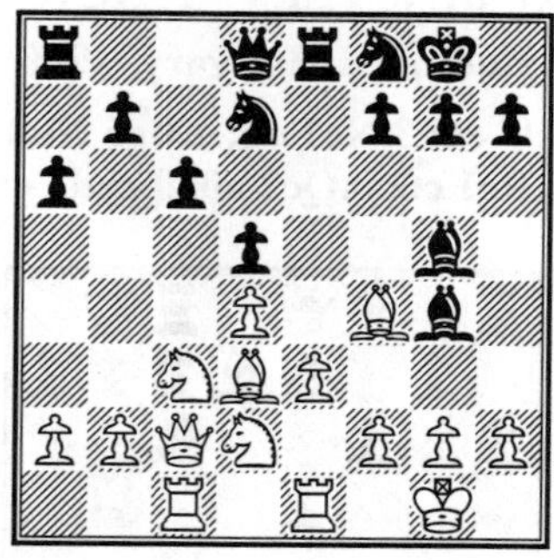

Black threatens to capture at f4, but Rubinstein comes up with a strong counterattack. **15.h3! Bh5.** 15...Bxf4 16.hxg4 Bg5; 17.f4 Bh4; 18.Re2 is better for White, who can play Nf3 and attack on the kingside. **16.Bh2 Bg6; 17.Bxg6 hxg6?!** 17...Nxg6 would have been more flexible. Making a little breathing space for the king is less important than flexible piece play. **18.Qb3 Qb6.** Black willingly enters an endgame in which the weakness of the queenside pawn structure is evident. Still, there were no appealing alternatives. **19.Na4 Qxb3; 20.Nxb3 Ne6.**

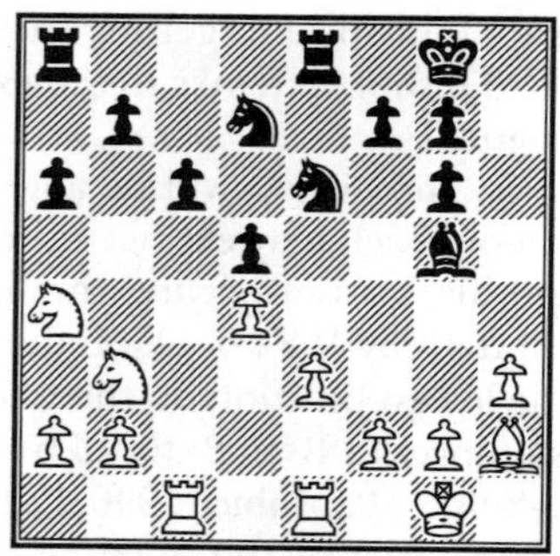

The endgame is very slightly favorable for White, but Black's knights keep the enemy horses at bay. The only tangible difference is the superior power of the bishop at h2 compared to the bishop at g5. **21.Na5 Ra7; 22.Kf1 Bd8; 23.b4!** This move is necessary if White is to make any progress. The endgame is typical of the Tempo variation and the Orthodox Variation in general. White has space and a strong bishop but too many lines are closed to make progress easily.

23...f5; 24.Nb2 g5; 25.Nd3 Kf7. Black should have exchanged bishops with ...Bc7 here. **26.Rc2 Bb6.** This is rather artificial, and in the end White gets into c5 anyway. **27.Bd6 Nd8; 28.Nc5.** White opts for a change of scenery. This move could have been prepared by Nb3, so that a recapture at c5 with a knight would be possible, but the plan is the recapture there with the b-pawn and open the b-file. **28...Nxc5; 29.Bxc5 Bxc5; 30.bxc5.**

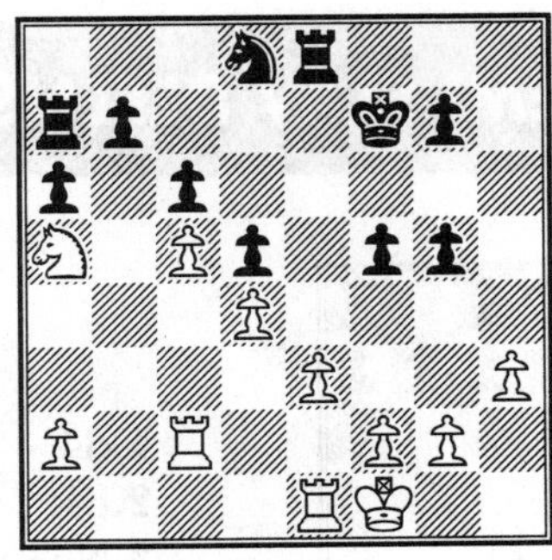

Now things have changed a bit. The pawn at b7 is weak, but can be defended by all three of Black's pieces, so White can't win it. However, the rook is now forced to remain at a7 for a while, and that is a very passive post. **30...Ke7.** The king comes to the queenside to take some of the defensive burden off his subjects. **31.Rb2 Kd7; 32.Reb1 Kc8; 33.Ke2 Re7; 34.Kf3.** The White king is more active, and White can now think about opening up the kingside. **34...Re4?** Black should have just played ...g6, because the rook is not well placed at e4, where it has no lateral movement. White now manages to open the g-file.

35.g4 g6; 36.Rg1 Nf7; 37.h4! The open file is worth a pawn. **37...gxh4; 38.gxf5 gxf5; 39.Rg7 Nd8; 40.Rg8.** This pin is annoying, and now White can maneuver the other rook to the g-file. **40...f4.** A rather panicky reaction. Breaking the pin with ...Kd7 made more sense. **41.Rh8! fxe3; 42.fxe3 Kd7; 43.Rg2! Re8.** 43...Re7 was correct, guarding the seventh rank. **44.Rxh4 Re7; 45.Rh8 Kc7; 46.Rgg8 Rd7; 47.Nb3 a5; 48.Nc1!** This knight is headed to c5! **48...Ra8; 49.Nd3.**

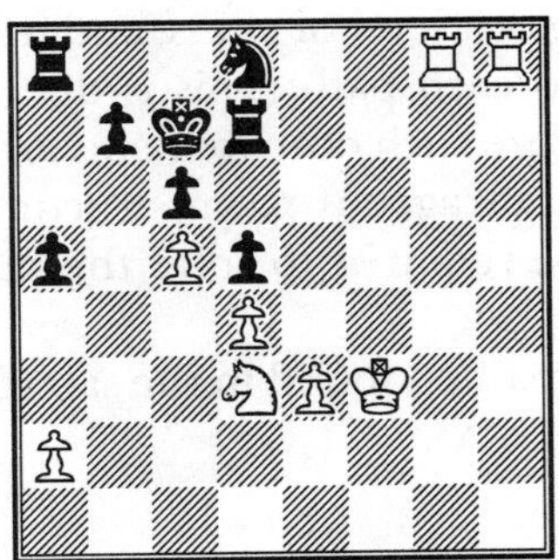

Black is running out of moves, because Ne5 is a serious threat. **49...b5.** 49...Rf7+; 50.Ke2 Rd7; 51.Ne5 Re7; 52.Kf3 and the King marches up the f-file. **50.cxb6+ Kxb6; 51.Nc5 Rd6; 52.a4!** Black has simply run out of moves. **52...Rc8; 53.Kg4.** Black resigned, since the White king is headed to e5, winning material. **White won.**

SEMI-SLAV DEFENSE

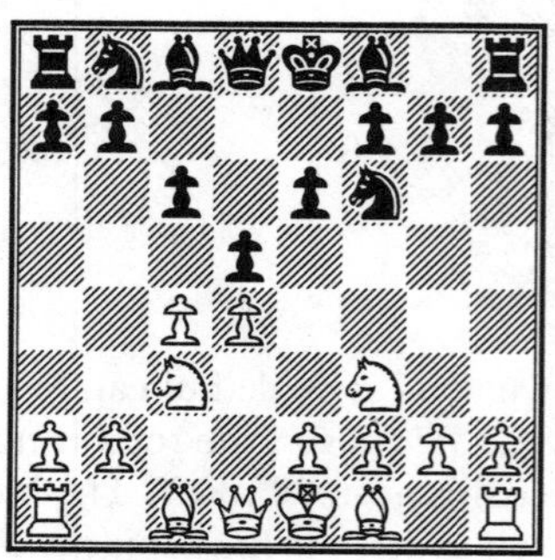

1.d4	**d5**
2.c4	**e6**
3.Nc3	**Nf6**
4.Nf3	**c6**

The positions which arise in the **Semi-Slav** are among the strategically richest in all of chess. Deep calculation is also required, as there are some very long forcing variations.

Black has a simple idea: capture the pawn at c4 and hold onto it by advancing the b-pawn to b5. The bishop at c8 can find a home at b7, and an eventual ...c5 will give it powerful scope on the long diagonal.

White can choose to preserve the pawn with 5.e3, at the cost of shutting in the bishop at c1, or allow Black to carry out the plan, receiving in return an ideal pawn center after advancing the pawn at e2 to e4. Both approaches have advocates at the highest level of chess, and hundreds of pages of analysis have been devoted to each path. This is due to the complexity of the positions, which can feature such obscure items as four queens on the board (two for each side) and outrageous pawn structures. Both tactical prowess and positional ability are required to solve the puzzles that lie in virtually every position.

The sharpest lines are often found in the sacrifice of the c-pawn, and we will start with that plan.

BOTVINNIK ATTACK

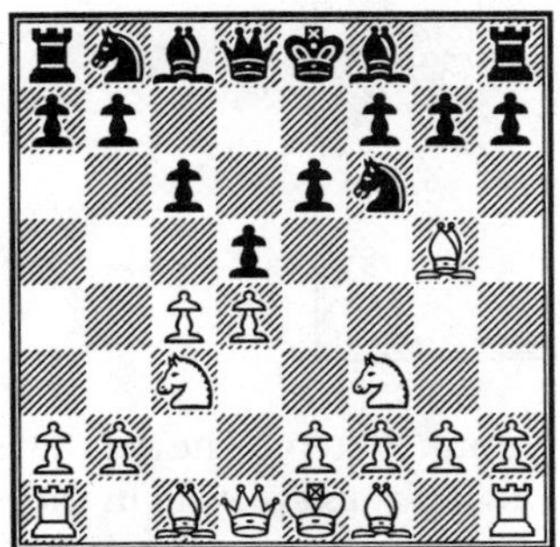

1.d4	**d5**
2.c4	**c6**
3.Nc3	**Nf6**
4.Nf3	**e6**
5.Bg5	

Mikhail Botvinnik was not afraid of complications, and it is only fitting that this complicated variation bears his name. Although the tableau is peaceful, for the moment, there is molten lava just beneath the surface. It usually explodes volcanically after Black captures the pawn at c4 and White creates the ideal pawn center with e4. Black then hold on to the pawn with ...b5, and White responds by smashing open the kingside with a piece sacrifice!

Fun for all, but the accumulation of theory has created a massive amount of work for anyone who wants to master its complexity.

(154) IVANCHUK - SHIROV [D44]

Wijk aan Zee, 1996

1.d4 d5; 2.c4 c6; 3.Nc3 Nf6; 4.Nf3 e6; 5.Bg5 dxc4; 6.e4 b5; 7.e5 h6; 8.Bh4 g5; 9.Nxg5 hxg5; 10.Bxg5.

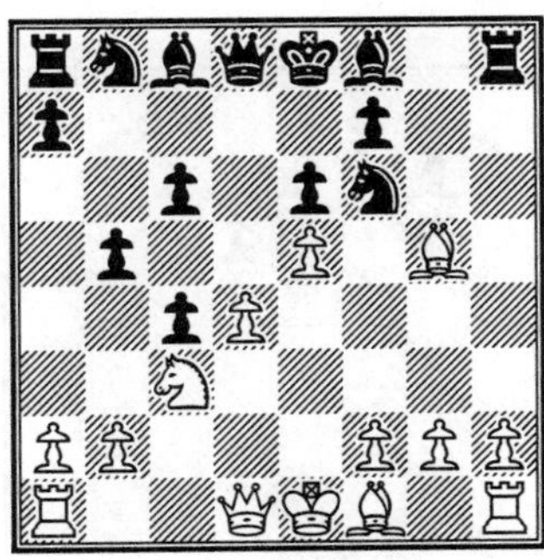

The old sacrificial lines in the Botvinnik System remain extremely topical and professional players are constantly introducing refinements to existing theory. In this game we will look at some recent developments. **10...Nbd7; 11.exf6 Bb7; 12.g3.**

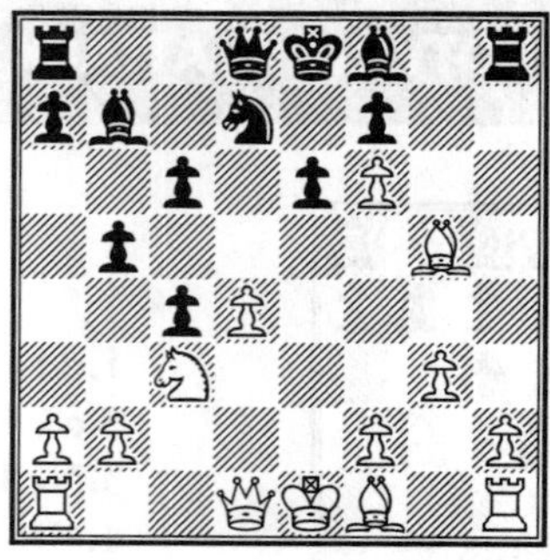

This is the modern handling of the Botvinnik System. The very latest theory is still unclear, and this game between two of the top rated players in the world shows why. **12...c5; 13.d5.** This is the only move which keeps White's initiative. It is important to keep in mind that Black has a menacing pawn phalanx on the queenside, so vigorous action is needed.

13...Qb6. Theory has settled on this move as best, after rejecting 13...Nb6, 13...Ne5, 13...Nf6 and 13...Bh6. I have always had a fondness for the last move, so let's consider what the authorities have to say. 13...Bh6; 14.Bxh6 Rxh6; 15.Qd2. White gets nothing out of 15.Bg2 b4!; 16.Ne4 Nf6!, as in Suba-Crouch, Wales 1984. 15...Rxf6; 16.Bg2 White must watch the center. Castling queenside is not likely to bring any advantage after Black responds ...d4, as in Langeweg-Kujpers, Hilversum 1984. 16...Ne5; 17.0–0 Nf3+; 18.Bxf3 Rxf3. This position was reached in Karpov-Ribli, Thessaloniki (Olympiad) 1988.

Black does not have any serious problems, even after the line given as best by Ribli: 19.Qh6 Bxd5; 20.Rad1 Qf6; 21.Qxf6 Rxf6; 22.Nxd5 exd5; 23.Rxd5 Admittedly, White does enjoy a small advantage because of the passed h-pawn, but Black has counterplay and I doubt that there is any danger of losing. Perhaps Black can just give up the c-pawn: 23...Rd8; 24.Rxc5 a6 and the rook infiltrates from d8 to d3. **14.Bg2 0–0–0; 15.0–0 b4.**

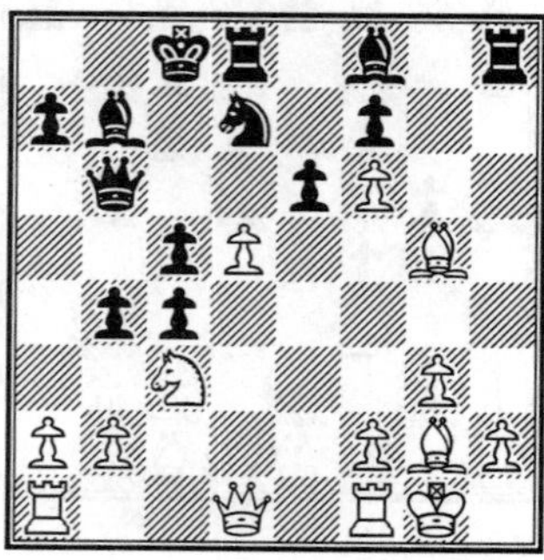

16.Na4. 16.Rb1 is an important alternative. 16...Qa6; 17.dxe6 Bxg2; 18.e7 Bxf1; 19.Qd5 White can try 19.Kxf1, as in Kramnik-Shirov, Monaco (blitz) 1996, and after 19...Qc6 Black eventually got into trouble. One alternative is 19...bxc3, as in Uhlmann-Alexandria, Halle 1981, which is not considered promising. Instead, Black can try 19...Be7, unveiled by Kramnik against Kamsky at Dos Hermanas 1996. 19...Bh6.

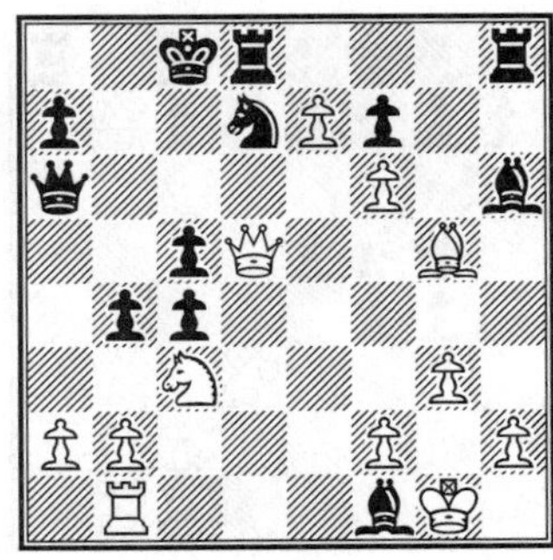

This position has been reached in many important games in the 1990s. (19...Bxe7; 20.fxe7 Rdg8 did not work out well for Black in a rapid game played between Kasparov and Kramnik in New York in 1994.) 20.Bxh6 Bd3; 21.Qa8+ If White captures at d8, Black can take back with the king, according to Yermolinsky. 21...Nb8; 22.exd8Q+ Rxd8; 23.Re1 bxc3; 24.Bf4 Qb6 The only move, since 24...Qb7? loses to the brilliant 25.Re7!, as pointed out by Shirov. 25.bxc3 Bf5; 26.h4 Qb7 White got a better game after 26...Be6; 27.Kh2! in Yermolinsky-D.Gurevich, from the 1994 United States Championship in Key West.

27.Qxb7+ Kxb7; 28.Re7+ Rd7; 29.Bxb8 Kxb8; 30.Rxd7 Bxd7. Black is up a piece, but the pawns are hard to stop. Azmaiparashvili-Shirov, Madrid 1996 concluded peacefully: 31.Kg2 Kc7; 32.Kf3 Kd6; 33.Kf4 Bc6! 34.Kg5 Bf3; 35.Kf5 Kd5; 36.g4 Kd6; 37.h5 Kd5; 38.Kf4 Bd1; 39.Kg5 Bf3; 40.Kf4 Bd1; 41.Kg5 Bf3; 42.Kf4. **16...Qb5.**

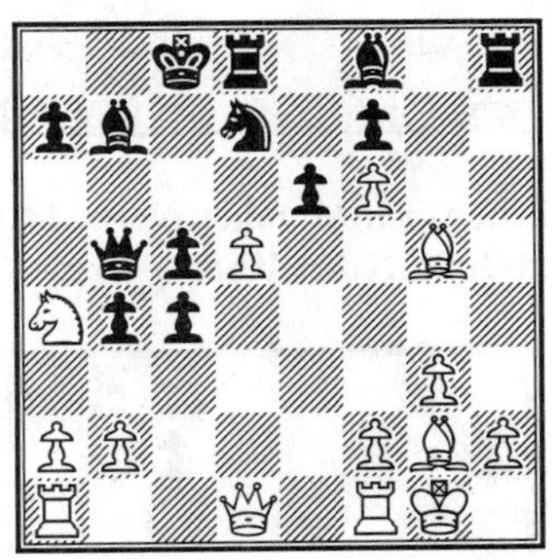

This position is important enough to have generated dozens of games. **17.a3.** 17.dxe6 Bxg2; 18.Kxg2 Qc6+; 19.f3 Qxe6. Black can be satisfied with this position, which has been reached in a number of games, most notably in Nikolic-Shirov, Wijk aan Zee 1993. **17...exd5.** 17...Nb8. The retreat of the knight is a popular alternative, but it is under a cloud at present. 18.axb4 cxb4; 19.Qg4! Bxd5; 20.Rfc1. White has a promising attack. This position has scored well for White, for example in I.Sokolov-Oll, Wijk aan Zee 1993. **18.axb4 cxb4; 19.Be3 Nc5; 20.Qg4+ Rd7; 21.Qg7.**

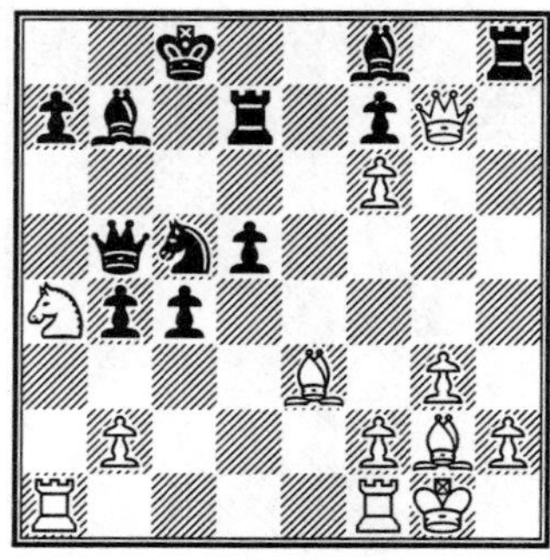

A new try. 21.Bxc5 Bxc5; 22.Qg7 Rhd8; 23.Nxc5 Qxc5; 24.Bh3. This analysis by German theoretician Rainer Knaak leaves no doubt about White's superiority. 21.Nxc5 Bxc5; 22.Bxc5 Qxc5; 23.Rfe1 Kc7. The position is unclear, according to analysis by Predrag Nikolic. **21...Bxg7; 22.fxg7 Rg8; 23.Nxc5 d4!**

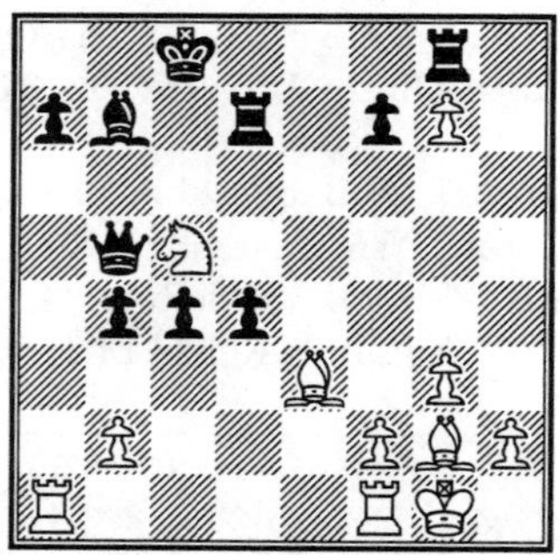

Now a simplification of the position takes place. **24.Bxb7+ Rxb7; 25.Nxb7 Qb6; 26.Bxd4 Qxd4; 27.Rfd1 Qxb2; 28.Nd6+ Kb8.**

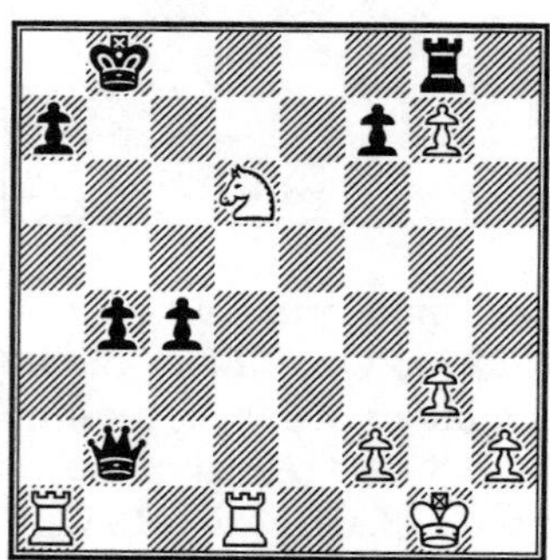

White has a rook and knight for the queen, and the g-pawn is falling. At the same time, however, the Black king has no safe home. **29.Rdb1 Qxg7; 30.Rxb4+ Kc7; 31.Ra6! Rb8.** An attempt to simplify further. **32.Rxa7+ Kxd6; 33.Rxb8.** The rooks are more powerful than the queen, and Black cannot avoid a losing endgame. **33...Qg4; 34.Rd8+ Kc6; 35.Ra1. White won.**

STOLTZ VARIATION

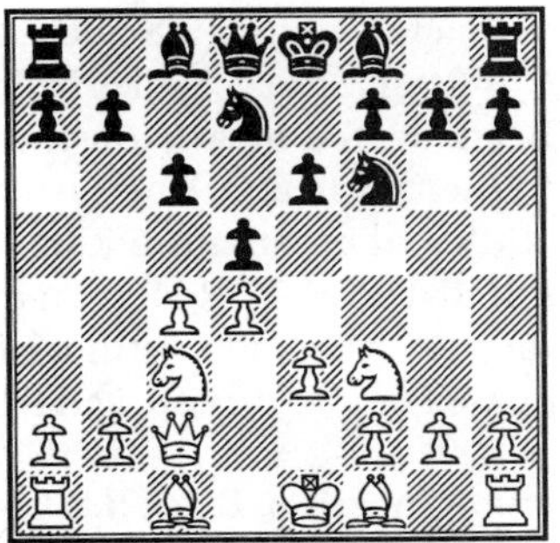

1.d4	d5
2.Nf3	Nf6
3.c4	c6
4.Nc3	e6
5.e3	Nbd7
6.Qc2	

The idea behind the **Stoltz Variation** is to battle for control of the e4 square and also to set up threats against h7 should Black castle short, as is customary in the Semi-Slav. The variation rested in obscurity for several decades before exploding onto the tournament scene in the mid–1980s. It has now become one of the main lines of the Semi-Slav but Black's defenses are holding and it may soon submerge again.

(155) STOLTZ - KOTTNAUER [D45]
Groningen, 1946

1.d4 d5; 2.Nf3 Nf6; 3.c4 c6; 4.Nc3 e6; 5.e3 Nbd7; 6.Qc2 Be7. This move has been replaced by the more vigorous 6...Bd6, which is now seen in almost every game. There does not seem to be any particular justification for abandoning 6...Be7, which is still quite playable. We will follow a game involving the oiginator of the line after an excursion to examine the more popular 6...Bd6.

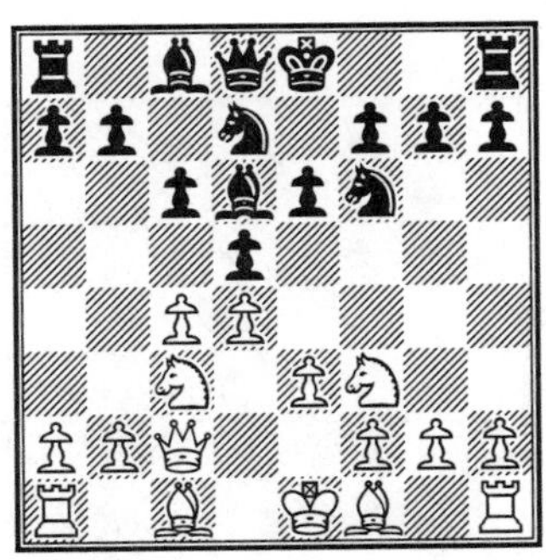

White continues to follow a variety of paths here.

A) 7.h3 0–0; 8.g4 Qe7; 9.g5 Nh5; 10.Bd3 g6; 11.Bd2 dxc4; 12.Bxc4 b5 gave Black excellent queenside play in Djurhuus-Shabalov, Oslo 1991.

B) 7.Bd2 0–0; 8.e4 c5; 9.cxd5 exd5; 10.exd5 cxd4; 11.Nxd4 Be5; 12.Nf3 Bxc3; 13.Bxc3 Re8+ with a fine game for Black in Banas-Dreyev, Capelle la Grande 1992. The bishop pair and passed d-pawn are not especially significant, because the pawn is weak and the bishops will find it difficult to maintain secure posts.

C) 7.e4 dxe4; 8.Nxe4 Nxe4; 9.Qxe4 c5; 10.Bg5 Be7; 11.Bxe7 Qa5+!; 12.Nd2 Kxe7; Black has a secure position and can "castle by hand" with ...Rd8 and ...Kf8, though the king can also remain at e7 for a while, Gorelov-Kishnev, Soviet Union 1984.

D) 7.b3. This positional treatment has been favored by Anatoly Karpov, among others. White will complete development and then try to attack in the manner of the Yusupov-Rubinstein Attack, with a bishop at d3 and eventually a knight at e5. The position after 7...0–0; 8.Be2 dxc4; 9.bxc4 e5; 10.0–0 Re8; 11.Rd1, seen in Karpov-M. Gurevich, Reggio Emilia 1991, is strategically very rich and continues to be scrutinized in the tournament arena. Black might do well now to capture at d4, but 11...Qe7 remains the main line.

E) 7.Be2 has remained the most popular continuation. Black has two plans, and must choose whether or not to accept an isolated pawn. 7...0–0; 8.0–0 e5 is the boldest line, heading toward structures reminiscent of the Tarrasch Defense. (8...dxc4 is more traditional but is also popular. 9.Bxc4 b5; 10.Be2 Bb7; 11.Rd1 Qb8!?; 12.Ne4 Nxe4; 13.Qxe4 c5; 14.Qh4 c4 led to a sharp struggle in Horvath-Wells, Budapest 1993. Black's chances are no worse.) 9.cxd5 cxd5; 10.Nb5 Bb8; 11.dxe5 Nxe5; 12.Bd2 Bg4; 13.Nbd4 Ne4 gave Black counterplay in Karpov-Korchnoi, Amsterdam 1991.

F) 7.g4 is the most ambitious line, but Black has found ways to counter the pressure, 7...Nxg4; 8.Rg1 Qf6; 9.Rxg4 Qxf3; 10.Rxg7 Nf6; 11.Rg5 Ne4; 12.Nxe4 dxe4; 13.Bd2 Bd7; 14.Bc3 0–0–0 as given by Wells. **7.b3.** This is the most logical plan. 7.Be2 0–0; 8.0–0 b6 is acceptable for Black, for example 9.cxd5 exd5; 10.b3 Bb7; 11.Bb2 Re8; 12.Ne5 c5 with counterplay for Black in Yepishin-Ljubojevic, Reggio Emilia 1991.

7...b6; 8.Be2. 8.Bd3! is more promising. 8...0–0 9.0–0 Bb7; 10.Bb2 Rc8 is still a solid defense, however. **8...Bb7; 9.0–0 0–0.** Both sides continue to develop logically. **10.Bb2 Rc8; 11.Rad1 Qc7; 12.Bd3 Bd6.** In effect, this admits that d6 is a better square for the bishop, but with both sides fully developed, repositioning forces is practical and there are no negative consequences. **13.e4.ßß** This is White's only plan, but achieving the goal does not bring any advantage for White. **13...dxe4; 14.Nxe4 Nxe4; 15.Bxe4 Nf6.**

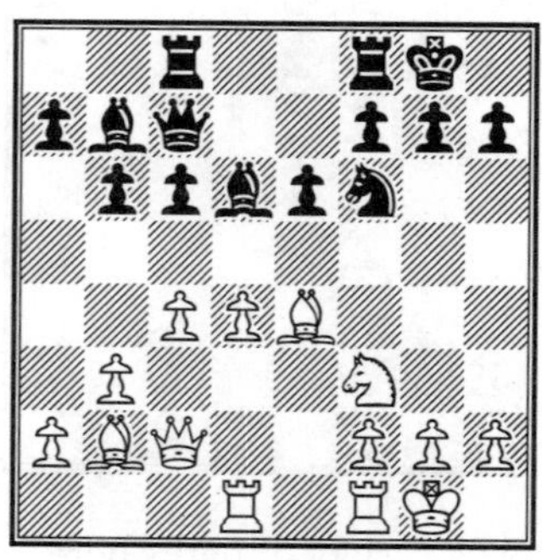

Now White decides to give up the bishop pair in return for securing the c5-square. Otherwise, Black could obtain a comfortable game by playing ...c5. **16.c5**

Nxe4; 17.Qxe4 Be7; 18.Bc1. The bishop has no future on the a1–h8 diagonal, now that the advance of the d-pawn to d5 is out of the question. **18...Rfd8; 19.Ng5 Bxg5.** It is safer to give up the useful bishop than to weaken the kingside pawn structure.

20.Bxg5 Rd5; 21.Bf4 Qd8; 22.Bd6 bxc5; 23.dxc5 Qa5; 24.Qg4 Qc3; 25.Rc1 Qd4; 26.Qg3 Ba6; 27.Rfe1 Qd3; 28.Qg4 h5; 29.Qh4 Re8; 30.h3 Qd4; 31.Re4 Qd2; 32.Rce1 Bd3; 33.R4e3 Qxa2; 34.g4 Bg6; 35.Be5 Qc2; 36.gxh5 Bf5; 37.Qg3 Rxe5; 38.Qxe5 f6; 39.Qd6 Kh7; 40.Qxc6 Rd8; 41.Qc7 Qd2; 42.Qg3 Rd5; 43.Ra1 a5; 44.Qc7 Qd4; 45.Rc1 Be4; 46.Rg3 f5; 47.c6 Rd6; 48.h6 Kxh6; 49.Qf7. White won.

WADE VARIATION

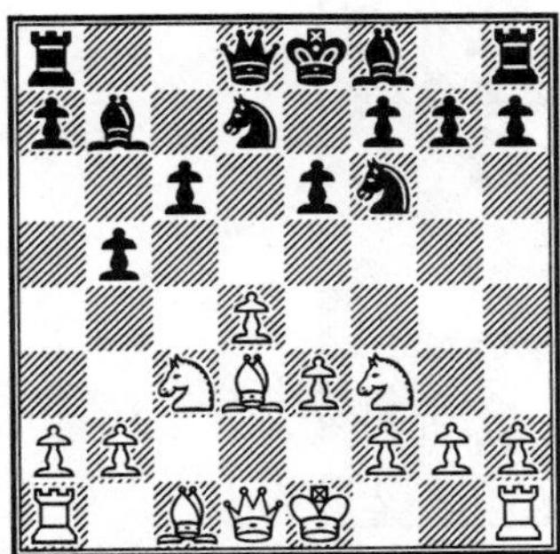

1.d4	**d5**
2.c4	**c6**
3.Nc3	**Nf6**
4.e3	**e6**
5.Nf3	**Nbd7**
6.Bd3	**dxc4**
7.Bxc4	**b5**
8.Bd3	**Bb7**

This is the **Wade Variation**, named after British theoretician Bob Wade. The most popular move is 9.e4, but the position takes on a more individual character after 9.a3, which has been rising in popularity. The bishop on b7 is not hiding. It is ready to take part in the action after an eventual ...c5.

(156) BAREYEV - AKOPIAN [D47]

Leon, 1995

1.d4 d5; 2.c4 c6; 3.Nc3 Nf6; 4.e3 e6; 5.Nf3 Nbd7; 6.Bd3 dxc4; 7.Bxc4 b5; 8.Bd3 Bb7; 9.a3. The idea behind this move is simple. White wants to play b4. Therefore Black should try to get there first. **9...b4.** This is considered best, but it is not the only move. 9...a5 is a reasonable alternative.

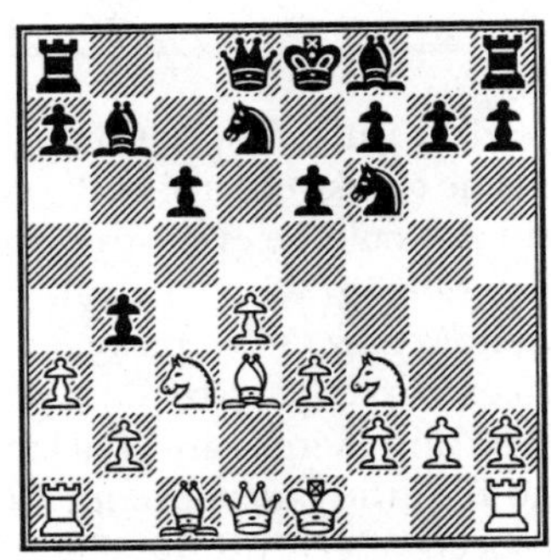

10.Ne4. This was introduced by Konstantin Sakayev, a former World under-18 Champion. It has been adopted by Gelfand and used at the highest levels of chess competition. **10...Nxe4.** 10...bxa3 is an obvious alternative. 11.bxa3 Be7 (11...Ba6 is suggested by Gelfand, and it deserves attention.) 12.Nxf6+ Nxf6; 13.0-0 0-0; 14.Rb1 White had a small advantage in Gelfand-Brenninkmeijer, Wijk aan Zee 1992. **11.Bxe4 bxa3.** Black might try 10...c5!? here, as in Dreyev-Illescas, Logrono 1991.

12.bxa3. 12.0-0 is an interesting gambit. Black can safely capture at b2. 12...axb2; 13.Bxb2 Nf6; 14.Bd3 Be7; 15.Qb1 Rb8; 16.Rxa7 Qb6; 17.Qa2 0-0; 18.Rb1 Ra8. The position holds equal chances, Ivanchuk-Kramnik, New York (PCA 25') 1994, which was eventually drawn. **12...Qc7.**

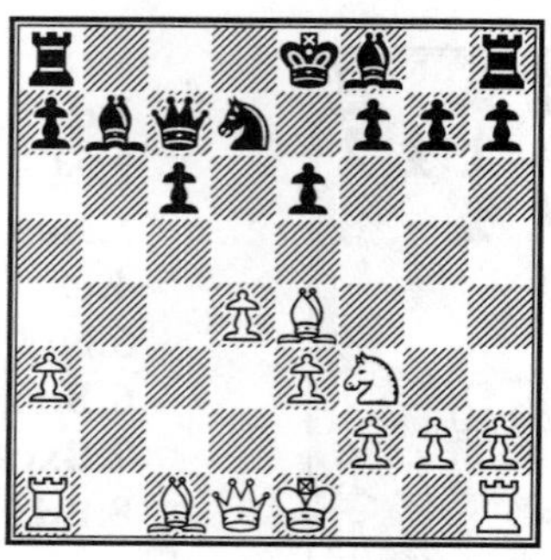

Although Black seems to have weaknesses in the pawn structure, Black can usually achieve a break at e5 or c5. 12...Bd6 is also an alternative plan for Black. 13.Bd2 Rb8; 14.Qa4 c5; 15.Bxb7 Rxb7; 16.dxc5 Bxc5; 17.Ba5 Qb8; 18.Rd1 0-0. The game Karpov-Kramnik, Dortmund 1995 ended in a draw. **13.0-0 Bd6; 14.Bb2 0-0; 15.Rc1.**

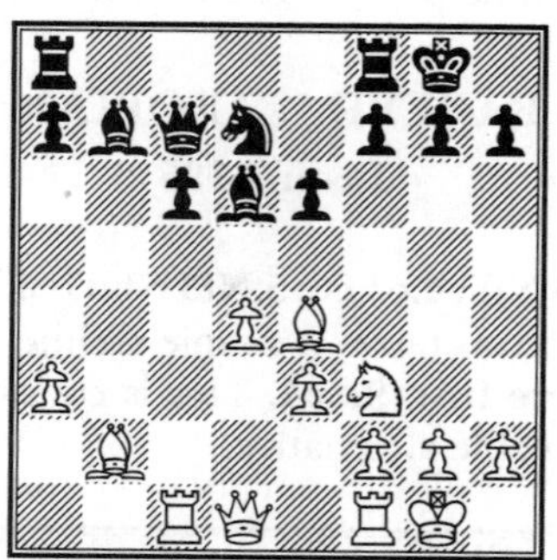

15...Nf6?! It was time to deal with the positioning of the rooks. **16.Bd3 Qe7; 17.e4!?** White felt that it was time to take control of the center, but one more preliminary move, 17.Qa4, the position would be even stronger.

17...Bf4. Could Black have safely grabbed the pawn at a3? 17...Bxa3; 18.e5! This sets up the threat of Bxh7+ followed by Qd3+, picking off the bishop at a3. So Black must take care. 18...Bxb2; 19.exf6 gxf6; 20.Rb1 Ba3. Black's position is precarious. The bishops are uncoordinated and there is are attacking possibilities for White on the kingside. It is not easy to find the best move for White here, but Akopian has pointed out some good prospects after 21.Re1!, which gives rise to additional options exploiting the pin on the e-file or lifting the rook to the third or fourth ranks.

Note that the sacrificial offering 21.Ne5 can be sidestepped by 21...f5!; 21.Re1! Rfb8! Akopian found this strange-looking defensive move. It makes sense if you consider two factors. First, Black wants a rook at a8 to help support the advance of the a-pawn. Second, Black needs to be able to slide the king along the back rank, if necessary, to deal with a White kingside attack. 22.d5!

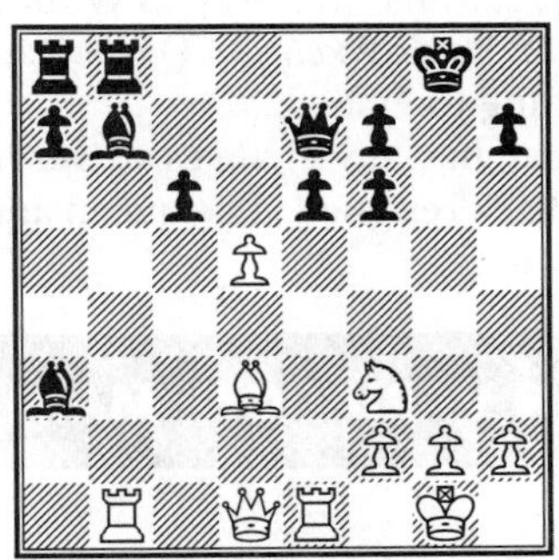

A classical breakthrough, underlying the importance of the rook at e1. 22...Bc8 An ignominious retreat, but there is nothing better. Black seeks to mitigate the pressure through exchanges. 23.Rxb8 Rxb8; 24.Nd4 Black may well be lost here. There does not seem to be an adequate defense. 24...Qf8 This breaks the pin, but White has other tools at his disposal. 25.Qf3! White is down two pawns, but the pressure is unbearable. For example: 25...Qg7; 26.Nxc6 Rb6; 27.Bxh7+ Kxh7; 28.Qh5+ Kg8; 29.Ne7+ Kf8; 30.Nxc8 Rb8; 31.Nxa7 with a winning position for White.

18.Rc2 Rac8. 18...c5; 19.dxc5 Rad8 fails to 20.c6 Ba6; 21.Bxa6 Rxd1; 22.Rxd1 White has too much material for the queen. **19.Qb1! Rfd8.** 19...c5 again loses, this time to 20.Rxc5 Rxc5; 21.dxc5 Qxc5; 22.Bxf6 gxf6; 23.Qxb7 **20.e5.** The timing of moves like this is critical in the Semi-Slav. Although this creates a gaping hole at d5, it takes the knight away from its important central post. **20...Nd7.** Occupying the outpost is, unfortunately, not really an option for Black. 20...Nd5; 21.Rc5! g6; 22.Bc1 Bxc1; 23.Rfxc1 Analysis by Ftacnik. **21.Bc1!** A beautiful move, preparing for the final assault on the enemy king. **21...Bxc1.**

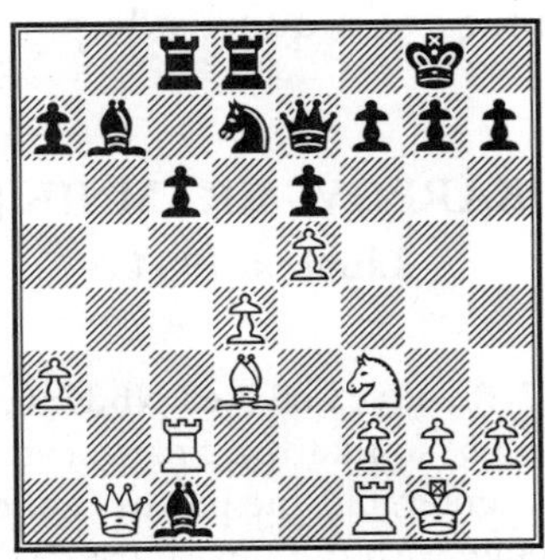

Now everything is ready for a sacrificial finish. **22.Bxh7+!** The Black king has almost no defense. **22...Kh8.** 22...Kxh7! Black may as well have captured, as there is no greater danger in these lines than in the retreat to h8. 23.Rcxc1+ Kg8; 24.Qxb7

Both a-pawns will leave the board, leaving White with a positional advantage thanks to Black's weakness at c6. 24...Qxa3; 25.Ra1 Qd3; 26.Qxa7 c5; 27.Rfd1 Qc4; 28.dxc5 Nxc5; 29.Rxd8+ Rxd8; 30.Qc7 and White will emerge with an extra pawn and a safe king, after playing h3.

23.Rfxc1 Ba6; 24.Be4 c5; 25.dxc5 Rxc5. 25...Nxc5 loses to 26.Qb4. **26.Rxc5 Nxc5; 27.Qb4!** This pin secures a winning position. **27...Rc8; 28.h4 g6; 29.Ng5 Kg7; 30.Rc3!** Now the Black king really has to worry, as White is setting up Bxg6. **30...Rc7; 31.Bxg6! Kxg6.** 31...fxg6; 32.Rxc5 Rxc5; 33.Qxc5 Qxc5; 34.Nxe6+ Kf7; 35.Nxc5. This wins for White, according to Ftacnik.

32.Qg4. Black no longer has any chances of survival. **32...Kh6; 33.Rf3 Be2; 34.Nxf7+ Qxf7; 35.Qg5+.** Black resigned. The queen and extra pawns are too much for Black's pieces. **White won.**

MERAN VARIATION: MAIN LINES

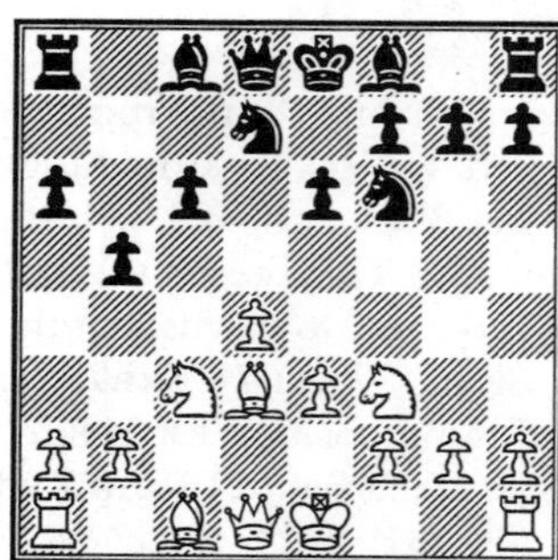

1.d4	**d5**
2.c4	**c6**
3.Nf3	**Nf6**
4.Nc3	**e6**
5.e3	**Nbd7**
6.Bd3	**dxc4**
7.Bxc4	**b5**
8.Bd3	**a6**

In the normal handling of the **Meran Variation**, Black will play ...a6 rather than ...Bb7. In this way the c-pawn can advance more quickly. Time is of the essence, since White is about to build the ideal pawn center with e4. Black has a number of weaknesses on the queenside, but if the minor pieces are well coordinated, than everything can be held together. If White is not careful, Black will take advantage of a queenside pawn majority created when the c-pawn reaches c4.

(157) KARPOV - KRAMNIK [D48]

Linares, 1994

1.d4 d5; 2.c4 c6; 3.Nf3 Nf6; 4.Nc3 e6 5.e3 Nbd7; 6.Bd3 dxc4; 7.Bxc4 b5.8.Bd3 a6. This provides support to b5, so that the c-pawn can safely advance. **9.e4.** White has achieved the ideal pawn center, but the pawns cannot remain at d4 and e4 after Black issues a central challenge with the next move. 9.0–0 is an older move, which Alekhine used against Bogoljubow in the 2nd game of their 1934 Championship match. Now it is considered more important to advance the pawn to e4.

9...c5; 10.d5. 10.e5 is a serious alternative which has been used by Botvinnik and Alekhine. For example 10...Nd5; 11.Ng5 cxd4; 12.Nxd5 exd5; 13.0–0 Be7; 14.e6 Ne5; 15.exf7+ Kf8; 16.Nxh7+ Kxf7; 17.Qh5+ g6; 18.Qxe5 Rxh7; 19.Qxd4 Rh4; 20.Qe3 Qh8; 21.Bxg6+ Kxg6; 22.Qxe7 Ra7; 23.Qxa7 Rxh2; 24.Qb6+ Kf5; 25.g4+ and Black resigned in Alekhine-Te Kolste, played in the famous tournament at Baden Baden Germany 1925 **10...c4.** This prevents White from playing 11.b3, which would otherwise hold up Black's queenside play.

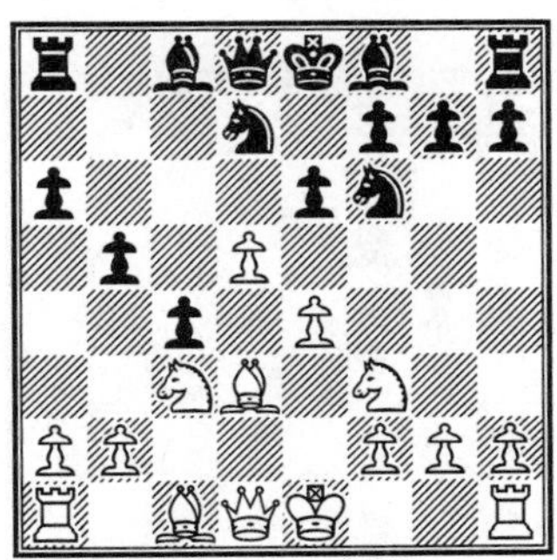

11.dxe6. 11.Bc2 is an acceptable alternative. Here is an example: 11.Bc2 e5; 12.0–0 Qc7; 13.Ne2 Rb8; 14.Ng3 h6; 15.Bd2 g6; 16.Rc1 Bd6; 17.h3 Kf8; 18.Bb1 a5; 19.b3 Ba6 with a complicated position which was eventually drawn in Karpov-Kamsky, Las Palmas 1994. **11...fxe6.** 11...cxd3; 12.exd7+ Qxd7 is also common, but Karpov has been very effective against it. 13.0–0 Bb7; 14.Re1 Bb4 (14...Be7! is better, but even so Karpov was able to gain an advantage after 15.e5 Nd5; 16.Ne4 0–0; 17.Qxd3 in Karpov-Lutz, Dortmund 1994.) 15.Ne5 Qe6; 16.Nxd3 Bxc3; 17.Nf4 Qd7; 18.bxc3 Nxe4; 19.Qxd7+ Kxd7; 20.Ba3 was eventually won by White in Karpov-Tal, Bugojno 1980.

12.Bc2 Bb7; 13.0–0 Qc7. Black has a weak e-pawn and an insecure king, but there is compensation in the form of queenside counterplay and potential use of the d-file. Indeed, Black's pieces deftly exploit that file in the course of this game. **14.Ng5.** 14.Qe2 is less ambitious and 14...Bd6 is a good reply. **14...Nc5.**

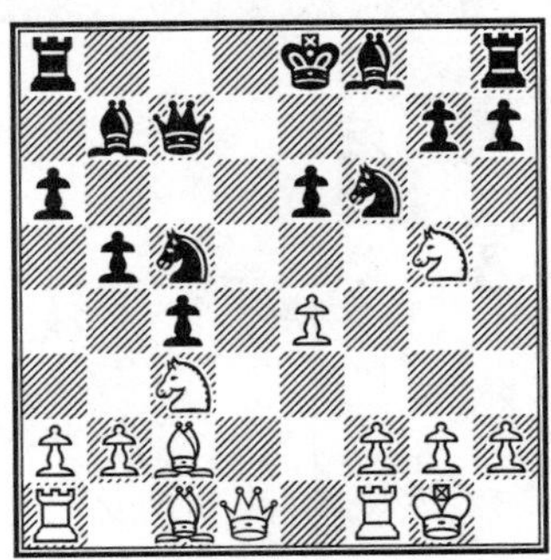

15.e5. 15.f4 is too slow after 15...h6!, driving back the enemy knight. **15...Qxe5!** A fearless capture, but one which seems safe at first. **16.Re1 Qd6.** Black, having eaten the pawn, is content to offer an exchange of queens, which is usually declined by 17.Be3. But Karpov has a surprise in store. **17.Qxd6! Bxd6; 18.Be3 0–0; 19.Rad1.**

White is content to play the position a pawn down for a while, counting on the well-placed forces to provide compensation.

19...Be7; 20.Bxc5 Bxc5; 21.Nxe6. Now White has the pawn back with beautifully placed pieces. **21...Rfc8; 22.h3 Bf8; 23.g4 h6; 24.f4.** White methodically advances on the kingside, seeking to establish a passed pawn there. **24...Bf3; 25.Rd2 Bc6; 26.g5 hxg5; 27.fxg5 Nd7; 28.Nxf8 Nxf8.** Now Black no longer even enjoys the advantage of the bishop pair and White owns the central files.

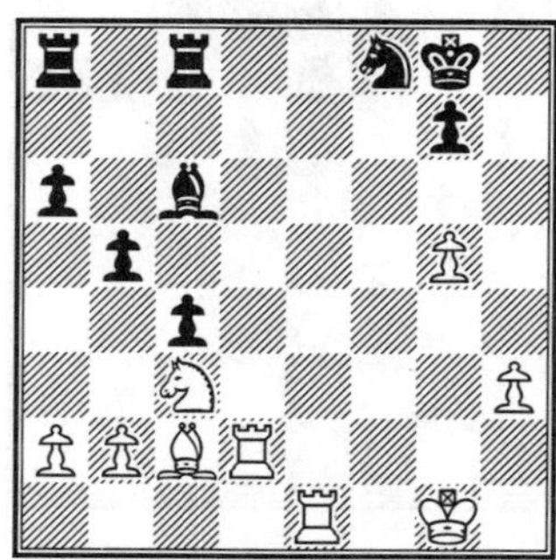

29.Rd6 b4; 30.Ne4. 30.Ne4 Be8; 31.Ng3 Rd8; 32.Nf5 Rxd6; 33.Nxd6 Bg6; 34.Bxg6 Nxg6; 35.Nxc4 Rd8; 36.Re4 b3; 37.axb3 Rd3; 38.Kg2 Rxb3; 39.h4 Nf8; 40.Re8 White won. Karpov-Kramnik, Linares Spain 1994 **30...Be8; 31.Ng3!** This knight is coming to d6 via f5. **31...Rd8; 32.Nf5 Rxd6; 33.Nxd6 Bg6.** Black offers up the extra queenside pawn to try to release the pressure. **34.Bxg6 Nxg6; 35.Nxc4 Rd8; 36.Re4 b3.** A temporary sacrifice. Black will regain this pawn quickly.

37.axb3 Rd3; 38.Kg2 Rxb3; 39.h4 Nf8 Not the best defense, though Black was probably lost anyway. **40.Re8** The pin cannot be broken because 40...Kf7 is met by 41.Nd6. The endgame is lost. **White won.**

TARRASCH DEFENSE

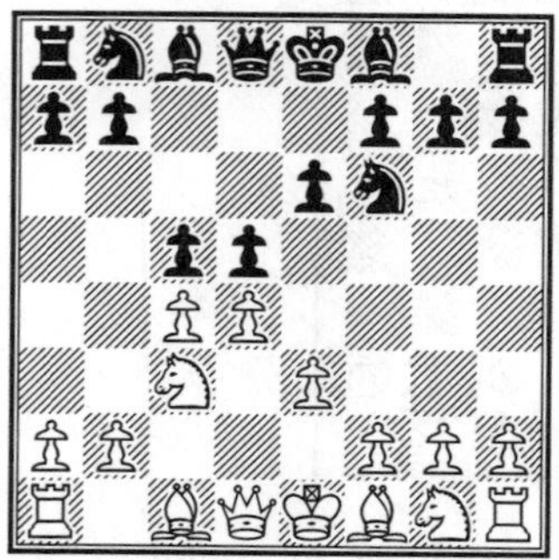

1.d4	**d5**
2.c4	**e6**
3.Nc3	**c5**

We were introduced to the **Tarrasch Defense** in our introduction to the topic of transpositions. Now we will examine the opening in more detail.

The Tarrasch Defense helped bring World Championship titles to Boris

Spassky and Garry Kasparov, but has not been a favorite of most top players. Siegbert Tarrasch, one of the greatest players of the late 19th century, loved the defense, and argued passionately on its behalf, claiming that active pieces compensate for the weakness of the isolated pawn.

You have to really value the dynamic piece play that Black obtains in return for being saddled with an isolated d-pawn which is typical in most variations. The main line continues 4.cxd5 exd5; 5.Nf3 Nc6; 6.g3 Nf6; 7.Bg2 Be7; 8.0-0 0-0; 9.dxc5 Bxc5; 10.Bg5 when it is clear that the battle must revolve around the isolated pawn at d5.

Endgame prowess is often required of both players. Black sometimes loses the d-pawn and must defend tenaciously. Superior endgame technique can often save a hopeless position. On the other hand, Black has abundant middlegame resources which give the opening a strong appeal to some players, and I am among them.

SCHARA GAMBIT

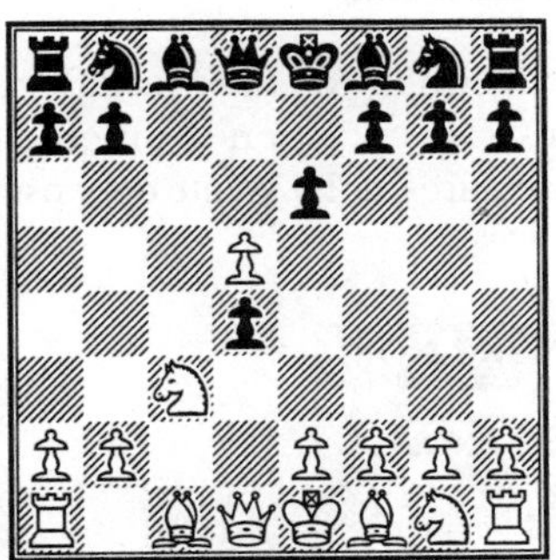

1.d4 d5
2.c4 e6
3.Nc3 c5
4.cxd5 cxd4

This is the **Schara Gambit**, a very interesting opening which leads to wild complications.There are two flavors of this gambit. In the one we will examine first, Black gives up a pawn and willingly enters an endgame, which is very unusual behavior for a gambit! Unfortunately, though it is still seen from time to time, it is probably unsound.

The funny thing is that Black often plays it anyway, because it only arises when White uses one particular move order, and the reasoning goes that if Black sees the opponent using it, then the opponent is probably not well prepared and will likely fall into one of the many traps that are available.

(158) SMYSLOV - ESTRIN [D32]

Leningrad, 1951

1.d4 d5; 2.c4 e6; 3.Nc3 c5; 4.cxd5 cxd4; 5.Qxd4. This move is considered suspect because it allows Black to play a gambit in the endgame. However, the endgame gambit is considered unsound, so it is not clear what is wrong with the direct capture at d4. Still, most players prefer to avoid the line by playing 5.Qa4+. Recently, an attempt has been made to revive the gambit, but I believe there is a resource for White which secures an advantage.

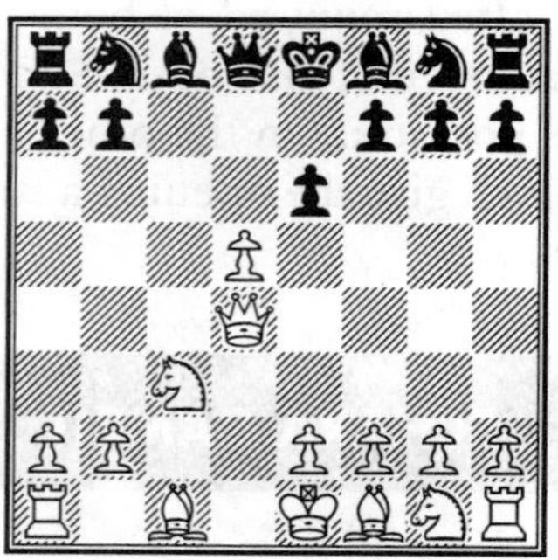

5...Nc6; 6.Qd1 exd5; 7.Qxd5 Be6. Usually when you have sacrificed pawns you do not want to exchange the mighty queens! This position is unique, however, in that the Black pieces can place tremendous pressure on the White queenside. **8.Qxd8+ Rxd8; 9.e3 Nb4; 10.Bb5+ Ke7; 11.Kf1.**

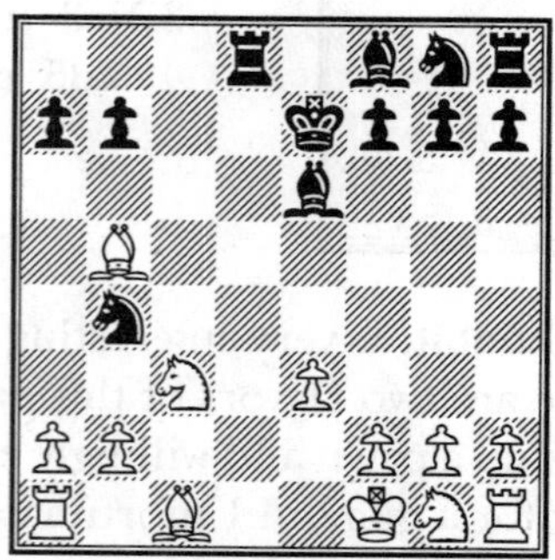

This is the move which has put the Von Hennig variation out of business, though as the database shows, it seems few players are aware of it! **11...Nf6.** Black can try 11...g5!?, recommended by Smith and Hall, in the hope of holding the line together, but I don't think it is good enough. White can reply 12.b3! and the opening of the long diagonal will create problems for Black. 11...a6 followed by ...g5 might be good, however. **12.Nf3 Nc2.** 12...a6!?; 13.Be2 Nfd5; 14.Nxd5+ Bxd5; 15.b3 g5!? might provide a little more counterplay than the game. **13.Rb1 Bf5; 14.Bd2 g5.**

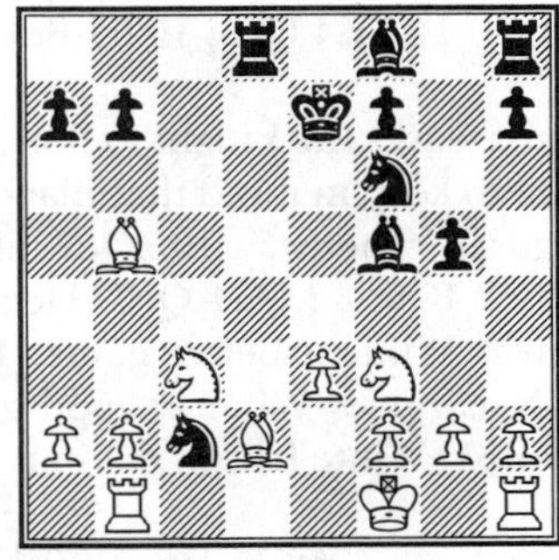

Amazingly, there is no way for Black to exploit a discovered attack on the rook at b1. **15.Rc1 h6; 16.e4 Nxe4; 17.Rxc2 Nd6; 18.Nd4!** White's pieces are just too active. The non-involvement of the rook at h1 is irrelevant because the enemy rook at h8 isn't doing anything either. **18...Nxb5; 19.Nxf5+! Kf6; 20.Nxb5 Kxf5; 21.Ke2. White won.**

(159) KARPOV - HECTOR [D32]
Haninge, 1990

1.d4 d5; 2.c4 e6; 3.Nc3 c5; 4.cxd5 cxd4; 5.Qa4+. This is the most accurate move, because it sidesteps the endgame gambit which is seen in the Smyslov-Estrin game. **5...Bd7; 6.Qxd4 exd5; 7.Qxd5 Nc6.** White has an extra pawn, but Black is developing quickly, and will soon drive the enemy queen back with ...Nf6. **8.e3** Unfortunately this move is needed now or at the next turn because Black intends to play ...Nf6, ...Bc5 and then the pawn at f2 can become vulnerable. **8...Nf6; 9.Qb3!?**

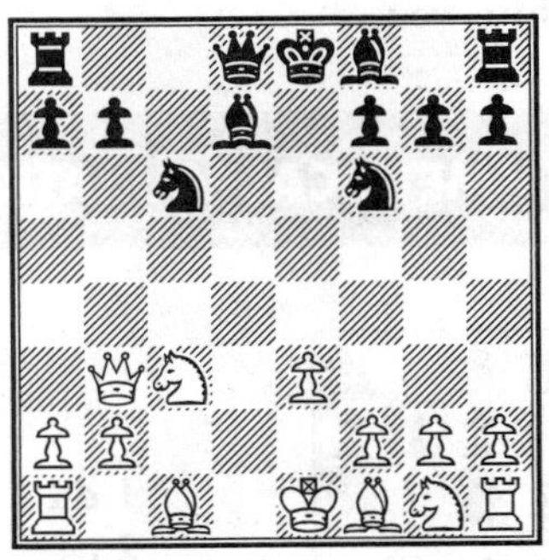

If Hector was trying to catch Karpov by surprise, he must have forgotten that Karpov has worked for years with Igor Zaitsev, who plays the gambit as Black. 9.Qd1 Bc5; 10.Nf3 Qe7 is normal, and now White will try to complete development and castle kingside. Black usually castles queenside and engages in a slugfest on the flanks, but recently kingside castling has been adopted as well. 11.Be2 (11.a3 0–0 is an example of Black's alternative approach. The idea is to take advantage of the open lines on the queenside to annoy the enemy queen.

For example: 12.Qc2 Rac8; 13.Be2 g6!?; 14.0–0 Rfd8; 15.Rd1 Bf5; 16.Rxd8+ Rxd8; 17.Qa4 Ne5; 18.Qh4! Kg7; 19.h3 Nxf3+; 20.Bxf3 h6; 21.Qa4 g5; 22.b4 Qe5!?;

23.Qb3 Bd6 with a strong attack for Black in Hovenga-Schiller, Groningen 1996.) 11...0-0-0; 12.0-0 g5; 13.a3 g4; 14.Nd4 Qe5; 15.b4 Bd6 points to the vulnerability of White's kingside.

9...Bc5 9...Na5 10.Qc2 just leaves the knight looking silly. **10.Nf3 0-0.** In evaluating this game it is important to keep in mind that Black chooses to castle kingside. An obvious alternative is to go the other way. 10...Qe7 intending queenside castling, is suggested by Karpov. **11.Be2 Be6; 12.Qa4 Qc7.** Hector's new move, hoping to improve on 12...a6 which gives White a better game. **13.0-0 Rad8; 14.Bd2 Ng4.** 14...Ne5; 15.Rfd1 Nfg4; 16.Nxe5 gives White a good game according to Karpov. **15.Rfd1 Bd6; 16.g3 Qe7; 17.Be1.** White has an obvious advantage here.

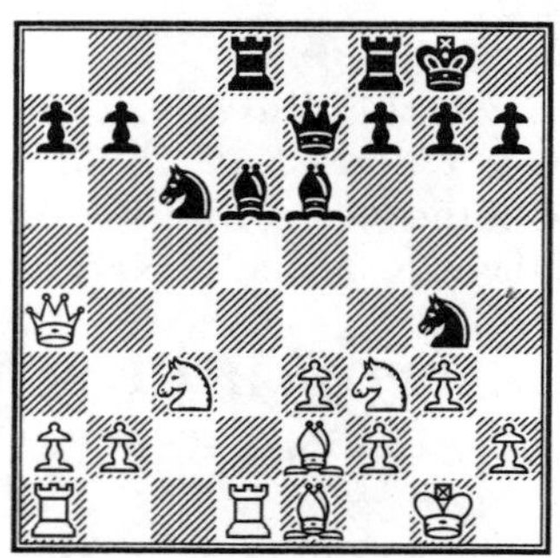

Black is running out of compensation for the pawn, as White is managing to complete development and has defended all of the weak squares near the king. **17...f5; 18.Nd5 Qf7; 19.Ng5 Qh5; 20.h4!** Now Black's attack is finished. **20...Bc8; 21.Nf4 Bxf4; 22.Rxd8 Nxd8.** 22...Rxd8 is no better: 23.Qc4+ Kh8; 24.Nf7+ Kg8; 25.Nh6+ Kh8; 26.Nxg4 fxg4; 27.Qxf4 and Black has no real chances of survival. **23.Qxf4 Nc6; 24.Qc7.** Black resigned. **White won.**

SYMMETRICAL VARIATION

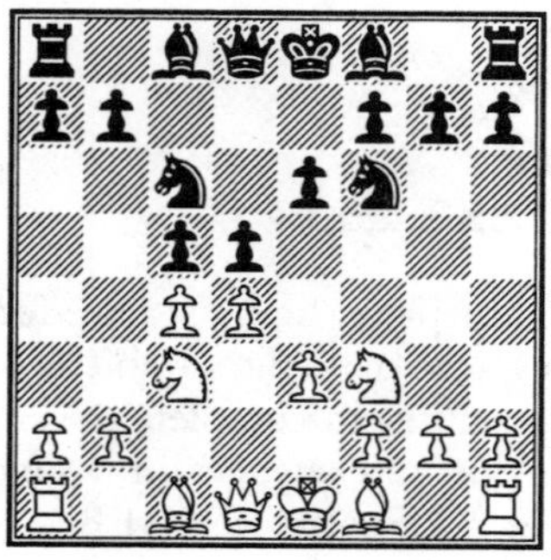

1.d4	**d5**
2.c4	**e6**
3.Nc3	**c5**
4.e3	**Nf6**
5.Nf3	**Nc6**

This is the **Symmetrical Variation** of the Tarrasch, also known as the "boring" line. Black must not undertake operations too early in the game, as White retains the advantage of the first move. Still, as the game progresses, chances will arise for Black, and this is the sort of opening where the stronger player usually prevails. In fact, far more games have been won in brilliant fashion by Black than as White in this opening.

(160) EVANS - LARSEN [D32]

Dallas, 1957

1.d4 d5; 2.c4 e6; 3.Nc3 c5; 4.e3 Nf6; 5.Nf3 Nc6.

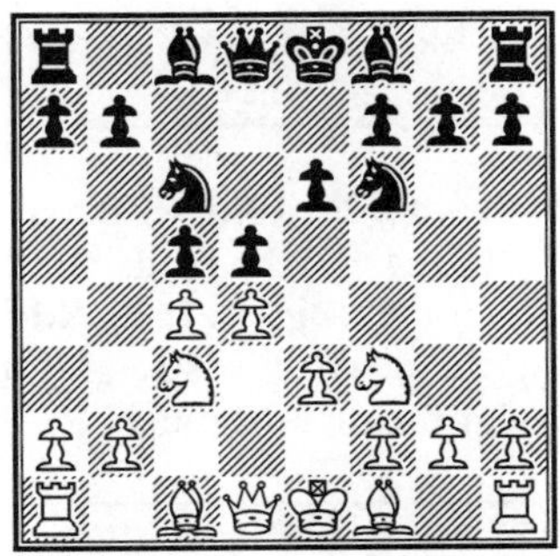

6.cxd5. 6.dxc5 led to one of the most famous games of all time. Since it is not so interesting from the point of view of the opening, just play through the moves until you reach the fantastic finish, or skip to the diagram. 6...Bxc5; 7.a3 a6; 8.b4 Bd6; 9.Bb2 0–0; 10.Qd2 Qe7; 11.Bd3 dxc4; 12.Bxc4 b5; 13.Bd3 Rd8; 14.Qe2 Bb7; 15.0–0 Ne5; 16.Nxe5 Bxe5; 17.f4 Bc7; 18.e4 Rac8; 19.e5 Bb6+; 20.Kh1 Ng4; 21.Be4 Qh4; 22.g3.

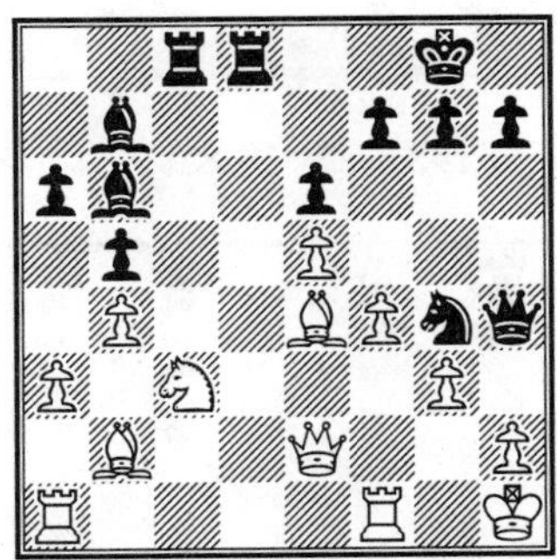

22...Rxc3; 23.gxh4 Rd2; 24.Qxd2 Bxe4+; 25.Qg2 Rh3 and there was nothing to do about mate at h2, Rotlevi-Rubinstein, Lodz 1907. 26.Bc3 **6...exd5.**

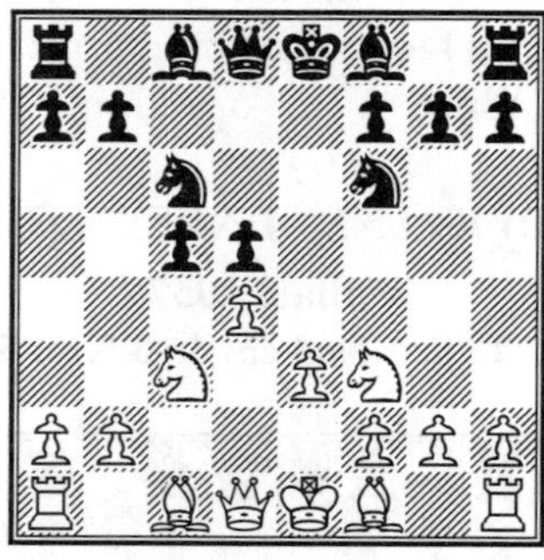

7.Bb5 a6; 8.Bxc6+ bxc6; 9.0–0 Bd6; 10.dxc5 Bxc5; 11.e4! Creating the famous isolated d-pawn. **11...0–0.** 11...Nxe4?; 12.Nxe4 dxe4; 13.Qxd8+ Kxd8; 14.Ng5 is a trick only a beginner would fall for. **12.Bg5 Be7; 13.Nd4 Qd6; 14.e5?** This is a much too clever method of isolating the pawn. The straightforward 14.exd5 cxd5; 15.Re1 would have brought White a significant advantage.

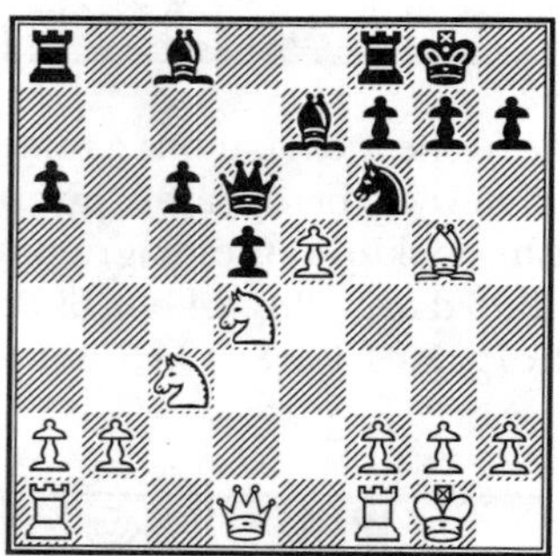

14...Qxe5; 15.Nxc6 Qxg5; 16.Nxe7+ Kh8.

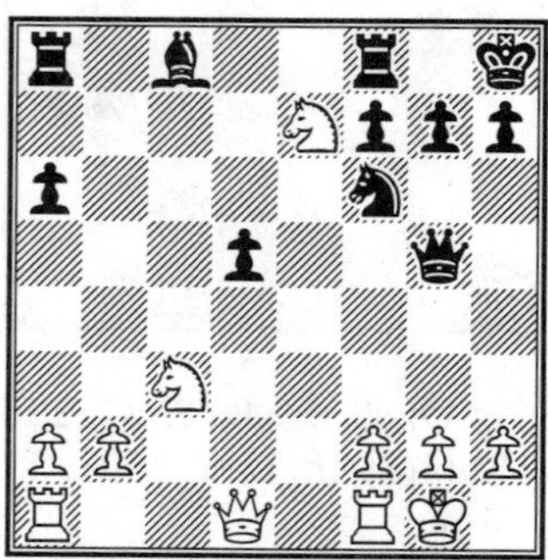

Perhaps Evans was counting on capturing at d5, but then 17...Rd8 would cause trouble, so instead he eliminates Black's bishop. **17.Nxc8 Raxc8; 18.Qd3.** This position is not easy to evaluate objectively. If Black plays passively, then White will dominate the e-file and go to work on the weak isolated pawn. But Larsen realizes that by giving up some material, he can get the e and c files. **18...Rfd8!?** So Black's plan is clear - give up the a-pawn and allow White to enjoy two connected passed pawns, but in return Black is going to take all of the files in the center and advance his own pawn. **19.Qxa6 d4; 20.Ne2 Rc2!; 21.Rad1.** White is of course prepared to give up his b-pawn for the powerful Pd4, but Larsen does not oblige. **21...Qe5!**

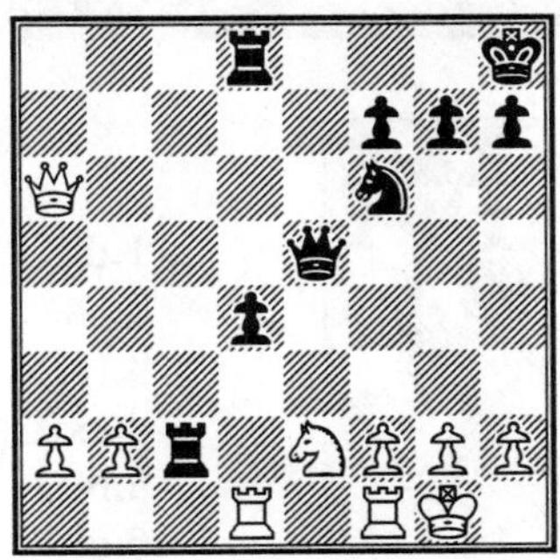

A powerful centralizing move which brings Black full compensation for his pawn since he now has kingside attacking chances in addition to the files. **22.Ng3.** 22.Nc1 Ng4!; 23.g3 Qh5; 24.h4 Nxf2!!; 25.Rxd4 Nh3+; 26.Kh1 Rdc8 was demonstrated by Brondum, in response to a published note that 22.Nc1 would have improved White's chances!

22...h5! Black has achieved complete control of the center of the board, and the laws of chess say that when you have the center, and the enemy forces (in this case the queen) are offside, a flank attack is in order. **23.Rfe1 Qd5; 24.Re2 d3!; 25.Re3.** And now we must look at the potential fork of f2 and e3 via Ng4. When we see this tactical idea, then Black's next move is obvious! 25.Rxc2 dxc2; 26.Rxd5 c1Q+; 27.Nf1 Rxd5 **25...Rxf2!; 26.Ne4.** Of course not 26.Kxf2 because then 26...Ng4+ picks up the stray rook with multiple threats. **26...Nxe4; 27.Rexd3.**

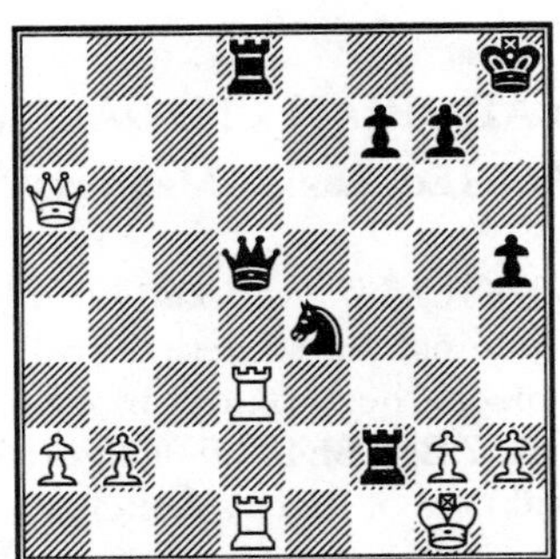

Now if the rook weren't in the way Qc5 check would be effective. And if the Rf2 were a knight we would have a fork. Put it all together... 27.Rdxd3 might have maintained equality - for example: 27...Qg5 (27...Rxb2; 28.Rxd5 Rb1+; 29.Qf1 Rxf1+; 30.Kxf1 Rxd5; 31.Rxe4 Ra5 is a theoretical draw.) 28.Rxd8+ Kh7; 29.Rh8+!! Kxh8; 30.Qa8+ Kh7; 31.Qxe4+ f5; 32.h4! Rxg2+; 33.Qxg2 Qxe3+ and Black draws.

27...Rf1+!!; 28.Rxf1. 28.Kxf1 Qf5+; 29.Kg1 (29.Rf3 Rxd1+; 30.Ke2 Nc3+!) 29...Qc5+. This is what Larsen had in his mind... 30.Kh1 Nf2+; 31.Kg1 Nh3+; 32.Kh1 Qg1+; 33.Rxg1 Nf2# and the knowledge of the familiar motif pays off. **28...Qc5+.**

and Evans resigned, because 29.Kh1 is met by Nf2+ and either the smothered mate or a backrank mate follows. **Black won.**

SWEDISH VARIATION

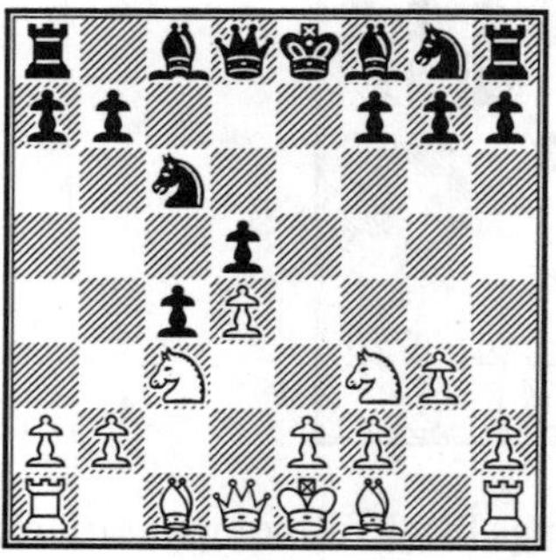

1.d4	**d5**
2.c4	**e6**
3.Nc3	**c5**
4.cxd5	**exd5**
5.Nf3	**Nc6**
6.g3	**c4**

The **Swedish Variation** is somewhat like the Schliemann Defense to the Spanish Game. It is never fully respectable, yet annoyingly, it refuses to go away. Just when the unbalanced positions seem to have been worked out in White's favor, Black's radical advance gets new support. While it is not fully deserving of credit as a "standard" open, the following encounter shows that professionals still use it from time to time.

The illustrative game was one of the most exciting of the 1981 international tournament in memory of Edward Lasker (not to be confused with Emanuel Lasker), a great American player who strongly influenced my own game in my youth.

(161) ADORJAN - TISDALL [D33]
New York (Ed. Lasker Memorial), 1981

1.c4 e6. This is a method of reaching various Queen's Gambit positions by transposition from the English Opening. It is sometimes called the Agincourt, because it is where the English, 1.c4, meets the "French" move 1...e6. **2.Nc3 c5; 3.Nf3 Nc6; 4.d4 d5; 5.cxd5 exd5; 6.g3 c4; 7.Bg2 Bb4; 8.0–0 Nge7; 9.e4.** This is the most effective move, exploiting the weakness of Black's center.

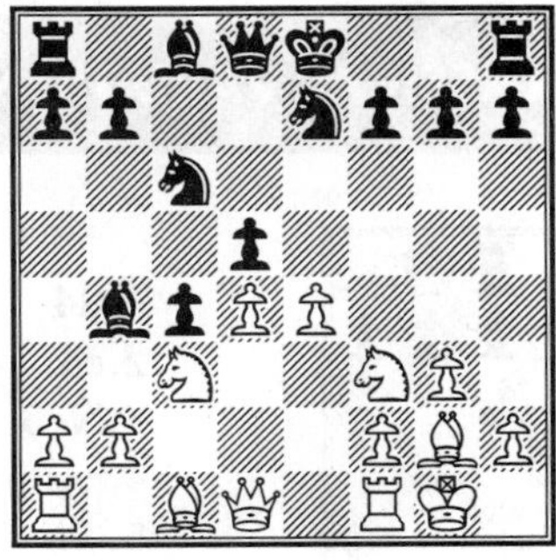

9.Ne1 Bf5; 10.Nc2 0–0; 11.Nxb4 Nxb4; 12.Bg5 f6; 13.Bf4 Qd7; 14.a3 Nbc6; 15.b3 cxb3; 16.Qxb3 Nxd4; 17.Qd1 Ndc6; 18.Nxd5 Rad8; 19.Bc7 Rde8; 20.Nxe7+ Nxe7; 21.Qxd7 Bxd7; 22.Bxb7 and White had a decisive advantage in Dao Thien Hai-Nenashev, Singapore 1995. 9.Bf4 0–0; 10.Ne5 Be6; 11.Nxc6 bxc6; 12.e4 Qd7; 13.Qa4 Bxc3; 14.bxc3 Rfe8; 15.Rfe1 dxe4; 16.Bxe4 Bd5 shows a typical equalizing maneuver by Black, exchanging pawns at e4 and bringing the bishop to d5, Zhukova-Fedorov, Yalta 1995.

9...0–0. 9...dxe4; 10.Nxe4 0–0 concedes the center. 11.Qe2 Bg4; 12.Rd1 Rc8; 13.Qxc4 Nf5; 14.Bg5 brought White the advantage in Xu Jun-Antonio Rogelio, Singapore 1995. **10.exd5 Nxd5; 11.Bg5 f6; 12.Nxd5 Qxd5; 13.Be3 Qf7; 14.d5.** This game created quite a stir when it was played, both because of the beauty of the finish and in addition the important alternative analyzed by Adorjan after the game: 14.a3 Ba5; 15.d5 Rd8; 16.Nd4 gives White a powerful position.

14...Rd8. 14...Ne7! would have equalized, according to Adorjan, who gave the example variation 15.a3 Bd6; 16.Nd2 Nxd5; 17.Nxc4 Nxe3; 18.Nxd6 Nxd1; 19.Nxf7 Nxb2; 20.Nd6 Be6 **15.dxc6 Rxd1; 16.Rfxd1 Ba5.** 16...bxc6; 17.Rd8+ Bf8; 18.Bc5 Bb7; 19.Rad1 Qc7; 20.R8d7! Qc8; 21.Bxf8 Kxf8; 22.Nh4 and Black is defenseless. **17.Nd4 a6; 18.b4 Bxb4; 19.Rab1.**

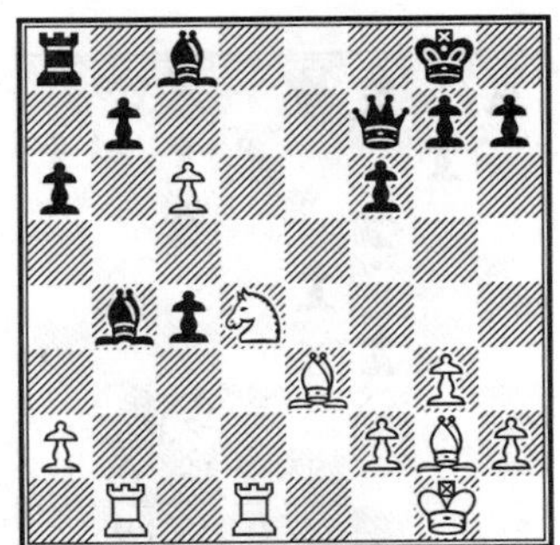

Black must lose a piece. **19...a5; 20.a3 bxc6; 21.axb4 axb4; 22.Nxc6 Bg4; 23.Nxb4. White won.**

CLASSICAL VARIATION

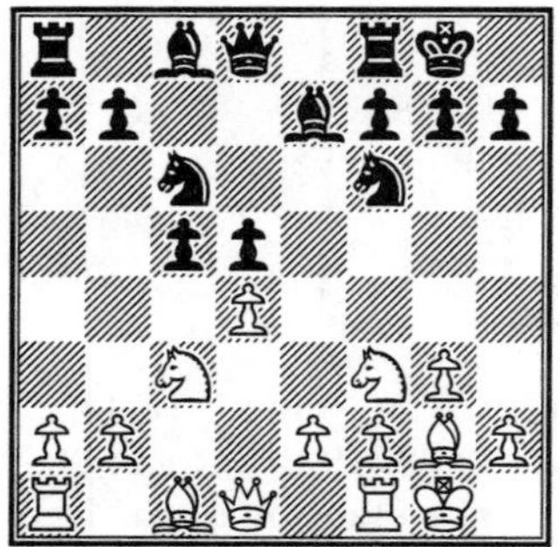

1.d4	**d5**
2.c4	**e6**
3.Nc3	**c5**
4.cxd5	**exd5**
5.Nf3	**Nc6**
6.g3	**Nf6**
7.Bg2	**Be7**
8.0–0	**0–0**

The **Classical Tarrasch Defense** is a particular favorite of mine. Black is willing to accept an isolated d-pawn in return for active piece play. This is a well investigated opening which has played a role in several World Championship matches, and leads to exciting middlegame and endgame play.

There is a great deal of internal diversity in the plans available to each side. White can exchange at c5, isolating the c-pawn, or allow it to advance to c4. If White does not capture at c5, Black also has the option of capturing at d4. So the isolated d-pawn games dominate.

(162) KASPAROV - HJORTH [D34]

World Junior Championship, 1980

1.d4 d5; 2.c4 e6; 3.Nf3 c5; 4.cxd5 exd5; 5.g3 Nc6; 6.Bg2 Nf6; 7.Nc3 Be7; 8.0–0 0–0; 9.Bg5 c4.

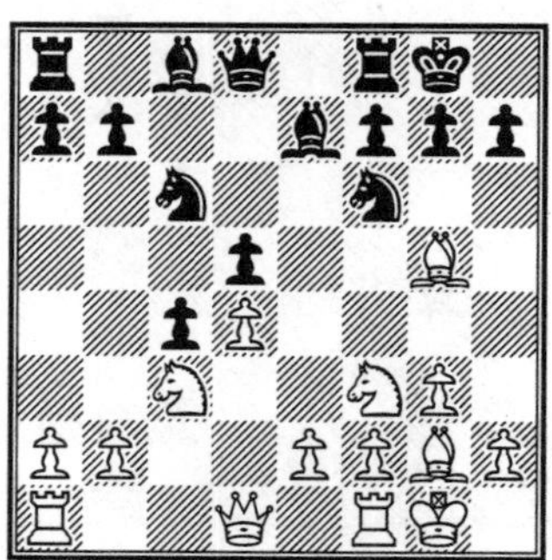

This leads to quite different positions than the normal Classical Tarrasch lines. Black's game plan is very simple: advance on the queenside. Of course White has something to say in the matter, too. **10.Ne5 Be6; 11.f4.** 11.Rc1 h6; 12.Bf4 Rc8; 13.b3 Ba3 gives Black a better game: 14.Rb1 Bb4; 15.Bd2 Bf5; 16.e4 dxe4; 17.bxc4 a5; 18.a3 Bxa3; 19.Rxb7 Nxd4; 20.Nb5 Bb2; 21.Na7 Rb8; 22.Nac6 Nxc6; 23.Nxc6 and now Black sacrificed the queen with 23...Rxb7!; 24.Nxd8 Rxd8 and after 25.Qc2 Bd4; 26.Bxa5 Rc8; 27.Bd2 Rb2 went on to win in Bjarnason-Schiller. Reykjavik 1986.

11.Nxc6 bxc6; 12.b3 Qa5; 13.Na4 is the older line, but it is still seen from time to time. 13...Rad8 had been considered sufficient, but recently suffered a serious fall, and Black should now turn to 13...Rab8 instead, with more pressure at b3. 14.e3 c5; 15.Bxf6 gxf6; 16.dxc5 Bxc5; 17.Nxc5 Qxc5; 18.Qh5 Qd6; 19.f4! looks very difficult for Black, Rogozenko-Lauber, Germany 1996. **11...Nxe5.**

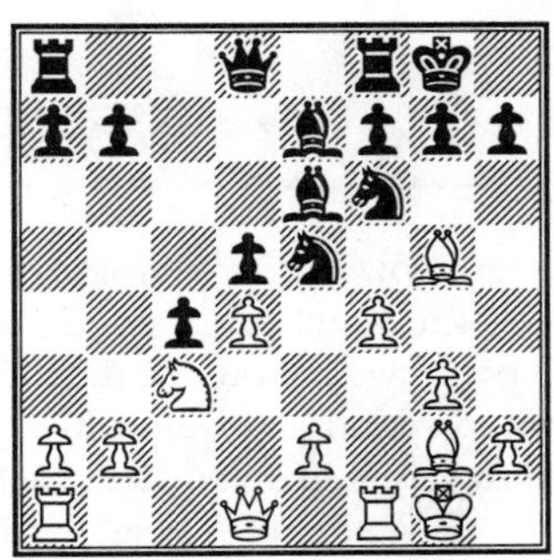

11...Ng4; 12.Nxg4 Bxg4; 13.Bxd5 Bxg5; 14.fxg5 Qxg5; 15.Rf4 Be6!? The idea is to drive the bishop back before playing Rd8, so that Qf1 will not put unbearable pressure at f7. The finesse seems to be good enough to offer strong prospects for equality. 16.Bg2 Rad8; 17.Kh1!? A clever move. The queen can now come to g1, defending the pawn and setting up eventual play on the kingside. 17...h6. The immediate Ne7 comes into consideration. 18.Qg1 Ne7; 19.e4. This is the other point of Qg1. The defense of the d-pawn enables the occupation of the center. The natural consequence of this is a sharpening of the game. 19...Ng6; 20.Raf1!? Offering up the exchange, but the sacrifice cannot be accepted. 20...Bg4; 21.h4 Qh5! was seen Salov-Lputian, Irkutsk 1986. Now the rook must retreat, since the pawn at h4 requires the services of the pawn at g3, and without the pawn phalanx the sacrifice of the exchange will not be effective.

12.fxe5. Kasparov introduced this move in the present game. The idea is that the f-file will be a useful asset in the attack and that a pawn at d4 may be helpful too. 12.dxe5 d4; 13.exf6 gxf6; 14.Bh6 dxc3; 15.bxc3 Qb6+; 16.e3 (16.Kh1 Rfd8; 17.Qc2 Bd5 dates back to Rubinstein-Perlis, St.Petersburg 1909. White has no advantage, and may even stand worse.) 16...Qxe3+; 17.Kh1 Rfd8; 18.Qh5 f5; 19.Bg5 Qc5; 20.Rae1 Rd2; 21.Re5 Qd6; 22.Rfe1 Kh8; 23.Bxe7 Qxe7; 24.Rxf5 Rxa2; 25.Rfe5 Qf6! and White could make no further progress on the kingside. The game continued 26.Be4 h6; 27.f5 Bd7; 28.Re7 Be8; 29.Bxb7 Bc6+; 30.Bxc6 Qxc6+; 31.R7e4 Rb8; 32.Qxf7 Qxe4+ and White resigned since capturing the queen allows a back rank mate, Azmaiparashvili-Lputian, Soviet Union 1980.

12...Ne4; 13.Bxe7 Nxc3; 14.bxc3 Qxe7. The only strategy available to White is to try to eliminate Black's pawn at d5 so that the central pawns can advance. Black will try to thrust the queenside pawns forward as quickly as possible. **15.e4! Qd7; 16.a4!** A very important move, restraining Black's queenside play. That accomplished, White can turn his attention to the kingside. **16...Rfd8; 17.Qh5 Rac8.**

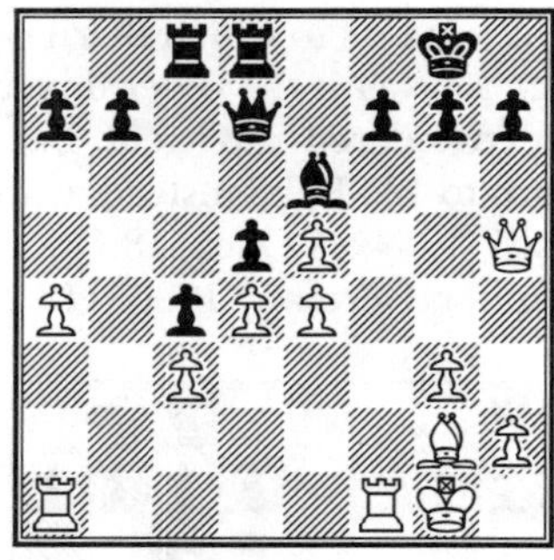

The battle lines are drawn. Now White doubles rooks on the f- file. This will leave the a-pawn hanging, but if the attack is fast enough it won't matter. **18.Rf4 Rc7; 19.Raf1 Qxa4?** Black should be worrying about the defense of his kingside, so 19...Qe8 was best, although White would retain a strong initiative. **20.exd5! Rxd5.** Forced, since otherwise f7 loses its most valuable defender. The f7-square is the cornerstone of Black's position, and obviously White would like to play Rxf7 as soon as feasible. **21.Bxd5 Bxd5.**

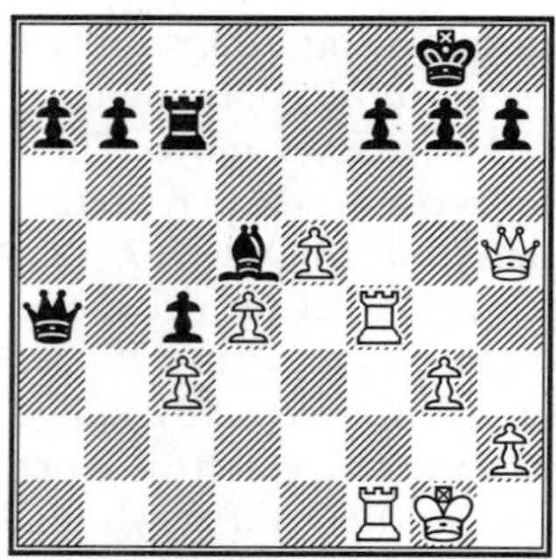

The material is not important. If White does not break through quickly Black will make a new queen on the other flank. The goal is achieved effectively. **22.e6!** What is surprising about this move is that it seems to contribute nothing to the task of deflecting the bishop from f7. In fact, however, it opens up the d5-square so that the White pawn can chase the bishop from the key square.

22...Bxe6; 23.d5 Qb5. 23...Rc5 loses to 24.Rxf7!; 23...g6 is met by 24.Qh4 with the threat of Qd8+. **24.Rh4!** The simultaneous threats at e6 and h7 force victory. **24...Qc5+; 25.Rf2 Bxd5; 26.Rd4!** This breaks the pin at f2 while exploiting the pin along the 5th rank. **26...Rd7; 27.Rf5. White won.**

(163) PETROSIAN - SPASSKY [D34]

World Championship, 1969

1.c4 e6; 2.d4 d5; 3.Nc3 c5; 4.cxd5 exd5; 5.Nf3 Nc6; 6.g3 Nf6; 7.Bg2 Be7; 8.0-0 0-0; 9.Bg5.

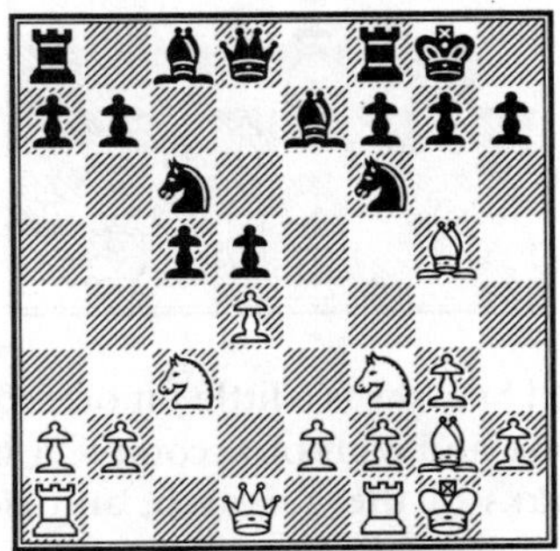

This is one of the main lines of the Tarrasch, with only 9.dxc5 as a very serious contender. Black has a choice of three very different plans here. In this game we examine the central exchange, which is far and away the most common move. Black accepts the permanent isolated pawn but mobilizes remaining pieces quickly and can put pressure on the soft points in White's position, for example at e2. White will try to win the weak pawn at d5, counting on a blockading knight at d4 to restrict the enemy forces.

9...cxd4. Spassky defended the Tarrasch five times in this match, drawing four and winning this game. That ranks as the greatest achievement the opening has had –so far! **10.Nxd4 h6; 11.Be3.** This is how all the match games began, except for the 16th. **11...Bg4.** This was one of Spassky's prepared novelties, and is known as the Spassky Variation.

12.Nb3 Be6; 13.Rc1 Re8. 13...Qd7; 14.Bc5 Rfd8; 15.Bxe7 Qxe7; 16.Nd4 Rac8; 17.e3 Ne5; 18.Nce2 Bg4; 19.Rxc8 Rxc8 gave Black equality in Andersson-Marjanovic, Banja Luka 1979. **14.Re1.** 14.Nb5 Qd7; 15.N5d4 Bh3; 16.Nxc6 bxc6; 17.Qd3 Bxg2; 18.Kxg2 a5; 19.Rc2 a4; 20.Nd2 Qb7 was eventually drawn in another game from this match. **14...Qd7; 15.Bc5 Rac8.** 15...Rad8!? comes into consideration. **16.Bxe7 Qxe7; 17.e3.** 17.Nxd5 does not get anywhere after 17...Nxd5; 18.Bxd5 Rcd8; 19.e4 Bxd5; 20.exd5 Qxe1+; 21.Qxe1 Rxe1+; 22.Rxe1 Rxd5 with full equality in the endgame.

17...Red8; 18.Qe2 Bg4; 19.f3?! White weakens the dark squares around his king, never a safe strategy in the Tarrasch. 19.Qf1 would have left Black with a slight initiative, but nothing too dangerous. **19...Bf5.** Black could have settled for equality with 19...Be6, but this is a much more active move. **20.Rcd1 Ne5.** The c-file belongs to Black now. **21.Nd4 Bg6.**

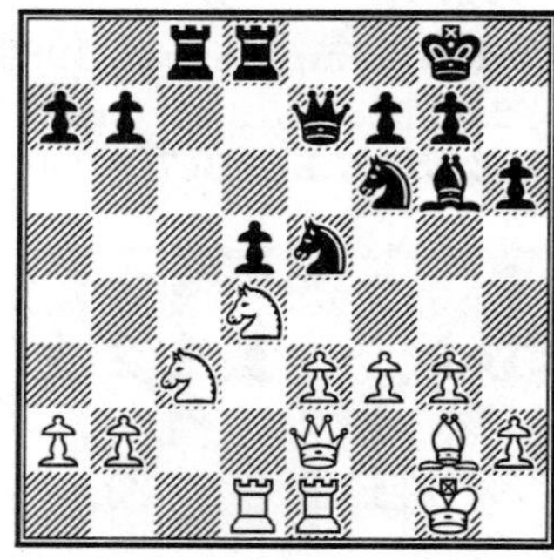

22.Bh3 Rc4; 23.g4 Rb4?! Spassky is a little bit overconfident here. The rook has no support on the queenside and cannot accomplish much. The coordination of pieces is one of the hallmarks of the Tarrasch, and isolated forays are rarely rewarded. 23...Rc5; 24.f4 Ned7; 25.f5 Bh7 and White must justify the weakening advances on the kingside. **24.b3?** White reacts prematurely. A better sense of timing would have produced the preliminary advance of the f-pawn. 24.f4 Nc4; 25.b3 Nd6; 26.f5 with a clear advantage for White. Black would have suffered from a misplaced knight at d6 and rook at b4, neither of which could be easily relocated to a more useful post.

24...Nc6; 25.Qd2 Rb6; 26.Nce2. The game is level again. 26.Na4 Ra6! maintains the balance. 27.Bf1 Nxd4; 28.Qxd4 (28.Bxa6?? loses to 28...Nxf3+; 28.exd4 Re6; 29.Nc5 Rxe1; 30.Rxe1 Qc7; 31.Re5 leaves the situation unclear.) 28...Rc6 (28...Re6; 29.Qxa7 d4!) 29.Qxa7 h5! and Black has a strong attack. **26...Bh7; 27.Bg2 Re8.** The flexible placement of the rooks in the Tarrasch allows Black to take advantage of weaknesses in the White camp. **28.Ng3 Nxd4; 29.exd4?**

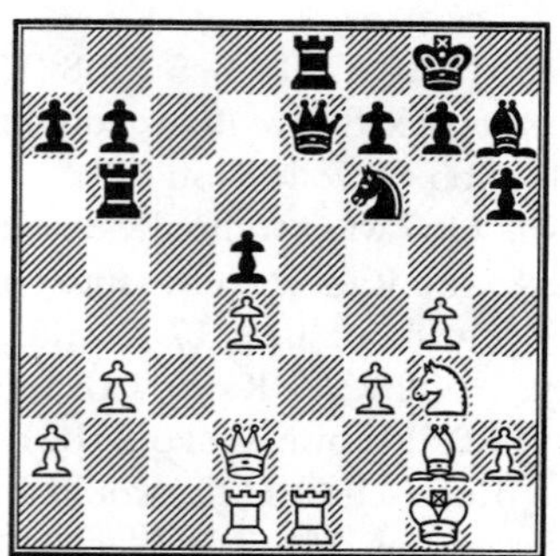

A natural, but fatal, move. After 29.Qxd4 White would have maintained an equal game, although Black might later exploit the weakness of the kingside. **29...Re6! 30.Rxe6 Qxe6; 31.Rc1 Bg6!** This introduces a maneuver which is not uncommon in the Tarrasch. **32.Bf1 Nh7!** Black threatens such moves as f7-f5 combined with Nh7-g5. With his next move White prevents this plan, but allows Black to reorganize in another effective manner.

33.Qf4 Nf8; 34.Rc5? White could have maintained some chances after 34.Qe5! **34...Bb1!; 35.a4 Ng6; 36.Qd2 Qf6; 37.Kf2 Nf4; 38.a5?** A final blunder, but Black was winning anyway. **38...Bd3; 39.Nf5 Qg5; 40.Ne3 Qh4+; 41.Kg1 Bxf1.** White resigned, since he is mated after 42.Nxf1 Re2 while 42.Kxf1 is met by 42...Qh3+ and White must lose at least a piece. **Black won.**

(164) KARPOV - KASPAROV [D34]

World Championship, 9th match game 1984
1.d4 d5; 2.c4 e6; 3.Nf3 c5; 4.cxd5 exd5;
5.g3 Nf6; 6.Bg2 Be7; 7.0–0 0–0; 8.Nc3 Nc6.

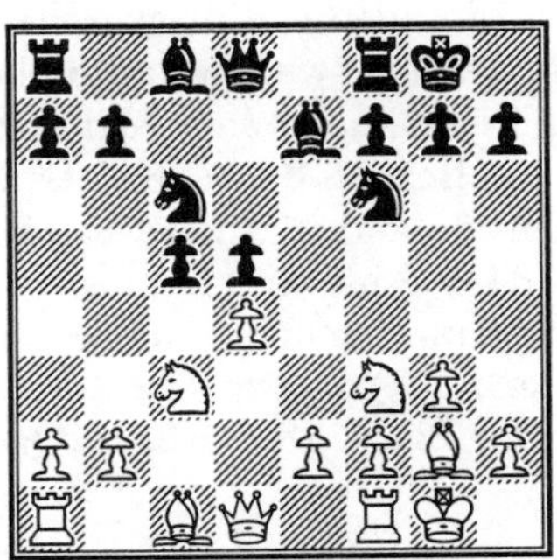

9.Bg5. This is the most ambitious move, and Black can respond by resolving the center with 9...cxd4, settling for passive but solid defense with 9...Be6, or with 9...c4!?, which leads to wild complications. **9...cxd4; 10.Nxd4.** Now Black can chase the bishop away, which is the most common plan, or play the quiet and trickily transpositional 10...Re8.

10...h6; 11.Be3 Re8; 12.Qb3. It is time for White to deploy the heavy artillery, and this move effectively adds pressure to d5, the weak point in Black's position. There are many other plans, including 12.Qa4, 12.Rc1, 12.Qc2 etc. but the general contour of the middlegame has been established by the pawn structure. **12...Na5.** Black must take the initiative in the Tarrasch, and this is well-timed. **13.Qc2 Bg4;** Best, because it places counter-pressure at e2, the typical plan for Black in such structures. **14.Nf5.** An interesting alternative is 14.h3 which can be met by retreating either to e6 or h5, with a dynamic game in either case. **14...Rc8.**

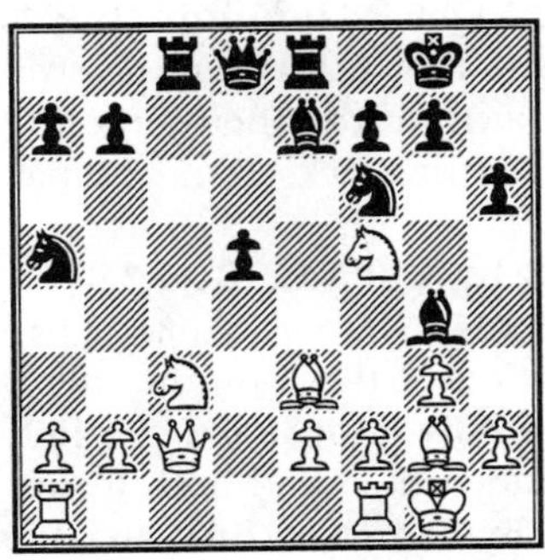

Black has tried a number of plans here, but two are of particular interest. 14...Bb4 is the most common move. 15.Bd4 Bxc3. Although Black does not want to part with the dark-squared bishop, here it seems to be necessary. 16.Bxc3 Rxe2! and now

White walks into a discovered attack with the bold 17.Qd1! d4! is the best reply. 18.Nxd4 Rxf2; 19.Qa4 Rxg2+; 20.Kxg2 Qd5+; 21.Kg1 is all forced, and after 21...Nc4; 22.Qb5 a6; 23.Qxd5 Nxd5. Black has enough compensation for the exchange, because his pieces are actively placed. 24.Rfe1 (24.Rac1 Rd8; 25.Rfe1 h5; 26.Kf2 Kh7; 27.Nf3 Nxc3; 28.Rxc3 Nxb2 and Black had more than enough compensation for the exchange in Ogaard-Rantanen, Oslo 1986.) 24...h5; 25.Ne2 Nxc3; 26.bxc3 Ne5; 27.Nd4 f6 and objectively Black should have enough compensation but White went on to win in Kasparov-Illescas Cordoba, Linares 1990.

15.Bd4. 15.Nxe7+ Rxe7; 16.Rad1 Qe8! Black is creating some counterplay, but White can maintain a small advantage with accurate play. 17.h3 Bh5; 18.Bxd5 Bg6; 19.Qc1 Nxd5; 20.Rxd5 Nc4; 21.Bd4 and White had greater control of the center in the 7th game of the match. **15...Bc5; 16.Bxc5.** 16.e3 Bxd4; 17.Nxd4 Qb6 gives Black some pressure on the queenside and it is hard to exploit the weak pawn at d5. **16...Rxc5; 17.Ne3 Be6.** 17...d4 doesn't work because of 18.Rad1.

18.Rad1! Karpov ignores tempting tactics and just increases the pressure. 18.b4 Rc7; 19.bxa5 d4; 20.Rad1 Rxc3; 21.Qxc3 dxc3; 22.Rxd8 Rxd8; 23.Rc1 Rd2; 24.Rxc3 Rxe2; 25.Bxb7 Rxa2 is fine for Black. **18...Qc8; 19.Qa4 Rd8; 20.Rd3 a6; 21.Rfd1 Nc4; 22.Nxc4 Rxc4; 23.Qa5.**

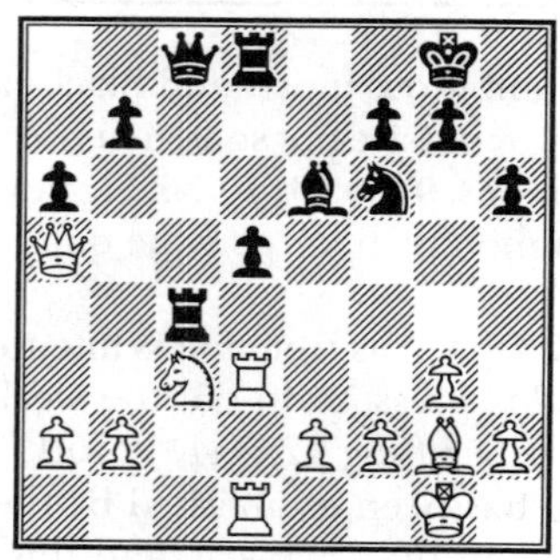

23...Rc5. 23...Rd7 was suggested by Yusupov immediately after the game. It later received a practical test. 24.Rd4 b5; 25.Rxc4 dxc4; 26.Rf1 Rd6 was agreed drawn, Morovic-Salazar, Santiago Zonal 1989, so we can conclude that the variation as a whole is playable for Black. **24.Qb6 Rd7; 25.Rd4 Qc7; 26.Qxc7 Rdxc7; 27.h3!** White is slowly improving the position, which is very passive for Black. Tarrasch players hate defending the weak d-pawn with all their pieces, waiting for White to liquidate pieces until a very unpleasant (for Black!) rook and pawn or minor piece endgame arises.

27...h5; 28.a3 g6; 29.e3 Kg7; 30.Kh2 Rc4; 31.Bf3 b5; 32.Kg2 R7c5; 33.Rxc4 Rxc4; 34.Rd4 Kf8; 35.Be2 Rxd4?! Kasparov, in time pressure, should have retreated to c5 instead. This clarification of the position only works to White's advantage. **36.exd4 Ke7; 37.Na2 Bc8; 38.Nb4 Kd6; 39.f3 Ng8; 40.h4 Nh6; 41.Kf2 Nf5; 42.Nc2.**

Here the position was adjourned and both teams returned home to analyze. **42...f6; 43.Bd3 g5; 44.Bxf5 Bxf5; 45.Ne3 Bb1; 46.b4 gxh4?** A big mistake. Clearly the Kasparov team failed to spot White's reply, something which would have been less likely had today's computers been available to assist. **47.Ng2 hxg3+; 48.Kxg3 Ke6; 49.Nf4+ Kf5; 50.Nxh5 Ke6; 51.Nf4+ Kd6; 52.Kg4 Bc2; 53.Kh5 Bd1.**

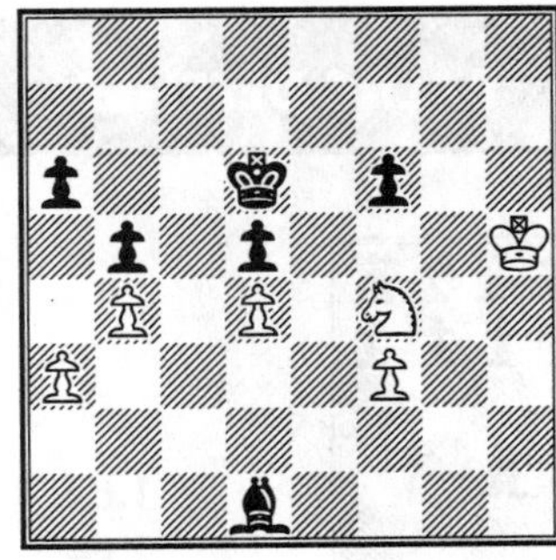

This endgame is winning for White, because Black has a bad bishop which cannot do any damage to the White pawns. **54.Kg6 Ke7.** 54...Bxf3; 55.Kxf6 and the winning plan is to move the Black king from d6, play Ke5, then arrange for Ne7+ to pick off the d-pawn, for example 55...Bg4; 56.Ng6 Bh5; 57.Ne7 Bg4; 58.Nf5+ Kc6; 59.Ke5 Bxf5; 60.Kxf5 Kd6; 61.Kf6 Kd7; 62.Ke5 Kc6; 63.Ke6 etc. **55.Nxd5+ Ke6; 56.Nc7+.**

The rest is simple: **56...Kd7; 57.Nxa6 Bxf3; 58.Kxf6 Kd6; 59.Kf5 Kd5; 60.Kf4 Bh1; 61.Ke3 Kc4; 62.Nc5 Bc6; 63.Nd3 Bg2; 64.Ne5+ Kc3; 65.Ng6 Kc4; 66.Ne7 Bb7; 67.Nf5 Bg2; 68.Nd6+ Kb3; 69.Nxb5 Ka4; 70.Nd6.**

A painful loss, which brought the match score to 5–0. Kasparov then dug in and Karpov could not win any of the subsequent 39 games before FIDE President Campomanes called a halt to the match. But after this game, the future Champion was not at all happy. Neither was I, since I had just published a book (with Grandmaster Leonid Shamkovich) on the Tarrasch and was delighted, at first, to see it play such a prominent role at the match, where I was present as a journalist, reporting for Associated Press and a variety of television programs. It was fascinating to see all the grandmaster analysts poring over Tarrasch positions that I had studied for months, but disappointed that the analysts were favoring White. **White won.**

QUEEN'S GAMBIT REFUSED

Black can accept or decline the Queen's Gambit, but there are still other approaches which are even more confrontational. In these, Black counterattacks immediately and challenges White in the center. These lines are sometimes called the **Queen's Gambit Refused**.

BALTIC DEFENSE

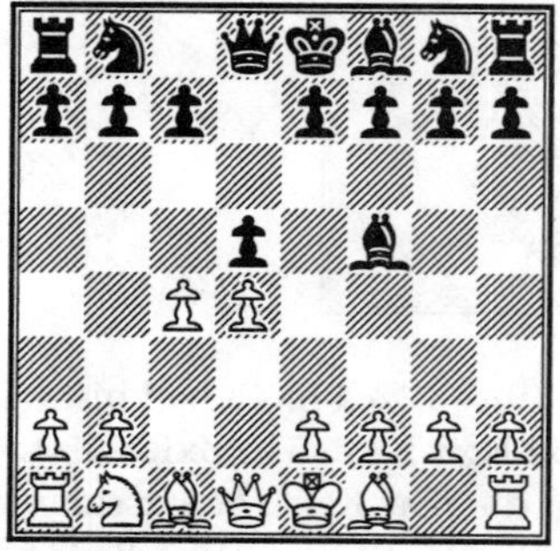

1.d4 d5
2.c4 Bf5

This defence enjoys partisan support at many levels of play, and is by no means unplayable, especially if White plays Nf3 before c4. Even in the illustrative game, Black gets a reasonable position before going astray. Black can aim for an early capture on b1, but the real point of the move is simply to battle for control of e4. The drawback is that the pawn at b7 is not defended, and Black must watch out for a timely Qb3.

(165) PORTISCH - LARSEN [D06]
Montreal, 1979

1.Nf3. In the present game, a typical position is reached via transposition. Indeed, the move order adopted by Larsen is probably best, as it avoids a lot of sidelines which can be problematic. **1...d5; 2.d4 Bf5. 3.c4.** 3.Bg5!? might be playable, intending to capture on f6 if Black plays 3...Nf6. **3...e6; 4.Qb3 Nc6; 5.c5.** 5.Bd2 is a reasonable alternative.

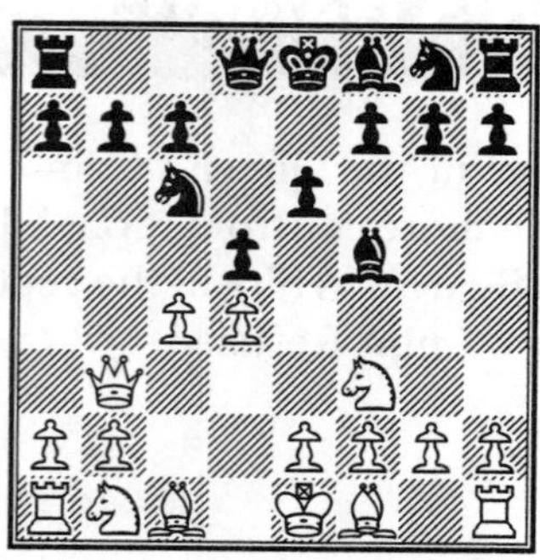

5...Rb8; 6.Bf4 h6; 7.e3 g5; 8.Bg3 Bg7; 9.Nc3 a6?! 9...Nge7! would have secured equality. **10.h4 g4; 11.Ne5 Nge7; 12.Nxc6 Nxc6; 13.Be2 0–0; 14.Qd1.** 14.0–0–0 is an aggressive alternative. **14...e5?!**

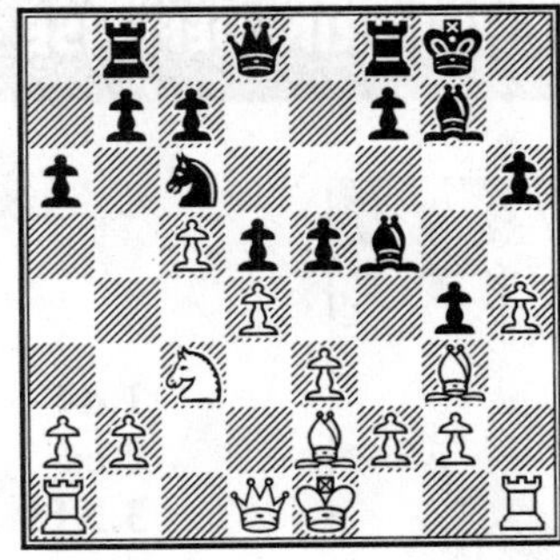

The slow openings like the Torre Attack and the present game require patience, and that is not one of Larsen's strong points. 14...h5 was called for. **15.dxe5 d4; 16.exd4 Nxd4; 17.0–0 Qd7; 18.Bc4 Bc2; 19.Qc1 Rbd8; 20.Re1 Bh7.** Black has created some threats, but the kingside is still vulnerable. That is why White should have played the knight to the center here.

21.Bd5?! 21.Nd5! Nc2; 22.Nf6+ Bxf6; 23.exf6 Nxe1; 24.Qxh6 and White should win without difficulty. **21...Qe7; 22.Be4 Qxc5; 23.Bxh7+! Kxh7; 24.Qf4.** The weakness of the kingside is still critical. **24...Qb6; 25.Rad1 Qxb2; 26.Rxd4! Qxc3; 27.Rde4 Kh8; 28.Qxg4.** Although the material is even, White has all the chances here.

28...Rd4; 29.Rxd4 Qxe1+; 30.Kh2 Qa1. 30...Bxe5?!; 31.f4! Qxg3+; 32.Qxg3 Bxd4; 33.f5 should be a pretty simple win. **31.Rd7 Qxa2; 32.Rxc7 b5.** 32...Qd5 is less accurate because of 33.Rd7 Qb5; 34.f4 a5; 35.h5! a4; 36.Bh4 a3; 37.Bf6 Bxf6; 38.exf6 Rg8; 39.Rd8! **33.f4 Qd5; 34.Rd7 Qe4; 35.Qh5.**

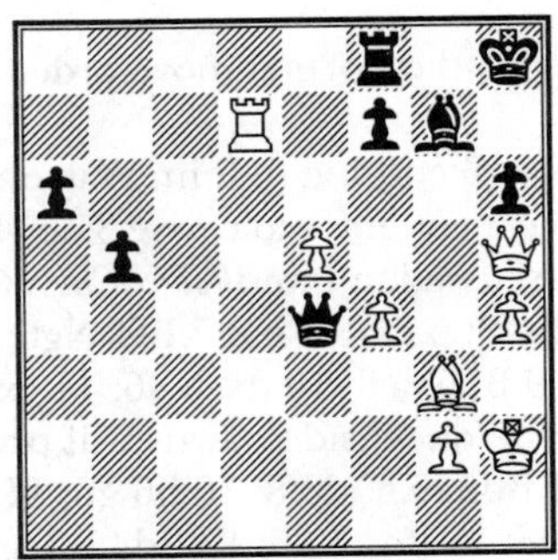

35...Kg8. 35...b4 looks obvious but there are problems: 36.f5 b3; 37.f6 b2 and now White has 38.e6! b1Q; 39.fxg7+ Kxg7; 40.Be5+ Kh7; 41.Rxf7+ Kg8 (41...Rxf7; 42.Qxf7#) 42.Rg7+ Kh8; 43.Qxh6+ Qh7; 44.Rxh7+ Kg8; 45.Qg7# **36.Re7 Qb4.** 36...b4; 37.f5 b3; 38.e6 fxe6; 39.Qg6 (39.Rxg7+ Kxg7; 40.Qg6+ Kh8; 41.Qxh6+ Kg8; 42.Qg6+ draws.) 39...Qd4; 40.Qxe6+ Kh8; 41.Rxg7! Qxg7; 42.Be5 and White wins. **37.Ra7 Qc5; 38.Rxa6 b4; 39.Qf3 Qb5; 40.Ra7 Rb8; 41.f5** This move was sealed after 35 minutes of thought, but it didn't take long to finish it off when the game was resumed. **41...Bxe5; 42.f6 Kh8; 43.Rxf7 Re8; 44.Qg4 Bxg3+; 45.Kh3!** and Black resigned, not wanting to face 45...Rg8; 46.Qe4. Notes after Tal. **White won.**

CHIGORIN DEFENSE

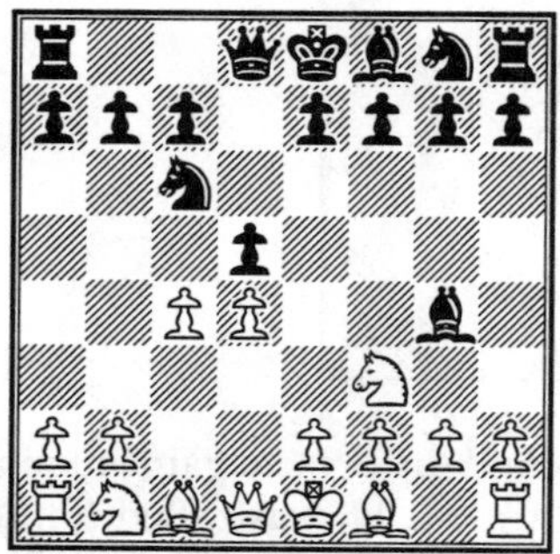

1.d4 d5
2.c4 Nc6
3.Nf3 Bg4

This is the **Chigorin Defense**, in its traditional form as employed by Mikhail Chigorin himself. Black is willing to part with the bishop pair early in the game, counting on rapid development and effective use of knights to compensate for the long-term disadvantage. The entire plan remains somewhat suspect, though there are strong grandmasters willing to defend the Black side.

(166) STEINITZ - CHIGORIN [D07]

World Championship 10th Match Game, 1889

1.Nf3. 1.d4 d5; 2.c4 Nc6 is the normal move order used to reach the Chigorin positions.

A) 3.Nc3 is the best move, according to John Watson, one of the major theoreticians in the line. 3...dxc4. Recent attempt to revive 3...e5 have not yet proven successful. This approach will be discussed in *Unorthodox Chess Openings*. 4.Nf3 is best here.

4...Nf6 (4...Bg4; 5.d5! Bxf3; 6.exf3 Ne5; 7.Bf4 Ng6; 8.Bxc4! is good for White, since 8...Nxf4 is refuted by 9.Bb5+ c6; 10.dxc6 a6; 11.cxb7+ axb5; 12.bxa8Q Qxa8; 13.Nxb5 Qa5+ 14.Nc3 and the queenside pawns will prove decisive.) 5.e4 (5.e3 e5; 6.d5 Ne7; 7.Bxc4 Ng6; 8.h4 Bd6; 9.h5 Nf8; 10.h6 g6; 11.e4 a6; 12.Bg5 N8d7; 13.a4 0–0; 14.Qe2 Be7; 15.Rd1 Ne8; 16.Bc1 Nd6; 17.Bd3 Bf6 gave Black a solid positon in Khalifman-Morozevich, Yalta 1995.)

5...Bg4; 6.Be3 e6 (6...Bxf3; 7.gxf3 e5; 8.d5 Ne7; 9.Qa4+ leaves Black with an awkward position, Flear-Bell, British Championship 1988.) 7.Bxc4 Bb4; 8.Qc2 0–0.

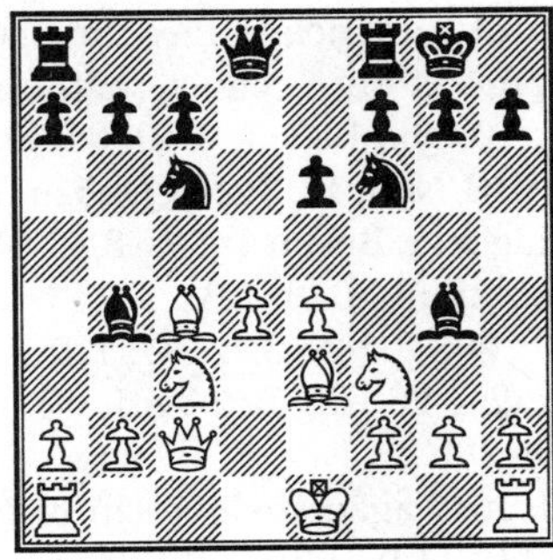

Now a rook will come to d1, either directly or via castling. (8...Qe7; 9.Rd1 is also good for White.)

A1) 9.0–0–0 Bxc3; 10.bxc3 Qe7; 11.h3 Bxf3; 12.gxf3 Rfb8; 13.Bd3 b5; 14.e5 Nd5; 15.Bxh7+ Kh8 (15...Kf8!? might have been safer). 16.Be4 b4; 17.Bxd5 exd5; 18.Kd2 Na5; 19.Ke2 Nc4; 20.Bd2 c5. I think that Black should have played ...Rb6 first, so that the rook could slide along the sixth rank. 21.Rhg1 Rb6; 22.Rg5 g6; 23.dxc5 Nxd2; 24.Qxd2 bxc3; 25.Qxc3 Ra6; 26.f4 Rc8; 27.Rxd5 Qe6; 28.Rd2 Rxa2; 29.Rxa2 Qxa2+ was eventually drawn in Shirov-Morozevich, Amsterdam (Donner Memorial) 1995.

A2) 9.Rd1 Ne7 (9...Qe7; 10.Bb5 e5; 11.Bxc6 bxc6; 12.dxe5 Nd7; 13.a3 Ba5; 14.Bf4 Bxf3; 15.gxf3 Nxe5; 16.Bxe5 Qxe5; 17.0–0 gave White the advantage in Piket-Morozevich, London (Intel) 1995.) 10.Be2 Bxc3+; 11.bxc3 c5; 12.0–0 Qc7; 13.Qb1 b6; 14.h3 Bh5; 15.g4 Bg6; 16.Bd3 Rfd8; 17.Ne5 Qb7;18.f3 cxd4; 19.cxd4 Rac8; 20.Rc1 Rxc1; 21.Rxc1 Nd7; 22.Nxd7 Qxd7; 23.Qb5 Qd6; 24.Kg2 h6; 25.h4 f5; 26.gxf5 exf5; 27.Qc4+ Kh7; 28.d5 Re8; 29.Re1 fxe4; 30.fxe4 Qd7; 31.Kg3 h5! 32.Kf2?! Qh3!; 33.Ke2 Nf5; 34.Kd2 Nd6; 35.Qc6 Nxe4+; 36.Bxe4 Rxe4; 37.d6 Qg2+; 38.Kc1 Qxa2; 39.Kd1 Rc4 and White resigned in Van Wely-Morozevich, Amsterdam 1995.

B) 3.cxd5 Qxd5; 4.Nf3 (4.e3 e5; 5.Nc3 Bb4; 6.Bd2 Bxc3; 7.bxc3 Nf6; 8.c4 Qd6; 9.d5 Ne7; 10.Qb1 0–0; 11.e4 Nd7; 12.Bd3 Nc5; 13.Ne2 f5 led to a complicated game in Khalifman-Morozevich, Amsterdam 1995.) 4...e6 (4...e5; 5.Nc3 Bb4; 6.dxe5 Qxd1+; 7.Kxd1 Bg4; 8.h3 Bxf3; 9.exf3 0–0–0+; 10.Kc2 Nxe5; 11.Be3 was a bit better for White in Steinitz-Chigorin, Vienna 1898.) 5.Nc3 Bb4; 6.a3 Bxc3+; 7.bxc3 Nf6; 8.e3 0–0; 9.c4 Qd8; 10.Bb2 is better for White, Gunsberg-Chigorin, Hannover 1902.

1...d5; 2.d4 Bg4; 3.c4 Nc6. We have transposed back to the main line.

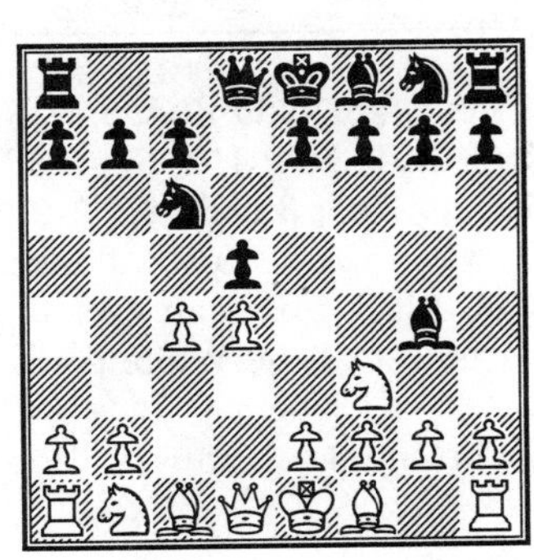

4.e3. 4.cxd5 Bxf3; 5.dxc6! Bxc6; 6.Nc3 is the most challenging continuation, and it has been difficult to find convincing lines for Black. 6...e6

A) 7.Bf4 is Teichmann's move, but Chigorin had no problems facing it. 7...Nf6 (7...Ne7; 8.e3 Ng6; 9.Bg3 a6; 10.Qb3 Be7; 11.0-0-0 0-0; 12.d5 exd5; 13.Nxd5 Qc8; 14.Be2 Bd8; 15.Bf3 Qe6; 16.Kb1 Ne5; 17.Bxe5 Qxe5 and the bishop pair gave Black the advantage Teichmann-Chigorin, Berlin 1897.) 8.e3 Bb4; 9.Qb3 Nd5; 10.Bg3 0-0; 11.Bd3 Qg5; 12.Qc2 f5; 13.Be5 Rf7; 14.0-0-0 Bxc3; 15.bxc3 b5; 16.Rhg1 Qe7; 17.Rdf1 Qa3+; 18.Kd2 b4; 19.c4 Ba4; 20.Qb1 Nc3; 21.Qa1 Rd8; 22.g4 Ne4+; 23.Ke2 Nc5; 24.Qb1 Nxd3; 25.Qxd3 Qxa2+; 26.Kf3 Bc2 and White resigned in Teichmann-Chigorin, Cambridge Springs 1904.

B) 7.e4 was used by Pillsbury against Chigorin in two games: 7...Bb4 (7...Nf6; 8.f3 Be7; 9.Be3 0-0; 10.Bd3 b6; 11.0-0 Bb7; 12.Qc2 and Black could not Pillsbury-Chigorin, Saint Petersburg 1895.) 8.f3 f5 (8...Qh4+!?; 9.g3 Qh5; 10.Be2 0-0-0; 11.Be3 f5! gave Black counterplay Granda Zuniga-Morozevich, Amsterdam (Donner Memorial) 1995.) 9.e5 Ne7; 10.a3 Ba5; 11.Bc4 Bd5 was fine for Black in Pillsbury-Chigorin, Saint Petersburg 1895.

4...e5. 4...e6 is the more conservative approach. 5.Nc3 Bb4; 6.Qb3 Bxf3; 7.gxf3 Nge7; 8.Bd2 0-0; 9.f4 White insures that Black will be unable to play ...e5. 9...Rb8

A) 10.0-0-0?! invites 10...dxc4; 11.Bxc4 b5; 12.Bd3 Bxc3; 13.Qxc3! Rb6; 14.Kb1 a5; 15.Rhg1 Nb4; 16.Be4 Ned5; 17.Qc5 Qa8! and Black had a solid position in Pillsbury-Chigorin, St. Petersburg 1895.

B) 10.h4 is useful preliminary move. 10...Nf5; 11.0-0-0 dxc4; 12.Bxc4 Be7; 13.Ne4 b5; 14.Bd3 Rb6; 15.Ng5 h6; 16.Bxf5 exf5; 17.Nf3 b4; 18.d5 Na5; 19.Qd3 Qd7; 20.Kb1 Rd8; 21.Bc1 Rd6; 22.Ne5 Qe8; 23.Qxf5 Bf6; 24.Rhg1 and Black resigned in Showalter-Chigorin, Nurenberg 1896.

5.Qb3! Bxf3; 6.gxf3.

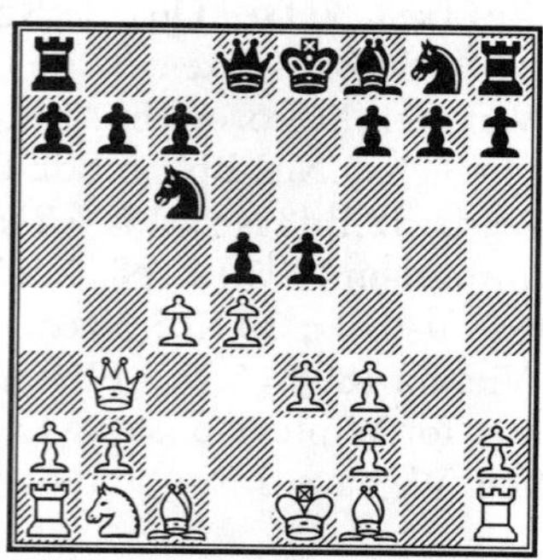

6...exd4. 6...Nge7; 7.Nc3 exd4; 8.Nxd5 Rb8; 9.e4 Ng6; 10.Bd2 Bd6; 11.f4 0-0; 12.0-0-0 Nce7; 13.f5 Nxd5; 14.cxd5 Nf4; 15.Qf3 gave White the advantage in the 14th game of the match. **7.cxd5 Ne5; 8.exd4 Nd7; 9.Nc3!** 9.Qxb7 Qe7+; 10.Be3 Qb4+; 11.Qxb4 Bxb4+; 12.Nc3 Ngf6 and Black will take advantage of White's weak pawns. **9...Qe7+; 10.Be3 Qb4.** Black offers an exchange of queens, which would permit him to exploit the weakness of the White pawn structure in the endgame. But White has better ideas.

11.Qc2! Ngf6; 12.Bb5. The simple 12.a3 was also interesting. **12...Rd8.** Black might have castled instead. **13.0–0–0 a6; 14.Ba4 Be7.** The immediate 14...b5 was possible, though it would not make much of a difference. Already Black's position is very bad. **15.Rhg1 g6.** 15...0–0 would have invited an attack with 16.Bh6 Ne8; 17.Qf5 for example 17...Ndf6; 18.Rxg7+!! Nxg7; 19.Rg1 and Black cannot defend.

16.Bh6! White immediately exploits the weakness of the dark squares. **16...b5; 17.Bb3 Nb6; 18.Rge1 Kd7.** This is the only way to break the pin on the bishop at e7, but the king is not particularly safe here. **19.Bf4 Rc8.** 19...Nh5; 20.Bxc7 Kc8; 21.Nxb5 Kb7; 22.Qc6+ is terminal. **20.a3 Qa5; 21.Bg5!**

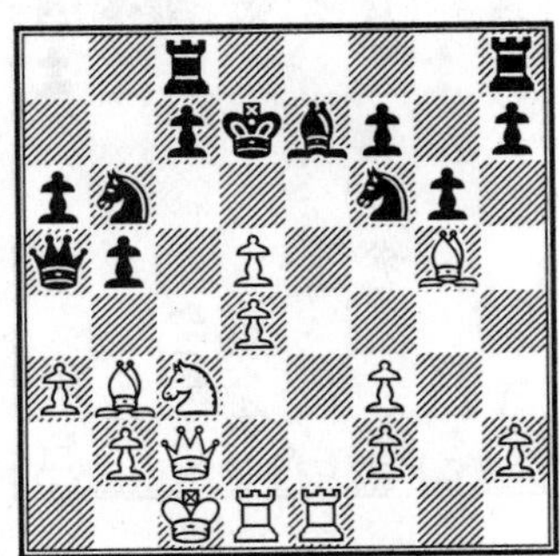

There is no way that Black can survive this position. **21...Ng8.** The pawn at d5 is still taboo: 21...Nbxd5 loses to 22.Rxe7+! while the other capture is also inadequate: 21...Nfxd5 is handled by 22.Bxe7. **22.Bxe7 Nxe7; 23.Ne4 Rb8; 24.Nf6+.** White closes in for the kill. **24...Kd8; 25.Rxe7 Kxe7; 26.Qxc7+ Nd7; 27.Qxa5.** Black resigned. **White won.**

ALBIN COUNTERGAMBIT

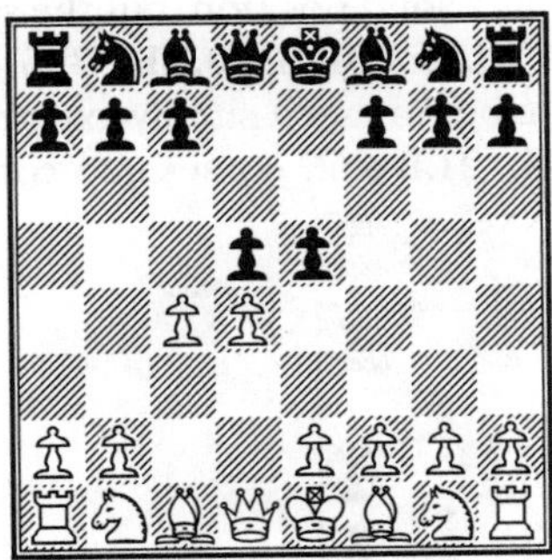

1.d4	**d5**
2.c4	**e5**

The **Albin** is a true countergambit. Black sacrifices a pawn but in return gains rapid development and will advance a pawn to d4, where it will remain a thorn in White's side. Castling on opposite wings is typical, and firestorms frequently fill the skies. Objectively speaking, the Albin falls just a wee bit short of respectability, but it is a useful weapon if applied on special occasions, especially against amateur players whose defensive and tactical skills are less polished.

(167) LINDBERG - SCHILLER [D08]

Postal, 1983

1.d4 d5; 2.c4 e5; 3.dxe5 d4; 4.Nf3 Nc6.

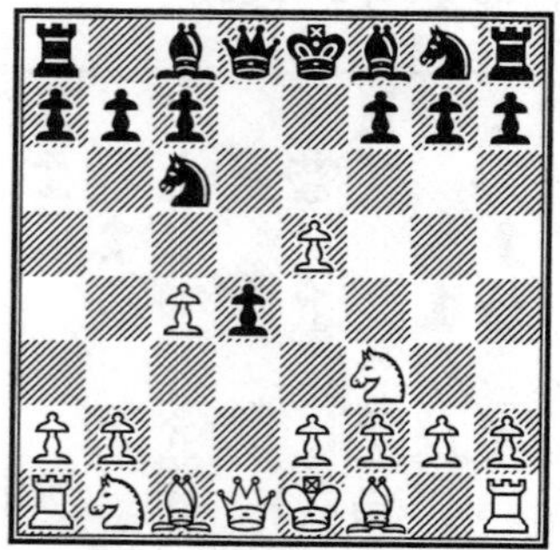

White usually plays a3, g3, Bg2, Nbd2 and 0–0 in some order. **5.Nbd2 Be6; 6.g3 Qd7; 7.Bg2 0–0–0 8.0–0 h5!** Black cannot waste any time, because White can also go on the offensive with such moves as a3 and b4. **9.h4 Nh6; 10.Ng5.**

I have faced 10.a3 a couple of times. 10.a3 Ng4; 11.Qa4 Kb8; 12.b4 Ncxe5 (12...Ngxe5; 13.b5 Nxf3+; 14.Nxf3 Ne7 and White enjoyed a small advantage in Carlsson-Schiller, Postal 1983.) 13.Qxd7 Rxd7; 14.Bb2 Nxc4; 15.Nxc4 Bxc4; 16.Nxd4 with unclear complications in Boness-Schiller, Postal 1983. **10...Bg4; 11.Ndf3 f6!** This regains the initiative and undermines White's center. **12.exf6 gxf6; 13.Ne4 Qe6; 14.Qc2.** 14.Nxf6 Qxf6; 15.Bg5 is possible but Black gains the upper hand with 15...Qd6; 16.Bxd8 Qxd8; 17.Ng5 Bg7; 18.Bxc6 bxc6; 19.Qa4 Kb8 with strong pressure at e2.

14...Nb4; 15.Qa4 a6; 16.c5 Nc6. Black has a solid position, but the same cannot be said for White. **17.Nfd2 Bxe2; 18.Re1 d3; 19.Nc3 Bxc5; 20.Nb3 Bb6; 21.Bf1?** An attempt to chase my bishop out of the parish, but in fact it simply extends an invitation for my an all-out assault on the monarch. 21.Bxc6!? comes into consideration. **21...Nd4! 22.Nxd4 Rxd4; 23.b4 Rxh4!; 24.Nxe2.**

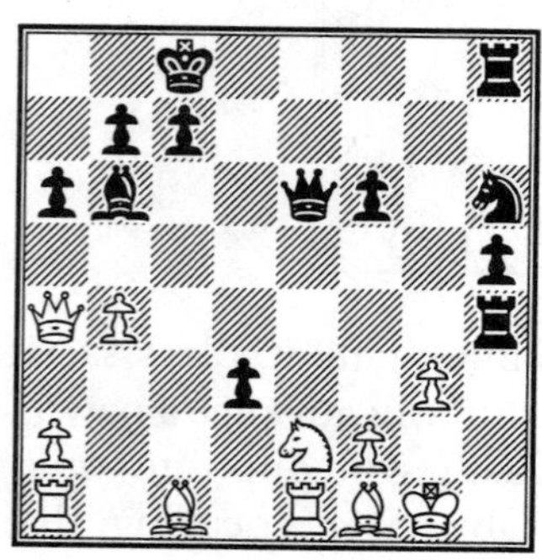

Now the game ends with a flourish! **24...Bxf2+!!; 25.Kxf2 Ng4+; 26.Kg1 Qb6+; 27.Nd4 Qxd4+; 28.Be3 Nxe3; 29.gxh4 Rg8+; 30.Kf2 Nd1+. Black won.**

SLAV DEFENSE

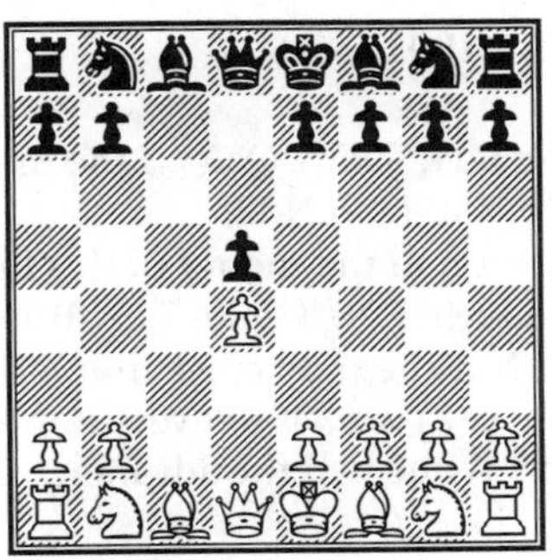

1.d4 d5
2.c4 c6

The full **Slav Defense** is an uncompromising opening, with a reputation for exciting chess–or a very dull draw. Black is ready to bring the bishop at c8 into the game at f5 or g4. There is also a direct threat–the capture of the pawn at c4 and subsequent support from a pawn at b5. This theme is seen in the main line of the Slav: 3.Nc3 Nf6; 4.Nf3 dxc4; 4.a4, where White eventually regains the pawn as in the Queen's Gambit Accepted.

The most serious drawback to the Slav is that after the boring 3.cxd5 cxd5; 4.Nf3 the game can be rather boring. White retains a minuscule advantage but the symmetry of the game, and the lack of weaknesses surrounding the king, limit any chances of excitement unless one side makes a serious error.

We begin our examination with a sharp gambit which White often avoids, by choosing 3.Nf3 rather than 3.Nc3.

WINAWER COUNTERGAMBIT

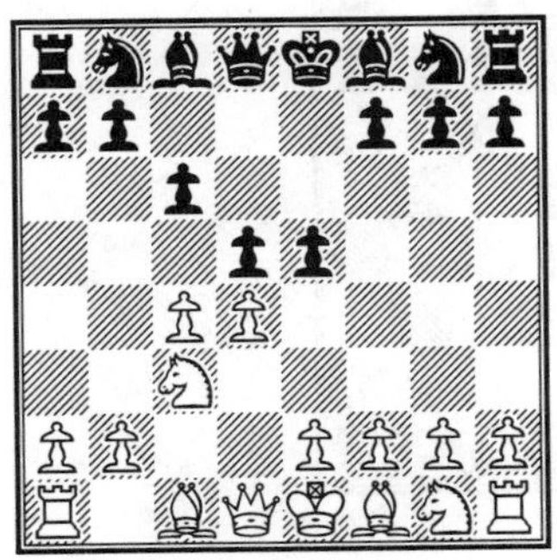

1.d4 d5
2.c4 c6
3.Nc3 e5

Winawer was a mediocre player, but his name has been attached to two very important openings, the Winawer Variation of the French Defense and this countergambit in the Slav. Here, Black gives up a pawn, usually temporarily, to obtain free piece play and restrict the enemy forces.

(168) MARSHALL - WINAWER [D10]

Monte Carlo, 1901

1.d4 d5; 2.c4 c6; 3.Nc3 e5; 4.cxd5. 4.dxe5 d4; 5.Ne4 Qa5+ is the most common line, and White has a choice of pieces to place at d2. 6.Nd2

(6.Bd2 Kasparov's choice led to an explosion in the theory of this line, not least because he managed to win so brilliantly. 6...Qxe5; 7.Ng3 Qd6; 7...Nf6 and 7...c5, are popular alternatives. 8.Nf3 Nf6; 9.Qc2 Be7. Not the only move, but a popular one. 10.0-0-0 0-0; 11.e3 dxe3; 12.fxe3! The weak pawn at e3 is not very important, but is in any case unavoidable. 12...Qc7; 13.Bc3 and White had the advantage in Kasparov-Nikolic, Manila Olympiad 1992.)

6...Nd7; 7.e6; 7.Ngf3 is the other option. 7...fxe6 8.g3. In return for the giving back the pawn, White disrupts Black's pawn structure. But White will have to exploit this quickly, as otherwise Black will develop and have a central pawnroller. 8...e5; 9.Bg2 Ngf6; 10.Ngf3 Be7; 11.0-0 Qc7; 12.Qc2 0-0; 13.b3 In Karpov-Bareyev, Linares 1992 White was able to aim a lot of firepower at d4, culminating in e2-e3.

4...cxd5; 5.e4. This is the most promising line for White. Fine attributes it to Alekhine, but clearly was not aware of this game, which gave the opening its name! **5...dxe4.** Other moves have failed to take root. 5...Bb4; 6.Nf3 Bxc3+; 7.bxc3 exd4; 8.Nxd4 dxe4; 9.Bb5+ Bd7; 10.Nf5 Qc7; 11.Qd4 Ne7; 12.Nxg7+ Kf8; 13.Ne6+ and Black resigned in Toth-Csaszar, Postal 1973. 5...exd4; 6.Qxd4 dxe4; 7.Qxd8+ Kxd8; 8.Bg5+ Be7; 9.0-0-0+ Bd7; 10.Nxe4 Bxg5+; 11.Nxg5 is better for White, despite the paucity of pieces. The Black king remains under attack and it is difficult for Black to get the minor pieces to useful posts and activate the rooks. White went on to win in Nei-Butnorius, USSR 1964.

6.d5?! We now know that the check at b5 is a better plan. 6.Bb5+ Bd7; 7.dxe5 Bb4 and now 8.Bxd7+ Qxd7; 9.Qxd7+ Nxd7; 10.f4 is interesting and awaits practical tests. **6...Nf6.** 6...f5 7.f3 exf3; 8.Nxf3 Bd6 is "of dubious value" according to Fine (1948). **7.Bg5.**

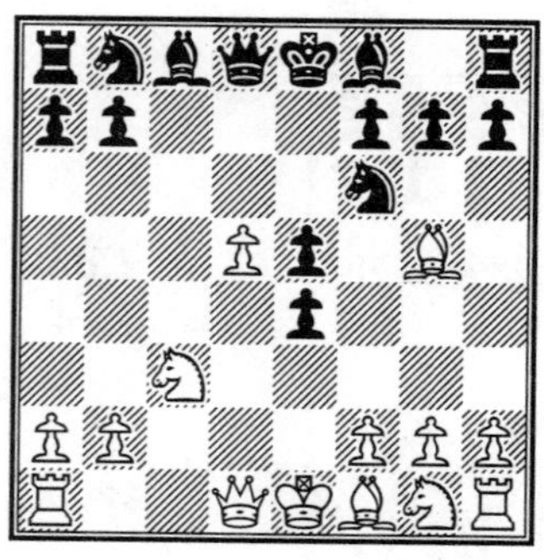

7...Qb6. 7...Nbd7 Messner-Schuster, Württenberg 1989, eventually won by Black at move 109 is a reasonable alternative. **8.Bxf6 gxf6.** Black's pawns make an ugly impression on the queenside, but are impressive in the center, and White's isolated d-pawn can become weak. **9.Bb5+ Bd7; 10.Bxd7+ Nxd7; 11.Nge2.** 11.Nxe4 Qxb2; 12.Rb1 Qxa2; 13.Rxb7 Qc4! and Black is clearly better. **11...f5; 12.Qa4 0-0-0!** The king will be safe enough on the queenside,. and Black's extra pawn is meaningful, even if there are two pairs of doubled pawns.

13.d6 Kb8; 14.Qc4 Nc5!; 15.0-0. 15.Qxf7 loses to 15...Nd3+. **15...Qxd6; 16.Qxf7 Qg6! 17.Qc4.** 17.Qxg6 hxg6 gives Black a tremendous pawn wedge and a clear advantage. **17...Rg8; 18.g3 Qe6! 19.Qxe6.** White must exchange queens, because otherwise Black advances the f-pawn to f3 and brings the queen around to mate at g2 via h3. But the endgame is hopeless.

19...Nxe6; 20.Rad1 Nd4; 21.Kg2 Bc5; 22.Na4 Be7; 23.Nac3 h5; 24.Nxd4 exd4; 25.Ne2 Bf6; 26.b3 Be5; 27.Rfe1 d3; 28.Ng1 h4; 29.Nh3 Rc8; 30.Rc1 hxg3; 31.Rxc8+ Rxc8; 32.hxg3 Rc2; 33.Nf4 Bd4; 34.Rf1 Bxf2; 35.Kh3 Rxa2; 36.Kh4 d2; 37.Rd1 Bd4. Black won.

SLAV-RETI HYBRID

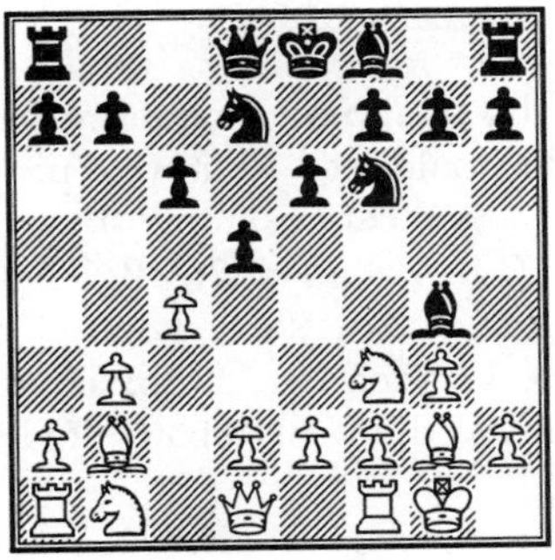

1.Nf3 d5
2.g3 Bg4
3.Bg2 Nd7
4.c4 e6
5.b3 c6
6.Bb2 Ngf6
7.0-0 (with d4)

This formation is a combination of the Slav Defense for Black with the Reti Opening for White, and will reach a true hybrid position when White plays d4. Neither of Whites fianchettoed bishops has great scope and the position is fairly harmless. Still, it is often seen when a strong player wants to avoid masses of theory and just play natural chess.

It is so innocuous that Black is sometimes tempted to transpose into it even with loss of time, but loss of time is the one thing Black cannot really afford. Still, even with a tempo less the position is solid, and it is easy to let the advantage go, as Hort almost does in our illustrative game.

(169) HORT - MALICH [D11]
Karlovy Vary, 1973

1.Nf3 d5; 2.g3 Bg4; 3.Bg2 Nd7; 4.c4 e6; 5.b3 c6. 6.Bb2 Ngf6; 7.0–0 Bc5. This is a serious waste of time, the sort of error one should avoid in all openings.

A more modest initiative is 7...Bd6, which has been seen in many games. Here is an example using a different move order: 1.c4 Nf6; 2.g3 c6; 3.Nf3 d5; 4.b3 Bg4; 5.Bg2 Nbd7; 6.Bb2 e6; 7.0-0 Bd6; 8.d3 0-0; 9.Nbd2 e5; 10.h3 Bh5; 11.e4 dxe4; 12.Nxe4 Nxe4; 13.dxe4 Qc7; 14.Qc2 f6; 15.Nh4 Rfd8; 16.Bf3 Bf7; 17.Nf5 Bf8 and Black had a solid position in Sher-Dautov, Geneva 1997.

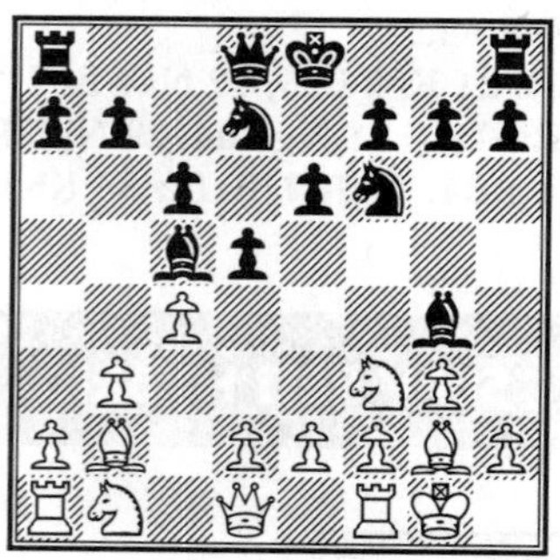

8.d4! White accepts the challenge with this tempo-winning move, which secures a lasting initiative. **8...Be7.** Retreating to d6 would lead to more typical positions, but Black does suffer from the loss of tempo. A recent example shows yet another transpositional path: 1.b3 d5; 2.Bb2 c6; 3.Nf3 Bg4; 4.g3 Nd7; 5.Bg2 Ngf6; 6.0-0 e6; 7.c4 Bd6; 8.d4 Qc7; 9.Nbd2 0-0; 10.Re1 Rfe8; 11.Rc1 Rac8; 12.a3 Qb8; 13.b4 e5; 14.cxd5 cxd5; 15.Rxc8 Qxc8; 16.dxe5 Nxe5; 17.Nxe5 Bxe5; 18.Bxe5 Rxe5; 19.Nf3 with a positional advantage for White thanks to the weak d-pawn, Odessky-Petrov, St. Petersburg 1996.

9.Nbd2 0–0; 10.Rc1. 10.h3 and 10.Ne1 are noteworthy alternatives suggested by Hort. **10...h6; 11.Ne1.** 11.Ne5 is more energetic, according to Taimanov. **11...Re8; 12.Nd3.** A preliminary 12.f3 Bh5 would have increased the force of this move, as the knight could then head for f4, for example 13.Nd3 Bd6; 14.Nf4 Bxf4; 15.gxf4 with advantage to White. **12...Bf5.**

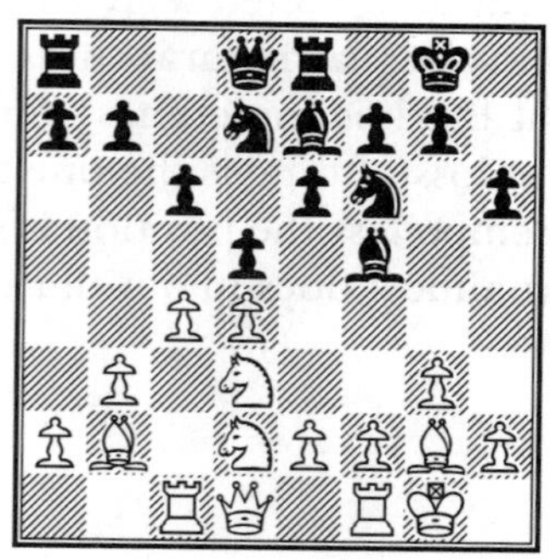

13.Nb1 Bd6; 14.Nc3. White has returned the gift of time presented by Black on his seventh turn. Black should now complete his development with 14...Qe7, leading to a balanced game. **14...Ne4?!; 15.Nxe4 dxe4; 16.Ne1 Qe7; 17.Nc2!** Perhaps Black overlooked the transfer of the knight to e3 when he initiated the central exchanges. **17...Bg6; 18.Qd2 Nf6; 19.Ne3 Red8; 20.Rfd1 Rd7; 21.Qc2.**

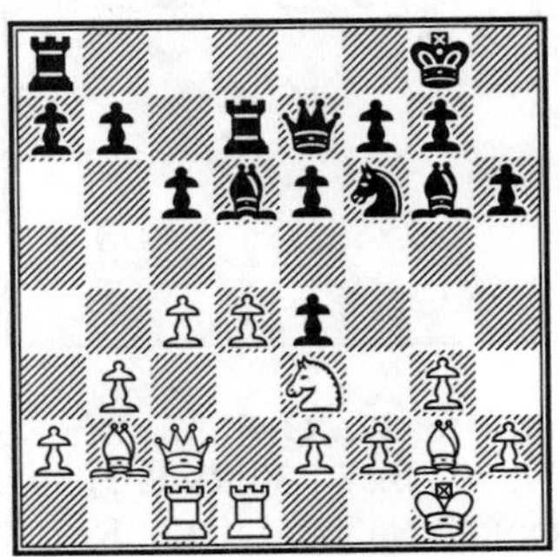

White's pieces are ideally placed. **21...Rad8; 22.Bh3!** Now that Black has locked in the d7-rook, this creates a powerful pin on the e6-pawn. **22...Ba3?** A gross positional blunder. 22...Nh7 allows 23.d5! as 23...Ng5; 24.Bg2 intending h2-h4 is clearly better for White. 22...b5 was perhaps best, so that on 23.cxb5 (23.d5! however, will secure a good game for White: 23...cxd5; 24.Bxf6 Qxf6; 25.cxd5 Rc7; 26.Qd2) 23...cxb5; 24.d5 Rc7. **23.c5! Bxb2; 24.Qxb2 Nh7; 25.Nc4.** Black's minor pieces are mere spectators. He must try to create some counterplay by advancing his e-pawn, but this will entail some structural weakness. **25...Ng5; 26.Bg2 f6; 27.Rd2 Nf7; 28.Rcd1 Rd5; 29.b4.**

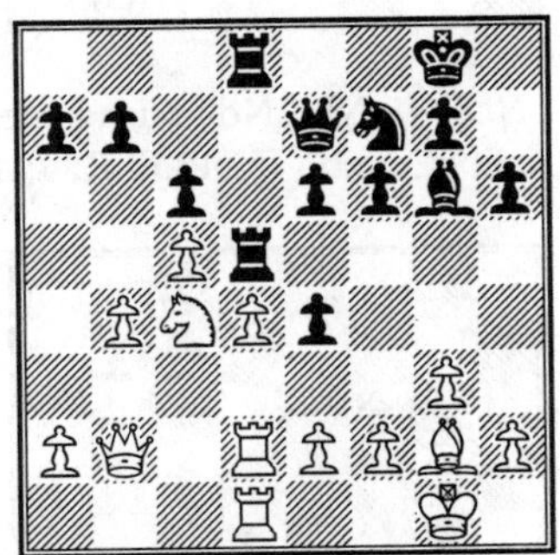

29...e5; 30.dxe5 Nxe5; 31.Nd6! White effectively disrupts the coordination of Black's pieces, maintaining his domination of the d-file. **31...Rxd2; 32.Rxd2 Nf7; 33.Qd4! Kf8; 34.h4! h5; 35.a4!** White is preparing for the inevitable decisive endgame. **35...b6; 36.a5 b5?**

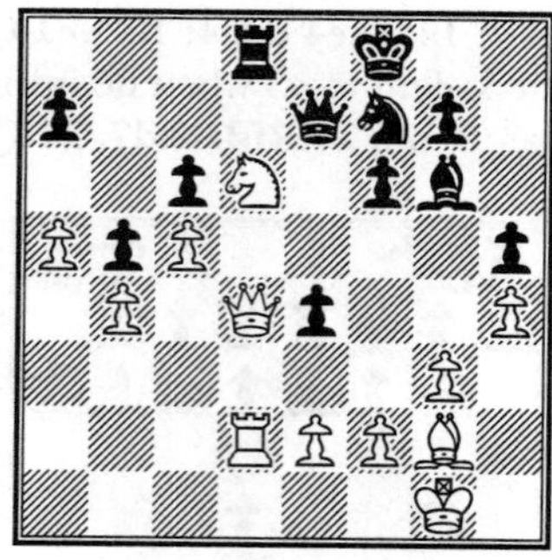

37.a6! The clamp is complete. **37...Qe6.** 37...Bf5 would have led to the brilliant combination 38.Nxf5!! Rxd4; 39.Nxe7! (39.Rxd4!?) 39...Rxd2 40.Nxc6 and now:

A) 40...Rd7; 41.Bxe4 Ne5; 42.Na5 and if 42...Ke7 (42...Rd4?!.

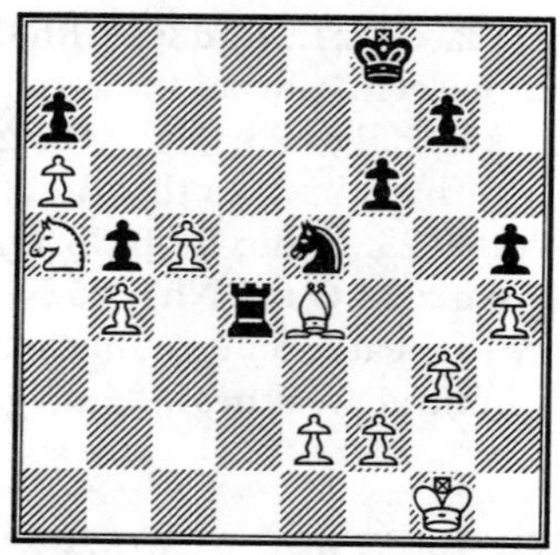

43.c6!) 43.c6 Rc7; 44.f4 Nc4; 45.Nb3 Nd4 with a clear advantage for White.

B) 40...Ra2; 41.Nxa7 Rxa6; 42.Nxb5 f5; 43.f3 Ra4; 44.c6 Rxb4.

45.c7 Rc4; 46.Bh3 Nd6; 47.Nxd6 Rxc7; 48.Nxf5 winning **38.Qe3! f5; 39.f3 Nxd6.** There is no choice now. **40.cxd6 Rd7.** 40...Rxd6 loses to 41.Qc5 **41.Kh2!** Ending all counterplay on the a7-g1 diagonal. **41...Kg8; 42.fxe4.**

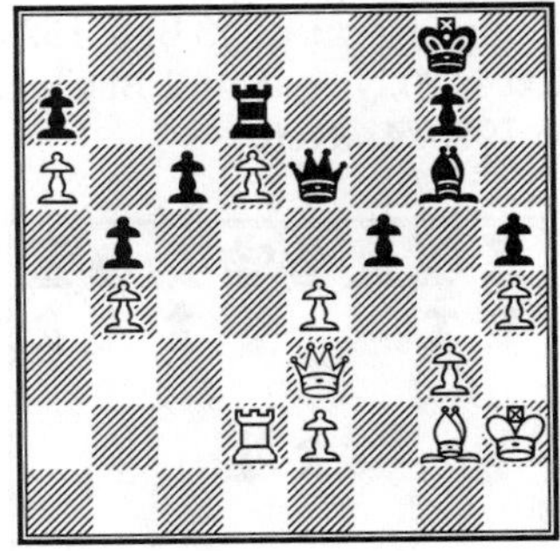

42...fxe4. 42...Rxd6; 43.Rxd6 Qxd6; 44.exf5 Bxf5; 45.Qxa7 wins. **43.Qc5 Qc4; 44.Bh3 Qxc5; 45.bxc5 Rd8; 46.d7 Bf7; 47.Rd6 Bd5; 48.Rxd5! White won.**

EXCHANGE VARIATION

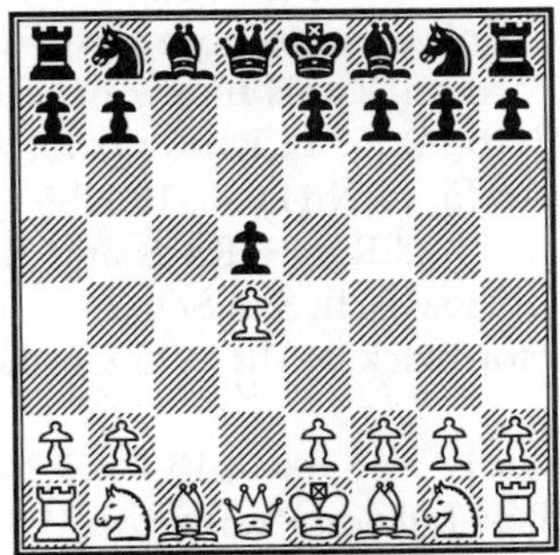

1.d4 d5
2.c4 c6
3.cxd5 cxd5

The **Exchange Variation** of the Slav has long annoyed players of the Black side, since it is very hard to effectively play with aggression in this rather sterile position. Indeed, Black can get into serious trouble if the symmetry is maintained for too long, or if care is not taken with regard to the weak square at c7. Nevertheless, it is not terribly difficult to equalize against the Exchange Variation. The problem is finding a way to win.

(170) MARSHALL - STOLTZ [D13]
Warsaw Olympiad, 1935

1.d4 d5; 2.c4 c6; 3.cxd5 cxd5; 4.Nc3. 4.Bf4 can lead to somewhat more interesting positions, but that does not mean that they favor White. 4...Nc6; 5.e3 Nf6; 6.Nc3 a6. This is a typical variation. By keeping enemy pieces off of b5, Black considerably eases the defense and can attend to development in comfort. 7.Bd3 Bg4; 8.Nge2 8.Nf3 and 8.f3 are also possible, but this is a very logical move. 8...e6; 9.Rc1 Be7; 10.0–0 0–0; 11.Na4 Nd7. Black guards the important c5-square. 12.f3 Bh5; 13.Qb3

Ra7. An awkward method of defending the pawn, but White's pieces are not coordinated and the discomfort is temporary. 14.Bg3 Bg6; 15.Nf4 Na5; 16.Qc3 b5; 17.Nxg6 hxg6; 18.b4 Nc4! 19.Bxc4 dxc4; 20.Nc5 a5 and Black had a queenside initiative in Kaidanov-Shabalov, Chicago 1993. **4...Nc6.**

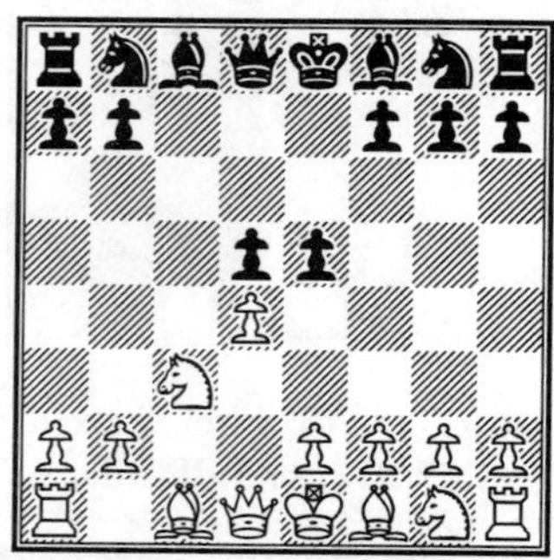

5.Nf3 Nf6; 6.Bf4. Here Black has tried many different plans, at least eight that I know of. But placing the queen at b6 is the most logical reaction to the evacuation of the queenside by the White bishop. **6...Qb6; 7.Na4.** 7.a3 Bf5; 8.Na4 Qd8; 9.e3 Ne4; 10.Bd3. White could try Ne5 here, but it doesn't seem to pose significant threats. 10...e6; 11.0–0 was agreed drawn in Dlugy-Portisch, Tunis Interzonal 1985.

7...Qa5+. 7...Qd8; 8.Rc1 Ne4; 9.a3 e6; 10.b4 Bd6; 11.Bxd6 Qxd6; 12.e3 Nxb4; 13.Nc5 Nc6; 14.Bd3 Nxc5; 15.dxc5 Qc7; 16.0–0 f5; 17.Nd4 0–0; 18.Nb5 Qe7; 19.Nd6 Ne5; 20.Qb3 b6; 21.Nxc8 Rfxc8; 22.cxb6 axb6; 23.Rxc8+ Rxc8 and Black's extra pawn was sufficient for a win. in Marshall-Nimzowitsch, San Sebastian 1912. **8.Bd2 Qd8** is a modern finesse which is even better for Black, as the White bishop does not belong on d2.

9.e3 e6; 10.Rc1 Bd6; 11.Bb5 Bd7; 12.0–0. 12.Nc5 Bxc5; 13.Rxc5 Ne4 is better, but Black still has at least an equal game, Velikov-Lukacs, Pamparovo 1981. **12...Ne4; 13.Nc5 Bxc5; 14.dxc5 0–0; 15.Bc3 Rc8; 16.a3 Ne5!** A wise decision to exchange minor pieces, after which the center can be occupied. **17.Bxd7 Nxf3+; 18.gxf3 Nxc3; 19.Rxc3 Qxd7; 20.Qd4.**

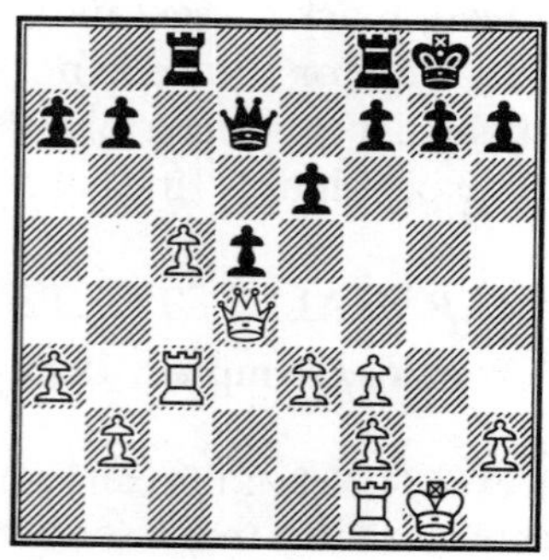

White seems to be ready to lock the center with f4, but Black has a surprise in store. **20...e5!** This pawn sacrifice allows Black to develop an attack against the White king. **21.Qxe5 Rc6; 22.e4 d4! 23.Rd3 Qh3; 24.Rxd4 Rg6+ 25.Qg3 f5!** Black is in no rush to grab the queen, which cannot be saved. **26.Rfd1 f4; 27.Qxg6 hxg6; 28.R1d3 g5; 29.e5 g4; 30.fxg4 f3** and White resigned. **Black won.**

GELLER GAMBIT

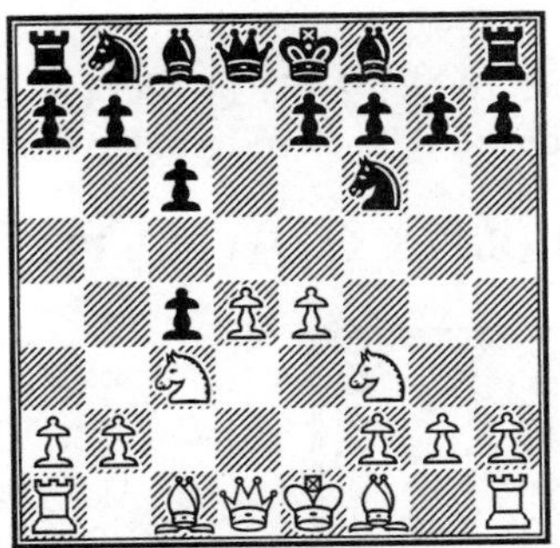

1.d4	**d5**
2.c4	**c6**
3.Nf3	**Nf6**
4.Nc3	**dxc4**
5.e4	

The **Geller Gambit** has become enormously popular and now has a vast body of theory supporting it. As with many variations of the Slav, White gives up the c-pawn for control of the center. This opening can also be reached via the Queen's Gambit Accepted (cf. 1.d4 d5; 2.c4 dxc4; 3.Nf3 Nf6; 4.Nc3 c6) and is equally popular there. Actually, the main ideas of the gambit were worked out by Tolush in 1947, but it is Geller who worked to establish the gambit as a respectable opening by playing it consistently and finding many improvements for White.

(171) GELLER - UNZICKER [D15]

Saltsjobaden Interzonal, 1952

1.d4 d5; 2.c4 c6; 3.Nf3 Nf6; 4.Nc3 dxc4; 5.e4 b5; 6.e5 Nd5; 7.a4 e6; 8.axb5.

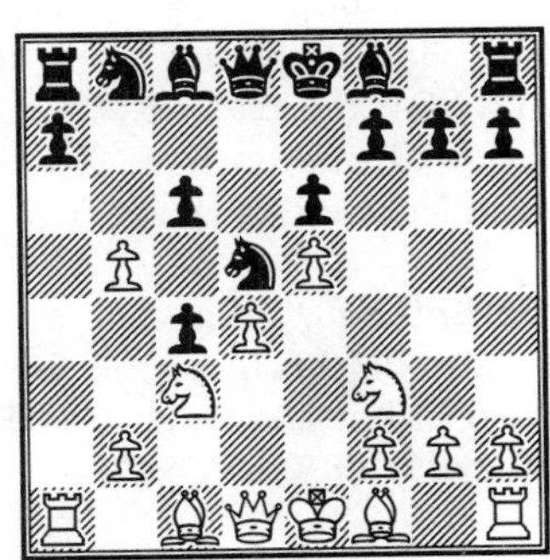

8.Be2 is a common alternative.

A) 8...Bb7; 9.0–0 (9.Bg5 Nxc3; 10.bxc3 Qc7; 11.0–0 h6; 12.Bh4 Nd7; 13.Nd2 Nb6; 14.Ne4 c5; 15.Bf3 cxd4; 16.Qxd4 Bxe4; 17.Qxe4 Nd5 was fine for Black in

Geller-Smyslov, Soviet Championship 1950.) 9...a6; 10.Ne4 Nd7; 11.Nfg5 Be7; 12.Bh5 0–0; 13.Qg4 Nc7 invited the piece sacrifice 14.Nxh7!? Kxh7; 15.Ng5+ Kg8 and after 16.Qh4 Bxg5; 17.Bxg5 f6; 18.Bg6 Rf7; 19.Qh7+ Kf8; 20.Ra3! Nd5; 21.Bh6. Black was barely able to survive 21...Ke7!; 22.Bxf7 Qh8; 23.Qxh8 Rxh8; 24.Bxg7 where fortunately for Black there was the resource 24...Rh7! yet after 25.Bxe6 Kxe6; 26.Bxf6 White had a material advantage. The continuation is interesting: 26...b4; 27.Rg3 c5; 28.dxc5 Nxc5; 29.f4 Nxf6; 30.Rg6! Ncd7; 31.exf6 Nxf6 and the game was eventually drawn in Geller-Smyslov, Budapest 1952.

B) 8...Nxc3; 9.bxc3 Na6?! is too passive: 10.Ng5 Nc7; 11.Bh5 g6; 12.Qf3 Qd7; 13.axb5 gxh5; 14.bxc6 Qe7; 15.Ne4 f5; 16.Nd6+ and Black resigned in Geller-Grozdov, Russia 1949.

8...Nxc3; 9.bxc3 cxb5; 10.Ng5 Bb7; 11.Qh5 g6; 12.Qg4 Be7; 13.Be2 Nd7.

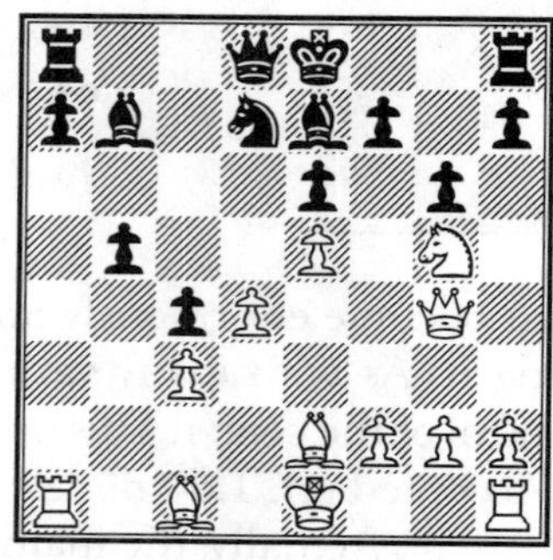

This was all established theory (after all, the moves are very logical) back in the 1950s. There are other ways to play the position, for example 13...a5; 14.0-0 a4, as in Pukkila-Aaltio, Espoo 1996. The advance of the h-pawn used to be almost obligatory, but it was eventually refuted. **14.Bf3.** A novelty, prepared for this game on the recommendation of several theoreticians. 14.h4? h5; 15.Qg3 Nb6; 16.0–0 a5!; 17.Rb1

(17.d5 was tried by Petrosian against Smyslov in the same tournament, during the same round! Petrosian had played more slowly, and after seeing what happened to Geller in the game against Flohr, decided to try another plan. Smyslov cooperated by capturing at d5 with the knight, conceding the e4 square and eventually losing. But had he taken with the bishop, Black would have had a fine game.)

17...b4; 18.f4 Qd7; 19.Ra1 b3; 20.f5 gxf5; 21.Nh3 a4; 22.Qg7 0–0–0 23.Bg5 a3; 24.Qxf7 Bxg5; 25.Nxg5 Qxf7; 26.Nxf7 a2; 27.Nxd8 Kxd8 and White's game was hopeless in Geller-Flohr, Soviet Championship 1951. 14.Rb1 Bd5; 15.Rxb4 Nb6; 16.0-0 a5 gave Black a powerful passed pawn in Trifunovic-Truran, British Team Championship 1997.

14...Qc7; 15.Ne4 Nb6; 16.Bh6 Rg8? What can one say about such a move? Better to sacrifice something than to do this to a rook! 16...Nd5; 17.Bg5 0–0; 18.Bxe7 Qxe7; 19.Nf6+ Kg7 is precarious, but about the best Black can hope for. **17.Bg5 Bxe4; 18.Bxe4 Nd5; 19.Bxd5 exd5; 20.Bxe7 Qxe7.**

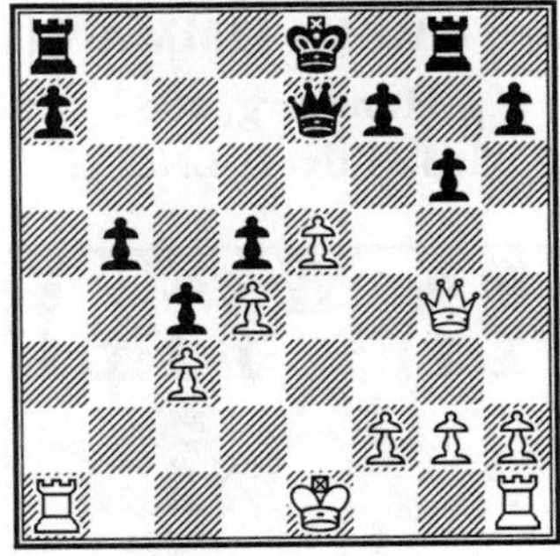

White has a tremendous advantage, because his rooks can more effectively exploit the open lines on the queenside. In addition, the Black king has no prospect of a secure home. **21.0–0 Kf8.** When the king can't hitch a ride to the kingside via castling, he has to walk! **22.Rfb1 a6; 23.Qf3.** 23.Rxb5 axb5; 24.Rxa8+ Kg7 would be quite difficult to win for White. Instead, Geller keeps piling on the pressure, and his opponent goes wrong immediately.

23...Qe6? 23...Kg7; 24.Qxd5 Qe6 would have been better, inviting endgames which can be held. White would have to retreat the queen and continue to play with heavy pieces. **24.Qf6! Qc8.** 24...Qxf6; 25.exf6 g5; 26.Rxb5 Rg6; 27.Rxa6!! is not the way Black wants to end the game! **25.f4 Qb7; 26.Ra5 Ke8; 27.Rba1.** Black could resign here, but tries one last desperate plan. **27...b4; 28.cxb4 Qxb4; 29.Rxd5! Qb7; 30.e6** and now it was time to put the pieces back in the box. **White won.**

CZECH VARIATION

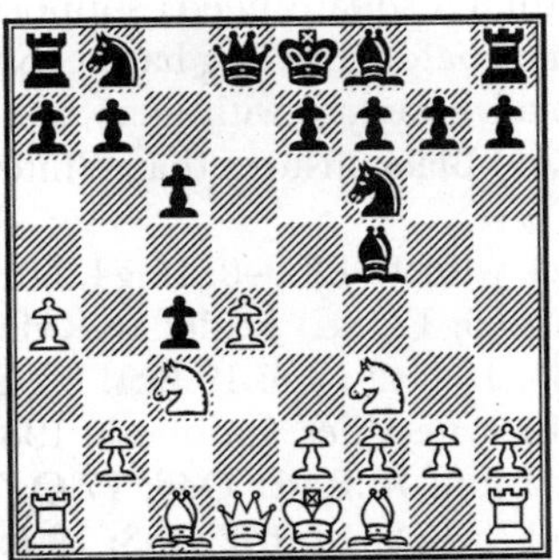

1.d4	**d5**
2.c4	**c6**
3.Nf3	**Nf6**
4.Nc3	**dxc4**
5.a4	**Bf5**

This is the main line of the Slav. White secures the b5-square so that the pawn at c4 can be captured later, after the e-pawn advances. White can also play Ne5 and capture the pawn with the knight. Black's position is fairly solid, but White can act in the center and also aim at the weak pawn at b7 which no longer has the support of a bishop.

(172) TORRE - TIMMAN [D17]

Hamburg, 1982

1.d4 Nf6; 2.Nf3 d5; 3.c4 dxc4; 4.Nc3 c6; 5.a4 Bf5; 6.Ne5.

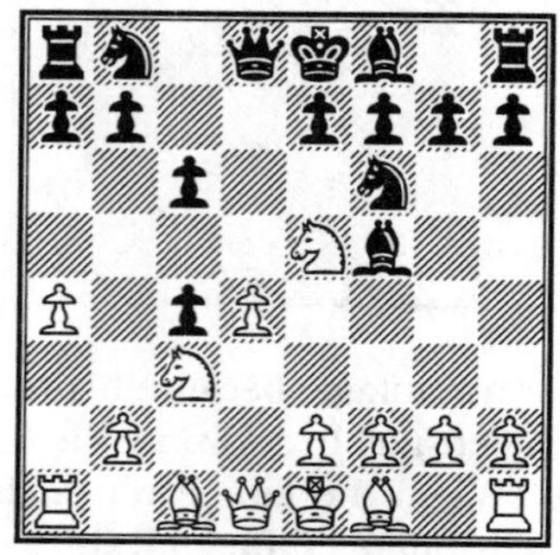

This was first seen in the 1929 match between Alekhine and Bogoljubow, and remains a very popular choice. **6...Nbd7.** 6...Na6; 7.e3 Nb4; 8.Bxc4 e6; 9.0–0 is bit better for White, Smejkal-Torre, Thessaloniki Olympiad 1984. **7.Nxc4 Qc7!** This move helps to control the important dark squares in the center. Black will try to get in an early ...e5. White usually responds by taking over the light squares, and exchanging pieces on the dark squares so that Black cannot maintain control of them.

8.g3. 8.Bg5 e5; 9.Bxf6 gxf6; 10.e3 is now considered about even, on the basis of a game Timman-Boouwmeester, Busum 1982. Timman has made great contributions to the Slav on both sides of the board! **8...e5; 9.dxe5 Nxe5; 10.Bf4 Rd8.** 10...Nfd7; 11.Bg2 Rd8; 12.Qc2 f6; 13.0–0 Be6; 14.Ne4 exploits the weakness of d6, but White is only a little better, Euwe-Alekhine, World Championship (1st match game) 1937.

11.Qc1 Bd6. This is the best move, even though it concedes the bishop pair. Black must make an effort to castle, and the e5 square needs support. **12.Nxd6+ Qxd6; 13.Bg2 0–0.** Retreating the queen to e7 before castling has become a normal continuation. **14.0–0.** White also obtains a small advantage with 14.a5, as in Tukmakov-Agzamov, Soviet Championship 1983. **14...a5!** Black insures that White will not advance the pawn to a5 now.

15.Qe3. White can also launch an attack with 15.h3 0–0; 16.g4, but that entails a bit of risk. **15...Nfd7.** 15...Nc4; 16.Bxd6 Nxe3; 17.fxe3 Rxd6; 18.Rxf5 and White wins. 15...Nfg4; 16.Qb6 Qb4; 17.Qxb4 axb4; 18.Na2 Ng6; 19.Bc1! b3; 20.Nc3 Bc2; 21.a5 Ra8; 22.Ra4 was better for White in Browne-Miles, Indonesia 1982. 1982 was a very important year in the life of this variation! **16.Rad1 Qe6; 17.Qa7.** The invasion of the queenside is typical of this line. **17...Bc2; 18.Rd2 Qb3; 19.Rc1 Bf5.**

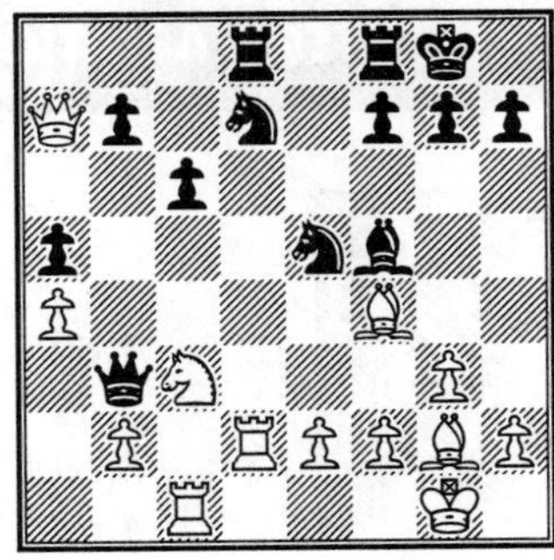

This is a critical position. White must play accurately in order to preserve any hope of an advantage. **20.Bxe5?!** 20.Ne4! Bxe4; 21.Bxe4 Qxa4; 22.Bf5 maintains the pressure, and White has compensation for the pawn, Gruenberg-Meduna, Sochi 1983. **20...Nxe5; 21.Rxd8 Rxd8; 22.Qxa5 Re8; 23.Nd1.** White hangs on to the pawn. Looking at the position, it is hard to believe that the Black queen will get to e1! **23...Bg4; 24.Bf1 f6; 25.Qc7.** Better was 25.Ne3, though Black still has the better prospects. **25...Qb4; 26.a5 Qe1; 27.Rb1.**

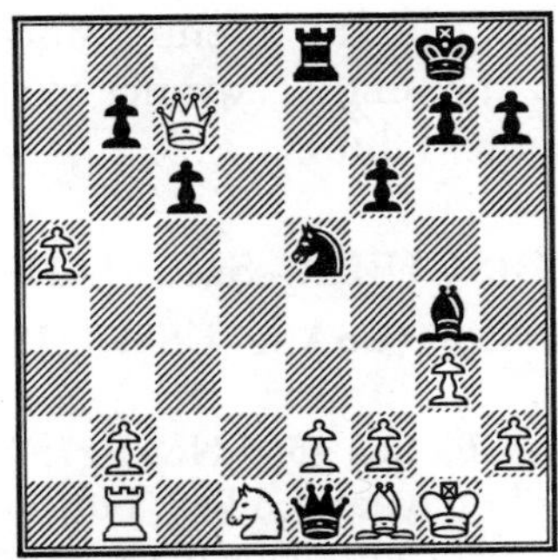

Now we have a big finish! **27...Nf3+!!; 28.Kg2 Qxf1+!!** and White resigned because of **29.Kxf1 Bh3#. Black won.**

SCHLECHTER VARIATION

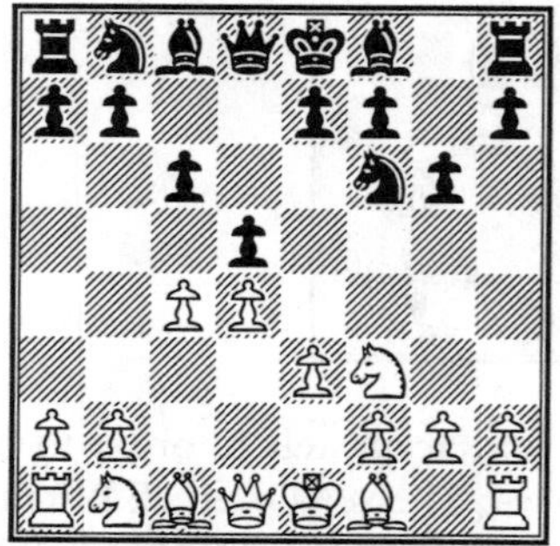

1.d4	**d5**
2.c4	**c6**
3.Nf3	**Nf6**
4.e3	**g6**

This is the **Schlechter Variation** of the Slav, a favorite with Smyslov. Black's strategy is similar to that of the Gruenfeld Defense. The White bishop at c1 is blocked by the pawn at e3, which it makes it harder to take advantage of any weakening of the dark squares on Black's kingside. Still, White has been able to obtain some advantage in the opening since Black's pawn at c6 often finds itself in the way, and an eventual advance to c5 represents a loss of time by comparison with Gruenfeld lines.

(173) BISGUIER - SMYSLOV [D94]
Moscow (USA vs. USSR), 1955

1.d4 d5; 2.c4 c6; 3.Nf3 Nf6; 4.e3 g6; 5.Nc3 Bg7; 6.Bd3. White has many tries here, including 6.Qb3, 6.Bd2, 6.b4 and 6.Be2, but the text remains the favorite. Since White always has the goal of advancing to e4 in the Closed Game, the position of the bishop at d3 is most logical.

6...0–0; 7.0–0. If White stations the queen at c2, then Black has counterplay on the queenside: 7.Qc2 Na6!; 8.a3 Nc7; 9.0–0 Be6; 10.cxd5 Ncxd5; 11.h3 Nxc3; 12.bxc3 c5 and Black can be fully satisfied with the position, which was reached in Bogoljubow-Alekhine, Vilnius 1912. **7...Bg4.**

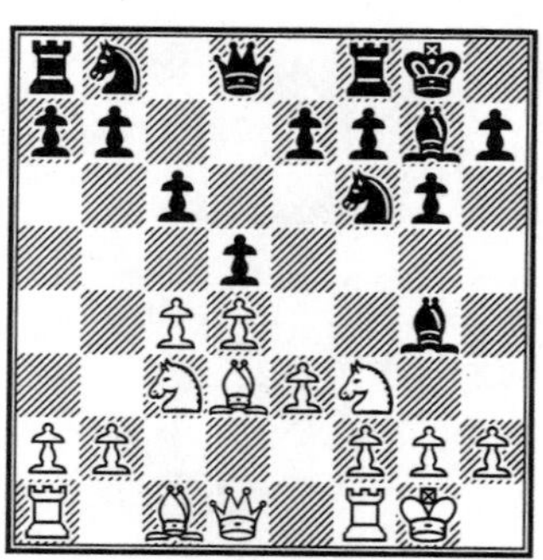

Smyslov's patent, introduced in this very game! 7...Bf5 is not good, despite the lock on the e4-square. 8.Bxf5 gxf5; 9.cxd5 cxd5; 10.Qb3 b6; 11.Bd2 Nc6; 12.Rfc1 Rc8; 13.Rc2 Qd7; 14.Rac1 and White had a strong initiative in Tarjan-Shamkovich, Lone Pine 1981.

8.h3 Bxf3; 9.Qxf3 e6. Although Black has given up the bishop pair, the position is very solid and White has no way of providing the bishop at c1 with an effective role in the game. There is another plan for Black, which Smyslov demonstrated over three decades later. 9...Qd6; 10.Rd1 Nbd7; 11.Qe2 e5; 12.dxe5 Qxe5; 13.cxd5 cxd5; 14.Bc2 Nc5 and in Hansen-Smyslov, Rome 1988, Black had enough piece activity to compensate for the isolated pawn.

10.Rd1 Nbd7; 11.e4. Timing is everything when it comes to the e4 advance in the Closed Games. Here it is premature, and 11.b3 is to be preferred. 11.Bf1 Re8; 12.b3 a6; 13.Bb2 e5! was fine for Black in Panno-Smyslov, Mar del Plata 1962. 11.b4 dxc4; 12.Bxc4 Nb6; 13.Bb3 Nbd5 is also quite nice for Black, as in Korchnoi-Smyslov, USSR 1967. 11.b3 Re8; 12.Bb2 (12.Bf1 e5 is another variation on the same theme, seen in Ribli-Smyslov from their 1983 World Championship Semifinal match.) 12...Qe7; 13.Rac1 (13.Qe2 dxc4; 14.Bxc4 Nd5; 15.Rac1 Nxc3; 16.Bxc3 Nb6 and here Petrosian and Smyslov agreed to a draw in the 1995 Soviet Championship.) 13...e5 is fully playable for Black, as in Bondarevsky-Smyslov, USSR 1951.

11...e5! An excellent counter-thrust. One would think that players of the White pieces would not give Smyslov a chance to repeat, but he has scored a lot of points as Black. **12.dxe5.** 12.exd5 exd4; 13.dxc6 (13.Ne4 Ne5; 14.Nxf6+ Bxf6 was better for Black in Simagin-Smyslov, Chigorin Memorial 1951.) 13...Ne5; 14.Qe2 Nxd3; 15.Rxd3 bxc6; 16.Bg5 Qa5; 17.Bxf6 Bxf6; 18.Ne4 Bg7 was better for Black in Polugayevsky-Smyslov, Moscow 1960. **12...Nxe5; 13.Qe2 d4; 14.Bc2 Nfd7; 15.Na4 Qa5; 16.Bd2.**

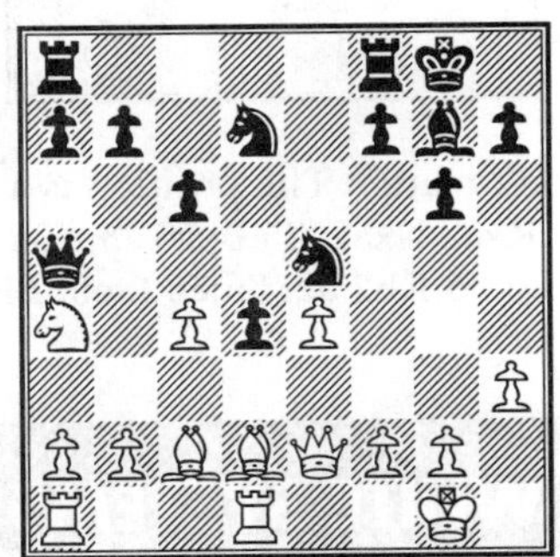

Now Smyslov exploits the clustered White formation with a bold advance. **16...d3!; 17.Bxa5?** 17.Qe3 Qa6; 18.Bb3 b5; 19.cxb5 cxb5; 20.Nc5 Nxc5; 21.Qxc5 Rac8 gives Black a lot of pressure. 17.Qxd3 Qxa4!; 18.Bxa4 Nxd3 and White remains a piece ahead. 17.Qf1 is best, but Black still enjoys a huge advantage. 17...Qa6; 18.Bb3 b5; 19.cxb5 cxb5; 20.Nc3 Nb6 and c4 beckons. **17...dxe2; 18.Re1 Nxc4; 19.Bc3 b5; 20.Bb3** A good move, according to Smyslov, because Bisguier plays vigorously. **20...Bxc3; 21.Nxc3.** 21.bxc3 Nd2; 22.Nb2 Nxe4; 23.Rxe2 Nxc3; 24.Re7 Nc5 and Black will win without difficulty. **21...Nxb2; 22.Rxe2 Nd3.**

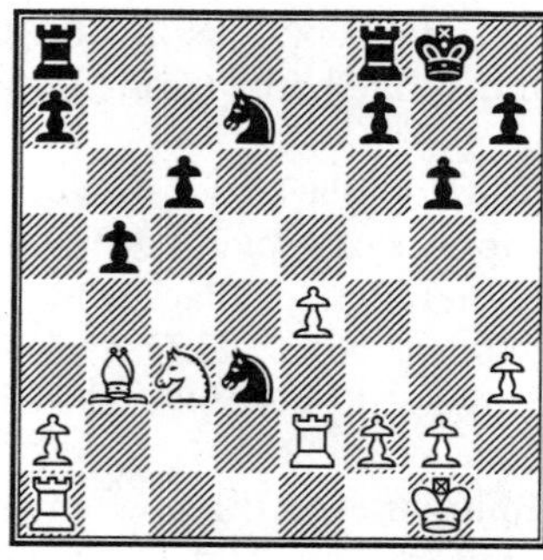

Black's extra pawn and queenside majority give Smyslov all he needs to bring home the point. **23.Rd1 N7c5; 24.Red2 Nb4; 25.f4 a5!** The march of the a-pawn brings home the point. **26.e5 a4; 27.Bc2 a3; 28.Be4 Na4; 29.Rc1 Rfd8; 30.Rxd8+ Rxd8; 31.Nxa4 bxa4.**

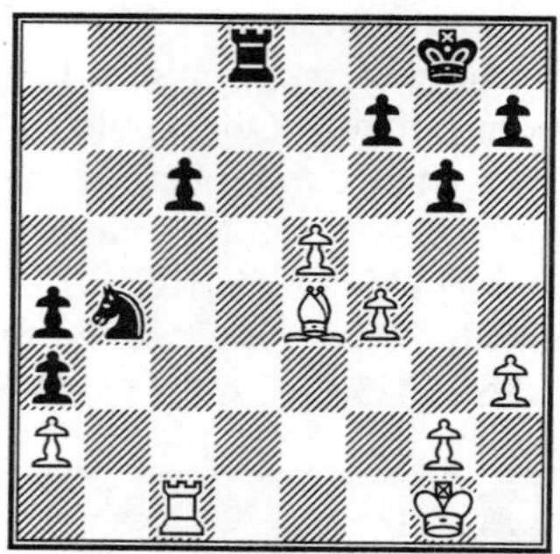

The doubled pawns don't matter. The position is a technical win. **32.Rc3 Rd2; 33.Bxc6.** 33.Rxa3 Rxa2; 34.Rxa2 Nxa2; 35.Bxc6 a3; 36.Bd5 Nc3 and White can give up. **33...Rxa2; 34.Bxa4 Ra1+; 35.Kh2 a2; 36.e6 fxe6. Black won.**

WHITE SYSTEMS

Sometimes White does not worry about move-by-move play in the opening, but instead chooses to simply set out the pieces in a particular configuration, concentrating more on general principles than on precise knowledge.

This strategy often works in amateur games, but at professional levels either the opening proves ineffective, being too easy to defend, as in the case of the Colle System, or turns into a major opening with a mass of theory, as has been seen in the Trompovsky attack, championed especially by British Grandmaster Julian Hodgson with a lot of support from his American colleague and competitor Joel Benjamin.

TROMPOVSKY ATTACK

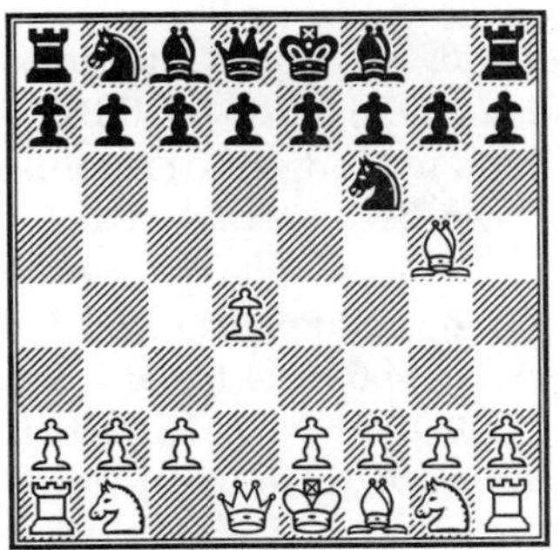

1.d4 Nf6
2.Bg5

This is known as the **Trompovsky Attack**, but British Grandmaster Julian Hodgson is the greatest exponent of the White side in the history of the variation. He has virtually single-handedly elevated what was once a sideline into a major opening which is seen at all levels of play. In America, 1997 U.S. Champion Joel Benjamin has taken up the cause.

Anyone who plays the Indian Defense by meeting 1.d4 with 1.Nf6 had best be prepared to do battle with this aggressive approach! White's idea is straightforward: a threat to capture the knight at f6 and fracture Black's pawn structure. It used to be thought that 2...Ne4 gave Black a good game, but Hodgson has put paid to that idea. In my opinion, the only truly promising defense is the one seen in this game, though Black does not manage to solve the opening problems.

(174) HODGSON - GRANDA ZUNIGA [A45]

Amsterdam (Donner Memorial), 1996

1.d4 Nf6; 2.Bg5 e6. 2...c5 is a common alternative. 3.Bxf6 gxf6; 4.d5 Qb6; 5.Qc1 f5 (5...Bh6; 6.e3 f5; 7.Ne2 d6; 8.c4 Nd7; 9.f4 Nf6; 10.Nec3 Bd7; 11.Bd3 e6; 12.0–0 0–0–0 led to a messy position in the clash of Trompovians Hodgson-Benjamin, New York (Marshall Chess Club) 1995.) 6.c4 Bg7; 7.Nc3 Qb4; 8.e3 d6; 9.f4!? Nd7; 10.Nf3 Nb6; 11.Nd2 Bd7; 12.Bd3 Bxc3; 13.bxc3 Qa5; 14.a4! Nxa4; 15.Qc2 Qxc3; 16.Rxa4 Qxc2; 17.Bxc2 Bxa4; 18.Bxa4+ Kd8; 19.Kf2 e6; 20.e4! allowed White to develop a strong attack in Hodgson-Schlosser, Horgen 1994. 2...Ne4 is the most confrontational move, and it is often seen.

A) 3.h4 is the wildest line, and Hodgson still plays it from time to time, though he also chooses somewhat quieter variations. 3...d5 (3...c5; 4.d5 g6; 5.Qd3 Nxg5; 6.Qc3 f6; 7.hxg5 Bg7; 8.Nd2 d6; 9.gxf6 exf6; 10.Qg3 0–0; 11.Qh4 h6; 12.Qg3 g5; 13.f4 and White was able to target the kingside weaknesses in Hodgson-Gufeld, London (King's Head) 1995.) 4.Nd2 Bf5; 5.e3 Nxd2; 6.Qxd2 Nd7; 7.Nf3 h6; 8.Bf4 e6; 9.Ne5 Bd6; 10.h5 Nxe5; 11.Bxe5 0–0; 12.Bxd6 Qxd6; 13.Bd3 Bxd3; 14.cxd3 led to an eventual draw in Hodgson-Tukmakov, Bern 1995.

B) 3.Bf4 is the positional approach. Black has a number of plans here, with the conservative approach of establishing a central pawn with ...d5 or the full court press with ...c5.

B1) 3...d5; 4.e3 e6 (4...Bf5; 5.f3 Nf6; 6.g4 Bg6; 7.h4 h5; 8.g5 Nfd7; 9.Nc3 c6; 10.Bd3 Bxd3; 11.Qxd3 g6; 12.e4 e6 and it is not easy for White to exploit Black's dark-square holes, Hodgson-Nunn, Bundesliga 1995.) 5.Bd3 b6; 6.Bxe4 dxe4; 7.Nc3 Bb4; 8.Qg4 0–0; 9.Qg3 Bxc3+; 10.bxc3 Nc6! and in Hodgson-Yermolinsky, Hastings 1995. White did not dare to capture the c-pawn because of 11.Bxc7 Qd5; 12.Qd6 Qc4; 13.Qa3 Ba6! with a tremendous attack.

B2) 3...c5. White can choose between the solid plans with e3 and the more ambitious ones with f3. 4.f3 Qa5+ (4...Nf6; 5.dxc5 b6; 6.e4 bxc5; 7.Nc3 Nc6; 8.Bc4 g6; 9.Nb5 d6; 10.e5 dxe5; 11.Qxd8+ Kxd8; 12.0–0–0+ Nd7; 13.Be3 a6; 14.Nc3 e6; 15.Ne4 gave White some compensation for the pawn in Hodgson-Shirov, Groningen 1996.) 5.c3 Nf6; 6.Nd2 cxd4; 7.Nb3 Qb6; 8.cxd4 d5 (8...e6 is the most common continuation, for example 9.Bd2 Nc6; 10.e3 Bb4; 11.Ne2 Bxd2+; 12.Qxd2 0–0 and the position posed problems for each of the light-squared bishops in Hodgson-Kengis, Bern 1995. 8...Nc6!?; 9.e4 e5; 10.dxe5 Bb4+; 11.Ke2 Nxe5 looked absolutely awful for White in Hodgson-Gelfand, Groningen 1996 and Black went on to win. I asked Julian about this position, and he admitted that it wasn't quite what he had in mind for White. We'll have to wait for future games to see more on 8...Nc6.) 9.e3 Nc6; 10.Ne2 e6; 11.Nc3 a6; 12.Bd3 Be7; 13.Bg5 provided White with an initiative in Hodgson-P.Cramling, Bern 1995.

3.e4 h6.

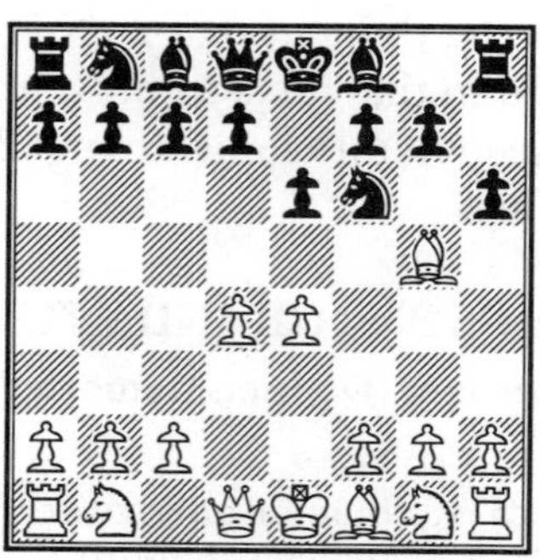

4.Bxf6 Qxf6. White has given up the bishop pair but has complete control of the center. **5.Nc3 Bb4.** 5...d6; 6.Qd2 g5; 7.0–0–0 Bg7; 8.g3 Nc6; 9.Bb5 Bd7; 10.Nge2 a6; 11.Bxc6 Bxc6; 12.f4 0–0–0; 13.Rhf1 and despite the bishop pair, Black seems to be suffering, because White's huge center keeps the bishops from gaining any scope, Hodgson-Gabriel, Switzerland (Horgen) 1995.

6.Qd2 d6. 6...c5; 7.a3 Bxc3; (7...cxd4; 8.axb4 dxc3; 9.bxc3 0–0; 10.Nf3 Nc6; 11.b5 Ne5; 12.Nxe5 Qxe5; 13.Qd4 Qxd4; 14.cxd4 d5; 15.exd5 exd5 gave White the better endgame in Hodgson-Pritchett, London 1996.) 8.bxc3 d6; 9.Nf3 0–0; 10.Be2 Nc6; 11.0–0 e5; 12.dxc5 dxc5; 13.Qe3 b6; 14.Bc4 Bg4 was drawn in Hodgson-De Firmian, Amsterdam (Donner) 1996. **7.a3 Ba5; 8.f4.** Now Black must do something to gain some counterplay, and now vigorous kingside action is called for.

8...g5!; 9.Nh3. 9.fxg5 hxg5 is better for Black, who has strong pressure on the h-file and control of f4. **9...gxf4; 10.Nxf4 c6?** Over optimistic. The correct move is to simply retreat the bishop. 10...Bb6; 11.0–0–0. This allows Black to get a good game, but after the better 11.Rd1 Black has no real problems, according to Hodgson. 11...Bxd4! and now White has nothing better than 12.Nfd5 exd5; 13.Qxd4 Qxd4; 14.Rxd4 Nc6; 15.Rxd5 Ne5 and Hodgson notes that the endgame is better for Black. **11.Bc4 d5; 12.e5 Qg5; 13.Be2.** White should have played b4 first, since now Black gets some counterplay.

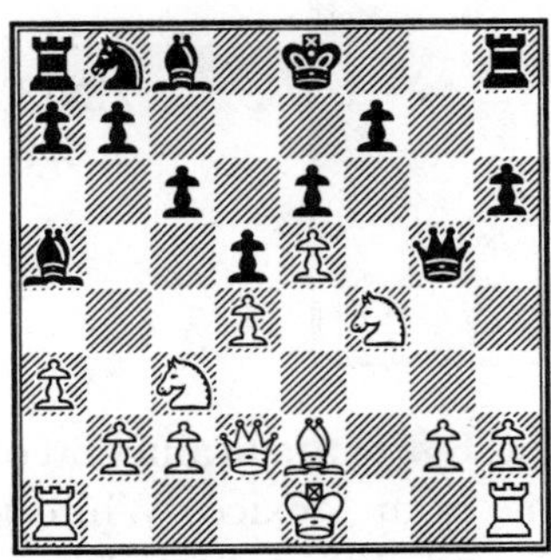

13...c5!; 14.b4 cxd4; 15.Nb5 Bb6; 16.Nd6+ Ke7. The Black king seems to be safe here, and the pawn at e5 is very weak. **17.Nxf7!?** Hodgson, realizing that White's position is desperate, decides to go for broke, and sacrifices his only active piece to expose the enemy king. **17...Kxf7; 18.Bh5+ Kg8; 19.0–0 Rh7; 20.Rf3 Rg7.** Black is erecting a defensive barrier, but pawns work better than pieces, and it is hard to bring the queenside forces to the kingside. **21.Raf1 Nd7.** 21...Nc6 allows the brilliant 22.Ng6 "when a white rook is landing on f8 with a huge, great thump!" as Hodgson puts it. **22.Rg3 d3+; 23.Kh1.**

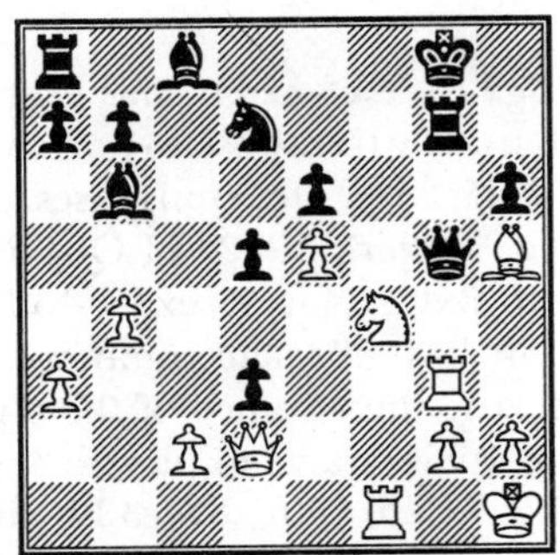

Here Granda Zuniga cracks under the pressure. **23...Qf5?** 23...Qxe5; 24.Bf7+ Kxf7; 25.Nh5+ Ke7; 26.Nxg7 and White is better, but the prognosis for Black's survival is not so dim. **24.Bg6! Qf8.** 24...Qxe5? comes too late now: 25.Nh5 Qe2; 26.Qf4 and the Black gravediggers can get to work. **25.Qxd3!** Granda Zuniga had simply overlooked this resource. **25...Nxe5; 26.Bh7+ Kh8; 27.Ng6+ Nxg6; 28.Bxg6 Qg8; 29.Rf6!** It is all over now. Black's pieces are just too far away. **29...Bd8; 30.Qe3 Bxf6; 31.Qxh6+ Rh7; 32.Bxh7 Bg7; 33.Qh5 Qf8; 34.Bd3+** and Black resigned because of **34...Kg8.** 34...Bh6; 35.Rg6 **35.Qh7+ Kf7; 36.Rf3+.** The notes to this game are based on Hodgson's excellent book *Attack with GM Julian Hodgson.* **White won.**

TORRE ATTACK

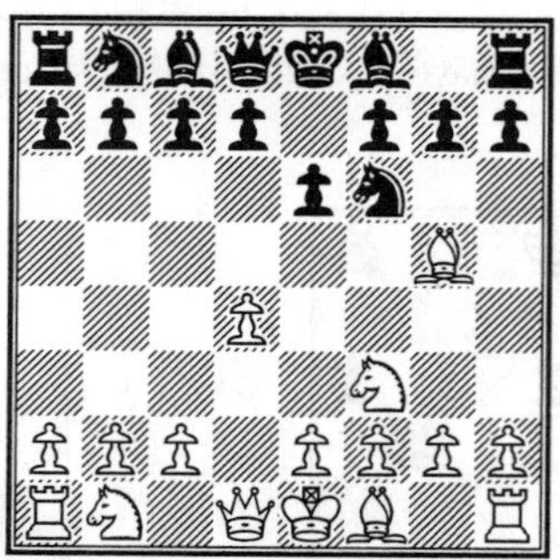

1.d4 Nf6
2.Nf3 e6
3.Bg5

The plan of d4, Nf3 and Bg5 is the brainchild of Carlos Torre, one of the few great players to come from Mexico. White will develop calmly, with kingside castling after e3 and Bd3, followed by c3, Nbd2 and eventually, when the time is right, e4. Black must take care not to allow White to slowly overwhelm the center. The Torre has been used by most of the top champions at some time or another. It is easy to play and often serves as a backup opening to be used when the first line of attack has just suffered a theoretical or practical reversal.

(175) TORRE - LASKER [A46]

Moscow, 1925

1.d4 Nf6; 2.Nf3 e6; 3.Bg5 c5; 4.e3 cxd4. This exchange may be thought to be premature, but in fact it will usually transpose to normal lines. **5.exd4 Be7.** 5...Qb6; 6.Nbd2 Qxb2; 7.Bd3 Qc3; 7...d5; 8.0-0 Qc3 transposes. 8.0-0 d5; 9.Rb1 Be7; 10.Rb3 Qc7, as in Hoi-Shamkovich, Esbjerg 1982. 11.Qb1 Nc6; 12.c4 is suggested by Shamkovich. 12...h6; 13.Bxf6 Bxf6; 14.cxd5 exd5; 15.Re1+ would seem to be the critical line. I think that White has sufficient compensation here.

5...b6 is interesting, because the advance of the d-pawn may not work as well here. 6.a3 is a useful move if White wants to play Nc3, since this deprives Black of ...Bb4 possibilities. (6.d5?! h6; 7.Bxf6 Qxf6; 8.Nc3 Bb4 is fine for Black. 6.g3 comes into consideration, though it leads to a quite different sort of game. 6...Bb7; 7.Bg2 Be7; 8.0-0 0-0; 9.c4 reaches a Queen's Indian.) 6...Be7; 7.c4 0-0; 8.Nc3 Bb7; 9.Bd3 d5 brought about a level game in I. Ivanov-D. Gurevich, United States Championship 1989. **6.Nbd2.**

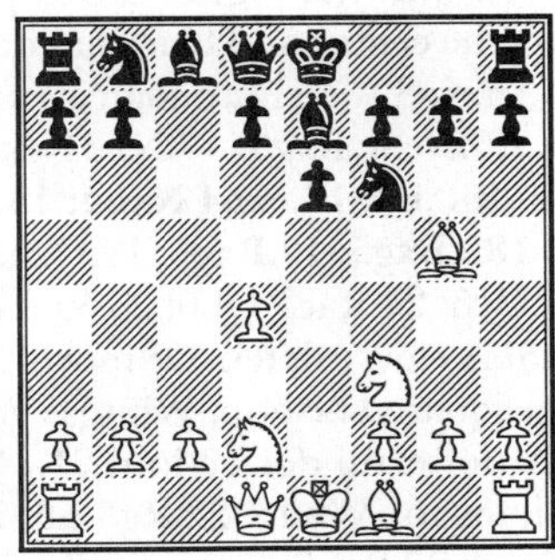

6...d6. 6...0–0; 7.Bd3 d6; 8.0–0 b6; 9.Re1 Bb7; 10.c3 Nbd7 reaches a typical position. 11.Qe2 Re8; 12.Rad1 Qc7; 13.Bc2 Rac8; 14.Bf4 Nf8; 15.h3 Bc6; 16.Bd3 Rcd8; 17.Bb5 Bxb5; 18.Qxb5 N8d7; 19.a4 Ra8; 20.Qb3 Bf8; 21.Re2 a6; 22.Rde1 h6; 23.Nc4 Rec8; 24.Ne3 and White was able to effectively exploit the advantage in McCambridge-Lau, Mendoza Teams 1985. 6...b6. Once again Black can adopt this move without fear of an immediate d5 by White. 7.Bd3 Bb7; 8.0–0 0–0 (8...d6 9.Re1 Nbd7; 10.Rc1 0–0; 11.h3 Re8; 12.c3 Qc7; 13.Bf4 is a little better for White, Berardi-Grosar, Olympiad 1994) 9.Re1 d6; 10.c3 Nbd7; 11.a4 a6; 12.Qe2 Re8; 13.Nc4 gave White more room to maneuver in Senkiewicz-Gurevich, Saint Martin 1991. **7.c3 Nbd7; 8.Bd3.**

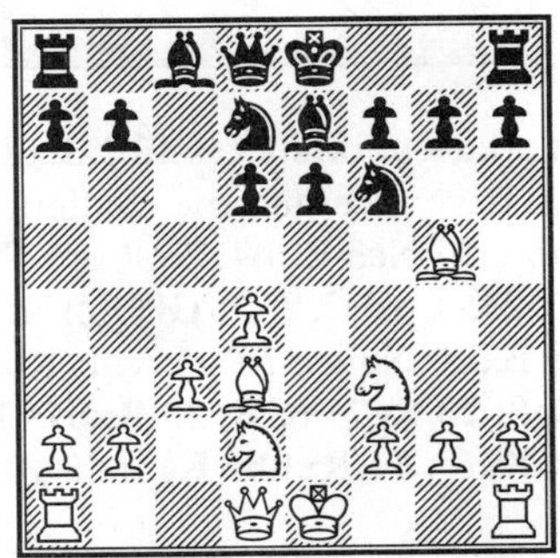

8...b6. Black has chosen a solid formation, but Torre was getting a lot of practice in these lines in 1925! **9.Nc4** or 9.0–0 0–0; 10.Re1 Bb7; 11.Nc4, which is perhaps a more reliable move order. **9...Bb7; 10.Qe2 Qc7; 11.0–0 0–0.**

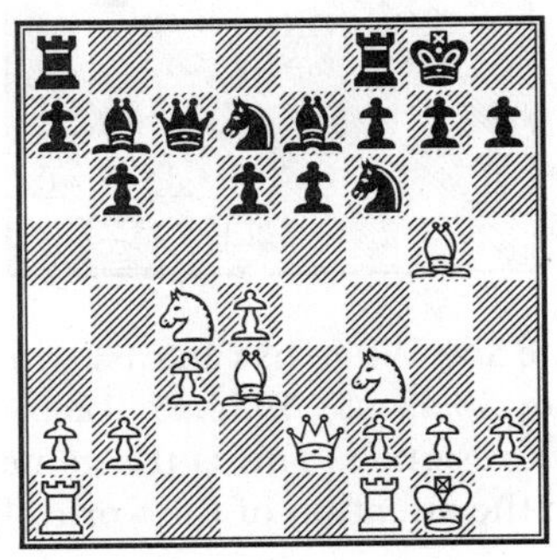

Both sides have continued with the logical development of their ideas. White has intensified the pressure on the center, and Black has dug in. **12.Rfe1 Rfe8; 13.Rad1 Nf8; 14.Bc1 Nd5; 15.Ng5?!** 15.Na3 was more logical, preventing Black's liberating maneuver. **15...b5!; 16.Na3.** 16.Ne3? Bxg5; 17.Nxd5 exd5!; 18.Qg4 Bxc1; 19.Rxc1 Ng6 provides equal chances. **16...b4; 17.cxb4 Nxb4; 18.Qh5?!** 18.Bb1 was the conservative and logical choice. **18...Bxg5; 19.Bxg5.** 19.Qxg5!? Nxa2; 20.Bd2 a5; 21.Ra1 Nb4; 22.Bxb4 axb4; 23.Nb5 Qc6; 24.Rac1 Qb6; 25.Re3 is an interesting alternative.

19...Nxd3; 20.Rxd3 Qa5! A clever defensive move, attacking the Re1 while pinning the Bg5. Without a light-squared bishop, White is going to have to work hard to whip up an attack. **21.b4!!** A powerful deflection! **21...Qf5?!** 21...Qd5! would have been best, with severe problems for White. 22.Rg3 h6; 23.Bf6 Ng6!; 24.Rxg6 fxg6; 25.Qxg6 Qxg2+!; 26.Qxg2 Bxg2; 27.Bxg7! Kxg7; 28.Kxg2 and White must fight for a draw. **22.Rg3 h6.**

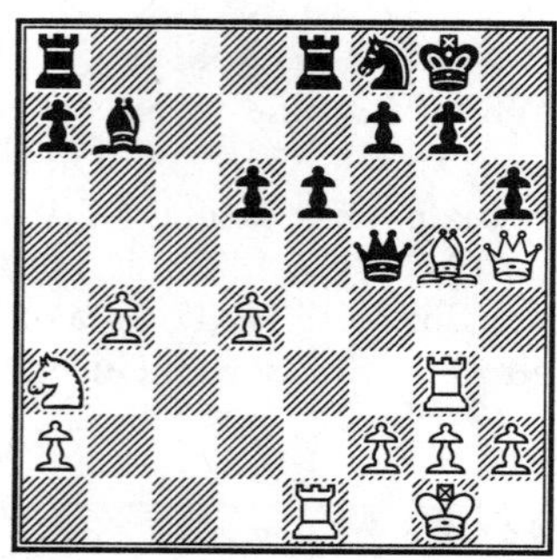

23.Nc4! In order for an attack to be successful, all of the pieces must get into the act! **23...Qd5?** Lasker should have accepted the challenge. 23...hxg5!; 24.Nxd6 Qg6; 25.Qxg6 Nxg6; 26.Nxb7 Rab8; 27.Nc5 Rxb4; 28.Rxg5 Nf4! and the game would still have been level. **24.Ne3 Qb5.** 24...Qxd4?; 25.Rd1! Qb2 (25...Qxb4; 26.Bf6 g6; 27.Qxh6 and checkmate follows.) 26.Bxh6 Ng6; 27.Bg5 with Rh3 to follow. **25.Bf6!! Qxh5; 26.Rxg7+ Kh8; 27.Rxf7+ Kg8; 28.Rg7+ Kh8; 29.Rxb7+ Kg8; 30.Rg7+ Kh8; 31.Rg5+ Kh7; 32.Rxh5 Kg6; 33.Rh3 Kxf6; 34.Rxh6+ Kg5; 35.Rh3.**

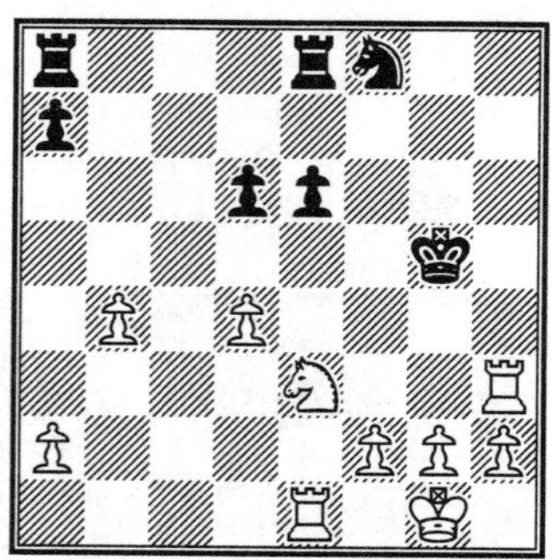

The carnage is complete and White has an easy win in the endgame. **35...Reb8; 36.Rg3+ Kf6; 37.Rf3+ Kg6; 38.a3 a5; 39.bxa5 Rxa5; 40.Nc4 Rd5; 41.Rf4 Nd7; 42.Rxe6+ Kg5; 43.g3.** Black resigned. This is the game that brought Carlos Torre and his opening strategy to the attention of the world. **White won.**

(176) KASPAROV - MARTINOVIC [A48]

Baku, 1980

1.d4 Nf6; 2.Nf3 g6; 3.Bg5 Bg7; 4.Nbd2 d6.

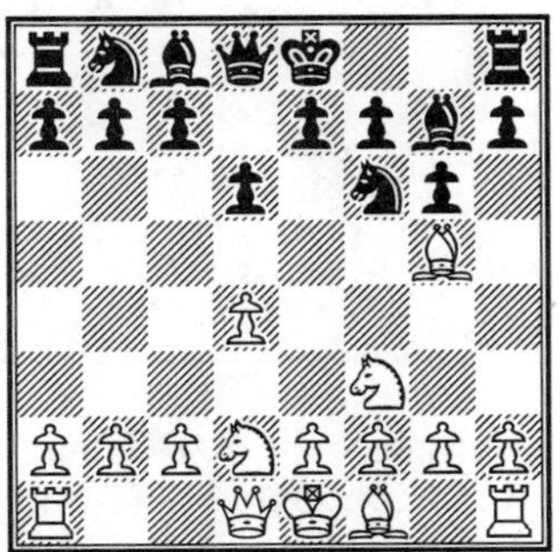

When Black adopts the King's Indian formation against the Torre Attack, White has the possibility of advancing the pawn to e4 in one go, and this creates a strong center which brings a small advantage. Black can of course try to play against the center with hypermodern techniques, but it is still rather difficult to equalize.

5.e4 0–0; 6.c3 Nbd7; 7.Be2 e5. This move is very much in the spirit of the King's Indian Defense. Black takes aim at the White center. If White is not careful, a timely exd4 will leave the Pe4 weak, while the advance d4-d5 will allow Black counterplay with f7-f5. 7...h6; 8.Bh4 g5; 9.Bg3 Nh5. Black is playing with great aggression, but his kingside will be weak. 10.Nc4!? An interesting idea, but White fails to follow it up correctly. 10...e6; 11.Nfd2. Forcing matters, but 11.Ne3 was a more solid approach. 11...Nf4; 12.0–0 b6! Suddenly the long diagonal is a promising target for the Bc8. 13.Bf3 Bb7; 14.Re1 Qe7; 15.a4 a5; 16.Nf1 Ba6! Black's bishop finds another useful post, and already it seems that his game is to be preferred, Seret-Nunn, Marbella Zonal 1982.

8.dxe5 dxe5. 8...Nxe5; 9.Nxe5 dxe5; 10.0–0 Qe8; 11.Qb3 Nd7; 12.Qa3 gives White control of the dark squares, Kagan-Speck, Australian Championship 1991. **9.0–0.**

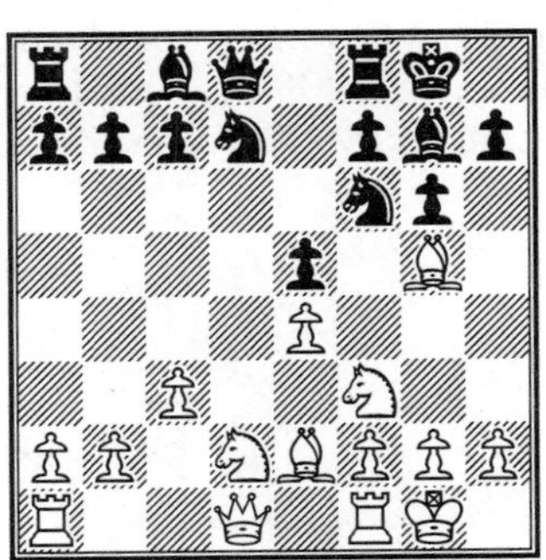

9...b6. 9...c6 leaves the d6-square too weak: 10.Nc4 Qe7; 11.Nd6 and the knight will prove difficult to dislodge. **10.Re1 Bb7; 11.Qc2 h6.** Black must do something to take the pressure off the pin. **12.Bh4.**

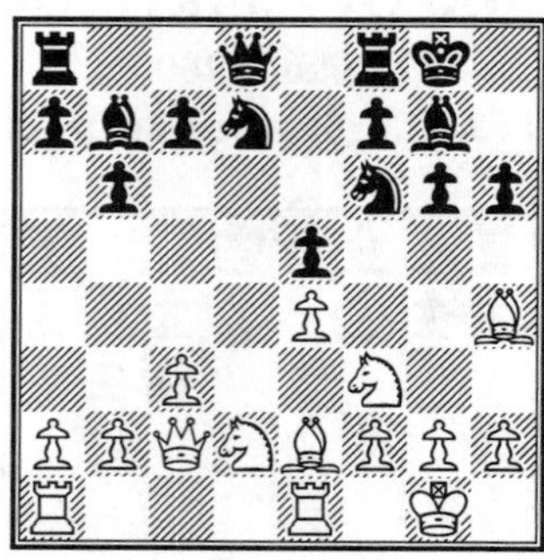

12...Qe7. 12...Qe8; 13.b4 Rausch-Stolz, German Championship 1993 **13.Bf1 Rfe8?!** Both sides have just about completed development and it is time to make a plan for the middlegame. With Black overprotecting the e-file, Kasparov shifts to the queenside.

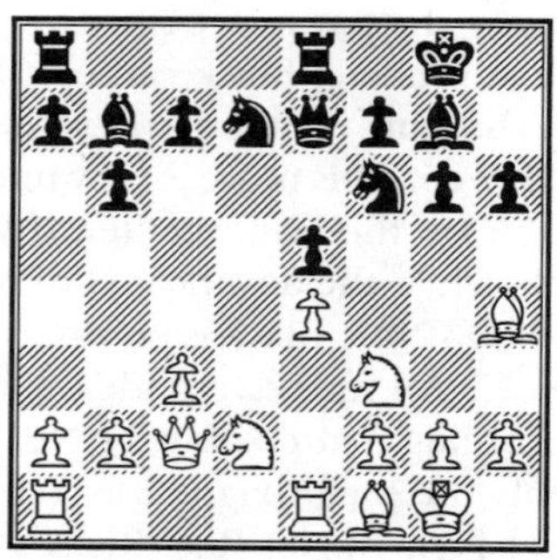

13...Rfd8 is the correct move, because the e-file is not going to be the location of any important activity. By misplacing his rook, Black conceded a valuable tempo to be forfeited at a later time. **14.b4!** This move gains important space on the queenside. Fooling around with the knights would have been less effective: 14.Nc4 Qe6; 15.Nfd2 Qg4!; 16.Bg3 (16.Bxf6 Nxf6) 16...Nh5; 17.f3 Qg5; 18.Bf2 Nf4; 19.Kh1 h5 with a formidable attack for Black. **14...a6.** 14...a5 would have challenged White's expansionist plans, but after 15.a3 Ra7; 16.Bd3 Rea8 the tempo lost with Rf8-e8 proves to be important, as white has time for 17.Qb2! after which he holds a small but significant advantage. **15.Nc4.**

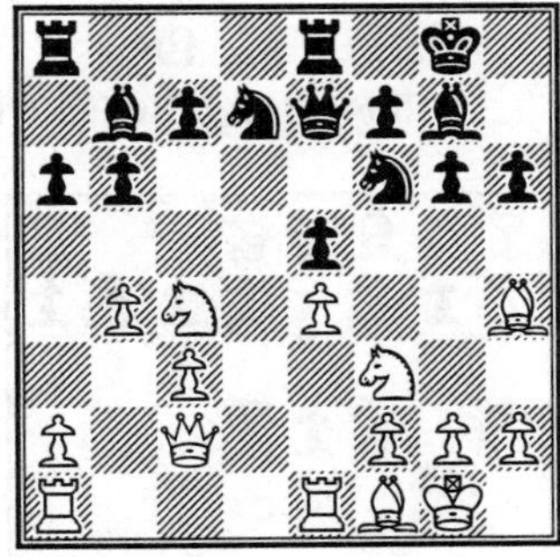

15...Rac8? A mistake in a difficult position. 15...c5; 16.Rad1 cxb4; 17.Nd6 Reb8; 18.Bc4! and the pressure is unbearable. 15...Qe6! breaks the pin with tempo. 16.Nfd2 c5; 17.Ne3 cxb4; 18.cxb4 Rac8; 19.Qb1 gives White a smaller, but still significant advantage. The battle will take place on the light squares, which White will occupy with Bc4, since 19...a5 is met by 20.a4! **16.a4!** Securing even more space on the queenside. **16...Qe6; 17.Nfd2 Nh5; 18.f3.** Now White's dark-squared bishop will be a full-fledged member of the army, controlling important dark-squares along the g1–a7 diagonal.

18...Bf6?! Because White is going to retreat the bishop anyway, this simply blocks a useful retreat square for the knight. **19.Bf2 Bg5.** More time-wasting. The bishop should have stayed at g7, where it could get to f8 more easily. **20.Ne3 Ndf6.** Black becomes more and more entangled in his own web. **21.c4! c6; 22.Nb3 Nd7.** 22...Bxe3?; 23.Bxe3 hitting pawns at h6 and b6. **23.c5 b5; 24.Red1.** Now we see why the bishop should have stayed home. The d6-square is now too vulnerable. **24...Be7.**

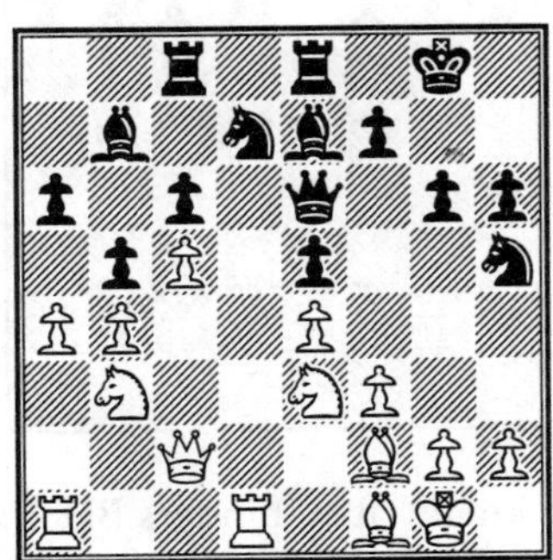

Observing that the Black queen has no place to run, Kasparov unleashes a shot! **25.Nc4! Rc7.** 25...bxc4? allows White to mop up with 26.Bxc4 Qf6; 27.Rxd7! Rb8; 28.Na5 Bc8; 29.Rc7 Rxb4; 30.Nxc6! Rb7; 31.Nxe7+ and White wins. **26.Nd6 Rb8; 27.axb5 cxb5; 28.Nxb7 Rbxb7; 29.Qa2!** and it is all over but the shouting. **29...Nb8; 30.Na5 Qxa2; 31.Rxa2 Ra7.** 31...Rd7 allows 32.Rd5. **32.c6 Ra8; 33.Rc2! Bxb4; 34.Rd8+ Kg7; 35.Bb6!** Black could resign here. **35...Bxa5; 36.Bxa5 Rxc6; 37.Rxb8 Rxb8; 38.Rxc6 b4; 39.Bc7. White won.**

(177) LEIN - HERNANDEZ [D03]

Saint John, 1988

1.d4 Nf6; 2.Nf3 g6; 3.Bg5 Bg7; 4.Nbd2 d5.

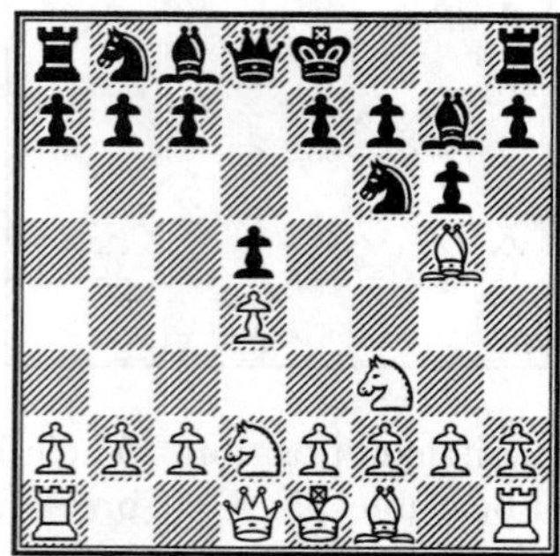

This is the normal reaction to the Torre Attack. Black sets up a Gruenfeld formation, with both strong control of the e4-square and a powerful bishop at g7. This is a very solid defense, but does not allow much scope for active play. Eventually, Black will try to play ...e5 and place pressure at d4. **5.e3 0–0.** 5...Bf5 allows White to expand on the queenside with 6.b4!? 0–0; 7.Be2 and now if Black tries to disrupt the queenside settlements with 7...a5 then after 8.b5 c5; 9.bxc6 bxc6; 10.0–0 Nbd7 White switches flanks with 11.Nh4! h6; 12.Nxf5! and after 12...hxg5; 13.Nxg7 Kxg7; 14.c4 e6; 15.Qa4 White had the advantage in Persitz-Kopylov, USSR 1976. **6.Bd3 Nc6.**

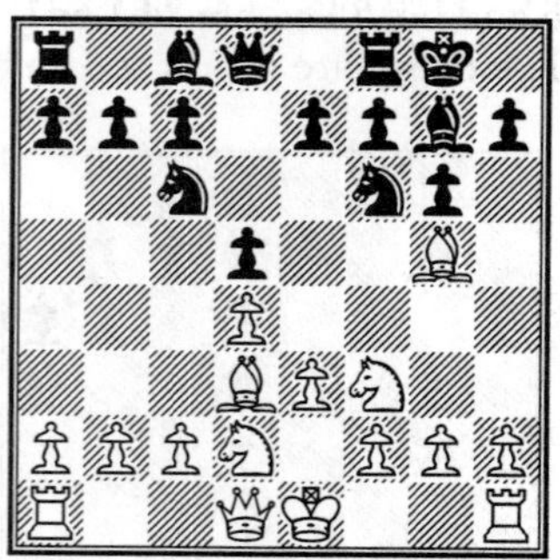

The deployment of the knight at c6 hinders Black's natural counterplay along the c-file. 6...h6 may be best. 7.Bxf6. I think that White must capture here. If the bishop retreats, it is vulnerable to a kingside pawnstorm. Black will play an early...c5 and then capture on d4. If White recaptures with the e-pawn, then control of f4 is lost. For example: (7.Bh4 c5; 8.c3 cxd4; 9.exd4 Nh5; 10.0–0 Nc6; 11.Re1 f5; 12.b4 a6; 13.b5 axb5; 14.Bxb5 g5) 7...exf6 (7...Bxf6; 8.c4 and White is likely to dominate the center.) 8.c4 and I think White has slightly better chances with good prospects of play on the queenside.

7.c3. The immediate 7.0–0 would allow 7...Nb4. **7...Re8.** 7...Qd7 is an odd-looking move, but in the only known example it worked out well, when combined with a rather interesting plan. 8.0–0 e5!?; 9.Nxe5 Nxe5; 10.dxe5 Ng4. The point of Qd7 was to break the pin in order to make this move possible. 11.Nf3 Re8; 12.Be2. 12.Bc2 is probably a better plan, supporting e4 and perhaps sliding to b3 to increase pressure at d5. 12...Nxe5; 13.Bf4 Nxf3+; 14.Bxf3 c6; 15.Re1 Qe7; 16.e4. Premature, but Black was ready to play Bf5, which would have been less good if the bishop were at c2. 16...dxe4; 17.Rxe4 Be6 with an equal game in Cifuentes-Pacis, Malta Olympiad 1980. **8.0–0 h6; 9.Bh4 Bf5?!** A poor plan. **10.Bxf5 gxf5; 11.Bxf6! Bxf6.**

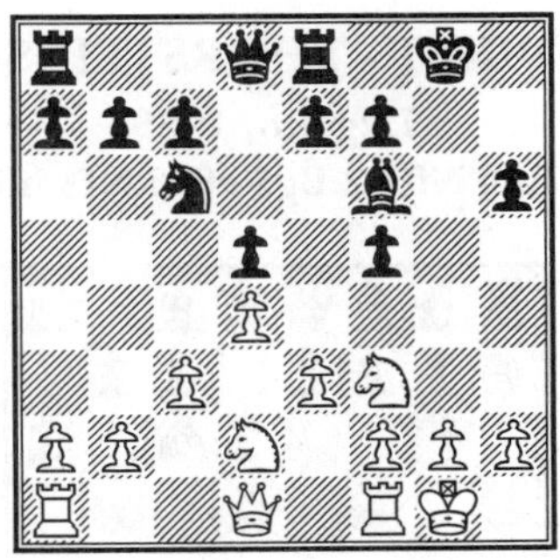

The weakness of Black's kingside cannot be repaired. **12.Kh1 e6; 13.Ne1 Ne7; 14.Nd3 Ng6; 15.f4 b6.** Black is seeking counterplay on the queenside, but White's position is too solid. **16.Rf3 h5; 17.Rh3 h4.** This was the only way to defend the h-pawn, but now it is exposed, despite having three defenders. **18.Ne5!** Well-timed! Getting rid of the invader will cost Black one of the h-pawn's guardians. **18...Bxe5.** 18...Nxe5; 19.dxe5 Be7; 20.Nf3 Kg7; 21.Qe1 Rh8; 22.Qf2 c5; 23.Rg g4. **19.dxe5 Kg7; 20.Qe2 Rh8; 21.a4!** With the Black pieces preoccupied on the kingside, White strikes at the other side of the board, inhibiting the advance of the Black pawns and keeping a4-a5 in reserve. But the real action remains on the kingside. **21...Qd7; 22.Nf3 c5; 23.Qf2 Qe7; 24.Rg1 Rh6; 25.Qe1 Rah8.**

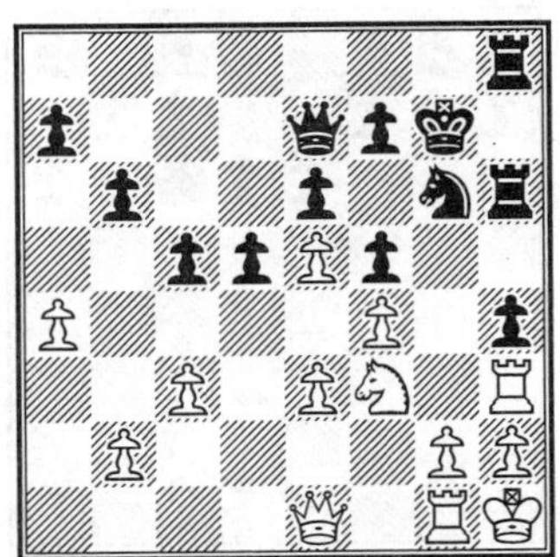

Black has put all of his power into the defence of the h-pawn, and both sides have evacuated the queenside. But now White launches a surprise attack. **26.b4!? Qd7; 27.Qa1!** A wonderful move in the style of Reti. **27...Rc8; 28.b5 a6?!** Black sees the coming threat of Rd1 and c4, or Rb1 and a5, but this reaction is not justified. **29.bxa6 Ra8; 30.Qe1! Qxa4.** 30...Qe7; 31.g4 hxg3; 32.Rxh6 Kxh6; 33.Qxg3 and if the Rook grabs the Pa6, it will take a long time to get home to the kingside. 33...Rxa6; 34.Qh3+ Kg7; 35.Ng5 Qe8; 36.Qh7+ Kf8; 37.Qh8+ Ke7; 38.Qf6+ Kd7; 39.Nxf7 Ne7; 40.Nd6.

31.Nxh4. Finally the pawn falls, and the king is further exposed. **31...Qe4.** Pinning the g-pawn, thus slowing White's attack. **32.Qg3 Rxa6; 33.Qg5 Rh8.** The threat was Nxf5+. **34.Rg3 Rh6; 35.Qf6+ Kg8; 36.Nxg6 Rxg6; 37.Rxg6+ fxg6; 38.Qxg6+ Kh8; 39.Qh6+ Kg8.** My guess is that Black lost on time here, but after Qxe6+; White wins easily. **White won.**

(178) PIKET - THORSTEINS [A46]

Lugano, 1989

1.d4 Nf6; 2.Bg5 e6; 3.Nf3 h6.

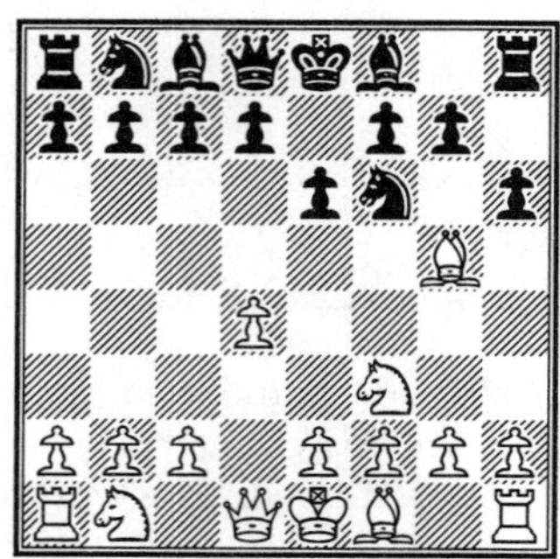

Our final example of the Torre features the Nimzowitsch Variation. Black immediately challenges the bishop. White does best to exchange at f6 here, keeping the initiative going. **4.Bxf6.** 4.Bh4 d6; 5.c3 Nbd7; 6.Nbd2 g5; 7.Bg3 Nh5; 8.e4 Bg7 is double-edged, as seen in Miles-Marin, Andorra 1995. The bishop at g3 can be captured at will. **4...Qxf6; 5.e4 d6.**

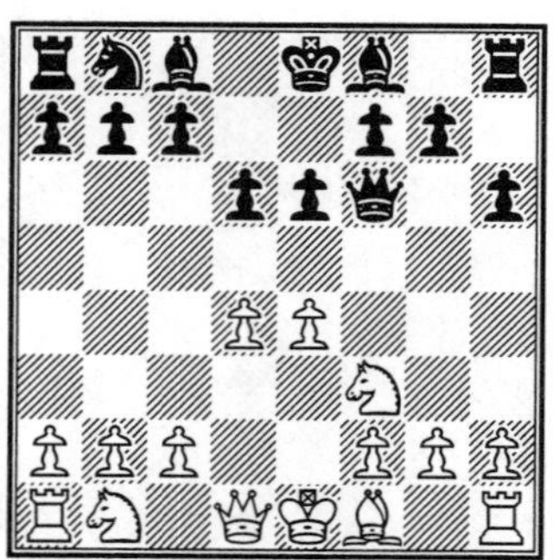

This is the normal continuation. White sets up the ideal pawn center, but Black has the bishop pair as a long-term asset. **6.Bd3.** 6.Nc3 Nd7; 7.Qd2 a6; 8.0–0–0 Qd8; 9.h4 b5 gave Black sufficient counterplay in Johansson-Marinkl Badalona 1994. **6...Nc6.** This is only one of many plans. 6...g6; 7.0–0 Bg7; 8.e5 Qe7; 9.Qe2 Nd7; 10.c4 c5; 11.Nc3 cxd4; 12.exd6 Qxd6; 13.Nb5 gave White the initiative in Sideif-Zade-A.Ivanov, Soviet Union 1985. 6...Nd7; 7.Qe2 e5; 8.c3 g6; 9.Nbd2 h5; 10.h3 Bh6; 11.0–0–0 0–0; 12.Kb1 Re8; 13.g4 led to a powerful attack for White in Dobosz-Kiss, Kecskemet 1987.

7.c3 g5; 8.Na3 Bd7; 9.Nc4 h5. 9...Bg7; 10.e5 gives White a strong initiative.

10.Ne3 a6; 11.Qe2 g4. Black seems to have some difficulty deciding which side of the board to play on, but of course also must determine a safe spot for the king. **12.Nd2 Rg8; 13.Rf1!** Now that Black has messed up the kingside, White correctly chooses to send the king to the queenside. **13...Bh6; 14.0-0-0 b5.** Black is intent on attacking the enemy king at all costs, so launches a queenside pawnstorm.

15.Kb1 b4; 16.e5! As is so often the case, the correct reaction to a flank attack is vigorous action in the center of the board. **16...dxe5; 17.Ne4! Qe7; 18.d5! Nb8.** 18...exd5; 19.Nxd5 Qd8; 20.Nef6+ wins quickly. **19.Bc4!** White just keeps piling on the pressure.

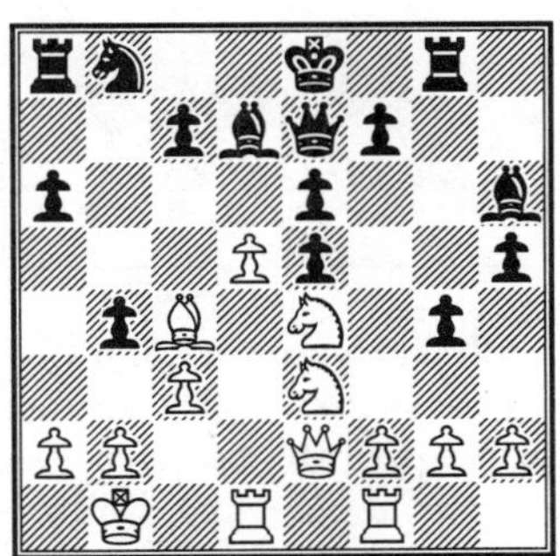

19...bxc3; 20.Nxc3 Kf8; 21.Qd3. White has complete control of the center, and the Black forces are scattered in useless positions. **21...c6; 22.dxe6 Bxe6; 23.Nf5 Bxf5; 24.Qxf5 Ra7; 25.Ne4 Nd7; 26.Rd6 Nb6; 27.Bb3 Rh8; 28.Rfd1 Nd5; 29.Rxc6** Black could resign here with a clear conscience. **29...Nf4; 30.Rcd6 Kg7; 31.Rd7 Rxd7; 32.Rxd7. White won.**

PSEUDO-QUEEN'S INDIAN

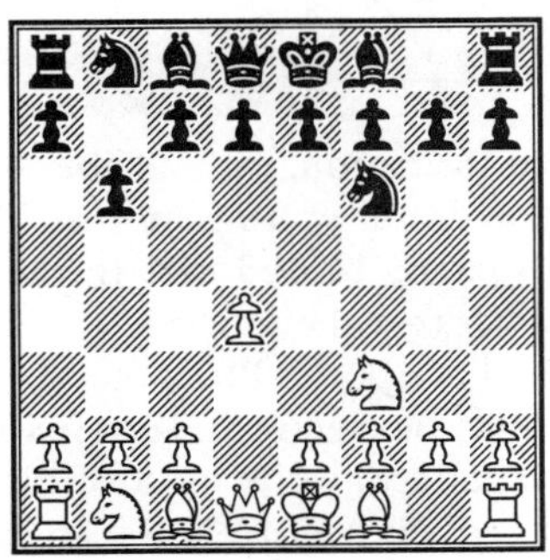

1.d4 Nf6
2.Nf3 b6

This is the Accelerated form of the Queen's Indian Defense. It will often transpose to normal lines, after, for example, 3.c4 e6 but White can adopt a more aggressive plan using Torre's idea of Bg5.

(179) TORRE - VERLINSKY [D03]

Moscow, 1925

1.d4 Nf6; 2.Nf3 b6. 3.Bg5 Bb7; 4.Nbd2.

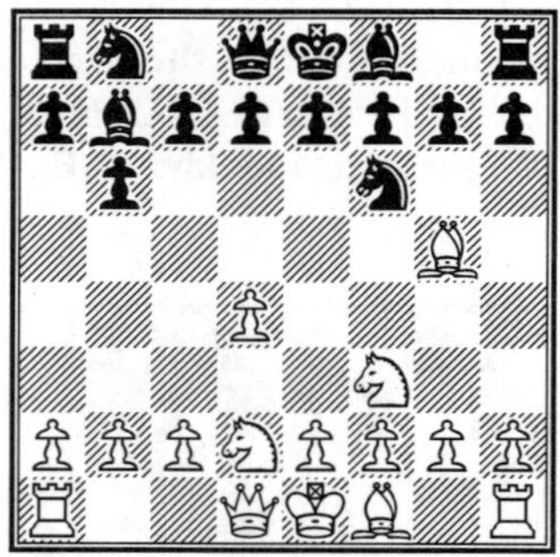

This structure can be handled in a number of ways by Black, with many transpositional possibilities. Verlinsky chose to overprotect the e4-square. **4...d5; 5.e3 Nbd7; 6.Bd3 e6; 7.Ne5!** Taking advantage of the fact that Black cannot afford to capture, White establishes a strong outpost at e5, which can be supported by an advance of the f-pawn. **7...a6.** 7...Nxe5?; 8.dxe5 h6; 9.Bh4 g5; 10.exf6 gxh4; 11.Qf3 is crushing, since Black has no knights to use to go after the Pf6. **8.f4 Be7; 9.0–0 c5; 10.c3.**

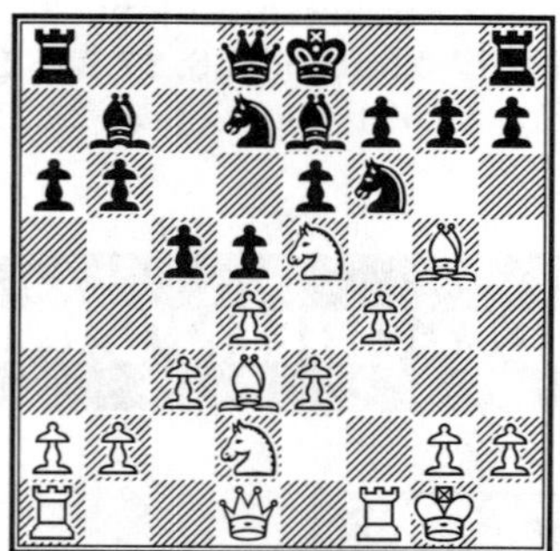

White has achieved a superior stonewall formation, with a "liberated" bishop. **10...0–0; 11.Qf3 Nxe5.** Black has run out of useful waiting moves. **12.fxe5 Nd7; 13.Qh3!** The attack is already dangerous. **13...g6; 14.Bh6 c4?!** In one sense, the move is merely irrelevant, since it does not address the kingside threats. But now even if White didn't come up with an inspired attack the Bb7 would be a spectator forever. **15.Bc2 b5; 16.Rf2 Qb6; 17.Raf1 f5.** Pretty much forced. **18.exf6 Rxf6; 19.Nf3!** All of White's pieces are participating in the attack, while most of Black's are off vacationing on the queenside. **19...Re8; 20.Qg3 Nf8; 21.Ne5.** Returning to the favored outpost. **21...Qd8; 22.h4.** The threat of h5 is so strong that Black tries to give up the exchange to reduce the pressure at g6. **22...Rf5; 23.Bxf5 Bxh4.**

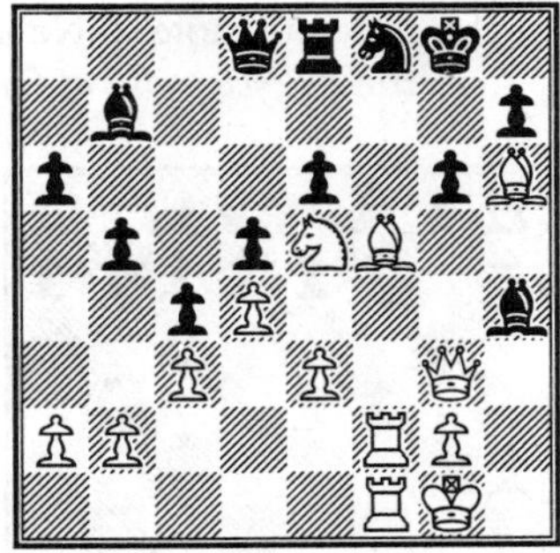

24.Bxg6!! A brilliant finish to a well-conducted attack. **24...Bxg3; 25.Bf7+ Kh8; 26.Bxe8 Bxf2+; 27.Rxf2. White won.**

PSEUDO-BENKO GAMBIT

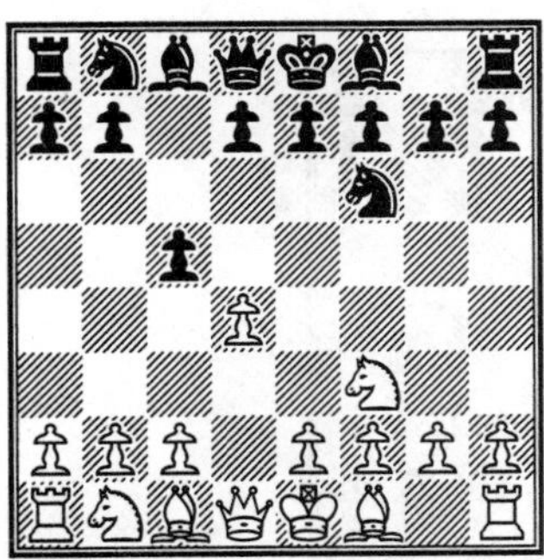

1.d4	**Nf6**
2.Nf3	**c5**

This choice by Black can radically alter the nature of the opening, if White chooses to advance the pawn. The advance 3.d5. Play is then similar to the Benko Gambit if Black replies ...b5, but without a pawn at c4, White can play along the lines of the Torre Attack.

(180) PIKET - POLGAR, J. [A43]

Brussels, 1987

1.d4 Nf6; 2.Nf3 c5; 3.d5 b5. A principled reply, preventing c2-c4 and gaining space on the queenside. 3...c4 is a strange reply from Buecker, who gave it the name Habichi (a form of a German phrase meaning "gotcha"! The following refute is by Joel Benjamin, in our 1987 *Unorthodox Openings* book. 4.Nc3 Qa5; 5.Nd2 b5; 6.e4 d6 (6...e6; 7.Be2!) 7.a4 Ba6; 8.axb5! Qxa1; 9.Bxc4 Nxe4; (9...Qa5; 10.bxa6) 10.Ndxe4 Bb7; 11.0-0 Nd7; 12.Qe2 Ne5; 13.Ba2 followed by f4 with advantage for White.

4.Bg5 Qb6. 4...d6 is considered a more reliable move. 4...d6; 5.e3 a6; 6.a4 b4!; 7.Bc4 Nbd7; 8.Nbd2 g6; 9.e4 Bg7; 10.h3 0-0; 11.0-0 Nb6 led to complications in Larsen-Browne, Hastings 1972. **5.a4 bxa4?!** This is generally a poor strategic choice, but it has the imprimatur of the *Encyclopedia of Chess Openings*. Black should probably advance the pawn, as in the previous note. **6.Nc3!** An obvious, but powerful gambit which is much better than the *Encyclopedia of Chess Openings*. 6.Bxf6?!

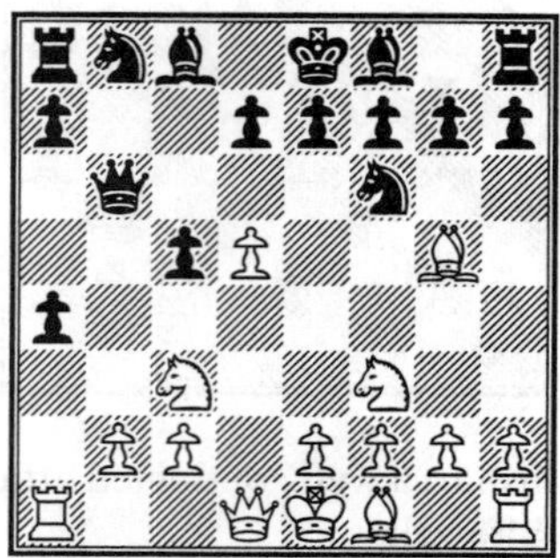

6...Qxb2; 7.Bd2 Qb7. The threat was Rb1 followed by Nb5. **8.e4 g6; 9.Rb1 Qc7; 10.e5!** In return for a couple of weak pawns White has a huge lead in development and absolute control of the center. **10...Ng4; 11.d6! Qd8.** 11...exd6; 12.exd6 Qd8; 13.Qe2+. **12.Nd5 exd6; 13.Bg5!**

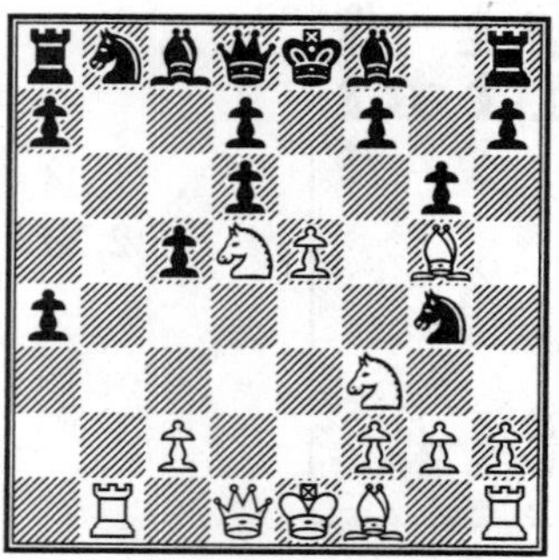

13...f6; 14.exf6 Qa5+; 15.Nd2 Ne5; 16.Rb5 and White won.

LONDON SYSTEM

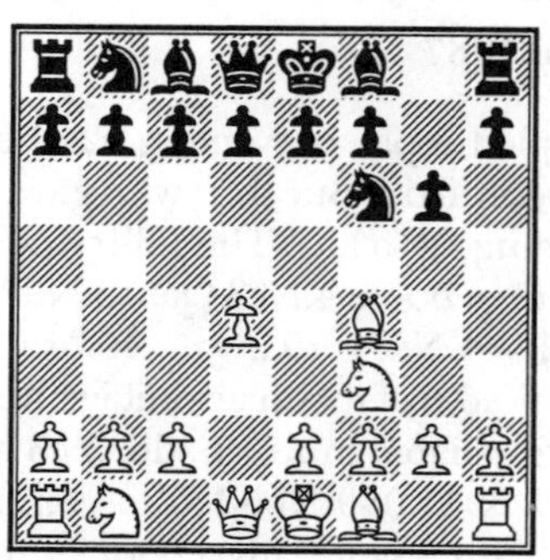

1.d4	**Nf6**
2.Nf3	**g6**
3.Bf4	

The **London System** is often chosen by players who want to avoid theory in the opening and just play chess or those who are simply too lazy to learn real openings! Unlike the Torre Attack, where the bishop at g5 plays a significant role, the bishop at f4 in the London system is simply a controller of the e5-square, and Black can often get rid of it with ...Nh5. It is important not to play such moves too early, however, and the first order of business for Black must be to comfortably develop the kingside pieces.

(181) BONDAREVSKY - BRONSTEIN [A48]

31st Soviet Championship, 1963

1.d4 Nf6; 2.Nf3 g6; 3.Bf4 Bg7; 4.e3 0–0; 5.Nbd2 b6; 6.c3 c5; 7.h3 d6.

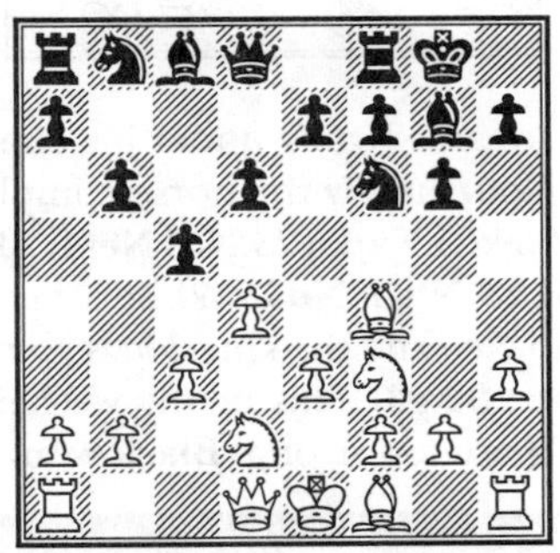

Bronstein adopts the King's Indian formation against White's London System. It is an interesting example of hypermodern play against a very solid center. **8.Be2 Ba6; 9.Bxa6 Nxa6.** Although this knight now sits on the edge of the board, it is headed for a more useful post, at c7, from which it can operate in the center at e6. **10.0–0 Qd7; 11.Qe2 Nc7; 12.dxc5 bxc5; 13.e4.**

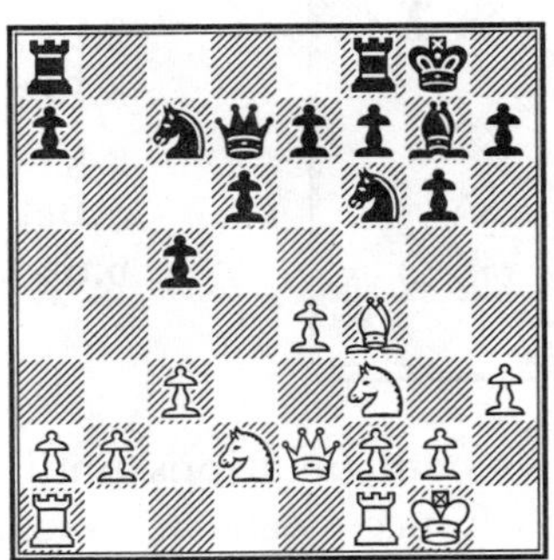

White seems to have a nice central position, and threatens to advance the e-pawn further. But Bronstein comes up with a surprising shot. **13...e5!?** This creates a temporary weakness at d6, but Bronstein appreciates that pawns which operate with hypermodern modesty in the opening can later be advanced with great effect. **14.Be3 Rab8; 15.b3 Qc6!** Even the powerful queen takes part in the pressure game. **16.Qc4 Nd7!** It seems strange, at first, to move this knight, which had supported the d5- square. But because of White's previous move, Black will be able to reposition the knight at b6, and then advance his d-pawn. **17.Nh2 Nb6!; 18.Qd3 d5!; 19.f3.** 19.exd5 Ncxd5 would give Black a great game. **19...Rbd8; 20.Qc2.**

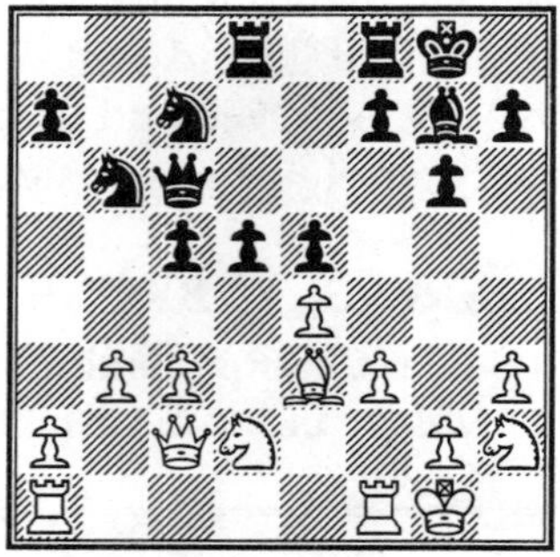

20...f5! With the dark squares firmly under his control, Bronstein now acts on the light squares. **21.Rad1 Ne6.** Finally the horse completes the ride from the edge of the board to the centre. **22.exd5 Nxd5; 23.Nc4 Nef4; 24.Rf2 Nxe3; 25.Nxe3 Rxd1+; 26.Qxd1 e4!; 27.Qc2 Bh6; 28.Nhf1 Nd3.** White's position is no longer tenable. **29.Rd2.** 29.Re2 exf3; 30.gxf3 Ne5 and the kingside is going to be demolished. **29...c4; 30.Nxc4 Qc5+; 31.Kh2 Bf4+; 32.g3.** This fatally weakens f3. **32...Ne1!** White now resigned, as the threats at f3 are too strong. **Black won.**

DOUBLE FIANCHETTO ATTACK

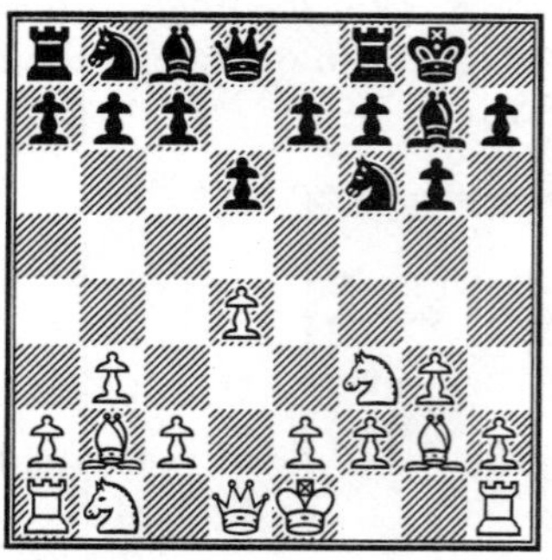

1.Nf3	**Nf6**
2.b3	**g6**
3.Bb2	**Bg7**
4.g3	**0-0**
5.Bg2	**d6**
6.d4	

This formation delays confrontations until the middlegame. Garry Kasparov used this approach successfully in his match against the Deep Blue computer in 1997. White remains flexible and will choose a plan based on the actions of the opponent. The slight advantage in the center insures that Black must be on guard for an eventual attack on either flank.

(182) RODRIGUEZ - HERNANDEZ [A49]

Granma Zonal, 1987

1.Nf3 Nf6; 2.b3 g6; 3.Bb2 Bg7; 4.g3 0–0; 5.Bg2 d6; 6.d4.

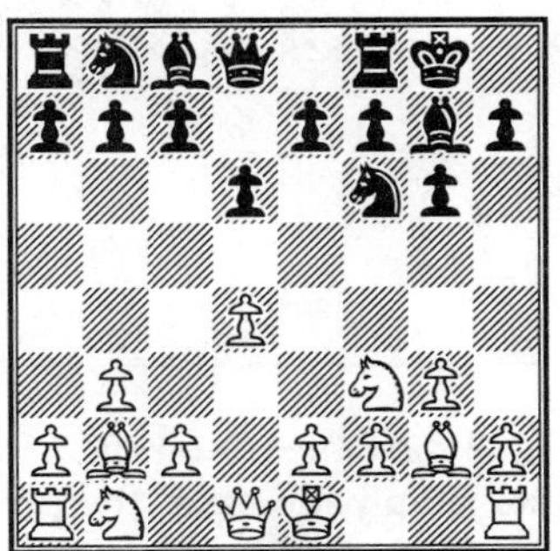

White combines the double-fianchetto with a pawn at d4. The pawn stands in the way of the Bb2, but can sometimes be effective if White can play Ne5. That is why Black usually places a pawn at d6. **6...c5.** 6...a5 is another source of counterplay, for example 7.0–0 a4; 8.c4 reaches, by transposition, Ribli-Bologan, Germany 1996, which continued 8...c5!; 9.Na3 Nc6; 10.Nb5 Ne4; 11.e3 axb3; 12.axb3 Rxa1; 13.Bxa1 Qa5 with a good game for Black. **7.c4 cxd4; 8.Nxd4 Qc7; 9.0–0 Bd7; 10.Nc3 Nc6; 11.Rc1.**

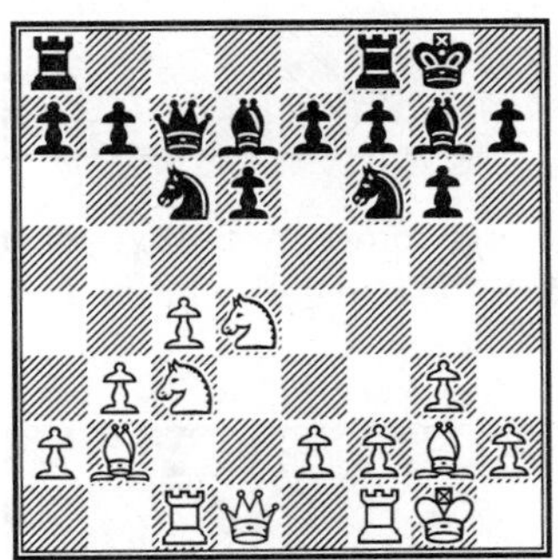

11...Nxd4. Both sides have developed their minor pieces and should now attend to the development of the heavy artillery. Instead, Black chooses to reorganize the central game, and this gives White a slight edge in development. **12.Qxd4 Bc6; 13.e4 e6; 14.Qd2 a6; 15.Rfd1 Rad8.** Without doing anything more than simply developing his pieces, White has achieved a dominating position. He completely controls the center and has a useful opposition Rc1 vs. Qc7 which is ready to be exploited. **16.Nd5!**

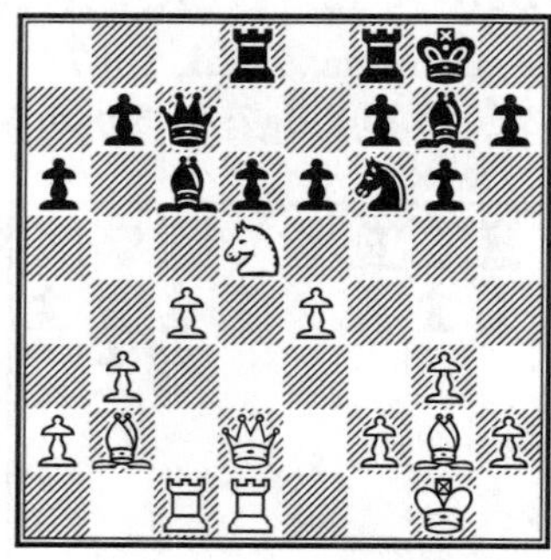

16...Bxd5; 17.cxd5 Qe7; 18.dxe6 fxe6. Now the hanging pawns provide a target for the White bishops. White simply increases the pressure until Black's position cracks. **19.Ba3 Ne8; 20.Qe2 Rd7; 21.Bh3.**

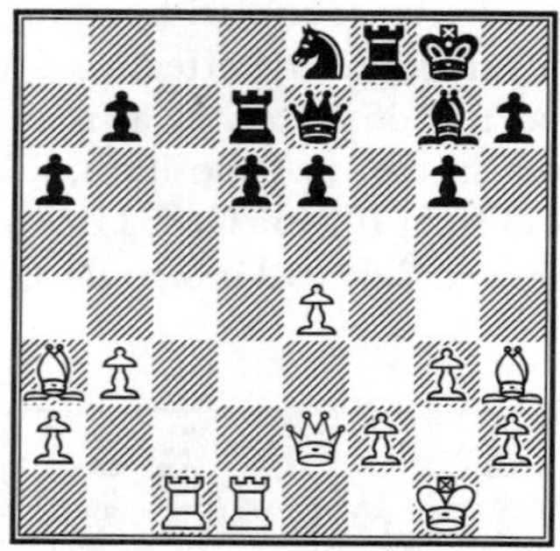

21...g5; 22.Qg4 Kf7. An ugly move, but otherwise the pawn at e6 falls. **23.Rd3 Be5; 24.Rf3+ Nf6; 25.Qxg5.** So White gets a pawn anyway. **25...Ke8; 26.Rc8+ Rd8; 27.Rxd8+ Kxd8; 28.Rd3.**

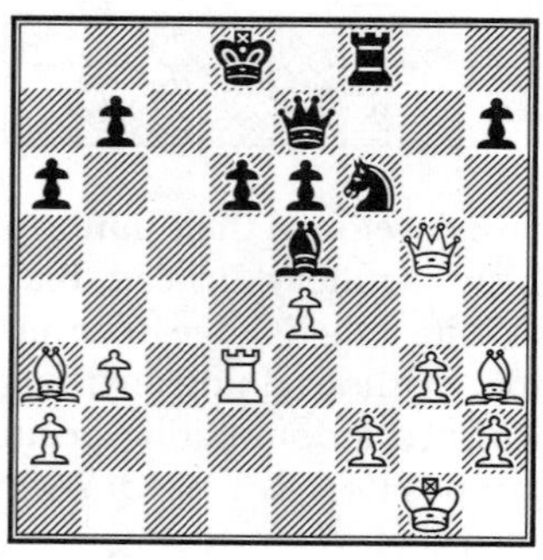

White won.

VERESOV ATTACK

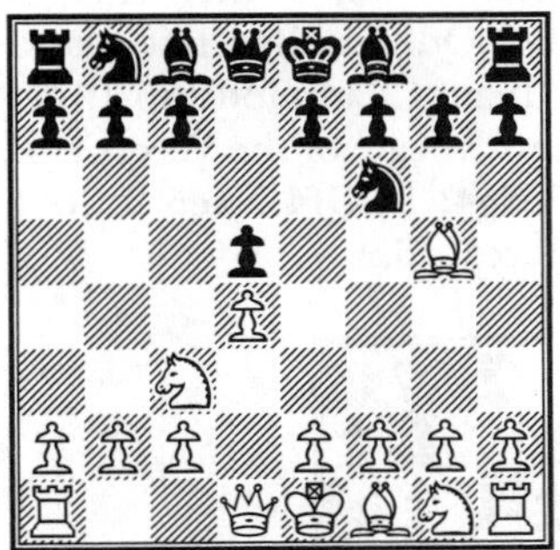

1.d4 Nf6
2.Nc3 d5
3.Bg5

The **Veresov Attack** has never attracted many followers in the international arena, but it can be dangerous if one is not well prepared. White plays a sort of left-handed Spanish Game, but the strategy is not as effective because Black's d-pawn is sufficiently defended. So White will have to aim for an eventual advance of the e-pawn to e4 if any progress is to be made in the center.

(183) VERESOV - BUNATIAN [D01]

Moscow, 1965

1.d4 Nf6; 2.Nc3 d5; 3.Bg5 Nbd7; 4.Nf3.

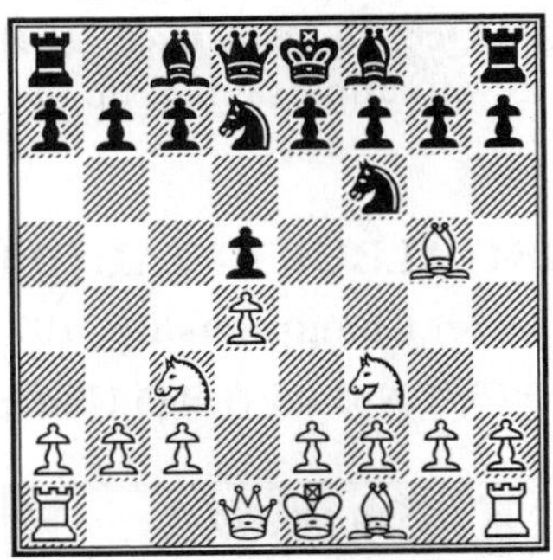

This is the original Veresov plan. White does not try to achieve the e4 break early in the game, but instead simply develops pieces rationally. **4...g6.** As with so many of the Queen Pawn games, a kingside fianchetto is the appropriate plan. **5.e3 Bg7; 6.Bd3 0–0; 7.0–0 c5.**

The difference between this opening and the Torre Attack is that White's knight is at c3, which is a bit inconvenient, because White usually chooses to support the center with a pawn on that square in most similar openings. **8.Ne5.** 8.Re1 b6; 9.e4 dxe4; 10.Nxe4 Bb7; 11.c3 cxd4; 12.Nxd4 creates an unusual center, with two knights sitting in the center. White has a little extra space, but Black can simplify the position with 12...Nc5!; 13.Bxf6 exf6; 14.Nxc5 bxc5; 15.Nb3 Qb6 as in Veresov-

Shagalovich, Byelorussian Championship 1957.

8...e6. 8...cxd4; 9.exd4 Nxe5; 10.dxe5 Ng4; 11.Be2 d4 is probably stronger. This resource was discovered by British theoretician Robert Bellin, and expert on the Queen Pawn Games.

9.Re1. 9.Bb5 is now considered strongest. 9...h6; 10.Bh4 cxd4; 11.exd4 Qb6; 12.a4 a6; 13.a5 Qc7; 14.Nxd7 Nxd7; 15.Bg3 Qd8; 16.Ba4 left Black with a very cramped position in Alburt-Gufeld, Soviet Team Championship 1974. Lev Alburt, former U.S. Champion, has been a long time advocate of the Veresov. **9...Qa5; 10.a3 a6; 11.Qd2 cxd4?; 12.exd4 Nxe5; 13.dxe5 Ng4; 14.Qf4 Nxe5.** It looks as though Black has simply won a pawn, but after **15.Rxe5! f6.**

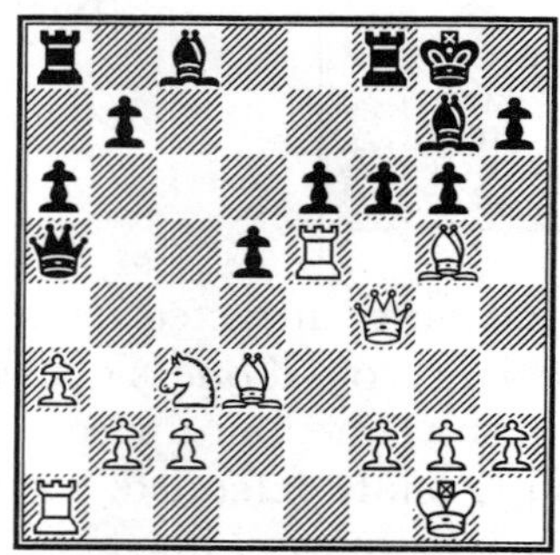

Of course, if Black takes the rook then White recaptures with the queen at e5 and has a much better game. Had White overlooked this possibility for Black? No indeed, for a brilliant combination is in store. **16.Nxd5!! exd5.** 16...fxe5; 17.Ne7+ Kh8; 18.Qh4 and Ng6+ or Bxg6 are following in short order. **17.Rxd5! Qb6.** 17...Qxd5 fails to 18.Bc4 and the pin wins. **18.Qc4 Be6; 19.Be3!** Black resigned here, unwilling to face the humiliation of **19...Qc6; 20.Qxc6 bxc6; 21.Rd6 Bd5; 22.c4 Bf7; 23.Rxc6** and White's queenside pawns will simply saunter up the board and turn into queens. **White won.**

(184) ALBURT - TAL [D01]

Soviet Championship, 1972

1.d4 Nf6; 2.Nc3 d5; 3.Bg5 Nbd7; 4.f3.

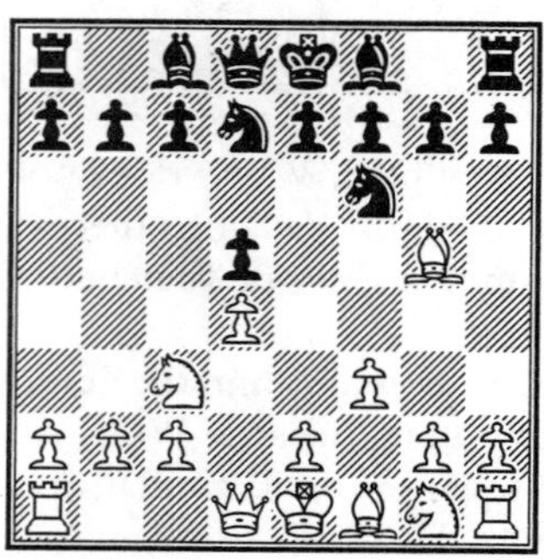

The most aggressive plan. In the previous game, we saw Veresov adopt the more positional 4.Nf3. **4...c6; 5.e4 dxe4; 6.fxe4 e5! 7.dxe5.** 7.Nf3 is countered by 7...exd4! 8.Nxd4 Bb4 and Black was equal in Schiller-Ligterink, Reykjavik 1986. Inferior is 7...Qa5; 8.Bxf6! Nxf6; 9.Nxe5 Nxe4; 10.Qf3! as in J.Brown-King, London 1978.

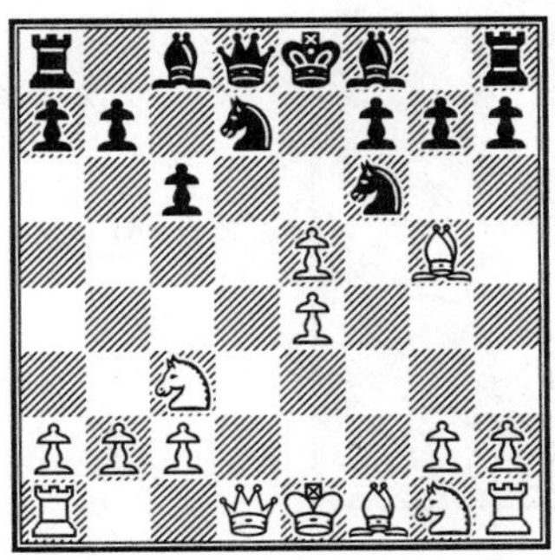

7...Qa5; 8.exf6. 8.Bxf6 gxf6; 9.e6 fxe6; 10.Bc4 Bb4; 11.Nge2 Ne5 and Black can be satisfied with the position. 12.Bb3 Rg8; 13.a3 Bxc3+; 14.Nxc3 Rxg2. Now things get very exciting! 15.Qh5+ Rg6; 16.Qh3! (16.Qxh7 Nf3+; 17.Kf2 Qg5!!; 18.Kxf3 Rh6 and Black wins.) 16...Ng4; 17.0-0-0! Nf2; 18.Qxh7 Qg5+; 19.Kb1 Rg7; 20.Qh8+ Rg8; 21.Qh7 Rg7; 22.Qh8+ Rg8 was agreed drawn in Rossetto-Gufeld, Camaguey 1974. **8...Qxg5; 9.fxg7 Bxg7; 10.Qd2** 10.Nf3? is a serious error because of 10...Qe3+ ;11.Be2 Bxc3+; 12.bxc3 Qxc3+; 13.Kf1 Nf6 and Black has a better game. **10...Qxd2+; 11.Kxd2 Nc5; 12.Bd3 Be6; 13.Nf3 0-0-0; 14.Ke2 b5; 15.a3 a5; 16.h3 Rhe8; 17.Rhd1.**

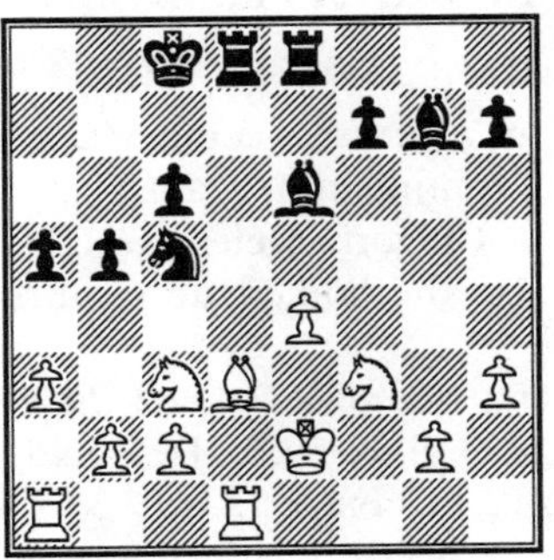

17...f5!; 18.e5 Nd7; 19.Re1 Bxe5; 20.Kf2 Bf6; 21.Re3 Nc5; 22.Rae1 Kd7. Black's pieces are much more active and the bishop pair is a tangible asset. Now White self-destructs, tempted by a sacrificial line which is too easily declined. **23.Nxb5? f4!; 24.Re5.** 24.R3e2 Nxd3+; 25.cxd3 cxb5 and White can resign. **24...Nxd3+; 25.cxd3 cxb5; 26.Rxb5 Rb8; 27.Ne5+ Kd6; 28.Rxa5 Bh4+. Black won.**

ANTI-TORRE

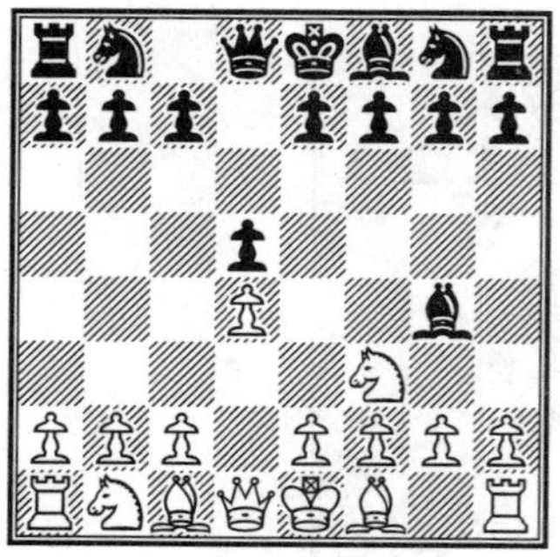

1.Nf3 d5
2.d4 Bg4

Systems like the Torre Attack, London System and Colle System are often considered annoying to meet, so Black sometimes uses this move just to steer the game into positions where White will have to start thinking early in the game. In a sense, Black is playing a reversed Trompovsky or Torre Attack, but the missing tempo means that a fight for equality still lies ahead. Note that this opening differs from the Wade Defense because the pawn is on d5, not d6.

(185) LOBRON - HODGSON [D02]
Haifa, 1989

1.Nf3 d5; 2.d4 Bg4 is an aggressive counter to the Torre Attack and London Attack. It is the most forcing continuation against 2.Nf3. **3.Ne5.** 3.c4 gives Black the choice between adopting the Chigorin Defense (3...Nc6) or continuing in Queen's Gambit fashion. There is also the immediate capture to be considered. 3...Bxf3; 4.gxf3 dxc4; 5.e4?!

5.e3 is evaluated by Cvetkovic and V. Sokolov (ECO II 1987) as better for White, but I am not convinced. 5...e5!?; 6.dxe5 Qxd1+; 7.Kxd1 Nc6; 8.f4 0-0-0+; 9.Bd2 f6; 10.exf6 Nxf6; 11.Bxc4 Bb4; 12.Nc3 Bxc3; 13.bxc3 Ne4 is just one example of Black's chances. I think the whole line needs practical tests.

5...e5!; 6.dxe5 Qxd1+; 7.Kxd1 Nc6; 8.f4 0-0-0+; 9.Bd2 Bc5; 10.Rg1 Nge7 and Black was much better in Steinitz-Chigorin (9), Havana 1889.

3...Bf5; 4.g4. 4.c4 f6 (4...c6 is probably wiser. This position requires practical tests, but I do not see any serious problems for Black.) 5.Nf3 e6; 6.Qb3! b6; 7.Nc3 c6; 8.a4 Na6; 9.cxd5 exd5; 10.e4! dxe4; 11.Bxa6 exf3; 12.0-0 and White was better in Lasker-Schiffers, Nurnberg 1896. **4...Bc8!**

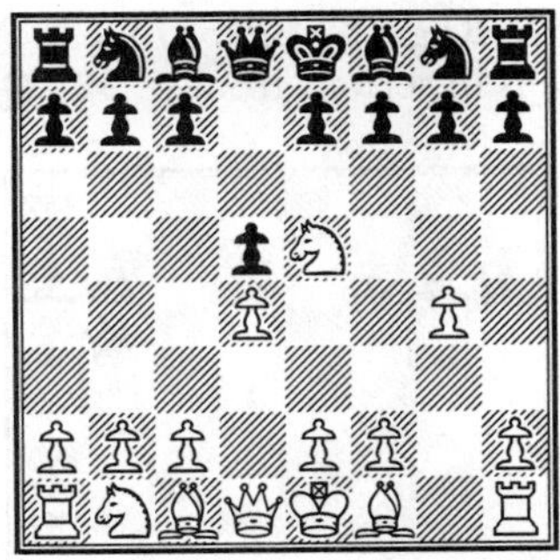

Having provoked the weakness, the bishop returns home. **5.g5.** 5.e3 f6; 6.Nd3 Nh6; 7.h3 Nf7; 8.f4 e5; 9.fxe5 fxe5; 10.dxe5 Qh4+ and Black has a strong attack. **5...Bf5.** Now that the pawn has advanced, Black returns to the outpost at f5. **6.c4 e6; 7.Nc3 Ne7; 8.Bg2 Nd7; 9.cxd5 Nxd5; 10.Nxd7.** 10.Nxd5 exd5; 11.Bxd5 Nxe5; 12.dxe5 Bb4+; 13.Kf1 Bh3+; 14.Kg1 c6; 15.Bb3 Qc8; 16.e3 Qf5 and Black is clearly better. **10...Qxd7; 11.e4.**

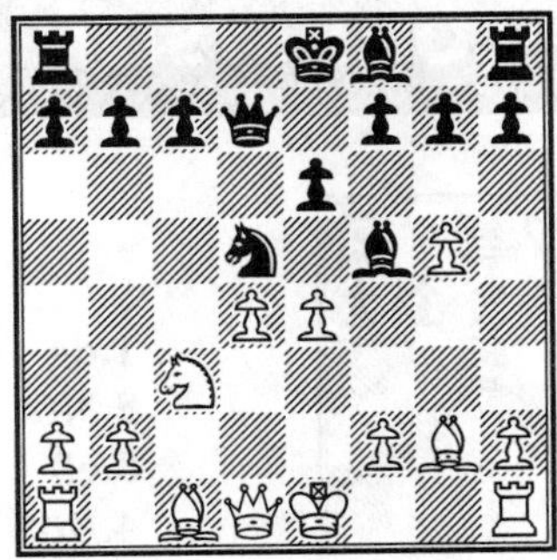

11...Nxc3; 12.bxc3 Bg6; 13.0-0 Be7; 14.Be3 0-0; 15.f4. Are the pawns strong or weak? **15...f6!; 16.h4 fxg5; 17.hxg5 Kh8; 18.Qd3 Rf7; 19.Rf2 Raf8; 20.Raf1.**

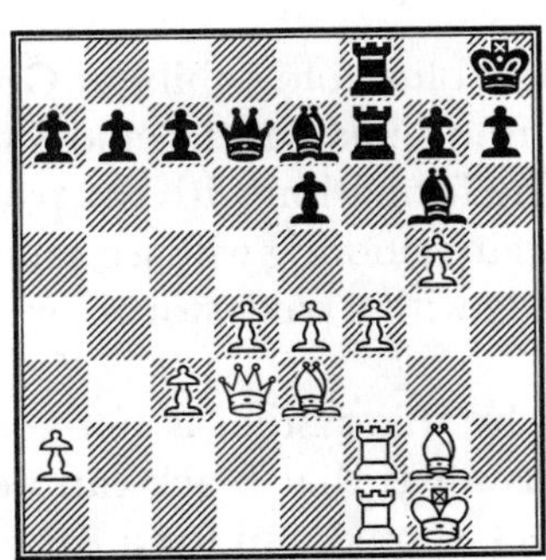

20...h6; 21.gxh6 gxh6; 22.Kh1 Rg8; 23.Rf3 Bh7; 24.Rh3 Bf8; 25.Bf3 Rf6. Black's position is solid enough. White has no real targets on the kingside. **26.Qd2 Rfg6; 27.Rg1 Rxg1+; 28.Bxg1 Qb5! 29.Qe1 Qd3; 30.Bg2 Qc2.** With just a Queen, Hodgson has been able to infiltrate effectively. **31.Bf3 Qxa2; 32.f5 exf5; 33.exf5 Qf7; 34.Bh2 Qxf5; 35.Be5+ Bg7; 36.Bxg7+ Rxg7; 37.Bg2.** 37.Qe8+ Rg8; 38.Qe5+ Qxe5; 39.dxe5 c6; 40.Rxh6 Rg3 and White is in serious trouble. **37...Qg6; 38.Bxb7?**

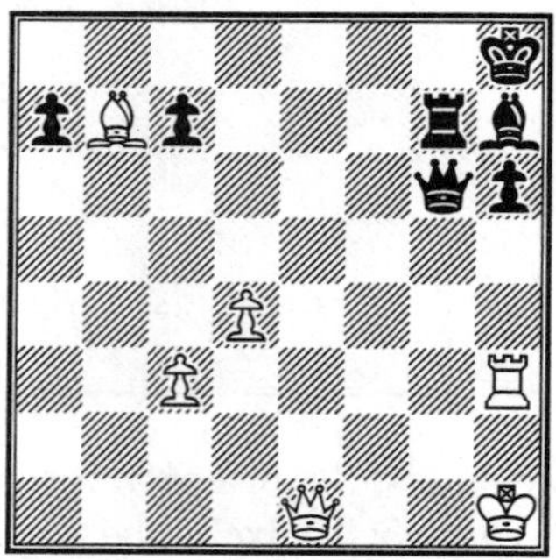

38...c6; 39.Qf2 Rxb7; 40.Qf8+ Bg8 and White resigned, since the capture at h6 would still leave him a piece down. **Black won.**

COLLE SYSTEM

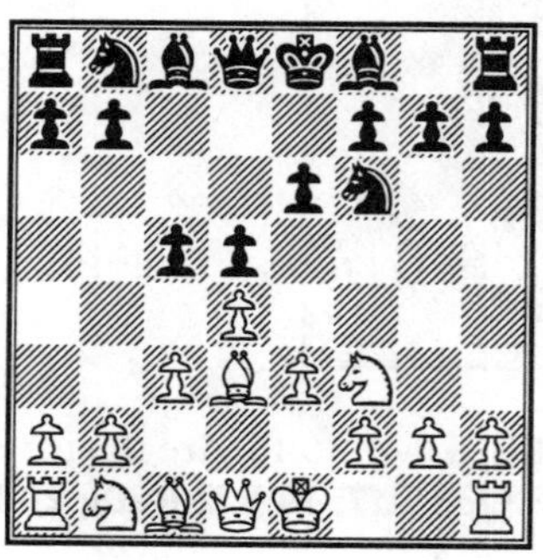

1.d4	**d5**
2.Nf3	**Nf6**
3.e3	**e6**
4.Bd3	**c5**
5.c3	

This is the way the great blindfold exhibitor George Koltanowski likes to play the Colle, and even in his 90s he still enjoys the attacking possibilities that White can obtain. The formation with the pawn at c3 is quite different than the Yusupov-Rubinstein handling with a queenside fianchetto. The idea here is go after the kingside with a pawnstorm, or advance the e-pawn to e4, as circumstances dictate.

One might wonder why this system is not seen more often in professional games, and the answer is that Black can deviate early in the game. After White plays e3, Black should aim for a King's Indian formation, and even "Kolty" admits that the setup is not so good against it.

When Black is ignorant enough to invite the position in the diagram, brilliant wins by White are the order of the day, especially when Koltanowski is handling the light pieces. Here we'll see just a few of his brilliancies.

(186) KOLTANOWSKI - LEU [D05]
Zurich, 1936

1.d4 d5; 2.Nf3 Nf6; 3.e3 e6; 4.Bd3 c5; 5.c3 Nbd7. The knight sits more naturally at c6, though that is no panacea, as Kolty demonstrates. 5...Nc6; 6.Nbd2.

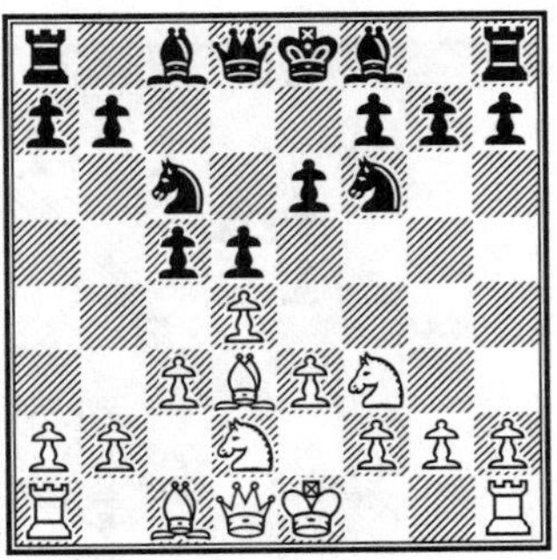

Here Black has tried a variety of defenses.

A) 6...Qc7; 7.0–0 Bd6; 8.dxc5 Bxc5 invites the standard thrust 9.e4! dxe4; (9...0–0 10.exd5 exd5; 11.Nb3 Bd6; 12.h3 Re8; 13.Nbd4 Nxd4; 14.Nxd4 left Black with a seriously weak d-pawn in Colle-Yates, Budapest 1926.) 10.Nxe4 Be7; 11.Qe2 0–0; 12.Bg5 Nxe4; 13.Qxe4 f5; 14.Qc4 Bxg5; 15.Nxg5 and Black suffered from the bad bishop and weak pawn structure in Koltanowski-Zavala, Mexico City (Simultaneous) 1939.

B) 6...cxd4; 7.exd4 Bd6; 8.0–0 Qc7; 9.Qe2 0–0; 10.Re1 Ne7; 11.Ne5 Ng6; 12.Ndf3 b6; 13.Ng5 Bd7; 14.f4 Ne7; 15.Ng4 Ng6; 16.Bxg6 hxg6; 17.Qf3 Nh7; 18.Nxh7 Kxh7; 19.Ne5 and White had the advantage in Colle-Prokes, Budapest 1929.

C) 6...Be7; 7.0–0 0–0; 8.dxc5 Bxc5 lets White carry out the thematic advance 9.e4! Qc7; 10.Qe2 and now what should Black do?

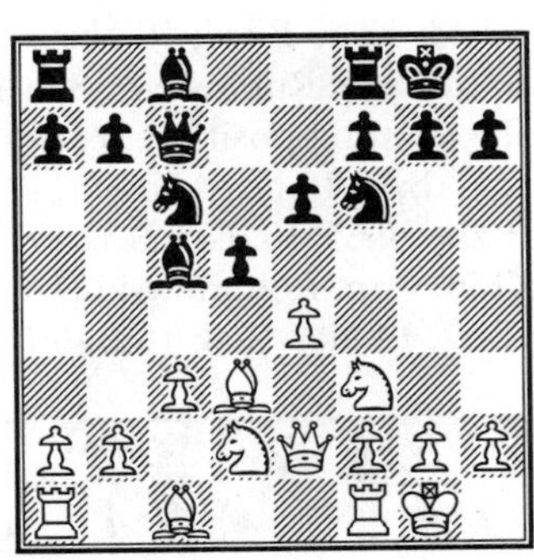

C1) 10...Re8; 11.e5 Nd7; 12.Nb3 Bb6; 13.Bf4 f6; 14.Rae1 Ncxe5; 15.Nxe5 Nxe5; 16.Bxh7+ Kf8 (16...Kxh7; 17.Qh5+ Kg8; 18.Qxe8+ Kh7; 19.Bxe5 fxe5; 20.Qh5+ Kg8; 21.Qxe5 is easily winning for White.) 17.Bg6 Rd8; 18.Qh5 Ke7; 19.Nd4 Bd7; 20.Rxe5 fxe5; 21.Bxe5 and Black resigned in Koltanowski-O'Hanlon, Dublin 1937.

C2) 10...h6; 11.b4 Bd6; 12.Bb2 e5; 13.a3 Re8; 14.c4 d4; 15.c5 Bf8; 16.Rac1 Bg4; 17.Nc4 Nh5; 18.g3 Qd8; 19.Kg2 Qc8; 20.Rg1 Re6; 21.h3 Rf6; 22.hxg4 Qxg4; 23.Kf1

Rxf3; 24.b5 Nxg3+; 25.Rxg3 Qxg3; 26.bxc6 bxc6; 27.Nxe5 Rf6; 28.Bxd4 Rd8; 29.Bb2 Qf4; 30.Ke1 Re6; 31.Nf3 Rb8; 32.Rc2 Rxb2 and in Ree-Polgar, Amsterdam 1995 White resigned because of the loss of material after 33.Rxb2 Qc1+; 34.Qd1 Qxb2.

C3) 10...Bd6; 11.Re1 Ng4; 12.h3 Nge5; 13.Nxe5 Nxe5; 14.exd5 exd5 forces Black to suffer because of the weak pawn at d5. 15.Nf3 Nxf3+; 16.Qxf3 Be6; 17.Be3 Rad8; 18.Bc2 b5; 19.Bd4 Bc5; 20.Rad1 b4; 21.Be5 Bd6.

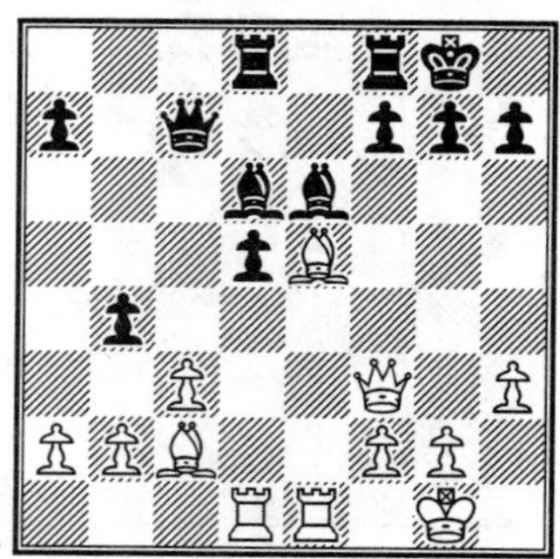

Koltanowski does not pass up the opportunity for a brilliant game: 22.Bxh7+!! Kxh7; 23.Qh5+ Kg8; 24.Bxg7!! Kxg7; 25.Qg5+ Kh7; 26.Rd4 and Black could only avoid checkmate by punting lots of material. 26...Bh2+ 27.Kh1 Qf4; 28.Rxf4 Bxf4; 29.Qxf4 Rg8; 30.Re5 and Black resigned in Koltanowski-Defosse, Belgian Championship 1936. 5...c4; 6.Bc2 is even worse for Black because when the e4 break comes it will undermine the entire pawn chain: 6...Nc6; 7.Nbd2 Bd6; 8.e4 dxe4; 9.Nxe4 b5; 10.0–0 Nxe4; 11.Bxe4 Bb7; 12.Qe2 g6; 13.a4 a6; 14.b3! cxb3; 15.axb5 axb5; 16.Rxa8 Qxa8; 17.Qxb5 0–0; 18.Qxb3 and that was the end of the pawn chain, and for all practical purposes the game, in a game Koltanowski played against an unknown opponent in 1936 in Zurich.

6.Nbd2 Be7. 6...Qc7; 7.0–0 Be7 is a variation on the same theme. 8.Re1 0–0; 9.e4 dxe4; 10.Nxe4 Nxe4; 11.Bxe4 Nf6; 12.Bc2 b6; 13.Bg5 Bb7; 14.Qd3 g6; 15.Ne5 Rac8; 16.dxc5 Rfd8; 17.Qh3 Rf8; 18.c6 Bxc6; 19.Nxc6 Qxc6; 20.Qh4 Kg7; 21.Bh6+ Kg8; 22.Bxf8 Kxf8; 23.Rad1 In Colle-Rubinstein, San Remo 1930, White actually found a way to lose this totally winning position. 6...Bd6; 7.0–0

A) 7...0–0; 8.e4 cxd4; 9.cxd4 dxe4; 10.Nxe4 Nxe4; 11.Bxe4 Nf6; 12.Bd3 b6 (12...h6; 13.Ne5 Bd7; 14.Qf3 Qc8; 15.Bxh6 Bxe5; 16.dxe5 Bc6; 17.Qg3 Ne8; 18.Rac1 f5; 19.exf6 Rxf6; 20.Bg5 Rf7; 21.Bg6 White won. Koltanowski-Danger, Santiago de Cuba Tournament Cuba 1940) 13.Re1 Bb7; 14.Ne5 Rc8; 15.Bg5 Be7; 16.Re3 h6.

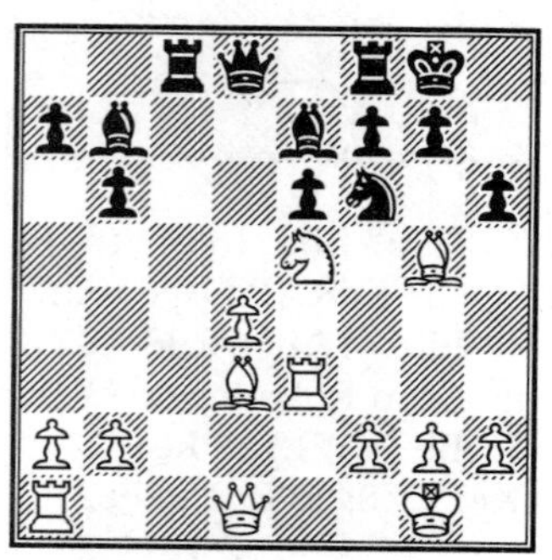

Here's another typical sacrifice: 17.Bxh6!! gxh6; 18.Rg3+ Kh8; 19.Qd2 Ng8; 20.Rxg8+! Kxg8; 21.Qxh6 f5; 22.Qxe6+ Kh8; 23.Qh6+ Kg8; 24.Qg6+ Kh8; 25.Bxf5 Rxf5; 26.Qxf5 and Black resigned, since further loss was inevitable. Koltanowski was playing a simultaneous exhibition blindfolded in Maine, 1939. 26...Qe8 (26...Qxd4; 27.Qh5+ Kg7; 28.Qf7+ Kh8; 29.Ng6#) 27.Re1! (Not 27.Ng6+? Kg7; 28.Re1 Bb4!! and Black comes out on top.) 27...Kg7; 28.Nd3 and the knight will be repositioned at f4 with a strong attack. In any case White has four pawns for the piece, which is more than sufficient.

B) 7...b6; 8.e4! dxe4; 9.Nxe4 Nxe4; 10.Bxe4 Rb8; 11.dxc5 Nxc5; 12.Bc6+ Ke7; 13.b4 Nb7; 14.Nd4 Qc7; 15.Qh5 Nd8; 16.b5 f6; 17.Re1 e5.

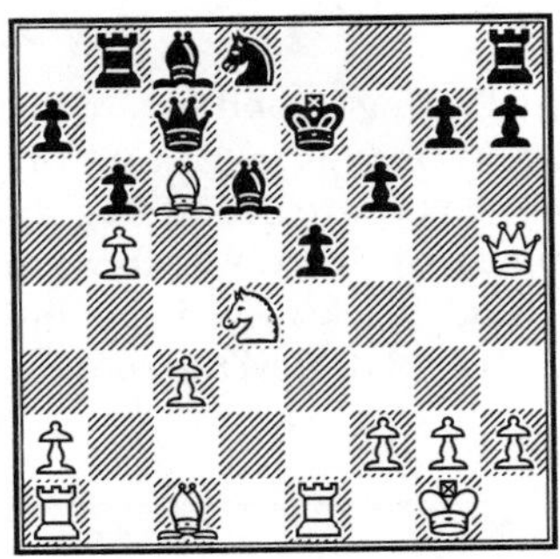

18.Rxe5+!! Bxe5; 19.Ba3+ Bd6; 20.Re1+ Ne6; 21.Nf5+ and it was mate in one, Koltanowski-Catala, Comtal Chess Club Tournament 1934. **7.0–0 0–0; 8.e4.**

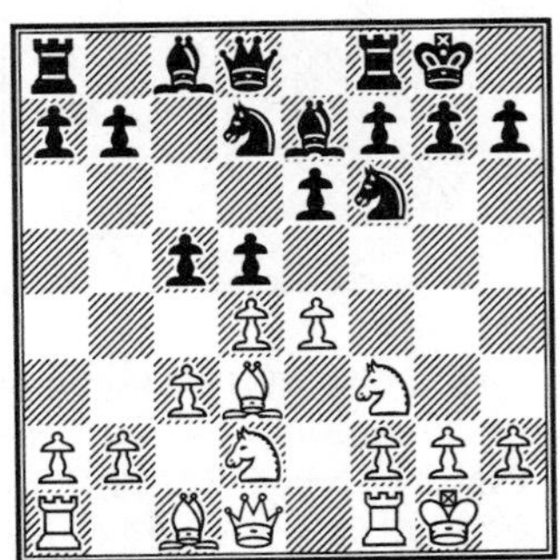

By now you get the idea. White's play is almost formulaic in the Colle, and the constant repetition of patterns makes it very easy to remember how to carry out the basic strategic and tactical operations. **8...dxe4; 9.Nxe4 cxd4; 10.cxd4 Nxe4; 11.Bxe4 Nf6; 12.Bd3.** White now has an isolated d-pawn, but this is not a bad one, because there are compensating factors in the availability of attacking forces n the kingside and the difficulty of getting the bishop at c8 into the game for Black. **12...b6; 13.Ne5 Bb7; 14.Re1 Qc7; 15.Bf4.** These are all natural developing move and a typical position has arisen.

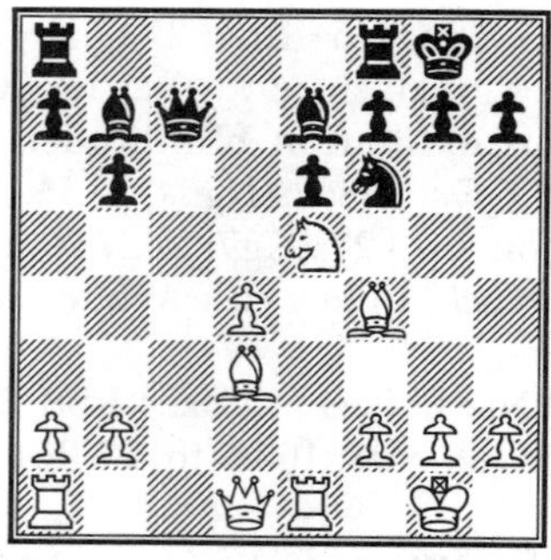

Black has some difficulty finding a good square for the queen, and cannot complete development until this problem is taken care of. Ideally the queen might be well-placed at a8, but first the rook has to get off that square and onto the c- or d-file. **15...Bb4.** This is a waste of time as the rook was about to move from e1 to e3 anyway. **16.Re3 Rfd8; 17.Rg3 Bd6.** Had Black played this instead of ...Bb4 a Black rook might already stand at c8. **18.Rc1 Qb8.** Now the rook at a8 has no future. **19.Qe2 g6; 20.Bg5 Be7.**

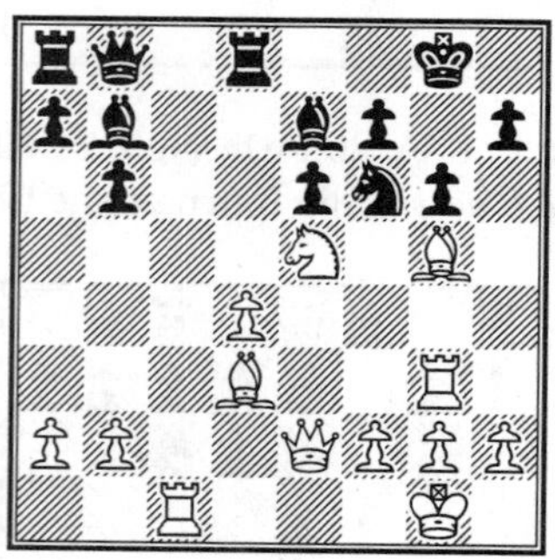

When calculating attacking force, we can eliminate the rook at a8 from the defensive side of the equation. Therefore sacrificing a piece is hardly a great risk. But it is still fun! **21.Bxg6! fxg6; 22.Nxg6 Kf7.** 22...hxg6; 23.Qxe6+ Kf8; 24.Bxf6 Qd6; 25.Bxe7+ Qxe7; 26.Qxg6 Bd5! (26...Qf7; 27.Qh6+ Ke8; 28.Re1+ Kd7; 29.Rg7 and White wins.) 27.Rh3 Qg7; 28.Qf5+ Bf7; 29.Rc7 Rxd4; 30.Rh8+! Qxh8; 31.Qxf7# **23.Ne5+ Kf8; 24.Bh6+ Ke8; 25.Rg8+ Bf8; 26.Rxf8+ Ke7; 27.Rf7+** and Black resigned as after **27...Ke8; 28.Rxf6** there is no point in continuing. **White won.**

QUEEN PAWN GAMES

Here we deal with some unrelated openings which do not fit into the standard categories, and so are simply known as **Queen Pawn Games.**

The Franco-Sicilian is known by many names, but the formation, usually reached via 1.e4 e6 2.d4 c5 3.d5, is suspect as White can defend the pawn at d5 with a knight at c3, and hold on to the spatial advantage it supplies. No strong players use it, but in amateur chess it is a popular opening among those who choose to stray just slightly off the beaten path.

The same idea of ...c5, allowing White to advance to d5, is seen in the Old Benoni, an opening known for its constricted positions with lack of room to maneuver.

The Keres Defense, 1.d4 e6 2.c4 Bb4+, can easily transpose into a Nimzoindian or Bogoindian. After 3.Nd2 or 3.Bd2, however, the play takes on a more original flavor.

White is not obliged to play a Queen's Gambit after 1.d4 d5, and there are alternatives such as the systems discussed in the previous section. White can also get radical by offering a pawn with 2.e4, the rather dubious Blackmar-Diemer Gambit. This opening has a legion of loyal fans in amateur circles because of the possibilities for quick and lethal attacks by White.

Finally, we deal with the Steinitz Countergambit which begins 1.d4 d5; 2.Bf4 c5. This opening has the usual drawback of being a tempo down on the usual Queen's Gambit by White.

FRANCO-SICILIAN

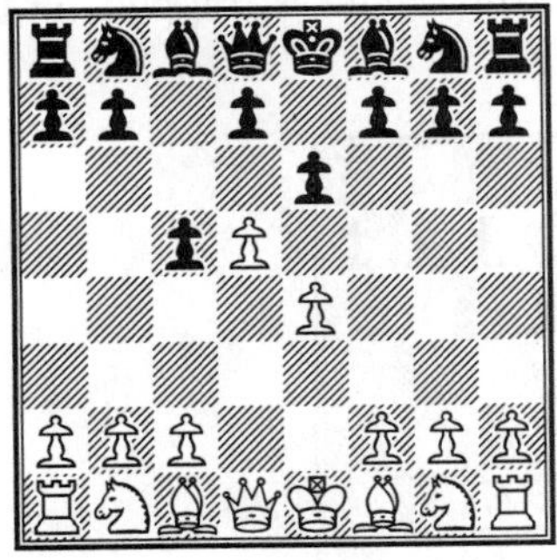

1.d4 e6
2.e4 c5
3.d5

This is a the **Franco-Sicilian** (1.d4 e6; 2.e4 c5), a variation which has never had a good reputation. Though unusual, it is by no means unorthodox, sharing standard concepts with the French Defense and Benoni. The problem is that White is able to establish a very strong center, against which counterplay will be hard to come by.

(187) KASPAROV - ILLESCAS CORDOBA [A43]

Madrid (active), 1989

1.d4 Nf6; 2.Nf3 c5; 3.d5 e6; 4.Nc3. Here the opening is reached via transposition. **4...exd5; 5.Nxd5 Nxd5; 6.Qxd5.**

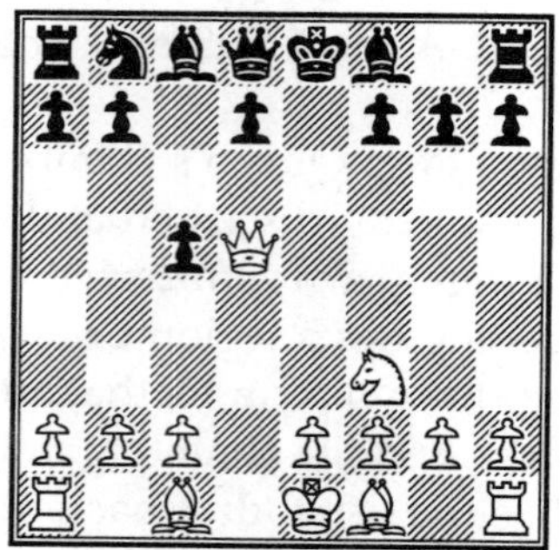

Black has traded off some pieces but is left with a serious backward pawn. **6...Nc6; 7.e4 d6; 8.Bc4 Be6; 9.Qd3 Nb4; 10.Bb5+! Ke7.** A rather bizarre solution. It is based on a tactical trick that does not bring the desired results. 10...Bd7; 11.Bxd7+ Qxd7; 12.Qc3! would prevent Black from fianchettoing his bishop. 12...Be7 but after 13.Qxg7 Nxc2+; 14.Kd1 Nxa1; 15.Qxh8+ Bf8. White continues the attack with 16.Bh6 Qe7; 17.Bxf8 Qxf8; 18.Qxf8+ Kxf8; 19.Kd2 and the knight is trapped. **11.Qe2 Nxc2+; 12.Qxc2 Qa5+; 13.Bd2 Qxb5.**

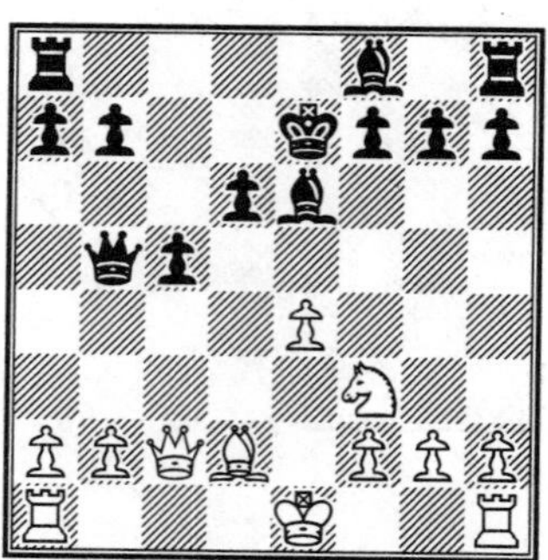

Black has an extra pawn, but his pieces are not functioning efficiently, save for the queen which is nicely posted at b5. **14.Bc3!** This will make it even more difficult to develop the kingside. **14...f6; 15.a4 Qb3; 16.Qe2 Qc4.** 16...Bc4 is met by 17.Qe3 and Nd2 is in the air. **17.Qe3 Kf7; 18.Nd2 Qa6; 19.f3.** Now the king will finally be able to shift position. **19...g6; 20.Kf2 Bg7; 21.Rhd1 Rhe8; 22.Qf4 Rad8; 23.Nf1.**

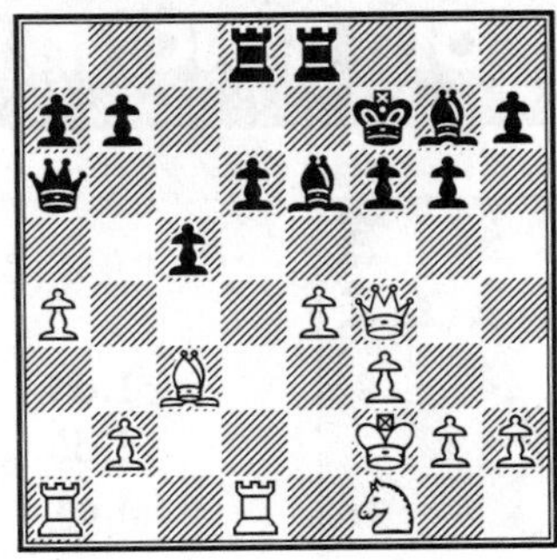

White still has strong pressure for the pawn, despite the fact that Black has developed and has the bishop pair. Black decides to eliminate the backward Pd6. **23...d5; 24.exd5 Rxd5; 25.Ne3 g5?!** This creates a serious weakness on the kingside. 25...Rxd1; 26.Rxd1 Qc6!? might be a better try. **26.Qc7+ Re7?** The Spaniard waves a red flag in front of Kasparov, who charges right at him!

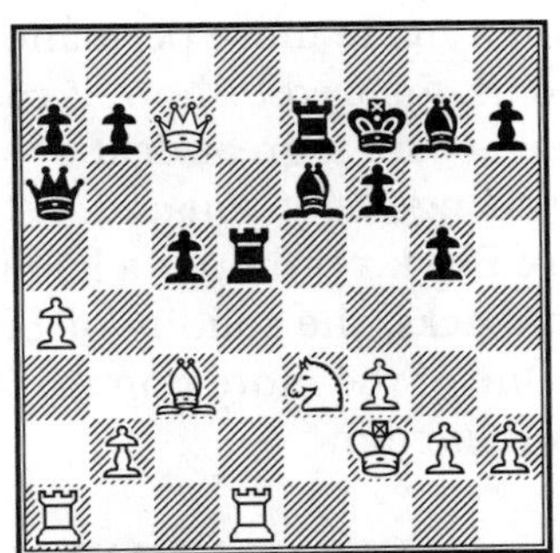

27.Qxe7+!! Kxe7; 28.Nxd5+ Kf7; 29.Nc7 Qc4; 30.Rd8. 30.Nxe6 Qxe6; 31.Re1 Qc6; 32.a5 was a reasonable alternative. **30...g4; 31.Re1 Bf5; 32.Ne8 Qxa4; 33.Nxg7 gxf3.** 33...Kxg7; 34.Re7+ Kg6; 35.Rf8 Qc2+; 36.Re2 and White wins. **34.Nxf5 Qc2+; 35.Kxf3 Qxf5+; 36.Kg3.** Black is attacking with just a queen, and soon eventually White's material superiority proves decisive. **36...b5; 37.Ree8 Qg5+; 38.Kf2 Qf4+; 39.Kg1 Qc1+; 40.Re1.** That takes care of the immediate checks. **40...Qc2; 41.Rd6 f5; 42.Rf6+.** Now White takes over the initiative and soon brings the game to a close. **42...Kg8; 43.Re8+ Kg7; 44.Rxf5+ Kg6; 45.Rf6+ Kh5; 46.Re5+ Kg4; 47.h3+ Kh4; 48.Be1+. White won.**

OLD BENONI

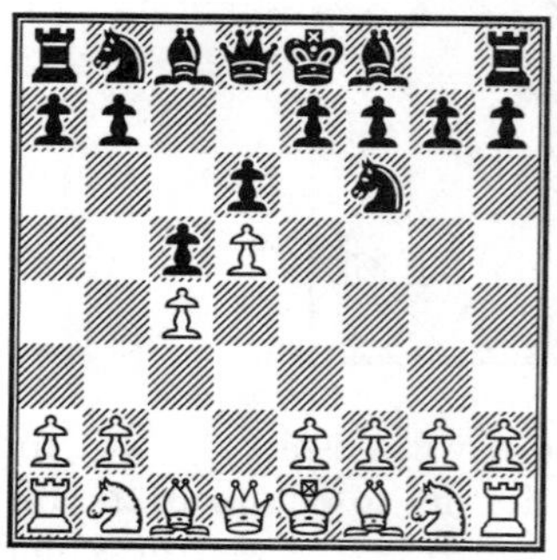

1.d4	**c5**
2.d5	**d6**
3.c4	**Nf6**

The **Old Benoni** is an inflexible formation for Black, who can at best hope for a transposition to the King's Indian Defense. Black suffers from lack of space, which is often made more permanent by an early ...e5. Black has two choices for the dark-squared bishop. It can go to g7 or e7. White's best replies are those that secure a great deal of space. If Black plays ...e5, sometimes White will exchange light squared bishops via Bh3 and go into superior endgames where Black's bishop is a liability.

Despite all these drawbacks, the solidity of Black's position appeals to some players even now. One of the more popular approaches is the Schmid Benoni, which we will examine now.

(188) HAYES - SCHMID [A43]
Postal, 1954

1.d4 c5; 2.d5 d6; 3.Nc3 g6; 4.e4 Bg7; 5.Nf3 Nf6. Lothar Schmid is one of the renaissance men of chess. He is a Grandmaster, International Arbiter, and owns one of the finest collections of chess sets and books in the world. He has also made significant contributions to opening theory, especially in the slower systems of the Benoni. This is one of his favorite lines.

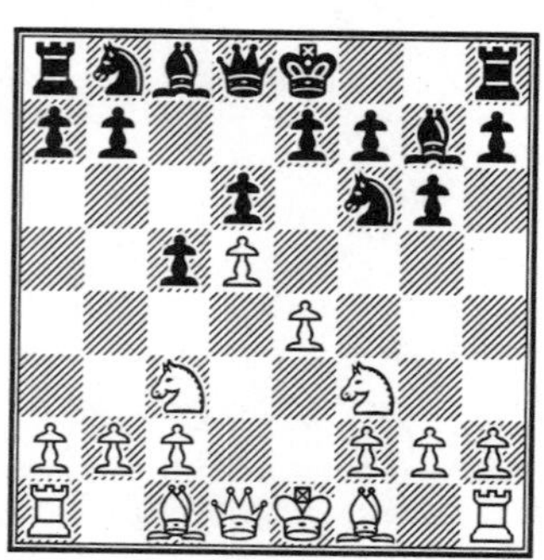

6.Be2. 6.Bf4 0–0; 7.Bc4 is met by 7...b5!; 8.Bxb5 Nxe4 as in Trifunovic-Schmid, Zurich 1954. 6.Bb5+ Nbd7; 7.a4 0–0; 8.0–0 a6 was fine for Black in Tal-Benko, Candidates Tournament 1959. **6...Na6.** Usually Black castles here and plays ...Na6 on the next move, but there is usually no significant difference between the lines. In the present game, however, Schmid postpones castling for another dozen moves! **7.0–0.** 7.Bg5 h6; 8.Bf4 Nc7; 9.e5 Nh5; 10.Be3 dxe5; 11.Bxc5 Nf4; 12.d6 Nxg2+; 13.Kf1 Bh3; 14.Kg1 led to a very messy position in Tal-Schmid, USSR vs. West Germany match, 1960. **7...Nc7.**

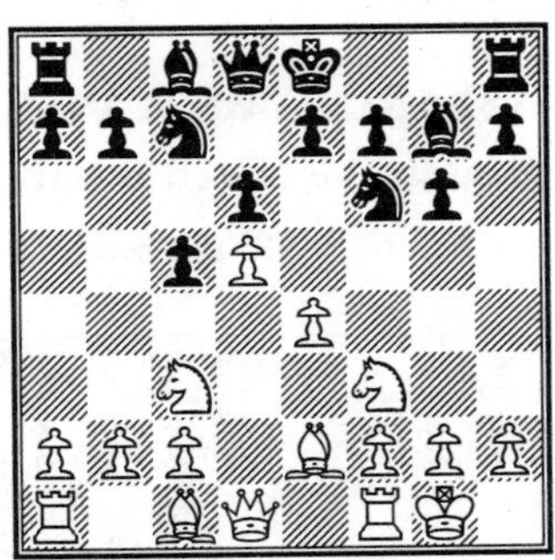

Schmid's idea is to initiate operations on the queenside as soon as possible, castling only if and when remaining in the center becomes dangerous, or if the rook at h8 is needed on the queenside. 7...0–0; 8.Nd2 Nc7; 9.a4 a6; 10.Nc4 b5; 11.axb5 axb5; 12.Rxa8 Nxa8; 13.Nxb5 Nxe4; 14.Bf3 Ba6; 15.Nba3 Nf6; 16.Re1 Re8; 17.Bd2 Nc7; 18.Ba5 Qc8; 19.Qd2 was agreed drawn in Malaniuk-Leko, Brno 1993. **8.Nd2 a6; 9.a4 Bd7; 10.Nc4.** 10.a5 Nb5; 11.Ncb1 0–0; 12.Bf3 Nd4; 13.Nc4 Bb5; 14.Nba3 Nd7; 15.Bg4 Ne5 is typical of the maneuvering nature of this opening. In Keres-Schmid, Vienna 1957, Black was no worse. **10...b5.**

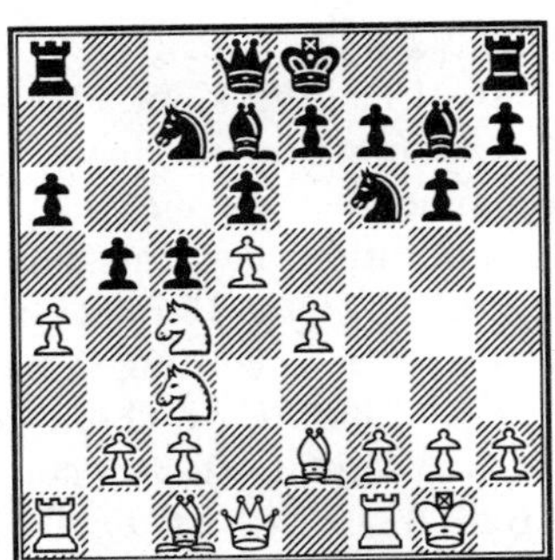

Now White must resist the temptation to infiltrate at b6, as Schmid has a surprise prepared. **11.Nb6?** 11.e5 is the correct move, for example 11...dxe5; 12.axb5 axb5; 13.Rxa8 Qxa8; 14.Nxe5 b4 where 15.d6 is a little better for White. Black must be careful, as Schmid found out against Botvinnik at the 1960 Olympiad in Leipzig: 15...bxc3?; 16.dxc7! and White had a winning position.

11...b4! Black sacrifices the exchange but has tremendous compensation on the queenside and in the center. **12.Nxa8 Qxa8; 13.Nb1 Nxe4; 14.Bf3 f5.** Black has secured the central outpost, and White has too many weaknesses in the position.

15.Nd2. 15.Re1 Qxd5; 16.Qxd5 Nxd5; 17.Bxe4 fxe4; 18.Rxe4 is fine for Black after 18...Bf5 or 18...a5, according to Soltis. 15.c4 bxc3; 16.Nxc3 Nxc3; 17.bxc3 Bxc3; 18.Rb1 0–0; 19.Qb3 Bg7 is also fine for Black.

15...Ng5; 16.Re1. Black now eliminates the defender of the weak pawn at d5. **16...Nxf3+; 17.Nxf3 Nxd5; 18.Nd2.** By now, this knight may be feeling a bit drunk, but it continues its peregrinations for a while. **18...0–0; 19.Nc4 Bc6.** Black's position is winning, and White's feeble attempt to launch a kingside attack is met with ruthless efficiency by Schmid. **20.h4 e5; 21.h5 Rf6; 22.Na5 Bd7; 23.Nc4 gxh5; 24.Qxh5 Rg6; 25.Qf3 e4; 26.Qd1 f4; 27.a5 Bg4. Black won.**

(189) KASPAROV - BELYAVSKY [A43]

Candidates, 9th Match Game, 1983

1.d4 Nf6; 2.Nf3 c5; 3.d5 d6.

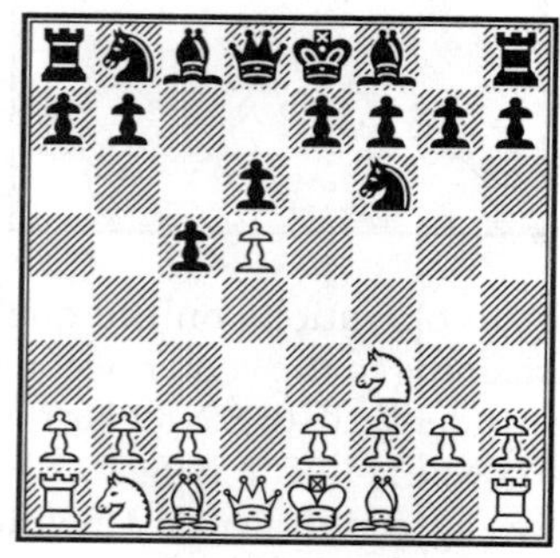

A solid move which allows the game to enter the pathways of the Benoni with 4.c4. But White doesn't have to cooperate. **4.Nc3!** This leads to the Russian System, which is structurally superior for White. **4...g6; 5.e4 Bg7; 6.Bb5+.** The simple 6.Be2 is also good. **6...Bd7.** 6...Nbd7; 7.a4 a6; 8.Be2 0–0; 9.0–0 leads to rich and unclear play. **7.a4 0–0; 8.0–0 Na6; 9.Re1!** Here it is not advisable to capture at a6, as the pressure on the b-file will compensate for the pawn structure. **9...Nb4; 10.h3 e6; 11.Bf4!? e5.** 11...Bxb5 was recommended by some commentators, but Kasparov points out that this would lead to complications favoring White. 12.Nxb5!

A) 12...a6; 13.Nxd6 Nh5; 14.Nxb7 Qb6; 15.Bd6! Qxb7 (15...Rfc8; 16.c3) 16.Bxf8 Rxf8; 17.c3 and White is clearly better, according to Kasparov.

B) 12...exd5; 13.Bxd6 dxe4; 14.Bxf8 Qxf8 (14...Qxd1; 15.Raxd1 Rxf8; 16.Ng5 Nxc2; 17.Re2) 15.Ng5 Re8; 16.Nc3 with insufficient compensation for the exchange.

12.Bg5 Bc8. 12...h6; 13.Bxf6 Bx f6; 14.Bxd7 Qxd7; 15.Nd2 Be7 might have provided more counterplay, according to Kasparov. **13.Nd2 h6; 14.Bh4 g5.**

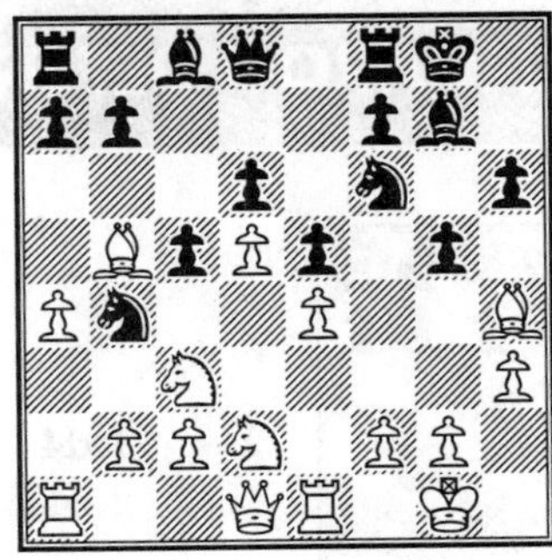

Black decides to go for broke. 14...Qc7; 15.Be2! Ne8; 16.Nc4 f5?!; 17.Nb5 Qd7; 18.exf5 gxf5; 19.Bh5 gives White very powerful pressure thanks to the bishops. **15.Bg3 g4?!** 15...h5!; 16.Be2 g4; 17.Bh4! gxh3; 18.g3! was given by Kasparov, and now Black has too many weaknesses on the kingside. **16.hxg4 Nxg4; 17.f3 Nf6; 18.Bh4 Kh8; 19.Ne2 Rg8; 20.c3 Na6; 21.Ng3.**

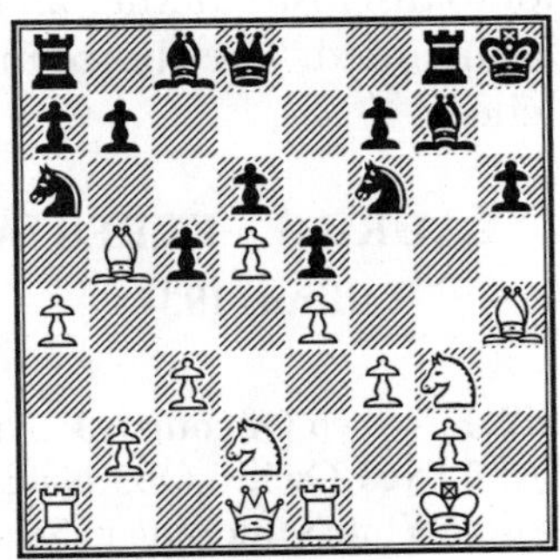

21...Qf8. 21...Bf8; 22.Ndf1 Be7 would have provided stiffer resistance, according to Kasparov. **22.Ndf1 Nh7; 23.Ne3 Bf6; 24.Bxf6+ Nxf6; 25.Ngf5.** With this infiltration Black is effectively lost, with White dominating the board. The rest is just a matter of technique for the future World Champion. **25...Nh5; 26.Kf2 Bxf5; 27.Nxf5 Nf4; 28.g3 Nh3+; 29.Ke2 Rxg3; 30.Nxg3 Qg7; 31.Rg1 Rg8; 32.Qd2. White won.**

KANGAROO DEFENSE

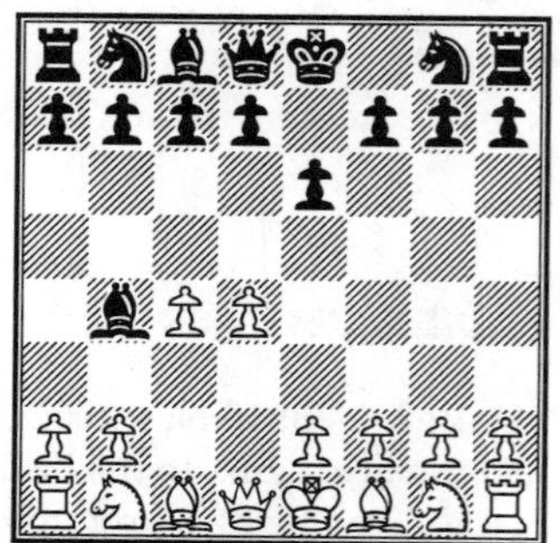

1.d4	**e6**
2.c4	**Bb4+**

This is the **Keres Defense**, more commonly known as the **Kangaroo Defense**. Black decides not to disclose whether an Indian formation, Closed Game or Dutch Defense is intended. The choice may depend on how White chooses to deal with the check.

(190) LAURINE - KERES [A40]
Tallinn, 1937

1.d4 e6; 2.c4 Bb4+; 3.Bd2. 3.Nc3 c5 Of course 3...Nf6 would be a Nimzo-Indian Defense. 4.e3 (4.dxc5 Bxc3+!; 5.bxc3 Qa5; 6.Qb3 Na6; 7.Qa3 Qxc5 and the weak doubled pawns eventually proved White's undoing in Schmidt-Keres, Estonian Championship 1936.) 4...d5; 5.cxd5 exd5; 6.a3 Bxc3+; 7.bxc3 Nf6; 8.dxc5 0–0; 9.Bd3 Nbd7; 10.Ne2 Nxc5; 11.Bb1 b6; 12.0–0 Ba6; 13.Re1 Rc8; 14.Bb2 Bc4 and Black had a fine position in Landau-Keres, Zandvoort 1936.

3...Qe7; 4.Nc3. 4.Bxb4 Qxb4+; 5.Qd2 Nc6; 6.e3 Qxd2+; 7.Kxd2 f5; 8.Nc3 Nf6; 9.Nb5 Kd8; 10.f3 a6; 11.Nc3 f4; 12.Nge2 fxe3+; 13.Kxe3 d5 gave Black sufficent resources in Graf-Keres, Prague Olympiad 1931. **4...f5; 5.Nf3 Nf6; 6.Qb3.** 6.Qc2 Bxc3; 7.bxc3 b6; 8.e3 Bb7; 9.Bd3 0–0 and now 10.0–0–0 was a big mistake: 10...c5; 11.h3 Rc8; 12.Ne1 d5; 13.cxd5 Bxd5; 14.Qb2 Ne4; 15.Bxe4 fxe4; 16.f3 Nc6 and White was in big trouble on the queenside in Kibbermann-Keres, Tallinn 1937. **6...b5.**

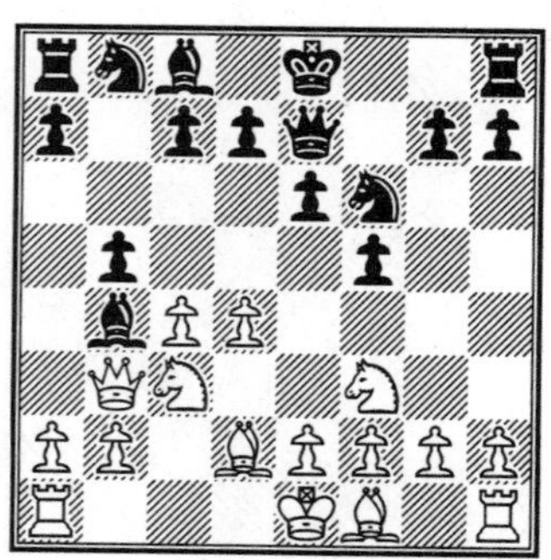

An interesting gambit idea, to open up the position on the queenside and try to gain control of d5. **7.e3?** I don't know why White declined the offer. 7.Nxb5! Threatens Nxc7+, but there is no simple defense, for example 7...Bxd2+ (7...Na6; 8.Bxb4 Qxb4+; 9.Qxb4 Nxb4; 10.Nxc7+ Kd8; 11.Nxa8 Nc2+; 12.Kd2 Nxa1; 13.Ne5 Ne4+; 14.Kc1 Rf8; 15.f3 Nf6; 16.c5 Bb7; 17.Nb6 axb6; 18.cxb6 Nb3+; 19.axb3 and White may not have three healthy pawns, but they are still three extra pawns!) 8.Nxd2 Kd8.

A) 9.e3 Bb7; 10.0–0–0 Nc6.

A1) 11.Nd6?! Qxd6; 12.Qxb7 Rb8; 13.Qa6 does not provide enough compensation for the pawn because 13...Rb6 is refuted by (13...Qb4!; 14.Qa3 Qxa3; 15.bxa3 Ke7; 16.Bd3 Rb7; 17.Nb3 d6; 18.f3 is only a little better for White.) 14.c5! **A2)** 11.Be2! Rb8; 12.Qa4 leaves Black with no compensation for the pawn.

B) 9.Nxa7!? Rxa7; 10.Qxb8 Rb7; 11.Qa8 Rxb2 gives Black too much counterplay.

7...Bb7; 8.Be2. 8.cxb5 a6; 9.bxa6 Nxa6; 10.a3 Bxc3; 11.Bxc3 Bd5; 12.Bc4 Rb8 also might be worth something to Black, with ...Ne4 as a follow-up. 8.Nxb5 Bxd2+; 9.Nxd2 Na6; 10.Nc3 Rb8 would now provide just a bit of compensation for the pawn, but not a lot. **8...0–0; 9.0–0 Bxc3; 10.Bxc3 Ne4.**

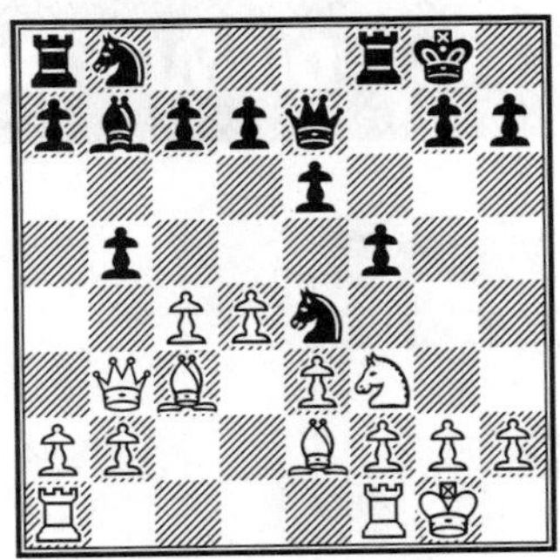

Black's strategy is now that of the Queen's Indian. Now White must be concerned with attacks on the kingside. Therefore White was obligated to take the pawn at b5 when it was still edible. Now it is getting dangerous. **11.d5?!** 11.a4! would have been awkward for Black. 11.Qxb5 Ba6; 12.Qa5 d5 provides some counterplay, though even here it is probably not enough. **11...Na6!; 12.Rad1.** 12.Qxb5 Nac5 and the Black knights are much more powerful than the White bishops.

12...d6; 13.dxe6. An interesting alternative is 13.Ba5!? **13...Nac5; 14.Qc2 Nxe6; 15.b4 a5.** This is much more aggressive than the capture at c3. **16.a3?** White's stubborn insistence on not capturing any pawns is becoming tiresome. 16.bxa5 was the correct move. **16...f4; 17.Rd3?** The reader is by now familiar with the pattern of the game. This was the last opportunity to finally snatch the pawn at b5! 17.cxb5 Nxc3; 18.Qxc3 axb4; 19.Qxb4 Nc5; 20.Bc4+ Kh8 would have White worrying about the kingside, but keeping the bishop at e2 would probably be wiser.

17...axb4; 18.axb4 N4g5! Now Black has the initiative, and pawns are no longer of any consequence. **19.exf4.** Now White had to take the other pawn (of course!) even though it would cost the exchange after 19.cxb5 Be4. **19...Nxf4; 20.Re3.**

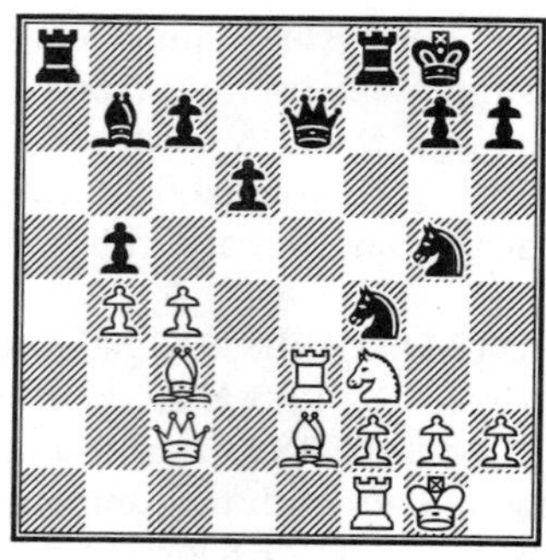

Here the walls start to crumble. **20...Nxe2+; 21.Qxe2 Nxf3+; 22.gxf3 Qg5+; 23.Kh1 Rxf3!!; 24.Rxf3 Qg4** and White resigned. Note that the Black pawn, offered up at move 6, is still sitting at b5! **Black won.**

BLACKMAR-DIEMER GAMBIT

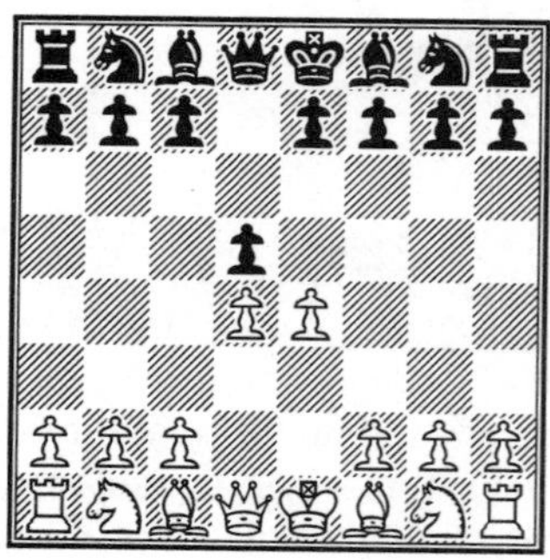

1.d4 d5
2.e4

The **Blackmar-Diemer Gambit** has never been considered respectable enough for use in professional events, and the few attempts that have been made to use it have often met with disaster for White. The opening remains popular in amateur chess games because it leads to very sharp games with opportunities for spectacular sacrifices.

If Black accepts the pawn at e4, White will develop the knight to c3 and then offer to make the gambit a permanent one by challenging the center with f3. The gambit can be declined, of course, and Black can transpose to the French Defense with 2...e6 or Caro-Kann with 2...c6, but of course those openings are only options if Black is well acquainted with them. In any case, anyone who plays the Blackmar-Diemer as White will likely continue with a lively gambit anyway.

The best defenses involve acceptance of the gambit pawns and rapid kingside development, setting up barriers that will weather the attacking storm that White will create with open lines and effective pawn advances. If the defenses are solid, the endgames will be a simple matter to win. The Euwe Defense with 5...e6 is the strongest available, in my opinion. Also good is 5...g6, the Bogoljubow Defense.

We will examine both of these approaches below.

(191) SAWYER - O'CONNELL [D00]

Correspondence, 1989

1.d4 d5; 2.e4 dxe4; 3.Nc3 Nf6. This position can also arise via 1.d4 d5; 2.Nc3 Nf6; 3.e4 dxe4. **4.f3 exf3; 5.Nxf3 e6.**

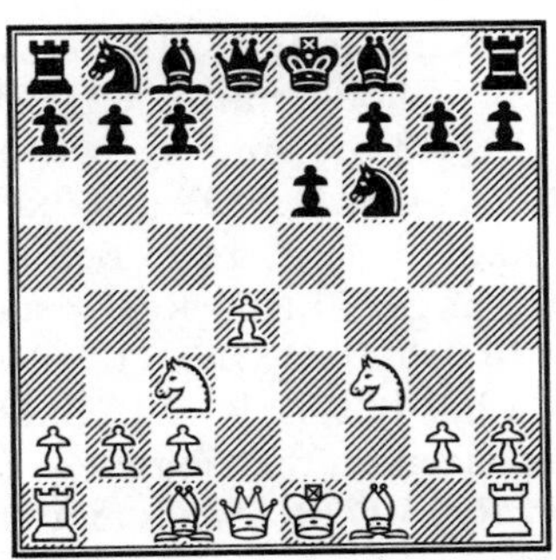

There are other playable options, but in those cases White gets real attacking chances for the pawn. **6.Bg5 Be7; 7.Bd3.** The standard move, though there are alternatives. 7.Qd2 h6; 8.Bh4 Nc6; 9.0–0–0 Ne4! 10.Nxe4 Bxh4; 11.g3 Be7; 12.h4 Qd5 and White has less than nothing for the pawn. 7.Bb5+ Bd7; 8.Qe2 Nc6!? (8...a6; 9.Bd3 0–0; 10.0–0 Nc6; 11.a3 h6; 12.Bd2 Bd6; 13.h3 gave White some compensation in Stummer-Kiesei, Correspondence 1958, and in my monograph on the Blackmar Diemer Gambit I suggested that this is the best path to follow for White. But now I think that the immediate knight move may be better.) 9.0–0–0 h6

A) 10.Bd2 a6

A1) 11.Bxc6 Bxc6; 12.Ne5 Nd7; 13.Nxc6 bxc6; 14.Qf3 Bf6; 15.Qxc6 0–0; 16.Bf4 e5; 17.dxe5 Bxe5; 18.Bxe5 (18.Rxd7 Bxf4+; 19.Kb1 Qg5; 20.g3 Be5÷) 18...Nxe5; 19.Rxd8 Nxc6; 20.Rxf8+ Kxf8; 21.Nd5 Rc8; 22.Re1 Nd4

A2) 11.Bd3 Nb4 and again White is hard pressed to justify the investment of the pawn.

B) 10.Bh4 Nb4 11.Bxd7+ Nxd7 and White's attack has run out of steam. **7...Nc6!**

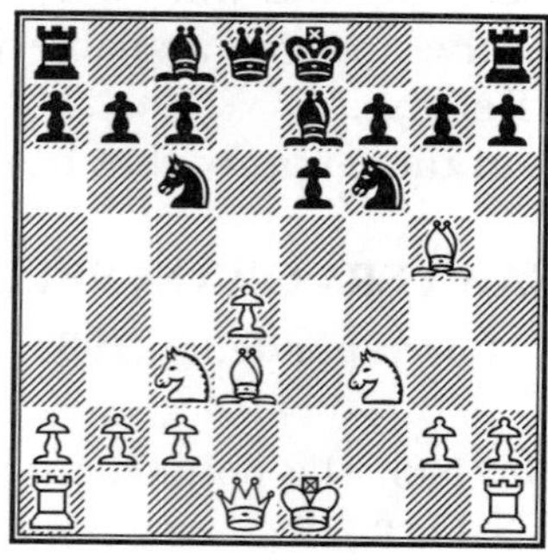

8.a3. 8.0–0 Nxd4; 9.Kh1 Nxf3; 10.Qxf3 (Fechner-Schneider, Correspondence n.d.) 10...Bd7! followed by ...Bc6. should suffice. 8.Qd2 be met by 8...h6; 9.Be3 Nd5; 10.Nxd5 (10.0–0–0 Nxe3; 11.Qxe3 Bf6 are both better for Black.) 10...exd5; 11.c3 (Sawyer-Riley, USA 1989) 11...Bg4; 12.Ne5 (12.0–0 Bxf3; 13.Rxf3 Qd7; 14.Qf2 Bf6; 15.Re1 0–0–0). 12...Nxe5; 13.dxe5 Bh4+; 14.g3 Bg5 and Black has a good game. **8...h6! 9.Bd2.** 9.Bf4 g5; 10.Be5 g4; 11.Nh4 Rg8 is suggested by Diemer. **9...0–0.** 9...Nd5!? might be stronger. **10.0–0.** 10.Qe2 a6; 11.0–0–0 b5 and Black's chances are no worse. **10...Nxd4; 11.Qe1 b6; 12.Kh1 Bb7; 13.Bxh6 Nxf3!; 14.gxf3 Qd4!** Now Black will be able to use his queen on the kingside – for both attack and defense! **15.Be4 Nxe4; 16.fxe4 f5!; 17.Rg1 Rf7.** Black has more than enough support for g7. **18.Rg2 fxe4. Black won.**

(192) DIEMER - DOPPERT [D00]

Worms, 1958

1.d4 d5; 2.e4 dxe4; 3.Nc3 Nf6; 4.f3 exf3; 5.Nxf3 g6.

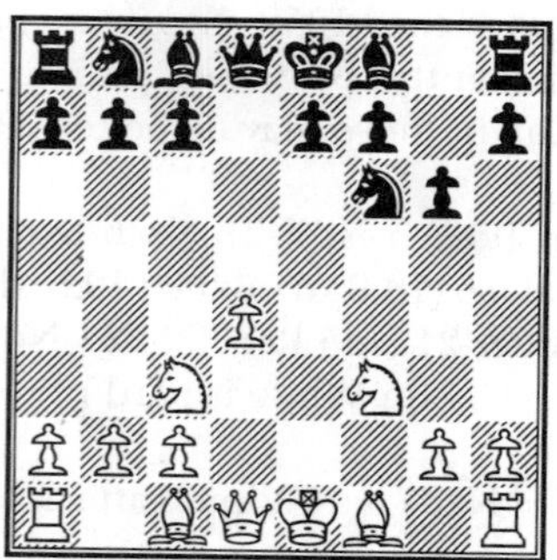

This is known as the Bogoljubow Defense, even though Bogoljubow was seen more frequently on the White side than the Black side. It is a popular defense to the Blackmar-Diemer Gambit, though it does require precise handling by Black. I think it is now fair to say that the Bogoljubow Defense is a fully playable reply to the Blackmar-Diemer Gambit, and is in many cases a more active plan of defense than 5...e6, the solid Euwe Defense. The main line of the Bogoljubow Defense runs 6.Bc4 Bg7; 7.0–0 0–0; 8.Qe1, which is known as the Studier Attack. Then 8...Nc6; 9.Qh4

Bg4 is the normal continuation, and it is examined in the present game. **6.Bc4 Bg7; 7.0–0 0–0; 8.Qe1 Nc6; 9.Qh4 Bg4; 10.Be3 Bxf3; 11.Rxf3.**

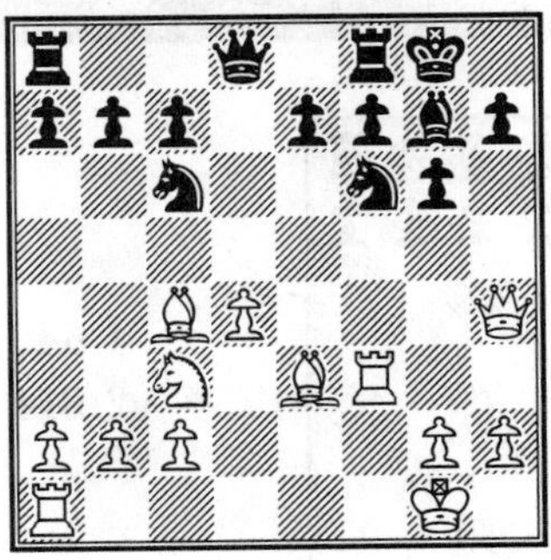

This capture is normal, as otherwise the knight becomes a strong attacking piece. Now Black has to choose a plan. **11...e5.** 11...Nb4; 12.Ne4 Nxc2 (12...Nxe4; 13.Qxe4 c6 followed by ...Nd5 is a better plan.) 13.Ng5 h5; 14.Raf1 Nxe3; 15.Rxe3 Nd5; 16.Ref3 and f7 is doomed, De Vore-Woll, Postal 1970. 11...Qd7; 12.Raf1 Rad8 is an interesting alternative. 13.Ne2 Qg4; 14.Qf2 Ne4; 15.Qe1 Nd6; 16.h3 Qh5; 17.Bb3 e6; 18.g4 Qb5; 19.c3 Na5; 20.Nc1 Nxb3; 21.axb3 Qd5 gave Black a solid game in Lagland-Frings, Postal 1975.

12.d5 Nd4; 13.Rf2 Nf5?! 13...Nd7; 14.Qxd8 Raxd8 is more solid. **14.Rxf5! gxf5; 15.Bg5.** White's powerful bishops provide adequate compensation for the exchange. **15...Qd6; 16.Rf1.** Now Black fell prey to material temptation, but this position may in fact be better for Black. **16...Qb6+.** 16...h6 is a move which definitely deserves consideration. **17.Kh1 Qxb2.**

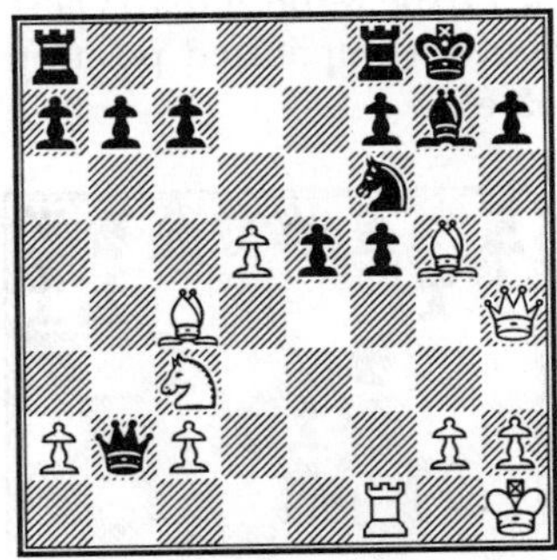

18.Bxf6 Bxf6; 19.Qxf6 Qxc2; 20.Rxf5 Qc1+; 21.Bf1. Black's attack has run out of steam, and now it is time to hand the initiative over to White. **21...Rfe8; 22.Qxf7+.** 22.Rg5+ Qxg5; 23.Qxg5+ Kf8; 24.Qf6 was simpler. **22...Kh8; 23.Qf6+ Kg8; 24.Rg5+ Qxg5; 25.Qxg5+ Kh8; 26.Qf6+ Kg8; 27.d6. White won.**

STEINITZ COUNTERGAMBIT

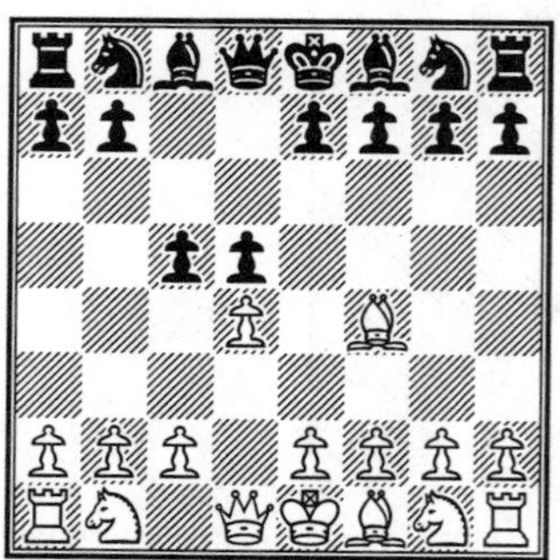

1.d4 d5
2.Bf4 c5

The **Steinitz Countergambit** has generally enjoyed a good reputation, but that may have to be re-evaluated now that 1.d4 d5; 2.c4 Bf5!?, the Baltic Defense, has achieved respectability for Black. Here White invites the same positions with an extra tempo. 2.Bf4 is the Sarratt Attack. It often transposes to the London System.

(193) MASON - STEINITZ [D00]
London, 1883

1.d4 d5; 2.Bf4 c5 3.dxc5. 3.Bxb8 Rxb8; 4.dxc5 Qa5+; 5.Nc3 e6; 6.e4 Bxc5; 7.Bb5+ Kf8; 8.exd5 Qb6 brings about a complicated position which seems no worse for Black. **3...Nc6; 4.Nf3 f6; 5.e3 e5.**

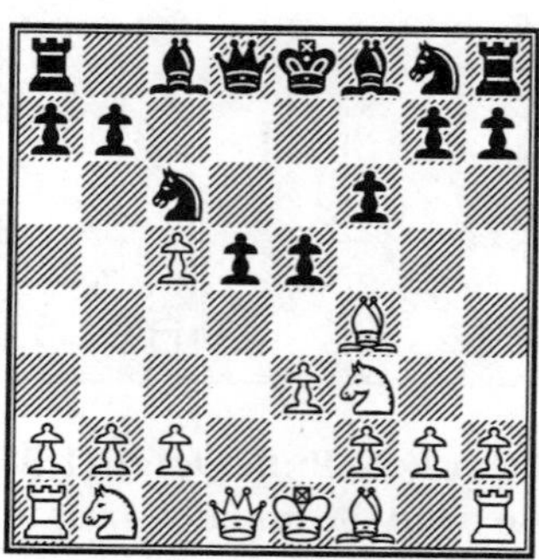

Black already has the advantage. **6.Bg3 Bxc5; 7.c3 Nge7; 8.Nbd2 Bb6; 9.Be2 0–0; 10.0–0 Nf5; 11.e4 Nxg3; 12.hxg3 d4!** Black is not concerned with the a2-g8 diagonal. The key action is on the dark squares, and the bishop at b6 will later play a major role when the pawn advances from d4 to d3. **13.cxd4 exd4; 14.Bc4+ Kh8; 15.Nb3 Bg4; 16.Bd5** 16.Be2 would have been safer. **16...Ne5; 17.Bxb7 Rb8; 18.Bd5 f5; 19.Nbd2 f4!** Black will crack open the f-file and descend on the kingside. **20.Qa4.**

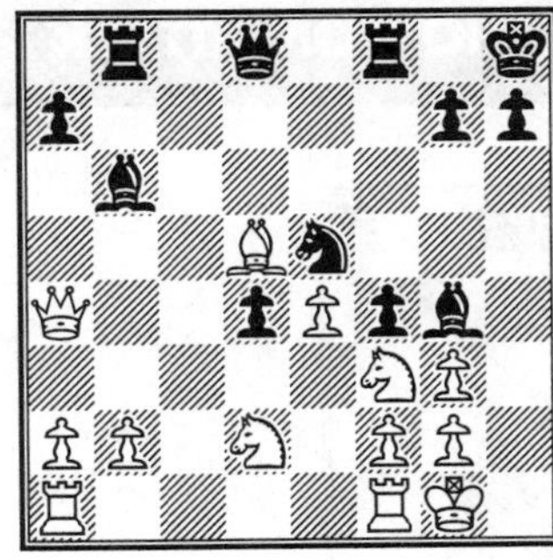

20...Nxf3+!; 21.Nxf3 fxg3; 22.fxg3 Qd6! This is stronger than the immediate discovered check. **23.Nh2 d3+; 24.Kh1 Be2; 25.Rxf8+ Rxf8; 26.Bb3 Qxg3; 27.Qd7 d2; 28.Qxd2 Bc7; 29.e5 Qxe5; 30.Nf3 Rxf3! Black won.**

DUTCH DEFENSE

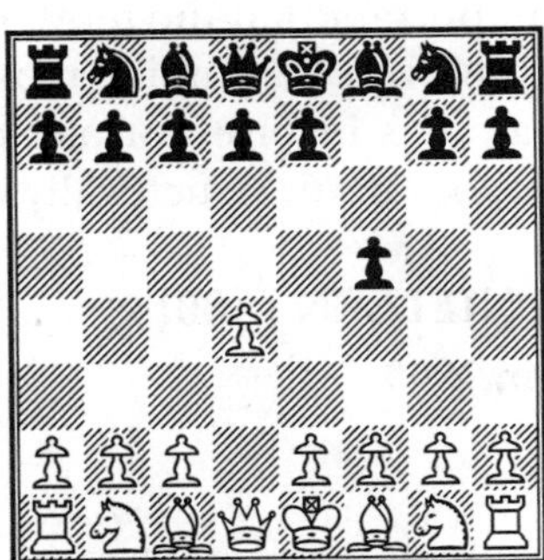

1.d4 f5

It almost makes no sense to talk of the **Dutch Defense** as a single opening. The style of play depends entirely on one fundamental decision on what to do after 1.d4 f5. If Black chooses to fianchetto the bishop at g7, then we have the Leningrad Variation, but if the bishop goes to e7 or d6 we have the Classical Variation. White usually tries to use pressure along the long diagonal with 2.g3, and the typical formation is achieved after 2...Nf6; 3.Bg2 e6; 4.Nf3 d5; 5.c4 c6; 6.0-0. Black used to play 6...Be7, but now 6...Bd6, the Modern Stonewall Dutch, is the overwhelming favorite.

There are great rewards for Black, especially if White does not take care to protect the king sufficiently. The pawns on the f-, g-, and h-files can come storming forward, aided by rooks, queen, knights, and even the famous bad bishop, which can emerge at h5 after visiting d7 and e8.

The Dutch Defense can be reached from 1...f5, but this direct approach invites White to try a lot of tricks. We start by examining some of the attempts to avoid the main lines.

HOPTON ATTACK

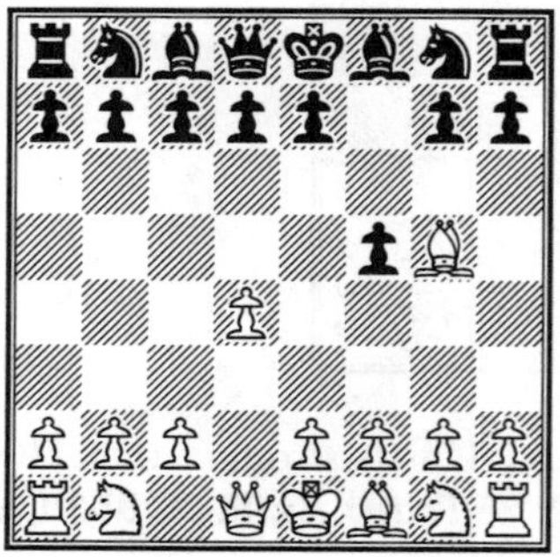

1.d4 f5
2.Bg5

This move looks very strange, but it has a serious point. If Black wants to play a Classical Dutch, then ...e6 is needed. This move prevents that. If Black tries to prepare it with ...Nf6, then White will capture the knight and really mess up the pawn structure. A World Champion will often steer into a sideline for psychological purposes. It isn't important that the move may be less ambitious than the main lines. Notice, however, that unlike most unorthodox openings, these diversions by Champions involve normal, developing moves. Played in a strange order, perhaps, but never structurally weakening.

(194) PETROSIAN - NIELSEN [A80]
Copenhagen, 1960

1.d4 f5; 2.Bg5 g6. The most principled reply, though it is noteworthy that this is not a formation which appeals to all Dutch players. 2...h6 is playable, but does weaken the kingside, something you don't want to do against Petrosian! 2...h6; 3.Bh4 g5; 4.e3! The bishop cannot be captured because of Qh5 mate! 4...Nf6; 5.Bg3 d6; 6.h4 and Black's kingside is overextended, for example 6...Rg8; 7.hxg5 hxg5; 8.Nc3 e6; 9.f3! and White is ready to open up the center quickly. 9...Qe7; 10.Qd2 Nc6; 11.0-0-0 Bd7; 12.e4! fxe4; 13.fxe4 0-0-0 and in Kasparov-Illescas, Dos Hermanos 1996, White could have secured the advantage with 14.Bc4 Bg7; 15.Nf3 Ng4; 16.Be2, according to Illescas.

3.Nd2. The premature attack with 3.h4 is not for Petrosian! 3.Nc3 is more accurate, perhaps, because Black might be able to work the long diagonal here. Andrew Martin, in his provocative and entertaining book on the Anti-Dutch, notes that "2.Bg5 leaves the b2 pawn wek so a quick ...c5 develops good counterplay." He has a point, but I am not sure that it applies to Petrosian's system, which is headed toward a Torre Attack.

3...Bg7; 4.c3 Nf6; 5.e3. White is going to adopt a Torre formation, but Black has a pawn at f5, so the d-pawn can be deployed at d6 instead of d5, as the e4 square is already guarded. **5...d6; 6.Ngf3 Nc6; 7.Qb3.** The weakness of the light squares will keep the Black king from escaping to the kingside. **7...h6; 8.Bxf6 Bxf6; 9.e4 e5.**

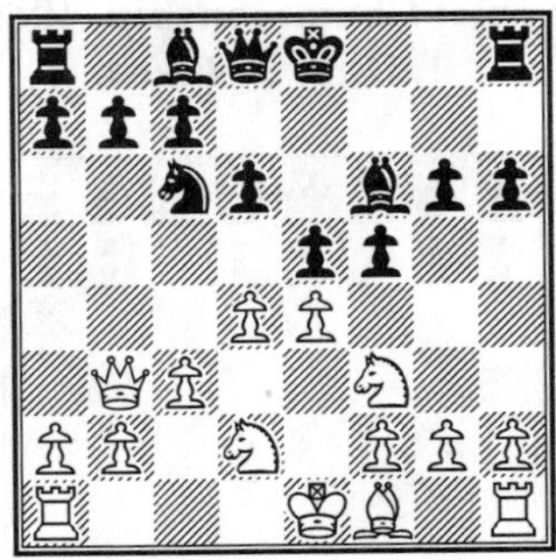

Black must have underestimated the power of the pin applied by Petrosian with his next move. **10.Bb5 Kf8.** 10...Bd7; 11.exf5 gxf5; 12.dxe5 dxe5; 13.0–0–0 Qe7; 14.Bxc6 Bxc6; 15.Nd4 Bxg2; 16.Nxf5 Qf7; 17.Nc4 sets up nasty threats at d6. **11.Bxc6 bxc6; 12.dxe5 dxe5; 13.Qa4.** Black's position is a mess. **13...Qd6; 14.Nb3 Bd7; 15.Rd1 Qe7; 16.Nc5! Be8.** 16...Qxc5; 17.Rxd7 Qb6; 18.Qc4 demonstrates the weakness of the Black king. **17.b4 Kg7.** Black has almost castled by hand.

18.0–0. White waited a long time to castle, but the position is now so overwhelming that Petrosian could take a bit of time out to get the remaining rook into the game. **18...Rf8; 19.Qa6!** The threat is primitive: Qb7! **19...fxe4; 20.Nd2 e3.** Black offers the pawn back. **21.Nde4!** This is much stronger than taking the pawn. **21...exf2+; 22.Rxf2 Bg5; 23.Rxf8 Kxf8; 24.Nxg5 hxg5.**

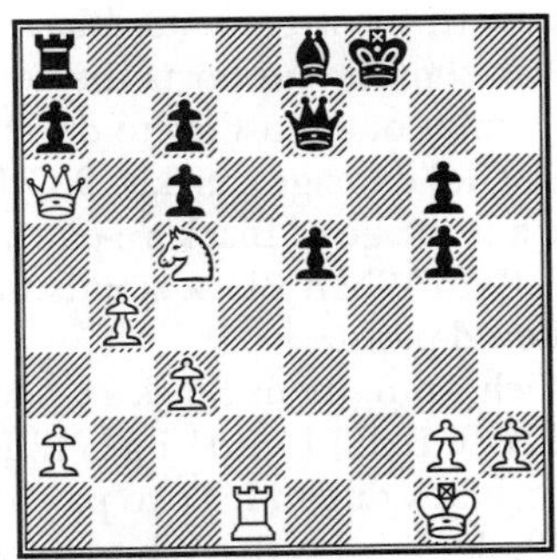

Black's extra pawn is a joke, and White now delivers the final blow. **25.Qb7** Black resigned. The rook has no escape: **25...Rd8; 26.Rxd8 Qxd8; 27.Ne6+. White won.**

(195) GULKO - GUREVICH, M [A82]

Soviet Championship, 1985
1.d4 f5; 2.e4 fxe4.

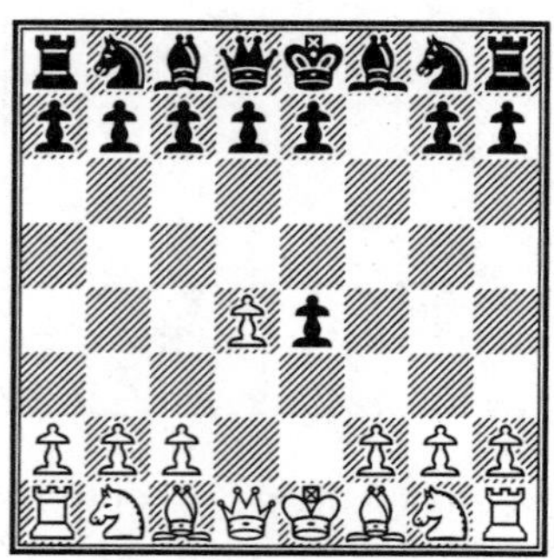

The Staunton Gambit is a typical 19th century attempt to control the initiative at the cost of a pawn. It is now considered relatively harmless, though Black should be prepared to meet it if the Dutch Defense is played on the first move. On the other hand, 1.d4 f5 is a relatively rare move order, because White has so many annoying minor lines, that Black will steer into the Dutch from other moves, such as 1...e6, 1...d5, 1...e6 or 1...g6, depending on which Dutch formation Black want's to erect.

Therefore the Staunton is a rare visitor, but at amateur levels it is found with somewhat more frequency. It is still topical enough that a Staunton Memorial tournament recently required this opening in all games.

3.Nc3 Nf6; 4.f3 d5. As with most gambits, Black should not get too greedy. **5.fxe4 dxe4; 6.Bg5 Bf5.** Black sensibly supports the center. **7.Nge2 e6; 8.Ng3 Be7.** When defending against a gambit one must try to develop as quickly as possible, so that White's forces cannot inflict damage quickly. **9.Qd2.** 9.Bxf6 Is a mistake since White will be unable to take advantage of Black's e-pawn due to the coming pressure on his own d-pawn after 9...Bxf6 When Black stands much better due to his extra pawn and pressure on White's d-pawn.

9...h6. A good move which strengthens Black's e-pawn by driving the bishop off of the f6 knight. **10.Be3.** 10.Bxf6 Bxf6; 11.Rd1 Bg4; 12.Be2 (12.Ra1 Bg5; 13.Qf2 e3; 14.Qg1 Qxd4. Is winning for Black due to his two pawn advantage and the exposed position of White's king.) 12...Bg5 Traps the White queen. **10...Nbd7.**

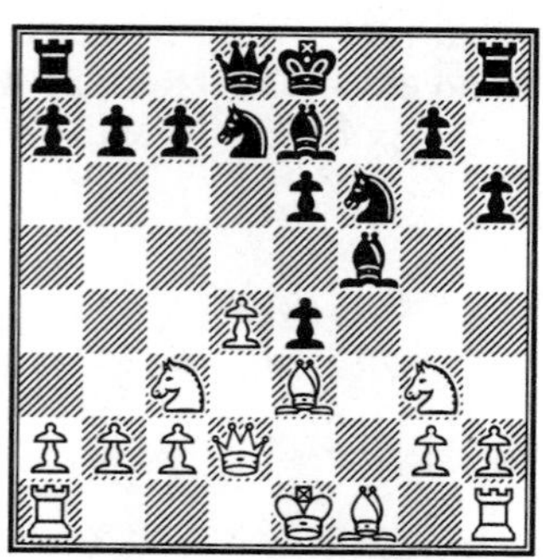

This position is better for Black due to his extra pawn and White's inability to gain a lead in development. **11.Be2 Nb6; 12.0–0 Qd7.** Black could bypass the coming tactics by covering his h5 square with 12... Bg6. Then Black would stand better since White has no play for the sacrificed pawn. **13.Nh5 Rg8.** Although this is not a bad move, the rook would be more active on f8 after 13...0–0. However, Black's king will no doubt be safer on the queenside due to his pawns having remained on their original squares.

13...0–0. Is also very strong since Black's pieces are well placed for any sacrifice that may be attempted for example 14.Nxg7 Kxg7; 15.Bxh6+ Kh7; 16.Qg5 (16.Bxf8 Rxf8. With a winning position for Black since his two pieces control more squares than his lost rook.) 16...Rg8; 17.Qh4 Rg6; 18.Bf8+ (18.Bg5+ Kg7; 19.Bh5 Rh8. When Black is able to take advantage of the pin on the h-file after 20.Bxg6 Rxh4; 21.Bxf5 exf5; 22.Bxh4 Qxd4+. is clearly winning for Black due to his material advantage.) 18...Kg8; 19.Bxe7 Qxe7. is winning for Black because of his extra piece.

14.Nxf6+ Bxf6; 15.Bh5+. A good move which provokes pawn g6 which weakens the Black pawn structure. **15...g6; 16.Be2.** Black must play carefully in this position since White is threatening to win material with g4 and Rxf6 or Nxe4 and Rxf6. **16...Qg7.**

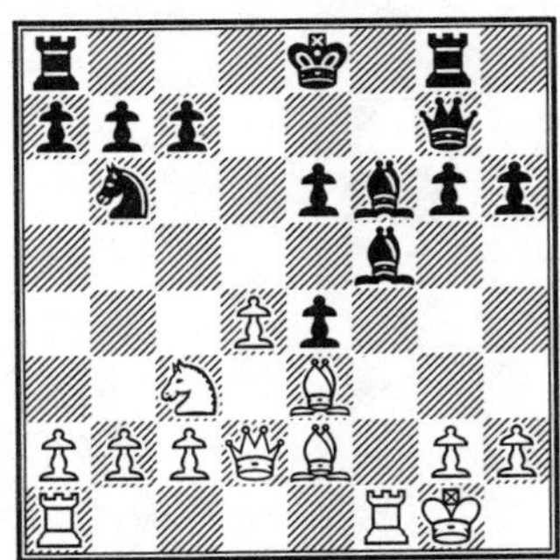

17.Bxh6. Although White temporarily wins back his pawn, Black's major pieces will use the opened h-file to launch an attack against the White king. 17.g4 poses no threat due to Black's pressure on the g-file for example. 17...0–0–0

A) 18.gxf5 gxf5+; 19.Kh1 (19.Kf2 Bh4#) 19...Qg2#;

B) 18.Rad1 is easily handled by 18...h5. **17...Bxd4+; 18.Kh1.** This intermezzo retains Black's material advantage. **18...Qh8; 19.Bf4 0–0–0; 20.Nb5 e5; 21.Be3 a6; 22.Nc3 Rg7.** The plan is to lift the rook over to attack White's king on the h-file. **23.Rf2 Rh7; 24.g3 Qe8; 25.Bf1 Qc6; 26.Qe2 Nd7.** The knight is heading to g4 where it will dominate White's dark squares and in particular the h2 square. **27.Nd1 Nf6; 28.c3 Bg4; 29.Rxf6.** 29.Qe1 Bf3+; 30.Kg1 (30.Rxf3 exf3; 31.cxd4 f2+; 32.Bg2 fxe1Q+) 30...Bb6; 31.Bxb6 Qxb6. is winning for Black due to his kingside initiative combined with his pawn advantage. **29...Bxe2; 30.Rxc6.**

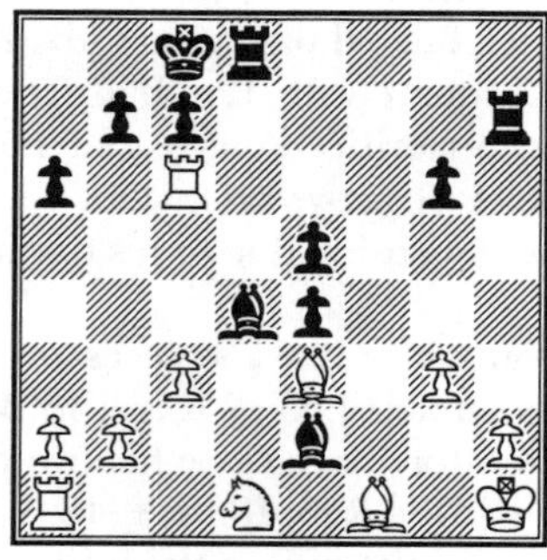

30...Bf3+. Another intermezzo which leaves Black with a winning material advantage. **31.Kg1 Bxe3+; 32.Nxe3 bxc6; 33.Bxa6+ Kb8; 34.Rf1 Rd2; 35.Rf2 Rxf2; 36.Kxf2 Rxh2+.** White resigned. **Black won.**

LENINGRAD VARIATION

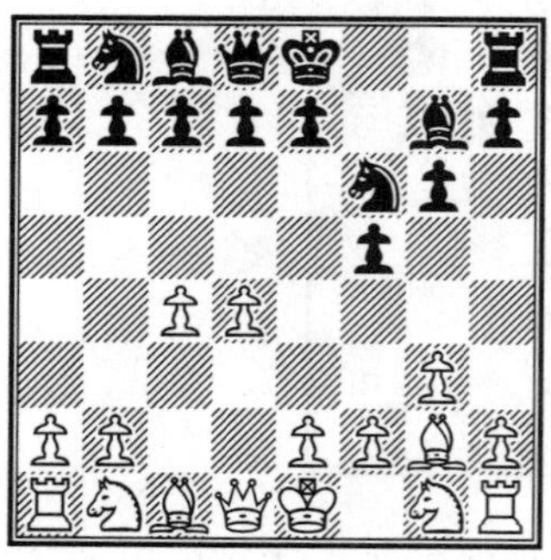

1.d4	**f5**
2.g3	**Nf6**
3.Bg2	**g6**
4.c4	**Bg7**

In the **Leningrad Variation**, Black concedes the center to White and hopes to be able to obtain counterplay later. In this game, Karpov takes on one of the leading specialists in the line.

(196) KARPOV - MALANIUK [A87]

Soviet Championship, 1988

1.d4 f5; 2.g3 Nf6; 3.Bg2 g6; 4.c4 Bg7; 5.Nf3 d6; 6.0–0 0–0; 7.Nc3.

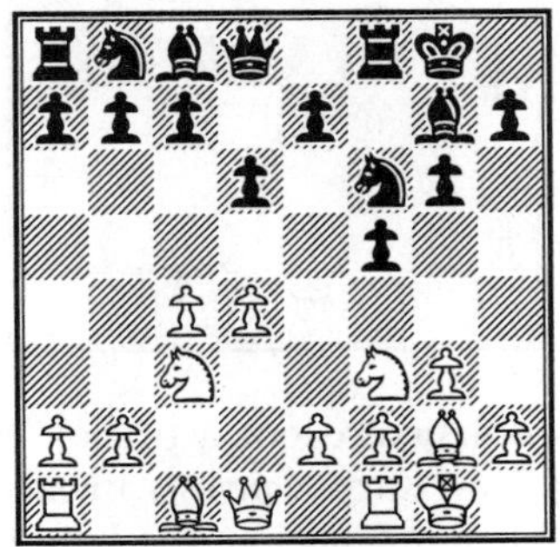

White can also play 7.b3 here, though play is likely to transpose after a couple of moves. **7...Qe8; 8.b3 Na6.** Not the most respectable plan. More common is an immediate strike in the center. 8...e5!?; 9.dxe5 dxe5; 10.e4 Nc6; 11.Ba3 Rf7; 12.Nd5 looks good, but Malaniuk has been able to defend this position against his fellow Grandmasters. Unfortunately, those games came after this one. **9.Ba3.** For some reason, authoritative publications mention only 9.a4 and 9.Bb2, but this move makes a lot of sense too. **9...c6; 10.Qd3 Bd7; 11.Rfe1 Rd8; 12.Rad1.**

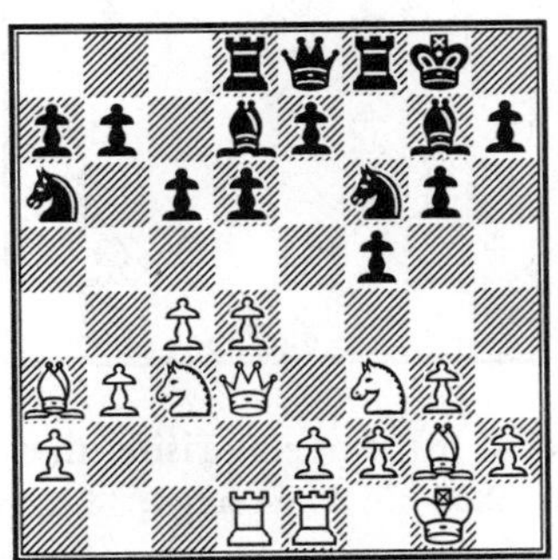

White has a magnificent position, and is ready for the central break at e4. **12...Kh8; 13.e4 fxe4; 14.Nxe4 Bf5.** The pin is defused immediately by Karpov. **15.Nxf6 Bxf6; 16.Qe3 Qf7; 17.h3 Nc7; 18.Re2.** White builds slowly, using a policy of restraining enemy pieces before trying to directly exploit the holes in Black's position. **18...Bc8; 19.Ng5 Qg8; 20.Qd2 Ne6; 21.Nxe6 Bxe6.**

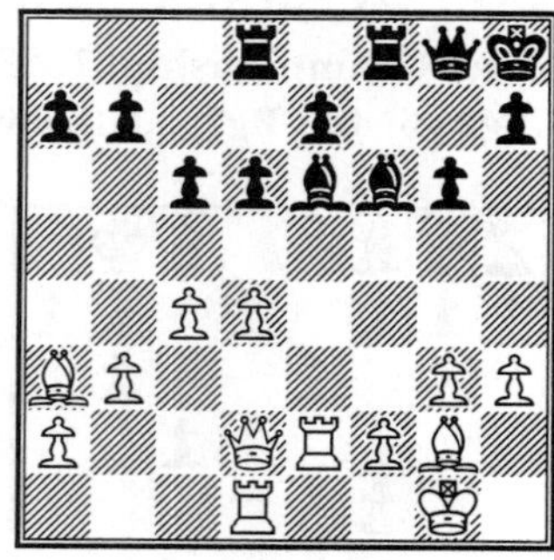

Black's bishops and pawn structure look artificial. White's bishops are dominating the board. **22.Rde1 Bd7.** Now Karpov invests an exchange to pick up the weak e-pawn, which is always a problem for Black in the Leningrad Dutch. **23.Rxe7 Bxe7; 24.Rxe7 Rf6.** Black can't afford to lose the d-pawn, too. **25.d5 Qf8; 26.Re3 Kg8; 27.Bb2 Rf5; 28.Qd4.** The dominate White battery on the a1–h8 diagonal is worth much much more than a little material. **28...Re5; 29.Rxe5 dxe5; 30.Qxe5 Kf7.** Black cannot hope to survive this position. Just look at White's bishops!

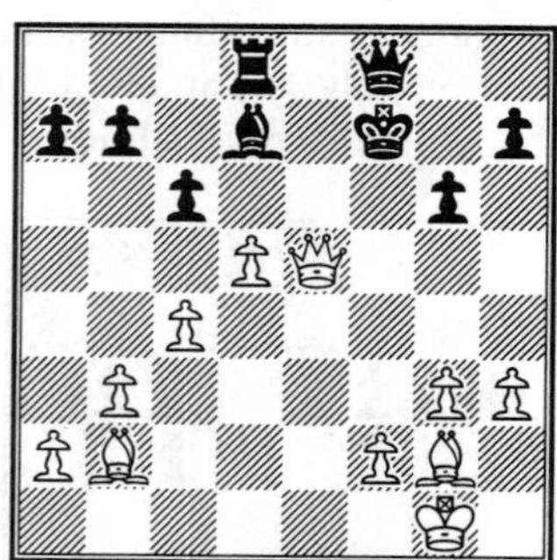

Just look at those bishops! It is not surprising that White owns the center and can attack at will. **31.d6 Bf5; 32.c5 h5; 33.g4 hxg4; 34.hxg4 Bd3; 35.Bd5+. White won.**

STONEWALL VARIATION

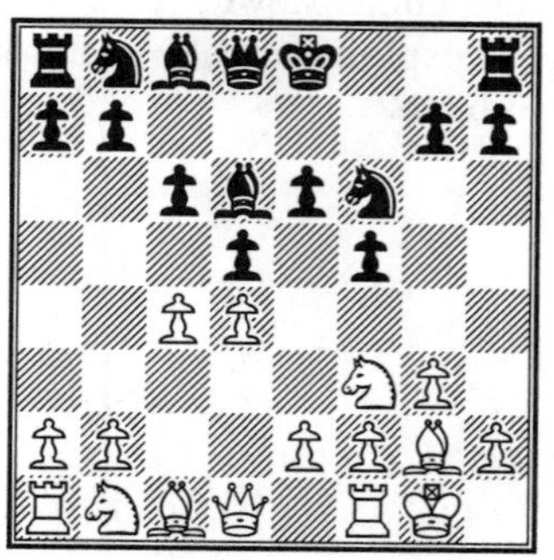

1.d4	**f5**
2.c4	**e6**
3.Nf3	**e6**
4.g3	**d5**
5.Bg2	**c6**
6.0-0	**Bd6**

The **Stonewall Dutch** is easy to understand. Black sets up a solid pawn structure, keeping the position closed. The modern handling places the dark-squared bishop at d6, keeping an eye on the important e5-square. The other bishop is a bit of a problem, however. If it gets stuck behind the pawns forever White will have a serious advantage. For this reason the Stonewall was not popular for many decades, but under the patronage of such fighting players as Nigel Short and Simen Agdestein it rose to a position of prominence in the late 1980s and early 1990s.

The movement may have been started in Sweden by Lars Karlsson, who convinced a number of strong players to take up the line. This group of players discovered that Black must keep an open mind regarding the bad bishop. It can squirm to the kingside via d7-e8-h5 or lie in wait at b7, depending on White's plan. White almost always reacts with a kingiside fianchetto, kingside castling, and the occupation of e5 by a knight.

(197) GUREVICH,D. - SCHILLER [D30]

Oak Brook, 1993

1.d4 d5; 2.c4 e6; 3.Nf3 c6; 4.Nbd2. 4.g3 f5; 5.Bg2 Nf6; 6.0–0 Bd6 is the most common move order. Now White has several plans. 7.Ne5 (7.b3 Qe7; 8.Bb2 0–0 9.Nbd2 b6 The bishop takes up a useful post on the queenside. 10.Ne5 Bb7; 11.Rc1 a5; 12.e3 Na6 and White was unable to make progress in Komarov-Gleizerov, Leeuwarden 1995.) 7...0–0; 8.Bf4. This plan can also be played at move 7, but this move order prevents the immediate exchange of dark-squared bishops. 8...Nh5; 9.e3 Nxf4; 10.exf4 Nd7; 11.Nxd7 Qxd7; 12.Nd2 b6 and Black had an acceptable position in Fominykh-Sherbakov, Russian Championship 1996.

4.Qc2 f5; 5.g3 Nf6; 6.Bg2 Bd6; 7.0–0 0–0 is another popular formation.

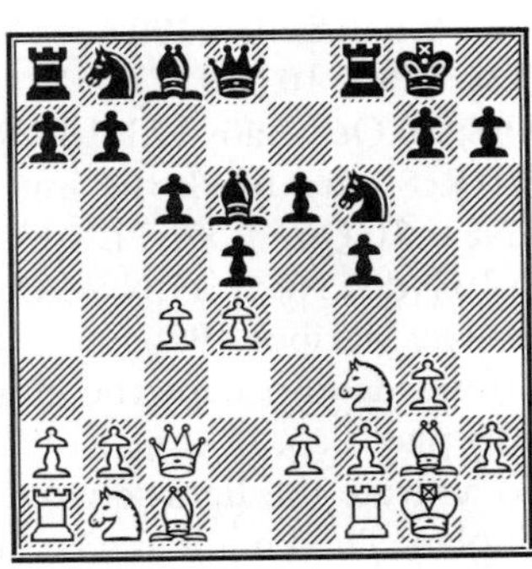

8.Bg5 (8.b3 Qe7; 9.Ne5 Na6; 10.Nd3 Nh5; 11.a4 f4; 12.Ba3 fxg3; 13.hxg3 Bxa3; 14.Nxa3 Qg5; 15.Qc1 was better for White in D. Gurevich-McClelland, New York Open 1995. The e-pawn is backward and weak, while White controls e5.) 8...h6; 9.Bxf6 Qxf6; 10.Nbd2 Bd7; 11.Qb3 Bc8; 12.e3 Kh8; 13.Ne1 Nd7; 14.Nd3 White often adopts this formation for the knights, but it allows Black to operate on the kingside. 14...g5!?; 15.f4 Qg7; 16.Rac1 Rb8; 17.Nf3 Nf6; 18.Nfe5 Ne4!; 19.Rc2 Bd7; 20.Kh1 Kh7; 21.Bf3 Be8; 22.Nf2 Rg8!?

In such positions White should not capture at e4, as this opens up more lines. 23.Nxe4?! dxe4; 24.Bd1 c5!; 25.Qc3 gxf4; 26.gxf4 Bxe5; 27.fxe5 (27.dxe5 Rd8 and White cannot prevent ...Rd3 with Be2, because of checkmate at g2.) 27...cxd4; 28.exd4 Bc6! The bad bishop is suddenly a mighty weapon! 29.Qe3 Rbd8; 30.b4 Black now finishes with a nice touch. 30...Rxd4!; 31.b5 (31.Qxd4 e3+ and Black wins.) 31...Rxc4! and White resigned, ackowledging that the weakness of g2 had become fatal, Akesson-Raaste, Finland 1996.

4...f5; 5.g3 Nf6; 6.Bg2 Bd6; 7.0–0.

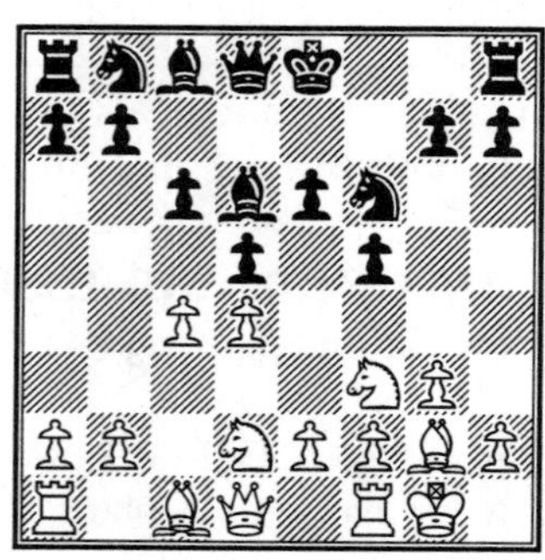

This position can be reached from many move orders, including 1.d4 d5; 2.c4 e6; 3.Nf3 c6; 4.g3 f5; 5.Bg2 Nf6; 6.0–0 Bd6; 7.Nbd2. **7...Qe7.** 7...Nbd7; 8.b3 Ne4 (8...0–0; 9.Bb2 Qe7; 10.Ne5 Bxe5; 11.dxe5 Ng4; 12.Nf3 b6; 13.h3 Nh6; 14.Qc1 gave Black problems on the a3-f8 diagonal in one of the earliest tests of the system, Dake-Santasiere, Philadelphia 1936.) 9.Bb2 Qf6; 10.Ne1 h5; 11.Nxe4 dxe4; 12.Qd2 Qg6; 13.f3 h4; 14.fxe4 fxe4; 15.Qe3 Nf6; 16.gxh4 Bxh2+!! and White resigned in Wiedermann-Dumitrache, Bad Woerishofen 1997.

7...0–0; 8.Ne5 (8.b3 b6; 9.Ne5 Bb7; 10.Ndf3 Qe7; 11.cxd5 cxd5; 12.Ne1 a5; 13.Bb2 Na6; 14.a3 Rac8; 15.Qd3 Nb8; 16.Qe3 Ba6; 17.N1d3 Rc2; 18.Rfc1 Bxd3; 19.Nxd3 Ng4; 20.Qf3 Rxc1+; 21.Bxc1 Rc8 gave Black the initiative in Miralles-Agdestein, Lyon 1988.) 8...b6; 9.Ndf3 Ne4; 10.Qc2 Bb7; 11.Nd3 Nd7; 12.Bf4 Bxf4; 13.Nxf4 Qe7; 14.Rfd1 g5; 15.Nd3 c5; 16.Nde5 Nxe5; 17.Nxe5 cxd4; 18.cxd5 Bxd5 and Black was better in Razuvaev-Pavasovic. Maribor 1996.

8.Qc2 0–0; 9.Ne5. White needs to occupy the e5 square at some point, since otherwise Black will eventually play ...e5. As long as White maintains control of e5, Black will find it difficult to activate the light-squared bishop. **9...Nbd7; 10.Ndf3** This is a standard anti-Dutch plan. The knight at e5 is supported by both a pawn at d4 and another knight at either f3 or d3. **10...Ne4.** Black can safely keep the knight here if an enemy knight is at f3, so that White cannot place a pawn there. In many cases the knight can sit at e4 even if the f3-square is not occupied, since the weakening of the a7-g1 diagonal can prove embarassing for White if the f-pawn advances. In addition, g3 can become vulnerable.

11.Bf4. White invites Black to advance the g-pawn. This is a double-edged strategy. **11...g5!?** Black accepts the challenge. **12.Nxd7 Bxd7; 13.Bxd6 Nxd6.**

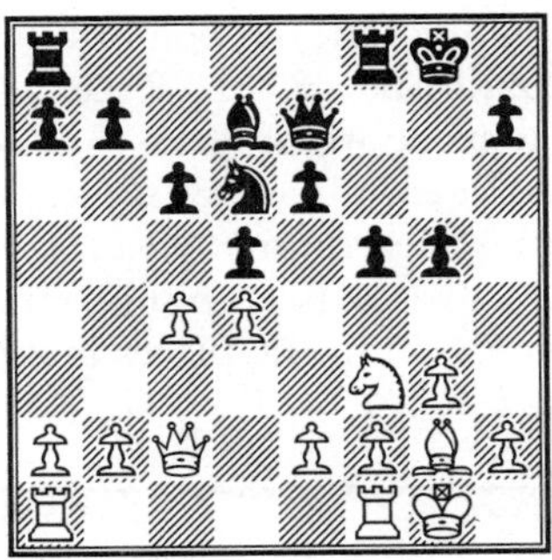

White now owns a superior bishop, but Black has plenty of room to maneuver. **14.Ne5 Be8.** There are two ways to activate the light-squared bishop in the Stonewall Dutch. Black can fianchetto it at b7 under some circumstances, most easily when the knight sits at b8 to defend the pawn at c6. The other plan, seen here, is to redeploy it on the kingside.

15.f4. 15.c5 Nf7; 16.Nxf7 Bxf7; 17.f3 Bg6; 18.e4 f4 leaves White with more problems to solve than Black. **15...Bh5; 16.Rac1 Rac8; 17.Kh1.** White takes care to get the king off the a7-g1 diagonal in case Black opens up the game with ...c5. **17...Nf7; 18.cxd5 exd5.** 18...cxd5 allows White to sacrifice the queen, though moving her to a safe square is also good. 19.Qxc8 Rxc8; 20.Rxc8+ Kg7; 21.Rfc1 Qb4; 22.fxg5 Nxe5; 23.dxe5 Qxb2; 24.R1c7+ Bf7; 25.Bf3! and White wins. **19.e3 Nxe5!** Although Black has a bad bishop, there is little to fear in most of the possible endgames. **20.fxe5 Bg6.**

White must now take seriously the threat of advancing the f-pawn. **21.Qd2 Kg7.** Black prepares to operate on the h-file. **22.b4 h5; 23.Rf2 Rh8; 24.Rcf1 h4! 25.Kg1** White gets the king off the dangerous h-file. **25...g4; 26.Rc1 Qg5; 27.Rf4.** White does not want to allow ...f4, even as a sacrifice. **27...Rh7; 28.b5 hxg3; 29.hxg3 Qh5; 30.Qf2?** This square is needed for the king. 30.Kf2 threatens Rh1, trapping the enemy queen. 30...Qh2; 31.Rh1 Forced, in view of the threat of ...Rh3. 31...Qxh1; 32.Bxh1 Rxh1; 33.Qb4 cxb5; 34.Kg2 (34.Qe7+ Kh6; 35.Kg2 Rcc1; 36.Qxb7 Rhg1+; 37.Kf2 Rgf1+; 38.Ke2 Rfe1+; 39.Kd2 Red1+ is a draw.) 34...Rch8; 35.Qe7+ Bf7; 36.Qf6+ Kf8; 37.Qd8+ Kg7; 38.Qf6+ would have drawn. **30...Qh2+; 31.Kf1 Rhh8!**

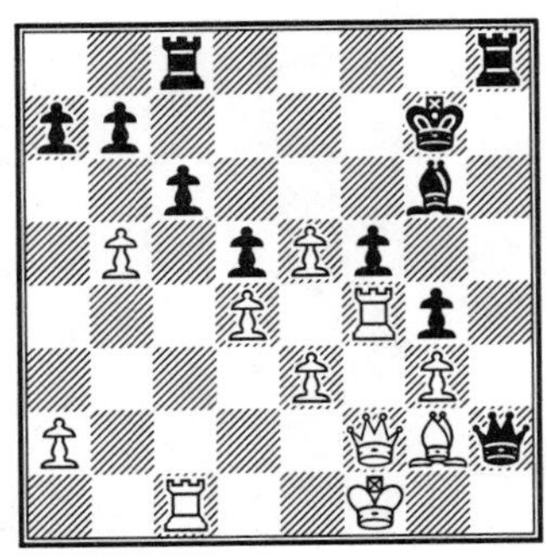

It looks as though Black cannot make further progress. It is true that I have exhausted the possibilities on the h-file, but there is another path to the enemy king, via the queenside, and with the next very subtle move I prepare a deep and long plan **32.bxc6.** Had Dmitry figured out the point of my last move, he never would have opened up the b-file. 32.Rb1 b6; 33.bxc6 Rxc6; 34.Bxd5 Rc2; 35.Qxh2 Rhxh2 and White is too tied down to make any progress. **32...Rxc6; 33.Rxc6 bxc6; 34.Qe1** 34.Qc2 Rb8; 35.Kf2 Rb6 and again White has no way to make progress. **34...Rb8; 35.a4 Rb3!** White is completely tied down. **36.Rf2.** Desperation. The rook should stay in its passive post at f4, as now the Black bishop enters the game. 36.a5 Rb7 and White is at a loss for a move, as all of the pieces must remain in place to defend. **36...f4!** The threat is ...Rb1.

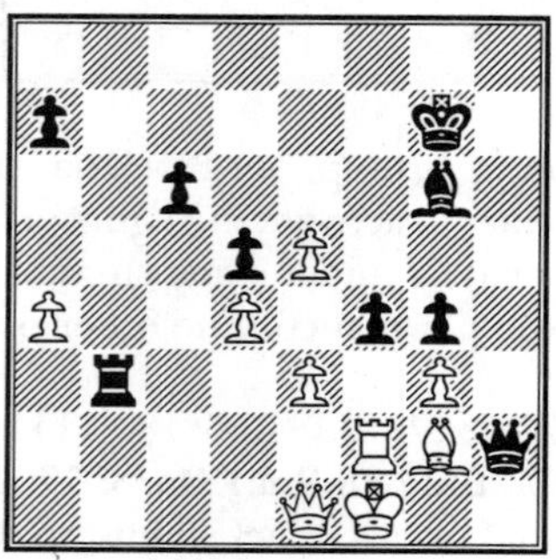

37.Rd2 Rxe3; 38.Qf2 Qxg3; 39.Qxg3 Rxg3; 40.Rf2 f3; 41.Bh1 Bd3+. Black Won.

7. THE INDIAN GAMES

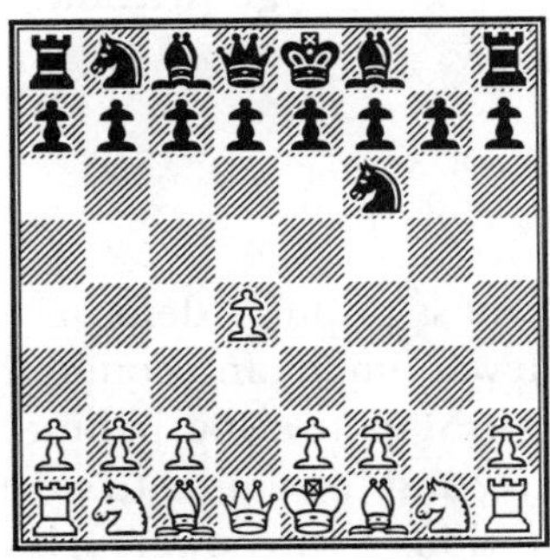

1.d4 Nf6

The Indian Games begin with 1.d4 Nf6, which also prevents White from achieving the ideal pawn center with 2.e4.

The Indian Games given their name by the great Savielly Tartakower, to replace the derogatory term "Irregular Opening" which no longer properly applied to the newly respectable openings such as the King's Indian and Queen's Indian defenses. These tend to be highly transpositional, and can lead right back into the Closed Games if Black chooses an early ...d5. But the distinctively Indian lines are those which involve the fianchetto of one bishop, either at g7 or b7. We sometimes call the ones with the kingside fianchetto the West Indians, and the ones where the action is on the queenside the East Indians, assuming that White is sitting on the North side of the board and that the battlefield and enemy Black forces are to the south.

The **Queen's Indian** and **Nimzo-Indian** are among the easiest Indians to play, though the **Benko Gambit**, a positional rather than aggressive gambit, is also quite straightforward. The sharp **Modern Benoni Defense** has attracted the interest of those who like to introduce tactics early in the game.

The **Old Indian** and **Bogo-Indian** suffer from having reputations from being boring, though we will examine some exceptions in our illustrative games.

The West Indians include the **Gruenfeld** and **King's Indian Defense**, both favorites of World Champions Fischer and Kasparov. These openings lead to complex struggles which require both positional and tactical skills, as well as a good memory to absorb the massive amount of theory which rivals even that of the Sicilian Defenses!

KING'S INDIAN DEFENSE

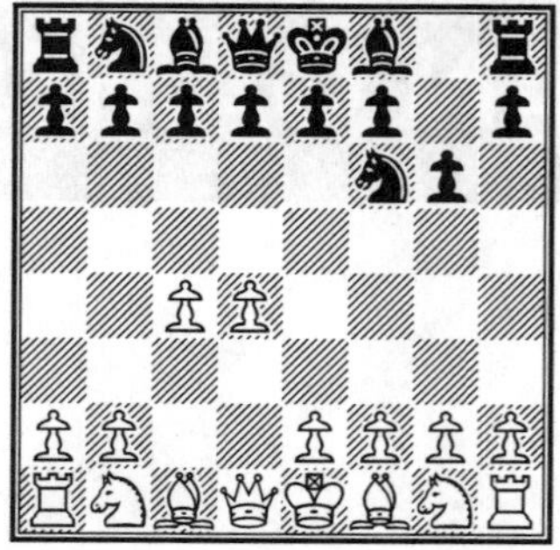

1.d4 Nf6
2.c4 g6 (without ...d5)

The **King's Indian** is currently the most popular defense to 1.d4 for Black. It is based on solid principles of development and counterattack that typify the Hypermodern school of chess. Maneuvering behind the ranks and vicious attacks are both commonplace, and the ability to calculate accurately is essential. Crucial to Black's aspirations is the powerful bishop at g7, which can exert a powerful influence in the center. Even if Black plays ...e5 and the center becomes closed, it can open up later and the bishop can wake up from its hibernation and inflict serious damage.

White has two fundamental approaches after 1.d4 Nf6; 2.c4 g6; 3.Nc3 Bg7. The straightforward occupation of the center with 4.e4 is generally met by 4...d6 or 4...0-0. In either case White can go for broke with 5.f4, but the more modest 5.Be2, 5.f3 and 5.Nf3 are all good moves.

The alternative plan involves an early kingside fianchetto, counting on play along the a8-h1 diagonal. We will start by examining this approach.

FIANCHETTO VARIATIONS

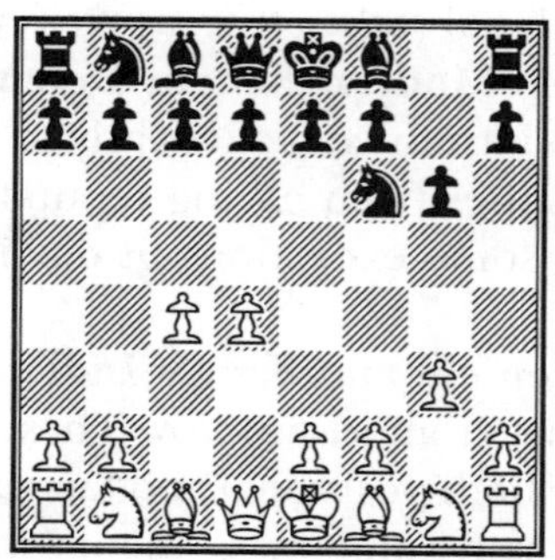

1.d4 Nf6
2.c4 g6
3.g3

The fianchetto approach is often used against the King's Indian and Gruenfeld Defenses. The two players ignore each other for a while, but White usually winds up with more control of the center. In time, Black can stage a counterattack against the central pawns.

(198) ROMANISHIN - CHIBURDANIDZE [E63]

Soviet Championship, 1980

1.d4 Nf6; 2.Nf3 g6; 3.c4 Bg7; 4.g3 0–0; 5.Bg2 d6; 6.0–0 Nc6; 7.Nc3 a6.

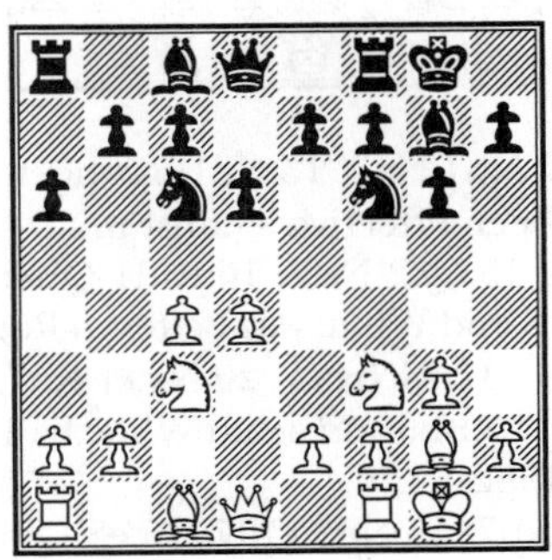

In the Panno Variation, Black aims for an early...b5, made possible by the fact that White's light-squared bishop is stationed at g2 and cannot operate on the f1–a6 diagonal. **8.b3.** White has many options here, but Romanishin's 8.b3 is one of the most popular. Kasparov prefers 8.Bg5, and 8.h3 is also seen frequently. Finally, White can close the center with d5. 8.h3 Rb8 (8...Bd7 has been gaining followers, but after 9.e4 White has been scoring well, and lately Black has been returning to the traditional 8...Rb8.) 9.e4 b5; 10.e5 Ne8 (10...dxe5; 11.dxe5 Qxd1; 12.Rxd1 Nd7; 13.e6! fxe6; 14.cxb5 axb5 and after 15.Bf4 White enjoys a much better pawn structure and a significant initiative, Vaganian-Sax, Lucerne 1985.

10...Nd7; 11.e6 fxe6; 12.d5 exd5; 13.cxd5 Nce5; 14.Nd4 gave White the better game in Aseyev-Tirard, St. Petersburg 1996.) 11.Qe2 Na5; 12.c5 b4; 13.Ne4 d5; 14.Ned2 f5; 15.Rd1 e6; 16.Nf1 h6; 17.Nh4 Kh7; 18.f4 with a kingside initiative in Larsen-Olafsson, Oslo (match)1955.

8...Rb8; 9.Bb2. White has several choices here, but only 9.Bb2 and 9.Nd5 see much action. The latter seems to be in decline, as Black has found ways to equalize. 9.Nd5 Ne4 (9...Bg4; 10.Bb2 Qd7; 11.Qd2 Ne4; 12.Qc1 e6; 13.Ne3 Bxf3; 14.exf3 Nf6; 15.d5 Ne7; 16.Bc3 e5 gave Black a solid game in Romanishin-Kosanovic, Stara Pazova 1988.) 10.Bb2 f5; 11.Qc2 Bd7; 12.Rfd1 b5; 13.Nf4 Qe8; 14.cxb5 axb5; 15.d5 Nb4; 16.Qc1 Bxb2; 17.Qxb2 g5; 18.a3! gxf4; 19.axb4 fxg3; 20.hxg3 c6; 21.dxc6 Bxc6; 22.Nd4 Bd7; 23.Ra7 with strong pressure for White in Romanishin-Zapata, Brussels 1986. **9...b5; 10.cxb5 axb5.**

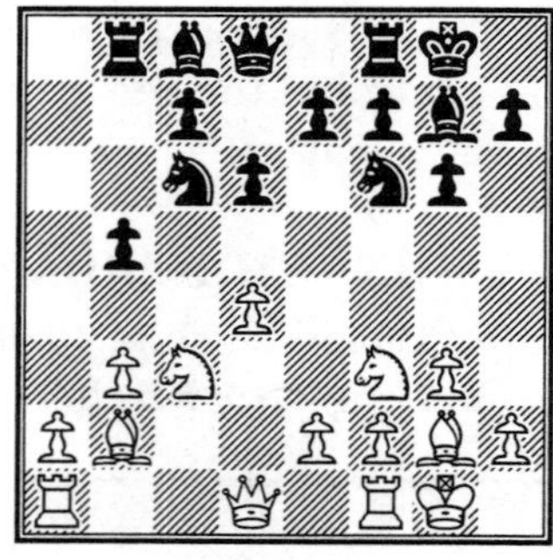

11.Rc1 Na5. 11...b4; 12.Nb1 Na7; 13.Ne1 has been seen on a number of occasions, but Romanishin has been effective against it.

A) 13...c6; 14.Nd3 Ba6; 15.Qc2 Nd7; 16.Rfd1 Qb6; 17.Nf4 Rfc8; 18.Bh3 Qd8; (18...Qb7; 19.Nd2 d5; 20.Nf3 and White was better in Romanishin-Keene, Dortmund Germany 1982, White won.) 19.a4 bxa3; 20.Nxa3 Rb7; 21.Nc4 c5; 22.dxc5 Bxc4; 23.Bxg7 Bxb3; 24.Qb2 Rxc5; 25.Bh6 and again White had the advantage, Romanishin-Tukmakov, Yerevan Zonal 1982;

B) 13...Bb7; 14.Bxb7 Rxb7; 15.Nd3 Qd7; 16.e3 Qf5; 17.Qe2 Ra8; 18.Rc4 Qa5; 19.Nd2 Nd5; 20.Qf3 e6; 21.e4 Nb6; 22.Rxb4 Nc6; 23.Nc4 Qxa2; 24.d5 exd5; 25.exd5 Nxb4; 26.Nxb4 Qa7; 27.Nc6 Qa6; 28.Nxb6 Bxb2; 29.Nxa8 Qxa8; 30.Re1. White won. Romanishin-Vaganian, Yerevan Zonal 1982

12.Qc2 Nd7. 12...Bb7 places the bishop on the wrong square, since it turns out that it is needed at a6. 13.Rfd1 Qd7; 14.e4 b4; 15.e5 bxc3; 16.Bxc3 Bh6; 17.exf6 Bxc1; 18.Qxc1 Bxf3; 19.Bxf3 Qf5; 20.fxe7 Rfe8; 21.Qe3 Rb6; 22.d5 Nb7; 23.g4. White won. Romanishin-Gruenfeld, Interzonal Riga Soviet Union 1979

13.Rfd1 c6; 14.Qd2 Ba6; 15.e4. White has control of the center and this is a permanent advantage. Black seeks counterplay on the queenside, but to no avail. **15...b4; 16.Ne2 e6; 17.Nf4 Qb6; 18.h4 Rfd8; 19.Nd3 d5; 20.Nc5 dxe4; 21.Nxe4 c5; 22.Qf4 cxd4; 23.Bxd4 Bxd4; 24.Rxd4 e5; 25.Nxe5 Nxe5; 26.Rxd8+ Rxd8; 27.Qxe5 h5; 28.Nf6+ Kf8; 29.Nd5. White won.**

(199) BOTVINNIK - SMYSLOV [E68]

World Championship (Game, 1954)

1.d4 Nf6; 2.c4 g6; 3.g3 Bg7; 4.Bg2 0–0; 5.Nc3 d6; 6.Nf3 Nbd; 7.0-0 e5. Black plants a stake in the center. **8.e4 c6.**

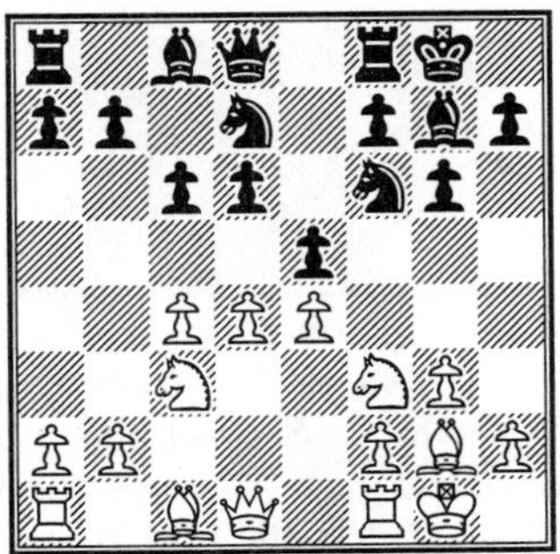

At the time, the Classical was already a familiar variation, featured in games by leading players for over a decade. **9.Be3.** It is more common to see 9.h3 here, in order to prevent Black's reply, but Smyslov had worked out an interesting plan for White. The advance of the h-pawn is covered in the next game.

9...Ng4; 10.Bg5 Qb6; 11.h3. This had already been seen in Grandmaster play, and 11...Ngf6 was expected. Smyslov had a nasty surprise planned, and sprung it now. **11...exd4!; 12.Na4 Qa6.**

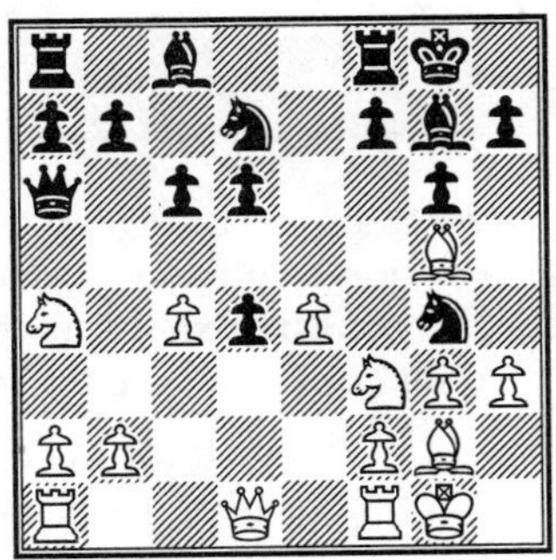

This was not anticipated by Botvinnik, and pointed to a severe flaw in his preparation. But like a true Champion he settled down at the board and worked out a way to lead the game into messy complications. After all, just because your opponent plays an unexpected move doesn't mean it is necessarily good!

13.hxg4 b5; 14.Nxd4. 14.Be7 Re8; 15.Bxd6 bxa4; 16.e5 (16.Nxd4 Ne5 was given by Smyslov as equal.) 16...Qxc4; 17.Re1 Bb7 is a very messy position, but the great Soviet theoreticians Boleslavsky and Lepeshkin combined forces deepen the analysis: 18.b3 axb3; 19.axb3 Qc3; 20.Rc1 Qa5; 21.Qxd4 c5; 22.Qf4 h6; 23.b4 Qxb4; 24.Qxb4 cxb4; 25.Rc7 Bxf3; 26.Bxf3 Rad8; 27.Bc6 Nxe5; 28.Bxe5 and here the authoritative *Encyclopedia of Chess Openings* gives 28...Rd6 and assesses the position as equal, but the rook on e8 is hanging, so they must have meant 28...Rxe5; 29.Rxe5 Bxe5; 30.Rxa7 which should be drawn. **14...bxa4; 15.Nxc6 Qxc6.**

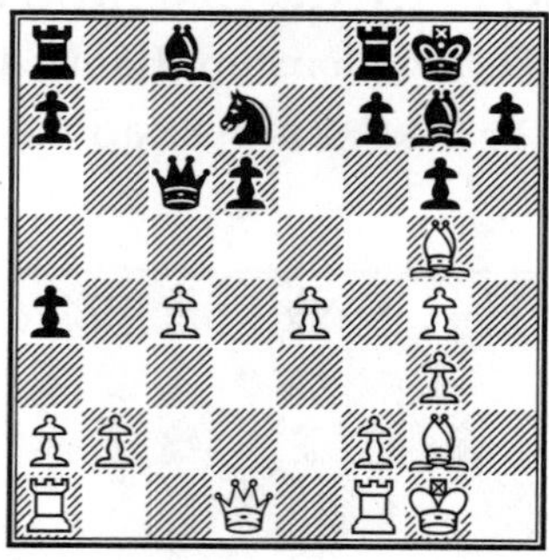

White now uses a simple tactic to win the exchange, but Smyslov had taken this into account. **16.e5 Qxc4; 17.Bxa8 Nxe5.** Black has more than enough compensation. Just look at the pawn at g4, the passed d-pawn and the general weakness of the light squares. **18.Rc1 Qb4; 19.a3 Qxb2; 20.Qxa4 Bb7.**

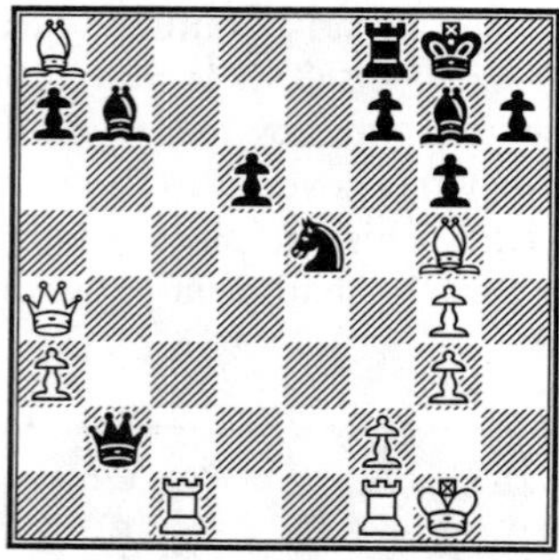

21.Rb1. 21.Bxb7 Qxb7; 22.Rc3 h6; 23.Bf4 Nf3+; 24.Rxf3 Qxf3; 25.Bxd6 Rd8; 26.Bc5 is given by Smyslov as superior, leading to a game with almost level chances. **21...Nf3+.** Now the carnage begins. **22.Kh1 Bxa8!** Smyslov parts with the queen, but gets a winning position as a result. **23.Rxb2 Nxg5+; 24.Kh2 Nf3+; 25.Kh3 Bxb2; 26.Qxa7 Be4.**

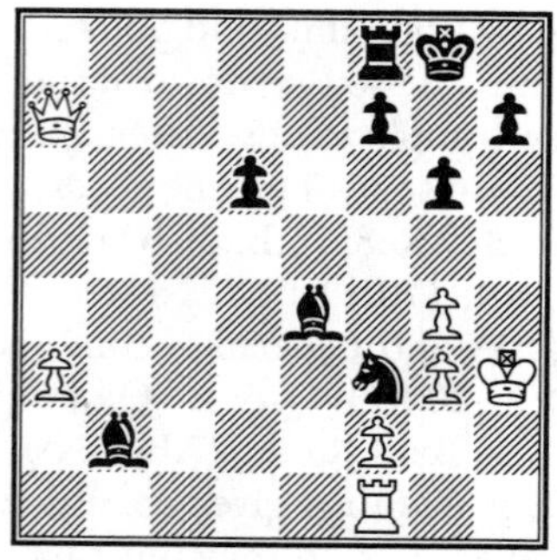

Black's three minor pieces are more than a match for the king. **27.a4 Kg7; 28.Rd1 Be5; 29.Qe7 Rc8; 30.a5 Rc2.** Everybody gets into the act! **31.Kg2 Nd4+; 32.Kf1 Bf3; 33.Rb1 Nc6.** White gave up. Even if Black can't organize an immediate checkmate, the advance of the d-pawn is inevitable. **Black won.**

(200) PORTISCH - STEIN [E69]

Sousse (Interzonal), 1967

1.d4 Nf6; 2.c4 g6; 3.Nf3 Bg7; 4.g3 0–0; 5.Bg2 d6; 6.Nc3 Nbd7; 7.0–0 e5; 8.e4 c6.

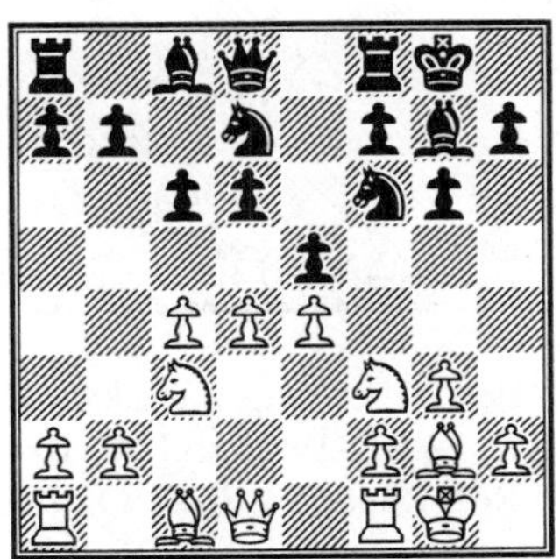

The Fianchetto Variation of the King's Indian Defense is not the choice of those who enjoy short games. The opening typically involves lengthy maneuvering battles with the position only occasionally blasting open into tactical brawls. White's center is very well supported and Black must rely on passive defenses for some time. The action will take place on the queenside, at first, where White will try to gain some space. Then an assault on the center with f4 will be possible. This game has a fascinating endgame. It has been analyzed many times and to great depth, and gives an idea of the richness one finds even when material is heavily unbalanced.

9.h3. 9.b3 can be played first, but eventually the h-pawn advances. 9...Re8; 10.h3 exd4; 11.Nxd4 Nc5; 12.Re1 a5 (12...Bd7; 13.Bf4 Qb6; 14.Bxd6! is a strong new idea for White: 14...Nfxe4; 15.Bxe4 Nxe4; 16.Rxe4 Rxe4; 17.Nxe4 Qxd4; 18.Qxd4 Bxd4; 19.Rd1 Bg7; 20.Bb8! Rxb8; 21.Rxd7 and White has a huge advantage because of the occupation of the seventh rank and strong centralized knight, Baburin-Littlewood, Dublin 1995.) 13.Rb1 h6 (13...Nfd7; 14.Be3 Ne5; 15.Re2 a4; 16.f4 axb3; 17.axb3 Ned3; 18.Rd2 Nb4 and Black's minor pieces are well-coordinated, Quinn-McShane, Hastings Challengers, 1995.) 14.Kh2 is still considered better for White, Marin-Groszpeter, Andorra 1995, or 9...Qb6; 10.d5 Nc5; 11.Qc2 a5; 12.h3 Bd7; 13.Be3 cxd5; 14.cxd5 Rac8; 15.Nd2 Qa6; 16.Rfc1 b5; 17.a3 Qb7; 18.Qb1 Nh5; 19.b4 axb4; 20.axb4 Na6; 21.Nb3 with a better game for White in Deng-Au, Honolulu (Outrigger Prince Kuhio) 1997.

9...Qb6. 9...Re8; 10.Re1 exd4; 11.Nxd4 is a popular alternative plan but new resources are still being discovered, for example 11...Qe7. This is probably not better than the older 11...a5; 12.Bf4 Nh5? Black could have limited the damage with (12...Ne5; 13.b3 Nfd7 where White is only slightly better thanks to superior control of the center, but the strong control of e5 makes it difficult to find a clear path into the Black position.) 13.Nf5! gxf5; 14.Qxh5 Nf6; 15.Qh4! Qe6; 16.e5! dxe5; 17.Bxe5 and White has better bishops and a superior pawn structure in Tukmakov-Almasi,

Hrvatska 1995. **10.Re1 exd4; 11.Nxd4 Re8.** 11... Nc5; 12.b3 Bd7; 13.Bf4 Qb6; 14.Bxd6 Nfxe4; 15.Bxe4 Nxe4; 16.Rxe4 Rxe4; 17.Nxe4 Qxd4; 18.Qxd4 Bxd4; 19.Rd1 and Black was slightly uncomfortable in Khalifman-Thipsay, Ubeda 1997. 9...Qb6; 10.c5 is very popular, for example Yusupov-Kasparov, Linares 1990 which continued 10.dxc5 11.dxe5 Ne8; 13.Bf4 Nc7; 14.Qc2 Ne6; 15.Rfd1 Re8! With counterplay for Black.

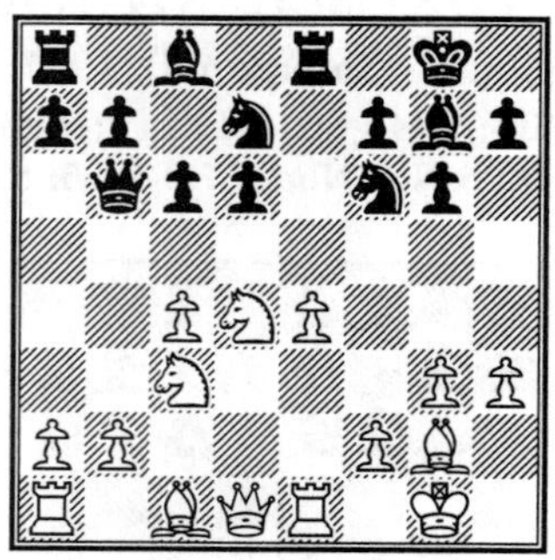

12.Nc2. 12.Nb3 Ne5; 13.Be3 c5! creates a backward pawn, but the hole at d5 is not easy to exploit for example 14.Bf1 Be6; 15.Nd5 Bxd5; 16.exd5 Ne4; 17.Kg2 f5; 18.Qc2 Nf7; 19.Bd3 Re7; 20.Re2 Rae8; 21.Rae1 Qa6 with a dynamically balanced game in Yepishin-Kasparov, Moscow (rapid) 1995. **12...Nc5.** Here White will take some action on the b-file, but there is a choice of plans. **13.b4.** 13.Rb1 Ng4; 14.hxg4 Bxc3; 15.Re3 Bg7; 16.b3 Be6; 17.Bd2 a5; 18.Bc3 Bxc3; 19.Rxc3 and Black's center was fragile in Nikolic-Kveinys, Yerevan Olympiad 1996. **13...Ne6; 14.Be3 Qc7; 15.Qd3 a5; 16.a3 Nd7.** Opening the a-file would just help White. **17.f4 Nb6; 18.Rad1 axb4.** Now the exchange is playable, since White no longer controls the a-file. **19.axb4 Na4; 20.Nxa4 Rxa4; 21.Qxd6 Qxd6; 22.Rxd6.**

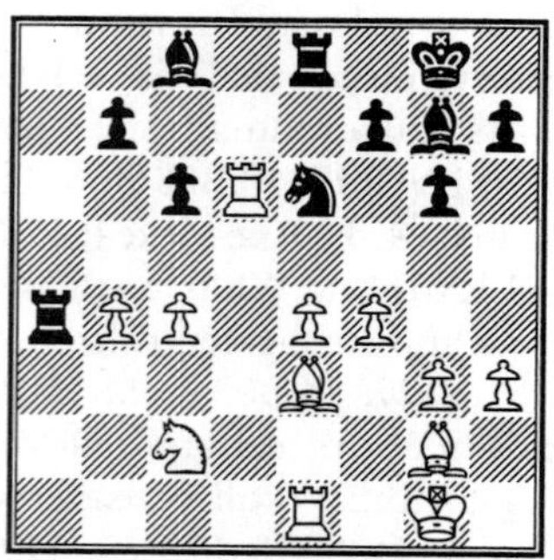

White has won a pawn, but Black heads for an endgame which is not so easy to win. **22...c5; 23.f5.** White miscalculates, missing the hidden dangers of the pin on the e-file. **23...Nd4; 24.Nxd4 cxd4; 25.Bxd4 Bf8!; 26.Bc5 Bxf5; 27.e5 Bxd6; 28.Bxd6.**

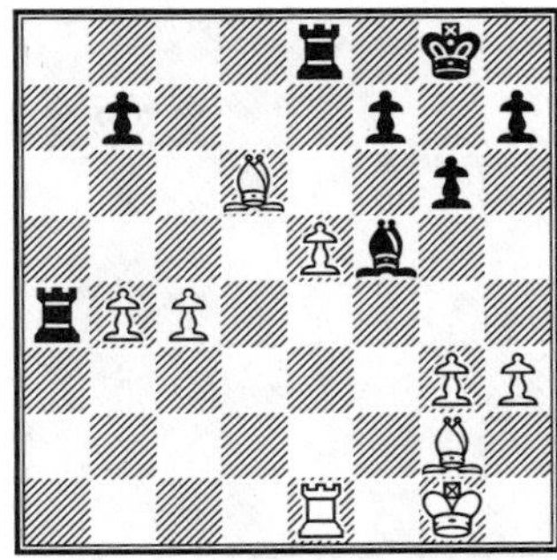

Black has the exchange, but White has powerful bishops. The next few moves are forced. **28...Bc8; 29.Rf1 Ra2; 30.Rf2 Ra1+;** 30...Rxf2; 31.Kxf2 and White has excellent prospects of making a queen quickly on the queenside. **31.Kh2 b6; 32.Bc6 Rd8; 33.b5 Be6; 34.c5 bxc5; 35.b6 Rb1; 36.b7 c4.**

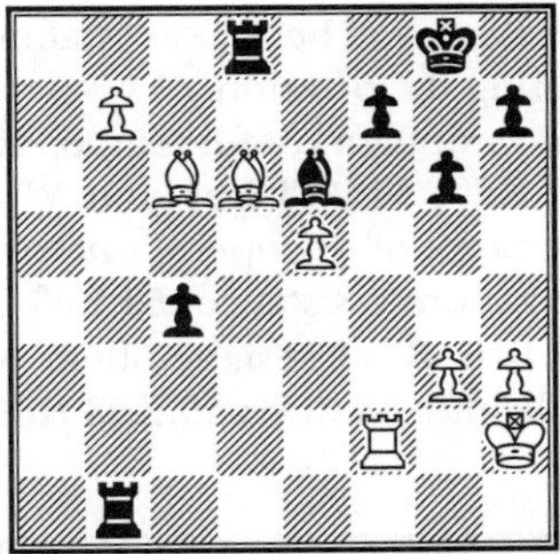

The endgame has become quite exciting, and accurate play is required. **37.Ra2!** The rook heads to a8. **37...Kg7; 38.Ra8 Rxd6.** There is nothing better, as the b-pawn was ready to promote. **39.exd6 c3; 40.Ra5.**

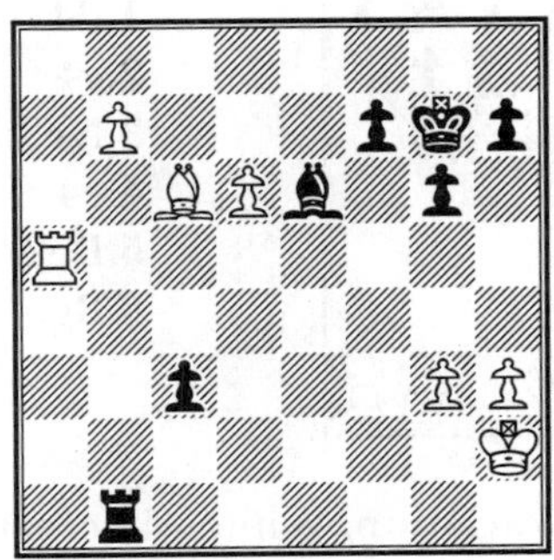

40...Rb2+?! 40...c2!; 41.Rc5 c1Q; 42.Rxc1 Rxc1; 43.b8Q Rxc6 and Black should hold. **41.Kg1 c2; 42.Rc5 Rb1+; 43.Kf2 c1Q; 44.Rxc1 Rxc1.**

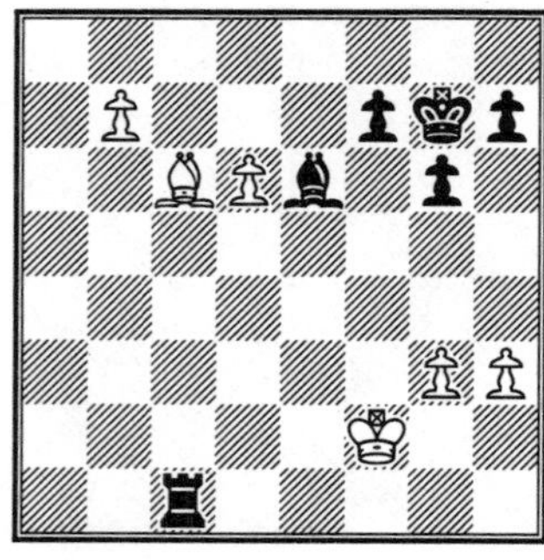

The goal here is not just to find the next few moves. There are pitfalls down the line, and the student must not relax for a moment, especially at move 49. **45.Bb5!** 45.b8Q Rxc6 offers Black excellent drawing chances of setting up a blockade. All that is needed is to bring the rook to d5, for example. **45...Rc8! 46.bxc8Q Bxc8; 47.d7 Bxd7; 48.Bxd7 Kf6.** The task here is to win despite having the wrong rook pawn and the possibility that Black will be able to establish a barricade that will keep the White king from infiltrating the position.

49.Be8! The best move, winning a useful tempo. **49...Ke7; 50.Bb5 f5; 51.Ke3.** 51.h4 h6; 52.Kf3 g5; 53.h5 Kd6; 54.Bd3 Ke5 and White cannot make progress. **51...Kf6; 52.Kd4.** This is the point of the operation: to get the king to d4. **52...h5?!** 52...Kg5! would have offered more resistance. **53.Ke3 h4; 54.g4 Ke5; 55.Bf1 Kf6; 56.Kf4 g5+; 57.Ke3 Ke5; 58.Ba6.** Black resigned here, after six and a half hours of play. But there is no way to defend. **58...f4+; 59.Kd3 Kd5; 60.Bb7+ Ke5; 61.Bf3** and the king gets in. **White won.**

AVERBAKH VARIATION

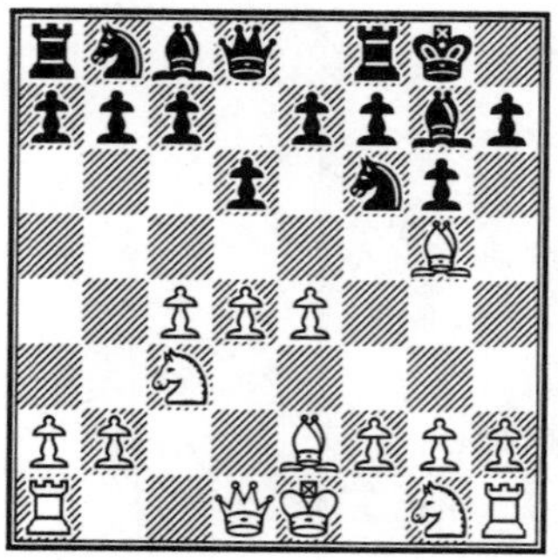

1.d4	**Nf6**
2.c4	**g6**
3.Nc3	**d6**
4.e4	**Bg7**
5.Be2	**0–0**
6.Bg5	

This is the **Averbakh Variation**. White will create a battery of queen and bishop along the c1–h6 diagonal and can attack along the h-file. Black should counter with pressure against d4, and this can be achieved in two ways, by advancing either the c-pawn or e-pawn.

(201) TUKMAKOV - KASPAROV [E73]

Soviet Championship, 1981

1.c4 Nf6; 2.Nc3 g6; 3.e4 d6; 4.d4 Bg7; 5.Be2 0–0; 6.Bg5 c5. There are several other approaches. Two reasonable alternatives involve the early development of the knight from b8. For example, 6...Nbd7; 7.Qd2 and now:

A) 7...c6 is the favorite of rising Russian star Peter Svidler. 8.Nf3 d5; 9.exd5 cxd5; 10.0–0 a6; 11.a3 (11.Ne5!? dxc4; 12.Bxc4 Qc7; 13.Bb3 Nxe5; 14.dxe5 Qxe5; 15.Rfe1 Qd6; 16.Qe2 gave White some compensation for the pawn in Gelfand-Svidler, Groningen 1996.) 11...dxc4; 12.Bxc4 b5; 13.Ba2 Bb7; 14.Ne5 Rc8; 15.Rad1 Nb6; 16.d5 Nfxd5; 17.Bxd5 Nxd5; 18.Nxd5 Qxd5; 19.Qxd5 Bxd5; 20.Rxd5 e6; 21.Rd6 Bxe5; 22.Rxa6 Bxb2; 23.a4 bxa4 and Black went on to win in Norri-Svidler, Yerevan Olympiad 1996.

B) 7...e5; 8.d5 Nc5 (8...a5; 9.h4 Nc5; 10.f3 Qd7; 11.g4 h5; 12.0–0–0 hxg4; 13.Bxf6 Bxf6; 14.fxg4 Kg7; 15.g5 Be7; 16.Nh3 Rh8; 17.Nf2 gave White a strong attack in Yermolinsky-J.Watson, San Francisco (Mechanics) 1995.) 9.f3 a5 (9...h6; 10.Be3 Kh7; 11.0–0–0 Nh5; 12.g3 Qe8; 13.Re1 b6; 14.Bd1 Bd7; 15.Nge2 a6; 16.g4 and the attack was underway in Averbakh-Zaitsev, Soviet Championship 1970.)

10.h4 c6; 11.Nh3 cxd5; 12.cxd5 Bd7; 13.Nf2. This is the prelude to a kingside pawnstorm. 13...a4; 14.g4 Qa5; 15.h5 Rfc8; 16.Ncd1! This knight will participate from e3. Queens are not needed to carry out the attack. 16...Qxd2+; 17.Bxd2 Ne8; 18.Ne3 with a better position for White, Averbakh-Fritsch, Graz 1987. 6...h6 is also popular, driving back the bishop before counterattacking in the center.

7.Be3 c5 (7...Nbd7; 8.Qc2 a6; 9.0–0–0 e5; 10.d5 Qe7; 11.Qd2 Kh7; 12.f3 Ne8; 13.h4 c5; 14.dxc6 bxc6; 15.h5 g5; 16.Na4 c5 and White's position looks preferable, since Black has a lot of pawn structure weaknesses, Gelfand - Van Wely, Groningen 1996.) 8.d5 e6; 9.Qd2 (9.h3 exd5; 10.exd5 Re8; 11.Nf3 Bf5; 12.g4 Be4; 13.Rg1 Nbd7; 14.Nd2 a6; 15.h4 b5; 16.g5 b4; 17.gxf6 bxc3; 18.Nxe4 Rxe4; 19.fxg7 Qxh4; 20.Kf1 cxb2; 21.Rb1 was drawn in Averbakh-Fischer, Interzonal 1958.) 9...exd5; 10.exd5 Kh7; 11.h3 Re8; 12.Bd3 a6; 13.a4 Nbd7; 14.Nf3 Ng8; 15.0–0 Ne5 and Black had a solid Benoni formation in Averbakh-Yukhtman, Soviet Championship 1959.

Another interesting try is 6...Na6.

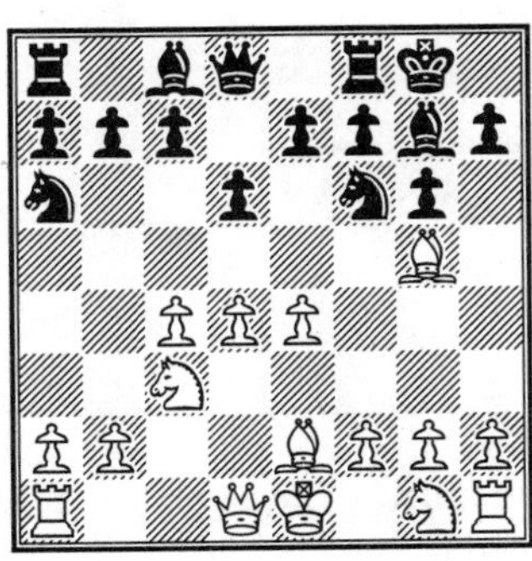

Once obscure, this defense has become a regular reply to the Averbakh Variation. Here White can continue on normal Averbakh lines with Qd2 or try the more aggressive plan with f4.

A) 7.f4!? c6; 8.Nf3 Nc7; 9.Qd2 d5; 10.Bxf6 exf6; 11.exd5 cxd5; 12.c5 is an interesting pawn strucutre. There are a number of holes in the pawn structure and it is difficult to see a future role for the bishop at g7. 12...Bf5; 13.0–0 Be4; 14.b4 Ne6; 15.Rad1 f5 (15...a6; 16.Nxe4 dxe4; 17.d5 exf3; 18.Bxf3 Nc7; 19.d6 Rb8; 20.dxc7 Qxc7; 21.Qd6 and White has a clear advantage, but the mitigating factor of bishops of opposite color allowed Black to escape with an eventual draw in Meins-Smirin, Groningen 1996.) 16.Ne5 Bh6; 17.Qe3 f6; 18.Nxe4 fxe5; 19.Nd6 e4; 20.g3 Rb8; 21.Qb3 Nc7; 22.Qa4 a6; 23.b5 axb5; 24.Nxb5 Nxb5; 25.Bxb5 g5 opened up the position but eventually the game was drawn, Meins-Kempinski, Groningen 1996.

B) 7.Qd2 e5 is a more traditional King's Indian plan, forcing White to close the center with 8.d5 and now Black breaks the pin with 8...Qe8! and if 9.h4 then 9...Nc5 where the attack on the e-pawn buys Black time to secure the knight's post with ...a5, preventing a later b4. White has yet to solve the puzzle, but here are three tries: 10.Qc2 (10.Bxf6 Bxf6; 11.Nf3 a5; 12.0–0–0 Bg7; 13.h5 f5; 14.hxg6 Qxg6; 15.Nh4 Qf6; 16.Nxf5 Bxf5; 17.exf5 a4; 18.g4 e4 with a very sharp game holding chances for both sides, Piket-J.Polgar, Aruba 1995. 10.Bf3 Ng4!? 11.Bxg4 Bxg4; 12.f3 Bd7 and in Rayetsky-Miles, Capelle la Grande 1995, White should have tried an immediate attack with h5.) 10...a5; 11.h5! Nxh5; 12.Bxh5 gxh5; 13.Be3 Na6; 14.Nge2 f5; 15.f3 c6 is analysis by Nadyrhanov, but this position is unclear and requires further investigation. 6...c6; 7.Qd2 e5; 8.d5 Na6 is similar to the 6...Na6 lines.

A) One logical continuation is 9.f3 Qa5 (9...cxd5; 10.cxd5 Bd7; 11.Bb5 Bxb5; 12.Nxb5 Qb6; 13.Nc3 Nc5; 14.Rd1 a5; 15.Nge2 Rfc8; 16.Be3 Qa6; 17.0–0 b5 gave Black active play on the queenside in Valdes-Cabreja, Cuba 1995.) 10.g4 h5; 11.h3 cxd5; 12.Nxd5 Qxd2+; 13.Kxd2 Nxd5; 14.cxd5 was eventually drawn in Yusupov-Smirin, Yerevan Olympiad 1996.

B) 9.h4 cxd5; 10.cxd5 Qe8; 11.f3 is a variation on the same theme. 11...Bd7; 12.Nh3 Nc5; 13.g4 h5; 14.Nf2 hxg4; 15.fxg4 Rc8; 16.Be3 Nh7; 17.Nd3 Nxd3+; 18.Qxd3 a6; 19.a4 and White had the more active position in Ivanchuk-Topalov, Yerevan Olympiad 1996.

7.d5 is the most common continuation.

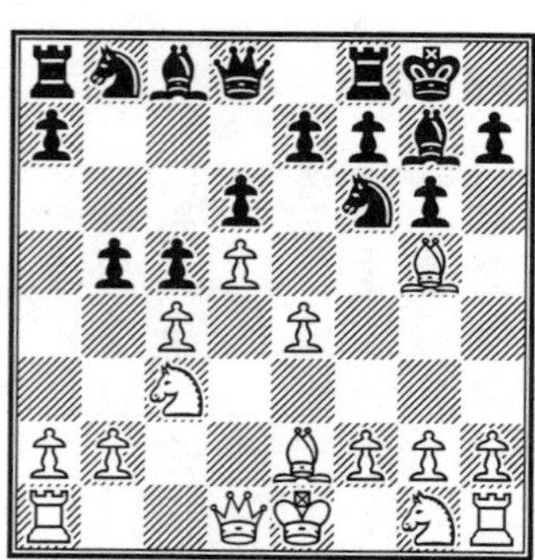

7...b5. This move is in the spirit of the Benko Gambit, and is one of Black's most ambitious plans, though objectively it is hard to fully justify the investment of a pawn. 7...a6 is the more conservative continuation. White now shuts down Black's counterplay with 8.a4 and then there are several plans.

8...Qa5 (8...e5; 9.Qd2 Qc7; 10.h4 h5; 11.f3 Nh7; 12.g4 hxg4; 13.fxg4 gave White good play on both flanks in Averbakh-Matanovic, Interzonal 1952. 8...e6; 9.Qd2 exd5; 10.exd5 Re8; 11.Nf3 Bg4 is a Modern Benoni position which has sufficient counterplay for Black. 12.0–0 Nbd7; 13.h3 Bxf3; 14.Bxf3 Qb6; 15.Qc2 Re5; 16.Bd2 Rae8; 17.Rae1 Rxe1; 18.Rxe1 Rxe1+ was agreed drawn in Sapis-Kempinski, Katowice 1995.)

9.Bd2 e5 (9...e6; 10.Nf3 exd5; 11.exd5 Qc7; 12.0–0 Bg4; 13.h3 Bxf3; 14.Bxf3 Nbd7; 15.Qc2 Rfe8; 16.Rfe1 Rxe1+; 17.Rxe1 Re8; 18.Rxe8+ Nxe8 and White's bishop pair and control of space were only partly offset by Black's control of the e5-square in Averbakh-Boleslavsky, Garga 1953.) 10.g4 Ne8; 11.h4 f5; 12.h5 f4; 13.g5 Rf7; 14.Bg4 and White's attack is powerful, Averbakh-Panno, Argentina vs Russia 1955.

7...e6 places the focus of attention on the center. 8.Qd2 exd5; 9.exd5 Re8; 10.Nf3 Bf5 (10...Bg4; 11.0–0 Nbd7; 12.h3 Bxf3; 13.Bxf3 h5 is an interesting plan. The advance of the h-pawn did not cause Black any problems in Trevelyan-Glek, Paris 1995.) 11.0–0 Qb6 (11...Na6; 12.Nh4 Bd7; 13.Qf4 h6; 14.Bxh6 Bxh6; 15.Qxh6 was better for White in White won. Hoang Thanh-Bolehradski, Budapest (Spring) 1995.) 12.Nh4 Ne4; 13.Nxe4 Bxe4; 14.f3 Qxb2; 15.Qxb2 Bxb2; 16.fxe4 Bd4+; 17.Kh1 Bxa1; 18.Rxa1 h6; 19.Bd2 Rxe4 and Black recovered even more material in Farago-Murdzia, Hamburg 1995.

8.cxb5 a6; 9.a4! This is the move that causes Black problems. Accepting the gambit by capturing at a6 would lead to normal Benko Gambit counterplay. **9...h6.** 9...Qa5; 10.Bd2 has been scoring well for White. 10...Nbd7 (10...e6; 11.dxe6 Bxe6; 12.Nf3 axb5; 13.Bxb5 Na6; 14.0–0 Nc7; 15.Re1 Nxb5; 16.Nxb5 d5; 17.exd5 Nxd5; 18.Ne5 Rfe8; 19.Rc1 Bf5; 20.Nc6 10...Qb4; 11.Bd3 c4; 12.Be2!? Nfd7; 13.Qc1 Nc5!, introduced in Kosanovic-Szuhanek, Belgrade 1995, may be the answer, after which it is White who has to struggle for equality.) 11.Ra3! gave White a large advantage in Kasparov-Spassky, Tilburg 1981.

10.Bd2 e6; 11.dxe6. If White allows Black to capture at d5 and open up the e-file, we will reach a Modern Benoni position with excellent counterplay for Black against White's weak pawn at d5 and on the queenside. **11...Bxe6.**

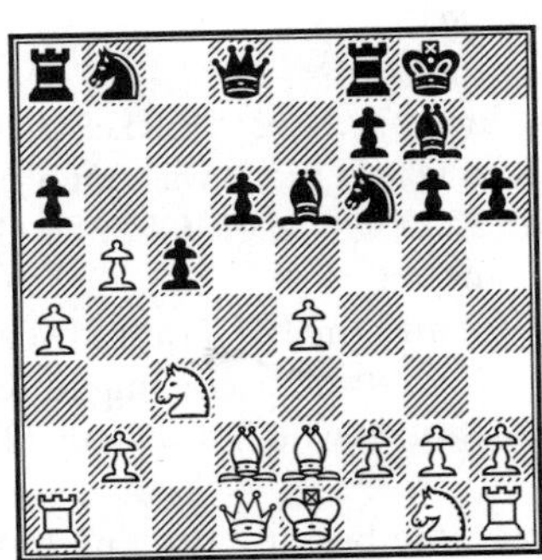

The structural contour of the middlegame is defined. White has an extra pawn of no great significance. Black will work in the center, aiming for an advance of the d-pawn. The bishops control important diagonals, and Black can already be satisfied with the position. **12.Nf3 axb5; 13.Bxb5.** 13.axb5 is not good because after 13...Bb3!; 14.Qc1 Rxa1; 15.Qxa1 Qe7; 16.e5 dxe5; 17.0–0 e4 White's position is a mess. 18.Ne1 Rd8; 19.Be3 Nbd7 and none of White's pieces are performing any useful functions.

13...Na6; 14.0–0 Nc7; 15.Re1. 15.Be2! is a sturdier test of White's strategy. If Black carries out the freeing maneuver 15...d5!; 16.exd5 Nfxd5; 17.Nxd5 Nxd5 then

White plays 18.Qc2 Qd6; 19.Bb5 keeping the b-file closed and holding on to a small advantage. **15...Nxb5; 16.Nxb5 d5!** This guarantees Black at least equality. **17.exd5 Nxd5; 18.Ne5! Re8.**

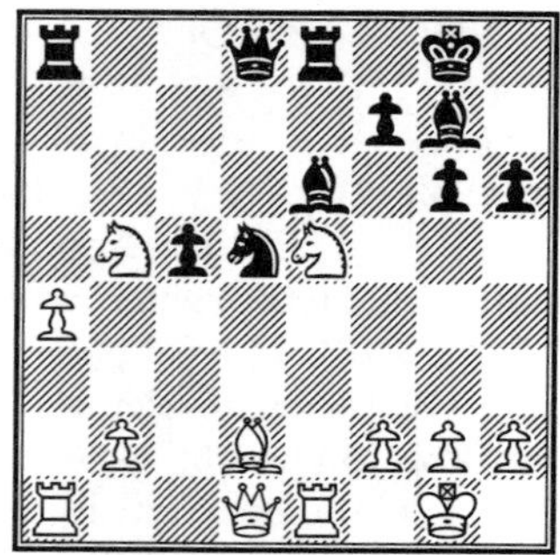

19.Rc1?! This is such a logical move that it is surprising that it turns out to be a mistake, but White had to play in the center with 19.Nc4, to be followed by an occupation of the d6-square, where a knight thoroughly disrupts the communication of Black's pieces. Now, however, Black gets a strong game by opening the e-file for the rook. **19...Bf5!; 20.Nc6.** It is too late for 20.Nc4 Rxe1+; 21.Bxe1 Nf4! 22.Qxd8+ Rxd8 with threats all over the light squares, especially at d3 and e2. **20...Qd7!** Kasparov appreciates that it is the light squares, not the dark squares, that need attention. **21.Rxc5 Rxe1+; 22.Qxe1 Re8; 23.Qc1 Nb6!**

In return for the c-pawn Black has a strong initiative, and White must be ever careful to guard the back rank. Black's bishops can operate on either side of the board, but the White knights are stuck on the queenside. **24.b3 Re2.** This is necessary preparation for Black's next move. **25.Ba5?!** White fails to appreciate Kasparov's plan. 25.Bc3!? was the difficult to evaluate, according to Kasparov, who provided the continuation 25...Rc2; 26.Qe1.

A) 26...Be4 and here:

A1) I prefer 27.Ne5, since 27...Bxe5; 28.Rxe5! f5 (On 28...Bf5; 29.Re8+ wins.) 29.f3 Bd5; 30.Re8+ Kf7; 31.Rh8 leaves Black without a plausible defense.

A2) Kasparov gives 27.Ncd4; 27...Qg4 28.g3 Qh3; 29.Qxe4 Rc1+; 30.Qe1! Rxe1+; 31.Bxe1 where White is much better.

B) 26...Bxc3!; 27.Nxc3 Qe6! and the back rank threats give Black some chances which should be good enough for a draw, according to Kasparov's analysis. 25.Be3?, on the other hand, is a terrible move which loses quickly to 25...Bb2!; 26.Qf1 Bd3; 27.Qd1 Bxb5!; 28.Qxd7? Re1#

25...Be4! This move is playable because the knight is taboo. **26.Ne5.** 26.Bxb6? Qg4; 27.Qf1 Re1!!; 28.Rc1 (28.Qxe1 Qxg2#) 28...Qxg2#; 26.Qf1! was therefore best, to guard the g2-square. 26...Rb2; 27.Bxb6 Bxc6 and Kasparov asserts that Black has good compensation for the pawns. Indeed, White probably has nothing better than to reduce the back rank mate threats with 28.h3; but after 28...Rxb3; Black is only one pawn down, and the bishop pair and better piece coordination are sufficient to balance the chances.

26...Qe7; 27.Nd4? Again White had to retreat the queen to f1 when a draw would still have been possible, e.g., 27.Qf1 Ra2; 28.Bxb6 Bxe5; 29.Nc3 Bxh2+; 30.Kxh2 Qh4+; 31.Kg1 Bxg2; 32.Kxg2 Qg4+; 33.Kh2 Qh4+, as given by Kasparov. **27...Ra2;**

28.Bxb6 Bxe5; 29.Qe3? White is in trouble, but there was still a fighting chance with 29.Qe1! where Black would have had to find 29...Qf6!; 30.Ne2 Ra1; 31.Rc1 Qg5!; 32.g3 Qg4!; 33.Nd4 Qh3; 34.f3 Ra2; 35.Nc2 Bxf3; 36.Qf2 Be4 and the powerful Black pieces provide not just compensation for the pawn, but real winning chances. **29...Qxc5!**

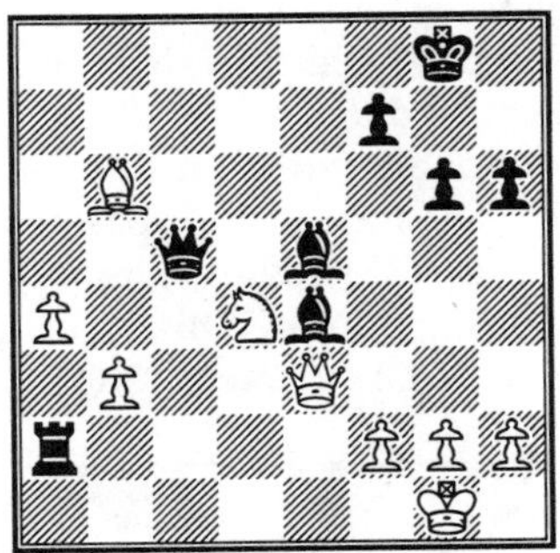

The queen cannot be captured because of ...Ra1+, so White resigned. This game secured the 1981 Soviet Championship, Kasparov's first. **White won.**

STEINER ATTACK

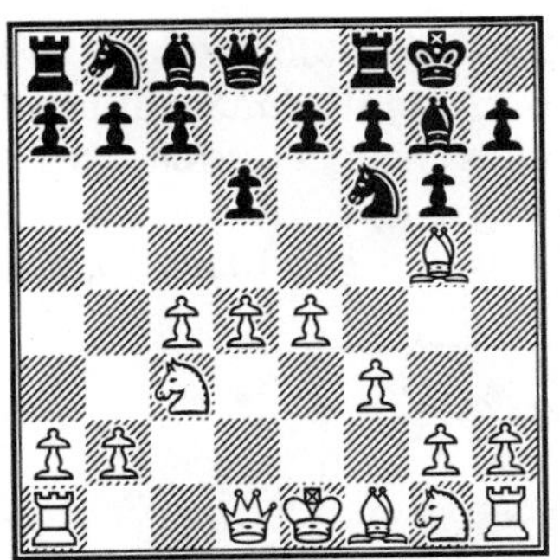

1.d4	**Nf6**
2.c4	**g6**
3.Nc3	**Bg7**
4.e4	**d6**
5.f3	**0–0**
6.Bg5	

Herman Steiner modified the standard Saemisch Variation by placing the bishop at g5. This plan is still frequently seen, but Black has been able to limit White's advantages to minimal ones at best. Counterplay is available on the queenside, usually with an advance of the c-pawn to c5, and if White pushes past to d5, then ...b5, in the spirit of the Benko Gambit, becomes available. White will use a battery of queen at d2 and Bg5 to try to attack the enemy king, often using an advance of the h-pawn as well. Our illustrative game features one of the developers of the line as White.

(202) STEINER - BOLBOCHAN [E81]

Mar del Plata, 1953

1.d4 Nf6; 2.c4 g6; 3.Nc3 Bg7; 4.e4 d6; 5.f3 0–0; 6.Bg5 c5; 7.d5 e6. The standard plan, though Benko Gambit-like approaches with an early ...b5 are also seen. 7...Nbd7 is an error, however, as it allows White to develop with Nh3 followed by Nf2, as in Schiller-Nakamoto, Hawaii International 1997. Now if 8.Nh3?! Black captures on d5 and then on h3. **8.Qd2 exd5; 9.Nxd5.**

Most modern games continue 9.cxd5, but this remains a popular alternative. **9...Be6; 10.Nc3 Nc6; 11.Rd1.** The loss of the d-pawn is nothing to worry about in such positions. Black has excellent play in the center. **11...a6!; 12.Qf4.** 12.Qxd6 Qa5; 13.Be3 Nd4! disrupts the coordination of White's pieces on the d-file. Soltis gives further 14.Bxd4 cxd4; 15.Qxd4 Nd5! **12...Ne5; 13.Qh4.**

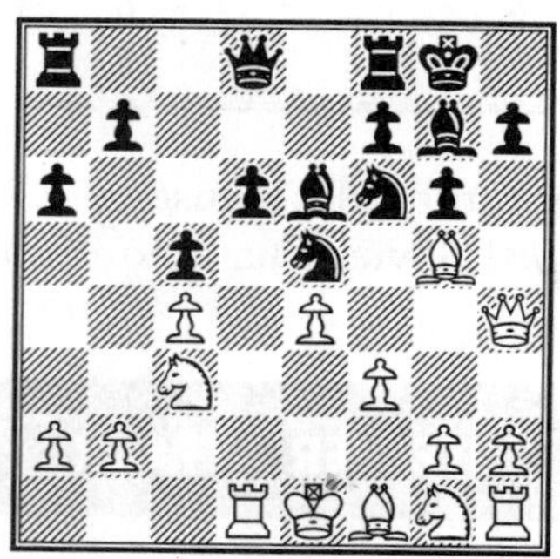

13...Re8! 13...Nxc4; 14.Bxc4 Bxc4; 15.e5! Re8; 16.Bxf6 Bxf6; 17.Qxc4 and White is a piece up. 13...Bxc4; 14.Bxc4 Nxc4; 15.Nd5 and the knight at f6 falls. **14.Nh3.** 14.f4 h6! gives Black excellent counterplay. Soltis analyzes the following line: 15.fxe5 (15.Bxf6 Bxf6; 16.Qxh6 Bg7; 17.Qg5 Qxg5; 18.fxg5 Nxc4 is clearly better for Black.) 15...hxg5; 16.Qxg5 Ng4!; 17.Qxd8 Raxd8; 18.exd6 Ne3! **14...h6; 15.Bxh6.**

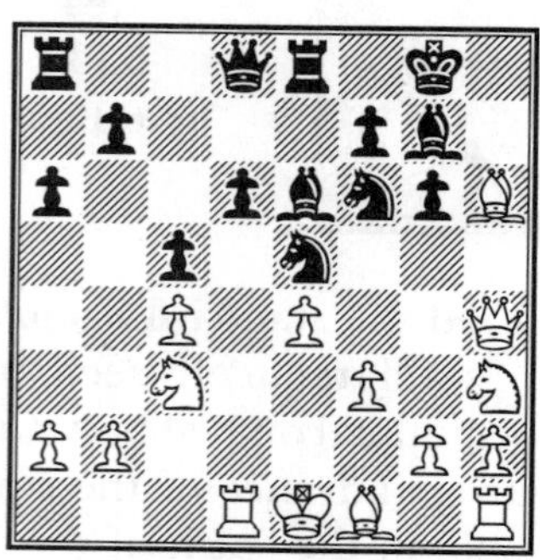

Black now forces an endgame where he holds all the trumps. **15...Nxe4!!; 16.Qxd8 Rexd8; 17.Bxg7.** 17.Nxe4 Bxh6; 18.Rxd6 Nxc4 (18...Bxh3; 19.gxh3 f5; 20.Rxd8+ Rxd8; 21.Nxc5 Bd2+ is given by Soltis, but I think the situation is still unclear. 22.Kf2 Bb4; 23.Nb3 and Black has compensation, but no more.) 19.Bxc4 Bxc4; 20.b3 Rxd6; 21.Nxd6 Bd5 and Black's bishops are better than the knights. **17...Nxc3!; 18.Bxe5**

Nxd1; 19.Bf6. 19.Kxd1 dxe5+; 20.Kc2 Bxh3; 21.gxh3 Rd4 is winning for Black. **19...Ne3; 20.Bxd8 Rxd8; 21.b3 Bxh3; 22.gxh3 d5; 23.cxd5 Rxd5.**

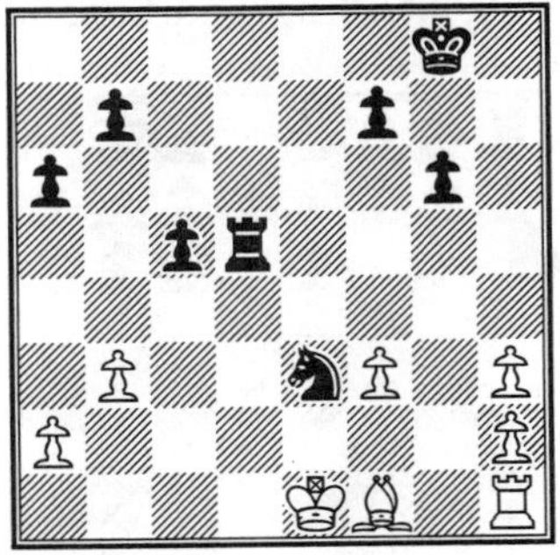

The rest of the endgame is just a matter to technique. In the end, White must lose against reasonably accurate play. **24.Be2 Nf5; 25.Bc4 Rd6; 26.Ke2 b5; 27.Bd3 Nd4+; 28.Ke3 f5; 29.Rc1 Re6+; 30.Kf2 Rc6; 31.h4 Kf7; 32.Ke3 Kf6; 33.Rg1 Ne6; 34.f4 Rd6; 35.Be2 Rd4; 36.h5 Re4+; 37.Kd2 Nxf4; 38.Bf3 Rd4+; 39.Ke3 Nxh5; 40.Rc1 f4+; 41.Ke2 c4; 42.bxc4 bxc4; 43.Bb7 a5; 44.Ba6 Rd3; 45.Rxc4 Rh3; 46.Ra4 Rxh2+; 47.Kf3 Rh3+; 48.Kf2 Kg5; 49.Bb7 Kh4; 50.Rxa5 g5; 51.Be4 Re3; 52.Ra4 Nf6; 53.Bf3 Ng4+ 54.Bxg4 Kxg4; 55.Ra8 Rh3; 56.a4 Rh2+; 57.Kf1 Ra2; 58.Ra5 Kh4. Black won.**

SAEMISCH VARIATION

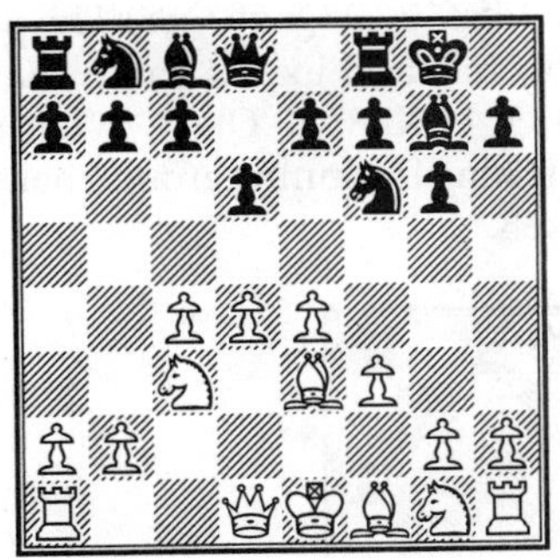

1.d4	**Nf6**
2.c4	**g6**
3.Nc3	**Bg7**
4.e4	**d6**
5.f3	**0-0**
6.Be3	

White builds a strong center with plenty of support, ready to withstand Black's hypermodern barrrage. The pawn at f3 also controls g4, allowing the advance of the g-pawn in an attacking mode, but more importantly securing the e3 square for the bishop. Normally, White continues with Qd2 and queenside castling, followed by a kingside attack. Black must take care to defend the kingside, so this makes the queenside a roughly level battleground and sometimes White can operate effectively on that side of the board as well. The Saemisch is a fighting opening which has produced many sparkling gems. Our next game is one of them.

(203) BAGIROV - GUFELD [E84]

Kirovabad, 1973

1.d4 Nf6; 2.c4 g6; 3.Nc3 Bg7; 4.e4 d6; 5.f3 0–0; 6.Be3.

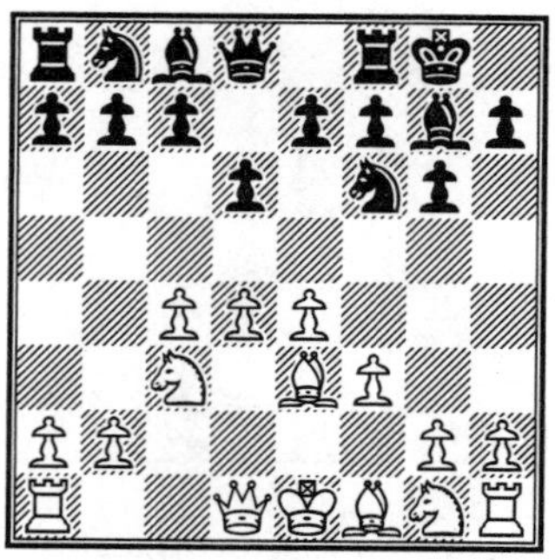

There are many ways for Black to meet the Saemisch, but the most interesting is the development of the knight at c6, where it has a great deal of influence on the center. **6...Nc6.** This is the Panno Variation. Black plans to play...Rb8, ...a6, and ...b5, with a lot of play on the queenside. That's important, because queenside castling is normal for White, who will try to march up the h-file and infiltrate with Bh6.

6...c5 is a good defense. It has become established that White does not get very far by capturing on c5, but fireworks can arise even when White adopts the normal plan. Here is an absolute gem of a game, played by the creative genius Tony Miles. Play it all the way to the end, because there is quite a surprise there! 7.Nge2 Nc6; 8.Qd2 e6; 9.Rd1 b6; 10.Bg5 Ba6; 11.d5 Ne5; 12.b3 h6; 13.Be3 exd5; 14.Nxd5 Nxd5; 15.Qxd5 b5; 16.cxb5 Bxb5; 17.Nc1 Bc6!; 18.Qd2 f5!; 19.Qxd6 Qe8! The point! There will be no exchange of queens. Miles is truly inspired in this game. 20.Qxc5 fxe4; 21.f4 Nd3+; 22.Nxd3 exd3; 23.Kf2 Rc8; 24.Qc4+ Kh8; 25.Qxd3. What now? Black has already invested two pawns, but the White king is running around naked. 25...g5!; 26.Rc1 Rd8; 27.Qe2 gxf4; 28.Bc5 f3!; 29.Qxe8.

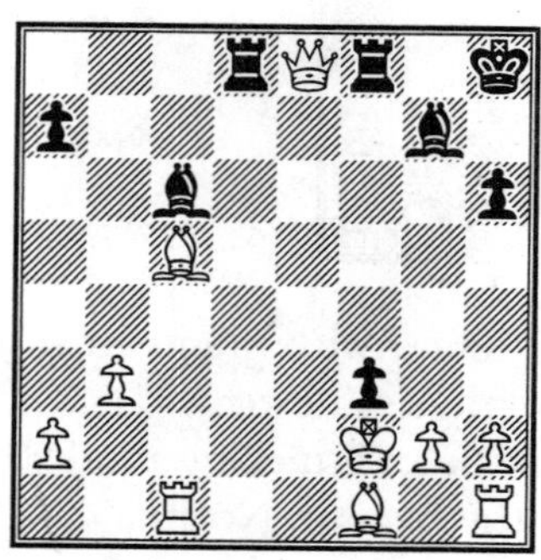

Can you believe this game ends in two moves? 29...fxg2+!; 30.Bxf8 gxh1N+!! and White resigned because of 31.Ke1 Rxe8+; 32.Be2 Bb5; 33.Bxg7+ Kxg7; 34.Rc2 Kf6 and the endgame is simple. 35.Kf1 Bxe2+; 36.Rxe2 Rxe2; 37.Kxe2 Ke5; 38.Kf3 Kd4; 39.Kg2 Kc3; 40.Kxh1 Kb2 etc.

7.Nge2. Although it seems, at first, that this just locks in the light-squared bishop, it turns out that the bishop is fairly happy at home. This knight can go to the kingside via g3, or it cand find a new home after a brief rest at c1. **7...a6; 8.Qd2 Rb8; 9.Bh6.** 9.h4 is also quite popular. 9...h5. Both sides are playing logically. Black can't allow White to play h5 too soon, and the last move is designed to slow the attack. Of course White can play an early g4 to open things up, but Black has a pawn, knight and bishop aimed at that square. Another typical reaction to the flank attack is an immediate counterblow in the center, while Black can even play on the queenside! 10.Bh6. Recently 10.Nc1 has found devotees at the top levels of chess.

(10.Nc1 e5; 11.d5 Nd4; 12.Nb3 c5; 13.dxc6 bxc6; 14.Nxd4 exd4; 15.Bxd4 has been used by Karpov, for example against Kindermann at Baden-Baden 1992.) 10...e5 This move was introduced by Spassky at this game. (10...Bxh6; 11.Qxh6 e5 is considered more accurate, for example 12.0–0–0 b5; 13.g4 bxc4; 14.Ng3 and now Black can try the sacrificial 14...Bxg4!; 15.Bxc4 Bxf3; 16.Qxg6+ Kh8; 17.Qh6+ Nh7; 18.Nxh5 with a complicated game in Lerner-W.Watson, Moscow 1985. Fischer was presumably familiar with this game.)

11.Bxg7 Kxg7; 12.d5 Castling might have been wiser. 12...Ne7; 13.Ng3 c6; 14.dxc6 Nxc6. An interesting move, but capturing at the pawn, intending to break through at d5, was also possible. Analysis by leading theoretician Leonid Shamkovich shows that life is not so simple: (14...bxc6; 15.0–0–0 Qb6; 16.Na4 Qb4; 17.Qxb4 Rxb4; 18.b3 d5; 19.Nc5! and the knight can redeploy at d3 with a good position for White.) 15.0–0–0 Be6! with a double-edged game in Spassky-Fischer, Sveti Stefan (8th Match Game) 1992.

9...b5; 10.h4 e5; 11.Bxg7 Kxg7; 12.h5. White presses the attack relentlessly, but after dealing with immediate threats on the kingside, Gufeld has a free hand on the kingside. **12...Kh8; 13.Nd5 bxc4; 14.hxg6 fxg6; 15.Qh6.**

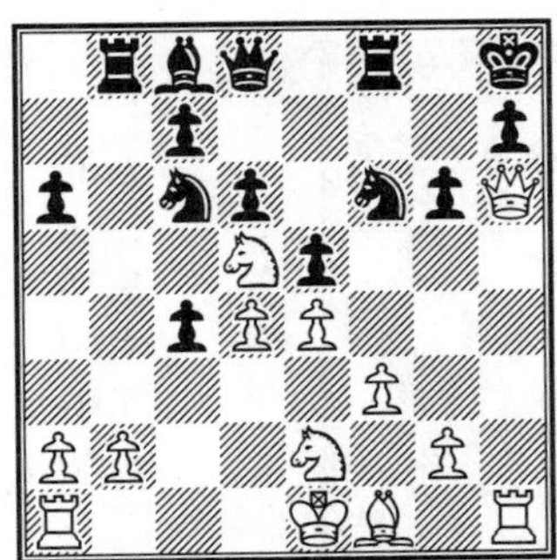

This leaves the queenside weak. White should simply have castled, with a superior game. **15...Nh5; 16.g4 Rxb2; 17.gxh5 g5; 18.Rg1 g4; 19.0–0–0 Rxa2; 20.Nef4.** 20.Bh3!! was the move White failed to spot. Of course the complications are tremendous, but Gufeld analyzed

20...Rxe2; 21.Bxg4 Rf7; 22.Bxc8 Qxc8; 23.Nf6 Qb8 where Black's mating attack can be held off by 24.Rg8+ Qxg8; 25.Nxg8 and now it is Black who has to save the game with 25...Nb4! threatening mate at c2, and so 26.Rd2 Re1+; 27.Rd1 Re2 with a draw. **20...exf4; 21.Nxf4?** 21.Bxc4 Ra1+; 22.Kb2 Rxd1; 23.Rxd1 Rg8; 24.Nf6 Rg7; 25.Bg8! Qe7; 26.Bxh7 Rxh7; 27.Nxh7 Qxh7; 28.Qf8+ Qg8; 29.Qh6+ with a miraculous draw, according to Gufeld's analysis. **21...Rxf4!; 22.Qxf4 c3.** The noose is tightening around White's neck. **23.Bc4 Ra3!** A temporary retreat, but keeping an eye on the a1-square. **24.fxg4 Nb4; 25.Kb1.**

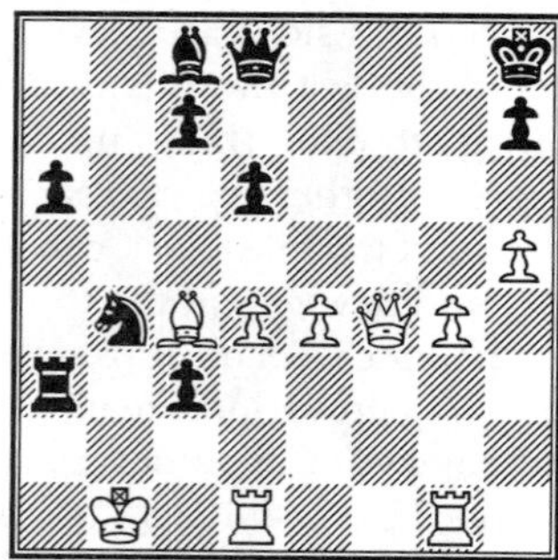

Now Gufeld unwraps one of the most beautiful combinations in chess literature. With his own king defenseless, every moment counts, so Gufeld removes the bishop from c4 by a most brutal method. **25...Be6!!** Advancing the pawn would have achieved nothing: 25...c2+; 26.Kb2 cxd1Q; 27.Rxd1 Ra5; 28.Rf1 and White's attack is worth a piece, for example 28...d5 (28...Bd7; 29.Qh6) 29.Qh6 Be6; 30.Rf8+ Qxf8; 31.Qxf8+ Bg8; 32.Qf6#. **26.Bxe6 Nd3; 27.Qf7 Qb8+; 28.Bb3 Rxb3+; 29.Kc2 Nb4+; 30.Kxb3 Nd5+; 31.Kc2 Qb2+; 32.Kd3 Qb5+** and White resigned, not wanting to bother with **33.Kc2 Qe2+; 34.Kb3 Qb2+; 35.Ka4 Qb4#. Black won.**

CLASSICAL VARIATION

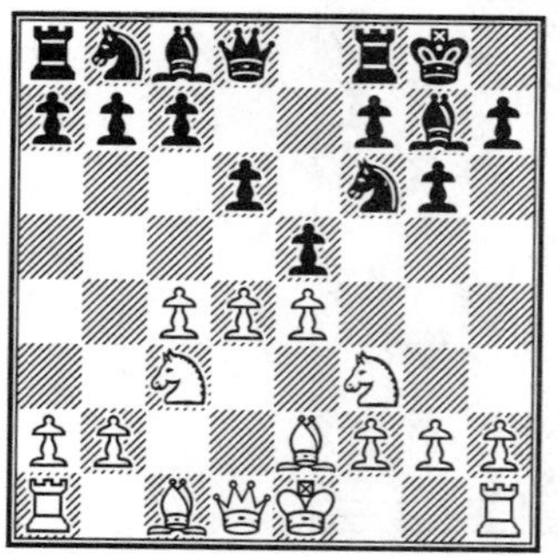

1.d4	**Nf6**
2.c4	**g6**
3.Nc3	**Bg7**
4.e4	**d6**
5.Be2	**0-0**
6.Nf3	**e5**

The **Classical Variation** sees straightforward development and conforms to logical opening principles, as befits its name. White occupies the center with pawns and supports it with pieces. Black has some pressure in the center, and after ...exd4 the bishop at g7 can become quite powerful.

Therefore, White often advances the d-pawn to d5, keeping the center closed. This can be done right away or later on in the opening. Once the center is closed, then play is limited to the flanks. White tries to bash open the queenside, while Black has eyes only for the enemy king. If Black's attack succeeds, then White is dead. But if White survives, the advantage on the queenside usually brings victory.

(204) PETROSIAN - YUKHTMAN [E92]

Soviet Championship, 1959

1.d4 Nf6; 2.c4 g6; 3.Nc3 Bg7; 4.e4 d6; 5.Be2 0–0; 6.Nf3 e5; 7.d5.

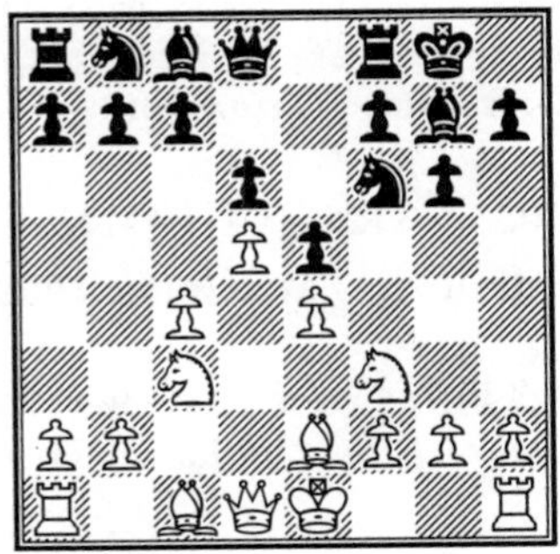

The idea behind the Petrosian Variation is to close the center, clamp down on Black's kingside counterplay, and then go to work on the queenside. Black must react vigorously, but the variation is considered harmless if handled with care. **7...Na6.**

7...Nh5 was tried at first, but it did not fare well, for example 8.g3 Na6; 9.Nd2 (9.0–0 f5; 10.exf5 Bxf5; 11.Ng5 h6; 12.Nge4 Nf6; 13.f3 Nxe4; 14.fxe4 Bd7; 15.Rxf8+ Qxf8; 16.Be3 gave White a comfortable advantage in space in Petrosian-Vukcevic, Leipzig Olympiad 1960.) 9...Nf6; 10.h4 c6; 11.Nb3 Nc7; 12.Bg5 cxd5; 13.cxd5 h6; 14.Bxf6 Qxf6; 15.Bg4 h5; 16.Bxc8 Raxc8; 17.Qe2 and in Petrosian-Gufeld, Leningrad 1960 White had the more comfortable position.

7...a5 is now considered stronger, so that the knight can come to c5 without having to worry about nagging attacks by the White b-pawn. 8.Bg5 h6; 9.Bh4 Na6; 10.Nd2 Qe8; 11.0–0 is the main line now, seen in Yusupov-Kasparov, Barcelona 1989. **8.Bg5.** This keeps Black's pieces tied down, unless Black is willing to weaken the kingside pawn structure. In fact, that is the only appropriate reply! **8...h6; 9.Bh4 g5; 10.Bg3 Nh5; 11.Nd2 Nf4; 12.0–0 Nc5.**

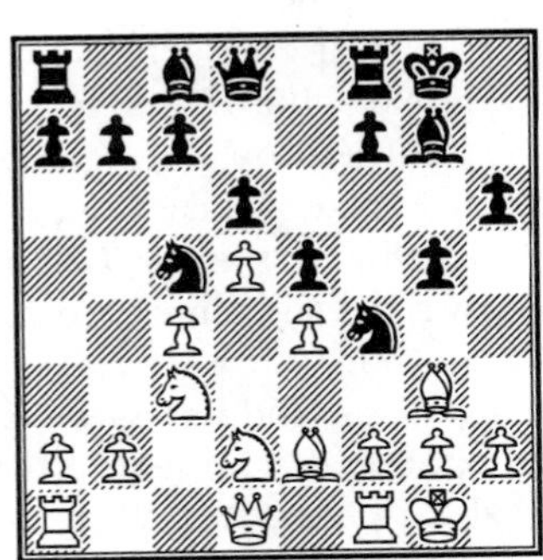

13.Bg4! This bishop will be exchanged for its Black counterpart in due course, but meanwhile it is a powerful force on the light squares. **13...a5; 14.f3 Ncd3.** This invasion really does not accomplish anything. 14...Bxg4; 15.fxg4 gives White an eternal lock on f5, which can one day be occupied by a knight. It also would doom the bishop at g7 to a very boring existence. 14...Ng6; 15.Bf2 Nd3; 16.Be3 Ndf4; 17.g3

Nd3; 18.Qc2 Nb4; 19.Qb1 is better for White.

15.Qc2 c6; 16.Kh1 h5. Now the bishop departs, its job done. **17.Bxc8 Rxc8; 18.a3 cxd5; 19.cxd5 Nc5.** Black hopes to both defend the queenside and attack on the kingside, but that is hard to do when White controls the center. **20.Bf2 g4; 21.g3! Ng6; 22.fxg4 hxg4.** Now Black's attacking prospects have disappeared. **23.Be3 b5.** Desperation. **24.Nxb5 Qb6; 25.a4 Qa6; 26.Nc4 f5; 27.Rxf5 Rxf5; 28.exf5 Qb7; 29.Qg2 Nb3; 30.Ncxd6 Qd7; 31.Rf1. White won.**

(205) LARSEN - TAL [E99]

Candidates Match (5), 1969

1.Nf3 Nf6; 2.c4 g6; 3.Nc3 Bg7; 4.e4 d6; 5.d4 0–0. By a transpositional route we have landed in the territory of the King's Indian Defense. **6.Be2 e5; 7.0–0 Nc6; 8.d5 Ne7.**

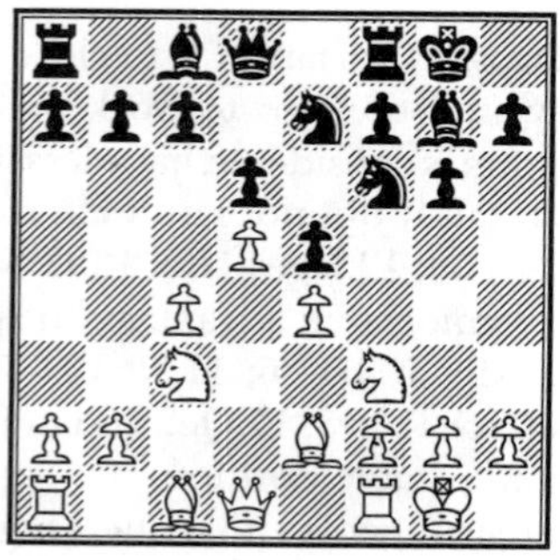

This is where the main lines of the Classical King's Indian diverge. The leading contenders are 9.Nd2 and 9.Ne1, and fashion tends to swing between them, with occasional spurts of popularity for 9.b4, too. **9.Ne1.** This is one of those openings where a horserace takes place. White will try to smash through on the queenside before Black gets to the White king on the kingside. The pace is brisk, and the closed center allows both sides to pursue their goals without much interference.

9...Nd7; 10.Nd3. 10.f3 f5; 11.Nd3 Nf6; 12.Bd2 f4 is the more normal method of reaching the position after the twelfth move in the game. 10.Be3 f5; 11.f3 f4; 12.Bf2 g5 is the rather crude plan which has now taken center stage. The entire line with 10.Be3 has surged in popularity during the last two decades, and in this critical position the advance of the a-pawn has suddenly become the subject of intense scrutiny.

13.a4. Here Black has many plans, and here are two samples: 13...Ng6 (13...a5 keeps White's a-pawn bottled up, but also presents a new target for White's operations. After 14.Nd3 b6; 15.b4 axb4; 16.Nxb4 and White has a light advantage, Kiriakov-Anapolsky, Alma Ata 1991.) 14.a5 a6; 15.Kh1 and in Krivoshey-Golubev, Alushta 1995, White had a flexible position with a lot of space on the queenside.

10...f5; 11.Bd2. The exciting 11.g4 remains an alternative for White. **11...Nf6; 12.f3 f4; 13.c5!?** This particular move order allows White to get the attack going right away. White could also play on the kingside with 13.g4, which gives you some idea of the strategic riches of the Classical King's Indian, even this far into the opening. **13...g5; 14.Rc1.** Current Women's World Champion Zsuzsa Polgar had defended this position as Black. 14.cxd6 cxd6; 15.Rc1 (15.Nf2 Ng6; 16.Qc2 h5; 17.h3 Rf7 was successful for Kasparov as Black against Yuferov at Minsk 1978.) 15...Ng6; 16.Nb5 Rf7; 17.Qc2 Ne8; 18.a4 h5 and Black had adequate counterplay in Ftacnik-Polgar, Trencianske Teplice 1985.

14...Ng6; 15.Nb5?! This is too slow. 15.cxd6 cxd6; 16.Nb5 Rf7 is a more accurate way of getting to the desired position. **15...Rf7.** Now 15...a6! is considered more accurate, but Tal had seen previous games by Larsen and had prepared a new move which would be revealed a bit later. **16.cxd6.** If Larsen had found 16.Ba5! then Tal might have had to reveal an answer which has so far eluded the theoreticians. **16...cxd6; 17.Qc2.**

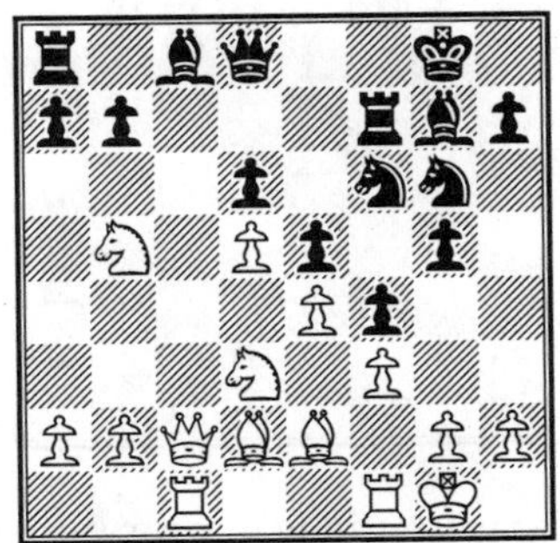

Now Tal unleashes his secret weapon. **17...g4!** This looks straightforward, but it is part of a deep and profound plan which involves sacrificing the rook at a8, and more! **18.Nc7 gxf3; 19.gxf3.** 19.Nxa8 fxe2; 20.Rf2 Bg4; 21.Nc7 Nxe4 is just too strong for Black. **19...Bh3; 20.Nxa8.** Larsen, the brave challenger to Bobby Fischer (a right earned in this match) fearlessly grabs the rook. It is not clear, however, that acceptable alternatives were at hand. 20.Ne6 Qb6+; 21.Rf2 Nf8!? (21...Bxe6; 22.dxe6 Re7; 23.Qa4 led to a draw in Podgayets-M.Gurevich, USSR 1984.) 22.Bf1 Bxe6; 23.dxe6 Nxe6 and the peripatetic knight lands eventually at d4. **20...Nxe4; 21.fxe4 Qg5+; 22.Kf2.**

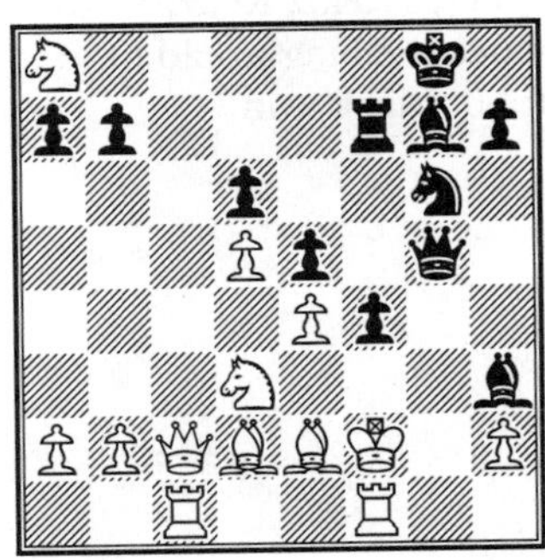

22...Qg2+. 22...Qh4+; 23.Kg1 Qg5+; 24.Kf2 would have led to a draw. In fact, that's how the game Averkin-Tal, played a bit later in the year in the Societ Championship, ended. **23.Ke1.** This position has been assessed as simply winning for White, but massive complications lie ahead. **23...Nh4; 24.Be3?** How easy it is to go wrong in a messy position! 24.Nf2 Nf3+; 25.Kd1 Nd4; 26.Qc3 f3; 27.Bd3 Bf6; 28.Be3 Bh4; 29.Bxd4 exd4; 30.Qxd4 would have put an end to Black's chances. That's why Tal took up the drawing line in his next game in this variation.

24...Qxe4; 25.Bf2. 25.Nxf4 loses, as pointed out by Larsen: 25...Qxe3; 26.Nxh3 Ng2+; 27.Kd1 Rxf1+; 28.Bxf1 Qe1#. **25...f3; 26.Bxh4 Qxh4+!** Tal attacks with relentless precision. Taking the bishop at e2 would have been inferior. 26...fxe2; 27.Rxf7 Qxh4+; 28.Rf2 and Black cannot continue the attack. 26...Bxf1; 27.Nf2! Qxe2+; 28.Qxe2 Bxe2; 29.Rc8+ Bf8; 30.Nc7 and the threat of Ne6 is strong. Black does not have enough pawns to compensate for the missing piece. **27.Nf2 fxe2; 28.Qxe2.**

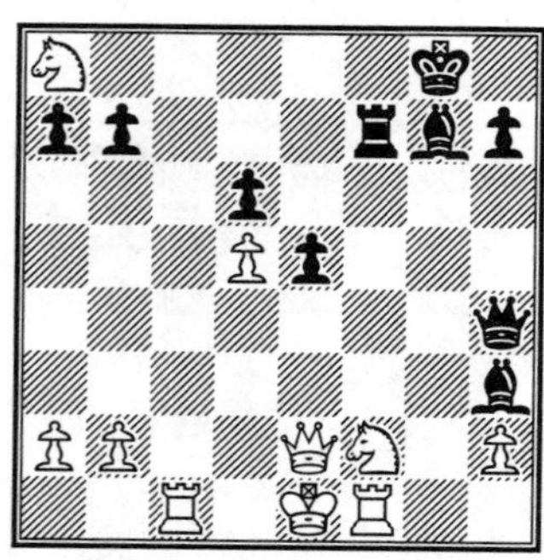

28...e4! A fine move. The pawn will march forward until it is captured, and that will open up yet another line against the White king. **29.Rg1?** 29.Rc7! was the final resource. If Black exchanges rooks then the knight returns to the game, but taking the rook at f1 leaves White a little better after 29...Bxf1; 30.Kxf1 Rf5; 31.Rc8+ Kf7; 32.Rc4 with a strong pin against the pawn at e4. To be fair, it is very hard to see this position when calculating back at move 29, especially the pin.

29...e3; 30.Qxe3 Re7. Now White, in time trouble, has to return some material. **31.Rxg7+ Kxg7; 32.Rc7 Bd7; 33.Rxd7 Rxd7; 34.Qxa7.** The last straw slips from Larsen's grasp. 34.Qc3+ Qf6; 35.Qg3+ Kf8 is better for Black, but it is not easy to get at the knight at a8 without allowing perpetual checks. **34...Re7+; 35.Kd1 Qc4!** A ruthlessly efficient move. Tal was also in tremendous time pressure yet did not fail to find the best move. **36.Qb6 Qf1+; 37.Kd2 Re2+; 38.Kc3 Qc1+; 39.Kd4 Qe3+; 40.Kc4 Rc2+** and Larsen resigned, since the king would have to move to the b-file, allowing ...Rxb2+ to win the queen at b6. **Black won.**

QUEEN'S INDIAN DEFENSE

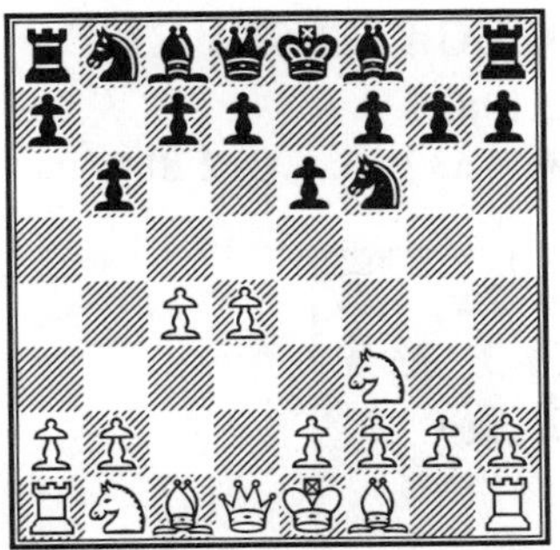

1.d4 Nf6
2.c4 e6
3.Nf3 b6

This is one of the most solid openings for Black, but it does not offer a lot of winning chances, and is often used when Black is satisfied with a draw. The simple plan of straightforward development with queenside fianchetto and a bishop at e7 and kingside castling is carried out without fear of any major White initiative in the opening.

For most of the last 50 years White had almost automatically fianchettoed the bishop at g2 with 4.g3, to which Black can reply with either 4...Bb7 or 4...Ba6. In the 1980s, a different approach, worked out by Tigran Petrosian and revived by Garry Kasparov, took over almost completely. This is the Kasparov-Petrosian Variation with Nc3 and a3 played in either order at moves 4 and 5.

KASPAROV-PETROSIAN VARIATION

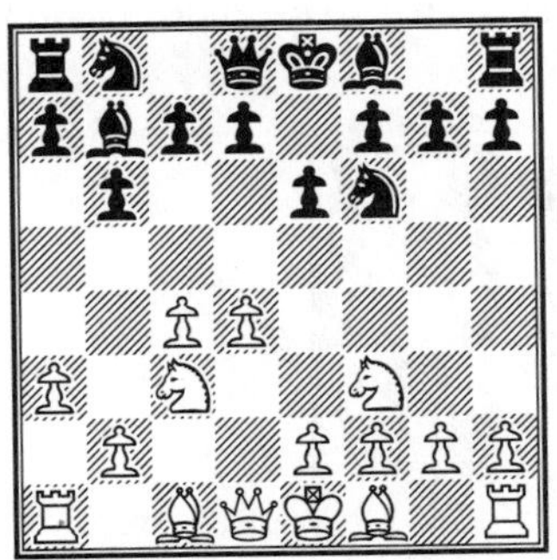

1.d4 Nf6
2.c4 e6
3.Nf3 b6
4.a3 Bb7
5.Nc3

Garry Kasparov has been a motivating force behind the popularity of the 4.a3 system since his first games as a Grandmaster, and he used it effectively throughout his climb to the World Championship. The idea behind this quiet move is to prevent the Nimzo-Indian Defense by controlling the b4-square. White cannot immediately advance to e4, creating the ideal pawn center, but this remains a major goal in the opening and after suitable preparation it becomes possible.

(206) PLASKETT - POLUGAYEVSKY E12

Lucerne, 1985

1.d4 Nf6; 2.Nf3 e6; 3.c4 b6; 4.a3 Ba6; 5.Qc2 Bb7.

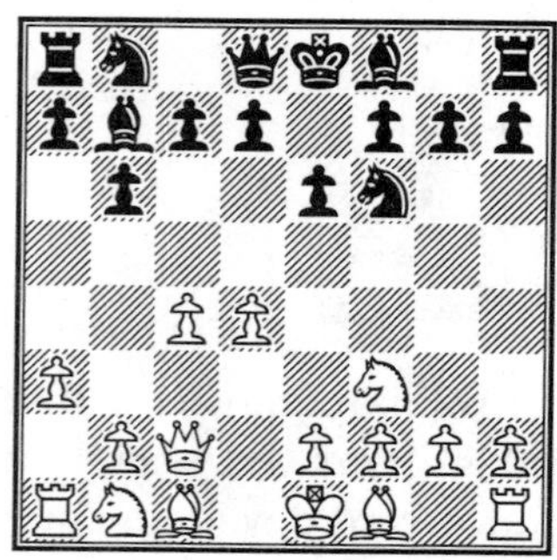

The Farago Variation is an interesting defense to the Kasparov-Petrosian Variation. Although Black has wasted time developing the bishop at a6 and retreating to b7, it is important to note that White has taken the queen off the d-file, so the pawn at d4 is not sufficiently supported. The battle for the e4-square is raging, and White has two plans: pin the knight at f6 or develop a knight to c3. In either case Black will respond by directly attacking the center with ...c5.

6.Nc3. This is considered the better plan. 6.Bg5 gained White a slight advantage in Plaskett-Skembris, Paris 1983: 6...c5; 7.d5 (7.dxc5 bxc5; 8.Nc3 Be7; 9.e3 h6; 10.Bh4 0–0; 11.Be2 d6; 12.0–0 a6; 13.Rfd1 Qc7; 14.h3 Nbd7; 15.Rd2 Rfb8; 16.Rad1 Bc6; 17.Bg3 Rb6 with an equal game, because Black has provided support for all of the weaknesses in his position, and White will not be able to make any progress in the center, Romanishin-Seirawan, Indonesia 1983.) 7...Be7!; 8.Bxf6 Bxf6; 9.e4 exd5?! (9...d6! would have equalized according to Plaskett.) 10.cxd5 d6; 11.Bd3 Nd7; 12.0–0 **6...c5.**

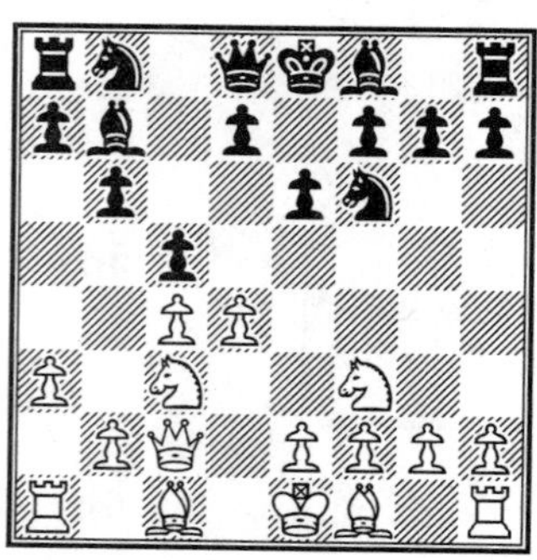

7.e3 7.e4! may be the most dangerous continuation for Black. Jan Timman has been investigating both sides of the position for some time. 7...cxd4; 8.Nxd4.

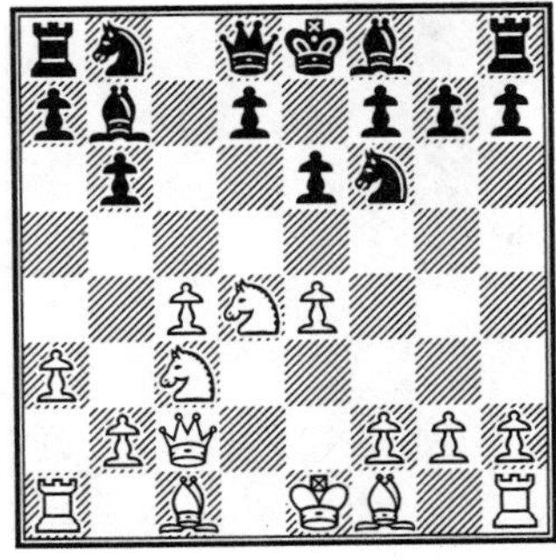

A) 8...Bc5; 9.Nb3 Nc6.

A1) 10.Bg5 h6 (10...Be7; 11.Be2 a6; 12.Bf4 d6; 13.0–0 Rc8; 14.Rac1 0–0; 15.Rfd1 Qc7 gave Black an acceptable hedgehog position in M.Gurevich-Farago, Budapest 1987.) 11.Bh4 Nd4; 12.Nxd4 Bxd4; 13.Bd3 Qb8; 14.Bg3 Be5; 15.0–0–0 0–0 and Black had every reason to be satisfied with the position in P.Cramling-Farago, Geneva 1989. Black has all the important central squares covered.

A2) 10.Nxc5 Nd4!? (10...bxc5; 11.Bd3 Nd4; 12.Qd1 d5; 13.exd5 exd5; 14.0–0 0–0; 15.cxd5 Nxd5 gave White a slight structural advantage in Portisch-Farago, Hungarian Team Championship 1993, but Black has great attacking potential on the kingside and has better development.) 11.Qd1 bxc5; 12.Be3. Although White does have a slight advantage in this position, Black has a playable game, Psakhis-Kjarner, Tallin 1983.

B) 8...Nc6; 9.Nxc6 Bxc6; 10.Bf4 Bc5 is an improved version of the same plan. 11.Be2 0–0; 12.0–0–0 (12.Rd1 a5; 13.0–0 Qe7; 14.Bf3 Ne8; 15.Qd3 e5; 16.Nd5 Qd6; 17.Bg3 Bxd5; 18.Qc3 Qc7; 19.Rxd5 gave White a superior pawn structure and the bishop pair in Dreyev-Timman, Wijk aan Zee 1996.) 12...Ne8; 13.Bg3 e5; 14.Kb1 Qe7 (14...Bd4; 15.Nb5 Bxb5; 16.cxb5 Qe7; 17.Rxd4 exd4; 18.Rd1 d5; 19.exd5 Nd6; 20.Bd3 where White's bishop pair and kingside attack provide a significant advantage, Lautier-Timman, Amsterdam (VSB) 1996.) 15.Rhe1 Bd4; 16.Nd5 Bxd5; 17.exd5 Qf6; 18.Bd3 g6; 19.Re4 Nd6 and now play became quite complicated after 20.Bh4 g5; 21.Rxd4 exd4; 22.Bxh7+ Kg7; 23.Bg3 Nxc4 but Black's defenses held in Timman-Tiviakov, Wijk aan Zee 1996.

C) 8...d6; 9.Be2 Be7; 10.0–0 0–0; 11.Be3 a6; 12.Rfd1 Nbd7 (12...Qc7; 13.f3 Nbd7; 14.Rac1 Rac8; 15.Bf1 Qb8; 16.Qf2 Bd8 and the hedgehog held up well in Stempin-Farago, Polanica Zdroj 1983.) 13.f3 Rc8; 14.Qb3 Kh8; 15.a4 Qc7; 16.Rac1 Rg8; 17.Qc2 g5 gave Black good counterplay in Timman-Ivanchuk, Amsterdam (Donner Memorial) 1996. 7.d5!? exd5; 8.cxd5 has been tried, even though it involves a pawn sacrifice after 8...Nxd5.

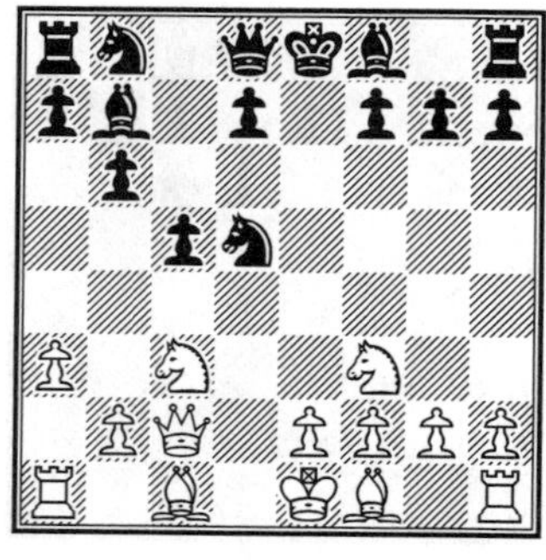

A) 9.Bg5 Be7 (9...f6; 10.Nxd5 Bxd5; 11.Bf4 Qe7; 12.0–0–0 Qe4; 13.Rxd5 Qxd5; 14.e3 Qe6; 15.Bd3 Nc6; 16.Rd1 was much better for White in Lputian-Farago, Marbella Zonal 1982. The advance of the f-pawn creates too many light-square weaknesses.) 10.Ne4 0–0; 11.Rd1 Nc7; 12.Nd6 Bd5; 13.h4 Nc6; 14.e3 Kh8; 15.Rxd5 Nxd5; 16.Qe4 Qb8; 17.Bd3 g6; 18.Nxf7+ Rxf7; 19.Qxd5 and here White's kingside attack is growing, so Farago invested an exchange to slow things down. 19...Rxf3; 20.Qxf3 Qd6; 21.Qe4 Rf8; 22.h5 Ne5. The Black pieces have rushed to the kingside to help with the defense. 23.Bb1 Bxg5; 24.hxg6 Nxg6; 25.Qxg6 Qxg6; 26.Bxg6 and the endgame was eventually drawn in Nascimento-Farago, World Team Championship 1985.

B) 9.Nxd5 Bxd5; 10.e4 Be6; 11.Bf4 Be7; 12.0–0–0 0–0 and Black had nothing to fear in Plaskett-Farago, Hastings 1982. 7.dxc5 bxc5 leaves White a bit better after 8.Bf4 with pressure on the h2-b8 diagonal.

A) 8.Bg5 Be7; 9.e3 d6 (9...0–0; 10.Be2 d6; 11.0–0 Nbd7 is another solid defense, Fahnenschmidt-Farago, Baden Baden 1990.) 10.Be2 Nc6; 11.0–0 h6; 12.Bh4 Nh5; 13.Bxe7 Qxe7; 14.b4 Nf6; 15.b5 Na5! with an equal game in Timman-Miles, Thessaloniki Olympiad 1984.

B) 8.Bf4 Be7; 9.Rd1 0–0; 10.e3 d6 (10...Qb6; 11.Be2 d6; 12.0–0 h6; 13.h3 Nbd7; 14.Nb5 e5; 15.Bh2 Ne4; 16.Nd2 Ndf6; 17.Bd3 a6; 18.Nxe4 Nxe4; 19.Bxe4 was agreed drawn in Shevelev-Farago, Hyeres Open 1992, though there was plenty of play left in the position.) 11.Rd2 Qb6; 12.Be2 Rd8; 13.0–0 Nbd7; 14.Rfd1 Nf8; 15.Ng5 Rd7; 16.Bf3 Bxf3; 17.Nxf3 Ng6; 18.Bg5 Rad8; 19.h3 h6; 20.Bxf6 Bxf6 gave Black a solid position in Stohl-Farago, Austria 1992.

7...cxd4; 8.exd4 Be7; 9.Bd3 Bxf3!?; 10.gxf3 Nc6. Polugayevsky's new idea rejuvenates the line. Black has parted with a very good bishop but has shattered the kingside pawn structure and seized the initiative by attacking the newly created weakness at d4. **11.Be3.** In case of 11.d5 Ne5; 12.Be2, Black should avoid 12...Rc8 (12...exd5; 13.cxd5 0–0 followed by Rf8-e8 with unclear complications is better.) 13.Qa4. **11...Rc8; 12.0–0.**

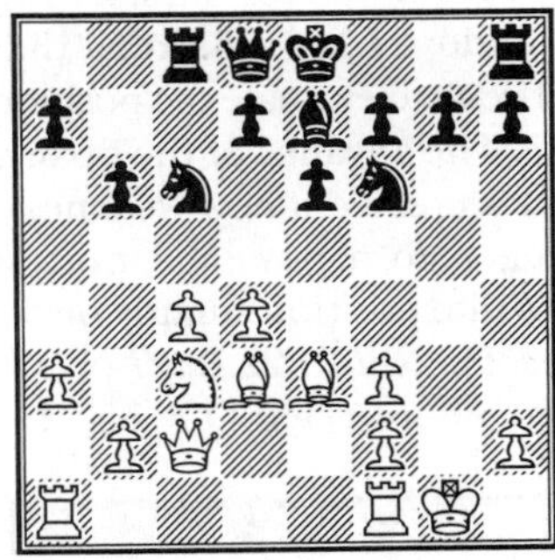

12...0–0. A bit routine. After 12...Na5! Black solves all his problems after 13.Qe2 (13.Qa4 0–0; 14.d5 would be met by 14...a6! intending to capture at d5 and then advance on the queenside with b6-b5.) 13...0–0 and now 14.b4? (14.d5 Nh5!; 15.f4 g6 followed by Bf6 with a clear advantage for Black.) 14...Nxc4!

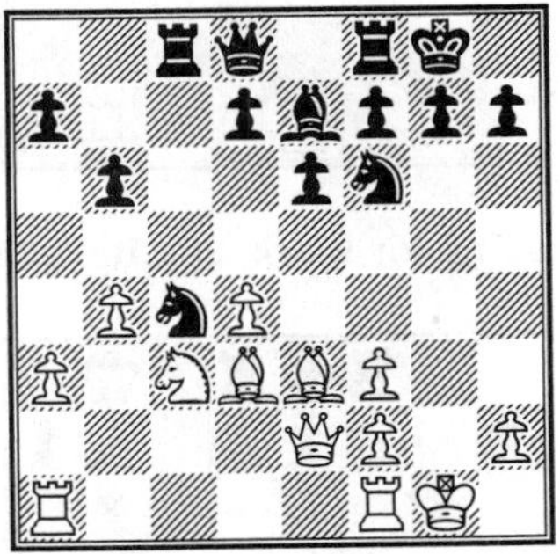

13.Rad1 Na5. It is already a bit late for this plan. 13...g6 with idea of of Nf6-h5 comes into consideration. 13...e5 does not bring equality, however, as White can continue 14.d5 Nd4; 15.Bxd4 exd4; 16.Nb5 with a better game. **14.d5 Re8.** 14...Nxc4 fails to 15.Bxc4 Rxc4; 16.d6 **15.Qe2 Nb7; 16.Kh1 Nd6.** The knight keeps an eye on c4 from a safer vantage point. **17.Rg1.**

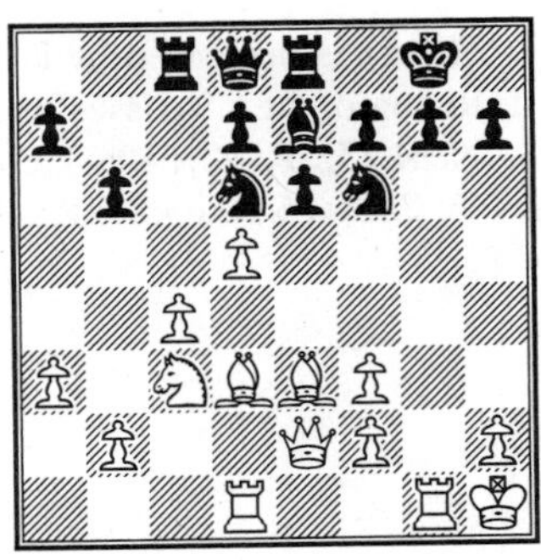

White has made his intentions clear: he will attempt to launch a mating attack with pressure along the g-file and with the bishops strafing the diagonals. **17...exd5.**

Black could not afford to sit idly and wait for the storm, for example 17...g6; 18.dxe6! dxe6; 19.Nb5! a6; 20.Nxd6 Bxd6; 21.Bg5 **18.cxd5.** 18.Nxd5 Nxd5; 19.cxd5 is possible, but after 19...Bf6 it is difficult to evaluate the position, according to Polugayevsky.

18...g6; 19.f4 Bf8; 20.f5?! The advance of the f-pawn is intended to rip open the kingside. But each advance has created a new weakness in the White camp. 20.Qf3 would have brought the queen to a powerful post, and after 20...Bg7; 21.Bc1 Polugayevsky considers the White position slightly better, but we feel that (21.Bd4!? is also possible, though after 21...Nh5!?; 22.Bxg7 Nxg7. Black can aim for Qd8-f6, exploiting the presence of the unprotected Qf3, e.g. 23.f5 Qf6) 21...Nh5; 22.f5.

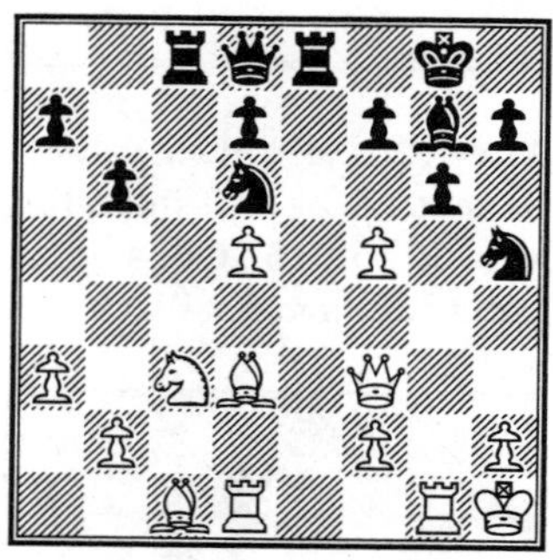

22...Qf6!; 23.Bg5 Qe5 is fine for Black. **20...Bg7; 21.Qf3 Nc4; 22.fxg6 fxg6.**

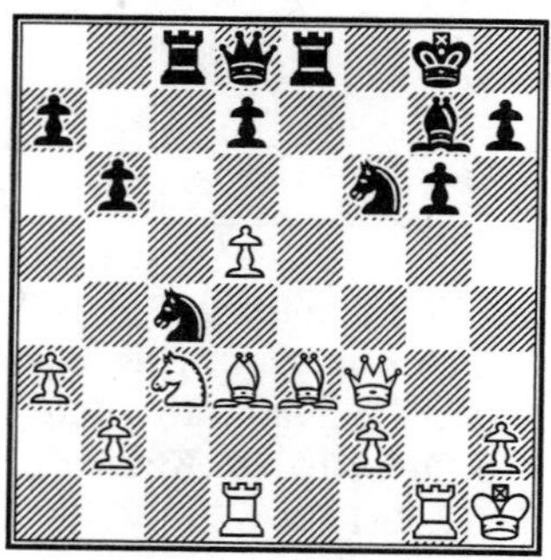

23.Bxg6? 23.Bxc4 Rxc4; 24.Bd4 is preferred by Polugayevsky in his comments in *Schach-Echo*, although in Informator he discusses only 23.Bd4 which leads to an advantage for Black after 23...Ne5! **23...Rxe3?!** Black could have secured his advantage with 23...hxg6; 24.Bd4 Ne5; 25.Bxe5 Rxe5; 26.Rxg6 Nh5 for example 27.Rdg1 Qf8; 28.Qg4.

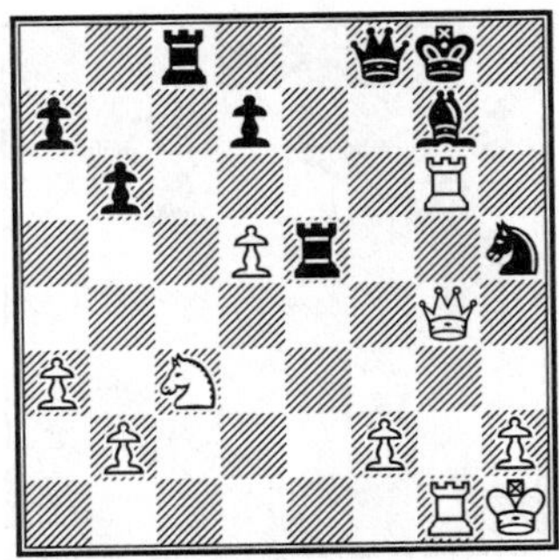

28...Rxc3!; 29.bxc3 Rxd5. **24.Bxh7+ Nxh7; 25.fxe3 Qf6; 26.Qh5.** 26.Qg3 is met by 26...Qe5! which leads to unclear complications after 27.Qxe5 Nxe5; 28.Ne4 Rf8. **26...Nxe3; 27.Rd3.**

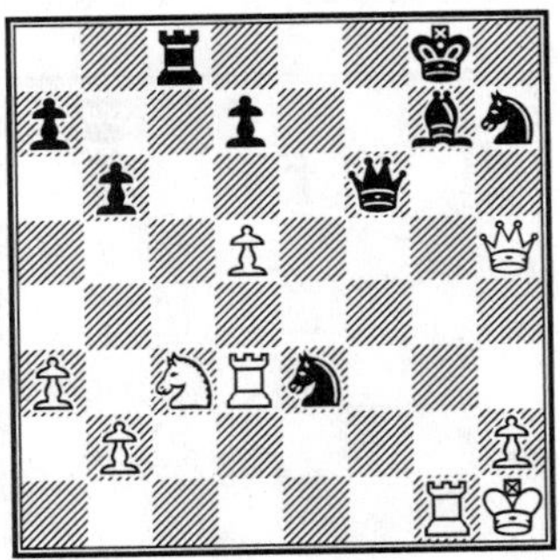

27...Qf5! Here Black holds a decisive advantage, according to Polugayevsky. **28.Qxf5.** White has little choice, since 28.Qe2 fails to 28...Rxc3. **28...Nxf5; 29.Rf3 Nd6?!** Black is letting his advantage slip. With 29...Rf8; 30.Rgf1 Nd6 he would have retained his commanding lead. **30.Rfg3 Ne8; 31.Ne4.**

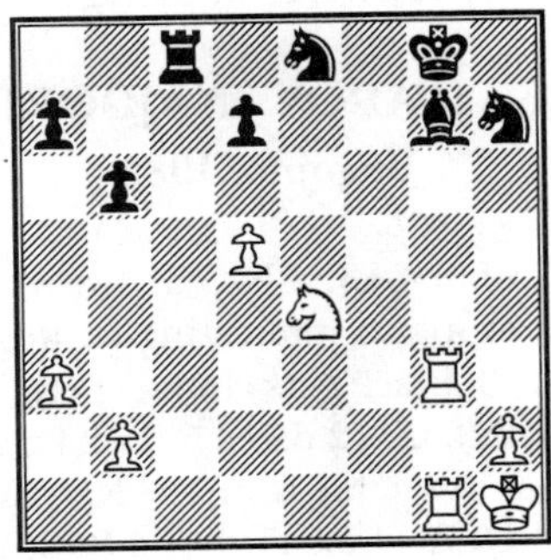

31.Nb5 Nhf6; 32.Nxa7 Rc5! would have led to an unclear position with chances for both sides. **31...Kf8; 32.Rf3+?** This hands the game back to Black. After 32.Rf1+ Nhf6; 33.Rg6 Rc2! (33...Kf7?.

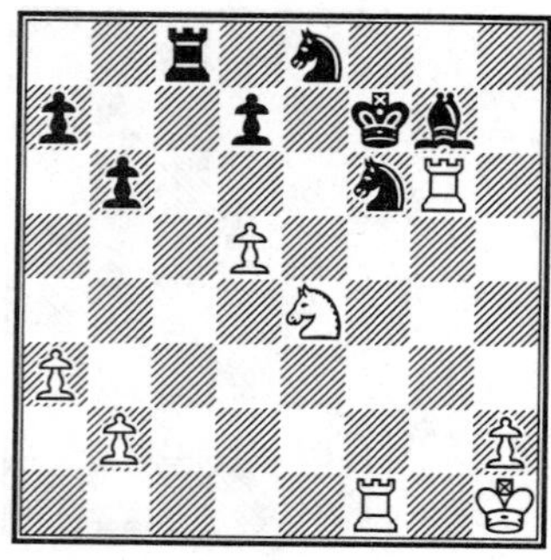

34.Rgxf6+ Bxf6; 35.Rxf6+!) 34.Nxf6 Nxf6; 35.Rgxf6+ Bxf6; 36.Rxf6+ Ke7. Black would still have some advantage, but there would also have been the chance to go wrong. **32...Nhf6; 33.Ng5** or 33.Rg6 Rc1+. **33...Rc5; 34.d6 Re5; 35.h4 Kg8; 36.Nh3 Rh5! 37.Rf4 Rd5; 38.Ng5 Rxd6; 39.Rf5 Rd4; 40.Nf3 Rd5.**

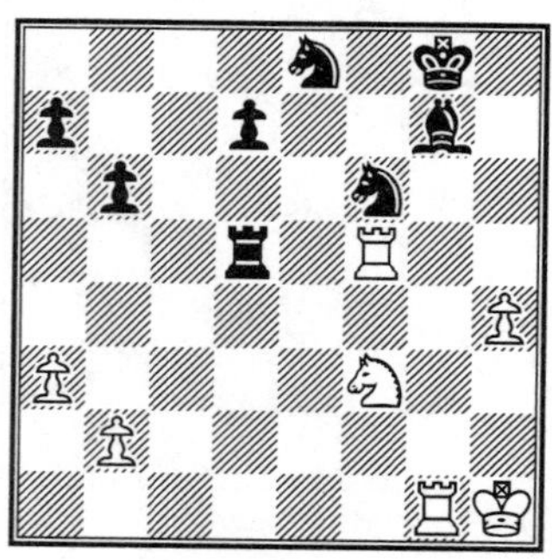

41.Rxd5. On 41.Rf4 Black would simply play 41...Rd3. **41...Nxd5; 42.h5.** 42.Rd1 would have been met by 42...Nec7. **42...Kf8; 43.Rg5 Ndf6; 44.Nh4.** Or 44.b4 Nd6. **44...Ne4!; 45.Rg6.** Black also wins on 45.Rg2 N8f6; 46.Nf5 Nxh5. **45...Bxb2!; 46.h6 N4f6!; 47.a4 Kf7; 48.Rg2 Bc1; 49.Nf5 Ke6; 50.Ng7+ Nxg7; 51.Rxg7 Bxh6. Black won.**

(207) KASPAROV - NAJDORF [E12]

Bugojno, 1982

1.d4 Nf6; 2.c4 e6; 3.Nf3 b6; 4.a3. 4.Nc3 allows 4...Bb4, but it is also seen frequently because White can adopt an interesting strategy with 5.Bg5 Bb7; 6.e3 h6; 7.Bh4, but after capturing at c3, Black gets counterplay. 7...Bxc3+ (7...g5; 8.Bg3 Ne4; 9.Qc2 Bxc3+; 10.bxc3 d6; 11.Bd3 f5; 12.d5 Nc5; 13.h4 g4; 14.Nd4 Qf6; 15.0–0 Nxd3; 16.Qxd3 and White was better in a game from the Kasparov-Timman match in 1985.) 8.bxc3 d6; 9.Nd2 g5; 10.Bg3 Qe7; 11.a4 a5; 12.h4 Rg8; 13.hxg5 hxg5 and Black had a fine game in game 18 of the 1986 Kasparov-Karpov World Championship match.

4...Bb7. 4...c5 is less effective. A good example is Kasparov's defeats of Van der Wiel and Fedorowicz at the 1981 World Youth Team Championship. 5.d5 Ba6; 6.Qc2 Qe7 (6...exd5; 7.cxd5 g6; 8.Nc3 Bg7; 9.g3 0–0; 10.Bg2 d6; 11.0–0 Re8; 12.Re1 Qc7; 13.Bf4 Nh5; 14.Bd2 Nd7; 15.Qa4 Bb7; 16.Qh4 a6; 17.Rac1 b5; 18.b4 Qd8; 19.Bg5 f6; 20.Bd2 f5; 21.Bg5 Qb6; 22.e4 cxb4; 23.axb4 Rac8; 24.Be3 Qd8; 25.Bg5 Qb6.

As team captain, I was very worried here, seeing the Black pieces drift away from the kingside. I had no idea how Kasparov would do it, but I expected a breakthrough soon. 26.exf5 Rxe1+; 27.Rxe1 Bxc3; 28.Re7 Rc4; 29.Qh3 Bc8; 30.fxg6 Ndf6; 31.Bxf6 Nxf6; 32.gxh7+ Kf8; 33.h8Q+ Kxe7; 34.Qg7+ and Fedorowicz resigned. The American team did manage to draw the match, thanks to a fine effort by Joel Benjamin.) 7.Bg5 exd5; 8.Nc3 Bxc4; 9.e4 h6; 10.Bxf6 Qxf6; 11.exd5 Bxf1; 12.Kxf1 d6; 13.Re1+ Be7; 14.Ne4 Qg6; 15.Qa4+ Kf8; 16.h4 and Van der Wiel eventually lost. The kingside pressure was just too much.

5.Nc3. This is the Kasparov-Petrosian variation, though now it is usually just called the Kasparov Variation, since he not only rehabilitated the line, but also set a good example by racking up many points as White.

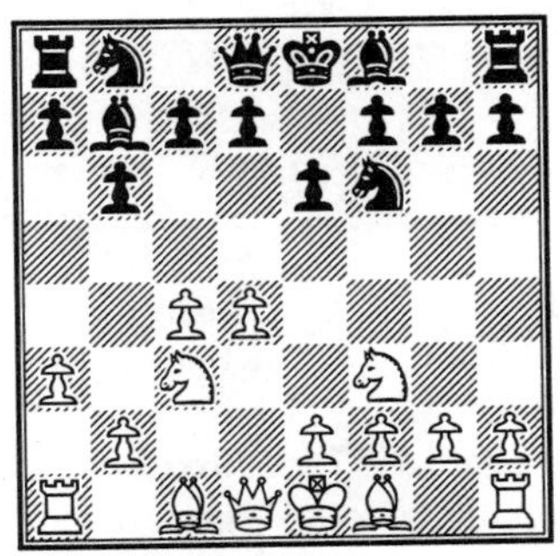

5...d5. His opponent, the great Miguel Najdorf (developer of the Najdorf Variation of the Sicilian) was not well prepared for this event. He was supposed to be the arbiter, but when one of the players couldn't make it the veteran gamely stepped in. Still, he plays well in the opening, following the main lines and improving on Petrosian's play.

5...Ne4 led to one of the most famous games in the variation, played by Kasparov against Ulf Andersson at the Tilburg Interpolis tournament of 1981. 6.Nxe4 Bxe4; 7.Nd2 Bg6; 8.g3 Nc6; 9.e3 a6; 10.b4 b5; 11.cxb5 axb5; 12.Bb2 Na7; 13.h4 h6; 14.d5 exd5; 15.Bg2 c6; 16.0–0 f6; 17.Re1 Be7; 18.Qg4 Kf7; 19.h5 Bh7; 20.e4! dxe4; 21.Bxe4 Bxe4; 22.Nxe4 Nc8; 23.Rad1 Ra7; 24.Nxf6 gxf6; 25.Qg6+ Kf8; 26.Bc1 d5; 27.Rd4 Nd6; 28.Rg4 Nf7; 29.Bxh6+ Ke8; 30.Bg7. Andersson resigned.

6.cxd5 Nxd5. Black usually captures with the knight, at after 6...exd5; 7.g3. White gets a superior position. **7.e3.** Kasparov has also been effective with 7.Qc2, especially against Karpov. 7.Qc2 Nd7; 8.Nxd5 exd5 allows White to play 9.Bg5! f6; 10.Bf4 c5; 11.g3 g6; 12.h4 with a better position in game 41 of the 1984- 85 World Championship. **7...Be7.** 7...g6 8.Bb5+ c6 creates holes in Black's pawn structure. 9.Bd3 Bg7 (9...Nxc3; 10.bxc3 Bg7 is an alternative, and how 11.h4 is the logical move, attacking on the kingside.)

10.Na4 has become popular, intending to advance the e-pawn to e4 without allowing Black a capture at c3 in reply. (10.h4 0–0; 11.h5 c5; 12.Ne4 cxd4; 13.exd4 Nc6; 14.hxg6 hxg6; 15.Nfg5 is too optimistic, for example 15...f5; 16.Qf3 fxe4; 17.Qxe4 Qf6; 18.Qh4 Rfd8; 19.Qh7+ Kf8; 20.Ne4 Qxd4 and Black was able to defend and win in Meyer-Lautier, Voba 1987.) 10...Nd7; 11.e4 Ne7; 12.0–0 (12.Bf4 c5; 13.dxc5 Nxc5; 14.Nxc5 bxc5; 15.0–0 0–0; 16.Rc1 c4; 17.Bxc4 Bxe4; 18.Qe2 Bxf3; 19.Qxf3 Bxb2 and White did not justify the investment of a pawn in Sadler-Psakhis, Yerevan Olympiad 1996.) 12...0–0; 13.Bg5 e5 (13...h6; 14.Be3 Kh7; 15.Rc1 f5; 16.exf5 exf5; 17.Bf4 Nd5; 18.Bd6 Re8; 19.Nc3 Qf6 gave Black counterplay in Khalifman-Short, Tallinn (Keres Memorial) 1996.) 14.dxe5 Nxe5; 15.Nxe5 Bxe5; 16.Nc3 and White had the better placed pieces in Lobron-De Boer, Amsterdam (Donner Memorial Open) 1995.

8.Bb5+ c6; 9.Bd3.

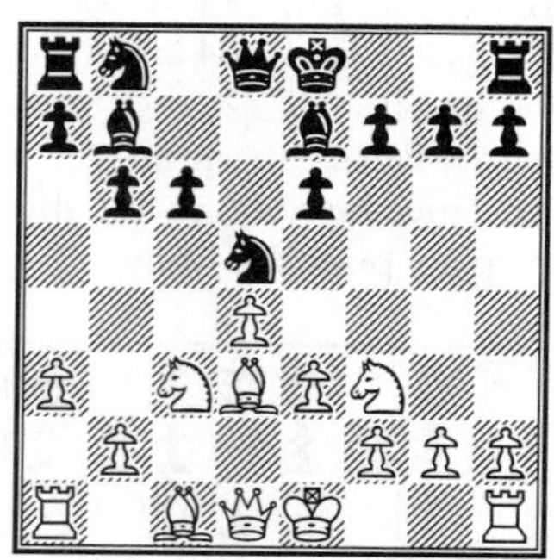

Now Black must decide whether to capture on c3, giving White's pawn at d4 more support, or keep the knight at d5, where it can be attacked by an enemy e-pawn. **9...Nxc3.** 9...0–0; 10.e4 Nxc3; 11.bxc3 was better for White in Kasparov-Marjanovic, Banja Luka Yugoslavia 1979. **10.bxc3 c5; 11.0–0 Nc6.** This is an attempt to improve on the simple castling, where White can get an advantage via rapid development. 11...0–0; 12.Qc2 g6; 13.e4 Nc6; 14.Bh6 and White had the advantage in Kasparov-Petrosian, Moscow 1981. Kasparov later blundered away the game in time pressure. **12.e4 0–0; 13.Be3 cxd4; 14.cxd4.**

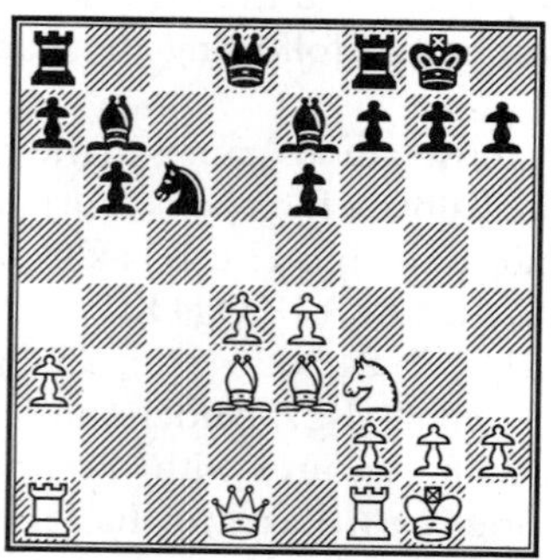

White has a good central position, but Black has no weaknesses. **14...Rc8; 15.Qe2 Na5; 16.Rfe1!** Kasparov realizes that the e-pawn will eventually need protection. 16.Rfd1 Rc7; 17.Bf4 Bd6; 18.Bg5 Be7; 19.Bf4 Bd6; 20.Be3 was drawn in Hernandez-Servat, Havana (Capablanca Memorial) 1995. **16...Qd6.** 16...Kh8; 17.h4 Bxh4; 18.Rad1 Be7; 19.d5 Bc5; 20.Bf4 led to a messy game in Kasparov-Groszpeter, also from the 1981 World Youth Team championship. **17.d5! exd5; 18.e5 Qe6; 19.Nd4! Qxe5; 20.Nf5.** White has plenty of compensation for the pawn, with active pieces and attacking changes on the kingside. Black's queenside forces are out of play.

20...Bf6; 21.Qg4 Rce8? I recall that as I watched this game from the audience (which was large, even in the bucolic little Yugoslav town) that this move made little sense to me. I had been concentrating on a different idea. 21...Qc3 was a good move, I thought. Another spectator pointed out to me that this could invite 22.Ne7+! Bxe7; 23.Bd4 but it wasn't hard to see 23...Qxd4; 24.Qxd4 Bf6; 25.Qg4 Bxa1; 26.Rxa1 with a small advantage for White. **22.Bd2.** Now the queen sacrifice fails for tactical reasons. **22...Qxa1; 23.Rxa1 Bxa1; 24.Nxg7 Bxg7; 25.Bh6.** Najdorf resigned. **White won.**

NIMZOWITSCH VARIATION

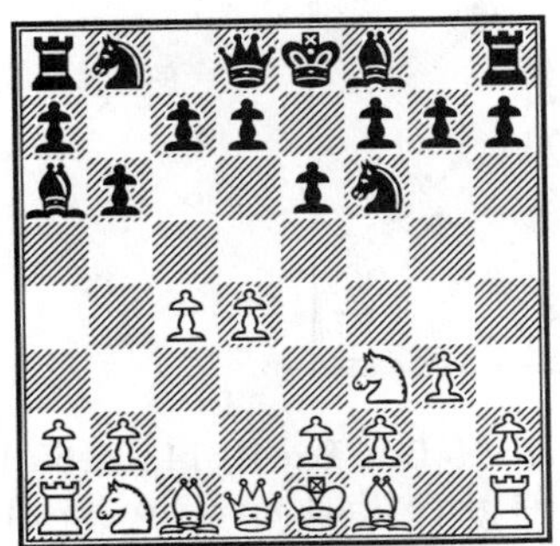

1.d4	**Nf6**
2.c4	**e6**
3.Nf3	**b6**
4.g3	**Ba6**

The development of the bishop at a6 was developed by Aron Nimzowitsch, the great opening theoretician of the period between the two world wars. The attack on the pawn at c4 is actually quite real, and White must defend the weak pawn. The bishop can later retreat to b7 if necessary, but can also stay at a6 and support actions such as ...b5. The plan still offers an acceptable alternative to the more normal positions with ...Bb7 played right away.

(208) SULTAN KHAN - NIMZOWITSCH [E15]

Liege, 1920

1.d4 Nf6; 2.c4 e6; 3.Nf3 b6; 4.g3 Ba6; 5.b3.

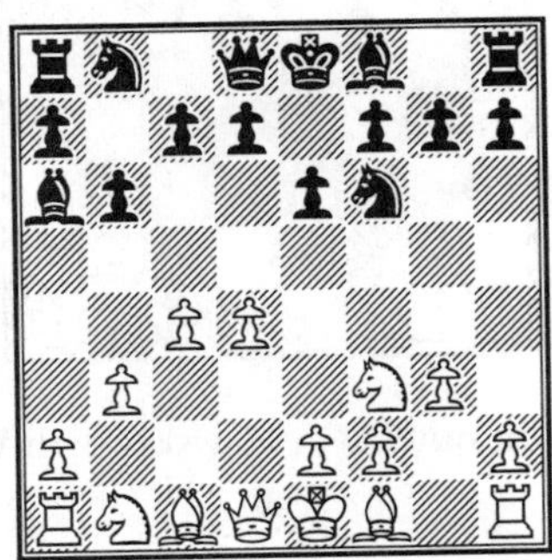

This has become one of the main lines of the Queen's Indian Defense. White defends his pawn and enables the development of his dark-squared bishop. **5...Bb4+.** White has protected his c-pawn in the most natural way, but in doing so, he has weakened his dark squares. Black therefore proposes to trade dark-squared bishops. Another more ambitious line is 5...b5. This variation has been researched by Henryk Dobosz and deserves to bear his name. Most of the analysis of the examples below is derived from his article in *Theory and Analysis*, 24 September 1984. 5...b5!?

A) 6.cxb5 Bxb5; 7.Bg2 c5!; 8.dxc5 Bxc5; 9.Nd4 Bxd4; 10.Qxd4 Bc6; 11.e4 0-0; 12.Ba3 e5!; 13.Qd3 Re8; 14.Bd6.

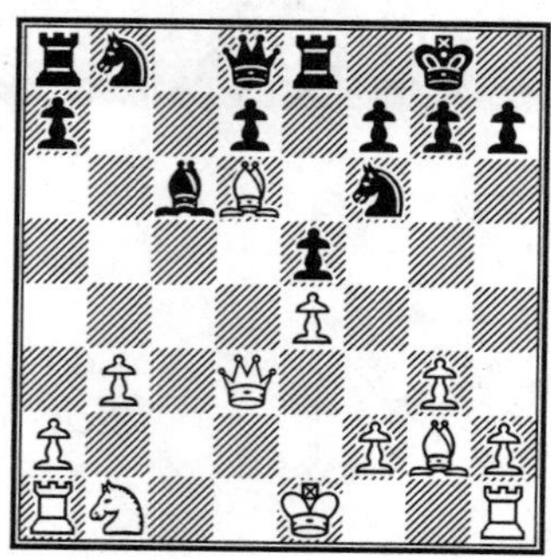

This is the critical position. (14.Nc3 Qa5; 15.Bd6 Bxe4!) 14...Re6!; 15.0-0 Ne8; 16.Bc5 (16.Ba3 Qa5; 17.Rd1 Na6; 18.Bb2 Nb4 gives Black an active position.) 16...d6 This is a significant improvement on Dobosz's (16...Qa5; 17.Qc3 Qxc3; 18.Nxc3 Na6; 19.Ba3 with the bishop pair constituting a significant advantage for White. The resulting position requires practical tests.) 17.Rd1 can be met by 17...Nd7, e.g. 18.Ba3 or (18.Be3 Nef6; 19.Nc3 Ng4; 20.Bc1 Qf6; 21.Qe2 Qg6 is less clear.) 18...Nb6 and Black is ready to play ...a5.

B) 6.Bg2 bxc4; 7.Ne5 Bb4+; 8.Kf1 d5!; 9.bxc4 0-0; 10.cxd5 (10.c5 Nfd7!; 10.Qa4 c5; 11.a3 Ba5; 12.dxc5 Nfd7!; 13.Nxd7 Nxd7 with a good game for Black in either case.) 10...Nxd5; 11.Qb3? c5!; 12.a3 Ba5; 13.dxc5 Bc7; 14.Nd3 Nc6; 15.Bb2 Rb8; 16.Qc2 Bxd3; 17.exd3.

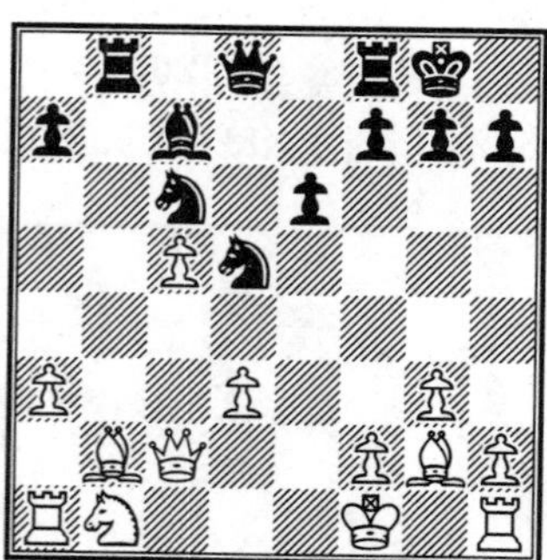

17...Rxb2! and Black won quickly in Hawsksworth-Wells, Oakham 1984. **6.Bd2 Bxd2+.**

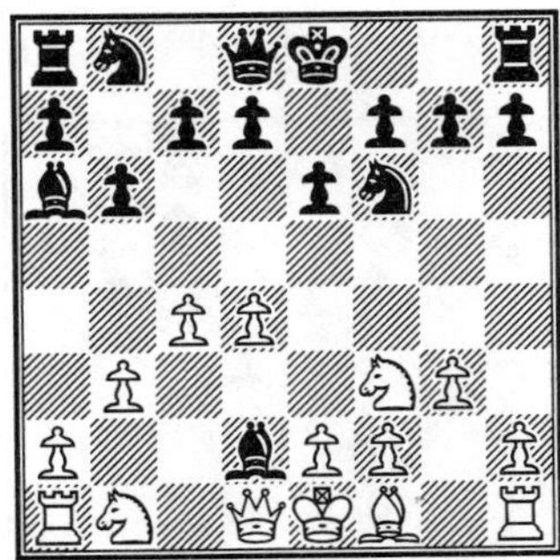

7.Nbxd2. White would have been better recapturing with the queen and developing the knight at c3. **7...Bb7; 8.Bg2 c5.** Black starts the first part of his plan he places his pawns on dark squares. **9.dxc5.** If 9.0–0 cxd4; 10.Nxd4 Bxg2; 11.Kxg2, Black has no problems. **9...bxc5; 10.0–0 0–0; 11.Re1 Qe7.** Black wants to answer 12.e4 with 12...e5, working on the dark squares. **12.Rc1 e5; 13.e4 Nc6; 14.Nb1.**

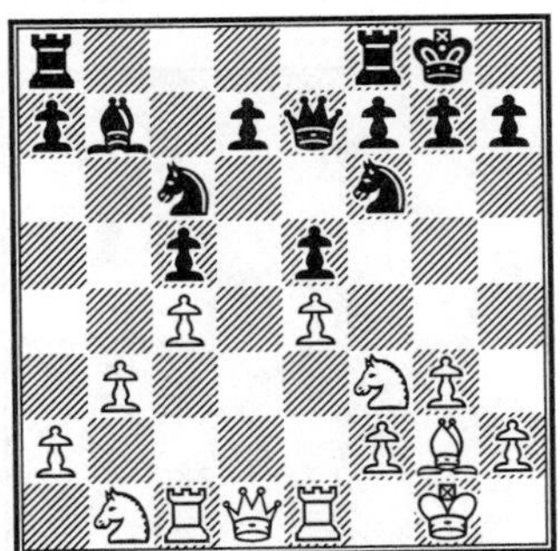

Black will play Nc6-d4, and White will counter with Nb1–c3-d5. The difference is that Black can exchange his bishop for White's knight while White can only take on d4 with a knight. This will lead to an ending where Black's knight is much stronger than White's bishop, which is blocked by its own pawns. **14...d6; 15.Nc3 a5; 16.Nd2 Nd4; 17.Nf1 Bc6; 18.Ne3 Qb7; 19.Qd3 a4; 20.bxa4 Bxa4; 21.Rb1 Qa7; 22.Rb2 Bc6; 23.Reb1 Qc7.**

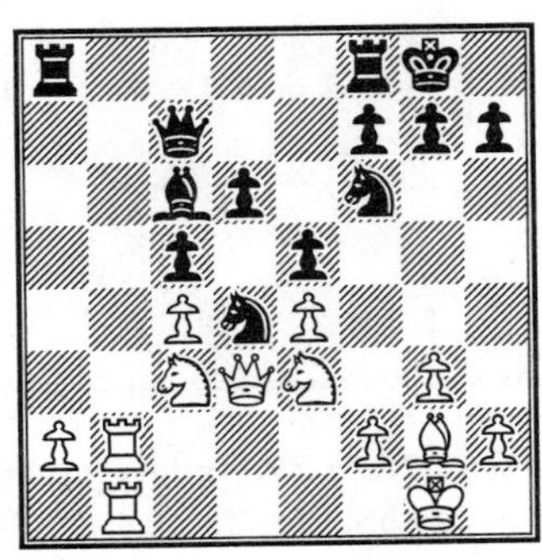

If Black can play 24...Ra3, White will be all tied up. **24.Nb5 Qd7; 25.Nd1 Ne8; 26.Ndc3 g6; 27.Nxd4 cxd4; 28.Nd5 Qa7; 29.g4.**

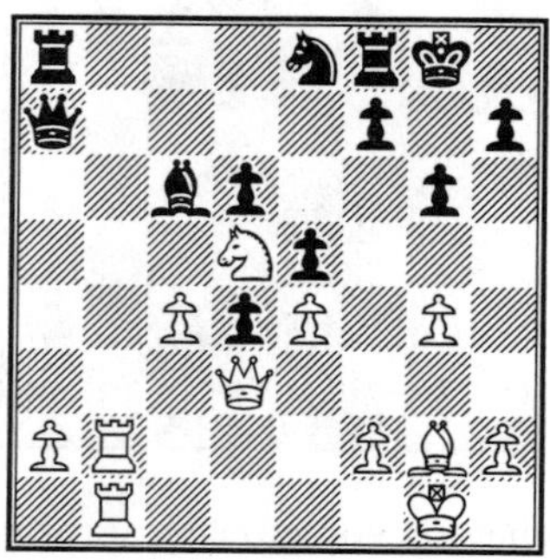

White wants to prevent f7-f5, but in this case the cure is worse than the disease, as this further weakens his dark squares. **29...Bxd5; 30.exd5 Nf6; 31.h3 Kg7; 32.Rb6 Rfd8; 33.R1b2 h6.** 33...Nd7?; 34.Rxd6 Nc5; 35.Qe2 Rxd6; 36.Qxe5+ Rf6; 37.g5. **34.f4 Nd7!; 35.R6b5.** Now if 35.Rxd6 Nc5; 36.Qe2.

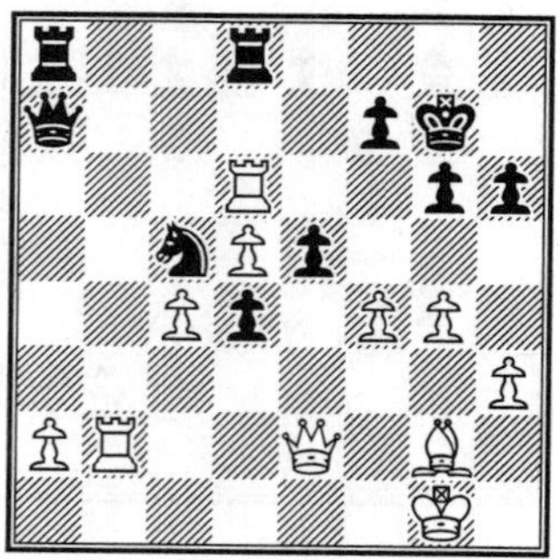

36...e4! (36...Rxd6?; 37.Qxe5+ Rf6; 38.g5) 37.Rxd8 Rxd8 as 38.Bxe4 would lose to 38...Re8. **35...exf4.**

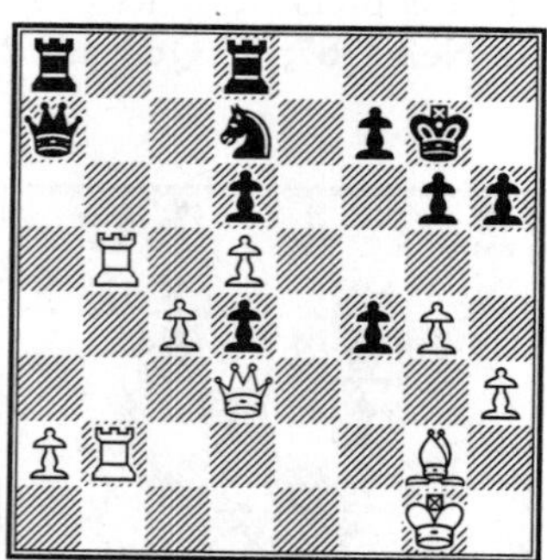

35...Nc5 was better. **36.Rd2 Ne5; 37.Qxd4 Qxd4+; 38.Rxd4 f3.** Again Black fails to play accurately. Better was 38...Rxa2; 39.Rxf4 Rc2 threatening both to take the c-pawn and to play Rd8-a8-a2. **39.Bf1 Ra4.** Not giving White any chances after

39...Rxa2; 40.c5! **40.Rd2 Nd7; 41.Kf2 Ra3; 42.Rb3.**

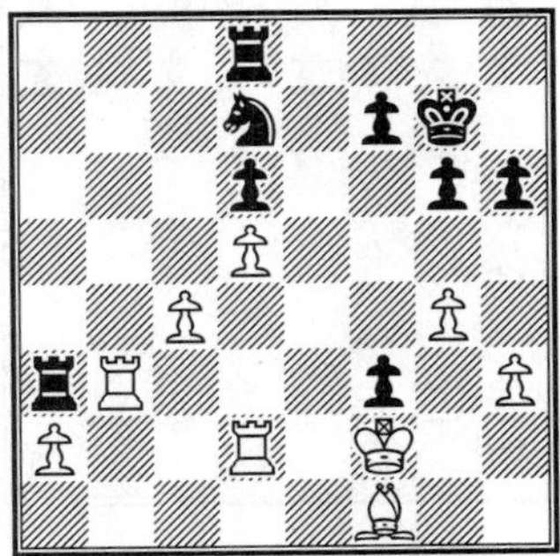

42...Rda8; 43.Rxf3 Nc5. White has won a pawn, but is still losing because of Black's bind on the position. **44.Rxa3 Rxa3; 45.Kg2 f5; 46.gxf5 gxf5; 47.Kg1 Kf6; 48.Rb2 f4; 49.Re2 Kf5; 50.Re8 f3; 51.Rh8 Kg5; 52.Rd8 Rxa2; 53.Rxd6 Ne4; 54.h4+ Kf4; 55.Rd8 Ra1; 56.Rb8 Ng3; 57.Kh2 Nxf1+; 58.Kh3 Ne3; 59.Rf8+ Nf5; 60.Rxf5+ Kxf5. Black won.**

(209) BENKO - KERES [E15]

First Piatigorsky Cup, 1963

1.c4 Nf6; 2.Nf3 e6; 3.d4 b6; 4.g3 Ba6; 5.Qa4.

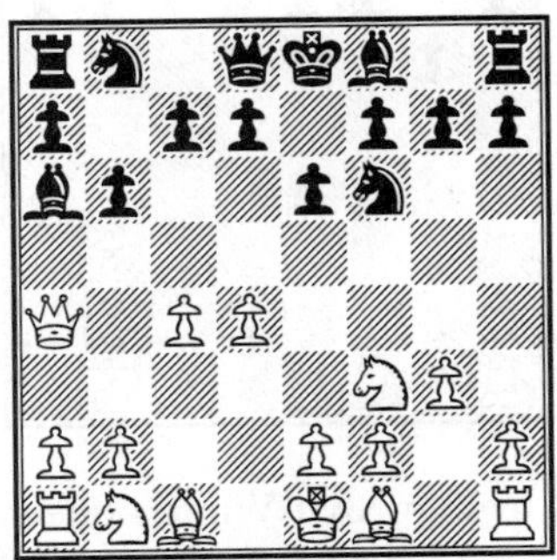

The Nimzowitsch Variation of the Nimzo-Indian is often met by this move. White defends his pawn with his most powerful piece, and yet this is considered the main line and White's most promising option. A less ambitious queen sortie is 5.Qb3 Nc6; 6.Nbd2, since 6...d5! gives Black good play, e.g. 7.Qa4 Bb7; 8.cxd5 (8.Ne5 allows Black to get a good game with 8...Bd6!; 9.Nxc6 Qd7!) 8...Qxd5 (8...exd5 may not be as strong with the knight on c6.) 9.Bg2 Qa5; 10.Qxa5 Nxa5; 11.0-0 Rc8; 12.a3 c5; 13.dxc5 bxc5; 14.b3 Rb8! and Black has nothing to complain about, Vainerman-Strokovsky, USSR 1987.

5...Be7. 5...Bb7; 6.Bg2.

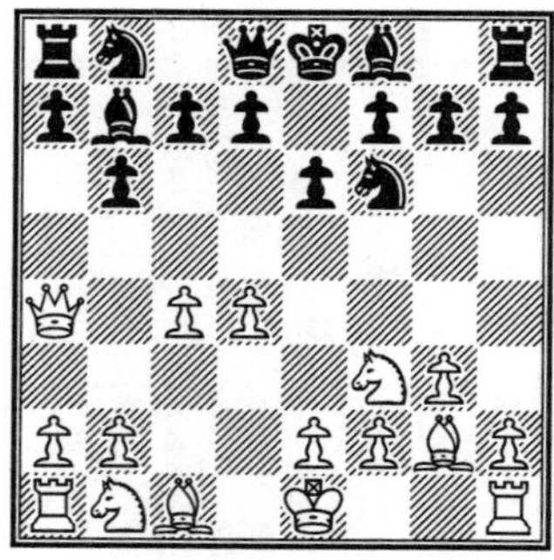

6...c5. Black takes advantage of the White queen's placement. With the queen on d1, White could now play 7.d5 ed; 8.Nh4. 7.0–0. A strong alternative is 7...cxd4; 8.Nxd4 Bxg2; 9.Kxg2 Be7; 10.Nc3 0–0; 11.Rd1 Qc7; 12.Bf4 Qb7+; 13.f3 a6; 14.e4 d6 was played in Browne-Andersson, Buenos Aires Olympiad 1978. Black sets up a hedgehog type position. White has more space, but will have trouble finding a breakthrough. **6.Nc3 Bb7; 7.Bg2 0–0; 8.0–0 Ne4; 9.Nxe4.** 9.Qc2 transposes to the main lines of the Queen's Indian, with White taking an extra move with Qd1–a4-c2 and Black with Bc8-a6-b7. **9...Bxe4; 10.Rd1 Qc8; 11.Ne1 Bxg2; 12.Nxg2.**

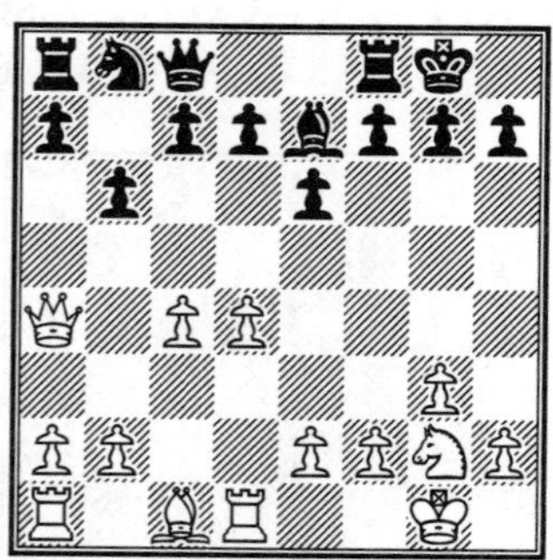

12...c5. Black attempts to show that White's queen is misplaced by striking in the center. For an early ...c5 see Browne-Andersson. **13.d5 exd5; 14.Rxd5.** White looks for pressure along the half open d-file. A good alternative is 14.cd with an eventual e2-e4. **14...Nc6; 15.Bd2 Bf6; 16.Bc3?** White understandably wants to get rid of Black's strong bishop, but the resulting isolated doubled pawns give Black an edge. **16...Bxc3; 17.bxc3 Re8; 18.Ne3?** 18.Nf4 was better.

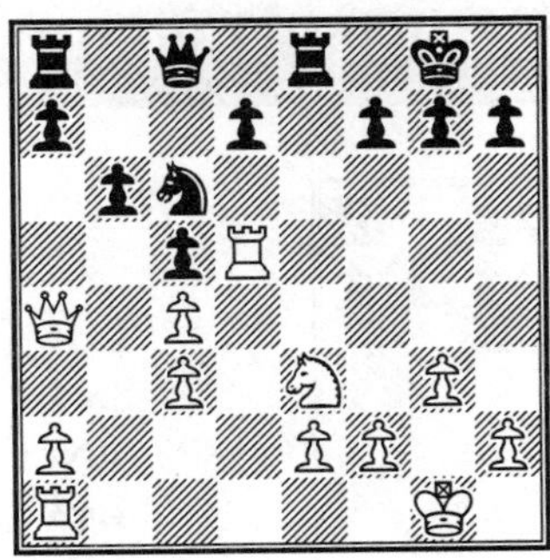

18...Rxe3! An excellent positional exchange sacrifice. Black has more than enough compensation due to White's horrible pawn structure and the e5-square that he gets for his knight. **19.fxe3 Qe8; 20.Qc2 Qxe3+; 21.Kh1 Ne5.** Black's position practically plays itself. **22.Rf1 Re8; 23.Rf4 f6; 24.Qe4 Ng6; 25.Qxe3 Rxe3.**

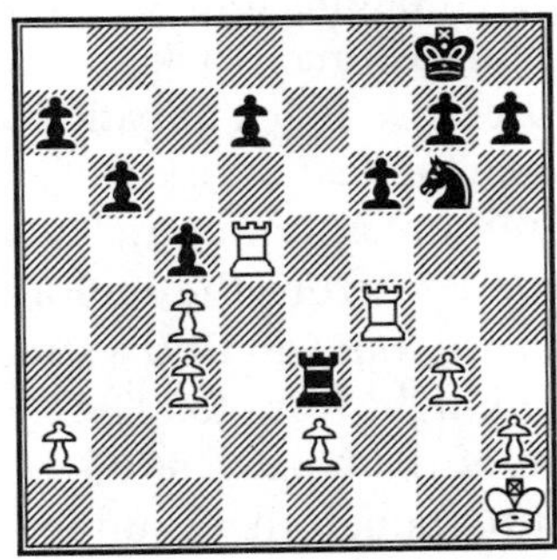

26.Rxd7. If 26.Rf3 Rxe2; 27.Rxd7 Ne5; 28.Rd8+ Kf7; 29.Rf1 Rxa2 and Black is winning. **26...Nxf4; 27.gxf4 Rxe2; 28.Rxa7 Rf2; 29.Rb7 Rxf4; 30.Rxb6 Rxc4; 31.Rb3.** With White's rook out of play, the rest is easy. **31...Kf7; 32.Kg2 g5; 33.Kf3 Ke6; 34.Ra3 h5; 35.Ke2.**

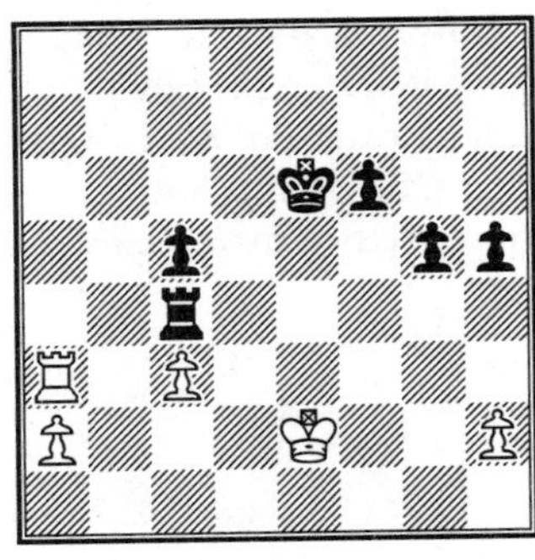

35...Rh4; 36.Ra6+ Ke5; 37.a4 c4; 38.Rc6 Rxh2+; 39.Ke3 Rh3+; 40.Kd2 Rd3+; 41.Kc2 h4; 42.Rxc4 Rd8. Black won.

SAEMISCH VARIATION

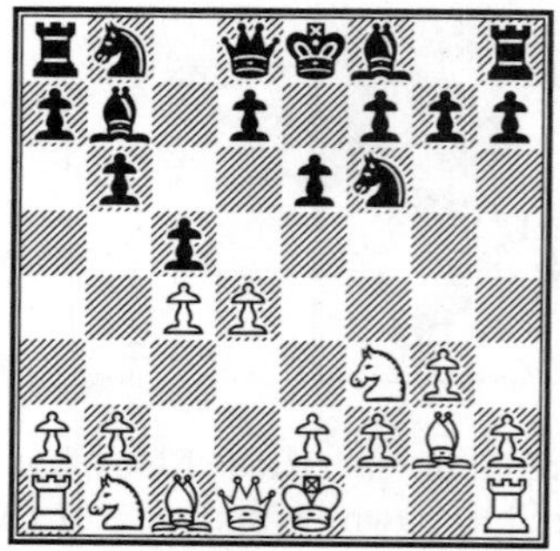

1.d4	**Nf6**
2.c4	**e6**
3.Nf3	**b6**
4.g3	**Bb7**
5.Bg2	**c5**

This old approach, played as both White and Black by Saemisch, has returned to an active role in the repertoire of top players. Instead of meekly continuing development and castling, Black immediately challenges White's central pawn formation. Because Black already controls the e4-square, this approach does not entail a great deal of risk, but it does allow for active play.

White is not without resources, however. The advance of the d-pawn to d5 threatens to cut off the Bb7 from the important e4 square. Black will then have to capture the pawn, but will find a strong pin on the long diagonal after White moves the knight from f3. The most aggressive defense involves the couner-sacrifice of the b-pawn at b5, but there is a solid alternative in a kingside fianchetto, though that is under a cloud at the moment.

(210) KARPOV-GAVRIKOV [E15]
Soviet Championship, 1988

1.Nf3 Nf6; 2.c4 b6; 3.d4 e6; 4.g3 Bb7; 5.Bg2 c5; 6.d5. This is the logical move. The alternatives, castling or capturing at c5, are not as effective. 6.dxc5 Bxc5; 7.Nc3 Ne4; 8.Nxe4 Bxe4; 9.0-0 0-0 gave Black no problems in Johner-Saemisch, Bad Pistyan 1922. No better was 6.e3 cxd4; 7.exd4 d5; 8.Ne5 Qc8; 9.Qf3 Nc6; 10.Nxc6 Qxc6, Prokes-Saemisch, Bad Pistyan 1922.

6...exd5; 7.Nh4. Now there are two main plans, as discussed above. **7...b5.**

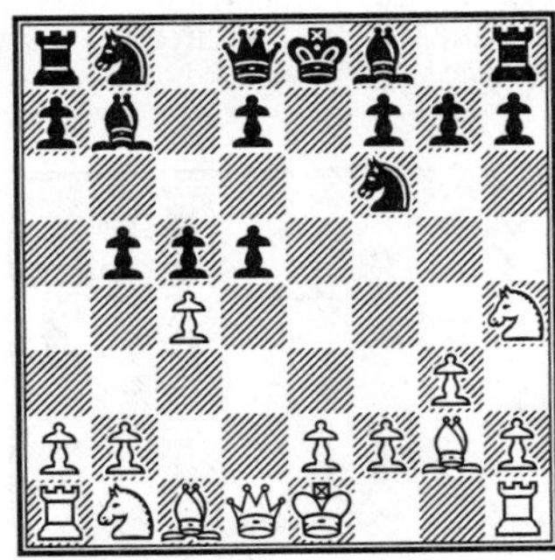

7...g6 is the main alternative. 8.Nc3 Bg7; 9.0–0 0–0; 10.cxd5 d6 transposes to Saemisch-Romanovsky, Moscow 1925, where after 11.e4 White was a little better, but not much. 10.Bg5 is considered better for White. 10...h6 was played in Capablanca-Marshall, Carlsbad 1929, but Belyavsky gives the simple (10...d6 is probably the best move. 11.Nxd5 Nc6; 12.Qd2 Rb8; 13.Rad1 Nd4!; 14.b3 b5!; 15.e3 Ne6; 16.Bxf6 Bxf6; 17.Nxf6+ Qxf6; 18.Bxb7 Rxb7; 19.cxb5 Rxb5 and White has good containment of Black's pawns, and an advantage of two pawn islands against three, Farago-Adorjan, Hungarian Championship 1995.) 11.Bxf6 Bxf6; 12.Bxd5 with an advantage for White. Possibly even stronger is (12.Nxg6! since 12...fxg6 is met by 13.Bxd5+.)

7...d6; 8.cxd5 g6; 9.Nc3 Bg7; 10.0–0 0–0; 11.e4 Nbd7; 12.f4 Re8; 13.Re1 a6; 14.a4 was a little better for White in Vajda-Monticelli, Budapest 1926.

8.0–0. White has also tried capturing at d5 with 8.cxd5 and Black usually responds by fianchettoing the other bishop. 8...g6; 9.0–0 d6 and here White has tried a variety of plans, but most logical is 10.a4 which immediately challenges the queenside pawn formation. 10...b4 Now White has the c4-square, so 11.Nd2 Bg7; 12.Nc4 where the most dynamic defense is Gavrikov's 12...Ba6!? 13.Qc2 0–0 for example 14.a5 (14.Rb1 Bxc4; 15.Qxc4 Nbd7; 16.e4 Nb6; 17.Qc2 a5; 18.b3 Rc8; 19.Bh3 Rc7; 20.f3 c4 and Black broke through in Gunawan-Gavrikov, Lugano 1988.) 14...Bxc4; 15.Qxc4 Nbd7; 16.Nf3 Re8; 17.Nd2 Qe7; 18.e4 h5; 19.h3 h4! 20.g4 Ne5 and the knight outpost brought Black the advantage in Novikov-Gavrikov, Lvov 1987.

8...bxc4; 9.Nc3 Be7; 10.Nf5. This eliminates Black's bishop pair. **10...0–0; 11.Nxe7+ Qxe7; 12.Bg5!** White gives up his own bishop pair to undermine the support of d5. **12...h6; 13.Bxf6 Qxf6.**

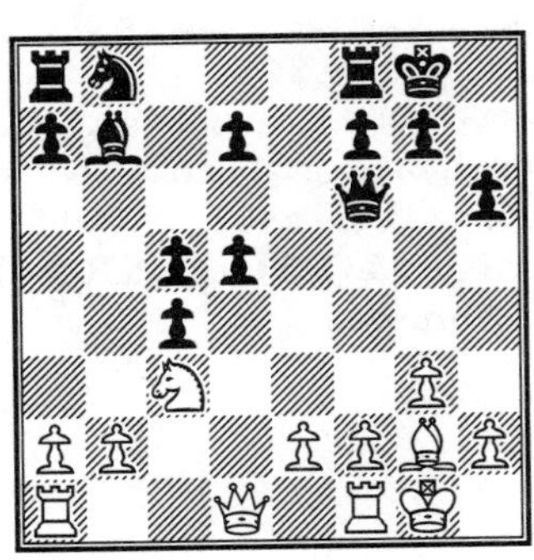

14.Nxd5. 14.Rb1 is a recent try. After 14...Nc6; 15.Nxd5 Qe5; 16.Ne3 Qe7 a tense position arises in which Black's chances are no worse, Itkis-Gevorgjan, Moscow 1995. **14...Bxd5; 15.Qxd5 Nc6.**

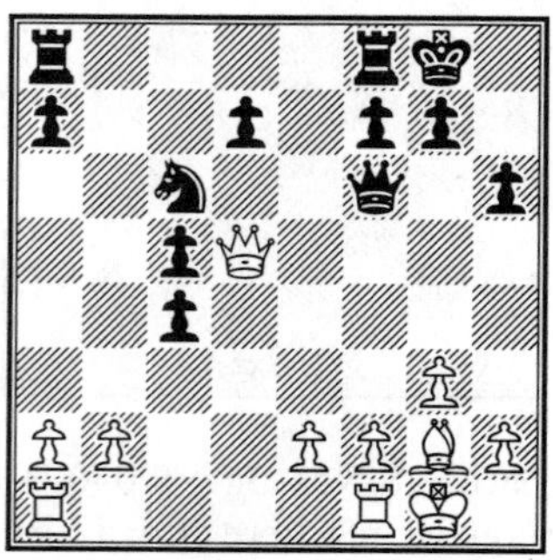

The White queen has a choice of three tasty morsels at c4, c5 and d7, but which one is best? **16.Qxc4!** 16.Qxc5 Rab8; 17.Rab1 Rxb2; 18.Rxb2 Qxb2; 19.Qxc4 was analyzed as better for White by Karpov and Zaitsev, and was confirmed in Gostisa-Yu, Yugoslavia 1987. **16...Qxb2; 17.e3 Rab8; 18.Qxc5 Rb6; 19.Rad1 Nb8; 20.Bd5** White has several advantages here. The pawn structure is superior, the bishop is better than the knight, and the pieces are better coordinated. **20...Qb5; 21.Qc7** White does not want to exchange queens, which would ease Black's defensive burden. **21...Qa6; 22.Rc1 Qa5; 23.Rfd1 Rb5; 24.Qd6 Qb6; 25.Qe7.** While Black aimlessly plays with queen and rook, White continues to improve the position of the heavy artillery. **25...Qg6; 26.Be4 Qe6.**

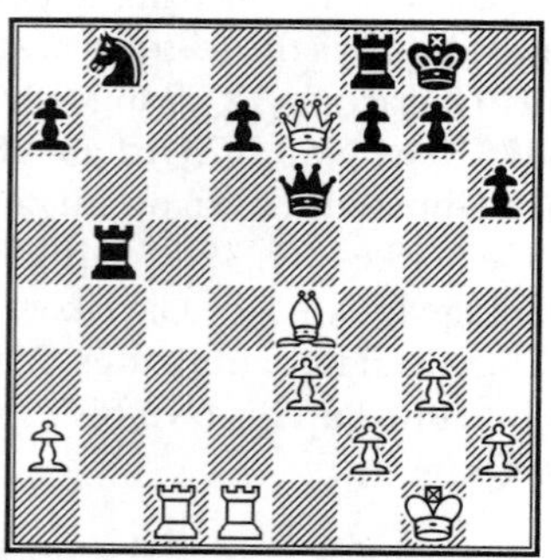

It seems as though an endgame is inevitable, but... **27.Bh7+! Kxh7; 28.Qxf8** won the exchange, and although Black grabbed a pawn with **28...Qxa2** , after **29.Qd6 a6; 30.Qd3+ f5; 31.Rb1 Qe6; 32.Rxb5 axb5; 33.Qxb5** the win was just a matter of technique. **33...Nc6; 34.Rd5 Kg6; 35.Qc5 Qe4; 36.Rd6+ Kh7; 37.Qd5 Qb1+; 38.Qd1 Qe4; 39.Qd3 Qg4; 40.Rd5. White won.**

CLASSICAL LINES

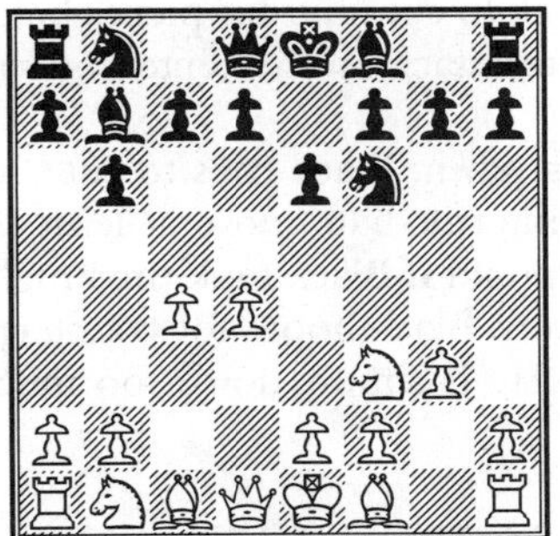

1.d4	**Nf6**
2.c4	**e6**
3.Nf3	**b6**
4.g3	**Bb7**

Despite the fact that two bishops will stare each other down on the long diagonal, the **Classical Lines** generally lead to very quiet play. Some players find it simply too boring, but others are content to try to win by a Steinitzian accumulation of small positional advantages. Black has a variety of defenses, but almost all involve straightforward development of the dark-squared bishop, kingside castling, and an eventual advance of one or more of the central pawns.

(211) EUWE - COLLE [E16]

Carlsbad, 1929

1.Nf3 Nf6; 2.d4 e6; 3.c4 b6; 4.g3 Bb7; 5.Bg2 Bb4+.

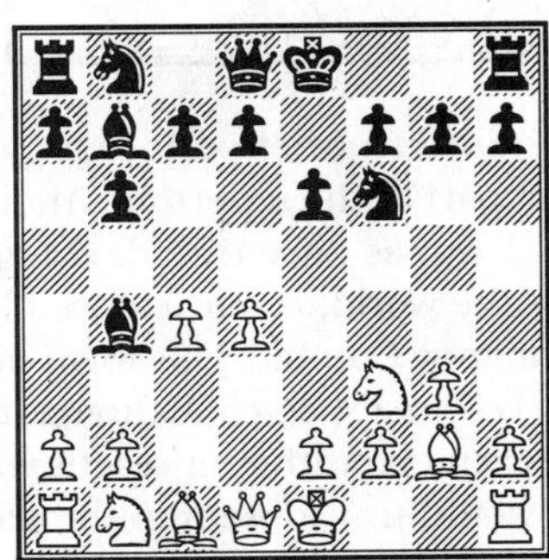

The idea behind this move is to exchange the dark-squared bishop before continuing with development, on the grounds that the White bishop would otherwise be guaranteed greater scope in the endgame. But that is not the case in most lines of the Queen's Indian, so it is a flawed logic. This is the Capablanca Variation.

6.Bd2 Bxd2+. This capture is by no means obligatory, or even recommended, these days. 6...a5; 7.0–0 0–0; 8.Bg5 Be7; 9.Qc2 h6; 10.Bxf6 Bxf6; 11.Nc3 g6 is a more solid defense, as seen in Kasparov-Karpov, World Championship (24th Match Game) 1986. 6...c5; 7.Bxb4 cxb4; 8.0–0 0–0; 9.Qb3 a5; 10.a3 Na6; 11.Nbd2 was a little better for White in Karpov-Korchnoi, Amsterdam 1987.

7.Nbxd2. Capturing with the queen is also possible, but Black can equalize, for example 7.Qxd2 0–0; 8.Nc3 d6; 9.Qc2 c5; 10.d5 exd5; 11.Ng5 Na6; 12.cxd5 Re8 with counterplay for Black in Psakhis-Larsen, Hastings 1987, 88. **7...d6; 8.0–0 0–0; 9.Re1** White prepares to take over the center by e4. **9...Nbd7; 10.Qc2.** White feels that, since e4 is inevitable he should wait for Black to committ his pieces before committing his own pawns. **10...e5.** A typical counterattack on the center, but it has a tactical flaw.

11.Nxe5. This discovered attack wins a pawn. Black tries to cut his losses, but only makes things worse. **11...Bxg2.** This intermediate move at least keeps White from taking over the a8-h1 diagonal as he would if Black took the knight. **12.Nxd7 Bh3**. This is one intermediate move too many. Black hopes for counterplay around White's king position, but after: **13.Nxf8.** He is simply down too much material. **White won.**

(212) TIMMAN - KARPOV [E17]

Tilburg, 1983

1.d4 Nf6; 2.c4 e6; 3.Nf3 b6; 4.g3 Bb7; 5.Bg2 Be7; 6.0–0 0–0; 7.d5 exd5.

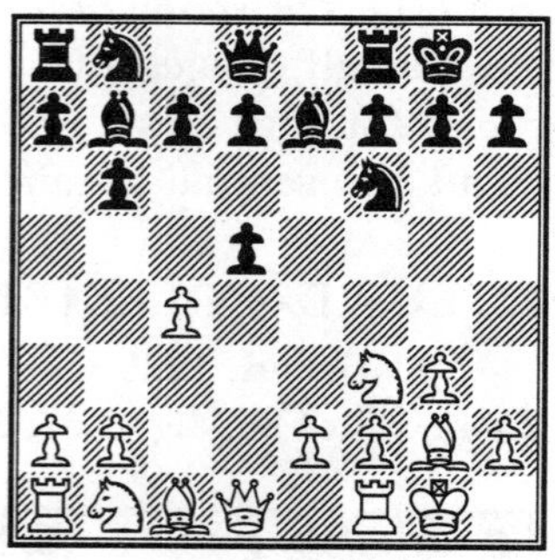

The gambit variations enjoyed a brief period of glory in the early 1980's, and have since been an important part of the repertoire, though they pose less danger to the player of the Black side than was once feared. Polugayevsky Gambit, where the knight heads for the edge of the world, is our featured line..

8.Nh4. 8.Nd4 is the Taimanov Gambit. This form of attack provides Black with a greater range of defensive resources. 8...c6 Although 8...Bc6 is a playable alternative, it makes little sense to learn two different reactions to the gambit plan. 9.cxd5 Nxd5; 10.e4 10. or 11. Nf5 would transpose into the game continuation. 10...Nc7; 11.Nc3 d6!; 12.Nf5 By delaying this move White has avoided some of the variations presented in the game. 12...Nd7; 13.Re1 (13.Qc2; 13.Qe2 comes strongly into consideration, after which White can place the rook on the d-file.) 13...Ne8 Bronstein-Balashov, USSR Cup 1980, with approximate equality. **8...c6; 9.cxd5 Nxd5; 10.Nf5.**

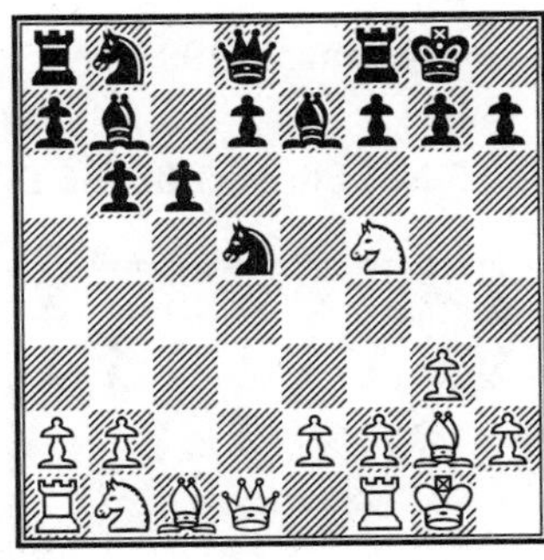

This gambit was popularized by Polugayevsky in 1980. It remains an interesting line for White, but Black has adequate defensive resources. **10...Nc7!** This is the best option at present. **11.Nc3.** The premature advance of the e-pawn will only get White into trouble as was demonstrated in Azmaiparashvili-Chernin, USSR 1980. 11.e4 Ne6; 12.Nc3 Na6; 13.e5 (13.Qg4 is a proposed improvement by Lepeshkin. Both 13...d6 and 13...Nac5 seem to be good replies.) 13...f6!

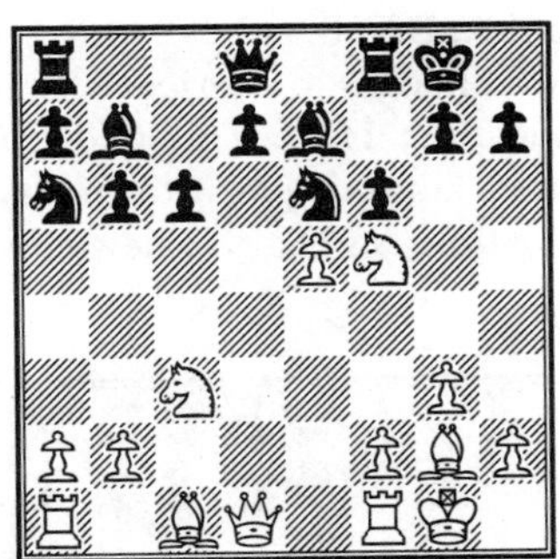

14.exf6 Bxf6; 15.Nd6 Nac5; 16.Qg4 Ba6; 17.Rd1 Bxc3; 18.bxc3 Qf6. **11...Ne8.** 11...d5; 12.e4 Bf6 with several options for White, including

A) 13.exd5 cxd5; 14.Bf4 (14.Qg4 Nc6; 15.Rd1 Ne5; 16.Qe2 Qd7; 17.Qc2 Rac8; 18.Nd4 Ne6; 19.Nxe6 fxe6; 20.Qe2 Kh8 gave Black a decisive advantage in Attqard-Guimares, Mediterranean Zonal 1981.) 14...Nba6; 15.Re1 Nc5!? was developed by Kasparov and tested in Douwen-Smith, Groningen 1980- 81, which continues below under A2. 16.Qg4 g6; 17.Nh6+ was played in Douwen-Pigusov, Groningen 1980- 81 17...Kg7 (17...Kh8 was best, although the game continuation was also acceptable for Black.) 18.Nf5+ Kg8; 19.Nh6+ Kg7; 20.Rad1 N5e6;

B) 13.Bf4; 13...Bc8!; 14.g4 Nba6; 15.Rc1 was seen in Kasparov-Karpov (second match game) 1984, which continued 15...Bd7 (15...Bxf5 gave Black a level game after 16.gxf5 Bg5; 17.Bxc7 Qxc7; 18.f4 Be7 Sosonko-Tukmakov, Tilburg 1984.) 16.Qd2 Nc5 and here 17.Bxc7 Qxc7; 18.exd5 Bxf5; 19.gxf5 Rad8; 20.b4 Nb7; 21.Ne4 would have given White a very good game.

12.Bf4 Na6; 13.Qd2 d5; 14.e4 Nac7; 15.Rad1 Bf6; 16.exd5 Nxd5; 17.Nxd5 cxd5; 18.Ne3 Nc7; 19.Bxc7 Qxc7 and with the d-pawn falling, the players agreed to a draw.

(213) KARPOV - SALOV [E18]

Linares, 1993

1.d4 Nf6; 2.c4 e6; 3.Nf3 b6; 4.g3 Bb7; 5.Bg2 Be7; 6.Nc3 Ne4.

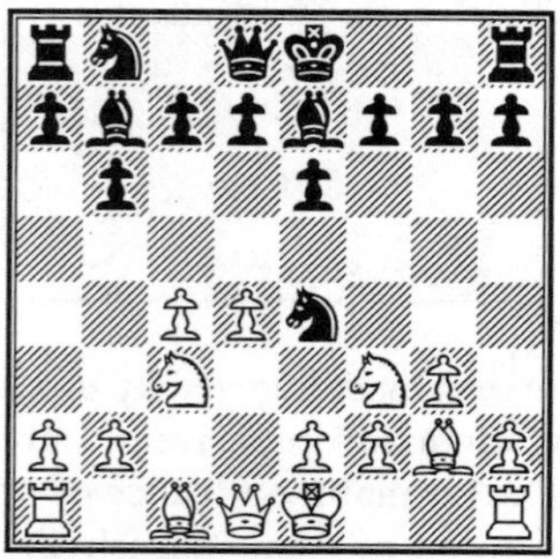

The point of putting the knight at e4 is to take control of the critical e4 square. This is the Opocensky Variation. **7.Bd2.** 7.Qc2 is the most common move, but this alternative is frequently seen. **7...Bf6; 8.0–0 0–0; 9.Rc1 c5.** It is already established theory that this is a good move. It leads to a series of exchanges. **10.d5 exd5; 11.cxd5 Nxd2; 12.Nxd2 d6; 13.Nde4 Be7; 14.f4.** This odd-looking move is actually best, because White's plans involve a kingside pawnstorm. **14...Nd7; 15.g4 a6; 16.a4 Re8;** All this was well-known at the time, and Salov's new move is just a logical alternative to 16...Nf6. **17.g5 Bf8.**

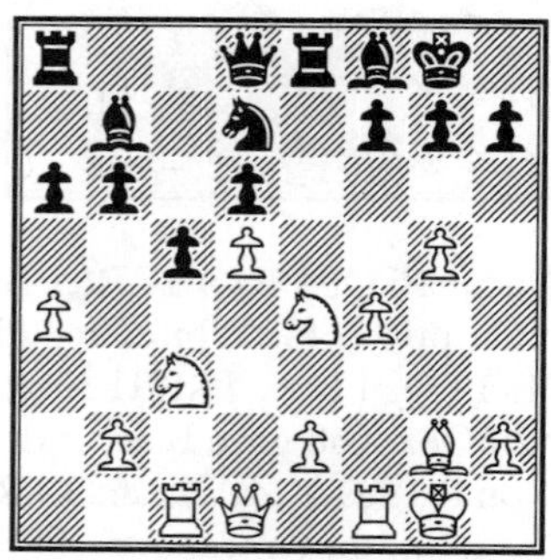

White's strategy has succeeded, since he now controls e4.**18.Kh1!** Karpov's prophylactic move insures that there will be no problems when Black later stations the queen at b6. **18...b5; 19.axb5 axb5; 20.Nxb5 Qb6.** This sacrifice would have been more effective if White's king still stood at g1! **21.Nbc3 Qb4.** Black has no time for maneuvers such as 21...Ba6 because the White rook quickly penetrates the kingside with Rf1–f3 and then it can operate on the g- or h-files. **22.Qd3 Nb6; 23.Qg3 Kh8; 24.Rcd1 Nc4; 25.b3 Nb6.** Now a surprising move cracks open the Black position.

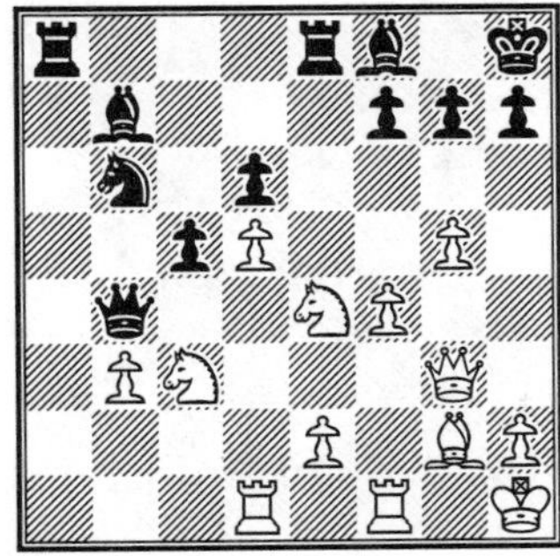

26.g6! fxg6. Taking with the other pawn also loses: 26...hxg6; 27.Qh4+ Kg8; 28.Ng5 and it is all over. **27.f5! gxf5; 28.Rxf5 Nd7.** Black cannot marshal the defensive forces in time. **29.Rdf1 Ne5; 30.R5f4 Qb6; 31.Ng5 Ng6.** Now for an elegant finish! **32.Nf7+ Kg8; 33.Qxg6!!** This brilliant sacrifice ends the game. There is no defense, for example **33...hxg6; 34.Rh4 Be7; 35.Rh8#. White won.**

(214) PANNO - KERES [E19]

Santa Monica (Piatigorsky Cup), 1963

1.c4 Nf6; 2.Nc3 e6; 3.Nf3 b6; 4.g3 Bb7; 5.Bg2 Be7; 6.0–0 0–0; 7.d4.

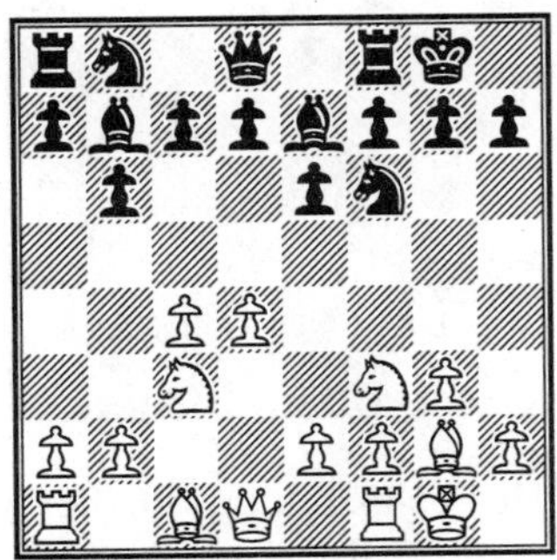

This is the main line of the Classical Queen's Indian. Black will now exchange a pair of knights and the battle for the e4-square will commence. White needs to have patience to slowly convert his slight central advantage into something meaningful. Most of the early middlegame is concerned with the center, and only after the central situation is resolved can either player try to accomplish something on the flank.

7...Ne4!; 8.Qc2 Nxc3; 9.Qxc3 f5. Now e4 cannot be controlled by White. **10.b3 Bf6; 11.Bb2.** 11.Be3!? should be met by 11...c5!?, according to Tukmakov, as 11...d6 is a bit passive. **11...d6.** Adventurous players might wish to investigate 11...a5 where 12.Rad1 Na6; 13.Qd2 Qe8; 14.Ne1 Bxg2; 15.Nxg2 g5 led to complications in Boleslavsky-Romanovsky, Kharlov 1956. **12.Rad1 Nd7.** Geller's 12...Qe8 deserves consideration as well as 12...a5 which was played in the second and fourth games of the Polugayevsky-Korchnoi Candidates match in Velden 1980. **13.Ne1 Bxg2; 14.Nxg2 Qe8.** Black intends to initiate play on the kingside with g7-g5 and Qg6 or Qh5. From g6 the queen also helps prevent e2-e4. **15.Qc2 g5; 16.d5.**

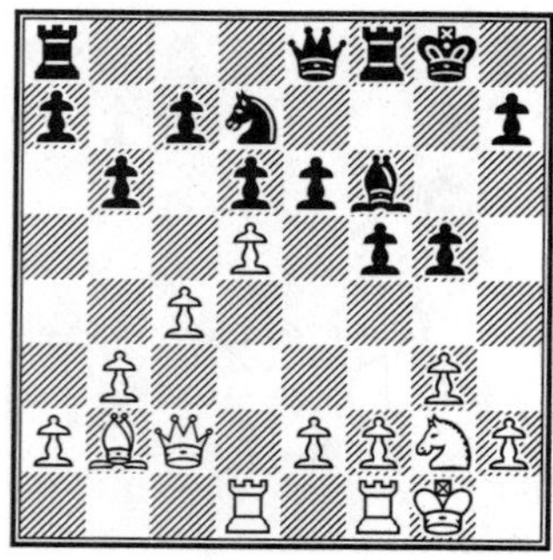

This move leads to problems for White. Better is 16.f4. Petrosian-Najdorf from the same tournament continued 16.f4 Qg6; 17.Rfe1 Rf7; 18.e4 fxe4; 19.Qxe4 Qxe4; 20.Rxe4 with a very slight edge to White, but Black had no difficulty holding on for a draw. 16.e4 f4; 17.gxf4 gxf4; 18.Nxf4 Bxd4 is also bad for White. **16...Bxb2; 17.dxe6 Qxe6; 18.Qxb2 Rae8.** Black's play throughout has been very thematic. From move 4 on he has had control of the e4-square, one of the main ideas in the Queen's Indian. The text forces 19.e3, increasing Black's grip on the position. **19.e3 Qh6; 20.f4.**

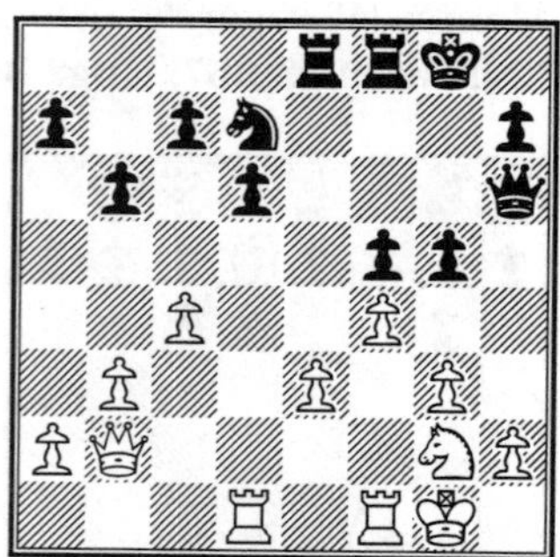

White wants to prevent Nd7-e5-f3, but this further weakens e4 and leaves White with a backward e-pawn. **20...g4; 21.Rd5 Qe6; 22.Rfd1 Nf6; 23.R5d3 Rf7; 24.Qd4 Rd7; 25.Nh4 a6; 26.Rc1.**

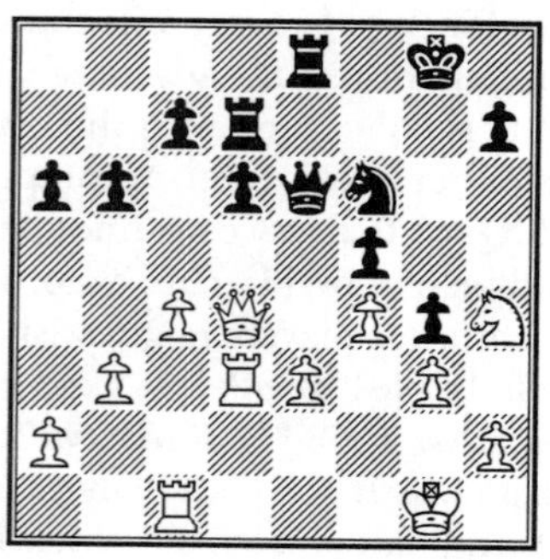

White can only play waiting moves while Black prepares d6-d5. **26...Kf7; 27.Qb2**

Red8; 28.Qe2 c6; 29.Rcd1 a5; 30.Qc2 Ne4; 31.Rd4 d5.

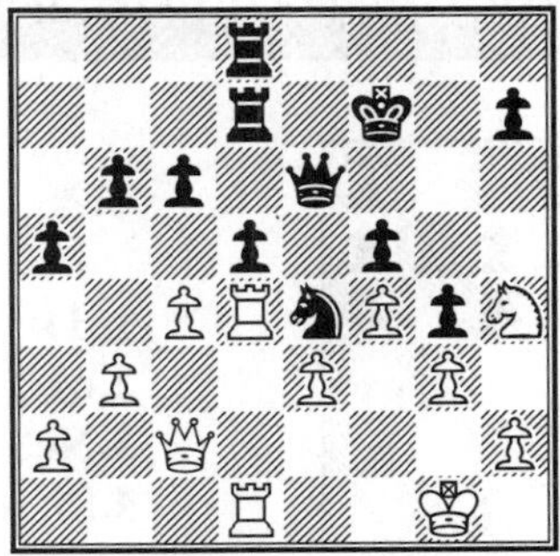

Black breaks open the position, trades off the rooks, and has a positionally won endgame. **32.cxd5 Rxd5; 33.Rxd5 Rxd5; 34.Rxd5 Qxd5; 35.Kf1 Ke6; 36.Ke1 Nc5; 37.Kf2 Qd3; 38.Qb2 Ne4+; 39.Kg2 Nc3; 40.Qc1 c5; 41.h3 Qe2+; 42.Kh1 Ne4. Black won.**

NIMZO-INDIAN DEFENSE

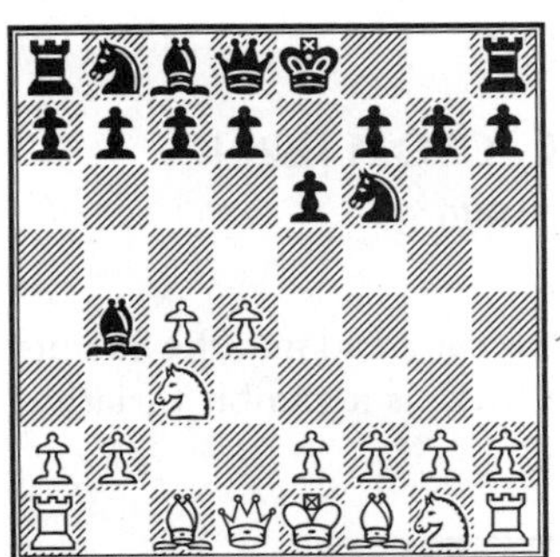

1.d4 Nf6
2.c4 e6
3.Nc3 Bb4

The **Nimzo-Indian Defense** is undoubtedly Aron Nimzowitsch's greatest contribution to opening theory. There is a clear battle for the e4-square. If White gets a pawn there without paying a penalty, then Black is in trouble. To prevent this, Black is willing to part with the dark-squared bishop to get rid of the knight at c3, and thereby undermine support of the e4-square. White gets the bishop pair, but Black has counterplay against the weak doubled c-pawns. An understanding of the hypermodern principles of Aron Nimzowitsch is essential to playing the Nimzo-Indian effectively.

As White, players can be divided into two camps. The first favors 4.e3 and the second are proponents of the Classical Variation with 4.Qc2, which avoids the doubling of pawn. Both plans remain popular.

Other plans are less ambitious, but nevertheless have some sting. We'll start with some of those, including the Kmoch Variation, Saemisch Variation and Leningrad Variation.

KMOCH VARIATION

1.d4 Nf6
2.c4 e6
3.Nc3 Bb4
4.f3

This move is tied in with Saemisch's plan of an early a3, and transpositions are often seen. There are independent paths to explore, however, and in the 1990s this became a hot opening for some time. White wants to build a strong center by advancing the e-pawn, but Black can react with either ...d5 or ...c5. Although theoretical battles still flare up from time to time, at present Black seems to be maintaining the balance.

(215) IVANCHUK - CSOM [E20]

Yerevan, 1990

1.d4 Nf6; 2.c4 e6; 3.Nc3 Bb4; 4.f3 c5. Play can head into the Saemisch Variation on 4...d5; 5.a3. **5.d5 Bxc3+.** 5...b5 has been tried as a gambit variation. 6.e4 bxc4; 7.Bxc4.

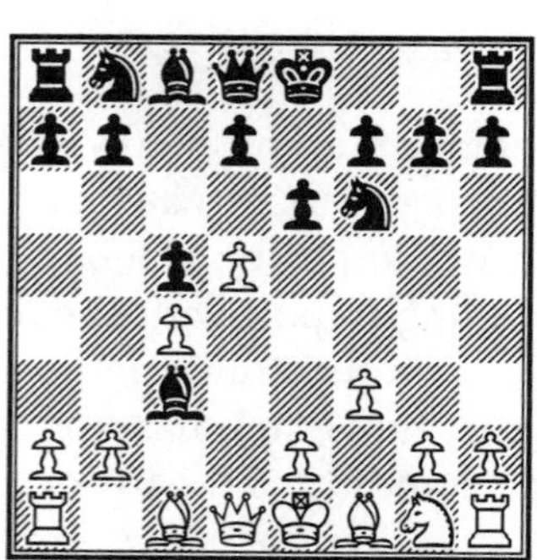

A) 7...Nxd5; 8.Bxd5 exd5; 9.Qxd5 Nc6; 10.Nge2 Ba6; 11.Kf2 0–0; 12.Rd1 and White is doing well: 12...Re8 (12...Bxc3; 13.bxc3 Bxe2; 14.Kxe2 Qb8; 15.h3 Kh8; 16.Kf2 f5; 17.exf5 Ne5; 18.Bf4 Rxf5; 19.Rab1 Qe8; 20.Qe4 g6; 21.Kg3 Rb8; 22.Rxb8 Qxb8; 23.Rxd7 Rxf4; 24.Rb7 Rxf3+; 25.gxf3. White won. Khenkin-Kotronias, Chalkidiki 1992) 13.a3 Re5; 14.Qxd7 Qh4+; 15.Ng3 Re6; 16.axb4 Ne5; 17.Qd5 Rae8; 18.b5 Bc8; 19.Kg1 Rg6; 20.Nce2 Bh3; 21.Rxa7. White won. Moskalenko-Zak, Germany

1992.

B) 7...d6; 8.Nge2 e5; 9.0–0 0–0; 10.Bg5 h6; 11.Bh4 Nbd7 leaves White with a lot of space and Black is tied down on the kingside, Malaniuk-Bronstein, Budapest 1989. 5...Nh5 is another recent try, trying to exploit the threat of ...Qh4+. 6.g3 d6 (6...f5; 7.Bg2 0–0; 8.f4 Nf6; 9.Nf3 Ne4; 10.0–0 Bxc3; 11.bxc3 b6; 12.Ng5 Nxg5; 13.fxg5 e5; 14.d6 and White had the advantage in Moskalenko-Long, Beijing 1991.) 7.e4 exd5; 8.cxd5 0–0; 9.Bg2 f5; 10.f4 Qe8 with an initiative for Black in Moskalenko-Howell, Belgorod 1990.

6.bxc3 Nh5. 6...d6 is an interesting alternative, for example 7.e4 e5; 8.Bd3 Nbd7; 9.Ne2 Nf8; 10.h4 h5; 11.Bg5 N8h7; 12.Bd2 Qa5; 13.a4 Bd7; 14.Nc1 Qc7; 15.Nb3 g6; 16.a5 0–0–0 and Black was about ready to counterattack in Malaniuk-Vladimirov, Moscow 1992. **7.g3.** Nobody falls for 7.g4? Qh4+ when the king must flee. **7...f5; 8.e4 f4; 9.dxe6 fxg3.** 9...Qf6 10.Ne2 fxg3; 11.Bg2 gxh2; 12.Rxh2 g6; 13.exd7+ Bxd7; 14.Qd5 and White has a huge advantage in space, with the much safer king, Moskalenko-Novikov, Lvov 1988. **10.Qd5.**

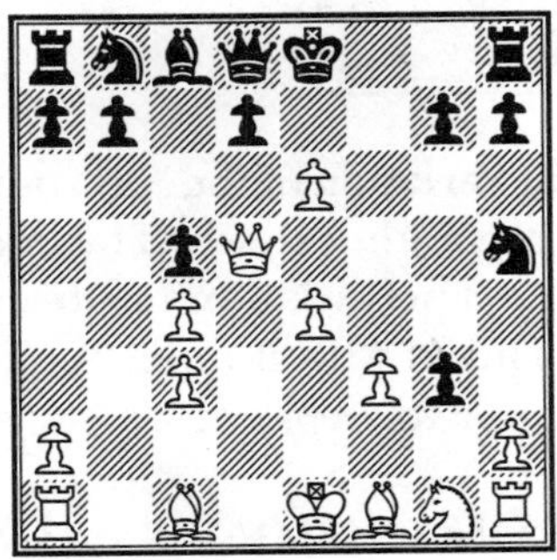

10...g2? 10...Nf6; 11.exd7+ Bxd7; 12.Qe5+ Kf7; 13.hxg3 Qa5; 14.Bd2 Nc6; 15.Qf4 Rae8 was the correct plan, according to Raymond Keene. **11.Qxh5+!** 11.Bxg2 Qh4+ would have given Black all the chances. **11...g6; 12.Qe5 Qh4+.** 12...gxh1Q?; 13.Qxh8+ Ke7; 14.Bg5+ and Black can resign. **13.Ke2 gxh1Q.**

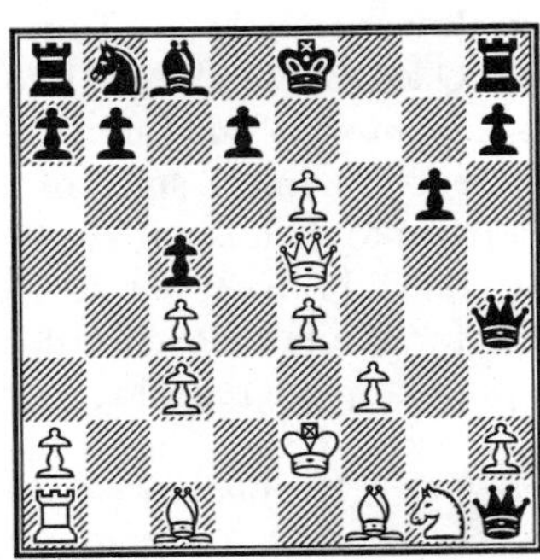

Black has an extra queen, and White has only a single queen. White's attack consists of queen and pawn, which should not be dangerous. In this case, however, it is fatal. **14.Qxh8+ Ke7; 15.Qg7+ Kxe6; 16.Bh3+ Kd6; 17.Qf8+ Kc7; 18.Bf4+.** The involvement of the bishops forces Black to sacrifice the queen, but even that is not enough to save the hapless king. **18...Qxf4; 19.Qxf4+ d6; 20.Rd1 Nc6; 21.Qxd6+ Kb6; 22.Qg3 h5; 23.Bxc8 Rxc8; 24.Nh3 h4; 25.Qf2** and Black resigned. A magnificent game! **White won.**

ROMANISHIN VARIATION

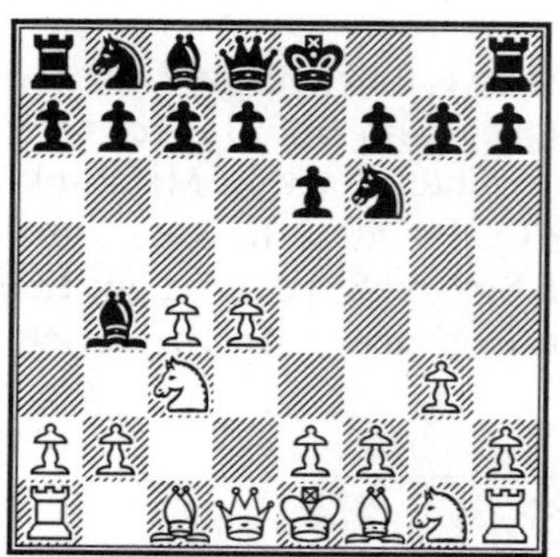

1.d4	**Nf6**
2.c4	**e6**
3.Nc3	**Bb4**
4.g3	

This is the **Romanishin Variation** of the Nimzo-Indian. White fianchettoes the bishop at g2 and will play rather slowly. The line can also be approached by 4.Nf3 and only later g3. The variation has been around for some time, but only when Kasparov flirted with it did it achieve the recognition it deserves as a serious alternative to 4.e3.

(216) ROMANISHIN - SAVON [E20]

Yerevan, 1976

1.d4 Nf6; 2.c4 e6; 3.Nc3 Bb4; 4.g3 0–0. 4...c5; 5.Nf3 is often seen.

A) 5...d5; 6.cxd5 Nxd5; 7.Bd2 cxd4; 8.Nxd4 0–0; 9.Bg2 Nb6; 10.Ncb5 Bxd2+; 11.Qxd2 a6; 12.Na3 e5; 13.Nb3 Qxd2+; 14.Nxd2 Nc6; 15.Bxc6 bxc6; 16.Nac4 and White had healthier pawns in Romanishin-Sydor, Dortmund 1976.

B) 5...Ne4; 6.Qd3 Qa5; 7.Qxe4 Bxc3+; 8.Bd2 Bxd2+; 9.Nxd2 Nc6; 10.d5 left Black feeling the pressure in Romanishin-Tal, Tallinn 1977.

C) 5...b5 is an interesting reaction, in the spirit of the Benko Gambit, but without White having advanced a pawn to d5 it is not so effective. 6.cxb5 a6; 7.Bg2 0–0; 8.0–0 d5; 9.bxa6 Bxa6; 10.dxc5 Bxc3; 11.bxc3 Ne4; 12.Qc2 Nd7; 13.c6! Ndc5; 14.Be3 Qc7; 15.Nd4 was clearly better for White in Romanishin-Vitolins, Riga 1981.

D) 5...b6; 6.Bg2 Bb7 is a popular plan, reaching a Queen's Indian position. 7.0–0 and now:

D1) 7...cxd4; 8.Qxd4 Nc6; 9.Qd3 has been used effectively by Van Wely. 9...Rc8 (9...0–0; 10.Bf4 Na5; 11.Nb5 Be4; 12.Qd1 d5; 13.Qa4 Be7; 14.cxd5 Bxd5; 15.Rac1 Qe8; 16.b3 leaves the Black position congested, Van Wely-Grooten, Belfort 1989.) 10.Bf4 Na5; 11.Rac1 Rxc4; 12.Nb5 d5; 13.a3 Be7; 14.Nc7+ Kf8; 15.Ne5 Rxc1; 16.Rxc1 Nd7; 17.b4 Nxe5; 18.Bxe5 Nc6; 19.Rxc6 Bxc6; 20.Qc3 and Black was already in deep trouble in Van Wely-Steingrimsson, Kecskemet 1991.

D2) 7...Bxc3; 8.bxc3 Nc6; 9.Ne5 Na5; 10.dxc5 Bxg2; 11.Kxg2 bxc5; 12.Qa4 places great pressure on the a4-e8 diagonal, Van Wely-Adamski, Lyngby 1989.

E) 5...cxd4; 6.Nxd4 transposes to the English Opening.

5.Bg2 d5.

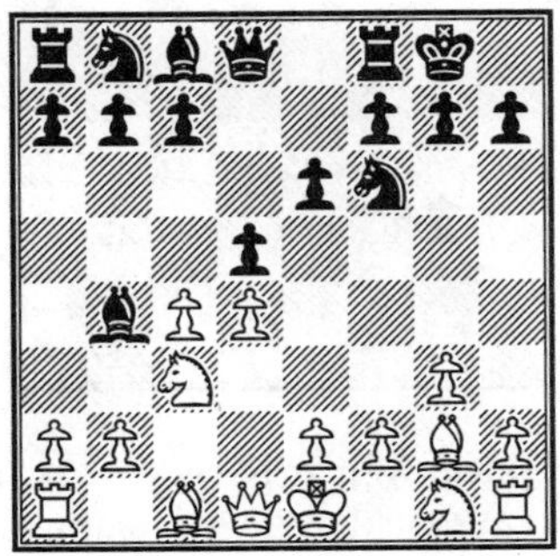

The position now takes on characteristics of the Catalan Opening. **6.Nf3 dxc4; 7.0–0 Nc6.** 7...Nd5; 8.Qc2 Be7; 9.Rd1 Nc6; 10.e4 Ndb4; 11.Qe2 Nd3; 12.Be3 a6; 13.b3! b5; 14.Rab1 Ba3; 15.bxc4 bxc4; 16.e5 with beautiful prospects for White, especially the e4-square, Romanishin-Damjanovic, Hastings 1976. **8.Re1 Rb8; 9.a3 Bxc3; 10.bxc3 Na5.** It is up to Black to demonstrate that parting with the bishop pair is justified. Black's extra pawn is weak, and White's central control alone is enough compensation. **11.Rb1 b6; 12.e4! Bb7; 13.Bg5 h6; 14.Bh4 Qe8.** Black has to do something about the threat of e5, but now the kingside pawn structure suffers the consequences. **15.Bxf6 gxf6; 16.Nd2.** Now Black has to worry about weak pawns at h6 and b5. **16...Kh7; 17.Bf1 b5; 18.Qf3.**

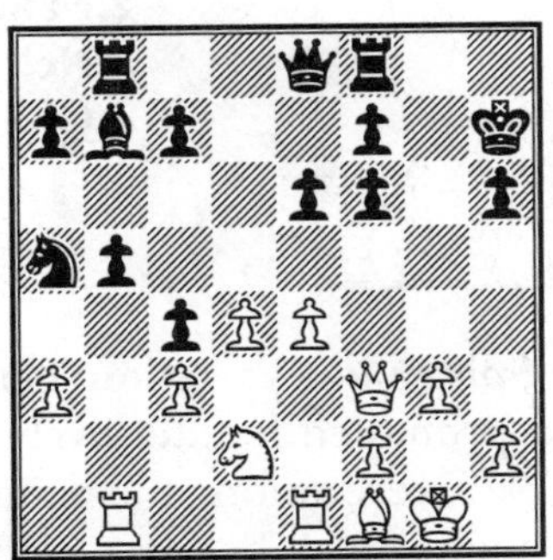

White just keeps piling on the pressure, keeping Black on the defensive. **18...f5; 19.Qf4.** Now c7 is the target. Black decides to simplify the position. **19...Nb3; 20.Nxb3 cxb3; 21.Bd3 fxe4; 22.Bxe4+ Bxe4; 23.Rxe4.**

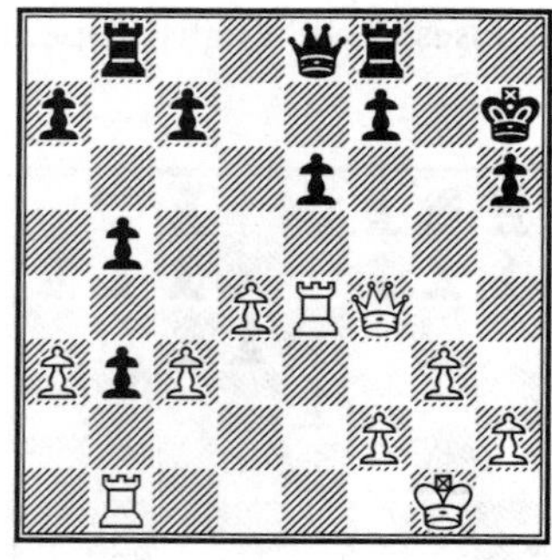

Black still has an extra pawn, but it is very weak, as is most of Black's pawn structure. Romanishin mops up quickly, playing against weaknesses on both sides of the board. **23...Qe7; 24.Re5 Rg8; 25.Rc5 c6; 26.Rxb3 Rbc8; 27.Qe4+ Rg6; 28.Rxc6 Rxc6; 29.Qxc6** faced with the loss of yet another pawn, Black resigned. **White won.**

SPIELMANN VARIATION

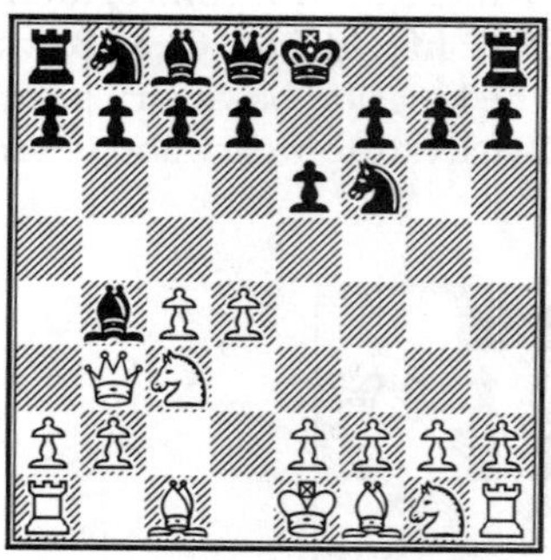

1.d4	**Nf6**
2.c4	**e6**
3.Nc3	**Bb4**
4.Qb3	

This is known as the **Spielmann Variation**, because the great romantic player both played it and promoted it extensively. His results at the great Carlsbad tournament of 1929 were among the main reasons. These days it is considered of negligible importance because Black can, as in the present game, transpose to the Classical Variation.

(217) WINTER - COLLE [E23]
Scarborough, 1930

1.d4 Nf6; 2.c4 e6; 3.Nc3 Bb4; 4.Qb3 c5! This is Blacks best move, if only for the reason than White has nothing better than leading the game into the channels of the Classical Variation by capturing on c5. Black can also play independently, for example 4...Nc6; 5.e3 0–0; 6.Bd3 a5 with a good game for Black in Stahlberg-Nimzowitsch, Goteborg (1st match game) 1934. 4...Bxc3+; 5.bxc3 d6; 6.f3 0–0; 7.Bg5

Qe7; 8.e4 e5; 9.Rd1 c5; 10.d5 Nbd7; 11.g4 Re8; 12.Bd3 Nf8 left Black with a very passive position in Nimzowitsch-Henneberger, Zurich 1934. **5.dxc5 Nc6.**

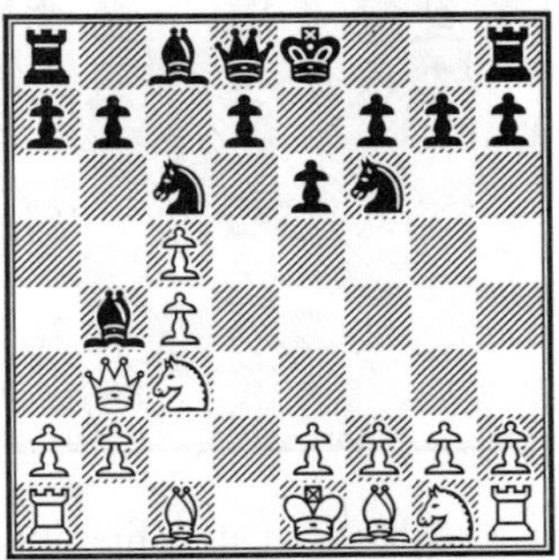

5...Na6 would lead to more traditional Classical lines after an eventual ...Bxc3, when White replies by recapturing with the queen. **6.Nf3 Ne4; 7.Bd2 Nxc5.** Already Black has a good game. 7...Nxd2 was played against Spielmann on several occasions. 8.Nxd2 f5 (8...0–0; 9.0–0–0 led to promising play for White in Spielmann-Johner, also from Carlsbad 1929.) 9.e3 Bxc5; 10.Be2 0–0; 11.0–0–0 b6; 12.Nf3 Ba6 Spielmann-Colle, Carlsbad 1929. Winter was no doubt familiar with this game.

8.Qc2. White would have saved time by playing the queen here on the fourth move. **8...f5; 9.e3 0–0.** Black has easy development and a comfortable position. **10.a3.** 10.Be2 b6; 11.0–0–0 a5; 12.a3 a4 gave Black a strong queenside attack in Bogoljubow-Nimzowitsch, San Remo 1930. **10...Bxc3; 11.Bxc3 b6; 12.Be2 Bb7; 13.0–0.**

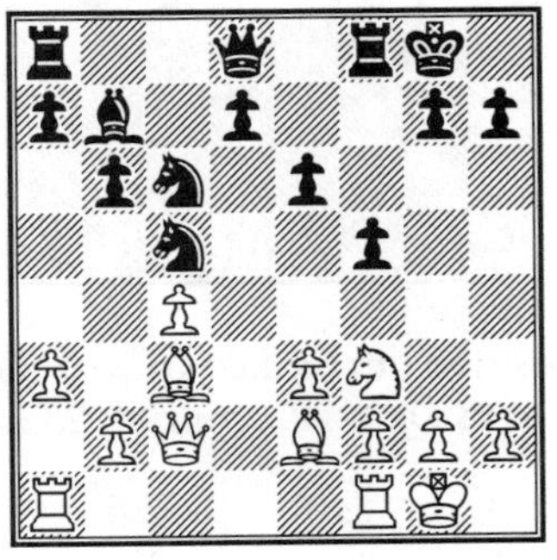

Clearly in this position Black is going to want to attack on the kingside. But first he takes time out to put some pressure on the c-file. **13...Rc8!** This rook could not be expected to take part in the attack. Therefore it lines up on the c-file, in order to keep some of White's potential defenders tied down. This makes the attack easier to achieve. **14.Rfd1 Qe7; 15.b4 Ne4; 16.Be1.** White preserves the bishop because his plan is to advance his b-pawn and then play Bb4, creating tremendous pressure on the dark squares. His king seems safe enough, since there are no attacking pieces in sight. **16...Rf6!** Simultaneously lessening the effect of Bb4 and starting the offensive. **17.Nd4?** White is oblivious to the danger - though in reality he has but a few moments left to live. 17.Bf1 would have defended the g2-square, and the defense of f3 could have been entrusted to a queen at e2. **17...Rg6!**

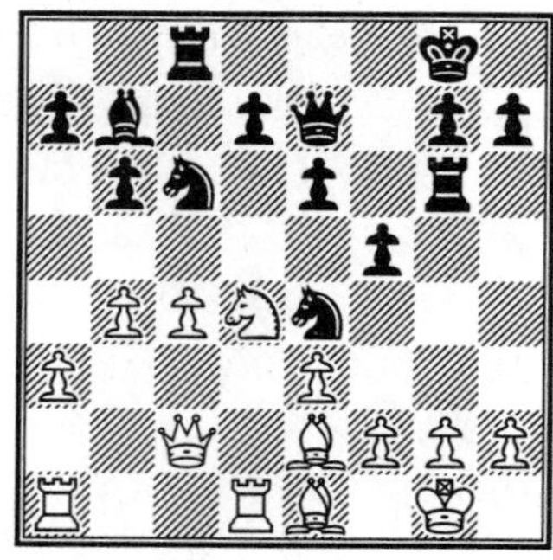

This position is winning for Black because his minor pieces can strike quickly and White is not able to defend in time. **18.Bf1.** Given that the Black queen can get to the kingside via h4, the presence of a Black knight at f3 should be decisive. Although the Pg2 is pinned, White can use his Nd4 to defend the square. But the Nd4 can be eliminated. 18.f3 is met by 18...Qg5!; 18.Bf3 meets refutation in 18...Ne5!; 18.g3 Ne5 is also good for Black, for example after 19.Qb3 Qh4! **18...Ng5!; 19.Kh1.** In order to avoid the check at f3. But Black doesn't need a check! **19...Nxd4; 20.exd4.**

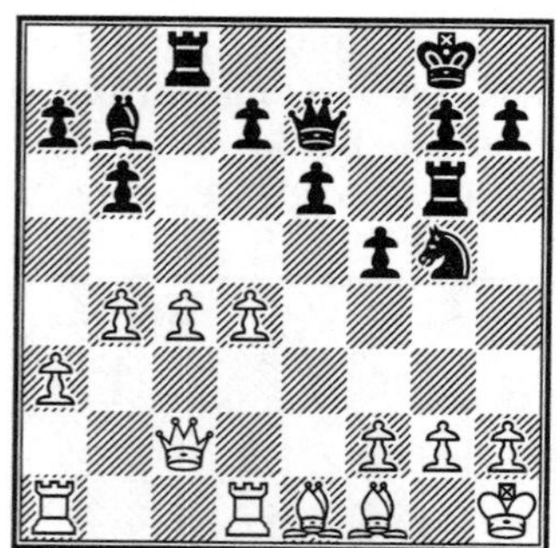

20...Nf3!! This is the position envisioned back at move 18. The threat is simply Qh4: 21.d5 Qh4; 22 h3 (22.gxf3 Qg5) 22...Qxh3+!; 23.hxg3 Rg1#. **Black won.**

LENINGRAD VARIATION

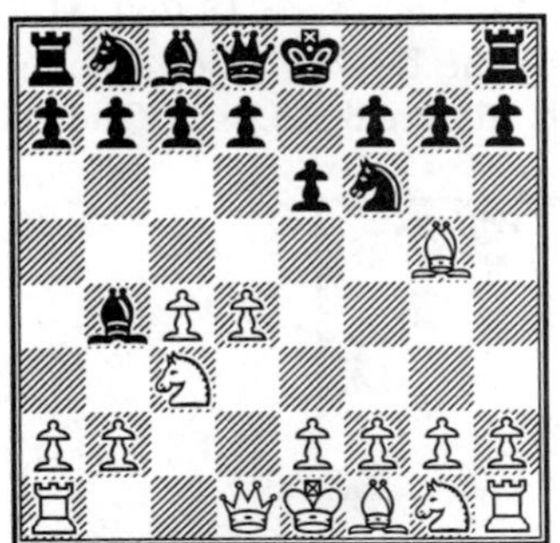

1.d4	**Nf6**
2.c4	**e6**
3.Nc3	**Bb4**
4.Bg5	

The **Leningrad Variation** was brought to prominence by Boris Spassky. White pins the knight and thus gains greater control of the c4-square. Play can get very lively, but Black need not worry, since many of the complications do not favor White.

(218) SPASSKY - SMYSLOV [E31]

Bucharest, 1953

1.d4 Nf6; 2.c4 e6; 3.Nc3 Bb4; 4.Bg5 h6; 5.Bh4 c5; 6.d5.

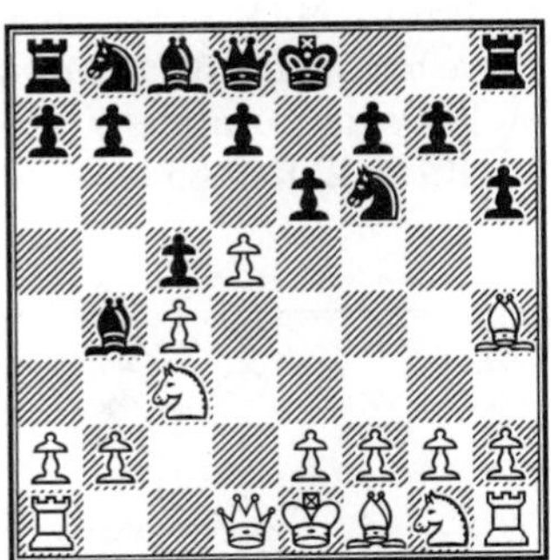

This reduces the flexibility of White's center and should not lead to any advantage for White. **6...d6.** 6...b5!? is also playable, but the text is the most principled move. 6...Bxc3+; 7.bxc3 d6; 8.e3 e5 is another solid plan for White, for example Dao Thien Hai-Tisdall, Yerevan Olympiad 1996 continued 9.Nf3 Qe7; 10.Nd2 g5; 11.Bg3 Bf5; 12.Qb3 Kd8!? 13.Be2 Kc7 with a dynamically balanced game.

7.e3 exd5. 7...Bxc3+; 8.bxc3 e5 is more in the spirit of the opening White can simply develop, but must always take into account the possibility that the Black pawn will advance to e4. That is why White often takes time to cover that square by playing 9.f3, yet Black can still counterattack, for example 9...g5; 10.Bg3 e4; 11.h4 g4; 12.h5 exf3; 13.gxf3 Qe7; 14.Bh4! gives White good play despite the investment of two pawns. 14...Qxe3+; 15.Qe2 Qxe2+; 16.Nxe2 Nxh5; 17.0–0–0 gxf3; 18.Ng3 Nxg3; 19.Re1+ and in this crucial position from Bareyev-Sax, Hastings 1990-91, Black should have played 19...Kd7!; 20.Re7+ Kd8 where, amazingly, no clearly favorable continuation is available for White.

8.cxd5 Nbd7; 9.Bb5 0–0. 9...Bxc3+; 10.bxc3 a6; 11.Bxd7+ Bxd7 would present no problems for Black. **10.Nge2 Ne5; 11.0–0 Ng6; 12.Bg3.** The bishop will not have time to rest at g3. **12...Nh5; 13.Bd3 Nxg3; 14.Nxg3 Ne5; 15.Be2.** Here Black has nothing better than to exchange at c3, since the bishop is not accomplishing anything at b4 and has no better home in sight. **15...Bxc3; 16.bxc3 Qh4; 17.f4.**

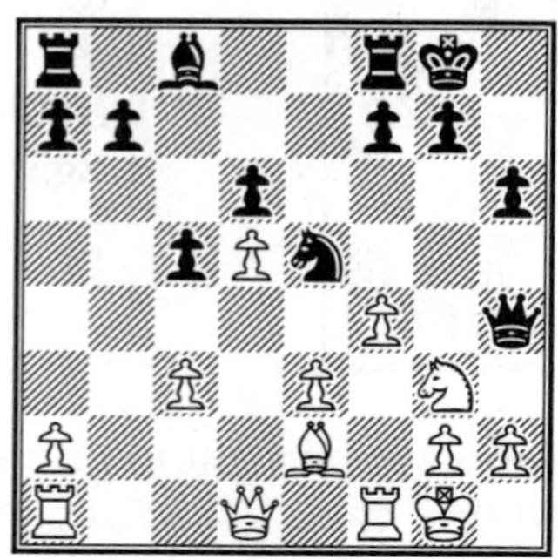

17...Ng4! The kingside attack forces White to part with his remaining bishop. **18.Bxg4 Bxg4; 19.Qa4!** Now the advance of the f-pawn could leave the bishop offside, so Black retreats to the only available square. **19...Bc8; 20.e4.** White has finally made progress in the center. **20...Qg4; 21.Qc2 h5; 22.Rf3 b5!** Black obtains some breathing room on the queenside. **23.e5 h4; 24.Nf1 Bf5; 25.Qd2.** White does not have any real advantage here, but Black must play very carefully. **25...dxe5?** 25...Rfe8; 26.exd6 Rad8; 27.Ne3 Rxe3; 28.Qxe3 Rxd6; 29.Qe8+ is much better for White. 25...Be4; 26.Re3 f5; 27.e6 Qxf4 would have been quite pleasant for Black. **26.fxe5 Bg6; 27.Re1 h3; 28.d6 Be4; 29.Ne3.** Now Smyslov commits a second, fatal error. **29...Qe6?** 29...Qd7; 30.Rf4 Bxg2; 31.Nf5 Rfe8; 32.Re3 g6 leaves the situation unclear. **30.Rf4 Bxg2; 31.Nf5 Rfe8.**

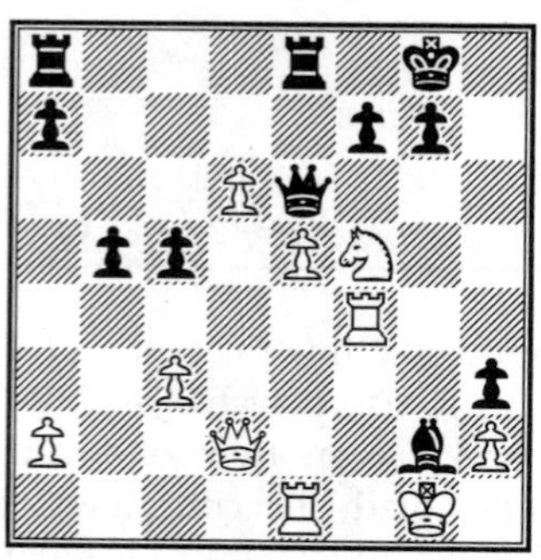

32.Re3! Rad8; 33.Nxg7 Rxd6; 34.Nxe6. White won.

CLASSICAL VARIATION

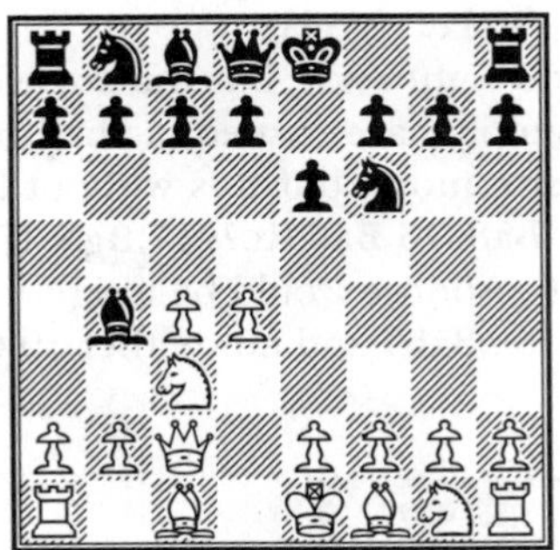

1.d4 Nf6
2.c4 e6
3.Nc3 Bb4
4.Qc2

The **Classical Variation** has become the main line of the Nimzo-Indian. White sensibly defends the knight at c3 so that if Black captures, the pawn structure will not have to be disrupted. The queen also serves to support control of e4. Unlike the Spielmann Variation, however, the queen is not in such a vulnerable position.

(219) LAUTIER - KARPOV [E32]

Linares, 1995

1.d4 Nf6; 2.c4 e6; 3.Nc3 Bb4; 4.Qc2 0–0. This is a conservative plan. In addition to 4...Nc6, 4...c5 and 4...d5, Nimzowitsch himself tried some other moves. 4...d6; 5.Bg5 Nbd7; 6.a3 Bxc3+; 7.Qxc3 h6; 8.Bh4 b6; 9.f3 Bb7; 10.e4 Nxe4; 11.Bxd8 Nxc3; 12.Bh4 Na4; 13.b3 c5; 14.bxa4 cxd4; 15.Ne2 e5 and the central pawn wedge gave Black compensation for the piece in Grunfeld-Nimzowitsch, Kecskemet 1927. 4...b6; 5.e4 Bb7; 6.Bd3 Nc6; 7.Nf3 Be7; 8.a3 d6; 9.0–0 e5; 10.d5 Nb8; 11.b4 Nbd7; 12.Bb2 0–0 gave Black a solid game in Opocensky-Nimzowitsch, Marienbad 1925. **5.a3 Bxc3+; 6.Qxc3 b6.**

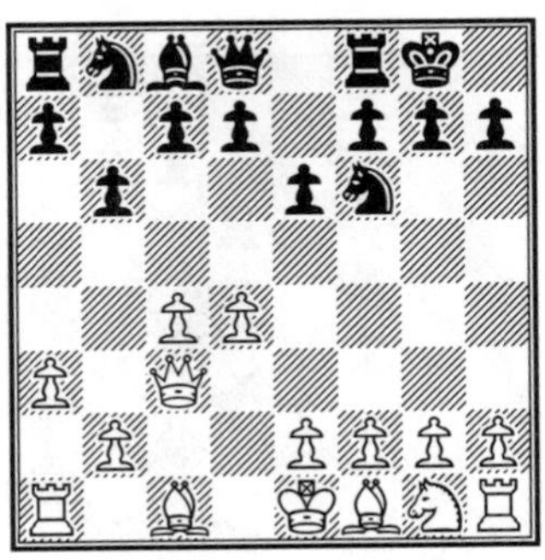

As usual, White has the bishop pair. On the other hand, Black has the lead in development. **7.Bg5 Bb7; 8.e3 d6; 9.f3 Nbd7; 10.Bd3 c5; 11.Ne2 Rc8.** This position is fairly typical of those which arise in the Qc2 lines. The most natural continuation is 12.b4, but that may lead to premature liquidation of pieces with a lot of drawing chances. Probably the best move is to retreat to d2. Lautier stations the lady at b3, but it proves to be an infelicitous post. **12.Qb3?! h6.** Better than an immediate capture at d4. This gives Black an opportunity to play ...g5 later.

13.Bh4 cxd4. Black can also play 14...d5 right away, but Karpov elects to capture. **14.exd4 d5; 15.c5?!** Lautier should simply have castled, as had been played back in 1993. This is a positionally aggressive move, but it is without foundation. 15.cxd5 Bxd5 should be fine for Black. **15...Ba8; 16.Ba6 Rc7; 17.Bg3.** If White captures at b6, Black must be careful. The best response would be to ignore the pawn and simply play 17.Rc6! since 18.b7 fails to 18...Bxb7 and now either 19.Qxb7 Qa5+ or 19.Bxb7 Rb6 picks off a piece.

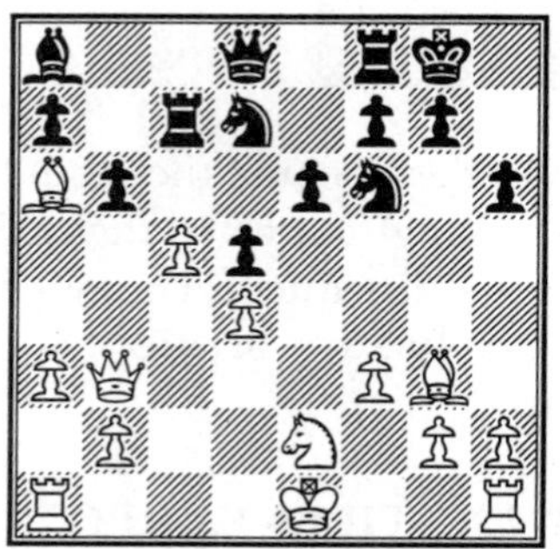

17...bxc5! Well timed! **18.Bxc7 Qxc7; 19.Qc3 e5!** Black's hypermodern opening has led to a powerful central counterattack and White is already in serious trouble. **20.Bd3.** Any capture by the d-pawn can be met by ...d4. **20...exd4; 21.Nxd4 Re8+; 22.Kf1.** White has to abandon hope of castling, and there are no further chances for survival. **22...Qb6; 23.Nf5 d4; 24.Qd2 Ne5; 25.Re1 Re6!** Black prepares to lop off the bishop at d3. This cannot be done immediately because of 26.Rxe8+ Nxe8; 27.Qxd3 Qxb2 when White can retreat the queen to e2 and it is hard to find a convincing line for Black. **26.Bb1 Bb7; 27.Kf2.** Perhaps 27.Ba2 would have held out longer. **27...d3; 28.Rhf1 c4+; 29.Kg3 Nh5+; 30.Kh3.** Black eventually gets mated if the king advances to h4. **30...Ng6!; 31.g3 Bc8; 32.Re4 Qc5; 33.g4 Ngf4+!**

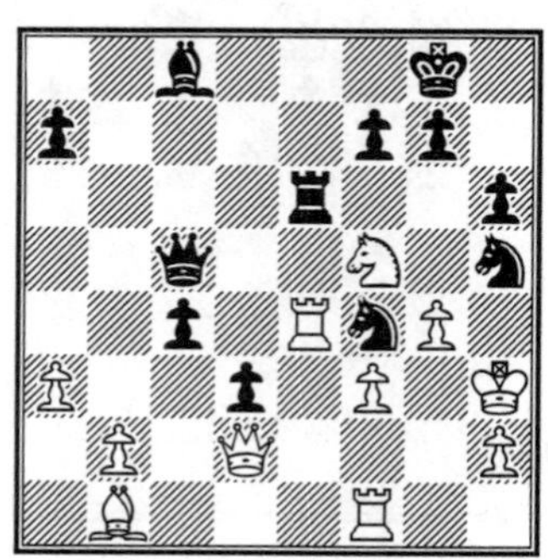

The decisive attack begins. **34.Rxf4 Re2; 35.Qc1 Nxf4+; 36.Qxf4 Bxf5; 37.gxf5 Rxb2.**

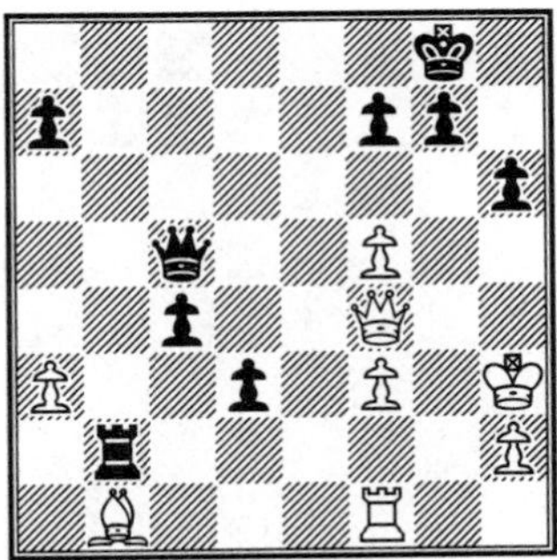

After most of the pieces have left the board, the advanced Black pawns are too difficult to stop. **38.Re1?** The only try was Qe4. but Black should still win. **38...Qf2; 39.Qg3 Qxg3+; 40.hxg3.** The queens are gone and White has a piece for two pawns. Given time, there might be some hope, but Karpov grants no extensions, and finishes the game by sacrificing the exchange and letting the pawns do the talking. **40...Rxb1! Black won.**

(220) KERES - EUWE [E33]

Holland, 6th match game, 1939

1.d4 Nf6; 2.c4 e6; 3.Nc3 Bb4; 4.Qc2 Nc6.

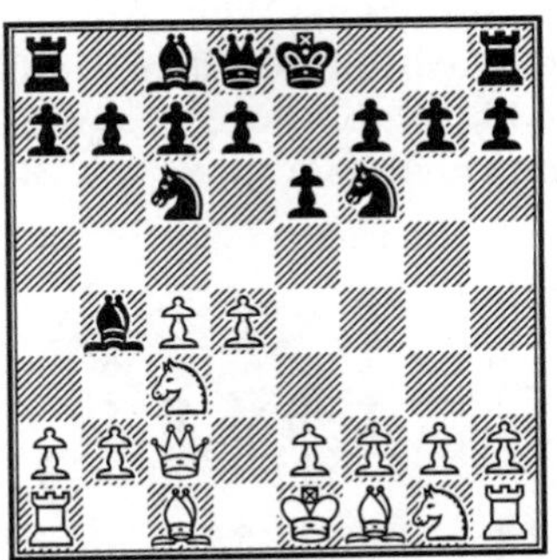

This is the Zurich Variation of the Classical Nimzo-Indian. The Black knight at c6 seems to occupy an artificial post, and it has few followers these days. **5.Nf3 0–0.** 5...d6; 6.a3 Bxc3+; 7.Qxc3 0–0 (7...Qe7; 8.b4 0–0; 9.Bb2 Re8; 10.e3 e5; 11.dxe5 Nxe5; 12.Nxe5 dxe5 was fine for Black in Flohr-Nimzowitsch, Bled 1931.) 8.b4 e5; 9.dxe5 Nxe5; 10.Nxe5 dxe5; 11.Qxe5 is a new gambit. 11...Re8; 12.Qb2 Ng4 (12...Qd3; 13.Bg5 Ng4; 14.f3 Qf5 is assessed as unclear by Browne. 15.Qd2 looks a little better for White.) 13.Qc3 a5; 14.Bb2 Qg5; 15.h4 Qh6; 16.Rd1 gave White the advantage in Browne-Orlov, Modesto (U.S. Championship) 1995.

6.Bg5! h6; 7.Bh4 d6. The pin may be annoying, but it cannot easily be broken, as Botvinnik pointed out: 7...g5?; 8.Bg3 g4; 9.Nh4 Nxd4; 10.Qd2! Nf5; 11.Nxf5 exf5; 12.Qxh6. 7...d5; 8.0-0-0 0-0; 9.a3 Be7; 10.e3 dxc4; 11.Bxc4 a6 prepared queenside counterplay for Black in Crouch-Stevenson, Scottish Championship 1997. **8.e3 Qe7; 9.Be2 e5.**

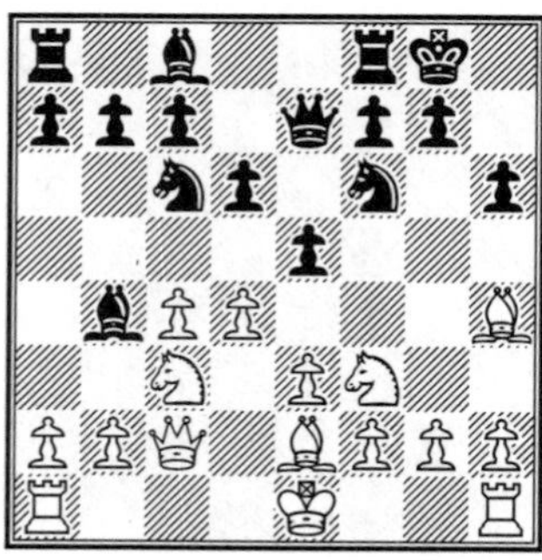

Black has treated the center with classical respect, and White must decide whether he should capture, advance, or maintain the status quo. **10.d5! Nb8.** The correct move. Now that White has conceded control of c5, that square will be the natural home for the knight. From b8 it only takes two moves to reach c5. **11.Nd2!** This move serves many purposes. It breaks the pin on the Nc3, and overprotects e4. Now if an eventual g7-g4, Black cannot gain more time with g5-g4. White will also be able to attack with a pawnstorm on the kingside.

11...Nbd7; 12.0–0 a5; 13.Rae1! The Rf1 should remain in place because it supports the advance of the f-pawn. There is no need to worry about action on the queenside, because White's pieces enjoy such freedom of movement that they can switch sides quickly.

13...Re8. This is aimed at preventing White from going after the weak square c7 with Nc3-b5. 13...Nc5 would have been consistent with Black's plans and might have been better than the text. **14.f4.** 14.Nb5 Bxd2; 15.Qxd2 Ne4; 16.Qc2 Qxh4; 17.Nxc7 Qd8; 18.Nxa8 Ndc5 and the knight is trapped. **14...Bxc3; 15.Qxc3 Ne4; 16.Nxe4 Qxh4; 17.g3 Qe7.**

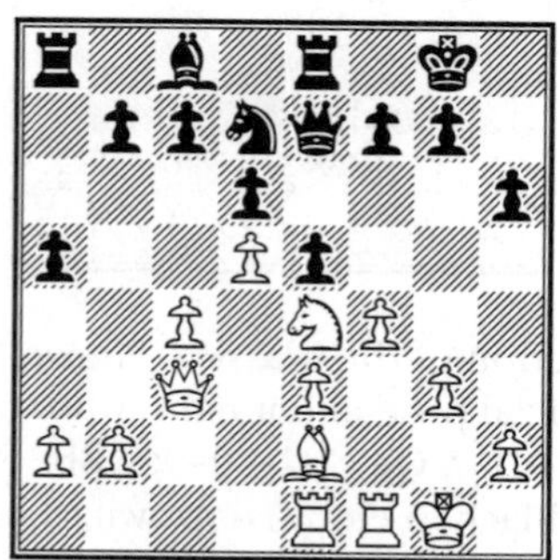

Now White must think of a long term plan. Clearly his bishop is not a long- term asset, and if Black plays f5-f5, it will be difficult to exchange. **18.Bg4!** This assures that the bishops will come off the board, and then the pawn structure will favor White. The threat of 19.Bxd7 Bxd7; 20.f5! is quite strong and therefore Black must exchange both sets of minor pieces. **18...Nf6.** 18...Nf8?; 19.Bxc8 Raxc8; 20.f5 secures a significant spatial advantage. **19.Nxf6+ Qxf6; 20.Bxc8 Raxc8.**

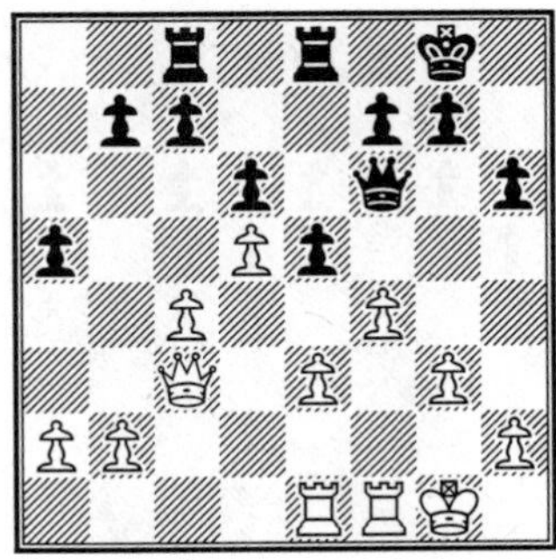

After avoiding 21.Qxa5? exf4! (... Qxb2), White must reconfigure his position so that his rooks will be effective on an open line. Which file? **21.Rf2!** This exploits the pin on e5, since the double-rook endgames favor White. Now Keres will gain more space on the kingside by playing f4-f5, after which he can concentrate on the queenside. **21...b6; 22.Ref1 Qg6; 23.f5! Qf6; 24.e4!** Given the fact that White's pieces enjoy superior mobility, it is possible for him to preserve chances on both sides of the board by locking the center. The threat of a kingside pawn storm will trouble Black for some time. **24...c6?!** This approach to the problem is too radical, or at least premature, since White has not yet weakened his queenside by advancing the pawns there. **25.dxc6 Rxc6.**

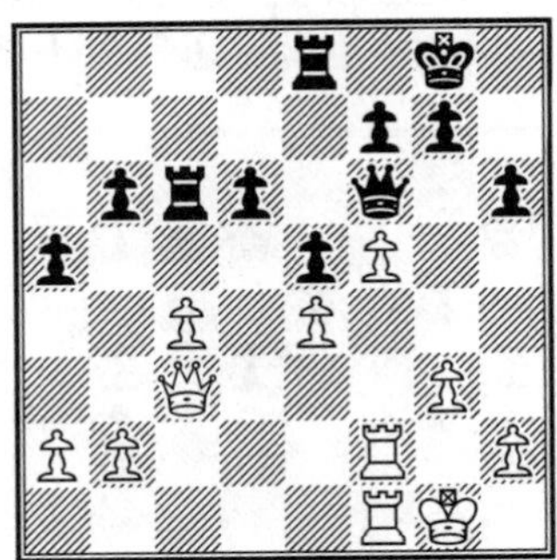

Now White has opened some lines and useful light squares, and Black now has to defend the weaknesses at b6 and d6. But Black threatens 26...b5! **26.a4! Kf8; 27.Rd1 Rec8; 28.b3 Ke7.** Black has now secured his queenside, but the kingside is defended only by the queen. Before undertaking action there, White will have to bring his own queen into play and ensure that his rooks can move freely on the f- and g-files. **29.Qf3 Kd7; 30.h4 Kc7; 31.Kf1!** The king crawls out of the way, so that the rooks can do their job. **31...Kb7; 32.Ke2 R8c7; 33.Rh2 Qd8; 34.g4 f6; 35.Rg2 Rc8.**

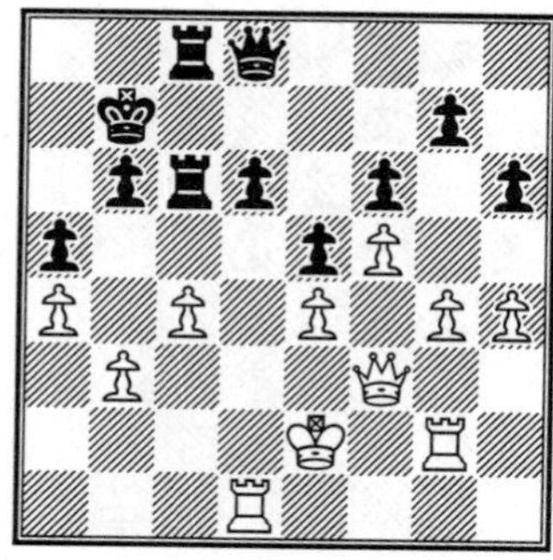

It is easy to see that the only way White can win is by a properly timed g4-g5 but at the same time he must make sure that Black is tied to the defense of d6. **36.Rg3 Qd7; 37.Qd3! Qf7; 38.Rh1 Rh8; 39.Rhh3 Rcc8!** Black now offers the d6-pawn as a sacrifice, since he will receive more than enough compensation if control of the d-file is granted to him. But White correctly keeps the position closed in the center, and breaks on the kingside. **40.g5! hxg5; 41.hxg5 Qc7.** 41...Rxh3; 42.Rxh3 fxg5 would allow White to capture at d6, since the d-file could not be contested.

42.Qd5+ Ka7; 43.Rd3 Rxh3. The sealed move. The alternative was to go into a rook endgame. 43...fxg5; 44.Rxh8 Rxh8; 45.Qxd6 Qxd6; 46.Rxd6 Rh4; 47.Kf3 Rh3+; 48.Kg4 Rxb3; 49.Rd7+ Ka6; 50.Rxg7 and the f-pawn decides. **44.Rxh3 fxg5; 45.Rh7!** The threat of f5-f6 forces Black to adopt a passive defense, and that allows the White king to take an active part in the game. **45...Qe7; 46.Kf3 Rf8; 47.Kg4 Rf7.**

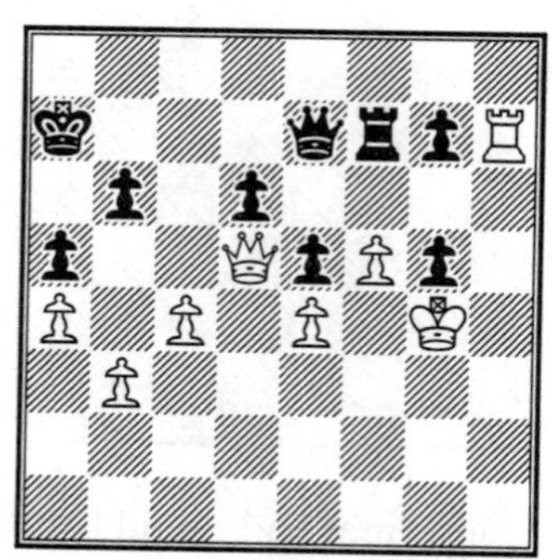

White has achieved a lot, but he must now find a way to exploit his spatial advantage. He needs open lines against the Black king! **48.b4! axb4.** 48...Qc7; 49.bxa5 bxa5; 50.Rh8; 48...Qb7; 49.Qxb7+ Kxb7; 50.b5 Rc7; 51.Kxg5 Rxc4; 52.Rxg7+ Kc8; 53.f6 Rxe4; 54.f7 Rf4; 55.Rg8+ Kd7; 56.f8Q Rxf8; 57.Rxf8 is hopeless for Black. **49.a5!** White relentlessly forces open lines, knowing that the rook on h7 only appears to be out of play. In fact, it can get to the queenside in two moves, via h8 or h1.

49...Qb7; 50.axb6+ Kxb6; 51.Qxd6+ Ka7; 52.Qxe5 b3; 53.Rh3! A fine move, which prevents the advance of the b-pawn because of Ra3+. Now Black cannot afford to exchange queens, as when the b-pawn falls the endgame is a trivial win for White. **53...Rf6; 54.Qd4+ Rb6; 55.Rxb3! White won.**

(221) GELFAND - ZVJAGINTSEV [E34]

Biel, 1995

1.d4 Nf6; 2.c4 e6; 3.Nc3 Bb4; 4.Qc2 d5; 5.cxd5 Qxd5; 6.Nf3 Qf5.

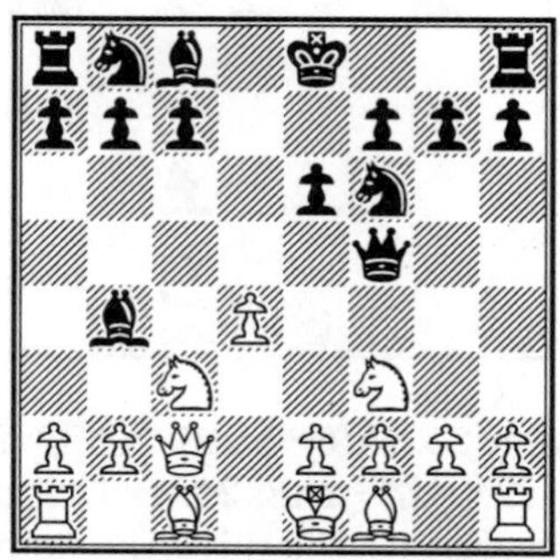

This is Romanishin's plan. The exchange of queens at f5 gives Black a doubled pawn, but this is rarely seen since Black gets a lot of open lines. The variation is highly topical, and new ideas are flowing steadily, as seen in this game. **7.Qd1.** 7.Qb3 has been suggested, but White finds that the queen will have to retreat at some point anyway, for example 7...c5; 8.e3 Nc6; 9.a3 Ba5; 10.Be2 cxd4; 11.exd4 Qd5; 12.Qd1 Qd6; 13.0-0 0-0 and the weakness of the d4-square gave Black the advantage in Kneldsen-Petursson, Valby 1995.

7...c5. This is one of the latest tries. 7...Ne4 is an interesting option. 8.Bd2 Nxd2; 9.Qxd2 c5; 10.a3 cxd4; 11.axb4 dxc3; 12.Qxc3 0-0; 13.e3 Qf6; 14.Qxf6 gxf6; 15.Be2 Na6; 16.b5 Nc7; 17.Rc1 Nd5; 18.Bc4 and White was slightly better in Sherbakov-Lukacs, Budapest 1995. **8.e3.** 8.a3 Bxc3+; 9.bxc3 b6 is solid for Black, e.g., 10.e3 Bb7; 11.Bb5+ Bc6; 12.Bd3 Be4; 13.Bb5+ Bc6; 14.Qa4 Bxb5; 15.Qxb5+ Nbd7; 16.Ne5 a6; 17.Qc6 Qe4; 18.Qxe4 Nxe4; 19.Nxd7 Kxd7 and Black had full equality in Dao Thien-Horvath, Budapest 1995.

8...cxd4; 9.exd4 0-0. 9...Ne4; 10.Bd2 Nxd2; 11.Qxd2 Bd7; 12.Bd3 Qf6; 13.0-0 0-0; 14.Ne5 gives White the advantage, with excellent attacking prospects in a typical isolated d-pawn position. Black is ill-equipped to protect the kingside. **10.Bd3 Qh5.** Perhaps the queen belongs at a5. **11.0-0 Nbd7; 12.Ne2!?** White preserves the knight so that it can go and bother the misplaced White queen. **12...Bd6; 13.Bf4 Bxf4; 14.Nxf4 Qh6.** 14...Qa5; 15.Re1 Rd8; 16.Ne5 Nf8; 17.Qf3 Rxd4; 18.Nh5 gives White a powerful attack. **15.g3!** 15.Qc1 b6; 16.Qc7 Rb8. **15...b6.** Black might try reconfiguring the knights here, using the b6-square. The weakness of the light squares quickly becomes significant. **16.Rc1 Bb7; 17.Rc7 Bxf3?** Black should have forgotten about the pawn at a7 and moved the rook from a8.

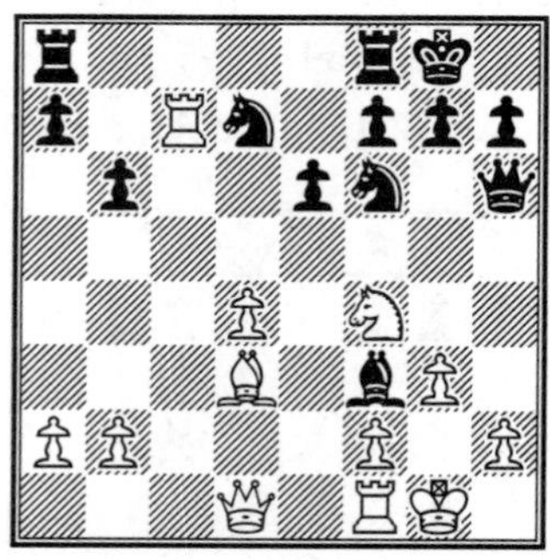

18.Qxf3 e5; 19.Nd5 exd4; 20.Nxf6+ Nxf6. 20...Qxf6?; 21.Qe4 and Black loses the knight at d7. 21...Rfd8; 22.Qxh7+ Kf8; 23.Rxd7 Rxd7; 24.Qh8+ Ke7; 25.Qxa8. **21.Re1.** Capturing at f7 was interesting, but this is the simplest path to a win. **21...Rae8; 22.Rxe8 Rxe8; 23.Rxa7 Qc1+; 24.Kg2 Qxb2; 25.Bc4 Kh8; 26.Ra8! Qb4; 27.Rxe8+ Nxe8; 28.Qa8!** Black resigned, since White will follow-up with Bb5, which at the very least wins the knight at e8. **White won.**

(222) BOGOLJUBOW - NIMZOWITSCH [E37]

Bled, 1931

1.d4 Nf6; 2.c4 e6; 3.Nc3 Bb4; 4.Qc2 d5.

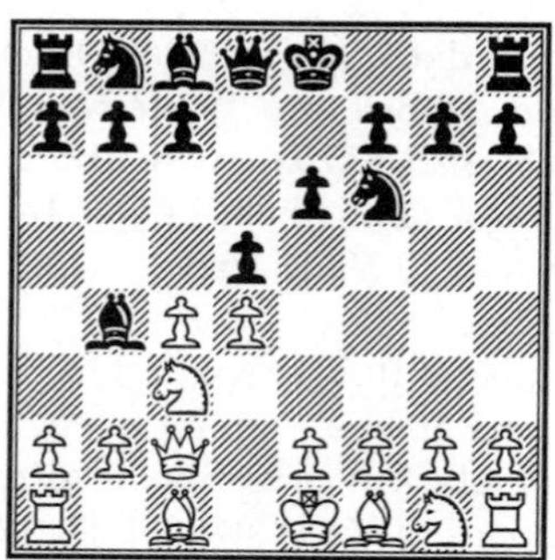

In this system Black immediately confronts White in the center, and sets up a formation which is also reached from the Ragozin Variation of the Queen's Gambit Declined. Black has a grip on the e4 square and will take care of castling a bit later. Ivan Sokolov, one of the leading theoreticians in the Classical Nimzo-Indian, points out in his book on the variation that you only find the variation with 4...d5 in old games, and that there has been a consistent view for several decades which gives the advantage to White. The best plan for White, objectively, is to capture at d5 and then play Bg5, so that we transpose into an Exchange Variation where the bishop at b4 is oddly placed. On the other hand, the lines after 5.a3 are a lot of fun and also pose problems to players on the Black side.

5.a3. 5.cxd5 Qxd5!? (5...exd5; 6.Bg5 h6; 7.Bh4 g5; 7...c5 is a popular alternative. 8.Bg3 Ne4; 9.e3 h5; 10.f3 Bxc3+; 11.bxc3 Nxg3; 12.hxg3 Nd7; 13.Kf2 and White had a flexible position in Bacrot-Smyslov, France (Match) 1996.) 6.Nf3 (6.e3 c5; 7.Bd2 Bxc3; 8.Bxc3 cxd4; 9.Bxd4 Nc6; 10.Bxf6 gxf6; 11.Ne2 Bd7; 12.a3 Qe5; 13.Nc3 f5; 14.0–0–0 0–0–0 allowed Black to equalize in Kasparov-Anand, PCA World Championship 1995.)

5...Bxc3+; 6.Qxc3.

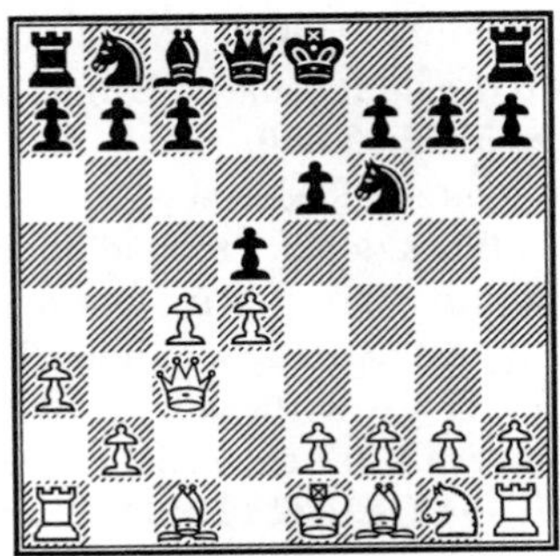

6...Ne4. Black takes over the initiative, but will suffer from the lack of the bishop pair, since White has not had to disrupt the pawn structure. **7.Qc2 c5.** 7...Nc6; 8.e3 e5; 9.cxd5 Qxd5; 10.Bc4 Qa5+; 11.b4 leads to an exciting game after the sacrifice 11...Nxb4!; 12.Qxe4 Nc2+; 13.Ke2 Qe1+; 14.Kf3 Nxa1; 15.Bb2 0–0. Black can slow down now. Eventually the rook at h1 will fall. 16.Kg3 Bd7!? (16...h6; 17.h4 is good for White.) 17.Nf3 Qxh1; 18.Ng5 g6; 19.Qxe5 Rae8; 20.Qf6 Sokolov's analysis ends here, but the players take up the challenge. 20...Rxe3+; 21.fxe3 Qe1+; 22.Kf3 Qd1+; 23.Kg3 Qe1+; 24.Kf3 Qd1+; 25.Kg3 Qe1+; 26.Kf3 and a draw was the result in Sadler-Tukmakov, Linares Open 1995. **8.dxc5 Nc6.**

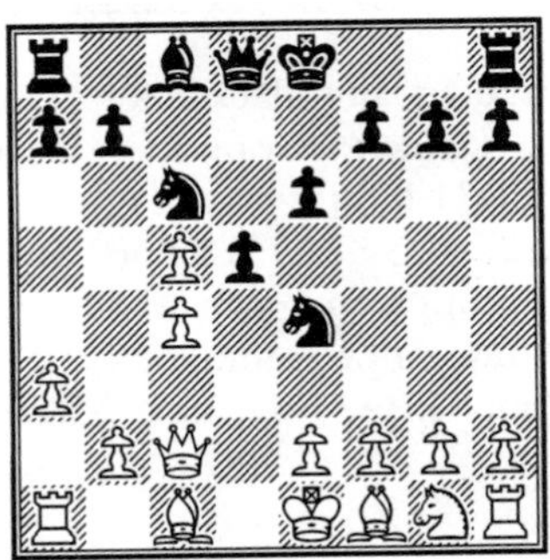

White has a choice of three plans here. Simple development with e3 or Nf3 is available, or White can play more ambitiously by capturing at e5. **9.Nf3.** 9.e3 Qa5+; 10.Bd2 Nxd2; 11.Qxd2 Qxc5; 12.b4 gave White the initiative in M.Gurevich-Portisch, Reggio Emilia 1989. 9.cxd5 exd5 (9...Qxd5 is not playable because of 10.Be3 and then Rd1 will prove most inconvenient.) 10.Nf3 Qa5+; 11.Bd2 Qxc5; 12.Qxc5 Nxc5; 13.Be3 which gave White the advantage in Kasparov-Georgiev, Thessaloniki Olympiad 1988.

It was generally assumed that Kasparov prepared hard for this game, planning to avenge a previous loss to Georgiev, but in fact he was so determined to win that he felt he didn't need to prepare, and when his second delivered his opening preparation the night before the game, Kasparov threw the notes down saying he didn't need anything to beat Georgiev. I happened to be in the room at the time and later asked if he was going to do some work before the game, and Kasparov explained that he was "simply going to smash him". He did!

9...Qa5+; 10.Nd2 Nxd2? Poor judgment. The endgame is certainly going to be worse for Black, so a sharper middlegame plan is needed. 10...Nd4; 11.Qd3 e5; 12.b4 Qa4! keeps pressure on the light squares, Bronstein-Boleslavsky, Saltsjobaden Interzonal 1948. **11.Bxd2 Qxc5; 12.e3 0–0.** 12...dxc4; 13.Qxc4 Qxc4; 14.Bxc4 Bd7; 15.Bc3 was clearly better for White in Reshevsky-Capablanca, AVRO 1938, thanks to the bishop pair. **13.Bd3 dxc4.** Black decides to take the c-pawn in return for the one at h7, but the latter plays an important defensive role. **14.Bxh7+ Kh8; 15.Be4 b5.** Black is reluctant to play ...f5 unless necessary, as it would create further holes on the kingside. **16.0–0 Bb7; 17.Bc3 f5.** Now the advance of the central pawns can be achieved, so this is a good move. **18.Bf3 e5; 19.Rfd1 Qe7; 20.Bxc6!** White wins the exchange here. **20...Bxc6; 21.Bb4 Qg5; 22.f4 exf4; 23.exf4 Qxf4; 24.Bxf8 Rxf8.**

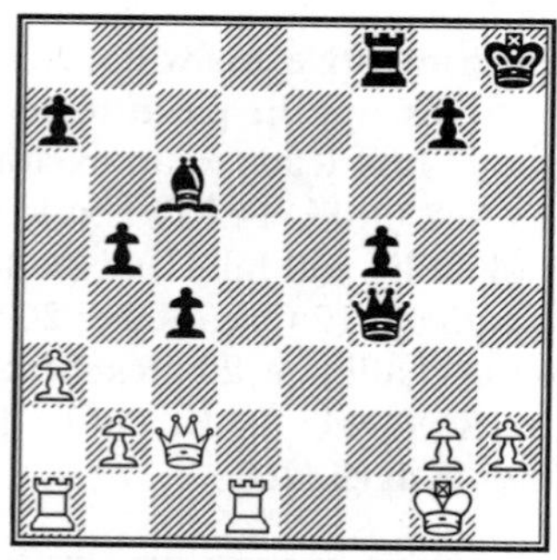

White has a material advantage but Black has good attacking possibilities. White wants to exchange queens, and makes his opponent an offer that cannot be refused. **25.Qf2! Qxf2+.** 25...Qg5; 26.Rd4 Kg8; 27.Rad1 would give White too strong an attack. **26.Kxf2 Rf6; 27.Rd4?** 27.Rd8+ Kh7; 28.Rad1 Rg6; 29.R1d6 would have won easily. Instead, we see a very sloppy endgame which, out of respect for the players, will be presented with a minimum of commentary. **27...Rg6; 28.g3 Be4; 29.Rad1 Bd3; 30.Re1 Be4; 31.Ke3 Rh6; 32.Re2 Bd3; 33.Rf2 Re6+; 34.Kd2 a5; 35.Rd8+ Kh7; 36.Ra8.**

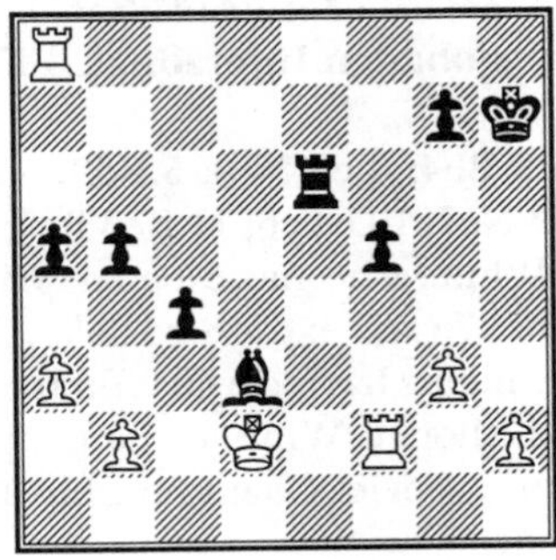

Bogoljubow had been bashing out moves in deep time trouble. The time control for this game was reached at move 36, but this last move was terrible. The simple 36.Rd5 would have won. **36...a4; 37.Rb8 Re5!; 38.Rb6 g6; 39.Kc3 Kh6; 40.Kd4.** 40.Kb4 Rd5; 41.Rxb5?? Rxb5+; 42.Kxb5 c3+! and Black wins!

40...Re4+; 41.Kc3 Re5; 42.Rd2 Re3; 43.Kb4? White should simply have taken the pawn at b5! **43...Kh5; 44.Rd6 Bf1; 45.Rf2 Rb3+; 46.Kc5? Bd3; 47.Rd8 Kg5; 48.Rd2?! c3! 49.bxc3.** 49.R2xd3?? c2; 50.Rxb3 axb3! and despite being rook down, Black wins! **49...Bc4; 50.Kd4 Rxa3; 51.Rd6 Ra1; 52.Kc5 a3.** Here the game was adjourned, and Bogoljubow could devote a day to analysis. But unfortunately it was too late, the position is already lost for White. **53.h4+ Kh5; 54.R2d4 Rf1; 55.Rd8 f4! 56.Ra8 a2; 57.Rxf4 Rxf4; 58.gxf4 Kg4; 59.Kd6 Bb3; 60.Ra3 Kxf4; 61.Ke7 Ke4; 62.Kf6 Kd3; 63.Kxg6 Kxc3; 64.h5 Kb2; 65.Ra8 Ba4.** White resigned. **Black won.**

TAIMANOV VARIATION

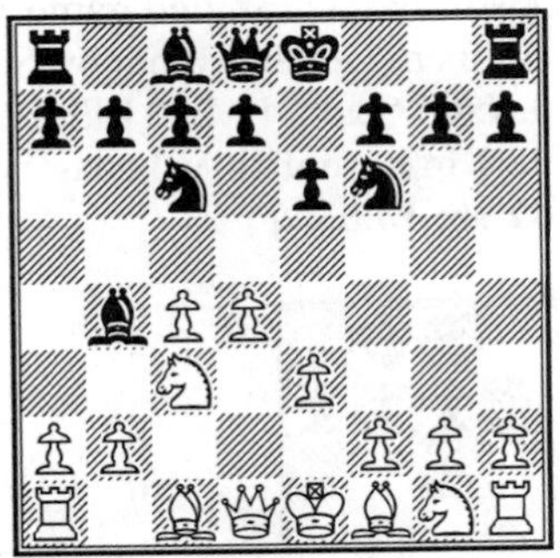

1.d4	**Nf6**
2.c4	**e6**
3.Nc3	**Bb4**
4.e3	**Nc6**

The **Taimanov Variation** has never enjoyed great popularity, but it is an interesting line which has attracted the attention of several strong players. The knight at c6 can support the advance of a pawn to e5, and this is the key idea in the line. Of course it is somewhat risky for Black to lose time with ...e6 followed by ...e5, but Black's rapid development makes up for this, to some extent.

(223) MATANOVIC - TAIMANOV [E40]

Saltsjobaden Interzonal, 1952

1.d4 Nf6; 2.c4 e6; 3.Nc3 Bb4; 4.e3 Nc6; 5.Bd3. 5.Nge2 d5; 6.a3 Be7 (6...Bf8; 7.cxd5 exd5; 8.Nf4 g6; 9.Qb3 Ne7; 10.e4 c6; 11.Be3 Bg7; 12.exd5 0–0; 13.dxc6 bxc6; 14.Bc4 is a little better for White, who has a better grip on the center, Uhlmann-Taimanov, Buenos Aires 1960.) 7.cxd5 exd5; 8.g3 0–0; 9.Bg2 Na5; 10.0–0 c6; 11.Na4 is an odd variation with two knights having a chat on the edge of the chess universe. Black's position is very solid, though White can attempt a minority attack on the queenside, Botvinnik-Taimanov, Soviet Championship 1952. **5...e5!?**

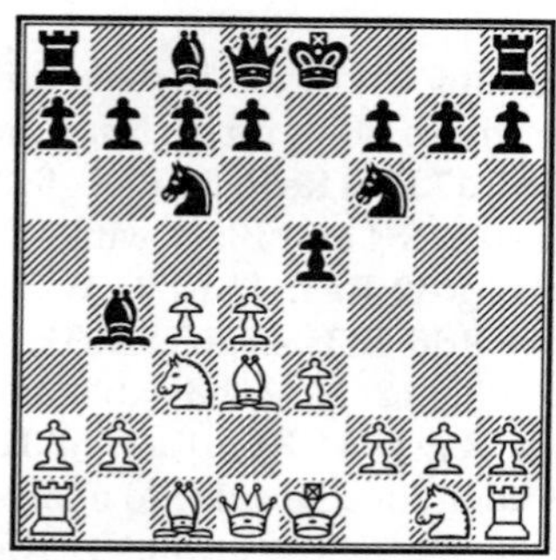

This is the move that gives the Taimanov Variation its own flavor. Instead of attacking d4 from c5, as is usual in the Nimzo-Indian, Black approaches it from the other side. This idea can also be carried out later in the opening, as we will see in game 226. **6.Nge2 exd4; 7.exd4 d5.** Now Black challenges the White center. White's best reply is to advance the c-pawn, because capturing at d5 would leave White with an isolated d-pawn. **8.cxd5.** 8.c5! is correct, for example 8...0–0 9.0–0 Bxc3; 10.bxc3 and now 10...b6?! (10...h6 is better, but Black still has a cramped game.) 11.Bg5 h6; 12.Bh4 bxc5; 13.dxc5 Ne5; 14.Nd4 gave Black fits in Geller-Taimanov. Soviet Championship 1952. **8...Nxd5; 9.0–0 0–0; 10.a3.** 10.Nxd5 Qxd5; 11.Be3 Bf5; 12.Bxf5 Qxf5; 13.Qb3 a5; 14.Rac1 a4 was much better for Black in Levenfish-Mikenas, Soviet Championship 1940. **10...Be7; 11.Qb3 Nf6; 12.Rd1 a6; 13.h3.**

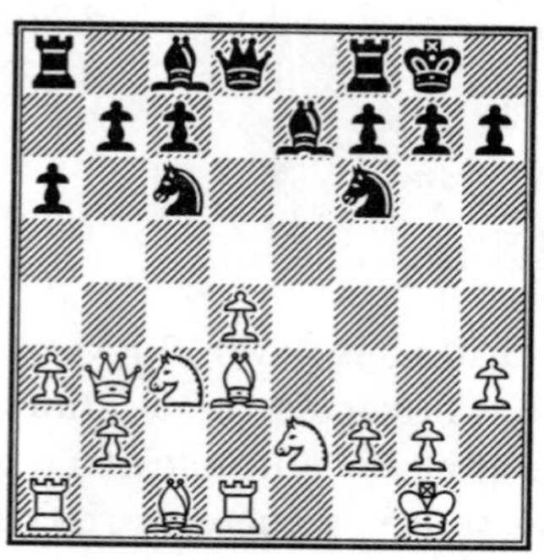

White is restricting the possibilities for the enemy pieces, and controls both the center and greater territory in general. **13...Bd6!** Black realizes that the correct strategy is not the exploitation of the isolated pawn, but rather a kingside attack. White tries to discourage this with a pin, but soon finds out just how serious Black's ambitions are.

14.Bg5 h6; 15.Bh4 g5! 16.d5. 16.Bg3 Bxg3; 17.fxg3 Qe7 leaves White with too many weaknesses. **16...Na5; 17.Qa4.** White will win the knight at a5, but the kingside lacks defenders. **17...Bd7; 18.Qc2.** 18.Qxa5?? loses the queen to 18...b6! **18...gxh4; 19.b4 Qe7!** The queen gets ready to take an active role in the attack on the dark squares. **20.bxa5 Qe5; 21.Kf1 Rae8.** The point behind this mobilizing move is that the queen is now free to invade, but the White king will not easily flee across the e-file. **22.Ng1 Qh2; 23.Bf5 Kh8; 24.Bxd7.**

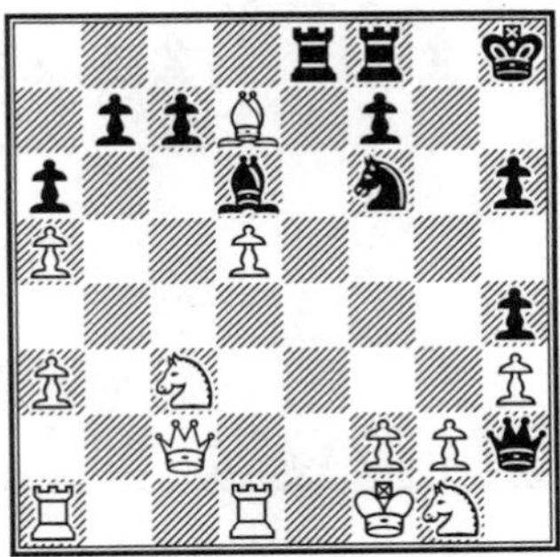

Black continues the attack without bothering about material. **24...Rg8!!; 25.Bg4 Nxg4; 26.Re1.** 26.hxg4 Rxg4; 27.f3 Bc5 and White cannot defend against the various mating threats. **26...Nf6; 27.Rxe8 Qxg2+!; 28.Ke2 Rxe8+; 29.Kd3 Qg6+ 30.Kd2.** 30.Kd4 Qxc2 and White can resign. **30...Bf4+; 31.Kd1 Qxg1#. Black won.**

HUEBNER VARIATION

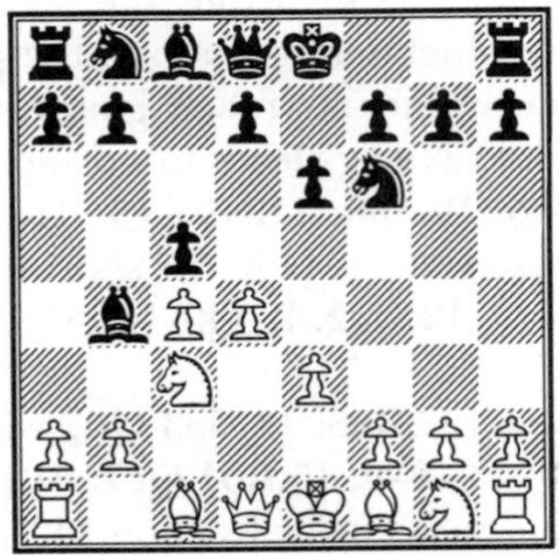

1.d4	**Nf6**
2.c4	**e6**
3.Nc3	**Bb4**
4.e3	**c5**

This is Robert Huebner's favorite line in this Nimzo-Indian, though Nimzowitsch himself also used it. The idea is to place pressure on the d4-square. Black can later advance the e-pawn to e5, and add a knight at c6 to the mix. Another common theme is the capture at c3 followed by ...d6 as a prelude to ...e5. With the center closed, the knights can maneuver on the flanks.

(224) NAJDORF - HUEBNER [E41]

Wijk aan Zee, 1971

1.d4 Nf6; 2.c4 e6; 3.Nc3 Bb4; 4.e3 c5; 5.Bd3 Nc6. Black can of course capture at c3 at just about any point. **6.Nf3.** 6.Nge2 Bxc3+; 7.bxc3 d6; 8.0–0 e5; 9.e4 is also possible, for example 9...0–0; 10.f3 b6; 11.d5 Ne7; 12.Ng3 where White enjoyed a considerable advantage in space in Christiansen-Anastasian, Yerevan Olympiad 1996. **6...Bxc3+; 7.bxc3 d6.**

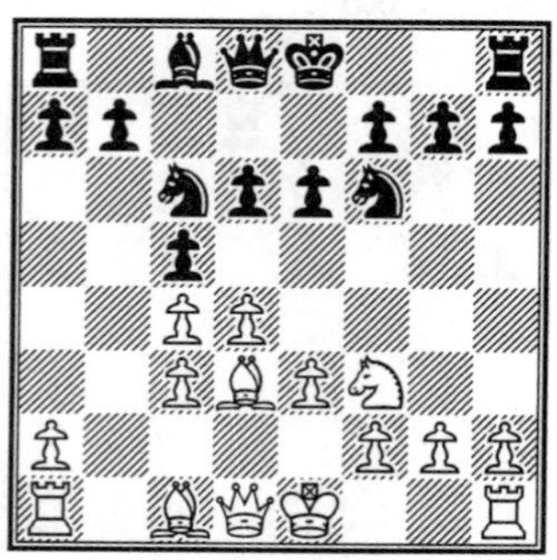

In this line, Black aims to keep the center closed with d6 and a timely e5 to restrict the power of the White bishops. White's doubled c-pawns can quickly become targets. **8.e4.** This is the logical reply, since Black has refrained from d7-d5. This gives Black the opportunity to create a totally blocked center, and that will favor the knights. That is why 8.0–0 is a more common move. **8...e5; 9.d5 Ne7!** Black prepares for a possible battle over the f4 and f5 squares. When the center is absolutely closed, it usually gives the advantage to the player who can push his f-pawn first to challenge the center. In the long run, the knight will likely return to the queenside (a5) to attack the weak c4-pawn.

10.g3?! Najdorf is in an experimental mood as he avoids the normal 10.Nh4 which leads to a complicated position. After Huebner's response, the game transposes into regular terrain though. 10.h3 is yet another approach, guarding g4 so that a bishop can settle in at e3. 10...h6; 11.Be3 b6; 12.Nd2 g5 leads to a complex struggle, as in Yusupov-Lalic, Yerevan Olympiad 1996. **10...h6; 11.Nh4 g5.** This aggressive move is the best continuation for Black and prevents f2-f4 in the short term. Black's king will likely find a safe haven on c7 if needed. **12.Ng2.** 12.Qf3 Nfg8!; 13.Nf5 Nxf5; 14.exf5 Nf6 would be very comfortable for Black.

12...Qa5. A decade later Huebner played 12...Bh3; 13.Ne3 Qd7 with an equal position against Timman. **13.Qb3 Bh3; 14.0–0 0–0–0; 15.Rb1 Qc7.** Black has nothing to fear on the b-file, as the best White can do is to play Rf2 and Rf2-b2. But with Kb8 and Bc8; Black will have an impenetrable fortress. **16.f3 Kb8; 17.Rf2.** 17.g4 h5 is bad for White. **17...Rhg8; 18.Ne3 Bc8.**

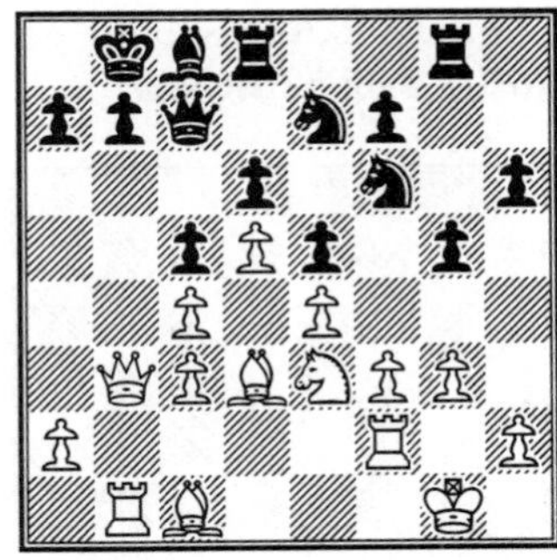

White has no attractive plans while Black will prepare to open a file on the kingside. Thus, he opts for a walk to a safer place in the center. **19.Kf1.** Black needs to carve a path into the White position. The best candidate for this is the f-file, which can be opened with f7-f5. White can prevent this, but that will only create opportunities on the e-file and h-file. **19...Rdf8!; 20.Ke1 Ne8; 21.Nf5** Else Black will take over the initiative with ...f7-f5. **21...Nxf5; 22.exf5.** White's pawn structure has further deteriorated. Black's focus now is to force White to play g4, and then open the h-file with ...h5. **22...f6; 23.g4 Rh8!; 24.Be3 h5; 25.Bf1 Rf7!** A multi-purpose move that allows Black to double rooks whenever he wants to. **26.h3 Qd7; 27.Kd2 Nc7; 28.a4?!** White was tired of waiting around doing nothing, but this move simply creates a weakness which will prove embarrassing later. **28...Re7; 29.Re1.**

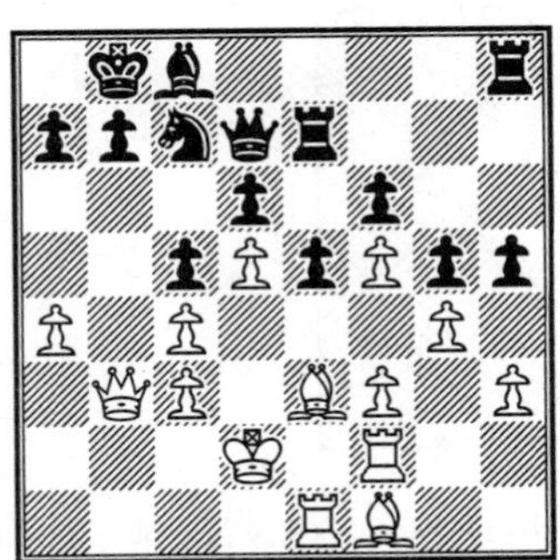

Now Black, recognizing the weakness at a4, comes up with a wonderful winning strategy. He will attack the pawn, lure it forward and exchange it for the Pb7. **29...Na8!** Provoking the a-pawn to advance. Huebner exploits the theme that an isolated pawn become weaker the further it advances. **30.a5 Qd8!; 31.Qa3 Rhh7.** Black is shifting all of his forces over to the queenside where he will open a file in spite of his king's position! **32.Rb1 b6!; 33.Bd3 Rb7; 34.axb6.** 34.a6 Rbd7 and Na8-c7 will pick up the pawn. **34...Nxb6; 35.Ra1 Qh8!** Black aims to exchange major pieces on the kingside while pushing his passed a-pawn only in the advanced state of an endgame. **36.Kc2 hxg4; 37.hxg4 Bd7; 38.Qa2 Rh2; 39.Kd2 Rxf2+; 40.Bxf2 Qh2; 41.Ke2 Na4; 42.Qd2.** Soon Queens will be exchanged after which Black will easily exploit his structural advantages.

42...Be8; 43.Rb1 Rxb1; 44.Bxb1 Qf4!; 45.Bd3 Qxd2+; 46.Kxd2 Nb6; 47.Kc1 Ba4; 48.Bc2 Bd7! Black for now avoids simplifications that would render White survival chances, e.g. 48...Bxc2; 49.Kxc2 Nxc4; 50.Kd3 Nb6; 51.c4 a5; 52.Be1 a4; 53.Ba5 a3; 54.Bc3 Ka7; 55.Ba1 Ka6; 56.Kc3 Ka5; 57.Kb3 Ka6; 58.Bc3 which draws! **49.Bd3 Kc7; 50.Kb2 Bc8; 51.Kb3 Ba6; 52.Be3.**

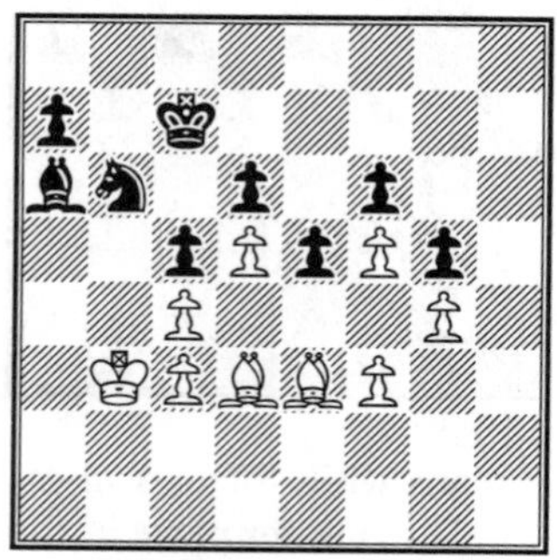

52.Kb2 Nxc4+; 53.Kb3 Nd2+; 54.Kc2 Bxd3+; 55.Kxd2 Bc4; 56.Ke3 Bxd5; 57.Be1 Kb6 and Black wins easily. **52...Nxd5! Black won.**

ST. PETERSBURG VARIATION

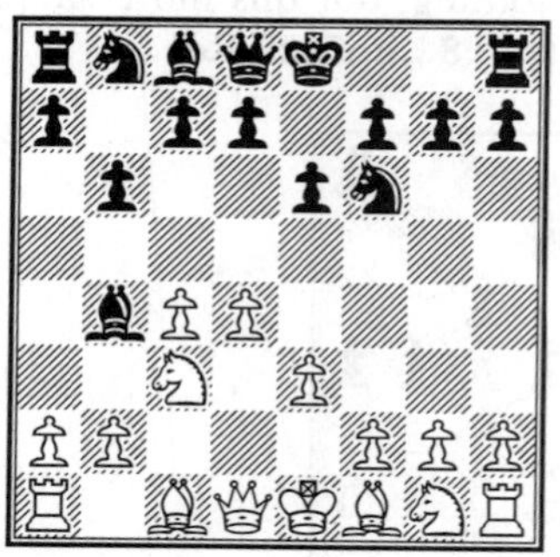

1.d4	**Nf6**
2.c4	**e6**
3.Nc3	**Bb4**
4.e3	**b6**

This line combines ideas from the Nimzo-Indian (...Bb4) and Queen's Indian (...b6). In the normal Queen's Indian with 1.d4 Nf6; 2.c4 e6; 3.Nf3 b6, we often see an early ...Bb4. Usually in the Nimzo-Indian the queenside fianchetto is delayed, or not played at all. In this line, however, the idea is not to place the bishop on b7, but to position it on a6, with pressure at c4, although in some cases the knight uses the a6 square and the bishop goes to b7. The variation got its name from the great St. Petersburg tournament of 1914, where both Nimzowitsch and Alekhine played it as Black.

(225) PORTISCH - FISCHER [E45]

Santa Monica 2nd Piatigorsky Cup, 1966

1.d4 Nf6; 2.c4 e6; 3.Nc3 Bb4; 4.e3 b6.

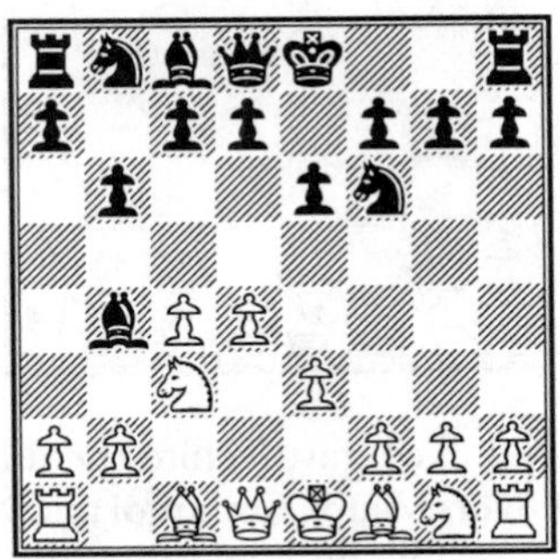

5.Nge2. The knight is not placed here to defend its colleague at c3. It is destined for g3, where it can operate on the kingside. 5.Bd3 Bb7; 6.Nge2 is the Pawn Sacrifice line in the Rubinstein Variation. White gives up a pawn at g2 in return for time, space and an open g-file. 6...Bxg2; 7.Rg1 Be4!, tempting White to capture the pawn at g7 because ...Bg6 will entomb the rook, is the most active plan for Black. 8.a3 Bxc3+; 9.Nxc3 Bg6; 10.e4 gives White compensation for the pawn. A recent attempt to disrupt the White center with 10...d5; 11.Bg5! dxe4 saw White obtain the better game after 12.Bxe4 in Rotstein-Lepelletier, France 1995.

5...Ba6. An alternative is 5...Ne4, for example 6.f3 (6.Bd2 and 6.Qc2 are also seen. 6...Nxc3; 7.bxc3 Be7 is a common continuation.

A) 8.Ng3 h5; 9.Bd3 h4; 10.Ne4 Nc6; 11.0-0 Ba6; 12.f4 Na5; 13.f5 exf5; 14.Rxf5 g6; 15.Rf2 0-0; 16.Nd2 d5; 17.Qe2 Nxc4; 18.Nxc4 Bxc4; 19.Bxc4 dxc4; 20.Qxc4 c5; 21.e4 cxd4; 22.cxd4 Bg5 was seen in Ashley-Adams, New York (CITS) 1996;

B) 8.e4 Nc6; 9.Ng3 Ba6; 10.Bd3 Na5; 11.Qe2 d6; 12.f4 Qd7; 13.f5 Bh4; 14.Bf4 0-0-0; 15.0-0 e5; 16.Be3 Bxg3 worked out well for Black in Sarfati-Johansen, Melbourne Masters 1995, which Black eventually won.

6.Ng3. 6.a3 is considered slightly more effective, but this move has always been popular, too.

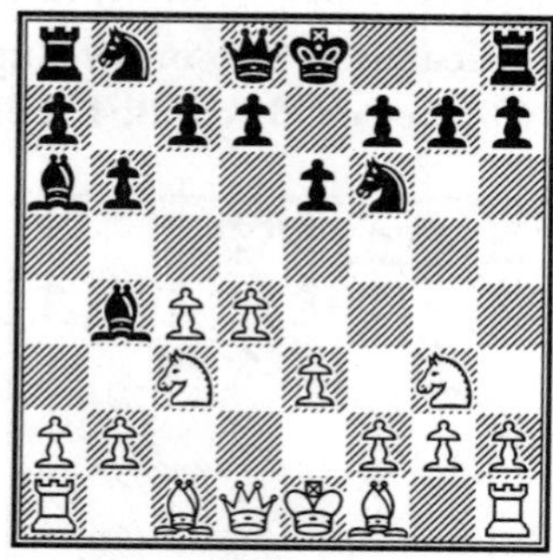

6...Bxc3+. 6...c5; 7.d5 0–0; 8.e4 gave White the advantage in a clash between World Championship challengers Viktor Korchnoi and Nigel Short, at Madrid 1995. **7.bxc3 d5.** A typical expression of the Hypermodern strategy. Even at this early stage White is forced onto the defensive. **8.Qf3.** Portisch noted the irony that found him on the White side of one of his favorite openings as Black. 8.cxd5 Bxf1; 9.Kxf1 Qxd5 was better for Black in Gligoric-Portisch, Torremolinos 1961. **8...0–0.**

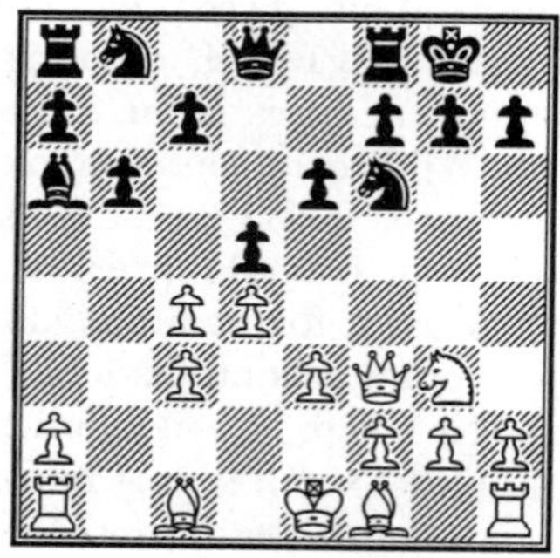

Now capturing at d5 is recommended, but thirty years ago the advance to e4 also looked promising. **9.e4.** 9.cxd5 Qxd5; 10.e4 Qa5; 11.Bxa6 Qxa6; 12.Ne2 (so that White can castle) led to an endgame with a very small advantage for White in Keene-Pritchett, London 1980. 12...Nbd7; 13.0–0 c5 gives Black sufficient counterplay. **9...dxe4; 10.Nxe4 Nxe4; 11.Qxe4.**

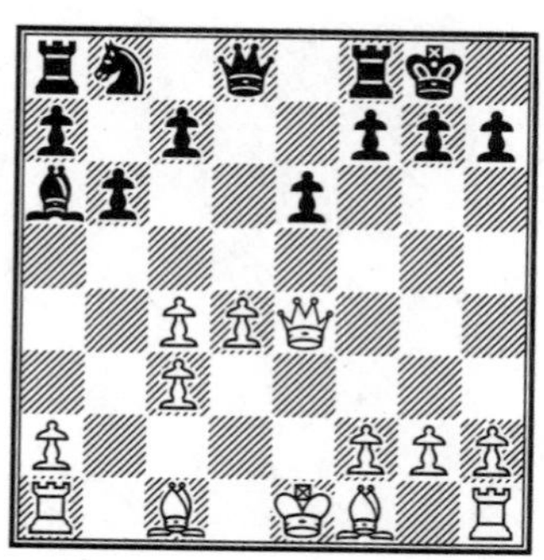

Now Fischer introduced a sacrificial plan, giving up both rooks for the White queen. Portisch admitted that it had come as a surprise-a very unpleasant one. **11...Qd7!**

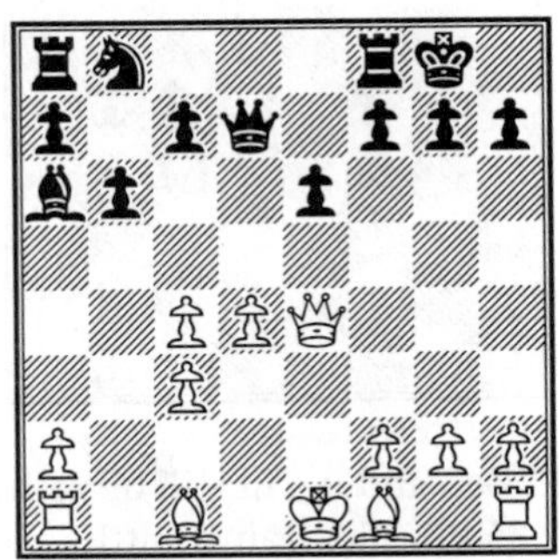

Black is going to develop his knight at c6 and put a lot of pressure on the central pawns. 11...Nd7; 12.Bd3 Nf6; 13.Qh4 gives White good attacking chances. **12.Ba3.** Portisch couldn't get the development of the other bishop to work: 12.Bd3 f5; 13.Qe2 Nc6; 14.0-0 Rae8 and the pawn at c4 is going to become a target. So Portisch decides to give up the queen for two rooks, usually about an even trade. 12.Qxa8?! Nc6; 13.Qxf8+ Kxf8 is better for Black, who will continue with the normal strategy of pressuring c4 with Na5. **12...Re8; 13.Bd3 f5.**

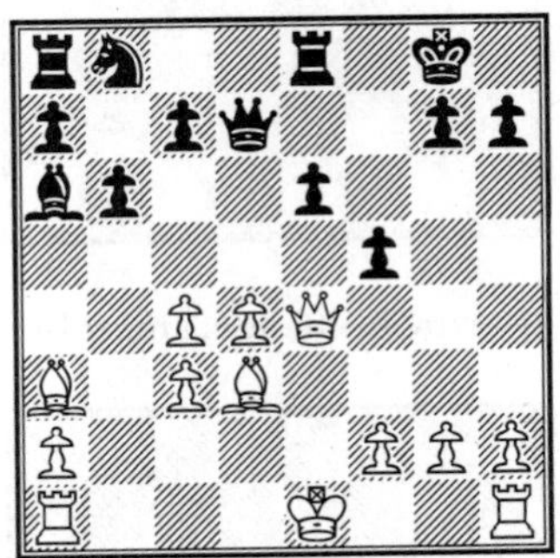

14.Qxa8. 14.Qe2 Nc6 gives Black a slight advantage, since the pressure is building on the center, but would not lead to the rapid disintegration of White's position seen in the game. **14...Nc6; 15.Qxe8+ Qxe8.** White has the bishop pair, but the pawn at c4 is weak and the king has not yet found a safe home. **16.0-0 Na5; 17.Rfe1 Bxc4; 18.Bxc4 Nxc4; 19.Bc1.** The knight completely dominates the bishop, and the rooks are uncoordinated. Black has a huge advantage. **19...c5; 20.dxc5 bxc5; 21.Bf4 h6; 22.Re2 g5.**

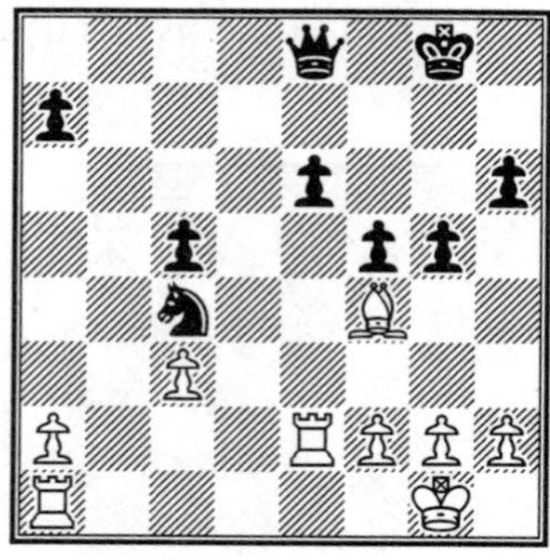

Now White must play 23.Be3 and it will still be rather difficult to win for Black. **23.Be5? Qd8!; 24.Rae1 Kf7; 25.h3.** This gains a little space for the bishop or king, as needed. But Fischer's next play shuts down all counterplay. **25...f4!; 26.Kh2 a6.** White is running out of moves. **27.Re4 Qd5; 28.h4.**

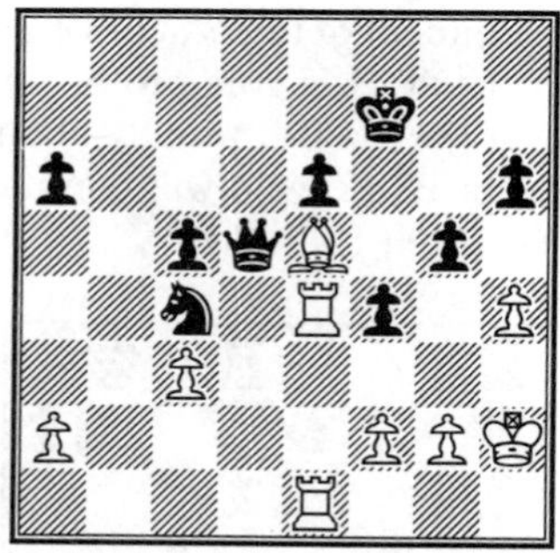

Now Black forces the win of the exchange, and subsequently the game. **28...Ne3!.**

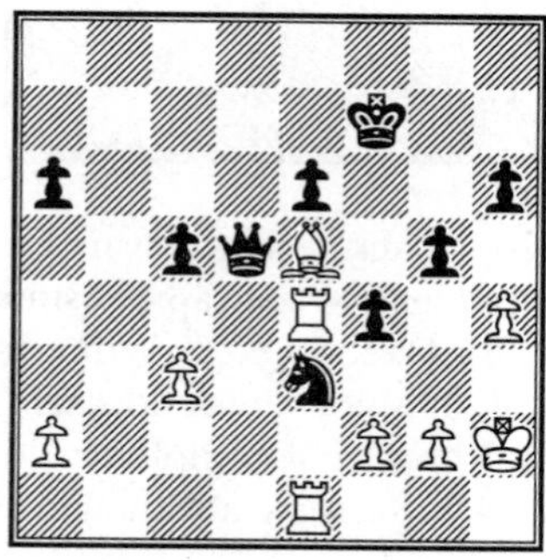

This wins more material, and leads to victory after a few more moves. **29.R1xe3 fxe3; 30.Rxe3 Qxa2; 31.Rf3+ Ke8; 32.Bg7 Qc4; 33.hxg5 hxg5; 34.Rf8+ Kd7; 35.Ra8 Kc6. Black won.**

RAGOZIN VARIATION

1.d4	**Nf6**
2.c4	**e6**
3.Nc3	**Bb4**
4.e3	**Nc6**

This approach usually transposes to the Ragozin Defense of the Queen's Gambit Declined. The knight sits somewhat unnaturally at c6, where it blocks the c-pawn. Nevertheless, the play can become quite dynamic and that has appealed to such fighting players as Tal and Fischer.

(226) GLIGORIC - FISCHER [E51]

Leipzig Olympiad, 1960

1.d4 Nf6; 2.c4 e6; 3.Nc3 Bb4; 4.e3 Nc6; 5.Nf3 0–0; 6.Bd3 d5; 7.0–0 dxc4.

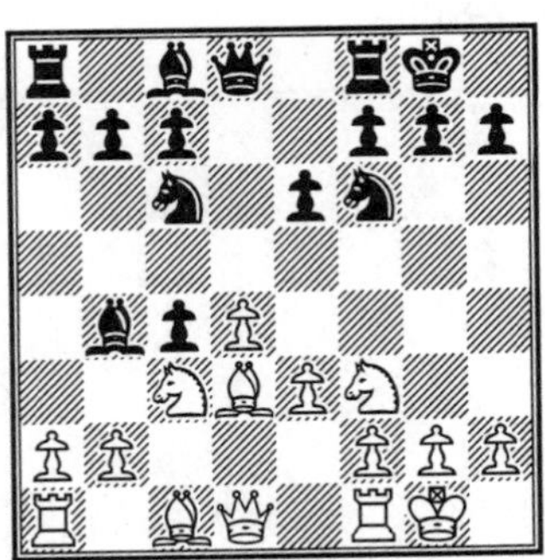

Black gives up the center, but can aim for an early ...e5, in the spirit of the Taimanov Variation. **8.Bxc4 Bd6.** 8...a6! is now considered best. This helps to protect the knight at c6, which is crucial to carrying out Taimanov's central break ...e5. 9.h3 h6; 10.Re1 Bd6; 11.e4 e5; 12.Be3 Bd7; 13.a3 and White has a more comfortable game, as White constantly threatens to expand in the center. 13...exd4; 14.Bxd4! Nxd4; 15.Qxd4 b5; 16.Ba2 left Black constantly worrying about the threat of e5 in Gligoric-Kovacevic, Pula 1981. 8...b6; 9.Qa4 Bxc3; 10.bxc3 Na5; 11.Ba3 Bd7! brought Black equality in Xu-Xie, Bejing 1997.

9.Nb5. 9.Bb5 is a logical alternative, threatening to disrupt Black's queenside pawn structure. 9...Qe7 (9...e5; 10.Bxc6 exd4; 11.exd4 bxc6; 12.Bg5 and White was eventually able to exploit the pawn weakness in Portisch-Andersson, Prague Zonal

Playoff 1970.) 10.Bxc6 bxc6; 11.e4 e5; 12.dxe5 Bxe5; 13.Nxe5 Qxe5; 14.Qf3 and again Black had no compensation for the weak pawns in Petrosian-Nei, Tallinn 1983. **9...Be7; 10.h3 a6; 11.Nc3.**

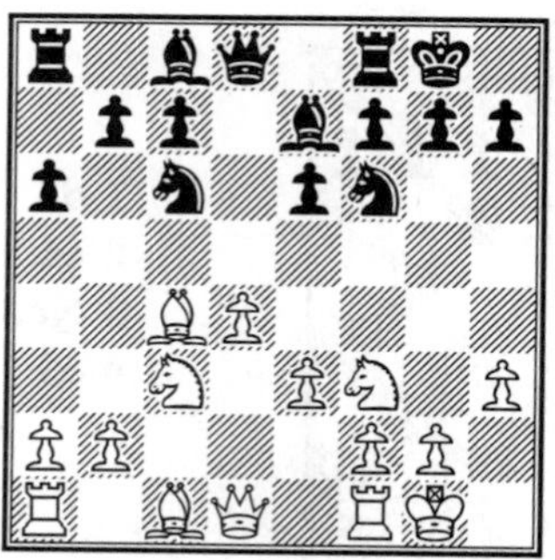

11...b5! This was an improvement on a previous game of Fischer's: 11...Bd6; 12.e4 e5; 13.Be3 kept strong pressure on the center in Taimanov-Fischer, Buenos Aires 1960. **12.Bd3 Bb7; 13.Qe2 Bd6; 14.Rd1 Qe7; 15.Bb1.** This retreat enables White to set up a bishop and queen battery later on, and also keeps the bishop from being hassled by ...Nb4. **15...e5; 16.d5!** This advance is justified by attacking possibilities which arise on the kingside as Black is preoccupied in the center. **16...Nd8; 17.Ng5 h6; 18.Nge4 Nxe4; 19.Nxe4 f5.** This changes the nature of the position, as a weakness is created at e6 and White has the advantage of the bishop pair, not a commonplace event in the Nimzoindian! **20.Nxd6 cxd6; 21.a4 bxa4; 22.Rxa4 Rf6; 23.Rc4 e4!** Black opens up the e5 square for use by the knight, which can arrive via a stopover on f7. **24.b4 Nf7; 25.Bb2.**

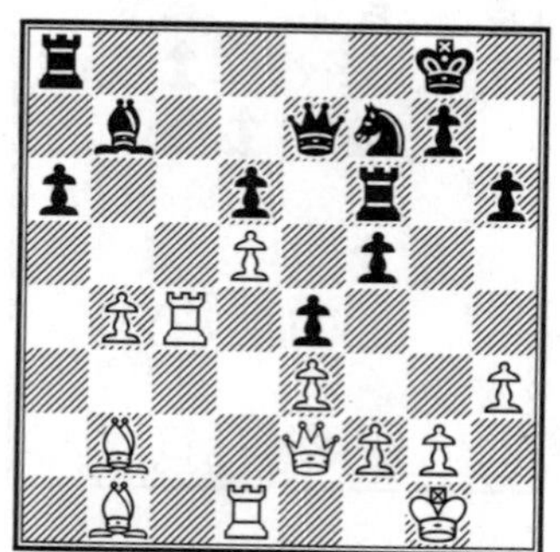

This is a critical position. Fischer now for some reason fails to follow through on his chosen strategy. He should swing the knight to e5, but instead embarks on an attack which is not justified by the position. **25...Rg6? 26.f3!** Some sources give this move as f4, but Gligoric's book on the Nimzo-Indian gives the text. It is an important difference, since here the pawn at e4 is threatened, so Black must capture. **26...exf3; 27.Qxf3** Now the pawn at f5 falls. **27...Rf8; 28.Bxf5 Ng5; 29.Qh5!** This is a most unusual manner of winning the exchange, with the queen playing a major role. **29...Rxf5; 30.Qxg6 Nxh3+.** Hoping that White will capture, losing the queen to ...Rg5+. **31.Kh2 Rg5; 32.Re4! Qf8.** 32...Rxg6; 33.Rxe7 and Black loses the bishop or the knight. **33.Qe8** Black resigned, since the knight is trapped. **White won.**

PANOV ATTACK

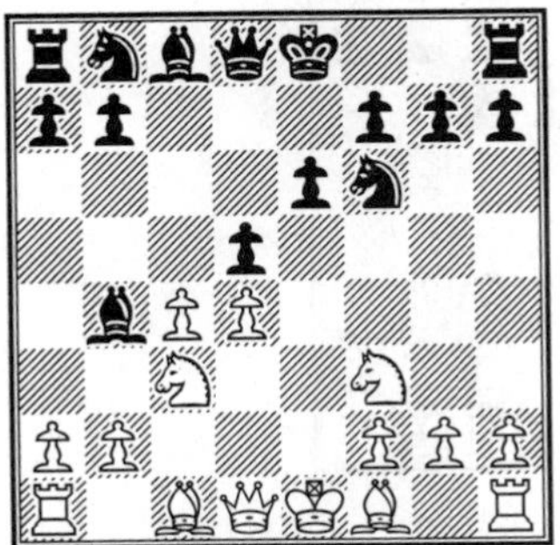

1.d4	**Nf6**
2.c4	**e6**
3.Nc3	**Bb4**
4.e3	**c5**
5.Nf3	**cxd4**
6.exd4	**d5**

In this system White gets an isolated d-pawn after ...dxc4, or after White captures on d5 and Black recaptures with a knight. In return for this, White achieves an advantage in space and good attacking chances on the kingside. Black must simultaneously guard the king and attack the pawn at d4. This can be achieved by repositioning pieces, for example by placing a bishop at f6. A knight on d5 blockades the isolated pawn.

The variety of attacking formations is great, and the following game is just a taste of the exciting play that can develop.

(227) ALEKHINE - BARATZ [E54]
Paris, 1933

1.e4 c6; 2.d4 d5; 3.exd5 cxd5; 4.c4. This is the famous Panov Attack of the Caro-Kann Defense. In the present game we will examine the strategy where Black steers the game into the deep waters of the Nimzo-Indian. **4...e6.** 4...Nf6 is considered slightly more accurate. **5.Nc3 Nf6; 6.Nf3 Bb4; 7.Bd3 dxc4.** Now that the White bishop has moved, this capture is appropriate. **8.Bxc4 0–0; 9.0–0.** 9.a3 Bxc3+; 10.bxc3 is also commonly seen.

9...b6. This is one of the most common formations for Black. The crucial element is the isolated d-pawn at d4. It is a little weak, but controls important squares. Black can try to blockade it with a knight, but that strategy is not as effective here as in the lines with ...Be7 (instead of ...Bb4) because in those lines the bishop can redeploy at f6, with effective pressure at d4. For that reason one often finds the bishop retreating to e7, usually in reaction to a White advance of the a-pawn to a3. **10.Bg5 Bb7; 11.Rc1 Nc6**. The alternative is 9...a6 followed by ...b5, as in Sadler-Emms, British Championship playoff 1997. **12.Qd3.**

White can also insert 12.a3 Be7 before playing the queen to d3. This was seen in Ibragimov-Supatapshuili, Russian Cup 1997.

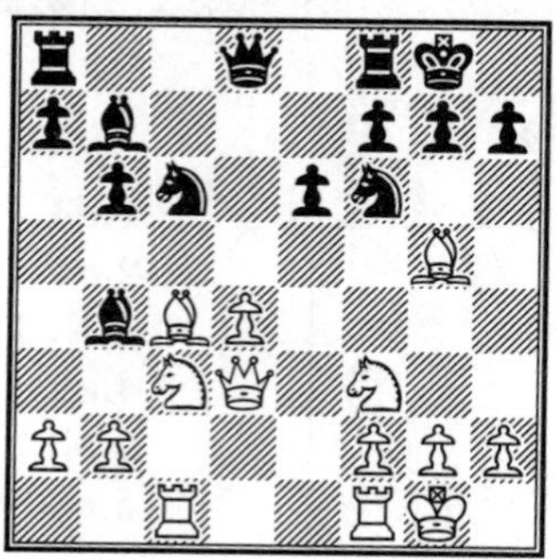

This is one method of setting up the battery of queen and bishop on the b1–h7 diagonal. The bishop will retreat to c2 via b3. Alternatively White can place the queen at b1, and let the bishop head the battery from d3. 12.d5? Na5; 13.Ne4 Be7! and the pressure at d5 gives Black a much better game. **12...Be7; 13.a3 Nd5.** The blockade is in place. Not a novelty, as claimed by Ivanchuk in *Informant*. As we have seen, it was played against Alekhine over a half century ago! 13...Rc8!? is Keene's preference. 14.Ba2 Nd5; 15.Bb1 g6; 16.h4!? is Ivanchuk's response. 13...h6 just forces the bishop back with 14.Be3 where it sits on a good square. **14.Bxd5 Bxg5.** Karpov prefers to capture with the pawn here. 14...exd5; 15.Bxe7 Nxe7.

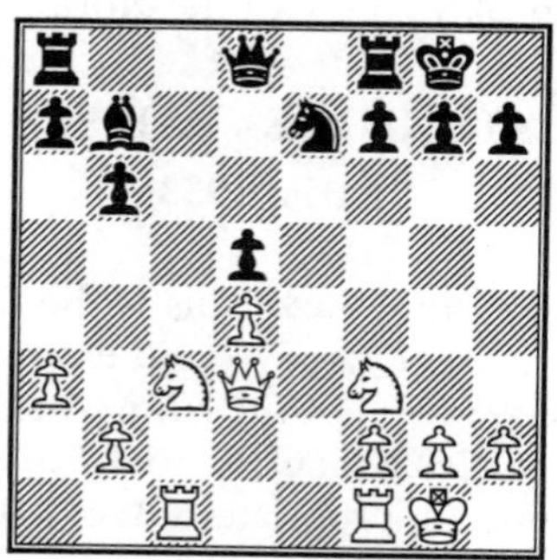

Black's bishop is pretty useless and there is no doubt that White has a much more comfortable game. 16.Rfe1 Rc8; 17.h4! An important advance. The h-pawn will sit at h5 and keep the Black King hemmed in. 17...h6; 18.h5 Rc7 a clever move by Karpov, who can now swing the Knight to d6 via c8. 19.Nb5?! (19.Ne5 might have been a strong preliminary move.) 19...Rxc1; 20.Rxc1 Ba6; 21.a4 Bxb5? A crucial strategic error. Analysis by Ivanchuk shows that Black was still in the game: (21...Qb8! 22.Ne5 Rc8; 23.Re1 Bxb5!; 24.axb5 Qd6; 25.Qf3 Qf6! 26.Qxf6 gxf6; 27.Ng4 Nf5; 28.Nxf6+ Kg7; 29.Nxd5 Nxd4) 22.Qxb5! (22.axb5 is met by 22...Qd6! and Black can swing the rook to c8 with full equality.) 22...Nf5; 23.g3! Ne7; 24.Ne5 and White had a small advantage in Ivanchuk-Karpov, Linares 1991, thanks to the better-posted pieces and control of the c-file, especially c6. **15.Nxg5 Qxg5; 16.Be4.**

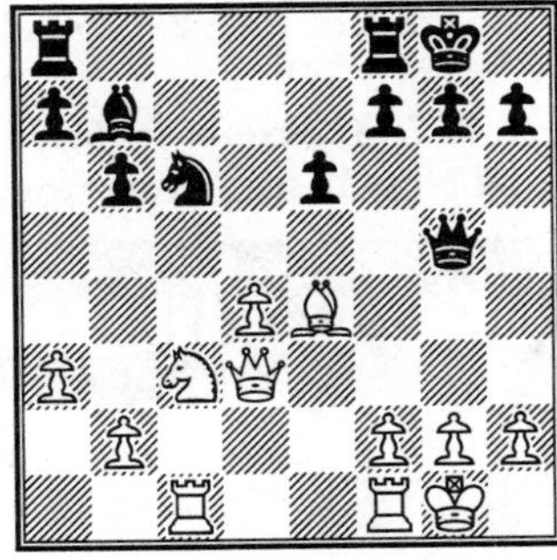

White has more control of the center and pressure on both light-squared long diagonals, with particular concentration at c6. **16...g6.** 16...Rfd8!; 17.f4 Qf6; 18.d5 gives White a strong initiative. **17.Qb5! Qxb5; 18.Nxb5 Na5.** There wasn't much choice, though this leads to an inferior position. 18...Rac8 would have been met by 19.Nd6 and White should win. **19.Bxb7 Nxb7; 20.Rc7.** We have a classic example of the devastating power of an invasion of the 7th rank. **20...Rfb8.** 20...Na5; 21.Nxa7 Nc4; 22.Rxc4 Rxa7; 23.Rb4 is clearly better for White, who has an extra pawn. **21.Re1!** Alekhine cleverly prepares to open up the e-file and bring a second rook to the 7th rank. The prosaic 21.Rc1 would have been less effective. **21...a6; 22.Nc3 Nd6; 23.d5!**

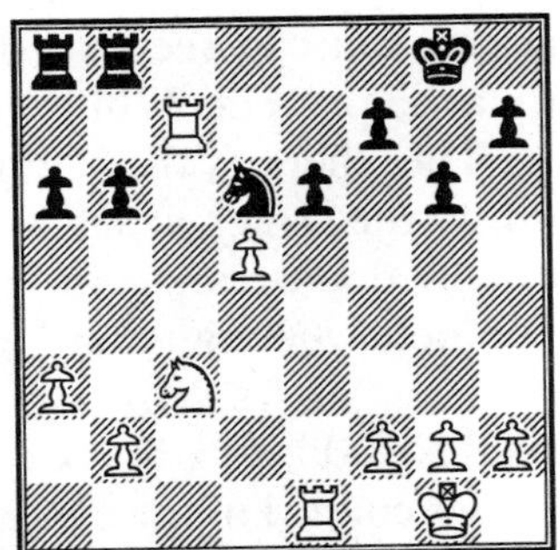

An important advance. Even though this seems to lead to simplification, the passive positions of the Black rooks gives White a big advantage. **23...Ne8; 24.Rc6 exd5; 25.Nxd5.**

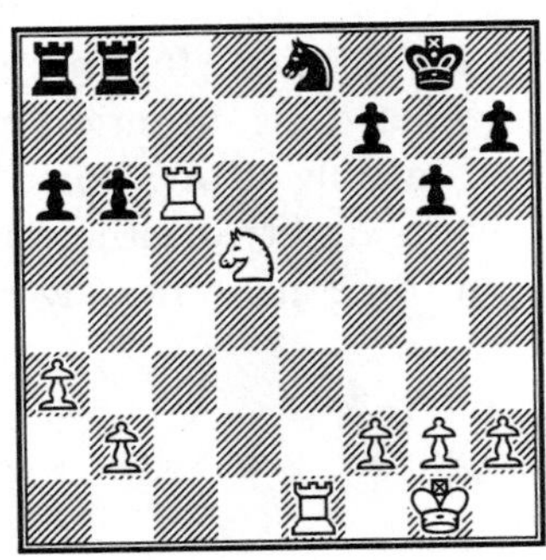

Now White wins material by force. **25...b5; 26.Nb6 Rxb6.** 26...Ra7; 27.Nc8! is a cute win for White. **27.Rxb6 Kf8; 28.Rc1 Ra7; 29.Rb8.** Black could have, and should have resigned here, especially since White was the reigning World Champion! **29...Re7; 30.Kf1 Re6; 31.Re1 Ke7; 32.Rxe6+ fxe6; 33.Rb7+ Kd6; 34.Rxh7 Kd5; 35.Rh6 Nd6; 36.Rxg6 a5; 37.h4 Nf5; 38.h5. White won.**

GRUENFELD DEFENSE

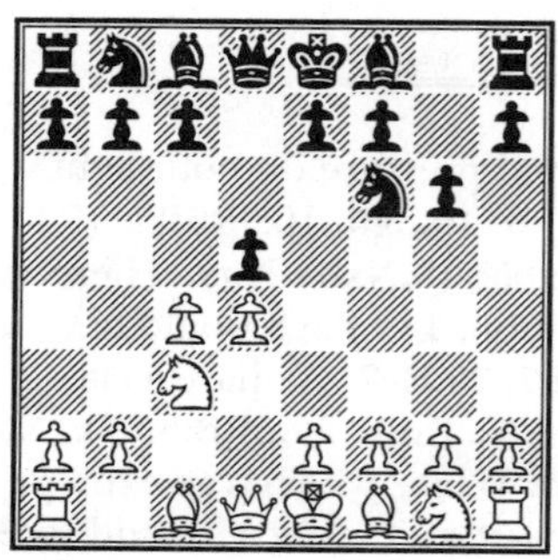

1.d4 Nf6
2.c4 g6
3.Nc3 d5

This seems a lot like the King's Indian. But if you compare the diagram above with the King's Indian, you can see that there is a very important difference. The Black pawn at d5 prevents White from establishing the ideal pawn center by playing e4. This changes the nature of the struggle, which will much more directly involve the center, which is often closed in the King's Indian. White can, and usually does, manage to get the ideal pawn center but must do so in an environment where it is hard to defend. Two main lines illustrate this.

After 1.d4 Nf6; 2.c4 g6; 3.Nc3 d5; 4.cxd5 Nxd5; 5.e4 Nxc3; 6.bxc3 (The Exchange Variation) White has control of the center, but Black will use ...c5, ...Bg7, and even ...Qa5 and ...Rd8 to undermine White's control.

In the Russian Variation (1.d4 Nf6; 2.c4 g6; 3.Nc3 d5; 4.Nf3 Bg7; 5.Qb3 dxc4; 6.Qxc4 O-O; 7.e4), White achieves the ideal pawn center by different means.

Again White has the center, but Black can chip away at the support by playing ...Bg4, moving the knight from f6, and acting on the queenside. When Ernst Gruenfeld introduced his invention in the early 1920s, such a White position seemed unthinkably strong, but ways have been found to create counterplay. White has a variety of other approaches too, including systems with Bg5 or Bf4, but these are generally held to be less dangerous for the second player.

EXCHANGE VARIATION

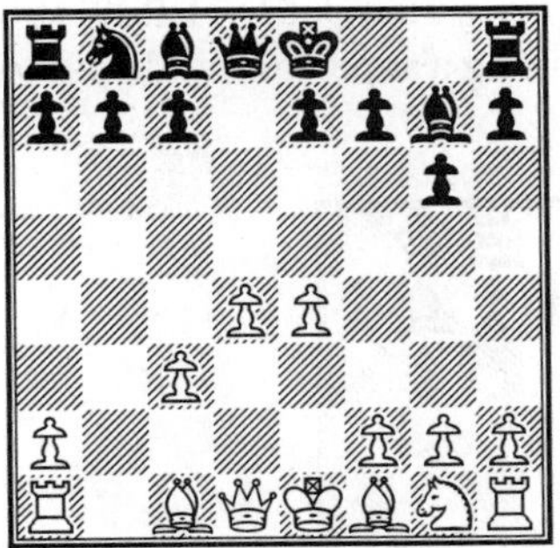

1.d4	Nf6
2.c4	g6
3.Nc3	d5
4.cxd5	Nxd5
5.e4	Nxc3
6.bxc3	Bg7

White must try to support the strong center, which will find itself under attack from a bishop at g7, queen at d8, pawn at c5 and knight at c6. As long as White controls the center, then it is possible to attack on the kingside. Sometimes White is willing to sacrifice the exchange by allowing the bishop at g7 to capture the rook at a1, but in return, the defense of the Black king becomes problematic.

There are two general plans for White. In the one we examine first, the knight moves from g1 to f3. This is the most popular continuation now, but previously White had preferred to station the knight at e2, so that if Black plays ...Bg4, White can interpose a pawn at f3.

(228) PETURSSON - SANCHEZ ALMEYRA [D85]

Lyon Zonal, 1990

1.d4 Nf6; 2.c4 g6; 3.Nc3 d5; 4.cxd5 Nxd5; 5.e4 Nxc3; 6.bxc3 Bg7; 7.Nf3.

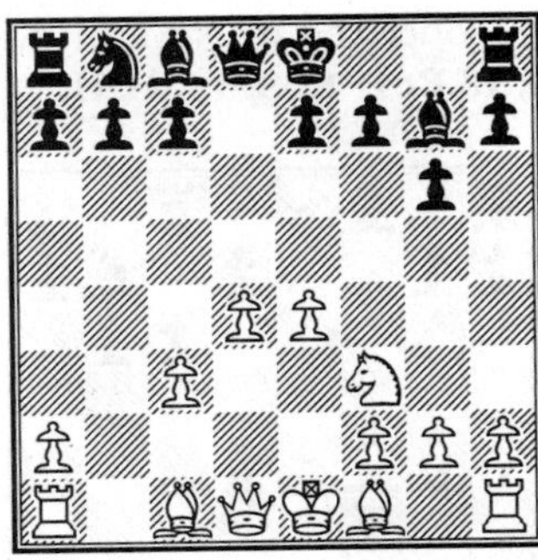

This is the modern handling of the Exchange Variation, which has been the main line for several decades. **7...c5. 8.Rb1.** This move, developed by theoretician Leonid Shamkovich, is a somewhat quiet move with very serious ramifications. It prevents the immediate ...Bg4, which would leave the b-pawn undefended, but at the same time, it leaves the a-pawn helpless, and Black can, if sufficiently emboldened, grab the pawn. The question is whether Black can do this and live, and the question is still open. Icelandic Grandmaster Margeir Petursson has contributed greatly to this line. **8...0–0; 9.Be2.** This nice, safe square is the appropriate home for the bishop. **9...cxd4; 10.cxd4.** Now Black can grab the pawn. **10...Qa5+; 11.Bd2!** White must try the gambit if there is to be any hope of obtaining a superior middlegame. **11...Qxa2; 12.0–0.**

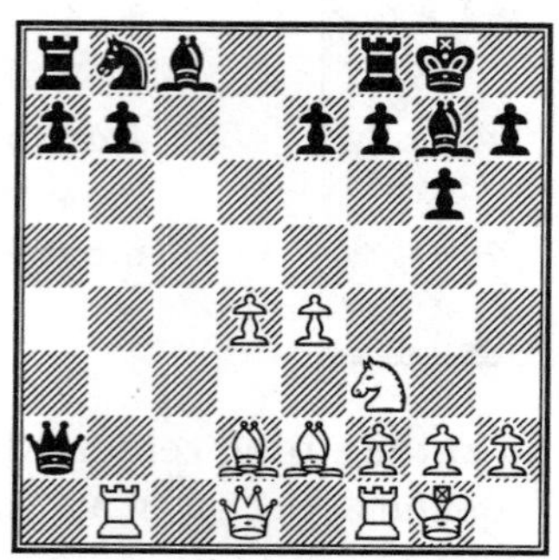

Here Black usually chooses between 12...Nd7 and 12...Bg4, though there are other tries. **12...Nd7.** 12...b6 has taken a pounding at the hands of Khalifman, for example 13.Qc1 Bb7 (13...Qe6; 14.Bc4 Qd7; 15.Ne5 Bxe5; 16.dxe5 Ba6; 17.e6 fxe6; 18.Bh6 Bxc4; 19.Rd1 Qc7; 20.Bxf8 Kxf8; 21.Rd4 and White eventually won in Khalifman-Komljenovic, Seville 1993) 14.Bc4 Qa4; 15.Bb5 Qa2; 16.Bc4 Qa4; 17.Bb5 Qa2; 18.Re1 Rc8; 19.Qd1 Qc2; 20.Qe2 Qc7; 21.Rbc1 Qd8; 22.Rxc8 Qxc8 and White had pressure in Khalifman-Dvoirys, Soviet Championship 1990.

13.Bb4 Nb6. enerally considered best, although again Black has explored some alternatives. 13...a5; 14.Ra1 Qe6; 15.Qc2 Nf6; 16.Ne5 N 16...Nd7; 17.Nf3 Nf6; 18.Ne5 Nd7; 19.Bc4 Qf6; 20.f4 Qb6; 21.Bxe7 Bxe5; 22.fxe5 Qxd4+; 23.Kh1 Nxe5; 24.Bd5! Bg4; 25.Bc5 (25.Bxf8 with a clear advantage for White) 25...Qd3; 26.Qb2 and White's bishops were powerful in Petursson-Ernst, Nordic Zonal 1995. **14.Ne5 f6.** 14...Bxe5; 15.dxe5 Qe6; 16.Qd4 Bd7; 17.f4 was better for White in Alterman-Rogozhenko, USSR 1989, where this plan, conceived by Neverov, was launched. **15.Nc4! Nxc4; 16.Ra1 Nb2; 17.Rxa2 Nxd1; 18.Bc4+ Kh8; 19.Rxd1.**

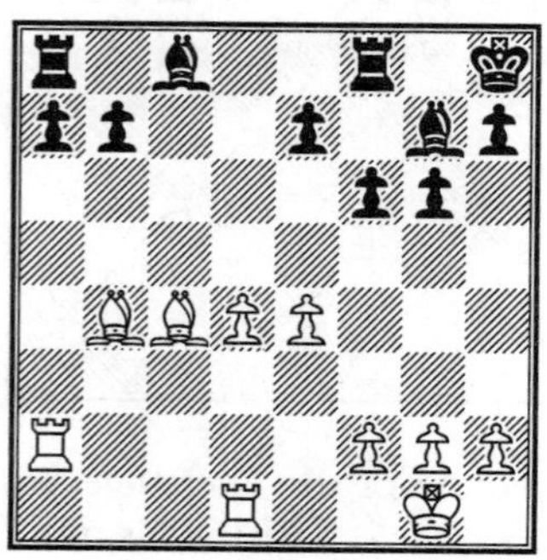

The endgame is better for White, despite the fact that Black has an extra pawn and menacing potential queens on the a-file and b-file. White owns the center, has better posts for the rooks, and active targets. Black's pieces are huddled on the back ranks. The remainder of the endgame is interesting, but unfortunately space constraints prevent us from giving detailed analysis.

19...Bd7. 19...Rd8 was recommended by Karpov, and it offers more prospects of a draw, for example 20.Bxe7 Re8; 21.Bc5 Rxe4; 22.Rxa7 Rxa7; 23.Bxa7 Bf8; 24.g3 Bd6; 25.Kg2 Kg7; 26.Bd5 Re7; 27.Bb6 and a draw was eventually agreed in Ivanov-Daniliuk, Russian Championship 1995. **20.Bxe7 Rfe8; 21.Bc5.** White also achieved a good position with 21.Bd6 in Polovodin-Maslov, Leningrad 1990. **21...b6; 22.Bd6 Be6; 23.d5 Bd7; 24.Bd3 f5; 25.exf5 gxf5; 26.Ba6!** Black is not tied down, and White can apply the slow squeeze. **26...Re4; 27.f3 Rd4; 28.Rxd4 Bxd4+; 29.Kf1 Re8; 30.Rc2 Be5; 31.Bc7 Bd4; 32.f4 Bc5; 33.Be5+ Kg8; 34.Rc3 Kf8; 35.Rh3 Re7; 36.d6 Rf7; 37.Bc4 Rg7; 38.Bxg7+ Kxg7; 39.Ba6 b5; 40.Rc3 Bb6; 41.Rc7 Bxc7; 42.dxc7 Kf6; 43.Ke2. White won.**

(229) GLIGORIC - SMYSLOV [D87]

Yugoslavia vs. USSR, 1959

1.d4 Nf6; 2.c4 g6; 3.Nc3 d5; 4.cxd5 Nxd5; 5.e4 Nxc3; 6.bxc3 Bg7; 7.Bc4 c5.

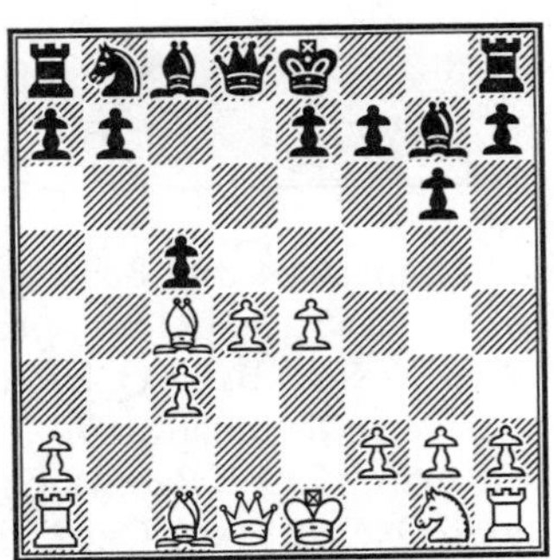

The Classical Exchange Variation is simple in appearance but subtle in play. The contour of the middlegame is clear. Black will train all of the guns at the center, especially at d4. The c3-square is also a target. White will try to maintain the ideal pawn center. **8.Ne2.** The plan with 8.Nf3 is another popular plan, and fashion shifts between the two. The advantage of Ne2 is that a pin with ...Bg4 can be broken by playing f3. Of course that is an asset only if the ...Bg4 plan is otherwise a good one.

8...0-0; 9.0-0 Nc6; 10.Be3 Qc7. This was Smyslov's contribution, and the system with 10...Qc7 now bears his name. Until this time, 10...cxd4 was preferred. 10...Bg4 was the focus of attention in the 1987 World Championship match. All three systems are in common use today. 10...Bg4; 11.f3 Na5; 12.Bxf7+ is known as the Seville Variation, after the memorable Karpov-Kasparov clashes in the 1987 World Championship. 12...Rxf7; 13.fxg4 Rxf1+; 14.Kxf1 Qd6 (14...cxd4; 15.cxd4 Qb6; 16.Kg1 Qe6; 17.Qd3 provided Karpov with a great position in the 9th game.)

A) 15.Kg1 Qe6; 16.Qd3 Qc4; 17.Qxc4+ Nxc4; 18.Bf2 (18.Bg5 is Yasser Seirawan's move, and it is a viable alternative to the text.) 18...cxd4; 19.cxd4 e5; 20.d5 was investigated in the 11th game, and that line is also still in use.

B) 15.Qa4 was introduced in later games and is still being explored.

C) 15.e5 Qd5; 16.Bf2 Rf8; 17.Kg1 Bh6; 18.h4 Qf7; 19.Bg3 Be3+; 20.Kh2 Qc4;

21.Rb1 b6; 22.Rb2 Qd5; 23.Qd3 Nc4; 24.Rb1 b5; 25.Kh3 a6; 26.Ng1 cxd4; 27.Nf3 Rd8; 28.a4 dxc3; 29.Qxc3 Qe6; 30.Kh2 bxa4; 31.Rb4 Nd2; 32.Rxa4 Nf1+ 33.Kh3 Rd1; 34.Qc2 Rc1; 35.Qe2 h5; 36.Be1 Qd7; 37.Qxa6 Ra1; 38.Qxg6+. White won. Karpov-Kasparov, Men's World Championship Seville Spain 1987; 10...cxd4; 11.cxd4 Na5; 12.Bd3 Be6; 13.d5 Bxa1; 14.Qxa1 is the well-known Exchange Sacrifice line, where White has a strong attack to compensate for the exchange, but if Black survives to the endgame, White will have a tough time defending.

11.Rc1. Capturing at c5 just weakens White's pawn structure and is not seen. **11...Rd8; 12.h3.** It is not necessary to prevent ...Bg4, so 12.Qd2 is more common. For example, 12...Qa5; 13.d5 Ne5; 14.Bb3 c4; 15.Bc2 e6; 16.f4 Nc6! which gave Black a solid game in Schneider-Mirumian, Cappelle la Grande 1997. **12...b6; 13.f4.**

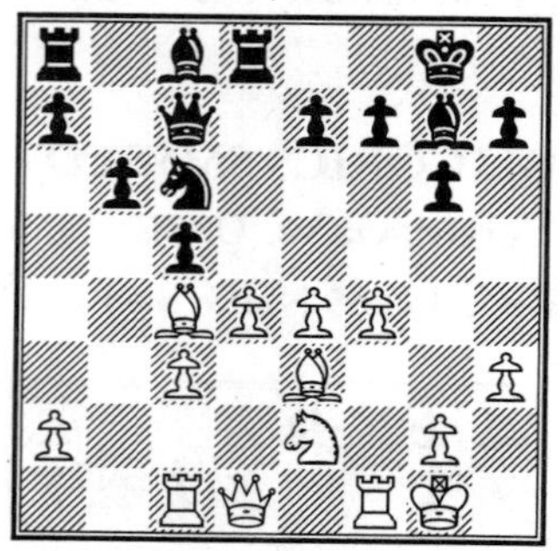

The White pawn mass looks impressive, but Black's pieces will soon start to chip away at it. **13...e6; 14.Qe1 Bb7.** 14...Na5 also holds appeal to Champions: 15.Bd3 f5; 16.g4 fxe4; 17.Bxe4 Bb7; 18.Ng3 Nc4; 19.Bxb7 Qxb7; 20.Bf2 Qc6 and Black had a good game in Spassky-Fischer, Siegen (Olympiad) 1970. **15.Qf2.** 15.f5 fails, as Smyslov demonstrated: 15...Na5; 16.Bd3 exf5; 17.exf5 Re8; 18.Qf2 because of 18...c4; 19.Bc2 Qe7 and Black wins a piece: 20.f6 Qxe3; 21.fxg7 Qxe2. **15...Na5; 16.Bd3 f5!** Smyslov correctly calculated the effect of this move, which is a typical one in structures like this. White's center collapses. **17.e5 c4; 18.Bc2 Nc6; 19.g4.** White could not just sit passively and wait for destruction, so Gligoric tries to open up some lines. **19...Ne7; 20.Kh2 Qc6; 21.Ng3.**

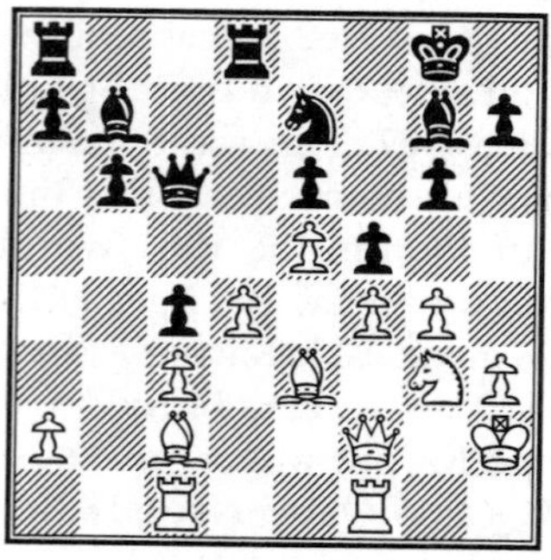

Smyslov realizes that the kingside is not the only area of operations, and starts an action on the other flank. **21...b5!; 22.a4 a6; 23.Rb1 Rab8; 24.Bd2 bxa4!** This is a move which required precise calculation. Smyslov already saw the resource at move

31, the next critical point in the game. **25.Ra1 Ba8; 26.Bxa4 Qc7; 27.Ra2 Rb6; 28.gxf5 exf5.** Black cannot afford to open the g-file, so the path for both the d-pawn and the e-pawn is cleared of pawn obstacles. Nevertheless, Black's pieces keep the situation under control. **29.Bc1 Nd5; 30.Ne2 a5! 31.Bc2.**

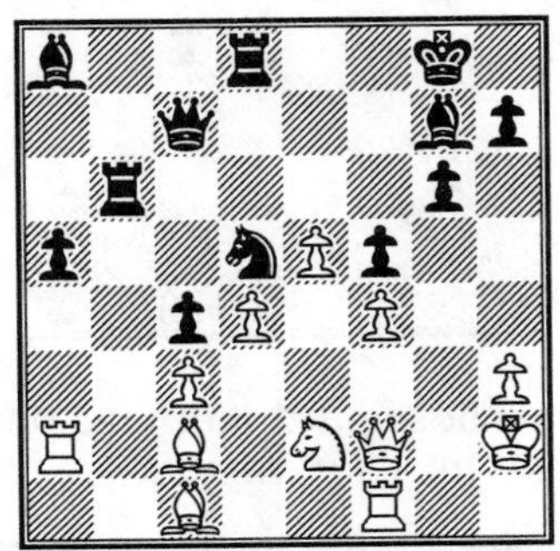

Recall that the entire opening strategy was initially built on the weakness of the White pawns at c3 and d4. Although everything looks fine now, the c-pawn is as weak as ever, as Smyslov shows with the plan launched by his next move. **31...Rb3!** The exchange is a small price to pay for two connected passed pawns on the queenside and a complete domination of the light squares. **32.Bxb3 cxb3; 33.Ra4 Bf8!** Capturing at c3 would have been a waste of time and energy. There is no hurry. 33...Nxc3? and the rook at a4 can return to the game. 34.Nxc3 Qxc3; 35.Bd2 Qb2; 36.Bxa5 Qxf2+; 37.Rxf2 Rc8; 38.Rb4 Rc2; 39.Rxc2 bxc2; 40.Rc4 Be4; 41.Rc8+ Kf7; 42.Bd2 and White will win without difficulty.

34.Bb2. Gligoric hopes to advance the pawn to c4 and get the central pawns rolling, but Smyslov's carefully prepared reply dashes all hopes. **34...Ne3!** When you have a good position, the tactics find themselves! **35.Rfa1.** 35.Qxe3 Qc6 leaves White with no defense to the threats at g2 and a4. For example: 36.d5 Rxd5!?; 37.Raa1 Rd2!; 38.Bc1 b2 and Black wins. **35...Nc4.** Again, there is no rush. Black's pieces are overwhelming their White counterparts. **36.Ng3!** 36.Rxc4 Qxc4; 37.Rxa5 Be7! and now Ng3 can be met by ...Bh4.

36...Be7!; 37.Nf1. Moving the queen to e2 was better, but the position was very difficult. Smyslov provided the following interesting possibility: 37.Qe2! Bd5; 38.Nf1 Ra8; 39.Ne3 Nxe3; 40.Qxe3 Bc6; 41.Rc4 Qd7; 42.Rxc6 Qxc6; 43.Qd3 a4; 44.d5 and it is difficult to evaluate the position. It seems to me that after 44...Qc5; 45.d6 Qf2+; 46.Kh1 Bh4. The Black king can find shelter at h6. The White queen must stay in the area, to prevent threats on the light squares. Black threatens ...Bg3 and ...Qh2#, as well as the bishop at b2. Just one sample: 47.Qd5+ Kg7; 48.Qxa8 Qxb2; 49.Rxa4 Bg3; 50.Qg2 Qc1+; 51.Qg1 Qxc3; 52.d7 b2; 53.d8Q Qf3+; 54.Qg2 b1Q+; 55.Qd1 Qbxd1#. **37...Qc6; 38.Rxc4 Qh1+!** 38...Qxc4 would allow White to get some counterplay with 39.Ne3. **39.Kg3 h5!** White resigned.

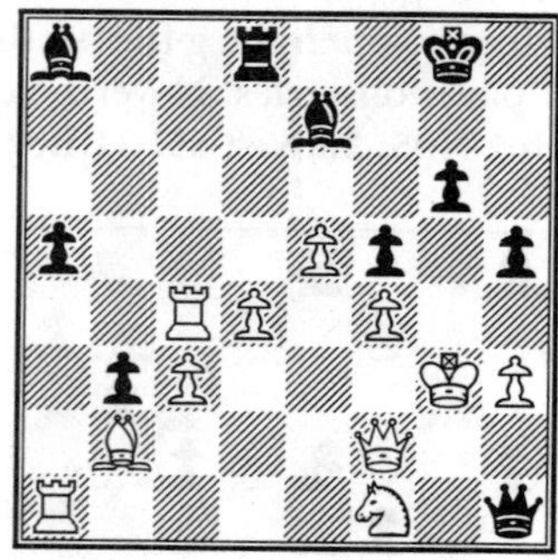

The threat of ...h4+ cannot be stopped, and if the White queen moves away then ...Qg1+ is available.39...h5; 40.Qh2 Qf3#. **Black won.**

RUSSIAN VARIATIONS

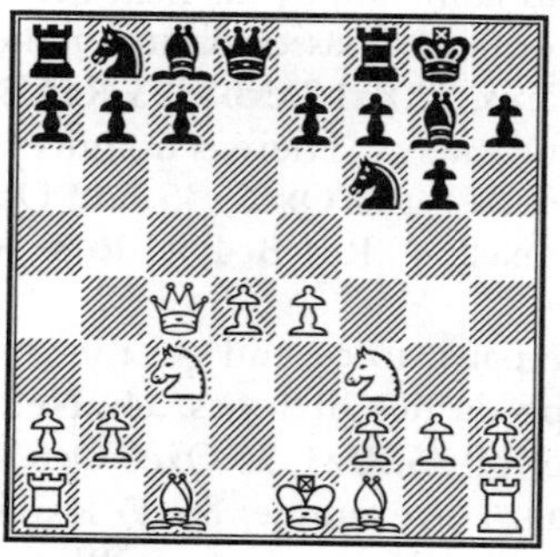

1.d4 Nf6
2.c4 g6
3.Nc3 d5
4.Nf3 Bg7
5.Qb3 dxc4
6.Qxc4 0-0
7.e4

In the **Russian Variations** White gets the ideal pawn center and Black must find some way to put pressure on the Black center. There are a number of ways in which this can be atttempted. Smyslov likes 7...Bg4, though he also played these positions as White. Black threatens to disrupt the kingside pawn structure by capturing on f3, so this places indirect pressure on the center. Alternatives for Black include the Hungarian Variation with 7...a6, the Korchnoi System with 7...Nc6 and the Najdorf-Prins Variation with 7...a6. We will examine Smyslov's system, but our illustrative game places him on the White side of the board.

(230) SMYSLOV - BOTVINNIK [D99]

World Championship Match , 1958

1.d4 Nf6; 2.c4 g6; 3.Nc3 d5; 4.Nf3 Bg7; 5.Qb3 dxc4; 6.Qxc4 0–0; 7.e4 Bg4.

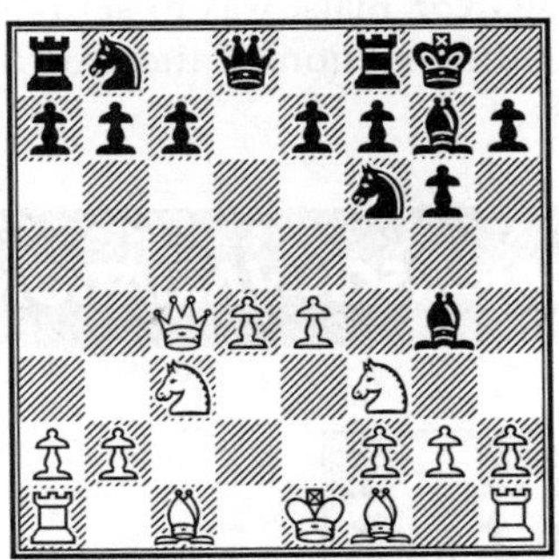

This is Smyslov's line in the Russian Variation of the Gruenfeld Defense. Black will try to undermine White's powerful pawn center by chipping away at the supporting cast. **8.Be3.** 8.Be2 should also be met by ...Nfd7, as 8...Nc6; 9.d5 has been successful for White. 9...Bxf3; 10.gxf3 Ne5 (10...Na5; 11.Qd3 c5; 12.f4 c4; 13.Qf3 e6; 14.dxe6 fxe6; 15.Qh3 gave White promising kingside play in Lilienthal-Smyslov, Moscow City Championship 1946.) 11.Qb3 c6; 12.f4 Ned7; 13.dxc6 bxc6; 14.e5 Nd5; 15.Nxd5 cxd5; 16.Qxd5 gave White an extra pawn in Kotov-Smyslov, Soviet Championship 1945. 8.Ne5 Be6; 9.Qb4 Nfd7; 10.Qxb7? is a trap: 10...Nb6; 11.Nc6 Qd6; 12.Nxb8 Rfxb8; 13.Qa6 Qxd4; 14.Be3 Qb4 leaves White in trouble.

8...Nfd7. This is the point of the variation. Black will use both knights on the queenside, supported by the long-range bishop at g7. **9.Rd1.** White has a choice here between developing with Be2, castling queenside, or occupying the d-file with Rd1. 9.0–0–0 should be met by 9...Nb6 or even 9...e5!?, but the straightforward development of the knight at c6 is problematic: 9...Nc6; 10.h3! Bxf3; 11.gxf3 and White had a grip on the center in Smyslov-Botvinnik, World Championship 1957.

9...Nb6. 9...Nc6 has taken over as the main continuation now. 10.Be2 Nb6; 11.Qc5 Qd6 has found White working hard to find a way to an advantage. 12.e5. This is a commitment by White, since any thoughts of controlling the light squares with pawns must be abandoned. (12.h3 Bxf3; 13.gxf3 Rfd8; 14.d5 Ne5; 15.Nb5 Qf6; 16.f4 Ned7; 17.e5 Qxf4!! was Fischer's spectacular creation against Botvinnik at the 1962 Varna Olympiad.) 12...Qxc5; 13.dxc5 Nc8; 14.h3! An improvement over the 15th game which saw 14.Nb5 Rb8!; 14...Bxf3; 15.Bxf3 Bxe5; 16.Bxc6 bxc6; 17.Bd4 Bf4; 18.0–0 and here Karpov-Timman, Tilburg 1986 saw 18...e5!; 19.Be3 Bxe3; 20.fxe3 Ne7 with an acceptable game for Black. Black can also play 10...Bxf3; 11.gxf3 Nb6, for example 12.Qc2 f5; 13.d5 Ne5 as in Khalifman-Illescas Cordoba, Ubeda 1997

10.Qb3 Nc6; 11.d5 Ne5; 12.Be2 Nxf3+; 13.gxf3. White trades a weakness on the kingside for control of the light squares in the center. **13...Bh5.** This remains a topical position. White's most promising options now are 14.Rg1 and 14.a4, but the winds of fashion shift frequently. The move 14.h4 transposes into the other two lines in most cases. **14.h4.** 14.Rg1 is now more popular. **14...Qd7; 15.a4.** Moving the rook is considered stronger. 15.Rg1 Qh3; 16.f4 Qh2; 17.Kd2! White's king is safer than Black's, Ehlvest-Ernst, Tallinn 1989.

15...a5; 16.Nb5 Nc8; 17.Bd4! White eliminates an important defensive piece. **17...Nd6; 18.Bxg7 Kxg7; 19.Nd4.** White has a complete grip on the position, and Black has no source of counterplay. The bishop at h5 is a mere spectator. **19...Kg8; 20.Rg1 Qh3; 21.Qe3!** The queen shifts to the kingside to take part in the attack. **21...c5; 22.dxc6 bxc6; 23.Qg5 c5?** Black was in serious trouble, but after **24.Nc6.** Botvinnik had to resign, as the invasion of the dark squares cannot be stopped. **White won.**

SAEMISCH VARIATION

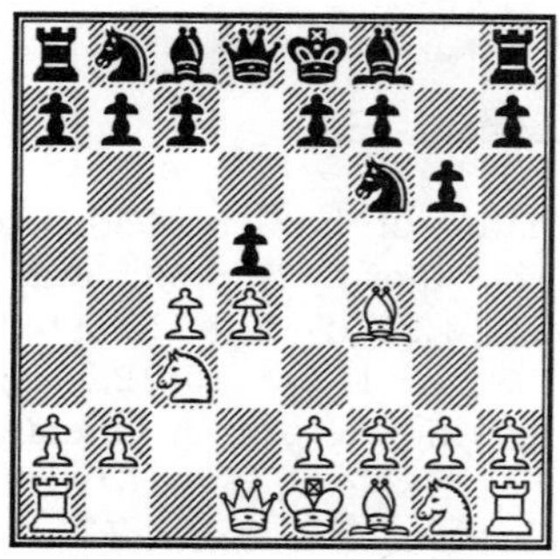

1.d4	**Nf6**
2.c4	**g6**
3.Nc3	**d5**
4.Bf4	

In this system Black must take care not to allow too much pressure at c7, so an early ...c5 is called for. The central pawns often leave the board early in the game, and White can enjoy a slight advantage if Black does not find a way to activate the bishop at c8.

4.Nf3 Bg7; 5.Bf4 is a common move order, for example 5...c5; 6.dxc5 (6.Bxb8 Rxb8; 7.Qa4+ Bd7; 8.Qxa7 cxd4; 9.Qxd4 0-0 gives Black sufficient compensation for the pawn.) 6...Qa5; 7.Rc1 dxc4; 8.e3 Qxc5; 9.Qa4+ Nc6; 10.Bxc4 0-0; 11.0-0 Bd7; 12.Qb5 Qxb5; 13.Bxb5 Rac8; 14.Rfd1 Rfd8; 15.h3 h6; 16.Kf1 a6; 17.Be2 Be6; 18.Rxd8+ Rxd8; 19.Ne5 Nxe5; 20.Bxe5 Rd2; 21.b3 and a draw was agreed in the first game of the match.

(231) KARPOV - KASPAROV [D93]

World Championship 11th Match (11), 1986

1.d4 Nf6; 2.c4 g6; 3.Nc3 d5; 4.Bf4 Bg7; 5.e3 c5; 6.dxc5.

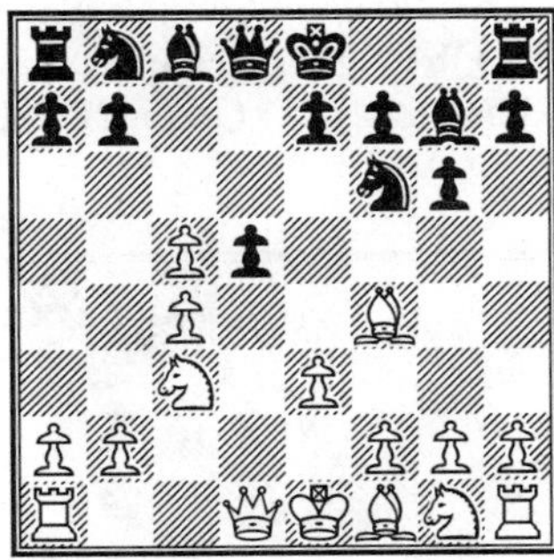

6.Bxb8 Rxb8; 7.Qa4+ Bd7; 8.Qxa7 gets White into trouble after 8...cxd4; 9.Qxd4 0–0; 10.cxd5 Qa5!; 11.Qd2 b5; 12.Bd3 b4; 13.Nce2 Nxd5 according to Karpov. **6...Qa5; 7.Rc1 dxc4.** 7...Ne4; 8.cxd5 Nxc3; 9.Qd2 Qxa2; 10.bxc3 Qxd2+; 11.Kxd2 Nd7; 12.Bb5 0–0; 13.Bxd7 Bxd7; 14.e4 f5; 15.e5 e6!; 16.c4 gave White a formidable pawn center in Karpov-Kasparov, World Championship (5th match game) 1986.

8.Bxc4 0–0; 9.Nf3 Qxc5. Black has the pawn back and development is progressing nicely. **10.Bb3 Nc6; 11.0–0 Qa5; 12.h3 Bf5.** Black has tried 12...Qa6 with some success. **13.Qe2.** White quickly fell into trouble after 13.e4 Bd7; 14.Rfd1 e5!; 15.Bg5 Nd4! in Reynolds-Baquero Continental Open 1997. **13...Ne4; 14.Nd5.** White got nothing out of 14.Nxe4 Bxe4; 15.Rfd1 h6; 16.Rd7 Rac8, Lukacs-Peter, Budapest 1997. **14...e5.**

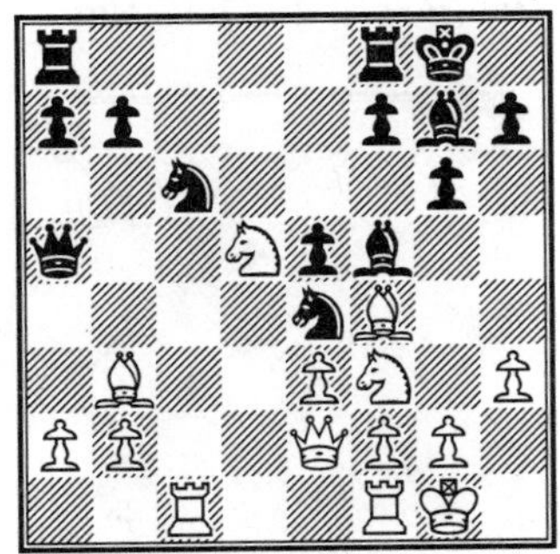

A critical moment. Karpov had prepared a new sacrifice here, trying to improve on 15.Bh2 Be6! as in Farago-Smejkal, 1985. As is often the case with innovations, the first try turned out well. Kasparov, caught by surprise, failed to find the best line, which was, however, noticed in the press room during the match by American Grandmaster Maxim Dlugy and the on-site analysis team. Black can play 14...Nc5, which provided equality in Rizhkov-Yepishin, Leningrad 1996. **15.Rxc6?! exf4?!** 15...bxc6; 16.Ne7+ Kh8; 17.Nxc6 Qb6; 18.Ncxe5 Be6; 19.Nc4 Bxc4; 20.Qxc4 Nc5 was the line the analysts discovered. Karpov never played the exchange sacrifice again!

16.Rc7 Be6!; 17.Qe1? 17.Ne7+ Kh8; 18.Rfc1 is a fairly obvious continuation, and it would have brought Karpov the advantage. The move he played invites an endgame which Kasparov wisely declined. **17...Qb5!** Karpov went into a long think here, obviously not being as well-prepared as he had thought. **18.Ne7+.** Kasparov analyzes the alternatives: 18.Bc4 Qxb2; 19.exf4 Ng3!; 20.fxg3 (20.Ng5 Nxf1; 21.Ne7+ Kh8; 22.Nxe6 fxe6; 23.Qxe6 Qf6) 20...Bxd5; 21.Bxd5 Qb6+; 22.Kh2 Qxc7 and Black wins. 18.Nd4 Bxd4; 19.Ne7+ Kh8; 20.exd4 Qb6; 21.Rc1 f5! and Black has the initiative. **18...Kh8; 19.Bxe6 fxe6; 20.Qb1 Ng5!** Black must play energetically, before White can coordinate his forces. **21.Nh4.** 21.Nxg5 Qxg5; 22.exf4 Rxf4; 23.Rxb7 Raf8 gives Black a strong attack.

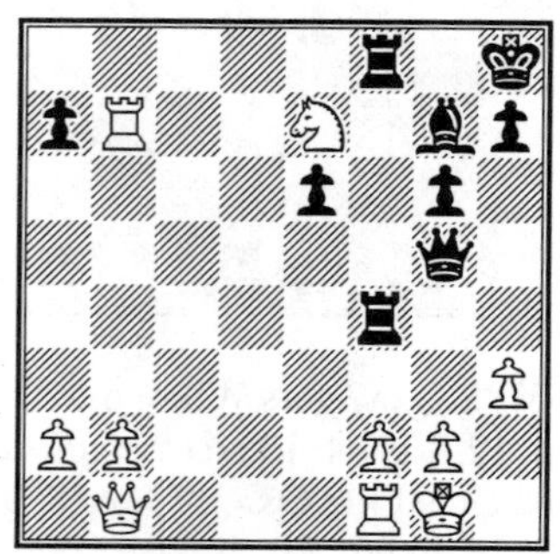

21...Nxh3+!? Kasparov could have played for a draw by capturing at e3, but was tempted by the flashy continuation of the game. **22.Kh2 Qh5; 23.Nexg6+ hxg6; 24.Qxg6?** 24.Nxg6+ Kg8; 25.Ne7+ Kh8; 26.Qg6 was much stronger and would have restored White's advantage. **24...Qe5!** The saving move! **25.Rf7?** Karpov is floundering, missing the best moves. In fact, Kasparov hadn't even considered this reply! 25.Rxb7 Nxf2; 26.Nf3 Qf6; 27.Qh5+ Qh6; 28.Qxh6+ Bxh6; 29.Rxf2 fxe3 is described by Kasparov as holding equal chances, and that is probably correct, though there would be plenty of play left. **25...Rxf7!; 26.Qxf7 Ng5.**

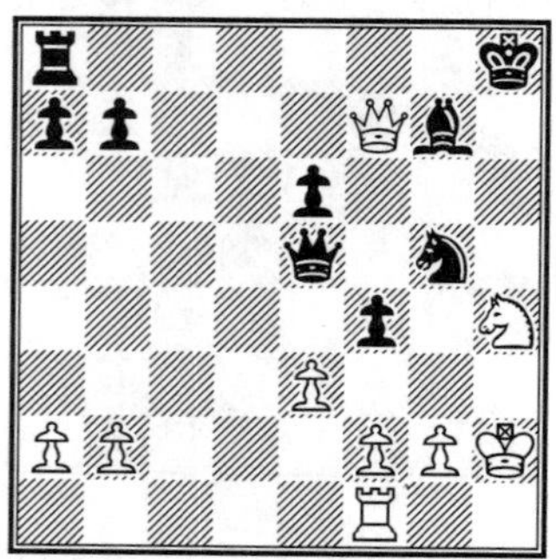

Black's initiative is serious, and Kasparov had worked out the complications correctly. **27.Ng6+ Kh7; 28.Nxe5 Nxf7; 29.Nxf7 Kg6!** The active king gives Black a serious advantage. **30.Nd6 fxe3; 31.Nc4 exf2; 32.Rxf2 b5; 33.Ne3 a5.** As the players head toward the time control, the play gets a bit ragged, but Kasparov manages to convert the advantage into a win. This game won the prize as the best game of the first half of the match, and the players split the prize of about $15,000 for this effort. **34.Kg3 a4; 35.Rc2 Rf8; 36.Kg4 Bd4; 37.Re2 Bxe3; 38.Rxe3 Rf2; 39.b3 Rxg2+; 40.Kf3 Rxa2; 41.bxa4** and at this point the titanic struggle came to a peaceful conclusion.

MODERN BENONI

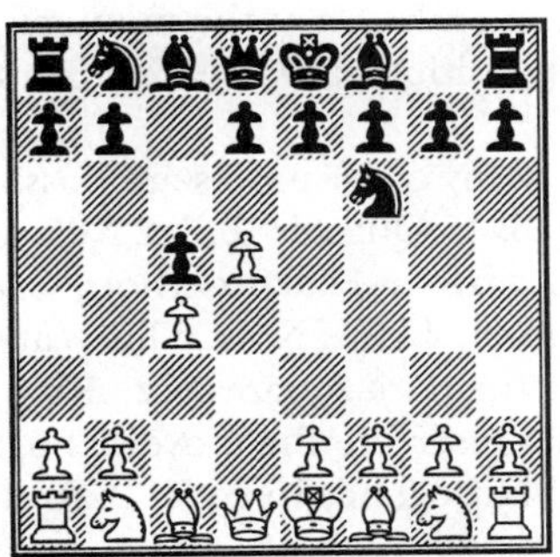

1.d4	Nf6
2.c4	c5
3.d5	

The **Modern Benoni** is a fierce and fiery defense. Black creates a central pawn structure that allows profitable use of the e5-square. Black will fianchetto the bishop at g7 and use the dark squares, especially e5, as staging posts for a kingside attack. White's firm control of the light squares usually provides an advantage in theory, but in practice the preponderance of tactics is decisive. The Benoni lends itself to miraculous escapes and swindling tactics.

PENROSE VARIATION

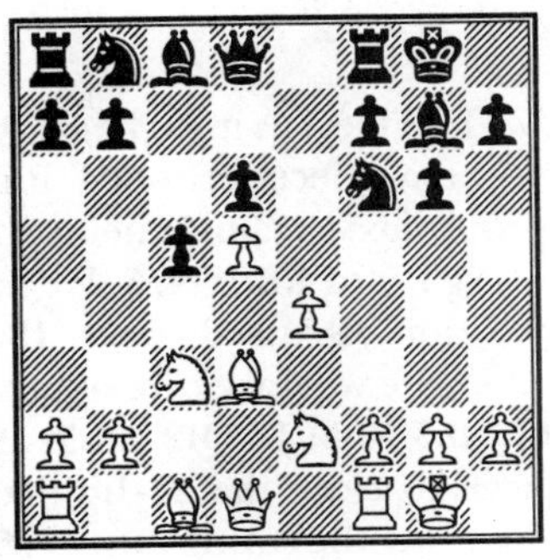

1.d4	Nf6
2.c4	e6
3.Nc	3 c5
4.d5	exd5
5.cxd5	d6
6.e4	g6
7.Bd	3 Bg7
8.Nge2	0–0
9.0–0	

The **Penrose Variation** of the Modern Benoni remains quite popular, because White essentially just sets up the formation in the diagram and then waits to react to Black's plans. This is mostly typical Benoni play, for example reacting to ...a6 with a4, playing f4 at just the right time to keep an enemy knight out of e5, and eventually organizing the advance of the e-pawn. This system can also be used against the King's Indian, though there of course Black is not obliged to advance ...c5.

(232) PENROSE - TAL [A65]
Leipzig Olympiad, 1960

1.d4 Nf6; 2.c4 e6; 3.Nc3 c5; 4.d5 exd5; 5.cxd5 d6; 6.e4 g6; 7.Bd3 Bg7; 8.Nge2 0–0; 9.0–0 a6. 9...Na6 is the strongest recommendation at the moment. As is often the case in the Benoni, the knight takes up a position at c7, where it can support the advance of the b-pawn. 10.h3.

10.Bg5 is the major alternative, though many other moves are possible. 10...h6; 11.Bh4 Re8; 12.f3 Bd7; 13.a3 Rc8; 14.Bf2 Qa5; 15.Qd2 c4; 16.Bc2 Nc5; 17.Bd4 Ba4; 18.Bxa4 Nxa4; 19.Qf4 and White had an initiative in Haik-Koerholz, Cannes 1996.

10...Nc7; 11.Ng3 (11.a4 a6; 12.Bg5 is more precise. Now White can play f4 followed by e5 with the bishop helping out on the dark squares. 12...Rb8; 13.f4 Qe8. Benoni specialist David Norwood thinks that inserting the moves ...h6, forcing the retreat Bh4, would improve Black's chances. 14.Bc2! h6; 15.Bxf6! Bxf6; 16.e5! dxe5; 17.f5 gxf5; 18.d6! is now possible and Black cannot reply 18...e4 because there is no bishop at d3 to attack.) 11...Rb8; 12.Bg5 b5 and Black had counterplay in Christiansen-Van Mechelen, Antwerp (Lost Boys) 1995. **10.a4 Qc7.**

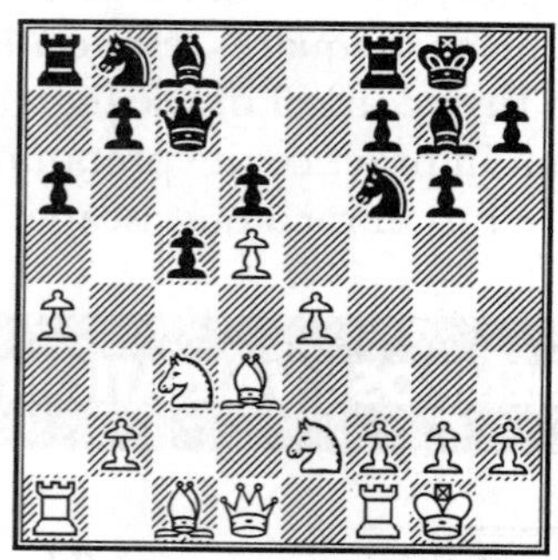

Black can go the other way with 10...Nbd7 11.h3 Qe7, as in Etchegaray-Azariants, 1997. **11.h3.** This is a typical strategy to keep enemy pieces off of g4. It is clear that in the Benoni, the Nimzowitschian idea of prophylaxis against enemy threats must guide White's hand. **11...Nbd7; 12.f4 Re8; 13.Ng3 c4; 14.Bc2 Nc5.** We have already seen this maneuver at work in the 9...Na6 variation discussed above. **15.Qf3 Nfd7; 16.Be3 b5.** Black achieves the flank break, but White will take care of business there and then respond, properly, in the center. **17.axb5 Rb8; 18.Qf2 axb5; 19.e5! dxe5; 20.f5.** A typical tactic. White sacrifices a pawn to close the a1–h8 diagonal and, more importantly, keeps an enemy knight from using the strong post at e5. **20...Bb7; 21.Rad1!** 21.Nxb5 Qb6 just gets the pawn back with a good game. **21...Ba8.** To defend the pawn at b5. **22.Nce4 Na4; 23.Bxa4 bxa4; 24.fxg6 fxg6; 25.Qf7+ Kh8.**

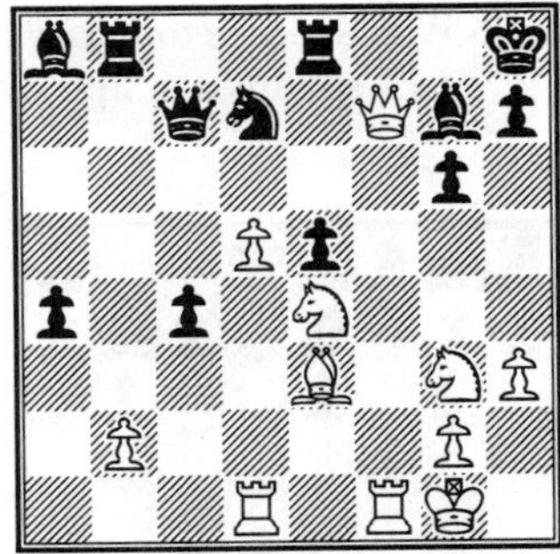

Now White forces a transition to a favorable endgame, but adding pressure to the pin along the seventh rank. **26.Nc5 Qa7; 27.Qxd7 Qxd7; 28.Nxd7 Rxb2.** Black has two pawns for the piece, but they don't last long. **29.Nb6.** This picks off one of the queenside pawns. **29...Rb3; 30.Nxc4 Rd8; 31.d6! Rc3; 32.Rc1 Rxc1; 33.Rxc1 Bd5; 34.Nb6 Bb3; 35.Ne4 h6; 36.d7 Bf8; 37.Rc8! Be7; 38.Bc5 Bh4; 39.g3** with the entire d8-h4 diagonal covered, Black had no choice but to resign. **White won.**

TAIMANOV VARIATION

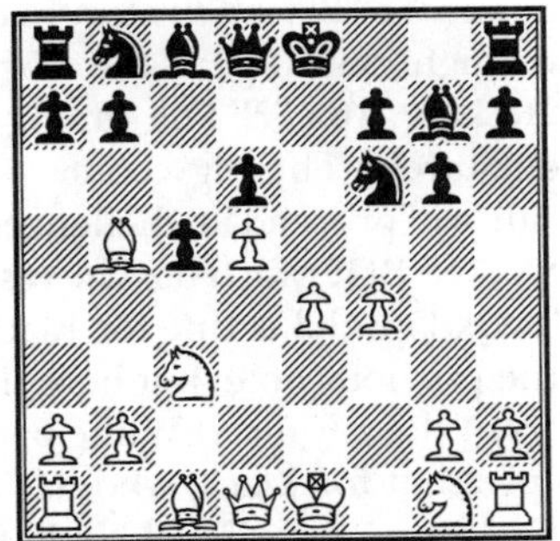

1.d4	**Nf6**
2.c4	**c5**
3.d5	**e6**
4.Nc3	**exd5**
5.cxd5	**d6**
6.e4	**g6**
7.f4	**Bg7**
8.Bb5+	

This is the **Taimanov Variation**, currently the most feared weapon in White's arsenal. In fact, many players have given up on the Modern Benoni because of it, though there are a few die-hards, notably English Grandmaster David Norwood, who stick by it.

(233) BORIK - HORT [A67]
Bundesliga, 1982

1.d4 Nf6; 2.c4 c5; 3.d5 e6; 4.Nc3 exd5; 5.cxd5 d6; 6.e4 g6; 7.f4 Bg7; 8.Bb5 Nfd7. 8...Nbd7. This alternative blocking move has been in the workshop of Norwood and Topalov for a while, but the refurbishing is far from convincing. The current main line is: 9.e5 dxe5; 10.fxe5 Nh5; 11.e6! Qh4+ 12.g3 Nxg3; 13.hxg3 Qxh1; 14.Be3

Bxc3+; 15.bxc3 a6; 16.exd7+ Bxd7; 17.Bxd7+ Kxd7 and now Ivan Sokolov greeted Topalov with 18.Qb3 at the 1996 Wijk aan Zee tournament, and it is hard to see how Black can survive. **9.Be2 Qh4+.** Black spends a tempo in order to weaken the White kingside. **10.g3.**

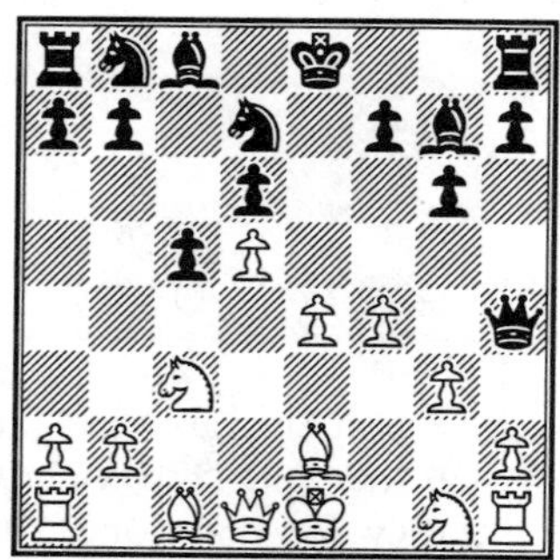

10...Qd8!? Hort's original idea. The positional basis is that the usual plan with Qe7 leaves the queen on the e-file, which will eventually be pried open with e4-e5 so her majesty returns home instead. **11.Nf3 0–0; 12.0–0 Re8; 13.Re1 Na6; 14.Bf1.** A logical move, since White will be attempting to advance his e-pawn and free the e4-square for occupation by a knight. In addition, it protects h3, which will be important if White wants to launch a pawnstorm on the kingside. **14...Nb6; 15.h3.** White might have productively inserted a2-a4 here, as suggested by Borik.

15...c4! This advance is an important component of Black's strategy in the Benoni. It frees the c5-square for occupation by the knight, and opens the a7-g1 diagonal which can be useful for attacks on the White king. **16.e5?!** The timing of this advance is critical, and here White acted prematurely. The big center will soon be liquidated, and Black's activity on the queenside will proceed unchallenged. 16.Be3!? Nb4; 17.a3 Nd3! takes advantage of the overworked Bf1, which has the responsibility of holding both d3 and h3. 18.Bxd3 cxd3; 19.Qxd3 Bxh3 is fine for Black.

16...Nb4. The ideas are the same as in the previous note, but here the simplification will bring into focus the lack of support of the advanced White pawns. **17.g4.** 17.a3 Nd3; 18.Bxd3 cxd3; 19.Qxd3 Bxh3 is pleasant for Black, who has the bishop pair and better coordinated pieces. **17...dxe5; 18.fxe5 N6xd5; 19.Nxd5 Qxd5!** The endgames are clearly better for Black, with or without the extra pawn. **20.Qxd5 Nxd5; 21.Bxc4.**

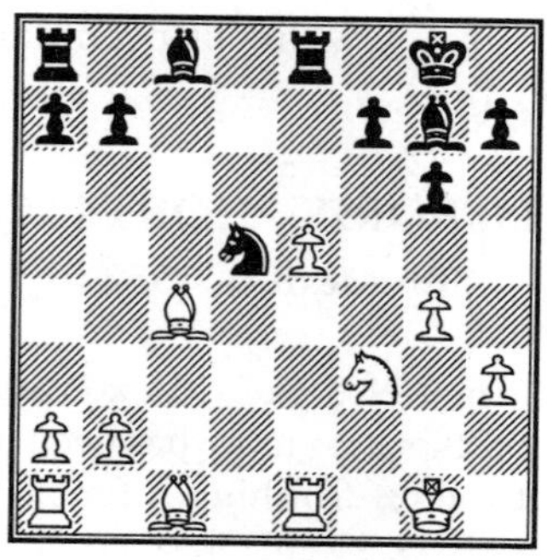

Material balance is restored, but White has a very weak pawn at e5, the result of his premature advance at move 16. **21...Nb6; 22.Bb3 Be6; 23.Be3 Nd7.** 23...Bxb3; 24.axb3 only works to White's advantage, since the open a-file ties down the Ra8 and the doubled pawns are not weak. In fact, the pawn at b3 limits the activity of the enemy knight. **24.Bxe6 Rxe6; 25.Bd4 Rae8; 26.Rad1.** 26.Bxa7 Nxe5; 27.Nxe5 Bxe5! creates the embarrassing threat of Bh2+ as well as Bxb2. **26...Nxe5; 27.Bxe5 Bxe5; 28.Nxe5 Rxe5; 29.Rxe5 Rxe5; 30.Rd7 Rb5.**

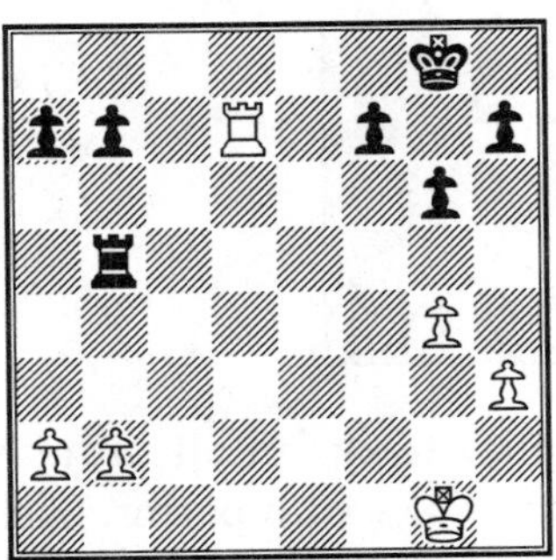

One extra pawn is often insufficient for a win in single rook endgames, but despite good play by White, Hort manages to win with good technique. **31.b3 Kg7; 32.Kf2 Kf6; 33.Kf3 a5; 34.Rc7 h6; 35.Kg3 Ke6; 36.Kf3 h5!** Black must try to create a passed pawn. **37.Kg3 hxg4; 38.hxg4 g5!** It is too soon to play f7-f5. The pawn at f7 limits the mobility of the White rook, while the pawn at g5 hinders the movement of the White king. **39.Kf3 f6; 40.Rh7 Rb4.** Since the Black pawns are located near the edge of the board, White does not have sufficient maneuvering room for his rook. Now the Black rook will be able to infiltrate. **41.Kg3 b6!** An essential move, as otherwise the Rb4 is tied down to the defense of the pawn. **42.Rh2 Rf4; 43.Rd2.**

This is an instructive endgame. Even though there are no obvious targets in the White position, the occupation of the back rank is critical. **43...Rf1!; 44.Kg2 Rc1.** Only in this way can Black insure that he will be able to defend both of this pawn chains with his rook, freeing the king. Endgames like this need the support of the monarch if one hopes to achieve victory. **45.Re2+ Kd5; 46.Rf2 Rc6; 47.Kg3 Kd4; 48.Kf3 Kd3** and White resigned, since Rc2 will be fatal. **Black won.**

FOUR PAWNS ATTACK

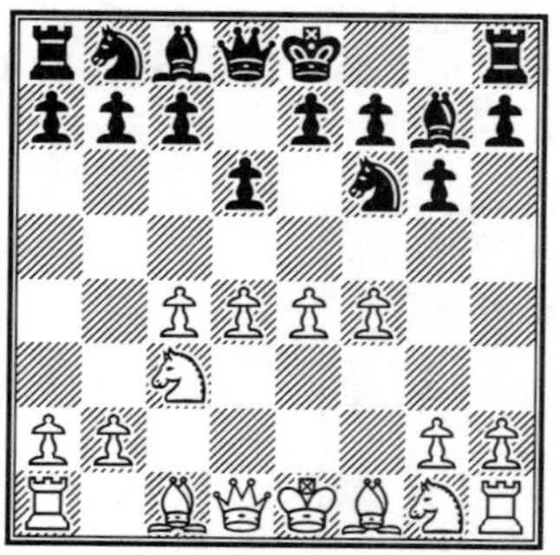

1.d4 Nf6
2.c4 g6
3.Nc3 Bg7
4.e4 d6
5.f4

This is the **Four Pawns Attack**, an all-out attempt to win early in the game. White populates the center with pawns, and controls most of the 5th rank. But these pawns are vulnerable to counterattacks by Black, and several systems are considered good enough to make Black eager to face this line. There is still much to be discovered, however, as Black and White have significant alternatives to the moves that were once held to be *de riguer*.

5...c5. The normal move is castling, but if Black wants to play ...c5 there is no harm in doing so now. 5...0–0 is explored in our other game. The Four Pawns requires both sides to be familiar with a number of different strategies, and therefore it is not recommended to players with poor memories!

(234) KERES - SPASSKY [A68]

Riga (Candidates Match game, 1965)

1.d4 Nf6; 2.c4 g6; 3.Nc3 Bg7; 4.e4 d6; 5.f4; 6.d5 0–0; 7.Nf3.

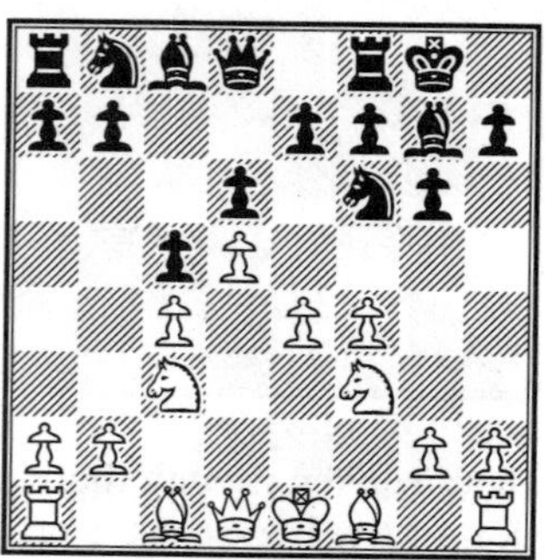

Black now has two basic approaches, which can even be combined. The first plan is to open the e-file by playing ...e6 and ...dxe5, while the other is the Benko Gambit-like ...b5 sacrifice on the queenside. In either case, it is the apparently strong pawn center which will be Black's target. **7...e6.** 7...b5; 8.cxb5 a6 has not yet been sufficiently explored. **8.Be2.** 8.dxe6 fxe6 is fine for Black, who can bring a knight to d4 via c6. **8...exd5; 9.cxd5.**

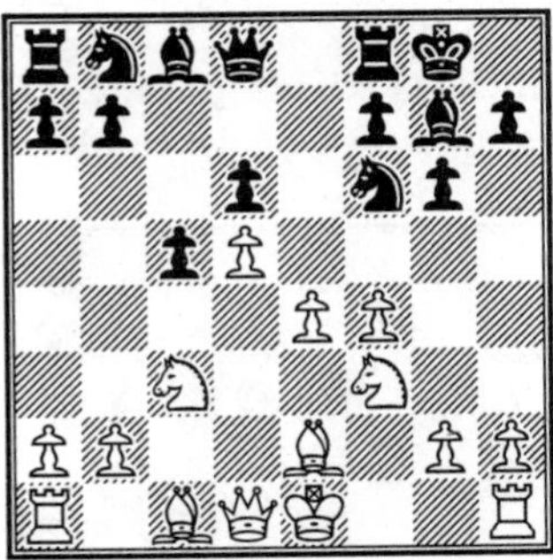

This position, is very complicated. The pawn at e4 is defended only by the knight at c3. It is important to keep that in mind. **9...b5.** At the time, this move was all the rage, but a decade later it had all but disappeared. Now Black prefers to work in the center. 9...Re8; 10.e5 dxe5; 11.fxe5 Ng4; 12.Bg5 f6; 13.exf6 Bxf6 remains controversial, but it is the approved formula at present. A recent example is 14.Qd2 Bxg5; 15.Qxg5 Bf5; 16.Qxd8 Rxd8 and Black had the better endgame in Twyble-Singleton, London 1997.

10.e5 dxe5; 11.fxe5 Ng4; 12.Bf4. 12.Bg5! is the move that put this line out of commission. 12...Qb6; 13.0–0 c4+; 14.Kh1 is better for White, since there is no smothered mate trick. 14...Nf2+; 15.Kg1 Nh3+; 16.Kh1 Qg1+; 17.Nxg1 but not 17.Rxg1?? 18.Nf2#. **12...Nd7.** 12...b4!; 13.Ne4 Nd7 is more accurate, for example 14.e6 fxe6; 15.dxe6 Rxf4; 16.Qd5 Kh8; 17.Qxa8 Nb6; 18.Qc6 Ne3 is still unclear, Martin-Botterill, Charlton 1978. Rather fitting that the game was played in Charlton, long-time home to one of Britain's great chess researchers Bob Wade, at whose home many important opening innovations were developed. **13.e6.**

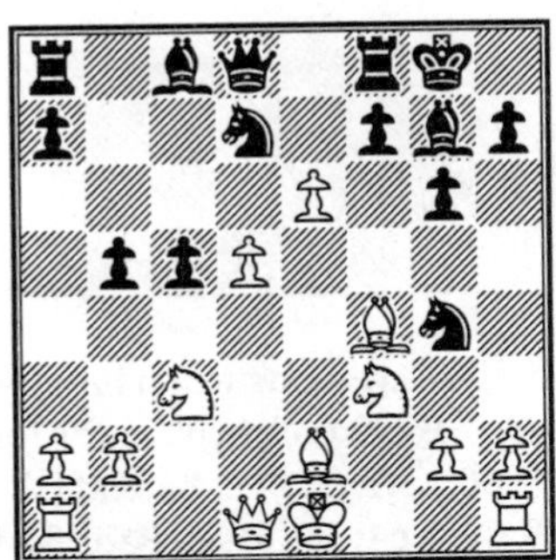

A typical motif, as we have seen. **13...fxe6; 14.dxe6 Rxf4.** Spassky consumed over half an hour, one fifth of his entire allotment (to move 40), contemplating this move. Thirty years later, superstars usually don't settle in for a long think until around move 20 in well analyzed openings, and sometimes they can rattle off prepared moves until their 30th turn! **15.Qd5.** The dual threats lead to the win of the rook.

15...Kh8; 16.Qxa8. 16.0–0–0 Rb8; 17.Qd6 Bh6 and it is Black who threatens the discovered check! **16...Nb6; 17.Qxa7.** 17.Qc6 Ne3 would be unpleasant for the White king who would be unable to castle to safety. **17...Bxe6; 18.0–0.** 18.Rd1 is ineffective because of 18...Bd4. **18...Ne3; 19.Rf2.** 19.Rad1 is interesting. Bernard Cafferty, long-time editor of the famous **British Chess Magazine** gives 19...Nxd1; 20.Rxd1 Bd4+ 21.Kh1 b4; 22.Nb5 (22.Ng5 Qxg5; 23.Qxb6 bxc3; 24.Qxe6 Qe5; 25.Qc8+ Kg7; 26.bxc3 Qxe2 and Black wins.) 22...Bd5; 23.Nbxd4 cxd4; 24.Nxd4 Rxd4; 25.Rxd4 Bxg2+; 26.Kxg2 Qxd4; 27.Qe7 h5 and a draw is likely. **19...b4.**

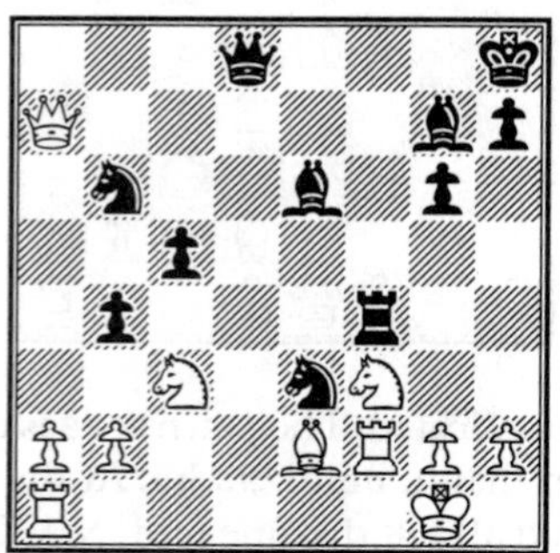

20.Nb5? 20.Nd1! would have given White a clear advantage. Instead, the position remains murky. **20...Rf7; 21.Qa5 Qb8!** This unpins the knight, freeing Black's pieces to pursue loftier goals. **22.Re1 Bd5.** 22...Ng4; 23.Bf1 Nxf2; 24.Rxe6 Nh3+; 25.gxh3 Rxf3; 26.Qxb6 Qxb6; 27.Rxb6 Bxb2; 28.Kg2 is a win for White. **23.Bf1.** This was not the best way to defend, but even after 23.Bd3, 12...Nbc4 would give Black the advantage. **23...Nxf1; 24.Rfxf1 Nc4; 25.Qa6 Rf6; 26.Qa4 Nxb2.**

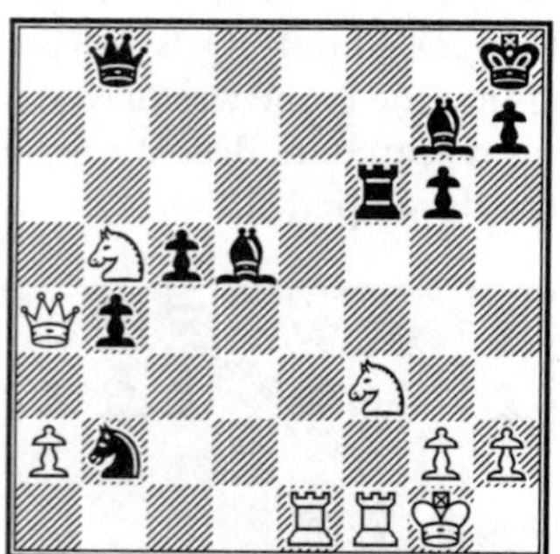

The final critical position. Keres retreats when he should have advanced. **27.Qc2?** 27.Qa5 Nd3; 28.Re7 Qf8; 29.Qa7 Bxa2 is clearly better for Black. **27...Qxb5; 28.Re7.** 28.Qxb2 Rxf3; 29.Qd2 Bd4+; 30.Kh1 Qxf1+; 31.Rxf1 Rxf1# was hardly an acceptable alternative. **28...Nd3; 29.Qe2 c4; 30.Re8+ Rf8; 31.Rxf8+ Bxf8; 32.Ng5 Bc5+; 33.Kh1 Qd7; 34.Qd2 Qe7; 35.Nf3 Qe3.** Keres didn't have to resign, because he ran out of time here. **Black won.**

UHLMANN KNIGHT TOUR

1.d4 Nf6
2.c4 c5
3.d5 e6
4.Nc3 exd5
5.cxd5 d6
6.e4 g6
7.Nf3 Bg7
8.Be2 0–0
9.0–0

The **Uhlmann knight Tour** is the Classical variation of the Modern Benoni. Black has a large number of plans, but most feature attempting to get a knight to e5 when supported by another piece, since in the event of an exchange Black does not want to have to recapture with a pawn. White will use the advantage in space to act on the queenside, bringing a knight to c4 and advancing the a-pawn, further cramping Black's position.

(235) TUKMAKOV - TAL [A77]

Soviet Championship, 1969

1.d4 Nf6; 2.c4 c5; 3.d5 e6; 4.Nc3 exd5; 5.cxd5 d6; 6.e4 g6; 7.Nf3 Bg7; 8.Be2 0–0; 9.0–0; Re8. 10.Nd2. A typical theme in the Benoni. White will be able to secure the center, at least temporarily, by playing f3. **10...Nbd7.** Black steers a knight toward the strong post at e5. **11.f3.**

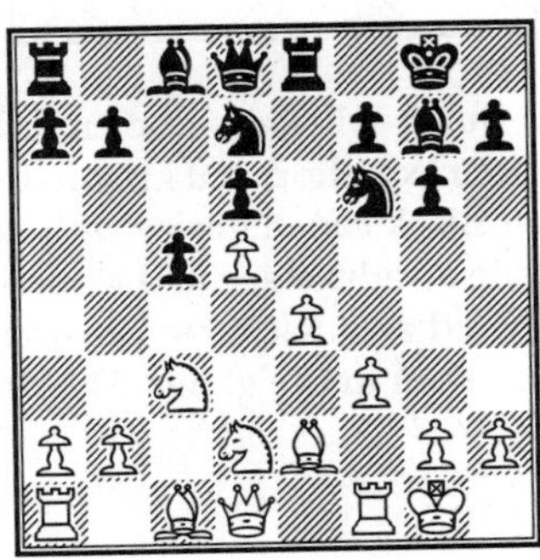

Now this is considered premature. 11.a4 a6; 12.Re1 (12.Qc2 b6; 13.f4 Bb7; 14.Bf3 Rb8; 15.Nc4 Qc7; 16.Be3 Ba8; 17.Bf2 b5; 18.axb5 axb5; 19.Ne3 b4; 20.Nb1 gave Black good counterplay in Krush-Epstein, Unites States Women's Championship 1995.) 12...Ne5; 13.h3 g5; 14.Nf1 h6; 15.Ne3 is perhaps a little better for White, who obtained a good game in Ivanchuk-DeFirmian, Biel 1989. But the situation remains murky and further investigations are likely. Note that the immediate 11.Qc2 is no good, e.g.) 12.h3 g5!; 13.Nf3 Nxf3+; 14.Bxf3 g4 with a strong attack in Dornauer-Soffer, Linz 1997. **11...a6; 12.a4.** This is an automatic response to ...a6 in the Modern Benoni. Black cannot be allowed to advance the pawn to b5. **12...Qc7; 13.Qb3 Ne5.** Black's knights must play an active role if the Modern Benoni is to succeed. **14.a5 Rb8; 15.Nd1 Nh5.**

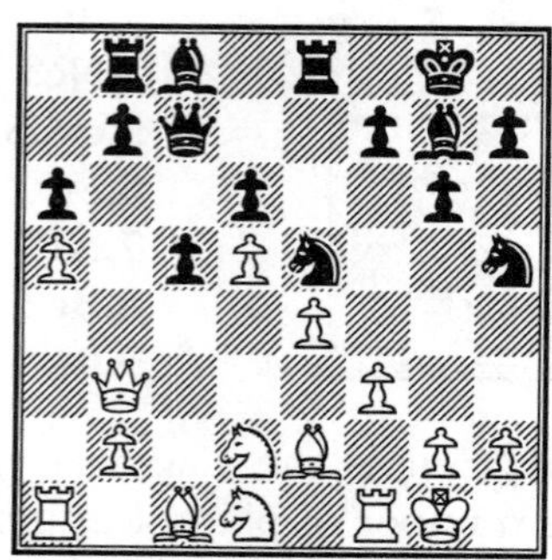

It is fair to say that the chances are equal here, which gives the advantage to the stronger player. **16.Nc4 f5; 17.exf5.**

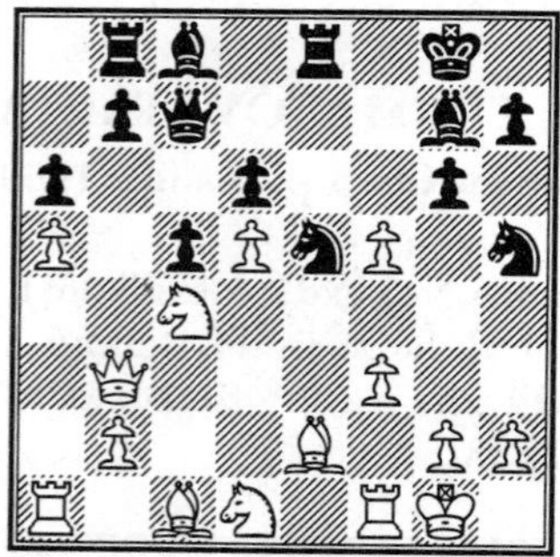

Now Tal invites a fork, but it will be some time before Tukmakov can eat! **17...Bxf5!; 18.g4.** The pawn attacks bishop and knight, but it is Black's turn to move. **18...Nxc4; 19.Bxc4 b5!** When Black can get away with this move, it is an indication that White has failed to maintain an advantage in the opening. **20.axb6 Rxb6; 21.Qa2.** 21.Qa3 Rb4; 22.b3 was evaluated as unclear by Petrosian, but Tal maintained that White has more chances there than in the game. **21...Bd4+; 22.Kg2 Qg7.**

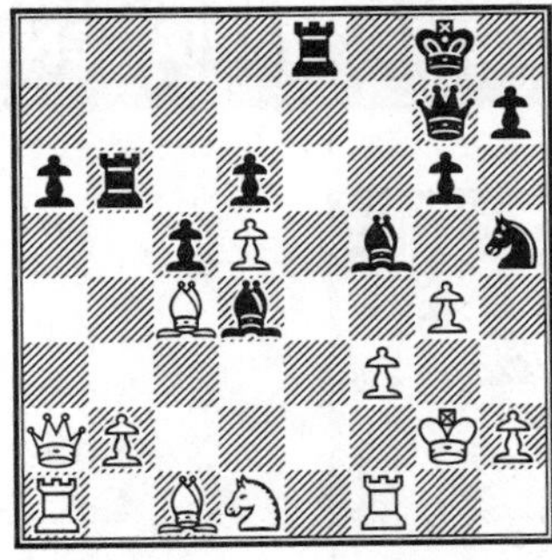

23.Nc3. The bishop is still taboo. 23.gxf5 gxf5+; 24.Kh1 Kh8! was pointed out by Petrosian. **23...Bd7; 24.Bd2.** Once again, the cleric is off-limits. 24.gxh5 gxh5+; 25.Kh1 Bh3. **24...Reb8; 25.Rab1 Nf6; 26.Rfc1 Qf7; 27.b3?** A final error, though the game was hopeless anyway. 27.Rf1 Bc8; 28.h3 Bb7 and the d-pawn will fall. **27...Nxg4!** Splendid, after luring the pawn to this square it is finally captured. Obviously White can't grab the knight because of the attack on the king. **28.Ne4.** 28.fxg4 Qf2+; 29.Kh1 Qf3# **28...Ne5. Black won.**

BENKO GAMBIT

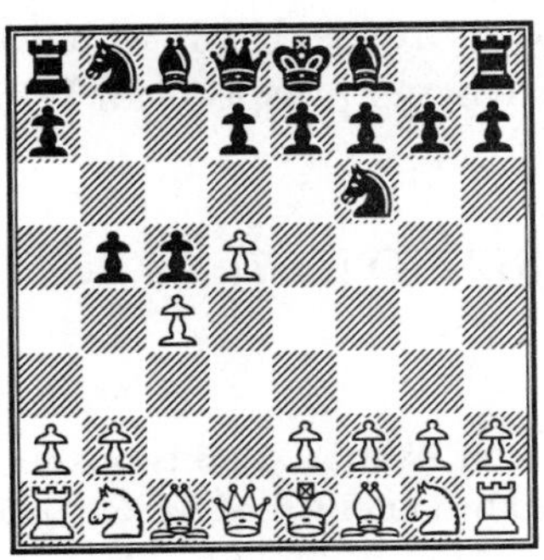

1.d4	**Nf6**
2.c4	**c5**
3.d5	**b5**

This is the **Benko Gambit**. Pal Benko developed the opening in the 1970s, and another United States Champion, Lev Alburt, has used it throughout his career. Black gives up a pawn to open up lines on the queenside, and will station a bishop at g7 to increase the pressure. The pawn at c5 remains very strong for Black. In fact, the endgames often favor the second player despite being a pawn down. For an endgame specialist like Pal Benko, the opening was perfect. This is not to say that tactics cannot erupt, especially in the sharp Zaitsev Variation but the play tends to be peaceful and more positional in nature.

ZAITSEV VARIATION

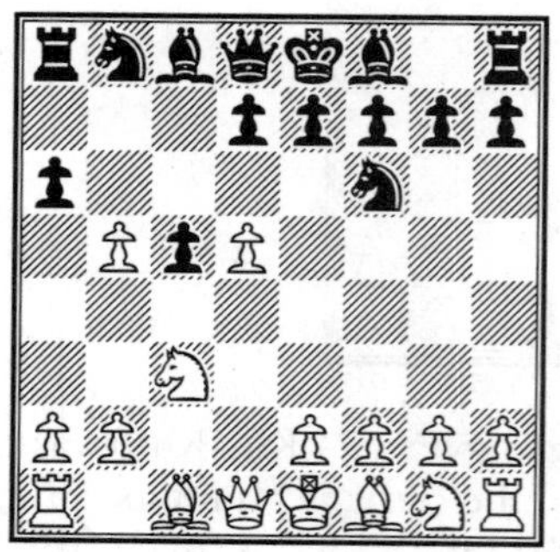

1.d4	**Nf6**
2.c4	**c5**
3.d5	**b5**
4.cxb5	**a6**
5.Nc3	

Given Benko's success on the Black side of the Benko Gambit Accepted, many players prefer to decline it in some fashion or another. It is generally agreed that White should capture at b5 but afterwards can decline the pawn at a6. Here, Benko faces another famous theoretician, Igor Zaitsev, who chooses an exciting line which has not been thoroughly evaluated even two decades later. The 5.Nc3 variation, the Zaitsev, now bears his name.

5.f3 is another way to decline the gambit, and it has been popular recently, for example 5...axb5; 6.e4 Qa5+; 7.b4!, seen in a number of recent games, including Shipov-Tzermiadianos, Greece 1996, which continued 7...cxb4; 8.Nd2 e5; 9.Nb3 Qb6; 10.Qe2 with better prospects for White. Black's light-squared bishop looks ill.

(236) ZAITSEV - BENKO [A57]
Szolnok, 1975

1.d4 Nf6; 2.c4 c5; 3.d5 b5; 4.cxb5 a6; 5.Nc3 axb5. 5...g6 is possible, but here White has resources. 6.e4 d6; 7.f4 is suggested by Gufeld. **6.e4 b4.** 6...Qa5; 7.Bd2 b4; 8.e5 bxc3; 9.Bxc3 is slightly better for White, for example 9...Qb6; 10.exf6 gxf6; 11.Nh3 d6; 12.Nf4 Bh6; 13.Nh5 with better prospects for White, Naumkin-Yanovsky, Soviet Union 1988. **7.Nb5.**

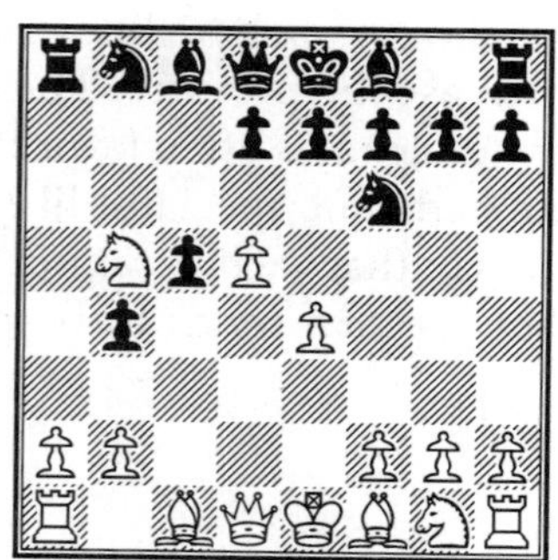

This looks like a precarious position for the knight, which has no escape route. **7...d6; 8.Nf3.** This is the normal continuation these days.

8.Bf4 g5!? is an interesting line. 9.Bxg5 Nxe4; 10.Bf4 Bg7 (10...Qa5 is also seen.) 11.Qe2 Nf6; 12.Nxd6+ Kf8; 13.Nxc8 Qxc8 has been established as a major continuation, but recently 14.Qf3! has caused problems, for example 14...e6; 15.d6 Nc6; 16.Qh3 h5; 17.Bc4 with an unclear position, Sokolov-Khalifman, Parnu 1996. Sokolov recommends 17...Nd5, when Black may have sufficient compensation. Time will tell.

8.Bc4. This is known as the Nescafe-Frappe Attack, as reported in Graham Burgess's monograph on the subject. It is a highly tactical line which requires attentive play from both players. 8...Nbd7 is now the recommended antidote. In fact, the latest (1996) edition of ECO doesn't mention any of the alternatives, this despite the fact that 8...Nbd7 was considered a fairly major line in Burgess's monograph in 1990. (8...Ra5!? is a very interesting option. 8...g6; 9.e5 dxe5; 10.d6! This is the point of the variation. Now the bishop at c4 can take an active part in the attack. 10...exd6; 11.Bg5 Ra5; 12.Nf3 gives White very good attacking chances, seen in many games.) 9.Nf3 Nb6; 10.Bd3 g6 and now curiously ECO gives only 11.Nd2, though 11.b3 is the main line. 11.b3 (11.Nd2?! Bg7; 12.a4 Bd7; 13.Qe2 0–0 and Black was clearly better in David-Votava, Duisburg 1992.) 11...Bg7; 12.Bb2 0–0; 13.0–0 Bb7 with a roughly even game.

8...Nbd7; 9.Bf4 Nh5. 9...Nxe4? is a serious mistake: 10.Bd3 f5; 11.Nh4 Ndf6; 12.f3 e5; 13.dxe6 Bxe6; 14.fxe4 fxe4; 15.Be2 and Black is busted, Milov-Kirilov, Soviet Union 1989. **10.Bg5 Nhf6; 11.Qe2?!** 11.e5! is better, for example 11...dxe5 (11...Nxe5; 12.Nxe5 dxe5; 13.Be3 and White has some targets, but Black's position is solid, C.Hansen-Fedorowicz, Amsterdam 1990.) 12.Qe2 Ba6; 13.Nxe5 Rb8?; 14.Nxf7!! Kxf7; 15.Qe6+ Kg6; 16.Bd3+ Kxg5; 17.h4+ Kh6; 18.Qe3+ and Black resigned in Van den Steen-Giordanengo, Biel 1976. **11...Ra5; 12.e5 Ba6; 13.exf6.** 13.Nxd6+ exd6; 14.exf6+ Bxe2; 15.fxg7 Bxg7; 16.Bxd8 Kxd8; 17.Bxe2 Bxb2 and Black should win. **13...Bxb5; 14.fxe7 Bxe7; 15.Bxe7 Qxe7; 16.Qxe7+ Kxe7.**

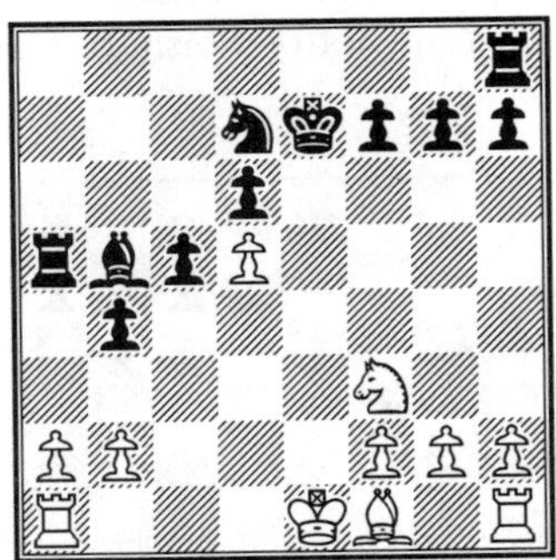

Black has a clear advantage on the queenside, which proves decisive in this endgame. **17.Bxb5 Rxb5; 18.0–0 Nb6; 19.Rfe1+ Kd7; 20.a4 bxa3; 21.Rxa3 Ra8!** The d-pawn is not going anywhere. **22.Rae3.** Any exchanges just increase Black's endgame advantage. **22...Nxd5; 23.Rd3 c4; 24.Rd4 Rc8; 25.Red1 Rcc5; 26.h4?!** White should have centralized the king to help with the defense. This move is irrelevant and just hastens the end. **26...Rxb2; 27.Nd2 Nc3; 28.Nxc4 Nxd1.** White resigned. **Black won.**

FIANCHETTO VARIATION

1.d4 Nf6
2.c4 c5
3.d5 b5
4.cxb5 a6
5.bxa6 g6
6.Nc3 Bxa6
7.Nf3 d6
8.g3 Bg7
9.Bg2 Nbd7
10.0-0

The long introductory sequence of moves in the **Fianchetto Variation** is very logical. Both sides develop forces rapidly and the attention soon turns to the queenside, where the real action will take place. The Black formation is solid, but White's queenside pawn will need protection as all of the Black army assembles to attack it.

(237) HORT - ALBURT [A58]
Decin, 1977

1.d4 Nf6; 2.c4 c5; 3.d5 b5; 4.cxb5 a6; 5.bxa6 g6; 6.Nc3 Bxa6; 7.Nf3 d6; 8.g3 Bg7; 9.Bg2 Nbd7; 10.0-0. The Benko Gambit is a deeply strategic opening, with Black simply putting as much pressure as possible on the queenside, using the two open files and the power of his fianchettoed bishop. Black can also target the pawn at d5. **10...Nb6.**

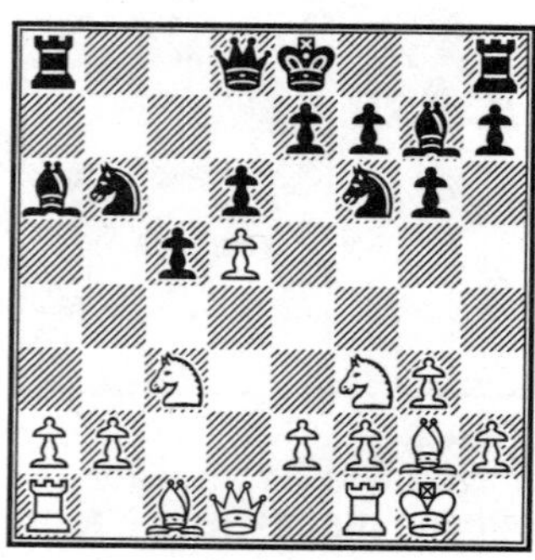

10...0-0; 11.Qc2 Qb6 is another approach, but in Vukic-Benko, Sarajevo 1967, we have an example that shows just how the endgames can turn out in Black's favor. 12.Rd1 Rfb8; 13.Rb1 Ne8; 14.Bg5 Qd8! Black retreats the queen so that the knight can use the f7-square while letting the queen defend the pawn at e7. 15.Bf1 h6; 16.Bd2 Nc7; 17.b3 Nb6; 18.e4 Bxf1; 19.Kxf1 Qd7; 20.Re1 Kh7; 21.Kg2 e6; 22.dxe6

Nxe6; 23.Ne2 d5! 24.Nf4 dxe4; 25.Rxe4 Nd4; 26.Nxd4 cxd4. Black's passed pawn is more active than White's connected passed pawns on the queenside. 27.a4? This is a good move strategically, but has a tactical flaw because Black can set up a threat against the a-pawn. 27...Qb7! There are two threats: ...f5 and ...Nxa4. 28.f3 Nxa4; 29.Rbe1 Qxb3; 30.Qxb3 Rxb3 and Black went on to win the endgame.

11.Re1 0–0; 12.Nd2. White needs to reorganize his pieces in order to protect the weak Pd5. But it is likely the straightforward 12 e4, suggested by Jon Speelman, is the most logical move. Schwarz's 12.Bf4 Nh5 leads to untested complications. 12.e4 Nfd7; 13.Qc2 Nc4; 14.Bf4 Qa5; 15.Rac1 Rfb8; 16.b3 Nce5; 17.Nxe5 Nxe5; 18.Bxe5 Bxe5; 19.Nb1!? c4; 20.Nd2 c3; 21.Nf3 led to unclear complications in Gunawan-Bellon, Lugano 1988. **12...Qc7; 13.Rb1 Qb7!** This leads to a profound queen sacrifice based entirely on positional factors which allow him to carry out his strategy effectively. **14.b3 Nfxd5!; 15.Nxd5 Nxd5; 16.Nf1.**

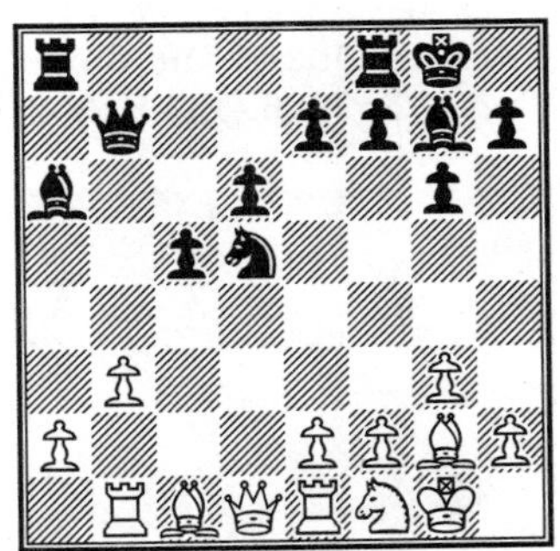

Black has eliminated the e-pawn and can go after the queenside bits. Naturally Black would like to play Nc3, and even though the queen hangs, he does! 16.Ne4 Rad8; 17.Bb2 Bxb2; 18.Rxb2 Qb4! is relatively best, and leads to unclear complications, according to Kasparov's evaluation of analysis by Bagirov. **16...Nc3!!; 17.Bxb7 Bxb7.**

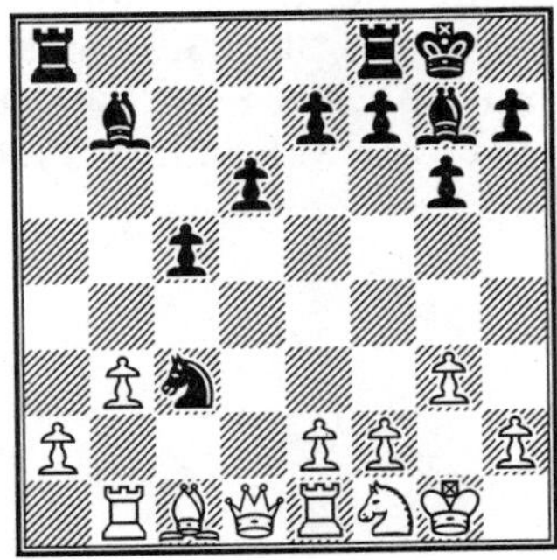

Black does not have full material compensation, but he has enough pieces to eliminate the queenside pawns, while White's forces sit idly on the back rank. **18.Qd3?!** 18.Qd2 might have been better, because it would have forced Black to capture at b1 because otherwise 19.Bb2 would threaten the supremacy of the Bg7. Now Black keeps the knight in its strong position at c3, using the Bb7 instead. **18...Be4!; 19.Qe3 Bd4!; 20.Qh6 Bxb1.**

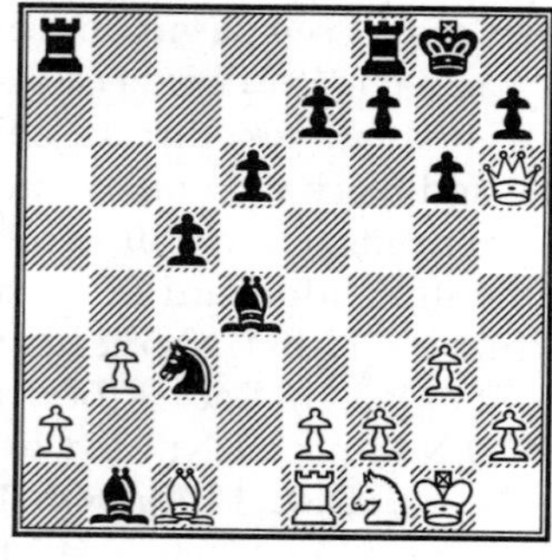

Almost all of Black's pieces are aimed at the White pawns, and the other rook will soon get into the act. White tries to preserve his pawns, but fails. **21.a3 Ba2; 22.Nd2.** 22.b4 cxb4; 23.axb4 Bc4; 24.Qd2 e5 and the pawn at e2 is gone: **22...Rfb8; 23.b4 cxb4; 24.axb4 Rxb4; 25.Nf3 Bg7; 26.Qh3 Be6; 27.Qf1 Bc4!**

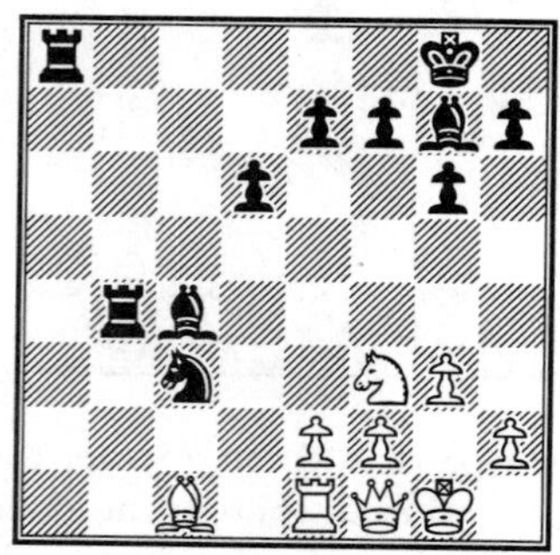

After demolishing the queenside and kicking the White forces back to the home rank, Black pins the e-pawn, completely paralyzing his opponent. **28.Kg2 Ra1!** An additional pin to cause White trouble. **29.Ng1 Rbb1; 30.Kh3.** White is almost in zugzwang, so Black reduces his options. **30...h5; 31.f4.** Now the pin at c1 means that the Black knight can head for e3. **31...Be6+!; 32.Kg2 Nd5; 33.Kf3 Bc3!** If 33...Bb2 immediately, then White could escape with 34.Bd2. **34.Rd1 Bb2. Black won.**

KING WALK VARIATION

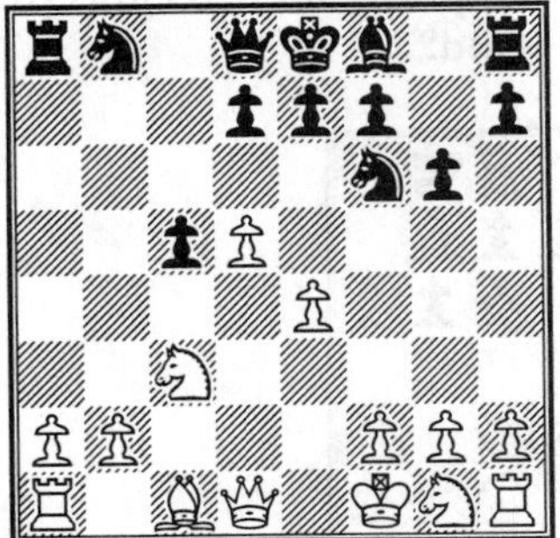

1.d4	**Nf6**
2.c4	**c5**
3.d5	**b5**
4.cxb5	**a6**
5.bxa6	**g6**
6.Nc3	**Bxa6**
7.e4	**Bxf1**
8.Kxf1	

It is rare for his majesty to budge so early in the game, but in the **King Walk Variation**, it is a common maneuver. The king will move to a safe home at g2 eventually, and Black cannot organize the army quickly enough to threaten his safety.

(238) KARPOV - GELFAND [A59]

Sanghi Nagar (6th match game), 1995

1.d4 Nf6; 2.c4 c5; 3.d5 b5; 4.cxb5 a6; 5.bxa6 g6; 6.Nc3 Bxa6; 7.e4 Bxf1; 8.Kxf1 d6; 9.g3 Bg7; 10.Kg2 Nbd7; 11.Nf3 0–0; 12.h3.

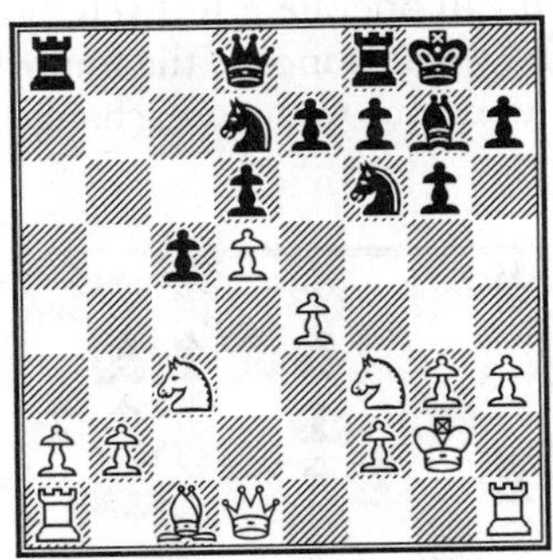

White takes measures to keep enemy forces off of the g4-square. There are many alternative, including 12.Nd2, 12.Re1, 12.Qe2 and 12.Qc2. Now Black will reorganize the queenside. The rook usually moves to either a7 or a6. Black will later be able to double on the a-file with either rook or queen creating a formidable battery.

12...Ra6. 12...Ra7; 13.Re1 Qa8; 14.Re2·Rb8 has been seen several times, and White has not been able to make much progress against it. 15.Bg5!? (15.Qc2 Ne8; 16.Bg5 h6; 17.Be3 Nc7 provided opportunity for both sides in Dumitrache-Palatnik, Baku 1988.) 15...Nb6; 16.b3 Nfxd5; 17.Nxd5 Nxd5; 18.exd5 Bxa1; 19.Qxa1 f6 and now too speculative is 20.Qd1, though if the bishop retreats the a-pawn falls. After 20...fxg5; 21.Nxg5 e5; 22.h4 Rb4! 23.h5 Rd4. White had a hard time justifying the material investment in Danner-Plachetka, Ostrava 1994.

13.Bg5. This is Karpov's invention. 13.Re1 is the normal continuation. 13...Qa8; 14.Qc2 Qb7 (14...Rb8; 15.Rb1! Nb6; 16.b3 led to a better game for White in I. Ivanov-Christiansen, Philadelphia 1990.) 15.Re2 Qb4; 16.Bd2 Rfa8; 17.Rd1 Ne8; 18.Bf4 and now 18...Bxc3; 19.bxc3 Qc4 brought Black equality after 20.Qd3 Qxd3; 21.Rxd3 in Marin-Nedobora, Ibercaja 1994. **13...h6; 14.Bd2.**

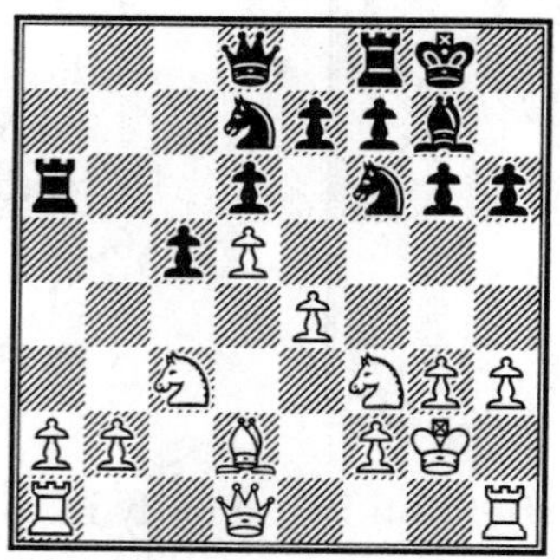

White has created a weakness in Black kingside by luring the h-pawn forward. **14...Qa8; 15.Re1 Rb8.** Black has alternative approaches here. The primary strategic question regards the e-pawn. Should it advance to e6 and confront the White pawn at d5? There is no consensus on the answer yet. **16.b3 Ne8.** The retreat opens lines for the bishop at g7, which threatens the knight at c3 which is needed for defense of the a-pawn. **17.Re2 Nc7; 18.Rc1 Ra7.** 18...Bxc3; 19.Rxc3 Rxa2; 20.Bxh6 and White comes out with the better of the deal, as the Black kingside is vulnerable. Black should hang on to the bishop as the sole defender of the king. **19.Qc2 Na6.** The knight heads for b4, where it can operate effectively against d3, c2 and a2. **20.Na4 Nb4; 21.Bxb4 Rxb4.** 21...cxb4 would concede the important d4-square to the White knight. **22.Qd3 Ra5.** Black does not want to exchange knights at b6 unless absolutely necessary.

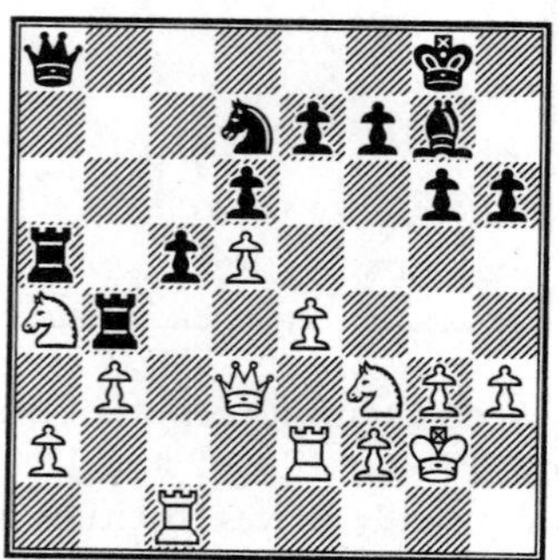

23.Rec2 h5; 24.Rc4 Rb8; 25.Qd2 Rab5; 26.R1c2 R5b7; 27.Qe2 Ra7; 28.Rd2 Ra5; 29.Rd1 Qa6. The pin on the rook at c4 keeps Black in the game for the moment. **30.Rd2.** But the pin is rendered harmless immediately. **30...Bh6; 31.Rdc2 Bg7; 32.Qe3 Qa8; 33.Rd2 Ra7; 34.Rd1 Rb5; 35.Qe2 Rb8; 36.Nd2.** Karpov plans to re-establish a knight at c4. **36...Nb6.** 36...Ne5 only temporarily takes control of c4. After 37.Rc2 Rab7; 38.f4 Nd7; 39.Nc4 the outpost remains forever.

37.Nxb6 Rxb6. With the departure of the knights, White's advantage has grown considerably. **38.a4 Bh6. 39.f4 h4.** This move undermines the f4-square, but is too weakening. **40.Qg4 hxg3; 41.h4!** Now White can apply double pawn pressure at g6. **41...Kh7; 42.h5 Qg8; 43.Rc3.** This rook will eventually capture the pawn at g3. **43...f5.** 43...gxh5; 44.Qxh5 Qg6; 45.Qh4 and there is no defense to Rxg3. **44.hxg6+ Qxg6; 45.Qh4 Qf6; 46.Rh1 fxe4; 47.Rxg3 Rb4; 48.Qg4 Ra8; 49.Rgh3!** and Black, having suffered long enough, resigned. **White won.**

ASSORTED INDIAN GAMES

Here we examine a few odds and ends that do not share common characteristics with the openings we have discussed above. All of the systems we discuss are commonly seen in tournament play. The Bogo-Indian is very popular even at the top level of play. The Budapest Defense is seen in the repertoires of several grandmasters, and the Janowski Indian and Old Indian are found from time to time in Grandmaster play.

BUDAPEST DEFENSE

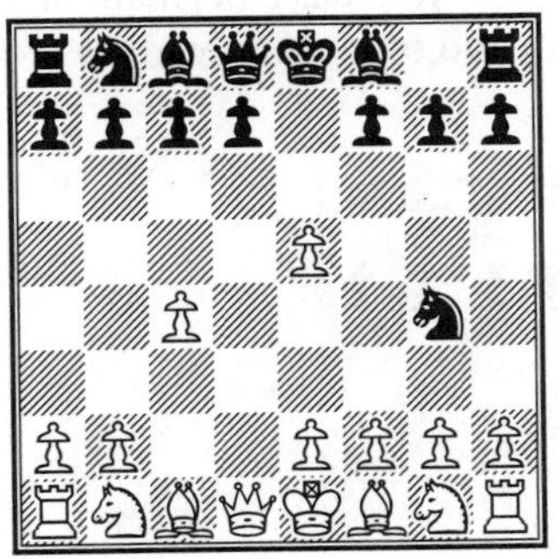

1.d4 Nf6
2.c4 e5
3.dxe5 Ng4

The **Budapest Defense** borders on respectability. If White overplays the position, Black can close in quickly for the kill. With a calmer approach, however, White can maintain an advantage in the opening.

(239) SMYSLOV - BLACKSTOCK [A52]

London (Lloyds Bank), 1988

1.d4 Nf6; 2.c4 e5; 3.dxe5 Ng4; 4.Nf3 Nc6; 5.Bf4 Bb4+; 6.Nbd2 Qe7.

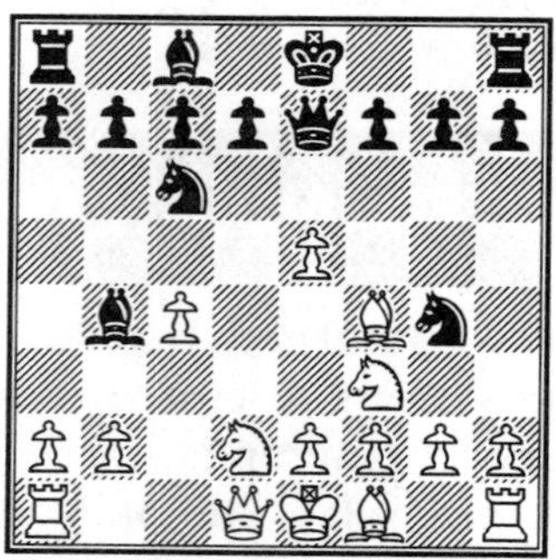

Black has developed quickly and will regain the pawn invested at the second turn. There is still some time needed to recover the pawn, and this gives White a chance to remedy the backward development. **7.e3.** 7.a3 Ncxe5; 8.Nxe5 Nxe5; 9.e3 Bxd2+; 10.Qxd2 0-0 is reasonable but White has the new move 11.c5! which causes some problems for Black, M.Gurevich-Miezis, Bad Godesberg 1996. **7...Ngxe5; 8.Nxe5 Nxe5; 9.Be2 0-0; 10.0-0 Bxd2; 11.Qxd2.** Now White has a permanent advantage in the form of the bishop pair, but that is not in and of itself enough to secure victory. **11...d6.**

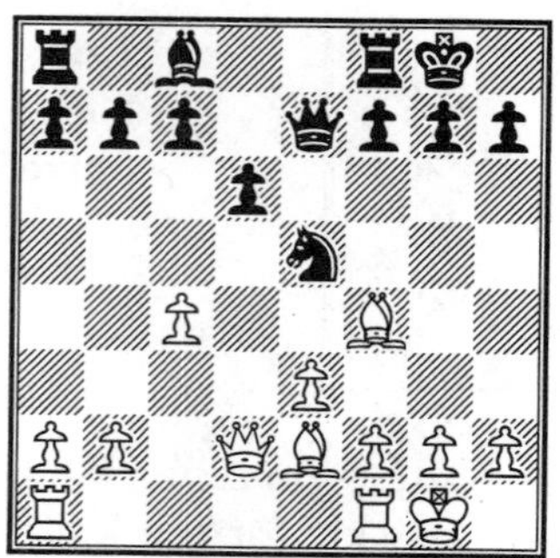

This position has been reached many times, and yet even some of the most respected authorities do not consider the move that Smyslov plays in this game! **12.b4!?** White usually plays this move in the early middlegame, so why not play it now? Smyslov really only had to take into account one additional reply, the one chosen in the game. **12...a5.** Black could try 12...b6, which would return to known paths after, say, Rfd1 or 13.Rac1 Bb7; 14.c5 dxc5; 15.bxc5 Rfd8 with a comfortable game for Black in Van Buskirk-Berman, National Open 1997. **13.a3 Rd8; 14.Qc3 f6; 15.Rfc1!?** This is the point of Smsylov's refined move order. Instead of going to d1, the rook operates from c1. Black must now always keep in mind the possible advance of the c-pawn. **15...Bf5; 16.f3 axb4; 17.axb4 b6; 18.e4 Bg6; 19.Rxa8 Rxa8.**

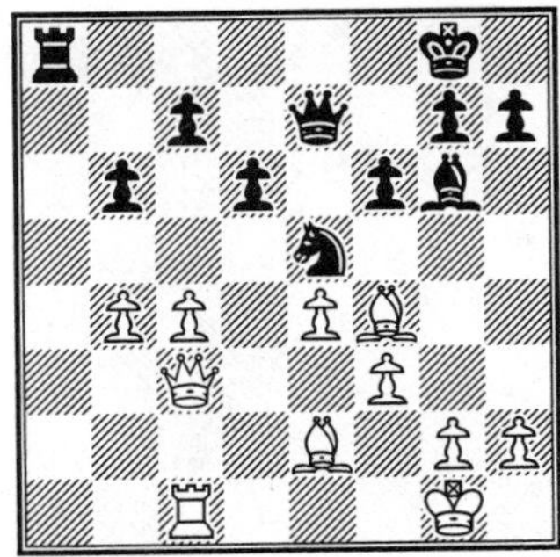

Now it is time for Smyslov to strike. **20.c5 bxc5; 21.bxc5.** The pressure on the c-file is still intense. **21...Bf7; 22.cxd6 cxd6; 23.Qd4.** Now White's advantages are clear. Smyslov holds the bishop pair and the pawn at d6 is weak. **23...h6; 24.Rd1 Rd8; 25.Qb6 Rd7; 26.Qb4 Kh7; 27.Bg3 Qe6; 28.f4 Qb3; 29.Qxb3 Bxb3.**

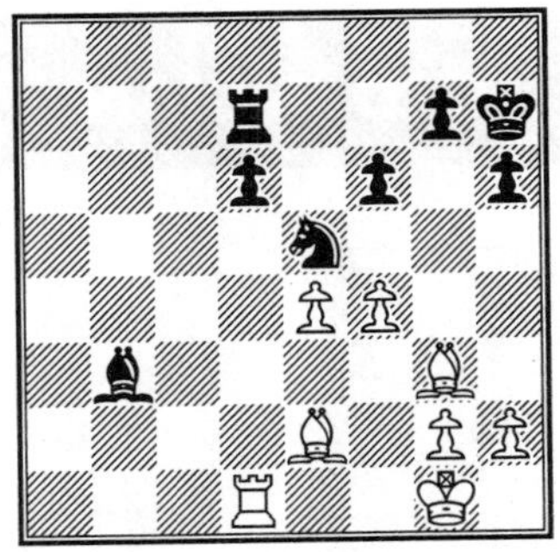

Here Smyslov wins two bishops for the rook, a substantial advantage. **30.fxe5 Bxd1; 31.e6 Re7; 32.Bxd1 Rxe6; 33.Bg4 Re8.** The e-pawn cannot be taken because of Bf5+. **34.Bxd6.** This position is a technical win, but requires good technique and will take some time. **34...g6; 35.Bf3 Kg7; 36.Kf2 Rd8; 37.e5 fxe5; 38.Bxe5+ Kh7; 39.Ke3 Re8; 40.Kd4 Rd8+; 41.Ke4 Rd2; 42.Bd4 Ra2; 43.Ke5.** White has managed to activate his king while not allowing any of the pawns to become vulnerable. The further advance of the king is now possible, with the aid of the two loyal clerics. The procession continues. **43...Ra6; 44.Bb7 Ra4; 45.Bc6 Rb4; 46.Bd5 Ra4; 47.Bc5 Ra5; 48.Bd6 Kg7; 49.Ke6 Ra6; 50.Bb7 Rb6; 51.Bc8 Kh7; 52.Ke7 Rb2.** Now it is time to get the pawns moving. **53.g4 Rf2; 54.Be6 Rf1; 55.Be5 Rf2; 56.Bf6.**

56...Rf4. 56...Rxh2 allows a mating net. 57.Kf8 Rf2; 58.Bg8#. **57.Kf7 Ra4; 58.Be5 Ra7+; 59.Kf6 Ra6; 60.h4 Rb6; 61.Kf7 Rb5; 62.h5.** Black resigned, for if the g-pawn moves, Bf5+ is mate. The only try is a check, but it bounces. **62...Rb7+; 63.Kf8 Rb6.** 63...gxh5; 64.Bf5#; 63...g5; 64.Bf5#. **64.Bg8#. White won.**

OLD INDIAN

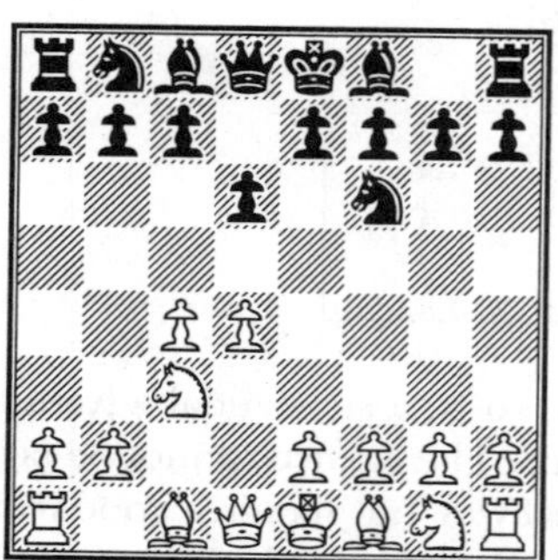

1.d4 Nf6
2.c4 d6
3.Nc3

The **Old Indian** is a solid opening, which often transposes into the King's Indian Defense, where Black invariably plays ...d6 early in the game.

Nyezhmetdinov did not care to play against the Saemisch Variation, which was considered a powerful weapon at the time. That's why he chose, in the second game we'll see, the pure Old Indian instead of the King's Indian, though we will see that a bishop winds up at g7 in the end, and plays a crucial role. Black can try 3...Bf5, the Janowski-Indian, which often transposes to a King's Indian. The more typical Old Indians see either 3...Nbd7 or an immediate advance of the e-pawn to e5. The main problem with the Old Indian is a lack of space.

The first illustrative game presents a rather extreme, but quite clear, example of how White can use this to great advantage. The second is a tactical brawl, showing the kind of excitement that can develop later in the game.

(240) ALEKHINE - KIENINGER [A54]

Poland, 1941

1.d4 Nf6; 2.c4 d6; 3.Nc3 e5.

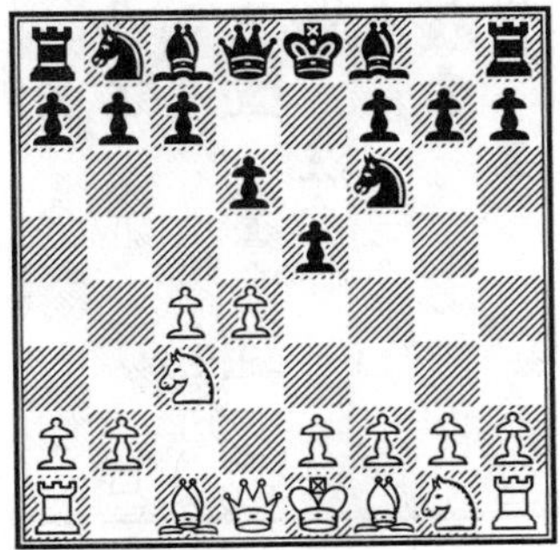

The main problem with the Old Indian is a lack of space. This game presents a rather extreme, but quite clear , example of how White can use this to great advantage. **4.Nf3.** 4.dxe5 dxe5; 5.Qxd8+ Kxd8 is not particularly advantageous for White because the pawn at c4 is just in the way, and weakens the a5-e1 diagonal. **4...Nc6.** This knight belongs at d7, though that blocks the bishop at c8. Developing the knight is therefore problematic in the Old Indian. 4...e4; 5.Ng5 Qe7 is an interesting alternative for Black. 6.Qc2 Nc6; 7.e3 Bf5; 8.d5 Nb8; 9.f3 Nbd7; 10.Ngxe4 Nxe4; 11.fxe4 Bg6; 12.Be2 Ne5; 13.0-0 a6; 14.Bd2 Qd7; 15.b3 Be7; 16.Bf3 0-0; 17.Ne2 Bf6; 18.Rac1 Rfe8; 19.Ng3 Re7; 20.Nf5 Bxf5; 21.exf5 and White had consolidated his material advantage in S.Ivanov-Vorotnikov, Russia 1997.

5.d5 Nb8; 6.e4. White has a large advantage in space, which will be expanded as the game goes on. **6...Be7.** Black might have tried getting the bishop to g4 before White prevented it with his next move. **7.h3 0–0; 8.Be3 Re8.** We can see Black struggling already. The idea behind this move is to free up f8 for use by a minor piece, for example ...Nd7-f8. We will discover that the e8 square needed to be kept available for a retreat by the knight at f6.

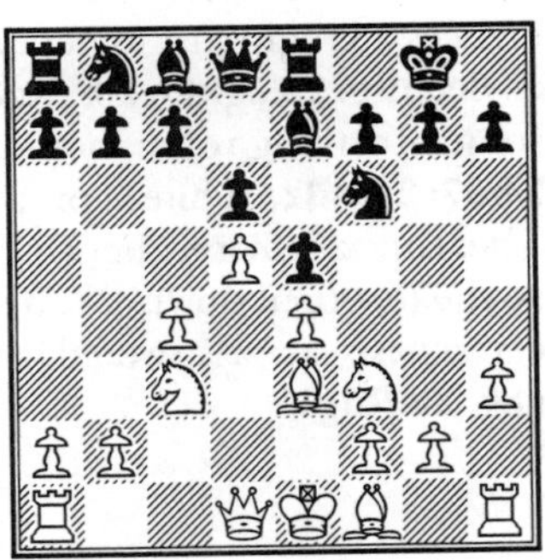

With a safe king and locked center, there is no need for White to hasten to castle. The time is already ripe for a kingside pawnstorm. The king can leap to the queenside later. **9.g4! c5.** This is a bad move, because it keeps the queenside closed. But Black was worried about a retreat square for the knight, since if it went to d7 while White could advance the c-pawn to c5, the d6-square could become quite a problem. Here we see the drawback of placing the rook at e8. **10.Rg1 a6; 11.g5 Nfd7; 12.h4 Nf8; 13.h5.**

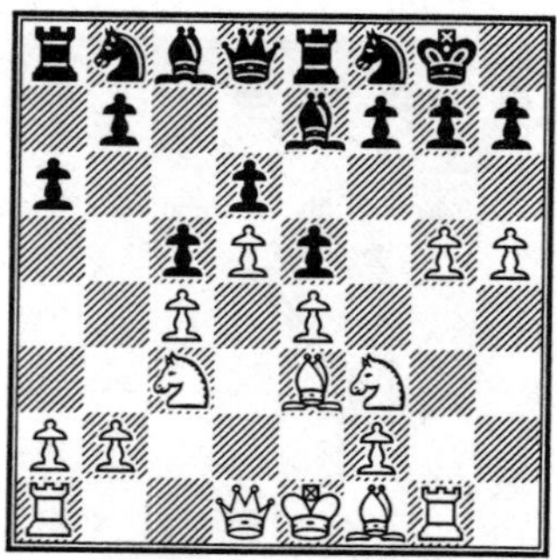

Black has just a single piece beyond the first rank, and that one is paralyzed with no available moves! **13...b6; 14.Nh4 g6; 15.Qf3 Ra7; 16.0–0–0.** White finally castles, and the end is within the horizon. **16...Qc7; 17.Bd3 Bd8; 18.Rg2 Kh8; 19.Rh1 Rb7.**

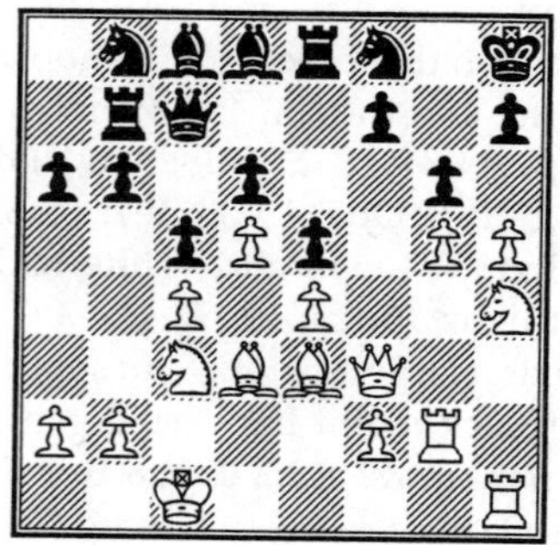

Black's pieces are almost comical. Alekhine may have had a hard time keeping a straight face here. He certainly could be forgiven a little smile when playing his next move. **20.Nf5!!** Alekhine sacrifices a knight just to get one pawn out of the way, but that pawn is the key to Black's defense. **20...gxf5.** 20...Kg8; 21.Nh6+ Kg7. **21.exf5 e4.** A desperate attempt to get some breathing room, hoping that the knight on b8 can find its way to e5. **22.Nxe4 Nbd7; 23.Bd2.** White is prepared for Black's jump to e5. The bishop will shift to c5, bearing down on the long diagonal and pinning the knight. So Black tries to close the diagonal down. **23...f6; 24.Bc3 Ne5; 25.gxf6 Qf7.** If Black had captured the queen, a nasty surprise would have been sprung by Alekhine: 25...Nxf3; 26.f7+ Ne5; 27.Rg8#. **26.Rhg1!**

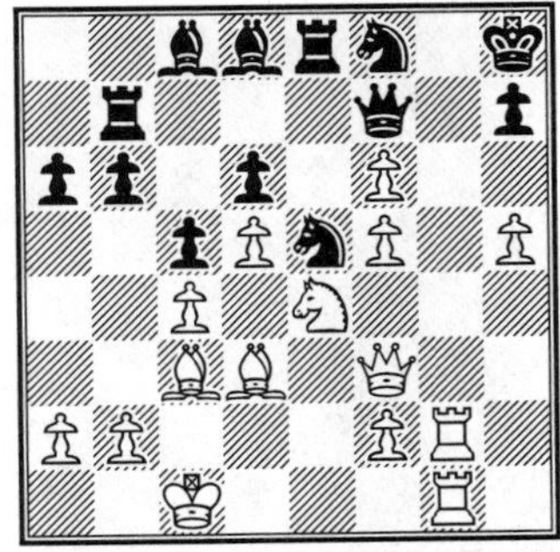

The queen is still taboo. **26...h6.** 26...Nxf3; 27.Rg8+ Qxg8; 28.f7+ Qg7; 29.Bxg7#. **27.Bxe5 Rxe5; 28.Rg7.** The rest is brutal. **28...Qxg7; 29.fxg7+ Rxg7; 30.Rxg7 Kxg7; 31.f6+. White won.** Black learned his lesson, and in the notes to the next game you'll find him on the White side.

(241) POLUGAYEVSKY - NYEZHMETDINOV [A53]

Sochi (Russian Championship), 1958

1.d4 Nf6; 2.c4 d6; 3.Nc3 e5.

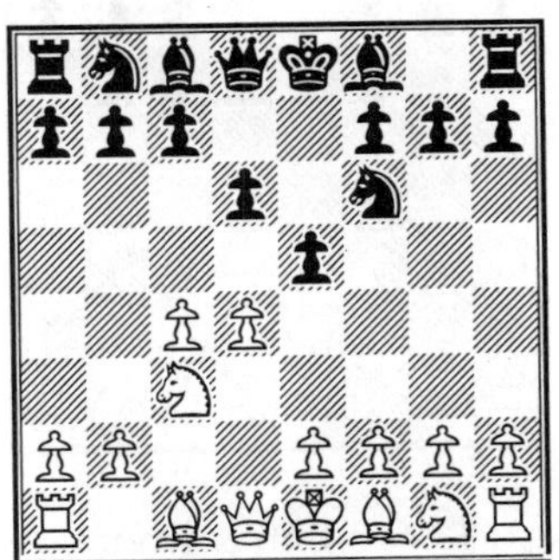

4.e4. Not a popular move anymore. The theory of the line hasn't changed much since this game was played. **4...exd4.** The most principled move, which concedes a bit of the center but gains time which can be used to develop quickly and place a dark-squared bishop on the long diagonal. **5.Qxd4 Nc6; 6.Qd2.** The logical retreat, since the Bc1 is going to be fianchettoed. 6.Qd1 g6; 7.Bd3 Bg7; 8.Nge2 0–0; 9.f3 creates a very bad bishop, which allows Black to gain the upper hand: 9...Ne5!; 10.Be3 c6; 11.0–0 Be6; 12.b3 d5! and Black had the initiative in Kottnauer-Simagin, Prague vs. Moscow 1946. **6...g6; 7.b3.** It is important to create counterplay along the long diagonal. 7.g3 Bg7; 8.Bg2 0–0; 9.Nge2 Ne5!; 10.b3.

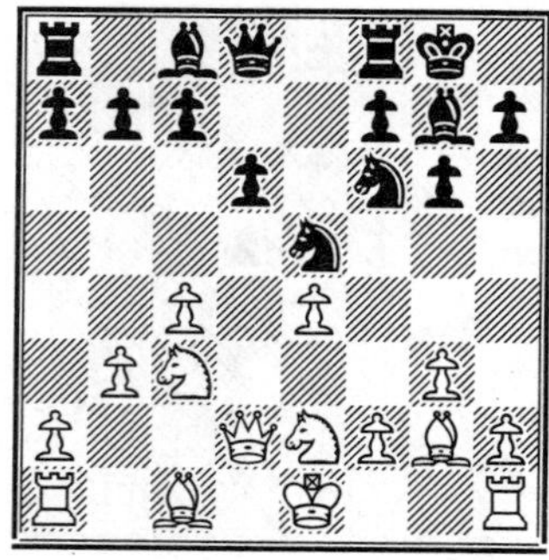

10...Bh3!!; 11.0-0 (11.Bxh3?? Nf3+) 11...Re8; 12.f3 Bxg2; 13.Kxg2 a5 and even though White has no bad bishop, the control of the dark squares gives Black the advantage, Martin-Trifunovic, Mar del Plata 1950. **7...Bg7; 8.Bb2 0-0.** Play has now transposed to a King's Indian where White is adopting a Maroczy Bind approach. **9.Bd3.** 9.f3 might be slightly better, although it does create an awfully bad bishop for White. 9...Re8; 10.Nge2 (10.h4 Be6; 11.g4).

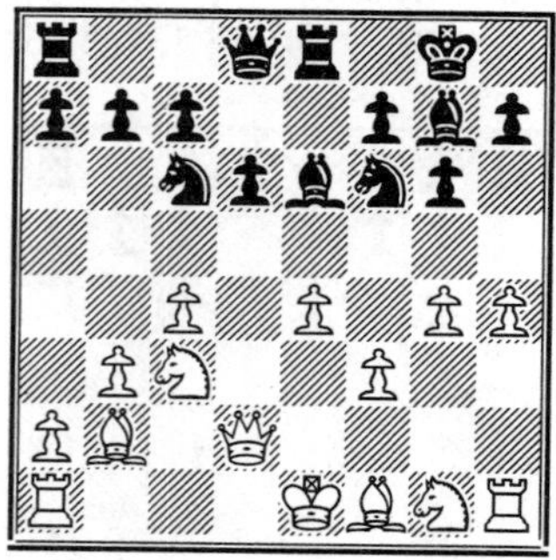

11...Bxg4!?; 12.fxg4 Nxg4; 13.Nf3 Bh6 is given by ECO (1979), with an evaluation of unclear.) 10...Be6; 11.0-0-0 Nd7; 12.Nd5 Nce5. This unclear position was reached in Kieninger-Heinicke, Hamburg 1955. After a properly timed capture at d5 Black should be able to equalize. **9...Ng4.** Black's strategy revolves around the e5-square. **10.Nge2.**

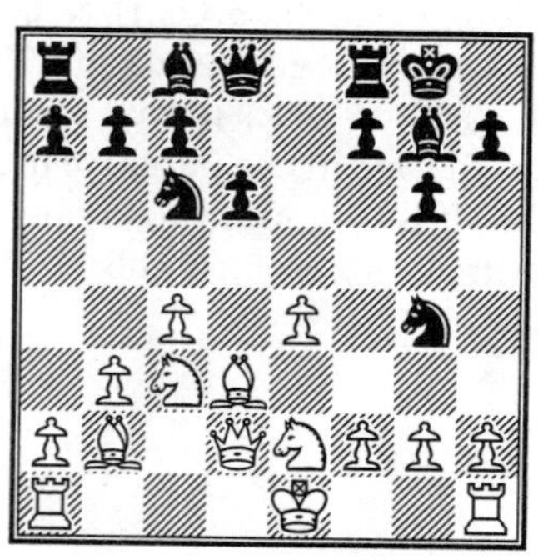

It is rather sad that ECO doesn't even mention this game! 10.Nf3 Nge5!; 11.Be2 (11.Nxe5 dxe5 concedes the d4-square, and Black's Bg7 is no less powerful than its counterpart at b2.) 11...Nxf3+; 12.Bxf3 Nd4 (12...Nd4 is also good for Black: 13.Be2 Qh4; 14.0–0 Bg4 and Black had a strong initiative in Penrose-Clarke, Southend 1957.) 13.Bd1? f5! gave Black the advantage in Alatortsev-Boleslavsky, 18th USSR Championship 1950. The White center is crumbling and the open e-file will be a source of discomfort for him.

10...Qh4! After 10...Nge5 Polugayevsky would have played 11.Bc2, which would have given support to the center. 10...Nge5; 11.Bc2 Bh3!?; 12.0–0! f4. The tactical trick at f3 deserves investigation. 12...Nf3+ (12...Qh4 allows White to obtain the advantage with 13.f4) 13.gxf3 Ne5; 14.Qf4! Bxf1; 15.Rxf1 and White has two pieces for the rook. **11.Ng3.** 11.Nd1 Nxh2! with the threat of Nf3+!; 12.Ng3 Ne5!; 11.g3 would have seriously weakened the light squares on the kingside. **11...Nge5.** 11...f5?!; 12.f4! Nxh2; 13.Nce2 and after castling queenside, White would have a strong initiative on the kingside.

12.0–0. White could not afford to delay castling for long. 12.Bc2 Nd4!; 13.Bd1 c5. The backward pawn is not weak because of the outpost at d4. 14.Nd5 Bh6!; 15.f4 Bxf4!; 16.Nxf4 Qxf4; 17.Qxf4 Nd3+; 18.Kd2 Nxf4; 19.Bf3 Nfe6 and Black has a clear extra pawn. **12...f5.** does not really weaken the a2-g8 diagonal, since White has piled up his pawns along it. The pawn will advance further, cramping the White kingside and reducing his ability to maneuver his pieces defensively there. 12...Ng4 is an obvious alternative, and indeed most players would find it very tempting. The refutation demands brilliant play on White's part. 13.h3 is the obvious move. Now Black can capture at f2. 13...Nxf2 (13...Nge5 runs into a simple counterproposal: 14.Be2 Nd4; 15.Nd5) 14.Qxf2! White's reply might come as a shock to Black, since he can now pin the queen: 14...Bd4.

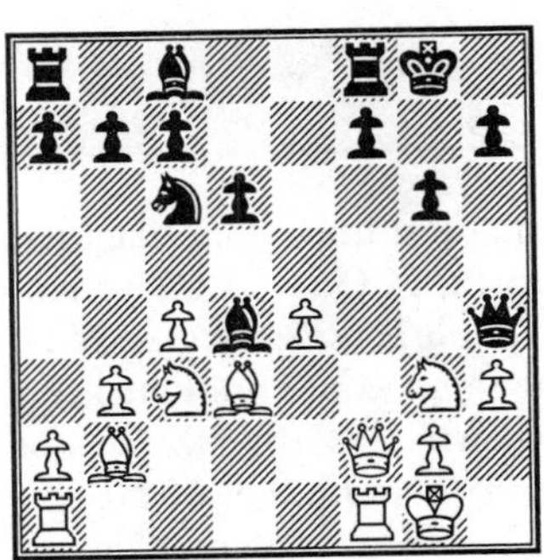

Looks pretty straightforward, doesn't it? But imagine Black's surprise when White simply removes the offensive cleric! 15.Qxd4!! And it would have been White who would have earned the brilliancy prize for this game! 15...Nxd4; 16.Nd5!

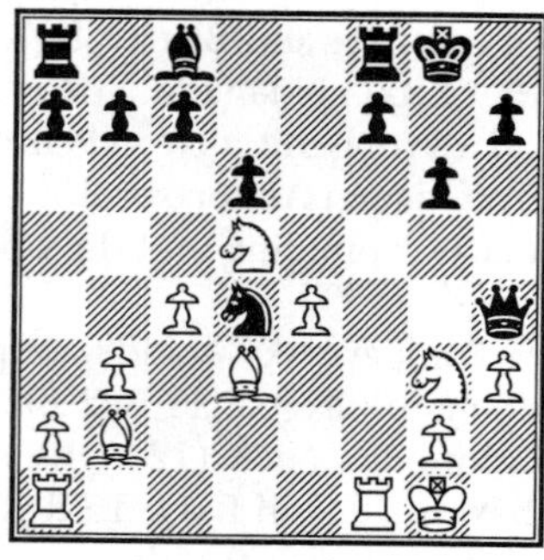

There are many defensive plans for Black here, and they are analyzed in depth in my monograph on this game. Here is just a taste: 16...Nc6; 17.Rf4 Qd8 (17...Qg5; 18.h4 Qd8 is even worse. 17...Qh6; 18.Nf6+ Kg7; 19.Ng4+ and White wins.) 18.Bf6 Qd7; 19.Be2 h5 and now 20.Nxh5!! gxh5; 21.Rh4 Kh7; 22.Bxh5 bring the game to a rapid conclusion. **13.f3!** Capturing at f5 just opens up the g-file when Black retakes with the pawn. **13...Bh6.**

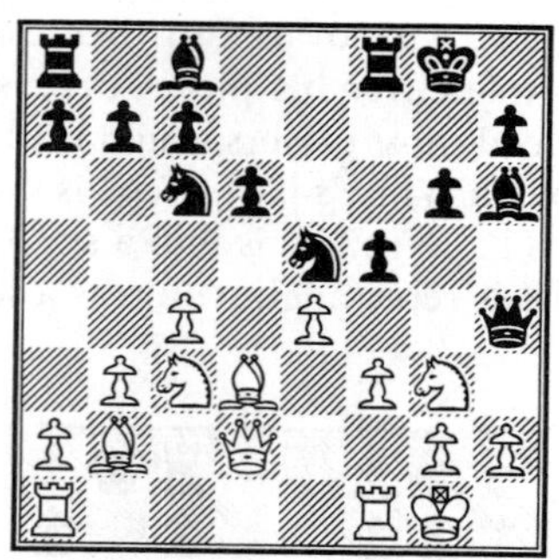

Black takes control of the most important diagonal. This adds tremendously to Black's forthcoming pawn storm. **14.Qd1.** 14.f4? Ng4 and Black wins: 15.Rf3 Qxh2+; 16.Kf1 Nd4; 17.Nd5 Nxf3; 18.Ne7+ Kf7; 14.Qe2 Nd4! brings the knight into the attack with gain of time. The same would hold on 14.Qc2. **14...f4; 15.Nge2.** 15.Nh1 is too passive. If Black gets a pawn to g3, then the knight is doomed to spend the rest of the game trapped in the corner. **15...g5; 16.Nd5.** This not only attacks the c7-square, but it also activates the Bb2 along the diagonal which Black abandoned at his thirteenth move. **16...g4; 17.g3!** Well timed! White's pieces are not well placed to defend the monarch, but he does have control of g3. 17.Nxc7? loses to 17...g3; 18.h3 Bxh3 and White cannot deal with ...Bxg2 and ...Qh2.

17...fxg3. This capture is necessary. 17...Qh3; 18.Ndxf4 Bxf4; 19.Nxf4 Nxf3+; 20.Rxf3! gxf3; 21.Nxh3 Bxh3; 22.Kf2 and Black has no compensation for the queen. **18.hxg3.** 18.Nxg3 Nxf3+; 19.Rxf3 gxf3 will win, because the dark-squared bishop will finally have its say, e.g., 20.Nxc7 Be3+; 21.Kh1 Bh3! (with the nasty threat of Bg2 mate!) 22.Bf1 Bg2+!; 23.Bxg2 fxg2+; 24.Kxg2 Rf2+ and mate next move. **18...Qh3.** Although the Black queen is a menacing figure, it cannot deliver mate on its own and at present only the Ne5 is poised to join the attack. If White can get in Rf1–f2-h2, his kingside attack will be stronger than Black's. **19.f4.**

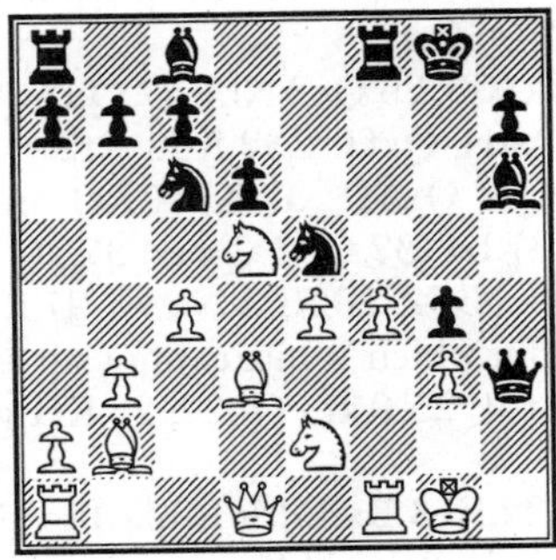

Here Polugayevsky probably let out a sigh of relief. But now it is time to start having fun! **19...Be6!** Of course the piece cannot be captured for tactical reasons, but the true power behind the move lies in the mobilization of all of Black's forces. 19...Nf3+; 20.Kf2 Qh2+; 21.Ke3 and the king is quite safe in the center, so White threatens Rh1 and an attack of his own. **20.Bc2?!** Nyezhmetdinov gives this move a full question mark, but that can be awarded only in hindsight. For no mortal could have seen all that is coming! 20.Bb1! is considered best but locking in therook at a1 would have taken real guts. And in any event, Black has plenty of threats even here, for example... 20...Bxd5; 21.cxd5 Ne7; 22.Kf2.

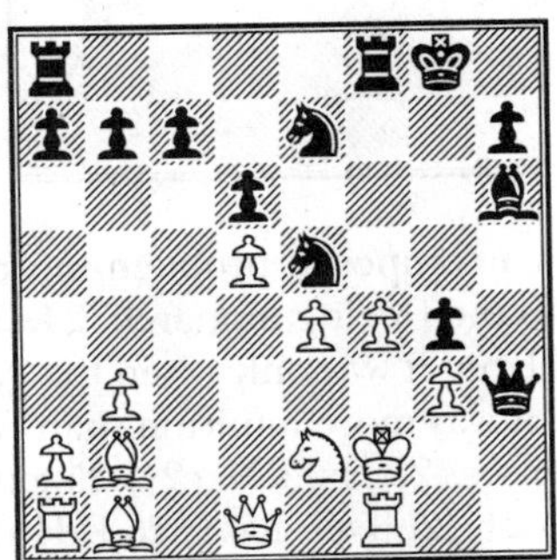

22...Rxf4+!!; 23.gxf4 (23.Nxf4 Qh2+; 24.Ng2 Rf8+; 25.Ke1 Qxg2; 26.Rxf8+ Kxf8; 27.Bxe5 dxe5; 28.Bd3 (or else Qb2) 28...Qxg3+; 29.Ke2 Qe3+; 30.Kf1 g3; 31.Qe2 Ng6; 32.Qxe3 Bxe3; 33.Ke2 Bd4; 34.Rf1+ Ke7!) 23...N7g6.

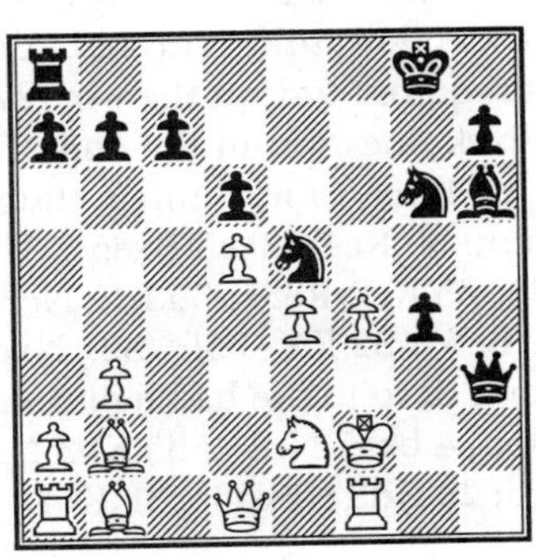

And despite the extra rook, White is in deep trouble, for example:

A) 24.fxe5 Rf8+; 25.Ke1 Qxf1#.

B) 24.Bxe5 Nxe5; 25.Qd4 Rf8; 26.Qe3 Nf3; 27.Qd3 Qh2+; 28.Ke3 Bxf4+; 29.Nxf4 Qxf4+; 30.Ke2 Nd4+!; 31.Qxd4 Qxf1+; 32.Kd2 Rf2+; 33.Kc3 Qc1+; 34.Kb4 a5+; 35.Kxa5 Qa3+; 36.Kb5 (36.Qa4 Qxa4+; 37.Kxa4 Rf1 and Black wins.) 36...Rf1 and then Qc5+ seals it, unless... 37.b4 (37.Qd3 Qa6+) 37...Qa6#.

C) 24.Rh1 Qf3+; 25.Kg1 Nxf4; 26.Rh2 Nh3+; 27.Rxh3 Be3+; 28.Kh2 Qxh3#; 20.Bc1 runs into 20...Nd4!! after which White cannot survive. 21.Nxd4 Qxg3+; 22.Kh1 Qh3+; 23.Kg1 g3; 24.Nf3 Nxf3+; 25.Rxf3 Qh2+; 26.Kf1 g2+; 27.Ke2 g1Q+ and mate follows.

20...Rf7; 21.Kf2 Qh2+; 22.Ke3 Bxd5! It is hard to find a role for the bishop in the attack on the White king, but the Nd5 could have come to the defense of the monarch, and it controlled the important squares e3 and f4, while simultaneously attacking c7. **23.cxd5 Nb4; 24.Rh1.**

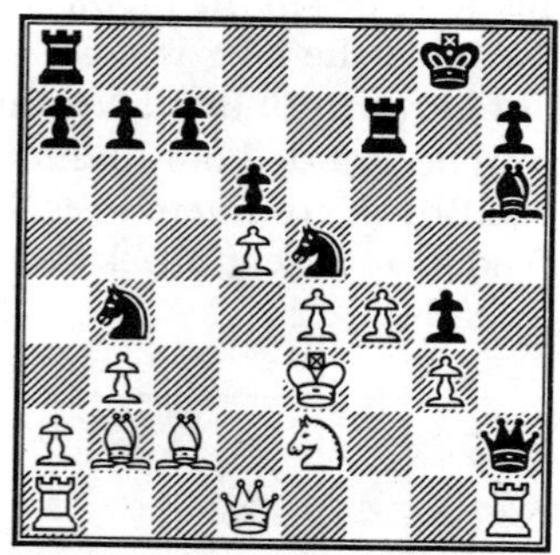

This position resembles a composed problem more than a tournament game. Black must find a way to trap the fleeing monarch. **24...Rxf4!!** Nyezhmetdinov had this planned back at move 19, but it was only when the game reached this point that he was sure of himself. Still, it was more intuition than calculation! **25.Rxh2.** There are no other workable defenses. 25.Nxf4 Nxc2+; 25.gxf4 Bxf4+; 26.Nxf4 (26.Kd4 Qf2+; 27.Kc3 Qc5#) 26...Nxc2+; 25.Bxe5 Rf3+; 26.Kd4 dxe5+; 27.Kc5 Bf8+; 28.Kc4 Qf2 with the threat of Qc5 mate. **25...Rf3+; 26.Kd4.** And what now? **26...Bg7!!** Black is a whole queen down, but he has his hands around White's neck! 26...c5+ was Nyezhmetdinov's original idea, but it doesn't work: 27.dxc6 bxc6; 28.Bd3! Nexd3; 29.Rxh6 Nxb2; 30.Rxd6 Nxd1; 31.Rxd1 and Black has no real chances for a win. 31...Nxa2; 32.Kc5! a5; 33.Rd8+ Rxd8; 34.Rxd8+ Kg7; 35.Kxc6.

27.a4. This allows a quick and beautiful finish, but the alternatives are fascinating in the depth of analysis required to find the win. 27.Ng1!? is perhaps the most challenging, even though Black does win in the end. 27...Rxg3! (Nyezhmetdinov's analysis shows this to lead by force to a winning endgame.) 28.Ne2 Rf3; 29.Ng1 Ned3+! is the correct solution. 30.Kc4 (30.e5 Bxe5+; 31.Kc4 Rf4+!; 32.Bd4 Rxd4+; 33.Kc3 Nxd5+; 34.Kd2 Bf4+; 35.Ke2 Re8+; 36.Kf1 Ne3+; 37.Ke2 Nxd1+; 38.Kxd1 Re1#) 30...Nxb2+; 31.Kxb4 Bc3+; 32.Ka3 b5!? (32...Nxd1; 33.Bxd1 Bxa1; 34.Nxf3 gxf3; 35.Bxf3 Rf8; 36.Rh3 and despite the bad light-squared bishop the position is likely to be drawn.) 33.b4 a5; 34.bxa5 Nc4+!; 35.Kb3 Nxa5+; 36.Ka3 Nc4+; 37.Kb3 Ra3#. **27...c5+; 28.dxc6 bxc6; 29.Bd3 Nexd3+; 30.Kc4.**

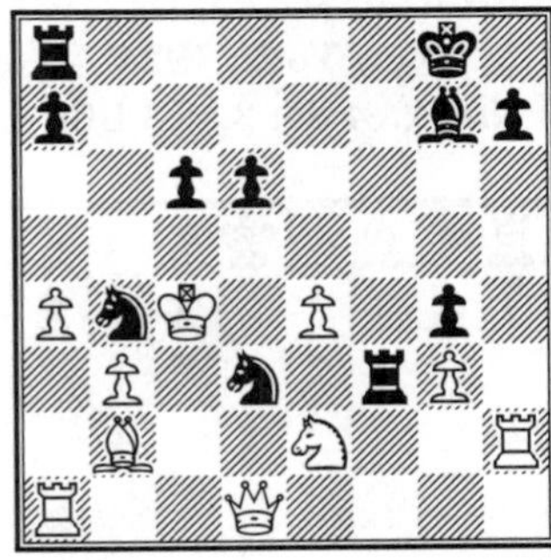

One more diagram is certainly justified, for the crowning blow: 30.e5 is a faster route to Valhalla: 30...dxe5+; 31.Ke4 Nc5#. **30...d5+!; 31.exd5 cxd5+; 32.Kb5 Rb8+; 33.Ka5 Nc6+** and Black resigned, not wanting to suffer the humiliation of 34.Ka6 Nc5 mate!

The reader will no doubt notice that a great deal of space has been devoted to this game, which takes place within a fairly rare opening. This is because although the game is one of the greatest ever played (Mikhail Tal told me it was his favorite!), it is not as well known as it should be. These notes are hardly exhaustive. I actually wrote a whole book on this one game, *The Chessplayer's Laboratory,* and studied and taught the game for over a year, before finally, with the help of no less than World Champion Kasparov, satisfying myself that I had discovered at least most of its secrets and beautiful treasures.

JANOWSKI INDIAN

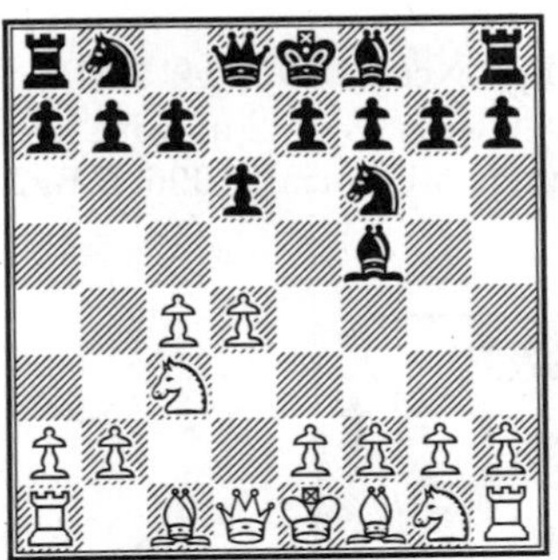

1.d4	**Nf6**
2.c4	**d6**
3.Nc3	**Bf5**

The **Janowski Indian** is a variation of the Old Indian which has remained somewhat obscure. The first monograph on the subject was my 1990 book. The idea is simple: Black turns the e4-square into a battleground. White can occupy the center with pawns, but only at the cost of considerable time, and Black obtains significant counterplay with rapid piece development. Should Black choose to fianchetto at g7, a King's Indian formation is established.

(242) ALEKHINE - JANOWSKI [A53]

New York, 1924

1.d4 Nf6; 2.c4 d6; 3.Nc3 Bf5; 4.g3.

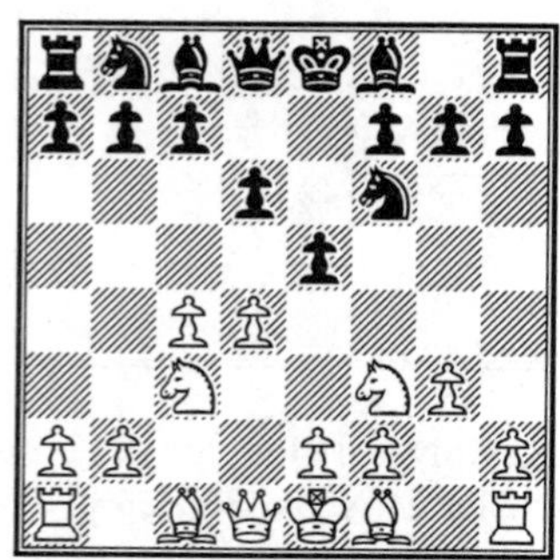

4.f3 is now the most challenging line. White can get the pawn to e4 quickly. 4...e5 (4...Nbd7 was Janowski's plan, but it is too passive. 5.e4 Bg6; 6.Bd3 e5; 7.d5 Nh5; 8.Be3 Be7; 9.Qd2 Nc5; 10.Bc2 and White has a much more comfortable game. Eventually the kingside pawns can be advanced in a strong attack, though White failed to exploit this opportunity in Norman Hansen-Janowski, Hastings 1926.) 5.e4 exd4; 6.Qxd4 Nc6; Black can delay this move and retreat to e6 right away.

7.Qd2. This looks unnatural, but since the dark-squared bishop is headed to b2 anyway it is the best retreat. 7...Be6; 8.b3 Be7. Alternatively, Black can adopt a fianchetto plan, which can led to interesting complications, for example (8...g6; 9.Bb2 Bg7; 10.Nge2 0–0; 11.g3 Ne5; 12.Bg2 Bxc4!? as in Ivkov-Sokolov, Kraljevo 1967, which continued 13.bxc4 Nxc4; 14.Qc2 c6; 15.Nd1 d5; 16.Bc3 b5; 17.Kf1 Re8 with considerable pressure for the minor material investment.) 9.Nge2 0–0; 10.Ng3 Nd7; 11.Nd5 Bh4; 12.Be2 f5 with strong central pressure for Black in Jovanovic-Kovacevic, Yugoslav Championship 1995.

4...c6. 4...e5 is a logical alternative. 5.Bg2 Nc6; 6.d5 Nd4; 7.e4 Bg4; 8.f3 Bd7; 9.Nge2 c5; 10.dxc6 Nxc6; 11.Be3 Be7; 12.0–0 0–0; 13.Qd2 a6 with a solid position for Black in Piket-Sokolov Amsterdam (Donner Memorial) 1996. **5.Bg2 Nbd7; 6.e4 Bg6; 7.Nge2 e5; 8.h3.**

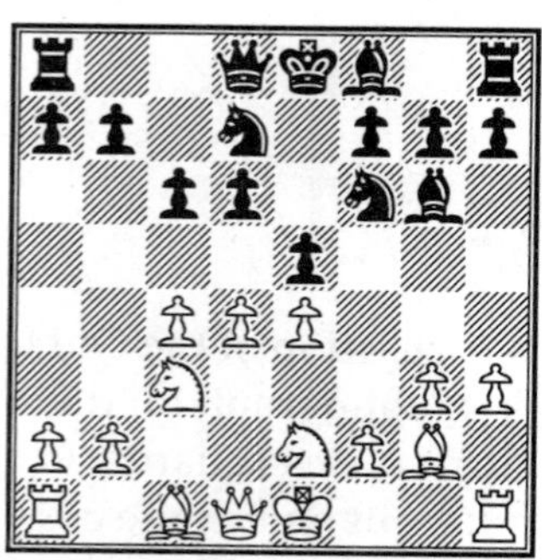

Alekhine claimed that White is already much better here, but a more modern player might not agree, as Black has no significant weaknesses and can develop quickly. **8...Qb6; 9.0–0 0–0–0.** This is simply to risky. Black should have headed for the kingside with 9...Be7; 10.Be3 QC7; 11.Qd2 0–0 with a reasonable game. Instead, Black simply provides White with a juicy target on the queenside. **10.d5 Nc5; 11.Be3 cxd5; 12.cxd5 Qa6; 13.f3.** White takes care of the center in preparation for b4. **13...Kb8.** 13...Qd3 14.Qc1 and the Black queen is simply misplaced. **14.b4 Ncd7; 15.a4 Qc4; 16.Qd2.** According to Alekhine, 16.Rb1 followed by Qd2 and Rfc1 would have won more easily. **16...Qxb4; 17.Bxa7+ Ka8.** 17...Kxa7 loses to 18.Nb5+. **18.Rfb1 Qa5; 19.Be3 Nc5; 20.Rb5 Qc7; 21.a5 Nfd7; 22.Nc1 Rc8; 23.Nb3.**

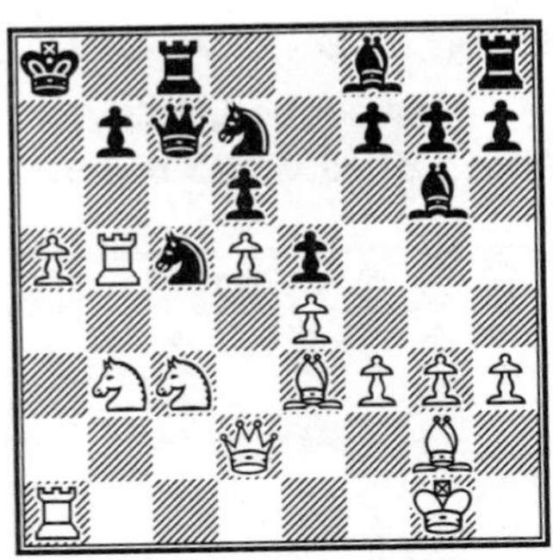

23...Na6. 23...Nxb3 allows the splendid finish 24.a6!! Nxd2; 25.axb7+ Kb8; 26.Ra8#. **24.Na4 Be7; 25.Nb6+ Kb8.** 25...Nxb6; 26.axb6 Qb8 gets swept away by 27.Rxa6+ bxa6; 28.b7+ Qxb7; 29.Rxb7 Kxb7; 30.Qb4+ Ka8; 31.Qb6 but after the test Black's fate is a miserable one and the remainder of the game needs no comment. **26.Rc1 Ndc5; 27.Nxc5 dxc5; 28.Nxc8 Rxc8; 29.Bf1 Qd7; 30.Rb6 c4; 31.Rxc4 Rxc4; 32.Bxc4 Qxh3; 33.Qg2 Qxg2+; 34.Kxg2 Bd8; 35.Rb2 Kc8; 36.Bxa6 bxa6; 37.Bb6 Bg5; 38.Rc2+ Kb7; 39.d6 f5; 40.d7. White won.**

BOGO-INDIAN

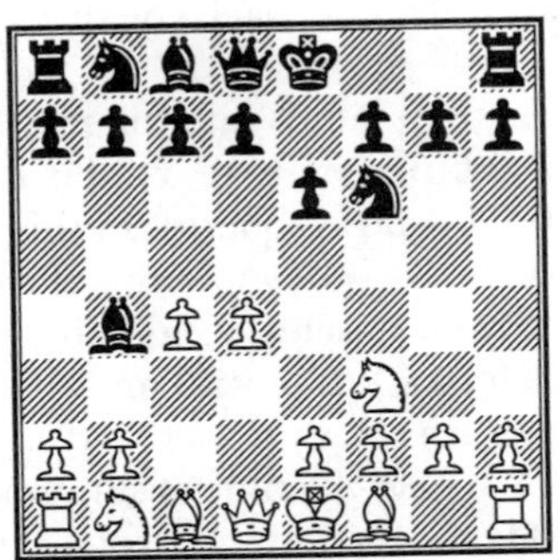

1.d4	**Nf6**
2.c4	**e6**
3.Nf3	**Bb4+**

The **Bogo-Indian**, or **Bogoljubow Indian**, is also known as the "Boring" opening. Black will develop on the queenside, with plans ranging from ...a5 and ...b6 to the more exotic ...c5 formations, with kingside castling and an eventual advance of the d-pawn. Against such a solid position it is generally hard for White to play with much aggression, though of course that can also be said for the Queen's Indian Defense.

If White wants a real fight, then 3.Nc3 must be played rather than 3.Nf3. That said, one would expect the check at b4 to be greeted by 4.Nc3, transposing to the Nimzo-Indian, but of course the Nf3 systems are not the most ambitious against the Nimzo-Indian, and in any case, if White wanted that sort of position, then 3.Nc3 would have been played.

(243) GRUENFELD - BOGOLJUBOW [E11]

Marienbad, 1925

1.d4 Nf6; 2.c4 e6; 3.Nf3 Bb4+; 4.Nbd2.

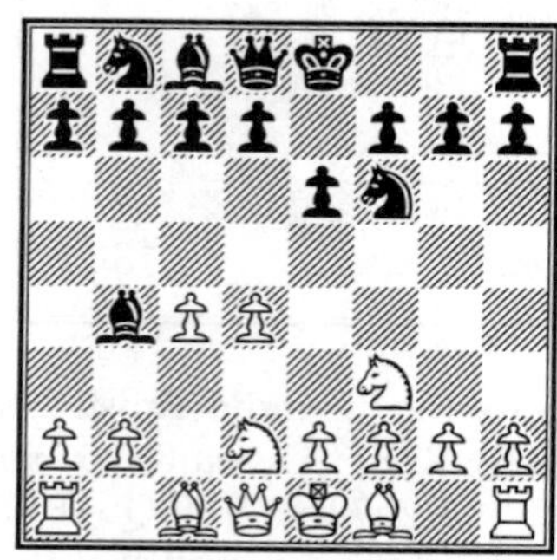

This is the Gruenfeld Variation. When White interposes the knight in response to Bogoljubow's check the play will develop more slowly, but Black must be careful. When the bishop is driven back from b4 by an eventual advance of White's a-pawn, White can seize the center. For this reason Black often tries to advance the d-pawn to d5 early in the game. **4...0–0.** This is perhaps not the most precise move order since Black needs to get a pawn to d5 quickly. 4...d5; 5.a3 Be7; 6.e3 0–0; 7.Bd3 c5 is an aggressive plan. For example 8.dxc5 can be met by 8...a5! and the pawn can be collected later. P.Cramling-C.Hansen, Malmo 1996, saw Black equalize quickly after 9.b3 Nbd7; 10.Bb2 Nxc5.

5.a3 Be7. 5...Bxd2+; 6.Qxd2!? is an alternative plan. White will play b4 followed by Bb2. **6.e3.** White could, and perhaps should, play e4 here. **6...d5; 7.Bd3 Nbd7; 8.0–0 c5!** Black immediately contests important central squares. In this highly symmetrical position White does not seem to have any way of exploiting the privilege of the first move. Notice that the bishop at c1 is just as useless as its counterpart at c8.

9.Qe2 cxd4; 10.exd4 b6; 11.cxd5!? This leaves White with an isolated d-pawn. **11...Nxd5; 12.Nc4 Bb7; 13.Bd2.** White's pieces are poorly posted and curiously ineffective. **13...Rc8; 14.Nce5 Bf6; 15.Qe4.** This feeble attempt at an attack is easily repulsed. **15...g6; 16.Qg4 Ne7; 17.Be4 Ba6.** There was nothing wrong with exchanging bishops, but Black is aware that the centralized bishop at e4 has no real effect, so the Black's bishop goes on a hunt for light squares. **18.Qf4.**

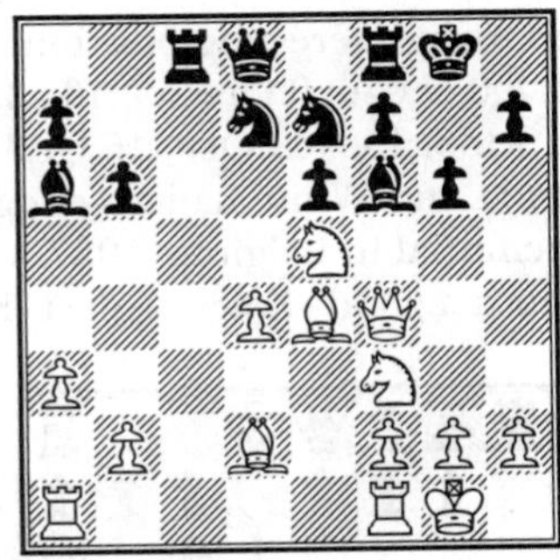

18...Bxe5! Excellent judgment! Black gives up a bishop for a knight and eliminates White's weakness at d4, but opens important lines. **19.dxe5 f5!** There is absolutely no reason to give up the bishop at a6 for the rook at d1 here. **20.Qh6.** 20.exf6 Rxf6; 21.Qd6 e5; 22.Qb4 Nc5 is much better for Black, since many White pieces are vulnerable. **20...Re8; 21.Bg5 fxe4; 22.Bf6 Nf5; 23.Qg5 Nxf6; 24.exf6 exf3; 25.Rfd1 Nd4** and White gave up. **Black won.**

(244) KASPAROV - YUSUPOV [E11]

Soviet Championship, 1981

1.d4 Nf6; 2.c4 e6; 3.Nf3 Bb4+; 4.Bd2.

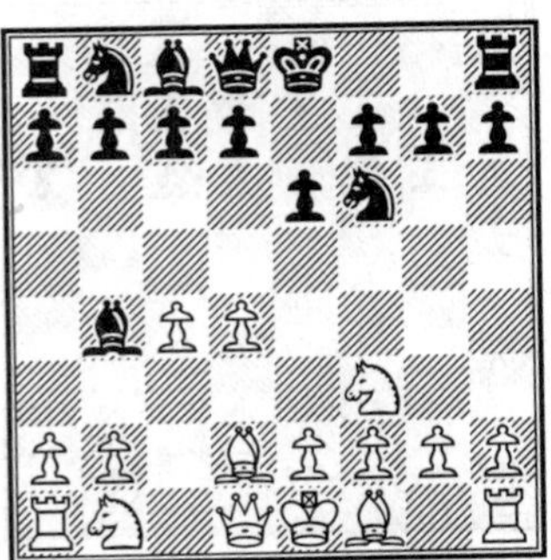

The normal reply. Now Black can exchange bishops, or defend with ...a5 or ...Qe7. **4...a5.** Here are some top-level encounters featuring the alternatives.

4...Bxd2+; 5.Qxd2 d5; 6.g3 0–0; 7.Bg2 Nbd7; 8.Qc2 has brought Karpov the advantage against Bogoindian specialist Ulf Andersson. 8...c6 (8...b6; 9.cxd5 Nxd5; 10.0–0 Bb7; 11.e4 N5f6; 12.Nc3 c5; 13.Rad1 cxd4; 14.Nxd4 Qe7; 15.Rfe1 Ne5; 16.f4 Nc6 and now Karpov unleashed 17.Nd5! exd5; 18.Nxc6 Bxc6; 19.exd5 Qxe1+; 20.Rxe1 Bxd5; 21.Bxd5 Nxd5; 22.Qa4 with a significant advantage for White in Karpov-Andersson, Enkoping (rapid) 1995.) 9.Nbd2 Qe7; 10.0–0 e5; 11.cxd5 Nxd5; 12.e4 N5f6; 13.Rfe1 Rd8; 14.Rad1 exd4; 15.Nxd4 Nb6; 16.N2b3 Bg4; 17.f3 Be6; 18.Qc5 and White won quickly: 18...Qe8; 19.e5 Nfd7; 20.Qc1 Nf8; 21.f4 Bxb3; 22.Nxb3 Ne6; 23.Rd6 Nc8; 24.Rxc6 Karpov-Andersson, Reykjavik (World Cup) 1991.

4...Qe7; 5.g3 Nc6; 6.Bg2 Bxd2+; 7.Nbxd2 d6; 8.0–0 0–0; 9.e4 e5; 10.d5 gives White too much space, as seen in the game between Euwe and Flohr, played at the famous AVRO tournament of 1938.

4...c5; 5.Bxb4 cxb4 leads to an interesting position, and again the fianchetto is correct. 6.g3 b6; 7.Bg2 Bb7; 8.0–0 0–0; 9.Qb3 a5; 10.a3 Na6; 11.Nbd2 d6; 12.Rfd1 Qe7; 13.Ne1 Bxg2; 14.Nxg2 Rfd8; 15.Ne3 Qe8; 16.Qd3 e5; 17.Ne4 Nxe4; 18.Qxe4 exd4; 19.Qxe8+ Rxe8; 20.Rxd4 and White had an endgame advantage in Karpov-Korchnoi, from the Euwe memorial in Belgium, 1987.

5.g3. The fianchetto plan is a good choice against the Bogo-Indian.

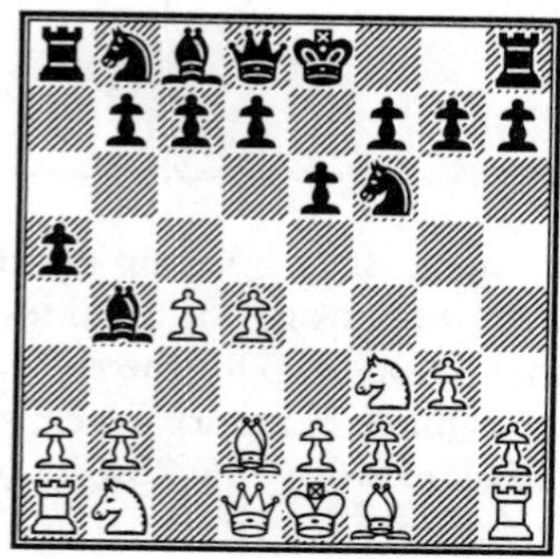

5...0–0; 6.Bg2 b6; 7.0–0 Ba6; 8.Bg5 Be7; 9.Qc2 Nc6; 10.a3. White keeps the enemy knight off of b4. **10...h6; 11.Bxf6 Bxf6.** Black's position is not bad. At present, only the h1–a8 diagonal looks dangerous. **12.Rd1 Qe7.**

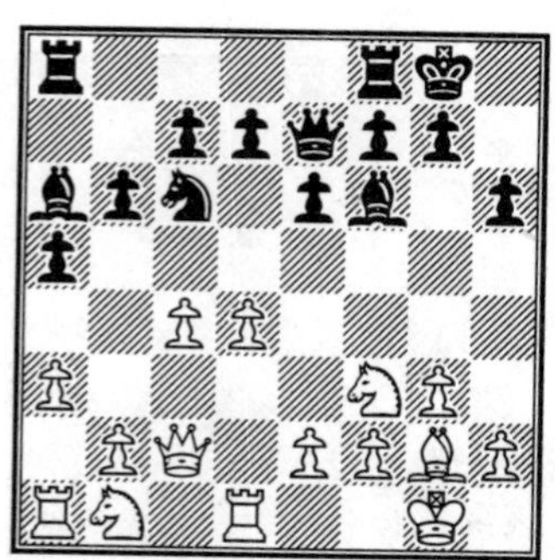

13.e3 Rae8?! In this slow opening, Black has actually outstripped White's development. But White controls the center, and d7-d5 will not be appropriate because of the position of the White queen, putting pressure on the c-file. **14.Nfd2.** A strong move which threatens to post the knight effectively at e4, while opening up lines for the Bg2 and threatening to disrupt Black's pawn structure. In addition, the pawn at c4 is guarded so that the other knight can enter the game. **14...g5?!** Black overreacts to the positional strength of White's game. 14...g6 would have been more solid. **15.Nc3 Bg7.** White should probably bring Black's extended fianchetto into question by playing 16.f4, but he is concentrating on the queenside, and in particular, on the c-file. **16.Nb5 Qd8; 17.f4.**

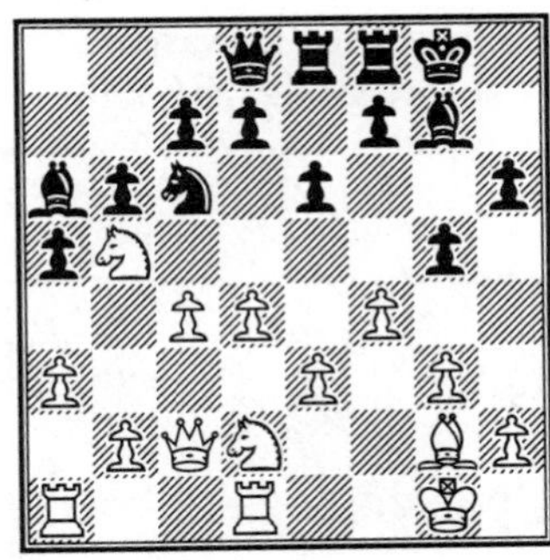

17...Ne7! Black has taken advantage of White's faulty plan by reorganizing his pieces so that the Ne7 can take part in the defense. Unfortunately, Yusupov soon forgets why he wanted the knight at e7. **18.Nf3 Nf5; 19.Qf2?!** Kasparov notes that this was not the correct square for the queen. It would have been better placed at e2, where it could protect the pawn at c4. **19...c6; 20.Nc3 gxf4; 21.gxf4 Bxc4.** Although White is a pawn down, he is at the same time almost a piece ahead, because Black's light-squared bishop is incapable of reaching the kingside to help in the defense. In addition, White now takes charge of the center.

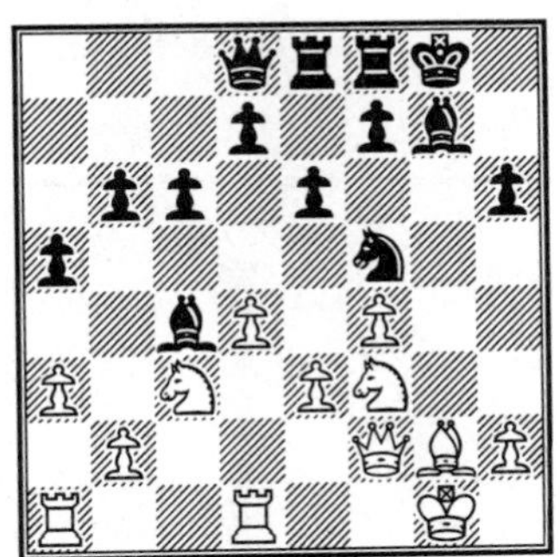

22.e4. Now Yusupov makes a major strategic error. He must return the knight to its defensive post at e7. **22...Nd6?** 22...Ne7; 23.Kh1! f5; 24.e5 brings White sufficient compensation for his pawn, because Black's kingside is very weak. The difference between this position and the game is that here the knight participates in the defense. In the game, it watches from c8. **23.Ne5 f5; 24.Nxc4 Nxc4.** Black does not mind parting with his bishop, but the problem is that the Nc4 is far away from the kingside. Kasparov now chases it to an utterly useless position on the back rank.

25.b3! Nd6; 26.e5 Nc8. White's goal is to infiltrate the kingside, and exploit the weak light squares. 26...Ne4; 27.Bxe4 fxe4; 28.Nxe4 is clearly better for White, with a SuperKnight at e4 and threats along the g-file. **27.Bf3!** Clearly the bishop must get involved in this task. **27...Kh7.** Black escapes the g-file, and hopes to use it to exchange rooks, lessening White's attacking force.

28.Bh5 Re7; 29.Kh1 Rg8?! Although this is consistent with Black's plan, he chooses the wrong rook. The correct strategy was 29...Bh8! followed by Re7-g7. 29...Bh8; 30.Rg1 Rg7; 31.Rxg7+ Bxg7; 32.Rg1 Qe7! The point. This square is now available for the queen, which can hold the position together until the other rook reaches g8. 33.Qg3 Rg8; 34.Nb1! is given by Kasparov, with the comment that White stands better, since he will be able to swing his knight to h4, while the Nc8 is still out of play. **30.Rg1 Bh8.** If White's queen stood on f5, and were not attacked, then mate in two.

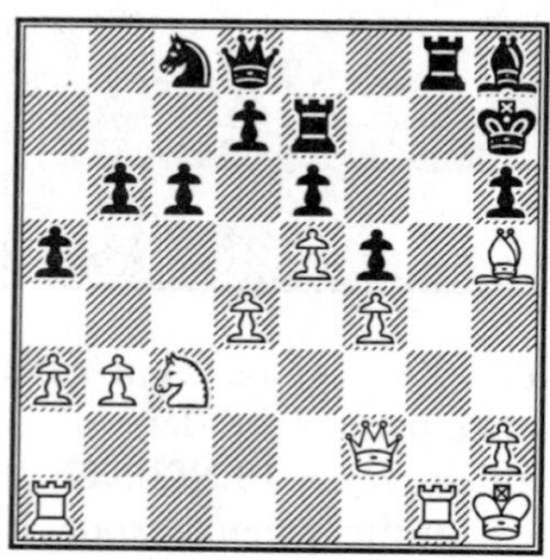

30...Bf8?; 31.Qh4 sets up a very nasty pin! **31.Ne4!!** Because of the threat of Nf6+, the knight must be captured. But this gives White access to the f5-square. The sacrifice of material is not so important because Black's knight is so out of play. **31...fxe4; 32.f5 Rg5?** An error in time pressure. According to Kasparov, Black should have brought the queen over to help with the defense: 32...Qf8; 33.Rxg8 Kxg8; 34.f6! Rg7! **33.Rxg5 hxg5; 34.f6.**

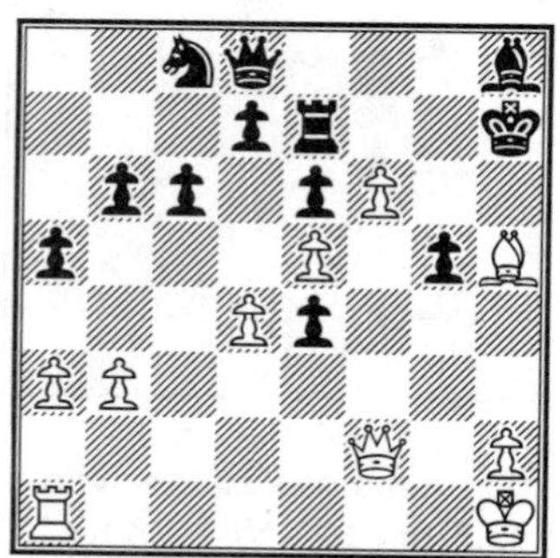

34...Kh6. 34...Qf8; 35.fxe7 Qxf2; 36.e8Q wins because Black has no checks. **35.fxe7 Qxe7. 36.Bf7! d6.** 36...g4; 37.h4! gxh3; 38.Rg1 Bg7; 39.Qf4+ Kh7; 40.Qxe4+ Kh8; 41.Qg6. **37.Rf1 g4.** White needs to get his queen and rook into the game in order to mate. The best route is via h4, but that is covered by the Black queen. 37...dxe5 allows 38.Qe2. **38.Bxe6!! Qxe6; 39.Qh4+ Kg7** and here Black resigned before Kasparov could play 40.Rf6. **White won.**

8. THE FLANK GAMES

In the Flank Games, White shirks the responsibility of building the ideal pawn center and instead tries to control that critical area of the board with piece pressure, usually involving a fianchetto at g2. The **Reti Opening,** 1.Nf3 d5 2.c4, is perhaps the purest version of this strategy. Developed by Richard Reti in the early decades of this century, it offers temporary custody of a pawn, which, if captured by 2...dxc4, can be regained later with Na3 or Qa4+. White can choose to fianchetto the other bishop as well, or independently as in the **Nimzo-Larsen Attack** (1.Nf3 d5; 2.b3).

White can also adopt the strategy of playing a defense with an extra tempo. This is the strategy behind the **English Opening**, which gives Black the opportunity to play the White side of a Sicilian formation after 1...e5. Another reversed opening is the **King's Indian Attack**. That is essentially a King's Indian Defense formation used against any Black opening plan.

RETI OPENING

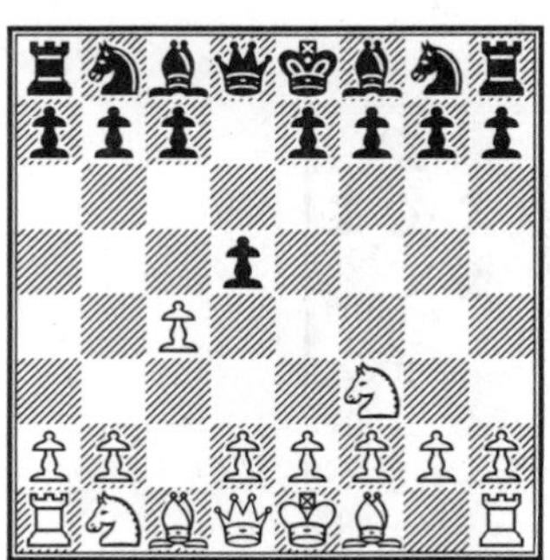

1.Nf3 d5
2.c4

The **Reti Opening** is thoroughly hypermodern. White's plan is to attack Black's central formation from the flanks, while also operating on the queenside with the help of a long-range bishop which will be stationed at g2.

(245) ROMANOVSKY - RABINOVICH [A12]

Moscow, 1924

1.Nf3 Nf6; 2.c4 c6; 3.g3 d5.

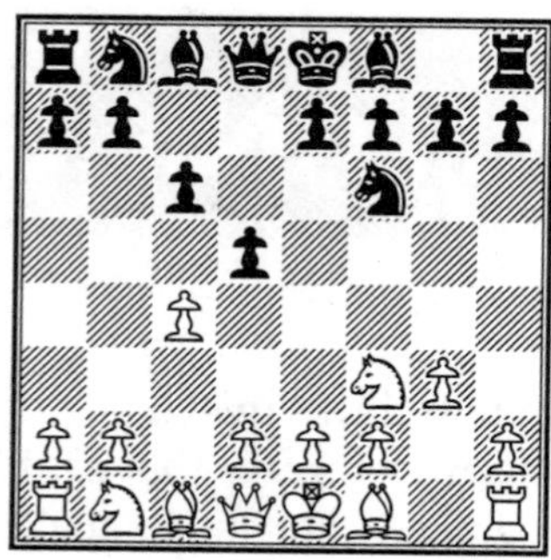

This leads to the conservative treatment of the Reti by Black, who supports the central pillar at d5. **4.b3.** With this move White declares the intention of remaining in the Reti Opening, rather than transposing elsewhere. **4...Bf5; 5.Bg2 e6; 6.0–0 Bd6; 7.Bb2 Nbd7; 8.d3 e5?!** Black gives in to the temptation and occupies the center, but this is just what White was hoping for. Objectively, there is nothing wrong with this approach, but from a psychological standpoint it makes sense only if Black really wants to play according to classical, rather than modern, principles. 8...0–0 is obvious and correct. The logical continuation then is 9.Nbd2 when it is appropriate to advance the e-pawn, for example 9...e5; 10.cxd5 cxd5; 11.Rc1 Qe7; 12.Rc2 a5; 13.a4 h6; 14.Qa1 Rfe8; 15.Rfc1 Bh7 when the White forces have no targets, Reti-Lasker, New York 1924.

9.e4! Be6. 9...dxe4; 10.dxe4 Nxe4??; 11.Nh4! **10.exd5 cxd5; 11.d4! e4.** White has wasted no time in punishing Black for his ambitious play. Black cannot afford to allow the e-file to be opened prior to castling, and the pressure in the center is unbearable. The only hope is to keep things closed. **12.Ng5! 0–0; 13.cxd5.** The central pawns are well supported by the bishops.

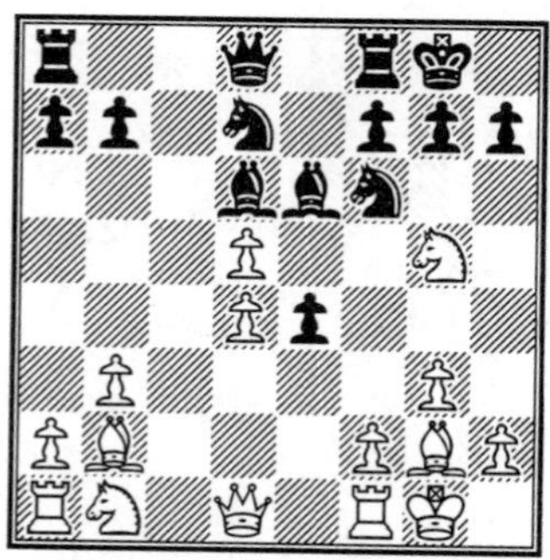

13...Bf5; 14.Nc3 Re8. White now finds a fine move, pinning the e-pawn to the bishop at f5. Although her majesty is rarely employed in such a capacity, here she provides nagging pressure which makes life uncomfortable for Black.

15.Qb1! Qe7; 16.Re1. By trading the doubled pawn for Black's remaining central pawn, White establishes a decisive advantage. **16...Nxd5; 17.Ngxe4 Nxc3; 18.Bxc3.** White has a secure extra pawn, and now demonstrates excellent technique as he grinds his opponent down. **18...Bb4; 19.Qb2 Ba3; 20.Qd2 Qf8.** White now tries to trap the enemy bishop at a3. **21.b4 Rad8; 22.Rab1 Nb6; 23.Rb3 Nc4; 24.Qd3.** White wins a piece, and Rabinovich capitulates after a few more moves. **24...a5; 25.Qxc4 Be6; 26.d5 Bxd5.**

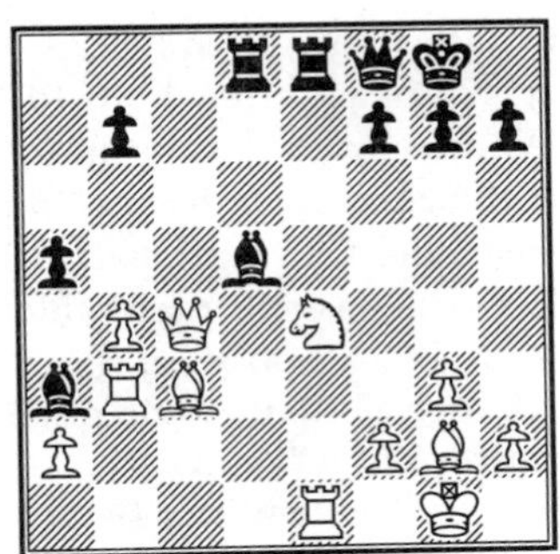

Romanovsky, a great combinative player, does not miss an opportunity to finish with a flourish. **27.Nf6+ gxf6; 28.Bxd5 axb4; 29.Rxe8 Qxe8; 30.Bxf6. White won.**

(246) RETI - BOGOLJUBOW [A13]

New York, 1924

1.Nf3 d5; 2.c4 e6. Accepting the Reti Gambit by capturing at c4 is considered unwise. White can in any case regain the pawn by moving the queen to a4, giving check, and then capturing at c4. The queen is not particularly exposed on that square, and is often found there in the Gruenfeld Defense (Russian Variations) and Catalan (Accepted). **3.g3 Nf6; 4.Bg2.** The contour of White's game is already established. Castling will take place on the kingside, and the d5-square is the focus of attention. **4...Bd6.**

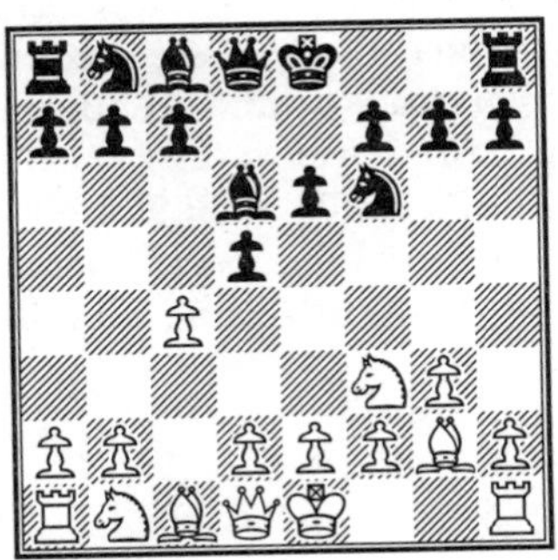

The idea behind this move is to play ...e5 at the appropriate moment. But it never comes to fruition and 4...Be7 is therefore better, so that after an eventual ...Ne4, Black can oppose the long diagonal with ...Bf6. **5.0–0 0–0; 6.b3 Re8.** Black continues with his plan, but it is going to seriously weaken the light squares in the center. Instead, he should be attending to his development on the queenside. 6...b6 ... Bb7 would be appropriate. **7.Bb2 Nbd7; 8.d4.** A strong move that gives White a grip on the center.

8...c6. Little good ever comes out of this Stonewall formation since the passive nature of the pawn structure constitutes and invitation to the opponent to gain control of most of the board. 8...dxc4!? was relatively best. 9.bxc4 c5 with counterplay for Black in the center of the board. **9.Nbd2 Ne4.** Though this leads to a number of exchanges it in no way reduces the pressure on Black's position. Still, it is difficult to find a satisfactory plan. 9...Qe7 was relatively best. **10.Nxe4 dxe4; 11.Ne5 f5.** This saves the pawn, but allows White to open dangerous lines. **12.f3 exf3; 13.Bxf3.** The bishop stands well here, and the e-pawn can have a future at e4.

13...Qc7. 13...Nxe5; 14.dxe5 Bc5+; 15.Kg2 Qxd1; 16.Raxd1 would have led to an inferior endgame for Black, but it was still preferable to the plan adopted in the game. **14.Nxd7 Bxd7; 15.e4 e5.** Black's position was already precarious, and there are no worthy alternatives, though perhaps some other moves might have delayed the inevitable for a bit. **16.c5 Bf8; 17.Qc2! exd4.** 17...f4; 18.gxf4 exd4; 19.e5 and the White pawns are a thorn which Black will not be able to remove. **18.exf5 Rad8; 19.Bh5!**

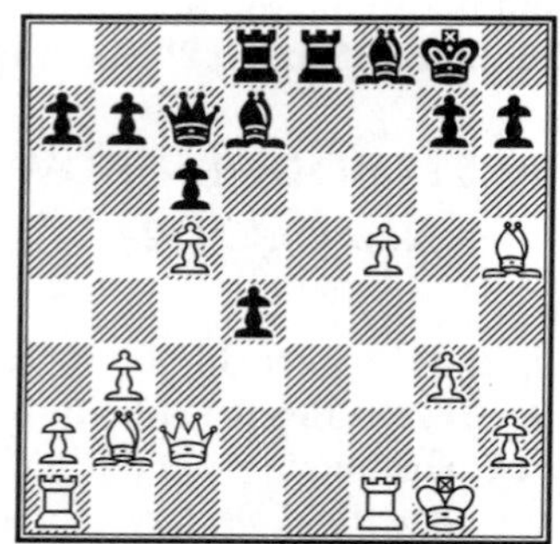

The coverage of the light squares, particularly at f7, prepare the way for an elegant finish. **19...Re5.** 19...Re7 20.Bxd4 Bxf5; 21.Qxf5 Rxd4; 22.Qxf8#. **20.Bxd4 Rxf5?!** 20...Rd5 would have been more resistant, remaining a pawn down but avoiding the sudden termination which Black now experiences. **21.Rxf5 Bxf5; 22.Qxf5 Rxd4.** Bishops of opposite colors lead to drawish endgames, but exciting middlegame! **23.Rf1 Rd8.** 23...Qe7 allows a pretty finish. 24.Bf7+ Kh8; 25.Bd5! Qf6; 26.Qc8 and the pin on the back rank wins. **24.Bf7+ Kh8; 25.Be8!** Mate is inevitable. This is a famous position, which can be found in most primers on tactics. **25...h6; 26.Qxf8+ Kh7; 27.Bg6+ Kxg6; 28.Qf5#.** This great game won the first brilliancy prize of the tournament. **White won.**

(247) CAPABLANCA - MARSHALL [A14]

Moscow, 1925

1.Nf3 Nf6; 2.c4 e6; 3.g3 d5; 4.b3 c5.

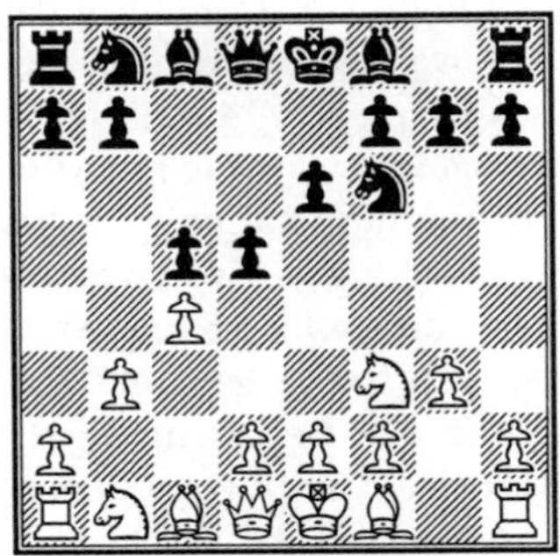

This is a common reply to the Reti. Once White declares the intention of fianchettoing on both flanks, Black can afford to play the standard White approach of advancing c- and d-pawns, since with colors reversed, the double fianchetto approach is rarely used by Black against 1.d4 and 2.c4. **5.Bg2 Nc6; 6.0–0 Be7; 7.d3 0–0; 8.Bb2 d4.** Marshall accepts Capablanca's hypermodern challenge. Alternatives include 8...a5, suggested by Golombek, and 8...Qb6. **9.e4.** Whether the pawn advances one square or two was of little consequence to the American, who would capture in any event. **9...dxe3?** This unleashes the power of the bishop on b2. Marshall should have fought against his love for open positions and played 9...e5!; 10.Ne1 Ne8; 11.f4 f6 with a solid game. **10.fxe3.**

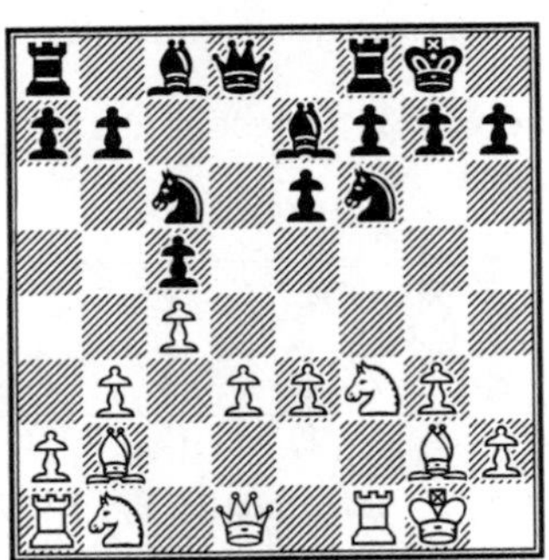

The pawns in the White forecourt may seem to be weak, but they are not. The pawn at e3 controls the d4-square, making it unavailable to the Black knight. Thus, the vista of the bishop on b2 is unimpeded. The White pieces can complete their harmonious development, while Black has significant problems developing the light-squared bishop.

10...Ng4; 11.Qe2 Bf6; 12.Nc3! Naturally White does not wish to part with his excellent bishop. **12...Qa5?!** The queen is not very useful on the edge of the board. 12...Bd7 was recommended by Bogoljubow and Nimzowitsch on the basis of 12...Bd7 but 13.Nd2 Nge5; 14.Nde4 Be7; 15.Rad1 is very good for White Tartakower. 12...Qe7 was perhaps best here, keeping the queen in the general vicinity of the king for defensive purposes while still transferring the f8-rook to d8. **13.Rac1.** Where to put the rooks? This is always a question which requires positional understanding to answer properly. If White's intention is to play on the queenside, then 13.Rfc1 comes into consideration, but this is clearly an inappropriate plan here. Note that the queen cannot be used to protect the knight because of the tactical trick Ng4xe3.

13...Rd8. Black seems to have little regard for the safety of the king, but then Marshall was always an attacking player. **14.h3! Nge5.** After 14...Nh6; 15.g4 Be7; 16.Ba1! White will be able to organize a strong kingside attack, e.g. 16...Bf8; 17.Ne4 Qc7; 18.Nfg5 f6 which allows the devastatingly brilliant 19.Rxf6!! gxf6; 20.Nxf6+ Kh8; 21.Ne8+. **15.Ne4!** White is willing to give up a little material in order to create a fatal weakness on the Black kingside. **15...Qxa2.** 15...Nxf3+; 16.Qxf3 Bxb2?; 17.Qxf7+ Kh8; 18.Qf8+ mates. **16.Nxf6+ gxf6; 17.Nxe5 Nxe5.** 17...fxe5; 18.Qh5! Qxb2; 19.Qxf7+ Kh8; 20.Be4! wins. **18.Be4.** Bringing the bishop into the battle from its base at g2 is one of the strategically important maneuvers in the Réti. **18...Bd7.** If 18...f5 then 19.Ra1! breaks the pin. 19...Qxb3; 20.Bxe5 fxe4; 21.Qg4+ Kf8; 22.Qg7+ Ke8; 23.Qxf7#. **19.Ra1 Qxb3.**

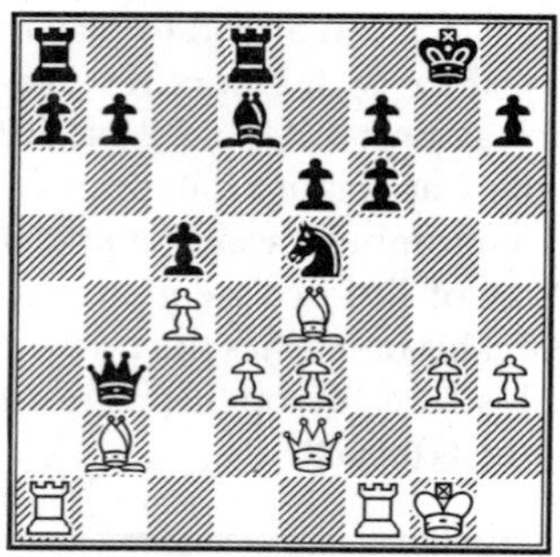

20.Rfb1. This forces the win of a piece, but right after the game Capablanca displayed 20.Bxe5 fxe5; 21.Qg4+ Kf8.

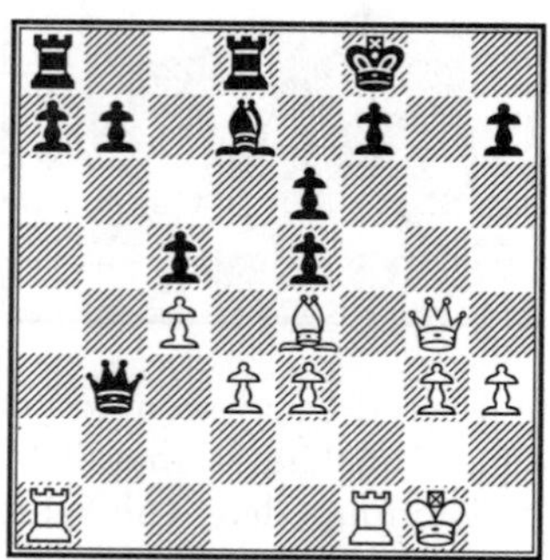

22.Rxf7+ Kxf7; 23.Qg5! Rf8; 24.Bxh7 Bc6; 25.Bg6+ Kg7; 26.Bf5+ Kf7; 27.Qg6+ Ke7; 28.Qxe6+ Kd8; 29.Qd6+ Ke8; 30.Bg6+ Rf7; 31.Rf1 Bf3.

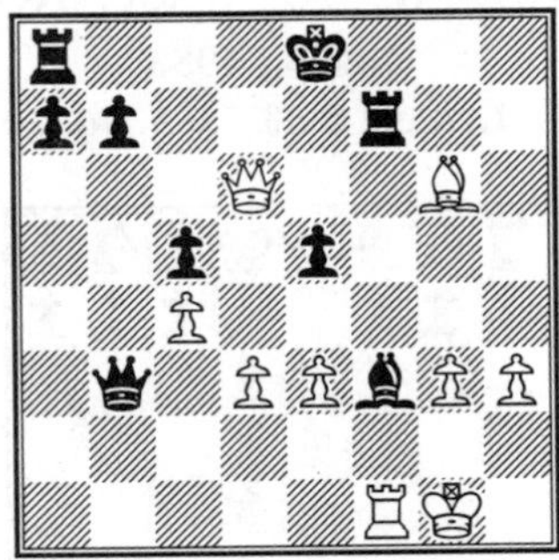

32.Qe6+ Kd8; 33.Qxf7 and White wins. Capablanca is said to have avoided this continuation because of its complications, but perhaps he didn't investigate it deeply enough because the text wins easily enough. **20...Qb4; 21.Bxe5 fxe5; 22.Rxb4 cxb4; 23.Bxb7 Rab8; 24.Rxa7 b3; 25.Qb2 Ba4; 26.Qxe5 Bc6; 27.Qg5+ Kf8; 28.Bxc6 b2; 29.Qe7+. White won.**

KING'S INDIAN ATTACK

Nf3
g3
Bg2
0-0
d3
e4
Nd2

Shows typical white formation; the order of moves is not relevant.

The **King's Indian Attack** is one of those openings where White stays behind the frontier line and sets up pieces, awaiting developments. White's play is almost formulaic, with all of the pieces destined for designated squares: knights at d2 and f3, bishops at c1 and g2, rook at e1, queen at e2, and an advance of the h-pawn. It really has little in common with a King's Indian Defense, because Black is already committed to ...e6, whereas White rarely chooses e3 against the King's Indian. For this reason the opening is most often approached from the Sicilian (1.e4 c5; 2.Nf3 e6; 3.d3) or French Defenses.

Few strong players use the opening with any regularity, but Bobby Fischer toyed with it and the swashbuckling Yugoslav Grandmaster Ljubojevic has always been a fan.

(248) LJUBOJEVIC - KASPAROV [C00]

Niksic, 1983

1.e4 e6; 2.d3 d5; 3.Nd2.

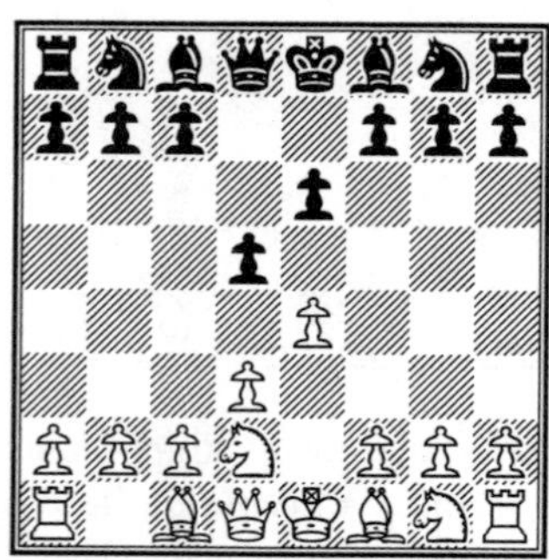

This is just one introductory sequence to the King's Indian Attack, which involves a kingside fianchetto by White and usually an attack on that flank. The game can also begin 1.Nf3 Nf6; 2.g3 and many other move orders are possible.

3.Qe2 is the modern handling, but it actually dates back to Chigorin, who used to play 2.Qe2 consistently against the French. The difference now is that instead of using the move to discourage Black from playing ...d5, it is now almost exclusively played after Black gets the d-pawn to d5. White then avoids a threatened exchange of queens after ...dxe4, dxe4. Former Soviet Champion and now Israeli Grandmaster Lev Psakhis is one of the leading exponents of this approach, even though he is also famous as a defender of the French Defense!

3...Nf6 (3...b6; 4.Nf3 dxe4; 5.Qxe4 c6; 6.d4 Nf6; 7.Qh4 Bb7; 8.Be2 Nbd7; 9.Nc3 Bd6 is an interesting solid option, seen in Christiansen-Bareyev, Yerevan Olympiad 1996.) 4.Nf3 b6; 5.e5 Ng8; 6.g3 c5; 7.Bg2 Nc6; 8.0-0 Nge7; 9.c4! illustrates White's key idea in this new approach. White wants Black to advance the d-pawn, turning the bishop at g2 into a monster. Black does not have to cooperate, but even in this case there will be difficulties because of the pressure at f5, for example 9...Nf5; 10.Nc3 Ncd4; 11.Nxd4 cxd4; 12.Nb1! Bb7; 13.Nd2 Be7; 14.cxd5 Bxd5; 15.Bxd5 Qxd5; 16.Qe4 and Black had no way to avoid problems on the light squares later in the game in Psakhis-Skomorokhin, Vienna 1996.

3...c5. 3...Nc6; 4.Ngf3 d4; 5.g3 e5 is another defense. Play can get quite lively after 6.Bg2 Bg4; 7.0-0 Qd7; 8.Qe1 0-0-0 as the kings sit on opposite wings. Pawnstorms on both sides can arise, for example 9.Nc4 f6; 10.a4 Bh3; 11.Bd2 Bxg2; 12.Kxg2 h5 where 13.h4! slowed down Black's attack and allowed White to take over on the queenside with 13...Nh6; 14.b4 Nf7; 15.a5 Be7; 16.b5 Nb8; 17.Qb1 Bc5; 18.b6! Na6! Black finds the best defense, and it is not easy for White to continue the attack. 19.Qb3 Nd6; 20.Rfb1 Rde8; 21.c3! and the Black pawn chain starts to collapse. 21...Kd8; 22.cxd4 exd4; 23.Nxd6 Qxd6; 24.bxa7 Bxa7; 25.Qxb7 Bc5; 26.Bf4 Qe6; 27.Rc1 Ke7 and now a small sacrifice finished things off nicely: 28.Rxc5! Nxc5; 29.Qxc7+ Nd7; 30.Nxd4 Qa6; 31.Bd6+!! and in Schiller-Draifinger, Eastern High School Championship 1971, Black resigned, since ...Qxd6 loses the queen to Nf5+.

3...Nf6; 4.g3 b6. French specialist John Watson prefers 4...Bd6 here, but this needs more tests. If Black wants to fianchetto on the queenside, however, that had better take place quickly. (4...c5 leads to the most common lines, seen above in notes to Ljubojevic-Petrosian.) 5.Bg2 Bb7; 6.e5 Nfd7; 7.Ngf3 c5; 8.0–0 Nc6; 9.Re1 Qc7; 10.Qe2 h6 Black refuses to castle, which would invite enemy pawn storms on either flank. With the center closed, one might think that the king could remain safe at e8, but in fact the lack of coordination of the rooks makes it impossible to find an effective plan of attack. 11.h4 g5!? Black throws caution to the wind in the hopes of building a kingside attack. 12.hxg5 hxg5; 13.Nxg5 Nd4; 14.Qd1 Nxe5; 15.c3 Nf5 and here White tried an interesting exchange sacrifice because the knight at e5 was just too strong. 16.Rxe5 (16.Ndf3 would have led to a more civilized equality.) 16...Qxe5; 17.Qa4+ Ke7; 18.Ndf3 Qc7; 19.Qg4 Ng7; 20.Nh4 Ke8; 21.c4. The thematic move again, but here it comes much too late to have any effect. 21...Rd8; 22.cxd5 Bxd5; 23.Ne4 Bxe4; 24.Bxe4 Nh5; 25.Qf3 Qe5 and Black had consolidated in Nyezhmetdinov-Antoshin, Sochi (Chigorin Memorial) 1964.

4.Ngf3 Nc6; 5.g3 Nge7. 5...Bd6; 6.Bg2 Nge7 is more natural, for example 7.0–0 0–0; 8.Re1 Qc7; 9.c3 Bd7; 10.Qe2 and now Black can equalize with 10...f6!, as in A.Zaitsev-Gufeld, Soviet Championship 1969. **6.Bg2 g6; 7.0–0 Bg7** is crucial, and there is no clear consensus on White's best move here.

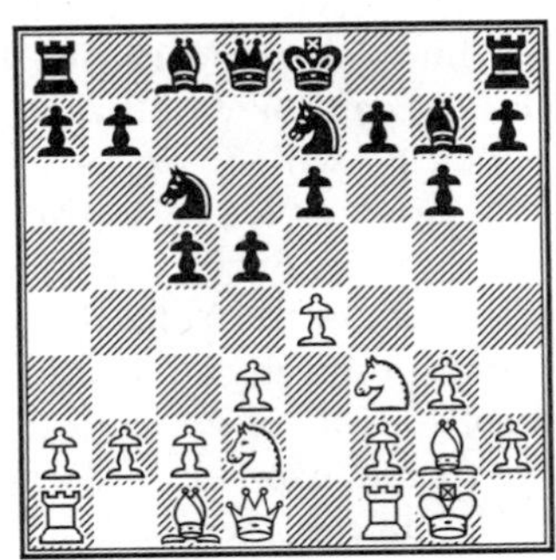

8.Re1. White has completed essential development and can start to work on the flanks. The bishop at c1 will eventually be activated at f4. 8.exd5 exd5; 9.d4 is the best move, according to the book on the King's Indian Attack by Smith and Hall. In my own book, 8.Re1 is the choice. Time for another installment in the debate! 9...cxd4; 10.Nb3 Qb6; 11.Bg5 is the critical move, on the basis of a game Dvoretsky-Vulfson, Soviet Union 1986. In my book, I suggested simply castling, but now I think that after 11...Be6 White has serious problems justifying the investment of a pawn. On 12.Re1 Black does not play ...Nf5, transposing back into the cited game, but instead plays 12...h6; 13.Bf4 and now Black can consider castling on either side, where I just don't see full compensation for the pawn.

8...b6. Smith and Hall claim that the plan used by Black in this game is very effective against 8.Re1, but I felt that too much emphasis was placed on the fact that Kasparov was Black. Let's look at the objective situation after **9.c3.** 9.a3 h6; 10.Rb1 a5; 11.h4 Ba6; 12.exd5 Nxd5; 13.Nc4 0–0; 14.Nce5. Black has not played with sufficient aggression, so White enjoys a comfortable game. 14...Rc8; 15.Nxc6 Rxc6; 16.c4! Again the thematic move which White must always take into consideration when forming strategic plans. The backward d-pawn is of no consequence, since it can always be advanced to d4 if necessary. The key is to shut down Black's queenside counterplay. 16...Ne7; 17.Bf4 b5; 18.Qc1 h5; 19.Ne5 Rc8; 20.b4! Now White smashes open the queenside. 20...cxb4; 21.axb4 a4; 22.Qe3 Nf5; 23.Qa7 Ra8; 24.Qc5 Rc8; 25.Nc6 Qd7; 26.cxb5 and White went on to win in Ljubojevic-Petrosian, Milan 1975.

9...h6; 10.h4 a5; 11.a4 Ra7! An excellent move, foreseeing the day when the rook will have a role elsewhere.

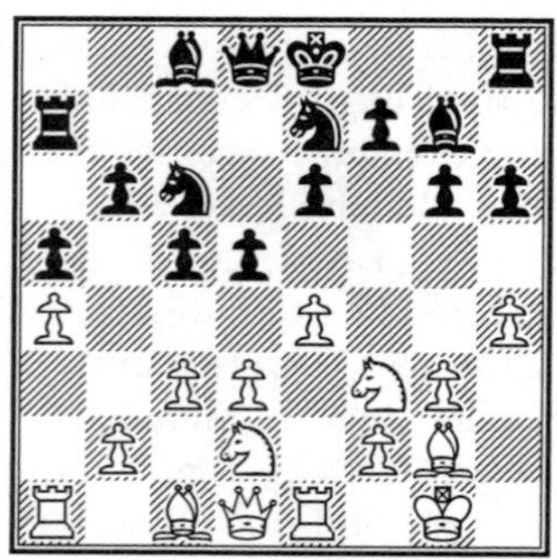

White has shut down Black's queenside counterplay and has the usual central and kingside formation. Here Ljubojevic chose an inferior plan and went down to defeat. The question is, can White do better? **12.Nb3?!** 12.exd5!? I had previously suggested 12.e5, but am no longer confident of that move because Smith and Hall, in the revised edition of their book, present some good arguments against it. 12...exd5; 13.Nb3 and now the pin on the open e-file is effective in rendering ...d4 harmless, for example 13...d4; 14.Nfxd4! cxd4; 15.Bxc6+ with a better game for White.

Of course this is hardly the last word in the matter. That's how chess theory develops, with one theoretician refining and contradicting proposals by other theoreticians and players until some sort of consensus is formed. Fortunately, it is rare that an opening has all of its secrets exposed, even after a few hundred years of examination, because that is what makes chess such a lasting game. Ken Smith and John Hall are constantly putting new ideas into the world, some of which are quite good. When one of us makes a mistake, it takes only another article or actual game to correct it, and even the World Champions have made lots of errors!

12...d4!; 13.cxd4 cxd4; 14.Bd2 e5. Now Black is in firm control of the center, and White has no compensation for the weak pawn at d3. **15.Nc1 Be6; 16.Re2 0–0; 17.Be1 f5.** Now Black simply slices open the White kingside. **18.Nd2 f4!; 19.f3 fxg3; 20.Bxg3 g5!** The pawns just keep on coming. **21.hxg5 Ng6!**

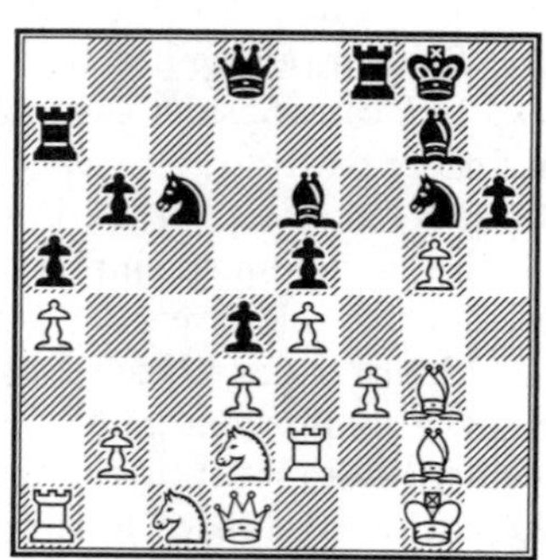

Black is not concerned with mere pawns. **22.gxh6 Bxh6; 23.Nf1 Rg7!** It is amazing that the rook took only two steps to reach this active square! **24.Rf2 Be3; 25.b3 Nf4.** White resigned. **Black won.**

CATALAN

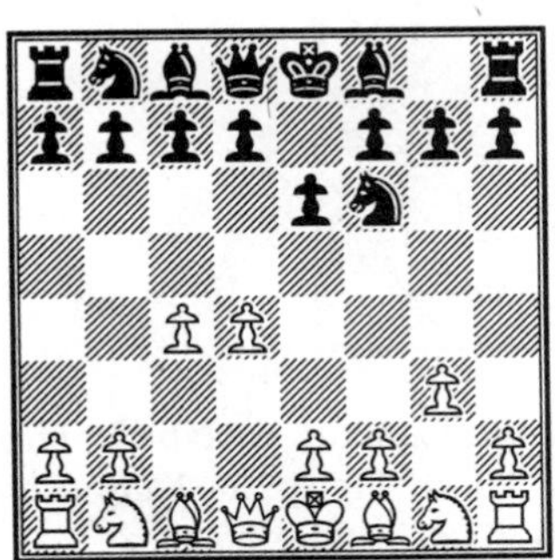

1.d4 Nf6
2.c4 e6
3.g3

The **Catalan** can arise out of many openings. The key elements are a kingside fianchetto by White with pawns at c4 and d4, and the moves ...Nf6 and ...e6 by Black.

Play normally continues 3...d5; 4.Bg2 Be7; 5.Nf3 0-0; 6.0-0.

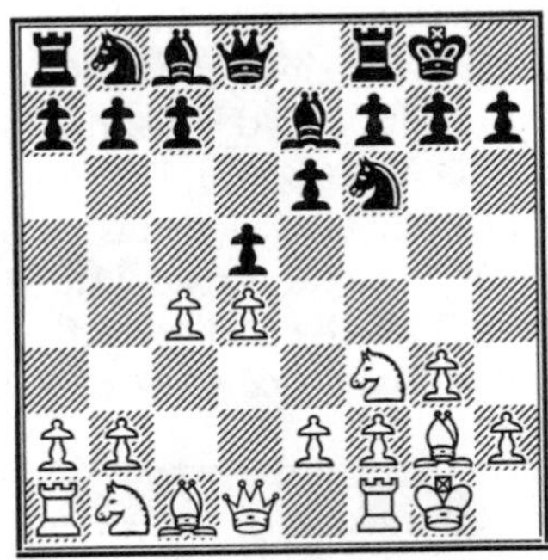

Black can choose between a closed game with ...c6 or accept the offer of the pawn at c4. In this game we examine the former plan. The latter plan has tended to result in so many draws that it has lost interest among top players. A typical line runs 6...dxc4; 7.Qc2 a6; 8.Qxc4 b5 followed by ...Bb7 with so much control over the a8-h1 diagonal that usually minor pieces leave the board quickly and a drawish endgame results. The closed systems give White a slight advantage in space, but there is much more scope for counterplay. There are additional possibilities, such as a transposition into the Tarrasch Defense after 6...c5; 7.cxd5 exd5.

(249) GELLER - LARSEN [E08]

Copenhagen, 1966

1.c4 e6; 2.g3 d5; 3.Bg2 Nf6; 4.Nf3 Be7; 5.0–0 0–0; 6.d4.

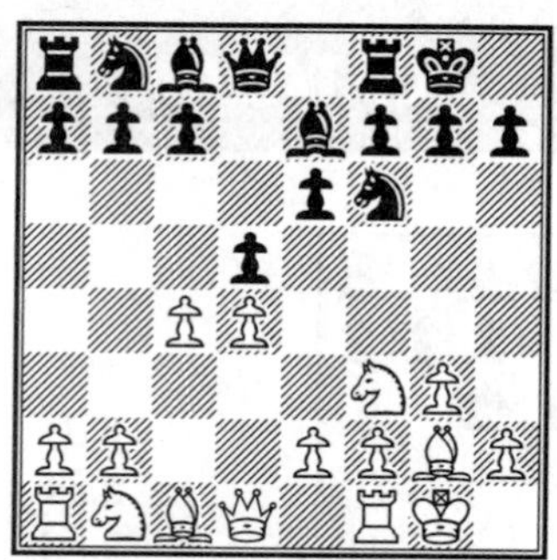

We have now reached the main line of the Catalan. **6...Nbd7.** The open lines with 6...dxc4 have a deservedly drawish reputation. Here, Black chooses the Closed Variation. **7.Qc2.** 7.b3 can be played without a preliminary 7.Qc2. Play will usually transpose to the main lines. 7...c6; 8.Bb2 b5!? 9.Nbd2 (9.c5 a5 should give Black sufficient counterplay.) 9...b4!? As far as I know, this move, given in the 1987 edition of my Catalan book, has still not been tried, but I like the look of Black's position.

7...c6; 8.b3. Now Larsen adds a bite to the position. 8.Rd1 b5; 9.c5 Ne4; 10.a4 b4; 11.Nbd2 f5; 12.Ne1 Bf6; 13.Nb3 a5; 14.Nd3. The *Encyclopedia of Chess Openings* (1991) claims a slight advantage for White, based on Gheorghiu-Gobet, Biel 1983, but if there is one, it is difficult to see after 14...Ba6. **8...b5!** Black applies the pressure to c4. This is a typical motif in the closed lines of the Catalan. **9.Nbd2.** 9.c5 Ne4; 10.Bb2 f5; 11.Ne1 Qe8!?; 12.f3 Nef6; 13.Nd3 a5! and the complicated position held chances for both sides in Van der Vliet-Bohm, Dutch Championship 1981.

9...bxc4!; 10.bxc4 Ba6; 11.Bb2. 11.Qa4 seems an obvious reply, but Black can respond with 11...Qc8! and Nb6 is a real threat. **11...Rb8; 12.Rab1 Qa5!** Black has achieved equality. **13.Bc3 Bb4; 14.Rxb4 Rxb4; 15.Rc1!** 15.a3?? Qa4! and White's position is hopeless. **15...Qa4; 16.Bxb4 Qxb4; 17.e3 Rc8; 18.Qb3 Qa5; 19.Bf1 h6.**

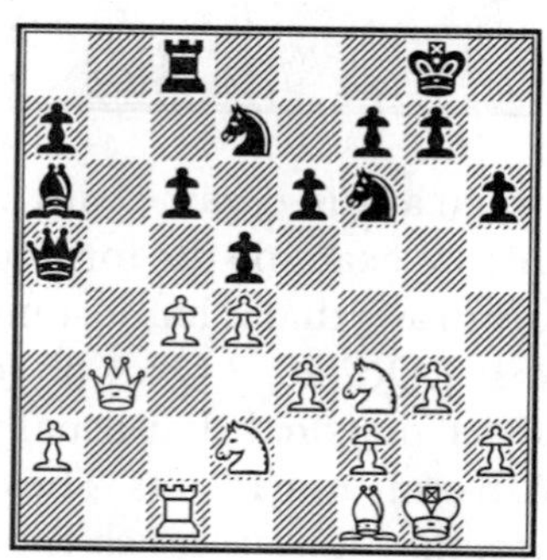

20.Rc3?! 20.Qc3 Qa4; 21.Qb3 might have led to a more peaceful conclusion. Now, however, the game becomes more interesting, in a manner which is more pleasant for Black. 21...Qa5!; 22.Qc3 Qa4 etc. **20...c5!; 21.cxd5 Nxd5; 22.Rc1.** 22.Bxa6

allows the powerful zwischenzug 22...Rb8! **22...Bxf1; 23.Nxf1.** Black's knight have more mobility and the pawn at c5 is not particularly weak. **23...Rb8; 24.Qc2 Nb4; 25.Qd2 Qxa2; 26.dxc5 Qxd2; 27.N1xd2.**

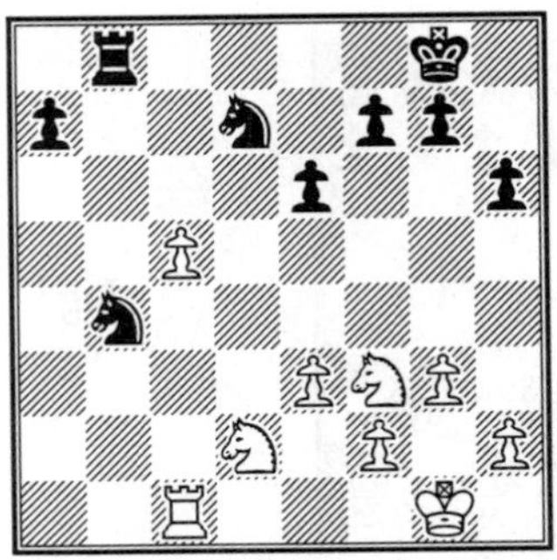

White is in trouble, since the pawn at c5 is exposed and there are serious holes in the kingside that will play a great role in the denouement. **27...Rc8; 28.Ra1 Rc7; 29.Nb3 e5; 30.Ra4 Nd3; 31.c6 Nb6; 32.Ra1 Nc4; 33.Ra4?** White needed to defend the c-pawn with Ra6 here, keeping some lines closed. **33...Rxc6! 34.Rxa7.**

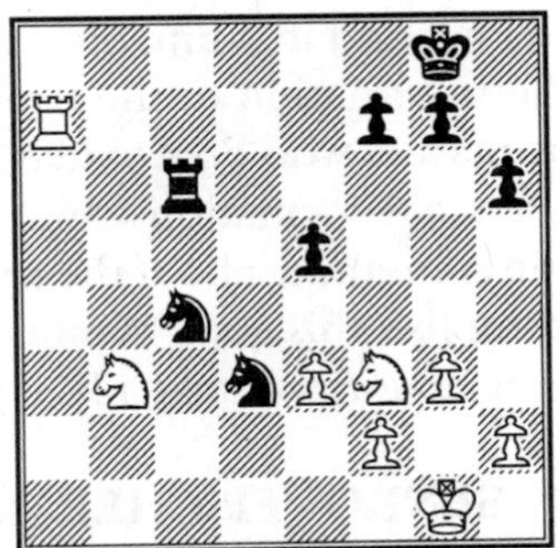

34...Rf6! Now the kingside weaknesses are ruthlessly exploited. **35.Rd7 Nxf2!; 36.Kxf2 e4; 37.Nbd4 Ne5!; 38.Rd8+ Kh7; 39.Re8 Nxf3; 40.Ke2.** 40.Nxf3 loses to 40...Rxf3+ 41.Ke2 f5 and slowly but surely Black will win. 40.Kg2 Nd2! and White cannot hold the endgame. **40...Nxh2; 41.Rxe4 Nf1; 42.Rg4 g5! 43.Nb5.** 43.Nf3? allows 43...Rxf3!; 44.Kxf3 Nh2+ and Black wins easily. **43...Kg6; 44.Nc3 h5.** In this hopeless position, White resigned. **Black won.**

HUNGARIAN ATTACK/PIRC FIANCHETTO

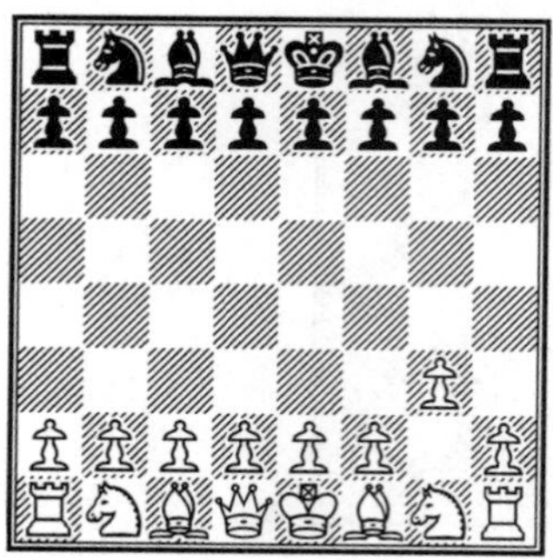

1.g3

The move 1.g3 allows Black a great deal of flexibility in chocie of replies, but White is preparing to follow a formula and doesn't really care. The Hungarian grandmaster Benko, Barcza and Barczay have been among the best known proponents of this system. This position also represents the fianchetto approach by White in the Pirc, and if White plays an early c4, the game can transpose into the Fianchetto Variation of the King's Indian Defense.

It has been favored by players who do not like an early confrontation in the center. White builds a solid formation while hanging on to the ideal pawn center. Black must do something about the center eventually, choosing either ...c5 or ...e5 to accomplish this goal. White will play primarily on the queenside, and much of the action will take place there.

(250) BENKO - FISCHER [A00]

Candidates Tournament, 1962

1.g3 Nf6; 2.Bg2 g6; 3.e4 d6; 4.d4 Bg7; 5.Ne2. Obviously White does not want to limit the scope of the bishop by placing a knight at f3. **5...0–0; 6.0–0 e5.**

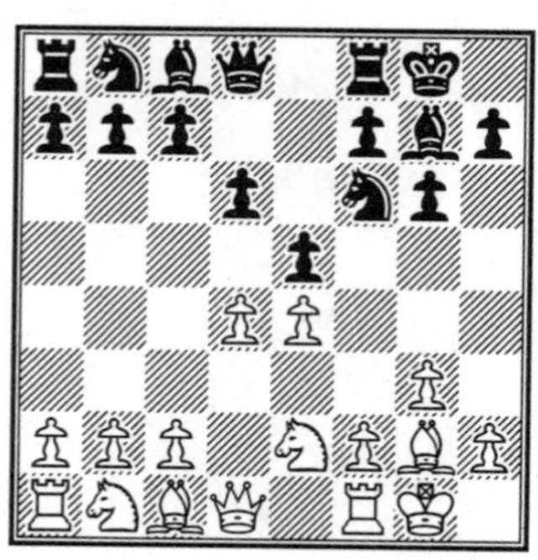

6...Nbd7; 7.Nbc3 c5 is the major alternative strategy. White must now take care to keep an enemy knight off of g4 before playing Be3. 8.h3 a6; 9.Be3 Qc7; 10.Qd2 Rb8; 11.Rad1 is a typical continuation, given by Grandmaster Andy Soltis, an authority on the line.

7.Nbc3. This keeps the position within the confines of the Pirc Defense. 7.c4 exe4; 8.Nxd4 leads into Kig's Indian territory, as in De Fotis-Popovych, New York 1972. **7...c6.** Another plan is 7...Nc6; 8.d5 Ne7, in the spirit of the King's Indian, but after 9.f4 exf4; 10.Bxf4. White opened up the game in Gulko-Gufeld, Soviet Union 1975. **8.a4 Nbd7.** Black should play ...a5 to prevent the further advance of the a-pawn. After 8...a5; 9.h3 Qc7; 10.Be3 Nbd7; 11.Qd2 Re8. Black has a solid position, Kislov-Voloshin, Frydek Mistek Open 1996.

9.a5! This makes it hard for Black to free the position on the queenside, as the b-pawn can no longer advance safely. 9.h3 exd4; 10.Nxd4 Re8; 11.Re1 a5 lets Black consolidate, as in Kveinys-Kempinsky, Polish Team Championship 1995. **9...exd4?** Conceding the center is a serious error here. Unlike the King's Indian, where there is a pawn at c4 that becomes a target, here Black has no source of counterplay.

10.Nxd4 Nc5; 11.h3 Re8; 12.Re1 Nfd7; 13.Be3. White simply continued developing, in firm control of the center except for the e5-square, but that will be dealt with shortly. **13...Qc7; 14.f4! Rb8; 15.Qd2.** The backward pawn at d6 is a vulnerable target and White is threatening to continue with Rad1, adding to the pressure. Fischer, never comfortable in cramped quarters, tries to liven things up on the kingside. **15...b5?!; 16.axb6 axb6; 17.b4 Ne6; 18.b5 Nxd4; 19.Bxd4 Bxd4+; 20.Qxd4 c5; 21.Qd2.**

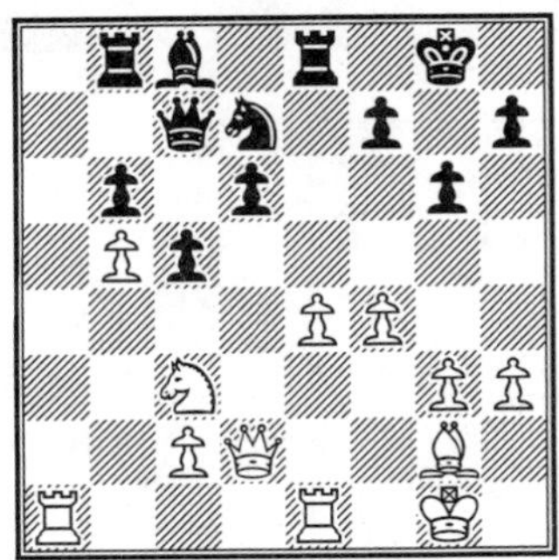

Black is positionally lost, because d6 cannot be held for long and all of White's pieces are more actively posted than there Black counterparts. **21...Bb7; 22.Rad1 Re6; 23.e5! Bxg2; 24.Kxg2 Qb7+; 25.Kf2 Rd8; 26.exd6.** White's king is not very exposed and the extra pawn is secure. **26...Nf6; 27.Rxe6 fxe6; 28.Qe3 Kf7; 29.Qf3!** Of course White wants an endgame! **29...Qb8; 30.Ne4 Nxe4+; 31.Qxe4 Rd7; 32.Qc6! Qd8.** Now White can make no further progress without the assistance of the king, but it is safe for his majesty to stroll up the board, as the Black forces have no scope.

33.Kf3 Kg7; 34.g4 e5; 35.fxe5 Rf7+. Black has finally succeeded in opening a line against the White king. **36.Kg2.** With another pawn in hand, the king retreats to a safer post. **36...Qh4; 37.Rf1 Rxf1; 38.Kxf1 Qxh3+; 39.Qg2 Qe3; 40.Qe2 Qh3+.** The time control reached, with no perpetual check in sight, meant that it was time to give up for Black. White's pawns are too far advanced. **White won.**

ENGLISH OPENING

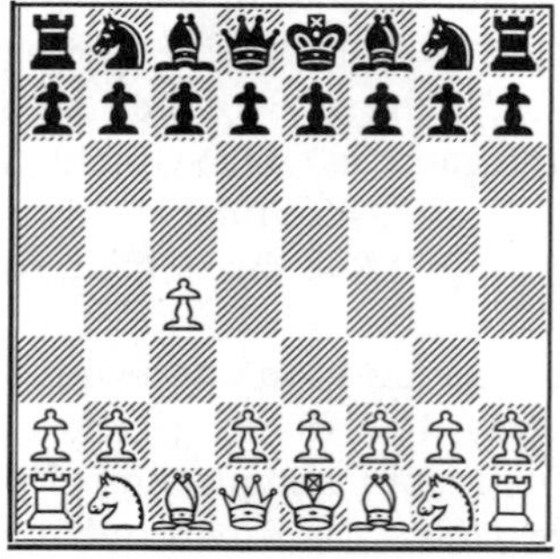

1.c4

The English Opening is the third most popular opening behind 1.d4 and 1.e4. It often transposes to closed games or Indian Games. Sometimes Black even dares to play 1...e5 inviting a reversed Siclian Defense where White enjoys an extra tempo.

ANGLO-INDIAN

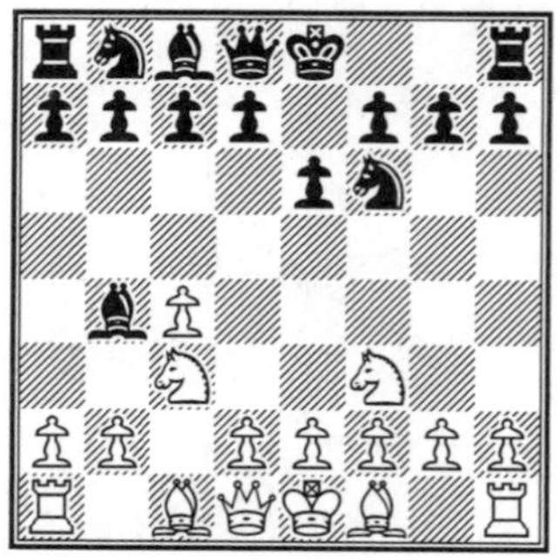

1.Nf3	**Nf6**
2.c4	**e6**
3.Nc3	**Bb4**

The Nimzo variation of the **Anglo-Indian** seeks to transpose into a Nimzo-Indian if White should venture an early d4, but in recent years it has taken on a life of its own and is seen frequently at the highest level of competition. The main difference between this line and a full Nimzo-Indian is that with an early ...e5 Black can slow down White's occupation of the center.

(251) KOMAROV - RAZUVAYEV [A17]
Reggio Emilia, 1997

1.Nf3 Nf6; 2.c4 e6; 3.Nc3 Bb4; 4.Qc2. The most popular reply, avoiding doubled pawns. **4...0–0.** 4...c5; 5.a3 Bxc3; 6.Qxc3 Nc6 should be met by 7.b4, since 7.g3 Qa5!

gave Black a good game in Ftacnik-Tong Yuanming, Beijing 1996. **5.a3 Bxc3.** Black should nevertheless part with the bishop, as seen in almost all top-level games. **6.Qxc3 d5.** 6...c5; 7.b4 b6; 8.g3 Nc6; 9.Bg2 Bb7; 10.0–0 d6; 11.Bb2 e5 gave Black a solid position in Kramnik-Ehlvest, Vienna 1996, but White maintained a slight initiative after 12.e3. **7.b4!?** This is the most promising plan. **7...dxc4; 8.Qxc4 b6; 9.Bb2 c6.**

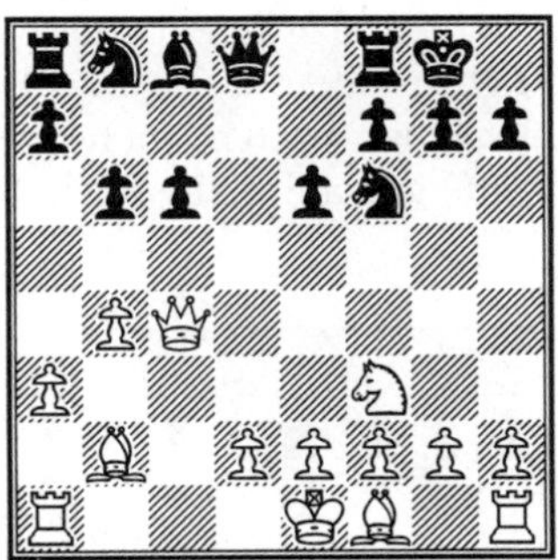

Black has a very passive position and White's bishop pair can be quite effective. Now Komarov opened up the game with **10.g4 a5; 11.g5 Nd5; 12.Rg1** and after **12...axb4** went right for the jugular with **13.Qd4! f6; 14.gxf6 Qxf6.**

This allows a fine combination: **15.Rxg7+!! Kxg7; 16.Qg4+ Kh8; 17.Bxf6+ Rxf6; 18.Ng5 Nd7; 19.Nxe6.** Materially, Black has a rook and a knight for the queen but White also has an extra pawn. **19...Rg6; 20.Qd4+ N7f6; 21.Nf4 Nxf4; 22.Qxf4 bxa3;** The a-pawn looks strong, but it cannot advance. Meanwhile Black's pieces are just too uncoordinated. **23.Qf3 Bg4; 24.Qxc6 Rc8; 25.Qa4 Re8; 26.Rxa3.** End of pawn, end of game! **26...Bxe2?** Not that Black could survive in the long run, but this makes it easy. **27.Re3! Rxe3; 28.fxe3 Bxf1; 29.Kxf1 h6; 30.Qd4.** The White pawns decide, especially since the pawn at b6 falls. **White won.**

TARTAKOWER-INDIAN DEFENSE

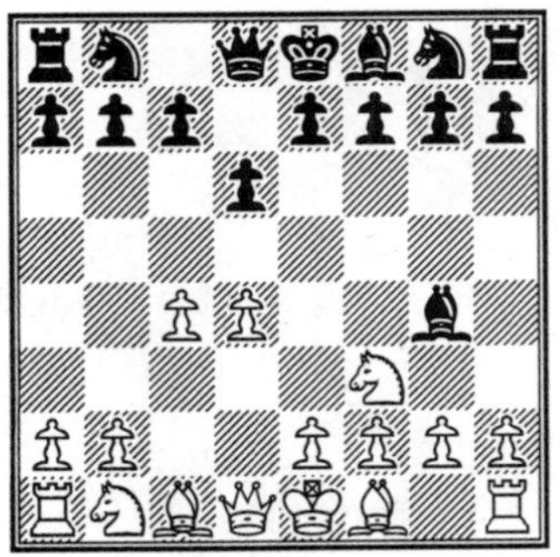

1.c4	**d6**
2.Nf3	**Bg4**
3.d4	

The **Tartakower-Indian Defense** was almost unheard of until quite recently in many Grandmaster games. It is a conservative defense, but it does grant White greater control of space and the center.

(252) TISDALL - GULKO [A21]

San Francisco (Pan-Pacific), 1995

1.d4 d6; 2.Nf3 Bg4; 3.c4. This is an invitation to the Tartakower-Indian, which would arise directly on 3...Nf6. **3...Nd7.** Because 3...Nf6; 4.Qb3! is considered better for White these days, Black adopts a different move order. **4.Nc3 e5.** The game might be classified in the English Opening, or as a Purdy Defense. **5.e3.** A solid move. Tisdall suggests a fianchetto approach might be appropriate: 5.g3!? Bxf3; 6.exf3 Ngf6; 7.Bg2 c6; 8.0-0 and White was a little better in Speelman-Bezold, Altensteig 1994. **5...Ngf6.**

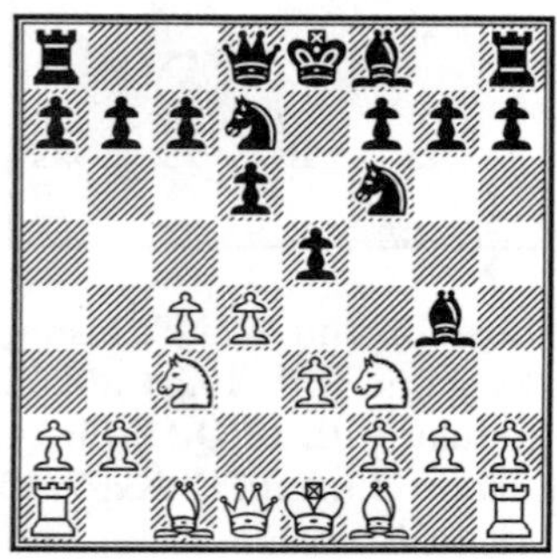

Now this is a position which is truly typical of the Tartakower Indian. The game will continue with quiet development for a while. Black has sufficient pressure on the center to prevent White from taking control. **6.Be2 Be7; 7.0-0 0-0; 8.b3.** At any point now, White can consider attacking the bishop by advancing the pawn to h3. 8.h3!? Bh5; 9.b4! Re8; 10.a4 exd4; 11.Nxd4 Bxe2; 12.Qxe2 Bf8; 13.Rd1 White has a clear advantage in space, and can play on either, or both, wings. This line was seen in I. Ivanov-Miles, New York Open 1994. **8...Re8; 9.Bb2 c6; 10.h3 Bh5; 11.g4?!** White plays with too much ambition and too little concern for the safety of his king. 11.Nh4 Bxe2; 12.Nxe2. White cannot claim any advantage here. **11...Bg6; 12.Nh4 Bf8.**

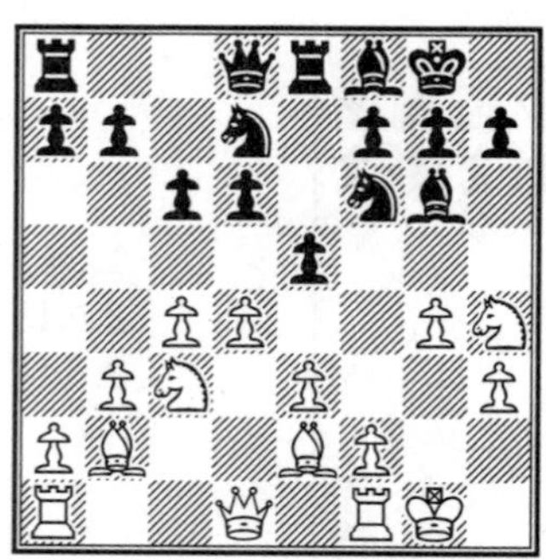

13.Nxg6. 13.dxe5 Rxe5!; 14.f4 Rxe3!; 15.f5 Rxh3!; 16.Ng2 d5. White's king is under serious attack in this piece of analysis by Jonathan Tisdall. **13...hxg6; 14.Bf3 e4; 15.Bg2 d5.** Black's opening play has succeeded. The kingside is solid, development is proceeding comfortably, and the pawn structure is sound.

16.f3?! Attacking the head of a pawn chain is always a double-sided operation. On the one hand, the pressure can be effective in opening lines. On the other, it entails weakening one's own pawn structure (here at e3) and once the pawn moves forward, there is no turning back. The timing of such "breaks" is an important factor in professional chess, and only the strongest Grandmasters fully understand it. In this case, the timing was bad. White should first at least chase the knight from f6 by advancing the g-pawn.

16...Bb4! The battle is for the e4-square. The knight at c3 defends e4. Therefore Black undermines control of e4 by attacking the knight which supports it. **17.g5.** Tisdall noted that f4! would have been a better, and safer, move. **17...Nh5; 18.h4 Ng3.** Gulko has cleverly managed to keep this knight involved in the battle for the crucial e4-square.

19.fxe4 Bxc3; 20.Bxc3 Nxe4! The center is more important than a minor amount of material. Taking the rook at f1 would have been much less effective. **21.Bb4.** 21.Bxe4? loses to 21...Rxe4; 22.Qf3 Qe7; 23.Bb4 Qe6; 24.Bd2 Rxh4 and White's king is in a real mess. **21...a5; 22.Ba3 a4!** Black continues to undermine the support of White's pawn chains. **23.Rf4 axb3; 24.axb3 Qc7; 25.cxd5.** White opens up the c-files in an attempt to harass the Black queen. **25...cxd5; 26.Rc1 Qa5; 27.Bxe4.** Sooner or later this capture had to be made, and the contour of the middlegame shifts as a result. **27...Rxe4; 28.Rxe4 dxe4.**

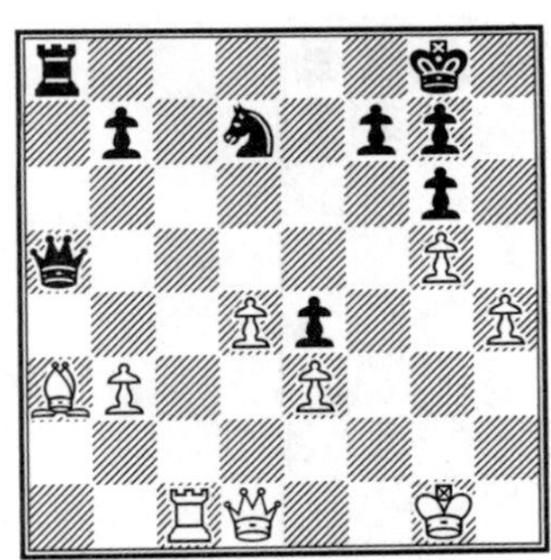

White has a rather weak bishop. The pawns are very hard to defend, as you can see if you mentally move the knight to f5. Black can defend the e-pawn with a rook at e8. All in all, Black's position is clearly superior. **29.Bd6 Qf5; 30.Bf4 Nb6!** and **Black wins. 31.Qe2 Nd5; 32.Bg3 Qh3; 33.Bf2.** 33.Qg2 Qxg2+; 34.Kxg2 Nxe3+; 35.Kf2 Nf5 is an easy win for Black. **33...Ra3?!** Tisdall pointed out that this was not necessary. The simple 33...Kh7 would have been good. **34.Qc4 Qg4+; 35.Kf1.**

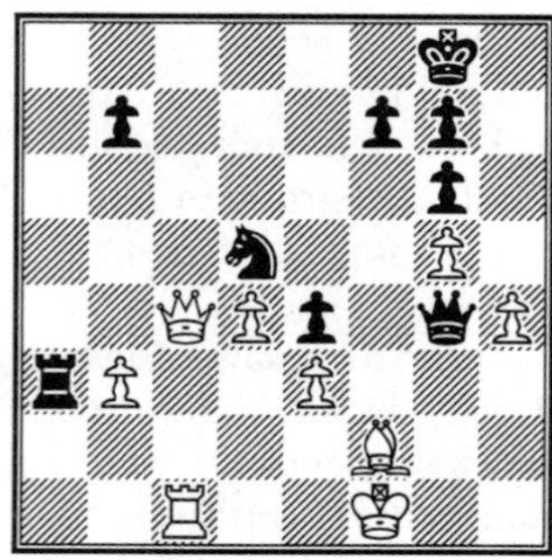

Here Gulko finishes with a nice combination. **35...Nxe3+; 36.Bxe3 Qf3+; 37.Bf2 Ra2.** White resigned, since Rc2 allows ...Qd1+. **Black won.**

KING'S ENGLISH

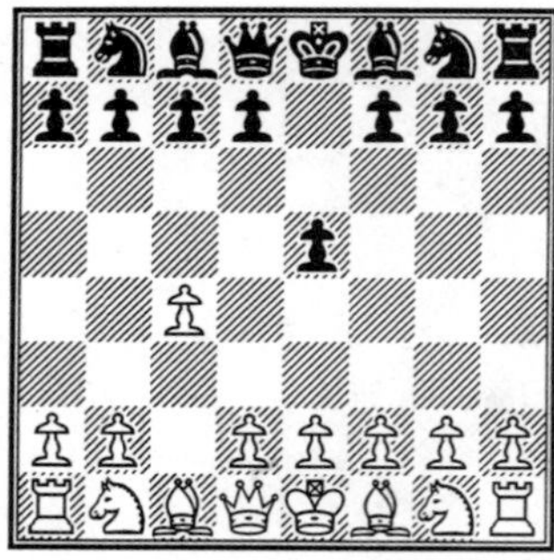

1.c4 e5

The **King's English** is a reversed Sicilian Defense. Black therefore does not want to open up the game too quickly with .d5, because then White has an extra tempo in some very sharp lines. Instead, Black chooses one of the closed lines in which the extra tempo is of less significance.

These include lines with ...Nc6 and ...f5 (a reversed Grand Prix Attack) as well as traditional Closed Sicilians with ...Nc6 and ....g6. Sometimes, as in the following game, Black places a bishop at e7 instead of using the fianchetto.

(253) CARLS - TORRE [A22]

Baden-Baden, 1925

1.c4 Nf6; 2.Nf3 e5; 3.Nc3 d6; 4.g3.

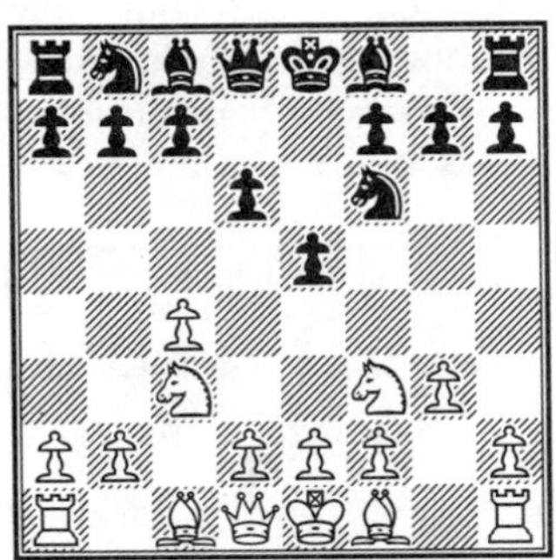

Black has chosen a reversed Closed Sicilian, but to be consistent should now fianchetto the dark-squared bishop at g7. Instead, Torre invites a transposition to the Old Indian. **4...Be7; 5.Bg2 0–0; 6.0–0 Nc6.** The problem with Black's formation is that it doesn't put any pressure on White. This passive approach is intended as a prelude to a kingside attack, as is common in the Closed Sicilian. But White's extra tempo is important. **7.d3?!** 7.d4!? is stronger, transposing to the Old Indian Defense.

7...Bd7. 7...Nd4! is the correct way to react to White's last move. 8.Nxd4 (8.Ne1 c5; 9.e3 Nc6; 10.f4 Bg4! 11.Qd2 Qd7 gave Black a fine game in Petrosian-Smyslov, Budapest 1952.) **8.h3!** White has enough time to get this in before Black plays Qc8. The h-pawn can be defended by both bishop and king. **8...h6; 9.Kh2 Nh7; 10.Ng1.** White remains a step ahead of his opponent. **10...f5; 11.f4!** Black's center is now under assault. **11...Nf6; 12.Nd5 Rc8; 13.Bd2!** The bishop will add more pressure at e5. **13...Qe8; 14.e3 Nd8; 15.Bc3 c6; 16.Nxe7+ Qxe7; 17.fxe5 dxe5; 18.Nf3! e4** forced, since after 18...Nf7 White plays 19.Nh4! and the weaknesses on the light squares are apparent. **19.Ne5 Re8; 20.dxe4 fxe4.**

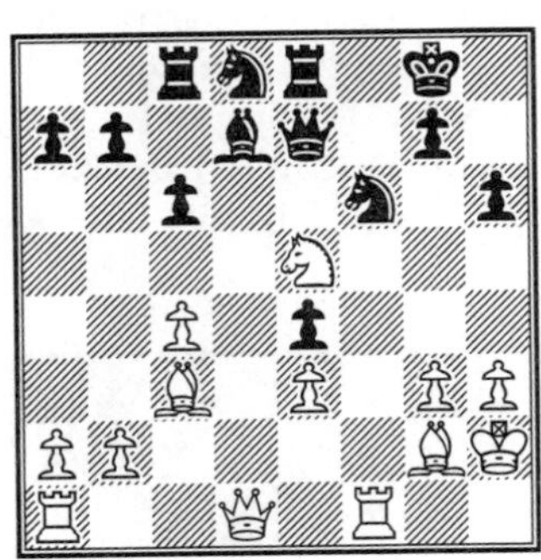

21.Rxf6! An obvious little combination, which leads to a decisive advantage. **21...Qxf6; 22.Qxd7 Nf7; 23.Ng4 Qg6; 24.Rf1 Rcd8; 25.Qxb7.** White maintains the pressure on the seventh rank, and will continue to munch on queenside pawns. The game is effectively over. **25...h5; 26.Nf2 Ng5; 27.h4 Nf3+; 28.Bxf3 exf3; 29.Qxa7 Rf8; 30.e4 Rf7; 31.Qe3 Rdf8; 32.Nh3 Qg4; 33.Ng5 Re7; 34.Bb4. White won.**

(254) SIGURJONSSON - SMYSLOV [A29]

Reykjavik, 1974

1.c4 e5; 2.Nc3 Nf6; 3.Nf3 Nc6. In the Four Knights Variation of the King's English. White has many different plans. The kingside fianchetto, aiming for a reversed Dragon Sicilian, has always been very popular. The extra tempo is not so important because it often forces White to prematurely reveal plans. **4.g3.**

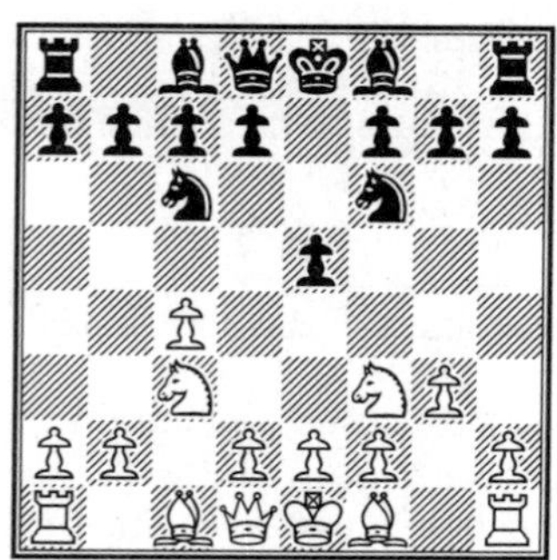

4...Bb4. This plan is more active than the one seen in the Carls-Torre game, where the bishop was hemmed in by ...d6. **5.Bg2 0-0; 6.0-0.** Now 6...d5 would lead to the reversed Dragon, but Smyslov plays more aggressively and denies White that opportunity. **6...e4!** This remains the main line. After the knight advances or retreats, Black will capture at c3. 6...Bxc3; 7.bxc3 Re8; 8.d3 e4 is a variation on the same theme. 9.Nd4 exd3; 10.exd3 h6; 11.Rb1 Nxd4; 12.cxd4 d5; 13.Bf4! brought plenty of pressure to bear on Black's center and queenside in Hodgson-Salov, Amsterdam 1996.

7.Ng5 Bxc3; 8.bxc3 Re8. Black has given up a bishop for a knight, but the strong pawn at e4 and uncoordinated White army is more than enough compensation. **9.f3.** Advancing the d-pawn instead would have been less risky. 9.d3 exd3; 10.exd3 h6; 11.Ne4 allows Black to exploit the blockage on the long diagonal by slipping in 11...b6! after which Black gets play on the light squares, as in Romanishin-Taimanov, Leningrad 1977. **9...exf3; 10.Nxf3 d5!** Only now is this an appropriate move. **11.cxd5 Qxd5.** A bold but correct capture. Discovered attacks by the Nf3 are not a problem. **12.Nd4 Qh5; 13.Nxc6 bxc6; 14.e3.** 14.Bxc6 would run into 14...Qc5+. **14...Bg4; 15.Qa4 Re6; 16.Rb1 Be2.**

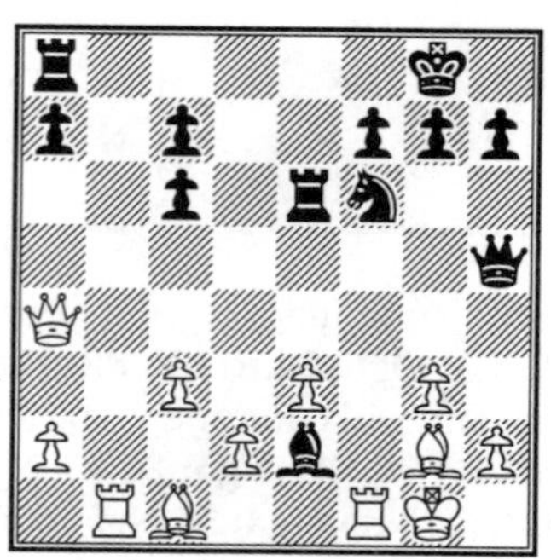

An annoying move. The rook must move, but has no happy destination. **17.Re1.** 17.Rf2 Ng4; 18.Bxc6 Nxf2; 19.Bxa8 Nh3+; 20.Kg2 h6 and with the back rank attended to, White's king will not survive for long. Analysis by Smyslov. **17...Ng4; 18.h3 Qf5.** The attack on the rook at b1 makes the threat at f2 unstoppable. **19.Rxe2 Qxb1; 20.Qxg4 Qxc1+; 21.Kh2 Rd8.** White has no compensation for the exchange. The d-pawn cannot advance because then the pawn at e3 would fall. **22.Qb4 h6; 23.c4 Qd1; 24.Rf2 Qe1.** The hunt is over. White resigned. **Black won.**

HEDGEHOG FORMATION

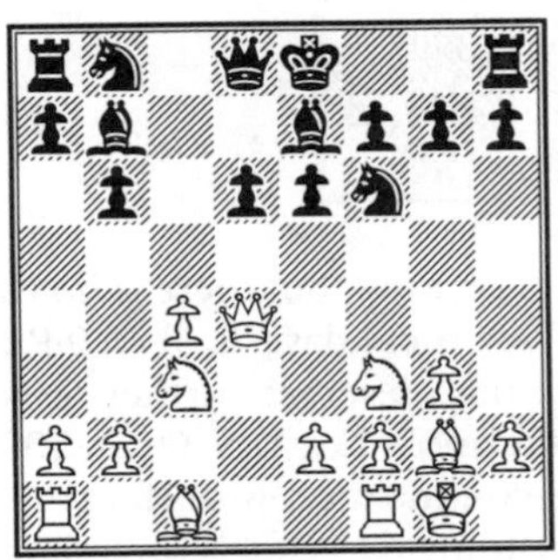

1.c4	**c5**
4.Bg2	**Bb7**
5.0–0	**e6**
6.Nc3	**Be7**
7.d4	**cxd4**
8.Qxd4	**d6**

The **Hedgehog Formation** can be reached from many different openings, but the most common is the method seen in this game, which applies the Symmetrical English. Black counters White's fianchetto plan with one of his own. From here on it is difficult to determine the very best moves, and a great deal of subtlety and foresight is needed.

Usually it is unwise to bring the queen to the center of the board so early in the game, but if White used the knight to capture, then the light-squared bishops would be exchanged at g2.Black now usually chooses between plans involving ...Nc6 and those with ...d6 and ...Nbd7. It is also possible to combine the two plans, as in this game. That strategy requires a deep knowledge of transpositional pitfalls.

(255) SMYSLOV - ANDERSSON [A30]

Biel (Interzonal), 1976

1.c4 c5; 2.Nf3 Nf6; 3.g3 b6; 4.Bg2 Bb7; 5.0–0 e6; 6.Nc3 Be7; 7.d4 cxd4; 8.Qxd4 d6.

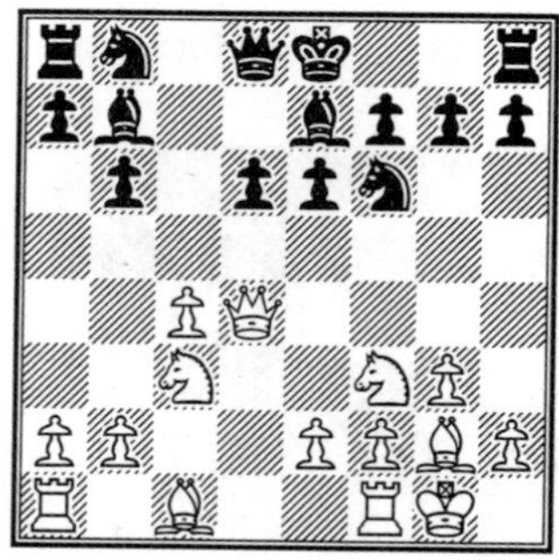

The queen can be driven away from d4 right away, but there is no rush. 8...Nc6; 9.Qf4 0–0 is considered a little better for White these days. 8...0–0; 9.Rd1 d6; 10.b3 Nbd7; 11.e4 Qc8 is a recent plan for Black that deserves further tests, but Black achieved a decent position in Schwartzman-Yermolinsky, U.S. Open 1996.

9.b3. Twenty years later, this is still the continuation with the best reputation. The bishop can come to either b2 or a3, depending on White's preference. 9.e4 a6 is very common, for example 10.b3 (10.Qe3 Nbd7; 11.Nd4 Qc7; 12.b3 0–0; 13.Bb2 Rfe8 is another typical formation, which Kasparov has defended as Black.) 10...Nbd7; 11.Rd1 Qc7; 12.Ba3 Nc5; 13.e5 dxe5; 14.Qxe5 Rc8 which has been successfully defended by six-time United States Champion Walter Browne in many professional encounters. **9...0–0; 10.Bb2.** 10.Ba3! is also seen. 10...Na6; 11.Rfd1 Nc5 gives Black a solid position, as in Miles-Adorjan, Riga (Interzonal) 1979. **10...a6; 11.Rfd1.**

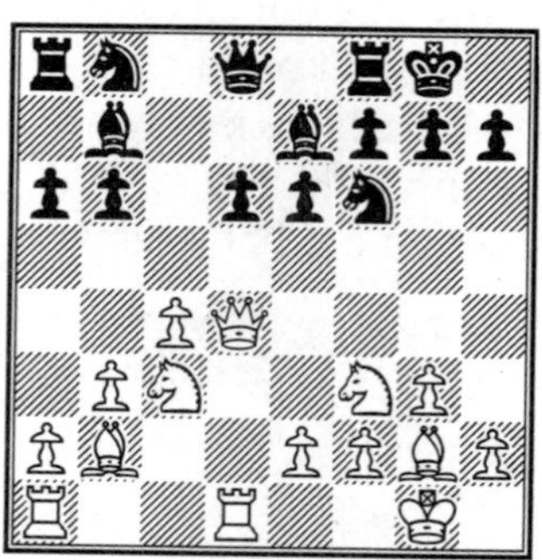

11...Nc6. 11...Nbd7 is the normal move, for example: 12.Qe3 Qc7; 13.h3 and now Black puzzles over 13...Rfc8, 13...Rac8, both played by Browne, or John Watson's preferred 13...Rfe8 after which Black can choose a position for the other rook. 12.e4 is also playable, for example 12...Qc7; 13.Qe3 (13.Ba3 Nc5; 14.e5 dxe5; 15.Qxe5 Qc8 with approximate equality in Cobb-O'Shaughnessy, British Team Championship 1996.)13...Rfe8; 14.Nd4 Rac8; 15.h3 Bf8; 16.Re1 Qb8 with a full hedgehog position in Dautov-Lehtivaara, Geneva Open 1997.

12.Qf4 Qb8. Black is adopting a normal strategy of having the queen support d6 from b8, with the possibility of bringing the rook from f8 to d8 for more support. As for the rook at a8, it can play a role at a7, defending along the seventh rank and making the a8-square available to the queen, which can team up with the bishop at b7 to slice down along the long diagonal. **13.Ng5!** A strong move. Notice how firmly White controls the e4 square. **13...Ra7.** 13...h6; 14.Nge4 Rd8; 15.h4 Ra7; 16.Rd2 Ba8; 17.Rad1 Ne8 is just too passive, and White can open up the game with 18.g4! Ne5; 19.Qg3 with a strong kingside attack in Kovacevic-Spassov, Virovitica 1976. **14.Nce4 Ne5!**

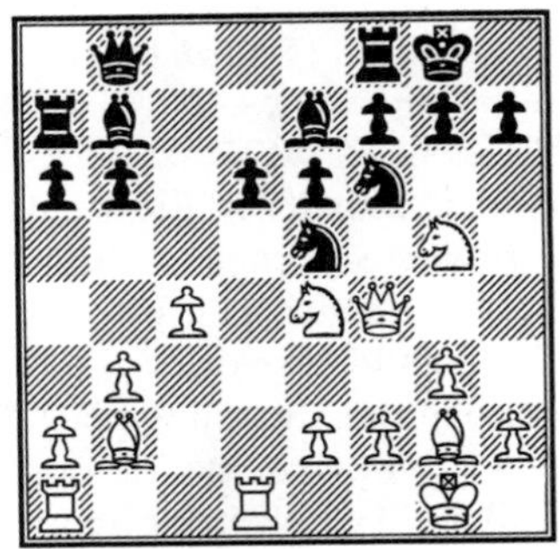

Andersson is one of the greatest exponents of the hedgehog defenses, and has an excellent sense of timing. Black is going to create counterplay by playing ...b5 and putting pressure on the pawn at c4. **15.Nxf6+ Bxf6; 16.Bxb7 Rxb7.** The exchanges have brought about a position where Black is going to need some counterplay. The pawn at d6 is now a real weakness. **17.Ne4 Be7; 18.Rd2 Ng6; 19.Qe3 Rd8; 20.Rad1 b5.** Now the game is a real fight. Smyslov and Andersson are among the greatest positional players ever. Smyslov shows his Championship mettle by forcing the Black b-pawn to advance, relieving pressure on the center. **21.Qc3!** First, a small weakness is created on the other flank.

21...f6; 22.Qe3 Nf8. 22...bxc4; 23.Nxd6 was given by Andersson. The point can be seen in the variation 23...Rxd6; 24.Rxd6 Bxd6; 25.Qxe6+ Rf7; 26.Rxd6 cxb3; 27.axb3 and White should win. **23.Ba3! b4; 24.Bb2.** Now Black has preserved the d-pawn, but has no source of counterplay. This does not mean the game is lost, just that no further mistakes can be made by Black. **24...Qc7; 25.Rd3 Qc6; 26.Qf3 Rc7; 27.Nd2 Qxf3; 28.Nxf3.**

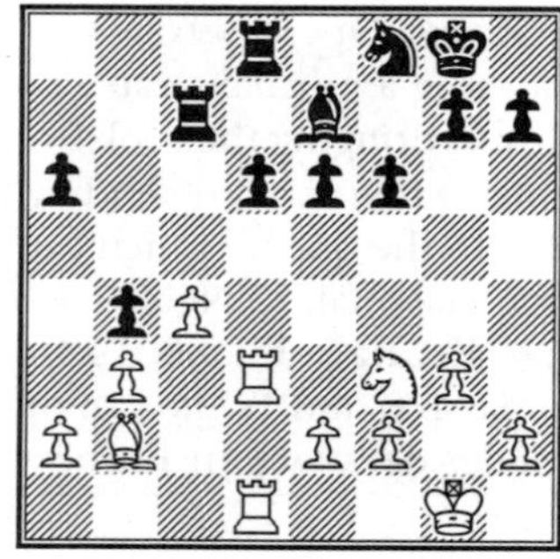

28...Kf7? Andersson probably didn't realize that he could get away with 28...Nd7, but he later published the following line. 28...Nd7!; 29.Rxd6? (I think that 29.e4!? is probably best, as after 29...Nc5; 30.Re3.) White has a lock on the center. But White's advantage would be pretty small. 29...Bxd6; 30.Rxd6 e5! the point being that 31.Rxa6 is met by 31...Nc5 and Black threatens to encircle the White bishop with ...Rd1+ and ...Rb1. **29.a3 bxa3; 30.Bxa3.** The pressure is just too much. Black's next move hastens the end. **30...Rc6?** 30...Rb8 would have offered more resistance. **31.Nd4.** White has enough advantages to put together a winning plan. **31...Rb6; 32.Nc2 Rc6; 33.c5 e5; 34.cxd6 Bxd6; 35.Ne3.** Now it is just a matter of mopping up. **35...Bxa3; 36.Rxd8 Ne6; 37.R8d7+ Kg6; 38.Nc4 Bb4; 39.e3 Nc5. White won.**

SYMMETRICAL VARIATION

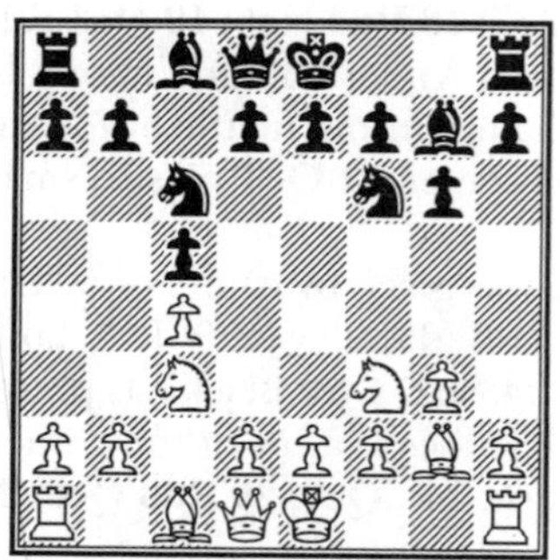

1.c4	**Nf6**
2.g3	**c5**
3.Bg2	**g6**
4.Nc3	**Bg7**
5.Nf3	**Nc6**

In most chess openings Black cannot afford to maintain symmetry for long. After all, if taken to extremes, White would checkmate Black one move before Black would checkmate White! In the English Opening, however, the lack of central confrontations makes it possible to start the game by adopting the same formation that the opponent chooses.

(256) TAL - IVANOVIC [A34]

St. John, 1988

1.Nf3 c5; 2.c4 Nc6; 3.Nc3 Nf6; 4.g3. Black can maintain the symmetry, but there is a stronger plan which opens up the game for lively counterplay. Here Black adopts the Rubenstein Variation. **4...d5; 5.cxd5 Nxd5; 6.Bg2 Nc7.**

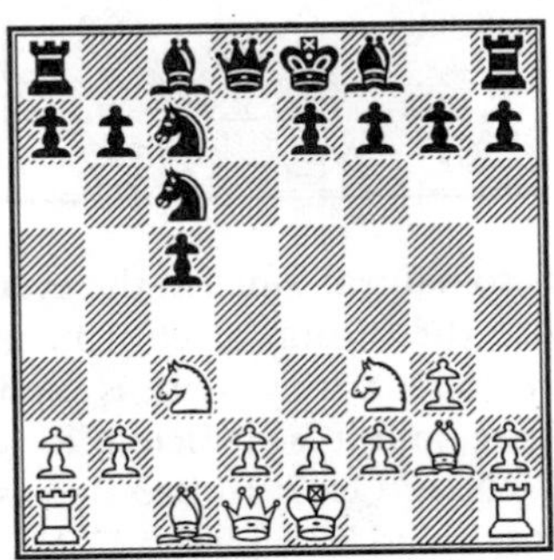

This is one of the key positions of the Rubinstein Variation. Black plans to secure the center with ...e5, creating a reversed Maroczy Bind formation, similar to the Accelerated Dragon Variation of the Sicilian Defense. There, the retreat of the knight is not considered particularly effective early in the game, but here Black is only trying to equalize, and the plan is considered acceptable. White will usually castle and then play d3, in order to maneuver a knight to c4. Black does not want to make any premature pawn moves on the queenside, as c5 is weak enough as things stand. Black will play ...e5, ...Be7 and castle kingside, then try to maintain control of the center.

7.0–0. 7.Qa4 Bd7; 8.Qe4 g6; 9.Ne5 Bg7; 10.Nxd7 Qxd7; 11.0–0 0–0 was equal in Vaganian-Polugayevsky, Soviet Championship 1971. **7...e5; 8.d3.** 8.a3 is not all that easy to meet. With b4 covered, White can undertake action in the center with e3 followed by d4, or switch back to the d3 plan, depending on Black's reply. Current theory holds that the awkward move 8...Qd7 is the best chance for reaching an equal position, for example 9.Rb1 f6; 10.d3 Be7; 11.Bd2 Rb8; 12.Qc2 b6; 13.Rfc1 Bb7; 14.Ne4 Nd5 with equality in Smyslov-Korchnoi, Soviet Championship 1967.

8...Be7; 9.Nd2 Bd7; 10.Nc4 f6. 10...0–0; 11.Bxc6 Bxc6; 12.Nxe5 is a pawn sacrifice which gives Black good counterplay, as long as the light-squared bishop is retained. 12...Be8!; 13.Be3 Ne6; 14.Qb3 Bd6; 15.f4 Bxe5; 16.fxe5 and with the knight at e5 out of the way, the bishop can return to c6, with excellent compensation for the pawn, Psakhis-Ehlvest, Tilburg 1992. **11.f4.**

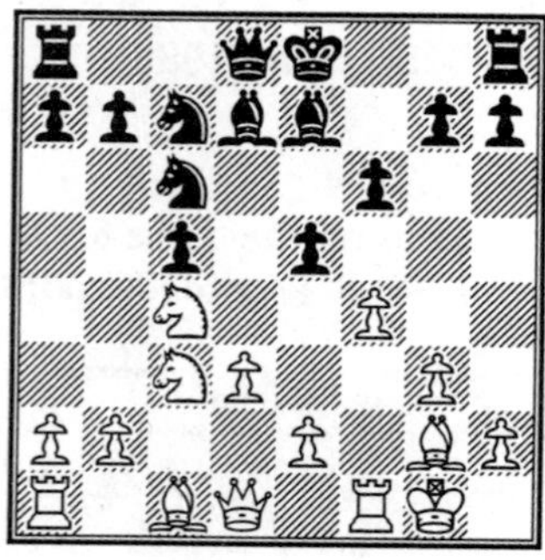

11...0–0? Castling seems so natural, since in the event of a check at d5 Black can either run to h8 or interpose the bishop at e6 if necessary. The center is under control and the defenses are solid. Surely there is plenty of defense on the f-file? 11...b5 is a more active defense, and it is sufficient for equality after 12.Ne3 exf4!; 13.gxf4 Rb8; 14.Ned5 0–0; 15.Nxc7 Qxc7; 16.Be3 Be6 as in Spiridonov-Pinter, Baile Herculane 1982, where White should have played 17.Nd5!, maintaining the balance, according to Pinter. **12.fxe5! fxe5; 13.Rxf8+ Bxf8; 14.Be3.** The pawns at c5, b7 and e5 are quite weak, and this presents White with adequate targets. **14...Kh8.** To lessen the effect of White's next move by getting off the dangerous diagonal. **15.Qb3 b5.** The only reply. It leads to some very complicated tactics which Tal had worked out well. **16.Nxb5 Rb8.**

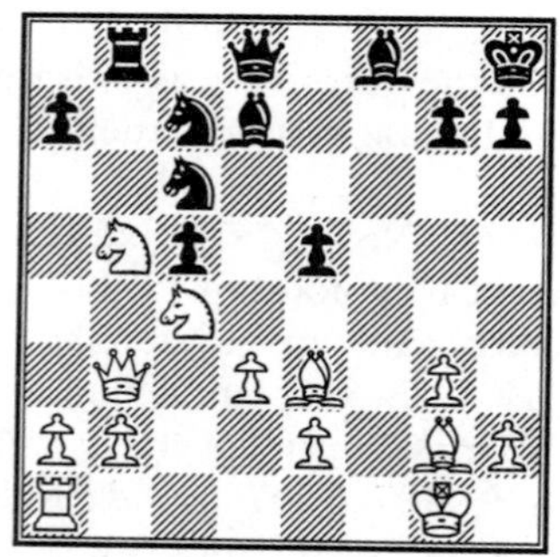

16...Nxb5; 17.Qxb5 Rb8; 18.Qa4 Nd4; 19.Qxa7 Nxe2+; 20.Kh1 Nd4; 21.Nxe5 and White wins. **17.Ncd6!** The pin on the knight at b5 is simply ignored! **17...Bxd6; 18.Nxd6 Qe7.** 18...Rxb3; 19.Nf7+ Kg8; 20.Nxd8 Rb6; 21.Bxc6 Bxc6; 22.Bxc5 Ra6; 23.Nxc6 Rxc6; 24.Bxa7 and White wins without difficulty. **19.Nf7+ Kg8; 20.Nh6+ Kh8; 21.Bg5! Qf8?** 21...Rxb3; 22.Bxe7 Rxb2; 23.Bd6 Nb5 (23...gxh6; 24.Bxc6 Bxc6; 25.Bxe5+ Kg8; 26.Bxb2 is a straightforward win.) 24.Nf7+ Kg8; 25.Bd5 Nb4; 26.Bxe5 Nxd5; 27.Nh6+ gxh6; 28.Bxb2 is better for White, who should not have much of a problem eliminating the weak c-pawn. 21...Qxg5?? drops the queen to 22.Nf7+. **22.Qf7 Qxf7; 23.Nxf7+ Kg8; 24.Bxc6 Bxc6; 25.Nxe5.**

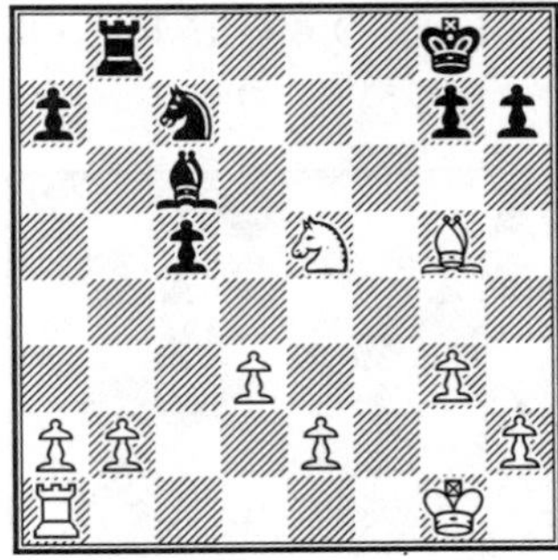

After a series of forced moves, Black's position is a shambles, with no compensation for the pawn. **25...Bd5; 26.e4 Be6; 27.b3 Bh3; 28.Rc1 Re8; 29.Nc6 Ne6; 30.Be7 Rc8; 31.Ne5 a5; 32.Kf2** and Black resigned in this hopeless position. **White won.**

(257) BLECHSCHMIDT - FLOHR [A38]

Zwickau, 1930

1.c4 Nf6; 2.g3 c5; 3.Bg2 g6; 4.Nc3 Bg7; 5.Nf3 Nc6; 6.0–0 d6. Black is content to declare the future of the d-pawn before White is committed to any particular plan. White can maintain the symmetry, but can also choose a different formation, as in this game. 6...0–0; 7.d4 cxd4; 8.Nxd4 allows Black to choose an interesting plan which repositions the knight from f6 to h6. 8...Ng4!?; 9.e3 Nxd4; 10.exd4 Nh6; 11.Bxh6. Otherwise the knight will wind up on f5! 11...Bxh6; 12.c5! d6; 13.b4 Bg7; 14.Rc1 Rb8 but White gains the upper hand on 15.Qa4!, as in Bakic-Petronic, Yugoslavia 1996.

7.h3 Bd7; 8.e3. The immediate 8.d4 was called for, opening up the game. The quiet 8.d3 would also have been reasonable, but the text simply creates weaknesses on the light squares. **8...Qc8; 9.Kh2.**

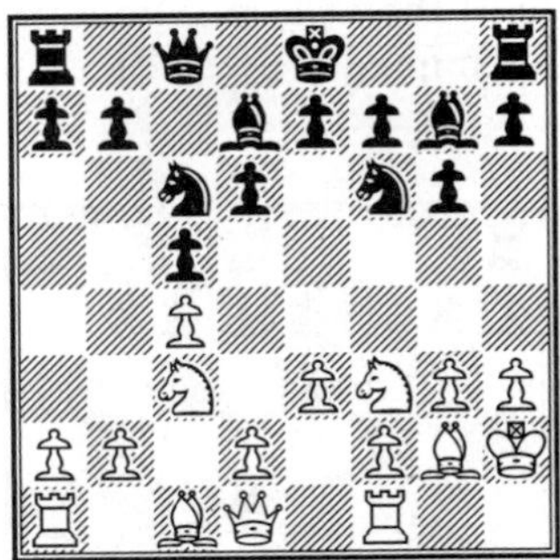

Many players would automatically castle here, but if so, then how would a kingside attack be carried out? Instead, Flohr counts on safety in the center. **9...h5!; 10.d4 h4!; 11.gxh4.** White must try to keep the h-file blocked in order to protect the king. 11.Nxh4? g5; 12.Nf3 Bxh3; 13.Kg1 Bxg2; 14.Kxg2 Qh3+; 15.Kg1 Qh1#. **11...g5!** And Black must strive to open up the h-file! The pawn cannot be captured. **12.Rh1.** 12.Nxg5

Rxh4 threatens the d-pawn as well as Bh6. 12.hxg5 Bxh3; 13.gxf6 (13.Bxh3 Qxh3+; 14.Kg1 Qh1#) 13...Bxg2+; 14.Kxg2 Qh3+; 15.Kg1 Qh1#. **12...g4; 13.hxg4 Bxg4; 14.Kg1 Qf5.**

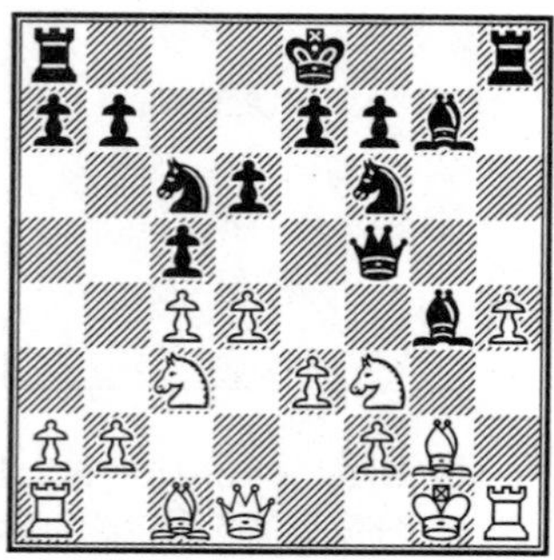

Black seems to have an unstoppable attack, but because his own king is stuck in the center his pieces do not coordinate well. White must stop 15...0-0-0. **15.d5! Ne5; 16.Qa4+ Nfd7; 17.Nxe5 Bxe5; 18.e4 Qg6; 19.Kf1.**

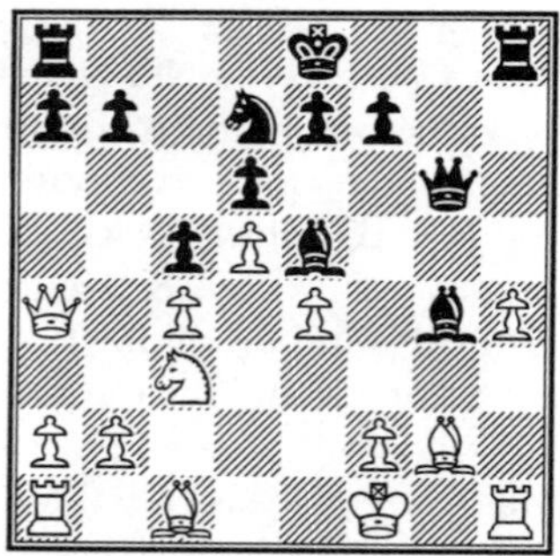

White has lost the initiative, as the threat of Bf3 had to be met. Now Black needs a plan. He can force the win of the e-pawn, a good first step. **19...Bxc3!; 20.bxc3 Be2+; 21.Kxe2.** 21.Kg1 loses immediately to 21...Bf3. **21...Qxg2; 22.Be3 Qxe4; 23.Rab1.**

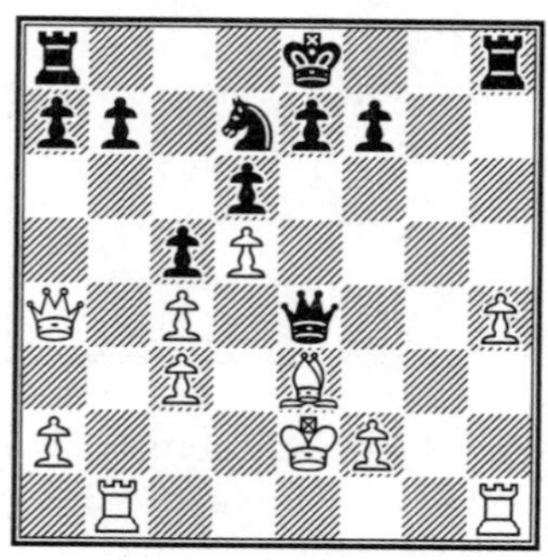

A deceptive position. White seems to be making real progress on the queenside.

But if Black can open a line on the queenside then the king is vulnerable. **23...b5!** Exploiting the pin at c4 and the pressure at h1. There is no need to go after the h-pawn when the enemy monarch is a much more attractive target. **24.Qxb5 Rb8; 25.Qc6.** 25.Qxb8+ Nxb8; 26.Rxb8+ Kd7; 27.Rxh8 Qxh1; 28.h5 Qe4; 29.h6 Qxc4+; 30.Ke1 Qxd5; 31.h7 Qh1+; 32.Ke2 f5 and the Black king emerges at e6, after which his pawns decide. **25...Qxc4+; 26.Kf3.**

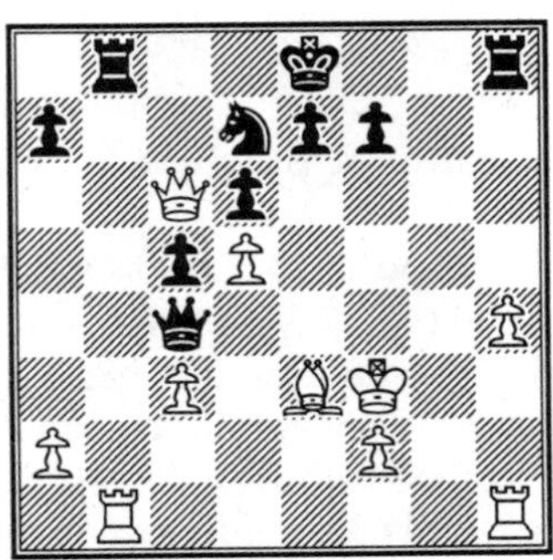

Black needs to find a way to continue attack without the participation of his rooks. He will require the services of the pinned knight. 26.Kd2 0–0!; 27.Qxd7 Qxa2+; 28.Kd3 Qxd5+; 29.Kc2 Qe4+. **26...f5!** The point of this move is not merely the threatened mate at g4, but more significantly, a flight square for the king, so that the pin can be broken. **27.Rxb8+.** 27.Rbg1 Qe4+; 28.Ke2 Rb2+ and Black wins. **27...Kf7.** Now White must attend to the threatened mate at g4. **28.Bd4 Ne5+!** The knight finally joins the attack - with decisive results. **29.Bxe5 Qe4+** and White resigned because of 30.Kg3 Qg4+; 31.Kh2 Rxh4 mate. **Black won.**

NIMZO-LARSEN ATTACK

1.b3
2.Bb2 (often with Nf3)

The immediate fianchetto on the queenside is not considered best, because Black can plant a stake in the center with 1...e5. So 1.Nf3 is often played as a prelude to the queenside fianchetto.

White hopes to play a reversed Queen's Indian or Dutch Defense with an extra tempo. Black does not have to cooperate, but even if the game does enter those paths White is unlikely to obtain any significant advantage. Nevertheless, Black must be careful not to drift into a position where the tempo is significant. One good plan for Black is to aim for ...e5 as soon as possible. The pawn at e5 limits the influence of the bishop at b2.

(258) LARSEN - KAVALEK [A36]

Lugano, 1968

1.b3 c5. 1...d5 can easily transpose but there are some independent paths after 2.Bb2.

A) 2...Nf6; 3.e3 e6; 4.f4 transposes to a Bird Opening, but Larsen has enjoyed using that strategy as well. 4...b6 (4...c5; 5.Nf3 Nc6; 6.Bb5 Be7; 7.Ne5 Qc7; 8.Bxc6+ bxc6; 9.c4 a5; 10.Nc3 Ba6; 11.Na4 0–0; 12.0–0 Rab8; 13.d3 Rb4; 14.Bc3 Nd7; 15.Qg4 provided White with a decisive advantage in Larsen-Pappa, Mar del Plata 1995.) 5.Nf3 Bb7; 6.Be2 c5; 7.0–0 Nc6; 8.Ne5 Be7; 9.d3 0–0; 10.Nd2 Nd7; 11.Ndf3 Ndxe5; 12.Nxe5 Nxe5; 13.fxe5 Bg5 gave Black an initiative in a rapid game played between Larsen and Karpov with both players blindfolded, at Monaco 1992.

B) With 2...c5. Black accepts White's hypermodern challenge.

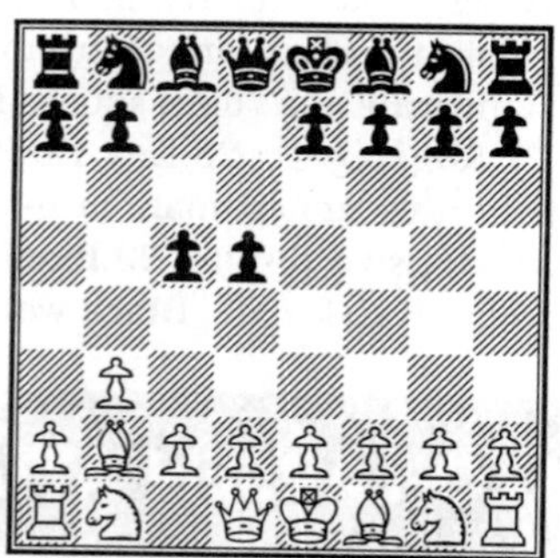

Now we have a reversed Queen's Indian Defense where the extra tempo is quite useful for White. Larsen and Nimzowitsch parted ways here, with Larsen preferring to defer the development of the Ng1.

B1) 3.e3 Nf6 (3...Nc6; 4.Bb5 a6; 5.Bxc6+ bxc6; 6.d3 Nh6; 7.Nc3 e5; 8.e4 f5; 9.Nf3 Nf7; 10.Na4 Bd6; 11.Qe2 0–0; 12.0–0–0 led to a double-edged game, Larsen-Dominguez Sanz, Las Palmas 1972.) 4.Bb5+ Bd7; 5.Bxd7+ Nbxd7; 6.Nf3 e6; 7.c4 Be7; 8.0–0 0–0; 9.Qe2 a6; 10.Nc3 Qa5; 11.cxd5 exd5; 12.d4 Rac8; 13.dxc5 Nxc5 and Black had the worse of the isolated d-pawn position, Larsen-Wade, Teesside 1972.

B2) 3.Nf3 Nc6. Black does not threaten to advance ...e5, as White has that square under control. 4.e3 Nf6 (4...Bg4; 5.h3 Bxf3; 6.Qxf3 e5; 7.Bb5 Qd6; 8.e4 d4; 9.Na3 f6; 10.Nc4 gave White a strong initiative which the progenitor of the variation exploited in fine fashion after 10...Qd7; 11.Qh5+! g6; 12.Qf3 Qc7; 13.Qg4 Kf7; 14.f4 h5; 15.Qf3 exf4; 16.Bxc6 bxc6; 17.0–0 g5; 18.c3 Rd8; 19.Rae1 Ne7; 20.e5 Nf5; 21.cxd4 Nxd4; 22.Qe4 Be7; 23.h4 Qd7; 24.exf6 Bxf6; 25.hxg5 and Black resigned in Nimzowitsch-Rosselli del Turco, Baden Baden 1925.) 5.Bb5 Bd7; 6.0–0 e6; 7.d3 Be7; 8.Bxc6!? (8.Nbd2 0–0; 9.Bxc6 Bxc6; 10.Ne5 Nd7; 11.Ndf3 Rc8; 12.Qe2 Nxe5; 13.Nxe5 Be8; 14.Qg4 f5; 15.Qe2 Bf6; 16.c4 Qe7; 17.f4 secured the center for White in

Nimzowitsch-Wolf, Carlsbad 1923.) 8...Bxc6; 9.Ne5 Rc8; 10.Nd2 0–0; 11.f4 Nd7; 12.Qg4 Nxe5; 13.Bxe5 Bf6; 14.Rf3 Qe7; 15.Raf1 a5; 16.Rg3 was the prelude to a magnificent attack by Bobby Fischer: 16...Bxe5; 17.fxe5 f5; 18.exf6 Rxf6; 19.Qxg7+!! Qxg7; 20.Rxf6 Qxg3; 21.hxg3 Re8; 22.g4 a4; 23.Nf3 axb3; 24.axb3 Kg7; 25.g5 e5; 26.Nh4 and White eventually scored the full point in Fischer-Mecking, Palma de Mallorca Interzonal 1970.

2.Bb2 Nc6; 3.c4 e5; 4.g3 d6. Black can try to get the pawn to d5 by playing ...Nge7 instead. **5.Bg2 Nge7; 6.e3 g6; 7.Ne2 Bg7; 8.Nbc3 0–0.** A routine move, but an error. Black should take advantage of the opportunity to fight for the d5-square with 8...Be6 since 9.Nd5 Bxd5; 10.cxd5 Nb4 wins at least a pawn. 11.Nc3 Nd3+; 12.Ke2 Nxb2; 13.Qc2 f5; 14.Qxb2 e4 and the d-pawn falls. **9.d3 Be6; 10.Nd5 Qd7; 11.h4!** The kingside assault begins. Black's pieces are not properly posted to help with the defense.

11...f5? This is a natural, but misguided, defensive strategy. 11...h5 was correct. **12.Qd2 Rae8; 13.h5 b5!** Black has to create counterplay somehow, and this is the fastest method. **14.hxg6 hxg6; 15.Nec3 bxc4; 16.dxc4.**

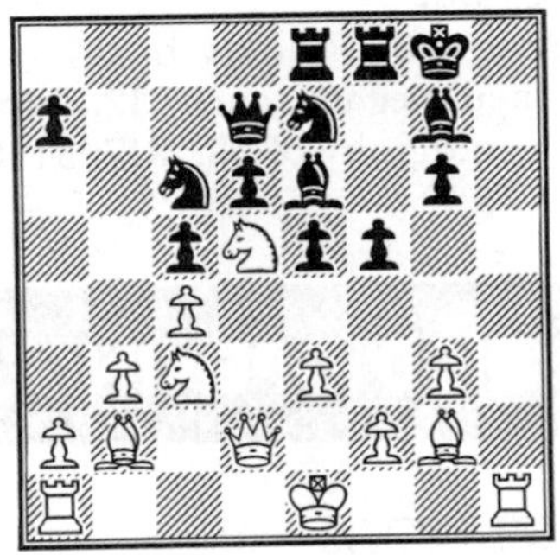

Now Kavalek plays a double-edged move, closing one diagonal and opening another. Later he will regret allowing White's dark-squared bishop an entryway to the kingside. **16...e4; 17.0–0–0 Ne5; 18.Nf4 Rd8; 19.Kb1.** White has time to attend to the invasion at d3. **19...Bf7; 20.g4!** Kavalek, down to his last 12 minutes, with enough problems, Larsen piles on the pressure. **20...Nxg4; 21.f3! exf3; 22.Bxf3 Ne5.**

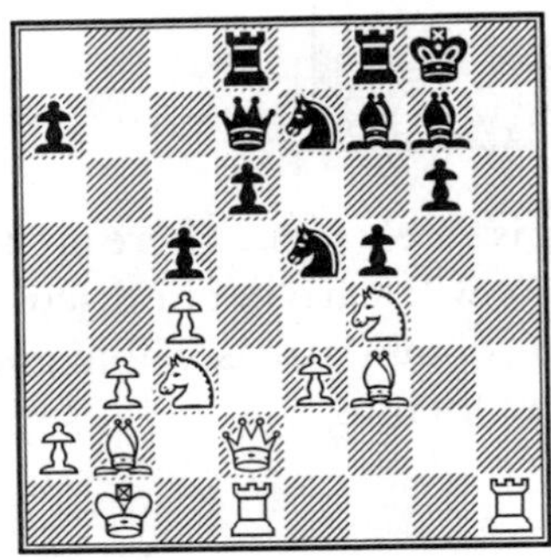

Larsen offers a piece to accelerate the attack. **23.Qh2! Bxc4.** 23...Nxf3; 24.Qh7#. **24.bxc4 Nxf3; 25.Qh7+ Kf7; 26.Ncd5 Rg8; 27.Nxe7 Rb8!** Black finds the only source of counterplay, an attack at b2. **28.Ka1 Qxe7; 29.Qxg6+ Kf8; 30.Ne6+!**

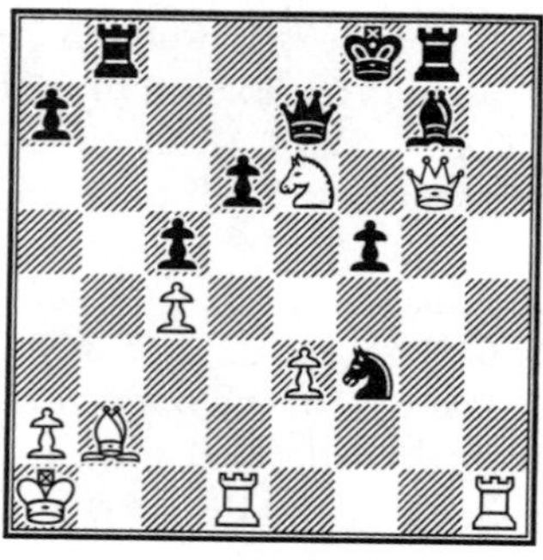

30...Qxe6! If White captures the queen, the game will end in a draw. **31.Bxg7+.** 31.Qxe6 Bxb2+; 32.Kb1 Ba3+.

A) 33.Kc2 Rg2+; 34.Kd3 Ne5+; 35.Kc3 (35.Qxe5 dxe5; 36.Rh8+ Kf7; 37.Rxb8 e4+; 38.Kc3 Bb4+; 39.Kb3 Rg3; 40.Rb7+ Ke6; 41.Rxa7 Rxe3+; 42.Kc2 Rc3+; 43.Kb2 Rxc4 and Black will win.) 35...Bb2#.

B) 33.Ka1; 33...Bb2+; 34.Kb1 Ba3+ holds the draw.

31...Ke7; 32.Bf8+!! A final elegant touch. **32...Rbxf8; 33.Rh7+** and Black resigned rather than suffer the indignity of 33...Rf7; 34.Rxf7+ Qxf7; 35.Qxd6+ Ke8; 36.Qd8#. **White won.**

BIRD OPENING

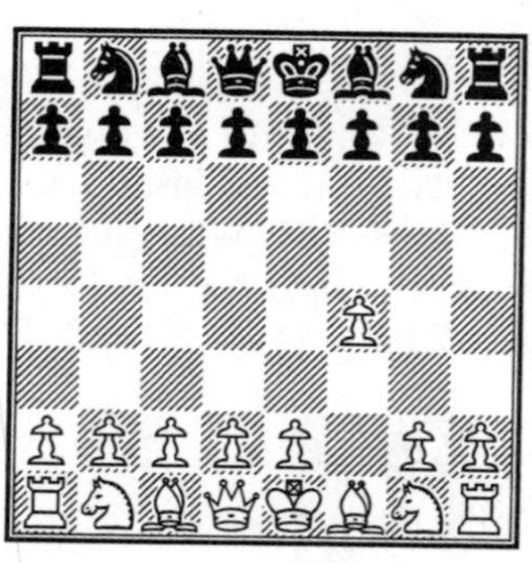

1.f4

Henry Bird's opening is rarely seen. There are two good reasons for this, and both begin 1...e5, as we will learn in our discussion of the From Gambit. In other cases, White can obtain a reasonably good version of a reversed Dutch Defense or English Opening.

REVERSED DUTCH

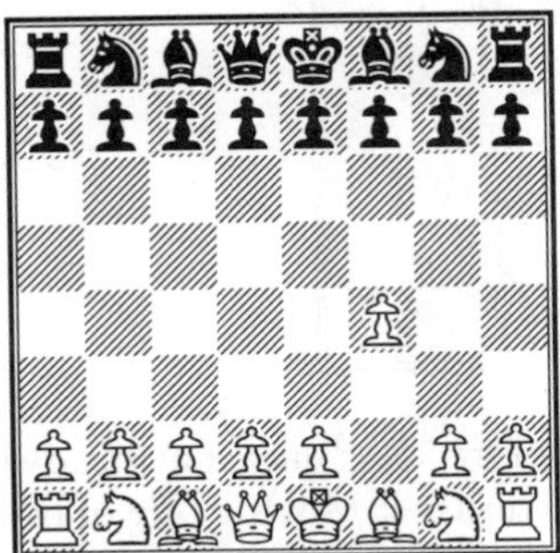

1.f4 d5

The **Reversed Dutch Defense** gives White a useful tempo, but at the same time this tempo forces White to declare the structure of the game earlier than usual and this gives Black time to react. Black can adopt the strategies used by White in the Dutch Defense, or try other plans. In our illustrative game Black's opening strategy works out well, but then disaster strikes.

(259) LASKER - BAUER [A03]
Amsterdam, 1889

1.f4 d5; 2.e3 Nf6; 3.b3 e6; 4.Bb2 Be7; 5.Bd3.

A somewhat artificial move, but not bad, because the c-pawn can advance to c4 and then the bishop can retreat to c2 or b1 as needed. Normal is 5.Nf3 Nbd7; 6.Be2, e.g., 6...a6; 7.0-0 c5 as in Rogers-Jonkman, Sonnevanck 1996. **5...b6; 6.Nf3 Bb7; 7.Nc3 Nbd7; 8.0–0 0–0.** Black has a solid position and White has no real advantage. **9.Ne2 c5.** Steinitz observed that 9...Nc5 was superior and would have led to an equal game, and the very latest evaluations confirm this. **10.Ng3 Qc7.**

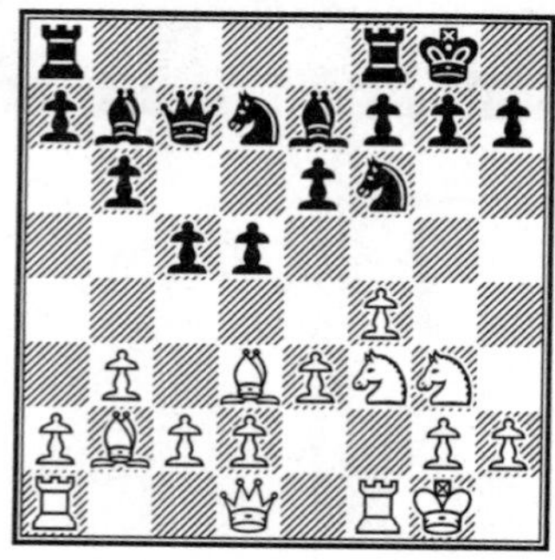

11.Ne5. White occupies this square before the Black pawn advances to e5. **11...Nxe5?** With just one move, Black invites disaster. Moving one of the rooks to c8 would have been better. **12.Bxe5.** Just compare the relative activity of the bishops Black is already in serious trouble. **12...Qc6; 13.Qe2 a6.** White has completed development and is ready to attack. The position of the rook at a1 cannot be improved, for the moment. Lasker starts by eliminating one of the few defenders of the Black king. But he doesn't part with the Be5. **14.Nh5 Nxh5.** White could simply recapture at h5 with a strong attack, but by sacrificing a piece the momentum is greatly increased. **15.Bxh7+! Kxh7; 16.Qxh5+.**

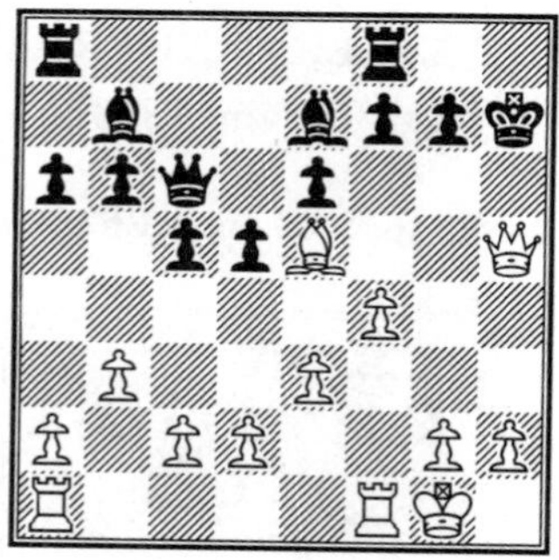

16...Kg8. Now White might like to transfer a rook to the h-file, but this is too slow, because Black is ready to play d5-d4 and threaten mate at g2. Then he could sacrifice some material in return and stay in the game. **17.Bxg7.** This threatens mate at h8. **17...Kxg7; 18.Qg4+ Kh7.** Now the queen guards g2 and White can threaten the sideways equivalent of a back rank mate. **19.Rf3 e5.** The only defense. Now the Black queen can come to h6. **20.Rh3+ Qh6; 21.Rxh6+ Kxh6.**

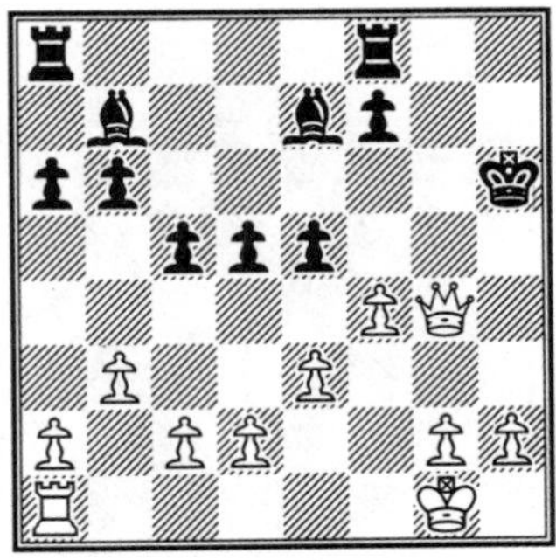

22.Qd7. This wins one of the bishops, and the game now is decisively in White's favor. **22...Bf6; 23.Qxb7 Kg7; 24.Rf1 Rab8; 25.Qd7 Rfd8; 26.Qg4+ Kf8; 27.fxe5 Bg7.** 27...Bxe5; 28.Qh5 f6; 29.Qxe5 shows another method of exploiting the pin on the f-file. **28.e6 Rb7; 29.Qg6.** White exploits the pin in the maximally efficient way. **29...f6; 30.Rxf6+ Bxf6; 31.Qxf6+ Ke8; 32.Qh8+ Ke7; 33.Qg7+.** Now the rook at b7 falls, so Black gives up. **White won.**

FROM GAMBIT

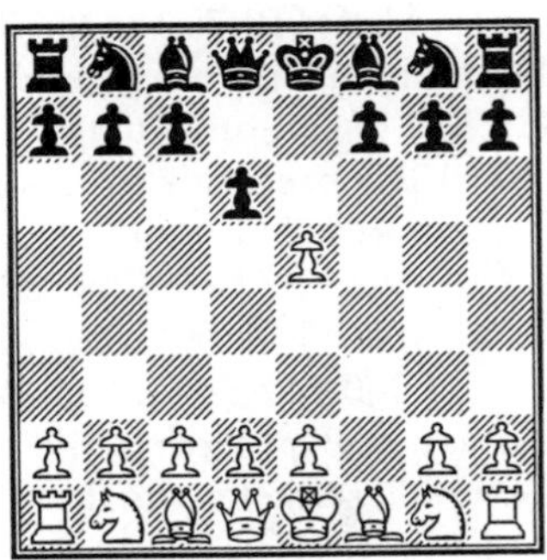

1.f4	**e5**
2.fxe5	**d6**

The **From Gambit** is the most dangerous reply to the Bird's Opening. Black gives up a pawn but gets to work on the weak dark squares on White's kingside. If White captures on d6, then after ...Bxd6 Black already has forces aimed at the weak White kingside. This is a sound gambit and White often avoids it by transposing to the King's Gambit with 2.e4.

(260) ANTOSHIN - PANCHENKO [A02]
Soviet Union, 1983

1.f4 e5; 2.fxe5 d6; 3.exd6. 3.Nf3 allows Black to keep the initiative by putting pressure on the knight at f3. 3...Bg4!?; 4.e4 dxe5; 5.Bc4 Nd7; 6.Nc3 Bc5; 7.d3 Ngf6; 8.Bg5 h6; 9.Bh4 c6; 10.h3 Bh5; 11.Qe2 g5; 12.Bf2 b5 and in Hayward-Nolan, Correspondence 1987, Black had an initiative on both sides of the board. **3...Bxd6; 4.Nf3 g5.**

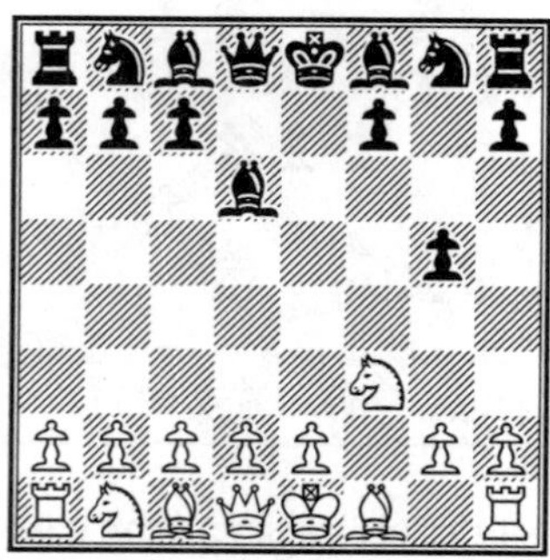

Such an outrageous advance of the g-pawn is not usually available to Black so early in the opening without severe penalties, but here, as in the King's Gambit, it is not only playable, but best! Black can also play 4...Nf6, and the situation in that line, as in the main continuation, is evaluated as "unclear" according to latest theory.

5.g3. 5.d4 g4; 6.Ng5 (6.Ne5 Bxe5; 7.dxe5 Qxd1+; 8.Kxd1 Nc6; 9.Nc3 Be6!; 10.Bf4 0–0–0+; 11.Ke1 Nge7; 12.e3 Ng6 and in Chigorin-Tarrasch, Vienna 1898, Black had solved the problems of the opening. Dogmatic old Tarrasch – who would have thought of him on the Black side of this opening!) 6...f5 Black will win the knight, but White gets compensation. These are wild lines!

7.e4 h6; 8.e5 Be7; 9.Nh3 gxh3; 10.Qh5+ Kf8; 11.Bc4 Rh7!; 12.Qg6 Rg7; 13.Bxh6 Nxh6. A well-studied alternative is 13...Bb4+, but this move is simpler and good enough for equality. 14.Qxh6 Bb4+; 15.c3 (15.Ke2 Qg5 returns to the complex line, though as a practical matter I think that 15.c3 is more likely in this move order. 16.Qxg5 Rxg5; 17.g3! and now Black must play carefully with 17...f4!; 18.c3 Bg4+! 19.Ke1 fxg3; 20.hxg3 Be7 for example 21.Nd2 Nc6; 22.Ne4 Rh5; 23.Nf2 Nxe5!; 24.dxe5 Rxe5+; 25.Kd2 Rd8+; 26.Kc2 Bf5+; 27.Kb3 b5!; 28.Bf1 Rd2. Daudswards-Gulbis, Latvia 1988.) 15...Qg5; 16.Qxh3 Nc6; 17.0–0 Nxe5!; 18.dxe5 Bc5+; 19.Kh1 Ke7; 20.b4 Be6! Black intends to activate the rook at a8 by playing Rh8. 21.Nd2 Rh8; 22.Nf3! Qg6; 23.Nh4 and now perhaps Black should settle for the draw by repeating the position. Instead, in Theiler-Ghitescu, Romania 1956, he tried for more and lost.

5...g4; 6.Nh4 Ne7.

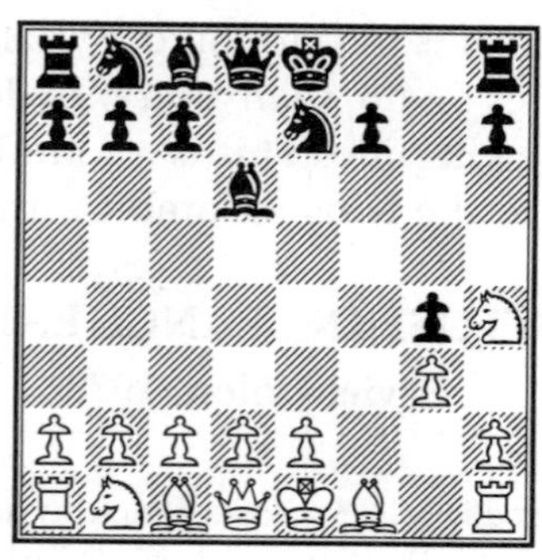

7.d4. This move has the advantage of staking out central territory. Others are too slow. 7.Bg2 Ng6; 8.Nxg6 hxg6; 9.0–0? allows a powerful and typical sacrifice: 9...Rxh2! 10.Kxh2 Qh4+; 11.Kg1 Bxg3; 12.Rxf7 Qh2+; 13.Kf1 Kxf7 and Black is clearly better. 7.e4 Ng6; 8.Nf5 (8.Nxg6 hxg6; 9.Bg2 Rxh2!; 10.0–0 Bxg3 and White was in serious trouble in Jacobsen-Petersen, Danish Championship 1970.) 8...Nc6 leads to some wild play: 9.Bg2! Bxf5; 10.exf5 Qe7+; 11.Qe2 Nd4!; 12.Qxe7+ Nxe7 and Black is better.

7...Ng6; 8.Nxg6. 8.Ng2 h5!? Not the most common move, but it seems good enough and avoids a lot of messy theory. 9.e4 h4; 10.e5 Be7!; 11.Rg1 Bf5; 12.Be3 Nc6; 13.c3 Qd7; 14.Bb5 0–0–0 and Black had a promising position in Genser-Jonassen, Correspondence 1979. **8...hxg6; 9.Qd3.** 9.Bg2? Rxh2; 10.Rxh2 Bxg3+; 11.Kf1 Bxh2 and Black is clearly better. **9...Nc6; 10.c3 Qe7.** 10...Bf5; 11.e4 Qe7; 12.Bg2 transposes to the main line. **11.Bg2 Bf5; 12.e4 0–0–0.**

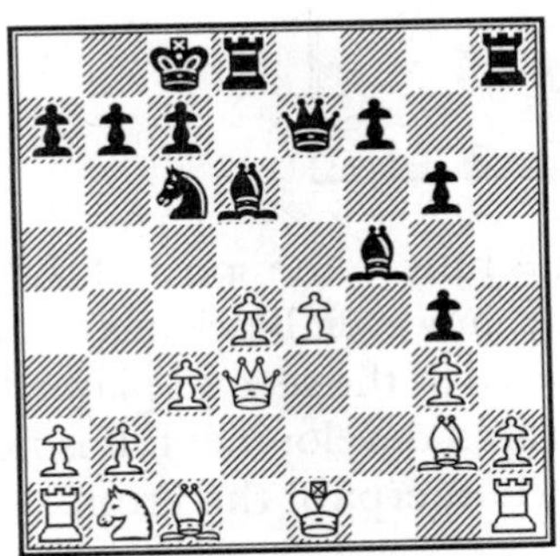

13.0–0?! 13.Be3! is best, but even so Black has resources in 13...Rde8! (13...Rxh2; 14.Rxh2 Bxg3+; 15.Kd2 Bxh2; 16.exf5 Ne5 is unclear. This analysis of mine is the concluding note on the From Gambit in the 1996 edition of the *Encyclopedia of Chess Openings*.) 14.Nd2 g5! and now White has nothing better than 15.exf5 Qxe3+; 16.Qxe3 Rxe3+; 17.Kf2 Rhe8; 18.Bd5 Ne7; 19.Bxf7 Rf8; 20.Be6+ Kd8 with a good game for Black in Langheld-Simchen, Correspondence 1990. **13...Ne5!; 14.Qd1.** 14.Qe3 Bd7; 15.Qg5 Nf3+; 16.Bxf3 f6 is unclear, according to Panchenko. **14...Nf3+!** This leads to a powerful combination. **15.Bxf3 gxf3; 16.exf5.**

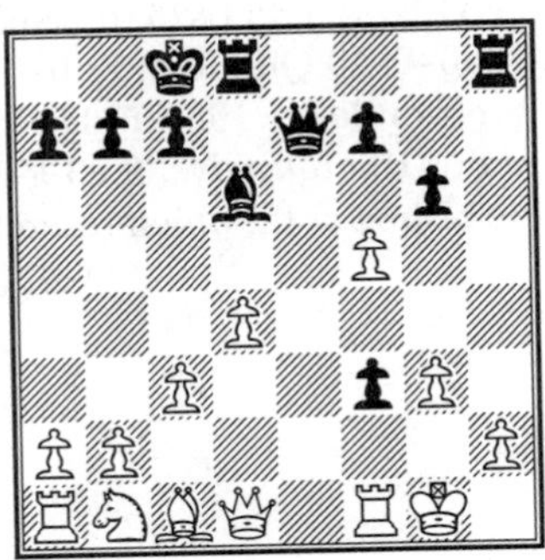

16...Rxh2!! The sacrifice cannot be accepted. **17.Qxf3.** 17.Kxh2 loses quickly to 17...Qh4+; 18.Kg1 Qxg3+; 19.Kh1 Qg2#. **17...Rh3.** Now White has only one reasonable way to try to defend the pawn at g3. **18.Bf4 Bxf4; 19.Qxf4 Rdh8.** The White king has no escape, since the e-file is cut off by the Black queen. **20.Qf3 Qg5; 21.Kf2 Rh2+; 22.Kg1 Rh1+. Black won.**

SCHLECHTER GAMBIT

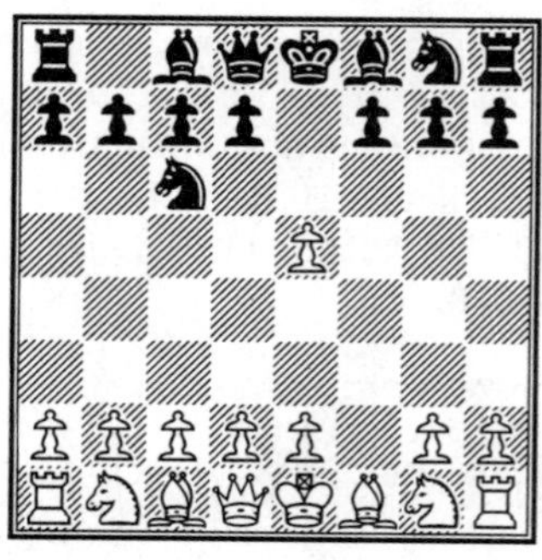

1.f4 e5
2.fxe5 Nc6

Schlechter's Gambit is fully in the spirit of the From, into which it often transposes. In recent years, however, Black has found additional resources to vary the plans at the disposal of the second player. The idea is classic gambit play–give up a pawn for rapid development. It is now considered as respectable as its more popular counterpart, the From.

(261) FRIED - SCHLECHTER [A02]
Vienna, 1894

1.f4 e5; 2.fxe5 Nc6; 3.Nf3 d6. Another way to continue the gambit is 3...g5, which leads to interesting complications. 3...g5; 4.h3 d6; 5.d4 dxe5; 6.dxe5! Qxd1+; 7.Kxd1 g4; 8.hxg4 Bxg4; 9.Bf4 Bg7. Schubert evaluates this as equal. 10.c3 Bxf3; 11.exf3 Nxe5; 12.Bxe5 Bxe5; 13.Bb5+ c6; 14.Re1 f6; 15.f4 cxb5; 16.fxe5 fxe5; 17.Rxe5+ Kd7; 18.Rxb5 Kc6; 19.a4 Rd8+ 20.Kc2 Ne7 is my own analysis.

4.exd6 Bxd6. 4...Qxd6; 5.d4 Bg4; 6.d5 Bxf3 (6...Ne5 comes into consideration.) 7.exf3 Ne5; 8.Nc3 Nf6; 9.Bf4 0-0-0; 10.Qd4 Re8; 11.0-0-0 b6; 12.Ba6+ Kb8; 13.Nb5. White won. Knorr-Plath, Correspondence 1989. **5.d4 Nf6; 6.Bg5 h6; 7.Bh4 g5; 8.Bf2 Ne4.** Black relentlessly maintains the initiative. **9.e3 g4!** There is no reason to give up the prize steed at e4 for the bishop at f2, which resembles little more than a pawn. **10.Bh4?**

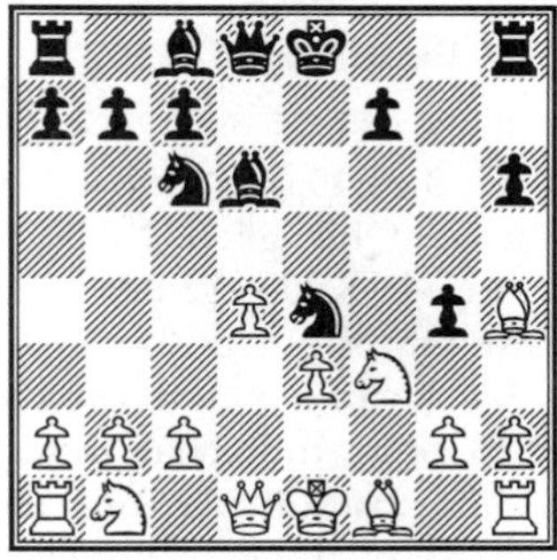

White fails to appreciate the danger, and is quickly demolished. **10...gxf3!!; 11.Bxd8 f2+; 12.Ke2 Bg4+; 13.Kd3 Nb4+; 14.Kxe4 f5#. Black won.**

VAN GEET OPENING

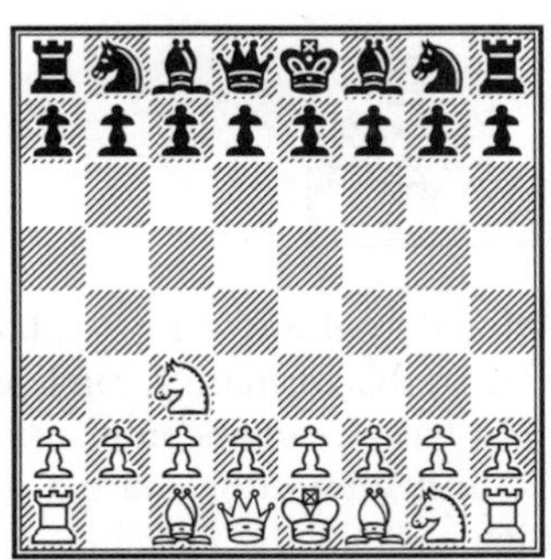

1.Nc3

This opening is traditionally known in America as the **Dunst**, but in Holland and most of Europe it is the **Van Geet**, named for Dick van Geet who has played and promoted it most of his life. It is a somewhat unorthodox opening but often transposes into such main lines as the French, Caro Kann or Closed Sicilian. The development of the knight at c3 is a normal move in and of itself.

This opening will be treated in greater depth in *Unorthodox Chess Openings*, but the present game is a sample of the unique plan with which van Geet is associated, and also contains a reference to a very famous game attributed to Napoleon.

(262) VAN GEET - GUYT [A00]
Paramaribo, 1967

1.Nc3 d5. 1...e5; 2.Nf3 d6; 3.e4 f5; 4.h3 fxe4; 5.Nxe4 Nc6; 6.Nfg5 d5 allows White to develop a strong attack. 7.Qh5+ g6; 8.Qf3 Nh6; 9.Nf6+ Ke7; 10.Nxd5+ Kd6 and now White mates with 11.Ne4+ Kxd5; 12.Bc4+ Kxc4; 13.Qb3+ Kd4; 14.Qd3#. This game was reportedly played by Napoleon Bonaparte against De Remusat at La Malmaison 1804! **2.e4.** Now Black can switch to the French with 2...e6, Caro-Kann with 2...c6, Alekhine via 2...Nf6, or Scandinavian Defense with just about any other move. If Black advances to d4, the position takes on a more original flavor, while the capture at e4 still leaves a variety of transpositional possibilities available. **2...d4; 3.Nce2 e5; 4.Ng3.**

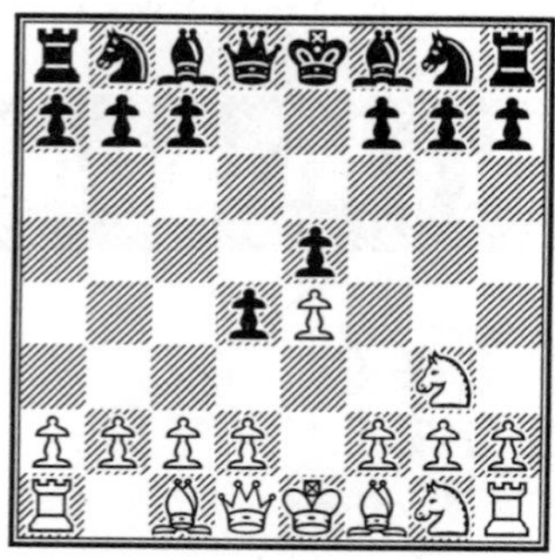

Looking at this position we see the rationale behind White's play. Although Black has occupied the dark squares in the center, this formation can later be undermined by such moves as c3 and f4. The knight has already been transferred to the kingside, where it can take part in an attack, and White does have a slight lead in development. **4...g6.** A logical reaction, which enables the fianchetto of the dark-squared bishop and denies access to f5 and h5 which might otherwise be useful to White.

5.Bc4 Bg7; 6.d3 c5; 7.Nf3 Nc6; 8.c3. White establishes a little tension in the center, though strictly speaking this is not the real point of the move. Instead, the idea is to be able to deploy the queen at b3, creating a powerful battery with the bishop, aiming at the vulnerable f7-square. **8...Nge7; 9.Ng5 0–0.**

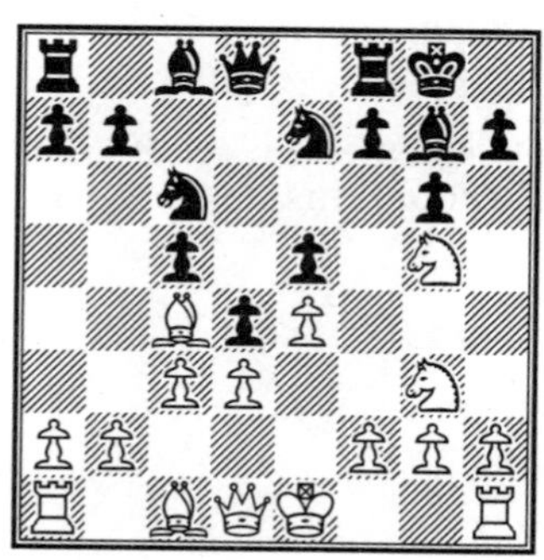

Now White has a surprising attacking move. **10.Nh5! Bh8.** Black tries to preserve the bishop, but this leads to disaster. 10...gxh5; 11.Qxh5 h6; 12.Nxf7 is obviously unacceptable. 10...Na5; 11.Nxg7 Nxc4!; 12.dxc4 Kxg7 is necessary. **11.Qf3 Qe8; 12.Nf6+ Bxf6; 13.Qxf6 dxc3?** This loses by force. Again it was necessary to harass the bishop at c4 by ...Na5. **14.Nxf7 Rxf7; 15.Bh6** and Black had no defense. **White won.**

9. BUILDING A REPERTOIRE

This section is a brief introduction to some opening repertoires that may work for your level of skill and style of play.

BEGINNER LEVELS

When just starting out in chess, you don't want to have to memorize lots of variations, or play positions with very complicated positions. The important thing is to get your pieces into the game and move your king to a safer position by castling.

White Repertoire

As White, you should start out with 1.e4. If the opponent plays 1...e5, then play 2.Nf3 and head for the Italian Game. After 2...Nc6; 3.Bc4 Bc5, use the Classical Variation with 4.c3, and if 3...Nf6, then just play 4.d3. Against the Sicilian Defense, use the Closed Variation with 2.Nc3, which is very easy to play because you just develop pieces and then attack.

In the other Semi-Open Games, play the Exchange Variation. This works well against the Caro-Kann and Alekhine, and against the French you can squeeze a little more out of the position by choosing the Delayed Exchange, forcing Black to break the symmetry of the position. If Black plays a Pirc or Modern setup, just develop your knights at c3 and f3, play Be2, and then castle (the Classical Variation).

Black Repertoire

With Black, it is important to choose openings which actively contest the center. The most suitable openings are the symmetrical ones against 1.e4 and 1.d4. The Classical Variation of the Spanish Game is a nice choice because it is simple and easy to execute. Defending the Queen's Gambit Declined can be handled in a number of ways, but the Orthodox Variation is the one which allows you to keep the most solid center. Against Flank Games, which are rarely seen at the beginner level, just set up the New York Defense.

INTERMEDIATE LEVELS

White Repertoire

After you have been playing chess for a while you will want to explore some of the other opening strategies, so why not switch to 1.d4 as White?

This will bring you into a whole new world of possible structures. In the Queen's Gambit, you can react to acceptance of the gambit with 3.e4, staking out important territory in the center and regaining the pawn quickly. If Black declines, or plays the Slav, then the Exchange Variations clarify the central situation quickly. Against the King's Indian, the Exchange Variation of the Classical Variation holds very little risk and creates some tactical possibilities for you. The Gruenfeld is a complicated opening, so the sideline 4.Bf4 is a good way of avoiding the most difficult and challenging lines. Similarly, the Benoni and Benko Gambit can be ducked after 1.d4 Nf6; 2.c4 c5 with 3.Nf3, the Anti-Benoni.

Finally, on 1.d4 Nf6 2.c4 e6 you invite the Nimzo-Indian with 3.Nc3, and on 3...Bb4 you select the main lines with 4.e3. It is not necessary to master the theory of these openings, because they are all rather quiet and as long as you develop your pieces on sensible squares you will achieve a decent position.

Black Repertoire

For Black, the French Defense offers a solid opening which can lead to favorable middlegame and endgame positions. If you haven't previously played the French or the Queen's Gambit Declined, then the French offers a good chance to learn all about "bad bishops", lessons that will serve you well as your skills increase. Against 1.d4, the Tarrasch Defense in the Queen's Gambit Declined is an excellent choice, providing good piece play and introducing you to another important middlegame formation: the isolated d-pawn position. Another advantage of the Tarrasch is that it can be played against all the Flank Games too.

ADVANCED LEVELS

White Repertoire

When you fully understand the dyanamics of the center, then it is possible to adopt a more hypermodern approach. As White, the English Opening and Reti are useful, but 1.e4 and 1.d4 are still the top choices. Now, however, it is time to master the main lines. If playing 1.e4, spend a lot of time on the Sicilian Defenses, since they can lead to a quick win for your opponent if you are not properly prepared. Against 1...e5, it is time to master the intricate Spanish Game, using your improved strategic, tactical and endgame technique to torture your opponents. If 1.d4 is your preference, concentrate on confronting the King's Indian and Nimzo-Indian in the main lines. The Queen's Gambits need less attention, except in ultra-sharp lines like the Botvinnik Variation of the Semi-Slav.

Black Repertoire

When facing 1.e4 as Black, choose one of the major Sicilian Defenses (Najdorf, Dragon, Scheveningen, Paulsen or Lasker-Pelikan) and learn it thoroughly, or adopt several (not just one!) variations of the Spanish Game. The French and Caro-Kann are acceptable alternatives. Against 1.d4, the King's Indian, Gruenfeld and Semi-Slav are excellent choices for everyday use.

PLAYING GAMBITS

If you are playing chess for fun, or want to sharpen your tactical skills, you can build a repertoire consisting of nothing but gambits. As White, play 1.e4 and against 1...e5 try the Göring Gambit or King's Gambit. Against the Sicilian, use the Smith-Morra Gambit. The Caro-Kann and French Defenses are more solid, but even there you can find gambits such as 1.e4 e6; 2.d4 d5; 3.Nc3 Bb4; 4.Nge2 and 1.e4 c6; 2.d4 d5; 3.Nc3 dxe4; 4.Bc4. In the Alekhine Defense, there are some gambits involving the advance e4-e5-e6.

As Black, you can meet 1.d4 with a number of gambits after 1...d5 2.c4, such as the Albin Countergambit and Schara Gambit. Against 1.e4, there is 1...d5; 2.exd5 Nf6, delaying the capture of the pawn at d5. The flank openings are more challenging, since White's refusal to engage in central confrontation makes gambit play risky, but you can aim for Benko Gambit type play when White eventually plays d4 by responding with ...c5, and if White advances to d5, then in some systems ...b5 is possible. Nevertheless, it is wise not to insist on a gambit in all circumstances, as sometimes there are no good gambit approaches available.

CHOOSING THE BEST REPERTOIRES

One easy and instructive way to develop a reperoire is to study the openings played by great players. There is a danger here that you may try to emulate a player whose chess understanding is much deeper than your own. Copying Kasparov's openings is a recipe for disaster if you lack his skills, and most of us do. You should copy players who represent styles that suit you own skills. While this sounds like a major research task, this is not the case. It turns out that for the most part, history recapitulates the learning path of the average player. The weaker the player, the more likely that an older master will provide a good model.

In the book *World Champion Openings,* I examined the repertories of all the world champions, and you can look there for advice, but here is a table that summarizes a wider range of players. The numbers in the Level column refer to standard ratings on the United States Chess Federation, World Chess Federation or Internet Chess Club scales, which vary slightly in their implementation but are close enough to be treated identically from our purposes.

You can learn about the opening repertoires of these players by reading game collections featuring their games, or using a software tool such as the Caxton Chess Database, or by downloading game collections from the Internet. You can also purchase books or disks devoted to the opening repertoires of great players from the publisher of this book (see the back pages).

REPERTOIRE GUIDE

Level	Attacking	Positional	Conservative	Unorthodox
Beginner (0-1000)	Morphy	Lasker	Tarrasch	Bird
Advanced Beginner (1000-1400)	Marshall	Schlechter	Tarrasch	Alapin
Intermediate (1400-1700)	Alekhine	Capablanca	Rubinstein	Tartakower
Advanced (1700-2000)	Tal	Petrosian	Fine	Mikenas
Candidate Master (2000-2200)	Larsen	Botvinnik	Euwe	Korchnoi
National Master (2200-2400)	Fischer	Smyslov	Yusupov	Hodgson
International Master (2400-2500)	Anand	Shirov	Spassky	Benjamin
Grandmaster (2500+)	Kasparov	Karpov	Kramnik	Miles

10. NEXT STEPS

After reading this book, you can go on to incorporate openings that you find interesting into your own repertoire. There are thousands of books available on specific opening strategies, and for proficiency, you'll need to turn to the extensive literature on each opening. You may be interested in the companion books to SCO as well, *World Champion Openings* and *Unorthodox Chess Openings*. WCO looks at the opening theory and moves of the major openings as played by all the World Champions, while UCO takes a look at the other side of the openings, the strange, unusual, and controversial ones.

A selection of recommended opening books from different publishers is available from Cardoza Publishing {www.cardozapub.com) as well as their own growing list. Armed with the knowledge you gain in this book, you can also deepen your understanding of the ideas behind the openings by examining collections of games by the strong players who use those openings.

ECO CODES INDEX

The following index contains the code used in the *Encyclopedia of Chess Openings*, *Chess Informant*, and many other important chess publications. Each code has a letter followed by two numbers. The letter refers to the volume of the *Encyclopedia of Chess Openings* in which the opening is treated, the numbers are used to identify the grid number in that book.

If you see a game in a publication which uses ECO codes (pronounced ee-see-oh), then you can use this index to find the relevant discussion in *Standard Chess Openings*. Note that transpositional openings can be covered in several different codes.

STANDARD CHESS OPENINGS

ECO	Opening	Variation	System	Page
B44	Sicilian Defense	Paulsen Variation	Kasparov Gambit	80
B47	Sicilian Defense	Paulsen Variation	Bastrikov Variation	82
B51	Sicilian Defense	Canal Attack		83
B52	Sicilian Defense	Canal Attack	Main Line	84
B57	Sicilian Defense	Classical Variation	Anti-Sozin Variation	85
B58	Sicilian Defense	Boleslavsky Variation	Variation	86
B62	Sicilian Defense	Richter-Rauzer Variation	Neo-Modern Variation	88
B76	Sicilian Defense	Dragon Variation	Yugoslav Attack	89
B77	Sicilian Defense	Dragon Variation	Yugoslav Attack	90
B79	Sicilian Defense	Dragon Variation	Yugoslav Attack	91
B80	Sicilian Defense	Scheveningen Variation	English Attack	92
B81	Sicilian Defense	Scheveningen Variation	Keres Attack	93
B81	Sicilian Defense	Scheveningen Variation	Delayed Keres Attack	94
B82	Sicilian Defense	Scheveningen Variation	Matanovic Attack	95
B83	Sicilian Defense	Scheveningen Variation	Modern Variation	96
B85	Sicilian Defense	Scheveningen Variation	Main Line	97
B87	Sicilian Defense	Sozin Attack	Flank Variation	98
B97	Sicilian Defense	Najdorf Variation	Poisoned Pawn	99
B99	Sicilian Defense	Najdorf Variation	Main Line	100
C00	Queen Pawn Game	Franco-Sicilian Defense		187
C02	French Defense	Advance Variation		101
C05	French Defense	Tarrasch Variation	Closed Variation	102
C05	French Defense	Tarrasch Variation	Pawn Center Variation	103
C07	French Defense	Tarrasch Variation	Open System	104
C10	French Defense	Rubinstein Variation		105
C11	French Defense	Classical Variation		106
C11	French Defense	Classical Variation	Steinitz Variation	106
C11	French Defense	Classical Variation	Burn Variation	107
C12	French Defense	MacCutcheon Variation		109
C12	French Defense	MacCutcheon Variation	Janowski Variation	109
C13	French Defense	Classical Variation	Richter Attack	108
C15	French Defense	Winawer Variation		110
C15	French Defense	Winawer Variation	Fingerslip Variation	110
C18	French Defense	Winawer Variation	Advance Variation	111
C19	French Defense	Winawer Variation	Advance Variation	112
C20	Bishop's Opening	Boi Variation		2
C22	Center Game	Normal Variation		12
C23	Bishop's Opening			1
C24	Bishop's Opening	Urusov Gambit		3
C25	Vienna Game	Steinitz Gambit		5
C26	Bishop's Opening	Vienna Hybrid	Spielmann Attack	4
C26	Vienna Game	Mieses Variation		6
C27	Vienna Game	Frankenstein-Dracula Variation		7
C28	Bishop's Opening	Vienna Hybrid		2
C29	Vienna Game	Vienna Gambit	Steinitz Variation	8
C29	Vienna Game	Vienna Gambit		8
C30	King's Gambit	Declined	Classical Variation	14
C31	King's Gambit	Declined	Falkbeer Countergambit	15
C33	King's Gambit	Accepted	Bishop's Gambit	17
C33	King's Gambit	Accepted	Breyer Gambit	16
C34	King's Gambit	Accepted	Fischer Defense	22
C34	King's Gambit	Accepted	Bonsch-Osmolovsky Variation	18
C35	King's Gambit	Accepted	Cunningham Defense	19
C36	King's Gambit	Accepted	Abbazia Defense	20
C37	King's Gambit	Accepted	Muzio Gambit	21
C39	King's Gambit	Accepted	Kieseritsky Gambit	23
C40	Elephant Gambit			10

STANDARD CHESS OPENINGS

ECO	Opening	Variation	System	Page
D00	Queen Pawn Game	Veresov Attack		183
D00	Queen Pawn Game	Steinitz Countergambit		193
D00	Queen Pawn Game	Blackmar-Diemer Gambit		191
D00	Queen Pawn Game	Blackmar-Diemer Gambit	Bogoljubow Variation	192
D01	Queen Pawn Game	Veresov Atack	Richter Variation	184
D02	Queen Pawn Game	Anti-Torre		185
D02	Queen's Gambit Refused	Baltic Defense		165
D05	Queen Pawn Game	Colle System		186
D07	Queen's Gambit Refused	Chigorin Defense		166
D08	Queen's Gambit Refused	Albin Countergambit		167
D10	Slav Defense	Exchange Variation		170
D10	Slav Defense	Winawer Countergambit		168
D15	Slav Defense	Geller Gambit		171
D15	Slav Defense	Schlechter Variation		173
D17	Slav Defense	Czech Variation		172
D20	Queen's Gambit Accepted	Saduleto Variation		140
D20	Queen's Gambit Accepted			140
D24	Queen's Gambit Accepted	Showalter Variation		139
D26	Queen's Gambit Accepted	Classical Defense		141
D32	Tarrasch Defense	Schara Gambit		159
D32	Tarrasch Defense	Symmetrical Variation		160
D32	Tarrasch Defense	Von Hennig Gambit		158
D33	Tarrasch Defense	Swedish Variation		161
D34	Tarrasch Defense	Classical Variation	Main Line	164
D34	Tarrasch Defense	Classical Variation	Spassky Variation	163
D34	Tarrasch Defense	Classical Variation	Advance Variation	162
D35	Queen's Gambit Declined	Exchange Variation	Positional Variation	142
D37	Queen's Gambit Declined	Harrwitz Attack		143
D38	Queen's Gambit Declined	Ragozin Defense		144
D40	Queen's Gambit Declined	Semi-Tarrasch Defense		145
D41	Queen's Gambit Declined	Semi-Tarrasch Defense	Exchange Variation	146
D42	Queen's Gambit Declined	Semi-Tarrasch Defense	Main Line	147
D44	Semi-Slav Defense	Botvinnik System		154
D45	Semi-Slav Defense	Stoltz Variation		155
D47	Semi-Slav Defense	Meran Variation	Wade Variation	156
D47	Semi-Slav Defense	Meran Variation		157
D52	Queen's Gambit Declined	Cambridge Springs Variation		148
D53	Queen's Gambit Declined	Lasker Defense		149
D55	Queen's Gambit Declined	Anti-Tartakower Variation		150
D58	Queen's Gambit Declined	Tartakower Defense		151
D60	Queen's Gambit Declined	Orthodox Defense	Botvinnik Variation	152
D64	Queen's Gambit Declined	Orthodox Defense	Rubinstein Attack	153
D82	Grünfeld Defense	Three Knights Variation	Saemisch Attack	231
D85	Grünfeld Defense	Exchange Variation	Modern Exchange Variation	228
D86	Grünfeld Defense	Exchange Variation	Classical Variation	229
D98	Grünfeld Defense	Russian Variation	Smyslov Variation	230
E00	Kangaroo Defense			190
E01	Catalan Opening	Closed Variation		249
E11	Bogo-Indian Defense	Grünfeld Variation		243
E11	Bogo-Indian Defense			244
E11	Queen's Indian Defense	Petrosian Variation	Farago Defense	206
E15	Queen's Indian Defense	Fianchetto Variation	Nimzowitsch Attack	209
E15	Queen's Indian Defense	Fianchetto Variation	Nimzowitsch Variation	208
E15	Queen's Indian Defense	Fianchetto Variation	Saemisch Variation	210
E16	Queen's Indian Defense	Capablanca Variation		211
E17	Queen's Indian Defense	Opocensky Variation		213
E17	Queen's Indian Defense	Kasparov	Petrosian Variation	207

ECO	Opening	Variation	System	Page
E17	Queen's indian Defense	Classical Variation	Polugayevsky Gambit	212
E17	Queen's Indian Defense	Classical Variation	Taimanov Gambit	212
E19	Queen's Indian Defense	Traditional Variation	Main Line	214
E20	Nimzo-Indian Defense	Kmoch Variation		215
E20	Nimzo-Indian Defense	Romanishin Variation		216
E22	Nimzo-Indian Defense	Spielmann Variation		217
E30	Nimzo-Indian Defense	Leningrad Variation		218
E32	Nimzo-Indian Defense	Classical Variation		219
E33	Nimzo-Indian Defense	Classical Variation	Zurich Variation	220
E34	Nimzo-Indian Defense	Classical Variation	Noa Variation	222
E35	Nimzo-Indian Defense	Classical Variation	Romainshin Variation	221
E40	Nimzo-Indian Defense	Normal Variation	Taimanov Variation	223
E41	Nimzo-Indian Defense	Huebner Variation		224
E43	Nimzo-Indian Defense	St. Petersburg		225
E46	Nimzo-Indian Defense	Ragozin Defense		226
E63	King's Indian Defense	Fianchetto Variation	Panno Variation	198
E67	King's Indian Defense	Fianchetto Variation	Classical Variation	199
E69	King's Indian Defense	Fianchetto Variation	Main Line	200
E73	King's Indian Defense	Averbakh Variation		201
E76	King's Indian Defense	Steiner Attack		202
E80	King's Indian Defense	Saemisch Variation		203
E92	King's Indian Defense	Petrosian System		204
E94	King's Indian Defense	Orthodox Variation		205

CHRONOLOGICAL INDEX

In order to appreciate the development and evolution of opening theory, you might wish to play through the games in this book in chronological order. This index will enable you to follow the development of opening strategy from the 19th century up to the present.

Year	Game #	Players
1834	65	McDonnell vs. De La Bourdonnais
1863	123	Steinitz vs. Mongredien
1865	21	Zukertort vs. Anderssen
1867	110	Steinitz vs. Winawer
1871	53	Mackenzie vs. Hosmer
1877	26	Göring vs. Paulsen
1883	19	Riemann vs. Tarrasch
1883	33	Blackburne vs. Steinitz
1883	193	Mason vs. Steinitz
1888	42	Ponce vs. Steinitz
1889	102	Tarrasch vs. Eckart
1889	166	Steinitz vs. Chigorin
1889	259	Lasker vs. Bauer
1892	6	Mieses vs. Blackburne
1894	261	Fried vs. Schlechter
1895	38	Steinitz vs. Von Bardeleben
1895	50	Lasker vs. Steinitz
1895	108	Mason vs. Bird
1896	40	Mikistga vs. Traxler
1896	139	Zukertort vs. Steinitz
1899	5	Steinitz vs. Liverpool Chess Club
1901	168	Marshall vs. Winawer
1904	148	Marshall vs. Teichmann
1906	1	Spielmann vs. Przepiorka
1906	4	Spielmann vs. Reggio
1907	30	Spielmann vs. Johner
1907	138	Maroczy vs. Spielmann
1907	149	Marshall vs. Lasker
1912	24	Spielmann vs. Marshall
1914	8	Spielmann vs. Flamberg
1914	29	Schlechter vs. Nyholm
1918	58	Marshall vs. Capablanca
1919	27	Spielmann vs. Rubinstein
1920	16	Spielmann vs. Moller
1920	208	Sultan Khan vs. Nimzowitsch
1921	14	Euwe vs. Maroczy
1921	127	Saemisch vs. Alekhine
1922	59	Capablanca vs. Bogoljubow
1924	242	Alekhine vs. Janowski
1924	245	Romanovsky vs. Rabinovich

Year	Game #	Players
1924	246	Reti vs. Bogoljubow
1925	175	Torre vs. Lasker
1925	179	Torre vs. Verlinsky
1925	243	Gruenfeld vs. Bogoljubow
1925	247	Capablanca vs. Marshall
1925	253	Carls vs. Torre
1926	15	Weltevreede vs. Euwe
1926	34	Spielmann vs. Yates
1926	153	Rubinstein vs. Takacs
1927	71	Yates vs. Nimzowitsch
1927	137	Spielmann vs. Nimzowitsch
1928	51	Reti vs. Capablanca
1929	117	Panov vs. Mudrov
1929	211	Euwe vs. Colle
1930	217	Winter vs. Colle
1930	257	Blechschmidt vs. Flohr
1931	222	Bogoljubow vs. Nimzowitsch
1932	87	Richter vs. Wagner
1933	227	Alekhine vs. Baratz
1934	144	Freiman vs. Ragozin
1935	170	Marshall vs. Stoltz
1936	152	Botvinnik vs. Vidmar
1936	186	Koltanowski vs. Leu
1937	146	Keres vs. Fine
1937	190	Laurine vs. Keres
1938	141	Alekhine vs. Book
1939	220	Keres vs. Euwe
1941	2	Alekhine vs. Rethy
1941	240	Alekhine vs. Keininger
1945	64	Verlinsky vs. Panov
1945	96	Smyslov vs. Rudakovsky
1946	70	Thomas vs. Devos
1946	155	Stoltz vs. Kottnauer
1948	72	Rossolimo vs. Romanenko
1948	83	Canal vs. Najdorf
1949	114	Smyslov vs. Gereben
1949	125	Estrin vs. Ufimtsev
1951	158	Smyslov vs. Estrin
1952	171	Geller vs. Unzicker
1952	223	Matanovic vs. Taimanov

Year	Game #	Players
1953	202	Steiner vs. Bolbochan
1953	218	Spassky vs. Smyslov
1954	10	Konstantinopolsky vs. Hove
1954	188	Hayes vs. Schmid
1954	199	Botvinnik vs. Smyslov
1955	9	Fischer vs. Pupols
1955	173	Bisguier vs. Smyslov
1957	76	Aronson vs. Gurgenidze
1957	160	Evans vs. Larsen
1958	86	Estrin vs. Boleslavsky
1958	192	Diemer vs. Doppert
1958	230	Smyslov vs. Botvinnik
1958	241	Polugayevsky vs. Nyezhmetdinov
1959	46	Krogius vs. Spassky
1959	78	Smyslov vs. Spassky
1959	204	Petrosian vs. Yukhtman
1959	229	Gligoric vs. Smyslov
1960	63	Unzicker vs. Tal
1960	100	Spassky vs. Eliskases
1960	101	Milner-Barry vs. Barden
1960	129	Fischer vs. Berliner
1960	194	Petrosian vs. Nielsen
1960	226	Gligoric vs. Fischer
1960	232	Penrose vs. Tal
1962	36	Ziulyarkin vs. Karpov
1962	250	Benko vs. Fischer
1963	37	Fischer vs. Fine
1963	181	Bondarevsky vs. Bronstein
1963	209	Benko vs. Keres
1963	214	Panno vs. Keres
1965	41	Estrin vs. Berliner
1965	49	Lehmann vs. Donner
1965	183	Veresov vs. Bunatian
1965	234	Keres vs. Spassky
1966	77	Larsen vs. Petrosian
1966	163	Petrosian vs. Spassky
1966	225	Portisch vs. Fischer
1966	249	Geller vs. Larsen
1967	3	Timoschenko vs. Karpov
1967	99	Fischer vs. Geller
1967	197	Gurevich D vs. Schiller
1967	200	Portisch vs. Stein
1967	262	Van Geet vs. Guyt
1968	105	Matulovic vs. Canal
1968	126	Baretic vs. Pirc
1968	134	Geller vs. Maric
1968	258	Larsen vs. Kavalek
1969	121	Botvinnik vs. Suttles
1969	205	Larsen vs. Tal
1969	235	Tukmakov vs. Tal
1970	45	Gilezetdinov vs. Tolush
1970	85	Kupreichik vs. Tal
1970	90	Pritchett vs. Soltis
1971	11	Hazai vs. Sax
1971	79	Fischer vs. Petrosian
1971	93	Karpov vs. Hort
1971	140	Gligoric vs. Portisch

Year	Game #	Players
1971	224	Najdorf vs. Huebner
1972	116	Browne vs. Larsen
1972	184	Alburt vs. Tal
1973	62	Karpov vs. Spassky
1973	104	Karpov vs. Uhlmann
1973	128	Vorotnikov vs. Kengis
1973	169	Hort vs. Malich
1973	203	Bagirov vs. Gufeld
1974	75	Karpov vs. Kavalek
1974	89	Karpov vs. Korchnoi
1974	254	Sigurjonsson vs. Smyslov
1975	236	Zaitsev vs. Benko
1976	103	Reshevsky vs. Vaganian
1976	109	Kurajica vs. Dvoretsky
1976	145	Petrosian vs. Peters
1976	216	Romanishin vs. Savon
1976	255	Smyslov vs. Andersson
1977	74	Korsunsky vs. Sveshnikov
1977	111	Bronstein vs. Uhlmann
1977	237	Hort vs. Alburt
1978	22	Arnason vs. Larsen
1978	66	Smith vs. McGuire
1978	113	Speelman vs. Larsen
1978	147	Larsen vs. Pomar Salamanca
1979	47	Schussler vs. Westerinen
1979	165	Portisch vs. Larsen
1980	57	Geller vs. Chekhov
1980	133	Karpov vs. Alburt
1980	162	Kasparov vs. Hjorth
1980	176	Kasparov vs. Martinovic
1980	198	Romanishin vs. Chiburdanidze
1981	31	Kupreichik vs. Belyavsky
1981	94	Schiller vs. Paolozzi
1981	130	De Wit vs. Nijboer
1981	161	Adorjan vs. Tisdall
1981	201	Tukmakov vs. Kasparov
1981	244	Kasparov vs. Yusupov
1982	115	Van der Wiel vs. Timman
1982	132	Ivanovic vs. Alburt
1982	172	Torre vs. Timman
1982	207	Kasparov vs. Najdorf
1982	233	Borik vs. Hort
1983	167	Lindberg vs. Schiller
1983	189	Kasparov vs. Belyavsky
1983	212	Timman vs. Karpov
1983	248	Ljubojevic vs. Kasparov
1983	260	Antoshin vs. Panchenko
1984	150	Kasparov vs. Timman
1984	164	Karpov vs. Kasparov
1985	7	Wybe vs. Bryson
1985	18	Spassky vs. Seirawan
1985	61	Timman vs. Kasparov
1985	80	Karpov vs. Kasparov
1985	195	Gulko vs. Gurevich M
1985	206	Plaskett vs. Polugayevsky
1986	112	Short vs. Korchnoi
1986	231	Karpov vs. Kasparov

Year	Game #	Players
1987	20	Illescas Cordoba vs. Murey
1987	92	Nunn vs. Marin
1987	180	Piket vs. Polgar J
1987	182	Rodriguez vs. Hernandez
1988	13	Makropoulos vs. Tolnai
1988	39	Speelman vs. Yusupov
1988	43	Georgiev vs. Inkiov
1988	177	Lein vs. Hernandez
1988	210	Karpov vs. Gavrikov
1988	239	Smyslov vs. Blackstock
1988	256	Tal vs. Ivanovic
1989	55	Astrom vs. Shirov
1989	120	Kupreichik vs. Lobron
1989	142	Karpov vs. Ljubojevic
1989	178	Piket vs. Thorsteins
1989	185	Lobron vs. Hodgson
1989	187	Kasparov vs. Illescas Cordoba
1989	191	Sawyer vs. O'Connell
1990	12	Goldsmith vs. Handoko
1990	159	Karpov vs. Hector
1990	215	Ivanchuk vs. Csom
1990	228	Petursson vs. Sanchez Almeyra
1991	28	Kasparov vs. Karpov
1991	84	Benjamin vs. Gurevich
1991	107	Garber vs. Lautier
1991	131	Howell vs. Kengis
1992	32	Valvo vs. Levit
1992	48	Fischer vs. Spassky
1993	98	Short vs. Kasparov
1993	118	Kamsky vs. Karpov
1993	196	Karpov vs. Malaniuk
1993	213	Karpov vs. Salov
1994	17	Westerinen vs. Ofsted
1994	106	Kasparov vs. Short

Year	Game #	Players
1994	151	Karpov vs. Georgiev
1994	157	Karpov vs. Kramnik
1995	23	Nunn vs. Timman
1995	44	Short vs. Piket
1995	52	Onischuk vs. Malaniuk
1995	54	Schiller vs. Arne
1995	56	Kasparov vs. Anand
1995	60	Anand vs. Kamsky
1995	73	Leko vs. Kramnik
1995	81	Kasparov vs. Kengis
1995	82	Kasparov vs. Lautier
1995	95	Polgar J vs. Van Wely
1995	97	Anand vs. Kasparov
1995	119	Khalifman vs. Seirawan
1995	122	Polgar J vs. Shirov
1995	135	Kasparov vs. Anand
1995	136	Illescas Cordoba vs. Miles
1995	143	Kasparov vs. Vaganian
1995	156	Bareyev vs. Akopian
1995	219	Lautier vs. Karpov
1995	221	Gelfand vs. Zvjagintsev
1995	238	Karpov vs. Gelfand
1995	252	Tisdall vs. Gulko
1996	25	Karpov vs. Kamsky
1996	67	Ekstroem vs. Dumitrache
1996	68	Benjamin vs. Wolff
1996	69	Anand vs. Gelfand
1996	88	Kasparov vs. Hracek
1996	91	Plaskett vs. Watson
1996	124	Belyavsky vs. Bezold
1996	154	Ivanchuk vs. Shirov
1996	174	Hodgson vs. Granda Zuniga
1997	35	Spassky vs. Xie Jun
1997	251	Komarov vs. Razuvayev

GAMES INDEX

In this index, players on the White side of the board, whose games are featured in this book, are listed alphabetically, followed by the Black player, when multiple games by the same player are included. Games in this book are listed sequentially, beginning with the first game, #1.

STANDARD CHESS OPENINGS

Game #	Players
154	Ivanchuk vs. Shirov
132	Ivanovic vs. Alburt
118	Kamsky vs. Karpov
133	Karpov vs. Alburt
210	Karpov vs. Gavrikov
238	Karpov vs. Gelfand
151	Karpov vs. Georgiev
159	Karpov vs. Hector
93	Karpov vs. Hort
25	Karpov vs. Kamsky
231	Karpov vs. Kasparov
164	Karpov vs. Kasparov
80	Karpov vs. Kasparov
75	Karpov vs. Kavalek
89	Karpov vs. Korchnoi
157	Karpov vs. Kramnik
142	Karpov vs. Ljubojevic
196	Karpov vs. Malaniuk
213	Karpov vs. Salov
62	Karpov vs. Spassky
104	Karpov vs. Uhlmann
56	Kasparov vs. Anand
135	Kasparov vs. Anand
189	Kasparov vs. Belyavsky
162	Kasparov vs. Hjorth
88	Kasparov vs. Hracek
187	Kasparov vs. Illescas Cordoba
28	Kasparov vs. Karpov
81	Kasparov vs. Kengis
82	Kasparov vs. Lautier
176	Kasparov vs. Martinovic
207	Kasparov vs. Najdorf
106	Kasparov vs. Short
150	Kasparov vs. Timman
143	Kasparov vs. Vaganian
244	Kasparov vs. Yusupov
220	Keres vs. Euwe
146	Keres vs. Fine
234	Keres vs. Spassky
119	Khalifman vs. Seirawan
186	Koltanowski vs. Leu
251	Komarov vs. Razuvayev
10	Konstantinopolsky vs. Hove
74	Korsunsky vs. Sveshnikov
46	Krogius vs. Spassky
31	Kupreichik vs. Belyavsky
120	Kupreichik vs. Lobron
85	Kupreichik vs. Tal
109	Kurajica vs. Dvoretsky
258	Larsen vs. Kavalek
77	Larsen vs. Petrosian
147	Larsen vs. Pomar Salamanca
205	Larsen vs. Tal
259	Lasker vs. Bauer
50	Lasker vs. Steinitz
190	Laurine vs. Keres
219	Lautier vs. Karpov

Game #	Players
49	Lehmann vs. Donner
177	Lein vs. Hernandez
73	Leko vs. Kramnik
167	Lindberg vs. Schiller
248	Ljubojevic vs. Kasparov
185	Lobron vs. Hodgson
53	Mackenzie vs. Hosmer
13	Makropoulos vs. Tolnai
138	Maroczy vs. Spielmann
58	Marshall vs. Capablanca
149	Marshall vs. Lasker
170	Marshall vs. Stoltz
148	Marshall vs. Teichmann
168	Marshall vs. Winawer
108	Mason vs. Bird
193	Mason vs. Steinitz
223	Matanovic vs. Taimanov
105	Matulovic vs. Canal
65	McDonnell vs. De La Bourdonnais
6	Mieses vs. Blackburne
40	Mikistga vs. Traxler
101	Milner-Barry vs. Barden
224	Najdorf vs. Huebner
92	Nunn vs. Marin
23	Nunn vs. Timman
52	Onischuk vs. Malaniuk
214	Panno vs. Keres
117	Panov vs. Mudrov
232	Penrose vs. Tal
194	Petrosian vs. Nielsen
145	Petrosian vs. Peters
163	Petrosian vs. Spassky
204	Petrosian vs. Yukhtman
228	Petursson vs. Sanchez Almeyra
180	Piket vs. Polgar J
178	Piket vs. Thorsteins
206	Plaskett vs. Polugayevsky
91	Plaskett vs. Watson
122	Polgar J vs. Shirov
95	Polgar J vs. Van Wely
241	Polugayevsky vs. Nyezhmetdinov
42	Ponce vs. Steinitz
225	Portisch vs. Fischer
165	Portisch vs. Larsen
200	Portisch vs. Stein
90	Pritchett vs. Soltis
103	Reshevsky vs. Vaganian
246	Reti vs. Bogoljubow
51	Reti vs. Capablanca
87	Richter vs. Wagner
19	Riemann vs. Tarrasch
182	Rodriguez vs. Hernandez
198	Romanishin vs. Chiburdanidze
216	Romanishin vs. Savon
245	Romanovsky vs. Rabinovich
72	Rossolimo vs. Romanenko
153	Rubinstein vs. Takacs

Game #	Players
127	Saemisch vs. Alekhine
191	Sawyer vs. O'Connell
54	Schiller vs. Arne
94	Schiller vs. Paolozzi
29	Schlechter vs. Nyholm
47	Schussler vs. Westerinen
98	Short vs. Kasparov
112	Short vs. Korchnoi
44	Short vs. Piket
254	Sigurjonsson vs. Smyslov
66	Smith vs. McGuire
255	Smyslov vs. Andersson
239	Smyslov vs. Blackstock
230	Smyslov vs. Botvinnik
158	Smyslov vs. Estrin
114	Smyslov vs. Gereben
96	Smyslov vs. Rudakovsky
78	Smyslov vs. Spassky
100	Spassky vs. Eliskases
18	Spassky vs. Seirawan
218	Spassky vs. Smyslov
35	Spassky vs. Xie Jun
113	Speelman vs. Larsen
39	Speelman vs. Yusupov
8	Spielmann vs. Flamberg
30	Spielmann vs. Johner
24	Spielmann vs. Marshall
16	Spielmann vs. Moller
137	Spielmann vs. Nimzowitsch
1	Spielmann vs. Przepiorka
4	Spielmann vs. Reggio
27	Spielmann vs. Rubinstein
34	Spielmann vs. Yates
202	Steiner vs. Bolbochan
166	Steinitz vs. Chigorin
5	Steinitz vs. Liverpool Chess Club
123	Steinitz vs. Mongredien
38	Steinitz vs. Von Bardeleben
110	Steinitz vs. Winawer
155	Stoltz vs. Kottnauer
208	Sultan Khan vs. Nimzowitsch
256	Tal vs. Ivanovic
102	Tarrasch vs. Eckart
70	Thomas vs. Devos
212	Timman vs. Karpov
61	Timman vs. Kasparov
3	Timoschenko vs. Karpov
252	Tisdall vs. Gulko
175	Torre vs. Lasker
172	Torre vs. Timman
179	Torre vs. Verlinsky
201	Tukmakov vs. Kasparov
235	Tukmakov vs. Tal
63	Unzicker vs. Tal
32	Valvo vs. Levit
115	Van der Wiel vs. Timman
262	Van Geet vs. Guyt
183	Veresov vs. Bunatian
64	Verlinsky vs. Panov
128	Vorotnikov vs. Kengis
15	Weltevreede vs. Euwe
17	Westerinen vs. Ofsted
217	Winter vs. Colle
7	Wybe vs. Bryson
71	Yates vs. Nimzowitsch
236	Zaitsev vs. Benko
36	Ziulyarkin vs. Karpov
21	Zukertort vs. Anderssen
139	Zukertort vs. Steinitz

OPENINGS INDEX

This index is organized alphabetically by openings, with the variations and subvariations listed within that grouping. The middle column shows the typical move order, while the far right column indicates the game number where the opening is featured or referenced. Many other variations not listed here can be found within the games and discussions themselves–and of course, the reader is directed to the table of contents for main opening and varations listings.

OPENING MOVES INDEX

1.e4 Openings

STANDARD CHESS OPENINGS

UCO INDEX

This index shows the list of openings for *Unorthodox Chess Openings* (UCO), the companion guide to this book. UCO is available direct from Cardoza Publishing, or at your local bookstores. Combined with SCO and WCO (*World Champion Openings*), these three opening guides contain more than 1700 pages of opening strategy!

UCO is an encyclopedic guide to every unorthodox opening used by chess players, and contains more than 300 weird, contentious, controversial, unconventional, arrogant and outright strange openings. You'll find that these openings are a sexy and exotic way to spice up a game – as well as a great tactical weapon to spring on unsuspecting and unprepared opponents.

Alekhine Defense
- Brooklyn Variation
- Krejcik Variation
- Mokele Mbembe
- Welling Variation

Amar Opening
- Gent Gambit
- Paris Gambit

Anderssen Opening

Barnes Opening
- Fool's Mate
- Hammerschlag
- Walkerling

Benoni Defense
- Cormorant Gambit
- Hawk Variation
- Modern Variation
- Nakamura Gambit
- Snail Variation
- Vulture Defense
- Woozle

Bird Opening
- Batavo-Polish Attack
- From Gambit
- Hobbs Gambit
- Horsefly Defense
- Lasker Attack
- Sturm Gambit

Bishop's Opening
- King's Gambit Reversed
- Kitchener Folly
- Lewis Gambit
- MacDonnell Gambit

Borg Defense
- Borg Gambit
- Troon Gambit

Canard Formation
- Double Duck Variation

Caro-Kann Defense
- Advance Variation: Bayonet Attack
- De Bruycker Defense
- Edinburgh Vatiation
- Goldman Variation
- Gurgenidze Counterattack
- Hector Gambit
- Hillbilly Attack
- Maroczy Variation
- Mieses Gambit
- Ulysses Gambit
- Von Hennig Gambit

Carr Defense

Catalan Opening
- Hungarian Gambit

Clemenz Opening

Creepy Crawly Formation

Dutch Defense
- Hevendahl Gambit
- Hopton Attack
- Janzen-Korchnoi Gambit
- Kingfisher Gambit
- Korchnoi Attack
- Krejcik Gambit
- Manhattan Gambit
- Senechaud Gambit
- Spielmann Gambit
- Staunton Gambit: American Attack
- Tate Gambit

Elephant Gambit
- Maroczy Gambit
- Paulsen Countergambit
- Wasp Variation

STANDARD CHESS OPENINGS

English Opening
- Anglo-Indian Defense: Flohr-Mikenas
- Anglo-Scandinavian Defense
- Anglo-Scandinavian Defense: Löhn Gambit
- Anglo-Scandinavian Defense: Schulz Gambit
- Anti-English
- Drill Variation
- English Defense
- English Defense: Hartlaub Gambit
- English Defense: Perrin Variation
- English Defense: Poli Gambit
- Halibut Gambit
- King's English Variation: Bellon Gambit
- Myers Variation
- Porcupine Variation
- The Whale
- Wade Gambit
- Wing Gambit

Englund Gambit
- Felbecker Gambit
- Mosquito Gambit
- Soller Gambit
- Soller Gambit Deferred
- Stockholm Variation

Four Knights Game
- Halloween Gambit
- Halloween Gambit: Oltimer Variation
- Halloween Gambit: Plasma Variation

Fred Defense
- and Mao Tse Tung

French Defense
- Advance Variation: Extended Bishop Swap
- Advance Variation: Nimzowitsch Attack
- Advance Variation: Nimzowitsch Gambit
- Alapin Gambit
- Bird Invitation
- Diemer-Duhm Gambit
- Exchange Variation: Canal Attack
- La Bourdonnais Variation
- Orthoschnapp Gambit
- Steinitz Attack
- Tarrasch Variation: Shaposhnikov Gambit
- Wing Gambit

Grob Opening
- Alessi Gambit
- Double Grob
- Grob Gambit
- Keene Defense
- London Defense
- Macho Grob
- Spike: Hurst Attack

Grünfeld Defense
- Gibbon Gambit

Guatemala Defense

Hippopotamus Formation

Horwitz Defense

Hungarian Opening
- Revesed Alekhine

Indian Game
- Anti-Grünfeld: Alekhine Variation
- Budapest Defense
- Devin Gambit
- Döry Indian
- Fajarowicz Defense: Bonsdorf Variation
- Fajarowicz Variation
- Gedult Attack
- Gibbins-Wiedehagen Gambit
- Gibbins-Wiedehagen Gambit: Maltese Falcon
- Gibbins-Wiedehagen Gambit: Oshima Defense
- Gibbins-Wiedehagen Gambit: Stummer Gambit
- Lazard Gambit
- Maddigan Gambit
- Medusa Gambit
- Omega Gambit
- Omega Gambit: Arafat Gambit
- Schnepper Gambit
- Trompowsky Attack: Borg Variation
- Trompowsky Attack: Raptor Variation

Italian Game
- Jerome Gambit
- Schilling Gambit
- Two Knights Defense: Fried Liver Attack
- Two Knights Defense: Traxler Counterattack

Kadas Opening

Kangaroo Defense
- Keres Defense: Transpositional

King Pawn Game
- Alapin Opening
- Beyer Gambit
- Clam Variation
- Clam Variation: King's Gambit Reversed
- Danish Gambit
- Dresden Opening
- King's Head Opening
- Macleod Attack
- Macleod Attack: Norwalder Gambit
- Maroczy Defense
- Napoleon Attack
- Philidor Gambit
- Portuguese Opening
- Tortise Opening
- Wayward Queen Attack
- Wayward Queen Attack: Mellon Gambit

King's Gambit
- Accepted: Allgaier Gambit
- Accepted: Basman Gambit
- Accepted: Breyer Gambit
- Accepted: Bryan Countergambit
- Accepted: Carrera Gambit
- Accepted: Dodo Variation
- Accepted: Double Muzio Gambit
- Accepted: Eisenberg Variation
- Accepted: Gaga Gambit
- Accepted: Leonardo Gambit
- Accepted: Muzio Gambit Accepted
- Accepted: Norwalde Variation
- Accepted: Orsini Gambit
- Accepted: Paris Gambit
- Accepted: Tumbleweed
- Declined: Keene Defense
- Declined: Mafia Defense
- Declined: Marshall Countergmbit
- Declined: Pickler Gambit

King's Knight Opening
Damiano Defense
Gunderam Defense
McConnell Defense
Latvian Gambit
Lobster Gambit
Poisoned Pawn Variation
Lemming Defense
Lizard Defense
Pirc-Diemer Gambit
Mexican Defense
Horsefly Gambit
Mieses Opening
Spike Deferred
Modern Defense
Beefeater Variation
Dunworthy Variation
Norwegian Defense
Pterodactyl Variation
Randspringer Variation
Nimzo-Larsen Attack
Norfolk Gambit 1
Norfolk Gambit 2
Paschmann Gambit
Ringelbach Gambit
Spike Variation
Nimzowitsch Defense
Kennedy Variation
Lean Variation
Neo-Mongoloid Defense
Wheeler Gambit
Williams Variation
Owen Defense
Matinovsky Gambit
Naselwaus Gambit
Smith Gambit
Polish Defense
Spassky Gambit
Polish Opening
Birmingham Gambit
Bugayev Attack
Karniewski Variation
Schühler Gambit
Tartakower Gambit
Tartakower Gambit: Brinckmann Variation
Wolferts Gambit
Queen Pawn Game
Anti-Torre
Bishop Attack: Welling Variation
Blackmar-Diemer Gambit
Blackmar-Diemer Gambit: Lemberger Variation
Blackmar-Diemer Gambit: O'Kelly Defense
Blackmar-Diemer Gambit: Ryder Gambit
Hübsch Gambit
Morris Countergambit
Veresov Attack: Shropshire Defense
Veresov Attack: Anti-Veresov
Zurich Gambit
Queen's Gambit Refused
Albin Countergambit
Austrian Defense
Austrian Defense: Gusev Countergambit
Baltic Defense: Argentinian Gambit
Chigorin Defense
Chigorin Defense: Lazard Gambit
Chigorin Defense: Tartakower Gambit
Rat Defense
Balogh Defense
San Jorge Defense
Reti Opening
Penguin Variation
Russian Defense
Cochrane Gambit
Damiano Variation
Saragossa Opening
Scandinavian Defense
Anderssen Counterattack
Bronstein Variation
Icelandic-Palme Gambit
Main Lines
Schiller Defense
Scotch Game
Göring Gambit: Double Pawn Sacrifice
Steinitz Variation
Semi-Slav Defense
Gunderam Gambit
Sicilian Defense
Accelerated Paulsen
Acton Extension
Brussels Gambit
Frederico Variation
Hyperaccelerated
Katalimov Variation
Mengarini Gambit
Mongoose Variation
Morphy Gambit
Snyder Variation
Snyder Variation: Queen Fianchetto
Wing Gambit
Sodium Attack
Celadon Variation
Chenoboskian Variation
Spanish Game
Alapin Defense
Brentano Variation
Vinogradov Variation
St. George Defense
St. George Gambit
Van Geet Opening
Anti-Pirc Variation
Battambang Variation
Napoleon Attack
Novosibirsk Variation
Reversed Nimzowitsch
Reversed Scandinavian
Sicilian Two Knights
Tübingen Gambit
Twyble Attack
Van't Kruijs Opening
Venezolana Formation
Vienna Game

JOIN THE INTERNET CHESS CLUB!

Welcome to the newest way to enjoy chess; on the Internet! The Internet Chess Club (ICC) is the longest running, most popular, and highest rated place to play chess on the Internet.

WORLDWIDE MEMBERSHIP - 30,000 GAMES A DAY!

ICC is rapidly becoming the largest organization of active chess players in the world. Nowhere else can you find as many chess enthusiasts ready for a quick round of blitz, a short chat, or an impromptu tournament. It is not uncommon to find nearly 1,000 chess players hanging out on ICC where over 30,000 games are played daily!

ICC IS FUN AND EASY TO USE

In addition to on-line games with players from around the world and daily tournaments, variations such as Bughouse, Kriegspiel, material and time odds, shuffle, and team games give you loads of options. Numerous on-line administrators offer helpful technical support, guidance, and adjudication.

A professional and caring staff provides helpful guidance to beginners.

ICC MEMBER BENEFITS
Play unlimited rated chess on the Internet
Exclusive handle and player profile
Extensive chat area
Personal game libraries
Over 20 tournaments a day
Master lectures
Broadcasts of major chess events
Access to vendors, teachers, and Grandmasters
Special discounts on chess products and services
Support World Wide Chess

FREE TRIAL OFFER!

To join the tens of thousands of regular users and qualify for a free trail:

1) Visit the www.chessclub.com/cardoza on the world wide web
2) Download the necessary software
3) Start playing!

SIGN UP NOW!

Membership fees are $49/year, $29/half-year, and $24.50/year for students. Pay by phone, fax, or online. For additional information, to obtain the necessary software by mail, or to pay by check or money order (drawn on US or Canadian bank) contact: Internet Chess Club, 5001 Baum Blvd., Suite 630, Pittsburgh, PA 15213 USA. Email: icc@chessclub.com.

FOR A FREE INTERNET CHESS CLUB TRIAL
Visit www.chessclub.com/cardoza

CARDOZA PUBLISHING CHESS BOOKS

STANDARD CHESS OPENINGS *by Eric Schiller* - The new definitive standard on opening chess play in the 20th century, this comprehensive guide covers every important chess opening and variation ever played and currently in vogue. In all, more than 3,000 opening strategies are presented! Differing from previous opening books which rely almost exclusively on bare notation, SCO features substantial discussion and analysis on each opening so that you learn and understand the concepts behind them. Includes more than 250 completely annotated games (including a game representative of each major opening) and more than 1,000 diagrams! For modern players at any level, this is the standard reference book necessary for competitive play. *A must have for serious chess players!!!* 768 pages, $24.95

UNORTHODOX CHESS OPENINGS *by Eric Schiller* - This all-inclusive guide to every major unorthodox opening references more than 300 weird, contentious, controversial, unconventional, arrogant and outright strange openings and variations. From their tricky tactical surprises to their bizarre names, these openings fly in the face of tradition. You'll meet such openings as the Orangutan, Macho Grob, St. George Defense, Woozle, Elephant Gambit and even the Reagan Attack! These openings are not only an exotic way to spice up a game - but a great weapon to spring on unsuspecting and often unprepared opponents. More than 750 diagrams illustrate the essential positions characteristic of each opening. 544 pages, $24.95

WORLD CHAMPION OPENINGS *by Eric Schiller* - This serious reference work covers the essential opening theory and moves of every major chess opening and variation as played by *all* the world champions. Reading as much like an encyclopedia of the must-know openings crucial to every chess player's knowledge as a powerful tool showing the insights, concepts and secrets as used by the greatest players of all time, *World Champion Openings (WCO)* covers an astounding 100 crucial openings in full conceptual detail (with 100 actual games from the champions themselves)! *A must-have book for serious chess players.* 384 pages, $16.95

WORLD CHAMPION COMBINATIONS *by Keene and Schiller* - Learn the insights, concepts and moves of the greatest combinations ever by the greatest players of all time. From Morphy and Alekhine, to Fischer and Kasparov, the incredible combinations and brilliant sacrifices of the 13 World Champions are collected together in the most insightful book on combinations written. Packed with fascinating strategems, 50 annotated games, and great practical advice for your own games, this is a great companion guide to *World Champion Openings*. 264 pages, $16.95.

BEGINNING CHESS PLAY *by Bill Robertie* - Step-by-step approach uses 113 chess diagrams to teach the basic principles of playing and winning. Covers opening, middle and end game strategies, principles of development, pawn structure, checkmate play, important openings and defenses, and how to join a chess club, play in tournaments, use the chess clock, and get rated. Two annotated games illlustrate strategic thinking for easy improvement. Includes beginner's guide to chess notation. 144 pages, $9.95

WINNING CHESS OPENINGS *by Bill Robertie* - Shows the concepts and best opening moves of more than 25 essential openings from Black's and White's perspectives: King's Gambit, Center Game, Scotch Game, Giucco Piano, Vienna Game, Bishop's Opening, Ruy Lopez, French, Caro-Kann, Sicilian, Alekhine, Pirc, Modern, Queen's Gambit, Nimzo-Indian, Queen's Indian, Dutch, King's Indian, Benoni, English, Bird's, Reti's, and King's Indian Attack. Includes examples from 25 grandmasters and champions including Fischer, Kasparov, Spassky. 144 pages, $9.95

MASTER CHECKMATE STRATEGY *by Bill Robertie* - Covers all the basic combinations, plus advanced, surprising and unconventional mates, and the most effective pieces needed to win. Players learn how to mate opponents with just a pawn advantage; how to work two rooks into an unstoppable attack; how to wield a queen advantage with deadly intent; how to coordinate movements by pieces of differing strengths into indefensible positions of their opponents; when it's best to have a knight, and when a bishop to win. 144 pages, $9.95

WINNING CHESS TACTICS *by Bill Robertie* - 14 chapters of winning tactical concepts illustrate the complete explanations and thinking behind every tactical concept. Players learn how to win using pins, single and double forks, double attacks, skewers, discovered and double checks, multiple threat tactics - and other crushing tactics to gain an immediate edge over opponents. Learn the powerhouse tools of tactical play to become a stronger winning player. Includes beginner's guide to chess notation. 128 pages, $9.95

THE BASICS OF WINNING CHESS *by Jacob Cantrell* - A great first book of chess, in one easy reading, beginner's learn the moves of the pieces, the basic rules and principles of play, the standard openings, and both Algebraic and English chess notation. The basic ideas of the winning concepts and strategies of middle and end game play are shown as well. Includes example games of great champions. 64 pages, $4.95.

GAMBIT OPENING REPERTOIRE FOR WHITE *by Eric Schiller* - Chessplayers who enjoy attacking from the very first move are rewarded here with a powerful repertoire of brilliant gambits. Starting off with 1.e4 and then using such sharp weapons such as the Göring Gambit, Smith-Morra Gambit, Alekhine Gambit, Marshall Gambit, and the Blackmar-Diemer Gambit to put great pressure on opponents, Schiller presents a complete attacking repertoire to use against the most popular defenses including the Sicilian, French, Scandinavian, Caro Kann, Nimzowich, Alekhine and a host of Open Game situations. 208 pages, $14.95.

GAMBIT OPENING REPERTOIRE FOR BLACK *by Eric Schiller* - For players that like exciting no-holds-barred chess, this versatile gambit repertoire shows Black how to take charge with aggressive attacking defenses against any orthodox first White opening move; 1.e4, 1.d4 and 1.c4. Learn the Scandinavian Gambit against 1.e4, Schara Gambit against 1.d4 and 1.c4, and the Schlechter Gambit against the Bird's Opening. Black learns the secrets of seizing the initiative from White's hands, usually by investing a pawn or two, to begin powerful attacks that if not handled correctly, can send White to early defeat. 208 pages, $14.95.

BASIC ENDGAME STRATEGY, Kings, Pawns and Minor Pieces *by Bill Robertie* - Learn the basic checkmating principles and combinations needed to finish off opponents and claim victory at the chessboard. From the four basic checkmates using the King with the queen, rook, two bishops, and bishop/knight combination, to the basic King/pawn, King/Knight and King/Bishop endgames, chessplayers learn the essentials of translating small edges in the middlegame into decisive endgame victories. Learnthe 50-move rule, and the combinations of pieces that can't force a checkmate against a lone King. 168 pages, $12.95.

301 TRICKY CHECKMATES *by Fred Wilson and Bruce Alberston* - Both a fascinating challenge and great training tool, this collection of two and three move checkmates is great for advanced beginning, intermediate and expert players. Mates are in order of difficulty, from the simple to very complex positions. Learn the standard patterns and stratagems for cornering the king: corridor and support mates, attraction and deflection sacrifices, pins and annihilation, the quiet move, and the dreaded *zugzwang*. Examples, drawn from actual games, illustrate a wide range of chess tactics from old classics right up to the 1990's. 192 pages, $9.95. Due February '98.

COMPLETE DEFENSE TO KING PAWN OPENINGS *by Eric Schiller* - Learn a complete defensive system against 1.e4. This powerful repertoire not only limits White's ability to obtain any significant opening advantage but allows Black to adopt the flexible Caro-Kann formation, the favorite weapon of many of the greatest chess players. All White's options are explained in detail, and a plan is given for Black to combat them all. Analysis is up-to-date and backed by examples drawn from games of top stars. Detailed index lets you follow the opening from the point of a specific player, or through its history. 240 pages, $16.95. Due March '98

COMPLETE DEFENSE TO QUEEN PAWN OPENINGS *by Eric Schiller* - This aggressive counterattacking repertoire covers Black opening systems against virtually every chess opening except for 1.e4 (including most flank games), based on the exciting and powerful Tarrasch Defense, an opening that helped bring Championship titles to Kasparov and Spassky. Black learns to effectively use the Classical Tarrasch, Symmetrical Tarrasch, Asymmetrical Tarrasch, Marshall and Tarrasch Gambits, and Tarrasch without Nc3, to achieve an early equality or even an outright advantage in the first few moves. 240 pages, $16.95. Due March '98

SECRETS OF THE SICILIAN DRAGON by *GM Eduard Gufeld and Eric Schiller* - The mighty Dragon Variation of the Sicilian Defense is one of the most exciting openings in all of chess. Each important variation is covered in detail, step-by-step, from the massive labyrinth of the Yugoslav Variation to the dark cave of the Anti-Dragon systems, with stops in the territory of the Classical Dragons and Levenfish Variation. The general strategies and tactics are introduced through examples of the most brilliant games of the most famous Dragoneers. You'll also learn how to keep the material up to date using internet resources. 160 pages, $14.95. Due April '98.

CARDOZA PUBLISHING CHESS BOOKS

ENCYCLOPEDIA OF CHESS WISDOM, The Essential Concepts and Strategies of Smart Chess Play *by Eric Schiller* - The most important concepts, strategies, tactics, wisdom, and thinking that every chessplayer must know, plus the gold nuggets of knowledge behind every attack and defense, is collected together in one highly focused volume. From opening, middle and endgame strategy, to psychological warfare and tournament tactics, the *Encyclopedia of Chess Wisdom* forms the blueprint of power play and advantage at the chess board. Step-by-step, the reader is taken through the thinking behind each essential concept, and through examples, discussions, and diagrams, shown the full impact on the game's direction. You even learn how to correctly study chess to become a chess master. 400 pages, $19.95. Due May '98.

BASIC ENDGAME STRATEGY: Rooks and Queens by Bill Robertie - The companion guide to *Basic Endgame Strategy: Kings, Pawns and Minor Pieces*, shows the basic checkmating principles and combinations needed to finish off opponents using the the Queen and Rook with King combinations.. You'll learn to translate middlegame advantages into decisive endgame victories, how to create passed pawns, use the King as a weapon, clear the way for rook mates, and recognize the combinations that appear in endgames. 144 pages, $12.95. Due June '98.

EXCELLENT CHESS BOOKS - OTHER PUBLISHERS

- OPENINGS -

HOW TO PLAY THE TORRE *by Eric Schiller* - One of Schiller's best-selling books, the 19 chapters on this fabulous and aggressive White opening (1. d4 Nf6; 2. Nf3 e6; 3. Bg5) will make opponents shudder and get you excited about chess all over again. Insightful analysis, completely annotated games get you ready to win! 210 pages, $17.50.

A BLACK DEFENSIVE SYSTEM WITH 1...D6 *by Andrew Soltis* - This Black reply - so rarely played that it doesn't even have a name - throws many opponents off their rote attack and can lead to a decisive positional advantage. Use this surprisingly strong system to give you the edge against unprepared opponents. 166 pages, $16.50.

BLACK TO PLAY CLASSICAL DEFENSES AND WIN *by Eric Schiller - Shows you how to develop a complete opening repertoire as black.* Emerge from *any* opening with a playable position, fighting for the center from the very first move. Defend against the Ruy Lopez, Italian Game, King's Gambit, King's Indian, many more. 166 pages, $16.50.

ROMANTIC KING'S GAMBIT IN GAMES & ANALYSIS *by Santasiere & Smith* - The most comprehensive collection of theory and games (137) on this adventurous opening is filled with annotations and "color" on the greatest King's Gambits played and the players. Makes you *want* to play! Very readable; packed with great concepts. 233 pages, $17.50.

WHITE TO PLAY 1.E4 AND WIN *by Eric Schiller - Shows you how to develop a complete opening system as white beginning 1. e4.* Learn the recommended opening lines to all the major systems as white, and how to handle any defense black throws back. Covers the Sicilian, French, Caro-Kann, Scandinavia; many more. 166 pages, $16.50.

HOW TO PLAY THE SICILIAN DEFENSE AGAINST ALL WHITE POSSIBILITIES *by Andrew Soltis* - Terrific book emphasizes understanding the ideas behind the Sicilian so that you'll not only play well against any sound White opening - you'll actually look forward to 1.e4! Learn to turn the Sicilian into a fighting offensive line. 184 pages, $13.95.

BIG BOOK OF BUSTS *by Schiller & Watson* - Learn how to defend against 70 dangerous and annoying openings which are popular in amateur chess and can lead to defeat if unprepared, but can be refuted when you know how to take opponents off their favorite lines. Greet opponents with your own surprises! Recommended. 293 pages, $22.95.

- ENDGAMES -

ESSENTIAL CHESS ENDINGS EXPLAINED VOL. 1 *by Jeremy Silman* - This essential and enjoyable reference tool to mates and stalemates belongs in every chess player's library. Commentary on every move plus quizzes and many diagrams insure complete understanding. All basic positions covered, plus many advanced ones. 221 pages, $16.50.

ESSENTIAL CHESS ENDINGS EXPLAINED VOL. 2 *by Ken Smith* - This book assumes you know the basics of the 1st volume and takes you all the way to Master levels. Work through moves of 275 positions and learn as you go; there are explanations of every White and Black move so you know what's happening from both sides. 298 pages, $17.50.

HANDHELD CHESS COMPUTERS!

KASPAROV EXPRESS™

SAITEK - The World Leader in Intelligent Electronic Games

VERSATILE AND FUN - An amazing 384 level/setting combinations includes fun levels for novices and challenging levels for experienced players. Economic powerful, and pocket size (approximately 5" x 61/2" x 1') this game is an unbeatable easy traveling companion.

GREAT INEXPENSIVE TRAVEL COMPANION! - Features different playing styles and strengths, 5 special coach modes, and teaching levels! Sensory-style chess board, peg type pieces, folding lid, LCD screen, take back and hint features, built-in chess clock that keeps track of time for both sides, and self-rating system. Memory holds an unfinished game for up to two years, gives you the complete package in an economical, handy travel-ready unit.

To order, send just $49.95 for the Express.

KASPAROV TRAVEL CHAMPION 2100

SAITEK - The World Leader in Intelligent Electronic Games

THE WORLD'S MOST POWERFUL HAND-HELD CHESS COMPUTER ANYWHERE! - This **super program** and **integrated training system** has an **official USCF rating of 2334**! This **awesome program** can beat over 99% of all chess players, yet it's still great for the novice. LCD shows principal variation, evaluation, search depth, and search mode counts.

64 SKILL LEVELS - 64 levels of skill and handicapping give you tons of **options** and **versatility**: Play against beginning, intermediate or advanced opponents (includes tournament time controls), play Blitz or Tournament, choose Active, Passive, or Complete style, or Tournament Opening Book, select **Brute Force** algorithm or the advanced Selective Search. Match your skill to the correct level for most **challenging** chess. You want it - it's all here!

To order, send just $129.95 for the Kasparov Travel Champion 2100.

TAKE THE CHESS COMPUTER ALONG WHEREVER YOU GO!

Saitek - the world leader in intelligent electronic games

Yes! I'm ready to take the Saitek Chess challenge and match my skills against these exciting handheld games! Enclosed is a check or money order to:

Cardoza Publishing, P.O. Box 1500, Cooper Station, New York, NY 10276

Call Toll-Free in U.S. & Canada, 1-800-577-WINS; or fax 718-743-8284

Please include $8.00 postage and handling for U.S. shipping; CANADA/MEXICO double; other countries 4X. Orders outside U.S., money order payable in U.S. dollars on U. S. bank only.

ITEM DESIRED ______________________

Kasparov Express ($49.95) Kasparov Travel Champion 2100 ($129.95)

NAME ______________________

ADDRESS ______________________

CITY ____________ STATE ____________ ZIP ____________

SCO

30 Day Money Back Guarantee!

TOURNAMENT CHESS CLOCKS

Tournament Player

Tournament Pro

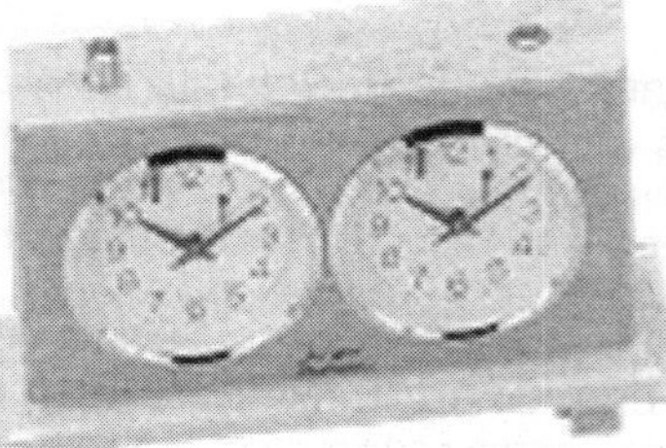

Saitek Chess Clock

TOURNAMENT-STYLE CHESS PIECES

Tournament Staunton *(Standard - Not Shown)*

TOURNAMENT-STYLE CHESS BOARD

Tournament Board *(Standard - Not Shown)*

CHESSWORKS UNLIMITED

Chess Software, Books, Tournaments, E-mail Instruction and Information

THE ONE STOP SOURCE FOR SERIOUS CHESS PLAYERS

Chessworks Unlimited, owned and operated by Eric Schiller, is a central information center where you can shop for high-quality chess software at affordable prices or find out about international chess events, editorials, and chess in general. You can also find out more information on Dr. Schiller's books and be the first to know about upcoming titles when they're hot off the press, and you can even arrange for online or email instruction and analysis!

Chessworks Unlimited organizes chess tournaments in Hawaii and Northern California.

Visit our web site to see the latest listings!

http://www.chessworks.com

THE CHESSWORKS UNLIMITED SOFTWARE SHOP

For serious players who own a chess playing application, we carry more than 100 different products that help you become a better chess player. There are software products on everything from openings, middle games, end games, and combinations, to chess studies and game collections. (Our PGN formatted software is compatible and works with virtually all chess programs.) For novices, *Dr. Schiller's How to Play Chess* and *Chess Game* provide instruction up to tournament level. They also include a chess playing program *and* database of 10,000 games!

CARDOZA PUBLISHING ONLINE

For the latest in Chess Software and Books by the World's Best Chess Writers

www.cardozapub.com

To find out about our latest chess and backgammon publications, to order books and software from third parties,or receive the Chessworks Unlimited Catalog:

1. Go online: www.cardozapub.com
2. Use E-Mail: cardozapub@aol.com
3. Call toll free: (800)577-9467
4. Write: Cardoza Publishing,132 Hastings Street, Brooklyn, NY 11235

We welcome your suggestions and comments, and are glad to have you as a customer. Our philosophy is to bring you the best quality chess books from the top authors and authorities in the chess world, featuring *words* (as opposed to hieroglyphics), *clear expanations* (as opposed to gibberish), *nice presentations* (as opposed to books simply slapped together), and authoritative information. And all this at reasonable prices.

We hope you like the results.

FREE!!! - Our New Free Online Chess Magazine

Subscribe to our free online chess magazine with articles, columns, gossip, and more. Go to www.cardozapub.com for details. *Chess is our Game!*